社会学·政治学·文化学·教育学·民族学·历史学

叶显恩 主编
王春煜 刘集林 副主编

陈序经全集

第二卷
现代主权论

Recent Theories of Sovereignty
Politology

中山大学出版社
·广州·

版权所有　翻印必究

图书在版编目（CIP）数据

陈序经全集 / 陈序经著；叶显恩主编；王春煜，刘集林副主编.
广州：中山大学出版社，2025.3. --ISBN 978-7-306-08274-9

Ⅰ．Z427

中国国家版本馆CIP数据核字第2024GE9169号

CHEN XUJING QUANJI: DI-RE JUAN

出　版　人：	王天琪
总　策　划：	王天琪
项目统筹：	嵇春霞　王延红
责任编辑：	卢思敏　蓝若琪
封面设计：	雅昌文化（集团）有限公司　曾　斌　周美玲
责任校对：	李昭莹　张陈卉子
责任技编：	靳晓虹
出版发行：	中山大学出版社
电　　话：	编辑部 020-84111901，84110283，84111997，84110779
	发行部 020-84111998，84111981，84111160
地　　址：	广州市新港西路135号
邮　　编：	510275　传　真：020-84036565
网　　址：	http://www.zsup.com.cn　E-mail：zdcbs@mail.sysu.edu.cn
印　　厂：	恒美印务（广州）有限公司
规　　格：	787mm×1092mm　1/16
总 印 张：	433
总 字 数：	8718千字
版次印次：	2025年3月第1版　2025年3月第1次印刷
定　　价：	1980.00元（全十四卷）

如发现本书因印装质量影响阅读，请与出版社发行部联系调换

凡 例

一、**编排方式**。《全集》总体上兼顾著述发表时间先后与研究领域的区别。第一卷以时间为序收录了陈序经的论文、时论、书评等,其中论文已收入其他卷者,原则上只存目;同题异文者,则均予以收录。第二卷至第十三卷收录了陈序经在不同研究领域的论文或专著。第十四卷收录了陈序经的遗稿《珠崖篇》,整理了其年谱、往来书信、照片等相关资料。底稿为直排繁体者,一律改横排简体,内容列举、引用位置指向用词,如"如左"径改为"如下"等。

二、**底本来源**。《全集》所收文献中有大量未曾整理的手稿、抄稿,其版本源流、底本选择等情况,皆写入"本卷说明"中。

三、**引文说明**。《全集》所引古籍或他人著述,有漏字、错字等现象者,一般参照现今中华书局、上海古籍出版社等相应版本径改,不另说明;引用古籍或他人著述时只取其大意,与原文不尽一致,凡此,照录,不予修改;手稿或抄稿中引用本人已发表文章,但内容与已发表的原文不尽一致,凡此,亦依手稿或抄稿。

四、**校订符号**。原稿中有漏字者,在〈 〉内补之。原稿中的错讹字,在其后〔 〕内补正。原稿中的衍字,用［ ］标示。原稿中漫漶不清、难以识别或残缺的字,用□表示;字数难以确定者,用▨表示。原稿中的小字夹注,置于（ ）内,字体、字号同正文。外文书名、刊名用斜体。

五、**历史用语**。《全集》保留作者文字风格及语言习惯,不按现行用法改动原文。历史时期若干字词表达与今有异,但不影响理解,为存当时之真,不改。如智识（知识）分子、澎涨（膨胀）、计画（计划）、瞭解（了解）、那（哪）、澈底（彻底）、那末（那么）、原故（缘故）等。凡行文中对少数民族的蔑称,根据国家相关民族政策一律改为规范称呼,如"猺"改为"瑶"、"獠"改为"僚"、"猓猡"改为"倮倮"等。

六、外文名词。译名不统一或与现今不一致，如拿破伦/拿破仑、哥仑布/哥伦布、菲洲/非洲等，均不改。外文人名、地名书写有误者，一般径改。外文专有名词在原稿中大小写掺杂，按现今规范格式统一。

七、内文标点。原稿正文无标点或仅有简单断句者，一律按照中华人民共和国国家标准《标点符号用法》（GB/T 15834—2011）予以修改。专名号从略。

八、文字规范。《全集》中的简体字以2013年6月国务院公布之《通用规范汉字表》为准。通假字，不改。繁体字、异体字，改为规范字；但专有名词中的繁体字、异体字等，依从其使用惯例，不改。作者笔误、排印舛误等明显错误，径改。

其余未规定事项，一般遵从作者原稿。

本卷说明

  本卷收录了陈序经先生1928年撰就的博士论文"Recent Theories of Sovereignty"（附汉译《现代主权论》，张世保译）。另收录《新政治》一书（英文），该书是陈序经先生对政治学领域深入研究和思考的成果。由方志彪校订。其中，《现代主权论》曾于2010年9月由清华大学出版社出版。

本卷目录

Recent Theories of Sovereignty ································· 1

现代主权论 ································· 311

Politology ································· 557

Recent Theories of Sovereignty

CONTENTS

PUBLICATION NOTE ·· 6
PREFACE ··· 7
INTRODUCTION ··· 9
CHAPTER Ⅰ   HISTORY OF THE THEORY OF SOVEREIGNTY ········ 12
  Ⅰ. Introduction ··· 12
  Ⅱ. Greek Conception of Sovereignty—Aristotle ································ 13
  Ⅲ. Roman Conception of Sovereignty ·· 14
  Ⅳ. Conception of Sovereignty During the Middle Ages ···················· 15
  Ⅴ. Early Modern Conception of Sovereignty ···································· 17
  Ⅵ. Reactionary Movement ·· 27
  Ⅶ. Conclusion ··· 36
CHAPTER Ⅱ   SOVEREIGNTY IN THE FEDERAL STATE ·················· 39
  Ⅰ. Introduction ··· 39
  Ⅱ. State Sovereignty ··· 39
  Ⅲ. Sovereignty of the Federal Government ·· 47
  Ⅳ. Compromise Theories ··· 51
CHAPTER Ⅲ   SOVEREIGNTY IN THE FEDERAL STATE（Continued）
           ·· 66
  Ⅴ. Conclusion ··· 89
CHAPTER Ⅳ   SOVEREIGNTY AND INTERNATIONAL RELATIONS:
           Characteristics of Sovereignty ··· 90
  Ⅰ. Introduction ··· 90
  Ⅱ. Sovereignty and International Law ·· 90
  Ⅲ. Nature of Sovereignty ··· 97
CHAPTER Ⅴ   SOVEREIGNTY AND INTERNATIONAL RELATIONS
           （Continued）: Location and Criticism ································ 116
  Ⅳ. Location of Sovereignty ·· 116
  Ⅴ. Recent Attacks on the Notion of Sovereignty ······························· 138
  Ⅵ. Conclusion ··· 141
CHAPTER Ⅵ   SOVEREIGNTY AND LAW ·· 142
  Ⅰ. Introduction ··· 142

  II. Analytical School ································· 143
  III. Natural Law School ································ 163
CHAPTER VII SOVEREIGNTY AND LAW（Continued） ············ 166
  IV. Historical School ·································· 166
  V. Economic School ··································· 175
  VI. Sociological School ································ 182
CHAPTER VIII SOVEREIGNTY AND LAW（Continued） ··········· 192
  VII. Conclusion ······································· 215
CHAPTER IX SOVEREIGNTY AND FUNCTIONAL GROUPS ············ 217
  I. Introduction ······································· 217
  II. German Writers ··································· 218
  III. English Writers ··································· 220
  IV. French Writers ··································· 240
  V. American Writers ································· 245
  VI. Conclusion ······································· 251
CHAPTER X LASKI AND OHTERS ························· 253
  I. Laski ·· 253
  II. Other Writers ····································· 269
CONCLUSION: A POINT OF VIEW ····························· 278
BIBLIOGRAPHY ··· 291
VITA ·· 310

RECENT THEORIES OF SOVEREIGNTY

BY
SU CHING CHEN, PH. D.

ASSISTANT PROFESSOR OF POLITICAL SCIENCE

LINGNAN UNIVERSITY

CANTON, CHINA.

1929

敬 献 家 严
继 美 先 生

TO
MY FATHER

PUBLICATION NOTE

The reader will be surprised to find out so many mistakes, and serious mistakes, either in spelling or otherwise, occurred in the following pages. The reason is partly due to the lack of facility in printing matters in English, to say nothing in German or French; and partly due to the inability of reading English or even distinguishing the English letters on the part of the printers. My carelessness and "busyness" should be counted also. In view of this fact, I take much pains to present this book to the public, and if there is any justification for me to publish it, it must be my trust in the genius and understanding of the readers.

I can hardly estimate how much I owe to Professor S. Y. Chen of Lingnan University in publishing this volume and I hope that my grateful appreciation will be a compensation for his long hours of silence.

S. C.
Canton, June 1929

PREFACE

The fundamental principles of the so-called traditional theory of sovereignty may be reduced into two propositions: (1) Sovereignty is, in its nature, indivisible; (2) Sovereignty is the source of law and consequently in order to be called law proper, there must be a sovereign behind it. The first proposition has been attacked in its application to the federal state, and particularly to international relations. The growth and development of functional groups within and across the boundary lines of the state have equally led many writers to deny the first proposition and its implied principle that sovereignty is the essential characteristic of the state. The second has long been challenged by advocates of the natural law school; but formally it has been criticized and discredited by historical jurists, writers of the economic school of jurisprudence and most important and recent of all, by the sociological jurists.

It seems the controversy to which the second proposition gave rise as to whether law is law in the strict sense of the term, if it is not backed by a sovereign, has ceased to have any practical interest. Few writers at the present day, if any, maintain or recognize that law is and must be the creature of sovereignty. The most recent discussion has therefore in the main, been on the question whether or not sovereignty, in its nature, is divisible. The answer given in the dissertation is affirmative. The response so given is based on historical evidence, existing facts, a generally accepted standard of morality, and a comparatively sound and adequate conception in philosophy.

The foregoing may serve as a brief summary of the study in the following pages. It is to be noted, however, that the order of the chapters in the study does not follow exactly the summary.

As the primary purpose of this dissertation is to give a general survey of recent theories of sovereignty, I have, from the first chapter to the last, confined myself to presenting as faithfully as possible what other writers have thought without attempting to criticize them. To attain this end, quotations have been freely used. My point of view will be found in the conclusion; but it is to be added that no originality is claimed for it.

The methods of approaching a subject like this are two: one is chronological and the other according to subject matter. The latter has been emphasized although the former has also been employed when it is in harmony with the latter.

A few works of value to this study have not been used. I regret very much that Hans Kelsen's *Das Problem der Souveranitat und die Theorie des Volkerrechts* has not been available. Professor Johannes Mattern's *Concepts of State, Sovereignty and International Law* and Paul W. Ward's *Sovereignty: A Study of a Contemporary Political Notion* were published after the thesis had been completed. But it is believed that the salient features of recent theories of sovereignty have been noted.

I am deeply indebted to many writers and scholars, particularly to members of the University of Illinois faculty. It is at Professor James W. Garner's suggestion that I have undertaken the present study. From their works, lectures, and personal counsel, Professor Edward C. Hayes of the Sociology Department, Professor Matthew T. McClure of the Philosophy Department, and Professor Clarence A. Berdahl of the Political Science Department have given me much help.

Above all, I wish to pay a tribute with gratitude and affection to Professor John A. Fairlie of the Political Science Department, without whose constant guidance and cordial assistance, the following pages would never have been written. It goes without saying that I am alone responsible for errors and shortcomings.

Su-Ching Chen
Illinois University
Urbana, Illinois
April 1, 1928

INTRODUCTION

Sovereignty, a term generally recognized as having been invented by Bodin in the sixteenth century, has recently been held by some authorities to have been first employed by other French writers notably by Beaumanoir and Loyseau in the fifteenth century.[①] There may be still other investigators who, delving in the literatures of antiquity, will tell us that it was invented before the fifteenth century. But let the inventor be who he may, the truth is that the concept of sovereignty has long been and is still one of the most important concepts in the history of human thought.

Look back to the time of Rome. When the Emperor was in his glorious day, he was regarded as the possessor of this very authority and therefore "the fountain of honor, the author of all legislation, and the referee in all disputes"[②]. He was Jehovah. His act was infallible and his word was final. Nearly a thousand years later, in the scene at Canossa, Henry, the king of one of the greatest countries then in Europe, had to kneel down before the Vicar of God, the ghost, say some of the scholars, of the Roman Emperor coming out from his grave.

On the other hand, men like Dante, the intellectual leader of the "Romans", declared strongly that this authority should be in the hands of the monarch. The keenness of his foresight was realized in the drama of Avignon. It was then the monarch who could do what the Emperor and the Pope had done, because he was then the possessor of sovereignty. The long fight between the Pope and the king ended; but the battle for sovereignty still continued. So came another between the king on the one hand and the people on the other. *Magna Carta*, the Declaration of Rights, it may be said, are only some of its manifestations. It is now well recognized that the day of Louis XIV has gone. This again does not mean that there is no more battle for sovereignty; yet enough has been shown how important it is.

---

① Carlyle: *A History of Mediaeval Political Theory*, Vol. III, *Political Theory from the Tenth Century to the Thirteenth*, 1916, pp. 50–84. See also Garner: *Political Science and Government*, 1928, Chapter VIII, p. 156. Viollet: *Etablissements de Saint Louis*, Vol. II, p. 370. Carre de Malberg: *Theory Generale de l'etat*, Vol. 1, pp. 73–74.

② Sumner: *Folkways*, 1913, p. 82.

This being so, we find that statesmen of our day are wont to speak of it as the vital interest, the soul and the life of their respective beloved countries. With it, they say, there is nothing to fear; without it, there is no hope. The militarists, looking at it as far more important than anything else, are willing to give up all the lives of their fellow-citizens to fight for it. Even the laymen, proud of living under its shadow, look down with contempt on their brothers, other than those who are within their own artificial national border, because they are so unfortunate as to be citizens of a half or partial sovereign state.

Moreover, its importance as such has brought it to the public forum and it has been discussed by learned men in many fields of human knowledge. Some of them claim that the problem of sovereignty is exclusively a subject of their respective fields, while others hold that the subject can never be solved without their help. Thus the lawyer, viewing it as the final power over litigants, declares that it is a legal problem and that only the lawyer can deal with it.① The political scientist, who considers its nature, location and results, claims that largely it is he himself who is qualified to talk about it. The philosopher, seeing its fundamental and universal basis as the ultimate foundation of the state, maintains that it is he who plays the leading role. The economist, seeing it simply as a result of economic conditions, tells us that unless we follow the light that he is bearing, we can never understand what it is.② The moralist, taking it as the inherent right of mankind,③ says that the problem is in its nature one of morality. The psychologist finds that it is nothing more than the unorganized, unconscious influence of public opinions—of the attitudes, impulses and ideas of the voting masses, the rival parties, classes, interests, holding that the problem of sovereignty is essentially a social-psychological problem.④ The sociologist, who approaches it by analyzing its development and the state in their joint evolution as a product of social forces, insists that it should be studied from the sociological point of view. ⑤

Such a wide discussion naturally gives rise to various opinions as to its origin, function, nature and location. To some, it has originated in the family. To some, it can not even be found in the hordes.⑥ To others, it has arisen in the confederacy composed

---

① Commons: "A Sociological View of Sovereignty" in *American Journal of Sociology*, Vol. V, pp. 1-3.
② Loria: *Economic Foundation of Society*. English translation by Lindley M. Keasbey.
③ Laski: *Authority in the Modern State*, pp. 28, 32-65.
④ Williams: *The Foundations of Social Science*, pp. 18-19.
⑤ Barnes: *Sociology and Political Theory*, p. 131.
⑥ Gumplowicz: *Outline of Sociology*, translated by Moore, p. 124.

of the tribes.① To still others, it did not come into light until the modern states came into existence.

As to its function, some say that it is the characteristic—the essential characteristic of the state, so that there can be no state if there is no sovereignty. On the other hand, some hold that the state is nothing more than one of the social institutions or organizations; a state may possess sovereignty, but so do other groups.

As to its nature, there are those who maintain that it is nothing more than power. Where there is power there is sovereignty. Then, there are those who declare that it is something more than a collection of powers; but without possessing power, it can not be realized. Again, there are those who regard it as reason or even God, and that it can not be found in human institutions. Still again, there are those who take it as nothing more than an empty vent through which the air and smoke come and go.

But this is not all, for further study has led many writers to ask whether or not it can be divided, limited, violated; and whether or not it is absolute, infallible, supreme and the like. To this question, some will say yes, and others no. As to its location, at one time it is placed in the Emperor, at another, it is in the monarch, and at another, in the hands of the people. Sometimes, it is located in the government as a whole, sometimes it is placed in the parliament, sometimes in the law-making bodies of the whole country, and sometimes in the electorate.

Sovereignty, then, is one of the most important concepts in the history of human thought, not only in the past, but even more so at the present. The recent attack on the traditional conception of sovereignty may be regarded by some as the death knell of the whole notion of sovereignty, but as a matter of fact, the more vigorous the attack, the wider the discussion tends to be. What will be the result, time alone can tell.

---

① Giddings: *Principles of Sociology*, p. 285.

CHAPTER I
HISTORY OF THE THEORY OF SOVEREIGNTY

I. Introduction

The purpose of this thesis is to give a general survey of recent theories of sovereignty. But no theory stands alone. One theory is always related to another theory or other theories even though they are radically in conflict with each other. We may call a certain theory new, but in order to understand the new theory, a knowledge of the theory or theories of the past as well as those which are contemporary to it is always desirable, and even necessary. The truth seems to be that any theorist who wishes to make an advance or deviation which is relatively new, it is necessary for him to have an adequate understanding of what other people or theorists have done in the held in which he is specializing. But before the new theory or idea comes into existence, usually if not always, he has been already influenced, consciously or unconsciously, by the ideas of others. The so-called idea of his may be different and radically different from those that influence his, but we may not understand his, if we want to understand it throughly, without understanding what has influenced him, although it may not be called his own. In fact, the so-called new theory is usually an outcome of the old theory or theories. One may be regarded as the mother and the other the child. Without the former, the latter seems to be impossible.

Let us take one instance for illustration. Generally speaking we usually say that the theory of the separation of powers was advocated and advanced by the fathers of the constitution of the United States. But when we think of the theory as advocated and defended by the fathers of the constitution; we may not understand it well if we only think of them alone, for we have to look back to Montesquieu, to Locke and even to Polybius and Aristotle. The reason is obvious. We cannot separate them, because they themselves were not separate. We cannot understand one of them without referring to another, because among them one was influenced by another.

In view of what has been said, it is desirable, and even necessary, for us to present a brief sketch of the history of the theory of sovereignty before we proceed to deal with our main subject.

Ⅱ. Greek Conception of Sovereignty—Aristotle

By virtue of his clear and systematic presentation of the subject, "western" writers on the history of the notion of sovereignty usually begin with Aristotle.① This does not mean, however, that before him, there was no theory of sovereignty.② It may even be safe to say that the notion of sovereignty is as old as human thought itself, for the simple reason that the former is a part of the latter, and that men, being the animals of the highest reason, must have some ideas, however crude they may be, concerning supreme authority, if there is such an authority, under which they live.

"Man is by nature a political animal."③ This is a statement upon which Aristotle's whole "political" system is built. Being a political animal he is bound to live within a "political" organization, or a state, because a state is an expression of human nature in its "political" aspect, and at the same time it is the means by which the highest good of human life can be achieved. But being an animal, he can not entirely free himself from doing things "brutal" which may be deemed as obstacles on the way to the highest good; and it is for this reason that a supreme authority, which can restrain the former and secure the latter, is justified and necessary for every "political" organization.

This supreme authority, or to use the proper term, "sovereignty", according to Aristotle's comparative study of the political institutions of his own time and of the past, may be in the hands of one, a few or many. But a philosopher will never be satisfied with what it was and is, so he proceeds to ask what it ought to be. This brings him to assert that authority should be in the mass of the "citizens". The reason is not hard to explain. "For the many, of whom each individual is but an ordinary person, when they meet together may very likely be better than the few good, if regarded not individually, but collectively, just as a feast to which many contribute is better than a dinner provided out of a single purse." ④

---

① I use the adjective "western" here to make it clear that the present study is purely Occidental.
② In fact, men like Mr. Barker have traced the notion of sovereignty to an earlier period than that of Aristotle.
③ I heard a well-known scholar say that to Aristotle the term "Politics" meant social. If this is the case, the term "political" here used in a few places should be changed to "social" in order to do justice to Aristotle, because the recent tendency has been to deny that the notion of sovereignty is purely a political question.
④ Aristotle: *Politics*, translated by B. Jowett, Ⅲ, ⅲ, p. 85.

But like Plato, his master, Aristotle had no full confidence in the mass of the "citizens", for they are easily led by their passions to seek particular and selfish aims and forget the general welfare and public good. In order to avoid such danger, reason alone must be their guide in their actions. What is reason then? It is "nothing else than law and it is therefore necessary if a state is to be normal and directed by unselfish rulers toward the general good, that it should have law for its ultimate sovereignty."① And the writer just quoted tells us in another place that law, to the Greeks in general as well as to Aristotle, "is thus the common spiritual substance in concrete form, and as such it is the cohesive force and the sovereign of society."②

It may be said that, to Aristotle, perhaps the sovereignty of law and that of the people are not two different things in the sense that one is always superior and the other inferior, for men are endowed with both reason and passion. They may act with both or either of them. So far as they act in accordance with their reason, their sovereign power can not be questioned.

Ⅲ. Roman Conception of Sovereignty

The Roman notion of sovereignty was crystalized in a well known statement: "The will of the prince has the force of law, since the people have transferred to him all their right and power."③ It seems that the statement quoted above has been interpreted in different ways under different circumstances. When the emperor or the king's power was at its zenith as it was in the time of Augustus, it was thought that it was he who bore the

---

① Barker: *Political Thought of Plato and Aristotle*, p. 33. See also Aristotle: *Politics*, Jowett's translation, Book Ⅲ, chapters Ⅶ and Ⅷ. See also Dunning: *Political Theories, Ancient and Mediaeval*, p. 71. Cf. Krabbe: *Die Moderne Stasts-ldee*, pp. 15 ff.
② Barker: *Greek Political Theory, Plato and His Predecessors*, 1918, p. 38, footnote.
③ *Institutes*, LI, Part Ⅱ, Section 6.

sovereignty.① But the conception was different before the power of the emperor had developed, or when it was waning. It was argued that the will of the emperor had the force of law because the people had delegated the supreme authority to him. While delegation does not mean alienation, the ultimate sovereignty must be in the hands of the people, and this view seems to have been widely entertained by the Roman jurists.②

Ⅳ. Conception of Sovereignty During the Middle Ages

Professor Figgis once remarked that "in the strict sense of the term, there is no

---

① Cf. Sumner: *Folkways*, 1913, p. 82. "A legal theory of sovereignty," says Professor Duguit, "dates only from the beginning of the Roman Empire. It was the profession of the people as a whole. Capable of being delegated to a single man it was confided to the princeps by the 'lex regia'. It was thus possible for the emperor to concentrate in his person all those powers the Republic had divided between the different magistracies. The imperial power was founded on a two-fold authority; on the one hand the proconsular impression derived from the system of prorogation, and on the other the tribunitian power derived from Plebeian constitutions. The emperor obtained the 'imperium' either from the Senate or from the Army. The people, by the 'lex regia' transferred to him the tribunitian power. In the course of a natural evolution the emperor came to possess both the 'imperium' and the 'postestas', as a right to command inherent in his position. It was no longer a right exercised by popular delegation; it had become a right inherent in his character. The development is achieved at the end of the third century under Diocletian and Constantine. If in the sixth century the Institutes of Justinian still speak of the 'lex regia', it is as a piece of antiquarianism, a phrase copied literally from a text of Ulpian. The fact was that the Roman Emperor equaled his will with law. 'Quod principi placuit legis habet vigorem' is a maxim derived from the fact that the emperor ⟨who⟩ now possesses full sovereignty, can, that is to say, impose his will on others as his right, just because it is his will, just because it therein possesses a quality entitling it to general obedience. So the genius of Rome created a legal theory of public power—later to be called sovereignty—which was to remain until the twentieth century the basis of public law in Europe and America."

See *Law in the Modern State*, translated by Laski, pp. 2-3.

② "The theory of the Roman Lawyers with respect to the people as the sole ultimate source of authority in the state seems to us to be clearly an undeveloped form of the theory of contract. We might call it the theory of consent which is not the same thing as the theory of contract in any of its forms, but is the germ out of which the theory of contract might very well grow... Few phrases in the *Digest* are more familiar than that of Ulpian, 'Quod principi placuit, legis habet vigorem'; some times at least it has been forgotten that Ulpian continues, 'utpote cum lege regia, quae de imperio ejus lata est, populus ei et in eum omne suum imperium et potestatem conferat'." Few phrases are more remarkable than this almost paradoxical description of an unlimited personal authority founded upon a purely democratic basis. The Emperor's will is law, but only because the people choose to have it so. Ulpian's words sum up in a single phrase the universal theory of the lawyers; so far as we have seen, there is no other view known to Roman jurisprudence. From Julianus, in the earlier part of the second century, to Justinian himself in the sixth, the Emperor is the source of law, but only because the people by their own legislative act have made him so: The matter is of much importance that we must justify this judgement by an examination of all the writers of the *Digest* who, so far as we have found, refer to the question.

Carlyle: *A History of Medieval Political Theory* Ⅰ, pp. 63-64.

sovereign in the Middle Ages."① While this may be true to a certain extent in an actual state, we must not be mistaken by concluding that the absence of the sovereign involves the absence of the notion of sovereignty. Generally speaking, the theories of sovereignty in the Middle Ages may be grouped into three schools: namely, the theory of the sovereignty of the church, that of the king or emperor, and that of the people.

The argument presented by the first is that there are two worlds, the temporal and the spiritual. The latter is like the sun, and the former, the moon. The moon gets its light from the sun, so the temporal world receives its power from the spiritual one. Since the church is the representative of the latter, it has authority over the temporal.②

The argument advanced by the second is that human nature, being twofold, demands two guides, emperor and pope. Both of them get their power directly from God. "Each had his sphere, and each abode in his sphere. The things that were Caesar's were rendered to Caesar and the things that were Peter's to Peter." They admit that the pope is supreme in handling things spiritual; but so far as temporal things are

---

① Figgsi, *Studies of Political Thought, From Gerson to Grotius*, p. 11. Professor Maitland expressed the same idea in his *Collected Papers*. "Above all things we must," says Carlyle, "if we are to make our way at all, discard the common conception of sovereignty, the conception that a law represents the mere command of a lawgiver, or even of a community. This conception, whose value in regard to modern times we cannot here discuss, is wholly foreign to the Middle Ages." A. J. Carlyle, *A History of Mediaeval Political Theory in the West*, Vol. Ⅲ, p. 41.

② The policy of the Hildebrandine school, and the politoecclesiastical thought which lies behind it, are of cardinal importance in mediaeval thought. The key-note of that policy was "justitia". "Justitia" meant, in the first place, the papal sovereignty over the Church. The Christ incarnate in a visible, historical, traditional church must have His visible representative as the head of that church on earth, the fountain of all ecclesiastical power, the exponent of all religious tradition. In the second place, "justitia" meant the liberation of the clergy from the lay world—from the social bond of matrimony, the economic bond of simony, and the feudal bond of lay investiture. In a sense, therefore, it meant the separation of the Church from the State. But the separation of the Church from the State was not the separation of State from the Church. The sovereign Pope might exclude the temporal power from things spiritual; he could not, being sovereign, exclude the spiritual power from things temporal. "Justitia", therefore, meant, in the third place, the right of the pope, as the sovereign exponent of the sovereign law of Christ, to judge and correct even kings and princes if they contravened that law or hindered its free operation. In principle, therefore, (I quote the words from Troltsch), "the state is subordinated to the Church, as an instrument under the control of the Church for the governance of temporal things, and for the bringing of temporal relations and values under the absolute spiritual purpose of which the hierarchy is guardian. The dogma of universal episcopacy involves for its completion the dogma of theocracy". *Mediaeval Political Thought* by E. Barker in F. J. C. Hearnshaw's *Social and Political Ideas of Some Great Mediaeval Thinkers*, p. 13, see also p. 15. See also Gierke, *Political Theories of the Middle Ages*, translated by Maitland, pp. 15 ff.

See also Carlyle, *ibid.*, Chapter Ⅹ, Vol. Ⅱ.

concerned, the emperor or the king alone must be regarded as sovereign. ①

The argument given by those who held the sovereignty of the people was largely based on the argument of Aristotle and of the Roman jurists. They insisted that the ultimate sovereignty was in the hand of the people on the ground, as one of the most conspicuous representatives said, that "men have come together into civil association for the sake of convenience and the resulting sufficiency of life, and in order to escape the opposite conditions"②. Thus "the undeveloped form of the theory of contract" as phrased by Professor Carlyle finds its higher significance here. ③

There is no doubt that from the time of Greece to the end of the Middle Ages, the theories of sovereignty are different in the writings of different writers as well as in different ages, yet there is a similarity among them, that is, all of the writers confine themselves to the question of where sovereignty is. No attempt was made to solve or even to ask the question of what it is. It was in the writing of Bodin that the answer given to this latter question was first found in the history of the theory of sovereignty. It is in the doctrine of sovereignty, as it is said, that Bodin made his most distinctive contribution to political theory. It is this doctrine, moreover, that has exerted a great influence on the theorits of latter generations. ④

V. Early Modern Conception of Sovereignty

A. Sovereignty of the King

1. Bodin

Bodin is not an absolutist as used to be thought. The starting point of his notion of the location of sovereignty is not different from those who maintained popular sovereignty. Originally, he thinks that sovereignty was in the hands of the people, and he even goes so far as to assert that if the people do not give up their sovereignty to some

---

① See Dante: *De Monarchia*. —Pierre Du Bois even went so far as to declare that the Pope should hand over his temporal authority to the French King and that the French King alone should rule the earth. But even he recognized that the Pope might exercise the spiritual authority. See E. E. Power: "Pierre Du Bois and the Domination of France" in Hearnshaw's *The Social and Political Ideas of Some Great Mediaeval Thinkers*, pp. 139-166.

② Marsiglio: *The Defensor Pacis*, Book I, Chapter XII. See Coker: *Readings in Political Philosophy*, p. 164.

③ The leading exponents of this school were Marsiglio of Padua, and William of Ockum. See Gierke: *Political Theories of the Middle Ages*, translated by Maitland, pp. 38-60.

④ Profesor Figgis writes: "His (Dodin) book is the first treatise on sovereignty in the strict sense and was used very shortly after for lectures at Cambridge. All subsequent writers from Hobbes to Sidgwick and Professor Holland go back to him." *From Gerson of Grotius*, p. 126. See also Pollock: *The History of the Science of Politics*, pp. 47 ff.

one or few for a considerable period of time, the sovereignty is still in the hands of the people. Thus he writes: "But suppose that supreme power, unlimited by laws, and without protest or appeal, be granted by the people to some one or few, shall we say that the latter have sovereignty? For he has sovereignty who, after God, acknowledges no one greater than himself. I hold that sovereignty resides not in such person, but in the people, at whose pleasure they hold their power, or to whom they must return their authority at the expiration of the period designated. The people cannot be considered as having divested themselves of their power when they intrust supreme authority, unrestrained by laws, to one or a few, if the commitment is for a certain period of time, or at the pleasure of the people; for in either case the holders of the supreme authority must render account of their doings to the prince or people, who, being sovereign, are required to give account to no one, save immortal God."①

But if the people give up their sovereignty to a person or persons for his or their whole life, then that person or those persons may be said to have and possess the real unconditional sovereignty. "If the power," says he, "is given unlimited by laws, and without the name of magistrate, deputy, governor, or guardian, and not at the pleasure of any one, certainly it must be confessed that sovereign rights have been conceded to such a one. The people in such ⟨a⟩ case have despoiled themselves of their authority, in order to give to another all the privileges of sovereignty, without conditions; in like manner as anyone might by pure gift surrender to another the ownership and possession of his property; such a perfect donation contains no conditions."② From what has been said and quoted, it may be gathered that it is by reason of his time and environment that made, or forced if you like, Bodin to attribute the sovereignty to the monarch or king. He thinks differently from those who hold that sovereignty is an inherent right of the king and therefore it is the king alone who receives it from God.③ Had he been born at a different time and under different circumstances, one may venture to say, he would have been no less a believer and advocate of the doctrine of popular sovereignty.

In reading Bodin's writings one is led to notice that he speaks of two kinds of sovereignty. One is spiritual and the other temporal. The former is called divine sovereignty; and the latter, originally vested with the people, he prefers to give to the king or prince. The sovereignty of the latter, particularly that of the prince, must be in conformity with the former, for divine sovereignty is superior to princely sovereignty. It

---

① Bodin: *De Republica*, p. 126. English translation, see Coker's *Readings in Political Philosophy*, p. 231.
② *Ibid.*, p. 128.
③ Cf. *ibid.*, p. 134.

is this premise that leads him to conclude that the sovereignty of the prince is limited by the law of God. "No one," he says, "who attempts to abrogate or weaken the law of God can escape the judgement of divine sovereignty."① Again he says, "If justice is the end of law, and law is the command of the prince, and the prince is the image of almighty God, then the laws of the prince should bear the stamp of divine laws."② Here we see that Bodin, being born in a time which was not far from, or, if you like, still a part of, the Middle Ages, could not free himself from the theological atmosphere and the dogma that human power is an emanation of God.

Having considered the location and the kinds of sovereignty, let us come to his conception of the nature or characteristics of sovereignty. This is certainly the heart and the corner-stone of his theory of sovereignty and therefore his political system as a whole. Sovereignty is defined as the supreme power over citizens and subjects, unrestrained by law.③ From this definition, there come the following principles. Sovereignty in the first place is absolute since it is the supreme authority in the commonwealth and it is wholly free from the law that it makes and subject to no conditions or limitations. Secondly, it is perpetual or unlimited in time, for as has been pointed out, the power given to a person only for a short time is not sovereignty.④ In connection with this, there comes a third principle, namely, that of inalienability and delegation. It seems, however, that Bodin is not clear on this point.⑤ He thinks that sovereignty is by no means inalienable, for sovereignty which is originally in the hands of the people may be given up to a person or a few persons just "as any one might by pure gift surrender to another the ownership and possession of his property"⑥. But alienation involves perpetuity of time, and if it is to be alienated, it must be so for the whole life, because delegation of powers for a short period is not a transfer of sovereignty. Fourthly, sovereignty is indivisible, for there can not be two supreme

---

① Bodin: *De Republica*, p. 134.
② *Ibid.*
③ *Ibid.*, p. 123.
④ *Ibid.*, p. 126. "What if supreme power be conferred for a period of ten years; as in Athens one archon, whom they called judge, stood thus preeminent in power in the city? Still the sovereignty of the state did not rest in him; he was rather curator or deputy for the people, and had to render account to them. What if the high power of which I speak be given to one or more for a year, with no requirement that account of their actions be given to any one? So the Cnidians every year chose sixty citizens whom they called 'amymones', that is, men superior to any limitation or censure. Sovereignty, nevertheless, was not in them, since they were compelled, at the expiration of the year, to surrender their authority."
⑤ See Merriam: *History of the Theory of Soverignty*, p. 14.
⑥ Bodin: *ibid.*, p. 128.

authorities within a state. It seems to Bodin, that power should be differentiated from sovereignty. Power may be divided, but not soverignty. Thus the power of making laws may some times be given to a magistrate or shared by an assembly or senate, but the sovereignty always remains one. ①

A few words remain to be said concerning the function of sovereignty. "The first and principal function of sovereignty," says Bodin, "is to give law to the citizens generally and individually…And under this supreme power of ordaining and abrogating laws, it is clear that all other functions of sovereignty are included; so that it may be truly said that supreme authority in the state is comprised in this one thing—namely, to give laws to all and each of the citizens, and to receive none from them."② In the language of Professor Dunning, "Legislation, then, is not only the chief function of the sovereign; it is practically the sole and all inclusive function."③ The declaration and making of peace, the appointment of magistrates; jurisdiction on final appeal; the pardoning power; the exaction of oaths of fidelity and obedience from all subjects; the coining of money; and the imposition of taxes, "though seeming to involve what is alien to the term law, are yet accomplished by law, that is by decree of the supreme power"④.

2. Hobbes

The theory of the sovereignty of the king or monarch as advanced in the writing of Bodin was developed to the utmost in the works of Hobbes. The starting point of Hobbes' theory is the state of nature in which there is no "people" and no king, in which might is right and in which everywhere, turbulence, confusion and anarchy are to be found. Thus the state of nature is a state of war where "men live without a common power to keep them all in awe, they are in that condition which is called war; and such a war, as is of every man against every man"⑤.

It is clear then that a common power is necessary for keeping men in awe, and

---

① Merriam: *History of the Theory of Sovereignty*, p. 134.
② *Ibid.*, pp. 240-243.
③ Dunning: *Political theories, from Luther to Montesquieu*, p. 103.
④ Bodin: *ibid.*, p. 243. Also Hancke: *Bodin: Eine Studie uber den Souverainetat*.
⑤ Hobbes' *Leviathan*. See *Collected Works*, by W. Molesworth, Vol. Ⅲ, pp. 112-113.

directing their actions to the common benefit.① But how can this power—sovereign power—be attained? Hobbes' own language in response to this question is plain: "The attaining to this sovereign," he "is by two ways. One by natural force; as when a man maketh his children, to submit themselves, and their children to his government, as being able to destroy them if they refuse; or by war subdueth his enemies to his will, giving them their lives on that condition. The other is when men agree amongst themselves, to submit to some man, or assembly of men, voluntarily, on confidence to be protected by him against all others. This latter may be called a political commonwealth, or commonwealth by 'institution'; and the former, a commonwealth by 'acquisition'."②

Sovereignty then may either be attained by force or by covenant.③ One is compulsory, while the other is voluntary. It is for fear of death, of bonds, of anarchy and the like that men, singly or collectively, come to submit to a common power or sovereignty. But in one case, i. e., in case of a commonwealth by acquisition, men are afraid of the force of the strongest; while in the other case, men submit to the sovereignty because they fear one another.④ Since sovereignty is an outcome of fear, whether it is the fear of one another or of a particular one, the sovereign so originated is

---

① *Collected Works*, Vol. II, p. 75.

"The only way to erect such a common power, as may be able to defend them from the invasion of foreigners, and the injuries of one another, and thereby to secure them in such sort, as that by their own industry, and by the fruits of the earth, they may nourish themselves and live contentedly; is, to confer all their power and strength upon one man, or upon one assembly of men, that may reduce all their wills, by plurality of voices, unto one man, or assembly of men, that may reduce all their wills, by plurality of voices, unto one will: which is as much as to say, to appoint one man, or assembly of men, to bear their persons; and every one to own, and acknowledge himself to be author of whatsoever he that so beareth their person, shall act, or cause to be acted, in those things which concern the common peace and safety; and therein to submit their wills, every one to his will, and their judgement to his judgement. This is more than consent, or concord; it is a real unity of them all, in one and the same person, made by covenant of every man with every man, 'I authorize and give up my right of governing myself, to this man, to this assembly of men, on this condition, that thou give up thy right to him, and authorize all his actions in like manner.'" *Works*, Vol. III, pp. 157-158.

② *Works*, Vol. III, pp. 158-159.

③ "A commonwealth is said to be instituted when a multitude of men do agree, and covenant, every one, with every one, that to whatsoever man, or assembly of men, shall be given by the major part the right to present the person of them all, that is to say, to be their representative; every one, as well as he that voted for it as he that voted against it, shall authorize all the actions and judgements of that man, or assembly of men, in the same manner, as if they were his own, to the end to live peaceably amongst themselves, and to be protected against other men. From this institution of a commonwealth are derived all the rights and faculties of him, or them, on whom sovereignty is conferred by the consent of the people assembled." *Works*, Vol. III, p. 159.

④ *Works*, Vol. III, p. 185.

outside and above the other persons whom we may call subjects. In the case of sovereignty by acquisition, the sovereign is outside and above all the others in the commonwealth, because by nature he is the strongest, for he may be the father of all or the victor in war. In the case of sovereignty by institution or covenant, it is the others who agree "among themselves" to give the very authority to him. In either sense, there is no contract between the sovereign and the other persons or subjects.

By reason of being outside and above other persons or subjects, the sovereign power ought to be absolute. Here we see the justification for the absolutism of Hobbes. The sovereign power, says he, "is as great, as possibly men can be imagined to make it."① And he has reason for this: "And though of so unlimited a power men may fancy many evil consequences, yet the [the] consequences of the want of it, which is perpetual war of every man against his neighbour, are much worse. The condition of man in this life shall never be without inconveniences; but there happeneth in no commonwealth any great inconvenience, but what proceeds from the subject's disobedience, and breach of those covenants, from which the commonwealth hath its being. And whatsoever thinking sovereign power too great, will seek to make less, must subject himself, to the power, that can limit it; that is to say, to a greater."②

What then are the rights and consequences of this absolute sovereignty? Here is an excellent summary: "His power can not, without his consent, be transferred to another: he cannot forfeit it: he cannot be accused by any of his subjects, of injury; he cannot be punished by them: he is judge of what is necessary for peace, and judge of doctrines: he is sole legislator; and supreme judge of controversies; and of the times, and occasions of war, and peace: to him it belongeth to chose magistrates, counsellors, commanders, and all other officers, and ministers; and to determine of rewards and punishments, honour, and order."③

The location of sovereignty. It remains to be considered ⟨that⟩ Sovereignty, according to Hobbes, may be in the hand of one, a few or many. But in either case, it is indivisible, and this is one of the essential characteristics of sovereignty.④ If it is in the hands of one, the form of the commonwealth is monarchy; if a few, aristocracy; and if many, democracy. While possibility or practice shows that sovereignty may be vested in the hands of one, a few or many, Hobbes strongly insists that it should be in the hands of one.

---

① *Works*, Vol. III, p. 195.
② *Ibid*.
③ *Ibid*., p. 186; also pp. 159 ff.
④ *Ibid*., p. 167; also p. 171.

B. Popular Sovereignty

1. **Monarchomachs**

Over against the theory of the sovereignty of the monarch held by Bodin and Hobbes and some other writers, [1] stood that of popular sovereignty held by a group of writers known as Monarchomachs at the end of the sixteenth century and the beginning of the seventeenth century, by Locke in the latter part of the seventeenth century and most important of all, by Rousseau in the eighteenth century. The leading Monarchomachs were widely spread over Europe, notably, Languet and Hotman in France, Buchanan in Scotland, and Althusius in Germany. "The central features of the doctrine were the original and inalienable sovereignty of the people, the contractual origin of government, the fiduciary character of all political authority, and the consequent right of the people to resist and destroy the existing rulers whenever found guilty of a breach of trust."[2]

2. **Locke**

The historical influence under which Locke wrote his *Two Treatises of Government* (1690) was that of the Revolution of 1688 in England. He agrees with Hobbes that there is a state of nature. But to him, the state of nature is not a state of war. The mark of the state of nature is the want of a common judge and authority. The absence of a common judge and authority leads to a state of inconvenience for individuals to maintain their natural rights against injustice. Accordingly, a body politic was formed by individuals by means of a compact.[3] In this body politic, the legislature is the supreme governmental power or sovereignty, because it is the representative body of the people. In a limited sense, the executive branch is also supreme when the legislature is not in session. But neither the executive nor the legislative department is the final authority of the body politic, for back of them stands the people who are the real sovereign which is active in

---

[1] The theory of the sovereignty of the king was defended also by men like James Ⅰ and Filmer. For the views of James Ⅰ, see his *Basilicon Doron, True Law of Free Monarchies and Remonstrance for the Right of Kings*. For Filmer's views, see his *Patriarcha, or the Natural Power of Kings* (1630) published in Morley's edition of Locke's *Two Treatises of Civil Government*. For the general discussion of the theory of James and Filmer, see G. P. Gooch: *Political Thought in England from Bacon to Halifax*; Figgis: *Divine Right of Kings*; Dunning: *Political Theories, from Luther to Montesquieu*; C. H. McIlwain: "The Political Works of James Ⅰ" in *Harvard Political Clasics*, Vol. Ⅰ; Lask: "Political Ideas of Tames Ⅰ" in *Political Science Quarterly*, ⅩⅩⅩⅣ.

[2] Merriam: *History of the Theory of Sovereignty*, p. 24. See also Dunning: "The Monarchomachs' Theories of Popular Sovereignty in the Sixteenth Centuary" in *Political Science Quarterly*, Vol. ⅩⅨ, pp. 277 ff. ; Figgis: *Studies of Political Thought, from Gerson to Grotius*, Lecture Ⅴ; Gierke: *Johannes Althusius* (1880); R. M. Treumann: *Die Monarchomachen* (1895); Gumplowicz: *Ceschichte der Staatstheorien* (1926 edition), pp. 182 ff.

[3] It is to be noted however, that the word "sovereignty" does not occur in Locke's *Two Treatises of Government*.

time of revolution and latent under normal conditions. ①

3. Rousseau

Just as the theory of the sovereignty of the monarch reaches its highest climax in the writings of Hobbes, so the theory of popular sovereignty develops to its extreme in the writings of Rousseau. Rousseau, Locke and Hobbes are the three leading exponents of the social contract theory. While the appearance of Rousseau's *Social Contract* was much later than both Locke and Hobbes, that he was influenced by these two writers is generally recognized by scholars. In the language of Professor Dunning, "he defined sovereignty with the fullness and precision of Hobbes, and gave it an abode an operation that satisfied the feeling of Locke"②.

Like Hobbes and Locke, he begins with a state of nature; but, to him, it is not a state of war or a state in which there is no common judge or authority. It is a state in which men are equal, self-sufficient and content, in a word, it is a state of ideal happiness. However, the increase of population and the advance of civilization brings evils. "Then this primitive condition can no longer subsist, and the human race would perish unless it changed its mode of existence."③

The mode of existence which men are forced to change is "to find a form of association which may defend and protect with the whole force of the community the person and property of every associate, and by means of which each coalescing with all, may nevertheless obey only himself, and remain as free as before"④. And then he writes: "If, then, we set aside what is not of the essence of the social contract, we shall find that it is reducible to the following terms: Each of us puts in common his person and his whole power under the supreme direction of the general will; and in return we receive every member as an indivisible part of the whole. Forthwith, instead of the

---

① While the pendulum was swinging from sovereignty of the monarch to that of the people or vice versa from the end of the sixteenth century to the close of the seventeenth century, another theory was developed by Grotius, and to a certain extent by his followers (I mean particularly Pufendorf) a compromise in its nature, and by no means insignificant. In contrast to Bodin and Hobbes, he holds that sovereignty may be divided. "Thus the Roman Imperial power," says he, "was often divided, so that one ruler had the East and another the West; even into three parts." Again in contrast to Bodin, he maintains that sovereignty is not perpetual and may be limited by time. On the other hand, he agrees with Bodin and Hobbes in denying that sovereignty belongs always to the people, and that it may be transferred to the king; unlike them, he believes that it is capable of being alienated; and once it is alienated, it cannot be taken back, for although such transfer is voluntary at first, it becomes compulsory afterwards. "Thus a woman accepts a person as her husband, whom afterwards she is obliged forever to obey."

② Dunning: *Political Theories, from Rousseau to Spencer*, p. 22.

③ Rousseau: *Social Contract*, trans. by H. J. Tozer, Bk. I, p. 109.

④ *Ibid*.

individual personalities of all the contracting parties, this act of association produces a moral and collective body, which is composed of as many members as the assembly has voices, and which receives from this same act its unity, its common self (son moi commun), its life, and its will. This public person, which is thus formed by the union of all the individual members, formerly took the name of 'city', and now takes that of 'republic' or 'body politic', which is called by its members 'state' when it is passive, 'sovereign' when it is active, 'power' when it is compared to similar bodies."①

It is clear then that out of the social compact comes a general will "which is the soul and the spirit, the sovereign in the state". The sovereignty or the general will, being a creation of the individuals, binds or favours equally all the individuals who are now the citizens of the state. It gives no special privileges to one or makes harm to another, but treats them all alike. "By whatever path we return to our principle we always arrive at the same conclusion, viz. that the social compact establishes among the citizens such an equality that they all pledge themselves under the same conditions and ought all to enjoy the same rights. Thus, by the nature of the compact, every act of sovereignty, that is, every authentic act of the general will, binds or favours equally all the citizens; so that the sovereign knows only the body of the nation, and distinguishes none of those that compose it." But the act of sovereignty "is not an agreement between a superior and an inferior, but an agreement of the body with each of its members; a lawful agreement, because it has the social contract as its foundation; equitable, because it is common to all; useful, because it can have no other object than the general welfare, and stable because it has the public force and the supreme power as a guarantee. So long as the subjects submit only to such conventions, they obey no one, but simply their own will; and to ask how far the respective rights of the sovereign and citizens extend is to ask up to what point the latter can make engagements among themselves, each with all and all with each"②.

Let us come now to some of the characteristics of sovereignty or general will. In the first place, sovereignty is inalienable. "Sovereignty," says he, "being nothing but the exercise of the general will, can never be alienated, and the sovereign power, which is only a collective being, can be represented by itself alone; power indeed can be transmitted, but not will."③ It is, secondly, indivisible. "For the same reason that

---

① Rousseau, *Social Contract*, trans. by H. J. Tozer, Bk. I, pp. 110–112.
② *Ibid.*, Book II, Chapter IV, p. 127.
③ *Ibid.*, p. 119.

sovereignty is inalienable it is indivisible."① To divide it is nothing more than "a fantastic story which, as is said, the Japanese conjurers cut up a child before the eyes of spectators, then, throwing all its limbs into the air, they make the child come down again alive and whole"②.

It is, thirdly, "always right and tends to the public advantage"③. "The sovereign," he maintains, "being formed only of the individuals that compose it, neither has nor can have any interest contrary to theirs; consequently the sovereign power needs no guarantee towards its subjects, because it is impossible that the body should wish to injure its members; and we shall see hereafter that it can injure no one as an individual. The sovereign, for the simple reason that it is so, is always everything that it ought to be."④ It is, fourthly, absolute. "As nature gives every man an absolute power over all his limbs, the social pact gives the body politic absolute power over all its members."⑤ Being absolute, it can not be judged, for it is as a matter of fact, the judge of all.⑥

It is, fifthly, not to be represented, because it consists essentially in the general will, and the will cannot be represented.⑦ "This being so, what is the position of the deputy of the people? To him, they are not and cannot be its representatives; they are only its commissioners and can conclude nothing definitely. Every law which the people in person have not ratified is invalid; it is not a law."⑧ Sovereignty, it is to be added, is sacred and inviolable.⑨

We have considered the origin, nature and characteristics of sovereignty or general will, but further questions may be asked. By general will, is it meant the will of all or the will of a majority? According to Rousseau, the answer given to this question should be two-fold, because it is necessary to make a distinction between the general will for forming a social compact and the general will for making law or doing any act after the

---

① Rousseau: *Social Contract*, trans. by H. J. Tozer, Bk. I, p. 121.
② *Ibid*.
③ *Ibid*., p. 123.
④ *Ibid*., Book I, Chapter VII, p. 113.
⑤ *Ibid*., Book II, Chapter IV, p. 125. In another place he says, "But the body politic or sovereign, deriving its existence only from the sanctity of the contract, can never bind itself, even to others, in any thing that derogates from the original act, such as alienation of some portion of itself, or submission to another sovereign. To violate the act by which it exists would be to annihilate itself; and what is nothing produces nothing." p. 112.
⑥ "Each one loses, by the social pact...only that part of his freedom the use of which is of importance to the community...But we must agree also that the sovereign is the judge of this important matter."
⑦ *Ibid*., Book III, Chapter XV, p. 187.
⑧ *Ibid*.
⑨ *Ibid*., Book II, Chapter IV, p. 127.

body politic has been established. In the former case, and only in the former case, the will of all is necessary, because "civil association is the most voluntary act in the world; every man being born free and master of himself, no one can, under any pretext whatever, enslave him without his consent"①.

On the contrary, sovereign and governmental acts may be determined by the majority in the latter case. "Excepting the original contract," he writes, "the vote of the majority always binds all the rest, this being a result of the contract itself. But it will be asked how a man can be free and yet forced to conform to wills which are not his own. How are opponents free and yet subject to laws they have not consented to? I reply that the question is wrongly put. The citizen consents to all the laws, even to those which are passed in spite of him, and even to those which punish him when he dares to violate any of them. The unvarying will of all the members of the state is the general will; it is through that that they are citizens and free. When a law is proposed in the assembly of the people, what is asked of them is not exactly whether they approve the proposition or reject it, but whether it is conformable or not to the general will, which is their own; each one in giving his vote expresses his opinion thereupon; and from the counting of the votes is obtained the declaration of the general will. When, therefore, the opinion opposed to my own prevails, that simply shows that I was mistaken, and that what I considered to be the general will was not so. Had my private opinion prevailed, I should have done something other than I wished; and in that case I should not have been free."②

VI. Reactionary Movement

The important role that Rousseau's theory has played in human history seems to be obvious.③ To say nothing of his influence other than in his own country, the French Revolution seems to demonstrate to the world its significance. And Henry Maine, a vigorous critic, tells us that "the world has not seen more than once or twice in all the course of history a literature which has exercised such prodigious influence over the minds of men, over every cast and shade of intellect, as that which emanated from

---

① Rousseau: *Social Contract*, trans. by H. J. Tozer, Book IV, Chapter II, p. 200.
② *Ibid.*, pp. 200-201.
③ See Paul Janet: *Histoire des Doctrines Politiques*, Second edition, Vol. II, p. 612. Cf. Duguit: "The Law and the State", *Harvard Law Review*, Vol. XXXI, pp. 27 ff.

Rousseau between 1749 and 1762"①.

Few deny Rousseau's influence on the French Revolution and perhaps none denies that the French Revolution was the most epoch-making event in the history of the world. But how much the French Revolution has done to the world is open to question. To some, who, regardless of the means, look only to the end, like St. Beuve, "it came like the law of Sinai, amid thunder and lightning—and foreigners loved it as much as we did". To others who do not care to think of its end and look only to the means, it is just miserable as the Great Deluge sent from Heaven. Mr. Burke is not the only one who holds this latter view,② and perhaps it may be said that this latter view has been widely accepted, especially during and right after the Terror.

To criticize the French Revolution, writers have gone a step further to review carefully the principles upon which the revolution was built. This new movement has sometimes been called the reactionary theory or anti-revolutionary theory. The writers in this new movement are many, yet they may be grouped into a few schools. Let us discuss briefly the leading schools of this new movement.

1. Kantian School—Idealist

Kant, the leader of idealism, was Rousseau's "legitimate successor". "He formally accepted the contract," says Professor Merriam, "but by his distinction between the ideal and real agreement damaged the revolutionary theory cause more than if he had directly opposed it."③

Being profoundly imbued by Rousseau, he started his theory just as Rousseau did. "The act by which the people organize themselves into a State, or rather the simple idea of this act which alone permits conceiving of its legitimacy, is the *original contract*, by virtue of which all the people set aside their freedom of action to resume it immediately thereafter as members of a commonwealth, that is, to receive back their liberty from the people, as a State. And we cannot say that the State, or that men in the State, have sacrificed for a certain end to be attained a part of their innate liberty of conduct. But each one has renounced entirely savage and unregulated liberty, in order to find his general liberty once more intact in a legal dependence, that is to say, in a juridical state, since this dependence results from his own legislative will."④

---

① Maine: *Ancient Law*, Chapter Ⅵ.
② Burke: *Reflections on the Revolution in France* (1790).
③ Merriam: *History of the Theory of Sovereignty*, p. 40.
④ See Kant's *Philosophy of Law*, trans. by W. Hastie, p. 169, English version, *Harvard Law Review*, Vol. XXXI, p. 44.

Besides agreeing with Rousseau that out of the social contract comes the political organization, he also agrees with him that a sovereign general will come into being as soon as the political organization is established. But Kant is radically different from Rousseau in that while the state and its sovereignty, in the mind of the latter are nothing more than human creation, they are, to the former, truly ideal or divine. Thus, to Kant, in an ideal state, there may be a political organization and a sovereignty created by compact, but this does not happen in an actual state. Criticizing those who hold that there is a social contract in a practical state, Kant writes: "Where there is no record of anything like a compact actually proposed to the commonwealth, or accepted by the sovereign, or sanctioned by both, these thinkers have assumed the idea of an 'original contract' which is always involved in reason, as a thing which must have 'actually' happened; but thus they supposed that the right was always reserved to the people in the case of any gross violation of it in their judgement, to resile from it at pleasure."①

In short, Kant makes a distinction between the ideal state and sovereignty and the actual state and sovereignty. In the former, sovereign power rests on the union of the wills of all, while in the latter it is in the hands of those who hold actual power. Thus he starts with the premise of Rousseau, but he ends like Hobbes. Like Hobbes, he attributes this practical sovereignty to the head of the state—the monarch. The origin of the supreme power of the monarch is inscrutable and all one can do is to obey it without resistance. "The origin of the supreme power", he writes, "is practically 'inscrutable' by the people who are placed under its authority. In other words, the subject need not 'reason too curiously' in regard to its origin in the practical relation, as if the right of the obedience due to it were to be doubted (jus controversum). For a people, in order to be able to adjudicate with a title of right regarding the supreme power in the state, must be regarded as already united under one common legislative will, it cannot judge otherwise than as the present Supreme Head of the state (summus imperans) wills."②

Undoubtedly Kant takes pains to distinguish between the ideal state and the practical state. But the reason is obvious. "It is hard," says Professor Dunning, "in the days of Frederick the Great and his successors for a royal subject of the Hohenzollerns to think of a king as merely a chief executive. Few philosophers were free themselves from the idea that something, at least, of sovereignty inhered in the monarch, no matter how peremptorily they preached the absolute supremacy of the people or the nation or the

---

① Kant: *Principles of Politics*, trans. by Hastie, p. 53.
② Kant: *Philosophy of Law*, p. 174. Also *Principles of Politics*, p. 55.

state."① But being an idealist, Kant thinks more of his ideal state, and he presumes that there is a tendency toward the realization of the ideal state and the ideal soverignty.② Here we see that Kant comes back to his master's position, at least in his future world.

As to the nature of sovereignty, Kant follows Rousseau to a certain extent. He holds that sovereignty is one and absolute, but at the same time it is three-fold. Each of three is sovereign, yet as there is only one state, there is one sovereignty. "Every state," he says, "contains within itself three powers, that is to say, the unity of the general will may be decomposed into three persons, 'trias politica'; the sovereign power (Herrschergewalt), which is found in the person of the legislator; the executive power (Vollziehendegewalt), in the person who controls the enforcement of the law, and judicial power (Rechtsprechendegewalt), in the person of the judge, who renders unto each that which belongs to him according to law. It is like the three propositions of practical syllogism: the major, which contains the law of a will; the minor, the command to act according to law, that is to say, the principle of subsumption of action according to law; and finally the conclusion, the judgement, which decides which is right in the case in question."③

2. Religious School

Another attack directed against the revolutionary theory came from the religious

---

① Dunning: *Political Theories, from Rousseau to Spencer*, p. 134.

② Kant: *Philosophy of Law*, pp. 257-258.

③ Duguit: "The Law and the State", *Harvard Law Review*, Vol. Ⅲ, p. 46. Cf. Hastie's translation, Kant's *Philosophy of Law*, pp. 161 - 162. Among the writers in the idealistic school, besides Kant, Fichte deserves our special attention. It seems that Fichte is not free himself from the inconsistency of his master's dual system, as he asserts that the actual state must be made to approximate more and more to the rational state. He rejects the idea of pre-political state of nature, yet admits the necessity of a social contract which must undergo three processes, namely, the property contract, the protection contract and the union contract. The last named completes the social contract and constitutes a sovereign with the duty of enforcing the previous agreements and to protect the rights of the citizens. The sovereign power so constituted must rest with the unorganized people, because the people as a unity cease to exist when the sovereign comes into being. Although the sovereign is in the hands of the people, they should not rebel against it, not because they cannot do so, but because to do so means to rebel against themselves. See J. G. Fichte: *Rudiment of Natural Right* (*Grundlage des Naturrechts*), 1796, 1797.

See also A. E. Kroeger's translation under the title *Science of Rights*. Cf. J. S. Beck: *Commentar uber Kant's Metaphysik der Sitten*, 1798. D. C. Reidnits: *Naturrecht*, 1803. T. Schmalz: *Handbuch der Rechtsphilosophie*, 1807. Bauer: *Leherbuch des Naturrechts*.

school, led by a group of writers in Germany and France.① The expression of this school is to be found in articles of the Holy Alliance of 1815, in which, among other things, it is declared that "the Christian nations of which they and their people are part, have no other sovereign than Him to whom alone belongs the power"②.

On its destructive side, the writers of this school deny the possibility of the creation of a sovereign power by human beings as the church fathers of the Middle Ages did. They attack the doctrine of sovereignty as a result of social contract. "If the people," one writer declares, "are legitimately sovereign, then, all laws made by them must be just, but justice rests upon a broader and deeper basis than this."③ Another exponent even goes so far as to say that democracy is an association of men without sovereignty.④

On its constructive side, it recognizes the sovereignty of the monarch, it advocates the relation of the church and the state, it even demands the restoration of Papal oversight of the secular power. In short it is thoroughly mediaeval in character.⑤

3. Patrimonial Theory

A third attack that deserves our attention is the patrimonial theory expounded by Ludwig von Haller.⑥ Like many other anti-revolutionary theorists, he denies the state of nature and the idea of a social contract. Men, according to him, are social animals and bound to have relation and intercourse with one another. Moreover, some are born to be strong and some weak. The strong are by nature to rule, and the weak to be ruled. "Naturliche Uberlegenheit istder grund aller Herrschaft; Bedurfnisse der grund aller Abhangigheit und Dienstbarkeit."⑦ Sovereignty can only exist in a state of inequality, and it is always in the hands of the strongest.

Although sovereignty is always in the hands of the strongest, it is not an inborn

---

① See De Maistre: *Etude sur la Souverainete*, 1794–1796. De Bonald: *Theorie du pouvoir politique et religieuse dans la societe civile*, 1796. Schelling: *System des transcendentalen Idealismus*, 1800. Muller: *Von der Nothwendigkeit einer theologischen Grundlage der gesammten Staatswissenschaften*, 1819. Schlegel: *Vorlesungen uber die Philosophie des Lebens*, 1828. Wagner: *System der Ideal-Philosophie*, 1804. Muford: *The Nation*, 1872.

② Article Ⅱ.

③ Merriam: *History of the Theory of Sovereignty*, pp. 55–56. Oeuvres de M. de Bonald: *Legislation Primitive*, Ⅲ, 21.

④ Maistre: *Etude sur la Souverainete*, p. 346.

⑤ Dunning: *Political Theories, from Rousseau to Spencer*, p. 187. See also Laski: "De Maistre and Bismarck" in his *Problem of Sovereignty*, Chapter Ⅴ. Also see *ibid.*, Chapters Ⅱ, Ⅲ, Ⅳ. Also Laski: "De Bonald" in his *Authority in Modern State*, Ch. Ⅱ.

⑥ *Restauration der Staatswissenschaft oder Theorie des Natürlaichgesellgen Zustandes der Chimaera des Kunstlichen-bürgerlichen entgegensetzt* (1816–1834).

⑦ *Ibid.*, Ⅰ, 342. Ci, Gumplowicz: *Outlines of Sociology*, trans. by Moore, also F. Oppenheimer: *The State*, trans. by J. M. Gitterman.

right. This leads him to work out his theory of the acquisition of sovereignty. According to him, there are many ways of acquiring sovereignty. Sovereignty, in the first place, may be a gift of fortune (Glucksgut). It may, secondly, be acquired by one's own force and exertion. Thirdly, it may be acquired by contract or gift from another possessor or by chance (Gluck). Fourthly and lastly it may be acquired by a combination of all the three ways just mentioned. ①

The sovereignty so based, i. e., on force, and so acquired is not bound by human law, but is limited, however, by the law of God. It has been pointed out that "on the surface Haller's sovereignty is based upon force—in contrast to the natural right upon which popular sovereignty rested; but in the last analysis, however, the basis proved to be not force, but an assumed 'natural right' to property"②. Thus the theory of sovereignty on force, as stated by Haller, ends as a theory of sovereignty on property right.

4. Utilitarian School

A fourth assault against the revolutionary theory is that of the utilitarian school, worked out by Bentham and afterwards developed to its full extent in the writings of Austin. The social contract, as seen by Rousseau and other writers, is merely a "fiction" to Bentham. ③ Men obey a political superior, according to Bentham, not because they agree to do so, but because they think that, for their interest and happiness, it is better for them to do so. Sovereignty is supreme and absolute because utility demands it. Therefore how far the supreme authority can extend, and what are the rights and duties of the individual members of society in respect to sovereignty, are questions that can be answered only by the application of utilitarian principles. ④

As a student of positive law, Bentham denies that legal sovoreignty is limited, but expressly admits, however, that it may be limited by convention or express agreement made by the governing body. Thus he says: "Let us avow then, in short, steadily but calmly, what our Author hazards with anxiety and agitation, that the authority of the supreme body can not, 'unless where limited by express convention' be said to have any assignable, any certain bounds—That is to say there is any act they 'cannot' do, —to

---

① *Restauration der Staatswissenschaft oder Theorie des Natürlaichgeselligen Zustandes der Chimaera des Kunstlichen-bürgerlichen entgegensetzt* (1816-1834), Vol. I, Chapter XIX.

② Merriam: *History of the Theory of Sovereignty*, p. 69.

③ Bentham: *Fragment on Government*, chapter I, par. XXXVII.

Professor A. R. Lord remarks that Bentham's *Fragment on Government* is in effect an eassy on Sovereignty, *The Principles of Politics*, p. 84.

④ See *Fragment on Government*, Chapter IV, par. XX.

speak of any thing of theirs as being 'illegal', —as being 'void'; —to speak of their exceeding their 'authority' (whatever be the phrase) —their 'power', —their 'right' —is, however common, an abuse of language."① Thus both of Bentham's absolutism and his recognition of the limitation upon sovereignty may be found in the passage just quoted.

Like his master, Austin negatively rejects the social contract theory and positively maintains that men are bound together in a political society by the habit of obedience. The keynote of his theory of sovereignty is to be found in the so-called classic and often quoted definition which reads: "If a determinate human superior, not in a habit of obedience to a like superior, receive habitual obedience from the bulk of a given society, that determinate superior is sovereign in that society, and the society, (including the superior) is a society political and independent."②

To Austin, in order to be called sovereign of a political society, four marks are necessary: In the first place, "the generality or bulk of its members must be in a 'habit' of obedience to a determinate and common superior"③. Secondly, "habitual obedience must be rendered, by the 'generality or bulk of its members', to one and the same determinate person, or body of persons"④. Thirdly, "the generality or bulk of its members must habitually obey a superior determinate as well as common"⑤. Fourthly and lastly, that "certain superior must 'not' be habitually obedient to a determinate human superior"⑥.

From the four marks just mentioned above, it follows that there are some salient features of the nature of sovereignty. In the first place, sovereignty is absolute and legally incapable of limitation. "A monarch or sovereign number bound by a legal duty, were subject to a higher or superior sovereign; that is to say, a sovereign number bound by a legal duty, were sovereign and not sovereign. Supreme power limited by positive law, is a flat contradiction in term."⑦ In another place, we find the following passage: "That the power of a sovereign is incapable of legal limitation, has been doubted and even denied. But the difficulty, like thousands of others, probably arose from a verbal ambiguity. —The foremost individual member of a so-called limited monarchy, is styled

---

① See *Fragment on Government*, Chapter IV, par. XXVI.
② *Jurisprudence*, Vol. I, p. 221.
③ *Ibid.*, p. 222.
④ *Ibid.*, p. 223.
⑤ *Ibid.*, p. 224.
⑥ *Ibid.*
⑦ *Ibid.*, p. 263.

improperly monarch or sovereign. Now the power of a monarch or sovereign, thus improperly so styled, is not only capable of legal limitations, but is sometimes actually limited by positive law. But monarchs or sovereigns, thus improperly so styled, were confounded with monarchs, and other sovereigns, in the proper acceptation of the terms. And since the power of the former is capable of legal limitations, it was thought that the power of the latter might be bounded by similar restraints. "①

It is obvious that sovereignty, to Austin, is supreme only in respect to positive law. He recognizes moral limitations and the influence of custom, and of habit. Thus the narrower the scope of the positive law, the more limitations there will be upon sovereignty. His denial of constitutional and international law as law in its proper sense may be regarded as his recognition of the limitation of these two upon sovereignty, although such limitation, from his point of view, is merely moral.

Secondly, sovereignty, legally speaking, according to him, is one and indivisible. By sovereign, he says, it is meant a monarch properly so called, or sovereign number in its collegiate and sovereign capacity. ② Sovereign is the supreme power of, and subject to none in a given political society. It is impossible to have two supreme powers within a state and "no government can be styled with propriety half or imperfectly supreme". The application of the epithet "half" sovereignty seems to be capricious.

We come now to the location of sovereignty. Sovereignty, according to Austin, may be vested in the hands of one or many. In actual practice, it is located in different places in accordance with different forms of state. In an absolute monarchical form of state, it is in the hands of the monarch. ③ In a state like Great Britain, however, it is in the hands of the king and the peers, and the electoral body of the Commons. In a supreme federal state, like the United States of America, the sovereignty rests with the state governments, "as forming one aggregate body", understanding however by the government, "the body of citizens which appoints the ordinary legislature"④.

We shall now point out Austin's conception of sovereignty in its relation to liberty. Political or civil liberty is the liberty from legal obligation, which is left or granted by a sovereign government to any of its own subjects. ⑤ As sovereignty is the mother of liberty, or in other words, liberty is granted by a sovereign, there can be no conflict

---

① *Jurisprudence*, p. 254.
② *Ibid.*, note.
③ Cf., p. 273.
④ *Ibid.*, p. 260. For location of sovereignty in a confederation, see p. 262.
⑤ *Ibid.*, p. 274. (I use all quotations from R. Campbell's edition.)

between these two as is sometimes thought. It is remarked that "the difficulty is not in seeing how liberty can exist with sovereignty, but how it could exist without sovereignty"①.

In conclusion, let us see how Maine, the so-called opponent of Austin, summarizes the latter's conception of sovereignty. The theory of sovereignty of Austin, in the language of Maine, "is as follows: There is, in every independent political community—that is, in every political community not in the habit of obedience to a superior above itself—some single person or some combination of persons which has the power of compelling the other members of the community to do exactly as it pleases. This single person or group—this individual or this collegiate sovereign (to employ Austin's phrase)—may be found in every independent political community as certainly as the centre of gravity in a mass of matter...This sovereign, this person or combination of persons, universally occurring in all independent political communities, has in all such communities one characteristic common to all the shapes sovereignty may take the possession of irresistible force, not necessarily exerted, but, capable of being exerted"②.

5. Historical School

Besides the idealistic school, the religious school, the patrimonial doctrine and the utilitarian school, the importance of the historical school in attacking the revolutionary theory should not be overlooked. To the writers of this school the social contract is only a creation of the imagination. From their practical investigations, they point out that social and political institutions are merely the products of many generations, not of an arbitrary will or the general will. Their development is gradual, unconscious and evolutionary rather than sudden, conscious and revolutionary.

The best exponent of the school was Henry Maine. In criticizing the social contract theory, Maine says, "This political speculation, of which the remote and indirect consequences press us on all sides, is of all speculations the most baseless. The natural condition from which it starts is a simple figment of the imagination. So far as any research into the nature of primitive society has any bearing on so mere a dream, all inquiry has dissipated it. The process by which Rousseau supposes communities of men to have been formed, or by which at all events he wishes us to assume that they were formed, is again a chimera. No general assertion as to the way in which human societies grew up is safe, but perhaps the safest of all is that none of them were formed in the way

---

① Merriam, *op. cit.*, p. 148.
② Maine, *Early History of Institutions*, pp. 349-350.

imagined by Rousseau."①

Having attacked Rousseau's theory of the social contract, he attacks also his theory of popular sovereignty. He has no confidence in democracy. He views it as a fragile form of government which is likely to result in mediocrity and stagnation. Endowed with an aristocratic mind, he holds that aristocracy is essential to all real progress. ②

It is to be noted, however, that there are few writers like Maine who attack the conception of popular sovereignty. In fact, many of the latter expounders of the historical school, while denying the social contract theory as an adequate theory for explaining the origin of the state, favor, nevertheless, the notion of popular sovereignty. ③

Ⅶ. Conclusion

Between the revolutionary theory of sovereignty and the reactionary theories, stood that of the sovereignty of reason and that of state sovereignty. The historical basis of the theory of the sovereignty of reason is to be found in the Constitutional Charter of 1814 in France in which a constitutional monarchy was provided. The writers of this school are

---

① Maine: *Popular Government*, pp. 158–159.

② This is the main thesis of Maine's *Popular Government*. For Maine's theory of sovereignty, see a section below under the title "Sovereignty and Law". See also his *Ancient Law*, pp. 98 ff; *Early History of Institutions*, Lectures, ⅩⅩⅠ and ⅩⅢ; *International Law*, pp. 54 ff. In the book last named, he writes, "The powers of sovereigns are a bundle or collection of powers, and they may be separated one from another", p. 58.

③ Cf. Lowell: "Theory of Social Contract" and "Limits of Sovereignty" in his *Essays on Government*. Cf. Wilson: *Congressional Government* (1835), *The State* (1839), *An Old Master and Other Essays* (1893), and various addresses.

Both the utilitarian school and the historical school are on the same side so far as they are against the social contract theory, though the methods of approach are different. But the utilitarians, particularly the Austinian doctrine, is contrary to that of the historical school. A new movement led by A. V. Dicey and D. G. Richie came as a compromise between the doctrine of Austin on one hand and the historical school on the other. They made a distinction between legal and political sovereignty. To them, the former is the sovereignty, —the only sovereignty recognized by the courts. Back of the legal sovereignty there is a political sovereignty. If the two are in conflict, they assert, the former must yield to the latter. For one has the characteristic of fixity, while the other, changeability. One represents the view of the past, the other the sentiment and public opinion of the present. Since political institutions as [as] well as other social institutions are subject to change as conditions change, the old view can no longer be maintained and the new one must be sustained in order to meet the changing conditions.

See Ritchie: "On Sovereignty" in *Annals of the American Academy of Political and Social Science*, Vol. Ⅰ; Dicey: *The Law of the Constitution* (1835).

characterized as Doctrinaires.① The French writers know very well that the sovereign power, before the revolution, was in the will of a divine right king, and after, in the general will of the people. Since they are not ready to think of the possibility of dividing the sovereign power, and since neither the king nor the people are supreme under the constitutional monarchy, these writers instead of placing it in a determinate human body, hold that it can only be found in reason. By reason, however, they do not mean human reason, or general, but the absolute reason which is always right and is alone the source of absolute right of sovereignty. Nowhere can one find this absolute reason on earth and one can only conceive it by an indirect means, namely the Constitutional Charter of 1814.

The theory so advanced aimed largely to meet the peculiar provisions of the constitution then adopted. As soon as this limited and quasi-constitutional monarchy of the restoration was overthrown by the Second Revolution in July 1830, which set up the monarchy of the House of Orleans, more constitutionally liberal than its predecessor; the sovereignty of "absolute reason", in order to meet the new situation, has been changed to national sovereignty, which is no longer abstract and inconceivable, but concrete and can be found in the government. Sovereignty, says one of the defenders, is a "melange of reason, justice and will, which represents at once what the nation believes, thinks and wishes, is in the people and no where else"②.

The ablest exponents of the theory of the state sovereignty are Hegel and Bluntschli. Hegel speaks of the state as a real person representing a phase of the historical world process. ③ It is in this person, or the state as a whole, that the sovereign power resides. The state, as an organism or a person, however, is the realized ethical idea or ethical spirit. ④ Unless it were made real and objective in some way, it would be only a pure abstraction. ⑤ How can this abstraction then be realized? It can be actualized, it is argued, only as a person, and this person, to Hegel, is the monarch who is the personification of the state.

In its abstract sense, sovereignty is attributed to the state; in its concrete sense, it

---

① The leading expenents of this school are undoubtedly Cousin, Guizot and Constant. See Cousin: *Cours d'histoire de la philosophie morale au dix-huitienme siecle* (1839–1840). Guizot: *Du gouvernement de la France depuis la Restauration et du ministere actuel* (1821). Constant: *Principes Politiques*, (1815); *Reflexiou sur les constitutions et les garanties* (1814–1818).

② Statemeat quoted by Merriam, *op. cit.*, p. 81.

③ Hegel: *Philosophy of Right*, Dyde's translation, p. 286.

④ *Ibid.*, p. 240.

⑤ *Ibid.*, pp. 285 ff.

is in the hands of the monarch. Here the modified form of Kant's dual system can be easily traced. But different from Kant, it seems that Hegel does not think that the sovereignty of the state and the monarchical sovereignty are two different things. They are one and the same. It is a thing with two phases. Without the latter it will be like a soul without a body and without the former, it will be like a body without a soul. In short there will be no sovereignty in the absence of either one.

Like Hegel, Bluntschli views the state as a person and this person itself is sovereignty. Thus he says, "Sovereignty is not something before or outside nor above the state, it is the power and majesty of the state itself. It is the right of whole, and as certainly as the whole is stronger than any of its parts, so certainly the sovereignty of the whole state is superior to the sovereignty of any member of the state."[①]

Independence, honor, power, supreme authority, and unity are the characteristics of sovereignty[②] and therefore are the elements that compose sovereignty[③]. Sovereignty, moreover, has two phases: It may be looked at from within and from without: from without, as the independence of a particular state in relation to others so far also in relation to the church; from within, as legislative power of the body politic.[④]

Besides the sovereignty of the entire state there is another sovereignty within the state, namely, the sovereignty of the monarch or the prince.[⑤] Here again Bluntschli seems to agree with Hegel and, to a certain extent, with Kant. But instead of following Hegel by saying that the sovereignty of the state is realized in the monarch, he asserts that these two may exist at the same time without being in conflict with each other. "There is no contradiction between them and there does not result a division of sovereignty, as if one half belonged to the people and the other to the prince, there are not two jealous powers striving for supremacy."[⑥]

---

① Bluntschli: *Theory of the State*, Oxford trans., pp. 500–501.
② *Ibid.*, p. 415.
③ *Ibid.*, p. 500.
④ *Ibid.*, p. 502.
⑤ *Ibid.*
⑥ *Ibid.*, p. 503.

CHAPTER II
SOVEREIGNTY IN THE FEDERAL STATE

I. Introduction

The application of the theory of sovereignty to a federal state has been and still is one of the most difficult and indeed one of the most interesting problems of political theory. This seems to be recognized by all students in political science. New theories have been worked out and old theories applied. Not only its richness in form, but also its importance as a transition from the old conception of sovereignty to the new in the history of the theory of sovereignty, have made it worthy of study.

Whether we are in favor of the traditional theory of sovereignty, or the new theory, is a question which no attempt will be made to answer at present. But if we want to know how the old theory has been questioned, criticized and even discredited, and how the new theory has come into light, a brief consideration of the theories of sovereignty as applied to the federal state should not be overlooked.

II. State Sovereignty

In his *Discourse on the Constitution and Government of the United States*, Calhoun begins by declaring that "ours is a system of governments, compounded of the separated governments of the several states composing the union and one common government of all its members, called the government of the United States. The former preceded the latter which was created by their agency."[1]

Shortly after the Civil War, Mr. Alexander H. Stephens, the Vice-President of the Confederate States, in a colloquial style, published *A Constitutional View of the Late War Between the States*,[2] in which he argued at length that sovereignty, under the

---

[1] Calhoun: *Discourse on the Constituion and Government of the United States*, p. 1.
[2] Two volumes, 1867–1869.

American system, resided with the several states; ① that the union was nothing more than a compact made by the several states for their respective benefits and that the latter could withdraw from it at will whenever they saw fit; and that the powers exercised by the federal union or the federal government were not the powers of its own, inherent to itself, but were delegated by the several states. ②

Following the premise of Bodin in France, Pufendorf in Germany and Calhoun in the United States that sovereignty is a thing that is not and can never be divided, Seydel, a Bavarian youth, declares that the separate states, i. e., the members of the German Empire alone have sovereignty. The Empire was not a possessor of sovereignty and consequently it was not a state in the proper sense. It was, in reality, a union based on a compact from which the several members may retire as soon as they desire. ③

Writers on International Law, like Vattel, seem to share the view of the writers just mentioned above when he says "Several sovereign and independent states may unite themselves together by a perpetual confederacy, without ceasing to be, each individually, a perfect state. They will together constitute a Federal Republic; their joint deliberations will not impair the sovereignty of each member, though they may in certain respects, put some restraint on the exercise of it in virtue of voluntary engagements"④. Halleck sees that there is a possibility for sovereign states to unite together by a federal compact, without acknowledging any common sovereign. ⑤ Twiss maintains that the states of North America which compose the Federal Union are all sovereign states, though the nationality of each is merged in the Nationality of the Union. ⑥

The *Kentucky Resolutions* drawn by Jefferson and passed by the legislature of that state in 1789 reveal the proposition that the members of the federal state are sovereign states, that each of them has the right to judge its own affairs and that "the several states, composing the United States of America are not united on the principle of

---

① *War between the States*, Vol. I, pp. 81, 147.

② See also P. C. Centz: *The Republic of Republics, or American Federal Liberty*, B. J. Sage ed., 1881, p. 305. Also G. Tucker, in an appendix to his edition of Blackstone's *Commentaries*. "This constitution of the United States is an original written, federal and social compact, freely, voluntarily and solemnly entered into by the several states and ratified by the people thereof respectively. In a federal compact, several sovereign and independent states may unite themselves together by a perpetual confederacy, without ceasing to be a perfect state."

③ *Kommentar zur Verfassung Kunde fur das Deutsche Reich*, 1st ed., pp. 6, 23. *Tubinger Staatswissenschaftliche Zeitschrift*, 1872, pp. 185. Also *Harvard Law Review*, Vol. XXXI, p. 148. Kruger: *Government and Politics of the German Empire*, pp. 35-36.

④ Vattell: *Laws of Nations*, p. 3.

⑤ Halleck: *International Law*, Vol. I, p. 77.

⑥ Twiss: *Law of Nations*, Second edition, p. 23. Cf. Baty: *International Law*, p. 332.

unlimited submission to their general government"①. In 1832 the people of South Carolina assembled in convention and declared that any attempt of the Federal Government to enforce within the limits of South Carolina will be "inconsistent with the longer continuance of South Carolina in the Union; and that the people of South Carolina will henceforth hold themselves absolved from all further obligation to maintain or preserve their political connection with the people of the others, and will forthwith proceed to organize a separate government, and do all other acts and things which sovereign and independent states may of right do"②.

Through the 1860 Association, a number of tracts were written for defending the sovereignty of the several states. Here is a statement which represents its position: "Our doctrine is that the states, before the adoption of the Constitution, were sovereign and independent; that the Federal Union is a Union of states, and that the Constitution is a covenant or compact between them and the fundamental law of their union; and that inasmuch as the covenant or compact was between sovereigns, and there is no umpire or common interpreter between them, each has the right to judge for itself of infractions of the contract, and to determine for itself the mode and measure of redress."③

The argument revealed in the statement quoted above was already elaborated in Senator Hayne's notable speech in the Senate Chamber in January 1820. United States senators like Hayne are by no means lacking in our own day. Thus in an eloquent speech delivered in October 1927 before the Texas Bar Association, Senator Reed of Missouri described the sovereignty of the several states as a principle once dear to the American people, but which has been retired into obscurity by modern statesmanship and modern agitators. ④ He declared that "the several states were created as absolute and unqualified sovereignties"⑤. It is in this way that the principle of local government can be maintained and it is by this principle that the liberty and natural rights of men can be secured. ⑥ "Let us bring this government back to its old fundamentals," says he in conclusion, "restore to these sovereign states the right to control their own affairs by a

---

① See Randall's *Life of Jefferson*, Vol. II, p. 449 and appendix D.

② Quoted by Willoughby, See his *Fundamental Concepts of Public Law*.

③ W. D. Porter: *State Sovereignty and the Doctrine of Coercion*, p. 6. See 1860 Association Tract No. 2.

④ *Proceedings of the Texas Bar Association*, Vol. XLVI (October, 1927), p. 74.

⑤ "Encroachment of the Federal Government". *Proceedings of the Texas Bar Association*, Vol. XLVI (October 1927), pp. 76-77. On the other hand, Senator Reed points out that the central Government "was not in the proposed sense of the term a sovereignty; it was a government created by specific grant of powers and those powers were expressly limited".

⑥ *Ibid.*, p. 77.

rebirth of Americanism as it was dreamed by the fathers of our country as it was made possible by an assemblage of the past about the watchfire of the revolution; by a rechristening and new patriotism of all our hearts in the doctrine of liberty and beauty and honesty in government."①

The Senate of the United States passed a series of resolutions, submitted by Jefferson Davis on the 24th of May, 1860, affirming the principle of the sovereignty of the several states. ② The first of these resolutions reads: "Resolved, that in the adoption of the Federal Constitution, the states adopting the same, acted severally as free and independent Sovereignties, delegating a portion of their powers to be exercised by the Federal Government for the increased security of each against dangers, domestic as well as foreign; and that any intermeddling by any one or more states, or by a combination of their citizens, with the domestic institutions of the others, on any pretext whatever, political, moral, or religious, with a view to their disturbance or subversion, is in violation of the Constitution, insulting to the States so interfered with, endangers their domestic peace and tranquility—objects for which the Constitution was formed—and, by necessary consequence, tends to weaken and destroy the Union itself."③

The courts, federal as well as state, in the United States, in many cases recognize the principle that the states are sovereign. In the well known case of Gibbons vs. Ogden in 1824, Chief Justice Marshall, in delivering the decision of the Supreme Court of the United States, says: "As preliminary to the very able discussions of the Constitution which we have heard from the bar, and as having some influence on its construction, reference has been made to the political situation of these States anterior to its formation. It has been said that they were sovereign, were completely independent, and were connected with each other only by a league. This is true."④

In the case of the City of New Orleans vs. Abbagnato, the Snpreme Court of Massachusetts declares that under the governmental system in this country the state is sovereign. ⑤ Only a few years ago, Chief Justice Taft, in the case of Bailey vs. Drexel Furniture Co., delivered the opinion of the Court, holding that to let Congress lay a tax of ten percent on the net annual income of a person who employed a child in any mine or factory of the United States, "would be to break down all constitutional limitation of the

---

① "Encroachment of the Federal Government". *Proceedings of the Texas Bar Association*, Vol. XLVI (October 1927), pp. 88–89.
② His position may be found in his *Rise and Fall of the Confederate Government*, 1881, 2 volumes.
③ Quoted by Stephens, in *The War Between the States*, Vol. I, p. 409.
④ 9 Wheaton 1; 207, 1824.
⑤ See Scott's *Cases on International Law*, 119.

powers of Congress and completely wipe out the sovereignty of the States"[1].

Not only statesmen, political writers, the Senate and the Courts in the United States affirm the theory of the sovereignty of the states, but it is also declared in the constitutions of several federal states. Thus the Swiss Constitutions of 1858 and 1874 contained the following words: "The Cantons are sovereign in so far as their sovereignty is not limited by the Federal Constitution, and rights which have not been delegated to the Federal Government."[2] The same idea may be found in the Mexican Constitution of 1917 which reads: "It is the will of the Mexican people to constitute a representative, democratic and federal Republic, composed of free, sovereign states in all that concerns their interior regimen; but united in a federation in compliance with the principles of this fundamental law."[3]

The starting point of those who hold that the several states in the federal state are sovereign is that sovereignty is, by its very nature, indivisible. It must be one or none at all. It is impossible to conceive, as stated by Calhoun, how sovereignty itself, the supreme power, can be divided and how the people of several states can be partly sovereign and partly not sovereign, partly supreme and partly not supreme.[4] "Sovereignty," says Calhoun, "is an entire thing; to divide is to destroy it."[5] "It is", as we are told by another well-known writer, "that inherent, absolute power of self-determination, in every distinct political body, existing by virtue of its own social forces, which, in pursuit of the well-being of its own organism, within the limitations of natural justice, can not be rightfully interfered with by any other similar body, without

---

[1] 259 U. S. 20. In the case of Lonsdale vs. Brown, the Circuit Court of the Eastern District of Pennsylvania pointed out that the difference between the Union of sovereignties of England and Scotland and the Federal Union of the states in the United States, saying: "How different is the Union of these States. They are, in their separate political capacities, sovereign and independent of each other, except so far as they have united for their common defence and for National purpose. They have each a Constitution and form of Government with all the attributes of sovereignty." Peters' Vol. II. app. pp. 689-699.

In the case of Lane County vs. Oregon, it was held that "the people of each state compose a state, having its own government and endowed with all the functions essential to separate and independent existence. The disunited might continue to exist without the states in Union. There could be no such political body as the United States". Wallace, pp. 71, 76, 1868.

See also A. H. Stephens: *A Constitutional View of the Late War Between the States*, Vol. I, p. 396.

[2] Constitutions of 1848 art. III, 1874 art. IV.

[3] Mexican Constitution of 1817 art. 41. See also the Constitutive acts of the Mexican federation of January 1824. "Its integral parts are free, sovereign independent states, in as far as regards exclusively its internal administration, according to the rules laid down in this act and in the general constitution."

[4] Calhoun: *Works*. Vol. I, p. 146. Also Vol. II, p. 232.

[5] *Ibid.*, Vol. I, p. 146.

its consent."① It is like the will and power of self action in the personal body and just as much so as the mind is in the individual organism.② It is absurd and indeed impossible to have two sovereignties within a state. Its location must then be in one place as a whole.

If sovereignty is indivisible, where is it to be found? It is held that it is to be found in the several states and the arguments given by its defenders may be briefly summarized as follows:

The defenders of the theory of the sovereignty of the several states maintain that the several states became, when they dissolved their connection with Great Britain, free, independent and sovereign.③ This must be so, it is contended, because it is declared in the Declaration of Independence, reaffirmed in the Articles of Confederation,④ stated in a treaty concluded with Great Britain,⑤ held by the Supreme Court of the United States⑥ and revealed by the prevailing opinion during the early history of the Republic.⑦

But this is not all. The several states must be sovereign, it is argued, because in the first place, the states came before the Union; secondly, the United States was created by the states jointly; thirdly, the several states can exist without entering the Union.⑧

Having shown that the several states were sovereign before the Constitution was

---

① *A Constitutional View of the Late War Between the States*, by Stephens, Vol. II, p. 22.

② *Ibid.*, p. 23.

③ See James Brown Scott, *Sovereign States and Suits*, p. 36. Also pp. 28, 46, 48, 143.

④ "Each state retains its sovereignty, freedom, and independence, and every power, jurisdiction, and right which is not by this Confederation delegated to the United States in Congress assembled." Articles of Confederation, Article II.

⑤ "His Britainic Majesty acknowledges the said United States, viz. New Hampshire, ...to be free, sovereign and independent states..." The Treaty was concluded on September 3, 1783. Quoted by Scott, *ibid.*, p. 39.

⑥ For example, in the case of McIvaine vs. Coxe, the court held that "on the 4th of October 1776 the State of New Jersey was completely a sovereign, independent state..." Peter's *Condensed Reports*, p. 86.

⑦ During Washington's Southern Tour, one of the toasts was "the perpetual union of distinct sovereign states under an effecient federal Head." A. Henderson, *Washing's Southern Tour*, 1791 (1923). This is cited as an example to show that the prevailing opinion at that time was that the states were sovereign. See Scott, *ibid.*, p. 48.

⑧ See J. B. Scott, *ibid.*, p. 69. Also Ogg and Ray, *Introduction to American Government*, p. 97. Also McLaughlin, "Social Compact and Constitutional Construction" in *American Historical Review*, April, 1900.

It must be borne in mind that those who maintain that the states were sovereign and independent after the Declaration of Independence are not necessarily those who maintain that the states are sovereign under the present Constitution. In fact, no fewer writers who deny that the several states are sovereign under the present Constitution, admit that they were sovereign under the Articles of Confederation. The latter position is taken by Willoughby and Wilson. See Willoughby, *Nature of the State*, p. 264. Wilson, *The State*, Sections 1372–1379. Hamilton also admitted that the State governments by their original Constitutions, were invested with complete sovereignty. See Ford, *Federalist*, p. 196. Also *Federalist*, No. 81. Webster, in a debate with Calhoun (1839), admitted as such.

adopted, they endeavor to show that they are still sovereign under the Constitution of 1787. In the first place, they contend that there is not much difference between a confederate state and a federal state; and if there is any, the difference is in degree rather than in kind. ①

To them, then the phrase "in order to form a more perfect Union" means to make more perfect "the Union" then existing, namely, the Articles of Confederation. A convention was called to revise and enlarge the powers under the Articles of Confederation. It did not change the nature of confederation. This is to be shown by the fact that even after the ratification of the Constitution, the term "confederation" was still employed in public documents and used by statesmen. ② It is only natural then, that the several states, being sovereign under the Confederation, are and must be sovereign under the present Constitution.

Secondly, it is argued that the Union is a compact between states and not between individuals or people. ③ This is obvious in the Constitution when it declares that "the ratification of the Conventions of nine states shall be sufficient for the establishment of this Constitution between the states so ratifying the same"④. It is also evidenced by the fact that the delegates signed their names by states.

Thirdly, even if it is a compact made between individuals or people, the term "people" means the people of the several states, not of the Union as a whole. It has been pointed out that the preamble of the Constitution passed by the Convention on the 7th of August, 1787, was in these words: "We, the people of the States of New Hampshire, Massachusetts, Rhode Island and Providence Plantations, Connecticut, New York, New Jersey, Pennsylvania, Delaware, Maryland, Virginia, North Carolina, South Carolina and Georgia, do ordain, declare, and establish the following Constitution." When this was changed into the present phrase: "We, the people of the United States..." it was not changed by the Convention, but by the sub-committee on style for the obvious reason that it was not known at that time, which of the states would ratify it. Hence it was exceedingly inappropriate to set forth in advance the states by

---

① Washington, in many public speeches, did not make a distinction between the confederate state and federal state. See also Stephens, *War Between the States*, Vol. I, pp. 167–170. When Calhoun attempted to make a distinction between the two, he at once gets into difficulties. See *Disquisition*, p. 163. See also Merriam, *History of the Theory of Sovereignty since Rousseau*, p. 170, footnote.

② See *Washington's Writings*, Vol. IX, p. 398. Also *Annals of Congress*, Vol. I, p. 38.

③ J. B. Scott, *op. cit.*, p. 69.

④ Article VII.

name. ①

Fourthly, it is contended that it is declared in the Constitution that "the Congress of the United States shall consist of a Senate and a House of Representatives,"② and "a majority of each shall constitute a quorum to do business"③. But there will be no Congress and consequently the union will be destroyed if a majority of the states refuse through their legislatures or their conventions to choose senators to Congress and that the executive of such states should in obedience to the will of their people respectively, decline to make temporary appointment. ④ Thus the federal government or the federal Union is not and can not be regarded as a sovereign body. ⑤ Its life is at the mercy of the sovereign states, and its powers are expressly limited and may be taken back when the states see fit.

Fifthly, it is maintained that the several states must be sovereign, because they can not be sued by their own citizens, or by citizens of another state, or by citizens or subjects of any foreign state. This principle, it is said, is recognized by the courts of modern states and it was reaffirmed by the Eleventh Amendment, adopted in 1798. ⑥

It must be added that almost all of those who hold the doctrine of sovereignty of several states attempt to distinguish between sovereignty and power. ⑦ Power may be divided, but not sovereignty. "There is no difficulty in understanding how powers appertaining to sovereignty may be divided, and the exercise of one portion be delegated to one set of agents, and another portion to another", ⑧ says Calhoun. So it is held by Stephens. "We must discriminate between the powers of sovereignty and sovereignty itself."⑨ The former are divisible while the latter is not. ⑩ While denying that sovereignty is the sum of powers, they recognize that the latter are the emanations or

---

① Stephens, *ibid.*, Vol. I, pp. 137–139.

② Article I, Section 1.

③ Article I, Section 5.

④ W. D. Porter, *State Sovereignty and the Doctrine of Coercion*, see 1860 Association Tract No. 2, p. 12.

⑤ "Encroachment of the Federal Government" by Senator Reed, in the *Proceedings of the Texas Bar Association*, Vol. XLVI (October, 1927), pp. 76–77.

⑥ "The judicial power of the United States shall not be construed to extend to any suit in law or equity, commenced or prosecuted against one of the United States by citizens of another State, or by citizens or subjects of any foreign State."

⑦ Some writers differentiate between attributes of sovereignty and sovereignty, e. g., Calhoun, and some like Stephens, distinguish between sovereign power and sovereignty.

⑧ *Discourse*, p. 146.

⑨ Stephens, *War Between the States*, Vol. II, p. 33.

⑩ Stephens, *ibid*.

outgrowths from the former.① This, as has been said, "is really the essence of Calhoun's argument."② The Same may be said of most of the writers who advocate the doctrine of sovereignty of the several states.③

How then is power divided? It is divided in a federal state, say the United States, in the first place, between the federal government and the governments of the several states; secondly, into three branches, namely, legislative, executive and judicial, both in the federal government and in the several state governments;④ and thirdly, between the central and several state governments on the one hand and local governments on the other.⑤ Town and cities may and do exercise sovereign powers, such as that of taxation; but they are not and can never be called sovereign bodies.⑥ This is also true of the federal government or federal union. What the federal government possesses is nothing more than the powers delegated by the several states, such as the power of declaring war and concluding peace which is by no means different in nature from the power of taxation exercised by the towns and cities.

III. Sovereignty of the Federal Government

Over against the doctrine of sovereignty of the several states in a federal state, is that of sovereignty of the federal union. The starting point of this theory is almost similar to that of the former. The leading expounders all agree that sovereignty can not be divided and must be one. But instead of locating it to several states, they find it to be in the federal union or federal government.

Treitschke, a well known German writer, distinguishes between a federal state and a confederate state in the location of sovereignty. While in the latter, it resides in the several states, it is to be found in the federal union in the former. "The various subordinate countries of Germany," he says, "are not genuine states; they must at any moment be prepared to see a right, which they possess at present, withdraw by virtue of imperial authority."⑦

---

① Merriam: *ibid.*, p. 171. Stephens: *ibid.*, Vol. II, p. 23.
② Merriam: *History of the Theory of Sovereignty since Rousseau*, p. 171.
③ Compare the opinion of the Court in the case of the Sapphire, 1781, 11 Wallace, p. 164.
④ Stephens: *ibid.*, Vol. II, p. 23.
⑤ Porter: *State Sovereignty and the Doctrine of Coercion*, p. 8.
⑥ *Ibid.*
⑦ *Politics*, Vol. I, p. 30.

In his *Studien zum deutschen Staatsrechte*,① Albert Haenel develops the "Competenz-competenz" doctrine which he considers as the characteristic feature of the theory of sovereignty. Sovereignty is the power which knows no superior and can do what it wills and wants. This power, as he sees it, resides in the Empire in Germany, for the Empire alone has the legal power of self-determination. "Acting in a wholly legal and constitutional way, the Empire may, as it chooses, increase its own powers, diminish those of the individual states, and determine their respective fields of governmental activity."② F. V. Liszt, in his treatise on International Law, while declaring that the sovereign power of the Empire or central government is supreme, admits that it is, nevertheless, limited.③

Other writers who, having taken more or less the same position, may be mentioned are: J. Held④, Zopfe⑤, Kaltenborn⑥, Ronne⑦, P. Resch⑧, and Zorn⑨.

There are writers who, on the one hand admit that sovereignty in a federal state resides in the federal union, while on the other hand refuse to recognize sovereignty as a characteristic feature of the state. This group of writers includes the following well known thinkers: Jellinek, Laband and Meyer. Meyer⑩ speaks of two kinds of state i. e., centralized state and a union of states. He sees no difficulty in locating the sovereignty in the former, but he is in doubt as to the latter. It seems to him that the members which compose the union are entitled to be called states, although they no longer possess sovereignty.⑪

Like Meyer, Jellinek holds that the member states in a federal state are states though they lose their sovereignty.⑫ The difference between a sovereign state and a non-sovereign state, according to Jellinek, is found in the fact that the former has the power

---

① 1923, Part Ⅰ. See Ⅰ, S. 240, his constitutional basis of argument.

② See Merriam, *History of the Theory of Sovereignty*, p. 192.

③ *Das Volkrecht*, p. 121.

④ *System des Verfassungsrechts der Monarchischen Staaten Deutschlands mit besanderer Rucksicht auf den Constitutionalesims*, Bk. Ⅰ, Sections 392–395, 1856.

⑤ *Grundzatz des gemeinen Deutschen Staatsrechts*, 5th ed., 1863, Bk. Ⅰ, Sections 63–64.

⑥ *Einleitung in das constitutionalle Verfassungsrecht*, section 159, 1863.

⑦ *Staatsrecht des deutsche Reiches*, Vol. Ⅰ, p. 65.

⑧ *Europaische Volkrecht* 1885, p. 39. "Die Staatsgewalt, welche das Gemeinsessen nach Aussen vertritt ist im Bundsstaate die Centralgewalt."

⑨ *Staatsrecht*, Vol. Ⅰ, section 73. See also Pozl, *Staatswarterbunch von Bluntschli und Brater*, Bk. Ⅱ, pp. 284–293.

⑩ *Lehrbuch des deutschen Staatsrechts*, 1878, pp. 2–3.

⑪ *Ibid.*, 4th ed., 1895, p. 8.

⑫ *Lehre von den Staatensverbindungen*, p. 36. Also *Allgemeine Staatslehre*, 2nd ed., pp. 470 ff.

of preventing the latter from exercising constitutional powers. ① Likewise Laband argues that the several states, combining together as a union of states and thereby losing the sovereign powers that they had before, retain the character of real states. ② The several states, according to both Jellinek and Laband, are, by virtue of its inherent right, to be called states. In short, it is not sovereignty, but right, which is the essential characteristic of a state. ③

It is generally recognized that French writers since Bodin have been accustomed to the indivisibility doctrine of sovereignty, and when this theory is applied to a federal state, most of them, being influenced by their own political ideas and experiences, and not wishing to take trouble to solve a problem which is not their own, do not hesitate to locate the sovereignty in the federal union. Thus according to E. Borel, sovereignty is the quality of a state by virtue of which it is not determined by its proper and free will. ④ This quality is absolute and exclusive. It implies the supreme power from within, and the complete independence without. ⑤ It is by nature one and indivisible, and this one and indivisible power is to be and must be found in the central government, for in the eyes of law, there is no difference between a decentralized area in a unitary state and a state in a federal state. ⑥

The point that Le Fur begins with reference to sovereignty in the federal state is similar to that of Borel. He holds that it is the federal government alone that possesses the sovereign power. To him, a federal state composed of the several states is no more than a unitary democratic state composed of many individual citizens. When a federal

---

① *Die Lehre von den Staatenverbindungen*, pp. 41–42. Compare his *Gesetz und Verodnung*, p. 203, where he maintains that the existence of the non-sovereign state as a state is therefore itself determined by the sovereign will of the superstate. The sovereign can exploit the non-sovereign state to an extent to which no formal *a priori* legal limit can be set. See Willoughby: *Nature of the State*, pp. 246–248.

② "Hieraus ergibt sich aber andererseits, dass die souverantat nicht zu den wessentlichen Eigenschaften des States gehart. Da der Ausdruck Souveranitat in Verschiedenem sinn gebraucht wird, so muss zur Vermeidung eines planlosen wortstreites, der ohne Ergebnis bleiben muss, zunachst festgestellt werden, was darunter zu verstehen ist." *Das Staatsrecht des deutschen Reiches*, 5th ed., Vol. I, p. 72. See also E. Nys: *Le Droit international*, p. 120.

③ See Jellinek: *Lehre von den Staatenverbingen*, p. 42; and Laband: *Staatsrecht*, Vol. I, p. 180. For the discussion of non-sovereign states, see Willoughby: *Fundamental Concepts of Public Law*, p. 254.

④ Etude sur la Souverainete et L'Etat federatif, p. 47.

⑤ *Ibid.*, p. 28. "Il est dans la nature meme du superlatif d'etre un et indivisible, c'est la une necessite logique absolue…De meme que L'Etat, la Souverainete est une et indisible."

⑥ *Ibid.*, p. 74 and p. 172. Professor Seeley, undoubtedly shares the view of Borel, although it seems that he does not expressly state where the sovereignty resides in a federal state. "I deny then," says he, "that between the unitary state and the federation or federal state there is any fundamental difference in kind; I deny that one is composite in any sense in which the other is simple." See his *Introduction to Political Science*, pp. 94–95.

state is created, a new sovereign personality takes place and the sovereign personality of the member states ceases to exist. ①

Turning to the American thinkers, we find men like Hamilton undoubtedly would like to have a strong union with a single sovereignty, although their time and environment forced them to share the view of those who held the doctrine of divisibility of sovereignty② and sometimes even went so far as to admit that the several states were sovereign. ③ If Hamilton was not at heart a monarchist who would like to realize the dream of Bodin and Hobbes, as has been claimed, it seems that it is not going too far to speak of him as a strong advocate of centralized republicanism who would like to see the sovereignty of the several states entirely destroyed and their status reduced to that of the counties of England and that the federal government alone had the right to do what it willed and wished. ④

The opinions of the Supreme Court of the United States during the early part of the nineteenth century as revealed from the pen of Marshall, tended in the same direction. And when Abraham Lincoln declared "The Union is older than any of the states, and in fact it created them as states,"⑤ he certainly had in mind that it was not the states, but the Union alone that was to be called sovereign.

Recent American writers are by no means lacking in taking the position under consideration. In *The State and Government*, Professor Dealey points out that if political unity established is so powerful that the parts obviously lose their sovereignties, which become merged into the sovereignty of the union, then it is a federation rather than a

---

① Le Fur, *L'Etat Federal*, pp. 697 ff.

Piedelievre, in his *Droit International Public*, Vol. I, p. 78, although recognizing that there are semi-sovereign states existing in the modern world, denies that it is divided in a federal state. Thus he says that the different constituents which make up the federal state cease to be entirely sovereign. They obey the supreme authority of the federal government which established by a compact, forms a new personality.

Other writers who hold the similar view are: Neumann, *Elements du Droit des gens modern Enropean*, p. 27. "L'Etat fédéral n'est pas une simple agglomeration de Souverainetes particulieres, il a lui-meme sa souverainete et par suit il possede, a L'encontre de la Confederation d'Etat, des autoricties central propres, executive, legislatives et meme judiciarie." See also Merignhac, *Le Droit de la Paix* (Droit Public International), 1907, pp. 25–26. Antoine Rougier, *Les guerres civiles et le droit des gens*, p. 47.

② Ford, *Federalist*, p. 207.
③ *Ibid.*, p. 196.
④ Cf. W. B. Munro, *The Government of the United States*, p. 37.
⑤ See A. Lincoln, Special Message to Congress, July 4, 1861,

confederation. ① W. Wilson hold the same position when he says, "We must be careful to distinguish between federal states and confederacies. Both of these have a central government and local governments, each of which exercises certain powers of sovereignty; but there is a very great difference between them. If we have a single sovereign which says what powers the government shall exercise, we have a single state, a federal state, or as Germans say, 'Bundesstaat'. If, however, sovereignty rests not in the large territory but in the smaller territorial divisions, we have many sovereignties, therefore many states, or a confederacy, a 'Staatenbund'. In other words, a confederacy is a union of states and the central government is nothing more than the agent of those states while in a federal state there is a real central united state, as well as central government."② But Wilson, like many German political writers, maintains that the member states in a federal state, are nevertheless entitled to be called states though they lose their sovereignties. ③

Ⅳ. Compromise Theories

Having outlined the two opposite theories, i. e., that of the sovereignty of the

---

① Dealey: *The State and Government*, pp. 152, 154. See also Willoughby: *Nature of the State*, pp. 253-254; and his recent book, *The Fundamental Concepts of Public Law*, p. 249. Cf. James Wilson's view, in *Madison Papers*, Vol. Ⅱ, p. 824.

② Wilson: *The State*, sections 1372-1379.

③ Wilson: *An Old Master and Other Essays*, pp. 3-94. "In the federal state, self-determination with respect to their law as a whole has been lost by member states. They can not extend, they cannot even determine, their own powers conclusively without appeal to the federal authorities. But they are still states because their powers are original and inherent, not derivative; because their rights are not also legal duties; and because they can apply to their commands the full imperative sanctions of law. But their sphere is limited by the presiding and sovereign powers of a state super-ordinated to them, the extent of whose authority is determined under constitutional forms and guaranteed by itself." Wheaton, as has been pointed out, admits the doctrine of the sovereignty of the several states, yet the following statement shows that he is also sharing with those who hold the theory of the sovereignty of the federal union. "The federal government created by the act of union, is sovereign and supreme, within the sphere of the powers granted to it by the act, and the government acts not only upon the states which are members of the confederation, but directly upon the citizens. The sovereignty both internal and external of each several state is impaired by the powers thus granted to the federal government, and the limitations thus impaired on from this League is alone a sovereign power." *International Law*, p. 74. English writers like Lawrence, take a similar position. See *Principles of International Law*, p. 63.

H. E. Willis, in an article published recently, advances the idea that in the early history of the Republic, sovereignty was divided between the several states on the ⟨one⟩ hand and the Union on the other, but the tendency had been that the states lost their sovereignty gradually and lost completely when they ratified the Eighteenth Amendment. At present, the federal union alone possesses sovereignty. *Kentucky Law Journal*, March, 1927, Vol. XV, pp. 175, 178.

several states and that of the sovereignty of the federal union, we come now to the third group of writers who hold what, for lack of a better term, may be called a compromise theory. The forms which it has taken have been numerous, yet roughly speaking they may be grouped into the following categories: (1) sovereignty of the people, (2) sovereignty of the nation, (3) sovereignty of the state, (4) sovereignty of the united states, (5) sovereignty of the electorate, (6) sovereignty as constitution-making power, (7) sovereignty as lawmaking power and (8) the divisibility doctrine of sovereignty.

1. Sovereignty of the People

The theory of the sovereignty of the people is not a modern enunciation.① It may be found in the writings of Aristotle. It was recognized by the Roman jurists, advocated by the writers of the school of Monarchomachs, and warmly accepted during the time of the French Revolution. In the language of Henry Maine, "this theory, which is known on the Continent as the theory of national sovereignty, has been fully accepted in France, Italy, Spain, Portugal, Holland, Belgium, Greece and the Scandinavian states. In Germany it has been repeatedly repudiated by the Emperor and his powerful minister, but it is to a very great extent acted upon. England, as is not usual with her, stands by herself"②. Its chief aim has been to overthrow the theory of the sovereignty of the king. But when it is applied to a federal state, it compromises, consciously or unconsciously, the theory of the sovereignty of the several states and that of the federal union.

The theory under consideration was advocated by James Wilson, one of the most industrious and useful members of the Constitutional Convention of 1787. Profoundly influnced by the contract theory of Pufendorf,③ Wilson advanced the idea that it was the people who, for their common benefit, formed an artificial person or body politic known as the United States which was to be considered as the highest and the noblest thing that the world had ever had.④ The people, being the founder of the union, alone possess the sovereignty. By people, according to Wilson, it is meant in the first place, the people of the United States and in the second place, the white male adults.⑤

---

① By "people", it is meant here the people of a whole federal state, in contrast to the people of the several states.
② Maine: *Popular Government*, p. 8.
③ Pufendorf's writings were extensively quoted by Wilson in his *Works*.
④ J. Wilson: *Works*, Vol. II, p. 6, also footnote.
⑤ The term "people" has two other different meanings as pointed out by J. Wilson. "The people of the United States must be considered attentively in two very different views—as forming one nation, great and united; and as forming, at the same time, a number of separate states, to that nation subordinate, but independent as to their own interior government." *Works*, Vol. II, p. 8.

Among the expounders of the theory under discussion, Daniel Webster is the ablest.① His argument is based mainly upon the Constitution of the United States and revealed in the Hayne-Webster debate, and in his contention made before the Supreme Court of the United States on the 27th of January, 1848, in the case of Martin Luther vs. Luther, M. Borden and others.

In the Webster-Hayne debate,② Webster argued that the Constitution is not a league between the several states, but is founded upon the adoption of the people. "No man," says he in his argument in the case of Martin Luther, "makes a question that the people are the source of all political power. Government is instituted for their good, and its members are their agents and servants."③ Therefore, "let all admit, what none deny, that the only source of political power in this country is the people. Let us admit that they are sovereign, for they are so; that is to say the aggregate community, the collected will of the People, is sovereign"④.

The basis upon which Webster built his argument, as he pointed out, is the preamble of the Constitution which reads: "We, the people of the United States, in order to form a more perfect Union, …do ordain and establish this constitution for the United States of America." It is established by the people of the United States, so runs the reasoning. It does not say "by the people of the several states". It is by all the people of the United States that the Constitution is established.⑤

Another reason for asserting the theory of the sovereignty of the people may be found in a statement made by Professor Holcombe. "The most conclusive evidence of the ultimate sovereignty of the people of any particular state is afforded by this provision that the United States shall guarantee to every state a republican form of government,

---

① Webster did not hold this theory firmly and he even admitted the theory of the sovereignty of the several states. In a letter to the Barings, London, 1839, he wrote: "Yonr first inquiry is, whether the Legislature of one of the states has legal and constitutional power to contract loans at home and abroad? To this I answer, that the legislature of State has such power; and how any doubt could have arisen on this point it is difficult for me to conceive. Every state is an independent, sovereign, political community, except in so far as certain powers, which it might otherwise have exercised, have been conferred on a General Government, established, under a written constitution, and exerting its authority over the people of all the states." See Niles: *National Register*, Vol. LVII, pp. 273–274.

Also see his speech made by him at Capon Springs, Virginia, June 28, 1851, cited by Stephens, *War Between the States*, Vol. I, pp. 404–405. See also his *Works*, Vol. XI, p. 222. "We usually speak of the states as sovereign states, I don't object to this. But the Constitution never styles them, nor does the Constitution speak of the government here as the general or federal government the United States; and it calls state government state governments."

② *Works*, Vol. I, pp. 82–92.
③ *Ibid.*, Vol. XI, p. 221.
④ *Ibid.*, p. 222.
⑤ Merriam: *American Political Ideas*, p. 285.

whether the people of every state wish such a government or not."① From the constitutional basis, Professor Holcombe advances to a logical basis, namely, the whole is greater than the parts and the parts are inferior to the whole. Thus the people of the several states are subject to the sovereignty of the people of the nation, though the people of each are equal to the people of any other state before the law of the federal constitution.②

The people then must be sovereign, for "without the people standing back of the skeleton… without the people, to teach, to stimulate, to guide, to correct and to punish—this complex machine of government would have gone to ruin a hundred years ago, and a hundred times since then"③.

2. Sovereignty of the Nation

Writers who advance the notion of the sovereignty of the nation④ are undoubtedly imbued by German and French ideas. It is from the Germans that they get their philosophical background, for German thought has always been colored with abstraction, seeing and explaining things outside of reality, and is not only philosophical, but even mystical. It is from the French that they get its form and substance. Thus Article 3 of the Declaration of the Rights of Man and the Citizen of 1789 proclaimed that "all sovereignty resides essentially in the Nation", and the Constitution of 1791 declared that "the sovereignty is one and indivisible, inalienable and imprescriptible. It belongs to the Nation".

Negatively, thinkers in this group deny the theory of the sovereignty of the people on the ground that it is too simple. The people, as they see it, is merely the aggregate of

---

① Holcombe: *State Government in the United States*, p. 11.

② *Ibid.*, p. 8.

③ Jameson: "National Sovereignty" in *Political Science Quarterly*, Vol. V, p. 211.

See also Burgess: *Political Science and Constitutional Law*, Vol. I, pp. 123–124. He held that the German people were the ultimate sovereignty in the later German Empire. Also R. L. Ashley: *American Government*, p. 7. He maintains that the people are sovereign, because the people alone can change their old constitution and make new ones. Cf. Story: *Commentaries*, Vol. I, Bk. I, p. 210; and Pomeroy: *Constitutional Law*, pp. 4–5; Treitschke: *Politics*, Vol. II, p. 352. The opinions of the courts in regard to the sovereignty of the people revealed in the following cases: Chisholm vs. Georgia 2 U.S. 419, 471. Spooner vs. McConnell, Federal Case No. 13, 249, and Yick Wo vs. Hopkins, 118 U.S. 356, 365.

Compare W. L. Clark: *Elementary Law*, 1909, p. 22.

④ The terms "Nation" and "People" have been loosely used. Maine and Jameson did not seem to distinguish between them. See Maine: *Popular Government*, pp. 7, 8; and Jameson: "National Sovereignty" in *Political Science Quarterly*, Vol. V, p. 198. The French word "Peuple" has been translated into "Nation". See League of Nations: *Provisional Verbatim Records*, 1920, I, p. 4.

the inhabitants of a territory without an additional idea, at least favorable idea.[1] "If the people," says one of the advocates, "are the sovereign by a union—a conglomeration of previously detached parcels of sovereignty—each member holds a share in the sovereignty."[2] It, i. e., the people, is not and can not be sovereign, as it is held by another able advocate, because in the first place, that theory asserts that a sovereignty is apart from an organic people; secondly, that it is an inorganic mass, or a formless crowd, which is "destitute of the consciousness of unity which is implied in the will and is the condition of sovereignty"; and thirdly, that "it can not make clear what the will of the many is, nor by what law its sovereignty or its reserved sovereignty is to be ascertained nor how it is to be exercised".[3]

While denying that the people are sovereign, they also deny that the federal union or federal government, or the several states are sovereign. "Government", it is declared by one, "is the institution in which the sovereignty of the nation is realized"[4]. The federal government is merely the creature of the federal constitution, and the federal constitution is the creature of the nation.[5]

The member-state, or to use Mulford's own term, the commonwealth, is not sovereign, because the commonwealth is of itself incomplete and presumes the being of the nation in which it subsists.[6] Moreover, the commonwealth of itself has no permanence, and in the nation alone it has its consistent end.[7] Furthermore, "the commonwealth has in itself no external relation, excepting only to the nation and to the other commonwealths through the nation. It comprehends no foreign relation, that is a relation to an international state. It can enter into no league nor alliance, nor any treaty"[8].

While the commonwealth has no real sovereignty which is in the nation,[9] it is, nevertheless, invested with a formal sovereignty which is "limited to a certain process and to the formal exercise of certain powers in the prosecution of that process"[10]. For the commonwealth has, in the historical development of the United States, its simplest and

---

[1] See Merriam, *History of the Theory of Sovereignty*, pp. 174-175. Lieber, *Miscellaneous Writings*, Vol. II, p. 228. Also H. P. Judson, *Our Federal Republic*, p. 2.

[2] Lieber, *Manual of Political Ethics*, Vol. I, pp. 219-220.

[3] E. Mulford, *The Nation*, 1872, pp. 134-185. Cf. Pomeroy, *Constitutional Law*, p. 5.

[4] Mulford, *ibid.*, p. 140.

[5] See *ibid.*, p. 300.

[6] *Ibid.*, p. 145.

[7] *Ibid.*

[8] *Ibid.*, pp. 303-305.

[9] Mulford, *ibid.*, p. 302.

[10] *Ibid.*

its highest organization.①

So much for the negative side of the theory ⟨is⟩ under consideration. Let us turn to its constructive side. A nation, according to one writer of this school, implies a homogeneous population, inhabiting an inherent territory; a population having a common language, literature, institutions, and "an organic unity with one another, as well as being conscious of a common destiny"②. "It exists," according to another writer, "as an organic and moral being; its existence is a fact, and the apprehension of its existence in its beginning, is in the conscious life of man."③

In holding that the nation is an organic and moral being with a conscious life, some writers even go so far as to maintain a position which is colored with the divine theory. Thus it is said, that nation "has also a divine foundation and has for its end the fulfillment of the divine end in history. It has its issue in the divine prevision, that is in the moral nature of man"④.

Having understood what is meant by nation, we come to the notion of sovereignty. Sovereignty, as has been said, is in the nation and in the nation alone. But what is sovereignty? Professor Lieber defines it as "the right, obligation and power which human society or the state has to do all that is necessary for the existence of man in society"⑤. It is defined by Mulford as existing in the nation as it is an organic and moral person, and in it and through it justice is asserted and realized in a moral order.⑥

---

① E. Mulford, *The Nation*, 1872, p. 291. In another place he declares that "the nation in its sovereignty is immanent in the commonwealth. Its determination is the supreme law; the law of the nation is the law in every commonwealth. The Constitution of the United States is the constitution of every state. The real sovereignty is in the nation, and the will of the people is prevalent through the whole". p. 302.

② Lieber, *Miscellaneous Writings*, Vol. II, p. 228.

③ Mulford, *ibid.*, p. 55.

④ Mulford, *ibid.*, p. 54. He continues: "It is not the continuance of the family, nor the product of force, nor the working of instinct, nor the result of the social compact, nor the creation of the sovereignty of the people; while the truths which underlie these otherwise false assumptions, in the course of providence, illustrate in a greater or less degree the rise and growth and conservation of the nation." Cf. Brownson, *American Republic*, 1865, p. 192.

⑤ Lieber, *Manual of Political Ethics*, Vol I, p. 216. In another place he defines sovereignty "as the selfsufficient source of all power from which all specific powers are derived. It can dwell, therefore, according to the view of freemen, with society, the nation only". See his *Civil Liberty and Self-Government*, p. 156. The words "nation" and "society" were used by Lieber to mean one and the same thing. Cf. J. Wilson, *Law Lecture*, Vol. I, ch., 2.

⑥ Mulford, *ibid.*, p. 113. Cf. Jameson, *A Treatise on Constitutional Conventions: Their History, Powers and Modes of Procedure*, 1866, sec. 18. A nation is "a political body one and indivisible, made up of the citizens of the United States, without distinction of age, sex, color or condition of life". Jameson, *ibid.*, sec. 57.

"Sovereignty resides in the society or body politic, in the corporate unit resulting from the organization of many into one, and not in the individuals constituting such unit, nor in any number of them, as such, nor even in all of them, except as organized into a body politic and acting as such." Jameson, *ibid.*, section 18.

The indices of sovereignty are independence, authority, supremacy, unity, and majesty; and its external manifestations are inalienable, indivisible, irresponsible to any external authority, and comprehensive of the whole political order. ①

3. Sovereignty of the State

Closely connected with the theory of the sovereignty of the nation is that of the sovereignty of the state② which has been well elaborated by Professor Burgess. Professor Burgess was under the influence of German writers such as Zorn and Seydel, of French writers, such as Bodin and Rousseau, of English writers such as Hobbes and Austin, and of American writers such as Calhoun and Stephens.

Sovereignty is defined by Professor Burgess as the "original, absolute, unlimited, universal power over the individual subject and over all associations of subjects"③. To him, it is not only the essential characteristic of the state, but also the first and the highest conceivable mark of the state. ④ Where there is no sovereignty there is no state. No one can exist without the other.

Following this premise, it is concluded that there is only one kind of state, namely, a state with sovereignty which he has defined. This again leads him to deny that "there is no such a thing as a federal state"⑤. What is really meant by the phrase federal state, is a dual system of government under a common sovereignty. The transition of the sovereignty from the several states which were once independent and sovereign is nothing more than "in the case of the transition of the sovereignty from monarch to aristocracy, and from the aristocracy to the democracy, when the preceding form in which the sovereignty was organized is not entirely abolished; i. e., the old states become parts of the government in the state, and nothing more"⑥. Once the several states enter into a union and form a federal state, they lose the character of being called as states, and consequently, their sovereignties. In common usage, they still may be called states, but they are states only in name or "a title of honor", without any corresponding substance. ⑦ "Confusion and inertia of thought support it for a long time. When new

---

① Mulford, *The Nation*, 1872, pp. 129–130.

② *Ibid.*, p. 131.

③ How the theory of the sovereignty of the nation is different from that of the sovereignty of the state in the last analysis, is hard to conceive. Professor Burgess distinguished between nation and state, yet Burgess's definition of nation is certainly different from that of Mulford or Lieber. See Burgess, *Political Science and Constitutional Law*, pp. 1–4. Mulford, *The Nation*, p. 145.

④ See *Political Science Quarterly*, Vol. VIII, p. 128.

⑤ *Political Science and Constitutional Law*, Vol. I, p. 79.

⑥ *Ibid.*, p. 80.

⑦ *Political Science and Constitutional Law*, Vol. I, pp. 79–80.

things proceed out of old ones, it is a long time before we invent the new names rightly describing the new character."①

While admitting that a federal state may be created by several independent and sovereign states, Burgess does not think that this was true in the case of the United States. He holds that a sovereign state existed at the time of the establishment of the first Continental Congress in 1764, two years before the Declaration of Independence. Thus he says, "Complete geographical separation and partial ethnical separation from the motherland, together with complete geographical unity, substantial ethnical unity, and almost complete identity of interests among themselves were the forces which conspired, at last, to awaken the consciousness of the people of these thirteen colonies to the fact that they had attained the natural conditions of a sovereignty, —a state. The impulse to objectify this consciousness in institutions became irresistible. Its first enduring form was the Continental Congress. This was the first organization of the American state. From the first moment of its existence there was something more upon this side of the Atlantic than thirteen local governments. There was a sovereignty, a state; not in idea simply or upon paper, but in fact and in organization."②

This being the origin of the sovereignty of the American state, it is only natural and logical that "with us the government is not the sovereign organization of the state"③. For "back of the government lies the constitution; and back of the constitution, the original sovereign state, which ordains the constitution both of government and of liberty"④.

Here we come to a special feature of Burgess's political theory which is widely accepted by his followers and American political writers. This is the distinction between the state and the government.⑤ "This", as he points out, "is the point in which the public law of the United States has reached a far higher development than that of any state of Europe."⑥ To Europeans, especially the German publicists, the state and the government almost mean one and the same thing, for in Europe, the distinction between these two is not yet as clear it is in the United States in objective reality. The state, as he conceives it, is a supreme organization which is above and outside of government. It is in the state alone, not in the government, that sovereignty resides. There may be different governmental powers within a state, but there is only one sovereignty. There

---

① *Political Science and Constitutional Law*, Vol. I, p. 80.
② Burgess, *ibid.*, p. 100.
③ *Ibid.*, p. 57.
④ *Ibid.*
⑤ This is of course not Burgess's invention. See Brownson, *American Republic*, p. 207.
⑥ Burgess, *op. cit.* p. 57.

are many governments in the United States, but there is only one state.

4. Sovereignty of the United States

The theory of the sovereignty of the United States is not easily differentiated from that of the sovereignty of the state or that of the sovereignty of the nation. Its best expounder, Brownson, uses the terms "state", "nation", and "united states" loosely. [1] Yet it seems that we must not be misled by terms and disregard the substance. In order to have a clear understanding of what is meant by the sovereignty of the united states, we may quote a statement from Brownson's *American Republic*. "The key to the mystery is precisely in this appellation, United States, which is not the name of the country, — for its distinctive name is America, —but a name expressive of its politcal organization. In it there are no sovereign people without states, and no States without union, or that are not 'United' States. The term 'united' is not part of a proper name, but is simply an adjective qualifying States, and has its full and proper sense. Hence, while the sovereignty is and must be in the States, it is in the States united and not in the States severally."[2]

A somewhat similar view is taken by John Hurd in these words: "The inhabitants of the United States constituted a nation in which sovereignty was manifested by the organized political people of the several states, being united as States, and was exercised by a general government as the instrument of that organized political people of such states, being so united, and by State governments as the instrument of the political people of each several State, being united with the other States."[3]

The thesis advanced by the defenders of this theory is that a sovereign state, or a group of sovereign states may, with or without its or their consent, lose its sovereignty or sovereignties, but only by being merged in or subjected to another sovereign state or states then existing. The logic is that sovereignty can only be given up by one party to another party which has already existed before the former gives up its sovereignty; in other words, a state can not part with its own sovereignty to nothing or to a non-existent body. "A prince can abdicate his power, because by abdicating he simply gives back to the people the trust he had received from them; but a nation can not, save by merging itself in another", says Brownson.[4]

Following this reasoning, sovereign states may, by agreement, unite in an alliance,

---

[1] See Brownson, *American Republic*, 1865, chapters VIII and IX. Also see Hurd, *Theory of Our National Existence*, p. 141.

[2] Brownson, *ibid.*, p. 221.

[3] Hurd, *Theory of Our National Existence*, p. 141.

[4] Brownson, *American Republic*, p. 194.

league or confederation and agree to exercise the whole or part of their sovereign power through a common agency; but in doing this, they do not lose their respective sovereignty; because, as has been pointed out, the organ or agency created by them was not in existence at the time or before they could part with their own sovereignty. "An independent state not merged in another, or that is not subject to another", so the argument runs, "can not cease to be a sovereign nation, even if it would".[1]

Applying this reasoning to the United States, the question that has to be asked is whether the several states of the Union were severally sovereign states or not. If they were, they must remain so now,[2] and "secession is, then an incontestable right; not a right held under the constitution or derived from the convention but a right held prior to it, independently of it, inherent in the State sovereignty, and inseparable from it"[3]. If the colonies have become severally sovereign states after their separation from Great Britain, a single or indivisible sovereign state could never have been created by them by agreement; for "no sovereignty is of conventional origin, and none can emerge from the convention that did not enter it"[4].

But this was not the case, for it is inconsistent with the historical fact. The several states had never been severally sovereign. Prior to the Declaration of Independence, they were under the sovereignty of Great Britain, and after that, they have existed and acted only as stated.[5] It is true that in the Declaration of Independence, they declared themselves independent states, but they were independent jointly, not severally. "They unitedly declared independence; they carried on the war for independence, won it, and were acknowledged by foreign powers and by the mother country as the 'United' States, not as severally independent sovereign states."[6] "While they declared and won their independence jointly, they exercised their sovereignty only as states united or the United States."[7]

It is no doubt that there was a possibility for Great Britain to pass the sovereignty to the states severally or separately and consequently each of them would become a distinct sovereign state, but she did not do so.

The whole question, argues the learned defender, is a question of fact, "and the

---

[1] Brownson, *American Republic*, p. 194. "The creature takes nothing from the Creator, exhausts not his creative energy, and it is only by his retaining and continuously exerting his creative power that the creature continues to exist." *Ibid.*, p. 194.

[2] Brownson, *American Republic*, p. 196.

[3] *Ibid.*

[4] *Ibid.*, p. 200.

[5] *Ibid.*, p. 208.

[6] *Ibid.*, p. 209.

[7] Brownson, *op. cit.*, p. 210.

fact is determined by determining who it was that assumed it, exercised it, and has continued to exercise it. As to this there is no doubt. The sovereignty as a fact has been assumed and exercised by the United States, the States united, and never by the States separately, or severally. Then as a fact the sovereigty that was before independence was in Great Britain, passed on independence to the States united, and reappears in all its vigor in the United States, the only successor to Great Britain known to or recognized by the civilized world"[1].

So there is no question of law or antecedent right involved in the case. It is useless to appeal to the language or provisions of the Federal Constitution.[2] The constitution is created by the sovereign and it is law for the citizens of a state only so long as the state remains one of the United States.[3]

5. Sovereignty of the Electorate

The theory of the sovereignty of the electorate was advanced by Austin.[4] We have already intimated that ⟨is⟩ his scientific and classic definition of sovereignty.[5] It is the heart and the central point of his whole system. But when this definition is applied to a federal state, or what he prefers to call a supreme federal state, difficulty at once arises. He is by no means unaware of this fact. Thus he says, "In a political society styled a composite state sovereignty is so shared by various individuals or bodies, that one sovereign body whereof they are the constituent members, is not conspicuous and easily perceived."[6]

Here neither the general government, nor the several states, may be called sovereign so far as he can conceive. It would be not a federal state, if any one of the two alone is sovereign.[7] "The political powers of the common or general government," says he, "are merely delegated to it by the several united governments, it is not a constitutent member of the sovereign, but is merely its subject minister."[8]

---

[1] Brownson, *American Republic*, pp. 212-213. The states were called "united" not confederated States, even in the very Articles of Confederation themselves, and officially the United States were called the "Union". *Ibid.*, p. 215.

[2] *Ibid.*, p. 198.

[3] *Ibid.* In regard to the theory of the sovereignty of the united states, compare also N. C. Butler, "Sovereignty in Modern State" in *American Law Review*, Vol. 39(1905), p. 393. J. Bigelow, *World Peace*, p. 221. Fang Yue Ting vs. U. S. 149 U. S. 698, 711. The Chinese Exclusion Cases, 130 U. S. 581, 604.

[4] Compare Blackstone, *Commentaries*, Vol. I, p. 171.

[5] "If a determinate human superior, not in a habit of obedience to a like superior, receives habitual obedience from the bulk of society, that determinate superior is sovereign in that society, and the society is a society political and independent." See his *Jurisprudence*, Vol. I, p. 226.

[6] Austin, *Jurisprudence*, Vol. I, p. 257.

[7] *Ibid.*, pp. 258-260.

[8] *Ibid.*

Although the political powers come from the several state governments, the several state governments are not severally or separately sovereign, for as he points out, if these several governments were severally sovereign, they would form a system of confederated states rather than a federal state. ①

In Austin's mind, there is a clear difference between a federal state and a confederated state, for one is a society political and independent, while the other is only a permanent alliance composed of two or more sovereign states. ② While the several states in a federal state are not severally sovereign, they were, it seems to Austin, as the members of a confederated state, sovereign in character before the federal state was created.

A state as such must have a sovereignty and the sovereignty must be somewhere. So ⟨is⟩ in a federal state. This was a line of thought firmly adhered to by Austin. There is a sovereignty in a federal state. But where is it? "I believe," says he, "that the sovereignty of each of the States, and also of the larger state arising from the federal union, resides in the States' governments, as forming an aggregate body; meaning by a state's government, not its ordinary legislature, but the body of its citizens which appoints its ordinary legislature, and which, the union apart, is properly sovereign therein."③

"The body of citizens which appoints the ordinary legislature is known as the electorate and it is in this body that the sovereignty resides." There is no doubt that Austin, realizing that the legal competence of the legislature of the several states, of the Congress of the federal union, and of both combined, is limited by written constitutions, as is different from the practice of Great Britain, was forced to place the sovereignty in the electorate. ④

6. Sovereignty as Constitution-Making Power

The theory of sovereignty as constitution-making power is summarized by an American political writer as follows: "The fundamental form of a state is called its constitution. This collection of principles creates government, outlines its powers, and adjusts the relation of the state to its citizens. Hence the government is limited in its powers by the constitution, and is inferior in authority to the body that may create or change this fundamental

---

① Austin, *Jurisprudence*, Vol. I, pp. 257, 259.
② *Ibid.*, p. 257.
③ *Ibid.*, p. 261.
④ Willoughby, *Nature of the State*, p. 296. Professor Ritchie pointed out that in placing sovereignty in the electorate, Austin no longer speaks as a lawyer. See *Annals of American Academy of Political and Social Science* (January 1891), Vol. I, p. 1392. Cf. Dicey, *Law of the Constitution*, pp. 68, 73, 424–425.

ducument. There is no higher authority possible than that which creates the constitution. That authority expresses the direct will of the state and is therefore sovereign."①

The best expounder of the theory of this school is perhaps Professor Dicey of England. Looking to the omnipotent powers exercised by the Parliament of his own country, Professor Dicey does not have any difficulty in locating its sovereignty. But the United States is different in her political structure from that of Great Britain. Here sovereignty is not vested in any ordinary legislature acting under the Constitution, for so to vest legislative sovereignty would be inconsistent with the aim of federalism, namely, the permanent division between the sphere of the national government and of the several states. ② The United States would become a unitary Republic instead of a federal state, if the changes were made to permit Congress, or the legislature of a single state alone, to legally alter the Constitution of the United States.

But there must be a sovereignty and only one sovereignty in a federal as it is in a unitary state, and there must be a place where sovereignty rests. "One may say," says Dicey, "with sufficient accuracy for our present purpose, that the legal sovereignty of the United States resides in the States' governments as forming one aggregate body represented by three-fourths of the several states at any time belonging to the union."③

It must be remembered that when Dicey considers sovereignty as constitution-making power, he speaks as a lawyer, for to him, besides the legal sovereignty, there is a political sovereignty and the location of one is not necessarily the same as of the other. But difference in location does not mean that they are in conflict, for they must be always in harmony with each other. "That the conduct of the different parts of the legislature should be determined by rules meant to secure harmony between the action of the legislative sovereign and the wishes of the political sovereignty, must appear probable from general considerations."④ Certainly this does not mean that there is no possibility of having conflict, for sometimes they do, and if they do, political sovereignty must take precedence over the legal sovereignty, because the latter "is limited on every

---

① Gettell, *Introduction to Political Science*, 1910, pp. 101–102. Also Foster, *On the Constitution*, 1895, p. 270; also an article in *American Law Review* for 1886, p. 519, under the title "The Subjection of the State to Law".

② Dicey, *The Law of the Constitution*, 1885, p. 144, 8th ed.

③ Dicey, *The Law of the Constitution*, 1885, pp. 144–145. Following here, he quotes Articles V of the Constitution of the United States which declares "Congress, whenever two thirds of both houses shall deem it necessary, shall propose amendments to the Constitution, or on the application of the legislatures of two-thirds of the several states, shall call a convention for proposing amendments, which in either case shall be valid to all intents and purposes as part of this Constitution, when ratified by the legislatures of three-fourths of the several states, or by conventions in three-fourths thereof, as the one or the other mode of ratification may be proposed by Congress". Cf. The amendment clause of the Swiss Constitution.

④ *Ibid.*, p. 425.

side by the possibility of popular resistance"①.

Professor Leacock may be regarded as an advocate of this theory. He argues that "the creation of the federal state annihilates the sovereignty of the component states, — not limits it or divides it, but annihilates it"②. Sovereignty, according to him, either is or is not. Not only that the several states by reason of being merged into a union lose their sovereignty and consequently are no longer sovereign, but that even the central government is not a sovereign either. Sovereignty can only be found in the body, wherever and whatever it may be, which has power to amend the constitution. ③

It is admitted by some of the writers in this group that such sovereignty as they conceive is not permanent in character, as Wilson calls it, "daily operative power". Nevertheless, "It is", says one of the writers, "clear that theoretically at any rate it exists, and may be looked upon as having a legal supremacy as complete as that of the British Parliament. "④

7. Sovereignty as Law-Making Power

Not satisfied with the theory of sovereignty as constitution-making power for the reason that sovereignty can not be considered as dormant or latent, that "sovereignty as a question of fact, deals with the organs that express the state's will now; not with the original revolutionary source of authority by which the people, in creating the state, established its government, that such bodies, when they do act, are really a part of the government"⑤. Another theory which is known as the theory of sovereignty as lawmaking power has been devised. This theory, like that of sovereignty as constitution-making power, is purely legal in its character and those who advocate it are writers from the

---

① Dicey, *The Law of the Constitution*, 1885, p. 70. The limitations, according to him, come from two sides, one is internal and the other is external. See pp. 74, 77.

② Leacock, *Elements of Political Science*, 2nd ed. , 1913, p. 240.

③ *Ibid.*, pp. 240-241.

④ Munro, *The Government of the United States*, 1925, pp. 66, 250. Professor Munro also denies both the theory of federal sovereignty and that of state sovereignty finding sovereignty only within the limits of the Constitution. The power or authority which can change the consititution is the only absolute sovereignty in the United States.

Lansing takes a somewhat similar view, though in a limited sense. Speaking of the sovereignty and its location in the United States, he says, "In time of domestic peace rests in those who, as units, adopt and amend the constitution. These are clearly political groups of individuals, each forms a separate state of the union, not the individuals. " See "Note on Sovereignty" in *American Journal of International Law*, Vol. 1, p. 126.

See also M. Bernard, *Neutrality of Great Britain During the American War*, p. 43. "Behind both general and local authorities, there is a power intricate in respect of its machinery and extremely difficult to set in motion, requiring the concurrence of three-fourths of the states acting by their legislature or in conventions which can amend the constitution itself. This power is unlimited, or very nearly so. "

⑤ Gettell, *Introduction to Political Science*, pp. 102, 103.

lawyer's point of view.

Among writers of this school, Professor Willoughby must be regarded as the most celebrated. ① As to the nature of sovereignty, Professor Willoughby is no more than a mouth-piece of Austin. As to its location, he differs from him. ② "Sovereignty", he holds, "is the vital principle in the life of the state. The validity of all law is dependent upon it, and all international relations are determined by it."③ "In a general way," he continues, "it is convenient to say that sovereignty is that term which denotes the highest power of the state, and that that person or number of persons, who possesses or possess this power, is or are sovereign."④

Taking the view that sovereignty is a power which can only be exercised through existing governmental organs, he proceeds to argue that this supreme power is exhibited whenever the will of the state is expressed. ⑤ As the will of the state is, and can only be expressed through the law-making bodies, this latter must be considered as the sovereignty of the state. "By whomsoever, or whatsoever body, therefore, the will of the state is expressed, and law created, there we have sovereignty exercised."⑥

By law-making bodies, however, he does not mean it in a narrow sense, applying it to those bodies by which formal statutory enactments are made, and these bodies include: (1) Legislatures, national, commonwealth, or local. (2) Courts; in so far as they create law, not when merely interpreting or applying existing law. (3) Executive officials, in so far as they create law, by ordinances, proclamations, etc. (4) Conventions, when acting legally as law-making bodies, as in the case of a constitutional convention properly assembled. (5) Electorate, when exercising powers of referendum or of plebiscite. ⑦

---

① Gettell is also one of its advocates.
② Willoughby, *Nature of the State*, 1896, pp. 182–183.
③ *Ibid.*, p. 185.
④ *Ibid.*, p. 185.
⑤ *Ibid.*, p. 302.
⑥ *Ibid.*
⑦ *Ibid.*, p. 303. Gettell, *Introduction to Political Science*, p. 103.

CHAPTER III
SOVEREIGNTY IN THE FEDERAL STATE
(Continued)

8. Divisibility Doctrine of Sovereignty

We have, so far, outlined nine theories of sovereignty as applied to the federal state. We have pointed out that the first two are opposite to each other while the last seven are different forms of a compromise of the first two. It remains now for us to consider the last one which is also one form of the compromise theory. It is to be borne in mind that while this last one, i. e., the divisibility doctrine of sovereignty, though similar to the other seven in form is by no means similar in nature. Here we find one fundamental similarity among the nine theories which we have already considered and a fundamental difference between the nine theories on one hand and the last one on the other. In spite of the differences between, or in conflict with, one another, as in the case of the theory of sovereignty of the several states and that of the sovereignty or the federal government, they are all similar in that their advocates agree that sovereignty is, in its nature, indivisible. Here lies the keynote of our study of the theories of sovereignty in the federal state. It implies both the old and the new theory or theories. Here, there is a monistic doctrine and here, also, there is a pluralistic theory. It is here that we find the combination, the complexity and the fruitfulness of the traditional theory; and it is here that we find the beginning and the development of the modern theory. ①

A. German Writers

The divisibility doctrine of sovereignty has been advocated by many German publicists. Waitz was one of the most conspicuous representatives. He was influenced by the well-known French writer, Tocqueville, whose doctrine of sovereignty was enunciated in a treatise entitled *Democracy in America*, which we shall have occasion to discuss a little later.

---

① Grotius had pointed out that sovereignty may be divided; but this was not developed by his successors, nor did it attract the attention of his opponents.

Waitz strongly denies sovereignty as the highest power in the state and therefore indivisible both in respect to sphere and objects. Sovereignty, he believes, may be restricted in extent but not in content.① "Sovereignty is to be considered, it appears, qualitatively rather than quantitatively. The question is not how far does the power extend, if it is sovereign, but in what manner is it exercised within the given limits. The sovereign need not be very extensive, but it must be intensive."②

Waitz conceives that independence and sovereignty are one and the same thing. ③ Where there is independence, there is sovereignty. As the several states are independent in their own sphere in certain respects, they must be sovereign in certain respects. To divide it, is not, as Colhoun would say, to destroy it. In applying this contention to Germany, he holds that there sovereignty is actually divided between the union-state and the member-state. Each is sovereign in its own sphere. "Both powers, that of confederation and that of separate states, must be independent (sovereign) in their own sphere; neither must receive delegated power from the other."④ In the language of Professor Dunning, "Sovereignty is here conceived as meaning authority that extends over all conceivable subject matter"⑤.

Such a division of sovereignty is necessary in theory as well as in fact in a "Bundesstaat" and it is from this that he distinguishes between a unitary state (Einheitsstaat) and a federal state (Bundesstaat). A unitary state is a state in which a single government exercises all the powers that are necessary to a state in every field, while a federal state is a state in which powers are exercised through two sets of governments. ⑥

---

① Georg Waitz, *Grundzug der Politik*, 1862, p. 166.

② See Merriam, *History of the Theory of Sovereignty*, 1900, p. 186.

③ Waitz, *ibid.*, p. 44. See also K. Gareis, *Volkerrecht*, second ed., pp. 48, 95. Also his *Allgemeine Staatrecht*, Bk. I, section 65.

On the other hand, Halleck distinguishes between sovereignty and independence and argues that a state may be sovereign but not independent. *International Law*, Vol. I, pp. 71, 72.

④ See Bluntschli, *Theory of the State*, p. 488, footnote.

⑤ Dunning, *Political Theories*, Vol. III, p. 284.

⑥ Waitz, *ibid.*, p. 163. For a further discussion of the theory of Waitz, see Brie, *Der Bundesstaat*, pp. 105-118.

Zacharia, in his early view, maintained that the central government alone is sovereign; but after the attempt of the reform of the Bundes (Bundesreformversuche) and his active life in the national convention, he changed his conception and shared the view of Waitz. He spoke of the subjective respect of sovereignty and the objective respect of sovereignty. The subjective respect of sovereignty, which the federal union shares with the separate states, is one or independent or sovereign within its own sphere and which tends to be a true sovereignty (Staatsherrschaft) over the member states. In its objective respect, on the other hand, in a federation as well as in a confederation, there is a division of common or federal affairs from the special affairs of the individual states; and the power of the states are superior in so far as belonging to them. *Deutsches Staats und Bundestrecht*, 1841, sec. 21, 27. Cf. the peculiar view of H. Escher, a Swiss writer; *Handbuch der praktischen Politik*, 1864, Bk. II, pp. 481, 553.

Bluntschli is another German writer who holds that sovereignty is divided in a federal state.① Sovereignty according to him, implies, in the first place, independence of the authority of any other state; secondly, public dignity—what the Romans called *majestas*; thirdly, plentitude of public as opposed to mere particular powers; fourthly, that it is the highest in the state; and lastly, unity, a necessary condition in every organism.②

In a unitary state, all elements composing sovereignty is in one place and sovereignty is one and indivisible. But in the compound states, which he divides into (1) states having colonies or vassal provinces, (2) states in personal unions, (3) confederacies, and (4) federal unions,③ the elements or characteristics of sovereignty are divided, and consequently sovereignty is divided between the union and the states forming the same. Independence, dignity, public power and unity must be understood as only relative.④ In a federal state or a federal empire, there is independence, and there is dependence, but neither independence nor dependence is absolute.⑤ There is an organized nation for the whole, but at the same time, the people of the particular states also possess organic unity.⑥ "Thus we speak of Americans, and also of Pennsylvanians sand Virginians; of a Swiss nation, and of Bernese and Genevese; of Germans, and of Prussians, Saxons, Bavarians, etc. The collective state is as free in its movements and as well provided with organs as the simple state. But the separate states are not at all vassals; within their sphere they are as independent as a simple state."⑦

Like Waitz, he maintains that sovereignty may be limited in extent, but not in content.⑧ The particular states, in forming the federal union, may surrender a certain portion of their sovereignty to the federal union, but the remaining portion is just as real as the part given up. Subjection and subordination of a state does not destroy its sovereignty completely.⑨ "Thus in Switzerland, cantonal sovereignty is distinguished from federal sovereignty, similarly, in North America and in the German Empire, there

---

① See also Chapter Ⅱ.
② Bluntschli, *Theory of the State*, 1892, p. 595.
③ *Ibid.*, p. 486.
④ *Ibid.*, p. 495.
⑤ "La Souverainete ne signifie ni l'independance absolue, ni la liberte absolue, car les etats ne sont pas des etres absolus, mais des personnes dont les droits sont limites." *Droit international Codifie*, par Bluntschli, traduit de L'Allemand par M. C. Lardy, 1886, p. 88.
⑥ Bluntschli, *Theory of the State*, p. 488.
⑦ *Ibid.*
⑧ *Ibid.*, p. 526.
⑨ *Ibid.*

is a difference between the sovereignty of the Union or of the Empire and that of the federated states."①

Those who held the theory of the sovereignty of the Empire have been wont to assert that, by Article 78 of the Imperial Constitution the Empire was given the right to extend its competency without any restriction against the will of the individual states. ② This assertion, as has been pointed out by Bornhak, was incorrect at least so far as Prussia was concerned, for the reason that she alone had seventeen votes in the Federal Council (Bundesrat) and could veto any measure introduced in the Council. ③

Neither the Empire nor the separate states were absolutely sovereign in Germany, as Bornhak insisted, yet both were sovereign in a limited sense. Sovereignty, according to him, has its positive and negative sense. ④ It is positive in regard to its extent and it is negative in regard to its content. A complete independence from any high authority in its own sphere or in the powers left to them, is a sovereignty exercised by the several states in its negative sense; and the right to send representatives to the Bundesrat is a sovereign power exercised by the several states in its positive sense. ⑤

Even Treitschke, while maintaining that the sovereignties of all other member states in Germany had been swallowed up in that of the Empire, was forced to admit that

---

① Bluntschli, *Theory of the State*, p. 526.

See also *Das Moderne Volkerrecht der civilisirtenals Rechtsbuch Dargestellt*, 1872, sec. 70, pp. 90-91. "In der Regel gibt es nur eine Souveranetat fur ein bestimmtes Volk und Land, wie nur Einen Stat, Ausnahmsweise zeigt sich in zusammengesetzten Staten (Statenbunden, Bundesstaten, Statenreichen, Bundesreichen) auf demselben Boden und fur dieselbe Bevolkerung eine Doppelsouveranetat wie eine zweifache Statenbildnng, die eine des Gesammstatus, die andere der Einzelstaten."

"Der Bundesstat (die Union) dagegen ist eine einheitliche Gestaltung des Gesammtstates, der scharfer unterschieden wird von den Einzelstaten und in sich als Stat vollstandig organisirt ist. Zuerst erscheint diese von Alexander Hamilton erdachte moderne Statsform ausgebildet in Nordamerika seit 1787, und ist in Schweiz 1848 nachgebildet worden. In der Union ist die Dopplesouveranetat klarer dargestellt als in der Confoderation, in welcher noch die Souveranitat der Einzelstaten vollig uberwiegt." It is to be noted that, to Bluntschli, the German Empire has a special character and it is better to call it as "Bundesreich". See *Volkerrecht*, p. 90.

② See C. Bornhak, *Preussisches Staatsrecht*, Vol. I, p. 71 (1888). See also Hanel, Aehnlich, *Studien zum deutschen staatsrechte*, 1873-1880, I, Section 240.

③ Imperial Constitution of 1871.

④ Bornhak, *ibid.*, pp. 69 ff.

⑤ *Ibid.*, p. 73, "Wenn man gefragt hat, wodurch sich Umfang und Inhalt unterscheiden, so ist zu erwidern, dass der Umfang das positive Begriffsmoment der Souveranitat, den Inbegriff der staatlichen Hoheitsrechte, der Inhalt das negative Begriffsmoment, die Freiheit von jeder hoheren Gewalt ausdruckt."

"Die deutschen Einzelstaaten geniessen daher tross ihrer Beschrankung auf einzelne Zweige der staatlichen Thatigkeit in der ihnen verbliebenen Sphare eine vollstandige Unabhangigkeit von jeder hoheren Macht, d. h. die Souveranitat in negativen Sinne."

Prussia still retained her sovereignty. Thus by implication if not by express recognition he admitted the divisibility doctrine by reason of his belief that there were two sovereignties existing in the German Empire. "What would happen to Germany if Prussia should cease to be?" He asked. "There could be no more German Empire. Out of this follows a truth, unpleasant to most people, but which contains no insult to a non-Prussian—namely, that Prussia is the former States within the German Empire who has preserved her sovereignty."① "Prussia, too", he went on, "is the only German State which is secure from any diminution of the limits of its sovereignty." This is to be proved by the fact that Prussia had 17 votes in the Federal Council which is more than enough "to hinder any curtailment of her sovereign rights"②.

B. Swiss Writers

Since their own country is federal in form, Swiss writers have different views. Those who hold the theory of sovereignty of the Cantons, base their argument on the express provision of the Federal Constitution,③ and those who maintain the theory of sovereignty of the Federal government argue on the ground of the extensive authority

---

① Treitschke, *Politics*, English translation, Vol. II, p. 373.

② *Ibid.*, p. 374.

The divisibility doctrine was also held by Robert von Mohl in his *Encyklopadie der Staatswissenschaften*, 1858, pp. 36-38, 96-97. Second edition, 1872, sections 49, pp. 366-367. "Die Zustandigkeit dieser Staatsgewalt (der bundesstaatlichen central Gewalt) ist aber wesentlich und nothwendig eine beschrankte und umfasst nicht die gesammte Aufgabe eines Rechtsstaates, denn ein bedeutender Theil dieser Zwecke verbleibt den einzelnen Bundesgliedern in selbstandigem Rechte. Es sind also zweierlei leitende und befehlende Gewalten neben einander: die uber das ganze Bundesgebiet sich erstreckende Centralgewalt, und die orlichen Gewalten der verschiedenen Gliederstaaten je in ihrem besonderen Gebiete. Beide sind iherm verfassungsmassigen Wirkungskreise unabhangig von einander, and beide haben, als virkliche Staatsgelalten, ihre eigenen Organe und ihre selbstandige Thatigkeit. Es besteht fur die Gliedstaaten keine beschrankte sondern eine getheilte Souveranetat." p. 367. "Die Gliederstaaten verlieren also einen entsprechenden Theil ihrer Souveranetat und es besteht neben der Staatsgewalt jedes Einzelstaates auch noch die hohere Bundesstaatsgewalt." *Ibid.*

See also Mohl, *Geschich und Literatur der Staatswissenschaften*, Bk. I, pp. 511-513, 515-517, 560.

In his Introduction to *Deutsche Staatsrecht* Schulze adopts the same position as Waitz with almost the same words. See Brie, *Der Bundesstaate*, p. 121. Schulze, *System des Deutschen Staatsrechts*, 1865, sections 206-207.

C. F. V. Gerber, *Grundzuge eines System Deutschen Staatsrechts*, p. 24. "Ein zwar auf einen gewissen Kreis beschrankte, innerhalb desselben aber wirkliche Staatsgewalt mit unmittelbarer Beherrschung des Volks." Appendix No. 3. Also *Der Norddeutsche Bund*, pp. 238-240, 244.

Blumer, *Handbuch des Schweizerischen Bundesstaatsrechtes*, 1863, pp. 141-147.

H. Ahrens, *Naturrecht, Oder Philosophie des Rechts und des Staate*, 6th ed., 1870, Bk. II, pp. 338-346. Compare also with Gareis, *Volkerrecht*, 2nd ed., 1901, p. 48. Also *Allegemeine Staatsrecht*, Bk. I, section 65. Von Adolf Arndt, *Das Staatsrecht des deutschen Reichs*, 1901, pp. 38 ff.

③ Constitution of 1848, Article III, of 1874, Article IV.

exercised by the Federal government, particularly by the legislative branch.① To compromise these two theories, there are also writers who adopt the divisibility doctrine. To the writers of the last group, Ruttiman has been the most conspicuous representative.②

Ruttimann vigorously attacks the position taken by Calhoun and his followers,③ and argues that each state gave up parts of her sovereignty by uniting herself to the Union and once she gave it up, the Union began an independent life, completely independent from the several states. "The statement that the creator stands above the creature in this case holds no truth."④

Having denied the proposition that the Union is not sovereign and that the several states alone are sovereign, he proceeds to discredit the indivisibility doctrine, for this, according to him, is inconsistent with facts.⑤ Sovereignty in its nature is divisible and in a federal government it is divided between the several states on the one hand and the federal government on the other. "Each part is supreme," says he, "in its own sphere with the freedom as if the other parts are not in existence."⑥ Here Ruttiman concurs with many German and French writers. The division of sovereignty, to him, is the characteristic of the federal state. The individual states are by no means subordinate to the federal government, or vice versa. They are co-ordinate to each other. "No body," he points out, "denies that the states are sovereign in many respects, yet nobody maintains that they are sovereign in all respects."⑦ The division of sovereignty is clear, for the sovereignty of the federal government refers to the general matters and that of the states to the local matters.

Contemporary statesmen, like M. Banjour, agree with Ruttiman in his conclusion, though their arguments are based on different grounds. Banjour raises the question as to whether there can be two sovereign powers or one sovereignty in Switzerland and whether

---

① In addition to the powers as conferred upon Congress in the United States, the powers given to the federal legislature may be found in Articles: 24, 25, 26, 32, 34, 37, 43, 49-57, 64, 69. etc. Cf. Dupriez, *Les Ministres dans les Principaux pays d'Europe et d'Amerique*, Vol. II, p. 175.

② Brie regarded Ruttimann as the best writer on the Swiss and the American Federation. Brie, *Der Bundesstaat*, p. 121.

③ P. Ruttiman, *Das Nordamerikanische Bundesstaat verglichen mit den politischen Einriehtungen der Schweiz*, Vol. I, p. 70 (1867-1782).

④ *Ibid.*, p. 70.

⑤ Ruttiman, *ibid.*, pp. 66, 71.

⑥ *Ibid.*, p. 48.

⑦ *Ibid.*, p. 54.

or not the term sovereignty can be applied to a cantonal autonomy.① To him these are the questions that the Swiss writers have to face. For his own part, he sees no reason why sovereignty is not divided in Switzerland.② Thus he says, "Confederation and Canton are alike sovereign in the particular spheres assigned to them by the Constitution."③ "I leave," he continues, "to others the task of fathoming a problem of purely theoretical interest, and confine myself to stating that the Constitution declares the Cantons to be sovereign wherever they have not delegated their powers to the Confederation."④

C. Dutch Writers

Political scientists in the Netherlands, such as J. R. Ferguson, also hold the theory under discussion. Like many other political scientists and international lawyers, Ferguson views sovereignty in two respects: the internal and the external. Internal sovereignty is the power exercised in conformity with the constitution of the state for purposes of government and internal policy, while external sovereignty, in the exercise of its functions for the maintenance of external relations, on the principles, of independence and equality with other states, is a subject of international law.⑤

Being an international lawyer, Ferguson inclines to the view that the term sovereignty would be more appropriate to the external attributes of the state. And in order to make a clear distinction in our mind, he suggests that the term "autonomy" may be employed as a substitute for the term internal sovereignty.⑥ But it is to be remembered that to use different terms does not mean that the two aspects of sovereignty are thereby different in kind.

Sovereignty, according to Ferguson, is represented by government; but the absence of a definite government or a condition of anarchy does not result in a state in which there is no sovereignty. The same is true as to a government which is not recognized by another state.⑦

What has been said is only a brief account of his theory of sovereignty in general. Let us turn to its application to a federal state. "When individual sovereign states form a federal union or a confederacy," says he, "the external sovereign functions are

---

① Banjour, *Real Democracy in Operation*, p. 3.
② *Ibid*.
③ *Ibid*. M. Banjour, however, admits that the sovereignty of the Cantons is now diminishing.
④ *Ibid*.
⑤ Ferguson, *Manual of International Law*, 1883, Vol. I, p. 81.
⑥ *Ibid*.
⑦ Ferguson, *ibid*., pp. 81-82.

delegated by all to one chief-government, in order to represent all or each of them (as the case may be) in the intercourse with other states outside the union, whilst also the internal sovereignty of the several component states of the union undergoes, at the same time, certain modifications, in conformity with the notion and conditions of the compact."①

It is clear then, sovereignty is divided into the internal and the external aspects and in a federal state one aspect of it, and in sometimes some parts of another aspect may be exercised by one government and the rest of it may be exercised by another. There is a possibility of division and there is a possibility of increasing and diminishing.②

D. French Writers

France is not and has never been a federal state, yet she has produced one of the greatest writers on the federal state, who is considered the father of the divisibility doctrine of sovereignty in continental Europe. This writer is none other than Tocqueville. To him, sovereignty is defined as the right of making laws.③ In France, he finds that the right of making laws is in one place,④ and the sovereignty is one and undivided. But this is not the case in the United States of America. "The Union", he says, "as it was established in 1789, possesses, it is true, a limited supremacy; but it was intended that within its limits it should form one and the same people. Within those limits the Union sovereign is sovereign. When this point is established and admitted, the inference is easy; for if it be acknowledged that the United States constitute one and the same people within the bounds prescribed by their constitution, it is impossible to refuse them the rights which belong to other nations."⑤

This being the case, the federal union must be regarded as a sovereign body. On the other hand, the sovereignty of the several states seems to suffer a severe blow as a result of the establishment of the Supreme Court of the United States, yet the dangers in this regard are less serious than they appear to be.⑥

The federal union is sovereign then in regard to the execution of the law of the

---

① Ferguson, *Manual of International Law*, 1883, Vol. I, p. 87. M. Ferguson points out also the difference between a federal state and a confederate state.

② In general, most of the writers take the German Empire, 1871–1918, Switzerland, and the United States as examples of federal states. M. Ferguson, on the other hand, groups both Switzerland and the German Empire as confederate states and the United States, Venezuela, Columbia, etc., as federal States. See *op. cit.*, p. 87, footnote.

③ De Tocqueville, *Democracy in America*, trans. by Henry Reeve, Vol. I, p. 122.

④ He thinks the king in France is sovereign. *Ibid.*

⑤ *Ibid.*, p. 144.

⑥ *Ibid.*, pp. 142, 146.

Union, and the relations of the nation with foreign powers; and the states are sovereign in regard to the regulation of the relations of the citizens amongst themselves. ① "The principal aim of the legislators of 1789," he says, "was to divide the sovereign authority into two parts. In the one they placed the control of all the general interests of the Union, in the other the control of special interests of the component states."② The difference between the sovereignty of the central government and that of the several states is pointed out more clearly in the following statement: "The sovereignty of the Union is an abstract being, which is connected with but few external objects; the sovereignty of the States is hourly perceptible; easily understood, constantly active, and if the former is of recent reaction, the latter is coeval with the people itself. The sovereignty of the Union is factious, that of the states natural and derives its existence from its own simple influence, like the authority of a parent."③

So far as theory is concerned, the distinction between the sovereignty of the federal union and that of the states is clear to every one. But there are difficulties none the less in drawing a hard and fast line between them. In the first place, it is difficult in its application; for "The sovereignty of the union is so involved in that of the states that it is impossible to distinguish its boundaries at the first glance"④. In the second place, it is difficult to know what matters belong to the states and what matters to the Union. ⑤ The solution of the former is dependent upon a people who has been long accustomed to the conduct of its own affairs or to one in which the science of politics has descended to the humblest classes of society. ⑥ The solution of the latter may be dependent upon the means of determining the jurisdiction of the Federal courts; for the jurisdiction of the tribunals of the Union extends and narrows its limits exactly in the same ratio as the sovereignty of the Union augments or decreases. ⑦

What are the advantages and the disadvantages of the application of the divisibility doctrine? This question, according to Tocqueville, can be answered in a given situation.

---

① Tocqueville, *Democracy in America*, trans. by Henry Reeve, Vol. I, p. 149.

② *Ibid.*, p. 145.

③ This point is elaborated by President Coolidge in an address on May 15, 1926, before William and Mary College at Williamsburg, Virginia. "If the federal government should go out of existence the common run of people would not detect the difference in their daily life for a considerable length of time but if the authority of the states were struck down, disorder approaching chaos would be upon us within twenty-four hours." See *Boston Univ. Law Review*. Vol. VII, p. 36.

④ *Ibid.*

⑤ *Ibid.*, p. 144

⑥ *Ibid.*, p. 166.

⑦ *Ibid.*, p. 144.

In other words, it will be advantageous to a people who can control their own affairs in good order and disadvantageous to those who do not. Thus the application of this principle in the United States has been a great advantage, while in the Mexican Republic, it made her the victim of anarchy and the slave of military despotism. ①

It is advantageous because in the first place, it "contributes to the well-being of each of the states which compose the the Union. In these communities which are never agitated by the desire of aggrandizement or the cares of self-defense, all public authority and private energy is employed in internal amelioration"②. In the second place, as the sovereignty of the Union is limited and incomplete, liberty may be secured; for it does not excite those insatiable desires of fame and power which have proved so fatal to great republics. ③

It is disadvantageous, because, in the first place, "two sovereignties are necessarily in presence of each other. The legislator may simplify and equalize the action of these two sovereignties, by limiting each of them to a sphere of authority accurately defined; but he can not combine them into one, or prevent them from coming into collision at certain points"④. In the second place, because of the relative weakness of the government of the union, for a divided sovereignty must always be less powerful than an entire supremacy. ⑤ Not only is the federal system deficient because its power is not centralized, but the central government itself is imperfectly organized, which is invariably an influential cause of inferiority when the nation is opposed to other countries which are themselves governed by a single authority. ⑥ And this is the third defect of the doctrine.

But Tocqueville is not the only French writer who has held the doctrine under consideration. Duguit, one of the most outstanding figures in the field of jurisprudence, takes the same position. He thinks it difficult to reconcile the notions of personality of the state and the indivisibility of sovereignty with the facts of communal, provincial and colonial decentralization. It is more difficult and in fact impossible, to recognize these ideas with the federal forms of the states. ⑦

---

① Tocqueville, *Democracy in America*, trans. by Henry Reeve, Vol. I , p. 166.
② *Ibid.*, p. 165.
③ *Ibid.*, p. 163.
④ *Ibid.*, p. 165.
⑤ *Ibid.*, p. 167.
⑥ *Ibid.*, p. 170.
⑦ Duguit, *L'État: Les Gouvernants et Les Agents*, 1903, p. 673. Also *Les Transformations du Droit Public*, 1913, pp. 20–21.

Federalism is common in the New World.① In Europe, Switzerland and the German Empire are already federal states and it is quite certain that the system is destined to be extended.② "Here the same territory and the same men are subject at the same time to the commanding power of the federal state and the member-states. The state, then, is not the superior collectively existing on a given territory, since on the same territory exist two states. The public power (Puissance politique) is not the right (droit) to give unconditioning orders, since they are public powers over the same territory, and that one is found to be conditioned by the other."③

The sovereignty, therefore, is not always the single and indivisible will of the nation.④ To assert that sovereignty in a federal state is one and indivisible is "the merest dialectic without relation to reality"⑤.

This view is also entertained by many international lawyers in France. Vattell found that in a federal state, the member-states alienate part of their sovereignty in order to form a federal authority.⑥ Frunck-Brentano and A. Sorel are of the same opinion.⑦ Rivier views sovereignty from its external and internal aspects. The federal government possesses the former and the member-states the latter.⑧ Other political writers such as Brunet⑨, and Foignet⑩ accept the same doctrine. Even Esmein, the well-known opponent of Duguit, while refusing to recognize that sovereignty is divisible, is willing to admit that it is divided in the federal state. Thus he says: "In unitary states sovereignty is one. The federal state, on the other hand, although corresponding to a real national

---

① The term federalism may be used in two senses: one is narrow and the other broad. The former is used here.
② *Les Transformations du Droit Public*, p. 21.
③ *L'État: Les Gouvernements et Les Agents*, p. 673.
④ *L'État: Le Droit Objectif et La Loi Positif*, 1901, pp. 324–325.
⑤ *Les Transformations du Droit Public*, p. 25. See also Duguit, *Droit Constitutionnel*, Vol. I, p. 437. Also pp. 134, 141.
⑥ Vattell, *Le Droit des Gens*, Vol. I, p. 133, footnote. "Dans les Etats federatifs, les Etates particuliers alienent une part de leur souverainete pour constituer l'autorite federale et lui conferer, en certains points. le droit de commandement direct sur les subjets de chaque partie du territoire. La Suisse et les Etats Unis d'Amerique offrent des exemples d'Etate federalifs."
⑦ Funck-Brentano, et A. Sorel, *Precis du Droit des Gens*, pp. 40–41. "Les Etats federatifs se distinguent des autres Etats en ce que les Etats qui font membres de la federation abdiquent tout ou partie de leur souverainete en matiere diplomatique et militaire; il y a un chef commun de l'Etat federatif, une representation commune de la federation, et le pouvoir federal a la droit d'etendre son action legislative, dans les cas prevus par le pact, jusqe dans les affaires interieures des Etats qui font partie de la federation." See also p. 42.
⑧ Rivier, *Principles du Droit des Gens*, Vol. I, p. 104–105.
⑨ Rene Brunet, *The New German Constitution*, trans. by J. Gollomb, 1922, pp. 76–77.
⑩ Foignet, *Droit International Public*, 1915, p. 87.

unity, divides its sovereignty...Certain attributes of sovereignty are constitutionally taken from the participating states and transferred to the federal union."①

E. English Writers

Crossing the channel, we find, in England, writers who accept the doctrine of divisibility of sovereignty as well as those who take the same view in Germany and France. Freeman, one of the most celebrated historians, has advanced this doctrine in the well-known treatise entitled *History of Federal Government*. He views the federal state as one which preserves to the several members their full internal independence, while it denies to them all separate action in relation to foreign powers.② Sovereignty is, as he says, in fact divided; the government of the federation and the government of the states have a co-ordinate authority, each equally claiming allegiance within its own range.③

Not only is sovereignty divided in actual facts in a federal union, but division of sovereignty, as he conceives it, is essential to a true federal state.④ The several states in a federal state are sovereign and must be sovereign, for they fix themselves the "law of jurisprudence, and even the details of its political constitution and they do this not as a matter of privilege or concession from any higher power, but as a matter of absolute right, by virtue of its inherent powers as an independent commonwealth"⑤.

Beyond the internal sovereignty, the sovereignty of the states ceases and that of the federal government begins. The making of peace and war, the sending and receiving of ambassadors, generally all that comes within the department of international relations, will be reserved wholly to the central or federal power and it is these powers, which constitute the sovereignty of the federal government.⑥

The examples of federal states, as Freeman points out, were not to have attained four or five times in the history of the world. They are: (1) the Achaean League, 281-146 B. C., (2) the Swiss Cantons, 1291-1862, (3) the seven united Provinces of the Netherlands, whose union arose in the war of independence against Spain, and lasted in a republican form, till the wars of the French Revolution, 1779-1795, (4) The United States of North America which formed a federal union after their revolt against the British Crown under George the Third, and whose destiny forms one of the most important, and

---

① Esmein, *Droit Constitutionnel*, 5th edition, p. 6.
② *Ibid.*
③ *Ibid.*, p. 15.
④ *Ibid.*, p. 5.
⑤ *Ibid.*, pp. 4-5.
⑥ *Ibid.*

certainly the most interesting of political problems in our time(1878–1862). ①

The next English writer who deserves mention is Professor Oppenheim. "A federal state," says he, "is a perpetual union of several sovereign states which has organs of its own and is vested with power, not only over the member-states, but also over their citizens."② He seems to disagree with some of the writers on International Law who think that in a federal state, the sovereignty of the federal government is more real than that of the several states.

To him, there seems to be no doubt that the member-states in a federal state are sovereign and the point to be considered is whether the federal union, or federal government, is a sovereign or not. Following Kent and Story in the United States he maintains that the character of the federal union as a sovereign is just as real as the member-states. "Now if a federal state is recognized as a state of its own, side by side with its member-states, it is evident that sovereignty must be divided between the federal state on the one hand and on the other, the member-states."③

How and in what manner, then, is sovereignty divided? It is divided, he points out, by transferring parts of the authority or competence of the member-states to the federal state, and after dividing, each is independent and sovereign in its own proper competence.④ Like many other international lawyers, he thinks that sovereignty may be divided into internal and external parts, but to him, either of these two may be exercised by one part alone; for actual facts show that, in the first place, as in Germany, the member-states of the federal union have retained competence to send and receive diplomatic envoys, not only in intercourse with one another, but also with foreign states;⑤ in the second place, the monarchs of member-states are treated in practice as heads of sovereign states; and thirdly, among themselves, they conclude international treaties without the consent of the federal state. ⑥

The member-states, then, are originally and really sovereign in their relations to the federal state, and are part-sovereign from the viewpoint of international law, or in their relations to foreign states. From this he goes a step further and classifies the federal state into two groups, namely: those in which the member-states have both external and

---

① Freeman, *History of Federal Government*, Vol. I, p. 5.
② Oppenheim, *International Law*, 3rd ed., Vol. I, p. 157.
③ *Ibid.*, p. 158.
④ *Ibid.*, p. 159.
⑤ *Ibid.*
⑥ *Ibid.*

internal sovereignty, and those in which the member-states have only internal sovereignty. Of the former, Germany and Switzerland are typical examples and of the latter, the United States of America. ①

Lord Bryce takes the same position as the writers just mentioned. In his earlier work, *The American Commonwealth*, he pointed out that for certain purposes, the federal government is sovereign. ② But the sovereignty of the federal government does not abrogate the sovereignty of the several states, since the states still possess a large portion of sovereign powers, and, most important of all, the immunity from being sued except by another state. ③ Thus Lord Bryce's argument for the part-sovereignty of the several states is built on this proposition: A sovereign state can not be sued without her consent except by another state. Since the several states are entitled to such privileges, they must be considered as sovereign.

But the duality of sovereignty can be proved from another angle. This is pointed out by Bryce in the following statement: "Thus every American citizen lives in a duality of which Europeans, always excepting the Swiss, and to some extent, the Germans, have no experience. He lives under two governments and two sets of laws; he is animated by two patriotisms and owes two allegiances."④

Sir Frederick Pollock, a distinguished student of jurisprudence, sees also the difficulty of the Engish doctrine of absolute sovereignty in its application to a federal state. He has no doubt that the federal government is sovereign in its own bounds, and, in speaking of the sovereignty of the several states in the United States and in Germany or of the Cantons in Switzerland, he remarks that "we can hardly say that it is in no sense sovereign, for within the bounds of its competence it knows no human superior, although we cannot attribute sovereignty to it in the same sense in which sovereignty is attributed to the British Parliament since its competence has assigned and known bounds"⑤.

Even Holland, a faithful student of Austin, has not followed his master in locating the sovereignty in the electorate in the federal state, but takes the same position with

---

① Oppenheim, *International Law*, 3rd ed., Vol. I, p. 159.
② Bryce, *American Commonwealth*, 1890, Vol. I, p. 409. See also *Modern Democracies*, Vol. II, p. 21.
③ *The American Commonwealth*, Vol. I, p. 409.
④ Bryce, *American Commonwealth*, Vol. I, p. 412. Cf. *Studies in History and Jurisprudence*, Vol. II, p. 508. See Also E. H. Hamilton, "The Alienation of Sovereignty", *Virginia Law Review*, Vol. XIII (May 1927), p. 523.
⑤ Pollock, *A First Book of Jurisprudence, for Students of the Common Law*, 1918, pp. 276–278. Also his article in *Fortnightly Review*, Vol. 110, 1918, pp. 813–815.

many international lawyers in asserting that sovereignty is divided into internal and external aspects and places the former in the several states and the latter in the federal government.① Other writers who share the view of divisibility of sovereignty are Sir S. Baker, Admas and Cunningham, and others.②

F. Canadian Writers

Federalism has been the main product of the New World. It is here that we see its growth and development more clearly. It is here that we get a more definite picture of its practice and experiment. It is here that we have the best examples of its success and its failure, and it is here that we learn the richness of its theory, particularly the doctrine of divisibility of sovereignty.

Professor Smith, a Canadian writer, in his *Federalism in North America*, makes a comparative study of federalism in the United States and in Canada. The difference between the former and the latter, he points out, is to be found in the location of sovereignty. In the former, sovereignty is divided while in the latter it is not. "The American conception," he says, "is that of two sovereign authorities dividing between themselves the various fields of political activity, while Canada proceeds upon the theory of a single sovereign power expressing itself through different agencies, some national and others provincial."③

The basis upon which he maintains that throughout the United States, there are two sovereignties in continuous operation, the sovereignty of the whole and that of each particular state within its own area,④ is to be found in the following statement: "The members of the Philadelphia Convention were faced with the problem of constructing a new sovereign state. This new entity could only derive the powers necessary to its existence by coaxing them out of the thirteen small states which were extremely unwilling to part with them. Hence it was necessary to make an accurate statement of the principle on which the new federal government was based, and the tenth amendment was added to

---

① Holland, *Elements of Jurisprudence*, 12th ed., pp. 50–51.
② Baker, *First Steps in International Law*, 1899, p. 31. Adams and Cunningham, *The Swiss Confederation*, pp. 25–26. Cf. Baty, *International Law*, p. 332; Phillimore, *International Law*, Vol. I, p. 156. Also Oppenheimer's view on the present German Republic, *Constitution of the German Republic*, 1923, p. 37.
③ H. A. Smith, *Federalism in North America*, 1923, p. 12.
④ Smith, *Federalism in North America*, p. 7.

the original document for this purpose."①

G. American Writers

So it is in the United States we find the full fruition of the divisibility doctrine. We may doubt the saying of Madison, the champion of the doctrine, that the theory of divisibility of sovereignty as applied to the federal state was an American creation, but we must at least admit that it is the most characteristic in the history of American political thought. The theory under consideration has been advocated, maintained and defended by different kinds of men; but for our purpose, a few representatives presented in the following pages will be sufficient.

Looking back to the fathers of the Constitution and the earlier statesmen, we find Hamilton, though he would like to have created a thoroughly centralized and aristocratic union, and tried, with all his powers, to extend the powers of the federal government, admitted that sovereignty was divided between the states and the union.② Samuel

---

① Smith, *Federalism in North America*, p. 9.

"On the other hand," says he, "The statesmen who met at Quebec to organize the Dominion of Canada were faced by no such problem. For them there could be no question of creating a new sovereign power. All parties at that time agreed that the entire sovereignty over all the provinces and territories in British North America was vested for all purposes in the Imperial Parliament." p. 9. "Canadian federalism is, herefore founded upon the unitary principle, as distinguished from the principle of dualism." p. 11.

② "The necessity of a concurrent judiction in certain cases results from the division of sovereignty." See Ford, *Federalist*, pp. 200, 650, footnote. Also Bryce, *Studies in History and Jurisprudence*, Vol. II, p. 550.

Hamilton, not only maintained that sovereignty was divided between the states and the Union, he even inclined to think that it might be divided between different departments within one set of government. Such idea is revealed in the following quotation: "It is well known that in the Roman Republic the legislative authority, in the last resort, resided for ages in two different political bodies—not as branches of the same legislature, but as distinct and independent legislatures, in each of which an opposite interest prevailed; in one, the patrician; in the other the plebeian." Ford, *ibid.*, p. 207.

The same view is maintained by Sir John Salmond, a distinguished student in the science of jurisprudence. He maintains that sovereignty or supreme power is that which is absolute and uncontrolled within its own sphere. He argues that in England, sovereignty is divided between a sovereign legislature, a sovereign executive, and a sovereign judicature. The sovereign legislature is the Crown in Parliament. The sovereign executive is the Crown. "Each is supreme within its own sphere; and the two authorities are kept from conflict by the fact that the executive is one member of the composite legislature. Until the passing of the Parliament Act, 1911, the British Constitution recognized a supreme judicature, as well as a supreme legislature and a sovereign executive. The House of Lords in its judicial capacity as a court of final appeal was sovereign." "The theory of Sovereignty" in Salmond's *Jurisprudence*, first edition, 1902, p. 468, Appendix II. See also B. R. Wise, *Outline of Jurisprudence*, pp. 31-32.

Compare W. W. Lucas' book entitled *The Coporate Nature of English Sovereignty*. The keynote of the book may be found in Professor MacIver's statement: "The ultimate conclusion arrived at by this method is that the English sovereignty is and always was co-operative. That in legal theory the king never could act alone in any department of state activity, but only in conjunction with other organs of the state which were always more or less independent of his control." *Political Science Review*, 1913, Vol. VII, p. 503. Cf. Davis, *Elements of International Law*, pp. 40-41.

Adams, in a letter to R. H. Lee, when the Constitution was still in preparation, praised the division of sovereignty between the states and the union as a means for the people to govern themselves more easily, the laws of each state being well adapted to its own genius and circumstances and the liberties of the United States more secure than they would be otherwise.① John Adams also remarked that "the government is an attempt to divide a sovereignty—a fresh assay at imperium in imperio"②. When Jefferson said that "the states are foreign to [to] each other, in the portion of sovereignty not granted, as they were in the entire sovereignty before the grant"③, he no longer spoke as a defender of the absolute sovereignty of the several states. The first Chief Justice of the Supreme Court of the United States was fully aware of the division of the sovereignty in this country, although he described it in an amusing manner.④

Even a strong supporter of the doctrine of indivisibility of sovereignty was compelled to come to a conclusion which is worth quoting. "For security against oppression from abroad, we look to the sovereign power of the United States to be exerted according to the compact of union; for security against oppression from within, or domestic oppression, we look to the sovereign power of the state. Now all sovereigns are equal, the sovereignty of the state is equal to that of the union, for the sovereign of each is but a moral person. That of the state and that of the union are each a moral person and in that respect precisely equal."⑤

In a message to Congress (1822), President Monroe said, "There were two separate and independent governments established over our union, one for local purposes over each state by the people of the state, the other for national purposes over all the states by the people of the United States. The whole power of the people, on the representative principle, is divided between them. The state governments are independent of each other and to the extent of their powers are complete sovereignties. The national government begins where the state governments terminate...This government is also, according to the extent of its powers, a complete sovereignty."⑥

But most important of all, as has been pointed out, is the work of Madison. The difficulty for those who do not see the possibility of dividing sovereignty, according to Madison, lies in the fact that they do not have clearly in mind "that all power in just and

---

① Samuel Adams, *Works*, Vol. IV, pp. 324-325.
② John Adams, *Works*, Vol. IX, p. 564.
③ See Madison, *Works*, Vol. IX, p. 352.
④ See D. Webster, *Works*, Vol. XI, p. 222.
⑤ See Madison, *Works*, Vol. IX, p. 572.
⑥ *Writings of Monroe*, Vol. VI, p. 223.

free government is derived from compact, when the parties to the compact are competent to make it"①.

The parties to this compact, as he pointed out, were not, as Webster would say, the people of the United States as a whole, but the people of the several states. By states, he meant the "people thereof respectively in their sovereign character, and they alone"②③. And further, by people, he meant the majority of them rather than all. Sovereignty, as he conceived it, is the will of the people, i. e. , the will of the majority of the people, in a given society. At this point, a question presents itself: How far can the will of a majority of the society, by virtue of its identity with the will of society, divide, modify or dispose of the sovereignty of society?④ This, according to Madison, may be answered under two headings: in the first place, "the majority has not only naturalized, admitted into society by actually dividing the society itself into distinct societies equally sovereign"⑤. The separation of Kentucky from Virginia, and Maine from Massachusetts, may be cited as examples of this operation. ⑥

Secondly, if it is true that the sovereignty can be divided into two. When a state divides into two, it is equally true that two sovereign states may combine into one sovereignty. Thus sovereignty is a thing which in its nature, can be divided or combined whenever the majority of the people of a society so desire.

Based on what has been said, it follows that "if two states, could thus incorporate themselves into one by a mutual surrender of the entire sovereignty of each; why might not a partial incorporation, by a partial surrender of sovereignty, be equally practicable if equally eligible"⑦.

What is true [as] to two states is also true to ten or twenty or more states, so the reasoning runs. ⑧ The possibility of dividing sovereignty is not only logical, but also in conformity with fact. "Thus a division of sovereignty is illustrated by the exchange of sovereignty rights often involved in treaties between independent nations, and still more in the several confederacies which have existed, and particularly in that which preceded

---

① Madison, *Works*, Vol. IX, p. 569; also pp. 383-394, a letter to Hayne.
② Madison, *Works*, Vol. IX, pp. 352, 600-602.
③ *Ibid.* , p. 571.
④ *Ibid.*
⑤ *Ibid.*
⑥ *Ibid.* Also Vol. IV, pp. 420-421.
⑦ Madison, *Works*, Vol. IX, pp. 571-572. *Ibid.* , pp. 568-569.
⑧ *Ibid.*

the present constitution of the United States."①

But this is not all. We now come to his main point. Even under the present constitution of the United States, "sovereignty is in its nature and in fact divided between the states in their united and the states in their individual capacities that as the states, in their highest sovereign character, were competent to surrender the whole sovereignty as form themselves into a consolidated state, so they might surrender a part and retain, as they have done, the other part, forming a mixed government with a division of its attributes as worked in the Constitution"②.

This being the case, it is difficult, then, to argue intelligibly concerning the compound system of government in the United States without admitting the divisibility of sovereignty.③

Sovereignty, in the United States, is then divided and must be so. But, it is to be borne in mind, the doctrine of divisibility was an American invention. It was under the peculiar conditions which were different from the countries of the past and the rest of the world that such a theory may come into being.④

One can not argue, on the other hand, that there was no such thing in the past or that there is no such instance which can be cited in the rest of the world, so that it cannot exist in this country. One cannot hold that because such a theory is contrary to the traditional theory, namely that sovereignty must be one, so it is invalid. For this would be to hold a theory regardless of fact. "Our political institution," he says, "is admitted to be a new creation—a real 'nondescript'. Its character must be sought within itself; not in precedents, because they are none, not in writers whose comments are guided by precedents."⑤

It was not only a creation which was new, but it was also a creation which was advantageous. Here is the point which Tocqueville developed in his famous treatise and which we have already pointed out. It was a remedy for the defects under the

---

① Madison, *Works*, Vol. IX, pp. 571-572. *Ibid.*, pp. 568-569.
② *Ibid.*
③ *Ibid.*, p. 572.
④ *Ibid.*, p. 551.
⑤ Madison, *Ibid.*, Vol. IX, p. 551. Such is the political system of the United States *de jure* and *de facto*, and however it may be obscured by the ingenuity and technicalities of controversial commentators, its true character will be sustained by an appeal to the law and the testimony of the fundamental charter. *Ibid.*, p. 600.

Confederation and a unitary state.① On the other hand, the danger of indivisibility can be easily seen in that it may lead to the dissolution of the union. "The main pillar of nullification is the assumption that sovereignty is a unit, at once indivisible and inalienable, that the states therefore individually retain it entire as they originally held it, and consequently that no portion of it can belong to the United States."②

The divisibility doctrine may be found in the decisions of the courts of the United States. As early as 1793, in his dissenting opinion in the case of Chisholm vs. Gerogia, Justice Iredell said: "Every state in the union in every instance where its sovereignty has not been delegated to the United States, I consider to be as completely sovereign, as the United States are in respect to the powers surrendered. The United States are sovereign as to all powers of government actually surrendered. Each state in the Union is sovereign as to all powers reserved, It must necessarily be so, because the United States have no claim to any authority but such as the states have surrendered to them, of course the part not surrendered must remain as it did before."③ It is clear, as the language shows, that sovereignty is governmental powers, that it is divided between the Union and the several states and that it is transferrable. Three years later, the same court, in the case of Ware vs. Hylton, made a distinction, as many international lawyers did, between internal and external sovereignty. The former remains in the several states and the latter is given to Congress.④ Even Chief Justice Marshall, while trying with all his efforts to extend the powers of the federal government, expressly declared, in the Case of McCulloch vs. Maryland, that "in America the powers of sovereignty are divided between the government of the Union, and those of the States. They are each sovereign with respect to subject committed to them"⑤.

Some writers have maintained that the Civil War cleared the dispute between the

---

① Madison, *Works*, Vol. IX, pp. 568-569. *Ibid.*, pp. 605-606. "Those who deny the possibility of a political system, with a divided sovereignty like that of the United States, must choose between a government purely consolidated, and an association of government purely federal. All republics of the former character, ancient and modern have been found ineffectual for order and justice within, and for security without. They have been either a prey to internal convulsions or to foreign invasions. In like manner, all confederacies, ancient or modern, have either dissolved by the inadequacy of their cohesion, or, as in the modern examples, continues to be monuments of the frailties of such forms. Instructed by those monitory lessons, and by the failure of an experiment of their own, the United States have adopted a modification of political power, which aims at such a distribution of it as might avoid as well the evils of consolidation as a defect of federation, and obtain the advantages of both."

② Madison, *Works*, Vol. IX, p. 599.

③ Dallas, 419, 435.

④ 3 Dallas 232.

⑤ 4 Wheaton 316. See also the case of Weston and others vs. City of Charleston, 1829, 2 Peters 449.

sovereignty of the federal government and that of the several states and affirmed the doctrine of indivisibility, yet it did not persuade the court to reverse its previous opinion. In the leading case of Collector vs. Day, decided in 1870, it was held that two sovereignties may exist in the same territorial limits. "They are distinct and separate sovereignties acting separately and independently of each other, within their respective spheres."① The same opinion was still held in 1922 in the case of Panzi vs. Fessenden et al. Chief Justice Taft, delivering the opinion of the Court, said, "We live in the jurisdiction of two sovereignties, each having its own system of courts to declare and enforce its laws in common territory."②

Many writers on constitutional law have accepted the theory of divisibility in its general principle though each of them may be different as to details. Story spoke of sovereignty in two senses: one is broad and the other limited. With the former, it was considered as "supreme, uncontrollable power, the jus summi imperii, the absolute right to govern". With the latter, it was regarded as such political powers as in the actual organization of the particular state or nation "are to be exclusively exercised by certain public functionaries without the control of any superior authority". It is indivisible in the former sense, but in the latter it is divided.③ Curtis, while denying that there can be two supreme powers in the community if both are to operate upon the same objects, maintained that there is nothing in the nature of political sovereignty to prevent its powers from being distributed among different agents for different purposes.④ "In all external relations and transactions with foreign nations," says Foster, "the sovereignty of the United States is absolute except in so far as it is limited by express

---

① 11 Wallace 113, 124.

② 258 U. S. 254. In the case of Kohl et al vs. the United States, 91 U. S. 368, 1875, the court said: "That government (federal) is a sovereign within its sphere as the states are within theirs. True its sphere is limited, certain subjects only are commited to it, but its power over those subjects to which it extends, is supreme." In this case the court thought that that sovereignty of the several states was more real than that of the federal government.

In the case of Ex Parte Siebold, 100 U. S, 371 (1879), also Evans' Case Book, p. 28, it was declared that "without the concurrent sovereignty, referred to, the national government would be nothing but an advisory government".

See also the following cases: Texas vs. White, 7 Wallace 700, 725 (1868); South Carolina vs. the United States 199 U. S. 437 (1905); Tenn. vs. Dayis 10 Otto 226; Ex parte Wells 59 U. S. 307 (1855) Progne vs. Pennsylvania, 41 U. S. (16 Peters) 539 L. ed. 1060 (1841); 5 How 504; 21 How 506; 92 U. S. 542; 13 Wallace 397; 20 Wallace 655.

③ *Commentaries on the Constitution of the United States 1833*, secs. 207, 208; Pomeroy, *Constitutional Law*, p. 26.

④ Curtis, *History of the Constitution*, Vol. II, p. 377.

language and implied restrictions of the constitution①...In other respects each State has full and complete jurisdiction and all the attributes of sovereignty over every thing and person within its borders."②

The theory under discussion was presented more clearly in the work of Judge Cooley. Sovereignty, in its full sense is here defined as "supreme, absolute and uncontrollable power by which any independent state is governed"③. Taking this definition as the starting point, he maintained that in the United States, the several states, being called sovereign, were never in their individual character strictly so, for the reason that their actions were always limited by some common authorities. ④ This is the characteristic of the political system in the United States. Thus he said, "In American constitutional law a peculiar system is established; the powers of sovereignty being classified, and some of them apportioned to the government of the United States for their exercise, while others are left with the states."⑤ "Under this apportionment," he continues, "the nation is possessed of supreme, absolute and uncontrollable power in respect to certain subjects throughout all the states, while the states have the like unqualified power, within their respective limits, in respect to other subjects."⑥

International lawyers like Wheaton and Halleck speak of international sovereignty and domestic sovereignty. While the former of the several states were destroyed and merged into the federal government, the latter are reserved to them. "A composite state or supreme federal government," says Halleck, "results from a grant of supreme federal powers to the government of the union with the consequent limitations imposed upon the separate governments of the several compact states may still subsist internal in respect to its co-ordinate states, and in respect to the supreme federal government in questions of power not expressly granted to it; but in all external relations its sovereignty is completely merged and destroyed."⑦ Contemporary writers, such as James Brown Scott, take the same position, so far as the general principle of the doctrine is concerned. He

---

① R. Foster, *On the Constitution*, 1895, p. 270.

② *Ibid.* In one place he called the term state sovereignty a misnomer, but the language seems to be plain to show his recognition of the divisibility doctrine.

③ Cooley, *The General Principles of Constitutional Law in the United States*, third edition, 1898, p. 16. "In theory sovereignty must be a unity, and the sovereignty of a state must extend to all the subjects of government within the territories occupied by the associated people who compose it, so that the dividing line between sovereignties must be a territorial line." See also *Constitutional Limitations*, pp. 1-2, 4. *Ibid.*, pp. 16-17.

④ *Ibid.*, pp. 21-22.

⑤ *Ibid.*, Also J. Taylor, *New View of the Constitution*, 1922, section 13.

⑥ Willoughby, *Fundamental Concepts of Public Law*, p. 189.

⑦ Halleck, *International Law*, 1908, 4th ed., Vol. I, p. 79. Wheaton, *Elements of International Law*, 1866.

argues that after the first day of the Constitutional Convention, the delegates of the several states were trying to create a new union to which a certain amount of sovereign power, formerly exercised by the several states, were given to the central government and to that extent the union is sovereign. On the other hand, the sovereign powers which the several states did not renounce, are still reserved to them. ①

What has been said has not exhausted the list of political writers who advocate the theory of the divisibility of sovereignty. Chipman remarks that experience has shown that sovereignty is capable of division. ② Grimke holds that it is a contradiction to assert that sovereignty is inalienable while in effect we impose limitations upon it. ③ Bliss, in his treatise on sovereignty, gives more strength to the theory under contemplation. In speaking of the subject of sovereignty, he says, "I am willing to treat it as destroyed or divided. "④ "Sovereignty, " he points out, "is nothing more than the supreme power which is exercised by governmental machinery; it is hard to see then, that there is a sovereignty without powers. "⑤ If powers may be divided and exercised by different sets of government, why not sovereignty? So the argument runs.

In order to form a federal union, the several states who were once full sovereign states may transfer part of their sovereign powers to the common government. In doing this, "each citizen is under the jurisdiction of two governments, two states, each with full machinery; and one is supreme as to one thing and the other is supreme as to another"⑥. "To say that a state cannot surrender a part of its sovereignty is a naked assertion: it is a conclusion of law and not a fact; and if the word has a tangible meaning, it is a conclusion contradicted by the actual and legal relations which states may and sometimes do assume. "⑦

The position may be presented more clearly from the legal relations between the states on the one hand and the union on the other. "The change of the legal relations in this country can not be made by any one party, not the people of the several states, no even the federal people, or aggregate of peoples, that can make the change. "⑧ The

---

① James Brown Scott, *Madison's Notes and a Society of Nations*, 1918, pp. 47-48.

② N. Chipman, *Principles of Government*, 1833, pp. 273 ff. Also E. D. Mansfield, *The Political Grammar of the United States*, 1834, pp. 520, 521.

③ Grimke, *Nature and Tendency of Free Institutions*, 1848, p. 527.

④ P. Bliss, *Of Sovereignty 1885*, p. 115.

⑤ *Ibid.*, pp. 113-114.

⑥ *Ibid.*, p. 113.

⑦ *Ibid.*, p. 115.

⑧ *Ibid.*, p. 114. See also Chapter IX.

truth remains that such a change must be made by two sovereignties together, namely, the federal state and the several states. ①

V. Conclusion

A word by way of conclusion seems desirable after having briefly and incompletely outlined the theory of sovereignty as applied to a federal state. Possibly, there are three theories in regard to the status of the federal state. The first is that it is a miniature of the family of the nations of the world. The second is that it is in fact a simple or unitary state. The third is that ⟨it⟩ is neither a miniature of the family of the nations, nor a unitary state, but something between these two.

The proposition of the first is that the establishment of a federal union by a group of states is not very different from an international organization, or union created by two or more states. The argument of the second is that the several states, or the constituents of the federal state, having lost their external relations with foreign states, their position is not far from a department of France or a county in England. While the third is in its nature a compromise, its view point is no more than a compromise of the other two. The way from the first to the second seems to be long, yet they are on the same way and their difference is in degree rather than in kind, and if one stands on the mid-way he can hardly draw a hard and fast line between the position that he is taking and that of any one of the other two.

In considering the theory of sovereignty in its application to the federal state as a connecting link between monism and pluralism, one is likely to commit himself to the position of the latter, yet this is by no means all true, for the simple reason that, although pluralism is a compromise, a compromise is not, in all cases, pluralism.

---

① Cf. D. J. Hill, *The Rebuilding of Europe*, pp. 179-180. Also, MacIver, *The Modern State*, 1926, p. 380.

CHAPTER IV
SOVEREIGNTY AND INTERNATIONAL RELATIONS:
Characteristics of Sovereignty

I. Introduction

How much similarity there may be between the federal state on the one hand and the family of nations on the other, the assertion that the federal state is a miniature of the family of nations does not lead us to concluding that international relations are no more than inter-state or inter-cantonal relations. Facts alone are sufficient to demonstrate that they are not so; and much less so if a moment's reflection is called to the application of the theory of sovereignty.

To a certain extent, the notion of sovereignty becomes more complicated and difficult and indeed more interesting in its application to international relations. The difficulty and intricacy have been and still are growing, as time goes on; chiefly if not wholly, because the commercial, industrial, and if you like, political interdependence of the states of the world continue to develop more strongly each day; and the result of this together with some other reasons has led some writers to deny that the conception of sovereignty can be applied to the field of international affairs.

It is intended, in this chapter and the following one, to deal briefly, but as comprehensively as is possible, with the most important phases of the theory of sovereignty as far as its international aspects are concerned.

II. Sovereignty and International Law

If it is true, as Dr. Buell remarks, that "a field of international relations exists which is almost as distinct from international law as the study of American government is from constitutional law"①; equally is it true, as it is said, that the conduct of international relations is based upon international law just as constitutional law is the basis of American government. This being the case, let us, in dealing with the present subject, examine first of all the notions of the writers on the subject of sovereignty in its relation to international law.

The idea that law is the expression of sovereign will may be traced back to the time of Rome when the power of the Emperor was at its zenith. As political thought was theological in character, it was held that the will of God, in whom alone sovereignty is vested, was law. The decline of the church and the rise of the national states made possible the theory that the king's will was law, because it was the king who was then the sovereign of each state. The sovereignty of the king was soon denied and the sovereignty of the people came instead. Here again the will of the people is law. The location of the sovereignty has been placed here and there, but the truth drawn from the account just given is that law is the expression of sovereign will.

The high watermark of this idea is to be found in the writings of Austin. In order to be called law, in its strict and proper sense, according to Austin, it must emanate from a sovereign. Having taken such a position, he does not hesitate to conclude that international law is not law at all, since it is not the command and expression of a sovereign. He holds therefore, that international law is nothing more than international morality which does not have any legal effect and which can be disregarded by a sovereign state at will.

Many German writers have taken the same position. Hegel, for example, can not see how a sovereign state can be submitted to international law without ceasing to be a sovereign. So he writes: "Since there exists no power that can decide against the state what is right itself, and which can assure the realization such of decision, we must consider that these relations always fall back on the moral duty (soll). The relations of states among themselves is the relation of autonomous beings which stipulate among themselves, relying at the same time upon these stipulations."② To him, as M. Duguit points out, there is in verity no international law, because there is no human power superior to the States which can formulate the jural principle applying to them and enforce their obedience to such principle. What exists in regard to the relations between

---

① Buell, *International Relations*, 1925, preface.

② Daguit, "The Law and the State", *Harvard Law Review*, Vol. XXXI (November, 1917), p. 97. Quoted by Duguit.

states is not law, but moral duty. ①

Mr. Robert Lansing shares the view stated above with some modifications. But the result of the modifications brings him to a conclusion which is not only different from, but contrary to that of Austin and Hegel. Like Austin and Hegel, he holds that law, in order to be law, must have sovereign authority behind it. Starting from this premise, he sees difficulty in applying this view to the field of international affairs, for the reason that "the community of Nations, being unorganized, that is, without a government, and therefore without an agent of the sovereign to formulate in terms and formally proclaim rules of human conduct, the will of the world sovereign can not find expression through the usual channel of enacted law, by which the sovereign will is announced in a state". ②

But the difficulty, as he sees it, does not seem to be so serious as may be thought, because there has been existing a world sovereign which, though not finding its expression in the positive sense as the sovereign in a state, has nevertheless revealed in its negative sense; and the tendency has been and is from the latter to the former. ③

The conclusion so reached may be proved from the standpoint of the origin and the character of the law of nations. ④ According to Mr. Lansing, the conditions which are necessary for the growth of law in a state and in the community of nations, are analogous. ⑤ It is evident that in a state in which "law arising through the decrees of judicial tribunals, when not interpreting enacted laws, is based upon the rational presumption that the sovereign of the state is persistently desirous of directing human conduct in accordance with the principles of natural justice"⑥. It is thus assumed, in the absence of enacted laws applicable to some cases presented before, a municipal court will apply the principles of natural justice which is equivalent to the sovereign will when so applied, although its character is passive rather than active. What is true for municipal law is also true as to international law. ⑦ "The principles of natural justice or

---

① Daguit, "The Law and the State", *Harvard Law Review*, Vol. XXXI (November, 1917), p. 97. Quoted by Duguit.
② Lansing, *Notes on Sovereignty, from the Standpoint of the State and of the World*, 1921, published by the Carnegie Endowment for International Peace, Division of International Law, Pamphlet No. 38, p. 68.
③ *Ibid.*, p. 69.
④ *Ibid.*, pp. 69-70.
⑤ *Ibid.*, p. 99.
⑥ *Ibid.*, p. 69. See also p. 51. "Justice is the great standing policy of civil society. In accordance with this truth it is assumed that a sovereign wills to be preeminently just, and that in controversies, to which enacted law does not apply, is sovereign will that principle of natural justice be applied."
⑦ *Ibid.*, pp. 69-70.

absolute justice or strict justice," says he, "are by civilized states assumed to be in accord with the dominant sentiment of the human race, that is, with the presumed will of the world sovereignty, except so far as repeated practice between governments has established a custom, in which case, as in that arising in a state, the custom overrules the abstract principle of natural justice."①

It is evident then that, although there is no central government to act for the world sovereign and to make formal declaration for the sovereign, it has a quality of legality which is recognized and acknowledged by civilized states. ② Where, then is the world sovereignty existing? It resides, according to Lansing, in the nature of human society and the constant intercourse between nations. ③ There is a sovereign before there is a state, so there is a world sovereign before there is a world organization. The organization of a state is an act of sovereignty, so the world central government will be an act of the world sovereignty. ④ Thus, to Mr. Lansing, both the state and law are the creatures of the sovereignty. Law may be anterior to, or created at the same time with, the state, while sovereignty is something above and superior to both of them. What has been true to a state and municipal law is or will be true to a world state and international law. In his mind, there had been a world sovereignty, however passive and negative it may be, before international law came into light, because international law, or "world law must emanate from the world sovereignty if indeed it ⟨is⟩ law properly so-called"⑤.

But Mr. Lansing does not stop at this point, for according to him, along certain lines of international conduct, that the world sovereign has already revealed its positive and active character. This is to be found in the case of the universal recognition of piracy as a crime against the world, and also in the case of the right and duty of all states to suppress the slave trade, which is a crime against humanity. ⑥ These are instances so recognized by the manifest will of the world sovereign that no one can deny at the present day. ⑦

What we have said is on the presumption that law, in order to be law, must have sovereignty behind it. When Austin sees that there is no world sovereignty in existence,

---

① Lansing, *Notes on Sovereignty, from the Standpoint of the State and of the World*, 1921, published by the Carnegie Endowment for International Peace, Division of International Law, Pamphlet No. 38, pp. 69–70.
② *Ibid.*, p. 72.
③ *Ibid.*, p. 68.
④ *Ibid.*, pp. 57–58.
⑤ *Ibid.*, p. 69.
⑥ *Ibid.*, pp. 72–73.
⑦ *Ibid.*, p. 74.

his conclusion follows that international law is not law. On the other hand, when Mr. Lansing sees that there is a world sovereignty, though its expression is not positive in character, he concludes that international law is no less law [is no less law] than municipal law.

Let us now turn to a group of writers who maintain that international law is law in spite of the fact that it is not the expression of sovereign will and that its existence means a limitation upon the sovereignty of the states. ① The view at issue is not a modern invention. Its origin may be traced back to the time when the notion of natural law was prevalent. It was recognized at that time that the command of the sovereign might be resisted, if it was contrary to the law of nature. ② Since the law of nations and the law of nature have been identified with each other and since the law of nature has been the fountain of the law of nations, as was held by the early writers on international law, there is no difficulty in transferring the idea from one domain to the other.

But not until the publication of Bodin's well known treatise, was it expressly declared that sovereignty is restricted by the law of nations. ③ So it has been declared in the epoch-making treatise of Grotius, the father of international law. ④ Although he did not say it expressly, Bentham would have shared the view with Bodin and Grotius when he stated that sovereignty might be limited by express convention. ⑤ With the development of international law since the time of Grotius and Bentham, the idea has been elaborated by many writers and has recently reached its high watermark. ⑥

Briefly the proposition may be stated as follows: International law, in order to be law as it is in the sense of municipal law, does not need to be the expression of sovereign will. Its origin is based, as it is held by some writers, on the solidarity of interests in the community of nations. Thus says Dr. Otfried Nippold, a well known writer on international law, "The solidarity which is founded on the community of

---

① This position is well stated in Professor Borchard's article entitled "Political Theory and International Law". See Merriam and Barnes, *Political Theories, Recent Times*, 1924, Chapter Ⅳ, pp. 120-140.

② See Pollock, *Essays in Law*, 1922, p. 51.

③ *Six Livres de La Republique*, 1576, Bk. Ⅰ, Ch. 8.

④ Grotius, *De Jure Belle ac Pacis*, English translation by Whewell, Ⅰ, 3, sec. 16.

⑤ Coker, *Readings in Political Philosophy*, 1914, pp. 549, 550.

⑥ See Garner, "Limitations on National Sovereignty in International Relations", *Political Science Review*, 1925, pp. 1 ff. Wehberg, *Problems of International Court of Justice*, pp. 113-114. J. L. Brierly, "The Shortcomings of International Law" in *British Year Book of International Law*, 1923-1924, pp. 12 ff. Fenwick, *Interternational Law*, 1924, pp. 44-45. W. H. Taft, "The Paris Covenant for a League of Nations", *American Political Sci. Review*, Vol. 13, 1919, p. 197.

interests of the states is the basis of modern international law. ① Because international law serves common interests, it is also able, in spite of all obstacles, to develop into real law in the full meaning of the term and to make possible the reign of law. "②

Since international law is something exterior to sovereignty, it is evident that the enforcement of international law means an impairment or limitation of the sovereignty of the states. It is said that English writers are illogical when they recognize the theory of sovereignty on one hand and the supremacy of international law on the other. ③ And when Kobler, a well-known German student on the science of jurisprudence, who likens the law of federal states to what he calls supernational law, by which he means international law, ④ he certainly has in mind that the sovereignty of the states is limited or impaired by the law of nations as the sovereignty of the several states are restricted by the federal constitution and federal law in a federal state. ⑤ Sovereignty, says a high authority, "implies nothing more than the legal right of the state to determine its own internal life, regulate its own purely domestic affairs and make law for its own subjects within its own territory. Its power ends at the frontier and even within the national territory it is limited by the rights which international law recognizes as belonging to the subjects of other states domiciled or engaged in business therein. "⑥

The assertion that the enforcement of international law is a limitation on the sovereignty of the states leads to the question of the sanction of international law. To this, it may be said that practically all the writers on international law hold that there are sanctions for the enforcement of international law no less real and substantial than those which secure obedience to municipal law. ⑦ One writer even goes so far as to declare that

---

① Nippold, *Die Fortbildung des Verfahrens in volkerrechlichen Streitigkeiten*, pp. 35 ff.
② Nippold, *The Development of International Law after the World War*, translated by Hershey, 1923, p. 39.
③ See Stallybrass, *A Society of States*, p. 26.
④ See J. M. Zane, *The Story of Law*, 1927, p. 422.
⑤ The position taken here is certainly not that of those who hold the theory of the sovereignty of the several states.
⑥ Garner, *op. cit.*, p. 6.
Professor Ritchie has a theory of his own though he may be classified under this group. "The recognition of international law may seem in a certain sense a limitation on the absolute sovereignty of the nation; but it is no 'legal' limitation, because it is a limitation which is self imposed. The independent nation, as Austin and his school rightly insist, has no legal superior. But the recognition on the part of a nation's representatives that the nation is one of a community of nations, with moral, though not legal, claims on one another, which are backed up by the irregular penalties of war, does impose a moral check on the unlimited independence of a nation, in the same sense in which the recognition of the will of the ultimate political sovereign imposes a moral check on the legal sovereign. " *Annals of Am. Pol, and Soc. Science*. Vol. I , p. 409.
⑦ Root, "The Sanction of Int. Law" in *Procs. Am. Soc. of Int. Law*, 1908, pp. 14 ff. Oppenheim, *International Law*, Vol. 1, sec. 3.

"interantional law is on the whole as well obeyed today as municipal law, and perhaps one would not go too far in saying that it is better observed, at any rate, in time of peace."① International law, then is the expression of some power which is external of or even above, the sovereignty of the states; and the submission of the nations to it means a limitation of their sovereignty. ②

It remains for us to say a few words concerning those who entertain the view that international law is neither a limitation upon the sovereignty of the states nor an expression of the sovereign will. They, i. e., international law and sovereignty, are conceived in fact to go hand in hand. This group, we may subdivide into two schools. Both schools recognize the fact that one can not exist without the other; but they are different in aim. One asserts that the sovereignty of the states is the true basis of international jurisprudence, that they are in harmony with each other and that the aim of both is to retain the existing status. This view is entertained by many English writers. ③ The other group maintains that so long as international law remains international, the sovereignty of the states will remain untouched. The aim of this school is to destroy national sovereignty, and to raise international law into a supernational law. In fact they want to have a world sovereignty whose will is to be the supreme law of the world. To this group most of the pacifists belong. ④

---

① Moore, "Law and Organization", *Am. Pol. Sci. Rev.*, Vol. IX, p. 11.
② Cf. D. J. Hill, *Rebuilding of Europe*, p. 182.
③ Stallybrass, *A Society of States*, p. 26.
④ See J. Bigelow, *World Peace*, 1916, pp. 217-218. "The crisis in the World's progress towards unity and peace will be a struggle between the idea of national sovereignty and that of world sovereignty. The contest of these two ideas for world supremacy has hardly begun. World nationalists are few, and have done little or nothing in the way of agitation. They are not welcomed or encouraged by the regular peace people, who with the advice and assistance of international lawyers, are laboring on a peace plan based upon, so-called international law and therefore on national sovereignty. International lawyers have the same interest in national sovereignty that soldiers have in war. National sovereignty is what they live and thrive on. Without national sovereignty the career of an international lawyer would be about as dark and void as that of a soldier without a prospect of a war. To abolish these things is to reduce the international lawyer to an attorney and the soldier to a policeman. For a longer time soldiers have been held up to popular opprobrium, for selfish disingenuousness in apologizing for war. It has apparently not occurred to any one to suspect the motive of international lawyers, who so earnestly defend national sovereignty."

"International Law can do nothing with national sovereignty, for there is no indication that Germany considers her invasion of France in 1870, or of Belgium in 1914 as a mistake." *Ibid.*, p. 56.

The sovereignty of law as advocated by Professor H. Krabbe in his *Die Moderne Staats-Idee* may be mentioned as another viewpoint on the subject of sovereignty in its relation to international law. See *Die Moderne Staats-Idee*, chapter X. Also below, the section on the discussion of the theory of sovereignty of Krabbe.

III. Nature of Sovereignty

The problem of sovereignty, so far as the present discussion is concerned, may be viewed in its two aspects: one is its nature and the other is its location. The former must not be confounded with the latter, for one is to decide the question of what it is whereas the other is to answer the question of where it is. It may be said that the former is the essential and proper problem, while the latter is merely its application. But this does not warrant us to conclude that the latter can not exist without the former. The history of the theory of sovereignty shows that the question of location had long been a matter of controversy among writers, even in the time of Greece or even earlier than that, while the problem of the nature did not come to the forum of discussion until the publication of Bodin's writings in the later part of the sixteenth century.

On the other hand, the modern tendency has been to affirm that the conception of location is usually determined by the notion of nature. Thus if one maintains that sovereignty is one and indivisible, his logical conclusion will be that it must reside in one determinate place. If he sees that there is a possibility of dividing it, he will place one part of it here and another part of it there.

What has been just said is the general consideration of the problem of sovereignty. Within the domain of international relations, there are certain salient features of both the nature and location of sovereignty which are different from that of a state or a federal state and to which our attention will be given.

1. Many and One

It is a generally accepted view that international relations are possible only where there are many sovereign states existing at the same time and treating each other on equal footing. Were there only one sovereignty on earth, it is said, international relations would no longer exist. While the minds of philosophers of all ages and of all of the countries usually expect to have one, and only one sovereignty dominating the whole world, facts have demonstrated that it has never been so. It is true that there was a time when Rome proclaimed herself mistress of the world and denied even a theoretical independence and equality to the other states. It is also true that there was a time when the Pope, the vicar of God, went so far as to boast, "I am Caesar: I am emperor." But to say that Rome or the Pope was the only sovereign of the world is to say no more than did the loyal minister of China who, having never taken a look further than the border of his own country, told his master with pride and confidence that all the territories and the subjects within the four seas and under the heaven belonged to his Majesty.

To the students of the history of the world, it is not hard to conceive, if a moment's attention is given, that two forces have been working all the time and everywhere, particularly at the time of crisis in the human world. One is centrifugal and the other centripetal. Thus whenever there is an upheaval, the tendency seems to be that many sovereign states or many sovereignties have merged into one, and that many sovereignties have emanated from one. By merely examining the result of the World War, we shall realize that this is true. What is true in fact is also true in theory. On the one hand, there has been a theory of balance of power, of equality of states, of the Monroe Doctrine and of self-determination defending the independence and sovereignty of each state and therefore holding the principle of many sovereignties. On the other hand there have been advocates of federation, dreamers of world empire, promoters of an American League, of an Asiatic League and of European confederation, and defenders of the League of Nations, having in mind that, in order to make mankind live a happy life and to save them from being troubled by the calamity of war, the principle of one sovereignty, or of very few under given circumstances, should be maintained and secured. ①

2. External and Internal Sovereignty

If it is true that many sovereignties or many sovereign states are the foundation of international relations, it must be also true that international relations are the pedestal upon which the idea of external and internal sovereignty has been developed. The terms under consideration are employed by many writers, but the meanings are by no means the same. To some, it is said, what is called external sovereignty is nothing more than

---

① In a very interesting article entitled "The Passing of National Sovereignty", Mr. Hamilton Holt, the editor of the *Independent Magazine*, wrote these words in 1917: "The powers have abandoned diplomatic isolation and neutrality, perhaps forever. (1) If Germany wins the War, or gains an inconclusive peace, there will be only two sovereign states in the world: the Pan-German Empire and a permanent defensive confederation of all the nations which Germany failed to conquer... (2) If the allies win and fail to use their victory right there will be four or five independent sovereignties (to this becomes Great Britain, Germany, France, the United States and probably Russia, because they alone can equip themselves with the might of artillery and ammunition to defend their territories against other powers), each with its attendant satellites of little nations. (3) If the allies are wise, they will pool their sovereignties into a common federation arising from the present Entente, which already includes, as President Wilson points out, four-fifths of the world. After the defeat of Germany there can arise no serious opponents to such a world league and there will therefore be but one great power on the planet. But nationality will still exist. By sacrificing sovereignty the small nations and the large as well will obtain eternal freedom and security." *The Independent*, 1917, Vol. 92, p. 120.

independence of a state from external control. ① To others, it is held that by external and internal sovereignty it is meant that sovereignty may be viewed from two aspects just as anything may be looked at from different sides, ② but remains one.

The most popular view, as it is held by many international lawyers and writers is that sovereignty may be divided into an internal part and an external part. ③ A state may lose the latter, yet retain the former. On the other hand, a state may possess the latter without having the former. But what is internal and what is external sovereignty? It seems that there is no consensus of opinion among writers concerning this point, for there can be no hard and fast line drawn between the two. In general it is recognized that the right of making war and peace, the right of concluding treaties, of sending and receiving representatives are considered to be external sovereign rights, and that the right of controlling and administering domestic affairs is regarded as internal sovereignty. ④

3. Partial and Full Sovereignty

Closely connected with, but different from, the notion of internal and external sovereignty is the conception of full and partial sovereignty. Full sovereignty means both the internal and external sovereignty combined. All states which only possess internal sovereignty are partial sovereign states, but not all partial sovereign states are states which only have internal sovereignty, because a partial state may be a state which has part of internal and part of external sovereignty or which may have all the internal sovereignty and part of external sovereignty.

There are writers who recognize the existence of partial sovereign states and therefore the possibility of having partial sovereignty, and also those who see the

---

① Compare Wheaton, *International Law*, p. 29. "Sovereignty is the supreme power by which any state is governed. This supreme power may be exercised either internally or externally. Internal sovereignty is that which is inherent in the people of any state, or vested in its rulers by its municipal constitution or fundamental laws. External sovereignty consists in the independence of one political society, in respect to all other political societies."

② Cf. Bluntschli, *Theory of the State*, p. 501. "This sovereignty of the state may be looked at from without and from within: from without, as the independence of a particular state in relations to others...from within, as the legislative of the body politic."

③ Cf. Westlake, *International Law*, pp. 20-21.

④ See Freeman, *History of Federal Government*, Vol. I, pp. 4-5, Also R. Foignet, *Manuel Elementaire de Droit International Public*, pp. 80-88. According to him, the consequences resulting from internal sovereignty are (1) from political and constitutional point of view, (2) from the viewpoint of application of penal laws, (3) from the viewpoint of application of civil laws, (4) from the viewpoint of the execution of judgments emanating from the foreign tribunal, (5) from the viewpoint of the immunity of jurisdiction of states. On the other hand, the consequences of external sovereignty are the right of legation, of concluding treaties and of making war.

possibility of dividing sovereignty into internal and external parts. Thus, says Professor Oppenheim, "A state in its normal appearance does possess independance and all round and therefore full sovereignty. Yet there are states in existence which certainly do not possess full sovereignty, and therefore named not full sovereign states."①

"If we find", says a well known student on jurisprudence, "that between the political community which is an independent state, and the political community which is only a part of an independent state there are other political communities more nearly allied to the former than to the latter, I do not see why we should allow any abstract doctrine of sovereignty to prevent us from applying to such states the obvious epithet of imperfectly independent, or even imperfectly sovereign. As Pradier Fodere remarked, metaphysically there ought not to be half-sovereign states but historically there have been and there may be again."②

It is said that even Austin recognized the possibility of partial sovereignty, though he admitted it with contempt. As Professor Markby points out, all that Austin postulates is that there can not be two independent sources of legal authority in one and the same community. Austin admits that the power of sovereignty may be distributed, and expressly notices that in half sovereign states, sovereignty is shared by two otherwise political societies.③

In the dispute between France and Great Britain as to the Nationality decree issued in Tunis and Morocco on November 8, 1921, the French Government contends that the public power by the protecting state, taken in conjunction with the local sovereignty of the protected state, constitute full sovereignty equivalent to that upon which international relations are based, and that therefore the protecting state and the protected state may, by virtue of an agreement between them exercise and divide between them within the protected territory the whole extent of the powers which international law recognizes as enjoyed by sovereign states within the limits of their national territory.④

---

① Oppenheim, *International Law*, Vol. I, p. 277.
② Brown, *The Austinian Theory of Law*, p. 142 note.
③ Markby, *Elements of Law*, p. 17.
④ See Advisory Opinion of the Permanent Court of International Justice, *Collection of Advisory Opinions*, No. 4, p. 28. The terms partial sovereignty have been identified with that of semi-sovereignty and half sovereignty. (According to Nys the term half sovereignty is invented by J. J. Moser, see Nys, *Le Droit International*, Vol. I, p. 358.) The fallacy of doing this can be easily conceived, for partial sovereignty is not necessarily semi-sovereignty or half sovereignty. If sovereignty can be divided into two parts as it is held, it is obvious that it can also be divided into four or five parts. To call a state which possesses one fourth or one fifth of the whole sovereignty a half sovereign or semi-sovereign state is undoubtedly absurd. Professor Westlake sees this fallacy, but he thinks that the change is unnecessary, "since no one will suppose that 'semi' implies an exact half, or that any quantitive division of sovereignty is possible". *International Law*, pp. 21-22.

It is obvious that the counsels of the French government had in mind that sovereignty is a thing which can be divided into many parts. Each part can do what it wishes within its own sphere and when all the parts combine together, in case of necessity, they become a full sovereignty and have the right to exercise it as any other full sovereignty.

4. Double Sovereignty

It is generally said that two or more full sovereign states on one and the same territory are a thing which by the nature of the case is impossible.[1] But this is not a universal principle unqualified by actual practice in international relations. Thus there may be an area which is placed under double sovereignty[2] or which is subject to a joint sovereignty of two sovereign states. This is one of the characteristic features in international relations and is recognized by high authorities on international law.

The most conspicuous example, as cited by Professor Hall for illustrating the point at issue, is the case of Trieste which was once under the joint sovereignty of Austria and the German Federation.[3] The case of Moresnet, (Kelnis) on the frontier of Belgium and Germany which was placed under double sovereignty of two states is cited by Professor Oppenheim.[4] The case of the Soudan which has been under the joint control of Great Britain and Egypt is cited by several writers. But, in the last case, as Professor Lawrence points out, it does not mean two sovereignties over the same territory, but that "the one is vested in a body made up of the government of the two powers that exercise the condominium"[5].

5. Acquisition and Extinction

It is a well recognized principle of international law that sovereignty can be acquired and lost in international dealings. Sovereignty, says Von Haller, is not an inborn right, but one which must be acquired by an individual or corporation. To him, there are four ways by which sovereignty may be gained. It may be gained, in the first place, by personal ability and exertion; secondly as the result of agreement with, or gift from, the former possessor; thirdly, by happy chance as many parts of a great empire become sovereign after the latter breaks into pieces; and fourthly as a combination of all

---

[1] Oppenheim, *International Law*, Vol. I, pp. 309–311.

[2] Double sovereignty differs from dual sovereignty which usually means that one sovereignty is divided into two and exercised by two sets of governments as it is held by some writers in case of federal state.

[3] Hall, *International Law*, p. 510.

[4] Oppenheim, *op. cit.*

[5] Lawrence, *Principles of International Law*, sec. 83. See also Pitt Cobbett, *Leading Cases on International Law*, 3rd ed., 1909, pp. 55, 115. See also the case of Samoa.

the three ways just mentioned. The last, it seems to him, is the most common one.① Having recognized that sovereignty may be gained by the ways mentioned above, it seems that he would imply that it may be lost in the same way.

Although Haller points out that sovereignty may be acquired by a corporation—and a state may be considered as such he, however, emphasizes more the individual side and therefore makes it an individual possession. This is quite different from the modern conception that sovereignty may be transferred from one state to another, without regard to individual ability or fortune; and consequently it is not the possession of an individual, but of a state as a whole.

Professor J. B. Moore, an outstanding figure in international law, points out three methods by which sovereignty may be gained or lost as the case may be, (1) by the transfer of territory, (2) by revolution, or (3) by internal development.② This seems to be recognized by all students of international law, of political science and by the courts of different countries. Without going into any detailed discussion, we shall briefly summarize the prevailing opinions of recent writers so far as these three methods are concerned.

It is generally admitted that sovereignty is inherent to, and must exist within, a particular territory. Sovereignty, says Judge Cooley, must be a territorial line.③ "Sovereignty," says another writer, "is thus conceived as inseparably connected with the possession of a fixed territory. So fundamental, indeed, is regarded the principle of territorial sovereignty in international law that at present it is deemed necessary to explain any exception to it as a fiction. No community is recognized in international law as a state that has no fixed and permanent territory."④

It follows then that the transfer of territory means a transfer of sovereignty. But how may territory or territories be transferred, i.e., acquired or lost? In the first place, sovereignty over a territory may be gained by occupation, the inchoate title of which is given by discovery. It is to be noted, however, that mere discovery is not sufficient for

---

① Von Haller, *Restauration der Staatswissenschaft oder Theorie des naturalich-geselligen Zustandes der Chimaera des Kunstlichenburgerlichen entgegensetzt*, 1825, Band Ⅵ. Also Mohl, *Geschichte und Literatur der Statswissenschaften*, Book Ⅱ. Dunning, Vol. Ⅲ, pp. 201-202. Merriam, *History of the Theory of Sovereignty* pp. 66-68.

② Moore, *International Law Digest*, Vol. Ⅰ, p. 258.

③ Cooley, *The General Principle of Constitutional Law in the United States*, third edition, by A. C. McLanghlin, pp. 1-2.

④ Crane, *The State in Constitutional and International Law*, p. 48. Cf. Rivier, *Principles du Droit des Gens*, Vol. Ⅰ, pp. 155-156. Levesque, *La Situation internationale de Dantzig*, p. 110.

the acquisition of sovereignty over a given territory. "It must be followed by some act of appropriation amounting to assertion of intent of holding the territory in question,"① says one of the high authorities on international law. Moreover, occupation can only take place in the so-called "no state" land, whether entirely uninhabited as, e. g., an island, or inhabited by natives whose community is not to be considered as a state, or even civilized individuals who "may live and have private property on a territory without forming themselves into a state proper which exercises sovereignty over such territory"②.

Secondly, it may be gained by cession which is different from occupation in that the latter is an original mode while the former is derivative. Through cession, says Oppenheim, the acquiring state receives sovereignty over the territory concerned from the former owner state. ③ Again, he says, the object of cession is sovereignty over such territory as has hither already belonged to another state. Thirdly, it may be gained by accretion, by which it is meant the slow addition made to land by the action of rivers flowing past it or by action of the ocean on the coast. ④ Fourthly, it may be gained by conquest. ⑤ But conquest alone does not give a state sovereignty over the conquered territory and it must be followed by subjugation if it is to be a legal one. Fifthly, it may be gained by prescription by which it is defined "as the acquisition of sovereignty over a territory through continuous and undisturbed exercise of sovereignty over it during such a period as is necessary to create under the influence of historical development the general conviction that the present condition of things is in conformity to international order"⑥.

In connection with this, a few words remain to be said concerning the grant by one state to another of a territory on a lease for a certain period of years. This is a question on which statesmen and international lawyers are still in doubt. The *Imperial Gazette* of Germany, after having leased Kiauchow from China, announced that, "the imperial Chinese government has transferred to the German government for the period of the lease

---

① L. B. Evans, *Cases on International Law*, 1922, second ed., p. 285 note.

② Oppenheim, *International Law*, 3rd ed., Vol. I, p. 384. In the case of Johnson and Graham's Lessee vs. McIntosh, chief Justice Marshall, delivering the opinion of the court, even went so far as to say that territories unknown to Christian states may be occupied by the latter by the right of discovery. Scott, *Cases on International Law*, p. 177.

③ Oppenheim, *ibid.*, p. 383.

④ *Ibid.*, p. 377.

⑤ Fenwick, *International Law*, p. 229.

⑥ Wheaton, *Elements of International Law*. Oppenheim, *Ibid.*, Vol. I, p. 401. Some writers do not recognize the existence of prescription as a mode of acquiring sovereignty over a territory. But as Lawrence points out more writers are in favor of Oppenheim's position.

all its sovereign rights in the territory in question"①. On the other hand, the language ⟨of⟩ the official communication sent to the Russian press styled the lease of Port Arthur and Talinwan as an arrangement "safeguarding the integrity of the sovereign rights of China, and satisfying the essential needs of Russia alike as a maritime power and territorial neighbor"②.

International lawyers, like Professor Lawrence, support the view of the German government. He maintains that the terms used in the Russian official statement are "mere diplomatic devices for veiling in decent words the hard fact of territorial cession"③. What China really parted with was sovereignty, only it was not convenient at the time to say so, and no power but Germany said it. ④ Professor Oppenheim takes the same position as Lawrence. ⑤ The former even classifies lease as one of the modes of cession, which is generally recognized as a transfer of sovereignty. ⑥

Professor Westlake, on ⟨the⟩ other hand, takes an opposite view. His argument is based on private law. Thus he says, "When property is leased, the lessor retains a proprietary right which runs concurrently with the lease right of enjoyment. If therefore the analogy were closely pressed, the state which grants a lease of territory would be held to retain all the time some sort of sovereignty over it. "⑦ This position is also held by Professor Fenwick. In speaking of the case of canal zone in Panama, says Professor Fenwick, "Technically, Panama retains sovereignty over the zone of the land and adjacent territory for the construction of an international canal, although it was expressly provided that the United States should be allowed to exercise over the territory 'all the rights, powers and authority' which it would possess if it were sovereign. "⑧

Having considered the acquisition (of course implying extinction) of sovereignty by transfer of territory, let us now come to the second mode, namely, acquisition of sovereignty by revolution. It is no doubt that when a group of individuals, under an organized political society, with the intention of forming a sovereign state, succeeds in a revolt against the government under which they formerly obeyed, they may acquire the right of sovereignty and therefore become a sovereign state. But the question is: at what

---

① Westlake, *International Law*, p. 136.
② *Ibid*.
③ Lawrence, *Principles of International Law*, p. 177.
④ Lawrence, *ibid*., p. 177.
⑤ Oppenheim, *ibid*., p. 310.
⑥ *Ibid*., p. 379.
⑦ Westlake, *ibid*., pp. 315-316.
⑧ Fenwick, *op. cit*., p. 244, also p. 243.

time does such political society gain the sovereignty? The answers given to this question are by no means in unanimity. Take the case of the United States. It is held by some that she gained her sovereignty and became a sovereign state when the treaty was concluded in 1783 between the United States on the one hand and Great Britain on the other. ① To others, it is maintained that she acquired it at the time when the Declaration of Independence was proclaimed. ② Still another would say that she was to be considered as a sovereign state at the time of the establishment of the First Continental Congress in 1774. ③

The question of the recognition by other states in the family of nations of the independence and sovereignty of a new state formed as the result of revolution is also a subject on which recent writers are in dispute. In some cases, a state has been recognized only by one existing sovereign state. In other cases, recognition of a state as a member of the family of nations and therefore a sovereign state has been given by a few sovereign states then existing. In some cases, a party of revolution has been recognized as a state before possessing even a single foot of territory, ④ or before the revolution has succeeded. In other cases, states have not been recognized by the members of the family of nations long after they have succeeded in revolution and established strong and well-organized governments. Each of these cases has its own defenders and each of the defenders has its own justification, arguments and reasons. All that can be said is that each case has to be judged by its own merits.

It remains for us to consider the third method by which sovereignty may be acquired, i. e., acquisition by internal development. Professor Moore regards the

---

① Brownson, *American Republic*, p. 213.

② This perhaps is the most accepted view. In the case of Johnson. J. Harcourt vs. Gaillard. the court says, "It has never been admitted by the United States that they acquired anything by way of cession from Great Britain by that treaty (of 1783). It has been viewed only as a recognition of pre-existing rights, and on that principle the soil and sovereignty within their acknowledged limits were as much theirs at the Declaration of Independence as at this hour." See Moore, *Digest*, Vol. I, p. 302.

③ Burgess, *Political Science and Constitutional Law*, Vol. I, p. 100. See Professor Willoughby's criticism on Burgess's view, *Fundamental Concepts of Public Law*, 1925. While no attempt will be made to set forth a new theory or even to criticize the three theories mentioned above, difficulties arising from them may be suggested. If the first and the second propositions are sound, then any group of individuals may gain its sovereign power at the moment when the revolution starts. This seems to be contrary, in many cases, to actual practice. If the second theory is sound, then can a political society become a sovereign state if the mother country refuses to conclude a treaty with her even she succeeds in revolution and if the mother country is entirely merged into the revolt-government with whom the latter has to conclude a treaty?

④ The recognition of the independence and sovereignty of the Czechoslovak nation by the United States in September, 1918, is one of the very best examples.

internal development of Japan as one of the most conspicuous examples in this connection. On the other hand it is pointed out that the admittance of Turkey to the Convention of 1856 did not give her the status of full sovereignty. ① How far the internal development of a state is required for gaining full right of sovereignty is certainly difficult if not impossible to determine.

6. Suspension and Restoration

Suspension and restoration of sovereignty should not be confounded with acquisition and extinction of sovereignty, although the difference is held to be a matter of time rather than that of kind. The character of the latter is permanent while that of the former is temporary. The question under discussion is usually connected with military occupation. As has been pointed out by Professor Hall, there was no distinction made between a mere occupation and a completed conquest before the middle of eighteenth century. ② It was first made by Vattel③ and a clear demarcation was not drawn until the publication of Heffter's Work. ④

Military occupation gives the right of sovereignty over the occupied territory. This view is usually held by belligerent governments and supported by many writers on international law. The reason for holding that the sovereignty is in the hands of the invader, although its character is only temporary, is summarized by a high authority in the following words: "The power to protect is the foundation of the duty of allegiance, when therefore a state ceases to be able to protect a portion of its subjects it loses its claim upon their allegiance; and they either directly pass under a temporary or qualified allegiance to the conqueror; or it is also put, being able in their state of freedom to enter into a compact with the invader, they tacitly agree to acknowledge his sovereignty in

---

① Burgess, *Political Science and Constitutional Law*, Vol. I, p. 303. The latter view is also taken by some writers in regard to the case of China, Persia and Siam. See Fenwick, *International Law*, pp. 83 – 104. Hall, *International Law*, p. 44. Lawrence, *Principles of International Law*, pp. 99–271.

The difficulty is in setting a standard by which the internal development can be measured. It is held by some writers (Hall, p. 44. Fenwick, p. 83), that semi-civilized states can not be regarded as full membership. This implies that such state is not a state in the strict sense, and therefore not a full sovereign state. But what is the basis of civilization? If the basis is physical force, army and navy (see Lansing, *Note on Sovereignty*, p. 63), then not a few or even one state can be regarded as sovereign states or state in the present world. Thus says Mr. Lansing, "It may be said then", after showing that there is not a single state which is really sovereign state in strict sense, "that every state, whether strong or weak, whether great or small, whether rich or poor, whether civilized or barbarous, is in a sense a protectorate." (Lansing, *ibid.*, p. 65) If, on the other hand, the basis is something other than physical force, then many states or most of the states in the world will be included in the list of sovereign states.

② Hall, *International Law*, sec. 153. Also Hershey, *Essentials of International Law*, p. 409, note.

③ *Le Droit des Gens*, Liv. III, sec. 197.

④ *Le Droit international de l'Europe*, fourth edition, par. F. H. Geffcken, sec. 131.

consideration of the relinquishment by him of the extreme rights of war which he holds over their lives and property."①

As the character of the invader's sovereignty over the occupied territory is not permanent, the sovereignty of the latter is merely suspended, not alienated. And when the demands of the invader are satisfied, sovereignty is usually restored. Instances of this kind are by no means lacking. As a result of the occupation of the German army in France during the Franco-German War in 1871, as it is shown by a brilliant student on the subject of sovereignty, the sovereignty of France was suspended. But it was restored by Germany, according to him, in exchange for the undertaking of the French government to pay a large war indemnity and the cession of Alsace-Lorraine.② The occupation of Peking during the time of the Boxer "outbreak", according to the same writer, is another instance. The sovereignty of China was suspended when Peking was occupied by the allies. "When at the close of that extraordinary event the Imperial Government was reestablished and Chinese sovereignty was restored by the victorious allies, that sovereignty was clearly dependent upon the consent of the various Powers, whose forces occupied Peking."③

It is to be noted, however, that recently some writers deny the fact that military occupation constitutes a suspension of sovereignty of the invaded territory. They maintain that "acts which are permitted to a belligerent in occupied territory are merely incidents of hostilities, that the authority which he exercises is a form of stress which he puts upon his enemy, that the rights of the sovereignty remain intact, and that the legal relations of the population towards the invader are unchanged"④.

Still other writers like Spaight, take a position somewhere between the two opposite views mentioned above. Thus he says, "War law recognizes that the occupying belligerent has a right of government which comes very near to the right of sovereignty."⑤

7. Limitations of Sovereignty

The traditional conception of sovereignty as it is well stated by a well-known writer

---

① Hall, *International Law*, eighth edition, pp. 557-558.
② Lansing, *Notes on Sovereignty*, p. 62.
③ *Ibid.*, pp. 63-64. Mr. Lansing even goes so far as to find the motives of the powers for restoring the sovereignty to China. "That they voluntarily surrendered the sovereignty to the Chinese was because they preferred that it should be retained within the Chinese state rather than that it should be held by one or more of their own number who would become thereby dominant in the Far East."
④ Hall, *ibid.* Looking to the uselessness of the illogical and oppressive fiction of substituted sovereignty, says Hall, the older theories may be unhesitatingly ranked as effete. sec. 154. Cf. Westlake, p. 84.
⑤ J. M. Spaight, *War Rights on Land*, 1911.

is that "it is legally unlimited and unlimitable. Being the supreme power in the state, there can not, legally speaking, be any authority above, and to speak of it as being limited by some higher power is a contradiction of terms"①. While the view revealed in the statement quoted above is still held by some writers, there are many writers at present who maintain that sovereignty is limitable and limited.

It has been pointed out that internationally, sovereignty is limited in various ways: In the first place, it is said, sovereignty is limited by the rules, principles and customs of international law. Secondly, it is limited by certain relations of suzerainty and vassalage or protection and dependence, which are supposed not to be in derogation of sovereignty. Thirdly, it is limited by treaties of alliance, guarantee, and protection, by which a state obligates itself to give aid to another under certain conditions or to assist in maintaining a certain state of affairs agreed upon. Fourthly, it is limited by the conventional law of treaties, subject to the clause of "rebus sic stantibus" which is generally implied. And fifthly, it is limited by state servitudes. ②

As to the first way of limitation of sovereignty in international relations, we have already discussed it in the previous section under the title, Sovereignty and International Law. As to the second and third ways of limitation of sovereignty, we shall consider them when we come to the subject of the location of sovereignty. Let us now examine briefly the last two ways by which the sovereignty of the states is considered to be limited.

The treaty between the Romans and the Carthaginians, in which it was provided that Carthage should not make war without the consent of Rome was cited by Grotius, the father of international law, as an example of a treaty impairing sovereignty.③ A treaty of this kind, as a matter of fact, is not very different from a command given by a superior to an inferior. An unequal treaty is not a treaty in its proper sense. What is meant by a treaty here is mainly that which is concluded by two or more parties on an equal footing and thereby binding on all of the parties.

We are told by a distinguished Senator of the United States that the majority of the Senate of the United States recognize again and again that in every treaty, there is some sacrifices of sovereignty. ④ And Professor Pollock, in order to calm the alarm about the

---

① Garner, *Political Science and Government*, 1928, p. 182, Ch. IX. Also his article in *Political Sci. Review*, Vol. XIX, p. 2.
② Hershey, *Essentials of International Law*, pp. 100–101.
③ See Dickinson, *Equality of States in International Law*, p. 55.
④ Lodge, *The Senate and the League of Nations*, Appendix 5.

interference with the sovereignty of independent states which it is alleged that the League of Nations will entail, says that few, if any, of the objectors have noticed that the parties to the League have already limited their freedom of action and consequently their sovereignty in many directions by these existing conventions. ①

Even Treitschke, while holding that "no state in the world is to renounce that egotism which belongs to its sovereignty", and that "even in its intercourse with other states, the preservation of its sovereignty is still the highest duty of the state," admits that "every state will for its own sake limit its sovereignty to a certain extent by means of treaties". Of course, the limitation so laid upon the sovereignty of the state, he conceives, is not a legal obligation, for the reason that "so long as there is an International Law, the moment that war is declared all treaties between the belligerent nations are cancelled." "Every treaty is a voluntary self-limitation of an individual power, and international treaties contain the proviso: rebus sic stantibus."② While this may be true, it is also true that self-limitation is a limitation: be it legal or moral or something else.

Other writers who will not go so far as to declare that every treaty is a limitation on the sovereignty of the states, hold that some of the treaties do but some do not. Thus Mr. Stallybrass, who does not think most of the conventions restrict the sovereignty of the states, maintains, however, that the international Sugar Union of 1902 did impose "a real restriction upon the sovereign powers of the members"③. And there are some who see the importance of distinguishing between an ordinary convention according to which the contracting parties undertake certain obligations under clearly defined circumstance, and a pledge to certain conduct or actions, as under the Covenant of the League of Nations or Protocol. While the sovereignty of the states in the former case is preserved, it is limited in the latter. ④ Senator Lodge expresses somewhat the same idea when he states that to say that in every treaty there is some sacrifice of sovereignty is not a

---

① Pollock, *League of Nations*, 1920, p. 86.
See also Wehberg, *Problem of an International Court of Justice*, p. 114. Garner, "Limitations of National Sovereignty in International Relations", *Political Science Review*, Vol. XIX, pp. 1 ff. Davis, *Elements of International Law*, p. 39.

② See H. W. C. Davis, *The Political Thought of Heinrich von Treitschke*, pp. 151–178. Also *Politik*, Vol. I, p. 39.

③ *A Society of States*, p. 86.

④ Montgomery, *Issues of European Statesmanship*, p. 117.

universal truth.①

Having considered the view that a treaty or convention is a limitation on the sovereignty of the states, we shall come now to the subject of servitudes in its relation to sovereignty. The existence of international servitudes as restrictions on sovereignty has been generally accepted by students of international law.② In the Dutch Mining case, the Supreme Court of Cologne held that the interest which the Dutch government had in the mine was to be regarded as an international servitude and consequently involves a derogation from sovereignty.③

In the North American Coast Fisheries Arbitration, Mr. Root, put forth the argument for the United States that "the liberties of fishery granted to the United States constitute international servertitudes in their favour over the territory of Great Britain, thereby involving a derogation from the sovereignty of Great Britain, the servient state, and that therefore Great Britain is deprived, by reason of the grant, of its independent right to regulate the fishery". It was further argued that if sovereignty itself was not limited then Great Britain was at least restricted in the exercise of its sovereignty in treaty waters.④

The tribunal, in its decision, while accepting the contention of the United States that the grant of an international servitude implies a derogation from the sovereignty of the servient state, declined to regard the grant in question as constituting an international servitude. The decision so reached was based on the assumption that an international servitude was by its nature a derogation of sovereignty.

But why did not fishery rights constitute a servitude and thereby a derogation of sovereignty? According to the tribunal, because, among other reasons, there was no satisfactory evidence to show that either British or American statesmen were familiar with the doctrine in 1818; because a servitude predicates an express grant of a sovereign right, whereas the treaty granted only a liberty to fish, which was purely an economic right; and because the notion of international servitudes originated among the quasi-

---

① Lodge, *The Senate and the League of Nations*, p. 407. Cf. Oppenheim, *Future of International Law*, p. 44. Also *American Journal of International Law*, Vol. XV, p. 8. See the statement made by Prince Arfa of Persia before the sixth Assembly of the League of Nations, on September, 12, 1925. *Records of Plenary Meeting*, VI, 1925, p. 57, and *Official Journal*, 1924, 1362, XXX.

② For example, Westlake, *International Law*, p. 61.

③ See A. E. McNair, "So-called State Servitudes", *British Year Book of International Law*, 1925, pp. 118–127.

④ *World Peace Foundation Pamphlet*, 1912, edited by J. B. Scott, p. 459. See also Root, *Address on International Subjects*, edited by J. B. Scott, 1916, pp. 181, 180, 295.

sovereignties of the Holy Roman Empire, whereas "in contradistinction to this quasi-sovereignty with its incoherent attributes acquired at various times, by various means, and not impaired in its character by being incomplete in any one respect or by being limited in favour of another territory and its possessor, the modern state, and particularly Great Britain, has never admitted partition of sovereignty, owing to the constitution of a modern state requiring essential sovereignty and independence", and therefore, the doctrine of international servitude is "little suited to the principal of sovereignty which prevails in States under a system of constitutional government such as Great Britain and the United States and to present international relations of sovereign state and has found little if any support from modern publicists"①.

It is clear from the passage quoted above that the whole doctrine of servitude was denied because of being inconsistent with the modern political principle, owing to the constitution of a modern state requiring essential sovereignty and independence. To this assumption, it has been pointed out that it is based upon theory rather than practical conditions. ②

It is to be added that the growing tendency, as Professor Higgins points out, seems to deny the term "servitude" to the numerous restrictions on sovereignty to which states had in many cases subjected themselves by treaty. ③ And Professor Fenwick, in pointing out the difference between the modern conception of a servitude and that of the earlier medieval one, which is based upon the relation between feudal lord and tenant, says "it would seem that servitudes, while involving a restriction upon the use of land or water, do not result in any loss of that theoretical jurisdiction and practical control on the part of the state over its territory which is the mark of sovereignty"④.

8. Violation of Sovereignty

Violation of sovereignty, says a writer on international law, is an international wrong and the injured country has the right of demanding redress. ⑤ In this respect, violation of sovereignty differs from limitation of sovereignty, for the character of the latter is more or less permanent, while that of the former is only temporary. Moreover, if a state admits that she has violated the sovereignty of another state, redress will be given to the latter. On the other hand, a limitation may be removed, but what has been lost or

---

① Scott, *Hague Court Reports*, pp. 159–161.
② Oppenheim, *International Law*, Vol. I, sec. 203.
③ Hall, *International Law*, edited by Higgins, p. 204, note added by the editor.
④ Fenwick, *International Law*, p. 261. Cf. Fauchille, *Droit International Public*, I, Paix, 1922, sec. 339.
⑤ W. E. Hall, *Rights and Duties of Neutrals*, p. 15.

injured as a result of the limitation, is rarely compensated.

It is said that no state may perform any acts of authority within the jurisdiction of another state unless the permission of the latter is secured, otherwise such acts will be a violation of sovereignty. ① Similarly it is held to be a violation of sovereignty if a state attempts through penal enactments to compel individuals while outside its own jurisdiction, to obey its commands in disrespect of the provision of the local law wherever they may be. ②

Instances of alleged violation of sovereignty in the history of international dealings are numerous. ③ As early as 1793, owing to the outrageous conduct of Citizen Genet, French Minister to the United States, in fitting out privateers and otherwise violating American neutrality, Jefferson, then Secretary of State, expressed the view that it was "the right of every nation to prohibit acts of sovereignty from being exercised by any other within its limits, and the duty of a neutral nation to prohibit such as would injure one of the warring powers" ④.

In the case of Crampton (1885), in inducing recruits to proceed to Canada for enlistment in the War against Russia, the act of the British Minister was regarded by Mr. Marcy, Secretary of State of the United States, as a violation of the sovereignty of

---

① Stowell, *Intervention in International Law*, p. 322.

② *Ibid*.

③ It seems that there are more cases arising from violation of the right of neutrality and the so-called intervention in this connection. "An independent state," says Professor Hershey, "has an inalienable right to remain neutral in a war, and a bellgerent is bound to respect this neutrality, more particularly its territorial sovereignty." *Essentials of International Law*, p. 445. "All states are sovereign," says Hall, "and in so far as neutrals are concerned, sovereignty is an attribute of community in the enjoyment of belligerent previleges." *Rights and Duties of Neutrals*, p. 15. "Intervention," says Hall, "is a hostile act, because it constitutes an attack on the independence of the state subject to it." *International Law*, 8th ed., p. 337. "Intervention is in the first instance a hostile act, because it constitutes an attack upon the independence of the state subjected to it. It is regarded by the state intruded upon, if not previously agreed so, as an act of war in that its sovereignty is impaired." H. G. Hodges, *The Doctrine of Intervention*, p. 5. See also Stallybrass, *A Society of States*, p. 60. Lawrence, *Principles of International Law*, p. 172.

④ Moore, *International Law Digest*, Vol. II, p. 446. Also, *ibid.*, p. 370. It is interesting to note that just a month after the case of Genet, George Hammond, the British minister to the United States, wrote: "The readiness I have evinced to anticipate a complaint of this kind, that has not yet been formally communicated to me, will, I hope, be regarded as a manifestation on my part that I will not countenance or protect any British subjects in any proceeding which may be considered as disrespectful to the sovereignty of the United States, or as an infringement on the neutrality which the executive government of this country has professed to adapt, and has recommended to its citizens rapidly to absence in the contest subsisting between France and the other belligerent powers." The Counter case of Great Britain as laid before the Tribunal of Arbitration at Geneva 1872. I am indebted to my friend, Dr. Charles S. Hyneman in informing me of this statement.

Compare also The Brig Alerta vs. Moran (1815), 9 Cranch 359, 365, 3L. Ed. 758, 760-766.

the latter.① In the Savarkar case, one of the arguments put forth by the French government before the Hague Arbitration Tribunal was that the seizure of Savarkar was a violation of French sovereignty.②

Numerous cases like these occurred during the World War. The attack of Japan upon Kiauchau in 1914 was alleged by the Chinese government and writers as a serious violation of her sovereignty. The same was alleged by the government of the United States in the case of Appam.③ More cases may be cited, but enough has been said to show that the notion of violation of sovereignty has existed for a long time and is one of the characteristic features in international relations.

9. Contempt of Sovereignty

Contempt of sovereignty is different, as it is pointed out by some writers on international law, from violation of sovereignty. In the case of the former, the acts committed against the sovereignty are not as serious as that in the latter. Foreign representatives who try to exert an indirect influence upon the government to which they are accredited for some desired policy are considered as examples of a contempt of sovereignty. During the World War, the German Ambassador, Mr. Bernstorff, giving a warning in the newspaper advising passengers not to embark upon the *Lusitania* was cited as a contempt of the sovereignty of the United States.④

It may be said that although, as has been shown, there is a difference existing between violation of sovereignty and contempt of sovereignty, it seems that the latter conception is not as well elaborated as the former, and acts of contempt of sovereignty have been alleged as violations.

10. Conclusion

Let us now briefly summarize the prevailing notion of the nature of sovereignty from the international law view point. We start by pointing out that there are those who would like to see the realization and objectification of one sovereignty for the whole world, and those who maintain the principle of many sovereignties. While the former has not yet come into existence, the latter has long been actualized. But this does not mean that there is no possibility for having only one sovereignty in the future. In theory as well as in practice, it has been shown that each of the many sovereignties which are to be

---

① Stowell and Munro, *International Law Cases*, Vol. Ⅱ, pp. 278 - 295. Also Stowell, *Intervention in International Law*, p. 332, note.

② Scott, *Hague Court Reports*, p. 279. Stowell and Munro, *op cit.*, Vol. Ⅰ, p. 418.

③ Stowell and Munro, *International Cases*, Vol. Ⅱ, p. 290.

④ Stowell, *Intervention in International Law*, pp. 323-324, note.

considered as the units of international relations may be divided into many sovereignties, and on the other hand, that many sovereignties may be combined into one, though not the only one of the world.

Each of the sovereignties of the world not only may be divided into many unique sovereignties, it may also be divided into internal and external parts. Each part of these is not necessarily in the same hands, for one part may vest in one state while the other in another state. Moreover, each sovereignty may be divided into parts without regard to internal or external part, and the number of parts may be two or more. While partial sovereignty is only one or more parts of a full sovereignty or the whole, all the parts of the whole combined together is equal to the whole, and therefore enjoys as much right as the whole. Furthermore, many sovereignties may rule jointly over a territory. It is called double sovereignty, if there are two sovereignties over that territory. ①

Looking from another angle, we find that it is held that sovereignty may be transferred from one state to another. The nature of a transfer may assume two forms: acquisition and extinction. Where sovereignty may be acquired by one way, it may be also lost in the same way. The methods of transfer are many. But in order to facilitate our understanding they have been grouped under three headings: (1) transfer of territory, (2) revolution, (3) internal development. As sovereignty may be acquired and lost, it also may be suspended and restored. Acquisition and extinction are different from suspension and restoration in that while the former have the character of permanence, the latter are merely temporary. It is to be added that sovereignty, as it is said, may be acquired, lost, suspended and restored either wholly or partly.

Further investigation has shown that, sovereignty not only can be combined and divided, acquired and lost, suspended and restored, but it also can be limited, violated, and condemned. Roughly speaking, there are five ways of limitation upon the sovereignty of the states so far as international dealings are concerned. Limitation is different from violation mainly in that the character of one is permanent while that of the other is temporary. Violation is not the same as contempt, for the former is to be considered as more serious than the latter.

From what has been said, it may be concluded that, from the viewpoint of international relations, sovereignty by its nature is a thing that is combinable and divisible. It is again a thing that can be acquired and lost. It is moreover a thing that

---

① The term "double sovereignty" is not proper when applied to a territory which is under the joint sovereignty of more than two sovereignties; yet it seems that there has been no writer who has suggested the term "co-sovereignty".

may be suspended and restored, It is furthermore a thing which is possible of diminishing and increasing. It is, finally, a thing that may be limited, violated or condemned.

CHAPTER V
SOVEREIGNTY AND INTERNATIONAL RELATIONS
(Continued): Location and Criticism

IV. Location of Sovereignty

We come now to the notions of the location of sovereignty from the viewpoint of international relations. As has been shown, although the nature of sovereignty and the location of sovereignty are different from each other, a given premise as to one always leads to a logical conclusion for the other. For this reason, it is hard to draw a clear and distinctive line during the course of our discussion. For example, regarding the lease of territory as a mode of transferring sovereignty from one state to another, this is taken from the viewpoint of the nature of sovereignty. ① On the other hand, if one looks at [as] a form or an organ through which international relations take place, it follows that it may be grouped under the heading of the location of sovereignty.

The notions as to the location of sovereignty from the international aspect take various forms with regard to different internationalized institutions. What is attempted here is to give an outline of those considered most important.

1. Sovereignty and Confederation

The terms confederation and federation have been loosely used. ② Many writers have not distinguished them and even those who have made the distinction, have not unanimously agreed as to the concrete examples. ③ How confusedly they may be used, the difference, or differences between the two is, or are, obvious, although the difference or differences may be merely in degree rather than in kind.

It seems that there has been very few, if any, who would go so far as to hold that the confederated union created by the member-states was a full sovereign union. On the other hand, there are writers who maintain that the confederated states were severally

---

① This does not imply that the writer is in favor of the theory that sovereignty is lost by lease of territory.
② See above. Chapters II and III.
③ Compare the classification of Ferguson and Freeman.

and fully sovereign. This position is taken by writers like Professor Oppenheim. He maintains that the sovereignty of the Diet did not affect the sovereignty of the member-states, ① and the agreement made by the several states for creating a union, was no more than an international treaty and that the union was not an international person. ②

The generally accepted view is that the confederated states were only partial sovereign states. This view is represented by Professor Lawrence. Thus be says, "Confederated union is a bundle of separated states, each of which retains some of the rights of sovereignty while it is deprived of the remainder. Accordingly, the states that compose it must be placed by international law among those part-sovereign communities which we regard as the second class among its subjects. They are something more than administrative districts of a larger whole. They are something less than sovereign states."③

There is no confederation existing at present, as has been pointed out. The last instance noted by Professor Oppenheim was the Major Republic of Central America which, composed of three sovereign states, [which] was ended in 1898. The question under discussion then is one which has only historical significance.

2. Sovereignty and the British Dominions

Within recent years, particularly after the World War, the question of sovereignty has become important and been widely discussed in connection with British Dominions. The old view has been that there is only one sovereignty in the British Empire. This position has been maintained by many English political philosophers and statesmen, ④ and even accepted by the Canadian Cabinet in 1918. ⑤

On the contrary, there are also statesmen and political writers who hold that the dominions are no longer under the sovereignty of Great Britain, for they are themselves sovereign. It has been pointed out that Prime Minister Hughes of Australia has spoken,

---

① Oppenheim, *International Law*, third edition, Vol. I, p. 156. Compare Hall, *International Law*, p. 28. Moore, *Digest*, Vol, I, Sec. 10. Garner, *Introduction to Political Science*, 1910, pp. 143–144.

② Oppenheim, *Ibid*.

③ Lawrence, *Principles of International Law*, p. 69, sec. 40.

④ "Metternich said that no sovereign could afford to give away a particle of his sovereignty. Professor Pollard neatly comments: We may not give away but we lease it to the Dominions and get a handsome return." Stallybrass, *A Society of States*, p. 177. The theory still has its defenders. In an article entitled "Sovereign Colonies", Professor T. Baty denies that the sovereignty of the Empire is divided. "The crown is one and indivisible, though it acts by different agents on different principles in different parts of the Empire." *Harvard Law Review*, Vol. XXXIV, pp. 837–861.

⑤ See *A History of the Peace Conference of Paris*, Vol. VI, p. 343, issued by the Institute of International Affairs, 1924.

not only once, but many times, of Australia as an independent state① and the same idea has been expressed by General Smuts,② an English hero during the World War and a man of creative mind as we are told. In his speech, following the admission of the Irish Free State as a member of the League of Nations at the Fourth Assembly, in September, 1923, President Cosgrave spoke of Ireland as joining "in a solemn covenant to exercise the powers of her sovereign status"③.

The arguments of those who hold that the dominions are sovereign, are based on different grounds. It is argued, in the first place, that, according to the Covenant of the League of Nations, it is presumed that only sovereign states can be the members of the League. Since the Dominions have been admitted as members of the League, it is taken for granted that they are sovereign.④ Secondly, it is maintained that Article 22 of the Covenant of the League expressly declares "those colonies which as a consequence of the late war have ceased to be under the sovereignty of the states which formerly governed them... will be entrusted to advanced nations". The Dominions must be sovereign, otherwise how can they be entrusted with the sovereignty of others? Thirdly, it is argued that the right of sending and receiving ambassadors is an inherent right of sovereignty. The Dominions would not have such right if they were not sovereign.

But most important of all is the argument based upon the declaration made by the Imperial Conference of 1926, which reads: "They, (the Dominions) are autonomous communities within the British Empire, equal in status, in no way subordinated one to another in any respect of their domestic or external affairs, though united by a common allegiance to the Crown, and freely associated as members of the British Commonwealth of Nations."⑤ It is held that Great Britain is a sovereign state, and if the Dominions are declared to be equal in status to Great Britain, they must be also considered as sovereign unless the former is not a sovereign herself.⑥

---

① Stallybrass, *A Society of States*, p. 176.
② *Ibid.*
③ League of Nations, *Records of the Fourth Assembly, Plenary Meeting*, p. 24. It is to be noted also that the treaty concluded between Ireland and Great Britain was refused to have sanction on the part of Great Britain because the term "sovereignty" was used in it.
④ The argument may also be supported on the ground that the Canadian representative is in the Council.
⑤ "World Peace Foundation Pamphlets," Vol. X, No. 6, 1927.
⑥ See J. S. Ewart, "Canada, the Empire and the United States", in *Foreign Affairs*, Vol. VI (1927), p. 127. He concludes that the tendency of the relations between the Dominions, (Canada) will be a personal union. "If Canada, as a sovereign state, continues to acknowledge as her sovereign the individual who occupies the British throne, the relationship will be that known to international law as a personal union, the old imperial relationship will have come to an end."

Another theory which is a compromise in character is that the Dominions are partial sovereign states. Professor M. M. Lewis is a conspicuous representative. After citing a statement made by Westlake that sovereignty is partible, Professor Lewis, in a well written article, entitled "The International Status of the British Self-Governing Dominions" concludes in these words: "By becoming partners in the British Empire they are pledged to persue a common partnership policy. They have the power to manage their own private affairs and to enter into relation with other international persons, but they are not fully sovereign states because their independence is necessarily limited by their obligations to the partnership."①

President Lowell of Harvard, a world known scholar, has a view of his own which is somewhat different from all that have been presented, but which is not very clear in expression. He seems to think that the Dominions are themselves sovereign when he says that they are not under control of Great Britain, or subject to her authority. But he also points out that the British use the term sovereignty in two different senses. Thus he says, "Popularly it is used for the wearer of the Crown; but among political philosophers it means the ultimate source of authority, and in that sense the sovereigty in Great Britain, although delegated to Parliament, resides in the last resort in the electorate, as from this time forth it will also ⟨be⟩ in the Dominions."②

3. Sovereignty and Protected States

It has been remarked that originally protected states were regarded as sovereign states. "The protection," says Professor Baty, "was little or nothing more than a form of guarantee. It did not affect in any degree the sovereignty of the protected power."③ This idea was entertained by the highest authorities, such as Grotius, Pufendorf and Vattell. Vattell says that a weak state which in order to provide for its safety places itself under the protection of a more powerful one and engages to perform in return several offices equivalent to that protection, without, however, divesting itself of the right of government and sovereignty, does not cease to rank among the sovereigns who acknowledge no other law than the law of nations.④ The Colonial Office of Great Britain, replying to the request of the Court of Appeal of England, in the case of Mighell vs. Sultan of Jahore in 1893, recognized that Jahore, though a protected state of Great

---

① *British Year Book of International Law*, 1922–1923, pp. 40–41.
② A. Lawrence Lowell, "The Imperial Conference," *Foreign Affairs*, Vol. V, pp. 275 ff. See also "World Peace Foundation Pamphlets", X, No. 6, p. 581.
③ Baty, "Protectorates and Mandates", *B. Y. B. International Law*, 1922, p. 109.
④ See Evans, *Cases on International Law*, p. 63.

Britain, is nevertheless a sovereign state. ① The view has been fully adopted by the court.

But the doctrine just mentioned has long been inconsistent with actual practice on account of the increasing desire on the part of the protecting states to control the foreign affairs of the protected states together with the weakness in power on the part of the latter. This according to Professor Baty has been true during and since the French Revolution. ②

Perhaps we shall not go too far in paying, that few, if any, writers at present will maintain that the protected states are sovereign states. The widely accepted idea is that a protected state is only a partial sovereign state. In a sense, says Professor Moore, it is true, every semi-sovereign may be regarded as a protected State; and protected states may be regularly classed as semi-sovereign. ③

4. Sovereignty and Neutralized States

A neutralized state is defined as a state whose independence and integrity have been guaranteed by the joint action of other states, and placed in a condition in which it is forbidden to engage, in offensive war. ④ There are several theories enunciated as to sovereignty in its relation to the neutralized state. The first that may be mentioned is that the neutralized state is just as fully sovereign as other sovereign and independent states in the family of nations. Westlake and Oppenheim are the conspicuous representatives of the theorists in this group. To Westlake, neutralization "does not carry with it the renunciation of any faculty of state life. It is merely an undertaking not to do certain things, and no more impairs sovereignty than does an undertaking not to interfere in a particular case…Besides, it is necessary that for every part of the civilized world the full powers of sovereignty should exist"⑤. "If sovereignty is nothing else than authority," says Oppenheim, "a neutralized state is as fully sovereign as any not-neutralized state."⑥ The act or treaty of neutralization which forbids a state to enter into any

---

① See Evans, *Cases on International Law*, pp. 205–207.

② Baty, *op cit.*, p. 111.

③ Moore, *International Law Digest*, Vol. I, p. 28.

In the case of Statham vs. Statham and his highness the Gaekwar of Paroda, 1911, the following language was used by the India Office in regard to the status of Baroda: "But though his Highness is thus not independent, he exercises as ruler of his state various attributes of sovereignty, including internal sovereignty, which chief of Baroda, subject, however to the suzerainty of His Majesty the King of England…" Evans, *Cases*, p. 62.

④ Garner, *Introduction to Political Science*, p. 164.

⑤ Westlake, *International Law*, p. 28. Cf. however, p. 61.

⑥ Oppenheim, *op cit.*, p. 173.

offensive war is nothing more than an arbitration treaty concluded by two or more sovereign states forbidding them to resort to war and requiring them to submit their differences to an arbitration tribunal. ① If it is true, then, that the sovereignty of a state is not impaired by entering to an arbitration treaty, it must be also true that a state does not lose a portion of its sovereignty on account of entering into obligations to abstain from hostilities. ②

Another view, which perhaps is the most prevailing one, is that the sovereignty of the neutralized state is limited and impaired. Thus King Albert, in a speech before the Belgian Parliament on November 22, 1918, said: "Belgium, victorious and free from the neutrality that was imposed upon her by states which have been shaken to their foundations by war, will enjoy complete independence." "Belgium," he continues, "reestablished in all its rights, will rule its destinies according to its aspirations and in full sovereignty."③ In reply to the proposition of Professor Oppenheim, Professor Hershey says: "It is true that a state does not lose any part of its sovereignty by concluding a treaty of arbitration, but if it were generally to arbitrate all or any class of international disputes, while other states retained the right to go to war, would such a state be fully sovereign?"④

A third view concerning the location of sovereignty in its relation to a neutralized state is that the sovereignty is in the hands of the guarantors. This was revealed in the opinion of the local lawyers of Luxemburg who maintained that Luxemburg was not neutralized by the will of the people, but by the will of the European Powers, when a demand arose in the grand Duchy for revising the constitution on the principle that all powers emanate from the nation. ⑤

A fourth view is that the sovereignty is in one of the guarantors alone but not collectively. This is the opinion of the Commission of the Rapporteurs, composed of

---

① Oppenheim, *International Law*, third edition, Vol. I, p. 174.

② *Ibid*. He also notes that "neutralization does not even exercise an influence upon the rank of a state. Switzerland is a state with royal honours and does not rank behind Great Britain or any other of the guarantors". "Belgium was a party to the treaty by which she was neutralized, although, by that act, her power and her freedom to make war were strictly limited, yet, because she was a party herself to the limitations imposed on her, she was expressly recognized in the Treaty and has since always been recognized in practice as an independent member of the family of nations." See Staliybrass, *A Society of States*, p. 67.

③ *New York Times*, November 23, 1918, quoted by Fenwick, *International Law*, 1924, p. 89, note.

④ Hershey, *Essentials of International Law*. Professor Garner seems to accept this view. See *Introduction*, p. 164. "In all other respects it (a neutralized state) is fully sovereign and independent."

⑤ Stallybrass, *op. cit.*, p. 67, note. Mr. Lansing seems to entertain this view with modifications. See "Notes on Sovereignty", *Am. Jour. Int. Law*, Vol. 15, pp. 18 ff.

three members appointed by the Council of the League of Nations in September, 1920, for examining the dispute between Sweden and Finland concerning the jurisdiction over the Aaland Islands. They held that the sovereignty of Finland over the islands is incontestable and "that to detach them would be an alteration of her status and deprive that country of what belongs to her"①. In spite of this contention, the Rapporteurs are in favor of neutralized action and demilitarization of the islands which are desired by Sweden and to which Finland was not adverse.② Moreover, while denying the sovereignty of Sweden over the islands, the commission affirms certain guarantees over and above the Finnish law, in the interest of the Swedish people, such as to language, schools, etc.

5. Sovereignty and International Administrative Areas under the League of Nations

(a) Danzig Free City

Six theories have been enunciated in regard to the location of sovereignty with reference to Danzig Free City. The first is that sovereignty over Danzig still remains in Germany. This theory is held by most of the German writers. They base their argument on article 192 of the treaty of peace, contending that Germany has never ceded her right of sovereignty to the powers. The second theory is that the sovereignty is in the hands of the Principal Allies. As in the case of mandates, the sovereignty of Germany over the territory in question was transferred to the Principal Allies. So it was in the case of Danzig. But the Principal Allies have never given up that sovereignty, for if they did, they would expressly renounce it as they did in the case of Memel where it was declared, in article 90 of the Peace Treaty, that they gave Lithuania the sovereignty over the latter.③

The third theory is that the sovereignty is in hand of the League of Nations, because, as it is argued, the latter has the authority over the territory and is charged with the protection and the defense of the city. It is argued moreover, that it is under the supervision of the League that the constitution of the city has been framed and under which it is guaranteed, and that the consent of the League must be given for modifying the constitution. Furthermore, the high commissioner representing the League of Nations

---

① Gregory, "The Neutralization of the Aaland Islands", in *American Journal of International Law*, Vol. XVII, p. 69.

② *Ibid.*, p. 75. The neutralization of the Congo Free State was somewhat peculiar, for it was recognized that the sovereignty was in Belgium. But the act of neutralization in this case was not perfect as it has been pointed out by Professor Oppenheim. See *International Law*, Vol. I, pp. 178-179.

③ G. Levesque, *La Situation Internationale de Danzig*, pp. 113-131.

manifests the actual sovereign power of the latter over the city.

The fourth theory is that the sovereignty rests in Poland. This is largely the idea of Polish writers. They maintain that sovereignty means the right of international existence. Since the power of conducting international affairs is given to Poland by virtue of article 104 of the Treaty of Versailles, the status of Danzig is no more than an autonomous territory of Poland.

The fifth theory is that the sovereignty resides in Danzig. It is asserted, mostly by the writers in Danzig, that no politically organized territory is without sovereignty. Danzig has a territory, a jurisdiction, a commercial flag. All these constitute the sovereignty of the city. It is argued moreover, that the relations between Poland and Danzig are no more than an international agreement between two sovereign states. ①

The sixth and the last theory is that the sovereignty has been divided between Poland, the League of Nations and Danzig, for each of them has exercised, to a certain extent, the sovereign powers of a state. ②

(b) Saar Basin

The problem of sovereignty was one of the most important problems for the so-called Big Three to solve in their settlement of the Saar Basin question. President Wilson, though willing to transfer the mines to France, opposed vigorously, not only once, but many times, both a change and a suspension of the sovereignty of Germany over the territory in question. ③ The French representatives, on the other hand, denied the view taken by President Wilson on the ground that if Germany would still retain the sovereignty over the territory, it would be impossible to apply French law in the matter of labor, recruiting, wages and similar matters, which France is entitled to do by virtue of the Treaty of Peace. ④ The representatives of France certainly had in mind that the right of enacting law is the right of sovereignty. To give one the former without giving the latter is a thing in its nature impossible. Lloyd-George, then the British Prime Minister, though more or less siding with France, took, however, a middle ground as he stated his view by saying: "I would give the Saar Basin its independence under the authority of the League of Nations." ⑤

---

① The best discussion of this subject may be found in Levesque's *La Situation internationale de Danzig*, p. 93.
② M. M. Lewis, "Free City of Danzig", in *British Year Book of International Law*, 1924, p. 90.
③ See Sidney Osborne, *The Saar Question, a Disease Spot in Europe*, 1923, pp. 56, 58. Also Donald, *A Danger Spot in Europe*, 1925, p. 13.
④ Osborne, *The Saar Question, a Disease Spot in Europe*, pp. 57, 59, 83; Donald, *A Danger Spot in Europe*, p. 14.
⑤ Osborne, *op. cit.*, p. 57.

The opinions of political writers also differ from each other. Professor Oppenheim thinks that the sovereignty is in the League of Nations, by virtue of the rights, duties, and powers attributed to the Governing Commission, the agent of the League of Nations. ① Mr. Corbett, on the other hand, supports the contention of President Wilson that it still remains in Germany. "What Germany renounces is not the sovereignty," says Mr. Corbett, "but the government of the Saar Territory."② To him, sovereignty must be differentiated from the powers exercised by governments. France and the League exercise the powers of sovereignty, but not sovereignty itself. ③ Some French writers have shared the contention of the French representatives. Still another view entertained by some thinkers is that the sovereignty is in the hands of the people of the Saar Basin. This argument is based on the ground that it is the people who have the right to decide, in the year 1935, under whose sovereignty they shall live.

6. Sovereignty and the Mandate System

It has been said that the mandate system is a new product of the World War. It is, moreover, a new departure in colonial administration, ④ and to some it is one of the most beneficent advances in international law. ⑤ For this reason, it follows, the problem of the mandates is one of the greatest and most valuable experiments made by the Covenant of the League of Nations. ⑥ In short, it is the test of the League of Nations. ⑦

Perhaps the most important and perplexing problem concerning the mandate system is that of sovereignty. Mr. Lansing, a well known authority on the subject of sovereignty, has sought in vain, its location in its application to the new system. ⑧ And when President Wilson was embarrassed by a number of questions put forth by Mr. Lansing as to the location of sovereignty in the mandate system, he laid them aside by characterizing them as legal technicalities and for that reason unimportant. ⑨ The members of the Permanent Mandate Commission have long been troubled with this question in connection with the work that they have been entrusted to do. And when M.

---

① Corbett, "What is the League of Nations", in the *British Year Book of International Law*, 1924, p. 121.
② *Ibid.*, p. 127.
③ *Ibid.*
④ See H. W. Harris, *What is the League of Nations?*, 1925, p. 104.
⑤ Statement of General Smuts, League of Nations, Permanent Mandate Commission, *Minutes*, Second Session Annex VI, p. 91. Also *ibid.*, p. 92, an extract from *Cape Times*, September 18, 1920.
⑥ League of Nations, *Records of the First Assembly*, 30th Plenary Meeting, Statement of Lord Balfour.
⑦ Hughan, *International Government*, p. 229.
⑧ Lansing, *The Peace Negotiations*, pp. 151 ff.
⑨ Lansing, *The Peace Negotiations*, p. 153.

F. d'Andrade, a member of the Commission, proposed that the question in regard to the status of Iraq might be referred to the Legal Section of the Secretariat, Professor Rappard, then the Director of the Mandates Section of the Secretariat, told the members of the Commission that the Legal Section would be placed in a very embarrassing position if the proposal of M. d'Andrade were adopted. The latter expressed the idea that he did not desire to press too much on this point for the moment. The discussion was then closed, yet the mystery remains unsolved. [1]

Under article 22 of the Covenant of the League of Nations, it is declared: "To those colonies and territories which as a consequence of the late war have ceased to be under the sovereignty of the states which formerly governed them..." The language here is clear enough to show that Germany can no longer claim sovereignty over the mandated territories, and it seems that it would go too far in asserting that the sovereignty is still in the hands of Germany. And in fact, the view has gained little if any support from the publicists.

The theory of Dr. Genevieve Levesque in regard to the sovereignty of Danzig may be applied to this case. [2] The theory is that Germany transferred the sovereignty over these territories to the Principal Allies and if the latter did not expressly give it up to any power, it still remains in the hands of the Principal Allies. The theory might not lack its defenders, but the criticism has been made that the Allied and Associated Powers, collectively speaking, is only a fiction which only had its existence for the time being. To some, it is said, it no longer exists; to others, it expresses its will and wishes through the League of Nations.

The latter viewpoint leads to a conclusion that the sovereignty is now in the League of Nations. This position is taken by writers like Wehberg and Schucking. Its logic is to be found in the following quotation: "These regions, though in fact each of them was conquered by some one or a few of the Allied and Associated Powers, are nevertheless, in contemplations of the law of nations, under the term of the alliance and association, the joint conquest of all; and the military occupation of any of these regions, though in fact established and maintained by one or a few of these powers, insures in law to the benefit of all and confers no individual sovereignty upon the state or states which actually made the conquest or which maintained the military occupation. The sovereignty of the

---

[1] League of Nations, *Minutes of the Permanent Mandate Commission*, seventh session, p. 123.
[2] Levesque, *La Situation Internationale de Danzig*, 1924, p. 121. See the letter sent by the Acting President of the Council to the Principal Allied Powers on June 15th, 1921. *Official Journal*, 1921, December, p. 645. See Baty, *op. cit.*, p. 117, note. Snow, *Proceedings of Academy of Political Science*, Vol. VII, p. 427.

former sovereigns of these territories has, as the article says, ceased, and the sovereignty of these regions is in the Allied and Associated Powers collectively. When, therefore, they unite themselves into a League, the League is regarded by them as succeeding to their collective sovereignty by operation of the law and their consent, so that no formal cession or quit-claim is necessary and a mere recognition of the passing of their collective title to the League is treated as sufficient."①

From the reasoning advanced in the statement quoted above, it is concluded that the sovereignty of the League over the mandated territories must be considered as the only and the true sovereignty, and that the League shall administer its trust for the tutelage of its dependent regions through the instrumentality of one of the civilized states, in every case where such administration is possible.

Moreover, turning to the legal side, the sovereignty of the League of Nations over the mandated territories can not be questioned, because the consent of the former is required for the transfer of mandates and also for the termination and modification of the terms of the mandates.② Furthermore, these territories are under the control of the League of Nations through its agent, the Permanent Mandates Commission, although such control is indirect rather than direct.③

On the other hand, there are many writers who deny the view just mentioned above for various reasons. "The League of Nations," says General Smute, "had nothing to do with the giving of mandates which were already settled as a fact by the Peace Treaty, quite apart from the League of Nations."④ Moreover, "the League of Nations is not a state, it owns no territory, governs no subjects and is not endowed with the attributes of sovereignty"⑤. Again, "the council of the League, which is the most important supervisory organ of the League over the mandated territories has expressly stated that it has no authority over the assignment of mandates,⑥ nor has it authority over the

---

① Snow, "The Mandatory System under the Covenant of the League of Nations", *Proceedings of the Academy of Political Science*, Vol. Ⅷ, p. 427.

② Article 22, paragraph (h).

③ See also the opinion expressed by M d'Andrade, in the first session of the Permanent Mandate Commission, *Minutes*, 1921, p. 41.

④ *Minutes*, Second Session, 1922, p. 92, In another place he declared: "Under the Peace Treaty, Germany had renounced her colonies not to the League of Nations, but to the Great Powers." Second Session, pp. 4-5, Annex Ⅵ, p. 92.

⑤ Of, Larnarde, *La Societe des Natious*, Paris, 1920. See also Levesque, *La Situation Internationale de Danzig*, p. 118,

⑥ Levermore, *Year Book of the League of Nations*, Vol. Ⅱ, p. 19. Also see League of Nations, *Official Journal*, 1920, Vol. Ⅰ, p. 343.

territorial limits"①.

Seeing that the League has no sovereignty over the mandated territories, some writers maintain that the sovereignty is in the hands of the Mandatory Powers. R. E. Rolin is one of the best expounders of this theory. ② Speaking from the legal point of view, he holds that the mandate system is nothing less than a system of annexation. ③ He asserts that "the colonial mandate appears as a convention 'sui generis' different from the civil mandate and implying the grant of a perpetual power over the thing administered. Viewed in this light, the colonial mandate is more in the nature of a sale than of an ordinary mandate"④. So it is concluded that the sovereignty belongs to the mandatory power whatever may be the terms of the Mandates. ⑤

The government of the South African Union has repeatedly declared that the mandated territory under her mandate may be incorporated as an integral part of the Union, and that as soon as this is done, the territory in question will no longer be under the supervision of the Permanent Mandates Commission. ⑥ In the preamble to one of the agreements concerning the boundary between the South African Union and Portugal, the

---

① Permanent Mandates Commission, *Minutes*, second session, p. 6, report of the Commission in regard to the Ruanda Boundary between Great Britain and Belgium.

② Permanent Mandates Commission, *Minutes*, third session, p. 218. Also, Millot, *Les Mandats internationaux*, pp. 107 ff. See *Revue de Droit international et de Legislation comparee*, 1920, Nos. 3-4, p. 350.

③ *Minutes*, third session, p. 218.

④ *Minutes*, third session, pp. 219-220.

⑤ *Ibid.*, p. 220. He further points out that the text does not contain any other reservation. The law of the mandatory power can have no meaning but actual sovereignty as denoted by its principle manifestation. This is an instance of a common rhetorical figure—the use of the part for the whole. Moreover, the words "integral portions of its territory" can have no other meaning than annexation. p. 219.

General Smuts also recognized that C Mandate communities are in effect not far from annexation. See a letter written by him, in League of Nations, Permanent Mandate Commission, second session, *Annex* VI, p. 91.

Professor Baty seems to be in favor of this theory. "It is exceedingly difficult to see in what respect such a state of affairs differs from annexation. If the entire administration of a territory is committed to you, you have entire control there. Let us imagine the case of a revolt. The territory is not sovereign, or even mi-sovereign; there is nothing to prevent the inflection by the mandatory of the penalties of treason on the people under its control. By Article 257 of the Versailles Treaty, the territory is to be 'transferred to' that power—so that it has a clear right to consider itself as entitled to their allegiance; though it is not so clear who is to make the transfer." "Protectorates and Mandates" in *British Year Book of International Law*, 1921-1922, p. 117.

Mr. Lansing remarks that the mandate system is a thin disguise for annexation. See Lansing, *Peace Negotiations*, pp. 155-156.

M. Sarrant has frankly said in the Washington Conference, that "our colonial Empire, though some would seem to be ignorant of it, really exists". See *Current History*, February, 1922.

⑥ League of Nations, Permanent Mandates Commission, *Minutes*, seventh session. Examination of the reports made by the Union of South Africa in the administration of South-West Africa.

Government of the former expressly declared that, subject to the terms of its mandate, it "possessed sovereignty over the territory of South-West Africa, lately under the sovereignty of Germany"①. The language quoted here is clear enough to show the conception of the statesmen in regard to the location of sovereignty concerning the mandate system.

But there are also writers who deny that the sovereignty is vested in the mandatory powers. The starting point of the argument may be found in the following quotation. "The two main pillars of the mandatory system as applied today are first, that the mandatory power is debarred from appropriating for its own peculiar purposes any of the resources of the territory, whether they be in the form of the labour or the persons of inhabitants or whether material values as expressed in mineral or vegetable products, and secondly, that the first duty of the mandatory is to foster the moral and material welfare of the people and of the territory whilst ultimate self-government will always be the goal towards which administrative effort must be directed. These basic principles preclude for all time the annexation of any mandated area."② As the adoption of the mandatory system has not involved the incorporation of German colonies in the territory

---

① The language so used is considered to be very serious. The Permanent Commission has again and again raised the question as to what is the exact meaning of the expression "possesses sovereignty". The matter has also been discussed in the Council and the Assembly. See *Minutes of Permanent Mandate Commission*, tenth and eleventh sessions. See also the *Monthly Summary of the League of Nations*, Vol. VII, No. 7, August, 1927, p. 227.

② League of Nations, Permanent Mandates Commission, *Minutes*, 3rd session, p. 217. The same view is expressed by M. de Caix, the accredited representative of France, the mandatory power of Syria, as follows: "The mandate is a provisional system designed to enable populations, which, politically speaking, are still minors to educate themselves so as to arrive one day at full self-government. This presupposes that the mandatory power will gradually create native organizations in the mandated territory such as may, when complete, be able to insure entirely the government of the country and such as may, if they carry out their duties in proper manner, render the intervention of the mandatory unnecessary. It appears from this that there should not be any intervention on the part of the organs of the mandatory power in the internal affairs of the native governments." *The Monthly Summary of the League of Nations*, Vol. VI, No. 3, March, 1926, p. 65.

of the mandatory powers, it is not intended to invest the latter with sovereignty. ①

Moreover, it is argued that the B and C Mandatory powers have not yet by any conscious act claimed sovereignty over the Mandated territories; ② none has shown signs of regarding these territories as its own, as inseparable; none appears to consider the natives as its own nationals. On the contrary, every one has given financial autonomy to their territories and the majority have granted them administrative autonomy. ③ In short, as Hicks says, the mandatories possess jurisdiction without possessing sovereignty. ④

---

① *Minutes of the Permanent Mandates Commission*, third session, p. 218. "The relations between a mandatory power and a mandated territory differ in kind from those between a sovereign state and its dependencies. The mandatory's status is not that of a proprietor, but of trustee, he is not free to govern in his own interest by right of conquest. Such authority as he exercises over the inhabitants of the territory is exercised on behalf of the League of Nations, and it is conferred upon him solely with a view to secure their well-being and development and to open the territory to the trade enterprise of all members of the League of Nations. In accepting a mandate he does not acquire the right of annexation. He assumes the duty of tutelage." A statement quoted by W. Rees from the British League of Nations Union in a volume entitled *A Plan for the Government by Mandate in Africa*, p. 7.

"The terms of mandates in themselves imply that the newly-acquired rights are not those of a proprietor but those of a trustee who is entrusted with the temporary administration of these countries in their interest and not in his own. A mandatory who wishes to fulfill his duties as a trustee is debarred from any right of appropriation; on the other hand he must protect the property of the people under his charge, foster its development, preserve its health, safeguard its liberty and its moral and material well-being. There is a sacred duty to be discharged and not a selfish profit to be gained." "Colonial Mandates and the League of Nations", in *Preliminary Document of the 12th Inter-Parliamentary Conference*, p. 76. *Minutes*, Third Session, p. 218.

W. Rees, the Vice-Chairman of the Permanent Mandates Commission for a few times, is certainly the best opponent of the theory of the sovereignty of the mandatory and at the same time the best advocate of the theory of the sovereignty of the League of Nations. In the third session of the Permanent Mandates Commission, he declared: "That which has been handed over to the mandatory state in virtue of Article 120 and 257, that which has 'passed' or 'been transferred' to the governor has been handed over to him as governor and not a state; consequently, there has been no final alienation and no real rights have been acquired by that state; the territory, property, possessions, and rights referred to in the two Articles do not belong to the mandatory state but have merely been placed at its disposal; it has been granted their use in order that it may carry out its duties as governor with which it has been entrusted." Therefore, he concludes, "That the sovereignty of Germany over her over-sea possessions has passed to the Principle Allied and Associated Powers. In virtue of their sovereign powers these states have appointed the mandatories entrusted with the administration of the territories ceded by Germany. In consultation with the other powers represented on the Council of the League of Nations, they have in accordance with the Covenant, determined the special conditions of each mandate, while the right of supervision appertaining to these powers as granters of mandates has automatically passed into the League of Nations. This supervision—which affects the entire fabric, and not merely certain given parts, of the administration of mandatory, who in any case acts merely on behalf of the League of Nations—excludes any supposition that the sovereignty over the territory is vested in the mandatory." See *Minutes of Permanent Mandates Commission*, third session, p. 221.

② Exception must be made in the case of the government of the South African Union, see above, pp. 128–129.

③ *Minutes of the Permanent Mandates Commission*, third session, pp. 218–219. Also second session, pp. 46, 58, 68. Cf. Lord Balfour's view. Levermore, *Year Book of the League of Nations*, Vol. II.

④ Hicks, *New World Order*, p. 125. See also *American Journal of International Law*, Vol. XVIII, p. 308.

So there are also writers who place the sovereignty in the mandated territories. Their argument is this: formerly, the sovereignty was in the hands of Germany, and Since Germany has renounced it, and since it has not been transferred to any other power, it must reside in the mandated territories.① This is certainly not a theory without some foundation. It is supported by the Organic Law of Iraq passed by the Constituent Assembly on July 10th, 1924. It is declared in that law, or constitution as it is called, that "Iraq is a sovereign state, free and independent. Its sovereign rights are indivisible and inalienable"②.

But this theory has also its opponents. In regard to the mandated territories of class A, it has been pointed out that "although the Covenant calls them 'independent nations', in fact it may be doubted whether the advice and assistance will not prove to resemble the sort of advice which the British residents soon convinced the Malay Sultans that they had undertaken to receive— 'advice namely' which must be taken"③. Needless to say the status of mandated territories of classes B and C is different for they "are in effect not far from annexations"④.

The extreme views and their difficulties in application, as have been shown, naturally bring a group of thinkers to advance another conception which is different from what has already been presented and yet is by no means a new theory in any sense. To this group of thinkers, the sovereignty is not to be placed in any one particular place, for to do this, as they argue, is not consistent with the actual facts and therefore difficulties can never be avoided. Professor Q. Wright, after making a careful study of the problem of sovereignty in connection with the mandate system, is forced to conclude with these words: "There will be a close approach to truth in ascribing the sovereignty of mandated territories to the mandatory acting with the consent of the Council of the League."⑤ So Professor Millot, an excellent student on the subject of the mandatory system, holds a somewhat similar idea, although he approaches it from another angle.

---

① See Albert Millot, *Les Mandats Internationaux*, Paris, 1924, pp. 116–117.

② Article Ⅱ. The expression of this article is certainly inconsistent with the terms of the mandate. In the seventh session of the Permanent Mandate Commission, M. Rees remarks: "Iraq was not a country governed by mandatory power nor was it a territory which engaged a certain autonomy. It was a veritable state, an independent kingdom undertaking to follow in certain points the advice and principles indicated to him by the British Government." *Minutes of the Permanent Mandates Commission*, seventh session, 1925, p. 12.

③ Baty, "Protectorates and Mandates", *British Year Book of International Law*, 1921–1922, p. 117.

④ Those who maintain the sovereignty of the mandatory powers or that of the League are naturally the opponents of this theory.

⑤ Wright, "Sovereignty of the Mandates" in *American Journal of International Law*, Vol. ⅩⅦ, p. 698. Also *ibid.*, Vol. ⅩⅡ, p. 315,

Like many political writers, Professor Millot divides sovereignty into its internal and external parts. The former may be located in one place and the latter in another. But no exact line can be drawn between the two. For example, in the A class mandates, first there is an external sovereignty which is exercised by the mandatory; but certain attributes of which have been passed to the hands of local authority. Then there are some attributes of eminent sovereignty also exercised by the former, but by the demands of the local population, they are exercised in accordance with the modality and the forms that they desire. Again there are attributes of internal sovereignty exercised by a limited cooperation of the two authorities, local and mandatory, which are given up by the latter. [1]

In order to make more clear the viewpoint under consideration, let us conclude by quoting a passage from a learned writer: "The effect of this is that the sovereignty of Syria and Mesopotamia, taken over by the Allied Powers, has been vested by these Powers in Syria and Mesopotamia themselves. In the recognition of the provisional mandate, because its continuance will depend on the development of these countries as political units, certain powers usually coupled with independence and sovereignty were reserved for exercise, under the supervision of the League of Nations, by a Mandatory to be chosen by the Allied and Associated Powers. That choice was the loss of sovereignty on the part of the allied Powers as such over the territories in question. Henceforward such powers as have not been transferred to the inhabitants of the territories themselves are divided between the Mandatory and the League."[2]

7. Sovereignty and the League of Nations

The world has come to a new era with the establishment of the League of Nations. It marks the highest watermark that has ever been reached in the history of the development of international or world organization. We are told that "the League of Nations is a series of engagements freely taken by 'many' sovereign or self-governing nations, each for itself and toward the others, in order to promote international cooperation and to achieve international peace and security"[3].

But whether the creation of the League has any effect on the sovereignty of these nations, or rather of its members, is one of the most interesting problems of political philosophy today which, undoubtedlly deserves our examination and attention.

No writer seems to be ready to go so far as to hold that the League of Nations is the

---

[1] A Millot, *Les Mandats Internationaux*. Paris, 1924, p. 96.
[2] Corbett, "What is the League of Nations?", *B. Y. B. of International Law*, 1924, p. 130.
[3] "World Peace Foundation Pamphlets", *Sixth Yearbook of the League*, 1927, Nos. 3-4, p. 137.

only sovereign body at present and that the status of its members has been reduced to that of a department in France or a county in England. While this seems to be true, it is also true that men of vision, in the past as well as at the present, remark that the world sovereignty has already planted its seeds and that it will not be long for us to see its realization and appearance. As early as in the year 1920, M. Motta, then the President of Switzerland, in his welcome speech to the first meeting of the Assembly of the League of Nations emphatically declared that "the League is not an alliance of governments, it is an association of peoples"①. Lord Robert Cecil, whose voice has been well heard by the members of the world assembly, said sometime ago these words: "In the process of time it (the League) will therefore absorb all the more important international questions. It will become the sole international authority in Europe and the world. All countries desiring to take part in international affairs will have to use the League machinery for that purpose, for there will be no other of importance."②

While none has said that the League is the only sovereignty, there are not only a few writers who assert that the League is one of the sovereignties of the world, or at least it is sovereign within its own sphere. Thus it is said: "A new international person has been created with enough sovereignty to make reasonable expectation…to the maintenance of international peace and security and the promotion of international cooperation through the development of international law."③

This position has been well defended by Professor Baldwin of Yale University. Professor Baldwin's starting point is revealed in the passage quoted below: "The general movement in human society is from the simple to the complex, the family, expanding into the tribe, is the first political unit, and the will of the patriarch is its rules of conduct. Gradually the operation of that will becomes in some measure limited. Several tribes come to constitute a nation…Society is still national in character, but each country enters into certain relations to other countries…As it is a natural step to proceed from the government of a family to that of a tribe, and thence to that of a nation, so it seems a not unnatural progress in social order to advance from the government of a

---

① *Provisional Verbatim Records*, 1920, Ⅰ, p. 4.

② Statement quoted by D. J. Hill. See E. S. Rakin, *The Dominion of Sea and Air*, p. 222. Cf. H. H. Powers, *The Great Peace*, p. 11.

③ See *Political Science Quarterly*, Vol. 36, p. 709. Also Harley, J. E. *The League of Nations and International Law*. Cf. Oppenheim, *International Law*, 3rd ed., Vol. Ⅰ, p. 268. "The League is the subject of many rights, which as a rule, can only be exercised by sovereign states. For instance, the League possesses rights (so-called) of legation; is able to exercise sovereign rights over such territories as are not under the sovereignty of any state; is able to declare war and make peace."

nation to the government of the ralations of nations to each other."①

The League of Nations is then no more than a result of the natural progress of the social order. As the nation has gained its sovereignty through the process of slow development, so it is with the League. The proposition that the League is sovereign, sovereign in its own sphere, is supported, according to Professor Baldwin, by the three great legal schools, namely, the historical, philosophical and pragmatic schools.

Historical evidences have shown that international associations have exercised sovereign powers. The Hanseatic League, the inter-state tribunal created by Article 105 of the Treaty of Vienna, the Postal Union, the German "Zollverein", the Holy Roman Empire; each of these exercised sovereign rights to a certain extent as a sovereign state, and indeed each was a sovereign body itself. This being the case, so it must be in the case of the League of Nations.

Turning to the philosophical school, Professor Baldwin finds its main thesis in that the right of a sovereign depends on the consent of the people. The people may give up part of their sovereignty and retain part of it. "If they can thus divide into parts, one vested in an active agent and one held back, why cannot a division be made on a basis of vesting part of the whole of sovereignty exclusively in one public agency and the rest of that whole in another agency?"② If a group of individuals can create a sovereign body, why not a group of nations? As to the pragmatic school, he finds its argument is based on facts. The American pragmatists do not have to look farther than his own country to give them a good example that a group of nations may create a sovereign, and the League of Nations, it seems to him, is no more than a federal union in its broader sense.③

Not so boldly as, but more widely accepted than, the view just stated, is that [that] the sovereignty of the members of the League of Nations is impaired or limited by the latter. It is idle, says Professor Pollock, to discuss the question whether the League as a whole could be properly called sovereign in any and what sense; but the sovereignty of a state may be limited just as a man's freedom is very seriously limited in the case of a marriage contract.④ The state, he says again, so far as internal sovereignty is

---

① "Vesting Sovereignty in a League of Nations", *Yale Law Review*, Vol. 28, 1919, p. 209.
② *Ibid.*, p. 217.
③ *Ibid.*, p. 218.
④ Pollock, "Sovereignty and the League of Nations", *Fortnightly Review*, 1918, Vol. 110, p. 814.

concerned, is in no way limited or impaired, but externally speaking, it is limited. ①

Dr. Manuel Diaz Rodriguez, the Venezuelan delegate, in a document submitted to the Assembly of the League of Nations on November 20, 1920, expresses the view that the different states are drawn closer together by the continuous development of the means of communication. This brings internationalization of interests. As "interests become more closely linked every day there results a corresponding interdependence of states". "Though it is true that interdependence in no way implies dependence," he adds, "it does none the less sometimes involve a real renunciation of sovereignty on the part of each state in favor of society at large in the interest of the common good." ②

It has been remarked that "the answer to the argument that sovereign rights can not be curtailed is the advocacy of a nebulous theory which would be little more than a pious vow…Machinery there must be; and for it to have any chance of keeping the peace, the Covenant must impose limitations on sovereignty"③. The same idea may be found in the following statement: "there will be no prohibition against any and all nations and rulers still believing in the divine right of kings, or the sovereignty of states, but the practical effect of a successful league of nations would be to limit the possible harm that these theories could do." ④

The statements quoted above show only the general expression of the statesmen and writers. Let us now examine how, in its actual working, the sovereignty of the members of the League is limited, as is held by some writers. It is argued that the right of conquest which is the sovereign right of an independent state, is abolished, so far as the members of the League are concerned, by Article X of the Covenant which forbids not only direct conquest as by external aggression against the territorial integrity of a member, but also veiled conquest as by external aggression against the existing political independence of a member. ⑤

The law of nations allows every sovereign state to make war upon another sovereign

---

① *Ibid.*, pp. 813 ff. "So long as state retains the usual attributes of supreme power within its own territory, and continues to exercise that power in its own government and affairs, there is no obvious necessity for denying it the name of sovereign." p. 814.

② *Provisional Verbatim*, 1920, November 20, 8th meeting, p. 5.

③ See Duggan, *League of Nations, the Principle and Practice*, p. 89.

④ Goldsmith, *A League to Enforce Peace*, p. 81.

⑤ "The Members of the League undertake to respect and preserve as against external aggression the territorial integrity and existing political independence of all members of the League. In case of any such aggression or in case of any threat or danger of such aggression the Council shall advise upon the means by which this obligation shall be fulfilled."

state. ① So this is stated in Lieber's code. ② And when a distinguished Senator of the United States declares that the right of war cannot be impaired, he views it as the essential characteristic of sovereignty. ③ But, again, this right can no longer exist under Article X of the Covenant just mentioned and under Article XI of the same which reads: "Any war or threat of war, whether immediately affecting any of the Members of the League or not, is hereby declared a matter of concern to the whole League, and the League shall take any action that may be deemed wise and effectual to safeguard the peace of nations."

Similarly Articles XII, XV, XVI, and XVII of the Covenant of the League of Nations have restricted the right of the members to war. "It is obvious that every state signing the Covenant of the League has pledged itself through the above provisions to surrender important sovereign rights."④ Therefore, "however much it may be denied that the Covenant affects the sovereignty of the States affiliated to the League, consideration of the above provisions of the document is sufficient proof that the sovereignty has been impaired"⑤.

Again, the draft Protocol for the Pacific Settlement of International Disputes adopted by the Fifth Assembly, means a "further intrusion upon the sovereignty of the States affiliated to the League—an intrusion all the more serious because it involves the supreme issues of life and death. To transfer the sovereign rights to decide over peace and war from the national parliaments to the Council of the League of Nations would be contrary to the fundamental principle of representative government. A nation might in this way be driven into a war contrary to its own desire and vital interests"⑥.

The right of every independent state to remain at peace while other states are engaged in war is an incontestable attribute of sovereignty. ⑦ "All states," says Hall, "are sovereign, and in so far as neutrals are concerned, sovereignty is an attribute of community in the enjoyment of belligerent privileges."⑧ But here again, as it has been pointed out, the right of neutrality is abolished by Article XVI of the Covenant of the

---

① Wright, "Effects of the League of Nations Covenant", *Political Science Review*, Vol. XIII, pp. 560–570.
② U. S. Army, *General Orders*, No. 100, 1863, Art, 67.
③ Lodge, *Senate and the League of Nations*, p. 407.
④ Montgomery, *Issues of European Statesmanship*, p. 123.
⑤ *Ibid.*, p. 124. Also *Pol. Sci. Rev.*, Vol. XIII, p. 563.
⑥ *Ibid.*, p. 138.
⑦ Wheaton, *Elements of International Law*, 8th ed., 1866, p. 509.
⑧ Hall, *Rights and Duties of Neutrals*, p. 15. See also Hershey, *Essentials of International Law*, p. 445.

League which declares: "Should any Member of the League resort to war in disregard of its covenants under Article XII, XIII, or XV, shall *ipso facto* be deemed to have committed an act of war against all other Members of the League, which hereby undertake immediately to subject it to the severance of all trade or financial relations, the prohibition of all intercourse between their nationals and the nationals of the covenant-breaking state, and the prevention of all financial, commercial, or personal intercourse between the nationals of the covenant-breaking state and the nationals of any other state, whether a member of the League or not. It shall be the duty of the Council in such case to recommend to the several Governments concerned what effective military, naval, or air force the Members of the League shall contribute to the armed forces to be used to protect the covenants of the League."①

We have already shown the view of those who see the League of Nations as being on the way of becoming the only sovereignty of the world, that of those who maintain that the League is a sovereign body, or at least that it is sovereign within its own sphere, and that the establishment of the League involves a limitation upon the sovereignty of its members. It remains now for us to consider the view of those who hold that the sovereignty of the states is not in any way limited by reason of being members of the League of Nations. This is not a new idea. William Penn seems to have had it in mind when he wrote "The Essay toward the Present and Future Peace". Thus he says, "I come now to the last objection, that sovereign princes and states will hereby become not sovereign—a thing they will never endure. But this also, under correction, is a mistake, for they remain as sovereign at home as ever they were…If this be called a lessening of their power, it must only be because the great fish can no longer eat up the little ones, and that each sovereignty is equally defended from injuries, and disabled from committing them."② M. Hymans, in a speech at the opening of the First Assembly, declared: "It is well that we should state once again that the League of Nations, is not, and must not, be a super-state which aims at absorbing national sovereignties or reducing them to bondage."③ Lord Curzon expressed the same view at

---

① See Q. Wright, "Effects of the League of Nations Covenant", *Political Science Review*, Vol. XIII, p. 571. Also "Sovereignty and Neutrality" in *International Conciliation*, 208. W. F. Taft and E. J. Bryan, *World Peace, a Written Debate*, 1917, p. 114. Cf. J. A. Hobson, *Towards International Government*, 1915, p. 127.

② Quoted by Pollock, *Fortnightly Review*, Vol. 110, p. 818.

③ *Provisional Verbatim*, 1920, p. 6.

the First meeting of the Council of the League.① So it is held by Bourgeois.② The main argument of this group of writers is that sovereignty is the essential characteristic of the state. Where there is a sovereignty there must be a state. But the League is not a state, for it lacks two essential elements of the state: namely, territory and people; consequently it possesses no sovereignty.③ The League, as they conceive it, can have nothing to do with the sovereignty of the states, for the reason that it is no more than a series of engagements freely taken by the sovereign states and the latter can withdraw from it at any time if they choose to do so.

8. Conclusion

What has been said as to the location of sovereignty from the standpoint of international relations is by no means exhaustive. There are many more items that may be added to our list,④ but enough has been given to show the difficulty and complications of the problem of the location of sovereignty in its application. Sovereignty has been placed here and there by different writers from different angles; but few theories can escape from difficulties and therefore criticism.

The increase of the facility of the means of communication has brought individuals as well as groups from different parts of the world more closely together than before. The interdependence of human activities and interests has become a matter of necessity rather than of choice. The more there will be of interdependnce the more organizations and conventions which are international in character will be needed. The more the latter are created in order to meet the needs and consequently the changing conditions, the more complicated the problem of the location of sovereignty will become. The creation of the mandatory system and the establishment of the League of Nations certainly demonstrate to us that what has been just pointed out, is not far from the truth.

---

① *Ibid.*

② Leon Bourgeois, *L'ouvre de la Saciete des Nations (1922-1923)*, p. 113.

③ M. Larnaude, *La Societe des Nations*, Paris, 1920. "La Societe des Nations n'est pas une societe d'Etat analogue soit a l'Etat federal, soit a la Confederation d'Etats, soit a l'Union, soit a tout autre forme d'Etat non unitaire. Elle est une formation d'un type absolument nouveau, avant tout et meme peut on dire exclusivement contractuelle, dans laquelle les Etats asument certaines obligations qui laissent intacte leur souverainete. La Societe n'est pas un super-Etat; elle resemble plutot a une association, a un syndicat d'Etats, a une cooperative d'Etats, mais, d'ailleurs, avec des caracteres speciaux qui depassent singulierement le droit contractuel proprement dit."

④ How the sovereignty of the states has been affected by the Hague Court of Arbitration, the Permanent Court of International Justice, International Labor Organization etc., may be cited as examples.

V. Recent Attacks on the Notion of Sovereignty

In its application to the field of international relations, the notion of sovereignty has been attacked from different angles. In the first place, there are those who even deny the use of the term sovereignty in international relations. They hold that sovereignty is a thing which only exists within the border of a state, not without it. "The idea of sovereignty," says Professor Willoughby, "as it is found in constitutional law, can find no proper place among international conceptions."① "It is futile," says another writer, "to introduce the conception of sovereignty into international law."②

Sovereignty, as it is argued by some, is a thing that has to be viewed from above to below or vice versa, that signifies the relation between the superior and the inferior and that can never be employed in relations or dealings between states, for the latter always stand on the same level and are treated by each other on an equal footing, whether they be strong or weak, great or small, rich or poor, therefore "a dwarf is as much of a man as a giant and Geneva is no less a state than Russia". So the reasoning runs.

What is popularly called the sovereignty of a state from the international standpoint is then nothing more than independence.③ And independence is, in its nature, negative, passive and latent rather than active, positive or affirmative.④ It merely means that a state has the right to exist for herself, and to deal with others just as much as the others are to her without being controlled, limited or restricted by the actions of the others. To mistake one for another would mean no more than to use a ladder for the purpose of walking from one end to the other on the level ground instead of climbing up and down, and the result of this is not only meaningless but also inconvenient and improper and even dangerous.⑤

Then there are other groups of writers who attack the notion in its application to the

---

① Willoughby, *Fundamental Concepts of Public Law*, p. 283.

② Statement made by P. A. Brown. See *American Journal of International Law*, Vol. IX, p. 326. See also Garner, "Limitations on National Sovereignty in International Relations", *Political Science Review*, Vol. XIX (1925), p. 6.

③ See Crane, *The State in Constitutional and International Law*, p. 65. The terms "sovereignty" and "independence" are frequently used by the writers to mean one and the same thing. Foulke, *International Law*, pp. 69-70, note.

④ Manning, *Law of Nations*, revised by Amos, p. 93. "Sovereignty represents the positive and independence the negative side." Cf. Brown, *International Reality*, pp. 64-65.

⑤ Cf. Garner, *op. cit.*, p. 2. Also R. Pound's view, see *Political Theory and International Law*, Merriam and Barnes, *Political Theories*, p. 121.

field of international relations from another standpoint. They say that the world of today is not the world of yesterday. The writers and statesmen of the past, they recognize, might go so far as to boast that sovereignty means the freedom of action and doing what you want and to act what you will, but the day of Hobbes has gone and the gulf between his theory and the actual practice of today has been and is becoming wider and wider and time alone has shown that they are not only irreconcilable, but even in conflict with each other and the existence of one would almost mean the extinction of the other.

Here is an eloquent passage illustrating the point at issue and worth while to be quoted: "As the world becomes economically more interdependent each day, new forms must be invented to forge the political side of our life into a shape which can meet and control these economic forces. In so far as a seventeenth or eighteenth or even nineteenth century theory of sovereignty does not conform to our present factual situation, it must fall into ground. There is abundant evidence that the term sovereignty has now become a term of confusion. The idea and the very word sovereignty threatened to hold up and postpone the final conclusion of the recent treaty between Great Britain and Ireland…What difference does it make? It may well be asked. The framers of the Covenant of the League of Nations ran up against the same problem. What state might be admitted? They decided to wholly discard the word sovereignty. Rather than 'sovereign state', membership is open to any 'self-governing' state dominion or colony. The word sovereignty is used only once in the entire Covenant and then only in a minor capacity. Other problems arising from new and novel forms might be suggested, but enough has been said to indicate that the word is becoming obsolete. At best it is but a theory by which we may classify results and situations, certainly not a reason upon which to base a conclusion."①

The passage just quoted is newly written, but the idea enunciated is old. Mr. Angel, the so-called pessimist would tell us that it is a great illusion to worship the sovereignty of the state. He certainly takes pains and says: "The outcome of purely modern conditions (rapidity of communication creating a greater complication and delicacy of credit system) have rendered the problems of modern international politics profoundly and essentially different from the ancient; yet our ideas are still dominated by the principles and axioms and phraseology of the old."② And he asserts that "society is classifying itself by interests rather than by state divisions; that the modern state is losing its homogeneity; and that all these multiple factors are making rapidly for the

---

① E. D. Hamilton, "In Re Alienation of Sovereignty", *Virginia Law Review*, Vol. XIII (1927), p. 524.
② Angel, *The Great Illusion*, p. 9.

disappearance of state rivalries"①.

Even thinkers brought up in the home land of Hegel are aware of the fact that the situation of the individual states have entirely changed since world economy has created countless modes between the hitherto isolated states, since commerce, industry, and the system of insurance, as well as numerous other institutions, have been built upon international foundations. This economic interdependence of the individual states has continued to grow stronger and greater with each day.② As a result of this change, "it is a matter of necessity and not of choice, that the states have come to enter into conventions, treaties and in turn the sovereignty of the states in the old sense has been strongly attacked and can no longer be maintained; for the interest of the community of the states must supersede the selfish interest of separate states"③.

The first attack mentioned above is purely from the legal standpoint and the second is mainly from the economical standpoint. Now let us come to a third one, which is chiefly from the moral standpoint. This conception has come into light as a result of the cataclysm of human wars of the past, particularly the World War.

It is to be remembered that the expounders of this idea usually do not attack sovereignty if it is only one for the whole world. They maintain that as sovereignty is supposed to be unaccountable, unlimitable, and infallible, such consequences as conflict, competition, rivalry and, worst of all, war, can never be avoided if there are many or even two sovereignties existing at the same time. They certainly share the view of Dante that peace can only be attainable by a unified governmental system under a single power; for a single power, as Dante sees it, having no rival to dread, and no further ambition to satisfy, could have no motive to rule otherwise than justly.

"The present war," says Faguini, "exhibits nationalism at its highest and at its worst. What is happening now must needs happen again unless the present independent, individual sovereign states surrender their sovereignty by becoming members of the federated states of the world."④ And Mr. D. A. Kingsley, the President of the New York Life Insurance Co., whether for the sake of his own customers or for that of mankind at large, has spoken to the world in such emphatic manner: "So long as there are even two great unconditioned sovereignties in the world, there can be no lasting

---

① Angel, *The Great Illusion*, p. 9.
② Wehberg, *The Problem of an International Court of Justice*, p. 1.
③ *Ibid.*, p. 3.
④ Quoted by Bigelow, *World Peace*, p. 219.

peace."① He sees that there is a possibility of having only one sovereignty under which the mankind of the whole world can live happily and peacefully, for "the United States has shown how so-called sovereign states can be merged into a larger state without losing their individuality and without parting with the principle of democracy". "If to do that the present doctrine of unconditioned sovereignty must be abandoned, if as a nation we must surrender what each colony seemed to surrender in 1789, we should stand for that, we should find when the time came—as our fathers did—that we had actually only surrendered a little false pride, a little hate, a little prejudice and a little fear, and had entered, as our colonies did, upon the only order that leads to peace and true happiness."②

VI. Conclusion

Traditionalists are not lacking in our age, but the traditionalists of the present day are different from those of the past. Many of them, instead of saying that sovereignty is unlimitable and indivisible without any qualification, say that the conception of sovereignty is one of constitutional, rather than of international law. It exists only within the border of a state rather than outside it. In fact they would like to see the term "sovereignty" no longer applied to international relations. Were such a view not far from the truth, the subject under consideration would be of little value, at most it would have only historical significance.

While not undertaking to test the validity of the view just presented, it seems desirable to conclude our discussion by pointing out the goal toward which recent thought is or rather has been directed. Whether this is wrong or that is right, is to us, of no significance here. The truth is that the doctrine of indivisible and unlimited sovereignty has been and likely will be discredited by most of the thinkers in its application to international relations. "The conception of the sovereignty of the state," says a learned student on the subject under discussion, "which admits the divisibility of the former belongs to what is here denominated the international theory, by reason of its acceptance by so many writers on international law."③ And if Professor Markby is not mistaken, Austin is no less than a believer in the divisibility doctrine of sovereignty, at least so far as its application to the field of international dealings is concerned.

---

① "The World's Fundamental Error", *The Independent*, Vol. 85, pp. 153–155.
② *Ibid.* See also Vol. 84, p. 376, 1915.
③ Crane, "The State in Constitutional and International Law", *Johns Hopkins University Studies*, 1907, No. 6–7, p. 41.

CHAPTER VI
SOVEREIGNTY AND LAW

I. Introduction

In considering the theory of sovereignty in its application to international relations, we have briefly presented different phases of the notion of sovereignty in its relation to international law. But international law, as has been pointed out, has not been or still is not recognized by some writers as law in its strict sense. Even we take for granted that international law is law, as we are told by many authorities, particularly authorities on international law, our previous presentation is too far from comprehensive for the simple reason that international law is only a branch in the field of jurisprudence. Accordingly it is proposed in this chapter and the two following to bring out the different aspects of the notion of sovereignty in its relation to law, not in any particular field, but in general.

The subject under discussion is at once an old and a new one. It is old because it was already discussed in the time of ancient Greece and even much earlier.[①] It is new because recently it has taken many forms, either as descriptions of new conditions, or as principles to be realized. Examining into extreme views, we find, on the one hand, those who hold that law is merely the creature of sovereignty and that it can not be called law unless it is backed by sovereignty; on the other hand those who maintain that law is above and therefore superior to sovereignty and that law can exist without being backed by sovereignty.[②]

Between these two poles, we find, some who insist that law is a limitation upon sovereignty. There are some who think that both may exist without being limited by each other. There are others who consider that in the earlier history of political and legal institutions, law is independent of, and exterior to sovereignty; but that the recent tendency has been to make law more and more the creature of sovereignty; again, there

---

[①] See Allen, *International Relations*, p. 12.
[②] Cf. K. C. Hsiao, *Political Pluralism*, 1927, pp. 9 ff.

are others who regard sovereignty as the chimney and law as the smoke; the chimney, they say, is useful because it is through it that the smoke comes out, but the fact is that if there is no coal or fuel in the stove, there will be no smoke. ① There are still others who argue that sovereignty is not independent or outside of law, but it is to be found in the law; thus the law itself is sovereign and where there is law, there is sovereignty.

The importance of the present subject can not be neglected. Perhaps it will not be too far-fetched to say that it is the central problem in the field of jurisprudence and therefore an important one in the field of political science or even in that of social science. Much ink and paper has been employed in discussing it since the time of Greece and particularly after the appearance of Bodin's *Les Six livres de la republique*, yet the discussion seems to have no end. But our review of what has been said will not be futile, not merely because it may lead us to see the light of the future, but also because it gives us a knowledge of the ideas of the past.

II. Analytical School

"A conception of sovereignty," says Professor Garner, "which has been the subject of wide discussion and which has exerted an important influence upon the legal thought of the last half century is that enunciated by the analytical school of jurists."② The term analytical school has long been connected with the name of John Austin, yet it has to be borne in mind that Austin is not the only writer in the analytical school, nor is he the first one who enunciated the doctrine. In order to make clear the notion of sovereignty in its relation to law as expounded by this school, some of its most conspicuous representatives will be presented here.

1. Analytical Jurists in France

Generally speaking the teaching of the analytical school has not been welcomed by the French, but it is in France that we find the father of the analytical school. ③ For it was Bodin who anticipated the analytical method of Hobbes and Austin, the so-called champions of the school. Sovereignty, according to Bodin, as has been pointed out, is

---

① Cf. Todd, *Theories of Social Progress*, 1918.

② Garner, *Political Science and Government*, Chapter VIII, p. 179. Also *Introduction to Political Science*, 1910, p. 268.

③ Cf. Dunning, *Political Theories, from Luther to Montesquieu*, p. 84. See also Merriam, Barnes and others, *Political Theories, Recent Times*, p. 146.

supreme power over citizens and subjects, unrestrained by law.① It is unrestrained by law, because law is the command of, and created by, the sovereign. It is difficult, then, to conceive that the sovereign should be subject to the command of his own or to the law which is made by him. Thus he says, "One may receive a command from another, but no man can command himself."②

Not only is the sovereign unrestrained by his own law, but also he is bound by no laws of his predecessor.③ Moreover, no consent of superiors, equals, or inferiors is required when the sovereign makes law, for "if the consent of superiors is required, then the prince (sovereign) is clearly a subject; if he must have the consent of the equals, then others share his authority; if the consent of inferiors…the people or the senate, is necessary; then he lacks supreme authority"④. This being so, it is only natural to conclude that the sovereign may abrogate, modify, or replace, a law made by himself and without the consent of his subjects, for such action is fully permissible where justice seems to demand it; but the abrogation, modification, or substitution, however, must not be obscure or ambiguous, but must be set forth in clear detail.⑤

While the sovereign is not bound by the law of his own or of his predecessor, he is nevertheless subject to the laws of God, of nature, of nations and what we call constitutional Law. "No one," says Bodin, "who attempts to abrogate or weaken the laws of God and of nature can escape the judgment of divine sovereignty."⑥ It seems to Bodin that there is no clear distinction between the laws of God and that of nature, nor that both of these are or should be different from the law of nations. Accordingly the sovereign is not bound by the law of nations if it is contrary to the laws of God and of nature. The sovereign, says he, is no "more bound by the law of nations than by his own laws, except in so far as the former are in agreement with the laws of nature and of God". And he adds: "If certain of the laws of nation are unjust, the prince may abrogate them and forbid his subjects to follow them. This we showed in relation to slavery; this institution was established in many states, by pernicious examples, yet in accord with the law of almost every nation; but through salutary decrees of several princes it has

---

① See above, Chapter Ⅰ.
② *De Republica*, p. 134; for part of English translation, see Coker, *Readings in Political Philosophy*, pp. 230 ff.
③ *De Republica*, p. 134.
④ *Ibid.*, p. 240.
⑤ *Ibid.*, p. 136.
⑥ *Ibid.*, p. 135. "If justice is the end of law, and law is the command of the prince, and the prince is the image of the almighty God, then the laws of prince should bear the stamp of divine law." *Ibid.*, p. 167.

been abolished, in conformity to the laws of nature."① Finally, "as to the laws concerning the supreme power, the prince can not abrogate or modify them, since they are attached to the very sovereignty with which he is clothed; such is the Salic law, which is the foundation of our kingdom"②.

As has been said, the first and principal function of sovereignty is to give law;③ and law is nothing else than a command of the sovereign.④ But can it be called law if it is not the command or the expression of the will, be it expressed or implied, of the sovereign? This question, does not seem clear to Bodin. It has been remarked that "the power to make law is not the proper mark of sovereignty, except we understand thereby the sovereign prince's law; for that a magistrate may also give law unto them (subjects) that are within his jurisdiction, so that nothing be decreed by him contrary to the edicts and laws of his sovereign prince"⑤. And Bodin writes: "The approval and promulgation of laws, which is commonly done in an assembly or senate, does not imply that the sovereignty of the realm resides in such assembly or senate, but only a species of authority without which laws issued by the king might be called in question at his death, or before the senate when it acts judicially."⑥

Recent French writers are by no means lacking who hold the notion of sovereignty in its relation to law as it is involved in the definition given by Bodin. Perhaps the greatest of them is Professor Esmein. In his *Droit Constitutionnel*, he declares: "The state is the legal personification of a nation: it is the subject and the basis of public authority."⑦ "This authority, which naturally recognizes neither a superior nor a competing power in the field it rules, is called sovereignty."⑧

"The basis of the public law is to be found in that it gives to the sovereignty outside and above the persons who exercise it at any given moment an ideal and permanent subject or title which personifies the whole nation: this moral person, is the state, which

---

① *De Republica.*, p. 167.
② *Ibid.*, p. 139.
③ See above, Chapter Ⅰ.
④ *De Republica*, p. 167. See also Dunning, *Political Theories*, Vol. Ⅱ, p. 103.
⑤ Crane, *State in Constitutional and International Law*, p. 29.
⑥ *De Republica*, p. 143.
⑦ Esmein, *Elements de Droit Constitutionnel*, 7th ed., 1921, Vol. Ⅰ, p. 1.
⑧ *Ibid.*

is identified with sovereignty, its essential quality."①

Since sovereignty is the supreme power of the state and recognizes no superior, there should be no limitation laid upon it. Thus he says: "It seems that sovereignty should (*soit*) not be limited and that consequently the right (*droit*) of the state should be limitless."② The sovereignty being supreme and unlimited, the law emanating from, and backed by, the sovereign must and should be obeyed and respected.③ To resist the law of the sovereign would mean to resist the sovereign itself. Thus it is an error to proclaim "that the citizen, without revolting by violence, can refuse to recognize the laws of his country which are contrary to his conscience and therefore refuse to submit to them"④. And he continues: "The primary duty of a citizen is to respect the laws of his country, particularly in a free country where one can always hope to win public opinion for securing the abrogation or modification of those laws which are offensive. It had been already said by Hobbes that those who profess the error pointed out put down human society so far as it is their power."⑤

2. Analytical Jurists in Germany

Among the German writers who uphold the doctrine of sovereignty are men like Hegel and Seydel. The views of Hegel in regard to sovereignty and law have already been noted.⑥ According to Seydel, the state is a certain number of men who occupy a definite portion of the earth's surface united under a superior will.⑦ This superior will, Seydel sees, belongs to the *Herrscher*. The will of the *Herrscher* is not in nor inferior to, but over the state. To Seydel, says Professor Duguit, "All such expressions as personality of the state, will of the state, the state as an organism are vacuous words devoid of meaning."⑧ The difference between the state and the *Herrscher* is that one is like property and the other the owner. This is obvious because the *Herrscher* can lose his

---

① Esmein, *Elements de Droit Constitutionnel*, 7th ed., 1921, Vol. I, p. 1. "Le fondement meme du droit public consiste en ce qu'il donne a la souverainete, en dehors et au-dessus des personnes qui l'exercent a tel ou tel moment, un sujet ou titulaire ideal et permanent, qui personnifie la nation entiere: cette personne morale, c'est l'Etat, qui se confond ainsi avec la souverainete, celle-ci e'tant sa qualite essentielle."

② *Ibid.*, p. 33, Vol. I.

③ Law must be backed by a sovereign power. International law having no sovereign behind it, can not be called law proper. "Le droit international public, faute de ce droit de contrainte qui reside dans l'Etat, est encore un droit incompletement forme." *Ibid.*, p. 39.

④ *Ibid.*, Vol. II, p. 534.

⑤ *Ibid.*

⑥ See above, Chapter III.

⑦ Duguit, "The Law and the State", *Harvard Law Review*, Vol. XXXI, page 150.

⑧ *Ibid.*, p. 153.

"Herrschaft"①. "Thus," says Seydel, "the will to 'Herrschen' is always and for all time a will over the state and not a will of the state; and it is because we have not recognized this relation that we have been led to the chimera of the personality of the state."②

Since the will of the *Herrscher* is superior, it is by nature a commanding will. In short it is the will of the sovereign. How will this be expressed? It is expressed in the form of law. "Law," says Seydel, "is nothing more than the collections by which the commanding will (the will of the *Herrscher*) governs that human grouping, the state. The source of law is therefore the will of the *Herrscher*."③ From what has been just said, it is concluded that: "It is thus an uncontrovertible truth that there is no law without the *Herrscher*; above the *Herrscher*, or on equal footing with the *Herrscher*. A law can exist only through a *Herrscher*."④

The logical conclusion of Seydel's notion of sovereignty and law within a state leads him to agree with Hegel in denying the validity of international law as law. Thus he says: "Since the legal command is a superior will as the source of the law, there can be no legal command between states. Did such a superior will exist, there would be a world state and the ideas of the Middle Ages would be realized in the lay *imperium mundi* or the spiritual sovereignty over states."⑤

So there can be no law between states. There is no such a thing as international law if the term is used in its strict sense. What exists in international dealings is might and might alone.⑥ "*Herrschers*," says Seydel, "can find it quite opportune for their interests to formulate, to establish certain rules as between themselves; but each one is bound by these rules only in so far as he so wills. Such a rule is evidently not a law. Just as there is no law between States, there is likewise no jurisdiction between them. Conflicts of interests find their last solution in war. Out of the complexity of the foreign relations of the State arises the most important function of the *Herrscher*: to defend the interests of the collectivity not only within but also against the other *Herrschers*. And since he may be compelled to use physical power as a last resort in preserving such collective interests, such power must be at his disposal at all times. This physical power resides in the army, which is, therefore, the instrument for the realization by material

---

① Seydel, *Grundzuge der allegemein Statslehre*, 1873, p. 5.
② *Ibid.*, pp. 7-8. (English translation, see Duguit, *ibid.*, p. 154).
③ *Ibid.*, p. 13. (Duguit, *ibid.*, p. 156).
④ *Ibid.*, p. 14. (Duguit, *ibid.*, p. 157).
⑤ Seydel, *Grundzuge der allegemein Statslehre*, pp. 31-32.
⑥ Seydel, *Grundzuge der allegemein Statslehre*, p. 32.

constraint (*Zwang*) of the will of the *Herrscher* at home and abroad."①

3. Analytical Jurists in England

The terms analytical jurists have been sometimes countered as identical with English jurists.② The error in so using can not be questioned, but it has to be admitted that the headquarters of the analytical school have been in England. As early as 1651, seventy-five years after the appearance of Bodin's famous treatise, Hobbes published *The Leviathan* in which the notion of sovereignty in its relation to law as enunciated by Bodin reached its highest elevation. Professor Dewey tells us that what has been put under the name of Austin is really not that of Austin but that of Hobbes and Lewis.③ There is no doubt that Austin was influenced by Hobbes, and in turn Hobbes was influenced by Bodin. In speaking of the latter case, says Professor Dunning: "It is no discredit to Hobbes to conjecture that the work of Bodin played some part in determining the type of his philosophy."④

We have already pointed out that, in the system of Bodin, sovereignty is limited by the law of God, the law of nature, and to a certain extent, the law of nations and what is called constitutional law. We have also noted that to Hobbes, there are no such limitations whatsoever. It is true that he speaks of the law of God as the highest of all, but that can not be realized unless there is a mediator between God on one hand and the individuals on the other. Thus he says: "And whereas some men have pretended for their disobedience to their Sovereign, a new Covenant, made, not with men, but with God; this also is unjust; for there is no covenant with God, but by mediation of some body that representeth Gods Person; which none doth but God's Lieutenant, who hath the sovereginty under God."⑤ God's Lieutenant, in the mind of Hobbes, is none other than the sovereign or the king himself.

Hobbes expressly declares that the law of nature is not law, but moral rule, because it is not the command of the sovereign. Thus says, "These dictates of reason, men use to call by the name of lawes; but improperly: for they are but conclusions, or theoremes concerning what conduceth to the conservation and defence of themselves;

---

① Seydel, *Grundzuge der allegemein Statslehre*, p. 32. (Duguit *ibid.*, p. 158.)
② See Pollock, *A First Book of Jurisprudence*.
③ Dewey, "Austin's Theory of Sovereignty", *Political Science Quarterly*, Vol. IX, p. 31.
④ Dunning, *Political Theories*, Vol. II, p. 84.
⑤ Hobbes, *Leviathan*, edited by E. Rhys, p. 91. But in another place, he declares: "But yet if we consider the same theorems, as delivered in the word of God, that by right commandeth all things; then are they properly called lawes." *Ibid.*, p. 83.

whereas law, properly is the word of him, that by right hath command over others."①

But living in an age in which the notion of the law of nature prevailed, and being an apologist of the king or kings who seek to have an absolute authority over the subjects within their dominion, he sees that there is a close relation between the law of nature and civil law, but attempts to distinguish one from the other: "The law of nature and the civil law contain each other, and are of equal extent."② Again he says: "Civil and natural law are not different kinds, but different parts of law; whereof one part being written, is called civil, the other unwritten, natural."③ Moreover, "the law of nature is a part of the civil law in the commonwealth of the world. Reciprocally, the civil law is a part of the dictates of the law of nature"④. Although the laws of nature are not written laws, they are equally obligating on all mankind if they be generally observed in all the provinces of a dominion, and no iniquity appear in the use thereof.⑤

Law, generally speaking, "is not counsel, but command; not a command of any man to any man, but only of him whose command is addressed to one formerly obliged to obey him."⑥ Law then is the command given by a legislator who is only the sovereign of a commonwealth. But the command of the sovereign may take many forms. It may be by voice, writing or some other sufficient argument of the same.⑦ It is clear that all laws, written or unwritten, have their authority and force from the will of the commonwealth, and by that he means the will of the sovereign, be he one man, in a monarchy, or an assembly of men, as in a democracy or aristocracy.⑧ This being so, it follows that none can make law save the sovereign of the commonwealth.⑨

Civil law, according to Hobbes, may be defined in this manner: "Civil law is to every subject those rules which the commonwealth hath commanded him, by word, writing, or other sufficient sign of the will, to make use of, for the distinction of right, and wrong; that is to say, of what is contrary, and what is not contrary to the rule."⑩

---

① Hobbes, *Leviathan*, edited by E. Rhys, p. 83.
② *Ibid.*, p. 141. But he continues: "For the lawes of Nature, which consist in equtity, justice, gratitude, and other moral virtues on these depending, in the condition of meer nature are not properly lawes, but qualities that dispose men to peace, and obedience."
③ *Ibid.*, p. 142.
④ Hobbes, *Leviathan*, edited by E. Rhys, p. 141.
⑤ *Ibid.*
⑥ *Ibid.*, p. 140.
⑦ *Ibid.*, p. 143.
⑧ *Ibid.*, pp. 140-141.
⑨ *Ibid.*, p. 140.
⑩ *Ibid.*, p. 140.

From this definition, the following principles may be derived: In the first place, it implies that in order to be law, it must be the will given by a superior to an inferior and the latter is obliged to obey. Secondly, that the sovereign is the sole legislator, i. e., he is the sole fountain of law. From the first and the second principles, comes a third one, namely that the sovereign is not subject to law, for he is above the law. The third principle, in turn, underlies a fourth one which is that there will be no law if there is no sovereign, for law is the creature of the sovereign. If law is merely the creature of the sovereign, it follows that it can not come before the existence of a sovereign. So comes a fifth principle, i. e., it is the will, and not the length of time of its being observed, that makes the authority of law. Sixthly, be it written or unwritten, that which has its authority and force from the will of the commonwealth is law. Seventhly, be it a man or a court of men, the command given by whomsoever is endowed with supreme power in the commonwealth concerning the future actions of his subjects is law. ①

These are the principles involved in his definition of civil law. It is to be borne in mind, however, that they are all correlated to each other and the keynote of them is that law is the expression of a sovereign will in the form of command.

The next English writer to be noted is Bentham. In his *A Fragment on Government*, Bentham vigorously attacks the "conservative temper and logical fallacies" of Blackstone's *Commentaries*. He criticizes the view of the latter that a sovereign is limited by the laws of God and of nature. To Bentham, the statement made by Blackstone that "if any human law should allow or enjoin us to commit it, we are bound to transgress that human law, or else we must offend both the natural and the divine," is dangerous so far as the Divine Law is concerned; and "as to the law of nature if it be nothing but a phrase; …if, in a word, there be scarce any law whatever but what those who have not liked it have found, on some account or another, to be repugnant to some text of scripture; I see no remedy but that the natural tendency of such doctrine is to impel a man, by the force of conscience, to rise up in arms against any law whatever that he happens not to like"②. And he adds: "What sort of government it is that can consist with such a disposition, I must leave to our Author to inform us."

Sovereignty, to Bentham, can not be limited then by the laws of God or of nature. But this does not mean, as has been pointed out, that there is no limitation whatsoever; because it is bound by express convention. ③ Following Bodin very closely, he declares

---

① Hobbes, *Leviathan*, edited by E. Rhys, Chapter XXVI.
② *A Fragment on Government*, see *Works*, collected by J. Bowring, Vol. I, p. 287.
③ *Ibid.*, p. 288.

that the characteristic function of sovereignty is to make laws. Law is that which is enjoined by the authority or sovereign which the members of the society habitually obey. It is defined as the expression of the sovereign will of a political society in the form of a command. [1]

In an often quoted article, Professor Dewey says that "A careful study of Austin's jurisprudence has convinced me that the theory which is ordinarily put forward under his name is not his at all." [2] He further points out that Maine misunderstands Austin on the historical side, Green mistakes it on the philosophical side, and Lewis, the so-called direct successor of Austin completely inverts Austin's conception. [3] In short, to Professor Dewey, Austin is a moralist rather than a legalist. Whether Professor Dewey is right or wrong in asserting this is open to question. But the generally accepted idea is that the notion that in order to be called law proper it must have a sovereign authority behind it is to find its high watermark and full explanation in the writings of Austin.

In the lectures on the Province of Jurisprudence determined, Austin begins by saying "that the matter of jurisprudence is positive law: Law, simply and strictly so called; or law set by political superiors to political inferiors"[4]. In another place, we find that positive law is defined in this manner: "Every positive law, or every law simply and strictly so called, is set by a sovereign or person, or a sovereign body of persons, to a member of the independent political society wherein that person or body is sovereign or supreme."[5] To change the expression, he continues, "It is set by a monarch, or sovereign number, to a person or persons in a state of subjection to its author."[6]

It is obvious, then, in order to be called law proper, it must be the command or emanation of a sovereign. But this is certainly not the final appeal of his system, for he adds immediately to the statements just quoted above that "even though it springs directly from another fountain or source, it 'is' a positive law, or a law strictly so called, by the institution of that present sovereign in the character of a political superior"[7]. Extremely stated as is the notion of positive law by Austin in the beginning, he comes back to the position of Hobbes. In the language of Hobbes, he quotes, "The legislator is he, not by whose authority the law was first made, but by whose authority it continues to

---

[1] *A Fragment on Government, Works*, collected by J. Bowring, Vol. I, p. 285, note (a).
[2] Dewey, "Austin's Theory of Sovereignty", *Political Sci. Quarterly*, Vol. IX, p. 31.
[3] *Ibid.*, p. 33,
[4] Austin, *Jurisprudence*, fifth edition by Campbell, 1911, p. 86, Vol. 1.
[5] Austin, *Jurisprudence*, fifth edition by Campbell, 1911, p. 220.
[6] *Ibid.*
[7] *Ibid.*

be a law."①

And here is a more accurate definition of positive law: "A positive law may be defined generally in the following: or the essential difference of positive law (or the difference which severs it from a law not a positive law) may be stated generally in the following manner...Every positive law (or every law simply and strictly so called), is set, directly or circuitously, by a sovereign individual or body, to a member or members of the independent political society wherein its author is supreme. In other words, it is set directly or circuitously, by a monarch or sovereign number, to a person or persons in a state of subjection to its author."② This definition, he adds, of positive law is assumed expressly or tacitly throughout the foregoing lectures, but it only approaches a perfectly complete and perfectly exact definition. ③

The definition of law so stated naturally excludes the laws of nature and of nations. "A man living in a state of nature," says he, "may impose an imperative law: though, since the man 'is' in a state of nature, he can not impose the law in the character of sovereign, and can not impose the law in pursuance of a legal right. And the law being 'imperative' (and therefore proceeding from a 'determinate' source) is a law properly so called: though, for want of a sovereign author proximate or remote, it is not a positive law but a rule of positive morality"④.

So an imperative law set by a sovereign to a sovereign, or by one supreme government to another is not a positive law or law strictly so called, "since no supreme goverment is in a state of subjection to another, an imperative law set by a sovereign to a sovereign is not set by its author in the character of political superior. Nor is it set by the author in pursuance of a legal right: for every legal right is conferred by a supreme government, and is conferred on a person or persons in a state of subjection to the granter. Consequently, an imperative law set by a sovereign to a sovereign is not a positive law or a law strictly so called. But being 'imperative' (and therefore proceeding from a 'determinate' source,) it amounts to a law in the proper signification of the term, although it is purely or simply a rule of positive morality"⑤.

Even constitutional law, according to Austin, can not be called law in its strict sense. "Against a monarch properly so called, or against a sovereign number in its

---

① Austin, *Jurisprudence*, fifth edition by Campbell, 1911, Vol. I, p. 220.
② Austin, *Jurisprudence*, fifth edition by Campbell, 1911, Vol. I, p. 330.
③ *Ibid.*
④ *Ibid.*, Vol. I, pp. 181-182.
⑤ *Ibid.*, p. 182.

collegiate and sovereign capacity, constitutional law and the law of nations are nearly in the same predicament."①

Austin certainly takes pains to decide the real character of constitutional law. He regards the latter as the compound of positive morality and positive law which determines the structure, organization or constitution of a given government. To quote his own words, constitutional law is defined as "the compound of positive morality and positive law, which determines the character of the person, or the respective characters of the persons, in whom, for the time being, the sovereignty shall reside: and, supposing the government in question an aristocracy or government of a number, which determines moreover the mode wherein the sovereign powers shall be shared by the constituent members of the sovereign number or body"②.

It seems that the expression "the compound of positive morality and positive law", in Auatin's mind, is that constitutional law is partly positive morality and partly positive law. It is different from the laws of nature and of nations which are purely positive morality and it is different from the positive law in that the latter is a thing which is given and backed by a sovereign. Thus consitutional law involves both the characteristics of the laws of nature and of nations on the one hand and of the positive law on the other.

It seems that it can be easily seen that it is ambiguous if not impossible to regard constitutional law as being partly positive and partly not law in its strict sense, and one would wonder how a man like Austin has committed himself to such ambiguity. But is there any explanation for that? And if so, how? In order to do that, first of all, Austin reminds us of the meaning of the word sovereignty that he employs. "By 'sovereign', " says he, "I always mean a monarch properly so called, or a sovereign number in its collegiate and sovereign capacity."③ "Considered collectively," he continues, "or considered in its corporate character, a sovereign number is sovereign and independent;" and therefore, "the power of a sovereign is incapable of limitation"④. It is in this sense that a sovereign is not legally bound or limited by constitutional law, and it is in this sense that "against a sovereign body in its collegiate and sovereign capacity, constitutional law is positive morality merely, or is enforced merely by moral sanction."⑤

---

① Austin, *Jurisprudence*, fifth edition by Campbell, 1911, Vol. I, p. 270.
② *Ibid.*, p. 267.
③ *Ibid.*, p. 269.
④ *Ibid.*, p. 269.
⑤ *Ibid.*, p. 267.

On the other hand, "considered severally, the individuals and smaller aggregates composing that sovereign number are subject to the supreme body of which they are component parts"①. "Consequently though the body is independent of legal or political duty, any of the individuals or aggregates whereof the body is composed may be legally bound by laws of which the body is the author."② The logic here is very simple. The whole is greater than the parts, so the parts are inferior to the whole. There are things that the component parts of the sovereign can not do in the capacity of not being united together, but it does not follow that [that] which the parts severally can not do the whole can not do. To violate the constitution in the capacity of the whole, i. e., a sovereign in its collegiate capacity, is not an illegal act.③ On the contrary, a breach of it by the component part would not be legal. It is in the latter sense that a constitution is regarded as a positive law.④

In conclusion, Austin's conception of sovereignty in its relation to law may be stated as follows: law, in order to be law in its positive sense, must be set directly or circuitously, by a sovereign. That which is not backed by that sovereign can not be called law in its proper sense. The word "sovereign" involves two senses: in one it means a collegiate capacity, in the other it is considered severally. In the former sense, it is legally incapable of limitation, because a sovereign is above the law if not outside of it, and consequently can not be restrained by the law of its own. On the other hand, the component parts may be subject to legal limitation and it is in this sense that the constitution is considered to be positive law. But by a sovereign, he always means sovereign in its collegiate capacity, so the constitution, as the reasoning runs, is always and merely a positive morality.

Perhaps Professor Dewey is right when he says that Austin is reasoning simply in a circle.⑤ And it may be added that Austin never reaches the point which Hobbes attains and he does not go beyond the line where Bodin stops. If Austin differs from Bodin, it must be in something else, and not in their conceptions of sovereignty and its "relation" to law.

How far the Austinian theory has been accepted by subsequent writers is hard to estimate, but perhaps it is safe to say that he has more successors in the English

---

① Austin, *Jurisprudence*, fifth edition by Campbell, 1911, Vol. I, p. 269.
② *Ibid.*
③ *Ibid.*, p. 278.
④ *Ibid.*, p. 270.
⑤ Dewey, *ibid.*

speaking world than in the other countries. ① Among his successors, George Cornewall Lewis deserves our special attention. Lewis has been said to be his true interpreter and most immediate successor. He was influenced more by Austin on account of their intimate relationship. But Lewis is not merely an Austinian, for in some respects, he seems to be more like Hobbes. ②

According to Lewis, "as long as a government exists, the power of the person or persons in whom the sovereignty resides, over the whole community, is absolute and unlimited"③. "The sovereign," he continues, "has the complete disposal of the life, rights and duties, of every member of the community. It has also power to modify or change the existing form of government. There is no law which it has not power to alter, repeal, or enact."④

Like his master, he considers that law properly signifies a general command of the sovereign, whether conveyed by the way of "direct" legislation, as in the case of statutes, or of "permissive" legislation, as in the legal rules established by courts of justice. ⑤ Since law in its strict sense is the creature of sovereign, the latter can not be bound by the former.

But law, according to him, must not be confounded with contract or compact. Following Blackstone, he conceives a compact as a promise proceeding from us and law is a command directed to us. The language of a compact is: "I will, or will not, do this;" that of law is: "Thou shalt, or shalt not, do it." Somewhat like Bodin, he holds that sovereignty may be constrained by a compact made with foreign powers, as then it is a party to a contract. ⑥

Like Austin, he places constitutional law outside of the field of law in its proper sense. A constitution, to him, signifies the arrangement and distribution of the sovereign power in the community, or the form of government. ⑦ Having started from the same point as his master, he goes on to declare that a "constitution, therefore, properly, expresses something which either has, or has had, a real existence"⑧. In short, constitution is little more than a vague term of praise, though it is calculated to deceive

---

① See also J. M. Lightwood, *Nature of Positive Law*, 1883, p. 295.
② See Lewis, *On the Use and Abuse of Some Political Terms*, edited by Thomas Raleigh, 1898, p. 40.
③ *Ibid.*, p. 41.
④ *Ibid.*, p. 41.
⑤ *Ibid.*, p. 36.
⑥ *Ibid.*, p. 42.
⑦ *Ibid.*, p. 20.
⑧ *Ibid.*

ignorant persons into a belief that a measure or law recommended to them is only a recurrence to ancient institutions and that the change is restoration, and not innovation.①

Professor Holland is another outstanding Austinian of recent times. "A law," says he, "in the proper sense of the term, is therefore a rule of human action, taking cognisance only of external acts; enforced by a determinate authority, which authority is human, and among human authority, is that which paramount in a political society."② To state it more briefly, law is defined as "a general rule of external human action enforced by a sovereign political authority"③. It has been remarked that by so defining it "he thus avoids the use of the Austinian command, but certainly indicates that it may be implied and expressed"④.

Having been influenced, or rather having the opportunity of observing the arguments presented by the historical jurists such as Sir Henry Maine, Professor Holland endeavors to avoid many of the dogmatic ideas or difficulties involved in the writings of his predecessors. Speaking for his own school, he points out that Maine has not done justice to the essential truth as to sovereignty and law.⑤ Giving credit to Maine, he says "Sir Henry Maine did good service by showing that it is a mistake to suppose that the obligation of law rests everywhere and at all times, as immediately and obviously upon a sovereign political authority as it does in England at the present day.⑥ And his own position is more clearly expressed in this statement: "It is convenient to recognize as law only such rules as can reckon on the support of a sovereign political authority, although there are states of society in which it is difficult to ascertain as a fact that rules answer to this description."⑦

Like Austin, he regards international law as being in reality no more than the moral code of nations.⑧ Besides what he thinks to be law proper as indicated in his definition of law, "all other rules for the guidance of human action are called laws merely by

---

① See Lewis, *On the Use and Abuse of Some Political Terms*, edited by Thomas Raleigh, 1898, p. 20.
② Holland, *Elements of Jurisprudence*, 12th ed., p. 41. "The sole source of laws, in the sense of that which impresses upon them their legal character, is their recognition by the state, which may be given either expressly through the legislature or the courts, or tacitly by allowance followed in the law resort by enforcement." 9th ed., p. 54. Cf. 12th ed., p. 55 ff.
③ *Ibid.*, 12th ed., p. 42.
④ Statement by Professor Patterson. See Merriam and Barnes, *Political Theories, Recent Times*, p. 147.
⑤ Holland, *Elements of Jurisprudence*, 12th ed., p. 53.
⑥ *Ibid.*
⑦ *Ibid.*, p. 54.
⑧ *Ibid.*, p. 134.

analogy; and any propositions which are not rules for human action are called law by metaphor only"①.

4. Analytical Jurists in the United States

Turning to the American writers, we find that Calhoun in his *Disquisition on Government* has "adopted, in general, the analytical-legal method, and viewed the state as an institution operating wholly through law and possessing an indivisible, legally omnipotent sovereignty"②. But the most distinguished of all is Professor Willoughby during the past thirty years. Professor Willoughby's views may be found chiefly in *The Nature of the State* (1896), *The American Constitutional System* (1904) and *The Fundamental Concepts of Public Law* (1924).

After repudiating Blackstone's conception of the laws of nature and of God as superior to human authority, Professor Willoughby writes: "If then, the only rules that possess legal validity are such as have received the sanction of the state, it follows as a logical deduction, that, since no one can be bound by one's own will, the sovereign political power must necessarily be incapable of legal limitation."③ Sovereignty, according to Professor Willoughby, belongs to the state as a person, and represents the supremacy of its will. ④ It includes and necessitates the possession of certain powers, such as taxation, contracting treaties, etc. , but it is something more than a collection of powers. ⑤ It is by nature a unity and indivisible. ⑥ "The logical impossibility of conceiving of a divided sovereignty is apparent from the impossibility of predicating in the same body two powers each supreme. "⑦ Powers certainly may be divided, but not will.

As it can not be divided, it can not be limited. Here again it is by its nature absolute, and here Calhoun's style is employed: "To place a legal limit upon it is, therefore, to destroy it. "⑧ So the Austinian expression that "supreme power limited by positive law is a flat contradiction of terms" is quoted. ⑨ It follows then that if a state is

---

① Holland, *Elements of Jurisprudence*, 12th ed., p. 42.
② Gettell, *History of Political Thought*, 1924, p. 396.
③ Willoughby, *Nature of the State*, pp. 181-182.
④ *Ibid.*, p. 105.
⑤ *The Fundamental Concepts of Public Law*, p. 72. *Nature of the State*, p. 194.
⑥ *Fundamental Concepts*, p. 72. *The Nature of the State*, p. 195.
⑦ *The Nature of the State*, p. 195.
⑧ *The Fundamental Concepts of Public Law*, p. 76.
⑨ *Ibid*. Sovereignty can not be limited by law, "since, 'ex hypothesi', its own sovereignty is the source of all law for itself, it can not by a law (except formally) limit itself, for, by an exercise of the same will that creates the limitation, the limitation may be removed". *Fundamental Concepts*, p. 77.

bound by legal restraint, that state can not be said to possess sovereignty. ①

Moreover, sovereignty is inalienable. A state, says he, is no more able to transfer its sovereignty, that is, its very life and personality.② But alienation must be differentiated from delegation. "Theoretically, indeed, a sovereign state may go to any extent in the delegation of the exercise of its powers to the governmental agencies of other states, those governmental agencies thus becoming 'quoad hoc' parts of the governmental machinery of the state whose sovereignty is exercised."③

So much for the general consideration of his conception of sovereignty, let us turn now to his idea of sovereignty in its relation to law. "The ascription of sovereignty to the state," says he, "and the definition of sovereignty as legal omnicompetence have made it necessary to view the state as the sole source of law in a positive or strictly juristic sense."④ It is clear that the statement quoted above shows that Professor Willoughby concurs with Austin in that, in order to be law in its strict sense, there must be a sovereign authority behind it.⑤ It is incorrect to say, according to him, that law of God is superior to human authority, as has been pointed out.

As to the character of international law, he writes: "When we forsake the field of constitutional or municipal law and enter that of international relations we no longer have to deal with legal superiors and legal inferiors. Here we find no supreme will but, legally speaking, a collection of equal wills, and the conflict or at least the interplay, of independent powers."⑥ From the proposition advanced in the statement just quoted, it follows that "clearly it can not be so regarded for it lacks the essential quality of embodying commands issued by political superior to political inferiors"⑦. But he continues: "This, however, does not mean, …that the title 'law' should not be given to these international rules if it be borne in mind that the term, when so employed, has a meaning different from that which it has when used by the analytical jurist when speaking of municipal laws."⑧

So far Professor Willoughby is no more than an Austinian. Considering that the word sovereignty used in international jurisprudence has a different meaning from that

---

① *The Fundamental Concepts of Public Law*, pp. 76–77.
② *The Nature of the State*, p. 221.
③ *The Fundamental Concepts of Public Law*, p. 74.
④ *The Fundamental Concepts of Public Law*, p. 129.
⑤ He frankly admits that he follows Austin to a certain extent, see *The Nature of the State*, p. 183.
⑥ *Fundamental Concepts of Public Law*, p. 282.
⑦ *Ibid.*, p. 298.
⑧ *Ibid.*, p. 298. *The Nature of the State*, pp. 198–204.

used in the municipal field, he suggests that "it would have been far better if some such term as Independence has been employed"①. But more radically different from Austin is his conception of constitutional law in its relation to sovereignty. We have already noted that the Austinian system denies to constitutional law the character of law in its proper sense. On the contrary, Professor Willoughby maintains that constitutional law is law, —law in its strict sense. The error of Austin in considering constitutional law as positive morality, according to him, is due to his failure to recognize the difference between the state and government.② Constitutional laws purport to control the government, but not the state, for it is the creature of the latter.③ Here Professor Willoughby follows Professor Burgess in asserting that back of the government lies the constitution; and back of the constitution, the original sovereign which ordains the constitution both of government and liberty.④ It is obvious that by pointing out the difference between government and the state, Professor Willoughby thus enlarges the scope of positive law, and narrows the limitations, be it moral or whatever else one may call it, on sovereignty. In this respect, Professor Willoughby brings the notion of sovereignty farther away from that of Austin and closer to that of Hobbes.

It may be added that the distinction between legal and political sovereignty made by Professor A. V. Dicey and Professor D. G. Ritchie does not seem to have any room in Professor Willoughby's system. Thus he says: "The characteristic that is essential to the State, and serves to distinguish it 'in toto genere' from all other human associations, is its possession of political sovereignty. By political sovereignty is meant, on the one hand, complete freedom from the legal control of any other power whatsoever, and, on the other hand, absolute and exclusive control over the legal rights and obligations of its citizens, individually considered or grouped into larger or smaller associations. The State is thus supreme not only as giving the ultimate validity to all laws, but as itself determining the scope of its own legal powers and the manner of their exercise."⑤

In another place, however, we find that, in speaking of the distinction made by Professor Ritchie, he says: "It is undoubtedly correct thus to make this distinction, but to the writer, it seems unfortunate that the same term 'soverignty' should be applied to

---

① *The Fundamental Concepts*, pp. 283, 315.
② *Ibid.*, p. 89, also *The Nature of the State*, p. 204.
③ *Ibid.*, pp. 84, 89. *The Nature of the State*, p. 204.
④ Burgess, *Political Science and Constitutional Law*, Vol. I, p. 57. Cf. his criticism of Burgess' distinction between the government and the state. *The Fundamental Concepts*, pp. 55 ff.
⑤ *American Constitutional System*, 1904, p. 4.

the two forces so radically different, even though distinguishing adjectives be prefixed."① And he adds: "In conclusion, then, of this point, it may said that, though legally absolute, sovereignty is to be considered in reference to the institutions, the character of the people governed, and other objective conditions."② The last sentence indicates that Professor Willoughby comes more closely to Austin.

In connection with what has been presented, it is desirable to turn a moment's attention to the position of Professor Garner. Professor Garner's position may be found in his own words: "We agree with Zorn and Burgess that sovereignty is not only an essential element, but the first and the highest conceivable mark of the state; and with Willoughby that it is one characteristic which serves to distinguish the state 'in toto genere' from all other human associations."③

Like Professor Willoughby, he does not accept the Austinian theory without any qualification. He sees that "Austin's chief error consisted in unduly emphasizing the purely legal aspects of sovereignty, and in ignoring the forces and influences which lie back of the formal law—a very natural mistake for a lawyer to make"④. He adds: "It may also be said that his theory is probably inapplicable to all states of society, such, for example, as those which Maine described in his work on the Early History of Institutions."⑤

But the criticism that he makes of the Austinian theory does not seem to be as much as the credit that he gives to this well-known jurist. To him, "as a conception of the strict legal nature of sovereignty, Austin's theory is, on the whole, clear and logical, and much of the criticism directed against it has been founded on misapprehension and misconception"⑥.

Seeing no mistake in Austin's strict legal nature of sovereignty, Professor Garner has been led to deny, what Willoughby and Lewis have denied, that legally sovereignty can be limited. There are limitations on the sovereignty, he admits, but "an examination of these limitations however, will show that 'legally' they are not restrictions on sovereignty at all"⑦. "The law of nature, the principles of morality, the laws of God,

---

① *Fundamental Concepts of Public Law*, p. 112.
② *Ibid.*, p. 113.
③ Garner, *Introduction to Political Science*, 1910, pp. 267–268.
④ *Political Science and Government*, 1928, Chapter 8, p. 181. Also *Introduction to Political Science*, p. 271.
⑤ *Ibid.*
⑥ *Ibid.*
⑦ *Political Science and Government*, Chapter 9, p. 184. "The inevitable conclusion, therefore, to which we are led, is that all attempts to place legal restrictions upon sovereignty are futile and useless." p. 185.

the dictates of humanity and reason, the fear of public opinion, and other alleged restrictions on sovereignty," he declares, "have no legal effect, except in so far as the state chooses to recognize them and give them force and validity."①

The doctrine of unlimited sovereignty which is sometimes attacked as leading to the legal despotism of the state is not accepted by Professor Garner, "It is difficult," he says, "to see how the doctrine of unlimited sovereignty is inconsistent with the idea of the widest liberty."② When the king has been identified with the state or sovereignty, few have advocated the theory of unlimited sovereignty. Unlimited sovereignty, in fact, as he conceives, develops with the tide of constitutionalism. While constitutionalism means a guarantee of right and liberty of the individuals and a limitation on the part of the government, "it became an easy matter to reconcile the doctrine of an unlimited legal sovereignty"③.

But Professor Garner does not stop here; for he does not think that the sovereignty of the state is unlimited in regard to international dealings. In this respect, he is no longer to be considered as an advocate of the Austinian theory, but standing on the same line with those who attack the traditional theory of absolute and unlimited sovereignty. "If we examine the facts relating to the intercourse of states today," he writes, "no other conclusion is possible than that the practice no longer corresponds to the traditional legal theory, and if usage and practice are sources of international law, it follows as a consequence that the absolute sovereignty of the state in its international relations is not only a legal fiction but a baneful and dangerous dogma which ought to be abandoned, and that the notion should be expunged from the literature of international law."④ And he continues, "Much indeed may be said in support of the thesis of Kohler, Pillet, Aplheus H. Snow and various others which today not only is international law superior in fact to the municipal law of every state, but its supremacy has even acquired a legal basis, from which it results that the limitations which it sets to the liberty of action of states are legal limitations and not merely self-imposed restrictions."⑤

Here Professor Garner differs radically from Professor Willoughby and therefore also from Austin. To Austin, as has been pointed out, international law is merely positive morality. To Professor Willoughby the term law may be applied to international rules.

① *Political Science and Government*, Chapter 9, p. 184.
② *Ibid.*, p. 187.
③ *Ibid.*
④ *Ibid.*, p. 193. See also *Political Science Review*, 1925, pp. 1 ff.
⑤ *Ibid.*

"If it be borne in mind that the term when so employed, has a meaning different from that which it has when used by analytical jurists when speaking of municipal laws."① To Professor Garner, on the contrary, international law is law in the sense of municipal law. Both Austin and Professor Willoughby consider that the limitations laid by international law upon sovereignty are not legal in the sense in which that term is used in positive or analytical jurisprudence.② It seems to Professor Garner that it is a legal limitation. The difference between these three writers is obvious. Austin is a municipal lawyer and Professor Willoughby is a constitutional lawyer. Professor Garner, on the other hand, is an international lawyer.

But it seems that there is a contradiction in maintaining that legally sovereignty can not be limited on the one hand, and that the limitation laid upon sovereignty by international law is a legal one on the other. In order to avoid this dilemma, Professor Garner is led to deny that the conception of sovereignty can be applied in international law, and therefore in international relations.③ In this point, Professor Garner again agrees with Professor Willoughby. But it is to be noted that the fundamental principle of Austin and of Professor Willoughby that in order to be called law, it must be backed by a sovereign and that law is the command given by a political superior to a political inferior, is turned down by Professor Garner. "The old controversy," says Professor Garner, "to which Austin's conception gave rise as to whether international law is law in the strict sense of the term, since it lacks certain of the ear-marks which municipal law possesses, or whether it is nothing more than international 'morality' or 'comity'—a controversy which has never been much more than a question of definition and terminology—has ceased to have any practical interest. All jurists now admit that the Austinian conception was too narrow and arbitrary, since it unduly emphasized the element of physical sanction, and ignored the large body of custom which the courts regard as law but which are never formally enacted by a legislative body. To deny the character of law to rules which all foreign offices and governments treat as law and to which they appeal in their controversies with one another, which have developed through judicial precedent or which have been formulated by international congresses, which have been elucidated and expounded by trained jurists, which are applied by national and international tribunals and which states in fact regard as binding upon them, is to

---

① Willoughby, *Fundamental Concepts*, p. 298.

② See Garner, "Limitations on National sovereignty in International Relations" in *Political Science Review*, 1925, p. 2.

③ Cf. Lansing, *Notes on Sovereignty*.

adopt a conception of the nature of international law which is in contradiction with the facts of international practice."①

The importance of the position of Professor Garner is obvious. His views serve as a departure from the theory of Austin and Willoughby and their adherents to that of those who criticise or discredit the theory of the former.

The Austinian Theory, formally or rather partly accepted by Professor Garner, has been, in fact, turned in another direction. In the following pages, we shall endeavor to show how far this movement has been advanced. There are many ways to go and one way is different from another, and some of them are as a matter of fact radically different from others, yet they all agree in one point: that law, in order to be law, is not necessarily the command given by a political superior to a political inferior.

III. Natural Law School

Writing in the evening of the nineteenth century, Lord Bryce, after making an excellent review of the history of the notion of the law of nature, says these words: "Except from the lips of the continental theorists—we now seldom hear the term law of nature."② But he adds immediately that "nevertheless the notion sometimes appears and properly appears, in unexpected places"③. And then he asks: "Who can say that an idea so ancient, in itself simple, yet capable of taking many aspects, an idea which has had so varied a history and so wide a range of influence, may not have career reserved for it in the long future which still lies before the human race?"④

Lord Byrce's keenness and foresight can not be questioned, but perhaps he would not have thought that his speculation would have come so fast; for, we have already seen, only ten years after he wrote that, a remarkable work entitled *La renaissance de droit naturel*, was published (1910).⑤ It must be admitted that the so called revival of natural law, is different from the old conception of natural law. But the difference is in the sense that "a new conception is taking its place besides the old, without supplanting

---

① Garner, *Recent Development in International Law*, 1925, pp. 3-4. Among American writers, the writings of Professor Coker in this connection, may be mentioned "Pluralistic Theories and the Attack upon State Sovereignty", in Merriam and Barnes, *Political Theories*, pp. 80-119. "The Technique of the Pluralistic State", *American Political Science Review*, Vol. XV (1921), pp. 186-213.

② Bryce, "Laws of Nature" in *Studies in History and Jurisprudence*, Vol. II, p. 604.

③ *Ibid.*, p. 605.

④ *Ibid.*, p. 606.

⑤ By Joseph Charmont.

it"①.

According to Dean Pound, the revival of natural law takes many forms. The first is an adaptation and broadening of Neo-Kantian juridical idealism; the second is a neo-scholastic philosophy of law and the third is a positivist-sociological philosophy of law philosophically akin to the mechanical sociology. ② Incidentally, we shall discuss some of these new forms in other connections; for our present purpose, we shall confine ourselves to the old conception of the law of nature in its relation to sovereignty.

The idea of natural law reached its high watermark in the writings of Cicero, although it was enunciated by the Greek writers. According to Cicero, "this law did not begin to exist when it was written, but when it was born, and it was born at the same time with the divine intellect. Wherefore, the true law, the primary law, the law which can fully command and forbid is the ever true mind of the supreme being, Jupiter"③.

"Speaking broadly," says Lord Bryce, "the law of nature represented to the Romans that which is conformable to reason, to the best side of human nature, to an elevated morality, to practical good sense, to general convenience. It is simple and rational as opposed to that which is artificial or arbitrary. It is universal as opposed to that which is local or national. It is superior to all other laws because it belongs to mankind as mankind, as is the expression of the purpose of the Deity or of the highest reason of man."④

As natural law is supposed to have the power to command and to be superior to all other laws, including, of course, the laws made by the human sovereign, it is logical for the defenders of natural law to maintain that the earthly sovereign is bound by the law of nature. This idea has been carried through the whole period of the Middle Ages and has been coloured with theological conceptions. "The doctrine that the law of nature," says Professor Pollock, "was entitled to paramount authority was universally held by the canonists down to the sixteenth century, and our common lawyers, who were mostly glad enough to leave speculation to the canonists, probably did more than echo their utterances."⑤

Bodin, though not a student of the law of nature, admits that the sovereign is

---

① *Modern French Legal Philosophy*, "Modern Legal Philosophy series", translated by Mrs. F. W. Scott and Joseph, P. Chamberlain, p. 110.
② Pound, "Jurisprudence", in H. E. Barnes, *The History and Prospects of the Social Science*, p. 456.
③ R. I. Holand, *Natural Law and Legal Practice*, pp. 51–52.
④ Byrce, *Studies in History and Jurisprudence*, Vol. II, p. 589.
⑤ Pollock, *First Book on Jurisprudence*, p. 26. See also his *Essays in the Law*, 1921, p. 51.

limited by the law of nature. Grotius, by tracing the laws of his country to their principles, was led to the contemplation of the law of nature, which he considered as the parent of all municipal law.[1] "Natural law," says Grotius, "is the dictate of right reason, indicating that any act, from its agreement or disagreement with the rational nature, has in it moral necessity or moral turpitude; and consequently that such act is commanded or forbidden by God, the author of nature."[2] The law of nature is immutable so that it can not be changed even by God himself.[3] It follows that the sovereign is bound by this law at all times.[4]

Blackstone, the well-known commentator, repeating Cicero, declares that "the law of nature being coeval with mankind, and dictated by God Himself, is of course superior in obligation to any other," and that, "it is binding over all the globe in all countries and at all times; no human laws are of validity if contrary to this; and such of them as are valid derive all their force and all their authority mediately or immediately from this original".[5]

The rise of the analytic school did not suppress the flame of the notion of natural law, for it still had its advocates and defenders. In criticizing the doctrine of the analytical school, a recent writer, says, "If the doctrine of Hobbes and Austin be true, any act of tyranny may become lawful, for both tell us in almost the same words that the power of the sovereign, from its very nature, is incapable of legal limitation; and as no other can be found in the absence of natural law, the power of the sovereign is strictly unlimited. Thus, granting that Herod was the legal sovereign of the Jews, he had the right to order the massacre of the little babes of Bethlehem, and the soliders were bound to carry out his infamous order. This illustration is not ours, it is supplied by Austin himself. We are not yet ready to prostrate ourselves at the feet of Hobbes' Leviathan; but let us also beware of sporting with theories which if carried into practice, would destroy every liberty, and give the whole world to absolute despotism."[6]

In short the argument of the defenders of the natural law school is very simple. Natural law, they hold, is not the creature of the sovereign. On the contrary, it is above the sovereign and therefore the latter is bound to observe it.

---

[1] See James Mackintosh, *A Discourse on the Study of the Law of Nature and Nations*, p. 23.
[2] See Coker, *Readings in Political Philosophy*, p. 267.
[3] *Ibid.*, p. 268.
[4] *Ibid.*, p. 274.
[5] Blackstone, *Commentaries*, Introduction.
[6] Holand, *Natural Law and Legal Practice*, pp. 68-69.

CHAPTER VII
SOVEREIGNTY AND LAW
(Continued)

IV. Historical School

Although the historical school of jurisprudence found its beginnings in the eighteenth century, or even earlier than that, [1] its high water-mark was in the nineteenth century. Dean Pound has remarked that it was the historical school that "divided the allegiance of jurists with the theory of law as command of the sovereign during almost the whole of the past century"[2]. The students of this school have been and are many, but the most conspicuous were undoubtedly Savigny in Germany, Maine in England and Carter in the United States.

1. Savigny

Written in reply to a pamphlet by Thibout urging a new civil code for Germany, Savigny, as early as 1814. In his *Vom Beruf unserer Zeit für Gesetzgebung und Rechtswissenchaft*, laid down the fundamental principles which have been accepted by the historical School as to the nature and orgin of law. The idea was restated in his *System des heutigen Romischen Rechts* (1840-1849). Speaking of the position occupied by him in the science of jurisprudence, says a well known writer: "He was to the science of law what Lessing was to litterature, what Niebuhr was to history, or Ritter to Geography."[3]

The name of the school under consideration signifies clearly the method employed by the students of the school. And Savigny was no exception. What the doctrine of the historical school teaches is, as he says, "that every age creates its world not for itself and arbitrarily, but in close communion with the wholy past. In consequence every age must recognize something that is given, which is necessary and free at the same time;

---

[1] The most distinguished forerunner of this school in the sixteenth century was Cujas.
[2] Pound, *An Introduction to the Philosophy of Law*, 1922, p. 65.
[3] E. Freund, "Historical Jurists in Germany," in *Political Science Quarterly*, Vol. V, 1890, p. 473.

necessary because not dependent upon the arbitrary will of the present; free because as little dependent upon a foreign command, but rather produced by the high nature of the people as a constantly growing and developing body"①.

And in the Preface of his *System des heutigen Ramischen Rechts* he writes: "The historcial view of legal science is completely mistaken and disfigured when it is frequently so conceived as if the legal culture sprung from the past were set up as something supreme to which the immutable government of the present and the future must be preserved."② "The essence of that view", he continues, "rather consists in the uniform recognition of the value and the independence of each age and it merely ascribes the greatest weight to the recognition of the living connexion which knits the present to the past, and without the recognition of which we recognize merely the external appearance, but do not grasp the inner nature, of the legal condition of the present."③ Having in mind what is revealed in the quotations presented above, Savigny has given to the world a new conception of the science of law which became rapidly dominant in the last century. The matter of law is regarded as the actual result of facts of human nature and history, not an ideal result of ethical or political analysis. ④

The origin and growth of law are just the same as the origin and growth of other social institutions, such as religion and language and the state. The forces which produce law produce also the state, as the state is sometimes identified with sovereignty by German writers, or at least they are said to have sprung from the same source. ⑤ But what is that force? Or to put it more plainly: What is the source of law? It is, to Savigny, the general spirit which animates all the members of a nation. So he writes: "In the general consciousness of a people lives positive law and hence we have to call it peoples' law."⑥

By people (volker,) it is to be noted, is not meant any particular one of them, but is meant the whole people of a given nation. "It is by no means to be thought," he declares, "that it was the particular members of the people by whose arbitrary will, law was brought forth; in that case the will of individuals might perhaps have selected the same law, perhaps however, and more probably, very varied laws. Rather is it the spirit

---

① Quoted by Freund, *ibid.*, p. 475.
② *System des heutigen Romischen Rechts*, 1840, Vol. I, p. XIV, English trans. by W. Holloway, pp. IV-V.
③ *Ibid.*
④ Pollock and Maitland, *History of English Law*, Introduction, p. XXIII.
⑤ Cf. J. M. Lightwood, *Nature of Positive Law*, p. 278.
⑥ Savigny, *System des Heutigen Romischen Rechts*, Sec. VII, p. 14. "In dem gemeinsamen Bewusstsein des Volkes lebt das positive Recht, und wir haben es daher auch Volksrecht zu nennen".

of the people living and working in common in all the individuals, which gives birth to positive law, which therefore is to the consciousness of each individual not accidentally but necessarily one and the same."①

The form (Gestalt) however, in which the law lives in the common consciousness or spirit of the people is not the abstract rule, but the living intuition (legendige Anschauung) of the legal institutions in their organic connection.② The longer the convictions of law live in a people, the more deeply they become rooted in it.③ The development of law is like the development of the life of an individual. What can be perceived is not a glimpse of a complete whole which stands still (Stillstandes) but a continual organic development.④ Thus the law is always in the process of development. To understand what it is today, one must find out also what it was yesterday. Its development is gradual rather than sudden. It is a thing which is found, not made.

From what has been considered, it is obvious that law is not the will of God, and much less is it the expression of the arbitrary will of a human sovereign. It is not the effect of chance, nor a "garment merely which has been made to please the fancy and can be taken off at pleasure and exchanged for another."⑤ It is as the matter of fact a part and parcel of the life of a nation. It comes as the nation comes and it grows as the nation does. As the nation has its own characteristic or characteristics which is or are different from that of another; so is the law. Where there is a political society, be it civilized or primitive, there will be law. The further we go back to primitive law or laws, the more clearly we will realize that law is not the command of the sovereignty but the crystalization of the spirit or consciousness of the people—the people as a whole, not severally or individually.

2. Maine

Lecture XII of Maine's *Early History of Institutions* begins with these words: "The historical theories commonly received among English lawyers have done so much harm not only to the study of law, but to study of history that an account of the origin and growth of our legal system, founded on the examination of new materials and the re-examination of the old ones, is perhaps the most urgently needed of all additions to

---

① Savigny, *System des Heutigen Romischen Rechts*, English translation, p. 12. In his *The History of the Roman Law During the Middle Ages*, he writes that "all laws depend more on the ever changing wants and opinions of those who obey them, than on the mere fiat of any legislator." Translated by E. Cathart, Vol. I, Preface, p. XII.
② *System des heutigen Romichen Rechts*, p. 16.
③ Ibid.
④ Ibid., pp. 16–17.
⑤ See Taylor, *Science of Jurisprudence*, 1908, p. 29.

English knowledge. But next to a new history of law, what we most require is a new philosophy of law."① This is undoubtedly the starting point of Maine's concept of sovereignty and its relation to law.

Criticizing the theory of the analytical school, particularly that of Austin, two objections were raised by Maine: "First of all", says he, "it is the history, the whole historical antecedents, of each society by which it has determined where, in what person or group, the power of using the social force is to reside. The theory of sovereignty neglects the mode in which the result has been arrived at, and thus is enabled to class together the coercive authority of the great king of Persia, of the Athenian Demos, of the later Roman Emperor, of the Russian Czar and of the Crown and Parliament of Great Britain."②

"Next," he continues, "it is its history, the entire mass of its historical antecedents, which in each community determines how the sovereign shall exercise or forbear from exercising his irresistible coercive power. All that constitutes this—the whole enormous aggregate of opinions, sentiments, beliefs, superstitions, and prejudices, of ideas of all kinds, hereditary and acquired, some produced by institutions and some by constitution of human nature—is rejected by the analytic jurists."③

Negatively, Maine endeavors to show that the Austinian definition of law is too narrow and that it excludes a great body of law which never had its source in the will of a determinate superior, or a sovereignty. Positively, according to him, law is produced by public opinion, sentiments, beliefs and the like social forces. The point at issue is that law, in order to be law, is not necessarily backed by a sovereign. But where is the evidence? Here is an instance, often referred to, which alone has meant so much to his system. "My instance", he points out, "is the Indian province called the Punjaub, the Country of the Five Rivers, in the state in which it was for about a quarter of a century before its annexation to the British Indian Empire. After passing through every conceivable phase of anarchy and dormant anarchy, it fell under the tolerably consolidated dominion of a half-military, half-religious oligarchy known as the Sikhs. The Sikhs themselves are afterward reduced to subjection by a single chieftain belonging to their order, Runjeet Singh. At first sight there could be no more perfect embodiment than Runjeet Singh of sovereigniy as conceived by Austin. He was absolutely despotic. Except occasionally on his wild frontier he kept the most perfect order. He could have

---

① Maine, *Early History of Institutions*, p. 342.
② Maine, *Early History of Institutions*, p. 360.
③ *Ibid.*

commanded anything. The smallest disobedience to his commands would have been followed by death or mutilation; and this was perfectly well known to the enormous majority of his subjects. Yet I doubt whether once in all his life he issued a command which Austin would call a law. He took, as his revenue, a prodigious share of the produce of soil. He harried villages which recalcitrated at his exactions, and he executed great numbers of men. He levied great armies; he had all material of power, and exercised it in various ways. But he never made a law. The rules which regulated the lives of his subjects were derived from their immemorial usages, and these rules were administered by domestic tribunals in families of villages—communities that is, in groups no larger or little larger than those to which the application of Austin's principles can not be effected on his own admission, without absurdity."①

Maine admits however that the existence of such a state of political society may not falsify the Austinian theory as a theory, because it may be still argued, according to the maxim that whatever the sovereign permits he commands, that the rules which have force in the Punjaub are laws because the tacit consent of the Sikh is given to the customary rules or to rules which are made by the heads of households or the village-elders. For this reason, these rules are his commands and consequently the true laws of the state, just as the common laws of England are to be called laws proper if the Crown and Parliament permit them or give their consent to them whether it is express or implied. But what is to be borne in mind is that while in England, the Crown and Parliament may change the common laws at their pleasure at any time and in fact they have done so quite often and particularly in our own day, the Runjeet Singh, on the other hand, never thought of changing the rules then existing in his own country and which his subjects obeyed. "An Eastern or Indian theorist in law," says he, "to whom the assertion was made that Runject Singh commanded these rules, would feel it stinging him exactly in that sense of absurdity to which Austin admits the appeal to be legitimate."② "The theory," he adds, "remains true in such case, but the truth is only verbal."③

While denying vigorously that the Austinian maxim that law is the command of a sovereign, can be extended to the early society or primitive society at present, he admits that the recent tendency has been that more and more law is to be the creature of sovereignty in modern society. To him, this tendency is very manifest in history. Its beginning is to be found in the time of the Roman Empire, for it is Rome that conquered

---

① Maine, *Early History of Institutions*, pp. 380-381.
② *Ibid.*, p. 382.
③ *Ibid.*

the states adjoining her, extended its territories, and centralized the political system, including of course the institution of law. Here we see, as Maine conceives, the first time in history that laws tended to be the command of the sovereign. It is more so in our day, in the day of Bentham and even in the time of Hobbes.

This observation and generalization has led him to conclude that in the world at large and to a certain extent in the past as well as at the present, there are two types of society. "In the more ancient of these," says he, "the great bulk of men derive their rules of life from the customs of their village or city, but they occasionally, though most implicitly, obey the commands of an absolute ruler who takes taxes from them but never legislates. In the other, and the one with which we are most familiar, the sovereign is ever more actively legislating on principles of his own, while local custom and ideas are ever hastening to decay."① And he adds: "It seems to me that in the passage from one of these political systems to another, laws have distinctly altered their character."②

Laying aside the first type of political society noted by Maine in the passage quoted above and confining oneself to his second type, one will realize that Maine is no less than a student of the analytical school in jurisprudence. As the world is going more and more toward the second type of political society, the theory of Maine is more and more to be Austinianized. And if eventually the first type is going to disappear, and if the second type alone will exist, the theory of Maine, so far as it is contrary to that of Austin, will have only historical significance, and then he will be a true and loyal Austinian. Perhaps it is viewing it through this light that Jameson was led to place Maine as a student of the analytical school.③ It was Maine who shook the root of the analytical school, and it was Maine who planted the seed and watered it.

To what extent Maine has made concession to the analytical school, the following quotation gives us a hint. "But, if the analytical jurists failed to see a great deal which can only be explained by the help of history, they saw a great deal which even in our day is imperfectly seen by those who, so to speak, let themselves drift with history. Sovereignty and law, regarded as facts, had only gradually assumed a shape in which they answered to the conception of them formed by Hobbes, Bentham, and Austin, but the correspondence really did exist by their time, and was tending constantly to become more perfect. They were thus able to frame a juridical terminology which had one virtue that it was rigidly consistent with itself, and for another that, if it did not completely

---

① Maine, *Early History of Institutions*, p. 392.
② *Ibid.*
③ Jameson, "National Sovereignty," *Political Science Quarterly*, p. 193.

express facts, the qualifications of its accuracy were never serious enough to deprive it of value, and tended, moreover, to become less and less important as time went on. No conception of law and and society has ever removed such a mass of undoubted delusion. The force at the disposal of sovereigns did in fact act largely through laws as understood by these Jurists, but it acted confusedly, hesitatingly, with many mistakes and vast omissions. They for the first time saw all that it was capable of effecting, if it was applied boldly and consistently. All that has followed is a testimony to their sagacity."①

3. Carter

We come now to Judge Carter, one of the influential students in the field of jurisprudence in the United States. Dean Pound speaks of his ideas as "those of the metaphysical historical jurispeudence which had been taught him in its first form by a student of Savigny when Mr. Carter was himself a student". In speaking of his position and his book, says Dean Pound, "the arguments of the late James C. Carter were no small factor in fashioning American judicial decisions of the last quarter of the nineteenth century and his posthumous book has in a measure kept his influence alive."

So far as the criticism against the theory of Austin is concerned, Judge Carter has fully shared the position of Maine. But to him, Maine does not go far enough. He admits, with Maine, that in primitive society custom plays an important role and that what is law is nothing else than custom. But he strongly questions Maine's defense of the Austinian theory that law as the command of the sovereign is destined to become truth in the future. ② He further challenges Maine's recognition of the Austinian theory that whatever the sovereign permits he commands. ③ In short, negatively, he denies absolutely the Austinian maxim that law is the command of the sovereign. ④

Positively, he maintains that all law is custom. This, however, as he points out, does not mean that all custom is law. ⑤ "There is a large range of human conduct of which the law takes no notice, though it is under the control of custom quite as much as

---

① Maine, *Ibid.*, pp. 396–397. Judge Carter writes, after citing this passage, "Sagacious indeed must those minds have been—and in a miraculous way—who, seeking to describe law as it was, failed only because they accurately described law as it was to become, and rose from the ashes of scientific failure into a glory of prophecy of which they had not dreamed!" *Law, Its Origin, Growth and Function*, by James Coolidge Carter, 1907, p. 220.

② Carter, *Law: Its Origin, Growth and Function*, 1907, p. 201.

③ *Ibid.*, p. 189.

④ *Ibid.*, p. 120.

⑤ Pound, *Interpretations of Legal History*, 1923, pp. 34–35.

that part which the law assumes to regulate."① After reviewing and criticising numerous definitions given by other writers, he regards law as "a body of rules for the regulation of human conduct."② But how is conduct regulate in the group politically organized such as the African kingdoms of Dahomey and Ashantee? "We do not find," says he, "any legislative bodies organized to enact laws, nor does the sovereign either by himself or through ministers declare any designers to affect the ordinary life of the people. The different tribes of the kingdom already, when conquered, had their customs, as we have seen, the silent growth of long periods of time, and these continue as before with all their sanctions. The tyrant could not change them, with all his power, even if he would, for as we have seen, they are unchangeable except in the ways by which they were formed; but he does not wish to change them. All tyrants are unqualified advocates, of the maintenance of things as they are. These barbarous sovereigns, indeed, are personally above the customs and plunder, rob, and murder at their will. Their tyrannical authority is sustained by favor and fear, but public peace and order beneath them it is their interest to promote. The ancient customs are supported by the ancient sanctions, except in the case of slaves who are left at the mercy of their masters. There is indeed an additional sanction. The state is organized, although rudely. It has a political form; the sovereign and his subordinate chiefs are clothed with power in the hands of warriors whom they command, and the weak, when injured, appeal to them, and they enforce redress. Violations of custom are punished by the public authority, and thus a beginning is effected in the public authority, and thus a beginning is effected in the public redress of private injuries; in other words, what we know as the public administration of justice begins, although in a very crude form. But whether an act is capable of being a public crime, or a private injury, depends as before upon its conformity, or nonconformity, to custom."③

  This is no more than another instance as was given by Maine in different words in the case of the Punjaub. And so far, as has been said, Mr. Carter is still within the circle of Maine. But he goes beyond the point where Maine stops. To Maine, as has already been seen, in the passage of the local communities like the instances just cited into an extended and centralized empire the laws distinctly altered their character. Seeing the change from one to another, Maine was led to assert that there are two types of society: (1) one where laws exist without being commanded by a sovereign; (2) the

---

① Carter, *Law: Its Origin, Growth and Function*, 1907, p. 120.
② *Ibid.*, p. 14.
③ *Ibid.*, pp. 24-25.

other where laws tend to be the command of the sovereign.

On the other hand, no such distinction is made in the system of Mr. Carter. What is true in the ancient or primitive society, to him, is also true in the modern states. "Taking the statute-books of any of the states of this country or of England," he declares, "we find, as have heretofore observed, that nearly all their contents consist of work of this character, which is not the making of law in any juristic sense. That part which does really deal with the government of conduct is, so far as it is valid and effective, so small that it may well be neglected in any inquiry concerning the main factor in our substantive law. It has been correctly described as a mere fringe upon the body of the common law. "①

What is true as to the English speaking countries, is also true as to Ancient Rome, to France, Germany and American states. The great codifications of the laws in the countries just mentioned may be thought at first sight to be the evidence of the supremacy of legislation over unwritten or customary law, "but I may remark here," he says, "that since all these codifications are, with certain exceptions not important to the present question, avowed re-enactments of existing law, they do not evidence any assumption of its functions but rather a confession that all that legislation can do in relation to it is to acknowledge and adopt. What is law without legislation cannot be made more law by enactment. "②

It is clear then that Maine's partial defence of Austin is only erroneous, and the Austinan assertion that law is the command of the sovereign is entirely wrong. Law is no more than custom, for it is custom that furnishes the rules which regulate human conduct. The role played by custom in this respect in our own day and in our own countries is just the same as it is in the so-called barbarous tribes and in the countries of the past. ③ What the legislatures of the different states at present can do is to supplement and aid the operation of custom, but not supplant it. ④

Custom in its simplest definition, is the "uniformity of conduct of all persons under like circumstances"⑤. The root of uniformity of conduct is to be found in human nature which is the same in every one in all places and in all stages of social progress. The field of investigation and the survey that he has made for human life "has embraced

---

① *Law: Its Origin, Growth and Function*, 1907, pp. 203–204
② *Ibid.*, p. 204.
③ *Ibid.*, p. 119.
④ *Ibid.*, p. 120.
⑤ *Ibid.*, pp. 122–123.

primitive man, the savage member of a wandering horde; man when he first adopts a fixed place of abode; man when he first consciously organizes a social state; man when he has first acquired the art of writing and when he first employs that art in the composition of laws; man as the subject of a conqueror imposing his dominion over realms not his own; man as the member of a conquered nation accepting submissively the rule of strangers; man in society where there is no power to protect him save his own right arm; man during the long period in which he seeks by the establishment of judicial tribunals to supplant the violence of self-help; man down to the period when judicial tribunals and legislatures have been established and perfected; man in the present enlightened age"[①].

While the time has been, is, and will be, changing steadily, "human nature is not like to undergo a radical change, and therefore, that to which we give the name of law always has been, and will forever continue to be custom"[②]. The past, future and present to Mr. Carter, are all the same in that respect. What is true as to the past and the present will be true as to the future. There may be more legislatures created in the world as time goes on, there may be more acts declared and passed by them, but what they do is a "mere fringe on the body of law".

V. Economic School

We come now to another field of discussion, namely, the conception of sovereignty in its relation to law from the economic point of view. This has been sometimes called a "money making law theory". It has to be borne in mind that the writers whose thories we are about to consider accept formally the dogma of the analytical school that law is the command of the sovereign. But the sovereign, as they see it, is no more than a vent or mouthpiece. "This doctrine, is of course true, but then it is also meaningless."[③] Viewing the Austinian "sovereign" as a vent or mouthpiece, the writers of the economic school damage the analytical theory more than if they directly opposed it.

The theory considered here may be traced back to the writings of Harrington (1656). "Dominion is property", says he, "as is the proportion or balance of Dominion

---

① *Law: Its Origin, Growth and Function*, 1907, p. 119.

② *Ibid.*, p. 120.

③ Common, "A Sociological View of Soveseignty," in *American Journal of Sociology*, Vol. V, p. 355.

or property, such is the nature of the Empires."① But more remarkable is the statement made by Toland, who says: "Those who possess money, have at all times and in all countries dictated the laws, and subjected the majority of the people to their power."② Arthur Young, a well known English writer, expresses somewhat the same idea. "The great line of division into which the people divides, is first, those who have property, and second, others that have none... It is not that the proprietors of property should have voices in the election proportioned to their property, but that men who have a direct interest in the plunder or division of property should be kept at a distance from power. Here lies the great difficulty of modern legislation, to secure property and at the same time to secure freedom to those that have no property."③ The writings of Marx during the last century, although themselves not legal in character, have exercised, however, an important influence in legal philosophy and given encouragement to those who consider economic conditians as the basis for studying legal institutions.

1. Loria

Most important of all, perhaps, is the works of Achille Loria, of Italy, and Brooks Adams of the United States. That work of Loria, which particularly draws our attention, is entitled *Economic Foundation of Society*, The fundamental idea of this book, as he tells us, is "that economic revenue is the basis of political sovereignty."④ The state, as he conceives it, is merely the political expression of the existing economic dominant class.⑤ Sovereignty has ever since sprung from property.

The position so taken by Loria has been vigorously criticized by Tarde, a well known sociologist and lawyer. The latter holds that logically and historically it is political power that determines economic influence, and he says that if we go back to a still more remote epoch we shall find that the "patria potestas," the primitive source of all authority, political, religious and judicial, preceded the property system and gave it birth.⑥ In answer to Tarde's criticism, says Loria, "It is...absolutely untrue that the 'patria potestas' was the original source of political authority; for sovereignty was established on the basis of mother right long before the patria potestas was known; and even among tribes recognizing the paternal line, political authority was already pretty

---

① Harrington, *The Oceana and Other Works*, collected by Toland, 1700, p. 39. Quoted by Loria, *The Economic Foundation of Society*, translated by L. M. Keasbey, 1899, p. 332.

② Loria, *ibid.*, p. 334.

③ Quoted by Loria, *ibid.*, p. 336.

④ *Ibid.*, p. 358.

⑤ *Ibid.*, p. 343.

⑥ *Ibid.*, p. 359.

well developed before the 'patria potestas' was recognized. Moreover, modern research into prehistoric conditions...has clearly shown that the 'patria potestas' was itself but the corollary of private property, and that during the period of communal property maternal authority exercised absolute sway."[1]

If political power be thus an emanation of economic revenue, the natural tendency of acts of sovereignty must be to facilitate the development of capitalistic income and favor its holders in every possible way.[2] Sovereignty, having originated from property, becomes naturally the creature and tool of property. As property has been accumulated into the hands of the few, sovereignty, consequently becomes the means for these few, or what we call the privileged and wealthy classes, for advancing their own interests. In short, a glance at the workings of the state is sufficient to demonstrate that "all the efforts of political authority converge toward one supreme end: to guarantee and augment the income from capital."[3]

But how have the capitalists or the propertied classes come into absolute supremacy within the state? According to Loria, they gain it by a double victory. First, they destroy the political supremacy of the feudal proprietors, and next they overcome the popular classes that originally lent them their support.[4] After having controlled this very authority, the capitalistic class or classes, in order to support itself or themselves "must furthermore have recourse to a series of, what may be called, connective institutions; whose special function it is to guarantee property against all reactions, on the part of those excluded from the possession of the soil"[5]. What are these connective institutions? Here we come to our very point. "The most important of these so-called connective institutions", says he, "are: morality, law and politics. These great social phenomena may, accordingly be regarded as organic products of capitalistic property—or property, at least, metamorphoses and adopt them to suit its own ends."[6]

It is clear then, in order to protect and promote their own interest or interests, it is essential for them to have the power, the real power to make law, for law is a means—and the most important means for regulating the order and peace of society or state, and so long the state or society is in a state of peace and order without having turbulence, the propertied or capitalistic class will enjoy the privileges that it has enjoyed. The

---

[1] Harrington, *The Oceana and Other Works*, collected by Toland, 1700, p.360.
[2] *Ibid.*, p.206.
[3] *Ibid.*
[4] *Ibid.*, p.317.
[5] *Ibid.*, p.9.
[6] *Ibid.*

capitalistic class has tried with all its efforts to gain this and it has gained what it wants. And "it is to this final conquest, constituting property's brightest crown and forming the most interesting page in its history"①.

If law is simply the necessary outcome of economic conditions, and if law has now come to be the creature of the capitalistic class, and merely as a means for promoting the interests of the latter, the idea that law is the chance result of the legislator's will is erroneous. Formally, it is still true that the law is passed in the legislative hall, but the legislative hall is only a mouthpiece, for back of the legislative hall, stands the real source of law, the propertied class. "The political science," writes Loria, "has heretofore been dominated by the idea that laws spring full born from the mind of the inspired legislator—*proplem sine matre creatam*—and that their function is to regulate social relations according to immutable principle of justice. This concept gave jurisprudence its former prestige, and made public law the foundation and keynote of social science. This was particularly true of the last century, but with a deeper insight into the composition of society a new concept has since arisen, and the law is now coming to be regarded as an organic product of economic conditions, rather than the chance result of the leglslator's will."② In short, law thus becomes the law of the capitalistic class, by capitalists and for the capitalistic class.

The definition of law given by Ihering "as a compulsion exercised upon individuals by the collective authority, with a view to deterring them from excesses that would turn to their own disadvantage, which they themselves are unable to foresee", may be applied to "the relations existing between the members of the capitalistic group, upon whom the law actually imposes a series of acts that are in conformity with their real interests; but it is not applicable to matters concerning the labourers, for they are obliged by law to act contrary to their real egoism."③

Not only is the conception of law of Ihering, one of the students of the analytical school, criticised, also the theory of Savigny, and therefore of the historical school which considers law as the product of national consciousness, or the result of the peculiar inheritance and habits of a people, is questioned.④ Law, as it has been shown by legal history, instead of being the product of abstract reason, or the result of national

---

① Harrington, *The Oceana and Other Works*, collected by Toland, 1700, p. 114.
② *Ibid.*, p. 327.
③ *Ibid.*, p. 76.
④ *Ibid.*, p. 79.

consciousness, or racial characteristics, is simply the necessary outcome of economic conditions. ①

If society all the time and everywhere contains one class living without working and the other working without living, and if sovereignty is only the machinery or vent which the former uses to issue decrees for the protection of their own rights, property, satisfaction, selfish desire and for the exploitation and suppression of the latter, the mere modification of the machinery would not bring a just law which is for the interests of the latter or both. ② Law being derived from economic conditions can only be changed as the economic conditions change. To the analytical jurists, as we have frequently pointed out, law is the creature of the sovereign and can only be changed by the sovereign or at least by its consent, be it express or implied. To Loria, the sovereign may still remain, if he be only meant as an agent which has no force of its own, but the actual force of power which creates or changes the law is the economic conditions. Economic conditions take place as a matter of necessity rather than a matter of choice. They develop, and change as human society does.

While insisting that law is not a creature of will and that economic conditions can not be modified by will, he does not preclude the possibility of ameliorating some of the economic conditions such as the sanitary condition of the poorer classes. Legislation of this kind does in no way affect the position of the capitalistic class. On the contrary, it gives the latter more advantages, ③ for better labor can render better services, and better services mean the real source of income. This is what we can do, and what we should do. Defending the position so taken, says our author, "Instead of leading toward fatalism, our theory, on the contrary, tends to encourage rational human activity, which alone can prevent, or at least mitigate, the confusion otherwise attendant upon social metamorphosis."④

2. Brooks Adams

Dean Pound remarks that "Brooks Adams puts economic determinism behind English analytical jurisprudence"⑤. Thus he continues as he summarizes the conception of the thinker: "Law is made by a sovereign or is recognized and applied by the organs of a sovereign. But in so making or recognizing or applying it they but register the self-

---

① Harrington, *The Oceana and Other Works*, collected by Toland, 1700, p. 84.
② *Ibid.*, p. 344.
③ *Ibid.*, pp. 334, 376.
④ *Ibid.*, p. 377.
⑤ Pound, *Interpretations of Legal History*, p. 97.

interest of the dominant class as it inevitably determines by economic laws. For purposes of formal juristic analysis we speak of a sovereign. When we look deeper we must speak of an economic conflict. Where Austin pictures a sovereign commands on the basis of utility, Brooke Adams would have us see a dominant class issuing commands, through the mask of the legal order, on the basis of its self-interest."①

"Sovereign powers", says Mr. Adams in his *The Theory of Social Revolution*, "are powers so important that the community, in its corporate capacity, has, as society has centralized, usually found it necessary to monopolize them more or less abolutely, since their possession by private persons cause revolt."② "These powers when vested in some official, as for example, a king or Emperor, have been held by him, in all Western countries at least, as a trust to be used for the common welfare." Punishment by means of deposition or death has been usually resorted to if this trust has been disregarded or breached by the king or emperor. The execution of Charles I is one of the examples cited to prove his contention. "In short, the relation of sovereign and subject has been based either upon consent and mutual obligation, or upon submission to a divine command; but, in either case, upon recognition of responsibility. Only the relation of master and slave implies the status of sovereign power vested in an unaccountable superior."③

The few statements quoted above from his *The Theory of Social Revolution*, represent his general conception of sovereignty. Here comes the point at issue. "Nevertheless", he continues immediately, after the statement last quoted, "it is in a relation somewhat analogous to the latter, that the modern capitalist has been placed, toward his fellow citizens, by the advances in applied science."④ It is the capitalist or capitalists now becoming "clothed with various attributes of sovereignty"⑤. But how do they get them? To Adams, "he (the capitalist) conceives sovereign powers to be for sale. He may, he thinks, buy them; and if he buys them; he may use them as he pleases"⑥. For sovereignty is apprehended as a "variable quantity of administrative energy, which, in civilization which we call advancing, tends to accumulate with a

---

① Pound, *Interpretations of Legal History*, pp. 97 – 98. Dean Pound depends for his source mainly on Mr. Brooks Adams's article in "Centralization and the Law" (1906). I regret that I do not have this book on hand.
② Books Adams, *The Theory of Social Revolution*, 1913, p. 13.
③ *Ibid.*, p. 14.
④ *Ibid.*
⑤ *Ibid.*, p. 13.
⑥ *Ibid.*, p. 209.

rapidity proportionate to the acceleration of movement"①.

If sovereign powers can be bought it is only natural that the capitalist can make the sovereign to make the law that he likes for his own interest or interests and to change those which are contrary to his desire. Thus says Mr. Adams, "If the capitalist has bought some sovereign function, and wishes to abuse it for his own behoof, he regards the law which restrains him as a despotic invasion of his constitutional rights, because, with his specialized mind, he can not grasp the relation of a sovereign function to the nation as a whole. He therefore, looks upon the evassion of a law devised for public protection, but inimical to him, as innocent or even meritorious. If an election be lost, and the legislature, which has been chosen by the majority, cannot be pacified by money, but passes some act which promises to be annoying, the first instinct of the capitalist is to retain counsel, not to advise him touching his duty under the law, but to devise a method by which he may elude it, or if he cannot elude it, by which he may have it annulled as unconstitutional by the courts."②

In short it is the capitalist who in fact makes law for his own interest, not the sovereign. The name of sovereign may still be used as indicating the spring from which law emanates, but it is not the real spring, for its soul and heart have gone. But can this still continue in the future? No. This is the answer of Mr. Adams.

"American society," he predicts, "as at present organized, with capitalists for the dominat class, can concentrate no further, and, as nothing in the universe is at rest, if it does not concentrate, it must probably begin to disintegrate."③ Here we may point out the difference between Loria and Brooks Adams. Both of them emphasize the importance of economic conditions in law making and deny the sovereign as the real source from which law comes; but while the former thinks that economic conditions can only change as a natural consequence, the latter goes a step further to declare that they are now going to change.

The collapse of capitalist supremacy and government is destined. And if it does, sovereignty is no longer to be unaccountable, for the exercise of sovereignty, as has been pointed out, involves the recognition of responsibility. And if responsibility is or should be taken into account in the exercise of sovereignty, the law given by the

---

① Books Adams, *The Theory of Social Revolution*, 1913, p. 20. "That is to say, the community, as it consolidates, finds it essential to its safety to withdraw, more or less, completely, from individuals, and to monopolize, more or less strictly, itself a great variety of functions."
② *Ibid.*, pp. 213-214.
③ *Ibid.*, pp. 226-227.

sovereign is no longer to be considered as a command of the superior to the inferior, as in the case of the relation between master and slave, but as a fulfillment of the responsibility for the common welfare of society as a whole. Here we come to the very point that M. Duguit advances and which will be presented more fully in our later discussion.

3. John R. Commons

In connection with the economic school of jurispridence, a few words need to be said regarding Professor Common's conception, which is set forth in a well-written and long article under the title "A Sociological View of Sovereignty". The title indicates that it is from a sociological view-point, but Professor H. E. Barnes aptly says that he lays more stress upon the economic factor in society. ①② Considering the Austinian theory of sovereignty and law, says Professor Commons, "This doctrine, of course, is true, but then, it is also meaningless, for by the very definition of law, custom is already excluded. In truth the doctrine only marks the complete breakdown of custom, and the subsequent injection of order into sovereignty". Sovereignty, as well as other social institutions had their origin in private property. "Private property is but another name for the coercive relation existing between human beings through which the proprietor commands the services of others. This is also sovereignty."③ Law is the criterion of a state, but the arbitrary, transient commands of a despot are not law. ④ Law then is something which is exterior to, if not above, sovereignty. For both law and sovereignty are the results of economic conditions.

Ⅵ. Sociological School

The appearance of Auguste Comte's *Positive Philosophy* directed human thought to a new field of investigation. This new field is known as sociology. The works of Spencer

---

① Barnes, *Sociology and Political Theory*, 1924, p. 131.
② Commons, "A Sociological View of Sovereignty," in *American Journal of Sociology*, Vol. Ⅴ, p. 355.
③ *Ibid.*, Vol. Ⅵ, p. 87.
④ *Ibid.*, p. 356. The prime aim of sovereignty is the protection of property. It is not absolute, unlimited or universal, for it is limited by the coercion which still remains in private hands. He denies the definition of sovereignty given by Professor Burgess. According to him, there are three constituents of sovereignty—coercion, order and right. "Coercion originates as private property. The struggle for existence causes this to survive in the form of monopoly and centralisation. Order emerges as a constitutent of sovereignty in place of caprice only when sovereignty has extended over wide areas and when subordinate classes have earned the veto power in determining the sovereign when freedom has displaced material and competitive necessity", See *Ibid.*, pp. 3, 359, 552, 824.

during the second half of the last century have given more encouragement to this new field. More or less contemporary to Spencer, we find Gumplowicz in Austria, Zimmer in Germany and Ward in the United States. All these men have done to the field of sociology what Darwin, Wallace, Wissman and Mendel have done to the field of biology.

The labor given to such investigations not only brings the new science into common understanding, but also throws a new light and exerts an important influence on other fields of human knowledge, including of course the science of law. Sociology itself is a new science, but sociology in its application to the study of law is now considered as the dominant conception in jurisprudence. As the approach to sociology takes different forms, the conception as to the origin and nature of law differs accordingly.

Thus during the earlier years of sociological development, the interpretation of sociology was based on physical conditions. So law was regarded as the product of physical—geographical, climatic—forces. It was argued that a certain kind of physical condition gives rise to a certain kind of law. There may be a sovereign—the legislator or the court—but all they do is to register the law which is actually the result of physical force.

There followed a period when a biological interpretation of sociology prevailed. The theory of struggle for existence as enunciated by Darwin was adopted by Gumplowicz who is generally known as a groupist. Social institutions are regarded as the result of social conflict. So it is for sovereignty and so it is for law. Equality can only be found in the simplest hordes. In them, there is no command and no obedience in the legal sense. ① State is defined as the organized control of the minority over the majority and sovereignty is supreme authority always exercised by the minority. ② Law is thus considered as the product of the ruling class or classes. "Thus the ruling class", says Gumplowicz, "through their parliaments exercise the legislative power and are able by legal institutions to further their own interests at the cost of others."③ On the other hand, Spencer, being an extereme individualist, denies strongly the authority of the state. In his *Study of Sociology*, he even condemns parliament for passing an act promoting the education of the people. He criticises the conception of Hobbes and Austin that law is the command given by superior to inferior. ④ He remarks that Austin, having been in the

---

① Gumplowicz, *Outline of Sociology*, Translated by Moore, p. 124.
② *Ibid.*, p. 118. Cf. Ward, *Pure Sociology*, pp. 30, 205–206.
③ *Ibid.*, p. 145.
④ Spencer, *Social Static and Man vs. State*, 1903, pp. 378–380.

army, confuses the distinction between civil and military authority. "It has been truly remarked," says he, "that 'the permanent traces left' may be seen in his Province of Jurisprudence."① Having confused the distinction, Austin is led to deduce the legal validity of its edicts which he calls positive. "The true question is: Whence the sovereign? What is the assignable warrant for this unqualified supremacy assumed by one, or by a small number, or by a large number, over the rest?" To this demand, as he sees it, there is no response.②

Thirdly, there has been a movement which we may call the economic interpretation of sociology. The relation of sovereignty and law is thus viewed from the economic standpoint. We have already discussed this in the previous section.

Fourthly, we come to the psychological interpretation of sociology. The best known writer in this movement is Tarde, a French sociologist as well as lawyer. Trade rejects the distinction made be Henry Maine between modern and ancient law and maintains③ that "law is only one form or outcome of man's inclination towards imitations."④ Imitation may pass from one people to another as well as from one class to another in the same people.⑤ So through the process of imitation, law may be transferred from one class to another or from one country to another.

German writers like Gierke deny the contention that law is the expression of the sovereign will of the state. Psychological factors must be taken into account. To understand the position of Gierke, the following passage may be quoted: "There is between law and the state a reciprocal penetration of a particularly close and intimate nature. The law is innate in the state. Law is no more begotten by the state than the state is begotten by law. But, although each has its own reasons for being, each is developed by the other, each is the complement of the other, …Today the state acts as an organ in the formation of law. But for that reason the state does not become either the ultimate source of law or the sole organ in its formation. The ultimate source of law resides rather in the common consciousness of social being. The common belief that something is right needs, for its external realization, materialization by a social expression, as for instance, in a rule of law… not unfrequently this expression takes place through and by means of the state, which has for its principal role the shaping of

---

① Spencer, *Social Static and Man vs. State*, 1903, p. 380.
② *Ibid.*
③ Tarde, *The Laws of Imitations*, trans. by Parsons, p. 314.
④ *Ibid.*, p. 61.
⑤ *Ibid.*, p. 201.

the juridical consciousness of the people in the form of law. But social organisms other than the state can formulate law ... Juridical life and the life of the state are two independent sides of social life. While power is a rational condition for the state because a state without omnipotence is not a state, it is immaterial, so far as the notion of law is concerned, that there exist for it means of External power; for law without power and without action always remains law."[1]

American writers like Professor Ellewood and Professor Williams emphasize strongly the psychological factor in law making. "Now law", says Professor Ellwood, "rests on custom, that is social habit". It is not something apart from social organization but springs from the psychological nature of society.[2] According to Professor J. M. Williams, lawyers have made the mistake of believing that law is the command of the political superior.[3] Jurists are lawyers and not scientists; the professional method of thinking of the lawyer is deductive, not the inductive method of the scientist.[4] A true definition of the nature of law requires valid social-psychological assumptions, which can be had only by an understanding of social-psychology.[5] It is manifest now that law is no longer to be expressed in the phrase to "lay down the law" which means to be given by a sovereign. Law, as a matter of fact, is essentially custom and there is an aversion to law-making.[6]

The modern tendency of sociology is to reject particularism and to work out a synthetic system. This movement may be traced back to the writings of Comte and Spencer and is developed in the works of Professors Small, Hayes and other recent writers. The synthetic movement in the field of jurisprudence itself, brings, in turn, the same effect in the field of jurisprulence. "In the present century", says Dean Pound, "jurists have become conscious that the distinction between the several social sciences are necessitated not by the nature of things, but simply by the requirements of division of labor. Indeed, except in the case of analytical jurists they had never wholly given up

---

[1] Gierke, "Die Grundbegriffee des Staatsrechts und die neuesten Staatstheorien," *Zeitschrift fur die gesammate Staatswissenschafte*, Tubingen, 1874, p. 179. Quoted by Duguit, "The Law and the State," in *Harvard Law Review*, Vol. XXXI, pp. 159–160.

[2] Ellwood, *Sociology in Its Psychological Aspects*, 1912, p. 37.

[3] Williams, *The Foundations of Social Science*, 1920, p. 210.

[4] Ibid., p. 209.

[5] Ibid., p. 211.

[6] Ibid., p. 219. See also his *Principles of Social Psychology*, 1922.

connections of jurisprudence with other sciences."① The leading representatives in this later movement are Kohler of Germany, Justice Holmes and Dean Pound of the United States, Salmond of Australia,② and most important of all, Duguit of France and Krabbe of Holland.

1. Kohler

According to Dean Pound, Josef Kohler is without question the first of living jurists.③ Berolzheimer, a well known student of the history of legal philosophy, also speaks of Kohler's legal philosophy as the most important and perhaps the most valid contribution to legal philosophy since Hegel.④ Like Hegel, Kohler holds that law is to be considered as a cultural phenomenon; but unlike Hegel's philosophy of law as the product of deduction, he proceeds empirically, leaning upon history and ethnology.⑤ It is in the latter case, that he concurs with Savigny. But besides believing that law is the product of the past, he asserts that this product can be consciously modified in order to fit it for the needs of the present. "The law of a people," says he, "can be interpreted only in the light of its entire culture; which, in turn, is to be interpreted, as extending beyond the material, economic factors, to include the ethical and religious views which the law reflects. Laws are not shaped consciously or unconsciously by considerations of utility. The general view of life influences the law, and from such composite cultural forces the law arose. The law establishes the channels through which the stream of culture flows, and the course and nature of the channels through which they take their character from the culture trends, which in large measure are sustained by prevalent beliefs in regard to the spiritual life and the divine rule."⑥

Law then is the product of civilization. But this is not all; for law is also a means toward civilization. In the language of Dean Pound, "we must look at it, therefore, in three ways; as to the past as a product of civilization, as to the present as a means of maintaining civilization, as to the future as a means of furthering civilization."⑦ The law so produced is certainly contrary to the view that law is created by the sovereign will. It is true that Kohler recognizes the conscious element in law making, but that does not

---

① Pound, "Sociology and Law," See Ogburn and Goldenweiser, *The Social Sciences, and Their Interrelations*, 1927, p. 323.
② It is rather in view of the importance of his theory that we take the opportunity to present his view here.
③ See *Harvard Law Review*, Vol. XXIV, p. 155.
④ Berolzheimer, *The World's Legal Philosophy*, English translation, p. 426.
⑤ *Ibid.*, p. 422.
⑥ Quoted by Berolzheimer, *ibid.*, p. 423.
⑦ Pound, *Interpretations of Legal History*, p. 143.

mean that it is a law given by the superior to the inferior; it means merely that it is made or modified for maintaining or promoting civilization.

2. Holmes

Justcie Holmes has been sometimes regarded as a historical jurist, [1] but as early as 1891, he has already shown that he is no longer a student of that school. [2] The acknowledgment of the indebtedness of Sir Frederick Pollock and Mr. Laski to him, makes his poition clear enough in the field of jurisprudence. [3] In a short preface to the *Collected Papers*, published in 1920, Justice Holmes, after expressing his thanks to Mr. Laski for collecting the articles together for printing, says: "A later generation has carried on the work that I began nearly half a century ago, and it is a great pleasure to an old warrior who can not expect to bear arms much longer, that the brilliant young soldiers still give him a place in their councils of war."[4] Even a layman can easily tell from this passage what kind of war has been fought and for what side he is fighting.

A student intimate with the works of Justice Holmes speaks of him as a great exception to the American judges. "Where others are guided through experience of life, he is led by divination of the philosopher and the imagination of the poet. He is indeed philosopher become king."[5] Justice Holmes is certainly more a philosopher than a lawyer. "Theory," says he, "is the most important part of the dogma of the law, as the architect is the most important man who takes part in the building of houses."[6]

As early as 1881, in his *Common Law*, Justice Holmes pointed out the failure of theories which consider the law only from its formal side. "You may assume", he declares, "with Hobbes and Bentham and Austin, that all law emanates from the sovereign, even when the first human beings to enunciate it are the judges, or you may think that law is the voice of the 'Zeitgeist', or what you like. It is all one to my present purpose. Even if every decision required the sanction of an emperor with despotic power and a whimsical turn of mind, we should be interested none the less, still with a view to prediction, in discovering some order, some rational explanation, and some principle of growth for the rules which he laid down. In every system there are such explanations and principles to be found."[7]

---

[1] See Taylor, *Science of Jurisprudence*, 1908, p. 30.
[2] See his article entitled "Agency" in *Collected Papers*.
[3] Pollock, *First Book of Jurisprudence*, Preface; Laski, *Problem of Sovereignty*, Preface.
[4] Holmes, *Collected Papers*, Preface.
[5] "Mr. Justice Holmes and the Constitution," *Harvard Law Review*, Vol. XLI, 1927, p. 128.
[6] Holmes, "The Path of Law," Vol. X, *Harvard Law Review*, p. 477. See also his *Collected Papers*.
[7] *Collected Papers*, p. 179. *Harvard Law Review*, p. 465.

The fallacy of the analytical school, according to him is the conception that the only force at work in the development of the law is logic. What is logic? It is nothing more than the assertion that law is the emanation of sovereignty. But "the life of law has not been logic, it has been experience."① While experiences are the accumulation of the human activities of the past, "the law embodies the story of a nation's development through many centuries, and it can not be dealt with as if it contained only the axioms and corollaries of a book of mathematics"②.

"The truth is", he declares, "that law is always approaching, and never reaching, consistency. It is forever adopting new principles from life at one end, and it always retains old ones from history at the other, which have not yet been absorbed or sloughed off, it will become entirely consistent only when it ceases to grow."③ In order to know what it is, we must know what it has been, and what it tends to become. ④

3. Pound

In his *Law and Morals*, three lectures ⟨are⟩ delivered at the University of North Carolina. 1923, Dean Pound summarizes a general survey of the history of legal philosophy as follows: "The Greeks put a theoretical moral foundation under law by the doctrine of natural rights. The Roman jurists made natural right into natural law…The Middle Ages put a theological foundation under natural law…The seventeenth and eighteenth centuries took out this theological foundation and replaced it or partially replaced it by a rational foundation…At the end of the eighteenth century Kant replaced the rational foundation by a metaphysical foundation…It remained only for the analytical jurists to argue that no foundation was needed; to urge that so far as concerns judge or jurist the law stands upon its own basis as a system of precepts imposed or enforced by the sovereign. If we felt inclined to go outside of the body of legal precepts so imposed or enforced, they referred us to the science of politics. Presently the analytical school in politics in America carried the movement for casting out ethics still further and limited the science of politics to a descriptive analytical method, leaving what ought to be to the philosophers as such. Thus the cycle is complete. We are back to the state as the unchangeable authority behind legal precepts. The state takes the place of Jehovah handing the tables of the law to Moses, or Manu dictating the sacred law, or the Sun-

---

① *Common Law*, p. 1. See also Taylor, *Science of Jurisprudence*, p. 30. Cf. his opinion in the case of the American Banana Co. vs the United States Co., 1909, pp. 213, 347, 356, 358.
② *Ibid*.
③ *Ibid*., p. 36.
④ *Ibid*., p. 1. See also *Collected Papers*, p. 185.

god handing the code to Mammurabi. Law is law by convention and enactment—the proposition, plausibly maintained by Sophists, which led Greek philosophers to seek some basis that made a stronger appeal to men to uphold the legal order and the security of social institutions."[1]

The point that Dean Pound wishes to emphasize here is that law has rarely been and should not be divorced from ethical custom and that the analytical dogma that law is mere command of the sovereign can no longer be maintained. Law, to him, is something more than the will of a sovereign and in fact much more.[2] For law is a sort of balance between individual and social interests. When we think of law we do not think of right, but interests, claims and demands.[3] "The task is one of satisfying human demands, of securing interests or satisfying claims or demands with the least of friction and the least waste, whereby the means of satisfaction may be made to go as far as possible."[4]

In the eyes of Dean Pound the world of today is no longer the world of yesterday. Conditions change as time goes on. Not only is the dogma of the analytical school not in harmony with the actual facts, even the doctrine of the historical school can not meet the demands of the time. "The possibilities of analytical and historical development of the classical materials," says he, "have been substantially exhausted. While jurists have been at these tasks, a new social order bas been building which makes new demands and presses upon the legal order with a multitule of unsatisfied desires. Once more we must build rather than merely improve; we must create rather than nerely order and systematize and logically reconcile details."[5] This change in the function of law is not only necessary, but also becomes a fact, because the present tendency has been to reject the absolute authority of the few, and the old conception that law is the command of these few is doomed to fall to the ground. In a word, present day jurisprudence is one for the welfare of the masses, as opposed to the welfare of the one class or a few at the cost of others.[6]

4. Salmond

The work of Professor Salmond marks a wide departure from the generally accepted view of sovereignty and law in England. He is not only a pluralist, but a radical

---

[1] Pound, *Law and Morals*, 1924, pp. 12–14.
[2] Cf. *Ibid.*, pp. 77–84.
[3] *Interpretations of Legal History*, p. 152.
[4] *Ibid.*, p. 157.
[5] Pound, *Introduction to the Legal Philosphy*, 1922, p. 57.
[6] See Pound, "Legislation as a Social Function," *Publications of American Sociological Society*, Vol. Ⅶ, pp. 153–154.

pluralist. He reduces the traditional theory of sovereignty to three propositions: (1) that sovereignty is essential to the state, (2) that sovereignty is indivisible and (3) that sovereignty is illimitable. As to the first, he really agrees with the old theorists. But he finds that no solid foundation can be maintained for the second and the third. ①

Sovereignty, according to him, is not only divided as is indicated by the terms "half" or "partial sovereignty," but it is also divided into as many parts within a state as is possessed by different departments. Thus in England, sovereignty is vested in three governmental departments, namely the legislature, executive, and judicial. Each of these departments is sovereign within its own sphere. ②

Moreover, sovereignty is not illimitable. "At no very remote period," says he, "it was considered to be the law of England, that a statute made by Parliament was void if contrary to reason and the law of God. The rule has now been abandoned by the courts, but it seems sufficiently obvious that its recognition involves no theoretical absurdity or impossibility however inexpedient it may be. Yet it clearly involves a limitation of the power of the legislature by a rule of law." "To take another example," he continues, "the most striking illustration of the legislative omnipotence of the English Parliament is its admitted power of extending the term for which an existing House of Commons has been elected. Delegates appointed by the people for a fixed time have the legal power of extending the period of their own delegated authority. It is difficult to see any theoretical objection to a rule of the opposite import. Why should not the courts of law recognize and apply the principle that an existing parliament is sovereign only during the limited time for which it was orginally appointed, and is destitute of any power of extending that time and in such a case would not the authority of the supreme legislature be limited by a rule of law."③

If the exercise of the legislative power of perliament is admittedly subject to legal conditions, it must be true that it is limited by a legal limitation. If the manner of the exercise of legislative power can be regulated by law, it must be true that its matter may be regulated by the law also. ④

But Professor Salmond does not stop here. Besides maintaining that sovereignty is limited by law, he goes on to show that law is something else than the command of the sovereignty. The assumption that law is merely the command of sovereignty can not be

---

① Salmond, *Jurisprudence*, sixth ed., p. 467.
② Ibid., pp. 467–474.
③ Ibid., p. 472.
④ Ibid., p. 473.

accepted, because it is based on the erroneorus conception of the essential nature of the administration of justice. The function of the state, according to him, is "to maintain right, to uphold justice, to protect rights, to redress wrongs"①. Its function to make law is secondary and unessential.

Law is simply the means for securing justice, and the means must not be defined without referring to its end.② "Law therefore, is defined as the body of principles recognized and applied by the state in the administration of justice or more shortly: The law consists of the rules recognized and acted on in courts of justice."③ From this definition, it follows that the administration of justice is perfectly possible without law at all. It is true, he admits, that what a man or litigant gets from a court in modern states is justice according to law, "but it is essentially and primarily justice and not law."④

---

① Salmond, *Jurisprudence*, sixth ed., p. 12.
② *Ibid.*, p. 9.
③ *Ibid.*, p. 14.
④ *Ibid.*, p. 13.

CHAPTER VIII
SOVEREIGNTY AND LAW
(Continued)

5. Duguit

In an article devoted to a discussion of the juristic conceptions of Professor Duguit, a student on political philosophy writes: "Just as in eighteenth century France and in the doctrines of Rousseau the intellectualist explanation of the nature of law found its classical statement, so in modern France once more and in the theory of M. Leon Duguit these doctrines meet their most elaborate rebuttal."① And another student on jurisprudence remarks: "In his *Transformations du Droit Public*...M. Duguit attempts for the science of law what Auguste Comte attempted for philosophy to emancipate it from theology and metaphysics."②

No one will deny the important position occupied by Duguit in the field of jurisprudence and no one will deny that he is the most conspicuous representative of the subject under consideration. In view of these reasons, we propose to examine his notion more fully.

a. Works

Professor Duguit has been Professor of constitutional law at the University of Bordeaux for nearly thirty years. The first treatise written by him is entitled *La Separation des Pouvoirs et L'Assemble' Constituante* (Paris), published as early as 1893. The second is *The Constitutions and Principal Political Statutes of France* written in collaboration with Henry Monnier in 1898. In 1901, he published *L'Etat: Le Droit Objectif et La Loi Positif* in which, he destructively criticizes Jellinek's famous work entitled *System der subjecktiven offentlichen Rechts* (1897); and constructively he advances his conception of sovereignty and its relation to law. This volume, says a writer, "Contains a comprehensive exposition of his leading principles, and is the best book to read to understand his general doctrine of the nature of law and its relation to the

---

① See *Political Science Quarterly*, 1922, p. 640, an article by Professor W. Y. Elliot.
② W. J. Brown, "The Jurisprudence of M. Duguit," in *Law Quarterly Review*, Vol. XXXII, 1916, p. 168.

state."①

The purpose of this book, according to Professor Duguit, is to accomplish a negative result—to show that the state is not that collective person invested with sovereign power; that the law is not that construction erected by the jurists on the unstable foundation either of individual right or of the omnipotence of the state; that this combination of fictions and abstractions disappears at the touch of the wand of reality.②

The view set forth in the volume just mentioned has been supplemented by another volume entitled *L'Etat: Les Gouvernants et Les Agents*, which appeared in 1903. Following these, a treatise on *Constitutional Law* has been written. This, according to Mr. Laski, "in the breadth of its analysis challenges comparison with Esmein's almost incomparable study, he has traced its ramifications throughout the field best fitted to display its import."③

His view was further elaborated in three lectures at the Ecole des Hautes Etudes Sociales, and published under the title *Le Droit Social, Le Droit Individual et L'Etat*, 1908. In 1912 he wrote a study of private law and as the result of this, his *Les Transformations Generales du Droit Prive*, was published. In 1913 he wrote *Transformations due Droit Public*. This latter may be regarded as the crystalization of his whole view. A long article was published in *Harvard Law Review* for November 1917 entitled "The Law and the State". In this, he restated his view and answered some of the criticism made against him.

This brief account shows that the writings of Professor Duguit are many, yet the trend of thought is one. More than twenty five years have elapsed since the appearance of his *L'Etat: Le Droit Objectiv et Loi Positif*, but the principle advanced in it is still the corner stone of his system at present. Thus after quoting his own words written in 1912, he wrote in 1917: "These lines, written before the war, are truer today than ever."④

b. Precursors

If one wishes to make a real advance in any line, he must know what other people have done in that line. But after he knows what other people have done and before he makes an advance, he is more or less influenced by other people who came before, or

---

① *Modern French Legal Philosophy*, "Modern Legal Philosphy Series," 1921, Vol. XLIV.
② Duguit, *L'Etat, Le Droit Objectif et La Loi Positive*, p. 1. Also *Modern French Legal Philosophy*, p. 238.
③ *Harvard Law Review*, Vol. XXXII, p. 189.
④ *Harvard Law Review*, Vol. XXXII, p. 185. Another book of Professor Duguit entitled *Sourveranete et liberte* (1922). I regret that I don't have this book in hand.

live at the same time with, him. This generalization may be said as a well established rule and Professor Duguit is not an exception. He has many precursors. From Philosophers like Comte, he grasps the idea that "there can only be a true right, so long as regular powers emanate from supernatural wills…In the positive state which does not admit of heavenly prerogative, the idea of right disappears absolutely."① From sociologists like Durkheim, he gets the notion of social solidarity which is the heart and soul of his juristic philosophy. From political writers like Seydel, he rejects the personality of the state and from jurists like Gierke, he sees that law is exterior to the state.

Without enumerating all the thinkers who have influenced or stimulated him, let us confine ourselves to a few whose theories Professor Duguit has taken into deep consideration. As early as the first half of the nineteenth century, Royer-Collard, a French statesman had denied the conception of sovereignty and maintained the authority of law.② According to Royer-Collard, there may be sovereignty in a state, but sovereignty is nothing more than despotism and "despotism means social death or at least organic disorder." Sovereignty then can only exist in a disordered state and it is not an ideal thing that statesmen and political thinkers should like to see.

If sovereignty should find no room in an ideal state, what is the essential thing that binds the individuals in a given society? "Law" is the response. Law, as he conceives it, is the foundation of legitimate interests and the corner stone of a state. It springs from justice or reason as contrary to sovereignty which is merely based on force.③

M. Charles Benoist is another writer who deserves mention. Professor Duguit regards him as one of the most authoritative representatives of the realistic conception of the state. He considers the notion of sovereignty as mystical and theological. "To us," he says, "it seems wiser and more just to abandon or, as we have been reproached for doing, to throw overboard the very notion of sovereignty; though certainly it is a very venerable and ancient notion, so ancient that it no longer has a place in contemporary political society any more than do the Assyrian or Egyptian gods in our museums…or the worm-eaten fetishes of the peoples of Central Africa. … Let us found our theories only on what is living in society. The idea of sovereignty is false and useless. It may have once

---

① Statement by Comte, *Systeme de politique positive*, edition published in 1890, Vol. I, p. 361, quoted by Duguit.

② For the theory of Royer-Collard, see especially, Laski, "Royer-Collard" in his *Authority in the Modern State*, Ch. IV.

③ A summary of Royer-Collard's theory, See Duguit, "The Law and The State," *Harvard Law Review*, Vol. XXXI, pp. 165-189.

been true and may have formerly served fashions which are dead today. But how long is modern Europe going to continue to believe in sovereignty after it can no longer be found in fact? No answer need be given; for these is not at present, nor will there ever be sovereignty among the nations of western Europe. Something else has everywhere arisen in its stead."①

But what is the thing that has everywhere arisen in its stead? "At present", he declares, "sovereignty does not exist, even among the nation of western Europe; but all about us there is something which is not intermittent, which is never arrested, which existed yesterday and will continue to exist tomorrow, which existed before us is, in us, and will be in existence after us; something which is not restrained, but embraces everything, and in which everything is epitomized; something which is not precarious, which can not be suspended by anything or anybody, can not be divided or destroyed, the extent or duration of which can not be measured by us and which is of supreme force and of supreme majesty."② And here comes the point: "This something is national life. Is the nation sovereign? One need not trouble himself to ask; it lives. Physically everyone lives in the nation. Accordingly, everyone has the right to live there politically, provided he has the means and to the extent that he has the means of so doing in obeying the law."③

It is clear that the idea of national life takes the place of sovereignty. And instead of obeying a sovereign law comes to be the authority of the state. Law and national life are two important elements of the state. "Let us not speak only of national life. Let us speak of legal authority; but with the understanding, of course that this authority has the national life as its perpetual source by which it is perpetually rejuvenated, in which it is continually merged, and from which it derives its ever recurring vigor. Let us speak of these two things togther: national life and legal authority. Neither the idea of life, the idea of law, the idea of order nor the idea of force—none of these are lacking; the legitimate attributes of sovereignty, coercive force, the power of constraining by law, and taxation, will be invested with legitimate authority. As for sovereignty, let us without remorse drop it from our political vocabulary, for time has set about to erase it."④

---

① Charles Benoist. *La Politique*. pp. 41, 42, quoted by Duguit, see *Harvard Law Review*, Vol. XXXI, p. 172.
② Charles Bennist. *Sophismes politiques de ce temps*, p. 161, quoted by Duguit, *ibid.*, p. 174.
③ *Ibid.*, quoted by Duguit, *ibid.*
④ Benoist, *La Politique*, p. 156, quoted by Doguit, *ibid.*, pp. 176-177.

c. Personality of the State

Having outlined the works and precursors of Duguit, we come now to his theory. Generally speaking, the proposition of the orthodox theory is this: Law is the command of sovereignty, and sovereignty is the essential characteristic of the state and the state is regarded as an organic whole having a personality of its own. To Professor Duguit, in order to show that law is not the expression of the will or command of sovereignty, it is necessary to show that the conception of sovereignty is erroneous and therefore not the essential characteristic of the state. In order to show that sovereignty is not the essential characteristic of the state and the conception of sovereignty of the old theorists, it is necessary to show that the state is not a person.

The conception of the personality of the state has been defended by many writers. And it takes many forms. There are those who hold that a state is a moral organism. Thus says Gerber: "The power of the state is the power of willing of a moral organism conceived of as a person. It is not an artificial and mechanical assemblage of several individual willings, but is the collective moral power of the people conscious of itself."① Then there are those who consider the state as a legal person. Thus says Jellinek: "The theoretical foundation of the legal conception of the state is the indubitable natural and historical reality of a people dominated by a power established in a definite territory… Personality is the capacity of being owner of rights—in a word, legal capacity. It does not belong to the world of things-in-themselves; it is not a reality, but a relationship of one subject to another, relationship of legal order…Personality is not the foundation, but the result of the legal community…The conception of personality of the state is confirmed by the fact that it alone can give a satisfactory explanation, from a legal point of view, of the manifestations of public law. It alone made it possible to conceive of international law in legal terms."②

All these doctrines, according to Professor Duguit, are merely hypotheses and fictions③—The "state person" has no more real existence than any other such abstract concept; all alike are qualified by what he calls the inanimity of the doctrines, whatever they may be, which wish to give a philosophical justification of political might. The truth is that political power is a fact which has in itself no character of legitimacy or

---

① *Die Grandbegriffs des deutschens*, p. 218, quoted by Duguit, *L'Etat Objectif et La Loi Positive*, p. 3. See also *Modern French Legal Philosophy*, p. 239.

② Jellinet. *System der offenntlichen subjectirvan Rechte*. pp. 20, 26, 27, 32, quoted by Duguit, in his *L'Etat, Le Droit Objectif et La Loi Positive*, pp. 3-4. English translation in *modern French Legal Philosophy*, p. 240.

③ Duguit. *L'Etat, Le Droit Objectif et La Loi Positive*, p. 5.

illegitimacy. It is the product of social evolution.① Only the individual man is a person.② There is no such a thing as personality of the state. Only the individual has a will, there is no such thing as collective will. The national conciousness is only a fiction, This being the case, the state as such has no reality apart from the individuals who compose it, and is not therefore endowed with personality.③

It is true that sometimes certain men have the same idea and wish, but that does not make a will or a consciousness. Even if we take for granted that all persons in a given group think and wish exactly the same thing and the same way, there will not result a will or a consciousness distinct from those of the individuals. Here Professor Duguit follows Durkheim very closely.

The state moreover is not a legal person. It can not be said that the state is a person, because the law has attributed to it the quality of personality and the state can only make law when it is considered as a person and therefore the personality of the state can not arise from the law.④

"Can it be shown," asks Duguit, "that public law is possible if the state is a person?"⑤ The defenders of the personality of the state maintain that in order to have a public law, there must be a subjective public right, and the state as a person possesses this subjective right. The idea of subjective right is a priori. But as a matter of fact, this subjective right really does not exist. Even Jellinek himself, Professor Duguit points out, recognizes that there is nothing behind what is called the organ or organs of the state. There is nothing but the organs and what is meant by organs are no more than the individuals who impose their wills on other individuals with the sanction of material coercion.⑥

d. State and Government

Having denied the personality of the state, what then is the state? Here we come to the constructive side of his theory. The state, says Professor Duguit, is only the manifestation of a force and it may be defined as "the man or the group of men who in fact in a given society are materially stronger than the others, or as the simple fact of the

---

① *Manuel de Droit Constitutionel*, 3rd ed., p. 23.
② Duguit, *L'Etat, Les Gouvernants et Les Agents*, p. 27.
③ Duguit, *L'Etat, Le Droit Ohjecif et La Loi Positive*, p. 242.
④ Duguit, *L'Etat, Les Goueruants et Les Agents*, p. 79.
⑤ Dougit, *L'Etat, Le Objectif et La Loi Positive*, p. 7.
⑥ *Ibid.*, pp. 7-8.

differentiation between the governor and the governed."①

The definition of the state so given has been explained by a student on political science as follows: "His definition of a state leaves no room for such a distinction, for the state is found wherever there is a differentiation between governors and governed, without regard to whether the governors are themselves subject to a higher power. This would make real states of Canada and the so-called states of the American Union, not to speak of less important communities."② And, in the language of Professor Laski, "for Duguit, the state is no more than a group of men between whom, through a variety of historical cirumstances, a differentiation between rulers and subjects has been introduced."③

The state so defined and so viewed is partially identified with government. A state is a combination of the governed and the governors, while a government on the other hand, is defined as the class or body which monopolizes the forces in a given society.④

e. Sovereignty

In his *Elements de Droit Constitutional*, Professor Esmein writes: "The state is the legal personification of a nation: it is the subject and the basis of public authority…This authority, which naturally recognizes neither a superior nor a competing power in the field it rules, is called soverignty…The ideal and permanent subject of possessor of this sovereignty, which personifies the whole—this moral person, is the state which is thus identified with sovereignty, its essential quality."⑤⑥

That the moral person which possesses the sovereignty, personifies the whole nation is the very idea that Professor Duguit strongly denies. "With rare exceptions there was no class or party in the nineteenth century which did not accept national sovereignty as religious dogma."⑦ He recognizes that it would be fruitless and futile to attack the theory of the sovereignty of nation if this theory can adapt itself to the facts of present. But this

---

① Dougit, *L'Etat, Le Objectif et La Loi Positive*, pp. 261, 350, 519. Cf. N. Wilde, "the Attack on the State," *Journal of International Ethics*, Vol. XXX, (1919–1920), p. 352.

② Mathews, "A Recent Political Theory," *Political Science Quarterly*, Vol. XXI, p. 289.

③ *Harvard Law Review*, Vol. XXXI, pp. 189–198. Also, *Law in Modern State*, trans. by Laski, Introduction.

④ Duguit, *L'Etat, Le Droit Objectif et La Loi Positive*, p. 311. Prof. Mathews seems only partially right when he says that Duguit makes no distinction between government and the state. *Ibid.*, pp. 290–291.

⑤ Duguit, *Lee Transformations du Droit Public*, p. 16, Laski's trans. under the title, *Law in the Modern State*, p. 15.

⑥ Duguit, *Ibid.*, p. 19. Laski, *ibid.*, p. 18.

⑦ Esmein, *Elements de Droit Constitutionnel*, p. 1, quoted by Duguit.

not the case, because "everything goes to show that it is in flagrant contradiction with the social and political changes that we are witnessing, and with the disappearance of its efficacy, it has become even harmful."①

The essential principles involved in the notion of national sovereignty are that (1) it implies an exact correspondence which in fact is often non-existent between state and nation; and (2) it is by definition one and indivisible; it implies the suppression in the national territory of all groups exercising independent control. ②

But such principles are no longer consistent with facts; for facts have shown in the first place, at the present time, that the state and nation are no longer coincident with each other. Sometimes, one government controls a few groups each of which is distinctly and undoubtedly another nation. These nations are, in many cases, in conflict with one another. This is (rather was) the case of the Austrian Empire. No one can say that the will of the Austrian state is one and indivisible and none can say that it is the Austrian nation in its political aspect. So it is in the case of the British Empire in spite of the fact that there is an English people. The United Kingdom is undoubtedly a state, but it is not a nation. ③

Moreover, there are men who are considered as the subjects of a government or a state yet they are not members of its constituent nation. This is true in the case of the inhabitants of colonies of different states. Professor Duguit can not see how this fact can be consistent with the theory of national sovereignty which implies that public power can be exacted only over the members of the nation which creates it. ④

Secondly, the contention that sovereignty, being inherent to the nation is one and indivisible and that no group within the same territory can exercise or share the sovereignty of the nation except one, is again inconsistent with actual practice. This is to be found in the tendency toward dencentralization and federalism. ⑤ Even in France, the tendency is very obvious. The French Commune holds real rights of sovereignty, such as police power, the power of taxation, and the privilege of eminent domain. ⑥

But this is not all. Still other facts may be mentioned, in order to show that the notion of sovereignty is on the way to eclipse. The principle of majority rule is intimately connected with the ideal of national sovereignty. But this principle is no longer

---

① Duguit, *opit. cit*. p. 19. Laski, *opit. cit*. p. 18.
② Duguit, *opit. cit*. p. 19. Laski, *opit. cit*. p. 18.
③ *Ibid*., pp. 19-20. Laski, pp. 18-20.
④ *Ibid*., p. 20.
⑤ *Ibid*. For his notion of federalism, see above. Chapter Ⅲ.
⑥ *Ibid*., pp. 20 ff.

fundamental in modern democracy.① Moreover, according to the old theory of sovereignty, a sovereign can not be sued. But such a contention falls to ground as not supported by the facts. Furthermore, the old theory is doomed to fall, because those who exercise the sovereign power of the state can not do some things as they wish to do, and on the other hand they must do some things which they do not like. This means there is a limitation upon sovereignty as opposed to the old idea that sovereignty is illimitable.

All these facts induce us to believe that the old notion of sovereignty has been eclipsed. And the eclipse of sovereignty certainly changes the notion of sovereignty in its relation to law. Let us now pass to the consideration of law.

f. Law

The relation of sovereignty and law as it is held by the old theorists is, as Seydel says, that there is no law without a sovereign; law exists through the sovereign. On the contrary, Professor Duguit says, "We think the law exists without the sovereign and above the Sovereign. We believe firmly that there is a rule of law above individual and the state, above the rulers and the ruled; a rule which is compulsory on one and on the other; and we hold that if there is such a thing as a sovereignty of the state, it is jurisdically limited by this rule of law."②

If law is not the emanation of sovereignty, where comes the law? Is it based on the natural right of the individual? No, says Professor Duguit. But why? Because the right of the individual is only a hypothesis, a metaphysical affirmation, not a reality.③ The natural right of the individual implies the idea that a society is formed by social contract; but the theory of social compact is nothing more than a phantom. The idea of contract can not come into men's mind until they live in a society. "Thus contract is born of society, not society of contract."④

But to deny the natural right of the individual as the basis of law does not mean that "the doctrine of natural rights of individuals did not appear at the proper time and did not render a great service." For it is this doctrine which declared that the sovereignty of the state is limited by law. This is the honor of French Revolution and such it will remain forever.⑤

---

① Duguit, *opit. cit.* pp. 35–36.
② Duguit, *L'Etat, Le Droit Objectif at La Loi Positive*, pp. 11–12. *Modern French Legal Philosophy*, p. 247.
③ *Ibid.*, p. 12.
④ *Ibid.*, p. 13.
⑤ *Ibid.*, p. 14.

But what is law and what is the basis of law? "Law", says Professor Duguit, "is not a power of the community any more than it is a power of the individual."① It is objective. In short, it is a rule of fact②—the fact of social solidarity.

g. Social solidarity—the basis of law

Men, according to Professor Duguit, are social animals. Being social animals, they must live in society and can live only in society. To Professor Duguit, the notion of the state of nature advanced by a group of writers, such as Hobbes, Locke and Rousseau, is only a fiction. ③ Society is not a product of human will. It begins as men begin. To live in society is not a matter of choice but of necessity. "We do not say society exists because man wants to live in society. Men have always lived and can only live in that manner."④ While holding that men are social animals, it does not follow that human society can exist without men. There will be no human society if there is no man. Men and society thus become a thing with two phases.

Being a man and being a social animal, he wishes and wants something as his fellow-men wish and want. And because they have the same wants and thoughts, they are able to live together and form a social bond. Every man wants to get as much happiness as possible and to avoid sufferings as much as he can. But one can only suffer less if he lives in a community, because it is only by living with other men that he knows that he suffers and wants to suffer less. ⑤ Having realized that he can not live in isolation, he realizes the value of living together. It is by this way that social solidarity increases. This is what is called solidarity through similitude.

But not all men in a given society think in the same way or want the same thing in all cases. But the differences between men in thinking or in wants do not tend to weaken the social bond. On the contrary, they tend to strengthen it. Only because men do not think and want and act in the same way, division of labor is possible. While division of labor gives rise to interdependence of one upon another, interdependence of one upon another binds men together in society.

When man thinks that his needs, thoughts and wills are different from others, he is conscious of his individuality. But his individuality is not an individuality that he possssses by nature, but an individuality with reference to other men. Thus he is not an

---

① Duguit, *L'Etat, Le Droit Objectif at La Loi Positive*, p. 16.
② *Ibid.*
③ *Ibid.*, p. 37.
④ *Ibid.*
⑤ *Ibid.*, p. 31.

individual because he is born to be so, but an individual as a social being. The more he thinks of himself, the more he will think of society. The more one desires and needs and the more he tries to do what he desires in order to meet his needs, the higher the society will be. The progress of civilization means the increase of division of labor. Civilization, says Professor Duguit, is nothing more than the accentuation of dissimilarities between individuals. ①

There are two processes working all the time in society; one is socialization and the other individualization. Socialization increases in direct proportion to division of labor and division of labor increases in direct proportion to individualization. ② Both of these processes are not contrary to each other, but the existence of one needs the help of the other. Division of labor, then, as a criterion for both socialization and individualization, is a means by which social solidarity takes place. This is what Durkheim calls solidarity through division of labor. ③

From what has been said, we come to the following conclusion: "In every grouping two elements constitute the social bond; two elements that may appear in infinitely variable forms, but the basis of which, reduced to its simplest terms is always the same. They are (1) the similarity of needs, which is the basis of solidarity either through mechanical interdependence or through similitude; (2) the difference in needs and in aptitudes which produces and makes necessary an exchange of services, and which found solidarity either by organic interdependence or by division of labor. "④

And Professor Duguit adds: "Thence is derived the following formula for the jural principle (la regle de droit) imposing itself on all the individuals of a social group, both great and small, both strong and weak, as well as the governing and the governed: Do nothing which can possibly infringe upon social interdependence, either through similitude or through division of labor; do all that is within your power, within your given situation and within your aptitudes, to insure and increase social interdependence both by similitude and by division of labor. "⑤

---

① Duguit, *L'Etat, Le Droit Objectif at La Loi Positive*, p. 43.

② *Ibid.*, p. 48.

③ *Ibid.*

④ Duguit, "The Law and the State," *Harvard Law Review*, Vol. XXXI, p. 178. "We do not say that man ought to cooperate in social solidarity because that cooperation is good itself, but that man ought to cooperate in social solidarity because he is a man, and because as such he can not live except by solidarity. We do not say that the act of cooperation in solidarity is good; we say, the act of cooperation has a social consequence." *Droit Constitutionnel*, p. 16.

⑤ *Ibid.*

h. Test and General Characteristics of Law

The test of law then is social solidarity. It will be called law if it is based on social solidarity. ① The law, as a product of social solidarity is modeled on this solidarity; "It appears with the same characteristics. Like solidarity, it includes the whole man; like solidarity, again, it is at the same time individual and social."② It is social, because it can only exist so long as men live in society. Since men have always lived and will live in society, the law has always existed and will exist. It is individual because in the first place it can only be a concept of individuals and in the second place it applies only to individuals. Because it is individual, it is diversified in its application. It is diversified in its application, because men are different in need, want and aptitudes. The greater the differentiation of the individuals, the more the diversity of the rule.

Law, moreover, applies to all individuals without regard to whether they are strong or weak. It requires every one to do everything in order to increase solidarity and to do nothing which may injure social solidarity. The stronger the individuals, the more they can do for the increase of solidarity by using their force. And only as it is so used are they acting legitimately in accordance with law. But to use force for making the law effective does not mean the law is based on force, for force is only a means. On the contrary, it means it is an obligation for the stronger to use their power at the service of the law. ③

Furthermore, law is both permanent and changing. It is permanent because it is the same in its content. "Every society is a solidarity. Every rule of conduct (law) for men living in society commands cooperation in this solidarity, all social relation of similarity or of division of labor, hence the rule of conduct and its general content are permanent."④ It is changing, because the forms of solidarity are various. Thus, there is a family, there is a clan, there is a horde, tribe, and nation, and what not. The difference in forms is revealed in time as well as in space. Since the basis of law is social solidarity, the change of the forms of social solidarity certainly brings the change in the forms of law. It changes as civilization changes. In a word, it changes as conditions change.

It is obvious then that the evolution of law corresponds to the evolution of social solidarity. "This rule is social in foundation, individual in application and in concept,

---

① Duguit, *L'Etat, Le Droit Objectif et La Loi Positive*, p. 105.
② *Ibid.*, p. 91.
③ *Ibid.*, p. 98.
④ *Ibid.*, pp. 98–99.

diversified because it is individual, general because it is social, permanent in principle, infinitely changing in application."①

i. Definition of law

Having considered the basis, test and the general characteristic of law, let us quote his definition of law as the conclusion of what has been said and as a starting point for our further discussion. Law is defined as "a rule of conduct in perpetual evolution, resulting from the continually changing forms of the social solidarity, and varying constantly to time and place."②

Thus we come back to the place where we start: Law is not the command of sovereignty; sovereignty is not the essential characteristic of the state and the state is not a person. But Professor Duguit does not stop here. Law, as so defined, is the law objective which is contrary to the so-called subjective law which is regarded as the command of sovereignty. "Neither has the state a subjective right to command", he declares, "nor have the individuals subjective rights of liberty and of property; but all, governing and governed, are submitted to the jural principle, founded on social interdependence; and by the application of this jural principle all individual wills—the will those who govern as well as the wills of those who are governed—find themselves placed in a certain situation which we call an objective or legal situation, implying in a general way the obligation upon everyone to co-operate according to his position in the maintenance of social solidarity in either of its two forms, and to do nothing which constitutes an interference with it."③

To submit to the law which is founded on social solidarity is to increase the social solidarity. Thus law is not only a product of social solidarity, but also a means for furthering social solidarity. The activity which is in conformity to the law for furthering or increasing the social solidarity is public service. The term "public service" is to the system of Professor Duguit what the term "general will" is to the conception of Rousseau. Before closing our discussion on Duguit, let us examine what is meant by public service.

j. Public Service

Professor Duguit tells us that the notion of public service itself is not a new notion. It is an old idea, as old as public service. The idea, according to Professor Duguit, was born as soon as the distinction between rulers and subjects was established. While the

---

① Duguit, *L'Etat, Le Droit Objectif et La Loi Positive*, p. 100.
② *Ibid.*, p. 428.
③ Duguit, "The law and the State," *Harvard Law Review*, Vol. XXXI, pp. 182-183.

notion of public service itself is not new, it is, however, new in the field of law. It seems to Professor Duguit, that it is a great service to introduce this idea to modern public law. Repeatedly, Professor Duguit tells us that the notion of public service comes to replace that of sovereignty. The latter rests on a subjective right to rule, a right which finds its justification in a metaphysical or theological basis. On the other hand, the former rests on the facts or knowable facts, i. e. , social solidarity. It is a means by which the governed as well as the governing must and can only use for the end it serves. Thus a law is not a law of a sovereign, but a law for public service.

Public service is defined in this manner: " Any activity that has to be governmentally regulated and controlled because it is indispensable to the realization and development of social solidarity is a public service so long as it is of such a nature that it can not be assured save by governmental intervention. "[1]

Governmental activities may increase as times go on, and history shows they did and do increase. But the increase of the activities does not mean the increase of powers. On the contrary, it means the increase of duties and obligation, and those who are entrusted with them are no longer masters of men imposing the sovereign will on their subjects and can no longer issue commands. "They are simply the managers of the nation's business. Their business increase, and their duties expand; but their right of control is extinct because no one any longer believes in it. "[2]

No definite rule can be laid down as to the nature and extent of public service. In the past it has been said that national defense, the maintenance of internal security and order and justice are public functions, or public services, but at present these are not sufficient. There are thinkers in our age who still maintain that what belong to a government are no more than those just enumerated, but facts have overcome such contentions; and when the modern minds come to realize these facts, their attitudes will change in consequence.

The fact is that the economic changes in recent years have created new governmental duties, and therefore increased its activities. This tendency is not only obvious in one country or in the countries in Europe alone, but over the whole world. No one can say that the public services tomorrow will be the same as they are today; for the reason that "the content of public services is always varying and in a state of flux"[3]. " It is even difficult to define the general direction of such change. All that can be said

---

[1] Duguit, *Les Transformations du Droit Public*, p. 51. Laski's trans. , p. 48.
[2] *Ibid.* , p. 55. Liski, p. 51.
[3] *Ibid.* , p. 47.

is that with the development of civilization the number of activities related to public need grows and as a consequence the number of public services grows also. That is logical enough. Indeed, civilization itself is simply the growth of all kinds of needs that can be satisfied in the least time. As a consequence, governmental intervention becomes normally more frequent with the growth of civilization simply because government alone can make civilization a thing of meaning."①

Having briefly outlined Professor Duguit's conception of public service, let us conclude by quoting a passage which Professor Duguit has repeatedly stated: "The principle underlying the whole system of modern public law may be summarized in the following proposition: Those who in fact hold the power do not have a subjective right of public power; but they are under the obligation to employ their power to organize public service, to assure and to control its development. None of their acts are of binding force or of political value, except when they tend toward this end. Public law is no longer a collection of principles to be applied to subjects of rights of different kinds—the one superior, the other subordinate; the one having the right to command, the other the right to obey. All wills are individual wills; all are equivalent in value; there is no hicrarchy of wills. All wills are equal if one considers the subject only. Their value can be determined only by the end which they pursue. The will of those who govern has no force as such, it has value and force only to the extent that it makes for the organization and the functioning of a public service. Thus, the notion of public service comes to replace that of sovereignty. The state is no longer a sovereign power which commands; it is a group of individuals having in their control forces which they must employ to create and to manage public service. The notion of public service becomes, therefore, the fundamental notion of modern public law."②

6. Krabbe

a. Works

Two important works have been written by Professor Krabbe: (1) *Die Lehre der Rechtssouveranitat* (1906); (2) *Die Moderne Staatsidee* (1919). The former, as has been remarked, is largely a critical and historical analysis of the conception of the state and of its relation to law.③ The latter is intended to explain the constructive side of his theory. The latter has been translated into English by Professors Sabine and Shepard and

---

① Duguit, *Les Transformations du Droit Public*, English translation. Laski, *ibid.*, p. 45.

② Duguit, "The Law and the State," *Harvard Law Review*, Vol. XXXI, 1917, pp. 184–185. See also *Les Transformations du Droit Public*, XXIII–XIX.

③ Krabbe, *The Modern Idea of the State*, trans. by Sabine and Shepard Translators' Introduction, p. XV.

Professor Willoughby has aptly remarked that the translators have increased its value by adding an extended and luminous note of introduction. ①

b. The Theory of Sovereignty of Law in History

Professor Krabbe designate his own theory as "the theory of sovereignty of law." It has been pointed out that this theory may be traced back to the time of Ancient Greece. Thus Professor Barker, a well-known student of political philosophy, says, "To the Greeks, law was the inherited substance of sanctions, both moral and legal which stood sovereign over a society."② According to Professor Barker, only Plato, in his "Republic" parts with this idea; yet the sovereignty of law is the fundamental principle of his "Law". ③

Professor Krabbe himself points out that, in a certain sense, Althusius may be called the father of this doctrine. To Althusius, there is no different foundation between the authority of sovereignty and that of law, for the former is rooted in the latter. But on the other hand, Althusius also speaks of a contract between the community and the sovereign. It is in this respect that Professor Krabbe differs from him. "Thus," says Professor Krabbe, "if Althusius had been more clearly conscious of the importance attaching to the social contract in his political theory, he might be called the father of the theory of the sovereignty of law, though with the reservation that the fiction of a social contract is no longer required as a basis for this sovereignty."④

In a sense, Grotius may by also regarded as a forerunner of this doctrine, but it was less clearly perceived by Grotius than Althusius. ⑤ And if the theory of Rousseau is not emphasized on the notion of social contract as it is commonly understood, the "modern idea of the state" may also be found in his system, for he too recognizes the community as the central fact and once one recognizes this fact, one arrives naturally at the basis of the state's authority, namely the law. ⑥ To Professor Krabbe, Rousseau confuses the authority of law and that of the sovereign, and thus unites ideas both old and new.

---

① Willoughby, "The Juristic Theories of Krabbe," in *The American Political Science Review*, Vol. XX, 1926, p. 509, note.

② Barker, *Greek Political Theory: Plato and His Predecessors*, p. 39.

③ *Ibid.*, pp. 39, 205. "Law is thus the common spiritual substance in concrete form, and as such it is the cohesive force and the sovereign of a society." *Ibid.*, p. 38, footnote. See Krabbe, *Die Moderne Staats-Idee*, p. 15. Dunning, *Political Theories*, I, p. 71.

④ Krabbe, *Modern Idea of the State*, p. 19. The English here and hereafter used are the translators. Original text, pp. 19-20.

⑤ *Ibid.*, pp. 19-21, Original Text, pp. 20-23.

⑥ *Ibid.*, pp. 28-30, O. T., pp. 30-32.

The reason for the confusion made by the earlier writers as to the authority of law and that of the sovereign is due to the actual conditions under which they lived. But if conditions or actual practice gave rise to the confusion, the confusion may be removed as conditions change. This change has taken place as constitutionalism has become widely spread. Contrary to the old historical sovereignty which was placed in the hands of the king, there comes a representative assembly composed of delegates of the people. At first this newly elected organ is considered as a coordinated organ of the governmental organs in order to prevent the abuse of or as a limitation on, the sovereignty of the king, and this practice is justified by the theory of separation of powers. But with the increase of the power of law-making together with the extension of legislation in different fields of human activities in recent years, the authority of law has gradually come to replace that of the sovereign.[1]

But constitutionalism is by no means fully realized. There are states where law is not actually in force and there are states where sovereignty is still independent of the law and even if we take for granted that the law has been well enforced, it still needs to be idealized. In other words, after the realization of the sovereignty of law, the improvement of the content of law should be taken into consideration. Viewed from this aspect, the theory of sovereignty of law may be considered as a description of the existing condition or as a principle that needs to be realized.[2]

c. The basis of law

Law itself is sovereign. But what is the basis of the binding force of law, or when can law be actually enforced? It is not, to Professor Krabbe, to be found in the will of God, nor in the will of a human sovereign, as it used to be held by the old theorists, but in the spiritual life of man, and specifically in that part of this spiritual life which operates in us as a feeling or sense of right,[3] (Rechtsbewusstsein).

d. Criticism of the theory of will

In order to have a clear idea of what is meant by the feeling or sense of right, it is desirable to point out the defect or defects of the notion of will as the binding authority of law. The theory of will as the basis of law takes two forms: one is that the authority is derived from the wills of the individuals subject to the law and the other is the will of a

---

[1] It is remarked that the supplanting of the authority of the sovereign by the authority of law is only a regain of what has been lost during the long period in history, for it has been pointed out that in practice as well as in theory it may be traced back to the past. Krabbe, *Modern Idea of the State*, p. 36. O. T., p. 38.

[2] *Ibid.*, p. 40. O. T., p. 37. O. T., p. 39.

[3] *Ibid.*, p. 41. O. T., pp. 43-44.

ruler who is regarded as sovereign. ① According to the former, the basis of law is to be found in man; and according to the latter, it is to be found outside of man either in God or inherent in nature along with the community. ② The former is erroneous, because the purpose of law is to control human will and therefore can not derive its binding force from that will. ③ The latter is wrong, because to assert that a sovereign is endowed with a subjective right to command whatever he pleases is apart from reality. ④

e. Feeling or sense of right

Having shown the untenableness of the theory of will as the basis of the authority of law, let us consider the idea of the feeling or sense of right. The first question that is to be asked is: what is the sense of right? "The sense of right," says Professor Krabbe, "is a universal human impulse which calls forth a specific reaction with respect to our own behavior and that of other men."⑤ The rules, originating from this reaction, are rules of right or law. There is no other source of law except the sense of right "which resides in man and has a place in his conscious life, like all the other tendencies that give rise to judgments of value."⑥ It is upon that that all law, be it positive, customary, or unwritten is based. ⑦ The sense of right, moreover, "is understood to mean the idea of justice, manifesting itself in statutes or ordinances, in custom or in unwritten law, directly applied to the solution of concrete conflicts of interests."⑧ Here, it may be pointed out, we come to an important point in Professor Krabbe's system, namely both morality and law have their common sources in the process of evaluating interests as the sense of right. ⑨

f. Further consideration of the sense of right

Going a step further, it is found that the strength of the feeling or sense of right is not merely to be regarded as the foundation of law, but it has demonstrated itself in many instances. It is the strength of the feeling or sense of right that produces the rise of rebellion and revolution. It is that which overthrows dynasties one after another. It is that which changes monarchy to democracy and modifies constitutions and statutes. It is

---

① Krabbe, *Modern Idea of the State*.
② *Ibid.*, p. 43. O. T., p. 46.
③ *Ibid.*, p. 44. O. T., p. 47.
④ *Ibid.*
⑤ *Ibid.*, p. 46. O. T., p. 49.
⑥ *Ibid.*, p. 47. O. T., p. 50.
⑦ *Ibid.*
⑧ *Ibid.*, p. 50. O. T., p. 54.
⑨ *Ibid.*, LXXIII.

like a thunderstorm that purifies a tained political atmosphere.①

g. Misunderstandings of the notion of sense of right

In order to reveal the truth of the notion of the sense of right, it may be approached from the negative side as well as from the positive side. For this reason, it is desirable to point out and to correct some of the misunderstandings of this doctrine.

In the first place, it is said that the sense of right lacks the normative character, for no one will be bound by his own feeling or sense of right and therefore it possesses no compulsion to action and judgment. To this it is replied that we are under the obligation to judge, think and act in accordance with some of the feelings which make up the content of our consciousness which are intrinsically normative in character, The sense of right involves, as has been pointed out, the idea of justice which is not "merely a matter for contemplation, but, as is shown by our common experience, is something that actuates what we do and forbear with obligatory force."②

Secondly, it is argued that the command given by the sovereign as has been maintained by the old theorists has retained its legal force and that the sovereignty of law is no more than the command of the sovereignty. But this again, as Professor Krabbe maintains, is not based on a solid foundation, for what has been accepted as law for centuries is not recognized as law at present. The so-called command of sovereignty has been and is superseded by the statutory law and new law has come as a result of new conditions. The difference between the two theories is obvious. In the one, the basis of law is in our spiritual life while in the other it is in a sovereign endowed with original authority or a natural subjection of the people to such a sovereign. The historical legal title of a sovereign has come to an end. To maintain it as the authority behind law is to say something contrary to fact.③

Thirdly, the new theory is criticized on the ground that it makes law lack the character of stability. The fallacy of this criticism, says Professor Krabbe, is that it ignores the fact that law, in its content, has a changeable value and "one can not ask that that should be immutable which by nature lacks fixity."④ "Stability of 'law' is a contradiction."⑤ Only the law which is issued by the "legal pope" has the character of absolute stability. "When one asks for 'stability' in a rule regardless of its content as a

---

① Krabbe, *Modern Idea of the State*, pp. 52 ff., O. T., pp. 57 ff.
② *Ibid.*, p. 55. O. T., p. 61.
③ *Ibid.*, pp. 56–61. O. T., pp. 61–67.
④ *Ibid.*, p. 61. O. T., p. 68.
⑤ *Ibid.*

principle of right, one is demanding something that can be secured only at the cost of its legal character."①

Fourthly, the theory of the sense of right is assaulted on the ground that it is "one-side because it deals with right, while the factor of force must also be taken into account."② To this, it is replied that "our theory in no way denies this. It merely denies, that in the light of the existing notions of law and of the state, there ought to be a place for a sovereign exercising authority in the enforcement of executions and the infliction of punishment, and in relation to whom the people are in a state of subjection, while at the same time there is another kind of subjection established by law."③

Thus the hypothesis of the old theory contains a dualism of power; that of the state and that of law.④ One denies the dualism, not simply because it is dualism, but "because it is now perceived that a natural relation of subjection to a sovereign is nothing but a fiction, because the conception of sovereignty is merely a logical construction which does not correspond to reality, because the basis of sovereign authority can nowhere be pointed out, and because a duty to without obey, which society would fall to pieces, can not be derived in this way from actual facts nor indeed be accepted as an hypothesis."⑤

Here we see the keynote of Professor Krabbe's work. Negatively, he sees that the old conception of sovereignty is contradictory to the actual fact, and that it is no more than a fiction. Constructively, he endeavors to show that if there is such a thing as sovereignty, it is only the sovereignty of law.⑥ Law is no longer the expression of the will of the sovereign, but the sense or feeling of right. The sense of right of men is not only the source of law, but it is also the obligatory force which makes law observed. ⑦

h. Sense of right and interest—source and subject matter of law

It has been already pointed out that by sense of right is meant the idea of justice directly applied to the solution of concrete conflicts of interests. It is clear that the basis of law is the sense of right, and the subject matter of law is interests. Here we see the necessity and the justification of the authority of law. The interests of one may be different from that of others, and the interests may conflict with one another in a

---

① Krabbe, *Modern Idea of the State*, p. 63. O. T., p. 70.
② *Ibid.*, pp. 63-64. O. T., p. 70.
③ *Ibid.*, p. 65. O. T., p. 72.
④ *Ibid.*, pp. 1-2. O. T., pp. 1-2.
⑤ *Ibid.*, p. 65. O. T., p. 72.
⑥ *Ibid.*, pp. 1-2. O. T., pp. 1-2.
⑦ *Ibid.*, pp. 68-69. O. T., p. 76.

community. The purpose of law is to adjust the conflicts of interests. But how can a law be based upon the sense of right and for the purpose of adjusting the conflicts of interests be secured? In order to answer this question, it is necessary to examine: (1) the unity of the sense of right and (2) the quality of the sense of right.

i. Unity of the sense of right—majority rule

The unity of purpose in a given community postulates the unity of the legal rule. It is therefore a desirable thing that the law or rule adopted will be supported by the sense of right of all the members of the community. But only in rare cases can this happen, and the only way for having a single rule which will bind all the members of the community is the rule which is approved by the sense of right of the majority. The rule so adopted is to be considered the best rule, "because the fact that it is accepted by the majority shows that it possesses a higher value than any other rule."① Here it is said that Professor Krabbe does not go beyond the circle of Rousseau.② The sense of right is the sense of the majority and the law which is based on the sense of right and which is regarded as sovereign is only the law of the majority.

j. Quality of the sense of right

The quality of the sense of right is the criterion by which we determine who is entitled to have a share in law-making. Youth and insanity will be excluded from taking part in law-making, because their natural qualities interfere with the operation of the sense of right.③ But exclusion must not be made of those who are poor, "for this would give effect to those derangements of the sense of right produced by the interests of the propertied class but not to those produced by the interests of persons who have no property. Legislation ought, however, to give equal weight to the interests of both classes."④

But to let every normal person have a share in law-making, "does not mean that every one ought to pass judgment on the legal value of 'all' the interests of the community."⑤ "A 'knowledge' of the interests involved is also needed. The sense of right can not be required to pass judgment upon the legal value of interests which are not present to consciousness or which occupy a very small part of it. The objection which can be brought against the existing legislative organization lies in the fact that men are

---

① Krabbe, *Modern Idea of the State*, p. 69. O. T., p. 77.
② *Ibid.*, p. 78. O. T., p. 87. See also Willoughby, "The Juristi Theories of Krabbe," *Political Science Review*, Vol. XX, p. 513.
③ *Ibid.*, p. 88. O. T., p. 99.
④ *Ibid.*, p. 88. O. T., p. 99.
⑤ *Ibid.*, p. 89. O. T., p. 100.

called upon to legislate for interests that lie beyond their intellectual horizon."① It is obvious now that the sense of right, the basis of law, is qualified by the interest of forming the community.② It is true that law can not be called a law if it is divorced from the sense of right. But it is also true that law can not be divorced from the interest which draws men together to form a community; for law represents an actually achieved evaluation of interests and the valuation of interests is the process of adjusting interests. In short, a law of a community is the law springing from the sense of right for adjusting the interests of having the community.

k. The extent of the sense of right—the extent of law

The extent of the sense of right extends from an individual to the world community. There is a sense of right of an individual; there is a sense of right of a community and there is a sense of right of the world community. The extent of the sense of right corresponds to the extent of law. Thus a rule which arises solely from the sense of right of an individual can only control the will of that individual and can not be applied to a group composed of many individuals. The rule arising solely from a group or community can only control the will of the group or community. Only the sense of right of the world can control the will of whole mankind.

l. The state

A state is defined by Krabbe in this manner: "The portion of mankind included within a community which is based upon such an independently operating sense of right is a state."③ It differs from other communities, for "its sole function consists in defining the legal value of public and private interests."④ One state "differs from another state because of the particular standard of legal value applied in the valuation of interests."⑤ Its reality is based on its control over legal value. Besides imputing legal value to certain interests, the state has no other function whatsoever. "We must insist," declares Professor Krabbe, "that the state is nothing except a legal community, that is, a portion of mankind having its own original legal standard, its own original source of law, and therefore a portion of mankind having its own independent body of legal relations. Hence the state performs no function whatever except to impute legal value to certain interests.

---

① Krabbe, *Modern Idea of the State*, p. 990. Willoughby, "The Juristi Theories of Krabbe," *Political Science Review*, Vol. XX, particularly ch. V.
② Ibid., LXXIV, also p. 209, O. T., p. 236.
③ Ibid., p. 211. O. T., p. 289.
④ Ibid., p. 213. O. T., p. 240.
⑤ Ibid., p. 209. O. T., p. 236. See especially pp. LXXIV ff.

The state can do nothing except to impose the obligation to serve public and private interests."①

m. World Community—international law

As national law is based on the sense of right of the members of the nation, so is international law based on the sense of right of the world. From this premise, it follows that "international law can not be built upon the unreal foundation of the sovereignty of the state."② International law differs from national law "not in respect to its origin and foundation, but in respect to the extent of the community to which its commands apply."③

If international law is not well observed as national law, it is not because "it rules over 'sovereign' states and is therefore rooted in the will of the state", but because it is due to the defective organization of the sense of right which tends to regulate the community of civilized nations."④ It has been remarked that we are still living in the Middle Ages, if we look at the organization of the international community.⑤ Until international law is expressed through a well organized organ of the world sense of right, international law will have the same weight as national law.

International law, as commonly called, is really a misnomer. It is better to speak of it as supernational law,⑥ for international law is in fact international constitutional law.⑦ The day of a supernational law is coming, "for every branch of law is now extending itself more and more into the field of supernational law."⑧ "International law can be elevated to the rank of a real science only when the mordern idea of the state is fully and clearly understood and when, as a result, the idea of sovereignty is discarded and all authority is traced back to the authority of law. In this way, international law, has or can have, the same foundation, the same content, and the same subjects as national law."⑨

n. Conclusion

The theory of the sovereignty of law denies the hypothesis of dualism of powers;

---

① Krabbe, *Modern Idea of the State*, p. 215. O. T., p. 243.
② *Ibid.*, p. 234. O. T., p. 265.
③ *Ibid.*, p. 236. O. T., p. 268.
④ *Ibid.*, p. 236. O. T., p. 268.
⑤ *Ibid.*, p. 237. O. T., p. 268.
⑥ *Ibid.*, p. 245. O. T., p. 278.
⑦ *Ibid.*, p. 246. O. T., p. 279.
⑧ *Ibid.*, p. 747. O. T., p. 280.
⑨ *Ibid.*, p. 248. O. T., p. 281.

namely that of the state and that of law. It insists that sovereignty is not independent, above or outside of law, for law is by nature sovereign[1] and besides law there is no sovereign. But in order to be called law it must receive the approval of the sense of right. By the sense of right is understood not necessarily the sense of right of all the members in a community, but the majority. The purpose of law is to adjust the different interests of the community, so law can not be divorced from the interest of the community. Thus the test of law is two-fold: one is the sense of right, the other is interest. The lack of either one means the lack of the character of law. Both must go hand in hand. The normal sense of right of a man is not necessarily the basis of law if he has no knowledge of the law which is to be adopted. "So the exclusion of such persons from law-making can not be taken as denying that the sense of right is the basis of law."[2]

VII. Conclusion

A general survey of the history of legal philosophy reminds one of the fact that the five schools considered above have by no means exhausted the list of the schools in jurisprudence. But it is safe to say that they are the leading ones and for our purpose they are the most important. The analytical school, with its maxim that law, in order to be called law in its strict sense, must be expressly or tacitly backed by a sovereign and that the chief function of the sovereign is to make law, stands alone on one side of the battle field as against all the others on the other side. The natural law school which in its old sense dominated legal thought from early history to the end of eighteenth century, insisted that sovereignty is limited by the law of nature. The historical school has side by side existed with the analytical school during the last century and even in our own day assaults the analytical dogma by declaring that law is not necessarily the command of a sovereign. Thus the analytical "sovereignty", the chief function of which is to make law, becomes a nonentity in the eyes of the historical jurists.[3] The economic school which views sovereignty as a mouth piece damages it more than if it directly opposed it. The sociological jurists, notably Professor Duguit and Professor Krabbe, make a vigorous attack on the old conception of sovereignty and therefore its relation to law. Although Professor Duguit declares repeatedly that the notion of public service comes to

---

[1] Krabbe, *Modern Idea of the State*, p. 232. O. T., p. 262.
[2] Ibid., p. 51. O. T., p. 56.
[3] The statement must be qualified to a certain extent in the theory of the writers such as Maine.

replace that of sovereignty, he seems to retain it and identifies it with the powers exercised by the ruler or rulers of a community. But in doing this, he places it under the authority of law and divides it into pieces. Professor Krabbe, on the other hand, maintains that law is by nature sovereign and sovereignty is not independent of, nor outside of, nor above, law. Thus to Professor Krabbe, sovereignty is law, and law is sovereignty. As law is different in extent and not in content, so must be sovereignty. From such a premise, the natural conclusion is, that the law of a commune is the sovereign of the commune, the law of a nation is the sovereign of the nation and the law of the world community is the sovereign of the world community.

CHAPTER IX
SOVEREIGNTY AND FUNCTIONAL GROUPS

I. Introduction

According to the so-called classical theory of sovereignty, it is held, generally speaking, that sovereignty is the essential characteristic of the state. The state and the state alone, it is argued, is the possessor of this very authority. That which does not possess sovereignty can not be called a state, and that which is not a state must not have the whole or any part of it. Where there is a state, then there must be sovereignty and only one sovereignty. This being so, it follows that all the groups or associations within the boundary of the state are under the absolute control, and therefore at the mercy, of the state.

The theory so advanced or so held has been and is discredited by many of the recent writers as being contrary to fact. The fact is, they say, that groups or associations, in their origin and existence, are independent of, though not above, the state. They have come and grown in the same way as the state. They maintain, moreover, that human interests are manifold, and interests may bring or rather have brought men to form different groups. Political interest, some say, as expressed through the state is only one form of these manifold interests. If a state can claim authority over its subjects for expressing and promoting political interest, why not a church or trade union claim the same authority for expressing and developing their respective interests? Without going into detailed discussion, we shall present the salient features of some of the most conspicuous representatives of this new movement in the following pages.

II. German Writers

The thinking of jurists has long been dominated by the so-called fiction theory[①]. It has been accepted by German and French writers and it is accepted almost fully by the courts in England and the United States and expressly or tacitly assumed by most of the jurists of these two countries. It is held by its defenders that a corporation may be treated as a person, but it is a person by fiction and only by fiction.[②] "It is capable of proprietary rights; but it is incapable of knowing, intending, willing, acting."[③]

Against this theory, came the realist school. The new movement, says Professor Maitland, began with Besler's criticism of Savigay, and the theory gradually took shape, especially in Dr. Gierke's hand. The works the aim of which is to overthrow the fiction theory and to construct a new one are Professor Gierke's *Genossenschaftrecht* (1868, 1873, 1881, 1913) and *Genossenschaftstheorie* (1887). The former is a treatise on the history of German fellowship law, and the latter, in the language of Professor Figgis, attempted to show how under the facts of modern life the civilian theory of corporations is breaking down on all hands, and that even in Germany, in spite of the deliberate adoption of the Romanist doctrine, the courts and sometimes even the laws are being constantly driven to treat corporate societies as though they were real and not fictitious persons, and to regard such personality as the natural consequence of permanent association, not a mere mark to be imposed or withheld by the sovereign power.[④]

The starting point of Professor Gierke is the individual. The individual or human being, as he conceives, is not merely a means, but an end itself. Being an end itself, all the political, social, religious associations or institutions are the means by which men seek to attain his end. To be a member of the state, one belongs only partly to it; besides the state, there are many organizations to which he belongs and by which his individuality may be realized. Thus he writes, "Human existence is not solved in the life of a species but it is at the same time an end in itself, we must recognize the individual and not the State as a primary essence, existing by itself, and finding its ultimate end in

---

① According to Professor Gierke, it was Innocent IV who first used the phrase "person ficta". On the other hand, H. A. Smith maintained that Innocent IV did not formulate this theory, See his *The Law of Associations*, pp. 152–156.

② CF. Holland, *Jurisprudence*, p. 82. Freund, *Legal Nature of Corporation*, pp. 10–12.

③ Maitland, *Introduction to Gierke's Political Theories of Middle Ages*, p. XX.

④ J. N. Figgis, *Churches in the Modern State*, 1913, pp. 55–56. See also Maitland, *Introduction to Gierke's Political Theories of Middle Ages*, p. XXVI.

itself. Only a part of the individual belongs to the State as a member thereof. The rest of what goes to constitute his being is completely independent of the collective life of the State, and forms the subject matter of his free individuality. The individual being and the being as a member of the State exist like two domains autonomous life beside each other, each one of which can not exist without the other, each finding its complement in the other, but each having, nevertheless, a direct end in itself."①

Although the individual is considered as the primary essence, and although the associations or groups are viewed as the means for attaining the end, the groups are not the products of the individuals, nor are they merely the sum of the individuals taken together. The groups, according to Professor Gierke, are natural products. They come into being just as the individuals are born. As every individual has his will, spirit and consciousness, so has a group. As the group is not merely the sum of the individuals or its members, so the will of the group is not simply the sum of the wills of its members. As has been said the group is an unconscious product, so the will of the group is a result of unconscious social instinct. But man is a social being. And as a social being, he has to live in one form or another of society and he is conscious of himself only as he knows that he is part of a group or groups. This being the case, the content of his will, his spirit, his consciousness are determined partly by the will, the spirit and consciousness of himself and partly by the wills, spirits and consciousness of others. ②

Having a will of its own, a group has a personality. This personality is not merely fiction but as real as the individuality of a physical person. It is not a fiction or artificial creation of the state or the law of the state as a subject of rights and duties as is held by the old jurists. The state or the law of the state "does not create the corporate person, but finding it in existence invests it with a certain legal capacity. The corporation rests upon a substratum of physical persons, but it is not identical with them, for out of the association of individuals the new personality arises, having a distinctive sphere of existence and a will of its own. If corporate rights are distinguished from individual rights it is because they are controlled by this distinctive will. The corporation as a

---

① Gierke, "Die Grundbegriffe des Staatsrechts und die neuesten Staatstheorien," *Zeitschrift fur die gesammte Staatswissenschafte*, Tubingen, 1874, p. 306. See *Harvard Law Review*, Vol. XXI, p. 159.

② Gierke, "Die Grundbegriffe des Staatsrechts und die neuesten Staatstheorien," *Zeitschrift fur die gesammte Staatswissenschafte*, Tubingen, 1874.

person distinct from its members is not a fiction, but a reality"①.

But the state must differ from other groups, otherwise it will not be called a state. And what are the differences? In the first place, the state differs from other groups by reason of being a political form of group life. But this is not the essential difference, for this is no more than to say that a trade union is different from other groups by reason of being an economic group. Secondly, and here is the important point, the State differs from the other groups in that its will is larger in extent than that of the groups which are within it.

The group, having a will and a personality of its own, has naturally an inherent authority or sovereignty of its own. Since will is not different in content, there is no difference in content in regard to sovereignty. Thus to Professor Gierke, sovereignty is not the essential characteristic of the state. It may exist in a group within the state. It is in this respect that Professor Gierke is regarded as one of the forerunners of the pluralistic theory of sovereignty.

But as will may be different in extent, so may be sovereignty. It follows that the state is greater in extent than the groups existing within it. By reason of being greater in extent the state's sovereignty may be superior to that of the groups when the common interests demanding the exercising of power for their existence.② The Leviathan of Hobbes may still be regarded as remaining in this case; but its foundation has been seriously shaken, for it is no longer to be a sacrosanct existing only in the state.

III. English Writers

1. Maitland

Professor H. A. L. Fisher, the editor of the *Collected Papers* of Professor Maitland, speaks of him in these words: "There is no annotation either here or elsewhere on the part of editor, for though much has been written on social or legal history during the last thirty years, it does not in any appreciable degree affect the permanent value of Maitland's work. He wrote little, perhaps nothing, in early manhood which he would

---

① *The Legal Nature of Corporations*, by Ernest Freund, 1897, pp. 13-14. "Our German Fellowship is no fiction, no symbol, no piece of the state's machinery, no collective name for individuals, but a living organism and a real person, with body and members and a will of its own. Itself can will, itself can act; it wills and acts by the men who are its organs as a man wills and acts by brain, mouth, and hand. It is not a fictitious person; it is a 'Gesammtperson', and its will is a 'Gesammtwille'; it is a group person, and its will is a group-will." Maitland, "Introduction to Gierke's *Political Theories of Middle Ages*", p. xxvi.

② Gierke, *ibid*., p. 308.

have cancelled in later years. He was always learned, always original, and in ninety nine cases of a hundred, he was transparently right."[1] And in the language of Professor Figgis, he is considered as "one of the three greatest minds which were occupied about historical matters during the nineteenth century."[2]

Professor Maitland was profoundly influenced by Professor Gierke. This has been repeatedly admitted by himself. To say nothing of the introduction written to the translation of Gierke's *Political Theories of the Middle Ages,* and to say nothing of some of the articles in his *Collected Papers,* we find, one section of the *History of English Law*[3], which in the first edition bore the title Fictitious Persons, was changed both in title and substance after "a repeated perusal of Dr. Gierke's great book, *Das Deutsche Genossenschaftsrecht.*"[4]

Like Gierke, he denies strongly the fiction theory which regards a corporation as a "persona ficta". The corporation, says he, is a person and is a person in fact. It has a personality of its own. It is a right-and-duty-bearing unit. "Not all the legal propositions that are true of man will be true of a corporation. For example, it can neither marry nor be given in marriage; but in a vast number of cases you can make a legal statement about X and Y which will hold good whether these symbols stand for two men or for two corporations, or for a corporation or a man."[5] A university can buy land, hire buildings, or borrow money from another corporation and these acts are treated, from the eyes of law, as if there were transaction between two men. What do we mean by this? It means that the university is a right-and-duty-bearing unit. But this is not all, for a transaction may also take place between a corporation and one of its members or any one outside of it. Thus one can contract with a university or vice versa.

What then is a corporation? It is, according to Professor Maitland, an organized group which has a personality of its own and is not merely a creature of the state or the law of the state. Corporations takes many forms. The Crown is a corporation. "Our sovereign lord is not a 'corporation sole', but is the head of a complex and highly

---

[1] Maitland, *Collected Papers*, editor's preface VIII.

[2] Figgis, *Churches in the Modern State.* Appendix II, "Three Cambridge Historians: Creighton, Maitland, and Acton", p. 227. Also see Justice Holmes' article in *Law Quarterly Review*, XXIII, p. 139 and also his *Collected Papers*.

[3] This work was written by Professor Maitland in collaboration with Professor Pollock. But largely, the work is Maitland's. See the acknowledgement of Pollock, a note below the preface to the first edition. The first edition published in 1895, second 1899.

[4] Maitland and Pollock, *The History of English Law*, Vol. I, p. 486, note.

[5] Maitland, *Collected Papers*, Vol. III, p. 307.

organized 'corporation aggregate of many'—of very many. I see no great harm in calling this corporation a Crown. But a better word has lately returned to the statute book. That word is commonwealth."①

A state in the United States may be regarded as a corporation. Agreeing, though not fully, with Dillon, the following passage was quoted by Professor Maitland: "Each one of the United States in its organized political capacity, although it is not in the proper use of the term a corporation, yet it has many of the essential faculties of a corporation, a distinct name, indefinite succession, private rights, power to sue, and the like. Corporations, however, as the term is used in our jurisprudence, do not include states, but only derivative creations, owing their existence and power to the state, acting through its legislative department. Like corporations, however, a state, as it can make contracts and suffer wrongs, so it may, for this reason and without express provision, maintain in its corporate name actions to enforce its rights and redress its injuries."②

A colony is a corporation. "We deny nowadays that a colony is a corporation—But can we—do we really and not merely in words—avoid an admission that the colony of New Zealand is a person."③ And if the borough is a corporation, and may be spoken of as having rights and duties, as breaking the law and being punished, this is also true of the county, the hundred and the township.④ So a church⑤ or a trade union⑥ may be regarded as a corporation. Even the institution of a trust, which originated in the early day for the protection of property from being taxed has long had a very close connection with corporations. This connection may be traced at least back to four centuries ago.⑦ And at present, hardly a line can be drawn between these two.

It may still be asked what the law of trusts has to do with the law of corporations? But "none the less, a branch of the law of trusts became a supplement to the law of corporations, and some day when English History is adequately written one of the most interesting and curious tales that it will have to tell will be that which brings trust and

---

① Maitland, *Collected Papers*, Vol. III, p. 259.
② Dillon, *Municipal Corporation*, Section 31, quoted by Maitland, *Collected Papers*, Vol. III, p. 266.
③ Maitland, *Collected Papers*, Vol. III, pp. 262–263.
④ Maitland, *The Constitutional History of England*, p. 54.
⑤ Maitland and Pollock, *The History of English Law*, 2nd ed., pp. 486 ff.
⑥ When Lord Balfour declared in the House that trade union is a corporation, a distinguished lawyer on the opposition benches interrupted him with "The trade unions are not corporations", "I know that," retorted Lord Balfour, "I am talking English, not law." Maitland, *Collected Papers*, Vol. III.
⑦ Maitland, *Collected Papers*, Vol. III, p. 395. For the origin of the trust, see *ibid.*, pp. 335 ff.

corporation into intimate connexion with each other."①

Thus the word trust has acquired a new sense in our day. "So nowadays the American 'trust' is almost always if not quite always a corporation."②

Considering that the trust is almost always a corporation, Professor Maitland is led to assert that the trust, like the corporation, has a personality of its own. So he writes: "The device of building a wall of trustees enabled us to construct bodies which were not technically corporations and which yet would be sufficiently protected from the assaults of the individualistic theory. The personality of such bodies—so I should put it—though explicitly denied by lawyers, was on the whole pretty well recognized in practice."③

In short, to Professor Maitland, the jurists may still make the distinction between a corporation and an unincorporated body, but in fact they are almost always one and the same thing. Any organized group which has a will and a personality of its own may be called a corporation. But what has this organized group to do with sovereignty? This is the point we want to know and here it is: "My organized group, says he, shall be a

---

① Maitland, *Collected Papers*, Vol. III, p. 272.

② *Ibid.*, Vol. III, p. 395.

③ And he adds: "That something of this sort happened you might learn from one simple fact. For somtime past we have had upon our statute book the term 'unincorporate body'. Supposed a Frenchman saw it, what would he say?" "Unincorporate body: inanimate soul. No wonder your prime minister, who is a philosopher, finds it hard to talk English and talk law at the same time." *Collected Papers*, Vol. III, p. 317, also see p. 367 "Not content, however, with permeating this region. The trust presses forward until it is imposing itself upon all wielders of political power, upon all the organs of the body politic. Open an English newspaper, and you will be unlucky if you do not see the word 'trustee' applied to the 'Crown' or to some high mighty body. I have just made the experiment, and my lesson for today is, that as the Transvaal has not yet received a representative constitution, the imperial Parliament is 'a trust for the the colony'. There is a metaphor here. Those who speak thus would admit that the trust was not one which any court could enforce, and might say that it was only a 'moral trust'. But I fancy that to a student of Staatswissenschaft legal metaphors should be of great interest, especially when they have become the commonplace of politicial debate. Nor is it always easy to say where metaphors begin. When a statute declared that the Herrschaft which the East India Company had acquired in India was held in 'trust' for the Crown of Great Britain, that was no idle proposition but the settlement of a great dispute. It is only the other day that American judges were saying that the United States acquired the sovereignty from Cuba upon trust for the Cuban." *Ibid.*, Vol. III, p. 403.

Speaking of the personality of the county, he writes: "It does not seem to me that a jurist is entitled to argue that the English county, being unincorporate, and having no juristic personality, can only be a 'passive' Verband, until he has considered whether he would apply the same argument to, let us say, the church of Rome (as seen by English law,) the Wesleyan 'Connexion', Lincoln's Inn, the London Stock Exchange, the London Library, the Jockey Club, and a Trade Union. Also it is to be remembered that making of grand theories is not and never has been our strong point. The theory that lies upon the surface is sometimes a borrowed theory which has never penetrated far. While the really vital principles must be sought for in out-of-the-way places." *Ibid.*, Vol. III, pp. 400-401.

See also Introduction to his translation of Gierke's *Political Theories of the Middle Ages*, p. XXVII.

sovereign state."① And he continues: "Let us call it Nunsquamia. Like many other sovereign states, it owns money."②

But like his master, Professor Maitland does not stop here. The groups having the same character as the state, possess also the high authority, or sovereignty. But the sovereignty of the state is larger in extent than that of the groups existing within it, for the state is a highly peculiar group-unit③.

When Professor Burgess says that the United States acquired her sovereignty during the time of the First Continental Congress, Professor Willoughby tells us that he is going too far. But it seems to Professor Maitland, he does not go far enough, for the sovereignty or rather sovereignties of the United States existed when there were organized groups coming into being. Where there is an organized group, there will be sovereignty. The sovereignty of a group, may exist within the sovereignty of a larger whole, but to exist within it does not mean that it ceases to be a sovereign body. It remains there as long as that group exists.

2. Figgis

As early as 1868, Lord Acton wrote: "The name of Ultramontanes was given in consequence of their advocacy of the freedom of the church against the civil power; but the characteristic of their advocacy was, that they spoke not specially for the interests of religion, but on behalf of a general principle, which, while it asserted freedom for the Church, extended it likewise to other communities and institutions."④

"Now," says Professor Figgis after quoting the passage just quoted above, "it is this recognition of the modern State which I desire to urge today." The view of Professor

---

① Maitland, *Collected Papers*, Vol. Ⅲ, p. 318.

② *Ibid*.

③ Maitland, Introduction to his translation of Gierke's *Political Theories of the Middle Age*, p. ix. "The State that Englishmen knew was a singularly unicellular state and at a critical time they were not too well equipped with tried and traditional thoughts which would meet the case of Ireland or of some communities, commonwealths, corporations in America which seemed to have will—and hardly fictitious wills—of their own, and which became States and United States. The Medieval Empire laboured under the weight of an incongruously simple theory so soon as lawyers were teaching that the Kaiser was the Princeps of Justinian's law-books. The modern and multicellular British State—often and perhaps harmlessly called an Empire—may prosper without a theory, but does not suggest and, were we serious in our talk of sovereignty, would hardly tolerate, a theory that is simple enough and insular enough, and yet withal imperially Roman enough, to deny an essentially statelike character to those 'self-governing colonies,' communities, commonwealths, which are knit and welded into a larger sovereign whole." Maitland, Introduction to his translation of Gierke's *Political Theories of the Middle Ages*, p. ⅹ.

④ See Figgis, *Churches in the Modern State*, pp. 110-112. See also note on page 111. Some passages written by Richard Simpson, on "The Individual, the Corporation, and State," in the *Rambler* for May 1862, were quoted. Cf. Acton, *History of Freedom*, p. 151.

Figgis may be found in his *Churches in the Modern State*, a series of lectures delivered in Gloucester in June 1921. The title and the materials used for illustration are chiefly ecclesiastical, but the principle implied is "concerned not with the details of ecclesiastical privilege or with the special position of Established Church, but with the very nature of the corporate life of men, and therefore with the true nature of state."①

Speaking to the churchmen, or rather giving them a warning, he says: "We cannot eat our cake and have it. We cannot claim liberty for ourselves, while at the same time proposing to deny it to others. If we are to cry 'hand off' to the civil power in regard to such matters as marriage, doctrine, ritual, or the conditions of communion inside the Church—and it is the necessary condition of a free religious society that it should regulate these matters, then we must give up attempting to dictate the policy of the State in regard to the whole mass of its citizens."②

The purpose of the book is more clearly stated in a passage in his Preface: "The author has been led to his present views not by the desire to defend Church rights, but by long brooding over the Austinian doctrine and the perception forced on him at last through Maitland and Gierke, that it is either fallacious or so profoundly inadequate as to have no more than a verbal justification. One begins be thinking Austin self-evident, one learns that many qualifications have to be made, and finally one ends by treating his whole method as abstract and theoretic."③ It is obvious then that negatively Professor Figgis denies the Austinian theory and positively he advocates what Gierke and Maitland have advanced.

According to Professor Figgis, the theory of sovereignty which more or less expressed the facts in the ancient Greek City state was applied to the great empire of Romans. It is recognized by the lawyers in later generations as a maxim that this authority is indivisible, inalienable, and incapable of legal limitation; and that besides the determinate body where it resides, no other real authority exists or should exist within the empire or the state. In the language of M. Emile Combes, one of the greatest statesmen of France, "There are, there can be no rights except the right of the State, and there are, and there can be no other authority than the authority of the Republic."④

This being the case, what Austin has formulated is little more than the theory of

---

① Figgis, *Churches in the Modern State*, pp. 49–50.
② *Ibid.*, pp. 112–113.
③ *Ibid.*, preface, ⅸ–ⅹ.
④ *Ibid.*, p. 56, quoted by Figgis.

sovereignty as advanced and elaborated by the Romans and statesmen or philosophers of the past. ① "The Great Leviathan of Hobbes, the 'plenitudo potesatis' of the canonists, the 'arcana imperii', the sovereignty of Austin, are all names of the same thing—the unlimited and illimitable power of the law-giver in the State, deduced from the notion of its unity."②

What is the natural consequence of such a theory? Here it is: It presumes that there are two social entities: one is the state and the other the individual. The rights or actions of the latter is private and the former public. "The state may be of any kind of structure, monarchic, aristocratic, or purely collectivist; but in all cases there are recognized by the law, no real social entities, no true powers, except the sovereign on the one hand with irresistable authority, and the mass of individuals on the other."③ Besides the individuals and the state, there may be associations—church, trade union, university and the like—but they are simply the creatures of law, the will of the sovereign, and at the mercy of the sovereign. They may be dissolved or modified at the sovereign's pleasure any time.

For the mere matter of convenient imagination on the part of law and in order to give a group the right to act, to hold property, to sue and to be sued, "it is necessary to treat them as what they are not, i. e. as persons; therefore the sovereign power by its own act grants to such bodies as it pleases the name of corporation, and with it endows with a 'fictitious personality'."④ These bodies, it is said, have the right to act as if they were persons, but their rights are merely the delegated rights of the sovereign authority and this is what has been called the concession theory of corporate life. ⑤

But the theory as has been shown above according to Professor Figgis, is contrary to the actual facts of social life. To illustrate this point, we may quote the following passage: "Throughout the education controversy much has been heard against the iniquity of privately managed schools receiving public money, at least in the form of rates (for the income-tax is not concerned with conscience). Now surely (except in the case of the one-man manager) this is a total misconception. As opposed to State management, perhaps the word private may be admitted, but when it implies, as it ought, purely individual management, a false view is suggested. These social bodies other than the

---

① Figgis, *Churches in the Modern State*, p. 38.
② *Ibid.*, p. 79.
③ *Ibid.*, pp. 67-68.
④ *Ibid.*, p. 60.
⑤ *Ibid.*, p. 25.

State are not only not private, but in their working they are more akin to the State than they are to the individual. I mean that both of them are cases of a society acting as one, to which the individual members are subject. The relations between the member and his society are more akin to those of a citizen to a state than to anything in the individual. It is very easy to say that universities, colleges, trade unions, inns of court &c. &c., are purely private, and in one sense it is true; they are not delegates of the State or parts of its machinery; but they are in a very real sense public, i. e. they are collective, not individual, in their constitution. The popular use of the word 'Public School' to denote a school under collective management is a far more reasonable and realistic habit, though I suppose that it is not technically justified. The point is that it is the public communal character of all such institutions that is the salient fact; and that we do wrong to adopt a rigid division into public and private, if we mean by the latter any and every institution that is not a delegation from the State. What we actually see in the world is not on the one hand the State, and on the other a mass of unrelated individuals; but a vast complex of gathered unions, in which alone we find individuals, families, clubs, trades unions, colleges, professions, and so forth; and further, that there are exercised functions within these groups which are of the nature of government, including its three aspects, legislative, executive, and judicial; though of course, only with reference to their own members. So far as the people who actually belong to it are concerned, such a body is every whit as communal in its character as a municipal corporation or a provincial parliament."①

The misunderstanding of the personality—real personality—of the social group or groups is due to the misunderstanding of the social fact. Man is a social animal, and he is born to be a man of group. What makes him as such is largely not what he has but what he is. He is under the influence of his family, school the group of profession that he joins. Each of these countless groups possesses a real personality. And "it is these that make up the life of the modern world, and to deny them all real existence or power, whether it be in the interests of legal theory or of an abstract economic collectivism, seems to me to be in principle false to the facts, and in practice to be steering straight for the rocks."②

The social facts are now before us. Whether we like them or not, we must recognize them as such. The judgment in the Taff Vale Case, so Professor Figgis remarks, is an instance in which facts are proving too strong for it. It was still held, in

---

① Figgis, *Churches in the Modern State*, pp. 68–70.
② *Ibid.*, pp. 72–73.

this case, that legally the trades unions were not corporate bodies, but the facts as they are were recognized. "Whatever other influences may have assisted in forming the minds of the judges, the truth is that the judgment bears witness to the fact that corporate personality, this unity of life and action, is a thing which grows up naturally and inevitably in bodies of men united for a permanent end, and that it can not in the long run be denied merely by the process of saying that it is not there. In other words, this personality is inherent in the nature of the society as such and is not a mere name to be granted or denied at the pleasure of the sovereign authority."①

What is true in educational and economical or other matters is also true in the case of religion. The first lecture entitled "A Free Religious Church in a Free State" discusses fully that a religious body or bodies are not created by the state. They have life and personality of their own. They have "arisen out of the natural associative instincts of mankind, and should all be treated by the supreme authority as having a life original and guaranteed to be controlled and directed like persons, but not regarded in their corporate capacity as mere names, which for juristic purposes and for these purposes only are entitled persons."②

The phrase "supreme authority" used here seems, to Professor Figgis, to indicate the authority of the state. If this is true, we see that he does not go beyond the point of Gierke or Maitland. He recognizes the sovereign power exercised by the groups is no less real than that of the state, yet the state authority may be supreme because it is a larger whole. Thus in addition to the sovereignty which is owned by the state, there are many small sovereignties within the state. The old dogma that sovereignty is supreme may still be accepted, but the contention that sovereignty is an essential characteristic founded by the state alone and that it is indivisible and illimitable, is denied.

Let us conclude by quoting the last paragraph of Professor Figgis' lectures: "Much that has been said in these lectures will seem commonplace, and some of it obvious. Yet it is plain that the principles here set out are not recognized, and where they are recognized are often disliked. Their purpose will be achieved if I have shown these facts: First, the problem of the relations of Church and State cannot be considered in isolation. It raises topics which go down to the root of all political philosophy, and forces us to face the whole problem of the true nature of civil society and the meaning of

---

① Figgis, *Churches in the Modern State*, p. 64.
② *Ibid.*, p. 47. The Kulturkampf in Germany, the Law of Separation in France, and the Free Church of Scotland case all emplify the arrogance of the claims of the sovereignty of the state to interfere with religious bodies. So stated Professor Figgis.

personality. If the view which is here suggested be the true one, we must get rid of our enslavement to doctrines never altogether true, but far less true to the facts now than has been the case at some periods, as, e. g., in a city state. We must seek to make our theories grow out of and coordinate with the life of men in society as it is lived. We must distrust abstract doctrines of sovereignty, with which the facts can be made to square only by a elaborate sophistry. Above all, we must be willing to put liberty above other ends as political goal, and to learn that true liberty will be found by allowing full play to the uncounted forms of the associative instinct. We are fighting not only our own battle but that of the liberty of all smaller societies against the tendency to mere concentration, which in one way is a marked feature of our time. Much has to be learned both by ourselves and others from the mediaeval guild system. Further we must learn to allow to others that liberty we claim for ourselves as a corporate society, and fairly face the fact which I have called "the religious heterogeneity of the modern State". Lastly, we shall see that the only basis on which a true defense of the English Church against Rome can be founded is precisely the same as that which we have been expounding. For Rome, as a church polity, simply embodies those seeming notions of omnipotent sovereignty which we saw had passed over from the antique State to the modern world. And thus we are forced to consider something of the nature of religious authority in general, and of life of the part in the whole. ①

3. Barker

Mr. Barker is certainly not a specialized student of the theory of sovereignty, nor is he the pioneer of pluralism. But perhaps it is not going too far to say that it was he who issued the formal declaration of war on the side of pluralism as against the traditional theory of sovereignty. The often quoted article written by Mr. Sarker on the subject under consideration is the one published in The Political Quarterly for February 1915 and entitled "The Discredited State". Attention may be called also to some passages in his *Political Thought in England: From Herbert Spencer to the Present Day* and other writings. ②

---

① Figgis, *Churches in the Modern State*, pp. 170-171.

② See also his essay on "Mediaeval Political Thought" in Hearnshaw's *The Social and Political Ideas of Some Great Medieval Thinkers*, pp. 1 f. Professor Coker points out in his "Pluralistic Theories and the Attack upon State Sovereignty" (Merriam and Barnes, *Political Theories; Recent Times*, p. 115) that Mr. Barker has modified his view recently. But the idea or ideas involved in the statements quoted by Professor Coker had been already expressed in 1915. See the note at the end of his "The discredited State". See also Gettell, *History of Political Thought*, 1924, p. 462, note. See also Barker, *A Confederation of the Nations*, 1918 and his recent book entitled *National Character and the Factors in its Formation*, 1927, pp. 131, 276. *Nietzsche and Treitschke* in "Oxford Pamphlets", No. 20, 1914.

Destructively, Mr. Barker, like Professor Figgis and other defenders of the pluralistic theory of sovereignty, assaults the dogma of Austin. "Austin," says he, "who, one is told, was not particularly skilled in English law, and could blunder shockingly in Roman law, may have theorized about 'majestas'; but his own difficulties in fitting his theory of sovereignty into the framework of English politics seem to show that it is fairly remote from the 'genius loci'. For in England, as Mr. Barker sees, the state has generally been discredited and there one can hardly find a singularly unicellular sovereignty. A sovereign and majectic state, a single and undivided 'imperium', lifted above the conflicts of society, neutral, mediatory, impartial, such as Hegel conceived and such as Germen theorists still postulate—this we have not known."① Neither in its executive nor in its legislative side can one find a supreme authority in England. What she has is "a bracket-enclosed bundle of officials, and a society tramelled legislature."②

This is the fact, and history and instances show it is true. The Magna Carta of 1215, the Revolution of 1688 are the most conspicuous examples. These are claims for the natural right to privilege, or property or work. Then there are claims for a right divine to worship free. "Robert Brown of Corpus Christi College," says Mr. Barker, "has little use for the Elizabethan State. Henry Barrow, of Clare, was of the same way of thinking."③

But these are not all. New conditions have brought new claims and new resistance. And the more it (the state) is resisted, the more it is discredited. But the problem of resistance is in actual life, not that of individuals but always that of groups, "Theorists may set limits to the State in the name of the individual; practical resistance is always a matter of group-consciousness."④ So writes Mr. Barker. Here it is that we see that Mr. Barker follows the path of Gierke, Maitland, and Figgis. ⑤

But what is a group? Has it a personality or a will of its own which is different from that of its members? We are told by Professor Gierke and his immediate successors that the question may be answered in the affirmative. And we shall see in our later

---

① Barker, "The Discredited State," *The Political Quarterly*, No. 5, 1915, p. 101.
② *Ibid.*
③ *Ibid.*, p. 103.
④ *Ibid.*, p. 110.
⑤ *Political Thought in England*, pp. 175 ff. "If we are individualists now, we are corporate individualists. Our 'individuals' are becoming groups. No longer do we write 'The Man versus the State: we write the Group versus the State.'" *Ibid.*, p. 181.

discussion, that a negative reply is given by some writers.[1] But Mr. Barker neither follows the former nor the latter in its extremity.[2] To him, it is something else. And what is it? "Let us call it an idea."[3] So he declares.

But what is idea or are ideas? "Ideas," says he, "are and are not fictions: they have hands and feet; but they are not persons, any more than they are fictions."[4] We may eliminate personality and will—transcendent personality and transcendent will—from associations; we may be content to speak of associations as schemes in which real and individual persons and wills are related to one another by means of a common and organizing idea. We may conceive the State as such a scheme based on the political idea of law and order; we may conceive it as containing, or at any rate co-existing with, a rich variety of schemes based on a rich variety of ideas. We are all members of one scheme and partakers of the one idea; most of us are also members of many other schemes, and partakers of many others. The ideas are in relation to one another; perhaps they are in competition with one another. It is so, it is a competition of ideas, not of real collective personalities. To apprehend this point of view is already a certain gain. We are rid of the idea of an internecine struggle between the real personality of the State and the real personality of other groups. We cease to feel murder in the air. Real ideas cannot be killed: they can only die by the suicide of their own excess, or the slow internal decay of their own life."[5]

But what have these ideas to do with sovereignty? The response is that the associating idea of a political community forms public opinion and public opinion may be regarded as sovereignty.[6] Thus Mr. Barker has made a turn and comes back to the position of Professor Ritchie. But further questions may be asked: can there be a graded hierarchy of associating ideas? Can there be a unique public opinion? "That it never is and that, some of us may hope, it never will be."[7] So argues Mr. Barker. A community is a community of conflicting ideas. The more human knowledge develops the richer will be such ideas—the conflicting ideas. One may argue that the sovereignty of England is unique in the day of Henry VIII, but "if to-day some may see a new Henry VIII in the guise of a sovereign public opinion, the syndicalist will none the less claim exemption from the

---

[1] Cf. Barker, *A Confederation of the Nations*, Oxford, 1918, p. 40.
[2] See *Political Thought in England*, p. 180.
[3] "The Discredited State," p. 111.
[4] *Ibid.*, p. 113.
[5] *Ibid.*, p. 113.
[6] *Ibid.*, pp. 114–115.
[7] *Ibid.*, p. 115.

bourgeois State for his idea of class, the nationalist will claim immunity from the denationalized State for his idea of the nation, and the right hand of the churchman will lose its cunning if he forgets Jerusalem."① A thorough Romanist may live in England, but his final allegiance does not lie with Westminister, but with Rome. ②

Admitting for the moment that the State idea is the broader and wider synthesis, it may, just because of its breadth, be an imperfect synthesis, which only achieves success by neglecting factors for which it should find room.③ Since ideas are never unique, sovereignty is in fact sovereignties. The monism of Austin thus becomes polyarchism in the hand of Mr. Barker. ④ A citizen like Hobbes may regard the state as a Leviathan; but it has to be remembered that what Hobbes sees is no more than when a churchman considers the church as the plenitudo "potestatis". The state may be an educator of citizens: the Church may also be an educator of churchmen with a right of entry as such. The State may have its Westminister Parliament: the nation may also have its Dublin Parliament. The State may be an area of political action: the trades union may also be a field of political action. ⑤ And he continues: "It hardly meets the point to urge that the Church will not have its right of entry, or Dublin its parliament, or trade unions a political levy, until the state has issued its permission."⑥ If the state can claim that she has the right to issue law, so may a trade union; and if the trade union is or should be bound by law, why not a state? Whether the law is the child or the parent of the state, makes no difference. But in either case, what is true for the state will be true for the trade union or a church. ⑦

4. Lindsay

"Ideals," says Mr. Lindsay, "are born of historical circumstances and fashioned to meet historical problems, and the would-be timeless ideals which political philosophers have put before us have always borne clear marks of the country and time of their origin. The ideal which men have set themselves in political organization has varied from time to

---

① "The Discredited State," p. 115.
② *Ibid.*, p. 114.
③ *Ibid.*, p. 116.
④ *Ibid.*, p. 120. See also his *National Character*, 1927, p. 131. "The life and actions of the modern State becomes more and more complicated. Theorists speak of its 'plurality', and abjure the notion any single centre of sovereignty. It is certainly a place of many loyalties. Besides the national groups with which we are concerned, there is also a range of professional groups, or occupations, which advanced their claims and profess their solidarity."
⑤ *Ibid.*, p. 119.
⑥ *Ibid.*
⑦ Concerning the theory of Mr. Barker, attention may be called to W. Y. Elliott's article entitled "Sovereign State or Sovereign Group?" in *Am. Pol. Sci. Review*, Vol. XIX, 1919, p. 475.

time."① Having such idea in mind, Mr. Lindsay goes on to point out that the political thought of Hobbes is different from that of Aristotle, not merely because one is right and the other is wrong, but because the political problems which they had to face were not the same. ②

Just as the theory of Hobbes is different from that of Aristotle, so individualism is different from collectivism. But neither individualism nor collectivism is now in conformity to the actual fact. Unless a new theory is formulated, political theory will be divorced from practice. What is the fact? To Mr. Lindsay, it is no more than the development and spread of group life. The multiplicity of the forms of social organization other than the state is becoming obvious day by day and any theory ignoring the fact that man's social nature expresses itself in many forms, ignores the chief point in political science. ③

Is there any such theory to justify such act? Yes, says Mr. Lindsay. It was enunciated by Gierke and reinforced by Maitland. It is a reflection of the political practice of the present day and it is not "mere theory in the air, but an attempt io make explicit principles realized and tried in practice."④ The new theory which is destined to come into prominence does not deny and can not deny man's social nature. What it aims to deny is the doctrine that the social nature of men can only find its expression through a single organization called the state.

It is the old theory which insists on the personality of the state and denies that of the groups existing within it. Mr. Lindsay cannot see how a state can be treated as a person and having a personality while a trade union or a church can not. ⑤ It seems to Mr. Lindsay, that the real issue is not the difficulty of admitting the existence of corporate personality in the sense that any men who work together express a will which is more than the sum of their several wills. It is the difficulty of finding any limit to the number of corporate personalities. "Once we admit the force of the arguments which claim that the state is a person and has a will of its own, we are faced with an infinite number of corporate personalities, and we have to determine how the state is to be distinguished from other corporate personalities and what should be its proper relation to

---

① Lindsay, "Political Theory", in F. S. Marvin, *Development in European Thought*, 1919, p. 164. See also his earlier article entitled "The State in Recent Theory" in *The Political Quarterly*, Vol. I, 1914, and also Proceedings of *Aristolelian Society*, June, 16, 1924.
② *Ibid.*, p. 165.
③ Lindsay, "The state in Recent Theory," *The Political Quarterly*, Vol. I, p. 132.
④ *Ibid.*, pp. 129–130.
⑤ *Political Theory*, p. 176.

them."①

Again it is the old theory that views the state alone as possessing the coercive power, or sovereignty. But this proposition can no longer be maintained for there is no organization which is born to have power or sovereignty. "The power of the state over its members depends upon the will of the members themselves, and on the fact that they allow the state to organize force which can indeed coerce individuals, but cannot coerce the whole community. The state, therefore, can have control over the corporations within it only if and in so far as the citizens are prepared to give such power."②

The state was once regarded as the largest organization but facts no longer allow us to believe such a conception, for groups in many cases extend over national or state lines. "It looks almost as though the state as it now exists were either too large or too small, for any principle in which we may try to rest its supremacy over other associations. If we choose the principle of consciousness of common interests, the feeling of mutual interdependence and relations, the state is too large. Intenser loyalties are easier in smaller, more homogeneous bodies. If we choose the principle of the need for regulating or controlling conflicting individuals and associations the state is too small."③

5. Cole

The works of G. D. H. Cole in recent years have received general attention. His name suggests guild socialism, although he is not the pioneer of this movement.④ It is generally considered that the guild socialist mainly takes interest in economic reform,

---

① "The State in Recent Theory," p. 131.

② "The State in Recent Theory," *Political Quarterly*, Vol. I, 1914, p. 134.

③ *Ibid.*, p. 136

④ For the origin and development of guild socialism, see Hobson's preface to his *National Guilds: An Inquiry into the Wage System and the Way Out*, 1919.

Cole's view in connection with our discussion may be found in the following books: *The World of Labour* (1915); *Self-Government in Industry* (1917); The Introduction to the edition of 1919 should be used; *Labour in the Commonwealth* (1919); *Social Theory* (1920); *Guild Socialism Re-stated* (1920 or American edition under the title *Guild Socialism*); *The Future of Local Government* (1921); *Organized Labour: An Introduction to Trade Unionism* (1924); And his Introduction to Rousseau's *Social Contract*, Everyman's ed. The general view of Mr. Cole may also be found in Ch. VII of Rockow's *Contemporary Political Thought in England* and an article by Miss Ellis entitled "Guild Socialism and Pluralism" in *American Political Science Review*, Vol. XVII, 1923, pp. 584-596. The former deals mainly with economic organization. The latter deals more with the Nature of the State; but the article is mainly based on a chapter entitled "The Nature of the State" in Cole's *Self Government in Industry*. The idea advanced in this book, according to Mr. Cole, is not fully held by him. Thus he says in the Introduction to the edition of 1919. "I am not satisfied with this book; but I do not know how to mend it... I do not today agree with every statement that is made in this book." See also note on pages 147-148.

but we find that in Mr. Cole's writings, the principles involved have been carried beyond the field of economics. This is true particularly of his *Social Theory*.

The ideas of Mr. Cole change as time goes on. Originally he was a Fabian. But as has been remarked, the danger of government by a "man behind a window" made him join the new movement① (guild socialism.) The introduction of the Soviet system in Russia exerted a great influence on Mr. Cole and he has been led to declare that "the soviet idea is the guild idea, or at least has very much in common with it."② Philosophically, Mr. Cole has been profoundly imbued by men like William Morris of England, Max of Germany and Maciver of the United States. ③

Negatively, Mr. Cole considers in theory as well as in practice that the sovereignty of the state is falling to the ground. ④ Positively, he thinks that sovereignty is in the hands of individuals or members of community. ⑤ He agrees almost fully with Rousseau on this point. ⑥ But he does not think that sovereignty is inalienable, for it may be exercised by social groups or associations⑦ since man can not live in isolation and he must be one of the members of these groups or some of these groups, and therefore he can not do, in many cases, what he likes to do.

As human interests are manifold, the forms of association are many. These forms are different in different times and at different places. ⑧ Generally speaking they may be grouped into two main divisions: one is essential and the other non-essential, ⑨ it is in the former that Mr. Cole takes special interest, because it is socially essential to organized society. ⑩ The essential forms of association may be classified according to (1) the content of the interest which the association sets before itself; and (2) its method of operation in relation to that interest. According to the first of these two ways of classification, the forms of association are political, vocational and appetitive, religious, provident, philanthropic, sociable and theoretic. ⑪ According to the second of the two

---

① Lewis Rockow, *Contemporary Political Thought in England*, 1925, p. 150.
② Cole, *Self-Government in Industry*, Introductory to the edition of 1919, p. 22.
③ Cole, *Labour in the Commonwealth*, p. 181. *Social Theory*, Ch. Ⅱ.
④ Cole, *Social Theory*, p. 102; *Labour in the Commonwealth*, p. 187; *Guild Socialism* (Am. ed.) p. 23. Cf. *Organized Labour*, p. 149.
⑤ He denies to use the term citizen, for being too closely connected with the state.
⑥ Cole, *Labour in the Commonwealth*, pp. 202, 205.
⑦ Cole, *Social Theory*, p. 133. Also Introduction to Rousseau's *Social Contract*, Everymen's edition.
⑧ *Social Theory*, p. 64.
⑨ *Ibid.*, p. 65.
⑩ *Ibid.*, pp. 65-66.
⑪ *Ibid.*, pp. 66-72.

principles of classification, each form of the associations as mentioned above, may be regarded as administrative, or propagandist. For example, under the religious form of association, we may have administrative associations such as the church and the propagandist associations such as the "Life and Liberty Movement". The administrative association is considered as the primary type while the propagandist is the secondary. ①

From the general considerations given above, we come to the position or status of the state. The state, according to Mr. Cole, is an association—a political association. It is defined as the machinery of political government in the commonwealth. ② It is "no more than the greatest and most permanent association or institution in society, and its claim even to any such position will have to be carefully considered."③ A state is certainly necessary, ④ but it is necessary just as a trade union is necessary. It has no more coercive power or sovereignty than other associations. ⑤ "Every association," says he, "by the mere fact of its existence, is endowed, with some coercive power, and actually exercises some such power in the course of pursuing its object."⑥

There are different kinds of coercion or sovereignty. "There is one kind of coercion which only affects a man's purse or property, that is coercion by fine... There is a second kind of coercion which affects a man's freedom of action by limiting pirectly his range of opportunity and self-expression, as, for instance, by disfranchising him or forbidding him to work in a particular factory or occupation... The third form of coercion is that which directly affects a man's body, by limiting his right of movement, interning him, imprisoning him, or, in the last resort, hanging him, or shooting him, or cutting off his head."⑦

The first form is employed by all kinds of association; the second is used by some associations, such as the Trade Union. The state, besides exercising the first and the second, alone possesses the third. Should the state continue to monopolize the third and share with other associations the second and the first? To this a negative answer is given.

---

① *Social Theory*, pp. 72–73.

② *Labour in the Commonwealth*, p. 50. For his conception of state and of commonwealth, see *ibid.*, pp. 57, 216. A commonwealth, it seems to him, involves all the associations within it, while the state is only a political association.

③ *Social Theory*, p. 81. Cf. *Self-Government in Industry*, p. 119.

④ *Labour in the Commonwealth*, p. 185.

⑤ Coercive power and sovereignty mean the same thing to Mr Cole. See *Social Theory*, Ch. Ⅷ.

⑥ *Social Theory*, p. 128. Also *Labour in the Commonwealth*, p. 191.

⑦ *Ibid.*, pp. 129–130.

It is the old theory of sovereignty that justifies the state to have an absolute power and to have it alone on the "assumption that the state, because it represents and includes everybody within its area, is necessarily superior to other associations, which only include some of the persons within its area."① But in what sense does the state represent and include everybody? Mr. Cole asks. "If our functional theory of representation is right, it may include everybody; but it does not include the whole of everybody; it may represent some purposes common to everybody, but it does not represent all the purposes common to everybody." And he adds, and this is the main point, "This being so, it can no longer lay claim to sovereignty on the ground that it represents and includes eyerybody; for the Sovereign, if there is one, must represent and include, as far as possible, the whole of everybody."②

If no particular functional association, not even the state, can possess this absolute power over the other associations, the natural consequence is that sovereignty is divided between functional associations. It is in this respect that Mr. Cole is one of the stronger advocates of pluralism. But this is not all, for difficulty may arise in case of conflicts between different functional groups. In our time functional groups are mostly national (states)③ in character, it is necessary then, within the border of the state, to have a unifying or co-ordinating body for the whole social life of the commonwealth. But the increase of the interdependence of the commonwealths and functional groups has made it necessary that there should be one unity or rather a co-ordinating body for the whole world It does not matter, however, whether it be a world-co-ordinating body or a co-ordinating body of the commonwealth; for the principle applied to both is the same. The co-ordinating body should be a body representing the functional associations.④

For settling the conflicts among the functional, this coordinating body should also have some coercive power. This leads Mr. Cole to introduce another sovereignty besides the sovereignty of the functional groups. It is to be noted, however, that this coordinating body should not be confounded with machinery of the modern state, for the state, in Mr. Cole's system, is only one of the functional groups.⑤ It possesses sovereignty just as a church or a trade union possesses it. Again it is to be noted that this coordinating agency "can only be a combination, not of all associations, but of all

---

① *Social Theory*, pp. 131-132.
② *Ibid.*, p. 132.
③ Both terms are inadequate. The term commonwealth seems to have been preferred by Mr. Cole.
④ *Ibid.*, p. 140.
⑤ *Ibid.*, p. 136.

essential associations, a joint Council or Congress of supreme bodies representing each of the main functions in society."① "Each functional association will see to the execution of its own function, and for the coordination of the activities of the various associations there must be a joint body representative of them."②

Thus far we have shown that Mr. Cole, on the one hand, opposes the old theory of state sovereignty. And maintains on the other, that sovereignty should be, and actually is, exercised by various functional groups, in its particular as well as coordinating capacity. There are many sovereignties, and there is one. Both may exist without being in conflict with one another, because each exercises it within its own sphere.

But Mr. Cole does not stop here, for he does not think that sovereignty is an essential thing for functional society. On the contrary, it is merely a manifestation of social disease. Its appearance implies the existence of a disorderly social phenomenon. It disappears or at least it is useless in a society where peace and order are adequately provided. "Having discovered where coercive power must reside in a functional society," he writes, "we are now in a position to give vent to our dislikes of it. One of the greatest results which, I believe, would flow from the full recognition of functional organization would be a substantial and immediate reduction in the use of coercion in society. For coercion is the consequence of social disorder, and the need for it largely comes, not of innate human wickedness, but of men's failure under existing social conditions to find their proper spheres of social service and to recognize clearly their rights and obligations in society. If we set our social house in order and make it easier for men to recognize their proper sphere of social service, the need for coercion will, I believe, speedily and progressively disappear."③

As we do not propose to consider the views of other guild socialists than Mr. Cole, we may quote some passages from the Introduction to the 1919 edition of Cole's *Self-Government in Industry*, on the difference between himself and Mr. Hobson. "Gradually, however, a clear divergence of view upon one fundamental point at least became manifest, and a prolonged controversy raged between Mr. S. G. Hobson and myself, with other Guildsmen joining in from time to time, on the question of State sovereignty. Mr. Hobson—and with him were Mr. Orrge and other New Age writers—insisted upon the sovereignty of the State as an essential point ot Guild doctrine. They refused to regard the State as in any sense the representative or protector of the consumer, and

---

① *Social Theory*, p. 135.
② *Ibid.*, pp. 135–136.
③ *Ibid.*, pp. 139–140.

insisted that its function was nothing other than the exercise of sovereignty, the ultimate representation of the 'civic' point of view of producer or consumer. They desired that the control of industry should be in the hands of Guilds of producers, and held that, in the normal case, the Guilds would adequately protect the interest of the consumer as well as the producer; but they desired to preserve the ultimate authority of the state as owner of the means of production, the state as owner representing men not as consumers but as citizens."①

"A curious position thus arose. Mr. Hobson and his supporters were firm in their insistence on State sovereignty in the economic as well as in other spheres; but they did not desire that the state should play any part at all in the normal conduct of industry, or recognize the need for any continuous representation of the consumer's point of view in relation to the organization. Theoretically, they claimed for the State an unlimited authority; but actually they wanted it to intervene considerably less than those of us who desire to place a strict limitation upon its theoretical sphere of authority.

"Those of us who took the other side urged that in the organization of the communal industries and services there were two distinct points of view to be considered—the point of view of man as a producer or renderer of services, and the point of view of man as a consumer or enjoyer of the services rendered. I argued that the Guilds—industrial and civil—represented men in the former aspect, while the State (and the local authority) represented them in the latter. I denied that either form of organization could be regarded as superior to the other, and insisted that each was complementary to the other. I therefore rejected the theory of State sovereignty, and insisted on the co-sovereignty of the Guilds and the State in the economic sphere, a co-sovereignty possibly to be shared with other bodies in other spheres of social action.

"I no longer believe that I was completely right, or that Mr. Hobson was completely wrong, in the controversy. I am strongly opposed as ever I was to the theory of State sovereignty; but I am no longer satisfied with the State as the final and only representative of the consumers."②

---

① *Self-Government in Industry*, 4th ed., pp. 4-5.
② *Ibid.*, pp. 5-6.
For Hobson's views, see his *National Guilds and the State* (1920), *Guild Principles in War and Peace* (1917), *National Guilds: An Inquiry into the Wage System and the Way out* (1915), ed. by Orage. See also A. R. Orage, *National Guild* (1914), A. J. Penty, *Old World for New* (1917), and *Guild and the Social Crisis* (1919).

Ⅳ. French Writers

1. Durkheim

In order to understand the view of Emile Durkheim more clearly, let us begin by considering his psychological analysis.① According to him, the interaction of the cerebral cells produces what we call sensations which are the primary elements of the individual's state of mind. The compounding of sensations produces images. By the same process, images may produce concepts and the concepts may compound into still more complicated products.②

This is the origin and development of the individual's consciousness may come into being as the result of the interaction of individual consciousness. Although the collective consciousness is a product of the consciousness of the individuals, the former is by no means identical with the latter. Collective consciousness is different from individual consciousness in two respects: (1) it is exterior to the individual consciousness and (2) it is constraint.

By exteriority of the social mind (consciousness or representation) as it is preferred by Gehlke, is meant that the property it possesses of coming to this mind from the outside and it is exterior to the individual mind because it is not derived from the individuals taken in isolation, but from their convergence and union. By constraint it is based on superiority of the social representation to the individual representation. The logic here employed is very simple: The whole is greater than the parts, so the former is superior to the latter. Moreover it is superior by virtue of its hierarchical position as it is at the top of the psychic scale.③

Having explained his fundamental concept, we come to his conception of society. The meaning of society, according to him, implies two senses: in the first place it means a group of concrete individuals. In the second place it is a psychic whole. But it is to the latter sense that more emphasis should be given. And in the latter sense the essential part of the relation of the individual mind to the group is the submission of the

---

① For Durkheim's view, see his *Le Suicide* (1897), pp. 434-450; and his *De la Division du Travail* (1902), preface. C. E. Gehlke's *Emile Durkheim's Contributions to Sociological Theory*, "Columbia Studies in History, Economics and Public Law," Vol. 63. H. E. Barnes' "Durkheim's Contribution to Political Theory," *Pol. Sci. Quarterly*, Vol. XXXV, 1928, pp. 236-254, and his "Some Contributions of Sociology to Modern Political Theory," *Am. Pol. Sc. Review*, Vol. XV, 1921, pp. 487-533.

② Gehlke, *ibid.*, pp. 19-27.

③ Gehlke, *ibid.*, Chs. Ⅰ and Ⅱ.

former to certain rule of moral conduct of the latter. Thus the submission of the individual mind to the group mind is the keynote of social solidarity. [1] The increase of social solidarity is necessary in human society, social solidarity can be best secured only in occupational groups; for it is here we find a solid bond and it is here we find that there is a common yet intimate interest that men are seeking for.

The importance of the functional groups increases with the industrial and economic changes of recent years, and the changes have witnessed the inadequacy of the omnipotence of the state to meet the present industrial situation. If we are going to have a better society in which to live, the occupational group should be taken as both the basis of political representation and the source of economic regulation. The state may still remain, but its power should be diffused and limited.

What then is the relation of the state to the other groups? The state, according to him, should make the general relations, but the details should be left to the functional groups in order to meet their particular and different needs and wants. Thus the formulation of specialized and diversified rules is the chief function of the functional groups and this should not be interfered with by the state.

While emphasizing the importance of functional groups in modern social life, and therefore the principle of functional representation, geographical divisions may still be employed to a certain extent. Thus the functional groups may be local and national in extent. While the national organization of each occupation should give the general principles for that occupation in the whole nation, matters purely local in character should be left entirely in the hands of the local organization.

Durkheim takes special interest in the industrial regulation between the employers and employees. This leads him to hold there should be separate functional groups for employees and employers. Each should be independent of the other in regard to its own policy within its own sphere and both should have representatives in a tribunal which is to apply the general regulations imposed by the state to the special needs of the industry in question.

2. Sorel

It is generally recognized that Georges Sorel is the most conspicuous representative of syndicalism. In a letter to Daniel Halevy, he writes: "I am neither a professor, a populariser of knowledge, nor a candidate for party leadership. I am a self-taught man

---

[1] Cf. above in connection to the discussion of Duguit's conception of social solidarity.

exhibiting to other people the note books which have served for my own instruction."① But Le Bon, a well known French writer tells us in his *La Psychologie du Socialismc*, that Sorel is "the most learned of French socialists".

Sorel was profoundly influenced by Karl Marx and he has called himself a Marxist.② But since the world of today is not that of yesterday, there are facts that we see which Marx did. Not see and for this reason the revision of Marxian theories is necessary. The revision is essential, "because, on the one hand, Marx was not always 'well inspired', and often harked back to the past instead of penetrating into the future; and because, on the other hand, Marx did not know all the facts that have now become known: Marx knew well the development of the bourgeoisie, but could not know the development of the labor movement which has become such a tremendous factor in social life."③

He calls his own theory a 'new school' or revolutionary syndicalism which is different from Parliamentary Socialism. The latter, according to him, justifies the existence of the state and therefore the exercise of power. "Experience has always shown us hitherto," he declares, "that revolutionaries plead reasons of State as soon as they get into power, that they then employ police methods and look upon justice as a weapon which they may use unfairly against their enemies. Parliamentary Socialists do not escape the universal rule; they preserve the old cult of the State: they are therefore prepared to commit all the misdeeds of the old Regime and of the Revolution."④

In another place, he writes: "It is impossible that there should be the slightest understanding between Syndicalists and official Socialists on this question; the latter, of course, speak of breaking up everything, but they attack men in power rather than power itself; they hope to possess the State forces, and they are aware that on the day when they control the Government they will have need of an army; they will carry on foreign politics, and consequently they in their turn will have to praise the feeling of

---

① Sorel, *Reflections on Violence*, trans by T. E. Hulme, 1912, p. 3. Besides the book just cited his views may be found also in the following books: *L'Avenir socialiste des Sydicats* (1898); *La Decomposition du Maxisme* (1908); *Introduction a l'economic moderne* (1922). Also see L. Levine, "Syndicalism in France", in *Columbia University Studies*, XLVI, No. 3, 1913; J. H. Harley, *Syndicalism*, Ch. Ⅵ; J. R. Macdonald, *Syndicalism*, Ch. Ⅲ; Kirkup. *History of Socialism*, pp. 293 ff; Mott, "The Political Theory of Syndicalism", in *Political Science Quarterly*, XXXIV, 1922, pp. 25–40.

② *Reflections on Violence*, p. 127.

③ Levine, *op. cit.* p. 143. See also *Reflections on Violence*, pp. 133, 155. He thought it was a mistake for Marx to live in England and he told us that he learned more from the trade unionists. See Sorel, *Avenir socialiste des syndicats*, p. 12.

④ *Reflections on Violence*, pp. 118–119.

devotion to the fatherland."①

On the other hand, the "syndicalists do not propose to reform the state, as the men of the eighteenth century did; they want to destroy it."② While sovereignty is regarded as inherent to the state, to destroy the state means to destroy sovereignty. This being the case, it is only natural that Sorel strongly denies the conception of sovereignty and the general will of Rousseau.③

The state, as he sees it, is no more than an organization of force. The state, "says he" has always been, in fact, the organizer of the way of conquest, the dispenser of its fruits, and the 'raison d'etre' of the dominating groups which profit by the enterprises—the cost of which is borne by the general body of society."④ But the day of the "God State" possessing limitless power for doing what she likes has gone and it should disappear at present.⑤

The disappearance of the state is necessary. We cannot endure to see it in existence any longer. And he strongly opposes those who would reason that "in the end the state must disappear—but this disappearance will take place only in the future so far distant that you must prepare yourself for it by using the state meanwhile as a means of providing the politicians with titbits; and the best means of bringing about the disappearance of the state consists in strengthening meanwhile the governmental machine."⑥ "This method, of reasoning," says Sorel, "resembles that of Gribouille, who threw himself into the water in order to escape getting wet in the rain."⑦

Thus the syndicalists want to destroy the state, and destroy it right away, "because they wish to realize this idea of Marx's that the Socialists revolution ought not to culminate in the replacement of one governing minority by another minority."⑧ To destroy it then we must destroy it at the heart, so that it will never exist again.

But how to destroy the state? What is the method that should be employed in abolishing it? The effective means, according to Sorel, is the general strike. "It was

---

① *Reflections on Violence*, pp. 123-124.
② *Ibid.*, p. 123.
③ *L'Avenir Socialiste des Syndicats*, p. 45.
④ *Reflections on Violence*, p. 190.
⑤ *Ibid.*, p. 116. "We are not perhaps better, more human, more sensitive to the misfortunes of others than were the men of 93; and I should even be rather disposed to assert that the country is probably less moral than it was at that time; but we are no longer dominated to the same extent that our fathers were by this superstition of the God State, to which they sacrificed so many victims."
⑥ *Ibid.*, pp. 128-129.
⑦ *Ibid.*
⑧ *Ibid.*, p. 123.

primarily in his conception of the general strike," says one writer, "that he made his contribution—a contribution not altogether accepted by his friends—to the syndicalist philosophy."① "The general strike, according to Sorel is the "social myth" of the working class longing for emancipation, and social myth is a means for social and moral development. Social myth is necessary to every revolutionary movement. History shows that this is true. The myth of the second coming of Christ was a powerful factor in early Christianity. "It must be admitted that the real development of the revolution did not in any way resemble the enchanting pictures which created the enthusiasm of its first adepts; but without those pictures would the revolution have been victorious?② Although we know that a general strike is a myth, "we are proceeding exactly as a modern physicist does who has complete confidence in his science, although he knows that the future will look upon it as antiquated."③

But "syndicalist violence, perpetrated in the course of strikes by proletarians who desire the overthrow of the state, must not be confused with those acts of savagery which the superstition of the state suggested to the revolutionaries of 93, when they had power in their hands and were able to oppress the conquered—following the principles which they had received from the church and from the monarchy."④

But suppose the myth of a general strike is actualized, and the state together with its power are destroyed, what is going to be done next? To some syndicalists, a constructive program may be worked out, but to Sorel the reply is: we have not completed our destructive task, what is the use of talking about a constructive program? Moreover, "it may be said, too, that the greatest danger which threatens Syndicalism

---

① H. W. Ladier, *A History of Socialist Thought*, 1927, p. 379.
② *Reflection on Violence*, p. 134.
③ Ibid., p. 167. "It is in strikes that the proletariat asserts its existence. I cannot agree with view which sees in strikes merely something analogous to the temporary rupture of commercial relations which is brought about when grocer and the wholesale dealer from whom he buys his dried plums cannot agree about the price. The strike is a phenomenon of war. It is thus a serious misrepresentation to say that violence is an accident doomed to disappear from the strikes of the future." "The social revolution is an extension of that war in which each great strike is an episode; this is the reason why syndicalists speak of that revolution in the language of strikes; for them socialism is reduced to the conception, the expectation of, and the preparation for the general strike, which like the Napoleonic battle, is to annihilate completely a condemned 'regime'." "Parlimentary socialists may be compared to the officials whom Napoleon made into a nobility and who laboured to strengthen the state bequeathed by the ancient regime. Revolutionary Syndicalism corresponds well enough to the Napoleonic armies whose soldiers accomplished such heroic acts, knowing all the time that they would remain poor. What remain of the empire? Nothing but the epic of the Grande armee. What will remain of the present socialist movement will be the epic of the strike." "Apology for violence." See *Reflections on Violence*, Appendix.
④ *Reflections on Violence*, p. 152.

would be an attempt to imitate democracy; it would be better for it to remain content for a time with weak and chaotic organization rather than that it should fall beneath the sway of syndicates which would copy the political forms of the middle class."①

The theory so based and so advanced seems to be pessimistic, but pessimism, says Sorel, is "a doctrine without which nothing very great has been accomplished in this world"②. "Pessimism is a philosophy of conduct rather than a theory of the world."③ "The pessimist regards social conditions as forming a system bound together by an iron law which cannot be evaded, so that this system is given, as it were, in one block, and cannot disappear except in a catastrophe which involves the whole. If this theory is admitted it then becomes absurd to make certain wicked men responsible for the evils from which society suffers; the pessimist is not subject to the sanguinary follies of the optimist, infatuated by the unexpected obstacles that his projects meet with; he does not dream of bringing about the happiness of future generations by slaughtering existing egoists."④

V. American Writers

1. Maciver

Concerning the subject under consideration, among the American writers, the most distinguished are Professor R. M. Maciver and Miss M. P. Follett. Professor Maciver's

---

① *Reflections on Violence*, p. 204. Sorel opposes strongly the so-called democracy advocated by statesmen, professors and thinkers at present day. See also his *Illussions du Progres*, 1911, p. 10. Although Sorel would not discuss the constructive program before the destructive work was completed, being a syndicalist, he certainly would think that the syndicatists or unionists of working men should handle the situation. And if there is still such a thing called power or sovereigty, it should be exercised by the syndicates.

② *Reflections on Violence*, p. 7.

③ *Ibid.*, p. 10.

④ *Ibid.* For Sorel's view, see also an article written by Professor W. Y. Elliott entitled "The Political Application of Romanticism" in *Political Science Quarterly*, Vol. XXXIX, 1924, pp. 234–264. For Syndicalism in general and the views of other writers, see the following books: Lagardelle, Huberts, and others, *Syndicalisme et Socialisme*, Paris, 1908; E. Berth, *Les nouveaux Aspects du Socialisme* (1908); E. Pataud and G. Pouget, *Syndicalism and the Cooperative Commonwealth*, trans by C. and F. Charles (1913); Fouget, Emile, *Sabotage* (1913); John Spargo, *Syndicalism, Industrial Unionism and Socialism* (1913); J. A. Estay, *Revolutionary Syndicalism* (1913); Louis Levine, *Syndicalism in America* (1913); F. G. Brooks, *American Syndicalism* (1913); P. F. Brissenden, *The I. W. W.: A Study in American Syndicalism* (1919); F. D. H. Cole., *World of Labour* (1917); Sidney Webb, and Beatrice, *What Syndicalism Means* (1912). For other French writers who advocate the power of sovereignty of the functional groups, see particularly M. Paul Boncour's *Le Federalisme Economic* and *Les Syndicats de Fonctionnaires*. According to Mr. Kirkup, Sorel has recently ceased to be a believer in Syndicalism, *History of Socialism*, 1920 ed., p. 294.

foundation of philosophy is laid in his earlier work entitled *Community: A Sociological Study* (1917). But his view is now fully developed in his recent book, *The Modern State*. This latter work has been highly praised by many well known scholars. ① "In his attack on the dogma of sovereignty," says Professor Jenks, "he is of course, not a pioneer. But it is seldom that the attack has been developed with such force, or with such a wealth of argument to support it."②

"The great difference between the political thought of our own time and that of the past," says Professor Maciver, "is the definite assertion of the limited and the relative characteracter of sovereignty."③ It is the old dogma which asserts that sovereignty of the state is the "final power, as free and unconditioned over human life as the will of an over-ruling God might be supposed to be."④ Such a theory as developed by the legalist "may be useful enough in its own place", but "it becomes not only inadequate but false when it is applied to explain the substantial nature of sovereignty."⑤

"Legally," he writes, "the state is unlimited, because it is itself the source of legal enactment; but it is no more absolute on that account than, say, the church, because it is the source of ecclesiastical law, or the Royal and Ancient Club, because it alone prescribes the laws of golf. We do not need to minimize the real and vital differences between political law and all other forms of social regulation. We merely insist that political law is but one form of social regulation. The state is 'one' of the organs of community, and we must reconcile with this cardinal fact both its great services and its greater claims."⑥

A state is defined an " [an] association which, acting through law as promulgated by a government endowed to this end with coercive power, maintains within a community territorially demarcated the universal external conditions of social order."⑦ And an association is defined as an organization of social beings for the pursuit of some common interest or interests.⑧ When an association is recognized by law as such, it becomes a corporation.⑨ An association, or a corporation comes into being just as a state comes

---

① Jenks, "Recent Theory of the State," in *Law Quarterly Review* (1927, April), p. 188.
② *Ibid.*, p. 192.
③ Maciver, *The Modern State*, p. 468.
④ *Ibid.*, p. 467.
⑤ *Ibid.*
⑥ *Ibid.*, pp. 467–468.
⑦ *Ibid.*, p. 22.
⑧ *Community*, p. 23. Also *The Modern State*, p. 6.
⑨ *The Modern State*, p. 473.

into existence. It may be said that an association exists within a community, but it is improper to say that it is within a state.① Here Professor Maciver agrees with Professor Gierke and Professor Maitland in that corporation is exterior to the state and therefore its character as a corporation need not require the permissive act of the state, for the state is bound to recognize it as such. "The state," says he, "is practically bound to acknowledge the corporate character, the rights and responsibilities of groups which operate as collectivities, and the formal recognition makes little difference to their character."② It is true, in a certain sense, that the state may dissolve a trust, or association, but at most "it is potent only to modify a mode of organization, and even so only with great difficulty, and under special conditions."③

But different from Professor Gierke and Professor Maitland, he denies the personality or will of the group. "We can not," he writes, "accept the attribution by Gierke and Maitland of a 'group mind' or a 'group will' or a 'group personality' to the corporation."④ A corporation is a unity, but not an integrity. It is simply an organization through which its members pursue a common purpose.⑤ In denying the personality of the group, he is logically led to deny the personality of the state. To him, to conceive the state as a personality of its own, is only an illusion.⑥

Since the state is only one of the association and since corporations or associations are on the same level with the state, the power of sovereignty exercised by the associations is just "as real as that exercised by the state; for sovereignty or power comes from the will of men and the will of men should not be confounded with the will of the citizens. It is a mistake to say, according to Professor Maciver, that power is merely the will of citizens, for the power is the will of social being."⑦

What then is the difference between the state and the other associations? The state is different from other associations in its regulative function: it settles the conflicts of the interests of different groups and marks "their boundaries and brings them into relation within a common order." But "it does not treat them as its own agencies, as subordinates which it commands." And "it does not and cannot determine their purposes

---

① *The Modern State*, p. 477, note.
② *The Modern State*, p. 475.
③ *Ibid.*
④ *Ibid.*, pp. 473-474. Cf. p. 490,
⑤ *Ibid.*, p. 247.
⑥ *Ibid.*, pp. 450-454.
⑦ *Ibid.*, p. 468, note.

or for the most part their methods."① In short, except as one group of interests encroaches on another, it does not deal with any of them in isolation from the rest. It does not say to the Trade Union, Go, and to the employer's association, Come, and to Church, Do this. These are the attributes of absolute sovereignty, and the state does not possess them."②

This being so, it follows that the sovereignty of the state is by no means superior to that of other associations. The interest of the state may be more extensive in range than many of the associations, but this does not give the state the character of superiority nor give it more right to claim loyalty from its members. On the contrary, interests are more closely connected and more intimate in the groups other than the state and a man's loyalty to a group is usually more than to a state. "On this account, the doctrine of absolute sovereignty, if actually practiced in the states of today with all their diversities of culture, would be fatal to the harmony of social life."③

Considering the state as one of the associations and considering the state and a corporation in their relation to law as the same, Professor Maciver comes almost to the position of Professor Krabbe in asserting the authority of law. The state, according to Professor Maciver, has the essential character of a corporation. If a corporation is subject to law, why not the state? The state, says he, is more the official guardian than the maker of the law.④

Regarding law as something exterior to the state and viewing it as the expression of the social sense, the sense of solidarity, the sense of common interest,⑤ he concurs with Professor Duguit, and particularly the latter's conception of public service. The power exercised by the state, to Professor Maciver as well as to Duguit, is only an instrument of service. "In the last resort," he writes, "it (power) is only an ability to render service which is recognized, constituted, and controlled by the kind of service it can render. It is possible of course to detach the means from the end. Men easily fall victims to that delusive habit of acceptance which makes them subservient to the institutions which should serve them. But they merely substitute in consequence a mystical for a real

---

① *The Modern State*, p. 476.

② *Ibid*.

③ *Ibid*., 477. "The claim of state supremacy… has often been successfully opposed, but it is never defeated by the opposition of unorganized individuals, only by individuals, organized into another association alongside or within the state." Maciver, "Supremacy of the State", *New Republic*, October, 1927, p. 304. In this respect, Professor Maciver agrees with Mr. Barker.

④ *Ibid*., pp. 478–479. Cf. pp. 263 ff.

⑤ *Ibid*., p. 481.

service. Always, in so far as they think at all, they must think of laws and other institutions as justified by their results. No one ever regards the service of the state as unlimited, and therefore the conception of unlimited sovereignty is dangerously false. To attribute power to government beyond the limit of its capacity for service is the grave error on which all tyranny is based."①

2. Follett

In her *The New State: Group Organization the Solution of Popular Government*. Miss Follett begins by presenting the following passages: "Our political life is stagnating, capital and labor are virtually at war, the nations of Europe are at one another's throats—because we have not yet learned how to live together. The twentieth century must find a new principle of association. Crowd philosophy, crowd government, crowd patriotism must go. The herd is no longer sufficient to enfold us."

"Group organization is to be the new method in politics, the basis of our future industrial system, the foundation of international order Group organization will create the new world we are now blindly feeling after, for creative force comes from the group, creative power is evolved through the activity of the group life."②

It is the group organization that should become the foundation of our social as well as political life and it is the group organization that hereafter our attention should be directed to. But by group organization is meant, mainly the neighborhood groups. "Our proposal," says she, "is that people should organize themselves into neighborhood groups to express their daily life, to bring to the surface the needs, desires and aspirations of that life, that these needs should become the substance of politics, and that these neighborhood groups should become the recognized political unit."③

Neighborhood groups are both necessary and desirable, because in the first place, it is there that fuller acquaintance and more real understanding between the people are possible and secondly neighborhood organization gives opportunity for constant and regular intercourse.④

While emphasizing the importance of neighborhood groups, she does not ignore entirely the occupational group.⑤ Both of these groups are necessary, because the

---

① *The Modern State*, p. 468. From Professor J. Dickson, the writer learns that Professor Maciver has written an important article on sovereignty in *Economica* for November, 1926. See "A working Theory of Sovereignty" in *Political Science Quarterly*, Vol. XLII, 1927, p. 524.
② Follett, *The New State*, 1918, p. 3. See also *Creative Experience*.
③ *Ibid.*, p. 192.
④ *Ibid.*
⑤ *Ibid.*, p. 320.

present industrial and economic conditions make them so. But it is better, however, to work out some machinery by which the neighborhood group can include the occupational groups. "All our functions," she insists, "must be expressed, but somewhere must come that coordination which will give them their real effectiveness."① It is for this reason that both the neighborhood and occupational groups either independently or one through the other, must both find representation in the state. In short, be it neighborhood, be it economic or any other kind, but the point that she emphasizes is that it is not the kind of group, "but that the group whatever its nature shall be a genuine group."②

By a "genuine group", Miss Follett means the genuine whole. But the idea of a genuine whole does not belong to the group alone. Thus there is a genuine whole of an individual, of a state and of the world as well as that of a group. And it is the genuine whole that possesses the supreme power or sovereignty. Thus wherever there is a genuine whole there is a sovereignty. "The individual is sovereign over himself as far as he unifies the heterogeneous elements of his nature. Two people are sovereign over themselves as far as they are capable of creating one out of two. A group is sovereign over itself as far as it is capable of creating one out of several or many. A state is soveriegn only as it has the power of creating one in which all are." "Sovereignty," she continues, "is the power engendered by a complete interdependence becoming conscious of itself. Sovereignty is the imperative of a true collective will. It is not something academic, it is produced by actual living with others—we learn it only through group life. By the subtle process of interpenetration a collective sovereignty is evolved from a distributed sovereignty. Just so can and must, by the law of their being, groups unite to form large groups, these larger groups to form a world-group."③

It is obvious that sovereignty is not absolute, for it is engendered by a complete interdependence. It may be different in extent, but not in content. The sovereignty of an individual is just as real as that of a group, of a state or even of the world state. Thus the old conception that sovereignty is the essential characteristic of the state finds no room in Miss Follett's system. Moreover, the collective sovereignty is only a product of the attributed sovereignty. The unit of attributed sovereignty starts from the individual. Without the attributed sovereignty, there will be no collective sovereignty. The sovereignty of a group is a collective sovereignty, because it is composed of many

---

① Follett, *The New State*, 1918, pp. 320–321.
② *Ibid.*, p. 323.
③ *Ibid.*, p. 271.

sovereignties of individuals or many attributed sovereignties; but in turn the collective sovereignty of the group may be considered as an attributive sovereignty, because it may be one of the many attributed sovereignties of a larger group. Only the collective sovereignty of the world as a whole may not, it seems to Miss Follett, or at least according to the logical consequence of her reasoning, be an attributive sovereignty.

Thus Miss Follett's whole system may be reduced to the problem of "one" and "many". By the subtle process of interpenetration, many sovereignties may become one sovereignty and perhaps it is equally true that one may become many. "The one and many," says she, "are constantly creating each other." But "when we say that there is one which comes 'from' the many, this does not mean that the one is 'above' the many. The deepest truth of life is that the interelating by which both are at the same time a-making is constant. This must be clearly understood in the building of the new state."①

From the passage quoted above, we may understand the position of Miss Follett more clearly. The sovereignty of the state may be a collective sovereignty of many attributed sovereignties, be they individuals or groups, but the sovereignty of the state is not superior to, or to use her own word, "above", the sovereignty of individuals or groups, for the sovereignty of a genuine whole of an individual or a group is just the same and has as much weight as that of the state.

And the salient feature of her conception of sovereignty is that she goes a step deeper to link up the sovereignty of the world as a whole to that of the individuals. Thus worldism, nationalism (ate) and individualism combine together in her system. ②

VI. Conclusion

All the writers mentioned above deny the old theory that sovereignty is one, indivisible, absolute and unlimited, and they all oppose the view that sovereignty is the essential characteristic of the state. Perhaps with the exception of the syndicalist whose main purpose is to destroy the state and therefore its sovereignty entirely, it may be said that all the other theorists recognize to a certain extent the existence of sovereignty. ③ Moreover, they seem to agree that sovereignty may be different in extent, but not in content. Furthermore, in their minds, there is a whole sovereignty for the whole world,

---

① Follett, *The New State*, 1918, p. 284.

② If I am not mistaken, Miss Follett has been profoundly influenced by Professor Cooley of Michigan (particularly his *Social Organization*).

③ Mr. Cole certainly likes to see the entire disappearance of sovereignty.

though it is not realized at present.

They all emphasize the importance of group life and therefore, the inherent power exercised by the group. On the one hand, some of them, like Mr. Barker and Professor Maciver would minimize the importance of the individuals in their relation to the sovereignty of the state. On the other hand, some, like Miss Follett, think that the sovereignty of an individual is just as real as that of other groups or states. Some of them like Professors Gierke and Maitland, emphasize the personality and will of the group and it is chiefly on that proposition that the sovereignty of the group is justified. But, some, like Professor Maciver and Mr. Cole, refuse to recognize the conception of group will or personality. Power, they seem to think, is necessary for the existence of a socially organized group. While a socially organized group may not be a conscious creation of human mind, this does not necessarily mean that the group has a personality or will of its own.

The principle involved in the writings of the theorists presented above are general and almost the same; but the methods of approach are different. Roughly speaking, it may be viewed from the legal, ecclesissastical, economical, psychological, social-psychological, and sociological standpoints. Professor Maitland approaches from the legal point of view, Professor Figgis from the ecclesiastical, Mr. Cole the economical, Professor Gierke the psychological, Miss Follett the social-psychological, and Professor Maciver the sociological. It is to be noted, however, the distinctions here made must not be pressed too far; for our purpose, it is the principle rather than the method, to which attention should be chiefly given.

CHAPTER X
LASKI AND OHTERS

I. Laski

1. Introduction

The name of Mr. Harold J. Laski has been intimately connected with the pluralistic doctrine of sovereignty. Perhaps it is not going too far to say that he is the most outstanding figure of this new movement. If the pluralistic doctrine of sovereignty will not be forgotten by the later generations, Mr. Laski will be long remembered by students of the history of the notion of sovereignty.

But Mr. Laski was not the first writer who enunciated this doctrine. In fact, the doctrine itself is not, comparatively speaking, a recent product. Looking back to the writings of the seventeenth century, we find the following passage written by Grotius, the so-called father of International Law, in his *De Jure Belli Ac Pacis*: "It is to be noted that sovereignty, though in itself a unit and indivisible, composed of those parts which we have enumerated, with the addition of irresponsibility, may be divided in possession. Thus the Roman imperial power, though one, was often divided, so that one ruler had the East, another the West; or even into three parts. So too it may happen that a people when it chooses a king may reserve certain acts to itself, and commit others to the king 'pleno jure'. This is not the case whenever the king is bound by certain promises, as we have shown above. But it is to be understood to happen when the partition of power is expressly instituted, concerning which we have already spoken; or if a people, hitherto free, lay upon the king some perpetual precept; or if anything be added to the compact, by which it is understood that the king can be compelled or punished. For a precept is the act of a superior, at least in the thing commanded. To compel is not always the act of a superior, for by natural law a creditor has the right of coercing his debtor; but to compel is at variance with the nature of an inferior. Therefore in case of such compulsion, a parity of powers, at least, follows, and sovereignty is divided." And he adds: "Many persons allege many inconveniences against such a two-headed sovereignty.

But in political matters nothing is entirely free from inconvenience."①

It is clear that Grotius begins with some doubt as to the divisibility of sovereignty, yet he is forced to end with an emphatic tongue in asserting that in practice it is divided. Viewed from this point, the father of international law may also be called the father of the pluralistic doctrine of sovereignty. The idea advanced by Grotius did not make much headway during the century following the appearance of his well known treatise. The reason seems to be simple. The nationalistic movement was then vigorous and the power of the king was at its high-water mark. The monarch of France could boast to the world that "I am the state". And the statement of James Ⅰ, that "kings are justly called gods, for they exercise a manner of resemblance of Divine power upon earth," had its best defenders. Filmer and Hobbes did not exhaust the list of them.

But the establishment of the American Union under the constitution of 1787 brought a new era in the history of the notion of sovereignty. Most of the fathers of the constitution of 1787 believed in the possibility of dividing sovereignty and that, under the American system, it is divided between the states on the one hand and the federal union on the other. This view was widely accepted by statesmen and various writers particularly during the early history of the Republic.

The American doctrine or rather the divisibility doctrine of sovereignty, advocated by De Tocqueville in his well known treaties, *Democracy in America*, has been adopted by many European statesmen and writers for explaining the location of sovereignty of the Swiss and German federations or confederations. The salient feature of the pluralistic theory as advocated by the European writers is that soverignty may be limited in extent, but not in content. They argue that the states, i.e., the members of the federation, are sovereign within their own sphere and so the federal union. They would be prepared to say that the sovereignty of the federal union is larger in extent than that of the several states, but that both are the same in content. It seems that Professor Gierke has grasped this idea quite closely and extended it into another form, which in turn has been followed by a group of writers whom we have considered in the previous chapter.

Generally speaking, those who hold that sovereignty is divided in a federal state, speak of sovereignty from its external and internal aspects. They maintain that although the several states lost their external sovereignty by becoming members of the federal state, they retain, however, their internal sovereignty. Thus while the federal union is sovereign in international affairs, the states are sovereign in things internal or local.

---

① Grotius, *De Jare Belli ac Pacis*, Book Ⅰ, ch. 3, see 17, also sec. 20. For the English translation here used, see Coker, *Readings in Political Philosophy*, p. 275.

The idea so advanced by writers on the federal state has been entertained by international lawyers and various writers on international reldations. While the theory of sovereignty in its application to international relations is more complicated than in regard to the federal state, the pluralistic doctrine has developed into various forms. Besides the conception of internal and external sovereignty, we have the so-called partial sovereignty which, being closely connected with the former, is nevertheless different from it. For, as has been pointed out, although all states which only possess internal sovereignty are partial sovereign states, not all partial sovereign states are states which have only internal sovereignty. The so-called double sovereignty limitations on sovereignty, violation of sovereignty and contempt of sovereignty, though not signifying that sovereignty is divided in the strict sense of the term, are nevertheless closely connected with it.

Side by side with the theory that sovereignty is divided in the federal state and in international relations, is the theory that sovereignty may be divided into many parts within one set of government in any form of state. Thus they may be what is called legislative, executive, and judicial sovereignty, as there is legislative, executive and judicial branches of government. Each is sovereign within its own sphere. It seems that this view was clearly entertained by Alexander Hamilton. The historical evidence that Hamilton employed to support it was the governmental system of the ancient Roman republic. The view was fully developed in the writings of Professor Salmond at the beginning of this century.

While admitting that sovereignty may be divided into parts within a state, whether it is a federal state or a unitary state, many thinkers insist that sovereignty is essential to the state. Only a state, they say, can be possessor of sovereignty and it is sovereignty that makes the state such. On the other hand, as has been pointed out, over against this argument comes a group of German writers who maintain that it is right rather than sovereignty that is essential to a state. The several states in a federal state, though losing their sovereignty by becoming members of the federal union, retain the characteristics of a state and therefore should be considered as states, in the proper sense of the term.

It seems that the position so taken is to harmonize the conflict between those who hold the doctrine of the sovereignty of the federal union and those who defend the sovereignty of the several states, and consequently to escape the criticism made against the divisibility doctrine of sovereignty. They are not willing to accept the view that sovereignty is divided between the states on the one hand and the union on the other, yet they are not prepared to reduce the status of the several states in the federal states to that of a commune of France or a county of England.

Approaching it from a different angle, the pluralistic doctrine of sovereignty and the view that sovereignty is not an essential characteristic of the state, have been combined and compromised, unconsciously or consciously, in the writings of Professor Gierke. Professor Gierks starts by denying the fiction theory of corporations which regards the corporation as a mere creature of, or a body which derives its rights and powers from, the state. A corporation, says Professor Gierke, exists as the state exists. It comes into being as the state does. It has a will and personality of its own, and, therefore, it exercises an inherent power which is the same in content as that of the state. Thus sovereignty is not a thing which can only be owned and exercised by the state, for it may also be owned and exercised by any organized group which has a personality and will of its own. Being owned and exercised by a number of organized groups which are within the boundary of the state, sovereignty is, as a matter of fact, divided and divisible.

The view advanced by Professor Gierke was introduced into the English world by Professor Maitland and elaborated by various writers from different standpoints. Among the leading exponents, Professor Figgis and Mr. Barker are undoubtedly the most conspicuous. And it is largely in the writings of these writers that Mr. Laski finds his source of inspiration. Mr. Laski acknowledges his indebtedness to numerous writers in different countries. From the preface to his *Problem of Sovereignty*, we read: "How much it owes to Maitland and Saleilles and Dr. Figgis, I dare not estimate; but if it sends anyone to their books (and particularly to Maitland's) I shall be well content. I owe much too, to the work of my friend and colleague, Professor McIlwain, from whose 'High Court of Parliament' I have derived a whole fund of valuable ideas. Nor have I, as I hope, failed to learn the lesson to be learned from the constitutional opinions with which Mr. Justice Holmes has enriched this generation. I would add that it was from Mr. Fisher that I first learned to understand the value of individuality, as it was from Mr. Barker that I first learned the meaning of community."

In the preface to his *Authority in the Modern State* he wrote: "Among the dead, I would like to emphasize how very much I have learned from Acton and Maitland; their writings have been to me a veritable store-house of inspiration. Among living men, I owe much to Professor Duguit of Bordeaux, to Dr. Figgis, and, in spite of, and perhaps because of, our differences, to Professor Dicey. My old tutor, Mr. Ernest Barker of New College, is the unconscious sponsor of this, as of my earlier book... My colleagues, Dean Pound and Professor McIlvain, have been untiring in their constant encouragement; and from Dean Pound's own writings, soon, one may hope, to be collected in some more permanent form, I learned the value of a pragmatic theory of state-function. My friends of the New Republic, particularly Mr. Francis Hackett, and Mr. Herbert Croly, have given me generous assistance. Mr. Graham Wallas has lent me great aid by friendly and suggestive counsel; and I found his 'Great Society' an invaluable guide to many difficult paths. To an unknown critic in the London Times I owe the debt that keen comment must always create."

Again we read in his *Foundations of Sovereignty:* "I believe profoundly that no attempt at reconstruction of our present institutions is likely to be successful save in so far as it is deeply rooted in historic knowledge. For that purpose we must go, not merely to men like Maitland and Gierke, Figgis and Mr. Justice Holmes, but to the actual texts themselves. In things like the Councilar Movement, the marvelous edifice of Edmund Burke, the struggle for the Charter, the early history of American federalism; in lesser men like John Taylor of Carolina no less than in the great thinkers like Hamilton himself will the clues to our problems be found. Nor does the literature of our own time lack suggestiveness. In law, men like Pound and Duguit; in economics, the superb edifice of Mr. and Mrs. Sidney Webb; in history, the work of Tawney and Hovell and Mr. and Mrs. Hammond; in administrative science, the books of Mr. Graham Wallas and the analysis of Lord Haldane; in politics, the brilliant, if too brief, suggestions of Mr. F. D. H. Cole; all of these, in their sum, are the marks of a movement which to the next generation will appear not less influential than the work done a century ago by the Utilitarians."

And lastly, in his recent book, *A Grammar of Politics*, we are told that, "my book owes an immense debt to friends. Among my colleagues, Professor L. T. Hobhouse and Graham Wallas, Mr. R. H. Tawney, both by their books and in conversation, have been endlessly helpful; and of others, I should like especially to thank Lord Haldane, Mr. Justice Holmes, Dr. Josef Redlich, Professor Felix Frankfurter and Dean Pound."

The writer has quoted these few passages freely, partly because all the names enumerated by Mr. Laski have more or less influenced him, and, therefore, may be regarded as his intellectual affiliations, and partly because the doctrines of some of the writers here named have not been and will not be presented in this study, although their conception of sovereignty are by no means less important than those we have discussed.

2. Works

Mr. Laski's first article on sovereignty which I have been able to discover was one entitled "Personality of the State" published in the *Nation* in July 1915. The proposition set forth in this essay may be regarded as the main thought of Laski. He attacks vigorously the monistic theory of sovereignty and the fictitious theory of the corporation. On the other hand, he follows the pluralistic doctrine of William James and the argument advanced by Professor Gierke and his successors. His *Studies in the Problem of Sovereignty*, published in 1917, consists of various essays. The first essay on "The Sovereignty of the Stare", read at the Fourth Conference on Legal and Social Philosophy at Columbia University November 27, 1915, largely restated the words as well as the ideas of the first article mentioned above. The four essays following the first are studies, largely suggested by Professor Figgis in his *Churches in the Modern State*, on the disruption of the Scotch Church (1843), the Oxford movement, the Catholic revival in England, in France following the French Revolution of which de Maistre was the most conspicuous exponent, and the "Kulturekamfpf" in Germany. The two appendixes entitled "Sovereignty and Federalism" and "Sovereignty and Centralization" set forth the idea that sovereignty is federal in nature and denied that the Austinian theory can find a place in a federal state such as the United States.

Another volume, entitled *Authority in the Modern State*, appearers in 1919. This volume, to use Mr. Laski's own language, "covered rather broader ground, since its main object is to insist that the problem of sovereignty is only a special case of the problem of authority, and to indicate what I should regard as the main path of approach to its solution". The first essay bears the title of the book restated, and develops his main argument. The studies of Bonald, Lamennais and Royer-Collard show a continuation of his earlier study of ecclesiastical history and of de Maistre. The last essay on "Administrative Syndicalism in France" goes to a new field of study. He inclines to think that the movement of the "functionaires" to organize syndicates as against the unconditional authority of the state is justified.

A third volume bearing the title *Foundations of Sovereignty*, consists of a numerous essays which, as he states in his preface, "are part of a scaffolding from which there is, I hope, eventually to emerge a general reconstruction of the state." A fourth volume which is entitled *A Grammer of Politics*, as he remarks, "is more positive and general, since it attempts to outline the institutions which my researches have suggested as desirable."①

A general survey of the writings of Mr. Laski shows that while his earlier writings are mainly destructive and critical, his recent works are more constructive. In the main, he gets inspiration from Mr. E. Barker, but he draws the substance chiefly from

---

① *A Grammar of Politics*, preface.

Professor Figgis. Recently he seems to be influenced more by the socialists who chiefly aim at an economic reconstruction of society. In short, it may be said that while Mr. Laski has used the ecclesiastical evidence to destroy the Leviathan, he builds his castle on an economic basis.

3. A Combination of the Pluralistic theories

Having been influenced by a number of writers as we have already indicated, the theory of Mr. Laski may be regarded as a combination of the pluralistic theories of various writers. He shares the view of those who hold that sovereignty is not a unity and is divided in a federal state. In speaking of the sovereign power in the United States, he says, "Had he commented with any fulness upon it, the Constitution of the United States would doubtless have provoked the vehement derision of John Austin, for nowhere, either in theory or in practice, has it chosen to erect an instrument of sovereign power… We do not know who rules. Certainly the president is not absolute. Neither to Congress nor to the Supreme Court is unlimited power decreed. And, as if to make confusion worse confounded, there cut athwart this dubiousness certain sovereign rights possessed by the States alone"[①].

He stands on the radical side with those writers whom we have grouped under our discussion on sovereignty and international relations. On the international side, he declares, the notion of an independent sovereign state is fatal to the well-being of humanity. "The common life of States," he writes, "is a matter for common agreement between states. International government, is therefore, axiomatic in any plan for international well being. But international government implies the organized subordination of States to an authority in which each may have a voice, but in which also, that voice is never the self-determined source of decision."[②]

As to the relation of sovereignty to law, he takes the same position as those who attack the Austinian dogma. He has been influenced particularly by such writers as Pound, Holmes, Duguit, and Krabbe. Like Pound he holds the pragmatic theory of law.[③] It is from Holmes that he is led to declare that law is written out of experience.[④] Somewhat like Krabbe he maintains that law itself is the final authority.[⑤] And he seems to share the view of Duguit that law is the law of public service rather than the law of

---

① *Studies in the Problem of Sovereignty*, p. 267. Cf. *A Grammar of Politics*, pp. 270 ff.
② *A Grammar of Politics*, p. 65, also Ch. XI.
③ See *Problem of Sovereignty*, p. 64. Also *Authority in the Modern State*, preface.
④ *A Grammar of Politics*, p. 278.
⑤ See *ibid.*, pp. 386 ff.

sovereignty.① "We are urging," he declares, "that law is, in truth, not the will of the state, but that from which the will of the state derives whatever moral authority it may possess. That is, admittedly, the abandonment of simplicity. It assumes that the ratoinale of obedience is in all the intricate facts of social organization and in no one group of facts. It denies at once the sovereignty of the state, and that more subtle doctrine by which the state is at once the master and the servant of law by willing to limit itself to certain tested rules of conduct. It insists that what is important in law is not the fact of command but the end at which that command aims and the way it achieves the end. It sees a society, not as a pyramid in which the State sits crowned upon the summit, but as a system of cooperating interests which, and in which, the individual finds his scheme of values. It argues that each individual scheme so found gives to the law whatever of moral rightness it contains. Law, that is to say, is made valid by my experience of it, and not by the fact it is presented to me as law. Such experience, indeed, is rarely separate in kind (though it is always unique in degree) because it is shared with others in the effort to make an impact upon society. It appears as an interest which seeks the objectivity of realization. It strives to suffuse the law with its sense of need. It judges the law by what it recognizes therein of that sense as satisfied. It therefore demands a system of social conditions in which the end capable of being achieved is both worthy of achievement and relevant to itself, therein appears the importance of the idea of rights. For these make the path of law a road which leads to the fulfilment of desire; and those who seek fulfilment are entitled to consider their needs equal in significance to the needs of others. Law then emerges as the evaluation of interests by the interests by the interweaving of interests. It is a function of the whole social structure and not of some given aspect of it. Its power is determined by the degree to which it aids what that whole social structure reports as its desire."② And one who is familiar with the theories of law of the so-called sociological school will not fail to see the sources from which the passage quoted above has been taken.

Law then is not the command of sovereignty. "Any attempt, as with Austin," says he in another place, "to discover the sovereign is a difficult, and often an impossible, adventure. It postulates for the sovereign the possession of qualities which can not in fact be exercised. It narrows down the meaning of vital terms to a content which, if maintained, would be fatal to the existence of the society. Political philosophy must,

---

① Cf. *A Grammar of Politics*, p. 27.
② *A Grammar of Politics*, pp. 286–287.

doubtless, consider law as an important factor in the life of the State. But it must also bear ceaselessly in mind that the method of approach to the nature of the law is, for itself, either akin to that suggested by Montesquieu, or else more likely to deceive than to assist. Law, for the student of politics, is built upon the general social environment. It expresses what are held to be the necessary social relations of a state at some given period. The organ by which it is declared to be law is, for politics, incomparably less important than the forces which made the organ act in the particular way."①

Thus it is obvious that no such thing as sovereignty exists at all in the Austinian sense. ② What is called legal sovereignty is in fact worthless. It has been sometimes pointed out that Mr. Laski recognizes the supremacy of legal sovereignty because he expressly declares that "legally, no one can deny that there exists in every state some organ whose authority is unlimited." The criticism so based seems to be unfair, for Mr. Laski adds immediately after the statement just quoted that "but that legality is no more than a fiction of logic."③ Thus it is said that in England, the sovereignty is the king in Parliament. But can the King and Parliament do what they like? No, Says Mr. Laski. Suppose Parliament chose to enact that no Englishman should become a Roman Catholic, argues Mr. Laski, it would certainly fail to carry out the statute into effect; ④ for "no sovereign has anywhere possessed unlimited power; and the attempt to exert it has always resulted in the establishment of safeguards. Even the Sultan of Turkey in the height of his power was himself bound down by a code of traditional observance, obedience to which was practically compulsory upon him. In law there was no part of the field of social fact he could not alter; in practice he survived only by willing not to will those changes which might have proved him the sovereign of Austinian jurisprudence."⑤

While denying the validity of the doctrine of legal sovereignty, Mr. Laski does not think that the solution offered by Professor Dicey to distinguish between legal and political sovereignty is satisfactory. To make such distinction "is at once to imply that the notion of sovereignty is the divisible which is entirely contradictory of the original definition."⑥ Equally the suggestion of Austin that the sovereign in England is the electoract can not be accepted; "for in the first place the Crown and the House of Lords

---

① *A Grammar of Politics*, p. 55.
② *Foundations of Sovereignty*, p. 236.
③ *Foundations of Sovereignty*, p. 236.
④ *Problems of Sovereignty*, p. 12.
⑤ *A Grammar of Politics*, p. 51.
⑥ *Ibid.*, p. 54.

are not representative of the Commons in any sense to which precision can be attached, and when Austin goes on to argue that the sovereign electorate may delegate its powers either subject to the trust or trusts or 'absolutely and unconditionally', he fails to remember the logical meaning of a definition which implies the impossibility of alienation. If the electorate merely created a trust, the latter would not be a sovereign body. If it created a sovereign body, in the sense Austin gave that term, it would itself cease to be sovereign."①

It is obvious that to Mr. Laski, the conception of sovereignty is something more, and much more, than that viewed by the lawyers; and Mr. Laski has expressly and freely admitted this fact.② What, then, in the mind of Mr. Laski, is the meaning of sovereignty? Here is the answer and here is one of the most important points, if not the most important point in the system of Mr. Laski. "We have," he declares, "therefore, to find the true meaning of sovereignty not in the coercive power possessed its instrument, but in the fused good-will for which it stands. Men accept its dictates either because their own will finds part expression there or because, assuming the goodness of intention which lies behind it, they are content, usually, not to resist its imposition. But then law clearly is not a command. It is simply a rule of convenience. Its goodness consists in its consequences. It has to prove itself. It does not, therefore, seem wise to argue that parliament, for example, is omnipotent in a special sense. The power parliament exerts is situate in it not by law, but by consent, and that the consent is, as certain famous instances have shown, liable to suspension… Where sovereignty prevails, where the state acts, it acts by the consent of man."③

It is the keynote of the theory of Mr. Laski that ultimate sovereignty rests with the individual and therefore it is sovereign in so far as the individual consents to obey it and recognizes it as such; for "sovereignty, after all, is no more than the name we give to a certain special will that can count upon unwonted strength for its purpose."④ The individual is always and everywhere the corner stone of social action.⑤ The individual is an end himself. He is not merely a means for attaining certain ends. If the individual is to be regarded as an end, all social institutions are simply the means. The state is not an end. "Every state," he declares, "is known by the rights that it maintains. Our

---

① *A Grammar of Politics*.
② *Problem of Sovereignty*, p. 16.
③ *Ibid.*, pp. 12-13.
④ *Foundations of Sovereignty*, p. 210.
⑤ *A Grammar of Politics*, p. 259.

method of judging its character lies, above all, in the contribution that it makes to the substance of man's happiness."① In insisting that the happiness of the individual is the end of social organization, Mr. Laski builds his system on the utilitarian basis. "The individual, that is to say, is to become increasingly the centre of social importance. Otherwise, in so vast a world, his claims may well suffer neglect. After all it was for his happiness that the state, at least in philosophical interpretation, existed from its origins; for if the good life does not bring happiness to humble men and women it is without meaning. So that it is upon the happiness he is able to attain that our judgment of its processes must be founded."②

To attain the happiness of the individual, the individual must have right or rights to demand and claim for what he thinks to be essential to his happiness. Freedom of speech, a living wage, and adequate education, a proper leisure, the power to combine for special effort, are all rights which are integral to the individual as a member of the state. Such rights are not rights which derived their validity from the authority of the state, for they are inherent rights. "They are natural rights in the sense that without them the purpose of the state can not be fulfilled. They are natural also in the sense they do not depend upon the state for their validity. They are inherent in the eminent worth of human personality. Where they are denied, the state clearly destroys whatever claims it has upon the loyalty of man. Rights such as these are necessary to freedom because without them man is lost in a world almost beyond the reach of his understanding. We have put them outside the power of the state to traverse; and this again must mean a limit upon its sovereignty."③ One may argue that such a theory countenances anarchy; but injustice is worse than anarchy.

The individual then is the center of social action, and sovereignty must be based on his will. In order to show whether sovereignty can be divided or not; we must, first of all, show whether or not will is divisible. Here we come to Mr. Laski's philosophical basis of pluralism.

In his *A Pluralistic Universe* William James declares: "Pragmatically interpreted pluralism or the doctrine that it is many means only that the sundry parts of reality 'may be externally related'. Everything you can think of, however vast or inclusive, has on the pluralistic view a genuinely 'external' environment of some sort or amount. Things are 'with' one another in many ways, but nothing includes everything, or dominates

---

① *A Grammar of Politics*, p. 89.
② *Authority in Modern State*, p. 120.
③ *Foundations of Sovereignty*, p. 246.

over everything. The word 'and' trails along after every sentence. Something always escapes. 'Ever not quite' has to be said of the best attempts made anywhere in the universe at attaining all-inclusiveness. The pluralistic world is thus more like a federal republic than like an empire or a kingdom. However much may be collected, however much may report itself as present at any effective center of consciousness or action, something else is self-governed and absent and unreduced to unity."①

One who reads the essays of Mr. Laski can easily see how much he has been inspired by this passage. For he believes, as James does, that the universe is pluralistic in nature. He refuses the monistic view that "everywhere the One comes before Many. All Manyness has its origin in Oneness and to Oneness it returns. Therefore all order consists in the subordination of Plurality and Unity, and never and nowhere can a purpose that is common to Many be effectual unless the One rules over the Many and directs the Many to the Goal." "We do not," he declares, "proceed from the state to the parts of the state, from the One to the Many, on the ground that the state is more unified than its parts; on the contrary, I contend that the parts are as real and self-sufficing as the whole. I do not know the United States before I know, say, New York, and Albany. It is from Albany and New York that I came to know the United States. Of course, the knowledge of them will lead to a knowledge of the Republic, simply because there is logical relation between them."②

Pluralism is almost pragmatism, and to Mr. Laski, pluralism is not only a fact, but it is a theory of progress. "It is from the selection of variations, not from the preservation of uniformities, that progress is born." To show more clearly the difference between the monistic and pluralistic views, let us read the following passages: "We start with a complex of impulses—all of them striving for the realization of personality. We find that the state such as our own can satisfy these strivings of relatively few of its members… The result is at every point repression with the manifold inversions that accompany it. The pluralistic state takes it rise from the need to satisfy those impulses in a better way. In a unified state the ultimate emphasis is upon authority, i. e. to disagree with the government is to be wrong. The pluralistic state emphasizes freedom by distributing authority in order that there may be channels through which the individual can find satisfaction he is unlikely to discover where one way of life only wins approval. The unified state, in short, implies repression with wastage; the pluralistic state endeavors to provide avenues of considered compensation. We must, of course, by a rigorous analysis

---

① James, *A Pluralistic Universe*, pp. 321–322.
② Laski, "Personality of the State," *The Nation*, Vol. 101, 1915, p. 115.

of history discover the types of avenue which are socially advantageous. We can not, in social life, wait, for instance, upon unanimity, but, where a rule is enforced by a majority against a minority, we seek to make the means of judgment and enforcement such that a balked disposition on that minority's part is not the result. We seek, that is to say, the means of a considered consent as the basis of political action. Anything else involves repression which is ultimately a denial of personality. Now personality is a complex thing and the institutions—religious, industrial, political, —in which it clothes itself are as a consequence manifold. The pluralistic state is an endeavor to express in terms of structure the fact we thus encounter. It asserts no primacy for any one of them because it cannot assign a priori significance to human acts without a knowledge of their background. It thus denies the logic of a sovereignty in its classical conception because that is a viciously abstract elevation of one aspect of human institutions where, at the given moment, some other man, for many, have a most poignant and compelling demand. It destroys, if you like, the sovereign state that it may preserve the personality of man."①

Thus in a pluralistic state, there is no room for sovereignty as conceived by the classical conception. Sovereignty, as has been noticed, must be based on the will of the individual. As the universe is pluralistic, so is the will. "For the starting point of every political philosophy is the inexpugnable variety of human wills. There is no continuity between them... The wills converge to a common purpose; but they are separate in everything save the substance of the thing willed."②

The theory so advanced naturally rejects the general will of Rousseau. "If the will itself is separate in each member of society," says Mr. Laski, "it is still more clear that it does not form a single and common will. Any one, indeed, who looks at the character of modern life would find its most distinguished feature in the existence of a multiplicity of wills which have no common purposes which drive them to identity."③

It is true that a man may submit his will to a state but equally is it true that he may submit his will to a church or other associations because he is a member thereof. If the state can claim sovereignty over him, because he submits his will to it, why not a church? "Sovereignty is, in its exercise, an act of will, whether to do or to refrain from doing. It is an exercise of will behind which there is such power as to make the expectation of obedience reasonable. Now it does not seem valuable to urge that a

---

① See *New Republic*, Vol. XIX, 1919, pp. 148–150.
② *A Grammar of Politics*, pp. 31–32.
③ *Ibid.*, p. 32.

certain group, the State, can theoretically secure obedience to all its acts, because we know that practically to be absurd. This granted, it is clear that the sovereignty of the State does not in reality differ from the power exercised by a Church or a trade union."①

If the wills of an individual are not a unity and if the personality does not cease to be personality because his wills are not unified, it follows that the personality of a church or a trade union is just as real as that of an individual, in spite of the fact that the wills of the church or the trade union are not unified. So too the personality of the groups is just as that of the state, for both the state and the groups come in the same way and depend upon the same basis, yet they are independent from each other, "because a group or an individual is related to some other group or individual it is not thereby forced to enter into relation with every other part of the body politic."② "When a trade union ejects one of its members for refusing to pay a political levy it is not thereby bringing itself into relations with the Mormon Church. A trade union as such has no connection with the Mormon Church; it stands self-sufficient on its own legs. It may work with the State, but it need not do so of necessity. It may be in relations with the State, but it is one with it and not of it. The State, to use James' term once more, is 'distributive' and not 'collective'. There are no essential connections."③

We are forced to personalize the association as well as the state, because man is an associative animal. In every sphere of human activity, there is some kind of association. Each of these associations has its own purpose which distinguishes it from the others and its purpose postulates its personality. Thus he writes: "Clearly when we take any group of people to whom some kindred idea or common purpose may be ascribed, we seem to evolve from it a thing, a personality, that, in a somewhat complex sense, is beyond the personalities of its elements. That personality is real for us; for when we assume its truth, the assumption leads to concrete differences in life."④ Such a personalized group is a distinctive self-governing body. It has its government or machinery through which the complex wills are expressed. It has its own power which is not derivative in the sense of the fictitious theory that it is granted by the state. This is the fact. And everywhere we find that the sovereignty of the groups challenges the supremacy of the state. In

---

① *Problems of Sovereignty*, p. 270.
② *Ibid.*, p. 10.
③ *Problems of Sovereignty*, p. 10. Also *Authority in the Modern State*, pp. 26-27.
④ See *The Nation*, Vol. 101, p. 115.

short, Mr. Laski is here insisting what Mr. Barker calls "polyarchism"①. A group may be in relations with the state, but that does not mean that it must do so; for if it has come into being without being related to the state, it will exist independently of the state. Part of it may be within the state, but not all of it, for it has its own interest, its own purpose and its own will which are different from those of the state.

What then is the position of the state? The state, says Mr. Laski, is a public service corporation. "It differs from every other association in that it is, in the first place, an association in which membership is compulsory. It is, in the second place, essentially territorial in nature. The interests of men as consumers are largely neighborhood interests; they require satisfaction, for the most part in a given place. And, at a given level, the interests of its members are identical interests. They all need food and clothing, education, and shelter. The state is the body which seeks so to organize the interests of consumers that they obtain the commodities of which they have need. Within the state, they meet as persons. Their claims are equal claims. They are not barristers or miners, Catholics or Protestants, employers, or workers. They are, as a matter of social theory, simply persons who need certain services they can not themselves produce if they are to realize themselves."②

And Mr. Laski adds: "Clearly, a function of this kind, however it is organized, involves a pre-eminence over other functions. The State controls the level at which men are to live as men. It is, in administrative terms, a government whose activities are shaped by the common needs of its members. To satisfy those common needs, it must control other associations to the degree that secures from them the service such needs require. The more closely a given function—education, for example, or the provision of coal—lies to the heart of the society, the more closely it will require to be controlled. Each function, that is to say, must be so organized in the interest of the consumer that it permits him access to a full civic life. There is a limit to the numbers of hours of labour a man can work and yet remain a human being. There is an income below which no man can be allowed to fall if he is to maintain himself as a decent citizen. The State is regulating, directly and indirectly, to secure common needs at the level which the society as a whole deems essential to the fulfilment of its general end."③

Thus the state of Mr. Laski is a state of consumers. As an artist, a man's interest is different from that of a farmer or a lawyer; but as a consumer, the interest of the former

---

① See *Foundations of Sovereignty*, p. 169.
② *A Grammar of Politics*, pp. 69–70.
③ *Ibid.*

is more or less the same as that of the latter. For an artist needs food, clothing and the like just as a farmer does. Since every man is a consumer, all men in a given territorial limit have more or less the same interest. Moreover, as a worker or a businessman may be regarded as merely a means by which his end may be secured. He works, not because he likes to be a worker, but because he realizes that he will suffer, suffer from hunger, from cold and the like, if he does not work. Happiness is the thing that every man is seeking; but one finds more happiness in being a consumer than being a worker. To protect him as a consumer, we find the essence of the state, for "it is necessary to safeguard his interests as a user of services he has no part in producing." But we must not go too far in this respect, for the reason that without producing the things which are essential to human wants, there will be nothing to enjoy.

To protect the interests of the consumers implies a presumption that a certain amount of power for regulating and controlling are necessary. And if the interests of the consumers are to be considered as essential, the machinery which aims to protect such interests needs a power which, obviously, should be higher than that of other associations. Here we see that the state of Mr. Laski is a federation of interests. The classical conception of sovereignty as being indivisible and absolute is denied, yet it seems that Mr. Laski does not propose to have a state in which all sovereignties are equal, for his state is a state of general interests which, according to him, should take precedence over the specific interests. Sovereignty, then, is regarded as federal, ① and federalism is pluralism.

It is clear that the state which deals with the general interests is a coordinating body. But the co-ordinating body of Mr. Laski is different from that which is proposed by the guild socialist. To the latter, as we have shown in our consideration of the theory of Mr. Cole, the co-ordinating body is an organization of organizations, i. e. a representative body of the essential functional groups. On the other hand, what Mr. Laski has in mind is a body which is directly responsible to the individuals without being intermediated by any connecting link. The reason is obvious. Mr. Laski is more of an individualist than a groupist and he would not like to see a body which is too remote from the individual's control. ②

---

① *A Grammar of Politics*, especially Ch. Ⅶ.
② *Ibid.*, pp. 72 ff.

II. Other Writers

Perhaps the saying that there are as many doctrines as there are doctors is not wholly true; but any one who reads the current literature will not fail to realize the richness of the variety of ideas of various writers. This is true in the case of the theories of sovereignty. It is impossible for us to discuss all the other writers on the subject of sovereignty whom we have not presented in our previous discussion. What is intended here is to point out, briefly, the intellectual affiliations of Mr. Laski in different countries.

Beginning with the English writers, we find a man like Professor Graham Wallas who has been repeatedly praised by Mr. Laski. The starting point of Professor Wallas' theory is psychological analysis. He maintains that politics is not the mere product of conscious reason, but largely a matter of subconscious processes, of habit and instinct, of suggestion and imitation. In politics, moreover, entities which are exactly alike are impossible, [1] and consequently the so-called general will resulting from wills which are exactly alike, is impossible. But there may be an organized will and the "organized will can only exist in a community provided with the necessary social machinery."[2] The need of such machinery in the Great Society is urgent at our age. He insists that the basis of organization of will in the future should be a compromise of the proposals as advocated by individualist, socialist and syndicalist. Each one alone is insufficient. For individualism is based on property-instinct and property-instinct can no longer be considered as coincident with social values. Socialism was a reaction against individualism in the nineteenth century, but the expansion of the state as advocated by the socialist is ineffective before a well organized machinery is provided. Syndicalism seems to reconcile the extremes of both individualism and socialism, yet in practice, no sufficient Will-Organization can be attained if we follow the scheme of syndicalism alone. A compromise, then, of the three is necessary, and it is only by compromise that the instinct of private property, the welfare of the whole community and the interest of professions can be adequately maintained.[3] A Will-Organization so proposed is undoubtedly hostile to parliamentarism, and the criticism of parliamentary government is the keynote of Professor Wallas's theory. It seems that, expressly, Professor Wallas may

---

[1] Wallas, *Human Nature in Politics*, Part I, Ch. IV.
[2] Wallas, *The Great Society*, p. XII, also p. 287.
[3] *The Great Society*, Part II, Ch. XII.

not be considered as a combatant in the battle on the subject of sovereignty, but it is he who manufactures the ammunition to support those who are at the front.

Another thinker who starts from the psychological standpoint is Bertrand Russell. Mr. Russell believes that human conduct is not determined by reason, but by impulses. There are two kinds of impulses: One is creative and the other is possessive. The former tends to seek knowledge and art, while the latter, the acquisition of exclusive ownership. One involves adding new things for all, while the other engenders conflict. "Possession means taking or keeping some good thing which another is prevented from enjoying; creation means putting into the world a [a] good thing which otherwise no one would be able to enjoy."①

"The State and Property are the great embodiments of possessiveness; it is for this reason that they are against life, and that they issue in war."② "The principal source of the harm done by the State is the fact that power is its chief end."③ At present, the power of the state is subject to two restrictions; one is internal and the other external. Internally, it is limited by the fear of rebellion, and externally, by the fear of defeat in war. Save these two limitations, it is absolute.④ "The excessive power of the State, partly through internal oppression, but principally through war and the fear of war, is one of the chief causes of misery in the modern world."⑤

This being the case, it follows that so long as there are many sovereign states, each with its own Army and Navy there can be no end of war and therefore misery can not be avoided. Thus what Mr. Russell has in mind is a world state which alone maintains an Army and Navy. So he writes: "There will have to be in the world only one Army and one Navy before there will be any reason to think that wars have ceased. This means that, so far as the military functions of the State are concerned, there will be only one State, which will be world-wide."⑥

On the other hand, so far as civil functions are concerned, they may be exercised by the states. Since civil functions are different from military functions, "there is no reason why both kinds of functions should normally be exercised by the same State."⑦ At our age the greater states are in fact too large for civil purposes. On the contrary,

---

① Russell, *Principles of Social Reconstruction*, p. 235.
② *Ibid.*
③ *Ibid.*, p. 63.
④ *Ibid.*, p. 64.
⑤ *Ibid.*, p. 65.
⑥ *Ibid.*, p. 101.
⑦ *Ibid.*, p. 102.

they are small for military purposes, because they are not world wide.

But if too many functions are given to the state, individual liberty is likely to be curtailed. Mr. Russell is an apologist for the liberty and freedom of the individual. In order to secure individual freedom, according to him, powers and functions must be extended rather than concentrated. "There is one way," he declares, "by which organization and liberty can be combined, and that is, by securing power for voluntary organizations, consisting of men who have chosen to belong to them because they embody some purpose which all their members consider important, not a purpose imposed by an accident or outside force."① "The state," he continues "being geographical, can not be a wholly voluntary association, but for that very reason there is need of a strong public opinion to restrain it from a tyrannical use of its powers. This public opinion, in most matters, can only be secured by combinations of those who have certain interests or desires in common."②

Thus Mr. Russell is, in a certain sense, an individualist, a worldist and a groupist. Being an individualist, he would like to reduce, if not to destroy entirely, the power of the state; and in order to do so, he proposes that, internally, powers should be distributed into voluntary associations, and externally, there should be a world state which alone possesses the physical power to restrain the aggressiveness of the states and, therefore, international anarchy. ③

Other writers such as R. P. Haldane maintain that there is no such thing as indivisible and absolute sovereignty in the British Empire, for the dominions are far from being under the absolute control of the Parliament in England. Like Mr. Laski, he holds that even within the British Isles, the Parliament's sovereign power is not absolute for there are many things that in practice it can not do. But Haldane is not, however, an extreme pluralist. Both the pluralistic and monistic views, according to him, are contradictory, for "within the province of each state, sovereignty may assume plural aspects; that is to say the general will may express itself distributively as regards

---

① *Principles of Social Reconstruction*, p. 71.

② *Ibid.*, p. 71.

③ See also his *Political Ideals* (1917); *Proposed Roads to Freedom* (1918); *The Practice and Theory of Bolshevism* (1920); and *The Prospects of Industrial Civilization*.

different phases of the common life."①

In America, thinkers such as Professor Giddings have attacked the classical theory of sovereignty from the sociological standpoint. He maintains that it is not the political theorist, but rather the sociologist who has adequately studied and better understood the conditions which determine the actual working of sovereignty.② According to him, "sovereignty is not, it never can be, 'an original, unconitional, universal, and irrestible power to compel obedience'." But he adds that "nevertheless, it is something very real and very great, for in all its forms and expressions it is—and in these words we may define it—the dominant human power, individual or pluralistic, in a politically organized and politically independent population."③

Sovereignty is not absolute, because it is restrained by [by] cosmic, international, and moral limitations and by limitations within, i.e. consent of the many. "Sovereignty," says he, "is subject to cosmic limitations, and sovereignty cannot transcend the laws of an orderly and ordering universe. Nor can it transcend the limitations imposed by the circumstances that mankind is politically organized in many nations, and that no nation can safely run amuck among its neighbors. Sovereignty, therefore, is subject, as the signers of the Declaration acknowledge, to 'a decent respect to the opinions of mankind.' Moreover, it is subject further to limitations imposed by human nature of its own subjects. Not only in democracies, but everywhere and always, rulers and ruling groups exist by the consent of the many. Finally, like every intellectual being the sovereign is subject, as Greek and Roman saw, to the rule of reason; and like every ethical being it is morally responsible to the intelligent conscience of all mankind, now living and hereafter to live."④

From his study of the history of the sovereignty, he discovers that there are four modes of sovereignty: (1) personal, (2) class, (3) mass, and (4) general sovereignty. All these four modes are related and therefore conditioned by the social environment. "Of four possible and familiar modes of that superior power which in political society actually secures the obedience of most men of the the time, one only is a power to

---

① R. P. Haldane, "The Nature of the State," in the *Contemporary Review*, Vol. 117, (1920, Jan. – June), p. 771.

From the economical standpoint, we find, in his *Servile State*, H. Belloc advocates a distributivism, a mediaevalist reaction from capitalism and centralized sovereignty. See also R. H. Tawney, *Acquisitive Society*, 1923.

② Giddings, F. H., *The Responsible State*, p. 45. See his article entitled "Sovereignty and Government," in *Political Science Quarterly*, Vol. XXI, p. 7.

③ *The Responsible State*, pp. 47–48.

④ *Responsible State*, 1918, pp. 46–47.

compel obedience, and that one is a power that is conditional upon obsession of the multitude. Personal sovereignty, the oldest and on the whole the commonest form, is not a power to compel, it is rather a power to command obedience. Class sovereignty, appealing through religion and tradition to human sentiment, or relying on superior wealth, is a power to inspire or to exact obedience. Mass sovereignty, the sovereignty of the overwrought and emotionally solidified multitude, is for the time being a true power to compel obedience, since, while it lasts and as far as it can reach, it is irresistible. And finally, the general sovereignty of an enlightened people that arrives at concerted volition through reason and discussion is a power, through its appeal to intelligence, to call forth, that is to say, to evoke obedience."①

In a lecture given in 1917, Professor A. W. Small declared: "We shall never separate the truth from vitiating error until we have broken utterly with all our traditional doctrines of the State in terms of that plausible philosophical conception of sovereignty."② It is the traditional doctrine of sovereignty that gives rise to war, the disease of the human world.

Professor Small's basic theory is the conception of interests. An interest is defined as "an unsatisfied capacity, corresponding to an unrealized condition, and it is predisposition to such rearrangement as would tend to realize the indicated condition."③ There are six kinds of interests: the health interest, the wealth interest, the sociability interest, the knowledge interest, the beauty interest, and the rightness interest.④ Each of these interests tends to be absolute and each seeks for its own satisfaction without regard to the others.⑤ As the result of this, interests may be in conflict with one another. The function of the state is to develop, to satisfy and to adjust interests. "The state," says he, "is the co-operation of the citizens for the furtherance of all the interests of which they are conscious."⑥ The state thus becomes a moral institution.⑦ If the furtherance of the interests of the people is the end of the state, the state is a state of

---

① Gidding. "Sovereignty and Government," in *Political Science Quarterly*, Vol. XXI, p. 12. See also Giddings, *Principles of Sociology*, 1896 (third edition, 1909), pp. 285, 314; *Inductive Sociology* (1914), pp. 133 ff; and *Descriptive and Historical Sociology* (1906), pp. 332.
② Small, *Americans and the World Crisis*, also published in *American Journal of Sociology*, Vol. 23, No. 2.
③ Small, *General Sociology*, p. 433.
④ Ibid., pp. 443 ff.
⑤ Ibid., p. 201.
⑥ Ibid., p. 226.
⑦ Ibid., p. 239.

responsibility rather than a state of power. ①

Somewhat like Professor Small, Arthur F. Bentley, in *The Process of Government* (1908), maintains that the essential factor for interpreting history is the pressure of interests, organized in the form of groups. To him, the place of sovereignty among the facts is merely trivial. "Sovereignty," he writes, "is of no more interest to us than the state. Sovereignty has its very important place in arguments in defense of an existing government, or in verbal assaults on a government in the name of the populace or of some other pretender, or in fine-spun legal expositions of what is about to be done. But as soon as it gets out of the pages of the lawbook or the political pamphlet, it is a piteous, threadbare joke. So long as there is plenty of firm earth under foot there is no advantage in trying to sail the clouds in a cartoonist's airship."②

Mr. Herbert Croly points out that "the essential evil arises from the attribution in all modern nations of moral sovereignty to physically powerful states without any sufficient assurance of the use of the power for genuinely social purpose."③ And he adds, "Unless I am much mistaken, states must, as a result of the war, consent to a diminution and a redistribution of authority as the one indispensable condition of an increase in grace."④

Walter Lippmann, like Mr. Laski, insists that man's allegiance is divisible and divided. It is not absorbed by the state alone. In order to meet the needs of human nature in this respect, a new and a more workable federalism should be maintained. How far Mr. Lippmann agrees with Mr Laski may be found in the following passage: "What Mr. Laski says about the necessary pluralism of modern sovereignty is an unanswerably accurate description of the demands that are placed upon us. He is right in saying that this the kind of world we live in, and much of the energy of political thought will have to go into a still more elaborate description and classification of the

---

① *General Sociology*, p. 240. See also his *Between Eras from Capitalism to Democracy*, 1913. Cf. E. A. Ross, *Social Control*.

② Bentley. *Process of Government*, p. 264. In another place, he says: "sovereignty is, indeed, but one legal theory grown luxuriant... We can not set the theories as insignificant, as was possible with the theory of sovereignty." *Ibid.*, p. 273.

③ Croly, "The Future of the State" in *New Republic*, Vol. XII, September 1917, p. 176.

④ *Ibid.*, See also his *The Promise of American Lite and Progressive Democracy*, 1914. See particularly a chapter entitled "Popular Sovereignty" in the latter volume.

varieties of political need. "①

Among the French writers, we find men like M. Berthelemy, M. Hauriou, M. Paul-Boncour and M. de Molinari, all of whom discredit the traditional theory of sovereignty from different standpoints. Somewhat like M. Duguit, M. Berthelemy holds that the notion of public service comes to replace that of sovereignty. Thus according to him, the sovereignty exercised by the state is a function rather than a subjective right to command. "A civil servant," says he, "who gives an order does not exercise the right of

---

① Walter Lippmann. "A Clue" in the *New Republic*, Vol. X (1917, April), p. 317. Cf. the issue of September 15, 97, pp. 119–192. Also Vol. XIX, 1919, pp. 147–148.

Other American writers, such as Professor McIllwain, Victor S. Yarros, Richard Roberts, also attack the classical theory of sovereignty from different points of view. Mr. Laski speaks highly of Professor McIllwain's *High Court of Parliament and Its Supremacy*. Professor McIllwain criticized parliamentary sovereignty in England as being unhistorical. "The theory now embodied in the doctrine of parliamentary sovereignty is mechanical, artificial insistent with natural growth, in a word, unhistorical." *The High Court of Parliament*, 1900, p. 370. See also *The American Revolution: A Constitutional Interpretation*, 1923.

In an article entitled "What shall we do with the State." (in *American Journal of Sociology*, XXV, 572–583; XXVI, 59–72) Victor S. Yarros writes: "War tends to tyranny. War is intolerent. War makes the state sovereign. Peace, plenty, opportunity economic justice, on the other hand, tend to weaken the state. Free and prosperous men do not need much government. To fight poverty, involuntary idleness and unmerited misery is, therefore, to fight the present state. Industrial freedom will pave the way for greater political freedom. This is why the enlightened libertarian is not today greatly interested in academic attacks on the metaphysical state or political state. He is interested in well-directed attacks on special privilege and shielded, protected monopolies, knowing that to get rid of these is to eradicate much poverty and much of the crime, vice, and brutality that poverty breeds. He who fights for economic and social reform fights for the emancipation of the soul of the individual as well, or for the curtailment of the authority of the state." Vol. XXVI, 1920–1921, p. 68.

I. A. Cornelison and Roberts attack the classical theory of sovereignty from the ecclesiastical standpoint. The former considers the theory of sovereignty as mystical theory. "Sovereignty," it is said, "is nothing but preponderating force, which among civilized peoples, is veiled from sight and powerfully restrained by a wondrously complex and firmly fixed system of institutions. There is no antecedent existence in which that ghost of kingship, sovereignty, resides. The state is not an eternal idea; nor is it an autocthonous something, sprung from the earth, as Aphrodite sprang from the foam of the sea; existing before all government, and imparting to government all its power." *The Relation of Religion to Civil Government*, 1895, p. 202.

"For the conception of sovereign authority of the state," writes bedded in his *The Church in the Commonwealth*, "It deeply embedded in the law of the land; and the claim of the state to interfere in the life of Churches is simply a logical development to the Austinian doctrine of sovereignty. Nothing will ever effectually free the Churches from the authority of the state but a changed doctrine of the state itself. Perhaps that change will come with the recognition of the inherent right of independent religious societies to live and grow within the commonwealth; for this will involve an an acceptance of diminished and qualified authority. It will be the end of the Sovereign state, and that event is not far off." pp. 102–103. Cf. William Prall, *The State and the Church* (1900), "Without the church, the state would break up into fragments." p. 259.

See also R. E. Turner, *America in Civilization*, 1925, Ch. IX.

sovereignty."① But he adds, however, that one may call the functions exercised by him as sovereign power. It seems to him, then, that we may still recognize that there is such a thing as sovereignty; but it is to be remembered that by sovereignty, it is no longer a power which is subjective, infallible and absolute without being conditioned by and limitation whatsoever.

M. Hauriou also holds that public service should be regarded as the foundation of a modern system of politics and sovereignty is no longer the essential element in the field of public law. ② As he puts it: "The whole social organization of a country, economic no less than political, derives from a mass of established situations kept constant by this power to compel… The real function of this power is to create and to protect certain states of fact. It is too often regarded as a simple form of command and constraint without due attention being given to purpose… The real function of power is to creats order and stability… This function it fulfils with more or less success. Power is legitimate when fulfilment is adequate."③

M. Paul-Boncour attacks the traditional theory of sovereignty mainly on behalf of the groups or associations. Like many other groupists, he holds that associations come spontaneously into being for the purpose of dealing with different interests of mankind. These groups at first are voluntary in character, but develop gradually into groups which are really obligatory and which exercise a power similar to that of the state. As associations develop to such an extent for all sorts of interests, it is better for the state to deal with only the general interest or interests of the whole nation, deaving the specific interests to the groups. And in so doing, he insists that there should be particular sovereigns of the groups, besides the general sovereignty of the state. ④

G. de Molinari attacks the classical theory of sovereignty from the standpoint of the individual. He maintains that the sovereignty of the individual should be the basis of the political system of the future society. According to him, the sovereignty of the individual may be delegated and may be exercised collectively through representatives or by direct treaty. ⑤ Other writers such as M. Maxine Leroy and M. Georges Cahen have been influenced by Duguit and they hold somewhat the same position with the latter. ⑥

---

① Berthelemy, *Droit Administratif*, pp. 41-42, 10th ed., Paris, 1923. Also his article entitled "Le Fondement de l'autorite Politique" in *Revue du Droit Public*, XXXII, 1915, pp. 662-682.

② Mauric Hauriou, *Principes de Droit Public*, 2d ed., 1916.

③ *Ibid.*, pp. 78-79. The English phrases are Mr. Laski's. See his translation of Duguit's *Les Transformation du Droit Public* (1901).

④ Paul-Boncour, *Le Federalisme economique* (1901) and his *Syndicats des Fonctionnaires* (1906).

⑤ G. de Molinari, *The Society of To-morrow*, trans. by P. H. Lee Warner. See also his *Theorie de L'Evolution* (1908).

⑥ M. Leroy, *Transformation de la Puissance Publique* (1907). M. Georges Cahen, *Les Fonctionnaires*. See also a Belgian sociologist, De Greef, *La structure generale des societes*.

Ramiro de Maezlu, an Italian writer takes a position similar to Duguit although he may not have been influenced by the latter. He considers war as a conflict between authority and liberty. To him both liberty and authority are fatal in our age. Liberty is merely the apotheosis of individualism, and individualism is mainly based upon human selfishness. Authority is nothing more than the use of force and the use of force is contrary to the moral principle. The history of authority may be regarded as the history of catastrophy and bloodshed. If our society can not be based on authority and liberty, what is the true foundation for its reconstruction? It should be based, says de Maeztu, on function and when the state and society is built on such a basis, the state is no more than a public service corporation. Here we see that this is the point which M. Duguit has emphasized in his writings. He further agrees with Professor Duguit that there is no such thing as the personality of the state, for it is merely a fiction. [1]

De Greef, a Belgian sociologist, thinks that it is the notion of absolute sovereignty which brings international anarchy and the catastrophe of war. In order to maintain peace and order, a world federation should be worked out and the traditional theory of sovereignty should be repudiated. [2] Franz Oppenheimer, a German writer, remarks that the old system of the state has been disappearing and that "the state of the future will be society guided by self-government."[3] Rudolf Steiner, seeing the defects of the present political system, proposes that social commonwealth should be divided into three divisions: i. e., an economic system, a political system, and a spiritual system. [4] Austrian writers like Gustav Ratzenhofer[5] take a position somewhat between Gumplowicz and Smalls J. Novicow, a Russian thinker, agrees with De Greef that the notion of absolute sovereignty can no longer be maintained for international relations. [6]

---

[1] Ramiro de Maeztu, *Liberty, Authority and Function*, English translation. See also Vaccaro, M. A., *Les Bases Sociologiques du droit et de l'etat* (1898).

[2] De Greef, *La structure generale des societies*.

[3] Oppenheimer, *The State*, translated by John M. Gitterman, p. 275.

[4] Steiner. *The Threefold State: The True Aspect of the Social Question* (1922), New York.
See Cf. Luwig Stein, "Autoritat ihr Ursprung, ihre Begrundung und ihre Grenzen," in Schmoller's *Jahrbuch fur Gesetzgevung, Verwaltung, und Volkswirtschaft im deutschen Reich* (1902); also "Die Trager der Autoritat," in *Archiv fur Rechts—und Wirtschaftsphilosophie*, Oct. 1907; and also his *Philosophische Stromungen der Gegenwart*, Ch. XV. (I owe these references to Professor H. E. Barnes; see his *Sociology and Political Theory*, p. 130).

[5] Ratzenhofer, *Wesin und Zweck der Politik*, 1893.

[6] Novicow, *War and its Alleged Benefits*, trans. by Seltzer, 1911. Also *La Federation de l'Europe*, 1901.

The movement so-called regionalism may be also mentioned as hostile to the traditional theory of sovereignty. See Brun, *La Regionalisme* (1911). J. Hennessy, *Recoganization Administrative de la France* (1919).

The doctrine of Communism and Anarchism are radically hostile to the state and therefore the authority of the state. The literature on these two theories is numerous, and needs no special mention.

CONCLUSION: A POINT OF VIEW

It is generally recognized that there is a close relation between theory and fact. On the one hand, a given theory may influence or modify a certain fact; and on the other a certain fact may give rise to a theory. While both theory and fact are interacting upon each other, history shows that the latter case seems to be more true. Numerous theories formulated by thinkers who lived a thousand years before us are still advocated in our day and, therefore, are not yet or will not be actualized. But once a given fact becomes obvious, thinkers are led to enunciate a theory or theories to explain and to justify the fact, or even to criticize it in the hope that it may be modified in order to meet our wants and needs. Thus whether we like it or not, we have to recognize it as such.

The history of the theory of sovereignty shows that it is not an exception to the reasoning so advanced. The mediaevalists were wont to speak of a single undivided sovereignty for the whole universe within their sight. John of Salisbury would locate it in the church; Dante wanted to turn it over to the monarch; and Pierre Du Bois put it in the hands of the French king. The rise of national states proved that one sovereignty for the whole world is only a fiction. Bodin noticed that; but he told us that within each state sovereignty is still one and indivisible. Then came Hobbes who told us that to divide Leviathan is to bring men back to a state of war. And Rousseau who realized that the day of Louis XIV had gone, placed it in the hands of the people.

So, we are told, within a state, no matter where it resides, sovereignty is and must be one and indivisible. Such a principle has been accepted without being questioned for centuries. But it received the first shot when the federal state came into existence. The increase of the interdependence of the states in their external relations, the development of international organizations and institutions, the growth of group life particularly with reference to human interests, the consciousness of the individuality of men and women together with many other factors have compelled us to believe that the state of Hobbes is nothing more than a phantom. Looked at from one angle, it is too big; from another, it is too small. It is for this reason together with some others that lead men with radical minds to demand the abolition of the state within twenty four hours.

It seems to us that if the state is one of the social institutions which spontaneously come into existence for developing human interests in their political aspect, we see no reason why it should be destroyed. But in taking such a position, we are forced to deny the state of Hobbes, possessing an indivisible and unified sovereignty for controlling everything within its boundaries and doing what it pleases in its relations with other states. There is no justification for the state to have such high power—to have it alone; for the simple reason that man is not merely a political animal and consequently our life should not be dominated by political organization alone. We are not merely preaching a moral principle. What we have insisted and pointed out are facts existing at the present day. We are by no means satisfied with all these facts as they are now existing; but we have to recognize them as such.

Sovereignty, we are told by some writers, is something more than, and therefore different from, power. They maintain that power may be divided; but not sovereignty. Let us not commit ourselves to the question whether or not sovereignty "should" be different from power, and confine ourselves to examine whether or not there is any satisfactory explanation in the writings of those who insist that sovereignty is different from power.

Bodin was the first writer who seemed to distinguish between sovereignty and power; but he starts with a definition of sovereignty as "the absolute and perpetual power of a commonwealth," or in the Latin edition, "supreme power over citizens and subjects, unrestrained by laws." It is hard to see how power is an entirely different thing from supreme, absolute and perpetual power. The most one can admit is that they are different in degree, but not in kind. If power, as Bodin thinks, can be divided,[1] why not the supreme power or sovereignty?

The most emphatic and often quoted statement in regard to the difference between sovereignty and power is that of Rousseau. "Power," says Rousseau, "may be divided, but not will." We shall not attempt here to examine whether will is divisible or not; but let us quote the following statement: "This public person, which is thus formed by the union of all the individual members, formerly took the name of 'city', and now takes that of 'republic' or 'body politic', which is called by its members 'state' when it is passive, 'sovereign' when it's active, 'power' when it is compared to similar bodies."[2] In fact, the language shows that the state, sovereign, and power are one and the same thing looked at from different points of view.

In his *Discourse on the Constitution and Government of the United States*, Calhoun

---

[1] Bodin, *De Republica*, pp. 143–144.
[2] Rousseau, *Social Contract*, Book I, Ch. VI, Tozer's translation, pp. 110–111.

writes: "The powers thus designated are divided into two distinct classes; those delegated by the people of the several states to their separate state governments, and those which they will retain, —not having delegated them to either government. Among them is included the high sovereign power, by which they ordained and established both; and by which they can modify, change or abolish them at pleasure. This, with others not delegated, are those which are reserved to the people of the several states respectively."①

The "high sovereign power" mentioned in the statement quoted above, is undoubtedly the sovereignty of the several states or the people of the several states which, ② according to Calhoun, is one and indivisible. But in putting this high sovereign power into one of the two distinct classes—i. e. , those which the people still retain—not having delegated them to either government, he committed himself to the position that sovereignty is power and acknowledged, at least unconsciously, that sovereignty was divided. Yet he followed the metaphor of Plotinus, ③ declaring that sovereignty is an entire thing and to divide it is to destroy it. ④

Calhoun admitted expressly that many sovereignties may be combined into one sovereignty. Thus he said: "If they (the several states) have, by ratifying the constitution, divested themsslves of their individuality and sovereignty, and merged themselves into one great community or nation, it is equally clear, that the sovereignty would reside in the whole."⑤ If sovereignties are combinable why can not one

---

① Calhoun, *Works*, Vol. I, p. 144.

② Calhoun maintained that the sovereignty is in the hands of the people of the United States severally, not collectively.

③ "All things that exist do so by virtue of 'unity' —in so far as they exist in any ultimate sense and in so far as they may be said to be real. For what would anything be if it were not 'one'? Without the unity of which we speak things do not exist. There can be no army which is not a unit, nor a chorus, nor herd, unless each is 'one'. Neither is there a household or ship without unity; for the house is a unit and the ship is a unit, and if one took away the unity the household would no longer be a household nor the ship a ship. Continuous magnitudes would not exist if there were no unity to them, when divided, in so far as they lose unity they lose existence." Plotinus. *Enneads*, IX, 1; I take this passage from Avey's *Readings in Philosophy* (1921).

④ "Among the first, is that which springs from the idea of divided sovereignty; involving the perplexing question, —how the people of the several States can be partly sovereign, and partly 'not' sovereign, —sovereign as to be reserved, —and not sovereign, as to the delegated powers? There is no difficulty in understanding how powers, appertaining to sovereignty, may be divided; and 'the exercise' of one portion delegated to one set of agents, and another portion to another: or how sovereignty may be vested in one man, or in a few, or in many. But how sovereignty itself—the supreme power—can be divided, how the people of the several States can be partly sovereign, and partly 'not' sovereign—partly supreme, and partly 'not' supreme, it is impossible to conceive. Sovereignty is an entire thing: —to divide, is, —to destroy it." *Works*, Vol. I, p. 146. Cf. pp. 275 ff.

⑤ Calhoun, *Works*, Vol. I, p. 122.

sovereignty be divisible and divided into many parts, or if you like, into many small entities?

Professor W. W. Willoughby follows Rousseau and Calhoun very closely. He declares that "sovereignty is something more than a collection of powers. It is something more than a mechanical aggregate of separate and particular capacities."① But he adds: "It does, indeed, include and necessitate the possession of certain powers, such as, for example, those of taxation, of contracting treaties, maintaining an armed force, etc." Then he turns around again and says: "But its content is not exhausted by an enumeration of these. It is an entity of itself, and represents the highest political power as embodied in the State."② We need not go deeper to point out that Professor Willoughby does not get clear in his own mind the difference between power and sovereignty. It is sufficient, for our purpose, to notice the title of Chapter IX in his *The Nature of the State* which runs like this: "The Power of the State: Sovereignty."③

The few leading writers mentioned above do not exhaust the list of those who hold that there is a difference between sovereignty and power and that power may be divided, but not sovereignty; yet enough has been shown that they never make clear the distinction between the two. We contend that there will be no sovereignty if there is no power. If power can be divided, so must be sovereignty. To maintain that power may be divided while sovereignty is not is to take refuge in mysticism.

But we are often told that sovereignty is a legal subject and that "legally" sovereignty is indivisible and is not divided. Laying aside for a moment the contention that sovereignty is a legal subject, we find that the argument that "legally" sovereignty is indivisible and is not divided has no weight at all. On the contrary, it only shows its

---

① Willoughby, *Nature of the State*, p. 194.
② *Ibid.*, pp. 194–195.
③ Cf. Willoughby, *The Fundametal Concepts of Public Law*, p. 27. Mr. Alexander Stephen even goes so far as to distinguish between sovereignty and sovereign power. "Sovereign powers," he says, "are divisible. Sovereignty itself, however, from which they all emanate, remains meanwhile the same indivisible unit." (*War Between the States*, Vol. I, p. 23.) But he never gives a satisfactory explanation in regard to the difference between these two, and he never speaks of sovereignty without referring to power. "By ultimate sovereignty," he says. "I mean that original, inherent, innate and continually rightful Power or 'will' of the several Bodies Politic, or state of our union—the source and fountain of all political power; which is unimpaired by voluntarily assumed obligations; and which at any time, within the terms stated, can rightfully resume all its delegated power—those to the federal government as well as to those to the several state government." *Ibid.*, p. 24. In another place, he says, "Allegiance and sovereignty are reciprocal. To whatever power a citizen owns allegiance, that power is sovereign." The citizenship of the United States is double and a citizen's allegiance is double. If allegiance is the basis of sovereignty, the division of the former postulates the division of the latter. (See *Ibid.*, Vol. II, p. 492)

weakness. The reason is very simple. Once one insists that "legal" sovereignty is indivisible, he admits, at least by implication, that besides "legal" sovereignty, there are other sovereignties—political, moral, economic, and etc.—each of which, therefore, may be divided. In other words, to insist that legal sovereignty is indivisible is to recognize that moral or political sovereignty is divisible; and to admit the divisibility of the latter and at the same time to hold the indivisibility of the former is a self-contradiction. In fact, to make a distinction between legal, political or moral sovereignty involves a recognition of the divisibility of sovereignty.

The proposition that legally sovereignty can not be divided is generally recognized as the lawyers' point of view. It is argued that men who do not specialize in law can hardly understand the meaning, significance and unity of sovereignty of the state. Perhaps it is unfair for an outsider to talk on things legal in their nature; but the fact is, that the indivisibility doctrine of sovereignty has never been recognized by institutions which are established to act and to act always in legal capacity. This is true at least in the case of the United States. To say nothing about the highest tribunal of the several states and the lower courts of both federal and state government, the Supreme Court of the United States, from its earliest history down to the present day, has repeatedly declared that sovereignty is divided in this country. It is true that that which is divisible may not be divided, but equally is it true that which is divided must be divisible. The Supreme Court of the United States is unquestionably recognized as the most powerful tribunal in the country; nor do we find any tribunal in other countries which is equal in power to it. In fact, it is the guide, if not the only source, of legality. Its decisions have been well observed and duly executed. And when it says that sovereignty is divided, it speaks legally. Unless the decisions of the Supreme Court in regard to the divisibility of sovereignty be overthrown, the contention that legally sovereignty can not be divided, is not only illogical as has been shown in the previous paragraph, but also contrary to the well established tradition and rule, and therefore the practice of the United States. ①

Sovereignty, as we understand it, is something much more than a legal thing. If a lawyer can speak of legal sovereignty, a political scientist can speak of political sovereignty, a moralist of moral sovereignty and so on. A lawyer may criticize an economist, a moralist or a sociologist for discussing sovereignty, but the notion of sovereignty has never been a legal notion alone. The idea exists in so-called primitive society as well as in so-called civilized society, and in the past as well as at present. We

---

① Lord Bryce in his *Studies in History and Jurisprudence* pointed out very positively that legal sovereignty is divisible. See the essay on "The Nature of Sovereignty", Vol. II, pp. 507-510, 520.

all know that in primitive society and in the remote past, division of labour is in its crudest form. No line, even in its approximation, can be drawn between legal and moral or any other notions. Even in our own day and in a highly developed society, no matter how minutely we divide our concepts according to subject matters, we have to recognize that there is a correlation, be it direct or indirect, and an overlapping in our concepts. An understanding of this point alone is sufficient to force us to deny the contention that the notion of sovereignty is exclusively a legal concept.

But we are told by some writers that the notion of sovereignty is a modern notion in its strict sense. This does not mean that sovereignty is exclusively a legal idea or a political idea. Even taking for granted that the modern conception of sovereignty is mainly a legal or political conception, because it is a reflection of the growth of legal or political institutions in the 16th century, we are not warranted to conclude that it is merely a legal or political notion; for the simple reason that if the legal or political institutions of the 16th century or the 17th century can produce a legal or political notion of sovereignty, why may not the economic institutions of the 19th or 20th century produce an economic conception of sovereignty. Thus once we admit, as we have pointed out in our early discussion, that a given condition of a given period can give rise to a certain kind of idea, we have to recognize that the idea is subject to change as conditions change.

Sovereignty then is divisible, and history demonstrates to us that this is true. Territorially speaking, the Europe of today is still the Europe of hundreds of years ago. History shows, however, that at the beginning of the 16th century, besides England, France, Spain, and some of the Italian city states, few were sovereign states. But the list of sovereignties has been increased by the middle of the 17th century when the Peace of Westphalia was concluded. More sovereignties came into existence in the 18th and 19th centuries, and particularly after the World War. Since the increase of sovereignties is still within the name territorial limits of Europe, the process of increase may be regarded as a process of division. The students of history will not fail to see that not only once, but many times, a sovereign unity was divided into many parts, each of which, usually if not always, in turn became a sovereignty itself. While sovereignty "is" not sovereignties, it does not mean that it "may" not be sovereignties. Thus grammatically Calhoun is right when he says that sovereignty is one. Nor is Calhoun wrong when he insists that to divide "sovereignty" is to destroy "it"; because it is only natural that the original entity of a sovereignty must be destroyed if we are going to make two or more out of it. Sovereignty is one; but one may be divided into two or many.

Not only does history support the divisibility theory of sovereignty, it has also the moral support. The indivisibility doctrine of sovereignty teaches us that sovereignty is the essential characteristic of the state; that it is supreme, absolute, and infallible: that internally it can injure any person or association without taking responsibility or paying damages and that externally it can do what it pleases. It is the sponsor of aggressive war. It is the justification for one state to drive the peaceful and unarmed inhabitants of another country out of their fatherland. In short, it is a doctrine for vindicating brutal acts. On the contrary, the divisibility doctrine teaches that the state is not the only possessor of sovereignty; that sovereignty is divided into different parts, or if you like, into different entities within and over the border of the state. The state has no more claim to do what it pleases than another organization to do that which is within its own sphere. It may be viewed as one of the human associations for advancing and caring for certain aspects of human interests. It is a means and not an end, and all that it can do is to secure the purpose of forming it. In short, the sovereignty that it possesses is not a right for doing what it pleases, but a power for developing human interests.

Is such a theory built on a comparatively sound, adequate and solid philosophical foundation? Our response to this question is at once affirmative. Pluralism is the widely accepted view in our age. It is backed by pragmatism and new realism. Its advantages are that, in the language of Professor James, "(1) It is more 'scientific', in that it insists that when oneness is predicated, it shall mean definitely assertainable conjunctive forms. With these the disjunctions ascertainable among things are exactly on a par. The two are coordinate aspects of reality. To make the conjunctions more vital and primordial than the separations, monism has to abandon verifiable experience and proclaim a unity that is indescribable. (2) It agrees more with the moral and dramatic expressiveness of life. (3) It is not obliged to stand for any particular type of plurality, for it triumphs over monism if the smallest morsel of disconnectedness is once found undeniably to exist. 'Ever not quite' is all it says to monism; while monism is obliged to prove that what pluralism asserts can in no amount whatever possibly be true—an infinitely harder task."[1]

As a matter of fact, if we are going to base the theory of sovereignty on metaphysics, pluralism is the only one that we can accept. Monism, as defended by Spinoza and his followers, is not the monism that is defended by those who hold that sovereignty is indivisible. We are told by Spinoza that there is only one thing in the

---

[1] William James, *Some Problems of Philosophy*, pp. 142–143.

universe, and this one thing is God. He is the only substance. He writes: "There does not exist more than one substance with a given attribute, and it belongs to the nature of that one to exist. It must, therefore, belong to its nature to exist either as finite or as infinite. But not as finite. For it would have to be limited by another of the same nature, and this, also would necessarily have to exist. There would, then, be two substances with the attribute, which is absurd. It, therefore, exists as infinite."①

If the view of Spinoza were adopted by those who hold that sovereignty is one and indivisible, they would have to insist that there can be only one sovereignty for the world or the whole universe. But this is not what they maintain. They recognize that the world is divided into many political entities each of which alone possesses an indivisible sovereignty and that each one is equal to another. In admitting or rather insisting that there are many sovereignties in the world, they are in fact pluralists. They, in fact, do not deny that sovereignty is divided and therefore divisible. What they insist on is that sovereignty of a state is not divided, and indivisible. If sovereignty itself is divided and divisible, we don't see how they can deny the divisibility of the sovereignty of a state.

Nor can the monistic reasoning that one is absolute and supreme without any limitation whatsoever be accepted as a sound argument.② If there is a sovereignty which is supreme and absolute without being limited, there can be only one for the whole world or universe. As long as we recognize that there are many sovereignties in the world, each sovereignty can not be said to be supreme and absolute in the absolute sense that it is illimitable. The most we can say is that it is absolute and supreme in a relative sense and within its own sphere. But to admit that is to admit that there is a limitation. The recognition of a limitation upon sovereignty, at least from the viewpoint of the extent of sovereignty, involves a recognition of divisibility; for in that sense, limitation means division.

Like Spinoza, Hegel insists that the universe is a whole or a unit. But to him, the one is not God and, therefore, it is not static. The ultimate one, according to Hegel, is essentially dynamic, it may evolve into a multitude of forms each of which is the partial expression of the ultimate one itself. Thus the principle that one may become many implies a recognition of the divisibility doctrine. The application, it seems to us, of Hegelian monism to the conception of sovereignty is not contrary to the divisibility doctrine of sovereignty.③

---

① *The Philosophy of Spinoza*, trans. Fullerton, p. 29.
② Cf. Bradley, *Appearance and Reality*, p. 140.
③ Cf. Hrgel's *Philosophy of the State and of History*, by George S. Morris, 1892, p. 105.

Monism, we are told, is on the wane in our day. It gives no support to those who maintain that sovereignty is indivisible. A man may be an advocate of monism, and yet admit that there is a possibility of dividing sovereignty. In other words, although pluralism involves a recognition of the divisibility doctrine, the divisibility doctrine is not always pluralism.

It has been noted, in the foregoing discussion, that the proposition that sovereignty is divisible is based on the existing facts, historical evidence, a generally accepted standard of morality, and a comparatively sound and adequate conception in philosophy. But this is not all, for etymologically speaking, our proposition is equally sound. It has been pointed out that it is well understood now that the term "sovereignty" was first enuciated by Beaumanoir; but when he used the term, he used it in two senses: one is that every baron is the "souverain" in his own barony and the other is that the king is "souverain" in all the kingdom.① In other words, besides the sovereignty of the king of the kingdom, there are many sovereignties of baronies within the kingdom. The sovereignty of the kingdom, it seems to Beaumanoir, may be larger in extent than that of the barony, but the existence of one does not interfere with or destroy the existence of the other; for the very simple reason that each is sovereign within its own sphere. If the foregoing interpretation of the term "sovereignty" as used by Beaumanoir is not mistaken, the proposition that sovereignty is one and indivisible and that it is the characteristic of the state within which no other sovereignties can be existing lacks its etymological basis.②

The word sovereignty is said to be derived from the medieval Latin word supremitas, i. e., suprema potestas, "supreme power".③ But the suprema potestas was

---

① Beaumanoir, *Les Coutumes du Beauvoisir*, ed. A. Salmon, Paris, 1899, XXXIV 1043. "Pour ce que nous parlons en cest livre, en pluseurs lieus, du souverain, et de ce qu'il peut et deit fere, li aucun porroient entendre, pour ce que nous ne nommons conte ne nommons conte ne duc, que ce fust du roi, mais en tous les lieus que li rois n'est pas nommes, nous entendons de ceus qui tienent en baronie, car chascuns barons est souverain en sa baronie. Voirs est que li rois est souverains par dessus tous, et a de son droit, la general garde de tout son roiaume, par quoi il pot fere teus establismens comme il li plest pour le commun pourfit, et ce qu'il establist doit estre tenu. Ei st n'i a nul si grant dessous li que ne puist estre tres en sa court par defaute de droit ou fous jugement, et peur tous les cas qui touchent le roi."

② Lord Bryce remarked, "The heads of monasteries seem to have sometimes familiarly described as Sovereign in the Middle Ages. The name Sovereign was down till very recent times used to describe the head of a municipality in several Irish boroughs." *Studies in History and Jurisprudence*, Vol. II, p. 505, footnote. See also James A. H. Murray, *A New English Dictionary*. It has been remarked that usage even permitted a husband to be "sovereign" to his wife. See *Oxford Dictionary*.

③ See Meyer, *Lehrbuch des deutschen Statrechts*, p. 15. Also Skeat's *Etymological Dictionary*. Cf. also Sir John Macdonell's article on sovereignty in the *Encyclopaedia Britannica*, eleventh edition.

international or supernational. It did not mean what Austin meant, far from that. Sovereignty in the Austinian sense, says Professor Figgis, was unknown in any single nation in the Middle Ages.①

The foregoing discussion shows that sovereignty is divisible. In holding that sovereignty is divisible, we hold also that is combinable. We do not deny that there is a possibility of having one sovereignty within a state or within the whole world. What we deny is that it is indivisible. The divisibility doctrine of sovereignty, as we understand it, may be considered either as a description of an existing condition or as a principle that should be applied at present. Facts have become too strong to prevent us from believing that sovereignty is indivisible and that there must be only one sovereignty within the boundary line of a state. The state has never been and perhaps will never be the only means by which the highest good of human life may be achieved. Many men of refinement and of high character have made little use of the state and men who love mankind of the world never think that the surface of the earth should be dominated by many Leviathans.

Thus our notion of sovereignty must change when facts demand; and if it does not, our dispute as to the location of sovereignty in different institutions existing at the present day can never be solved. A concrete example may be taken for illustrating this point. It is argued by some that the sovereignty of mandates is in the League of Nations. It is maintained by others that it vests in the mandatory power. Still others hold that it retains in the mandated territory. Who are right and who wrong? We think that they are all right and meanwhile that they are all wrong. In other words, they are partially right and partially wrong. It can be easily seen that if the indivisibility doctrine of sovereignty is to be maintained, the sovereignty of the mandate must be in one place. But it is well understood that it is not the League of Nations alone, it is not the mandatory power alone, and it is not the mandated territory alone, which possesses an indivisible

---

① Figgis, *Divine Right of the Kings*, p. 13 and footnote. Maitland, *Lectures on Constitutional History*, pp. 101–102, read as follows: "While we are speaking of this matter of sovereignty, it will be to remember that our modern theories run counter to the deepest convictions of the Middle Ages—to their whole manner of regarding the relation between Church and State. Though they may consist of the same units, though every man may have his place in both organisms, those two bodies are distinct. The State has its king or emperor, its laws, its legislative assemblises, its courts, its judges; the Church has its Pope, its prelates, its councils, its laws, its courts. That the Church is in any sense below the State no one will maintain, that the State is below the Church is a more plausible doctrine, but the general conviction is that the two are independent, that neither derives its authority from the other. Obviously, while men think thus, while they more or less consistently act upon this theory, they have no sovereign in Austin's sense; before the Reformation Austin's doctrine was impossible."

sovereignty. Unless the divisibility doctrine is applied, our dispute over the location of sovereignty of the mandates will never end so long as existing conditions continue.

The increase of international relations proves that it is futile to hold an indivisibility doctrine of sovereignty. When this is realized, it is argued that the notion of sovereignty is not a conception of international relations. We do not see how it is not a notion of international relations. We do not need to go further to point out the difficulty of those who entertain such a view. We only need to give a moment's contemplation to the dispute among themselves. Austin followed Hobbes very closely; but the absolute and illimitable sovereignty of the latter was narrowed by the former to a "municipal sovereignty". Then Professor Willoughby, though a confessed Austinian, opposing strongly the narrow notion of sovereignty of his master, extends it into a "constitutional sovereignty"; yet he refuses to go a little further so as to accept the conception of sovereignty as applicable in international relations!

Having insisted that there is no such thing as sovereignty in international dealings, Professor Willoughby proposes to use the term "independence" instead of "sovereignty". Here again we can not see how he can avoid the difficulty by merely changing a term. The trouble lies, so far as we can see, in the misunderstanding of the notion itself, not the term employed. It may be added that the term "sovereignty" has been loosely employed with other terms, such as "independence", "jurisdiction", "dominion", "prerogative", etc.① In many cases these terms have been used to mean one and the same thing. Moreover, it seems that it is safe to say that there has been no unanimity of opinion with regard to the meaning of "sovereignty" from the time that it was first employed until the present day. All that we can say is that it means power and we have already noticed that no writer talks about sovereignty without referring to power. Power exists everywhere in human society. To deny the application of the notion of sovereignty in international relations is to deny the notion of sovereignty itself, and if the notion of sovereignty itself has been discredited, there will be no such thing as the sovereignty of the state. It remains for us to say a few words concerning the basis of sovereignty. Sovereignty, we contend, is based upon no other ground than the consent or consents of individual or individuals. Those who deny the proposition so set forth may argue that, for instance, a Filipino is under the sovereignty of the United States, because he is forced to do so even if he is not willing. He who entertains such a view, undoubtedly, does not go into the bottom of things. It is inconceivable that there can be a sovereignty

---

① See W. G. Miller, *The Data of Jurisprudence*, 1809, pp. 102, 113, 118, 122. Also Dicey, *Conflict of Law*, p. 38.

over an individual without his consent. We shall not here undertake to examine the motive or motives that make him consent to live under the sovereignty of the United States; but it can not be denied that if a Filipino does not consent to do so, he may get away, or even overthrow it at anytime and by many means. He may persuade his followers to follow him and start a revolution. He may leave the Philippine Islands and go elsewhere. If he does not succeed in doing this, or if he is prevented from doing this, he may commit suicide or he may be killed. But as soon as he commits suicide or is killed, the sovereignty of the United States over him ceases at once.

History is the store-house in which numerous instances may be found for illustrating our point. Revolution after revolution has taken place in different places, and in different ages. Men who did not like to live under the sovereignty of their fatherland went to another country and ended their lives. And many cases may be cited to show that men preferred and chose death instead of submission to a sovereignty to which they did not consent.

To maintain that the basis of sovereignty is consent involves, however, a recognition that sovereignty, in the last analysis, is the sovereignty of the individual and that it is possible to delegate. The individual is sovereign because he alone can act as he sees fit. From the moral standard of a given period in a given place, his act or acts may be regarded as wrong, but no external force can prevent him from doing wrong if he chooses to do so.

But in a sense, man is a social and socialized animal. He may, of course, be a Thoreau who, ① acting from his own will, lives in isolation; or he may end his social life by killing himself. But usually he consents to be a member of some sort of social organization. Consenting to be a member of an association, he thereby delegates his sovereignty to that association. There are many ways of delegating sovereignty: Delegation may be direct or indirect. It may be express or tacit. It may be entire or partial. It may be temporary or perpetual. It is to be noted, however, that usually these ways interweave into each other.

An organization of men or individuals usually exercises a sovereignty which is directly delegated. We are not prepared to go so far as M. Motta, the President of Switzerland in 1920, who declared at the first meeting of the Assembly of the League of Nations that the latter is a League of peoples; but in holding that sovereignty may be delegated in an indirect way, we agree with those who maintain that the League of

---

① The case of Po-i and Shu Chi is another conspicuous example. See *Confucian Analects*, Book V, Ch. XXII, note.

Nations does possess sovereigty in the affairs with which it is competent to deal.

An individual who is born within the sphere of an existing sovereignty usually delegates his sovereignty by tacit means. On the other hand, the sovereignty of a newly established organization is usually delegated by express means. Delegation is temporary when an individual consents to transfer his sovereignty to a certain association or organization for a short period, and it is perpetual when he consents to give it up for a long period of time or even for life.

It is wholly delegated when one's sovereignty is not divided and is delegated to a particular organization for a particular purpose alone. The proposition so advanced does not deny that, for instance, Germany may have a unified and undivided sovereignty if she can make all her citizens or rather members consent to do all that she pleases. Thus if "all" the individual members of the German state consent to give up their families, their business and everything else only to fight for the so-called prestige, honor or what not of Germany, the sovereignty of Germany, in this case, is undoubtedly one and undivided; but not, however, indivisible; for as has been said, although things which are divided must be divisible, things which are divisible may not be divided. But it is to be borne in mind that if Germany can have a unfied and undivided sovereignty in such a case, a church or a trade union may have the same thing under the same conditions.

Human interests are manifold. One may devote himself to one and only one interest, consenting to give up his whole sovereignty to an organization for advancing that interest; but ordinarily he has many interests. He may be a member of a church and at the same time a member of a trade union and the like. He consents to be a loyal member to every one of these associations, or his loyalty or loyalties to these associations may be different in proportion to his taste of interests. In either case he is partially under the sovereignty of one association and partially under the sovereignty of another.

It may be added that to hold that the basis of sovereignty is consent, we may make a distinction between original and delegated sovereignty. The original sovereignty, strictly speaking, is the sovereignty of the individual while the delegated sovereignty is the sovereignty of the social organization. [①] But it is to be remembered that both of them have the same weight, for the simple reason that when I consent to let the church exercise power over me, it is the same as to say that it is I who exercise the power for myself.

---

① Relatively speaking, we may go as far as to say that, for example, the sovereignty of the member-states of the League of Nations is original while that of the League of Nations is delegated.

BIBLIOGRAPHY

Acton, J. E. E. D., The History of Freedom and other Easays, edited by J. N. Figgis, 1919.

Adams, B., Centralization and the Law, 1906.

Adams, B., The Theory of Social Revolution, 1913.

Adams, F. O. and Cunningham, C. D., The Swiss Confederation, 1894.

Adams, J. Q., Writings, edited by Worthington Chauncey Ford, 1913.

Adams, Samuel, Writings, edited by H. A. Cushing, 1904.

Advisory Opinion of the Permanent Court of International Justice, Collection of Advisory Opinions, No. 4.

Ahrens, H., Naturrecht oder Philosophie des Reichs and des Staats, 1870.

Allen, S. H., International Relations, 1920.

Angell, N., The Great Illusion, 1913.

Aristotle, Politics, translated by B. Jowett.

Arndt, V. A., Das Statsrecht des Deutschen Reiches, 1901.

Ashley. H. L., American Government.

Austin, J., Lectures or Jurisprundence, edited by R. Campbell, 1911.

Baoer, G. S., First Steps in International Law, 1899.

Baldwin, S. E., "Division of Sovereignty", in International Law, note, July, 1918.

Baldwin, S. E., "Vesting of Sovereignty in League of Nations", in Yale Law Journal, Vol. 28, 1919.

Barker, E., "Political Thought of Plato and Aristotle", 1906.

Barker, E., "The Discredited State", in Political Quarterly, No. 5, 1915.

Barker, E., "Political Thought in England from Spencer to Today", 1915.

Barker, E., "The Superstition of the State", in London Times Literary Supplement, July, 1918.

Barker, E., Greek Political Theory, Plato and his Predecessors, 1918.

Barker, E., A Confederation of the Nations, 1918.

Barker, E., National Character, 1927.

Barnes, H. E., "Durkheim's Contribution to Political Theory", in Political Science Quarterly, Vol. 35, 1920.

Barnes, H. E., "Some Contributions of Sociology to Modern Political Theory", in American Political Science Review, Vol. 15, 1921.

Barnes, H. E., Sociology and Political Theory, 1924.

Barnes, H. E., The History and Prospects of the Social Sciences, 1925.

Baty, T., International Law, 1909.

Baty, T., "Protectorates and Mandates", in British Year Book of International Law, 1923.

Baty, T., "Sovereign Colonies", Harvard Law Review, Vol. XXXIV, pp. 837 ff.

Beale, J. H., "Jurisdiction of a Sovereign State", Harvard Law Review, Vol. 36, January, 1923.

Belloc, H., The Servile State, 1912.

Benoist, C., L'Organisation de la Démocratie, 1900.

Bentham, J., Works, collected by J. Bowring. See particularly Fragment on Government, 1776.

Bentley, A. F., The Process of Government: A Study of Social Pressures, 1908.

Bernard, M., A Historical Account of the Neutrality of Great Britain During the American Civil War, 1870.

Berolzheimer, F., The World's Legal Philosophy, translated by R. S. Jastrow, 1912.

Berthelemy, N., Droit administratif, 10th ed., 1923.

Berthelemy, N., "Le Fondement de l'autorité politique", in Revue du droit public, XXXII, 1915, pp. 662–682.

Bigelow, J., World Peace: How War Cannot Be Abolished; How It May Be Abolished, 1916.

Blackstone, W., Commentaries on the Laws of England, 1765–1769.

Blakey, R., 〈The〉 History of Political Literature, 1855.

Bliss, P., Of Sovereignty, 1885.

Blummer, J. J., Handbuch des Schweizerischen Bundesstaatsrechtes, 1863.

Bluntschli, J. K., Das moderne Völkerrecht der Civilisirten als Rechtsbuch Dargestellt, 1872.

Bluntschli, J. K., Allgemihes Staatsrecht, 6th ed., 1885.

Bluntschli, J. K., Theory of the State, English translation, 1892.

Bluntschli, J. K., Le Droit international, Codifié Traduit d'allemand par M. C. Lardy, 1886.

Bluntschli, J. K., Geschichte der Neueren Staatswissen schaft, 1881.

Bodin, J., De Republica Libri Sex, 1575.

Bonald, de., Théorie du pouvoir politique et Religieux dans la société civile.

Bonjour, F., Real Democracy in Operation, 1920.

Borel, E., Étude sur la Souveraineté et L'état Fédératif, 1886.

Bornhak, C., Preussisches Staatsrecht, 1888.

Bosanquet, B., Philosophical Theory of the State, 1899.

Bourgeois, L., La Solidarité, 1897.

Bourgeois, L., L'Œouvre de la société des nations, 1920-1923.

Bradley, A. C., Aristotle's Conception of the State, Hellenica, edited by Abbott, 1898.

Bradley, F. H., Appearance and Reality: A Metaphysical Essay, 1908 ed.

Brierly, J. L., "The Shortcomings of International Law", in British Year Book of International Law, 1923-1924.

Brie. S., Der Bunderstaat, 1874.

Brooks, J. G., American Syndicalism, 1919.

Brown, I. J. C., English Political Theory, 1920.

Brown, P. M., International Reality, 1917.

Brown, W. J., "The Jurisprudence of M. Duguit", in Law Quarterly Review, April, 1916.

Brown, W. J., Austinian Theory of Law, 1906.

Brownson, O. A., The American Republic 1866.

Brun, C., Le Régionalisme, 1911.

Brunet, R., The New German Constitution, translated by J. Gollamb, 1922.

Bryce, J., The American Commonwealth, 1890.

Bryce, J., "Laws of Nature", in Studies in History and Jurisprudence.

Bryce, J., Modern Democracies, 1921.

Bryce, J., Studies in History and Jurisprudence, 2 volumes.

Buchanan, G., On the Sovereign Power among the Scots, 1579.

Buell, R. L., International Relations, 1925.

Burgess, J. W., Political Science and Comparative Constitutional Law, 1902.

Burgess, J. W., Recent Changes in American Constitutional Theory, 1923.

Burns, C. D., Political Ideals, 1919.

Calhoun, J. C., Works, ed. by R. K. Cralle, 1883. See especially his Disquisition on Government and Discourse on the Constitution and Government of the United States,

Works, Vol. I.

Carter, J. C., Law, Origin, Growth, and Function, 1907.

Carlyle, R. W. and A. J., A History of Mediaeval Political Theory, 1903-1922, 4 volumes.

Centz, P. C. (Bernard J. Sage), The Republic of Republics, 1865.

Charteris, A. H., "League of Nations and the Doctrine of Sovereignty", in Scots Law Times, February, 1920.

Chipman, N., Principles of Government, 1853.

Chipman, W., "Sovereignty", in Canadian Bar Review, Vol. 3, pp. 530 ff and 607 ff, 1925.

Clark, W. L., Elementary Law, 1909.

Clute, W. K., "Home Rule System of Municipal Government—City Sovereignty Versus State Sovereignty", in Central Law Journal, Vol. 77, Nov., 1913.

Cobbett, P., Cases and Opinions on International Law, 1909.

Coker, F. W., Readings in Political Philosophy, 1914.

Coker, F. W., "The Technique of the Pluralistic State", in American Political Science Review, Vol. 15, May, 1920.

Cole, G. D. H., The World of Labour, 2nd and rev. ed., 1915.

Cole, G. D. H., The Meaning of Industrial Freedom, 1918.

Cole, G. D. H., Self-Government in Industry, 1919 ed.

Cole, G. D. H., Labour in the Commonwealth, 1919.

Cole, G. D. H., Chaos and Order in Industry, 1920.

Cole, G. D. H., Social Theory, 1920.

Cole, G. D. H., The Future of Local Government, 1921.

Cole, G. D. H., Guild Socialism: A Plan for Economic Democracy, 1921.

Cole, G. D. H., Workshop Organization.

Cole, G. D. H., Introduction to Rousseau's Social Contract, Everyman's edition.

Commons, J. R., "A Sociological View of Sovereignty", in American Journal of Sociology, Vol. V, pp. 1 ff, 347 ff, 544 ff, 683 ff, 814 ff, and Vol. 6, pp. 67 ff.

Constant, B., Réflexions sur les constitutions et les garanties, 1814-1818.

Constant, B., Principes potitiques, 1815.

Cooley, T. M., A Treatise on the Constitutional Limitations Which Rest upon the Legislative Power of the States of the American Union, 1871.

Cooley, T. M, The General Principles of Constitutional Law in the United States of America, 1880.

Corbett, J., "What is the League of Nations?", in British Year Book of International Law, 1924.

Cousin, Coursd' histoire de la philosophie morale au dix-huitième siècle, 1839-1840.

Cornelison, I. A., The Relation of Religion to Civil Government, 1895.

Crane, R. T., The State in Constitutional and International Law, 1907.

Croly, Herbert, The Premise of American Life, 1909.

Croly, H., Progressive Democracy, 1914.

Croly, H., "The Future of the State", in the New Republic, Vol. XII, September 17, 1917.

Current History, February, 1922.

Curtis, G. T., History of the Origin, Formation and Adoption of the Constitution of the United States, 1861.

Dente, De Monarchia, trans. by A. Henry, 1904.

Davis, G. B., The Elements of International Law, 1916, 4th ed.

Davis, H. W. C., The Political Thought of Heinrich von Treitschke.

Davis, J., Rise and Fall of the Confederate Government, 1881, 2 volumes.

Dealey, J., "Austin's Theory of Sovereignty", in Political Science Quarterly, Vol. IX, pp. 31 ff.

Dewey, J., "Social Absolutism", in New Republic, Vol. XXV, pp. 315-318.

Dickinson, E. D., Equality of States in International Law, 1920.

Dickinson, J., "A Working Theory of Sovereignty", in Political Science Quarterly, December, 1927, and March, 1928.

Dicey, A. V., The Law of Constitution, 1885.

Dicey, A. V., Law and Public Opinion, 1925.

Donald, R., Danger Spot in Europe, 1925.

Douglas, P. H., "Occupational Versus Proportional Representation", in American Journal of Sociology, Vol. XXIX, pp. 129-157.

Dowdall, H. C., "The Word 'State'", in Law Quarterly Review, Vol. XXX-IX, January, 1923.

Duggan, S. P. H., The League of Nations, the Principle and the Practice, 1919.

Duguit, L., L'État, le Driot objectif et la Loi positive, 1901.

Duguit, L., L'État, les Governants et les Agents, 1903.

Duguit, L., Le Driot social, le Droit individuel et l'État, 1911, 2nd ed.

Duguit, L., Traite de driot constitutionnel, 1911.

Duguit, L., Les Transformations du Driot Public, 1913.

Duguit, L., "The Law and the State", translated by F. J. de Slovere, in Harvard Law Review, Vol. XXXI, No. I, Nov., 1917.

Duguit, L., Manual de droit constitutionnel, 3rd ed., 1918.

Duguit, L., Souvereineté et Liberté, 1922.

Duguit, L., "Concept of Public Service", in Yale Law Journal, Vol. XXXI, March, 1923.

Dunning, W. A., Political Theories: Ancient and Medieval, 1902.

Dunning, W. A., Political Theories: From Luther to Montesquieu, 1925.

Dunning, W. A., Political Theories: From Rousseau to Spencer, 1920.

Dunning, W. A., "Jean Bodin on Sovereignty" in Political Science Quarterly, Vol. XI, 1896, pp. 82 ff.

Dunning, W. A., "The Politics of Aristotle", in Political Science Quarterly, Vol. XV, pp. 273 ff.

Dunning, W. A., "Political Theories of Jean Jacques Rousseau", in Political Science Quarterly, Vol. XXIV, 1909, September.

Durkheim E., Le Suicide, 1897.

Durkheim E., De la Division du Travail, 1902.

Elliott, W. Y., "Sovereign State or Sovereign Group?", in American Political Science Review, Vol. XIX, 1919.

Elliott, W. Y., "The Metaphysics of Duguit, Pragmatic Conception of Law", in Political Quarterly, December, 1922.

Elliott, W. Y., "The Pragmatic Politics of Mr. H. J. Laski", in American Political Science Review, May, 1924.

Ellis, E. D., "The Pluralistic State", in American Political Science Review, Vol. XIV, August, 1920.

Ellis, E. D., "The Pluralistic State", in American Political Science Review, Vol. XVII, November, 1923.

Ellwood, Sociology in Its Psychological Aspects, 1912.

Esmein, Droit Constitutional, 5th edition.

Estey, J. A., Revolutionary Syndicalism, 1913.

Evans, L. B., Leading Cases in International Law, 2nd ed.

Evans, L. B., Leading Cases on American Constitutional Law, 1925.

Ewart, J. S., "Canada, the Empire and the United States", in Foreign Affairs, Vol. VI, 1927.

Fauchille, P., Traite de Droit International Public, 1921-1926.

Fenwick, C. G., International Law, 1924.

Ferguson, J. H., Manual of International Law, 1884.

Fichte, J. G., Right, 1796-1896.

Figgis, J. N., From Gerson to Grotius, 1907.

Figgis, J. N., Churches in the Modern States, 1913.

Figgis, J. N., The Divine Right of the Kings, 1914.

Figgis, J. N., The Will of Freedom, 1917.

Filmer, R., Patriarcha, or Natural Power of Kings, 1680.

Filmer, R., Observations Concerning the Original of Government, 1652.

Foignet, R., Droit International Public, 1915.

Follet, M. P., The New State, 1918.

Ford, P. L., The Federalist, 1898.

Foster, R., On the Constitution, 1895.

Foulke, R. R., A Treatise on International Law, 1920.

Freund, E., "Historical Jurists in Germany", in Political Science Quarterly, Vol. V, pp. 473 ff.

Freund, E., The Legal Nature of Corporations, 1897.

Freund, E., Empire and Sovereignty, 1903.

Gareis, K., Alligemein Staatrecht.

Gareis, K., Volkerrecht, 2nd.

Garner, J. W., Introduction to Political Science, 1919.

Garner, J. W., Recent Developments in International Law, 1925.

Garner, J. W., "Limitations on National Sovereignty in International Relations", in Political Science Review, 1925, Vol. XIX, p. 1 pp.

Garner, J. W., Political Science and Government, 1928.

Gehlke, C. E., Emile Durkheim's Contribution to Sociological Theory, 1915.

General Orders of the United States Army, No. 100, 1863.

Gettell, R. G., Introduction to Political Science, 1910.

Gettell, R. G., Readings in Political Science, 1911.

Gettell, R. G., Problems of Political Revolution, 1914.

Gettell, R. G., History of Political Thought, 1924.

Geza, Englemrnn, Political Philosophy from Plato to Bentham, translated from German by K. F. Geiser, 1927.

Giddings, F. H., The Principle of Sociology, 1896.

Giddings, F. H., Readings in Descriptive and Historical Sociology, 1906.

Giddings, F. H., Inductive Sociology, 1909.

Giddings, F. H., The Responsible State, 1918.

Gierke, O., Die Grundbegriffe des statsrechts und die Neuesten Staatstheorien, Zeitschrift fur die gesammte Staatswissenschafte, Turbingen, 1874.

Gierke, O., Johannes Althusius, 1880.

Gierke, O., Das deutsche Genossenchaftsrecht, 1868-1913.

Gierke, O., Political Theories of Middle Ages, trans. Maitland.

Gilchrist, R. N., Principles of Political Science, 1921.

Gooch, G. P., Political Thought in England from Bacon to Halifax, 1914-1915.

Graham, W., English Political Philosophy, 1899.

Greef, De la Structure Générale des Sociétiés.

Gregory, "The Neutralization of the Asland Islands", in American Journal International Law, Vol. XVII.

Grotius, De Jure Belli ac Pacis, 1625.

Guizot, Du Government de la France depuis la Restauration et du Ministère Actuel, 1821.

Gumplowiez, L., Geschicte der Staatstheorein, 1927 ed.

Gumplowiez, L., Outline of Sociology, trans. by Moore.

Haldane, R. P., "The Nature of the State", in Contemporary Review, CXVII, June, 1920.

Hall, W. E., Rights and Duties of Neutrals, 1874.

Hall, W. E., A Treatise on International Law, 8th ed., 1924.

Halleck, H. W., International Law, 4th ed., 1908.

Haller, L. V., Restauration der Staatwissenschaft order Theorie des Naturalichgesellgen Zustandes der Chimaera des Kunstlichen-burgerlichen entgegensetzt, 1816-1834.

Hamilton, A., Works, edited by J. C. Hamilton, 1850.

Hamilton, E. D., "In Re Alienation of Sovereignty", Virginia Law Review, Vol. XIII, p. 524, 1927.

Hancke, E., Bodin: Eine Studie über den Begriff der Souverainetat.

Hanel, A., Studien zum Deutschen Staatsrechte, 1873-1880.

Harley, J. E., The League of Nations and the New International Law, 1921.

Harley, J. E., Syndicalism, 1912.

Harris, H. W., What is the League of Nations, 1925.

Hart, A. B., Introdaction to Federal Government, 1891.

Hauriou, M., La Souverainete Nationale, 1912.

Hauriou, M., Principes de Droit Public, 2nd ed., 1916.

Hearnshow, E. J. C., The Social and Political Ideas of Some Great Mediaeval Thinkers, 1923.

Hearnshow, E. J. C., The Social and Political Ideas of Some Great Thinkers of the Renaissance and the Reformation, 1925.

Held, J., System des Verfassungsrechts der Monarchischen Staaten Deustchland Mitbesanderer Rucksicht auf den Constitutionalesimes, 1856.

Hegel, G. W., Grundlinien der Philosophie des Rechts, 1821, trans. by S. W. Dyde.

Henderson, A., Washington's Southern Tour, 1923.

Hennessy, J., Récoganization Administrative de la France, 1919.

Hersey, A. S., The Essentials of International Public Law and Organization, Rev. ed., 1927.

Hicks, F. C., The World Order, 1920.

Hill, D. J., World Organization as Affected by the Nature of the Modern State, 1911.

Hill, D. J., The Rebuilding of Europe, 1919.

History of the Peace Conference of Paris, 1924. Issued under the Auspices of the Institute of International Affairs.

Hobbes, T., Leviathan, edited by Rhys.

Hobson, J. A., Towards International Government, 1915.

Hobson, S. G., National Guilds: An Inquiry into the Wage System and the Way Out, 1919.

Hobson, S. G. Guild Principles in War and Peace, 1917.

Hobson, S. G. National Guilds and the State, 1920.

Hocking, William E., Man and the State, 1926.

Holaind, R. I., Natural Law and Legal Practice, 1899.

Holcombe, A. N., State Government, 1916.

Holland, T. E., The Elements of Jurisprudence, 12th ed., 1917.

Holmes, O., Common Law, 1881.

Holmef, O., Collected Papers, 1921.

Holt, H., "The Passing of National Sovereignty", in The Independent, 1917, Vol. XCII, pp. 120 ff.

Hotman, F., Franco-Gallia, 1573.

Hsiao, K. C., Political Pluralism, 1927.

Hughan, J. W., A Study of International Government, 1923.

Hurd, J. C., The Theory of Our National Existence, 1881.

Hurd, J. C., The Union State, 1890.

James, I., True Law of Free Monarchies, 1598.

James, W., Pragmatism, 1907.

James, William, A Pluralistic Universe, 1909.

James William, Some Problems of Philosophy: A Beginning of an Introduction to Philosophy, 1911.

James, W., Essays in Radical Empiricism, 1912.

Jameson, J. A., A Treatise on Constitutional Convention, 1866.

Jameson, J. A., "National Sovereignty", in Political Science Quarterly, Vol. □, pp. 193 ff.

Janet, P., Histoire de la Science Politique.

Jefferson, T., Works, ed. by P. L. Ford, 1892–1899.

Jellinek, G., Lehre von den Statenverbingungen, 1882.

Jellinek, G., Allegemeine Staatslehre, ed.

Jenks, E., "Recent Theories of the State", in Law Quarterly, 1927, April.

Johnston, F., "Some Modern Aspects of the Public Power", in Massachusetts Law Quarterly, Vol. VIII, May, 1923.

Judson, H. P., Our Federal Republic, 1925.

Kaltenborn, C. V. B., Einleitung in das Constitutionalle Verfassungercht, 1862.

Kant, I., Principles of Politics, trans. by Hastie.

Kant, I., Metaphysical First Principles of the Theory of Law, 1796, trans. by W. Hastie.

Kant, I., Perpetual Peace, 1795, trans. by M. C. Smith.

Kelsen, H., Das Problem der Souveranitat und die Theorie des Volkerrechts, 1920.

Kent, J., Commentaries on American Law, 12th ed., 1884.

Kent, J., Commentary on International Law, 1865, ed. by J. T. Abdy.

Kingsley, D. A., "The World's Fundamental Error", in The Independent, Vol. LXXX, pp. 153–155.

Kirkup, T., A History of Socialism, 1920 ed.

Korff, S. A., "The Problem of Sovereignty" in American Political Science Review, Vol. XVII, August, 1923.

Korkunov, N. M., General Theory of Law, trans. by Hastings, 1922.

Krabbe, H., Die Lehre der Rechtssouveranitat, 1906.

Krabbe, H., Die Moderne Staatsidee, 1919, also English translation by G. H. Sabine and W. J. Shepard.

Kruger, F. K., Government and Politics of the German Empire, 1915.

Laband, P., Das Staatsreacht des Deustches, 1880-1882.

Lagordelle, Huberts and others, Syndicalisme et Socialisme, 1908.

Laing, B. M., "Aspects of the Problem of Sovereignty", in International Journal of Ethics, Vol. XXXII, pp. 1 ff.

Lansing, R., Notes on Sovereignty: From the Standpoint of the State and the World, 1921.

Lansing, R., The Peace Negotiation, 1920.

Larnaude, La Sociétédes Nations, 1920.

Laski, H. J., "Personality of the State", in The Nation, July, 1915.

Laski, H. J., Studies in the Problem of Sovereignty, 1917.

Laski, H. J., Authority in the Modern State, 1919.

Laski, H. J., Political Thought in England, from Locke to Bentham, 1920.

Laski, H. J., The Foundations of Sovereignty and Other Essays, 1921.

Laski, H. J., A Grammar of Politics, 1925.

Laski, H. J., Communism, 1927.

Laski, H. J., "Democracy at Crossroads", in Yale Review, Vol. IX, pp. 788 ff.

Laski, H. J., "The State in the New Social Order", Fabian Essays, 1922.

Lawrence, T. J., International Law, 7th ed., by P. H. Winfield, 1923.

League of Nations, Provisional Verbatim Records, 1920.

League of Nations, Records of Plenary Meeting, 1925.

League of Nations, Records of the 4th Assembly, Plenary Meeting.

League of Nations, Monthly Summary.

League of Nations, Official Journal.

League of Nations, Minutes of the Permanent Mandate Commission.

League of Nations, Records of the First Assembly, 80th., Plenary Meeting.

Lee, R. W., "On Sovereignty", in Canadian Law Times August, 1915.

Le Fur, L., L'État Federal, 1897.

Le Fur, L., "La Souveraineté et le Droit", in La Revue du Droit public et de la Science Politique en France et a L'étranger, No. 3, 1908.

Leroy, M., Transformation de la Puissance Publique, 1907.

Levermore, C. H., Year Book of the League of Nations.

Levesque, G., La Situation internationale de Dantzig, 1924.

Lewis, G. C., On the Use and Abuse of Some Political Terms, edited by Thomas Raleigh.

Lewis, M. M., "Free City of Danzig", in British Year Book of International Law, 1924.

Lieber, F., Manual of Political Ethics, 1829.

Lieber, F., On the Civil Liberty and Self-Government, 1853.

Lieber, F., The Miscellaneous Writings, 188.

Lightwood, J. M., Nature of Positive Law, 1883.

Lindsay, A. D., "The State in Recent Theory", in the Political Quarterly, Vol. I, 1914.

Lindsay, A. D., "Political Theory", in Marvin's Development in European Thought, 1919.

Lippmann, W., Politics, 1913.

Lippmann, W., "A Clue", in the New Republic, Vol. X, April, 1917.

Liszt, F. V., Das Volkenrecht, 12th ed. 1925.

Levine, L., Syndicalism in America, 1913.

Levine, L., Syndicalism in France, 1913.

Locke, J., Two Treatises of Government, 1690.

Lodge, H. C., The Senate and the League of Nations, 1925.

Lord, A. R., Principles of Politics, 1921.

Loria, A., The Economic Foundation of Society, trans. by M. Keasbey, 1890.

Lowell, A. L., Essays on Government, 1897–1899.

Lowell, A. L., "The Imperial Conference", in Foreign Affairs, Vol. V, pp. 375 ff.

Lucas, W. W., "Legal Status of sovereignty", in Juridical Review, October, 1912.

Lucas, W. W., "The Corporate Nature of English Sovereignty".

MacIver, R. M., Community: A Sociological Study, 1917.

MacIver, R. M., "Society and State", in Philosophical Review, Vol. XX, pp. 30 ff.

MacIver, R. M., The Modern State, 1927.

Mackintosh, J., A Discourse on the Study of the Law of Nature and Nations, 1835.

Madison J., The Writings of Madison J., ed. by Gaillard Hunt, 1900-1910.

MacDonald, J. R., Syndicalism, 1912.

Maeztu, R. de, Authorship, Liberty and Function, 1916.

Maine, H., Ancient Law, 1861.

Maine, H., Early History of Institutions, 1874.

Maine, H., Early Law and Custom, 1883.

Maine, H., Popular Government, 1884.

Maine, H., International Law, 1887.

Maistre, de, Etude sur la Souverainete, 1796.

Maitland, F. W., Introduction to Gierkie's Political Theory of the Middle Ages, 1900.

Maitland, F. W., The Constitutional History of England, 1908.

Maitland, F. W., Collected Papers, 3 volumes, edited by A. L. Fisher.

Manning, W. O., Commentaries on the Law of Nations, 1875.

Mansfield, E. D., The Political Grammar of the United States, 1834.

Markby, W., Elements of Law, 6th ed., 1905.

Martens, G. F., de, Précis du Droit des Gens Moderne de L'Europe, 1788.

Mathews, J. M., "A Recent Development in Political Theory", in Political Science Quarterly, 1909, Vol. ☐, pp. 284 ff.

Martin, J., Concepts of State, Sovereignty, and International Law, 1928.

Mallwain, C. H., The High Court of Parliament and its Supremacy, 1910.

Mallwain, C. H., "The High Court of Parliament", 1910.

Mallwain, C. H., "The Political Works of James I", Harvard Political Classics, Vol. I.

Mallwain, C. H., The American Revolution, 1923.

McLlaughlin, "Social Compact and Constitutional Construction", in American Historical Review, 1900.

McNair, A. E., "So-called State Servitudes", in British Year Book of International Law, 1924.

Merignhac, A., Traite de Droit Public International, 1905.

Merriam, C. E., A History of American Political Theories, 1903.

Merriam, C. E., American Political Ideas, 1920.

Merriam and Barnes, A History of Political Theories: Recent Times, 1924.

Merraim, C. E., History of the Theory of Sovereignty since Rousseau, 1900.

Mexican Constitution of 1924 and 1917.

Meyer, H. V., Lehrbuch des deutschen Staatsrecht, 1914 ed.

Millot, A., Les Mandats internationaux, 1914.

Modern French Legal Philosophy, Modern Legal Philosophy Series, translated by Mrs. F. W. Scott and J. P. Chamberlin.

Mohl, R. V., Encyklopadie der Staatswissenschaften, 1959.

Mohl, R. V., Geschichto und Literatur der Staatswissenschaften.

Molinari, G. de, Théorie de l'évolution, 1908.

Molinari, G. de, The Society of Tomorrow, trans. by P. H. Lee-Warner.

Montegomery, B. G., Issues of European Statesmanship, 1926.

Moore, J. B., Intarnational Law Digest, 1906.

Moore, J. B., "Law and Organization", in American Political Science Review, Vol. IX.

Morris, G. R. and M., A History of Political Ideas, 1924.

Morris, G. S., Hegel's Philosophy of the State and of History, 1887.

Mott, "The Political Theory of Syndicalism", in Political Science Quarterly, Vol. XXXVII, 1922, pp. 25 ff.

Mulford, E., The Nation, 1872.

Munro, W. B., The Government of the United States, 1919.

Nippold, Die Fort bildung des Verfohrens in Volkerrechlichen Stritigkeiten.

Nippold, The Development of International Law after the World War, trans. by Hershey, 1913.

Nobicow, La Fédération de l' Europe, 1901.

Nobicow, War and Its Alleged Benefits, trans. by Seltzer, 1911.

Nys, E., Le Droit International, 1904-1906.

Sppenheim, L. F. L., International Law, 3rd ed.

Sppenheim, L. F. L., The League of Nations and Its Problems, London, 1919.

Sppenheim, L. F. L., The Future of International Law, 1921.

Sppenheimer, H., The Constitution of German Republic, 1923.

Sppenheimer, Franz., The State: Its History and Development Viewed Sociologically, trans. by J. M. Gitterman, 1914.

Orage, H. R., National Guild, 1914.

Osborne, S., The Saar Question: A Disease Spot in Europe, 1923.

Panunzio, S., Syndicalisme et Souveraineté, Le Mouvement Socialiste, 34, Nos. 253-254, pp. 59 ff.

Pataud, E. and Pouget, G., Syndicalism, Industrial Unionism and Socialism,

1913.

Paul-Boncour, J., Syndicats des Fonctionnaires, 1906.

Paul-Boncour, J., Le Fédéralisme économique, 2nd, 1901.

Penty, A, J., Old World for New, 1917.

Penty, A, J., Guilds and the Social Crisis, 1919.

Pergler, C., "Sovereignty in Judicial Interpretation", in American Bar Association Journal, Vol. XII, April, 1926.

Phillimore, R. J., Commentaries upon International Law, 1879−1889.

Pollock, F., "Locke's Theory of the State", in Proceedings of British Academy, Vol. I.

Pollock, F., An Introduction to the History of the Science of Politics, 1902.

Pollock, F., A First Book of Jurisprudence for Students of Common Law, 1918.

Pollock, F., "Sovereignty and the League of Nations", in Fortnightly Review, 1918, Vol. CX.

Pollock, F., League of Nations, 1920.

Pollock, F., Essays in Law, 1922.

Pomeroy, J. N., An Introduction to the Constitutional Law of the United States, 1886.

Porter, W. D., State Sovereignty and the Doctrine of Coercion, Association, No. 2, 1860.

Pound, R., "Legislation as a Social Function", see Publications of American Sociological Society, Vol. VII, pp. 153 ff.

Pound, R., "Scope and Purpose of Sociological Jurisprudence", in Harvard Law Review, Vol. 24, June, December 1911, and April, 1912.

Pound, R., The Spirit of Common Law, 1921.

Pound, R., Interpretations of Legal History, 1923.

Pound, R., An Introduction to the Philosophy of Law, 1922.

Pound, R., "Jurisprudence", in Barnes' The Philosophy and Prospects of the Social Science.

Pound, R., "Sociology and Law", in W. F. Ogburn and A. Colderweisser's The Social Sciences and Their Interrelations, 1927.

Pound, R., Law and Moral, 1924.

Pound, R., "Theory and Law", in Yale Law Journal, Vol. XXII, pp. 114 ff.

Powers, A. H., The Great Peace, 1918.

Prall, W., The State and the Church, 1900.

Preuss, H., Gemeinde, Staat Reich, 1889.

Pufendorf, S., De Jure Naturae et Gentium, 1672, translated by B. Kennett.

Rankin, E. S., The Dominion of Sea and Air, 1925.

Ratzenhofer G., Wessen and Zweck der Politik, 1893.

Ratzenhofer G., Die Sociologische Erkenntnis, 1898.

Reed, James A., "Encroachment of the Federal Government", Proceedings of Texas Bar Association, Vol. XLVI, October, 1927.

Resch, P., Europaische Volkerrecht, 1885.

Ritchie, D. G., "On the Conception of Sovereignty", in Annals of American Academy of Political and Social Science, January, 1891.

Riviers, A. P. O, Principes du Droit des Gens, 1896.

Roberts, R., The Unfinished Program of Democracy, 1919.

Roberts, R., The Church in the Commonwealth, 1918.

Rockow, L., Contemporary Political Thought in England, 1921.

Roune, L. V., Staatsrecht des Deustche Reiches, 1876–1877.

Root, E., "The Sanction of International Law", in Proceedings of American Society of International Law, 1908, pp. 14 ff.

Root, E., Address on International Subjects, edited by J. B. Scott, 1916.

Ross, E. A, Social Control, 1904.

Rougier, A., Les Guerres Civiles et le Droit des Gens, 1903.

Rousseau, J. J., The Social Contract, English translation by Toler.

Russell, B. A. W., The Prospects of Industrial Civilization, 1923.

Russell, Bertrand, A. W., Bolshevism: Practice and Theory, 1920.

Russell, B. A. W., Proposed Road to Freedom: Socialism Anarchism, and Syndicalism, 1919.

Russell, B. A. W., Principles of Social Reconstruction, 1918.

Russell, B. A. W., Political Ideals, 1917.

Ruttiman, P., Das Nordamerikanische Bundesstaat Verglichen mit den Politischen Einrichtungen der Schweiz, 1867–1872.

Ryan, J. A., "Proper Function of the State", in Catholic World, Vol. CXIII, pp. 169 ff.

Sabine, G. H., "The Concept of the State as Power", in The Philosophical Review, July, 1920.

Sabine, G. H., "Pluralism, a Point of View", in American Political Science Review, Vol. XVII, Febuary, 1923.

Salmond, J. W., Jurisprudence, sixth ed., 1920.

Savigny, F. K. V., Von Beruf unserer Zeit fur Gesetzgebung und Rechtswissenchaft, 1814.

Savigny, F. K. V., The History of Roman Law, trans. by E. Cathcart.

Savigny, K. V., System des Heutigen Romischen Rechts, 1840-1849.

Schulze, G. H., System des Deutschen Staatsrechts, 1881-1886.

Scott, J. B., James Madison's Notes of Debates in the Federal Convention of 1787 and their Relation to a more Perfect Society of Nations, 1918.

Scott, J. B., Cases on International Law, 2nd ed., 1922.

Scott, J. B., Sovereign States and Suits before Arbitral Tribunals and Courts of Justice, 1925.

Scott, J. B., The Hague Court Report, 1916.

Seeley, J. R., Introduction to Political Science, 1896.

Seydel, M. V., Xommentar zur Verfassung Kunde fur das Deutsche Reich, 1897.

Seydel, M. V., Grundzuge der Allgemein Staatslehre, 1873.

Small, A. W., Between Eros from Capitalism to Democracy, 1913.

Small, A. W., General Sociology, 1905.

Smith, H. A., The Law of Associations, 1914.

Smith, H. A., Federalism in North America, 1923.

Snow, "The Mandatory System under the Covenant of the League of Nations", in Proceedings of Academy of Political Science, Vol. VII, p. 427.

Sorel, G., Introduction à l'économie Moderne Composition du Maxisme, 1908.

Sorel, G., L'Avenir Socialiste des Syndiactes, 1898.

Sorel, G., Les Illusions du Progres, 2nd ed, 1911.

Sorel, G., Reflections on Violence, translated by T. E. Aulme, 1912.

Spargo, G., Syndicalism, Industrial Unionism, and Socialism, 1913.

Spaight, J. M., War Rights on Land, 1911.

Spencer, H., Man versus the State, 1884.

Spencer, H., Social Statics, 1851.

Stallybrass, W. T. S., A Society of States, 1919.

Steiner, R., The Threefold Commonwealth, 1922.

Stenphens, A. H., A Constitutional View of the Late War Between the States, 2 volumes, 1867-1869.

Story, J., Commentaries on the Constitution of the United States, 1883.

Stowll, E. C., Intervention in Intervention Law, 1927.

Stowell and Munro, International Cases, 1916.

Sumner, W. G., Folkway, 1913.

Taft and Bryan, World Peace: A Written Debate, 1917.

Taft, W. H., "The Paris Covenant for a League of Nations", in American Political Science Review, Vol. XIII, 1919.

Tarde, G., The Laws of Imitation, 1903.

Taylor, J., New View of the Constitution, 1822.

Taylor, Science of Jurisprudence, 1903.

Treitschke, Undesstaat und Einheitsstaat, 1864.

Treitschke, H. G. V., Politik, 1899–1900, also English translation by Dugdale and T. de Bille, 1916.

Treumann, R. M., Die Monarchomachen, 1895.

Tucker, G., His Edition of Blackstone's Commentaries.

Tuft, J. H., "The Community and Economic Groups", in Philosophical Review, Vol. XXVII, pp. 89 ff.

Turner, R. E., America in Civilization, 1925.

Twiss, T., Law of Nations, 1884.

Vaccaro, M. A., Les Bases Sociologiques du Droit et de L'état, 1898.

Vattel, E. de, Le Droit des Gens, 1863 ed.

Waitz, G., Grundzug der Politik, 1862.

Wallas, Human Nature in Politics, 1909.

Wallas, G., The Great Society: A Psychological Analysis, 1914.

Wallas, G., Our Social Heritage, 1921.

Ward, P. W., Sovereignty: A Study of a Contemporary Political Nation, 1928.

Washington's Writings, Collected and edited by W. C. Ford.

Webb, S. and B., A Constitution for the Socialist Commonwealth of Great Britain, 1920.

Webster, D., Works, 1851.

Wehberg, H., Problems of International Court of Justice, trans. by C. G. Fenwick, 1918.

Westlake, J., International Law, 1904–1907.

Wheaton, H., Elements of International Law, 1899, 3rd edition.

Whitfield, J. B., "Sovereign Power of Constitutional Governments", in Central Law Journal, Vol. XCI, August, 1920.

Wickersham, G. W., "Confused Sovereignty", Illinois Law Review, November,

1916, Vol. XI.

Wilde, N., The Ethical Basis of the State, 1924.

Williams, D. R., "Is Congress Empowered to Alienate Sovereignty of the United States", in Virginia Law Review, Vol. XII, pp. 1 ff, 1925.

Williams, G. H., "Sovereignty", in Central Law Journal, Vol. XCVIII, pp. 385 ff, 1925.

Williams, J. M., The Foundations of Social Science, 1920.

Williams, J. M., Principles of Social Psychology, 1922.

Williams, H. E., "Dual Government", in Kentucky Law Journal, March, 1927.

Willoughby, W. W., The Nature of the State, 1896.

Willoughby, W. W., Political Theories of the Ancient World, 1903.

Willoughby, W. W., The American Constitutional System, 1904.

Willoughby, W. W., "The Juristic Conception of the State", in American Political Science Review, Vol. 12, pp. 192-208.

Willoughby, W. W., "The Political Theories of John W. Burgess", in Yale Law Review, Vol. XVII, May, 1908.

Willoughby, W. W., The Fundamental Concepts of Public Law, 1924.

Willoughby, W. W., "The Juristic Theories of Krabbe", in American Political Science Review, August, 1926.

Wilson, J. Works.

Wilson, W, An Old Master and Other Political Essays, 1893.

Wilson, W., The State, 1898.

Wise, B. R., Outline of Jurisprudence, 4th ed., 1925.

World Peace Foundation Pamphlet, 1912.

World Peace Foundation Pamphlets, sixth Year Book of the League of Nations.

World Peace Foundation Pamphlet, Vol. X, No. 6, 1927.

Wright, Q., "Effects of the League of Nations Covenant", in Political Science Review, Vol. XIII, p. 569.

Wright, Q., "Sovereignty of the Mandates", in American Journal of International Law, Vol. XVII.

Yarros, V. S., "What Shall We Do with the State", in American Journal of Sociology, Vol. XXV, pp. 572-583 and XXVI, pp. 58-72.

Zane, J. M., The Story of Law, 1927.

VITA

The writer of this dissertation was born in 1903 at Hainan Island, China. He attended the primary school in his native place in 1908–1915. From 1916–1919 he studied in Yu Ling High School, Singapore. In 1920–1922 he was a student at Lingnan University, Canton, China. He was graduated from Futan University, Shanghai, in 1925 with the A. B. degree. He was a member of the Board of Editors of the *Futan Review* at Futan University. He came to the United States in August, 1925, and attended the University of Illinois. He received here the degree of A. M. in 1926. He continued his study for the degree of Doctor of Philosophy in Political Science in the Graduate School of the University of Illinois.

现代主权论

目　录

内容简介 …………………………………………………… 314
出版说明 …………………………………………………… 316
前　言 …………………………………………………… 317
引　语 …………………………………………………… 318
导　论 …………………………………………………… 319
第一章　主权理论的历史 ………………………………… 322
　　一、导论 ……………………………………………… 322
　　二、古希腊的主权概念——亚里士多德 …………… 322
　　三、罗马时期的主权概念 …………………………… 324
　　四、中世纪时期的主权概念 ………………………… 325
　　五、近代的主权概念 ………………………………… 326
　　六、反动运动 ………………………………………… 334
　　七、结论 ……………………………………………… 340
第二章　联邦国家中的主权 ……………………………… 343
　　一、导论 ……………………………………………… 343
　　二、州主权论 ………………………………………… 343
　　三、联邦主权论 ……………………………………… 349
　　四、各种妥协理论 …………………………………… 352
第三章　联邦国家中的主权（续） ……………………… 363
　　五、结论 ……………………………………………… 379
第四章　国际关系中的主权　主权的特征 ……………… 380
　　一、导论 ……………………………………………… 380
　　二、主权和国际法 …………………………………… 380
　　三、主权的本质 ……………………………………… 385
第五章　国际关系中的主权　归宿和批评（续） ……… 399
　　四、主权的归宿 ……………………………………… 399
　　五、近来对主权观念的攻击 ………………………… 414
　　六、结论 ……………………………………………… 416
第六章　主权与法律 ……………………………………… 418
　　一、导论 ……………………………………………… 418

二、分析学派 ………………………………………… 419
　　三、自然法学派 ……………………………………… 434
第七章　主权与法律（续） …………………………… 436
　　四、历史学派 ………………………………………… 436
　　五、经济学派 ………………………………………… 442
　　六、社会学学派 ……………………………………… 448
第八章　主权与法律（续） …………………………… 455
　　七、结论 ……………………………………………… 473
第九章　主权与职能组织 ……………………………… 474
　　一、导论 ……………………………………………… 474
　　二、德国学者 ………………………………………… 474
　　三、英国学者 ………………………………………… 476
　　四、法国学者 ………………………………………… 491
　　五、美国学者 ………………………………………… 496
　　六、结论 ……………………………………………… 500
第十章　拉斯基和其他 ………………………………… 502
　　一、拉斯基 …………………………………………… 502
　　二、其他学者 ………………………………………… 513
结论：一个观点 ………………………………………… 521
参考文献 ………………………………………………… 531
译名对照表 ……………………………………………… 550
译后记 …………………………………………………… 556

内容简介

《现代主权论》为陈序经1928年撰就的博士学位论文。本书以主权可分论立论,对主权理论的历史、主权在联邦国家、国际关系、法律、功能组织中的运用作了全面深入的考察,对传统的主权一元论和现代的主权多元论之间的关系作了详尽探讨。全书除导论与结论外,正文包括十章,第一章论述主权论的历史,第二章、第三章探讨联邦国家中的主权问题,第四章、第五章论述主权与国际关系,第六章、第七章、第八章分析主权与法之间的关系,第九章论述主权与职能组织之间的关系,第十章讨论拉斯基及其他学者的主权理论。

该书内容深刻、材料丰赡,有很高的学术价值,对于理解中国近代政治哲学史乃至主权论本身都有参考价值。

敬献家严继美先生

出版说明

读者在本书中或许会发现一些错误,这原因是出在当时打印的环节上,我的粗心和"忙碌"或许也是原因之一。以此观之,我将拙著公之于众,如果有一个出版理由的话,那是我对读者智力和理解的信任。

在出版这本书中,岭南大学陈受颐(S. Y. Chen)教授所作的贡献难以估量。我希望我的衷心感谢对他的长时期的期待是一个补偿。

陈序经
1929年6月于广州

前　　言

　　许多有价值的著作在这个研究中没有被运用。我非常遗憾没有找到凯尔森（Hans Kelsen）的《主权问题和国际法理论》（*Das Problemder Souveranitat und die Theorie des Völkerrechts*）。马特恩（Johannes Mattern）教授的《国家、主权和国际法的概念》和沃德（Paul W. Ward）的《主权：近代政治观念的考察》是在本书完成之后出版的。但我确信有关现代主权论的主要方面都已论及。

　　我深深感激许多作者和学者，特别是伊利诺大学的一些老师们。是在加纳（James W. Garner）教授的建议下，我才从事这项研究的。社会学系的海耶斯（Edward C. Hayes）教授、哲学系的麦克卢尔（Matthew T. McClure）教授、政治学系的伯代尔（Clarence A. Berdahl）教授，从他们的著作、演讲和个人建议中，我都得到了很多帮助。

　　更重要的是，我要感激政治学系的费尔赖（John A. Fairlie）教授，没有他的持续指导和热情帮助，本书是不可能完成的。当然，这并不是说本书的错误与缺点不由本人单独负责。

陈序经（Su-Ching Chen）
伊利诺大学
1928 年 4 月 1 日

引　语

　　所谓传统的主权理论的基本原则大致可以归结为两点：①主权在本质上是不可分的。②主权是法律渊源，因此正当的法必须有最高主权者在后面做支撑。在主权于联邦国家，特别是于国际关系的运用之中，第一条原则已经受到批评。那些无论是在国内还是在国际上增长和发展的职能组织都导致许多学者否认第一条原则以及该原则暗含的主权是国家的基本特征的原则。第二条原则则长时期地被那些自然法学派的拥护者所挑战和怀疑；但是，在形式上，它主要受到来自历史法学家，法理学中的经济学派，最主要的，来自社会法学家们的批评和怀疑。

　　关于第二条原则的反对意见认为，法律如果不是最高主权者做后盾，在严格的意义上就不能称之为法的说法，已经没有实际的意义。现在已经很少有人（即便有）认为法是且一定是主权的产物。最近的讨论一直主要关乎主权在其本质上是否可分这一问题。这种讨论的答案是肯定的。这有历史方面的证据、现存的事实、普遍接受的道德标准，还有哲学中的比较合理和充分的观念。

　　以下的内容或许可以为这方面的研究作一个简单的概括。必须提到的是，章节的顺序并不一定与概括严格保持一致。

　　本论文的主要目的是对现代主权论做一鸟瞰。从第一章到最后一章，我都必须尽可能如实地对那些作者的思想予以描述而不对其做出批评。要达到这个目的，引用是非常自由的。我自己的观点则在结论中；但是必须补充的是，这些观点并没有什么独创性。

　　达到这个主题的方法有两种：一是按时间顺序论述；二是根据主题论述。主题是更被强调的，在同一主题下再采用按时间顺序论述的方法。

导　论

主权这一概念，一般认为是布丹（Bodin）于16世纪最先使用的。但最近一些权威人士证明早在15世纪，法国的一些作家就开始使用了，特别是在波马诺（Beaumanoir）及诺索（Loyseau）的著作中。① 也许还有一些人在古代的文学作品中也发现了这一概念，并宣称在15世纪之前已经有人使用主权这一概念。不管是谁最先使用这一概念，一个无可争辩的事实是：主权这一概念已存在很久，并一直以来是人类思想史上最为重要的概念之一。

让我们回到罗马帝国时代。当皇权鼎盛时，皇帝被认为是主权的所有者，并且是"荣誉的源泉，法律的制订者，争端的裁判者"②。他就是上帝。他的行为是不会出错的，他的话就是最后的决断。将近千年后，在卡诺莎（Cannossa）发生的一幕中，亨利（Henry），那个时候欧洲最伟大的国家的国王，也必须跪在主教的面前。一些学者甚至宣称，罗马皇帝的幽灵正从他的坟墓里走出来。③

另一方面，浪漫派的知识分子们，例如领袖但丁（Dante），则坚信这种权威应当在君主的手上。他的这种预见在亚威农（Avignon）上演的一幕中被明确地反映出来。④ 君主可以做上帝和教皇所做的一切，因为他就是主权的拥有者。君主和教皇之间的长期的战斗结束了，但关于主权的战斗仍在继续。不过战斗的双方变成了国王和人民。《大宪章》《权利宣言》仅仅是几个明显的例子。人们现在清楚地意识到，路易十四的时代已经过去，但这并不意味着关于主权的战斗就已结束，相反，它充分显示出这种战斗的重要性。

---

① Carlyle, *A History of Mediaeval Political Theory*, 第三卷, *Political Theory from the Tenth Century to the Thirteenth*, 1916, 50～84页。也参见 Garner, *Political Science and Government*, 1928, 第八章, 156页。Viollet, *Etablissements de Saint Louis*, 第二卷, 370页。Carré de Malberg, *Théory générale de l'État*, 第一卷, 73～74页。

② Sumner, *Folkways*, 1913, 82页。

③ 格列高利七世（Gregorius Ⅶ, 1021—1085）宣扬教皇权力高于一切，不仅有权任命主教，而且可以废除君王。为了与神圣罗马帝国皇帝亨利四世争夺主教任免权，1076年宣布革除亨利教籍。亨利无奈，于次年1月亲赴卡诺莎（Cannossa, 意大利北部城堡）向教皇"悔罪"。1084年亨利进占罗马，格列高利出走，死于萨莱诺城（Salerno, 意大利南部西岸港口）。——译者注。

④ 公元1309年，教皇宝座从罗马被迁到靠近法国的亚威农（Avignon），教廷留在该地，直到1376年，这段时期在历史上被称为"教皇巴比伦被掳时期"（Babylonian Captivity）。"被掳"是因为这时期的教皇都在法王控制之下；"巴比伦"是因为前后持续约七十年之久，正如旧约时代以色列人被掳到巴比伦一样。这段时期，所有教皇都是法国人。继法王腓力给教皇制强烈的打击之后，"巴比伦被掳"更进一步削弱了教皇的特权。因为在亚威农的教皇们，完全听命于法国国王，其他各国人民不再尊重教皇。——译者注。

正因为如此，当代的政治家习惯于把主权当作头等大事来讨论，用最大的热情来谈论主权，视主权为他们深爱的祖国的灵魂和生命。他们说，人们有了它，就没有什么可以畏惧的；没有它，则没有希望。军事家们，把它看得比任何东西都要重要，他们愿意用所有臣民的生命去捍卫它。就连普通的民众，也为主权的荫庇而感到自豪，他们轻视国外那些不幸生活在主权残缺的国度里面的人们。

更为重要的是，主权是如此重要，以至于它被当作公众话题，并被各个领域的博学之士讨论。许多学者都宣称主权问题是他们各自的研究领域中一个专有的主题，还有一些学者则宣称如果没有他们的参与，主权问题就不可能得到解决。法学家把主权视为诉讼终审权（final power），认为主权问题是一个法律问题，只有他们才能处理它。① 政治学家们，从主权的特征、归宿和结果考虑，宣称他们最有资格研究它。哲学家们，把主权的最为基本的和一般的原理作为国家存在的最终依据，认为他们才是解决主权问题的关键角色。经济学家们将主权看作仅仅是经济现象的结果，认为如果不从他们所从事的领域去考察主权问题，我们将永远不可能理解它。② 伦理学家们，把主权作为人类的固有权利来谈论③，认为主权就其本质来说，是一种道德问题。心理学家认为主权不过是一种对公共观念，即选民、各反对党、各阶层、各利益团体的态度、冲动与观念的无序的、潜意识的影响，因此他们认为主权问题在本质上是一个社会心理学问题。④ 而那些社会学家，把主权作为各种社会势力的一个产物，以此来分析主权的发展和状况，坚持认为主权问题必须从社会学的观点来加以研究。⑤

如此之多的争论，也导致在关于主权的起源、作用、本质和归宿等的问题上出现了形形色色的观点。在起源上，有的人认为主权起源于家庭；有的人认为在原始游牧部落里面没有主权的存在；⑥ 有的人认为主权在部落联盟时期才产生；⑦ 更有人甚至认为主权的观念直到现代国家产生的时候才出现。

关于主权的作用，许多人认为主权是国家的特征，并且是最为基本的特征，如果没有主权，就没有国家可言。但另一方面，许多人却坚持认为国家只不过是一种社会组织方式，一个国家可以拥有主权，其他组织也可以拥有。

关于主权的本质，很多人坚信主权仅仅是一种权力，哪里有权力，哪里就有主权。然而，有的人却宣称主权不仅仅是权力的集合，因为权力只不过是实现主权的手段。另外有些人把主权看作理性甚至上帝，认为在人类组织中是不能发现

---

① Commons, "A Socoiological View of Sovereignty", *American Journal of Sociology*, 第5卷, 1~3页。
② Loria, *Economic Foundation of Society*, Lindley M. Keasbey 翻译。
③ Laski, *Authority in the Modern State*, 28页, 32~63页。
④ Williams, *The Foundations of Social Science*, 18~19页。
⑤ Barnes, *Sociology and Political Theory*, 131页。
⑥ Gumplowicz, *Outline of Sociology*, Moore 翻译, 124页。
⑦ Giddings, *Principles of Sociology*, 285页。

主权的。还有人认为主权不过是一个虚构的、空洞的东西。

不仅如此。随着研究的深入，许多学者已经开始探讨主权是否可以被分割、被限制和被侵犯，是否是绝对的、有效的和至上的，如此等等。对于这些问题，各方观点并不一致。至于主权的归宿，有的时期，它在皇帝手里，而有的时期在君主那里，有的时期还在人民手里。有时候，它完整地存在于一个政府中，有时候存在于议会中，有时候它存在于国家的立法机构那里，有时候它在选民手中。

总之，不仅是在过去，更是在现在，主权一直是人类思想史上的一个最为重要的概念之一。最近，对传统主权概念的攻击，也许被一些人看作是整体主权观念的丧钟，但事实是，有力的攻击越多，讨论也就越为宽广。至于结果如何，则只有时间才能告诉我们。

第一章 主权理论的历史

一、导论

本论文的主要目的是对现代主权理论作一纵览。但是没有任何一种理论能够孤立地存在。一种理论往往和另外一种或几种理论联系在一起，甚至这些理论相互之间有激烈的冲突。如果我们把其中一种理论称为新的理论，那么要理解这种新的理论，那些相关的背景知识是必要的，也是必需的。一个明显的事实是：许多理论家希望对一种理论进行改进或修正，从而使这种理论相对而言成为新的理论，那么对该领域其他人的研究工作有一个完整的理解对他而言就是必需的。在一个学者提出一种新的理论之前，不论他是否意识到，都已经受到了其他观念的影响。一个人的观念可能同影响他的观念不同，甚或有很大的不同，但如果我们不去研究一下那些影响他的观念，则想真正理解他的观念是不可能的。事实上，所谓新的理论一般都出自那些旧的理论。旧的理论和新的理论是一种母子关系，没有母，就没有子。

让我们举一个例子来证明。一般认为分权理论是美国的宪法之父们提出和推动的。但如果我们仅仅研究他们是不能很好理解这种理论的，我们还必须研究孟德斯鸠、洛克，甚至波利比奥斯（Polybius）和亚里士多德。道理很明显，我们不能分开他们，因为他们是密切相关的。他们彼此影响，如果不研究其他的学者，我们就不能理解其中任何一个观点。

正如前文所述，在我们处理主题之前，对主权理论的历史作一个纵览是必要的，也是必需的。

二、古希腊的主权概念——亚里士多德

由于他对该主题作了清晰和系统的表述，所以西方学者一般认为主权观念的历史始于亚里士多德。① 这并不是说，在亚里士多德之前，就没有主权的理论。② 说主权观念与人类思想自身一样久远可能更为合适，很明显，这是因为前者是后者的组成部分。人作为具有最高理性的动物（或万物的灵长），必有一些关于最

---

① 我在这里使用"西方的"这一形容词，是为了清楚地表明目前的研究纯粹是西方的。
② 事实上，像巴克（Barker）先生等人就把主权的观念追溯到比亚里士多德更远的历史时期。

高权威的观念这些观念或许是粗糙的,但如果有这样一个权威,人们就生活在他的统治下。

"人天生是一种政治动物。"① 这是亚里士多德整个"政治"系统建立的基础。正因为是一种政治动物,他就必定会生活在政治组织即国家里面,因为国家是人类本性在政治方面的表现,与此同时,这也是人类生活达到至善的手段。但同时因为人类也是动物,他们就不会完全摆脱掉一些野蛮的行为,这些行为被看做是通向最高的善(至善)的障碍,因而他们就不是完全自由的。因此,在任何政治组织里面,最高权威的存在就是合理的和必须的,因为它可以限制人们野蛮的行为,保护最高的善。

这种最高的权威,用一个合适的词语表示,就是"主权"。根据亚里士多德对他当时及以前政治组织的比较研究,主权可以是在一个人手中,也可以是在少数一些人或许多人手中。但是作为一个哲学家,他不会满足于知道主权在现实中是什么,他还要进一步地追问它应当是什么。这就导致他断言权威应当在"公民"那里。这不难解释。"当许多人在一起的时候,其中的每一个个体仅仅是平庸的个人,如果不是作为相互独立的个体而是作为集体存在,就比那些少数精英更好。就像众人集资准备的晚宴要比一个人自掏腰包准备的晚餐丰盛得多。"②

亚里士多德不像他的老师柏拉图那样对"公民"报以十足的信心,因为他们很容易受感情的驱使,去追求个人的和自私的目的,而忘记了公共福利(the general welfare)和公益(public good)。为避免这种危险,就必须有理性来引导他们的行动。什么是理性呢?那就是法律。"如果一个国家是正常的,并且是受一个无私的统治者引导通向一般的善(the general good),就应该有保证最终的主权的法律。"③ 亚里士多德在其他的论述里也说过,法律无论是对所有的希腊人,还是对亚里士多德个人而言,"是具体形式的精神实质,通常它还是核心动力和社会的统帅"④。

也许可以说,在亚里士多德看来,法律的主权和人民的主权在某种意义上不是两种不同的东西,只不过一种是优越的,另一种是低级的,因为人也被看作集理性与感性于一身。法律的主权和人民的主权可以共同也可以单独行动。只要它们的行为与理性保持一致,它们的至高无上的权力就不能被质疑。

---

① 我听一个知名学者说过,亚里士多德的"政治"的含义是社会。如果这是事实的话,这里多处使用的"政治"一词应当变成"社会",以更适合亚里士多德的思想,因为最近的趋势已经否认主权的观念是一个纯粹的政治问题。

② Aristotle, *Politics*, B. Jowett 翻译,第三章,第三节,85 页。

③ Barker, *Political Thought of Plato and Aristotle*, 33 页。也见 Aristotle, *Politics*, B. Jowett 翻译,第三卷,第七、第八章。也见 Dunning, *Political Theories, Ancient and Mediaeval*, 71 页。参见 Krabbe, *Die Moderne Staats-Idee*, 15 页以下。

④ Barker, *Greek Political Theory, Plato and His Predecessors*, 1918, 38 页脚注。

三、罗马时期的主权概念

罗马时期的主权观念在一句广泛流传的名言中得到了体现:"既然人民将所有的权利和权力都交给了国王,那国王的意志就具有法律的效力。"① 看起来上面引用的这段话在不同的语境中有不同的解释。当皇帝和国王的权力处于顶峰的时候,如在奥古斯都(Augustus)的时期,国王被认为拥有主权。② 但当罗马皇帝的权力还在上升或衰弱的时候,这个概念的含义是不同的。一方面,既然人民委托给他最高的权威,因此皇帝的意志就具有法律效力,但是,另一方面,委托并不等于放弃,最终的主权还是在人民手中。这样的观念在古罗马法学家那里被广泛地接受。③

---

① *Institutes*, LI, 第二部分,第六节。

② 参见 Sumner, *Folkways*, 1913, 82 页。Duguit 教授说:"主权的法律理论只能溯源到罗马帝国开始的年代。主权为全体人民共同拥有。为了使某一个人能够代表全体人民行使主权所包含的权力,罗马人民通过'王权法'(lexregia)将主权委托给'元首'。这样,皇帝便有可能将共和国时期分属不同机构的权力集于一身。皇帝的权力基于一种双重的权威;一方面是元老院和地方总督的权威;另一方面是源自平民宪法的护民官权威。皇帝从元老院或军队那里获得了'治权'(imperium)。而任免则通过'王权法'把护民官的权力转让给了皇帝。通过一个自然演进的过程,皇帝逐渐有了'治权'和'保护权'(postestas)。这两种权力结合成一种皇帝这一职位所固有的发布命令的权利。这种权利不再是一种通过人民的授权来行使的权力,而成了皇帝的天赋权利。这一发展到公元 3 世纪末也就是戴克里先(Diocletian)和康斯坦丁(Constantine)皇帝统治的时代——得以完成。虽然公元 6 世纪的《查士丁尼法学阶梯》中仍然提到了'王权法',但这只是一种好古癖的体现,只是从乌尔比安那里逐字照搬过来的一个词组。事实上的情况是,罗马皇帝将自己的意志等同于法律。'皇帝的决定具有法律效力'(Quod prinsip iplacuit legis habet vigorem)是一句法律箴言,它源自这样一个事实:皇帝享有完全的主权,也就是说,他有权利将自己的意志强加于他人,仅仅因为这是他的意志,仅仅因为他的这种权利具有一种要求普遍服从的属性。这样,罗马的天才们就创造出了一种后来被称为主权理论的公共权力理论,这种理论直到 20 世纪仍然是欧洲和美国公法的基础。"见 *Law in the Modern State*, Laski 翻译,2～3 页。

③ "罗马法学家关于人民是国家中权威的唯一的最终来源的理论对我们来说显然是契约论的原初形态。我们可以称之为'同意的理论'(the theory of consent),它在许多方面跟契约论不是同一个东西,但它是契约论的萌芽状态,契约论在它的基础上才得以形成……在《罗马法律汇编》中有几个句子同乌尔比安(Ulpian)的句子是类似的,'元首喜欢之事具有法律效力(Quod principi placuit, legis habet vigorem)'。起码在很多时候人们忽略了乌尔比安接下来的话,'因为根据赋予他权力的王权法,人民把他们的全部权威和权力移转给他(utpote cum lege regia, quae de imperio eius lata est, populus ei et in eum omne suum imperium et potestaem confertat)。'很少有比'建立在纯粹民主基础之上的不受限制的个人权威'这种几乎自相矛盾的描述更为明显的句子了。皇帝的意志是法律,但仅仅是因为人民选择让他这样。乌尔比安的话概括了法学家们的一般理论;就我们所见到的,罗马法学家们没有其他的观点。从公元 2 世纪早些时候的尤利安(Julianus),到 6 世纪的查士丁尼(Justinian)本人,皇帝都是法律的渊源,但这是因为人民根据其法律行为使他们成为这样的;更重要的问题在于必须就《罗马法律汇编》中我们所发现的作者对这一问题的考察来证明这一判断。"Carlyle, *A History of Mediaeval Political Theory*,第一卷,63～64 页。

四、中世纪时期的主权概念

菲吉斯（J. N. Figgis）教授曾评论道："从严格的意义上讲，中世纪没有主权者（sovereign）。"① 在一个具体的国家里面，在一定的范围内，这也许是正确的。不过我们不要认为主权者的缺失就意味着主权观念的缺失。一般而言，中世纪时代的主权理论可以分为三个派别：教会主权论、君主主权论和主权在民论。

第一种主权论认为有两个世界：世俗的和神圣的。后者就像太阳，前者就像月亮。世俗世界从神圣世界那里得到权力，就像月亮从太阳那里得到光亮。既然教会是神圣世界的代表，那么它对世俗世界就具有权威。②

第二种主权论认为人类的本性有两个层面，需要两个引导者，即国王和教皇。他们都直接从上帝那里得到权力。"他们二者有各自的领域，并且限定在这个领域内。恺撒的事归恺撒，彼得的事归彼得。"他们认为教皇在处理精神领域的事情时是至高无上的，但在处理世俗领域里面的事情中，皇帝或君主作为最高主权者的权威必须被承认。③

主权在民论主要建立在亚里士多德和罗马法学家的研究基础之上。他们坚持认为最终的主权在人世间的人民手中。他们中的一个杰出代表这样写道："人们

---

① Figgsi, *Studies of Political Thought, From Gerson to Grotius*, 第 11 页。Maitland 教授在他的 Collected Papers 中也表达了同样的观点。Carlyle 说："如果要更进一步讨论，我们首先必须抛弃掉那种主权的通常观念，这种观念认为法律仅仅是法律制定者或甚至是一个共同体的命令。这种观念在现时代的价值如何我们暂且不论，但它与中世纪的观念是完全不同的。" A. J. Carlyle, *A History of Mediaeval Political Theory in the West*, 第三卷, 41 页。

② "Hildebrandine 学派的政策及其背后的教会思想，是中世纪的首要思想。这种政策的主题是'正义'（Justitia）。首先，'正义'意味着教皇对教会拥有主权，在有形的、历史的、传统中的教会中的基督的化身必须有其有形的代表，以作为地上教会的头（head），所有教会权力的源泉，所有宗教传统的支持者。其次，'正义'意味着神职人员从俗世（the lay world）的解放——从婚姻的社会约束、买卖圣职的经济约束以及俗世授衣权（lay investiture, 所谓授衣权，即由俗王任命主教——译者注）的封建约束中解放出来。因此，从某种意义上讲，它意味着教会从国家分离出来。但是教会从国家中分离出来并不是国家从教会中分离出来。教皇的主权也许被排除于精神世界的世俗权力之外，但他作为主权者不能被排除于世俗社会中的精神权力之外。再次，'正义'意味着作为基督的最高律法的最高支持者，如果国王或君主违背或妨碍它的自由实施，教皇也可以加以裁断和修正。因此，从原则上说，（我引用 Troltsch 的话）'国家臣属于教会，作为教会控制以管理世俗世界的工具，国家是绝对精神目的下的世俗关系与价值的守护者。主教统辖制度（episcopacy）意味着神权政治的实现。'" E. Barker 的 "Mediaeval Political Thought", 收录于 F. J. C. Hearnshaw 的 *The Social and Political Idea of Some Great Mediaeval Thinkers*, 13 页, 也见 15 页。也可参见 Gierke 的 *Political Theories of the Middle Ages*, Maitland 翻译, 15 页以下。也可参见 Carlyle, *A History of Mediaeval Political Theory in the West*, 第二卷, 第五章。

③ 参见 Dante, *De Monarchia*. Pierre Du Bois 甚至走得更远，他宣称教皇应该把他的精神的权威交给法国国王，法国国王应该单独统治世界。但是他认识到教皇可以实施精神权威。参见 E. E. Power, "Pierre Du Bois and the Domination of France", 收录于 Hearnshaw 的 *The Social and Political Ideas of Some Great Mediaeval Thinkers*, 139~166 页。

聚在一起，形成一个城市共同体，是为了求得生活的便利和充裕，避免与此相反的情况发生。"① 在卡莱尔（Carlyle）教授所称作的"契约论的原始形式"（the undeveloped form of the theory of contract）里，它获得了更高的意义。②

毫无疑问，从古希腊到中世纪的结束，主权理论在不同年代、不同的著作中是不同的。但是，在它们中间有一点是相似的，即所有的学者都把问题限定在主权在哪里这一问题。他们没有试图解决甚至提出主权是什么的问题。在主权理论的历史上，这个问题是布丹首次在他的著作中提出来并加以回答的。也就是说，在主权论方面，布丹对政治理论做出了突出的贡献。并且，布丹的主权理论，对于后世的理论家也产生了深远的影响。③

五、近代的主权概念

（一）君主主权论

1. 布丹（1530—1596）

布丹并不是一个我们通常认为的那样的绝对主义者。他的主权归宿的观念的出发点同那些主权在民论者并无不同。他认为起初主权在人民手中，并且在相当长的时期内，如果人民不将他们的主权转让给某一个人或某些人，主权还会在人民手中。他这样写道："假设至高无上的权力，在不受法律限制，也没有抗议和申诉的情况下，被人民授予某一个人或某些人，我们就能说后者拥有主权吗？有些人一旦大权在握，就认为除了上帝，没有人比他更伟大。我认为主权不在这样的人手中，而在人民手中。他的权力是人民给的，在任期满后，他必须把权力还给人民。主权在愿意掌管主权的人民手中，或者说在有一定任期的人手中。在他们掌管这一至高无上的权威之时，我们不能认为人民的权力就被剥夺了。如果契约有一定的期限，并且出于人民自愿，那么人民在不受法律限制的情况下，把最高权力委托给一个人或一些人，就不能被认为是放弃了自己的权力。因为无论在哪种情况下，主权的代理者都必须向国王或人民及其他主权的所有者解释自己的所作所为，而国王或人民除了向不朽的上帝，无须向其他人作解释。"④

但是如果人民把他们的主权让渡给某一个人或某些人，且让他或他们终身拥

---

① Marsiglio, *The Defens or Pacis*, 第一卷，第七章。见 Coker, *Readings in Political Philosophy*, 164 页。

② 这一派的最为重要的代表是 Maisiglio of Padua 和 William of Ockum。参见 Gierke, *Political Theories of the Middle Ages*, Maitland 翻译，38～60 页。

③ Figgsi 教授写道："在严格的意义上，他（布丹）的著作是关于主权的第一篇著作，在坎布里奇的演讲后的很短的时期就被运用。后来的学者从 Hobbes 到 Sidgwick 和 Holland 教授都回到了他那里。" *From Gerson to Grotius*, 126 页。也见 Pollock, *The History of the Science of Politics*, 47 页以下。

④ Bodin, *De Republica*, 126 页。英译本，见 Coker, *Readings in Political Philosophy*, 231 页。

有这一主权，则那个人或那些人可以说拥有了真正无条件的主权。他说："如果权力不受法律限制，也不以行政长官、代表、政府官员、保护者的名义来行使，也没有任何人的授权，我们可以说主权集中到一个人手里。在这种情况下，人民已经完全放弃了他们的权力，无条件地将他们的主权给了他人，就像一个人无保留地将自己财产的所有权和控制权交给另一个人一样。这样的捐赠是完全没有任何条件的。"① 从上面所引用的话中可以看见，布丹是根据他那个时代的环境，将主权的归属划给了君主或国王。他的观点与那些认为主权是君主或国王的固有权利，故独获于上帝之处的观点不同。② 如果他生活在另外一个时代，处在另外一个环境中，也许有人会大胆地说，他是一个主权在民论的信奉者和鼓吹者。

阅读布丹的著作，我们会发现他谈到了两种类型的主权。一种是神圣的，一种是世俗的。前者被称为神性主权，后者则来源于人民的授予，它被授予国王或君主。后一种主权，特别是君主的主权，必须和前一种主权保持一致。因为神性主权要比君主主权高级。这样的前提导致布丹得出君主的主权必须为上帝的法则所限制的结论。他说："那些想废止或削弱上帝的法则的人，是不能逃脱神性主权的审判的。"③ 他又说："如果正义是法律的目的，法律又是君主的行为准则，君主又是全能的上帝的影子，那么，君主的法律必然打上神性法律的印迹。"④ 在这里，我们可以看到，由于布丹生活的年代离中世纪还不是太远（或者也可以说是中世纪的一部分），他还没有完全摆脱神学的氛围和人类权力来自上帝的教条。

在论述了布丹关于主权的归宿和类型的观念之后，让我们再来看看他关于主权的本质和特征的看法。这是他的主权理论以及整个政治体系的核心和基石。主权被定义为在公民（citizens）和属民（subjects）之上的至高无上的权力，它不受法律的约束。⑤ 从这个定义出发，就可以推导出如下原则。首先，主权既然在国家中是至高无上的权威，同时它又完全独立于法律，不受任何限制，因此它是绝对的。其次，它具有永久性或者说不受时间的限制，因为正如前文所述，如果只是短时期把权力交给某人，就不是这样的主权。⑥ 与此相关，就导致了第三个原则，主权不能转让（inalienability）和代表（delegation）。在这点上，布丹论述

---

① Bodin, *De Republica*, 128 页。
② Bodin, *De Republica*, 134 页。
③ Bodin, *De Republica*, 134 页。
④ Bodin, *De Republica*, 134 页。
⑤ Bodin, *De Republica*, 123 页。
⑥ Bodin, *De Republica*, 126 页。"如果最高权力被授予长达十年，如雅典的执政官（archon），也被称为士师（judge），在城邦中拥有特别的权力，情况又如何呢？城邦的主权还是不在他那里；他更是一个管理者或人民的代理，必须向他们负责。如果这种最高权力给予一人或多人长达一年时间，且其行为不需要向任何人负责，情况又如何呢？于是克尼德族（Cnidians）每年选出六十位公民，他们被称为阿密蒙尼（Amymones，即岁举长官——译者注），这些统治者很少受到限制和责备。既然他们在一年期满后，就必须被迫放弃其权威，主权毫无疑问不在他们那里。"

得并不清楚。① 他认为主权是绝对不能转让的，因为主权本来在人民手中，"被作为礼物送到别人手中"②，但是转让包含时间的永久性，如果它被转让，它必须是整个生命，因为某个人在短时期内掌握主权并不意味着主权的转换。最后，主权是不可分的，因为在一个国家里面没有两个至高无上的权威。权力可分，但主权不能。制定法律的权力有时可以在地方法官手中，有时可以被议院所分享，但主权只能保存在一个人手中。③

关于主权的作用，布丹也有论及。他说："主权首要和基本的作用，就是在总体上和具体领域中给公民提供法律……在这种颁布或废止法律的至高无上的权力下面，主权包含的其他作用就很明显了。因此，在一个国家内，至高无上的权威可以归结为一个整体，也就是说，为全部或每一个公民提供法律，但却不指望从他们那里得到任何回报。"④ 用邓宁（Dunning）教授的话说就是："立法，不仅仅是主权的主要作用，实际上也是唯一的、包含一切的作用。"⑤ 宣战、媾和以及缔结合约的权力，官吏的任免权，最高裁判权，赦免权，要求所属臣民忠诚和效忠的权力，货币铸造的权力，征税权，这些权力"看上去可以和法律分割开来，但都是靠法律来实现，也就是靠至高无上的权力的信念来实现"⑥。

2. 霍布斯

布丹发展了君主或国王主权的理论，而它在霍布斯的著作中则达到了顶峰。霍布斯理论的起点是自然状态，在这个自然状态的里面，没有"人民"和国王。在那里，武力就是正义，骚动、纷乱和无政府状态随处可见。这样一种自然状态乃是处于战争的状态，在这里，"在没有一个共同权威使大家慑服的时候，人们便处在战争状态之下。这种战争是每一个人对每个人的战争。"⑦ 人们感到敬畏，而这种共同权力也可以引导人们去实现公共的福利。⑧ 但是这种权力——最高主权

---

① 见 Merriam, *History of of Sovereignty*, 14 页。
② Bodin, *De Republica*, 128 页。
③ Bodin, *De Republica*, 134 页。
④ Bodin, *De Republica*, 240～243 页。
⑤ Dunning, *Political Theories, from Luther to Montesquien*, 103 页。
⑥ Bodin, *De Republica*, 243 页。也可参见 Hancke, *Bodin, Eine Studie uber den Souverainetat*。
⑦ Hobbes, *Leriathan*. 参见 *Collected Works*, by W. Molesworth, 第 3 卷, 112～113 页。
⑧ *Collected Works*, 第二卷, 75 页。"如果要建立这样一种能抵御外来侵略和制止相互侵害的共同权力，以便保障大家能通过自己的辛劳和土地的丰产为生并生活得很满意，那就只有一条道路——把大家所有的权力和力量付托给某一个人或一个通过多数的意见把大家的意志化为一个意志的多人组成的集体。这就等于是说，指定一个人或由多人组成的集体来代表他们的人格，每一个人都承认授权于如此承当本身人格的人在有关公共和平或安全方面所采取的任何行为、或命令他人所做出的行为，在这种行为中，大家都使自己的意志服从于他的意志，使自己的判断服从于他的判断。这就不仅是同意或协调，而是全体真正统一于唯一人格之中；这一人格是大家人人相互订立信约而形成的，其方式就好像是人人都向每一个其他的人说：'我承认这个人或这个集体，并放弃我管理自己的权利，把它授与这人或这个集体，但条件是你也把自己的权利拿出来授与他，并以同样的方式来承认他的一切行为。'"（*Collected Works*, 第三卷, 157～158 页。）

者的权力——如何获得？霍布斯对于这个问题的回答相当直率："取得这种主权的方式有两种：一种方式是通过自然之力获得的，例如一个人使其子孙服从他的统治就是这样，因为他们要是拒绝的话，他就可以将之处死；这一方式下还有一种情形是通过战争使敌人服从他的意志，并以此为条件赦免他们的生命。另一种方式则是人们相互达成协议，自愿地服从一个人或一个集体，相信他可以保护自己来抵抗所有其他的人。后者可以称为政治的国家，或'按约建立'的国家；前者则称为'以力取得'的国家。"①

因此主权可以通过武力或契约获得。② 一种是强迫性的，一种是自愿的。人们由于恐惧死亡、奴役、无政府状态，等等，而（单个的或集体的）顺从于一个共同权力或主权之下。但是，在一种情况下，比如，在"以力取得"的国家下面，人们恐惧最强者的暴力，但在另外一种情况下，人们彼此相互恐惧。既然主权是恐惧的产物，那么无论是恐惧另外的人还是某一特殊的人，最高主权者都应该是有别于那些一般臣民而居于其之上的。在"以力取得"的国家中，最高主权者在共同体中位居其他所有人之上，因为他天生是最强者，他是一切人之父，或是战争的胜利者。在"按约建立"的国家中，是其他人在"他们中间"同意给他以最高权威。不论在哪种意义上，在最高主权者与其他人或臣民之间都没有契约。

因为既然最高主权者位居其他人或臣民之上，那他的权力就应当是绝对的。在这里，我们可以看到霍布斯为专制主义的辩护，他说最高主权者的权力，"是人们能想象得到它有多大，它就有多大"③，原因是："像这样一种无限的权力，人们也许会觉得有许多不良的后果，然而缺乏这种权力的后果却是人与人之间长久相互为战，而这种后果更是坏多了。人们在这种状况下的生活是不可能没有弊端的，然而任何国家之中最大的弊端却莫过于由于臣民不服从并破坏建立国家的信约而产生的弊端。不论是谁，要是认为主权过大，想要设法使它减小，他就必须服从一个能限制主权的权力，也就是必须服从一个比主权更大的权力。"④

那么这种绝对主权的权利和后果是什么？对此霍布斯有简单的说明："主权者的权力，不得其允许不能转让给他人，他的主权不能被剥夺，任何臣民都不能控诉他侵害自己，臣民不能惩罚他，保持和平所必须的事项由他审定，学说由他审定，他是唯一的立法者，也是争执的最高仲裁者，他是和战问题的时间与方式

---

① *Collected Works*, 158～159 页。

② "当一群人确实达成协议，并且每一个人都与每一个其他人订立信约，不论大多数人把代表全体的人格的权利授予任何个人或一群人组成的集体（即使之成为其代表者）时，赞成和反对的每一个人为了在自己之间过和平生活并防御外人的目的，都将以同一方式对这人或这一集体所作的一切行为和裁判授权，就像是自己的行为和裁判一样。这时国家就成为按约建立了。由群聚的人同意授与主权的某一个或某些人的一切权利和职能都是由于像这样按约建立国家而得来的。" *Collected Works*, 159 页。

③ *Collected Works*, 第三卷, 195 页。

④ *Collected Works*, 第三卷, 195 页。

的最高审定者,地方长官、参议人员、将帅以及其他一切官员与大臣都由他甄选,荣衔、勋级与赏罚等也由他决定。"①

在霍布斯看来,主权可以在一个人手中,也可以在少数人或多数人手中,但不论是哪种情况,主权都是不可分的,并且认为这是主权的一个最基本的特征。②如果是在一个人手中,国家的形式就是君主制,如果在少数人手中,就是贵族制,如果在多数人手中,就是民主制。虽然可能性或实践表明主权可能被授予一个人、少数人、多数人,但霍布斯还是强烈地主张主权应当在一个人手中。

(二) 主权在民论

1. 反暴君论者(Monarchomachs)

与布丹和霍布斯等人的君主主权论相左的③,还有主权在民论,提出这一主张的人有16世纪末、17世纪初的被称作反暴君论者的一批学者。这里面有17世纪晚期的洛克和最为重要的18世纪的卢梭。作为开创者,反暴君论者在欧洲有广泛影响。著名的有:法国的朗格特(Languet)和霍特曼(Hotman),苏格兰的布坎南(Buchanan),德国的阿尔杜秀斯(Althusius)。"这种主张的最核心特征是人民主权的本原性和不可转让性,政府的契约起源,政治权威的忠诚,当发现统治者背信弃义之后人民可以推翻他。"④

2. 洛克

正是在光荣革命(1688年革命)的影响下,洛克写下了他的《政府论两篇》(1690)。他同意霍布斯的看法,认为有一个自然状态。但是,他认为,在这个自然状态里,不是充斥着战争。这个自然状态的一个特征是缺乏一个公共法官和权威。因为公共法官和权威的缺失,使得个人在维护他们在遭到不公平的待遇时处于不利的状况。因此,政治组织就由社会中的所有个体以契约的方式建立起来

---

① *Collected Works*,第三卷,186页。也可参见159页以下。

② *Collected Works*,第三卷,167页。也可参见171页。

③ 君主主权论也为诸如James Ⅰ和Filmer等人所拥护。James Ⅰ的观点,见他的 *Basilicon Doron*, *True Law of Free Monarchies and Remonstrance for the Right of Kings*. Filmer的观点见他的 "Patriarcha, or the Natural Power of Kings" (1630),该文见Morley编辑的Locke的 *Two Treatises of Civil Government*。对James Ⅰ和Filmer理论的一般讨论,见 G. P. Gooch, *Political Thought in England from Bacon to Halifax*。Figgis, *Divine Right of Kings*。Dunning, *Political Theories, from Luther to Montesquien*。C. H. Mellwain, "the Political Works of James Ⅰ", *Harvard Political Clasics*,第一卷。Laski, "Political Ideas of James Ⅰ" in *Political Science Quarterly*,第34卷。

④ Merriam, *History of Theory of Sovereignty*,第24页。也可见 Duniu, "The Monarchomachs' Theories of Popular Sovereignty in the Sixteenth Century", *Poligical Science Quarterly*, XIX,第277页以下;Figgsi, *Studies of Political Thought, from Cerson to Grotius*,第五讲;Gierke, *Johannes Althusius* (1880);R. M. Treumann, *Die Monarshomschen* (1895);Gumplowicz, *Geschichte der Staatstheorien* (1926),182页以下。

了。① 在这个政治组织里，立法权是最高的政府权力即主权，因为它是人民的代表机关。在一定意义上讲，在立法机关没有工作的时候，行政机关也可以看作最高的权力机关。但不论是行政机关还是立法机关，都不能看作这个政治组织的最后权威，因为在它们后面的才是真正的主权者——人民，他们在革命时期相当活跃，在和平时期，则显得很温顺。②

3. 卢梭

正如君主主权论在霍布斯那里达到最高峰一样，主权在民论在卢梭那里也达到了顶峰。卢梭、洛克、霍布斯是社会契约论的三个最重要的代表。卢梭的《社会契约论》的出现要比洛克和霍布斯的契约论晚得多，许多学者也都认为卢梭受到了二者的影响。邓宁教授就写道："他的主权定义的完整性和准确性来自霍布斯，但对主权的定位和操作的观念，则来自洛克。"③

卢梭像霍布斯和洛克一样，也是从自然状态着手的，但是，卢梭的自然状态，既不是霍布斯充斥战争的自然状态，也不是洛克的没有公共法官和权威的自然状态。在这个自然状态里，人人都是平等的，人人都感到充足和满意，一句话，这是一个理想的幸福状态。但是，人口的增加和文明的发展带来了罪恶，"于是，那种原始状态便不能继续维持；并且人类如果不改变其生存方式，就会毁灭"④。

这种人类被迫改变的生存方式就是："要寻找出一种结合的形式，使它能以聚合起来的全部力量来维护并保障每个成员的人身安全和财富，并且由于这一结合而使得每一个与全体相联合的个人又只不过是在服从其本人，因而他仍然像以往那样的自由。"⑤ 然后他写道："因而，如果我们撇开社会公约中一切非本质的东西，我们就会发现社会公约可以简化为如下的词句：我们每个人都将其自身及自身全部的力量共同置于公意（general will）的最高指导之下，并且我们在共同体中接纳每一个成员作为全体之不可分割的一部分。只是一瞬间，这一结合行为就产生了一个道德的与集体的共同体，以代替每个订约者的个人；组成共同体的成员数目就等于大会中所有的票数，而共同体就以这同一个行为获得了它的统一性、它的公共的大我，它的生命和它的意志。这一由全体个人的结合所形成的公共人格，以前叫'城市'，现在叫'共和国'或'政治体'，就其被动意义来讲，他的成员称之为'国家'，就其主动意义来讲，其成员称之为'主权者'，而跟其他

---

① 然而必须指出的是，"主权"一词并没有在 Locke 的 *Two Treatises of Government* 中出现。
② 从 16 世纪末到 17 世纪末，在君主主权论和人民主权论之间进行摇摆的时候，另一种理论为 Grotius 所发展，且在相当程度上为他的后继者（我想特别指出 Pufendorf）所阐发，这种理论在本质上是复合的，绝对跟与 Hobbes 的主权理论相反对，他认为主权可以分离。
③ Dunning, *Political Theories, from Rousseau to Spencer*, 22 页。
④ Rousseau, *Social Contract*, H. J. Tozer 翻译, 109 页。
⑤ Rousseau, *Social Contract*, H. J. Tozer 翻译, 109 页。

与之类似的组织相区别的时候,就称之为'政权'。"①

很明显地,从社会契约之中产生出了一个"公意"。"公意"是"一个国家的主权,是灵魂和精神"。主权或公意,由于是所有个体的组合,因此它对现在已经成为公民的每一个个体都是平等的。它不给任何人以特权,也不给任何人以伤害,而是同等对待。"无论从哪方面来说明这个原则,我们总会得到同样的结论,即,社会公约在公民之间确立了这样一种平等,它使大家全都遵守同样的条件并且全都应该享有同样的权利。于是由于公约的性质,主权的一切行为——也就是说,一切真正属于公意的行为就都同等地约束着或照顾着全体公民;因为主权者就只认得国家这个共同体,而不区别对待构成国家的任何个人。"但是主权的行为"不是上级和下级之间的一种约定,而是共同体和它的各个成员之间的一种约定。它是合法的约定,因为它是以社会契约为基础的;它是公平的约定,因为它对一切人都是共同的;它是有益的约定,因为它除了公共的福利之外就不能再有任何别的目的;它是稳固的约定,因为它有着公共的力量和最高权力作为保障。只要臣民遵守的是这样的约定,他们就不是在服从任何别人,而只是在服从他们自己的意志。要问主权者与公民这两者相应的权利限制究竟达到什么限度,那就等于是问公民对于自己本身——每个人对于全体以及全体对于每个人——能限制到什么地步"②。

让我们再来看看主权或公意的一些特征。第一,主权是不可转让的。卢梭说:"主权既然不外是公意的运用,所以就永远不能转让;并且主权者既然只不过是一个集体的生命,所以就只能由他自己来代表自己;权力可以转移,但是意志却不可以转移。"③ 第二,不可分割性。"同不可转让的原因一样,主权是不可分割的。"④ 分割主权就像一个荒诞的故事,"这个故事是这样的,一些日本的幻术家在观众的面前将一个小孩肢解,然后将他所有的肢体一一扔向空中,然后就能再掉下一个完整无缺的活生生的孩子来"⑤。

第三,"一般都是公正的而且永远以公共利益为最终目的"⑥。卢梭坚持认为:"主权既然只能由组成主权者的各个人所构成,所以主权者就没有,而且也不能有与他们的利益相冲突的任何其他利益;因此,主权权力就无需对于臣民提供任何保证,因为共同体不可能想要损害它的全体成员;而且我们以后还可以看到,共同体也不可能损害任何个体的人。主权者正由于他是主权者,便永远都是他所当

---

① Rousseau, *Social Contract*, H. J. Tozer 翻译,110～112 页。
② Rousseau, *Social Contract*, H. J. Tozer 翻译,第二卷,第四章,127 页。
③ Rousseau, *Social Contract*, H. J. Tozer 翻译,第二卷,第四章,119 页。
④ Rousseau, *Social Contract*, H. J. Tozer 翻译,第二卷,第四章,121 页。
⑤ Rousseau, *Social Contract*, H. J. Tozer 翻译,第二卷,第四章,121 页。
⑥ Rousseau, *Social Contract*, H. J. Tozer 翻译,第二卷,第四章,23 页。

然的那样。"① 第四，具有绝对性。"正像自然赋予每一个人支配他的四肢的绝对权力一样，社会公约也赋予了政治体支配他的成员的绝对权力。"② 正因为绝对性，它是不能被判断的，它就是事实，它判断一切。③

第五，主权不能被代表，因为它的本质体现在公意之中，公意是不能被代表的。④ "那么，人民的议员处于一个什么地位？"对它来说"人民的议员不是、也不可能是人民的代表，他们只不过是人民的办事员罢了；他们并不能做出任何有效力的决定。凡是不曾为人民所亲自批准的法律，都是无效的；那根本就不是法律。"⑤ 这儿要再加一句，主权是神圣的，不可侵犯的。⑥

我们已经讨论了主权或者说公意的起源、性质和特征，但是更进一步的问题也需要说明。公意，是所有人的意志呢，还是大多数人的意志？根据卢梭的观点，关于这个问题的答案有两个层面，因为在达成社会契约的公意和制定法律或政治体建立之后采取某种行为的公意之间做出区分是必要的。在前一种情况下，也只有在前一种情况下，必须是所有人的意志，因为"政治的结合乃是全世界上最自愿的行为；每一个人既然生来是自由的，并且是自己的主人，所以不能在任何可能的借口之下，都不经本人的允许就役使他"⑦。

与此相反，在后一种情况之下，主权者和政府的行为可以由大多数人来决定。卢梭写道："除去这一原始的契约之外，大多数人的投票是永远可以约束其他一切人的；这是契约本身的结果。但是，人们会问：为什么既然一个人是自由的，却又要被迫遵守那些并非自己的意志呢？反对者怎么能够既是自由的，而又要服从他们不赞同的那些法律呢？我要回答说，这些问题的提法是错误的。公民是同意了一切法律，即使是那些违反他们意愿的法律，即使是那些他们若胆敢有丝毫违反都要受到惩罚的法律也不例外。国家全体成员的普遍意志就是公意；正因为如此，他们才是公民并且是自由的。当人民代表大会提议制定一项法律时，他们向人民所提问的，精确地说，并不是人民究竟是赞成这个提议还是反对这个提议，而是它是不是符合公意；而这个公意也就是他们自己的意志。每个人在投票时都说出了自己对这个问题的意见，于是从票数的计算里就可以得出公意的宣告。因此，与我相反的意见若是占了上风，那并不证明别的，只是证明我错了，只是证明

---

① Rousseau, *Social Contract*, H. J. Tozer 翻译，第一卷，第七章，113 页。
② Rousseau, *Social Contract*, H. J. Tozer 翻译，第二卷，第四章，125 页。
③ "每一个人由于社会公约而转让出去的自己的一切权力、财富、自由，仅仅是全部之中其用途对于集体有重要关系的那部分；但是也必须承认，唯有主权者才是这种重要性的裁判者。"（第二卷，第四章——译者注）
④ Rousseau, *Social Contract*, H. J. Tozer 翻译，第三卷，第十五章，187 页。
⑤ Rousseau, *Social Contract*, H. J. Tozer 翻译，第三卷，第十五章，187 页。
⑥ Rousseau, *Social Contract*, H. J. Tozer 翻译，第二卷，第四章，127 页。
⑦ Rousseau, *Social Contract*, H. J. Tozer 翻译，第四卷，第二章，200 页。

我所估计的并不是公意。假如我的个别意见居然压制了公意，那么我就是做了另一桩并非我原来所想要做的事；而在这个时候，我就不是自由的了。"①

六、反动运动

卢梭的理论在人类历史上扮演的重要的角色是显而易见的。② 单就这种理论在其祖国的影响来讲，法国大革命似乎已向世界表明了它的光辉。亨利·梅因（Henry Maine），一个严厉的批评者，这样告诉我们："在人类历史上，极少有像卢梭在1749—1762年间的著作那样对人类的思想产生如此大的影响。"

很少有人否认卢梭的思想对法国大革命的影响，也许没有人否认法国大革命是人类历史上一个划时代的事件。但是法国大革命给世界到底带来了什么，还是一个激烈争论的问题。有些不看手段，只关注目的的人，像圣佩韦（Sainte-Beuve）就说："它就是西奈的律法（指《十诫》）一样，在雷光闪电之中，外人就像我们一样地热爱它。"另外一些人，不关心它的目的，只看它的手段，则认为它是一个可怕的灾难。柏克（Burke）就是许多持这种观点的人之一。③ 也许可以说后一种观点已被广泛地接受，特别是在恐怖（Terror）时期及之后。

为批评法国大革命，人们已经对产生革命的基本原理进行了仔细的考察。这种新的运动有时被称为反动运动，或者反革命运动。支持这种运动的学者是很多的，但是他们只归属于几个学派。现在我们就对这个新运动的几个主要学派作一些简单的探讨。

1. 康德学派——理想主义者

康德，理想主义的代表人物，是卢梭的"合法继承者"，"他在形式上接受了契约理论"，梅里亚姆教授说，"但是，他对理想契约和现实契约的区分对革命理论带来的破坏，比直接反对革命理论带来的破坏要更大。"④

因为康德受卢梭的思想影响很深，所以他的理论开始也和卢梭的理论一样。"人民组织一个国家，这个行为的基本观念要求人民接受它的立法，也就是原始契约。这时所有个人都把他们的行动自由放在一边，当成为共同体的成员后就又立即恢复。也就是说，从人民那里，或者说从国家那里，要回他的自由。我们不能说国家，或国家的人民，为了一个特定目的，已经牺牲了，从而获得了一部分行动的内在自由。而是，每个人都放弃了原始的、不受限制的自由，来得到以法律作

---

① Rousseau, *Social Contract*, H. J. Tozer 翻译, 第四卷, 第二章, 200~201页。
② 参见 Paul Janet, *Histoire des doctrines politiques*, 第2版, 第2卷, 612页。参见 Duguit, "The Law and the State", *Harvard Law Review*, 第3卷。
③ Burke, *Reflections on the Revolution in France*, 1790。
④ Merriam, *History of Theory of Sovereignty*, 40页。

后盾的完整自由,也就是说,在法治国家中,他们的这种后盾源自他们自己的法律意志。"①

康德除了同意卢梭的政治组织是从社会契约中产生的之外,还同意在政治组织建立之后,最高的"公意"就形成了。但是康德和卢梭的观点还是有很大的不同。卢梭认为,国家和主权就是人民的创造物,而康德认为,国家和主权是理想的产物、是神圣的。这样,对康德来说,在一个理想的国家里,政治组织和主权都是通过契约产生的,但这不可能发生在现实的国家里面。为了批驳那些认为在现实的国家里面有社会契约的人,康德写道:"从来没有一种像契约一样的记载导致共同体的出现,或为主权者所接受,或者被二者所许可。这些人假设'原始契约'的观念是理性的,就像一件已经实际发生的事情一样。他们假设权利总是为人民服务的,当他们依据自己的判断违背它的时候,他们也这样认为。"②

简单地说,康德对理想中的国家与主权的关系和现实中的国家与主权的关系作了区分。前者是所有意志的联合,后者则掌握在拥有实际权力的人手中。这样,康德就是以卢梭的逻辑出发,却得出了同霍布斯一样的结论。像霍布斯一样,康德把实际的主权交给国家的首领——君主。君主的最高权力的起源是不可测知的,任何人都必须彻底遵守。康德写道:"由人民的权威产生的最高权力,确实是不可测知的。也就是说,在实际关系中,人民对于它的产生不需要'太过惊奇',就好像不应怀疑对它的顺从的正确性一样。要想在一个国家中享有权利,就必须成为这个国家的成员,遵守共同的法律意志,除非他是代表国家意志的首脑。"③

毫无疑问,康德花了很大的力气去区分理想的国家和现实中的国家。道理很简单,邓宁(Dunning)教授说:"在腓特烈大帝及其继任者的时代,将国王仅仅作为行政首脑的想法是很艰巨的。很少哲学家能从主权至少有一部分是君主天生就有的观念中解放出来。无论他们多么强烈地鼓吹人民、民族或国家的绝对最高权力,都不能。"④但是作为一个理想主义者,康德对他的理想国家考虑得更多,他也设想有一个实现理想国家和理想主权的趋势。在这里我们又看到了康德回到了他的前人的立场上,至少对他来说,未来的世界是如此。⑤

关于主权的本质,康德跟卢梭的观点是一致的,但作了一定的拓展。他认为主权是单一的,也是绝对的。但是,同时它有三个方面,其中的每一个方面都是主权者,然而,只有一个国家,一个主权。他说:"每一个国家包含三个方面的权力,公意的联合体分解为三个单位,即三权分立(Trias Politica)。它们就是立法

---

① 参见 Kant, *Philosophy of Law*, W. Hastie 翻译, 169 页。
② Kant, *Philosophy of Politics*, W. Hastie 翻译, 53 页。
③ Kant, *Philosophy of Law*, W. Hastie 翻译, 174 页, 或 *Principles of Politics*, 55 页。
④ Dunning, *Political Theories, from Rousseau to Spencer*, 134 页。
⑤ Kant, *Principles of Law*, 257~258 页。

权、行政权和司法权。立法权力在一个国家中为立法者代表；行政权力为执行法律的统治者代表；司法权力为法官代表，他的职务是根据法律来裁决哪些东西归哪些公民所有。这三种权力可以和实践的三段论的三个命题作对比：大前提，包含着意志的普遍法则；小前提，就是根据法律而颁布的行政命令，或者可以说是根据法律而提出的行动准则；结论，就是判决，它对具体案件中的是非曲直做出判断。"①

2. 宗教学派

另一个直接攻击革命的理论来自宗教学派，它由一些德国和法国的学者所领导。"② 这个派别的主张可以在1815年神圣同盟（Holy Alliance）的条约里找到，同盟宣称："在他们以及他们的人民所属的基督教国家中，除了占有全部权力的上帝之外没有其他的主权者。"③

它的批判性的一面在于这派学者否认人类有中世纪教会的神父那样的创造最高权力的可能性，他们反对主权是社会契约结果的信条，他们宣称："如果人民是合法的主权者，那么，他们所制定的法律就一定是正义的；而正义要有比这更宽广和深入的根基。"④ 另一位反对者走得更远，他认为民主就是没有主权的人类联合。⑤

在它的建设性的一面，它承认君主主权，它为教会和国家的关系辩护，它甚至要求教皇放弃对世俗权利的占有。总之，这个学派是一个彻头彻尾的中庸学派。⑥

---

① Duguit, "The Law and the State", *Harvard Law Review*, 第3卷, 46页。也见Kant, *Philosophy of Law*, W. Hastie 翻译, 161～162页。在理想主义学派的学者当中，除了Kant以外，Fichte值得我们特殊的关注。Fichte没有完全摆脱其前辈的二元结构的不一致性，他断言现实的国家必须最大限度地接近理想的国家。他拒绝前政治的自然状态的观念，但他承认社会契约的必要性。社会契约必须经历三个阶段：财产契约（the property contract）、保护契约（the protection contract）和联合契约（the union contract）。联合契约完成了社会契约并组织一个负责执行先前协议及保护公民权利的最高统治者。如此形成的最高权力必定归于没有组织起来时的人民，因为当最高统治者形成的时候，作为一个整体的人民就不存在了。尽管最高统治者出于人民之手，但人民却不应该反抗它，不是因为他们不能反抗它，而是因为他们反抗它就意味着反抗他们自己。参见 J. G. Fichte, *Rudiment of Natural Right*（*Grundlage des Naturrechts*）1796, 1797。

② 参见 De Maistre, *Étude sur la souverainete*, 1794—1796; De Bonald, *Théorie du pouvoir politique et religieuse dans la societe civile*, 1796; Schelling, *System des transcendentalen Idealismus*, 1800; Muller, *Von der Nothwendigkeit einer theologischen Grundlage der gesammten Staatswissenschaften*, 1819; Schlegel, *Vorlesungen uber die Philosophie des Lebens*, 1828; Wagner, *System der Ideal-Philosophie*, 1804; Muford, *The Nation*, 1872.

③ 第二章。"这三个联合起来的君主，把自身看作来治理同一家族的三个分支的上帝的代表；他们理解奥地利、普鲁士和俄罗斯；他们承认，他们及其人民是基督民族的部分，而且除了那个权力严格的唯一归属者外，这基督民族实质上没有其他的主权者" 等——译者注。

④ Merriam, *History of Theory of sovereignty*, 55～56页。Bonald, *legislation primitive*, *Oeuvres*, 第三卷, 21页。

⑤ De Maistre, *Étude sur la Souverainete*, 346页。

⑥ Dunning, *Political Theories*, *from Rousseau to Spencer*, 187页。也可参见Laski, "De Maistre and Bismarck", 收录于Laski的 *Problem of Sovereignty*, 第五章。也可参见Laski, "De Bonald", 收录于Laski的 *Authority in Modern State*, 第二章。

3. 世袭制理论（Patrimonial Theory）

第三种反对革命的理论是由路德维希·冯·哈勒尔（Ludwig von Haller）提出的世袭制理论。① 像其他许多反对革命的理论家一样，他拒绝自然状态的国家和社会契约的观念。在他看来，人类是社会动物，他们之间有密切的关系。而且，在他们中间，有的天生强大，有的天生弱小。强大者就是统治者，弱小者就是被统治者。"自然优势是一切规则的原因，需求是一切依赖关系与臣属关系的原因。"② 主权只能存在于不平等的状态之中，它往往掌握在最强者手中。

尽管主权往往掌握在最强者手中，但也不是天然的权利。由此产生了哈勒尔的主权获得的理论。在他看来，得到主权，有许多方法。第一，主权可以凭运气得到；第二，主权可以运用暴力和争取得到；第三，也可能通过契约或受赠与他人或偶然的机会得到；第四，也是最后，是上述三者兼而有之。③

主权的建立和获得不受人类法律（人法）的束缚，但受上帝法律（神法）的限制。有人指出："哈勒尔的主权表面上建立在暴力的基础上——与人民主权论建立的基础'自然权利'形成对照。不过，归根结底其基础并非暴力，而是假定对财产的'自然权利'。"④ 这样，哈勒尔的强权主权理论，最终产生了财产权的主权理论。

4. 功利学派

第四种反对革命理论的是功利学派。这个学派是由边沁（Bentham）所开创，后来由奥斯丁（Austin）在其著作中加以全面发展。对边沁来说，卢梭以及其他人的社会契约论，只是一个虚构的东西。⑤ 根据边沁的观点，人们服从最高政治权力，不是出于自愿，而是因为他们认为只有这样做才能最好地保障他们的利益和幸福。主权是最高的和绝对的，因为它是实用（utility）的。因此最高权威应该扩展到多远，相应主权的每个社会成员的权利和义务是什么，答案只能通过功利原则的运用来回答。⑥

作为实证法的研究者，边沁否认法律主权是受限制的，但是他也坦率地承认，它也可以受到习俗或政府机关的文件的限制。他这样写道："让我们用简单的话，

---

① *Restauaration der Staatswissenschaft oder Theorie des naturlaichgesellgen Zustandes der Chimaera des kunstlichen-burgerlicher entgegensetzt*（1816-1834）.

② *Restauaration der Staatswissenschaft oder Theorie des maturlaichgesellgen Zustandes der Chimaera des kunstlichenburgerlicher entgegensetzt*（1816—1834），第一卷，342 页。参见 Gumplowicz, *Outline of Sociology*, Moore 翻译，也可参见 F. Oppenheimer, *The State*, J. M. Gitterman 翻译。

③ *Restauaration der Staatswissenschaft oder Theorie des maturlaichgesellgen Zustandes der Chimaera des kunstlichenburgerlicher entgegensetzt*（1816—1834），第一卷，第 14 章。

④ Merriam, *History of Theory of Sovereignty*, 69 页。

⑤ Bentham, *Fragment on Government*, 第一章，第 37 段。A. R. Lord 教授认为 Bentham 的 *Fragment on Government* 实际上是关于主权的论文。见 *The Principles of Politics*, 84 页。

⑥ 见 *Fragment on Government*, 第四章，第 20 段。

坚定而平静地说出那些该理论的创始者谨小慎微地说出的话，那就是，最高权力组织的权力，除非被惯例所限定，就不能说是可明确被指定或者说有确定的界限。也就是说，没有什么是它不能做的。你可以说权力的任一部分是违法的、无效的，说它们的所作所为超出了它们的权威或权力，或权利，随你怎么说。"① 通过以上的所引的话，可以看出边沁的绝对主义和他对主权限制的认识。

奥斯丁同他的前辈一样，从批判的角度否认社会契约理论的正确性，从肯定的角度坚持认为人们在一个政治社会里联合在一起是出于服从的习惯。他的主权理论的主要点体现在这句经常被引用的话："如果某个明显占优势的人没有服从于其他类似优势者的习惯，而获得特定社会中大部分人的习惯性服从，那么这个明显占优势的人就是这个社会的主权者。同时，这个社会（包括优势者在内）也是一个独立的政治社会。"②

对奥斯丁来说，要成为一个政治社会的主权者，需要有四个特征：一、一个社会的大部分成员必须习惯性服从于一个既定的公认最高权力；③ 二、习惯性服从必须得到一个社会的"大部分"或"大多数"人的服从；④ 三、一个社会的大多数成员必须习惯于服从一个特定的权力如同服从共同的最高权力；⑤ 四、那个特定的最高权力不必服从比它更高的权威。⑥

从以上四个特征可以看出，主权的特征有一些明显的特质。第一，主权是绝对的，且不受法律限制。"如果一个君主或最高统治者受法律义务所束缚，服从于更高的权力者，也就是说，统治者受法律义务的束缚，则等于说他既是主权者又不是主权者。因此说最高权力受实证法所限制，绝对是矛盾的。"⑦ 另一方面，我们发现这样的话："最高权力不受法律的限制，是受到怀疑甚至否认的。困难出在词语的模糊性上。最先的受限制的君主单个个体，被称为不合适的君主和统治者。现在君主和统治者的权力，不仅被法律所限制，而且实际上还被实证法所限制。但是君主和统治者在适当的称谓下与不适当的自诩相矛盾。既然前者的权力是受到法律限制的，则后者的权力也受到类似限制的束缚。"⑧

对于奥斯丁来说，显然地，主权仅仅是关于实证法的最高权力。他承认道德限制和习惯、风俗的影响。这样，实证法的范围越窄，对于主权的限制就越多。他对宪法和国际法是恰当意义上的法律的否认可以看作是他对这两者乃是对主权

---

① *Fragment on Government*，第四章，第 20 段，第 26 节。
② *Jurisprudence*，第一卷，221 页。
③ *Jurisprudence*，第一卷，222 页。
④ *Jurisprudence*，第一卷，223 页。
⑤ *Jurisprudence*，第一卷，224 页。
⑥ *Jurisprudence*，第一卷，224 页。
⑦ *Jurisprudence*，第一卷，263 页。
⑧ *Jurisprudence*，第一卷，254 页。

的限制的认识，尽管从他的观点来讲，这种限制仅仅是道德性的。

第二，根据奥斯丁的说法，主权，从法律上讲，是单一的、不可分的。他说，主权者，就是平常所谓的君主，或具有主权者能力的主权者成员。主权者是最高权力者，在一个特定的社会里面，他不臣服于任何人。在一个国家里面有两个最高权力者是不可能的，"一半的或不完全的最高权力的政府是不存在的"。形容词"一半的"主权的运用是不稳固的。①

我们现在来看主权的归宿。主权，根据奥斯丁的看法，可以授予一个人或一些人。在实际操作中，主权根据不同的国家形式而有不同的归宿。在一个绝对君主制国家里，它在君主手中。②但在像英国这样的国家中，则在国王、贵族和下议院的选举团中。在最大的联邦制国家如美国，主权在"形成一个集合体"的各个州的政府手中。③

我们现在可以指出主权概念和自由的关系。政治自由或公民自由是来自法律义务（legal obligation）的自由，它是由主权政府留给或授权给他的任何一个臣民的。④ 主权是自由之母，用另外的话说，自由由主权者授予，这两者并不像通常人们认为的那样是矛盾的。"困难之处不在于理解自由如何与主权并存，而在于没有主权自由如何存续。"⑤

在结论中，让我们看看奥斯丁的反对者——梅因是如何总结奥斯丁的主权观念的。奥斯丁的主权观念，用梅因的话说："是这样：在每一个独立的政治共同体中，一些个体或许多人的联合体有迫使其他人按他们的意愿去行事的权力。这个个人或组织可以在每一个独立的政治共同体中找到，就像万物必有引力一样。这种主权，这个个人或人们的联合，经常发生在所有独立的政治共同体中。在所有共同体中，主权的所有面相中一个特征是具有不需要发挥，但可以发挥的不可抵抗的暴力。"⑥

5. 历史学派

在反对革命的学派中，除了理想主义学派、宗教学派、世袭理论和功利学派之外，历史学派对革命理论攻击的重要性也不应被忽视。这一派的学者认为社会契约论只不过是空想的产物。从他们的实际的研究来看，他们指出社会组织和政治组织仅仅是历史的产物（the products of many generations），而不是恣意（专断）的意志（arbitrary will）或公意的产物。它们的发展是逐步的、无意识的和渐进的，而不是突然的、有意识的和革命性的。

---

① *Jurisprudence*，第一卷，254 页。
② *Jurisprudence*，第一卷，273 页。
③ *Jurisprudence*，第一卷，260 页。关于邦联中主权的归宿，见 262 页。
④ *Jurisprudence*，第一卷，274 页。（上文引述都来自 R. Campbell 编辑的版本）
⑤ Merriam, *History of Theory of Sovereignty*，148 页。
⑥ Maine, *Early History of Institutions*，349～350 页。

历史学派的最好的说明者是亨利·梅因（Henry Maine）。在批评社会契约论时，梅因写道："这种政治推断，虽对我们各方面多少有点影响，但却是所有推断中最没有根据的。这个理论开始的自然状态是这个设想的一个简单虚构。迄今，任何对原始社会性质的研究（结果），都与原始状态无关，原始状态仅仅是一个设想，所有的研究结果都在反对这个设想。卢梭所假定的人类共同体形成的进程，或者说他所希望我们假定它们形成的所有事情的进程，又是一个妄想没有任何关于人类社会发展的断定是可靠的，但是它们中的任何一个都比卢梭的设想要可靠。"①

除了反对卢梭的社会契约论，梅因还反对他的主权在民论。他对于民主没有信心。他把它看成是一种虚幻的政府形式，这种政府容易产生平庸和停滞。由于受贵族观念的影响，他认为贵族制度是最有益于进步的。②

然而，必须提到的是，很少有像梅因那样反对主权在民论的人。实际上，历史学派后来的许多拥护者，虽然否认社会契约论作为解释国家起源的完整理论，但却同时又比较喜欢主权在民论。③

七、结论

在主权的革命理论和各种反动运动的理论之间，还有理性主权论和国家主权论。理性主权论的历史基础在 1814 年法国宪章中可以找到，这个宪章规定了君

---

① Maine, *Popular Government*, 158～159 页。

② 这是 Maine 在 *Popular Government* 中的主要论题。关于 Maine 的主权理论，见标题为"主权与法律"的章节。也可以参见他的 *Ancient Law*, 93 页以下；*Early History of Institutions* 第二十一讲和第十三讲；*International Law*, 54 页以下。在最后一本书中，他写道："主权者的权力是权力的集合，一个权力可以从另外的权力中分离出来。" 58 页。

③ 参考 Lowell, *Essays on Government* 中的 "Theory of Social Contract" 和 "Limits of Sovereignty"。还参考 Wilson, *Congressional Government*, 1885；*The State*, 1889。

功利主义学派和历史学派在反对社会契约论这一点上是相同的，尽管他们达到的方法不一样。但是，功利主义者们，特别是 Austin 的理论，和历史学派的理论是相反的。由 A. V. Dicey 和 D. G. Richie 所领导的一种新的运动对这两者作了一个综合。他们在法律的主权和政治的主权之间作了一个区分。对他们来说，前者是被法院所承认的唯一主权。在法律的主权背后有一个政治的主权。他们断言，如果这两者是矛盾的，则前者必须服从于后者。它们中间一个具有稳固性的特征，一个具有可变性的特征；一个代表过去的观点，一个代表当前的感受和公共意见。既然政治机构同其他社会机构一样，是随着环境的变化而变化的，则为了适应变化了的环境，旧有的观念不能再被坚持，而新的观念必须得以认可。

参见 Richie, "On Sovereignty", *Annals of the American Academy of Political and Social Science*, 第一卷；Dicey, *The Law of the Constitution*, 1835。

主立宪制。这一派的学者以纯理论家的特征示人。① 法国学者们非常清楚地知道在革命前，最高权力存在于神圣的国王的意志；在革命后，则存在于人民的公意中。既然他们没有准备去思考分开最高权力的可能性，既然在君主立宪制下，君主和人民都不是主权者，这些学者不是把主权放在一个特定的人身上，而是认为只有在理性中才能发现它。然而，他们并不认为人类的理性或整体理性，而是永远正确的绝对理性才是主权绝对正确性的唯一来源。在现实中没有人能够找到这种理性，只有通过一种不直接的方式，也就是在1814年的宪章中找到。

这种理论得到很大的发展，很大程度上是由于宪法被采用这样一个特殊的条件。随着1830年7月第二次革命推翻这种复辟王朝有限的准君主立宪制，建立了奥尔良家族的君主制，比前任有了更多的宪法自由，"绝对理性"的主权，为了适应新的形势，变成了国家主权，不再是抽象的和不可改变的，而是具体的和能在政府中找到的。主权，这种理论的一个支持者说，是"理性、正义和意志的混合物。它适时地代表着国家的信念、思想和愿望，它仅仅存在于人民之中"②。

国家主权论的最好的解释者是黑格尔和伯伦知理。黑格尔把国家作为一个象征着世界历史进程的一个阶段的一个真人。③ 最高权力就存在于这样一个人，或作为一个整体的国家那里。这样，国家就如同一个有机体或一个人，是伦理观念或伦理精神的实现。④ 除非它通过某种方式变成现实和成为客体，它就仅仅是一个纯粹抽象的东西。⑤ 这样一个抽象的东西如何实现？它只能被一个人，这个人，在黑格尔看来，也就是这个国家的人格化的君主来实现。

从抽象上讲，主权属于国家；但在现实中，它在君主手中。这从康德对两层系统的区分也很容易得出。黑格尔的观点与康德的观点的不同之处在于，黑格尔认为国家的主权和君主的主权不是两回事，而是同一个东西。它是一个事情的两个方面。没有君主的主权，就像没有肉体只有精神；没有国家主权，就像没有精神只有肉体。简单地说，它们二者缺少了任何一个就谈不上主权。

伯伦知理的观点同黑格尔类似，也把国家作为一个人，而这个人就是主权。他这样说道："主权不在国家之前或之外，也不在国家之上。国家本身的威严和权力就是主权。它是全体，全体就要比它的部分强大。因此，一般而言，整个国

---

① 无疑地，这派的主要成员有 Cousin、Guizot、Constant。参见 Cousin, *Cours d'histoire de la philosophie morale au dix-huitienme siecle*（1839–1840）。Guizot, *Du gouvernement de la France depuis la Restauration et du ministere actuel*（1821）。Constant, *Principes Politiques*（1815）；*Reflexiou sur les constitutions et les garanties*（1814–1818）。

② 转引自 Merriam, *History of Theory of Sovereignty*, 81页。

③ Hegel, *Philosophy of Right*, Dyde 翻译, 286页。

④ Hegel, *Philosophy of Right*, Dyde 翻译, 240页。

⑤ Hegel, *Philosophy of Right*, Dyde 翻译, 285页以下。

家的主权要比这个国家一些成员的主权高级。"①

独立、荣誉、权力、最高权威和统一是主权的特征②,也是主权构成的要素。③ 并且,主权有两个方面:可以从外部看,也可以从内部看。从外部看,主权是指一个特定国家在与其他国家的关系上保持独立性,在某种程度上在与教会的关系上也如此;从内部看,主权是政治实体的立法权。④

在国家中,除了完全国家的主权之外,还有一个主权,也就是君主的主权。⑤ 这里伯伦知理好像同意黑格尔的观点,在某种程度上,又与康德的观念一致。但是与黑格尔所说的国家主权在君主那里得到实现不同,伯伦知理断言国家主权和君主主权同时存在且不发生冲突。"在它们之间没有矛盾,也不能产生主权分离的后果,即一半属于人民,一半属于君主,没有两种相互争夺最高权力的力量。"⑥

---

① Bluntschli, *Theory of the State*, 牛津译本, 500 页。
② Bluntschli, *Theory of the State*, 牛津译本, 415 页。
③ Bluntschli, *Theory of the State*, 牛津译本, 500 页。
④ Bluntschli, *Theory of the State*, 牛津译本, 502 页。
⑤ Bluntschli, *Theory of the State*, 牛津译本, 502 页。
⑥ Bluntschli, *Theory of the State*, 牛津译本, 503 页。

第二章 联邦国家中的主权

一、导论

主权理论在联邦国家中的运用一直是政治理论中一个最难的，实际上也是最有趣的问题。这似乎已被从事政治学的所有学者所认可。新的理论被提出，旧的理论也还存在。不仅仅是形式上的丰富性，而且它的重要性在于，它是主权理论史上从旧主权观念到新主权观念的一个过渡。

我们是应该赞成传统的主权理论，还是新的主权理论，我在此不便作答。但是如果我们想知道旧的理论是如何被提出，如何被批判以及如何衰落的，新的理论又是如何出现的，就不应轻视已经运用到联邦国家中的主权理论。

二、州主权论

卡尔霍恩（Calhoun）在他的《合众国宪法和政府论文集》中，开始就这样宣称："我们的政府是一个政府的系统，是州的分散的政府的混合物，这些州组成一个联合体和一个政府，称为合众国政府。州是在合众国之先的，后者是它们的代表组成的。"①

在国内战争结束不久，斯蒂芬（Alexander H. Stephens）先生，南方联邦国家的副总统，以一种口述的方式，出版了《宪法观念下的战后各州间的关系》②，讨论了主权的问题。他认为在美国的制度下，主权存在于州③，合众国只不过是州出于各自的利益而达成的一个契约，后者可以随时在它们认为适当的时候从这个合众国中脱离；由合众国或联邦政府实施的权力并不是它自己的固有权力，而是州委托给它的权力。④

与法国的布丹、德国的普芬道夫（Pufendorf）一样、美国的卡尔霍恩认为主

---

① Calhoun, *Discourse on the Constitution and Government of the United States*, 1页。
② 两卷本，1867—1869。
③ Alexander H. Stephens, *A Constitutional View of the Late War Between the States*, 第一卷，81页, 117页。
④ 也可参见 P. C. Centz, *The Republic of Republics, or American Federal Liberty*, B. J. Sage 编辑，305页, 1881。也可参见 G. Tucker 在编辑 Blackstone 的 Commentaries 时所写的附录。"合众国的这种状况是一个原始的、联邦的和社会的契约。州自由地、自愿地且正式地加入联邦并被各州的人民批准。在联邦契约中，具有主权且独立的州可以通过一个永久的联邦结合在一起，但不丧失其作为一个完整州的权力。"

权是不能分离的。赛德尔（Seydel），一个巴伐利亚州的青年，宣称分散的州，也就是德帝国的各个州，都有其独自的主权，帝国不是主权的拥有者。因此，从严格意义上讲，它不是一个国家。实际上，它只是几个成员建立在协议上的联合体，在它们愿意的时候，又可以随时解散。①

国际法方面的专家，像瓦泰勒（Vattel）的观点，同上面提到的观念类似。他说："几个拥有主权的独立的州可以组成一个永久的联邦，但并不因此丧失完整州的地位。它们可以组成一个联邦共和国；虽然由于自愿加入，在任何行为上受到一些限制，但这不会损害它们的主权。"② 哈勒尔克（Halleck）也看到了若干有主权的州通过联邦协议组成联邦的可能性，但并不承认有一些共同的主权者。③ 特威斯（Twiss）认为虽然美国的每一个州的民族性已经融入整个联盟的民族性之中，但它们仍然都具有独立的主权。④

1798年由州立法机关通过杰弗逊起草的《肯塔基决议案》（The Kentucky Resolutions）表明了组成联邦的各个州都具有主权⑤，它们都有权决断自己的事务，"州不是按绝对地屈服一个共同的政府的原则组成美利坚合众国的"⑥。1832年，南卡罗来纳州的人民在议会集会中宣称，联邦政府施于南卡罗来纳州的任何强迫性意图都会影响到未来"南卡罗来纳州是否会继续留在联邦里。南卡罗来纳州人民也强烈认为他们有从保留与其他州政治联系的义务中解放出来的权利。他们可以组织一个独立的政府，可以做其他主权和独立国家可以做的一切事情"⑦。

经过1860年的合作，保护州的主权的一些宣传册子陆续出版。这是这种观点的一种表述："我们的原则是在宪法面前，州是具有主权和独立的，联邦是州的联合，宪法是它们之间的一个协议，也是这个联合的基本法；协议只是州之间做出的，它们之间没有唯一的解释，每一个州都有权判断协议的违反与否，从而决定它修改的方式和尺度。"⑧

---

① *Kommentar zur Verfassung Kunde fur das Deutsche Reich*，第一版，6页、23页。*Tubinger Staatswissenschaftliche Zeitschrift*，1872，185页，也见 *Harvward Law Review*，第31卷，148页。Kruger, *Government and Politics of the German Empire*，35~36页。

② Vattell, *Laws of Nations*，3页。

③ Halleck, *International Law*，第1卷，77页。

④ Twiss, *Laws of Nations*，第2版，23页。参照 Baty, *International Law*，332页。

⑤ 1798年6~7月间，联邦党人控制的国会通过了《惩治叛乱法》（Sedition Act）等四项反对同情法国大革命的法律，一些民主共和党人首当其冲，受到迫害。时任副总统的杰弗逊匿名为肯塔基州议会起草了一项遭资和抗议这些法律的决议案，史称《肯塔基决议案》。在决议案中，他强调，只有州才有权裁定联邦法律是否违宪。据此，他认为《惩治叛乱法》违反了宪法第一条修正案所保护的言论自由和出版自由，宣布它们无效（void and no force）。——译者注。

⑥ 见 Randall, *Life of Jesserson*，第二卷，449页和附录D。

⑦ 引自 Willoughby，见他的 *Fundamental Concepts of Public Law*。

⑧ W. D. Porter, *State Sovereignty and the Doctrine of Coercion*，6页。参见1860年 Association Tract No. 2。

在1820年1月，海恩（Hayne）在其著名的演讲中就讲了这种观念。① 像海恩这样的参议员在现时代已经很少了。1927年10月，在得州律师协会（the Texas Bar Association）上，密苏里州的参议员里德（Reed）发表了著名的演讲。这种描述州主权的理论，曾经吸引过美国人，但已经被现代的政治家和演说家们弃之不理。② 他宣称："州是作为绝对的、不受任何限制的主权组成联邦的。"③ 在这种方式下，地方政府的权力得以保存。通过这种权力，人民的自由和自然权利可以得到保证。"让我们把这种政府带回到它原有的原则，"④ 在结论中他说，"通过美国的新生，保留这些主权州处理它们各自事务的权利。而这是我们国家的先驱者们所梦想的。"⑤

1860年5月24日，美国参议院通过了一系列由杰斐逊·戴维斯（Jefferson Davis）提出的决议案，肯定了州的主权原则。⑥ 这些决议案首先就写道："决议如下：各州遵守联邦宪法，应该各自行使自由而且独立的主权，并将一部分权力让渡给联邦政府，以便更好地保障安全，抵御内患和外敌；但凡有一个或多个州或其公民联合起来干涉其他各州的州内事务，妄图破坏或颠覆其他各州，无论其借口是政治的、道德的、宗教的或任何其他的理由，都违背了联邦宪法，侮辱了被干涉的各州，危害了各州内部的和平与安宁——这本是制定联邦宪法的初衷，而且其结果必然削弱和破坏合众国本身。"⑦

在美国，联邦和州的法院在许多案例中都是认同州具有最高权力的原则的。1824年的吉本斯诉奥格登案（Gibbons v. Ogden）中，大法官马歇尔就表明了最高法院的决定："州的政治地位先于它的形式。它们是主权者，是完全独立的。只有通过一个联盟，它们才相互联系起来。这是事实。"⑧

在新奥尔良城诉阿比嘉托（Abbagnato）案中，马萨诸塞州最高法院宣称在这

---

① 应当是1830年。当时美国关于联邦主权与州主权的争论极为激烈。南卡罗来纳参议员海恩（Robert Hayne）说道"自由最贵重，联盟在其次"（the Union is next to our Liberty the most dear），而西部参议员韦伯斯特（Daniel Webster）则驳斥宪法是州之间的契约的说法，然后说出了激励美国几代人人心的话："自由和联盟，现在到永远，统一而不可分割。"（Liberty and Union, now and forever, one and inseparable.）——译者注

② "Encroachment of the Federal Government", *Proceedings of Texas Bar Association*, 第XLVI章（1927年10月），74页。

③ 同上书，76～77页。另一方面，参议员Reed指出中央政府"不是通常意义上的主权词汇，它是由一些专项的权力产生的，这些权力受到明确地限制。"

④ "Encroachment of the Federal Government", *Proceedings of Texas Bar Association*, 第XLVI章（1927年10月），77页。

⑤ "Encroachment of the Federal Government", *Proceedings of Texas Bar Association*, 第XLVI章（1927年10月），88～89页。

⑥ 他的观点可以在其 *Rise and Fall of the Confederate Government*, 1882, 两卷本。

⑦ Stephens引用，见 *The War Between the States*, 第一卷，409页。

⑧ 9 Wheaton 1, 207页，1824。

个国家的行政系统下，州是主权者。① 就在几年前，在贝利（Bailey）诉德雷克赛尔家具公司（Drexel Furniture Co.）的案件中，塔夫提（Taft）大法官阐明了最高法院的立场。他坚持认为，让议会对雇佣童工在美国的矿井和工厂中劳动的人征收其年纯收入的10%的税款，"会打破宪法对议会权力的限制，并且会彻底损害州的主权"②。

不仅仅政治家、政治学者、参议员和美国法院赞成州具有主权的理论，一些联邦国家的宪法中也这样宣称。瑞士的1848年和1874年宪法就有这样的内容："各州是最高权力的主体，它们的主权不受联邦宪法所限制，它们的权利也没有委托给联邦政府。"③ 同样的观点出现在1917年的墨西哥宪法中："由自由的、有最高权力、保留其内在政权的州组成一个代议的、民主的联邦共和国是墨西哥人民的意愿。因而，组织联邦需同这个基本法的原则保持一致。"④

那些认为州在联邦国家里是主权者的观点的出发点是，主权的本质是不可分的。它要么是一个整体，要么什么都不是。如同卡尔霍恩所主张的，他们也不可能认为主权是可分的，州的人民在有些部分上是主权者，在有些部分上不是主权者，在有些部分有最高权力，在有些部分没有最高权力，是不可能的。⑤ 卡尔霍恩说："主权，是一个完整的东西，分离它就是毁坏它。"⑥ 另外一位著名的学者宣称："它是一种自我决定的内在的、绝对的权力。在每个不同的政治组织，依据它自己的社会力量而存在，以寻求在自然正义的范围内保护它自身的有机体免受其他类似组织的打扰。"⑦ 它就像每一个个体的自我行动的意志和权力，也就像单个有机体的精神。⑧ 在一个国家里有两个主权是荒谬的和不可能的。它必须作为一个整体而存在。

如果主权是不可分割的，那么在哪里找到它？一种说法是主权在州那里。这

---

① 参见 Scott 的 *Cases on International Law*，119页。
② 259 U. S. 20. 在 Lonsdale 诉 Brown 的案件中，宾夕法尼亚东区巡回法庭指出了英国和苏格兰的联邦与合众国的联邦之间的不同："合众国的联邦不同在于，各州在其各自的政治能力内，都是主权者和彼此独立的。除非它们为了共同的防御和民族的目的而联合起来。它们都有各自的宪法，并具有所有主权特征的政府形式。" Peters 第二卷，附录，689～699页。
在 Lane County 诉 Oregon 的案件中，法庭认为"每一个州的人民组成了一个州，每一个州都有它自己的政府，作为一个单独的、独立的存在被赋予了所有本质的功能。没有联邦也可以继续存在。可以没有向合众国这样的政治实体。" Wallace，71页、76页，1868。也可参见 Stephens，*A Constitutional View of the Late War between the States*，第1卷，396页。
③ 1848年宪法第三章，1874年宪法第四章。
④ 墨西哥1917年宪法第41章。也可参见1824年1月的墨西哥联邦基本法。"根据该基本法和一般宪法的规则，就单独的内部管理而言，联邦的各部分都是自由的、独立的具有最高主权的州。"
⑤ Calhoun，*Works*，第1卷，146页，也见第2卷，232页。
⑥ Calhoun，*Works*，第1卷，146页。
⑦ Stephens，*A Constitutional View of the Late War between the States*，第2卷，22页。
⑧ Stephens，*A Constitutional View of the Late War between the States*，第2卷，23页。

种理论的拥护者的观点可以用以下的话简要地指出：

州主权理论的拥护者认为自从它们从大英帝国解放出来之后，州就变成自由的、独立的和拥有主权的实体。① 这是必然的，因为这已经被《独立宣言》、《邦联条例》(The Article of Confederation)②，同大英帝国的条约③和美国的最高法院承认④，从而成为共和国早期历史中的普遍观念。⑤

但这还不是全部。州拥有最高权力，还有几个原因。第一，州在合众国之前成立；第二，合众国是各州加入而成的；第三，州不加入联邦也可以存在。⑥

在表明宪法被采用之前州就是主权者之后，它们还竭力表明在1787年宪法之下，它们仍然是主权者。第一点，他们认为在邦联与联邦之间没有太大区别。如果有，也只是程度上的区别，而不是种类上的区别。⑦

对他们而言，"为了组织一个更完善的联邦"意味着使更为完善的"一个联邦"存在。根据《邦联条例》召开的会议改变和扩大了邦联的力量，但没有改变它的性质。这被宪法批准之后的事实所证实。"邦联"一词仍然出现在公开的文件中并被政治家所使用。⑧ 州不仅在（原来的）邦联体制下是主权者，在现代宪法规定下也是主权者。

第二点，有人认为联邦是州之间契约的产物，而不是单个人或人民之间的契

---

① 参见 James Brown Scott, *Sovereign States and Suits*, 36 页。也可参见 28 页、46 页、48 页、143 页。

② "每一个州都保留自己的主权、自由和独立，且保留任何权力，司法权以及没有被邦联委托给大陆会议的权利。" The Article of Confederation, 第二章。

③ 这个条约签订于1783年9月3日。"尊贵的英国皇帝认识到……各州都是自由的、独立的主权者。"见 Scott, *Sovereign States and Suits*, 39 页。

④ 举例来说，在 Mcivaine 诉 Coxe 的案例中，法院就认为："在1776年10月4日新泽西完全是一个独立的拥有主权的州。" Peter 编 *Condensed Reports*, 86 页。

⑤ 在 Washington's Southern Tour 中，把联邦说成是"在一个完美联邦首脑下的完全拥有主权的州的永久联邦"。A. Henderson, *Washington's Southern Tour*, 1791 (1923)。这个例子很好地说明了州是主权者在那个时代是最为流行的观点。参见 Scott, *Sovereign States and Suits*, 48 页。

⑥ Scott, *Sovereign States and Suits*, 69 页。也可参见 Ogg 和 Ray 著 *Introduction to American Government*, 97 页。也见 McLaughlin, "Social Compact and Constitutional Construction", *American Historical Review*, 1900年4月。必须记住的是，那些认为在《独立宣言》下州是独立的和具有主权的人，并不一定是那些认为在现行宪法下州也是具有主权的人。事实上，很多学者否认在现行宪法下州是具有主权的，但认为在《邦联条例》下州是具有主权的。后一种观点为 Willoughby 和 Wilson 所支持。参见 Willoughby, *Nature of the State*, 264 页。Wilson, *The State*, 1373~1379 节。Hamilton 也认为在其最初的宪法下，各州政府都被赋予了完全的主权，见 Ford, *Federalist*, 196 页。也见 *Federalist*, 81 页。Webster 在与 Calhoun 的论辩中（1839）也持这样的观点。

⑦ 华盛顿在许多公开演讲中，没有对同盟国和联邦国家做出区分。参见 Stephens, *A Constitutional View of the Late War Between the States*, 第1卷, 167~170 页。当 Calhoun 试图对这两者做出区分的时候，他也立刻陷入了困境。参见 *Disquisition*, 163 页。也可参见 Merriam, *History of Theory of Sovereignty since Rousseau*, 170 页之注释。

⑧ 参见 Washington 的 *Writings*, 第9卷, 398 页。也可参见 *Annals of Congress*, 第一卷, 38 页。

约的产物。① 这一点在宪法中表现得最为明显。当宪法宣称:"宪法必须由九个州同时批准才能生效。"② 而且代表们签字时签州名,也可以看出这一点。

第三点,就是即使说这样的协议是在人民之间达成的,"人民"也是指州的人民,而不是作为一个整体的联邦的人民。在1787年8月7日通过的宪法的序言中,"我们,新罕布什尔州、马萨诸塞州、纽约州、新泽西州、宾夕法尼亚州、马里兰州、北卡罗来纳州、南卡罗来纳州和乔治亚州等州的人民宣布制定以下宪法",这样的话已经被修改成:"我们,美利坚合众国的人民……"含义并没有改变,但是起草委员会在那时并不知道有哪个州会修改它,所以在前面加上州的名字就是极为不合适的。③

第四点,在宪法里面有这样的表述,"美国的国会由参议院和众议院组成"④和"多数党组织日常事务的讨论"⑤。但是,如果大多数州拒绝通过它们的立法或派遣它们的议员到国会,就不存在国会,联邦也就被破坏了。⑥ 因此,联合政府或联邦不能被看作是一个主权者。⑦ 联邦的生命完全受各主权州支配,它的权力是明显受到限制的,且这种权力可以被各州在认为适当的时候收回。

第五点,州是主权者,是因为它们不能被它们自己的公民所控诉,也不能被其他州和其他国家的公民所控诉。这一个原则,已经被州法院所确认,并且在1798年通过的宪法第十一修正案中得到重新肯定。⑧

另外还必须指出的是,那些认为州拥有主权的观念的人试图区分主权和权力之间的区别。⑨ 权力可分,但主权不能。卡尔霍恩说:"认为主权的权力是可分的观点是不难理解的。权力的不同部分委托给不同的机构来操作。"⑩ 斯蒂芬也有同样的主张:"我们必须在主权的权力和主权本身之间做出区分。"⑪ 前者是可分的,而后者是不可分的。⑫ 他们否认主权是权力的总和,而认为权力是由主权产

---

① James Brown Scott, *Sovereign States and Suits*, 69页。
② 宪法第7章。
③ Stephens, *A Constitutional View of the Late War between the States*, 第1卷, 137~139页。《合众国宪法》与《联邦条例》有根本性的差异,此处当是Stephens为维护州主权论而做的曲解。——译者注
④ 宪法第1章第1节。
⑤ 宪法第1章第5节。
⑥ W. D. Porter, *State Sovereignty and the Doctrine of Coercion*, 参见1860年 *Association Tract* No. 2, 12页。
⑦ Senator Reed, "Encroachment of the Federal Government," *the Proceedings of Texas Bar Association*, 第XLVI章(1927年10月), 76~77页。
⑧ "合众国的司法权,不得被解释为可以扩展到受理由他州公民或任何外国公民或臣民对合众国一州提出的或起诉的任何普通法或衡平法的诉讼。"
⑨ 有些学者区分主权与主权的特征,如Calhoun,一些学者如Stephens在最高权力和主权之间进行区分。
⑩ Calhoun, *Discourse on the Constitution and Government of the United States*, 146页。
⑪ Stephens, *A Constitutional View of the Late War between the States*, 第2卷, 33页。
⑫ Stephens, *A Constitutional View of the Late War between the States*, 第2卷, 33页。

生的。① 这被认为是"卡尔霍恩观点的实质"②，同样的观点也被大多数拥护州主权论的学者支持。③

那么权力如何分？它只能在联邦国家中分。以美国为例，它首先在联邦政府和州的政府之间分；其次，它在联邦政府和各州政府中又被分为三个分支，也就是立法权、行政权和司法权；④ 最后，在中央以及各州政府和地方政府之间分。⑤ 镇和城市也可以行使最高权力，比如征税；但是它们不能且永远不能被称为主权的主体。⑥ 对于联邦政府和联邦来说，也是如此。联邦政府仅仅拥有州所委托的权力，像宣战、媾和等，但这些权力与乡镇和城市的征税权在本质上并没有什么不同。

三、联邦主权论

在联邦国家，与州主权论相反的是联邦主权论。这种理论的出发点和前一种理论基本上相似。他们都赞成主权是不能分的，必须是完整的。但是与州主权论者认为主权在州那里不同，他们认为主权在联邦或联邦政府那里。

著名德国学者特赖奇克（Treischke）对主权在联邦国家和同盟国家中的地位作了区分。在后者中，主权存在于几个国家，而在前者中，主权在联邦那里。"那些德国的从属国不是真正的国家。它们必须随时准备帝国权威收回它们现在所拥有的权利。"⑦

海内尔（Albert Haenel）在他的《德国国家法研究》（"Studien zum deutschen Staatsrechte"）⑧ 一文中，根据主权理论的特征发展了他的"决定一切职权的职权（Competenz-competenz）"理论，他认为这是主权理论的典型特征。主权，是一种自认最高的并且可以按它自身的意志和愿望行事的权力。按他的看法，这种权力在德国的皇帝手里，因为只有皇帝才有自我决断的合法权力。"皇帝完全按符合法律和宪法的方式行事，可以增加他自身的权力，减少那些下属国家的权力，并控制政府各个领域的行为。"⑨ 弗兰茨·冯·李斯特（F. V. Liszt, 1851—

---

① Merriam, *History of Theory of Sovereignty since Rousseau*, 171 页。Stephens, *A Constitutional View of the Late War Between the States*, 第 2 卷, 23 页。

② Merriam, *History of Theory of Sovereignty since Rousseau*, 171 页。

③ 比较在 Sapphire 案中法庭的观点, 1781, 11 Wallace, 164。

④ Stephens, *A Constitutionul View of the Late War Between the States*, 第 2 卷, 23 页。

⑤ W. D. Porter, *State Sovereignty and the Doctrine of Coercion*, 8 页。

⑥ W. D. Porter, *State Sovereignty and the Doctrine of Coercion*, 8 页。

⑦ *Politics*, 第 1 卷, 30 页。

⑧ 1923, 第 1 部分。参见第 1 部分, 240 节, 他对宪法基础的讨论。

⑨ 参见 Merriam, *History of Theory of Sovereignty*, 192 页。

1919），在其国际法的论文中，宣称皇帝和中央政府的权力是至高无上的，然而却是有限的。[1] 其他多少对该观点加以关注的学者，有如下这些人：赫尔德（J. Held）[2]、佐夫（Zopf）[3]、卡登朋（Kaltenborn）[4]、郎恩（Roune）[5]、里斯奇（P. Resch）[6] 和佐恩（Zorn）[7]。

也有一些学者，一方面承认联邦国家的主权存在于联邦中；另一方面又拒绝承认主权是国家的特征。这些学者有：耶利内克（Jellinek）、拉班德（Laband）、麦耶（Meyer）。麦耶认为有两种类型的国家，中央集权国家和联邦国家。[8] 他发现在前者中弄清主权的归宿没有困难，但是在后者中主权的归宿却容易让人产生疑问。对他而言，组成联邦的各成员尽管不再拥有主权，但还是被称为国家。[9]

耶利内克像麦耶一样，也认为联邦中的成员虽然失去了它们的主权，但仍然是真正的国家。[10] 在耶利内克看来一个主权国家和非主权国家的区别在于前者有权阻止后者实施宪法的权力。[11] 拉班德认为，当几个国家组成一个联邦国家后，就失去了它们曾经有过的主权。但仍然保留有真正国家的性质。[12] 根据耶利内克和拉班德的说法，这几个国家是由于其固有的权利，才被称之为国家的。简而言之，国家的本质特征不是主权而是权利。[13]

人们一般认为自从布丹以来的法国学者倾向于主权不可分的理论。当他们中的大多数把这种理论应用到联邦国家中的时候，由于受到其自身的政治观念和经验的影响，不希望自找麻烦，就毫不犹豫地把主权置于联邦政府之中。这样一来，根据波莱尔（E. Borel）的看法，主权是一个国家的特质。[14] 这种特质是绝对的、

---

[1] *Das Volkerrecht*，121 页。

[2] *System des Verfassungsrechts der Monarchischen Staaten Deutschlands mit besanderer Rucksicht auf den Constitutionalesims*，第一卷，392～395 节，1856。

[3] *Grundzatz des gemeinen Deutschen Staatsrechts*，第 5 版，第一卷，第 63～64 节，1863。

[4] *Einleitung in das constitutionalle Verfassungsrecht*，第 159 节，1863。

[5] *Staatsrecht des deutsche Reiches*，第 1 卷，65 页。

[6] *Europaische Volkerrecht*，39 页，1885。

[7] *Staatsrecht*，第 1 卷，第 73 节；也可参见 Pozl, *Staatswarterbunch von Bluntschli und Brater*，第二卷，284～293 页。

[8] *Lehrbuch des deutschen Staatsrechts*，2～3 页，1878。

[9] *Lehrbuch des deutschen Staatsrechts*，8 页，1895。

[10] *Lehre von den Staatenverbindungen*，36 页；也可参见 *Allgemeine Staatslehre*，第 2 版，470 页以下。

[11] *Die Lehre von den Stautenverbindungen*，41～42 页。比较他的 *Geselz und Verodnung*，203 页，在这里他认为非主权国家的存在，是由超国家的主权者的意志所决定的。主权者能利用非主权国家去扩大其能设定的非正式的先验的法律限定。参见 Willoughby, *Nature of the State*，246～248 页。

[12] *Das Staatsrecht des deutsche Reiches*，第 5 版，第 1 卷，72 页。也可参见 E. Nys, *Le Roit international*，120 页。

[13] 参见 Jellinek, *Lehre von den Staatenverbindungen*，42 页；Laband, *Staatsrecht*，第 1 卷，180 页。关于没有主权的国家的讨论，参见 Willoughby, *Fundamental Concepts of Public Law*，254 页。

[14] *Étude sur la souveraineté et l'État federatif*，47 页。

有排他性的。从内部看,它是最高的权力;从外部看,它是完全独立的。① 它是唯一的、不可分割的。这种唯一的、不可分割的权力必须掌握在中央政府手中。从法律上来说,中央集权国家的地方政府和联邦国家的州之间没有区别。②

乐福尔(Le Fur)关于联邦国家的主权问题的观念同波莱尔的比较类似。他认为只有联邦政府拥有主权。在他看来,几个州组成联邦国家,就如同许多单个的公民组成民主国家。当一个联邦产生之后,一个新的主权实体就出现了,州的主权就不存在了。③

再看一看美国思想家,我们发现像汉密尔顿那样的人非常向往一个强大的具有完整主权的联邦,虽然他们所处的时间和环境使他们不得不认同主权可分论的主张④,有时甚至不得不去承认州是主权者。⑤ 如果汉密尔顿不是如他所宣称的从内心想实现布丹和霍布斯的梦想,他就不会说自己是一个中央集权的强烈拥护者,想看见州的主权完全消失,而只有联邦政府有权按自己的意志去做任何它想做的事。⑥

在 19 世纪早期,从马歇尔大法官的笔下透露出的美国高等法院的观点也有同样的倾向。当林肯宣布"联邦比每一个州的历史都更悠久,事实上是联邦使得它们成其为州"⑦ 的时候,他内心一定是认为只有联邦而不是州,才可以成为主权者。

最近的许多美国学者都持这样的观点。在《州与政府》一书中,迪利(Dealey)教授指出如果所建立政治联合体的权力大到使其成员的主权完全融入联合体的主权当中,那么这个联合体就是联邦而不是邦联。⑧ 威尔逊(W. Welson)也持同样的观点。他说:"我们必须仔细区分联邦和邦联之间的差

---

① *Étude sur la souverainete et l'État federatif*, 28 页。

② *Étude sur la souverainete et l'État federatif*, 74 页、172 页。Seeley 教授,毫无疑问分享 Borel 的观点,尽管他没有明确表明联邦国家的主权归属于哪里。他说:"我否认在单一制国家和联邦制国家之间有任何性质上的基本不同;我否认说其中一个在某种意义上是复合的,另外一个是单一的。"参见他的 *Introduction to Political Science*, 94~95 页。

③ Le Fur, *L'État federal*, 697 页以下。Piedelievre 在他的 *Droit International Public* 中,尽管认为在现代世界中有半主权的国家存在,但他也否认联邦国家的主权是可分的。(第1卷,78 页)这样,构成联邦国家的各组成部分就不再是完全的主权者了。它们服从于那个通过契约、形成的一个新的人格的联邦政府。其他持类似观点的学者有:Neumann, *Élements du droit des gens modern Europeun*, 27 页;Antoine Rougier, *Les Guerres civiles et le Droit des gens*, 47 页。

④ Ford, *Federalist*, 207 页。

⑤ Ford, *Federalist*, 196 页。

⑥ 参见 W. B. Munro, *The Government of the United States*, 37 页。

⑦ 参见 A. Lincoln, *Special Message to Congress*, 1861 年 7 月 4 日。

⑧ Dealey, *The State and Government*, 152 页、154 页。也可参见 Wiloughby, *Nature of the State*, 253~254 页和他最近的著作 *The Fundamental Concepts of Public Law*, 249 页。参见 James Wilson 的观点, *Madison Papers*, 第 2 卷, 824 页。

别。它们都有一个中央政府和若干地方政府,其中每一个政府都实施主权的一部分权力;但是,它们之间有很重要的差别。如果一个国家的中央政府可以行使完整的主权,它就是联邦国家,或如德国人所说的'Bundesstaat'。如果一个政治联合体的主权不在一个完整的领域内,而是分散在比较小的领域内,就是说有多个主权,也就是有多个国家,那它就是邦联,或如德国人所说的'Staatenbund'。也就是说,邦联是许多国家的联合,中央政府只不过是这些国家的代理人;而联邦国家却是有一个真正的中央政府。"[1] 但是威尔逊同其他许多德国政治学者一样,坚持认为,虽然州在联邦中失去了它们的主权,但是都还有作为国家的权利。[2]

四、各种妥协理论

在对州主权论和联邦主权论这两种相反的理论进行陈述之后;我们来看第三种观点。这种观点没有更好的名称可以用,暂且称之为"妥协理论"。这种理论的形式有很多种。粗略地分,有以下几类:①主权在民论,②民族主权论,③国家主权论,④合众国主权论,⑤选民主权论,⑥主权是宪法制定的权力,⑦主权是法律制定的权力,⑧主权可分论。

1. 主权在民论

主权在民论并不是现代才出现的。[3] 在亚里士多德的著作中就可以找到。它曾经被罗马法学家所认可,被反暴君论者(Monarchomschs)学派的学者所支持,在法国大革命期间也被热烈地接受。用梅因的话说,"这种理论,如同民族主权论一样被欧洲大陆的人们熟知。它在法国、意大利、西班牙、葡萄牙、荷兰、比利时、希腊以及斯堪的纳维亚国家被全盘接受;在德国却被皇帝和权臣不断地否决,但也产生了很大的影响;在英国,则没有多大的市场"[4]。这种理论的主要目

---

[1] Wilson, *The State*, 1372~1379 节。

[2] Wilson, *An Old Master and Other Essays*, 3~94 页。"在联邦国家,各成员国家已经失去了作为一个整体所具有的自我决定其法律的权力。如果不求助于联邦权威,它们不能扩展,甚至不能决定它们最终的权力。但是,它们依然是国家,因为它们的权力是最初的和内生的,而不是派生的;因为它们的权利也不是法律义务;还因为它们的命令完全得到了法律的强制认可。但是它们的权力受到了它们之上的那个国家的最高权力的限制,这个国家的权威的范围是在宪法程序和保证下自我决定的。" 正如上文已经指出的,Wheaton 认可州主权论,但是下面的陈述表明他已经认同了联邦主权论的观点:"联邦政府是由联邦的法案产生的,是最高主权者,在法案许可的权力范围内,政府的行为不仅在作为联邦的成员州之上,也在公民之上。联邦政府的权力已经损害了每一个州的对内和对外的主权,来自于联邦的这种限制就是最高权力。" *International Law*, 74 页。英国学者如 Lavrence 也持相似的立场,见 *Principles of International Law*, 63 页。H. E. Willis 在最近发表的篇文章中提出这样一种观点:在共和国的早期历史上,主权是在州与联邦之间分离的,但是州在逐步地失去它的主权,直到它们签订第十八修正案之后就完全失掉了主权,现在,联邦单抽拥有主权。*Kentucky Law Journal*, 1927 年 3 月, 第 15 卷, 175 页、178 页。

[3] 这里的"人民"指整个联邦的人民,以与州的人民区别开来。

[4] Maine, *Popular Government*, 8 页。

的是推翻君主主权论。但是当它被运用到联邦国家的时候却自觉不自觉地成了州主权论和联邦主权论妥协的产物。

我们现在研究的这种理论是詹姆斯·威尔逊提出的,他是1787年制宪会议上的最有名的并发挥了至关重要作用的成员。由于受到普芬道夫的契约理论的深刻影响①,威尔逊提出这样的观点:人民,为了他们的共同利益,而组成了一个法人或政治实体合众国。它被认为是这个世界上最高级、最高贵的事物。② 因为人民是联合体的建立者,所以他们拥有全部的主权。威尔逊认为,这里的人民,首先,是指合众国的人民,其次,是指男性白种人。③

在所有对这种理论的解释者中,丹尼尔·韦伯斯特的表述是最完美的。④ 他的理论主要立足于美国宪法并在海恩-伟伯斯特(Hayne-Webster)辩论中,和他在1848年1月27日联邦最高法院马丁·路德诉路德·M. 波登等的事件进行审判之前作的评论中以及其他场合得到体现。

在海恩-伟伯斯特辩论中⑤,韦伯斯特认为宪法不是州之间的一个联合,而是建立在人民承认的基础之上。"没有人,"韦伯斯特在马丁·路德事件中说,"怀疑人民是所有政治权力的源泉。政府是为他们的利益服务的,政府的成员仅仅是他们的代理人和仆人。"⑥ 因此,"我们应该承认,这个国家的政治权力的源泉是人民。我们应该承认他们是主权者,因为他们本来就是。也就是说,人民意志的集合,集合的共同体,就是主权者。"⑦

韦伯斯特的理论的论据,正如他已经指出的,是宪法序言中的这些话:"我们,合众国的人民,为了组成一个更为完善的联合体……制定美利坚合众国宪法。"他的理由在于,宪法是由合众国的人民制定的,而不是说由"州的人民"。

---

① Pufendorf 的著作被广泛地在 Wilson 的作品中引用。

② J. Wilsom, *Works*, 第 2 卷, 6 页。也可参见脚注。

③ J. Wilson 指出"人民"有另外两种不同的含义。"合众国的人民必须要从两种非常不同的观念来看待——作为组成一个伟大的和合众的国家的人民和州的人民,州臣属于国家,但在内部管理上是独立的。"*Works*, 第二卷, 8 页。

④ Webster 并不强烈坚持这种观点,他甚至赞同州主权论。在 1839 年给 Barings 的一封信中,他写道:"你的第一个问题是,州的立法机构是否是有对内对外协议贷款的法律和宪法权力,我的回答是州的立法机构也有这样的权力,对这一点产生疑问对我来说是很困难的。每一个州都是独立的,拥有主权的政治团体,除非有一些权力以及委托给中央政府实施,这个中央政府是在成文宪法下建立起来的,对所有州的人民实施其权威。"参见 Niles, *National Register*, 第 57 卷, 273~274 页。

也可参见他在 1851 年 6 月 28 日在弗吉尼亚 Capon Springs 所作的演讲, Stenphens 在 *War between the States* 第 1 卷, 404~405 页引用。也可看其 *Works*, 第 11 卷, 222 页。"我们通常说州是拥有主权的州,我不反对这一点。但是宪法从不这样称呼它们,宪法也从来不像称呼联邦政府那样称它们为政府;它就是称呼州政府。"

⑤ *Works*, 第 1 卷, 82~92 页。

⑥ *Works*, 第 6 卷, 221 页。

⑦ *Works*, 第 6 卷, 222 页。

是由合众国的全体人民共同制定宪法的。①

支持主权在民论的另一个理由可以在荷尔卡姆（Holcome）教授的论述中找到："下面这一条款最能证明合众国的人民有最终的主权，'合众国将保证每一个州的政府的共和形式，而不管这个州的人民想不想要这样一个政府。'"② 基于宪法的原则，荷尔卡姆提出了一个逻辑：整体大于部分，部分低于整体。这样，州的人民就必须服从整个国家人民的主权，尽管在联邦宪法面前，国家人民和州人民之间，各州人民之间，都是平等的。③

人民必须是最高权力者，"如果没有人民支持这个体制……如果没有人民去教导、去规划、去指导、去纠正、去惩罚政府，这个复杂的机器早就万劫不复了"。④

2. 民族主权论

提出民族主权论⑤的学者无疑是受到了德国和法国学者观念的影响。这种理论从德国人那里获得哲学的根基，因为德国思想总是打上抽象的色彩，在现实之外看待和解释事情，它不仅仅是哲学的，甚至是神秘的。它又从法国人那里获得它的形式和本质。1789年《人权宣言》的第三条宣称："所有的主权都本质地存在于民族中"，1791年宪法也宣布"主权是唯一的，不可分割的，不可转让的，它属于整个民族"。

在批判性方面，这一群思想家否认主权在民论，原因是它太简单了。人民，在他们看来，仅仅是没有一般观念的一定区域的居民的集合。⑥ 他们中的一位拥护者说："如果人民通过联合成为主权者，则他们每一个人都要分享这一主权。"⑦

---

① Merriam, *American Political Ideas*, 285 页。
② Holcome, *State Government in the United States*, 11 页。
③ Holcome, *State Government in the United States*, 8 页。
④ Jameson, "National Sovereignty", in *Political Science Quarterly*, 第 5 卷, 211 页。

也可参见 Burgess, *Political Science and Constitutional Law*, 第 1 卷, 123～124 页。他认为德国人民是德意志帝国的最终主权。也可参见 R. L. Ashley, *American Government*, 7 页。他坚持认为人民是最高主权者，因为只有人民才能改变旧有的宪法和制定新的宪法。参见 Story, *Commentaries*, 第 1 卷, 210 页；Pomeroy, *Constitutional Law*, 4～5 页。Treitschke, *Politics*, 第 2 卷, 352 页。法庭的如下一些案例揭示了人民主权论：Chisholm 诉 Georgia, 2 U. S. 419、417；Spooner 诉 McConnell, 联邦案例第 13、第 249。Yick Wo 诉 Hopkins, 118 U. S. 356、365。

比较 W. L. Clark, *Elementary Law*, 22 页, 1909。

⑤ "民族"和"人民"这两个词用得比较松散。Maine 和 Jameson 在它们之间没有进行什么区分。参见 Maine, *Popular Government*, 7 页、8 页；Jameson, "National Sovereignty", *Political Science Quarterly*, 第 5 卷, 198 页。法语"人民"（peuple）被翻译为"民族"（nation），参见"League of Nations", *Provisional Verbatim Records*, 卷 1, 4 页, 1920。

⑥ 参见 Merriam, *History of Theory of Sovereignty*, 174～175 页。Lieber, *Miscellaneous Writings*, 第 2 卷, 228 页。也可参见 H. P. Judson, *Our Federal Republic*, 2 页。

⑦ Lieber, *Manual of Political Ethics*, 第 1 卷, 219～220 页。

也就是说，人民不是主权者或不能成为主权者。这种观念也被另外一个著名的拥护者证明，第一，这种理论宣称主权从有机的人民那里分离出来；第二，它是一个无机的集合，或者说是没有形式的群体；第三，它不能使许多人的意志变得清楚。①

否认人民是主权者的同时，他们也否认联邦主权论或联邦政府主权论，也否认州主权论。其中一人宣称："政府是民族主权得以实现的机构。"② 联邦政府仅仅是联邦宪法的产物，联邦宪法仅仅是民族的产物。③

成员州，或者是用马尔福德（Mulford）自己的词语，共和国不是主权者，因为共和国是不完整的。④ 并且，共和国不是永久的，只有民族与它的目的保持一致。⑤ 更进一步，"除了与民族和通过民族与其他共和国保持联系之外，共和国没有外部的联系。它没有同外国的联系，也就是没有同国际上其他国家的联系。它不能加入同盟、联盟，什么国际组织也不能加入。"⑥

尽管共和国没有如同一个民族那样拥有真正的主权⑦，但它有形式上的主权，这种形式上的主权"对有些程序进行限定，在诉讼程序中形式上执行某些权力"⑧。因为在合众国的发展历史上，共和国有它的最简单和最高级的组织。⑨

在讨论了这种理论的批判性之后，我们再来看看它的建设性的方面。根据支持该理论的一个学者的看法，一个民族，即世代居住在固定的领土内，有共同的语言、文学、习俗的人们，"由于认识到他们具有相同命运，而组成一个有机体"⑩。另外一位学者认为，"它存在，如同有机体和道德实体的存在一样，是一个事实。在其开端处认识到它的存在，是人类有理智的生活的开始"⑪。

在认识到民族是有意识生命的有机体和道德实体后，有些人走得更远，给民族加上神圣理论的色彩。也就是说，民族"有神圣的根基，在历史上有它自己神

---

① E. Mulford, *The Nation*, 134～185 页, 1872. 参见 Pomeroy, *Constitutional Law*, 5 页。
② E. Mulford, *The Nation*, 140 页, 1872.
③ E. Mulford, *The Nation*, 300 页, 1872.
④ E. Mulford, *The Nation*, 145 页, 1872.
⑤ E. Mulford, *The Nation*, 145 页, 1872.
⑥ E. Mulford, *The Nation*, 303～305 页, 1872.
⑦ E. Mulford, *The Nation*, 302 页, 1872.
⑧ E. Mulford, *The Nation*, 302 页, 1872.
⑨ E. Mulford, *The Nation*, 291 页, 1872. 在另外的地方他宣称："民族的主权内在于共和国。它的决定是最高法律；民族的法律是每一个共和国的法律。合众国的宪法是每一个州的宪法。真正的主权在民族，人民的意志是通过整体而普遍存在的。" 302 页。
⑩ Lieber, *Miscellaneous Writings*, 第 2 卷, 228 页。
⑪ E. Mulford, *The Nation*, 55 页, 1872。

圣的目的。在人类的道德本质中,它具有神性的预见"①。

在理解了民族这个概念之后,我们回到主权观念。主权,据他们说,存在于民族中且仅仅存在于民族。但是什么是主权?利伯(Lieber)教授这样定义:"在人类社会和国家中为了人类的存在所必须具有的权利、责任和权力。"② 马尔福德则认为主权存在于民族如同存在于一个有机体和一个道德人格。通过它,正义在道德秩序中被伸张与实现。③

主权的本质包括独立性、权威性、至高无上性、统一性和神圣性,它的外部特征是不可转让性,不可分割性,不需要对任何外部权威负责,统摄所有的政治秩序。

3. 国家主权论

跟民族主权论有密切关系的是由柏格斯(Burgess)教授所创立的国家主权论。柏格斯受到了德国人(如佐恩和赛德尔)、法国人(如布丹和卢梭)、英国人(如霍布斯和奥斯丁)和美国人(如卡尔霍恩和斯蒂芬)的影响。

柏格斯把主权定义为"最初的、绝对的、不受限制的、个体和个体的所有联合体之上的普遍权力"④。对他来说,主权不仅是国家的本质特征,而且是国家最明显的和最高的特征。⑤ 没有主权,就没有国家。两者是互为依存的。

在这种前提下,这种理论认为只存在一种国家,也就是拥有他定义的主权的国家。这又导致他否认"没有像联邦国家这样的事物"⑥。联邦国家的真实含义,在于它有共同主权下的两层政府系统。当组织主权的前一种形式没有被完全放弃的时候,主权在曾经是独立的和拥有最高权力的国家内部的转换只不过是"主权从君主(制)转向贵族(制),从贵族(制)转向民主(制)。不过从形式上来说,在前一种形式中主权被重新组织,并没有完全消失。也就是说,旧国家变成

---

① E. Mulford, *The Nation*, 54 页, 1872。他继续写道:"它不是家庭的延续,不是暴力的产物,也不是本能的运行,不是社会契约的结果,也不是人民主权的产物;真理在这些错误的假设下面,在天道运行中,或多或少地昭示了民族的上升、成长和保护。"参见 Brownson, *American Republic*, 192 页, 1865。

② Lieber, *Manual of Political Ethics*, 第 1 卷, 216 页。在另外的地方,他这样定义主权:"主权是所有权力自足的源泉,从主权那里所有的专门权力得以派生。因此,从自由人的观点来看,它只能和社会、民族交织在一起。"参见他的 *Civil Liberty and Self-Government*, 156 页。在 Lieber 这里,"民族"和"社会"这两个词是同一个意思。参见 J. Wilson, *Law Lecture*, 第 1 卷, 第 2 章。

③ E. Mulford, *The Nation*, 113 页, 1872。参考 Jameson, *A Treatise on Constitutional Conventions: Their History, Powers and Modes of Procedure*, 第 18 节, 1866。民族"是一个不可分的政治实体,由众国的公民组成,这些公民不分年龄、性别、肤色和生活状况"。Jameson, *A Treatise on Constitutional Conventions: Their History, Powers and Modes of Procedure*, 第 57 节。

④ 民族主权论与国家主权论有何不同,是很难区分的。Burgess 教授区分了民族与国家,但他对民族的定义显然与 Mulford 和 Lieber 不同。参见 Burgess, *Political Science and Constitutional Law*, 1～4 页。Mulford, *The Nation*, 145 页。

⑤ 参见 *Political Science Quarterly*, 第 8 卷, 128 页。

⑥ Burgess, *Political Science and Constitutional Law*, 第一卷, 79 页。

了新国家政府的一部分，仅此而已"。几个国家联合组成联邦国家，它们就失去了称做国家的性质，因而，失去了主权。一般情况下，它们还被称为国家，但这在很大程度上是名义性的，而没有任何实质意义。"当新事物取代旧事物的时候，思想的混乱和惰性支持会让旧事物存在很长一段时间，我们发明一个新的名称来描述新的特征往往需要花很长的时间。"①

柏格斯认为联邦国家可以由几个独立的、拥有主权的国家组成但同时他又认为美国的情况并不是这样的。他认为在《独立宣言》两年之前的1764年第一次大陆会议的时候，就存在一个主权国家。他这样说："同母国完全从地理上的分裂和部分的种族上的分裂，到完全地理上统一，种族本质上的统一，利益上的完全认同，是最后唤醒十三个殖民地人民意识到他们已经获得一个主权的自然状态国家的动力。将这种意识目标化为组织的冲动是不可抗拒的。它的第一个持久的形式就是大陆会议。这是美国的第一个组织。从它存在的那一刻起，大西洋的这边就不再仅仅是十三个地方政府，而是有了美国，这不是纸上的简单观念，而是实际的组织。"②

这就是美国国家主权的起源，"政府不是国家的最高权力组织"是自然的、合乎逻辑的。③ 因为"在政府后面有宪法，在宪法后面，有最初的主权国家存在，它委任了政府和自由的宪法"④。

这里我们回到柏格斯的政治理论中的一个被他的追随者和美国学者广泛接受的特殊地方，这就是他对国家和政府的区分。⑤ 他说："这是美国公法的发展达到了一个比欧洲国家的公法高得多的阶段的关键。"⑥ 对欧洲人，特别是对德国的公法学家来说，国家和政府几乎就是同一个东西。在欧洲，这两者的区分不如在美国清楚。他意识到国家是独立政府的最高组织，主权只存在于国家里面，而不是存在于政府里面。在一个国家里面也许有不同的政府权力，但是只有一个主权。在美国有许多政府，但只有一个国家。

4. 合众国主权论

合众国主权论不容易同国家主权论和民族主权论区分清楚。最重要的阐释者，布朗森（Brownson），就随意的运用"国家""民族"和"合众国"。⑦ 然而，我们不必受名词的误导而忽视它的实质。为了对合众国主权论有一个清楚的理

---

① Burgess, *Political Science and Constitutional Law*, 第一卷, 80 页。
② Burgess, *Political Science and Constitutional Law*, 第一卷, 100 页。
③ Burgess, *Political Science and Constitutional Law*, 57 页。
④ Burgess, *Political Science and Constitutional Law*, 57 页。
⑤ 这当然不是 Burgess 的发明，参见 Brownson, *Amercian Republic*, 207 页。
⑥ Burgess, *Political Science and Constitutional Law*, 第一卷, 57 页。
⑦ 参见 Brownson, *Amercian Republic*, 1865, 第八、第九章。也可参见 Hurd, *Theory of Our National Existence*, 141 页。

解，我们可以引用布朗森在《美国共和国》中的一段话："理解这个奥秘的关键在这个名称的使用上，'合众国'，不是这个国家的名字——它的确切的名字是美国这是一个能体现它的政治结构的名字。在它里面，没有拥有主权的人民，就没有州；没有州，就没有联邦，或者说没有'合众'国。'合众'一词不是固有名称（proper name）的一部分，而是修饰'国'的形容词，有它完整和适当的意义。因此，主权必须存在于国家中，存在于国家联邦中，而不是存在于单个的州中。"①

约翰·赫德（John Hurd）也提出了类似的论点。他是这样说的："美国的居民组成了一个国家。它的主权由成员州联合起来组成的合众国所有，并由作为合众国的工具的联邦政府和作为州的工具的州政府共同行使。"②

这种理论的阐释者提出的一个主要观点是，一个拥有最高权力的国家，或者是一组拥有最高权力的国家，不论有没有它或它们的同意，都失去了它或它们的主权，仅仅因为融入另外一个拥有最高权力的国家，合众国于是就存在了。这个理论的逻辑是主权只能交给一个在主权被交出前就已经存在的团体，也就是说，一个国家不能把它的主权交给一个根本就不存在的东西。"君主可以放弃他的权力，因为他的放弃仅仅是把人民委托给他的权力交还给人民，他正是从人民那里得到的权力。但是，一个民族却不能，因为它们是融合在一起的。"③

按这种理由，具有主权的国家，通过协议，可以组成一个联盟、同盟并且同意由一个共同的代理人来执行它们的全部或部分主权；但是在这样做的时候，它们并没有失去相应的主权，因为，正如前文所述，当它们放弃主权的时候，通过它们产生的代理人还不存在。"一个独立的国家没有融入另一个的时候，它作为一个国家拥有的主权就不会停止。"④

将这种理论运用到合众国，就必须提出这样的问题：联邦的州还是不是各自拥有主权的州呢？如果是，它们现在一定还是这样。⑤ "州可以从联邦中脱离出来是无可置疑的权利；这不是宪法下的权利，也不是协议派生出来的权利，而是先在的、独立的、内在的、不可分立的权利。"⑥ 如果殖民地在从大英帝国分离出来之后，变成了各自拥有政权的国家，一个单一的、不可分割的主权国家就不可能通过它们之间的协议而产生，因为"协议不是主权的起点，没有主权能从协议中产生"⑦。

---

① Brownson, *Amercian Republic*, 221 页。
② Hurd, *Theory of Our National Existence*, 141 页。
③ Brownson, *Amercian Republic*, 194 页。
④ Brownson, *Amercian Republic*, 194 页。"产物没有从创造者那里夺走什么，没有耗尽创造者的创造能量，它只是通过固定地和持续地运行创造者的创造力量，而让自身持续存在。"
⑤ Brownson, *Amercian Republic*, 196 页。
⑥ Brownson, *Amercian Republic*, 196 页。
⑦ Brownson, *Amercian Republic*, 200 页。

但是并非如此,因为这与历史事实并不一致。州并没有各自的主权。在《独立宣言》之前,它们在大英帝国的主权之下,之后,它们仅仅作为合众国而存在和行动。在《独立宣言》中,它们宣称是独立的国家是真实的,但它们是共同的独立,而不是各自的独立。"它们联合在一起宣布独立,它们为独立而从事战争,也就是说,它们被外部力量和母国看作是'联邦'国家,而不是各自独立的拥有主权的国家。"① "当它们宣战并赢得独立的时候,它们只能作为联合州(states united)或合众国(United States)执行它们的主权。"②

毫无疑问,还有一种可能性,那就是大英帝国把主权各自地、分散地传给每一个州,则每一个州都会变成一个明显的主权国家。但是大英帝国并没有这样做。

那些博学的辩护者所争论的整个问题,就是一个事实问题。"由主权由谁来承担它、实施它和已经继续实施它的事实来决定。毫无疑问,主权事实上由合众国来承担和实施,是合众国,从来不是州。事实是,以前在大英帝国独立的主权,已经传递给了合众国,在合众国那里重现了它的所有生机,大英帝国的唯一继承者是合众国,这已经为文明世界所承认。"③

因此,在这种情况下,没有什么法律问题和先前权利问题。诉诸联邦宪法的术语(language)和条款(provision)是无用的。④ 宪法只能由主权者产生,它是适合一个州所有公民的法律,只要这个州还是合众国的一个州。⑤

5. 选民主权论

选民主权论由奥斯丁提出。我们对于他的科学、经典的主权定义已经很熟悉。⑥ 这是他整个学说的核心和中心点。但是当这个定义应用到联邦中的时候,或者是他喜欢称做的最高权力的联邦的时候,问题马上就出现了。他对这个事实绝不是没有注意到。因此他说,在一个政治社会里如此多的个人和团体分享着它所构建的复合主权,以至于选民作为主权者并不显著,不容易被发现。⑦

在他所能认识到的范围内,中央政府、州都不能称为主权者。如果联邦政府

---

① Brownson, *Amercian Republic*, 209 页。

② Brownson, *Amercian Republic*, 210 页。

③ Brownson, *Amercian Republic*, 212～213 页。"被称为'合众'的国家不是邦联国家,甚至在《邦联条例》那里也是这样。正式地讲,合众国被称为'联邦'。" Brownson, *Amercian Republic*, 215 页。

④ Brownson, *Amercian Republic*, 198 页。

⑤ Brownson, *Amercian Republic*, 198 页。相关合众国主权论,还可以比较 N. C. Butler 在 *Amercian Law Review*(1905,第 39 卷)上的"Sovereignty in Modern State",以及 J. Bigelow, *World Peace*, 221 页。Fang Yue Ting vs. U. S. 149、U. S. 698、711。排华案,130, U. S. 581, 604。

⑥ "如果一个确定的人类优胜者不习惯性地服从于一个类似的优胜者,而得到社会大多数的服从,则这个确定的优胜者就是社会的主权者,这个社会就是一个政治社会且是独立的。"参见奥斯丁的 *Jurisprudence*, 第 1 卷, 226 页。

⑦ *Jurisprudence*, 第 1 卷, 257 页。

或者州政府二者中的任意一个是主权者,它就不能称之为联邦。① "联邦政府的政治权力,"他说,"只是由几个联合起来的政府委任给它的。它不是主权者的一员,而仅仅是主权的管理者。"②

虽然政治权力来源于州政府,但州政府并不是单独的和分裂的主权者,因为正如他指出,如果州政府是单独的主权者,则它们所组成的就是一个同盟,而不是一个联邦国家。③

在奥斯丁的观念里,联邦与同盟之间有一个清楚的区别,联邦是一个独立的政治实体,同盟则仅仅是由两个或更多的主权国家组成的一个稳定的联合。④ 在联邦中,州不是单独的主权者。在奥斯丁看来,它们只是在组成联邦之前,在特征上和联盟的成员一样,是主权者。

一个国家必须有一个主权,这个主权一定有所归宿。在一个联邦国家也是如此。这是奥斯丁牢牢遵循的一个思想主线。在联邦国家中有一个主权。但主权在哪里?他说:"我相信,每一个州的主权都产生于联邦中,而为州政府所有,这些州政府组成一个联合体;在这里说州政府,不是指它是一个一般的立法机构,而是指它是任命立法机构的公民的代表,而联邦的主权就存在于这些公民之中。"⑤

"任命一般立法机构的市民组织就是选民,也就是主权的所在。"毫无疑问,奥斯丁认识到州立法机构的法律权限,联邦国会的法律权限以及这二者联合的法律权限,是受成文宪法的限制的。由于这跟英国的现实是不同的,于是只好把主权放在选民那里。⑥

6. 主权作为制宪权

主权作为制定宪法的权力的理论被一位美国学者作如下概括:"一个国家的基本原则是它的宪法。这个原则的集合体产生政府,划定它的权力,调节国家与公民之间的关系。政府在权力方面要受到宪法的限制,因此在权威方面,就要比制定或改变宪法的组织要低。没有比制定宪法的组织更高的权威组织了。这个权威组织表达国家的直接意愿,因此是国家的主权者。"⑦

这个学派的理论的最好的解释者或许是英国的戴雪(Dicey)教授。考虑到

---

① *Jurisprudence*, 258~260 页。
② *Jurisprudence*, 258~260 页。
③ *Jurisprudence*, 第 1 卷, 257 页、259 页。
④ *Jurisprudence*, 257 页。
⑤ *Jurisprudence*, 261 页。
⑥ Willoughby, *Nature of the State*, 296 页。Ritchie 教授指出把主权放在选民那里,奥斯丁已经不能被看作是一个法学家了。参见 *Annals of American Academy of Political and Social Science*(1891 年 1 月), 第 1 卷, 1392 页。也可参见 Dicey, *Law of Consititution*, 68 页、73 页、424~425 页。
⑦ Gettell, *Introduction to Palitical Science*, 1910, 101~102 页。也可参见 Foster, *On the Constitution*, 1895, 270 页;或在 1886 年 *American Law Review* 上的名为 "The Subjection of the State to Law" 的文章。

他自己国家的全能的议会，戴雪教授很自然会认为主权在议会那里。但是，美国与英国在政治结构方面是有不同之处的。在美国，依据宪法，主权并不授予立法机构，主权授予立法机构与联邦主义的宗旨是不一致的，联邦主义对国家政府与州政府之间有一个永久的区分。① 如果容许联邦的国会，或者是一个州的立法机构合法地改变联邦宪法的话，美国会成为一个单一制的共和国而不是一个联邦国家。

但是，在一个联邦国家内必须有一个且只有一个主权，且必须有一个主权所在的地方。戴雪教授说："一个人也许会说，美国的立法主权在于由各州政府组成的联合政府，在任何时候只要四分之三的州同意，就适用于整个联邦。"②

必须记住，当戴雪说主权作为制定宪法的权力的时候，他是作为一个立法者来说的，因为在他看来，在立法主权之外，还有一个政治主权，立法主权和政治主权的归宿不一定是相同的。但是归宿的不同并不意味着它们是相冲突的，因为它们必须相互协调一致。"立法机构不同部门的行为必须保证立法主权的行动和政治主权的愿望之间的协调一致，必须尽可能地体现总体关切。"③ 当然也不是说它们之间没有冲突的可能性，因为在有些时候它们之间确实有冲突，如果它们之间有冲突，政治主权必须优先于立法主权，因为后者"在任何方面都可能受普遍阻力的限制"④。

里柯克（Leacock）教授可以看作是这个理论的积极拥护者。他认为"联邦的产生完全废止了所有组成国家的主权，不是限制，也不是分离，而是废止"⑤。不仅仅是州因为融入一个联邦而失去了主权，而不再是一个主权者，中央政府也不是一个主权者。主权只能在修订宪法的组织那里才能找到，无论这个组织在哪里，是什么。⑥

该学派的一些显赫者承认他们所设想的主权在特征上是不稳定的，就像威尔逊所说的那样，是"日常行使权"；不过，其中的一个学者说道："很明显从理论上来说，它是绝对存在的，并且被认为具有和英国议会一样完整的至高无上的法

---

① Dicey, *Law of Consititution*，第 8 版，144 页，1885。
② Dicey, *Law of Consititution*，第 8 版，144～145 页。在这里，Dicey 接着引用了美国宪法的第五条："国会在两院各有三分之二议员认为必要时，应提出本宪法的修正案；又如有各州三分之二州议会提出请求，亦应召开制宪会议提出修正案。不论哪种方式提出的修正案，经各州四分之三州议会或四分之三州制宪会议的批准，即实际成为本宪法之一部分而发生效力；具体采用这两种批准方式中的哪一种，须由国会提出建议。"也可参考瑞士宪法的修正条款。
③ Dicey, *Law of Consititution*，第 8 版，425 页。
④ Dicey, *Law of Consititution*，70 页，1885。根据 Dicey，这种限制来自两个方面，一是内部的，一是外部的，参见 74 页、77 页。
⑤ Leacock, *Elements of Political Science*，第 2 版，240 页，1913。
⑥ Leacock, *Elements of Political Science*，第 2 版，240～241 页。

定权力。"①

7. 主权作为制定法律的权力

由于认为主权不能被看做是潜在的原因,"主权是一个事实问题,是关于表达国家当下意志的机构,而不是关于权威的最初的革命性的来源。"② 由此不满意主权作为制定宪法的权力的理论,另外一种可以称做主权作为制定法律的权力理论被构思出来。这种理论,同主权作为宪法制定者的权力的理论一样,在特征上纯粹是法律性的,其拥护者也是从法学家的角度来看问题的。

在这派理论的所有学者中,韦罗贝教授一定是最出色的。③ 对于主权的本质,韦罗贝不像奥斯丁一样仅仅是一个辩护士。对于主权的归宿,他的观点也同奥斯丁不同。④ 他认为,主权"是一个国家生命中的关键原则,所有法律的效力要依靠它,所有国际关系要由它决定。""在一般意义上,"他继续说,"简单地说,主权这个词意味着国家的最高权力,占有(掌握)这个权力的一个人或许多人就是主权者。"⑤

在持有主权是只能通过现存的政府机构来实施的一种权力的观点的基础上,他进一步指出这种最高权力伴随着国家的意志的表达。⑥ 因为国家的意志的表达,只能通过法律制定机构,后者必须被看作是国家的主权。"不管通过任何人或任何主体,只要国家的意志得到表达,法律得到制定,主权也就得到了行使。"⑦

然而,立法机构,不是在狭义下的立法机构,而是适用于形式法律的制定机构,这些机构包括:①国家、共和国或地方的立法机关;②法院,它们不仅仅解释和应用法律,它们也制定法律;③行政机关,它们一般通过法令、文告等制定法律;④全国代表大会,在宪法会议召开的情况下,它合法地扮演法律制定者的角色;⑤全民公决(referendum)和人民自决主权公投(plebiscite)时的选民。⑧

---

① Munro, *The Government of the United States*, 66 页、250 页, 1925。Munro 教授也是既否认联邦主权论,也反对州主权论,他在宪法的范围内找到了主权。在美国能修改宪法的权力或者说权威只有绝对的主权。Lansing 也持类似的观点,不过是从更狭窄的意义上。在他谈到美国的主权及其位置的时候,他说:"在国内和平时期,(主权)存在于那些能制定并修改宪法的法人的手里。他们是一些由个人组成的政治团体,每个这样的团体而不是个人组成了合众国的一个州。"见 "Note on Sovereignty", *American Journal of International Law*, 第一卷, 126 页。
也见, M. Bernard 的 *Neutrality of Great Britain during the American War*, 43 页。"在联邦政府和地方政府的背后都有一种错综复杂的力量,这种力量很难通过动议来确立。因为动议需要在立法会上或者在本身能修宪的大会上由四分之三的州同意。这个权力是不受限制的,或者说几乎是不受限制的。"
② Gettell, *Introduction to Political Science*, 102 页、103 页。
③ Gettell 也是这派理论的支持者之一。
④ Willoughby, *Nature of the State*, 182~183 页, 1896。
⑤ Willoughby, *Nature of the State*, 185 页。
⑥ Willoughby, *Nature of the State*, 185 页。
⑦ Willoughby, *Nature of the State*, 302 页, 1896。
⑧ Willoughby, *Nature of the State*, 303 页。也可参见 Gettell, *Introduction to Political Science*, 103 页。

第三章　联邦国家中的主权（续）

8. 主权可分论

我们已经对应用于联邦国家的九种主权理论进行了总体上的讨论。我们也已经指出头两种主权理论是相对立的，后七种主权理论则是头两种主权理论的复合体的不同表现形式。现在让我们来讨论最后一种主权理论，它也是复合理论。这最后一种主权理论，也就是主权可分论，虽然在形式上与其他七种复合理论相似，但在本质上却绝不相同。在这里，我们可以发现在我们已经讨论的九种主权理论的基本相似之处，也可以发现在这九种主权理论和最后一种主权理论之间的基本不同之处。虽然在诸如州主权论和联邦政府主权论之间有不同，甚或冲突的地方，但是它们的拥护者都一致赞同，主权，在本质上，是不可分的。这可以说是我们研究的联邦国家的主权理论的主题。包括旧的和新的理论，有一种一元主义理论，也有一种多元主义理论。在这里，我们发现了传统理论的综合性、复杂性和多样性，也是在这里，我们发现了现代理论的开端与发展。①

（1）德国学者

许多德国公法学家拥护主权可分论。其中魏茨（Waitz），是最为引人瞩目的代表之一。他受著名的法国学者托克维尔的影响，托克维尔的主权理论在《论美国的民主》一书中体现出来，我们稍后要对其进行一些讨论。

魏茨强烈反对把主权看作是一个国家中最高的权力，因而反对不论是在范围上还是在目的上主权都是不可分的看法。他相信主权在范围内受到限制，但在内容上不受到限制。②"看来应当以定性的方式而不是定量的方式来考察主权。问题不在于权力的范围有多大，而在于如果这一权力是最高的，它在特定的范围内以什么方式行使。至高无上并不需要非常宽泛，但必须非常集中。"③

魏茨认为独立与主权是一码事。④哪里有独立，哪里就有主权。州在某种程

---

① Grotius 曾指出主权是可分的；但是这一点并没有为他的继承者所发展，也没有引起他的反对者的注意。

② Georg Waitz, *Grundzuge der Politik*, 166 页, 1862。

③ Merriam, *History of Theory of Sovereignty*, 186 页, 1900。

④ Georg Waitz, *Grundzuge der Politik*, 44 页, 1862。也见 K. Gareis, *Volkerrecht*, 第 2 版, 48 页、95 页。也见他的 *Allgemeine Staatrecht*, 第 1 卷, 第 65 节。

另一方面，Halleck 在"主权"和"独立"二者之间进行了区分，并且认为一个国家可以没有独立而拥有主权。*International Law*, 第 1 卷, 71 页、72 页。

度上有它们的独立性,则相应地成为某种主权者。分离主权,不像卡尔霍恩所说的等于破坏主权。将这种理论应用到德国,他认为主权确实可以在联邦和成员州之间分离,在它们各自的范围内,它们都是主权者。"同盟和州的权力,在它们各自的范围内都是独立的;二者都不需要对方授予的权力。"① 用邓宁教授的话说,"主权在这里是作为扩展到所有可以被想象到的主体事物之上的权威。"②

在联邦国家(Bundesstaat)里,这种主权的分离在理论上和在现实上都是必须的,从这里他区分了单一国家(unitary state, Einheitsstaat)和联邦国家(federal state)。单一国家就是一个单一政府实施一个国家在每一个领域都需要的所有的权力的国家;但是联邦国家是一个权力通过两套政府系统实施的国家。③

伯伦知理(Bluntschli)是另一个认为主权在联邦国家可以分离的德国学者。④ 按他的说法,主权首先意指独立于任何其他国家的权威;第二,公共的威严,罗马人称之为最高权力(majestas);第三,作为反对特殊权力的充裕的公共权力;第四,它在国家中居最高地位;最后,它是一体的,这对每个有机组织都是必须的。⑤

在一个单一国家里,构成主权的所有要素是一体的,主权是统一的,是不能分离的。但是在复合国家(他分为四种,有殖民地或隶属国的国家、在人员上联合的国家、同盟和联邦⑥),主权的要素或特质是可以分离的,因此主权可以在联邦和组成联邦的州之间分离。独立、威严、统一只能被相对地理解。⑦ 在一个联邦国家和联邦帝国,有独立的部分,也有不独立的部分,但独立与不独立都不是绝对的;⑧ 有作为一个整体的国家,同时,作为其部分的州的人民也拥有组织机

---

① 参见 Bluntschli, *Theory of the State*, 488 页脚注, 1892。

② Dunning, *Political Theories*, 第三卷, 284 页。

③ Georg Waitz, *Grundzuge der Politik*, 1862, 163 页。对 Waitz 的理论的进一步讨论,参见 Brie, *Der Bundesstaat*, 105~118 页。

Zacharia, 在其早期观点中, 他还坚持中央政府单独拥有主权的观点; 但是在经历联邦改革(Bundesreformversuche)和积极参与国家大会之后, 他改变了其观点并赞同 Waitz 的观点了。他论及主权的主观方面和客观方面。一方面, 主权的主观方面, 是联邦与各州分享的, 在其自身的范围内是唯一的、独立的和最高的, 而且趋向于在各州之上而成为真正的主权。另一方面, 主权的客观方面, 同在邦联中一样, 在联邦中, 各州的特殊事务导致了联邦事务的分类, 在属于它们的事务中, 州的权力要更高。*Deuisches Staats und Bundesrecht*, 第 21、27 节, 1841。参见瑞士学者 H. Escher 的奇特观点: *Handbuch der praktischen politik*, 第二卷, 481 页、553 页, 1864。

④ 参见第 2 章。

⑤ Bluntschli, *Theory of the State*, 595 页, 1892。

⑥ Bluntschli, *Theory of the State*, 486 页。

⑦ Bluntschli, *Theory of the State*, 495 页。

⑧ "主权既不意味着绝对的独立, 也不意味着绝对的自由, 因为政府不是绝对的存在物。但是人的权利是被限定的。"(原文为法文——译者注) *Droit International Codifie*, 由 Bluntschli 编著, 由 M. C. Lardy 从德文翻译过来, 88 页, 1886。

构。① "因此，合众国有主权，宾夕法尼亚和弗吉尼亚也有主权；瑞士有主权，伯尼尔和日内瓦也有主权；德国有主权，普鲁士、萨克逊、巴伐利亚也有主权，等等。一个复合国（collective state）在行动上和一个单一国（simple state）在行动上一样自由。但是，州绝不是隶属物，在其范围内它同单一国家一样独立。"②

伯伦知理像魏茨一样坚持认为主权在范围上可以受到限制，但在内容上不受限制。③ 成员国家，在组成一个联邦的时候，可以将一部分主权委托给联邦，但是保留的部分和它所放弃的部分一样真实地存在着。一个国家的臣属与隶属完全不会毁坏它的主权。④ "因此，在瑞士，州的主权和联邦主权不同；同样，在北美和在德国，在联邦或帝国的主权与各州之间的主权也不同。"⑤

那些持君主主权论的人已经习惯于宣称按照《帝国宪法》（Imperial Consititution）第78条，赋予德皇在与州意志相反的情况下，不受限制地扩展其权限的权力。⑥ 这个判断，正如波伦哈克（Conrad Bornhak）已经指出的，起码在考虑到普鲁士的时候，是不正确的，因为它在联邦参议院中有十七票表决权，可以表决会议中的所有提案。⑦

在德国，皇帝和州都不是绝对的主权者，如波伦哈克所坚持的，但两者在某种意义上都是主权者。主权，按他的说法，有肯定的和否定的意义。⑧ 在外延方面，它是肯定的；在内涵方面，它是否定的。在否定的意义上，在其有效范围内它对于其他权威是完全独立的，它是通过州实施的主权；在肯定的意义上，州有

---

① *Droit International Codifie*，由 Bluntschli 编著，由 M. C. Lardy 从德文翻译过来，488 页。

② "主权既不意味着绝对的独立，也不意味着绝对的自由，因为政府不是绝对的存在物。但是人的权利是被限定的。"（原文为法文——译者注）*Droit International Codifie*，由 Bluntschli 编著，由 M. C. Lardy 从德文翻译过来，88 页，1886。

③ *Droit International Codifie*，由 Bluntschli 编著，由 M. C. Lardy 从德文翻译过来，526 页。

④ *Droit International Codifie*，由 Bluntschli 编著，由 M. C. Lardy 从德文翻译过来，526 页。

⑤ Bluntschli, *Theory of the State*，1892。也可参见 *Das Moderne Volkerrecht der civilisirtenals Rechtsbuch Dargestellt*，90～91 页，第70节，1872。"一般来说，在一个特定的民族或一片特定的土地上只有一个主权，正如单一制国家。但也有例外的情况，即在一个特定的民族或一片特定的土地上有两个主权，如复合制国家，其中一个是邦联的主权，而另一个是成员国家的主权。"

"与此相对，联邦是联盟的一种统一形式，它与邦联有很大的不同，它完全是以一个国家的形式进行组织的。这种形式首先出现在由 Alexander Hamilton 所构想的现代国家形式中，他从1787年起在北美进行实验。1848年，这种形式在瑞士也被模仿过。"（原文为德文——译者注）对 Bluntschli 来说，日耳曼帝国有一种特殊的特点，最好称之为"联邦帝国（Bundesreich）"。参见 *Volkerrecht*，90 页。

⑥ Conrad Bornhak，*Preussische Staatsrecht*，第1卷，71 页，1888。也可参见 Hanel，*Aehnlich*，*Studien zun deutschen staatsrechte*，第1卷，第240节，1873—1880。

⑦ 1871年的《帝国宪法》。

⑧ Conrad Bornhak，*Preussische Staatsrecht*，第1卷，69 页以下。

权派出代表。①

甚至像特赖齐克（Treitschke），坚持认为所有成员国的主权都被皇帝的主权所吞并，也被迫承认普鲁士仍然保存着它的主权。在日耳曼帝国中存在两个主权的看法也就意味着他承认了主权可分论。"如果普鲁士不是一个主权国家了，将会导致什么情况？"他问道，"可能日耳曼帝国就不能继续存在。大多数人民可能对这一事实不乐意，但是这也并不是对非普鲁士人民的侮辱——也就是说，在日耳曼帝国，普鲁士是在前拥有它的主权的。"② 他继续说："普鲁士也是唯一一个能从对其主权的限制中摆脱出来的日耳曼国家。"这可以从普鲁士在联邦议会中拥有 17 席得到证明，17 票已经足以"阻止对其最高权力的削弱"③。

（2）瑞士学者

因为他们自己的国家在形式上是联邦的，瑞士学者之间有不同的观点。持州主权论的人以联邦宪法条款作为他们讨论的基础④，持联邦政府主权论的人则以联邦政府，特别是立法机构实施广泛的权威为基础。⑤ 作为这两种理论的综合，也有一些学者采用主权可分论。在这一组学者中，鲁提曼（Ruttiman）是其中最为引人注目的一个代表。⑥

---

① Conrad Bornhak, *Preussische Staatsrecht*, 第 1 卷, 73 页。"如果要问如何区分范围与内容的话，可以这样回答：范围指的是主权概念的积极表达，指国家最高权力的全部；内容则是主权概念的消极表达，指的是不受制于强制性权力的自由。"

"因此，尽管有一定的限制，但是德意志邦国们在其独自的领域，在国家性行为之外享有完全的独立性，不受制于最高权力，也就是负面意义上的主权。"（原文为德文——译者注）

② Treitschke, *Politics*, 第 2 卷, 373 页。

③ Treitschke, *Politics*, 第 2 卷, 374 页。17 票即可否决议案——译者注。

主权可分论也被 Robert von Mohl 在他的 *Encyklopadie der Staatswissenschaften* 中阐明, 1858 年版, 36~38 页, 96~97 页, 1872 年, 第二版, 第 49 节, 366~367 页。"国家强制性权力是受限制的，这是根本的、必要的。因为该目标的重要一点就是要留给联邦成员以自主权力。也就是一种双重领导和命令下的权力：即在整个联邦内有威慑力的中央权力和不同成员国及其中一些特殊区域的地方性权力。"（原文为德文——译者注）同上。

也可参见 Mohl, *Geschich und Literur der Staatswissenschaften*, 第一卷, 511~513 页, 515~517 页, 560 页。在 *Deusche Staatsrecht* 的导言中，Schulze 采用了同 Waitz 同样的立场，甚至用语都一样。参见 Bre, *Der Bundesstaate*, 121 页。Schulze, *System des Deutchen Staatsrechts*, 206~207 节, 1865。

Blumer, *Handbuch des Schweitzerischen Bundestaatsrechtes*, 141~147 页, 1863。

H. Ahrens, *Naturrecht, Oder Philosophie des Rechts und des Staate*, 第二卷, 338~346 页, 1870 年, 第 6 版。也同意同 Gareis 的 *Volkerrecht*（48 页, 1901 年, 第 2 版）和 *Allegemeine Staatsrecht*（第一卷, 第 65 节）进行比较。

Von Adolf Arendt, *Das Staatsrecht des deutschen Reichs*, 38 页以下, 1901。

④ 1848 年宪法第三章及 1874 年宪法第四章。

⑤ 除了合众国会给予的权力外，给予联邦立法机构的权力还可见宪法 24、25、26、32、34、37、43、49~57、64、69 等章。参见 Dupriez, *Les Ministres dans les principaux pays d'Europe et d'Amerique*, 第二卷, 175 页。

⑥ Brie 认为 Ruttiman 是关于瑞士和美国联邦领城最好的学者。见 Brie, *Der Bundesstaat*, 121 页。

鲁提曼强烈反对卡尔霍恩及其追随者的观点①，他认为每一个国家通过将其自身加入联邦而放弃了它的部分主权，既然它放弃了部分主权，联邦就开始成为一个独立的生命，从州中完全独立起来。

在否认了联邦不是主权者，州才是主权者的观点之后，他进一步地对主权是不可分的观点提出疑义，因为根据他的看法，这跟事实是不相符的。② 主权在其本质上是可以分离的，在一个联邦政府内，它可以在联邦政府和州之间分离。"每一个部分都是最高的，"他说，"在它自己的范围内是自由的，如同其他部分不存在一样。"③ 在这里鲁提曼与一些德国和法国的学者的意见较为一致。主权可分，在他看来，是联邦国家的一个特征。州绝对不是联邦政府的附庸或隶属物，它们是彼此平等的。他指出："在许多方面没有人否认州是主权者，然而也没有人坚持认为它们在所有的领域都是主权者。"④ 主权可分是非常清楚的，因为联邦政府的主权是针对一般性的事务，而州的主权是针对地方性的事务。

当代的一些政治家，像伯杰尔（M. Banjour）在结论上同意鲁提曼的观点，虽然他们的观点来自于不同的理论根基。伯杰尔提出了这样一个问题，无论主权这个词可否应用到州自治上，无论瑞士存在两个最高权力或只有一个主权。⑤ 在他看来，主权不可分是没有任何理由的。⑥ 他说："在特定的范围内，根据宪法，联邦和州都是主权者。"⑦

（3）荷兰学者

荷兰的政治学家，像福格森（J. R. Ferguson）也坚持主权可分论。像其他政治学家和国际法学家一样，福格森也是在两个方面考察主权：内部的和外部的。对内的主权是一种在遵从国家宪法的原则下，来实现政府的目的和对内政策的一种权力；对外主权是在与其他国家独立与平等的原则下采取的平衡对外关系的行动，是国际法的主体。⑧

作为一个国际法学家，福格森倾向于把"主权"这个词应用到国家的对外关系中。为了在我们的观念中有一个清楚的区别，他建议用"自治"这个词来代替

---

① Ruttiman, *Das Nordamerikanische Bundesstaat verglichen mitden politischen Einriehtungen der Schweiz*, 第1卷, 70页, 1867—1782。

② Ruttiman, *Das Nordamerikanische Bundesstaat verglichen mitden politischen Einriehtungen der Schweiz*, 第1卷, 66页、71页。

③ Ruttiman, *Das Nordamerikanische Bundesstaat verglichen mitden politischen Einriehtungen der Schweiz*, 第1卷, 48页。

④ Ruttiman, *Das Nordamerikanische Bundesstaat verglichen mitden politischen Einriehtungen der Schweiz*, 第1卷, 54页。

⑤ Banjour, *Real Democracy in Operation*, 3页。

⑥ Banjour, *Real Democracy in Operation*, 3页。

⑦ Banjour, *Real Democracy in Operation*, 3页。不过 Banjour 认为州的主权现在正在消失。

⑧ J. R. Ferguson, *Manual of International Law*, 第一卷, 81页, 1883。

国家的对内主权。① 但是必须记住使用两个不同的词语并不意味着主权的两个方面是两种不同种类的东西。

根据福格森的看法，主权由政府所代表。但是，一个特定政府的缺失或无政府状态，并不导致一个国家没有主权。一个政府没有被其他的国家所认同的时候，也是如此。②

总体上说，我们在上面所谈的只是他的主权理论的一个简要说明。再让我们回到这种理论在联邦国家中的应用。当单一的作为主权者的国家组成一个联邦和同盟的时候，他说，"对于外部的主权就由所有的成员国家授予中央政府，以代表全体去和联邦外的国家打交道，与此同时，联邦下的成员国家的对内主权也要发生变更，以便和契约的观念和条件相一致"③。

很显然，在联邦国家内，主权可以分为对内的和对外的两个方面。在有的时候，主权的某一方面可以被一个政府实施，另外的部分可以被另一个政府实施。主权存在分离的可能性，也存在增加和消失的可能性。④

（4）法国学者

法国从来就不是联邦国家。但是在法国却产生了一位最伟大的论述联邦国家的学者，他被称为欧洲大陆的主权可分论之父，他不是别人，就是托克维尔。对他来说，主权被定义为制定法律的权利。⑤ 在法国，他发现制定法律的权利集中在某个机构⑥，因而主权是单一的、不可分的。但是美国却不是这种情况，他说："不错，按1789年通过的宪法建立的联邦，只享有有限的主权，但宪法又欲使联邦在这个范围内成为一个单一制的统一国家。即主张在这个范围内，它是一个主权国家。这一点一经提出和得到同意，其余问题就迎刃而解了，因为如果承认美国是由宪法规定的拥有主权的国家，就得给它以一切国家所具有的权利。"⑦

在这种情况下，联邦国家必须被看成是一个主权者。另一方面，由于建立了联邦的最高法院，州的主权似乎遭到了严重的削弱，然而这种危险事实上要小得多。⑧

---

① J. R. Ferguson, *Manual of International Law*, 第一卷, 81页, 1883。

② J. R. Ferguson, *Manual of International Law*, 第一卷, 81～82页, 1883。

③ J. R. Ferguson, *Manual of International Law*, 第一卷, 87页, 1883。Ferguson 也指出了联邦国家与邦联国家之间的不同。

④ 一般来说，大部分学者把日耳曼帝国、瑞士和美国作为联盟国家的例子。J. Ferguson 有所不同，他把瑞士和日耳曼帝国作为一组，看作邦联国家。而美国、委内瑞拉、哥伦比亚等被看作联邦国家。参见 Ferguson, *Manual of International Law*, 第一卷, 87页注释, 1883。

⑤ De Tocqueville, *Democracy in American*, Henry Reeve 翻译, 第1卷, 122页。

⑥ 他认为国王是法国的主权者。De Tocqueville, *Democracy in American*, Henry Reeve 翻译, 第1卷, 122页。

⑦ De Tocqueville, *Democracy in American*, Henry Reeve 翻译, 第1卷, 144页。

⑧ De Tocqueville, *Democracy in American*, Henry Reeve 翻译, 第1卷, 142页, 146页。

在关于法律的执行、与外国的关系上,联邦是主权者;而在关于国内事务的管理方面,州是主权者。① "在1789年,立法者们的主要目的,是把主权分成两个不同的部分。让其一掌管联邦的一切共同利益,让其一掌管各州的一切自身利益。"② 联邦的主权与州的主权之间的不同在如下的表述中得到了更为清楚的说明:"联邦的主权是抽象的,它很少与现实联系在一起,但州的主权是能够随时地感受到的③,不难理解,它还是持续保持活力的。如果说前者是最近的产物,那么后者本身就是始终和人民处于同时代的。联邦的主权是随着概念的划分而产生的,而州的主权却是直接通过它的影响力来证明自己的存在的,就像家长的权威一样。"

　　就理论上说,联邦主权和州主权的区别是很清楚的,但是,在它们之间划一条明显的界线是很困难的。第一,在应用方面,因为"联邦主权与州主权纠缠在一起,因此很难划清它们的界线"④。第二,很难知道哪些事务由州来处理,哪些事务由联邦来处理。⑤ 前者的解决办法依赖于长期习惯于其自身事务的人民和政治学,而且已经延伸至社会最底层的社会。⑥ 后者的解决办法依赖于联邦法院决定司法权的方式,因为随着联邦主权的扩大或减少,联邦法院的司法权也以完全相同的比率扩展或缩减其限制。⑦

　　主权可分论有哪些利弊?对于这个问题,根据托克维尔的看法,只有在特定的条件下才能回答。也就是说,对于能够很好地持续控制他们自己的事务的人民就是有利的,反之就是不利的。这样主权可分论在美国就很有利,而在墨西哥,则使她成为无政府的牺牲品和军事独裁主义的奴隶。⑧

　　它是有利的,乃是因为:第一,"它能使联邦中的成员得到健康的发展,这些社区从来就不会被欲望的扩张和自我防卫的事情所扰乱,所有的公共权威和私人力量都用于内部的改进。"⑨ 第二,由于联邦的主权是有限制的和不完整的,自由可以得到保证。

　　它是不利的,乃是因为:第一,"两个主权的存在都是必要的,立法者可以通过把它们限定在一定的权威范围内而将两个主权的行动简化和平等化,但是他不

---

① De Tocqueville, *Democracy in American*, Henry Reeve 翻译,第1卷,149页。
② De Tocqueville, *Democracy in American*, Henry Reeve 翻译,第1卷,145页。
③ 1926年5月15日柯立芝(Coolidge)总统在弗吉尼亚州威廉姆斯堡的威廉姆和玛丽学院发表的演说中也表达了这个观点。"如果联邦政府不存在了,人们在很长时间内也不会感觉到日常生活有什么不同,但是如果州政府消失了,社会马上就会陷入混乱。"参见 Boston Univ, Law *Review*,第7期,36页。
④ De Tocqueville, *Democracy in American*, Henry Reeve 翻译,第1卷,145页。
⑤ De Tocqueville, *Democracy in American*, Henry Reeve 翻译,第1卷,144页。
⑥ De Tocqueville, *Democracy in American*, Henry Reeve 翻译,第1卷,166页。
⑦ De Tocqueville, *Democracy in American*, Henry Reeve 翻译,第1卷,144页。
⑧ De Tocqueville, *Democracy in American*, Henry Reeve 翻译,第1卷,166页。
⑨ De Tocqueville, *Democracy in American*, Henry Reeve 翻译,第1卷,165页。

能将二者合为一个，不能阻止它们在某些点上发生冲突。"① 第二，因为被分了一部分主权，因此就没有一个完全的主权那么有权力，因此也成为联邦政府相对的弱点。不仅仅联邦系统是不充分的，因为它的权力没有集中，而且中央政府的组织也不完善，这是这个理论的第三个不足之处。

但是，托克维尔不是唯一支持这种理论的法国学者。法理学领域的杰出人物狄骥（Duguit），也支持这种理论。②

联邦主义在新大陆被普遍接受。③ 在欧洲，瑞士和德意志帝国已经是联邦国家，而且可以确定的是这个体系注定还要扩大。④ 这样，同一个国家的人民同时服从联邦和州的权力。只要一个国家内存在两个州，其中任何一个就不再是最高权威。既然这些公共权力是同一个国家内部的权力，并且它们是相互制约的，它们就没有权力发布绝对的命令。⑤

因此，主权并非总是国家的单一不可分的意志。⑥ 宣称联邦国家的主权是单一的和不可分的主张是"跟事实没有关联的低级辩证法"⑦。

这个观念也被法国的一些国际法学者所支持。瓦泰勒（Vattell）发现在一个联邦国家，成员州让渡一部分主权以建成一个联邦权威。⑧ 布伦塔诺（Frunck Brentano）和索雷尔（A. Sorel）也持同样的观点。⑨ 里维尔（Rivier）从对外和对内两个方面来看主权，联邦政府拥有前者，成员州拥有后者。⑩ 其他一些政治学者像布鲁纳⑪（Brunet）和富瓦涅⑫（Foignet）接受同样的主张。甚至埃斯曼（Esmein），一个狄骥的重要反对者，拒绝承认主权是可分的，但也认为在联邦国家中，主权是可分的。他这样说道："在单一国家主权是单一的。另一方面，联邦国家，虽然相当于一个真实的国家统一体，但主权是可以分离的……依照宪法将主权的一部分从成员州那里转移给联邦。"⑬

---

① De Tocqueville, *Democracy in American*, Henry Reeve 翻译，第 1 卷，165 页。

② Duguit, *L'Etat, Les Gouvernments et les Agents*, 673 页，1903。也见 *Les Transformations du droit public*, 20~21 页，1913。

③ "联邦主义"一词有广义和狭义之分，此处是在狭义的意义上使用的。

④ *Les Transformations du droit public*, 21 页。

⑤ *L'État, Les Gouvernments et les Agents*, 673 页。

⑥ *L'État, Le Droit Objectif et la Loi positif*, 324~325 页，1901。

⑦ *Les Transformations du droit public*, 25 页。也可以参见其 *Droit constitutionnel*, 第 1 卷，437 页，或 134 页、141 页。

⑧ Vattell, *Le Droit des gens*, 第 1 卷，133 页脚注。

⑨ Frunck Brentano, A. Sorel, *Precis du droit des gens*, 40~41 页。

⑩ River, *Principles du droit des gens*, 第 1 卷，104~105 页。

⑪ Rene Brunet, *The New German Consititution*, J. Gollomb 翻译，76~77 页，1922。

⑫ Foignet, *Droit international public*, 87 页，1915。

⑬ Esmein, *Droit constitutionnel*, 第 5 版，6 页。

(5) 英国学者

在海峡的彼岸，我们发现在英国也有像德国与法国的学者那样持主权可分论的学者。著名的历史学家弗里曼（Freeman）在他的著作《联邦政府的历史》一书中发展了这种理论。他认为联邦国家是一个整体，虽然保留了州的完整的内部独立，但却取消了它们在对外关系中的独立性。① 根据他的说法，主权，在事实上是分离的，联邦政府和州政府有平等的权威，在它们各自的范围内可以平等地要求人民的效忠。②

在联邦国家主权可分不仅仅是一个事实，而且，正如他已经意识到的，主权可分对一个真正的联邦国家来说必不可少。③ 联邦国家的州是且必须是主权者，因为它们"可以立法，并且可以决定自己的政治体制的细节，它们这样做并不是因为某个更高权力的恩惠或特许，而是因为它们有这样的绝对权利，这样的权利来自于它们作为一个独立的利益体的固有权力"④。

在对内主权之外，州的主权就没有了，联邦政府的主权开始了。和平与战争的决定，派出和召回大使，国际关系部门的所有事务都是交给联邦政府的权力，正是这些权力组成联邦政府的主权。⑤

联邦国家的范例，如弗里曼所指出的，在世界历史上有四到五个历史时期。它们是：①公元前281—公元前146年的亚该亚联盟（Achaean League），②1291—1862年的瑞士联邦，③荷兰的七省共和国，这个联邦从对西班牙的独立战争中兴起，一直以共和国的形式存在到法国革命战争时期（1779—1795）。④反对英王乔治三世后而形成的美国，英王乔治三世也是我们时代最重要、同时也是最有趣的一个政治问题。⑥

另外一个应当注意的英国学者是奥本海（Oppenheim）教授。"一个联邦国家，"他说，"是几个主权国家组成的联合，它有自身的组织和被授予的权力，不仅仅在成员国家之上，也在公民之上。"⑦ 他好像不赞同那些认为在联邦国家内，联邦政府的主权比成员国家的主权更为真实的国际法学家的观点。

对他来说，联邦国家中的成员国家是主权者是不容置疑的，而不管联邦国家或联邦政府是不是一个主权者。他坚持认为作为主权者的联邦与成员国家一样真实。"现在如果一个联邦国家被视为与成员国家一样的国家，很显然，主权在联邦

---

① Freeman, *History of Federal Government*, 第一卷。
② Freeman, *History of Federal Government*, 第一卷, 15页。
③ Freeman, *History of Federal Government*, 第一卷, 5页。
④ Freeman, *History of Federal Government*, 第一卷, 4~5页。
⑤ Freeman, *History of Federal Government*, 第一卷, 4~5页。
⑥ Freeman, *History of Federal Government*, 第一卷, 5页。
⑦ Oppenheim, *International Law*, 第3版, 第一卷, 157页。

和成员国家之间分享。"①

那么，主权采取一种什么方式分离？他指出，通过把成员国家的部分权威或能力转移给联邦来分离。在分离之后，双方在各自的权限内都是独立自主的。②像许多其他国际法学者一样，他认为主权可以分为对内和对外两部分。但是，他认为这两者都可以由联邦或成员国单独实施，因为事实已经表明，第一，比如在德国，联邦的成员国保留有派遣和召回外交使节的能力，不仅仅与同联邦内的其他成员国，而且与联邦之外的国家；第二，成员国家的国王被看作是主权国家的首脑；第三，它们可以没有联邦的同意而签订国际协定。

成员国家在其与联邦的关系中是最初的、真实的主权者，从国际法的观点或与外国的关系看也是部分主权国家。从这里，他进一步把联邦国家分为两类：一类是成员国家既拥有对内主权，也拥有对外主权；一类是只拥有对内主权。在前者，德国和瑞士是典型的例子，后者则以美国为典型。

布里斯爵士（Lord Bryce）持与上述学者相同的观点。在他的早期著作《美利坚合众国》中，他指出为了一定的目的，联邦政府是主权者。③ 但是联邦政府的主权并没有废止各州的主权，因为各州还拥有一大部分主权，最重要的是，拥有在联邦内免受起诉的豁免权。④ 这样，布里斯公爵士就在这样的原则上建立他的州部分主权论：除非另外的州起诉，否则如果没有其同意，它不得被起诉。既然各州有这样权利，因此它必然是主权者。

但是，主权的双重性可以从另外的角度来证明。布里斯爵士在如下的论述中阐明这一点："每一个美国人同欧洲人（除了瑞士，在某种程度上，也除了德国）一样，其生活都具有双重性。他生活在两个政府和两套法律体系下；他有两个爱国主义，要具有两种忠诚。"⑤

弗里德利希·普罗克爵士（Sir Frederick Pollock），一个著名的法理学家，也看到了英国的绝对主权论在应用到联邦国家中的困难。他不怀疑联邦政府在其范围内是一个主权者，在谈到美国、德国的州以及瑞士的州的主权的时候，他写道："在其范围内，我们不能说它没有主权，因为它知道在其能力范围内没有更高的权力，虽然我们不能像英国把主权归于议会一样归于它，既然它的主权已经被划定。"⑥

甚至像霍兰得（Holland），一个奥斯丁的忠实信徒，也不像他的老师一样把

---

① Oppenheim, *International Law*, 第3版, 第一卷, 158 页。
② Oppenheim, *International Law*, 第3版, 第一卷, 159 页。
③ Bryce, *American Commonwealth*, 第1卷, 409 页, 1890。也见 *Modern Democracies*, 第2卷, 21 页。
④ Bryce, *American Commonwealth*, 第1卷, 409 页, 1890。
⑤ Bryce, *American Commonwealth*, 第1卷, 412 页, 1890。
⑥ Pollock, *A First Book of Jurisprudence for Students of the Common Law*, 1918, 276～278 页。也可参见他在 *Fortnightly Review*（第110卷, 1918）上的文章, 813～815 页。

联邦国家的主权放置在选民那里，而是同许多国际法学者一样，认为主权可以分为对内和对外两个方面，前者归于州，后者归于联邦政府。① 其他持主权可分论的人还有贝克（S. Baker）、亚当斯（Admas）、坎宁翰（Cunningham）以及其他。②

（6）加拿大学者

联邦主义是新世界的主要产物。在这里，我们更为清楚地看到它的成长和发展；在这里，我们得到一个它的实践和经验的更为清晰的图画；在这里，我们看到了它的最为成功和失败的例子；也是在这里，我们获得了的丰富的理论特别是主权可分论。

史密斯教授，一个加拿大学者，在《北美的联邦主义》一书中对美国和加拿大的联邦主义作了一个比较研究。这两者之间的不同，他指出，可以在对主权的归宿的不同中得到理解。在美国，主权是可分的；而在加拿大，主权是不可分的。他说："在美国，两个最高权威分享政治活动的不同领域，但在加拿大只有一个主权，这个主权通过国家的或省的机构来表达。"③

他讨论的基础是认为在全美国有两个主权：一个是整个联邦的主权，一个是在其区域内成员州的主权。④ 这种观点的基础可以在以下的说明中得到："费城会议的成员面临一个建立一个新主权国家的问题。这个新的统一体只能从十三个极不情愿分离权力的州那里获得使它可以存在的必要权力。因此，制定一个新的联邦政府建立的原则申明就是必须的，第十修正案就是为了增加这个最初的文件的目的而来的。"⑤

（7）美国学者

在美国我们可以发现主权可分论的最丰硕的成果。我们也许可以怀疑这种理论的领袖麦迪逊所说的将主权可分论应用到联邦国家是美国的独创，但是我们起码得承认主权可分论是美国政治思想史上的最重要特征。这种理论被许多不同类型的人所提出、拥护、坚持，但是为了我们的目的，我们将充分论述一些代表人物的理论。

---

① Holland, *Elements of Jurisprudence*, 第12版, 50~51页。

② Baker, *Frist Steps in International Law*, 31页, 1899。Adams 和 Cunningham, *The Suiss Confederation*, 25~26页。参考 Baty, *International Law*, 332页；Phillimore, *International Law*, 第1卷, 156页。Oppenheimer 论当今德国共和国的观点见 *Consititution of the German Republic*, 37页, 1923。

③ H. A. Smith, *Federalism in North American*, 1923, 12页。

④ H. A. Smith, *Federalism in North American*, 1923, 7页。

⑤ H. A. Smith, *Federalism in North American*, 1923, 9页, 12页。他指出："另一方面，相聚于魁北克组织加拿大自治领的政治家们没有遇到类似的问题。因为对他们来说建立一个新的主权政体是没有任何问题的。那个时候的各派别都认为在英属北美的所有省和领土之上有一个完整的主权，这是大不列颠国会所授予的。"9页。"因此，加拿大的联邦主义是建立在一元论的原则之上，而与建立在二元论原则之上的联邦主义区分开来。"11页。

让我们回头看看宪法之父、早期的政治家汉密尔顿,虽然他希望建立一个中央集权的和贵族式的联邦,而且竭尽全力来扩大联邦政府的权力,但他也承认联邦和州分享主权。① 当联邦正在酝酿成立的时候,亚当斯(Samuel Adams)在一封给李(R. H. Lee)的信中,赞扬在联邦和州之间分享主权,从而使人民更容易地自治,每个州的法律能够更好地适应它们自身的特质和环境,合众国的自由也更为有保证。② 亚当斯也评论道:"政府的目的就在于分享一个主权。"③ 当杰弗逊说"州彼此之间如同与外国之间的关系一样,它们的一部分主权没有被授予,正如它们以前有完全的主权一样"④ 的时候,他不再是州绝对主权论的捍卫者了。联邦最高法院的首任大法官完全意识到这个国家主权的分离,虽然他用含糊的方式来描述它。⑤

一个主权不可分论的支持者被迫得出一个结论,是值得我们引述的:"为了反对外部侵犯,我们希望依据联邦的契约扩大联邦的主权;为了反对内部侵犯我们寻求州的主权。现在,所有的主权者都是平等的,州的主权和联邦的主权是平等的,因为每一个主权者都是一个道德人格。州的主权和联邦的主权都是一个道德人格,在这个角度上,它们是绝对平等的。"⑥

在给国会的一封信中,门罗(Monroe)总统说道:"在我们的国家有两个分离而独立的政府,一个是在每个州的人民之上的为了管理各州地方事务的政府,一个是所有联邦的人民之上的管理联邦事务的政府。人民的整个权力,根据代议

---

① "并行管辖权(concurrent jurisdiction)的必要性归因于主权可分。"参见 Ford,*Federalist*,200 页,650 页注释。也可参见 Bryce,*Studies in History and Jurisprudence*,第 2 卷,50 页。

Hamilton 不仅认为主权可以在州和联邦之间分离,甚至还倾向于认为主权在行政机关的不同部门之间分离。这种观念在以下的引言中得以揭示:"众所周知,在罗马共和国,法律权威归属于两个不同的政治实体不是同一立法机构的两个分支,而是分开而独立的两个立法机构,其中每一个都代表着不同的利益;一个代表贵族的,另一个代表平民的"。参见 Ford,*Federalist*,207 页。著名法学家 John Salmond 坚持同样的观点。他坚持认为主权在它自己的范围内是绝对的和不受控制的。他认为在英国主权分为立法、行政、司法三个部分。立法主权归属国会中的王权,行政主权归属王权"每一个最高主权都有其范围;这两个最高权威因为行政机关是立法机构的成员而避免了冲突。直到 1911 年《英国国会法案》通过,英国宪法才接受与立法主权、行政主权鼎立的司法主权。司法主权归属于作为最高终审司法机构的上议院。"见 Salmond 的 *Jurisprudence* 中的"The Theory of Sovereignty",1902 年,第一版,468 页,附录二。也可参见 B. R. Wise,*Outline of Jurisprudence*,31~32 页。

比较 W. W. Lucas 的 *The Cooperate Nature of English Sovereignty* 一书。这本书的主体可见于 MacIver 教授的如下评论:"通过这种方法达到的最后结论就是英国的主权是且一直是复合的。从法理上讲,国王从来不能单独在国家机构的任一部门采取行动,而仅仅是在与其他或多或少独立于其控制的机构联合之后才能采取行动。"*Political Science View*,1913,第 7 卷,503 页。参见 Davis,*Elements of International Law*,40~41 页。

② Samuel Adams,*Works*,第 6 卷,324~325 页。
③ John Adams,*Works*,第 9 卷,564 页。
④ 参见 Madison,*Works*,第 9 卷,352 页。
⑤ 参见 D. Webster,*Works*,第 6 卷,222 页。
⑥ 参见 Madison,*Works*,第 9 卷,572 页。

原则，是在它们之间分离的。州政府是相互独立的，它们的权力范围是具有完全主权的。联邦政府在州政府结束的地方开始……根据它的权力范围，这个政府也是具有完全主权的。"①

但是所有最为重要的，正如前文所述，是麦迪逊的成果。根据麦迪逊的看法，那些无视主权可分论的人们的困难在于，他们没有分清楚这样一个事情："所有正义和自由的政府的权力都来源于契约，当契约的各方有能力制订它的时候。"②

契约的各方，正如他所指出的，不是一个整体的联邦的人民，而是州的人民。通过州，他的意思是"人民由此相应的有了主权者的特征"③。更进一步，他是说大部分人民，而不是全部。一个特定社会里的主权，正如他所意识到的，是人民的意志，也就是说，是大多数人的意志。在这一点上，有一个问题自动出现了：根据它对社会意志的认同，这个社会的大多数人的意志能在多大程度上分离、修正社会的主权？④ 根据麦迪逊的观点，答案在两个方面：第一，"通过把社会本身分离为具有相同主权者的不同的社会。"⑤ 肯塔基从弗吉尼亚分离，梅因从马萨诸塞分离就是例子。⑥

第二，一个州分成两部分，主权可以一分为二是真实的，则两个州的主权组合成一个主权也就是真实的了。这样，主权在本质上是可以分离或组合的，只要一个社会的大多数人民想这样做的时候。

在这样的基础上，就导致"如果两个州可以通过相互完全放弃各自的主权从而联合成一个，为什么不能通过放弃部分的主权，而达成部分的联合"⑦？

两个州如此，十个、二十个甚至更多的州也是如此。⑧ 分离主权的可能性不仅在逻辑上成立，也跟事实相一致。"主权的分离在独立国家之间的条约中所包含的主权权利的交换中得到显示，在几个邦联中更是存在，更特别的是在当前的美国宪法中得到显现。"⑨

不仅仅如此。我们现在来看他的关键点。在美国的现行宪法下，"主权按其本质是可以分离的。根据最高主权者的特征，州有能力放弃它们全部的主权而组成一个联合国家，它们也可以放弃一部分，而保留另一部分，组成一个像在宪法

---

① *Writings of Monroe*，第6卷，223页。
② Madison，*Works*，第9卷，569页。也可参见383～394页，"*A Letter to Hayne*"。
③ Madison，*Works*，第9卷，352页，600～602页。
④ Madison，*Works*，第9卷，571页。
⑤ Madison，*Works*，第9卷，571页。
⑥ Madison，*Works*，第9卷，571页。
⑦ Madison，*Works*，第9卷，571页。也可参考第6卷，420～421页。
⑧ Madison，*Works*，第9卷，571～572页。
⑨ Madison，*Works*，第9卷，568～569页。

中所表明了的分离主权的混合政府"①。

在不承认主权是可分的前提下，要清楚的讨论美国政府的复合制度是很困难的。②

在美国，主权是分离的，而且必须是分离的。但是，在人民的观念中，主权可分论是美国的发明。它是在与过去其他国家不同的特殊的条件下形成的。③

另一方面，一个人不会认为世界其他地方过去没有这样的东西或没有这样的例子，因此就不能在这个国家（美国）存在。一个人也不会坚持认为这个理论是与传统理论（认为主权是唯一的）相反的，因此它是无效的。因为它是不顾事实得出的理论。"我们的政治制度，"他说，"允许成为一个新的创造个真正的'无特征的东西'，它的特征必须在它自身中寻找，不是在前辈中，因为根本就没有前辈，也不在受前辈指导的学者中寻找。"④

这种理论不仅是一种新的理论，也是一种实用的理论。这是托克维尔在他的名著中指出的，正如前文所述。它是对同盟和单一国家的缺点的补救。⑤ 一方面，主权不可分论的危险在可能导致联邦解散的事实中容易看到。"使联邦废弃的关键点是这样一种假设，主权是一个单位，既然它是不可分的和不可让渡的，因此州也就拥有它起初完全的主权，结果它就不能将其一部分主权交给联邦。"⑥

主权可分论在美国的许多法院的判决中可以看到。早在1793年，在齐舍尔蒙（Chisholm）诉佐治亚州（Georgia）案中，艾尔德尔（Iredell）法官在反对意见中说道："联邦中的每一个州在任何情况下，其主权都没有授予联邦，它同联邦一样都是主权者。联邦是所有政府权力的主权者，各州的所有权力也都保留着。这样是必须的，因为合众国仅仅宣布拥有州让与给它的权威，而没有让与的就必须如同以前那样得以保存。"⑦ 很显然，主权是政府的权力，在联邦和州之间分离，也是可以转移的。三年后，还是在同一个法院，在韦耳（Ware）诉海尔顿

---

① Madison, *Works*, 第9卷, 568~569页。
② Madison, *Works*, 第9卷, 572页。
③ Madison, *Works*, 第9卷, 551页。
④ Madison, *Works*, 第9卷, 551页。"这正是合众国政治制度的法律（dejure）与事实（defacto），然而它也可能被那些好争论的评论家们的巧妙言辞和技术所掩盖，它的真实特征要通过诉诸法律和宪法来得到支持。" Madison, *Works*, 600页。
⑤ Madison, *Works*, 第9卷, 605~606页。"那些否认像美国的政治制度中的主权可分的人，必须在纯粹联合的政府（a government purely consolidated）和纯粹的政府联盟（an association of government purely federal, 即邦联——译者注）之间选择。前者的所有共和国，无论是在古代还是近代，在应对内部秩序和正义及外部安全的时候都是没有多大效果的。它们是国内动乱和外敌入侵的牺牲品。所有的邦联，无论是在古代还是近代，也都因为缺乏凝聚力而分解，或者说近代类似的组织显得非常脆弱。出于对这些教训的警戒和自身经历的失败，美国对政体进行了修正，目标就是既避免了联合政府和邦联的缺点又得到二者的优点。"
⑥ Madison, *Works*, 第9卷, 599页。
⑦ Dallas, 419页, 435页。

(Hylton)案中，对主权做出了一个如同许多国际法学家所做的一样的区别，即对内和对外主权。前者保留在州，后者则归属于国会。① 甚至马歇尔大法官，尽他所能扩大联邦政府的权力，也在马卡洛（McCulloch）诉马里兰州（Maryland）案中强烈宣称："美国的主权在联邦政府和州政府之间分离。它们在各自的范围内是主权者。"②

许多学者坚持认为南北战争清楚地表明了联邦政府和州政府之间的主权的争论，从而肯定了主权不可分论，但是仍没有说服法院改变原来的观点。在著名的、裁定于1870年的Collector诉Day案中，已经表明两个主权可以同时存在于同一个地区。"它们是相互区别的、分散的主权，在它们各自的范围内，彼此分散地、独立地行动。"③ 同样的观点在1922年的潘慈（Panzi）诉福森登（Fessenden）案件中仍被提出。大法官塔夫脱，也向法院表达这样的观点："我们生活在两个主权的司法管辖权中，在共同的区域内，每一个都有它的自己的法院系统宣布和实施它的法律。"④

虽然在具体方面有所不同，许多宪法学者在总体原则上接受了主权可分的理论，斯托尼（Joseph Story）在两层含义上讨论主权，一是广义的，一是狭义的。从前者说，主权是"最高权力，不受控制的权力，绝对的统治权"。对于后者，则是特殊州或国家的实际组织的政治权力，"是没有最高权威控制的公共机构执行的"。在广义上讲，主权是不可分的，在狭义上讲，主权是可分的。⑤ 柯蒂斯（J. Curtis）否认在针对同一目标的时候，一个共同体中有两个最高权力，而坚持认为政治主权的本质就是防止它的权力为了不同的目的在不同的机构中被分散。⑥ 佛斯特（Foster）则说："在外部关系和同外国的关联中，联邦的主权是绝对的，除非受到宪法的限制⑦……另外，州在其领域内，对每一事和每一人都拥有

---

① Dallas，232页。
② 4 Wheaton 316，也可参见 Weston and others vs. City of Charleston 的案例，1829, 2 Peters 449。
③ 11 Wallace 113, 124。
④ 258 U. S., 254. Kohletal vs. the United States 的案例中（91 U. S. 368, 1875），法院判决道："联邦政府在其范围内是主权者，州在其范围内也是主权者。联邦的主权确实受到限制，但对臣属于它的人民来说，它是主权者。"在这个案例中，法院认为州的主权比联邦政府的主权更为真实。
在 Ex Parte Siebold 的案例中（100 U. S. 371, 1879），有这样的话："没有共同存在的主权，也就是说，联邦政府仅仅是一个建议性的政府。"还可以参见下列一些案例：Texas vs. White, 7 Wallace 700, 725 (1868); South Carolina vs. the United States 199 U. S. 437 (1905); Teen. vs. Davis 10 Otto 226; Ex parte Wells 59 U. S. 307 (1855) Progne vs. Pennsylvania. 41 U. S. (16 Peters) 539 L. ED. 1060 (1841); 5 How 504; 21 How 506; 92 U. S. 542; 13 Wallace 397; 20 Wallace 655。
⑤ *Commentaries on the Constitution of the United States*，1833，第207～208节。Pomeroy, *Constitutional Law*，26页。
⑥ Curtis, *History of Constitution*，第2卷，377页。
⑦ R. Foster, *On the Constitution*，270页，1895。

完全和完整的司法权,和主权的所有方面。"①

主权可分论在库利法官(J. Cooley)的著作里得到了更为清楚的说明。主权,在其完整的意义上被定义为"任何独立国家拥有的最高的、绝对的、不受控制的权力"②。以这个定义为出发点,他坚持认为在合众国,州被称做主权者,不是从个体特征上来说的,因为它们的行动要受到共同权威的限制。③ 这是合众国政治体系的特征。这样,他说:"在美国,宪法这一特殊系统一建立,主权的权力就加以分类,它们中有的部分归属联邦政府执行,有的则归州政府执行。"④ 他继续说道:"在这种约定下,联邦在所有州的某些事务拥有最高的、绝对的和不受控制的权力,但是州在其相应的范围内对于其他事务也有无条件的权力。"⑤

像惠顿(Wheaton)和哈勒尔克那样的国际法学家,则从国际主权和国内主权来讨论主权问题。州的国际主权已经被融入联邦政府中了,国内主权则保留下来。⑥ 当代的学者,如斯科特(Scott)持相同的观点。他认为从制宪会议的第一天起,州的代表就尽力去创立一个新的联邦,在这个联邦里,原来由州执行一部分最高权力交由中央政府执行。另一方面,州的最高权力并没有放弃,它们依然属于州。⑦

上面所讲的并不是所有拥护主权可分论的政治学者。奇普曼(Chipman)评论说,实践已经证明主权是可以分离的。⑧ 葛罗米柯(Grimke)认为断定主权是不可转让的却对其加以限制是一个矛盾。⑨ 布利斯(Bliss)在他评论主权的文章中,对主权可分论进行了更强有力的说明。在讨论主权的主体时,他说:"我情愿把它看成是被破坏的和分离的。"⑩ 主权,他指出,就是由政府机构执行的最高权

---

① R. Foster, *On the Constitution*, 270 页, 1895。他在有个地方称"主权"这个词是个误称,这清楚地显示了他对主权可分的承认。

② Cooley, *The General Principles of Constitutional Law in the United States*, 1898 年第三版, 16 页。"理论上说,主权必定是单一的,一个国家的主权必然扩展至所有属民,因此主权的分界线必定是领土的分界线。" 也可参见 *Consitution Limitations*, 1~2 页、4 页。*The General Principles of Constitutional Law in the United States*, 16~17 页。

③ Cooley, *The General Principles of Constitutional Law in the United States*, 1898 年第3版, 21~22 页。

④ Cooley, *The General Principles of Constitutional Law in the United States*, 1898 年第3版, 21~22 页。也可参见 J. Taylor, *New View of the Constitution*, 1922, 第 13 节。

⑤ Willoughby, *Fundamental Concepts of Public Law*, 189 页。

⑥ Halleck, *International Law*, 1908 年第四版, 第 1 卷, 79 页。Wheaton, *Elements of International Law*, 1866。

⑦ James Brown Scott, *Madison's Notes and a Society of Nation*, 47~48 页, 1918。

⑧ N. Chipamn, *Principles of Government*, 273 页以下, 1833。也可参见 E. D. Mansfield, *The Political of the United States*, 520~521 页, 1834。

⑨ Grimke, *Nature and Tendency of Free Institutions*, 527 页, 1848。

⑩ P. Blis, *Of Sovereignty*, 115 页, 1885。

力，没有权力，就很难说有主权。① 既然权力可以由政府的不同部门分开执行，主权为什么不能？

为了成立一个联邦，曾经拥有完全主权的国家可以把它们的一部分最高权力转让给联邦政府。在这样做的时候，"每一个公民都服从两个政府的管辖权，每一个州都有完整的机构，每一个州都对自己的事务具有最高权力"②。"说一个州不能放弃它的一部分主权其实仅仅是一个法律结论而不是事实。"③

从州与联邦之间的法律关系上可能看得更为清楚。"这个国家的法律关系的改变，既不能由一个政党做出，也不能由州的人民做出，甚至联邦的人民或者说全体人民也无权作这个改变。"④ 现实上，这种改变必须由联邦和州两个主权者一起来做出。⑤

五、结 论

大体勾画了应用于联邦国家的主权理论之后，应该有一个结论性的表述。关于联邦国家的主权理论可能有三种。第一种就是世界民族家庭的一个小模型，第二种是单一国家，第三种则是介于这两者之间的一个东西。

第一种主张是联邦国家由一群国家建成，或者是由两个或多个国家建成，这与国际组织没有什么差异。第二种主张是指州失去了同外国的外部联系，它们的地位同法国的一个省和英国的一个郡一样。第三种，在本质上是复合的，也就是另外两者的复合。从第一到第二的道路看似很长，但是它们在同一条道路上，它们只是程度的不同，而不是种类的不同，如果一个人的思想出于两者之间，则他很难在他的观点和这两种观点之间划清界线。

我们所讨论的应用于联邦国家的主权理论就像是一元主义和多元主义之间的一个连接，一个人可能认为他自己是多元主义的立场，但这又绝对不是完全正确的，一个简单的理由是，尽管多元主义是一个复合体，但一个复合体并不是在所有的情况下都是多元主义。

---

① P. Blis, *Of Sovereignty*, 113~114 页。
② P. Blis, *Of Sovereignty*, 113 页。
③ P. Blis, *Of Sovereignty*, 115 页。
④ P. Blis, *Of Sovereignty*, 114 页，1885。也可参考第九章。
⑤ 参考 D. J. Hill, *The Rebuilding of Europe*, 179~180 页。也可参考 MacIver, *The Modern State*, 380 页，1926。

第四章　国际关系中的主权　主权的特征

一、导论

无论联邦和国际社会（the family of nations）之间多么相似，我们都不能仅仅因为联邦国家就是国际社会的小模型，就倒过来得出国际关系也只不过是和州（邦）之间的关系一样的结论，事实就足以说明不是如此。更不用说对主权理论的运用稍加考虑，就会更加明白这种说法（即国际关系只不过是州或邦之间的关系）是不对的。

在某种程度上，主权的观念在应用到国际关系的时候，变得更为复杂，更为困难，同时也确实更为有趣。随着时间的流失，其困难性和复杂性与日俱增；在很大程度上，由于各国商业的、工业的，还有政治的独立性的日益增强，和其他一些原因共同导致一些学者否认主权观念能够运用到国际事务中。

本章和下一章，将主要是简要地、但尽量全面地考察主权理论的几个最为重要的阶段。最后再谈一下它在国际关系领域的运用。

二、主权和国际法

正如标厄尔（Buell）博士所言——"要研究国际关系领域的问题，就必须从国际法入手，这就如同研究美国政府必须从其宪法入手一样"①，也就是说，就像宪法是美国政府的基础一样，国际法是国际关系的基础。出于这种考虑，就让我们先来论述一下那些探讨主权与国际法关系的一些学者的观念。

法律是主权者意志的表现这一观念可以追溯到古罗马时代的皇权鼎盛时期。当时的政治思想带有神学的性质，以为上帝是唯一的主权者，上帝的意志就是法律。教会的衰落和民族国家的兴起使得认为国王的意志就是法律的理论成为可能，因为国王是每个国家的主权者。国王主权论很快被否认，继之而来的是主权在民论。它认为人民的意志就是法律。主权的所有者虽然不断变更，但正如前所述，法律是主权者的意志的体现这一论断是不变的。

奥斯丁的著作中有对这种观点的成熟表述。在奥斯丁看来，从严格和普遍的

---
① Buell, *International Relations*, 前言, 1925。

意义上来说，法律只能出自主权者。由于持有这种观点，他确信：国际法根本不是法，因为它不是主权者的命令和意愿。继而他认为国际法仅仅是一种国际道德，它没有任何法律效力，因而主权国家可以随意轻视它。

许多德国学者持有相同的看法。例如，黑格尔就认为一个主权国家在没有丧失主权的情况下是不会屈服于国际法的。因此他写道："既然在国际关系中不存在一种能够改变一个国家的现状，并能使自己的意图成为命令的权力，我们就必须承认国际关系只能依靠道德来保障。国家之间的关系是在它们独立自主的情况下，通过签订条约而建立的。同时，这种关系又依赖于这些条约而存在。"① 对他来说，正如 M. 狄骥所指出的，根本就不存在国际法，因为这世界上不存在一种凌驾于国家之上的并能制定施用于国家的法律的权力，并强迫它们服从。国际关系中不存在法律，存在的仅仅是道德义务。②

罗伯特·兰辛（Robert Lansing）也持上述观点，但略有变更。但是变更的结果使得他得出与奥斯丁和黑格尔截然相反的结论。同奥斯丁和黑格尔一样，他认为一项法律要成为真正意义上的法律，就必须得到主权者的支持。从这个前提出发，他发现很难把这种观念应用到国际事务领域中，原因在于："国际社会，由于没有组织，也就是没有一个政府，因此就没有一个主权者的代理机关去规划人类行为的规则，世界最高权力的意志也就不能通过制定法律这样的一般渠道来实现。"③

但是他也认识到困难也不像想象中的那样严重，因为世界主权已经存在，它尽管不能如国家主权那样主动发挥影响，但却在潜移默化地发挥影响，并且这种趋势一直是由不自觉到自觉地发展着。④

从国际法本源的立场和国际法的特征上来看也可以得出这个结论。⑤ 根据兰辛的看法，国家的法律和国际社会的法律产生的必要条件是类似的。⑥ 很明显，在一个"当没有成文法可使用时，法庭（judicial tribunal）的判决就是法律，这是基于这样一个合理的推断，即国家的主权者一直渴望以自然正义的原则来指导人们的行为"⑦。也就是说，如果在审判中遇到的问题没有成文的法律能够施用，那么，法院将直接采用自然正义的原则来审理。这种原则被施用时，它也就等于是

---

① Duguit, "The Law and the State", *Harvard Law Review*, 第31卷（1917年11月），97页。Duguit 所引用。
② Duguit, "The Law and the State", *Harvard Law Review*, 第31卷（1917年11月），97页。Duguit 所引用。
③ Lansing, *Notes on Sovereignty, from the Stand Point of the State and of the World*, 68页, 1921。
④ Lansing, *Notes on Sovereignty, from the Stand Point of the State and of the World*, 69页。也见51页。"正义是公民社会政策的最大的立足点。主权者的意志一定是正义的。符合自然正义的主权者意志才能在法律制定中得以运用。"
⑤ Lansing, *Notes on Sovereignty, from the Stand Point of the State and of the World*, 69~70页。
⑥ Lansing, *Notes on Sovereignty, from the Stand Point of the State and of the World*, 99页。
⑦ Lansing, *Notes on Sovereignty, from the Stand Point of the State and of the World*, 69页。

主权者的意志，尽管这种施用是被动的，而不是主动的。国内法是这样，国际法亦如此。① 他说："文明国家承认自然正义或绝对正义或严格正义的原则和人类的主要情感是一致的。这就是在世界主权的意志的指导下，国家之间的重复的实践逐渐形成了一种习惯。这种情况，就像法律在国家中产生的情形一样，习惯（法）逐渐取代了抽象的自然正义原则。"②

很明显，虽然没有一个中央政府去执行世界最高权力，也没有一个对这个最高权力的正式的宣言，但是在文明国家，它被承认有合法性。③ 那么，世界主权存在哪里？根据兰辛的看法，它存在于人类社会的本质和不断的国家交往中。④ 在一个国家之前有一个最高权力，因此在一个世界组织之前有一个世界主权。一个国家的组织是主权的行为，因此世界中央政府也将是世界主权的行为。⑤ 这样，对兰辛来说，国家和法律都是主权所创造的。法律可以在之前，也可以同时与国家产生，但是主权高于二者，在二者之上。现在国家和国内法是这样，将来国际社会和国际法也会这样。在他的观念中，在国际法出现之前，有一个也许是被动和消极的世界主权，因为国际法，或者"世界法如果要成为真正意义上的法律，它就必须来源于世界主权"⑥。

但是兰辛并没有到此为止，因为根据他的看法，从国际行为的某些趋势来看，世界的最高权力已经显露了它的主动的和积极的特征。这从将海盗作为一种犯罪已成为全世界的共识就可以看出，从废止奴隶贸易成为每一个国家的权利和义务也可以看出。⑦ 这些例子都表明世界最高权力的意志是当今任何人都不能否认的。⑧

我们所说的是建立在这样的假设上：法律要成为法律，必须有主权为其支撑。当奥斯丁说没有世界主权存在，他的结论必然是国际法不是法律。另一方面，当兰辛认为有一个世界主权存在，虽然没有明确表达其特征，但认识到了国际法和国内法一样，都是法律。

现在让我们回到那些认为国际法尽管不是主权者意志的表达，但它依然是法，且它的存在也意味着对国家主权的限制的学者的观点。⑨ 这种观念不是现代

---

① Lansing, *Notes on Sovereignty, from the Stand Point of the State and of the World*, 69～70 页, 1921。
② Lansing, *Notes on Sovereignty, from the Stand Point of the State and of the World*, 60～70 页。
③ Lansing, *Notes on Sovereignty, from the Stand Point of the State and of the World*, 72 页。
④ Lansing, *Notes on Sovereignty, from the Stand Point of the State and of the World*, 68 页。
⑤ Lansing, *Notes on Sovereignty, from the Stand Point of the State and of the World*, 57～58 页。
⑥ Lansing, *Notes on Sovereignty, from the Stand Point of the State and of the World*, 69 页。
⑦ Lansing, *Notes on Sovereignty, from the Stand Point of the State and of the World*, 72～73 页。
⑧ Lansing, *Notes on Sovereignty, from the Stand Point of the State and of the World*, 74 页。
⑨ 这种观念在 Borchard 教授的名为 "Political Theory and International Law" 的文章中得到了很好的表述。参见 Merriam 与 Barnes, *Political Theories, Recent Times*, 第四章, 120～140 页。

才有的。它的起源可以追溯到自然法观念盛行的时候。那时人们认为当主权的意志与自然法抵触时，主权的意志会被限制。① 既然国际法和自然法是一致的，既然自然法是国际法的基础，正如一些国际法的早期学者所指出的，将这种观念从国家领域转到国际关系领域中就不困难了。

但是直到布丹的著名的著作发表之后，主权受国际法的限制的观念才得以明确表达。② 国际法之父格劳修斯在其引起很大反响的著作中也才宣明。③ 虽然边沁没有明确的说明，但当他指出主权受专门条约的限定的时候，他也赞同布丹和格劳修斯的观点。④ 自从格劳修斯和边沁之后，随着国际法的发展，这种观念已经被许多学者所主张，最近达到了它的顶峰。⑤

这种主张可以简要总结如下：国际法，要成为国内法意义上的法律，不必是主权者意志的表达。正如许多学者已经证明，它起源于国际社会中利益的一致性。著名的国际法学者奥特福瑞德·内庞德博士（Dr. Otfried Nippold）这样说道："国家共同体的利益的一致性是现代国际法建立的基础。⑥ 因为国际法服务于共同的利益，虽然有很多障碍，它也能发展成真正意义上的法律，也让法律的治理成为可能。"⑦

既然国际法是外在于主权的，很显然国际法的效力意味着对国家主权的损害或限制。有人说英国的学者一方面坚持主权理论，另一方面承认国际法的至高无上的地位是毫无逻辑的。⑧ 著名的德国法理学者克布勒（Kobler）认为联邦国家的法律类似于超国家的法律即国际法。⑨ 因此，他当然认为州的主权受到联邦宪法和联邦法律的限制，同样国家的主权也受到国际法的损害和限制。⑩ 一个权威学者说道：主权"就是一个国家决定自己内部生活、管理自己的纯粹的内部事务、对自己领域的属民进行立法的合法权力。它的权力止于国界，甚至在本国范

---

① 参见 Pollock, *Essays in Law*, 51 页, 1922。
② *Six Livres de La Republique*, 第 1 卷, 第 8 章, 1576。
③ Grotius, *De Jure Belle ac Pacis*, Whewell 翻译, 第 16 节。
④ Coker, *Readings in Political Philosophy*, 549 页, 550 页, 1914。
⑤ 参见 Garner, "Limitations on National Sovereignty in International Relations", *Political Seience Review*, 1 页以下, 1925; Wehberg, *Problems of International Court of Justice*, 113～114 页。J. L. Brierly, "The Shortcomings of International Law", *British Year Book of International Law*（1923-1924）, 12 页以下; Fenwick, *International Law*, 44～45 页, 1924; W. H. Taft, "The Paris Government for a League of Nations", *American Political Science Review*, 第 13 卷（1919）, 197 页。
⑥ Nippold, *Die Fortbildung des Verfahrens in Volkerrechlichen Streitigkeiten*, 35 页以下。
⑦ Nippold, *The Development of International Law after the World War*, Hershey 翻译, 39 页, 1923。
⑧ 参见 Stallybrass, *A Society of States*, 26 页。
⑨ 参见 J. M. Zane, *The Story of Law*, 422 页, 1927。
⑩ 持这种观点的人显然不是持州主权论的人。

围内,当国际法认为有些事务涉及他国的事务时,也会受到国际法的限制"①。

国际法的实施是对国家主权的限制,这引出了国际法的约束力问题。对这一点,实际上可以说所有国际法的学者都认为国际法的约束力应该得到如同国内法的约束力一样的认可。② 一个学者甚至宣称:"如今国际法在总体上同国内法一样得到遵守。但并不能说在任何和平时期国际法都得到很好的遵守。"③ 国际法,是外在于甚至高于国家主权的权力的表达,国家对它的服从就意味着对它们自身主权的限制。④

我们还必须对那种认为国际法既不是对主权的限制,也不是主权者意志的表达的观点说几句。这种观点认为,它们,也就是国际法和主权,在事实上是联系在一起的。我们可以把这些学者分为两派。两派都认为国际法和主权两者缺一不可、相辅相成,但是他们的目的是不一样的。一派宣称国家主权是国际法的真正基础,它们是彼此协调的,它们的目的是维持现状。这种观念主要由一些英国学者提出。⑤ 另一派则坚持认为既然国际法是国际性的,那么世界主权就是至高无上的。这一派的目的是消灭国家主权,把国际法提升为一个超国家的法律。实际上他们希望有一个世界主权,这个世界主权的意志就是世界的最高法律。这一派大多属于和平主义者。⑥

---

① Garner, "Limitations on National Sovereignty in International Relations", *Political Science Review*, 6 页, 1925。Ritchie 教授虽然也可以归入这类,但他有其自己的理论。"国际法的确认看似在一定程度上对国家绝对主权的限制,但是这种限制不是'合法的'限制,而是一种自我施加的限制。独立的国家,如同奥斯丁及其学派所强烈坚持的,没有更高的合法的主权者。但是国家作为国际社会的一员,虽然不是法律的限制,但是受道德的限制,将不受限制的独立国家置于道德评判之下,同样的意义上,最终的政治主权者的意志将法律主权者置于道德评判之下。" *Annals of Am. Science*, 第 1 卷, 409 页。

② Root, "The Sanction of International Law", in *Process of American Science of International Law*, 14 页以下, 1908。Oppenheim, *International Law*, 第 1 卷, 第 3 章。

③ Moore, "Law and Organization", *American Political Science Review*, 第 9 卷, 11 页。

④ 参见 D. J. Hill, *Rebuilding of Europe*, 182 页。

⑤ Stallybrass, *A Society of States*, 26 页。

⑥ 参见 J. Bigelow, *World Peace*, 217~218 页, 1916。"世界朝向统一与和平的进程的危机在于国家主权和世界主权两者之间的较量。关于世界主权的这两种观念的竞争已经激烈地进行了。世界国家主义者(world nationalist)是很少的,在这场运动中也少有作为,他们不为那些爱好和平的人民所欢迎和鼓励,后者在国家法学家的建议和帮助下,开始了一个建立在国际法、因而也是在国家主权基础上的和平运动。国际法学家也对国家主权感兴趣。国家主权是他们生存和兴盛的所在。没有国家主权,国际法学家的生涯就是暗淡的和了无生气的,就像一个战士没有对战争的渴望一样。取消国家主权,就是使国际法学家变成律师,战士变成警察。""没有国家主权,国际法什么都不能做。没有任何征兆显示德国承认它在 1870 年入侵法国和 1914 年入侵比利时是一个错误。" Stallybrass, *A Society of States*, 56 页。

H. Krabbe 在他的 *Die Moderne Staats-Idee* 中所提倡法律主权论或许是与国际法相关联的主权问题的另一种观点,参见 *Die Moderne Staats-Idee*, 第六章。也可参见下面讨论 Krabbe 的主权论时的内容。

三、主权的本质

就我们目前的讨论而言，主权问题可以从两个层面来分析：一是它的本质；一是它的归宿。不能把两者混淆。因为前者是回答主权是什么的问题，而后者是回答主权在哪里的问题。也可以说，前者是一个本质的和普遍的问题，而后者仅仅是它的应用。但是这并不足以说明：没有前者，后者就不会存在。主权理论的历史表明主权的归宿问题是学者激烈讨论的一个问题，在希腊时期，甚至更早就出现了。但是主权的本质问题却直到16世纪晚期布丹的著作出版之后才成为人们讨论的对象。

另一方面，现代的趋势也表明主权的归宿的定义一般由主权的本质的定义来决定。这样一来，如果一个人坚持认为主权是唯一的、不可分的，则他自然会得出这样一个结论，即主权一定存在于一个确定的地方。如果他看到了主权分离的可能性，则他会认为主权可以分散地放在不同的地方。

上面所说的是主权问题的概论。在国际关系的领域，主权的归宿和本质都有其显著特征，这个主权不同于国家或联邦中的主权，对此应该给予关注。

1. 多与一

一种被广泛接受的观点是：只有同时有许多主权国家存在，在平等的基础上签定协议，国际关系的存在才是可能的。也就是说，如果世界上只有一个主权，则国际关系是不存在的。但是所有时代所有国家的哲学家都通常期望只有一个主权统治整个世界，而现实中却从来没有出现过。的确，罗马帝国曾宣称她是世界的主人甚至否认其他国家理论上的独立和平等；教皇也宣称过"我是恺撒，我是皇帝"。但是说罗马或教皇是唯一的世界主宰，不过和那些眼光从来没有超出过国界的中国大臣自大地对他们的皇上说"普天之下，莫非王土；率土之滨，莫非王臣"没有什么区别。

熟悉世界历史的人稍加注意就会意识到有两种力量无时无地不存在，特别是在人类社会处于危机的时候。一是离心力，一是向心力。这样，无论什么时候的变动，趋势总是许多主权国家融为一个主权国家；或许多主权国家从一个主权国家中分离出来。只要看看世界大战的结果，我们就可以知道此言不虚。在现实中是真实的东西，有关它的理论就是正确的。如此一来，一方面，有权力制衡理论、国家平等理论、门罗主义以及每个国家的独立和主权自决的理论，这些都是坚持多个主权的理论；另一方面，又有联邦的支持者，世界帝国的追求者，美洲联盟的推动者。亚洲、欧洲联盟的推动者都认为，为了使人类生活得更好，使人类免于战争的灾难，应该坚持和实现一个主权的理论，或在特定环境下的少数几个主权的理论。①

2. 对内与对外主权

如果说主权国家是国际关系的基础，那么国际关系就是对外和对内主权观念的基石。对内和对外主权的概念被许多学者使用过但每个人的意思却不尽相同。有些人认为，对外主权只不过是意味着一个国家不受外部控制。② 有些人却认为，说对外主权和对内主权，就是意味着从外部和内部两个方面来看主权，就像我们可以从不同的方面来看同一个事物一样③，而它实际上还是一个整体。

一个为许多国际法学家和学者所认同的流行观念是，主权可以分为对内和对外两个部分。④ 一方面，一个国家可以失去后者，但保留前者；另一方面，一个国家也可以没有前者而拥有后者。但是什么是对内主权和对外主权？好像在这一点上学者们就众说纷纭了，因为在这两者之间没有明确的界限。一般而言，决定战争与和平的权力、签定条约的权力、派出和接受大使的权力被认为是主权者的对外权力，而处理国内事务则是主权者的对内权力。⑤

3. 部分的和完全的主权

完全和部分的主权观念跟对内和对外主权的观念不同，但是二者又有紧密关联。完全主权意思是把对内和对外主权结合在一起。所有只拥有对内主权的国家是部分主权国家，但并不是所有部分主权国家都是仅仅拥有对内主权的国家，因为一个部分主权国家也许是一个拥有部分对内主权和部分对外主权的国家，或者是一个拥有完全对内主权和部分对外主权的国家。

有一些学者认为既然存在部分主权国家，因此也就存在有部分主权，也有一

---

① 在一篇标题为"The Passing of National Sovereignty"的有趣文章中，*Independence* 杂志的编辑 Hamilton Holt 在1917年写到："列强已经使得外交孤立与中立变得不可能，也许永远不可能。(1) 如果德国赢得战争，或者获得非明确结果的和平，在世界上将只有两个主权国家：一个是德意志帝国，一个是德国没有征服的其他所有国家的永久的防御性联盟……(2) 如果协约国获胜，但是不能使用它们的胜利权，则将有四到五个主权国家（英国、德国、法国、美国，也许还有俄国，因为它们能够单独武装自己以保卫它们的疆域，防止其他国家的侵犯），每一个主权国家都有一些小卫星国家。(3) 如果协约国明智的话，它们应当共同把其主权变成一个共同联盟，这个联盟，如同威尔逊总统已经指出的，包括四个到五个领导国家。德国战败之后，这样一个世界联盟将没有一个严重的敌人，由此地球上将出现一个大的强权。但是国家依然存在。小国家通过牺牲其主权而获得永久的自由与安全。" *Independence*，第92卷，120页，1917。

② 比较 Wheaton，*International Law*，29页。"主权是国家统治的最高权力。这种最高权力的执行可以是对内的，也可以是对外的。对内主权在于国家的人民之中，或者被国内宪法或基本法所赋予。对外主权则存在于相应其他所有政治社会的某个政治社会的独立性。"

③ 参见 Bluntschli，*Theory of the State*，501页。"这种国家主权可以从内外两个方面看：从外部看，它是一个独特国家的独立性……从内部看，它是这个政治实体的立法者。"

④ 参见 Westlake，*International Law*，20～21页。

⑤ 参见 Freeman，*History of Federal Government*，第1卷，4～5页。也可参见 R. Foignet，*Manuel élémentaire de droit international public*，80～88页。在他看来，对内主权的后果就是：(1) 从政治和组织的角度；(2) 从刑法应用的观点；(3) 从国内法应用的观点；(4) 外国特别法庭的裁决的执行的观点；(5) 从国家的司法豁免权的观点。另一方面，对外主权的后果是设立公使馆、缔结条约和宣战的权力。

些学者认为可以把主权分为对内和对外主权。这样，奥本海（Oppenheim）教授说道："一般来说，一个国家如果拥有各方面的独立，就是完全的主权国家。但是现实中有一些国家并没有拥有完全主权，因此称之为非完全主权国家。"①

一个著名法理学家说道："既然我们发现处在绝对独立的国家与部分独立的国家之间的许多政治实体与前者联系得更为紧密，那么，我不明白我们为什么允许那些抽象的主权理论阻止我们将主权理论应用到这些不完全独立或没有完整主权的国家上。正如普瑞德·福德瑞（Pradier Fodere）所评论的那样，虽然理论上不存在半主权的国家，但现实中却一直存在着这样的国家。"②

据说奥斯丁也认识到了部分主权存在的可能性，虽然他是带有轻视的意味去肯定它。正如麦克白（Markby）教授指出的，奥斯丁只是假设在同一个共同体中不能有两个独立的法律权威的来源。奥斯丁承认主权的权力可以分配，也充分认识到在一个半主权国家里，主权被两个不同的政治实体分享。③

1921年11月8日，在英、法关于突尼斯和摩洛哥国籍法令的争端中，法国政府认为将保护国所有的公共权力和被保护国所有的地方主权合并在一起，组成完全的主权，而这种完全的平等主权是国际关系的基础。因而保护国和被保护国依据它们之间的协定可以在它们之间分享被保护区域内的全部权力。④

很显然法国政府认为主权是一个可以分为多个部分的东西。每一部分在其范围内可以做其想做的事情。当有必要的时候，所有部分联合在一起，它们就成了一个完全的主权，并且同其他完全主权国家一样有行使主权的权利。

4. 双重主权

一般而言，同一个领域内有两个或更多的主权国家在本质上是不可能的。⑤但在国际交往的实践中，这却是现实存在的。一个地区可能在双重主权统治之下⑥，或者臣服两个主权国家建立的联合主权。这是国际关系中的特征之一，也被国际法的权威认可。

---

① Oppenheim, *International Law*, 第一卷, 277页。
② Brown, *The Austinian Theory of Law*, 142页之注释。
③ Markby, *Elements of Law*, 17页。
④ 参见 *Advisory Opinion of the Permanent Court of International Justice, Collection of Advisory of Opinions*, 第4卷, 28页。部分主权和半主权已经被区分。（根据Nys的说法，半主权一词是J. J. Moser所发明的，参见努斯Nys, *Le Droit International*, 第一卷, 358页。）混淆部分主权和半主权的错误是显而易见的，因为部分主权并不必然是半主权。如果主权可以被分为两部分，则很明显地它也可以被分为四部分或五部分。称呼一个拥有四分之一或五分之一主权的国家为一个半主权国家无疑是荒谬的。Westlake教授发现了这种错误，但他认为没有必要加以改变。"既然没有人假设'半'意味着绝对的一半，则主权的许多量的划分就是可能的。" *International Law*, 21～22页。
⑤ Oppenheim, *International Law*, 第1卷, 309～311页。
⑥ 双重主权和"dual sovereignty"不同，后者一般指一个主权被分成两部分而被政府的两个不同部门执行，如一些作者在分析联邦国家时所证明了的。

一个明显的例子——是霍尔（Hall）教授用来证明这一观点的——就是曾在奥地利和德国联邦的联合主权统治下的里雅斯特（Trieste）。① 还有奥本海教授引用的被比利时和德国双重主权统治的两国边境上的莫雷内（Moresnet）。② 还有学者提到英国和埃及联合主权控制下的苏丹。但是，对于最后一个例子，正如劳伦斯（Lawrence）所指出的，它并不意味着同一个区域之上有两个主权，而是，主权存在于一个由两个大国组建的实行共管的政府所建立的政体中。③

5. 主权的获得与消失

国际法中一个公认的原则就是在国际交往中主权能够获得和失去。哈勒尔（Von Haller）说，主权不是天生的权利，而是可以获得的权利。对他来说，获得主权有四种方式。第一，通过个人的能力和努力；第二，以前拥有者同意或馈赠的结果；第三，机遇，如帝国分裂后其原来的组成部分都成为了主权者；第四，以上三种方式的结合。在他看来，三种方式的结合是最为普遍的一种。④ 既然他认为主权可以通过以上方式获得，那他也就意味着主权也可以以同样的方式失去。

尽管哈勒尔指出主权可以由一个组织获得——他认为国家就是这样的一个组织，但是他主要是强调个体的一面，因而使得主权成为个体的所有物。这同现代观念非常不同。现代观念认为主权可以从一个国家转移到另一个国家，而不考虑个人的能力与运气；因此主权不是被个人占有，而是被作为一个整体的国家所占有。

国际法领域的杰出人物莫尔教授，指出了获得或失去主权的三种途径。第一，通过领土的转移；第二，通过革命；第三，通过内部的发展。⑤ 这似乎被所有国际法学者、政治学家和不同国家的法庭所认同。我们不在这里进行具体的讨论，而是从上面三种途径的角度来简要地概括一下当代学者们的思想。

第一，一般认为主权是一个国家所固有的，并必须存在于这个国家内部。考

---

① Hall, *International Law*, 510 页。Trieste 今为意大利北部城市，在第一次世界大战之前一直属于奥地利。Trieste 当时是奥匈帝国的唯一出海口，重要性不言而喻。由于 Trieste 作为出海口的重要性，奥匈帝国对于 Trieste 的建设和当地居民的福利一直非常重视。一战以后，Trieste 被划给了战胜国的意大利。第二次世界大战中又被德国人和奥地利拿了回去。"二战"后盟军及苏军将 Trieste 像柏林一样一分为二，占领到 1954 年，美军才将自己占领部分交给意大利，苏军部分交给了南斯拉夫，现在属于斯洛文尼亚。不过 Trieste 古城区部分都划在了意大利这边，所以 Trieste 没有像柏林那样在城中间一分为二。——译者注。

② Oppenheim, *International Law*, 第 1 卷, 309~311 页。

③ Lawrence, *Principles of International Law*, 第 83 节。也可见 Pitt Cobbett, *Leading Cases on International Law*, 第 3 版, 55 页、115 页, 1909。也可参见 Samoa 的案例。

④ Von Haller, *Restauratiou der Staatswissenschaft oder Theorie des naturalicl-reselligen Zustandes der Chimaera des Kunstlichenburgerlichen entgegensetzt*, 1825。也见 Mohl, *Geschichte und Literature der Statswissenschafien*, 第 2 卷。Merriam, *History of the Theory of Sovereignty*, 66~68 页。

⑤ Moore, *International Law Digest*, 第一卷, 258 页。

莱（Cooley）法官说，主权就是领土的边界线。① 另外一个学者说："主权被认为与一个确定的领土的占有不可分割地联系在一起。因此，领土主权的原则在国际法中实际上是最为基本的，任何违背这个原则的例外都是不可能存在的。在国际法中一个没有固定和永久的领土的共同体不会被看作为国家。"②

领土的转换意味着主权的转换。但是，领土是如何转换的，也就是说，是如何获得或失去的？对一个领土的主权可以通过占领获得，或是通过发现的名义而获得。然而，仅仅通过发现，对于一个领土的主权的获得是不充分的。"必须有一些相应的行动表明拥有这个领土"③，一个国际法的权威如是说。

并且，占领只能发生在所谓"非国家"的地方，无论是完全的毫无人烟的地方（如岛屿），或有本土居民居住但没有成为一个国家的地方，或者是文明的个体"拥有的私有财产，但没有组成一个能实施主权的国家的地方"④。

第二，通过割让的方式获得主权，这与占领有所不同。占领是基本的方式，割让是派生的方式。奥本海（Oppenheim）说，通过割让，获得领土的国家从以前对该领域拥有主权的国家那里获得对该领域的主权。⑤

第三，主权可以通过领土增加而获得，如通过河流流过之后的陆地的缓慢增加，或海岸的增加。⑥

第四，通过征服而获得主权。⑦ 但是仅仅征服还不足以对被征服的地区拥有主权，要成为一个合法的主权，必须使被征服的地区服从。

第五，通过长期实际行使主权而获得合法性。这可以这样描述："持续而充分地行使一个地区的主权，以致随着历史的发展，人们普遍认为目前的状况是与国际秩序相一致的。由此而获得主权。"⑧

与此相关，必须谈到一个国家被允许从另一个国家租借一个地区一定年限从而获得对该地区的主权的问题。对这个问题，政治家和国际法学家还有争议。从中国租借到胶州半岛之后，德国的《帝国公报》（*Imperial Gazette*）就宣称："中

---

① Cooley, *The General Principle of Constitutional Law in the United States*, 第3版, A. C. MeLanghin 编, 1～2页。

② Crane, *The State in Constitutional and International Law*, 48页。也可参见 Rivier, *Principles du droit des gens*, 第一卷, 155～156页; Levesque, *La Situation internationale de Dantzig*, 110页。

③ L. B. Evans, *Cases on International Law*, 第2版, 285页注释, 1922。

④ Oppenheim, *International Law*, 第三版, 第一卷, 384页。"在 Johoson 和 Graaham's Lessee 诉 MeIntosh 案中，Marshall 法官通过法庭表达了这样的观点，基督教国家可以通过发现的权利而占有未知的领土。" Scott, *Cases on International Law*, 177页。

⑤ Oppenheim, *International Law*, 第三版, 第一卷, 383页。

⑥ Oppenheim, *International Law*, 第三版, 第一卷, 377页。

⑦ Fenwick, *International Law*, 229页。

⑧ Wheaton, *Elements of International Law*.

华帝国政府已经将该领域的所有主权在一定时期内转移给德国政府。"① 另一方面，俄国通过俄通社发表的官方声明称，对旅顺港和大连湾的租借，"既保证了中国的主权完整，又满足了作为海军强国，同时又是它的邻国的俄国的迫切需要"②。

国际法学家，如劳伦斯（Lawrence）教授，赞同德国政府的观点，他认为俄国的官方申明仅仅是"用外交辞令掩盖领土割让的残酷事实"③。中国真正分离出去的是主权，但在当时不便这样说，列强中也只有德国这样说了。④ 奥本海（Oppenheim）教授同劳伦斯持同样的观点⑤，但奥本海教授把租借看作割让的一种方式，而割让通常被看作是主权的转让。⑥

另一方面，韦斯特莱克（Westlake）教授持相反的观点。他的观点建立在私法的基础上。他这样说道："当财产被租借的时候，租借者同时保留所有权而同时暂时失去了使用权。与此相似，一个国家租借一个地区给其他国家后，仍一直拥有对它的主权。"⑦ 冯为柯（Fenwick）教授也持类似的观点。在谈到巴拿马运河的时候，他写道："严格从法律上来说，巴拿马保留对运河和运河周围地区的主权，但事实上美国拥有在这个地区的作为主权者应该有的所有权利、权力和权威。"⑧

在讨论了主权通过领土的转移而获得（当然也意味着失去）之后，现在让我们来讨论第二种获得方式，也就是通过革命来获得主权。毫无疑问，一群同属于致力于建立一个新国家的政治团体的人，在推翻现政府之后，可以获得主权的权利，而建立一个主权国家。但问题是：这样一个政治团体在什么时候获得主权？对这个问题的答案不一而足。以美国为例，有的人认为1783年美国与英国签订和约之后，它才拥有了主权并成为一个主权国家；⑨ 但有的人认为是在《独立宣言》发表之后；⑩ 还有的人认为1774年的第一次大陆会议之后美国就成了一个

---

① Westlake, *International Law*, 136 页。
② Westlake, *International Law*, 136 页。
③ Lawrence, *Principles of International Law*, 177 页。
④ Oppenheim, *International Law*, 第三版，第一卷，310 页。
⑤ Oppenheim, *International Law*, 第三版，第一卷，310 页。
⑥ Oppenheim, *International Law*, 第三版，第一卷，379 页。
⑦ Westlake, *International Law*, 315～316 页。
⑧ Fenwick, *International Law*, 244 页，也见 243 页。
⑨ Brownson, *American Republic*, 213 页。
⑩ 这也许是最广为接受的观点。在 Johnson、J. Harcourt 诉 Gaillard 一案中，法庭说："合众国从来不认为通过1783的协定而从大不列颠那里获得什么，是那个时候的《独立宣言》让合众国获得了对业已存在的权利的承认。"参见 Moore, *Digest*, 第一卷，302 页。

主权国家。①

一个通过革命而建立的新国家的独立性和它的主权被国际社会承认也是最近学者们讨论的一个主题。有些情况下，一个国家只被一个已存的主权国家承认；有些情况下，只被少数几个国家承认为主权国家并接纳为国际社会的一员；有些情况下，革命的政党尚未占领一寸土地或革命尚未成功，就被承认为主权国家。② 还有些情况下，尽管革命早已成功，并建立了强有力的、组织完备的政府，但仍久久不能被接纳为国际社会的一员。每一种情况都有它的拥护者，每一个拥护者都有他的推理、论断和原因。可以说每种观点都有可取之处。

现在要谈一谈第三种获得主权的方式，也就是通过内部改良。莫尔教授认为日本的内部改良是一个最为引人注目的例子。另一方面，又指出土耳其参加1856年会议并没有带给它完全主权的地位。③ 一个国家的内部改良要发展到何种地步才能获得主权是很难确定的。

6. 主权的中止和恢复

不应该把主权的中止和恢复与主权的获得和失去相混淆，因为它们之间的不同是在时间上，而不是种类上的。后者是永久性的，前者是暂时性的。我们现在所讨论的一般与军事占领有关。正如霍尔（Hall）教授指出的，在18世纪中期以前，一个简单的占领与完全的统治是没有区别的。"④ 这种区别是由瓦泰勒（Vattel）⑤ 最先指出的，直到赫福特（Heffter）的著作⑥出版之后才对之有一个清楚的区分。

军事占领带给占领者对占领地的主权。这种观点为交战国政府所支持，也为

---

① Burgess, *Political Science and Constitutional Law*，第1卷，100页。参见 Willoughby 教授对 Burgess 的批评，*Fundamental Concepts of Public Law*，1925。在这里，没有必要提出另外一种新的理论，也没有必要对上述三种理论进行批评，但由之产生的困难却可提及。如果第一和第二种主张是合理的，则当革命开始的时候个体组织就获得了它的最高权力，这在许多实际的事例中是相反的。如果第二种理论是合理的，则当母国拒绝签订条约或母国在革命中获得了胜利，则一个政治社会能变成一个主权国家吗？

② 1918年9月，美国承认了捷克国家的独立与主权，就是一个最好的例子。

③ Burgess, *Political Science and Constitutional Law*，第1卷，303页。后一种观点也为那些论及中国、波斯、暹罗等国的学者们所赞同。参见 Fenwick, *International Law*，83～104页。Hall, *International Law*，44页。Lawrence, *Principles of International Law*，99～271页。

提出一个可以衡量的内部改良的标准是困难的。学者（Hall，44页；Fenwick，83页）认为半文明国家不是国家社会的完全成员。这意味着在严格的意义上，这些国家不是国家，因而不是一个完全的主权国家。但是文明的基础是什么？如果基础是物质力量、军队和海军舰队（参见 Lansing, *Note on Sovereignty*，63页），则很少有国家甚至没有国家能被看作主权国家。Lansing 在表明在严格意义上没有一个单一国家是主权国家后这样说："可以这样说，一个国家，无论强弱、大小、贫富、文明与野蛮，在一定意义上都是保护国（protectorate）。"（Lansing, *Note on Sovereignty*，65页。）另一方面，如果文明的基础是除了物质力量之外的东西，则世界上的许多国家或大多数国家都可被列入主权国家。

④ Hall, *International Law*，第153节。也可参见 Hershey, *Essentials of International Law*，409页注释。

⑤ *Le Droit des gens*，第三卷，第197节。

⑥ *Le Droit international de l'Europe*，第四版，第131节。

许多国际法的学者所支持。他们认为主权在侵略者手中，但这是暂时的。一个权威学者由此总结道："国家为它的国民提供保护是它获得效忠的基础。当一个国家不能再保护它的国民的命运时，国民就不必对它效忠。这时，国民要么直接在这种无保护的状态下持续生活一个时期，要么去效忠占领者；要么还可以在保持自由的前提下与侵略者合作，并承认侵略者拥有该国的主权。作为交换，侵略者将最大限度地避免对他们使用战争手段，而这关系到他们的身家性命。"①

一个研究主权的杰出学者认为既然侵略者对占据地的主权只是暂时的，因此后者的主权只是中止，而不是让渡。当侵略者的要求满足之后，主权一般又得到恢复。这方面的例子并不缺乏。在1871年普法战争中，德国军队占领了法国，法国的主权中止了。但是后来主权又由德国恢复了。而作为交换，法国政府赔了一大笔军费并放弃了阿尔萨斯-洛林地区。② 这位学者还认为，在义和团运动时期，对北京的占领是另一个这样的例子。当联军占领北京的时候，中国的主权被中止了。"当事件结束的时候，帝国政府得到了重建，中国的政权被恢复，很显然中国的政权的恢复依赖于占领北京的列强的同意。"③

近来也有一些学者不认为军事占领会导致被侵入地区的主权的中止。他们坚持认为："对在占领区的敌国只能采取敌对行为。它行使的权威只是对敌国施压的一种方式。主权者的权利仍是完整的，并且人民和侵略者之间原有的法律关系并没有因为入侵而改变。"④

也有像斯潘特（J. M. Spaight）一样的一些学者，他们所持的观点居于上述两种观点之间。他这样说道："战争法承认占领国有非常类似主权的政府权利。"⑤

7. 主权的限制

传统的主权观念正如一个著名的学者充分的表述那样："主权是不受法律限制，也不能被法律限制。因为作为一个国家的最高权力，从法律的角度说，没有任何其他权威在主权之上。说它被更高的权力所限制，在词语上就是矛盾的。"⑥上面的观点为一些学者所支持，但目前许多学者坚持认为主权是能够限制的，并已经被限制。

---

① Hall, *International Law*, 557～558页。

② Lansing, *Notes on Sovereignty*, 62页。

③ Lansing, *Notes on Sovereignty*, 63～64页。Lansing甚至去探究列强把主权归还中国的动机："它们自愿地把主权归还给中国，是因为它们希望主权在中国手里，而不是在它们中间的一个或几个手里，因为那样的话，它们中的一个或几个就会成为远东的统治者（而这是它们谁也不愿看到的）。"

④ Hall, *International Law*, 557～558页。Hall说，看看替代的主权混乱的和不公正的谎言，旧的主权理论毫无疑问变得微弱了。参考Westlake, 84页。

⑤ J. M. Spaight, *War Rights on Land*, 1911。

⑥ Garner, *Political Science and Government*, 128页，第四章，1928。也可参见他在*Political Science Review*第19卷第2页上的论文。

在国际关系中，主权被不同的方式限制：第一，通过国际法的规则、原则和惯例来限制。第二，通过宗主国与附属国、保护与依附之间的关系来限制。第三，通过同盟的条约来限制。第四，根据条约的习惯法来限制。第五，通过地役权来限制。①

在国际关系中对主权的限制的第一种方式，我们已经在前面的章节"主权与国际法"中进行了讨论。第二、第三种方式我们将在讨论主权的归宿的时候进行讨论。我们现在简要地讨论一下后两种方式。

国际法之父格劳修斯举了一个例子，即罗马人和迦太基人之间的条约要求迦太基在没有罗马的同意的情况下不能发动战争，就是一个损害主权的条约。② 这一类的条约，在事实上，与上级对下级的命令并没有什么不同。不平等的条约并不是真正意义上的条约。条约在这里的意思是指由两个或多个实体在平等的基础上订立并对各方都有约束效力的条约。

一个著名的美国参议员告诉我们，参议院的大多数议员一再承认："每一个条约，都意味着在一定程度上牺牲了主权。"③ 普罗克（Pollock）教授为了平息国联将要干涉独立主权国所带来的恐慌，指出参与到国际联盟的各国已经限制了它们的行动自由，因而它们的主权在许多方面都受到了现存协定的限制。④

甚至主张"世界上没有国家自愿放弃它的主权中的自身的属性"，"甚至在与其他国家的交往中，保持主权的完整也是这个国家的最高义务"的特赖奇克（Treischke），也承认"每一个国家都会为了自身的利益而通过条约在某种程度上限制自己的主权"，当然，他认为这种对国家主权的限制并不具有法律效力，原因在于"国际法规定，战争一开始就宣告了敌对国家之间的所有条约都被取消"，"每一个条约都是单个国家的自愿的自我限制，国际条约都包含有一个条件：即情势变更原则（rebus sic stantibus）"。⑤ 这或许是真实的，另外一种情况也是真实的：自我限制也是限制：无论这种限制是法律的、道德的还是其他方面的。

另外一些学者尽管不认为所有的条约都是对国家主权的限制，但他们认为有的条约限制了，而有的条约却没有限制。这样，认为多数条约并不限制国家的主

---

① Hershey, *Essentials of International Law*, 100～101 页。

② 参见 Dickinson, *Equality of States in International Law*, 55 页。

③ Lodge, *The Senate and the League of Nations*, 附录 5。

④ Pollock, *League of Nations*, 86 页，1920。也可参见 Wehberg, *Problem of an International Court of Justice*, 114 页。Garner, "Limitations of National Sovereignty in International Relations", *Political Science Review*, 第 19 卷, 1 页以下。Divis, *Elements of International Law*, 39 页。

⑤ 参见 H. W. C. Davis, *The Political Thought of Heinrich von Treitschke*, 151～178 页。也可参见 Polilik, 第一卷, 39 页。所谓情势变更原则，即缔约国在缔约时有个假定，即假定当时的基本情势不变，以后如果情势发生根本变化，任何缔约国都可要求修改或废除条约。因为条约的有效性是以缔约时基本情势的继续存在为条件的。——译者注。

权的斯塔利布拉斯（Stallybrass）反而认为1902年的国际糖业联盟实施了"对成员国主权的真正限制"①。还有些人注意到在成员国在明确的特定背景下承担某种义务的条约和如在《国际联盟盟约》下某种行为的保证之间进行区分的重要性。在前者，国家的主权得到了保存，而在后者，国家的主权受到了限制。② 洛奇参议员在某种程度上也持相同的观点，他认为并不是所有的条约都意味着主权的牺牲。③

在讨论了条约对国家主权的限制之后，我们再来讨论地役权④与主权的关系问题。国际法学者普遍认为国际地役权存在对主权的限制。⑤ 在荷兰矿业的案例中，科隆最高法庭认为荷兰在矿产方面的利益是一种国际地役权，因而也就意味着对主权的贬损。⑥

在《北美海岸渔场仲裁》中，鲁特（Root）认为美国"对美国保证渔业开采的自由包含有对英国领土的国际地役权，因而也就意味着对英国主权的贬损，当然，英国的管理渔业开采的独立权利也就被剥夺了"。更进一步的讨论认为如果说即便英国的主权自身没有受到限制，但起码在渔场水域的主权的实施受到了限制。⑦

这个裁定中，实际上接受了美国的这样的观点：国际地役权的认可意味着对被使用地域的国家（承役国，the servient state）的主权的贬损。这样的裁决建立在这样一个假设基础上：国际地役权在其本质上就是对主权的贬损。

但是渔业权并不是地役权的一部分，也没有对主权造成损害。为什么呢？在特别法庭看来，无论是英国还是美国的政治家都对1818年法案一无所知。因为

---

① Stallybrass, *A Society of States*, 86页。

② Montgomery, *Issues of European Statesmanship*, 117页。

③ Lodge, *The Senate and the League of Nations*, 407页。也可参见Oppenheim的*Future of International Law*, 44页。*American Journal of International Law*, 第15卷, 8页。参见1925年9月12日国联第六次大会上波斯的Arfa王子所做的陈述。*Records of Plenary Meeting*, Ⅵ（1925）, 57页, *Official Journal*,（1924）1362, XXX。

④ 所谓"地役权"（servitudes），即指一国为实现本国利益在一定条件下涉及的在他国领土上的权利。国际地役的构成要件包括：（1）依条约而产生。（2）主体只能是国家。（3）客体是国家领土。（4）为他国的目的或利益服务。（4）国际地役一般分为积极的地役和消极的地役两种。有的学者还认为，积极的地役的要素是"容忍"，而消极的地役的要素是"不作为"。（5）主权国为实现对飞地的管辖权完全有理由取道他国领土，对方也完全有责任为该国提供合适的通道并保障其过境权。而前者也须像《海洋法公约》中的关于领海通过所规定的"无害通过权"原则那样，"连续不停地迅速过境"，从而不对后者的领土主权及固有利益造成危害或干涉，并也有义务偿付合理的费用。——译者注。

⑤ 举例来说，如Westlake的*International Law*, 61页。

⑥ 参见A. E. McNair, "So-called State Servitudes", *British Years Book of International Law*, 118～127页, 1925。

⑦ *World Peace Foundation Pamphlet*, 1912, J. B. Scott编辑, 459页。也见Root, *Address on International Subjects*, J. B. Scott编辑, 180页、181页、295页, 1916。

地役权是一种明确的主权权利。而这个条约仅承认捕鱼的自由，而这充其量不过是一种经济权利。况且，国际地役权的概念起源于隶属于神圣罗马帝国的几个半主权（quasi-sovereignty）国家。"为了避免这种半主权国家的出自多方的不甚清楚的主权特征，为了不因主权的某方面缺失而使其特征受到损害，也为了不使主权因为满足它国及其所有者的利益而受到限制，现代国家尤其是英国从来就不承认主权可分，因为现代国家的体制要求实质的主权和独立。因此，国际地役权的学说与像英、美这些宪政体制国家的主权原则不相适应；也与现代的国际关系不相协调，因而也就得不到现代政治家的支持。"①

从上述所引可以很清楚地看出整个地役权的理论是被否定的，因为它与现代的政治原理是不一致的，因为现代国家需要本质上的主权与独立。这种理论不是建立在事实基础之上，而是建立在理论基础之上。②

补充一点的是，如海因斯（Higgins）教授指出的，有一种趋势否认"地役权"这个词对国家主权的诸多限制，因为在许多情形下主权是通过条约而限制其自身。③ 冯为柯（Fenwick）教授指出了作为现代概念的"地役权"与作为中世纪概念的"地役权"之间的不同，后者是建立在封建领主与雇佣之间的关系，"地役权虽然意味着对土地和水源的使用进行了限制，但这并不会导致国家对其领土的理论上的司法权和实际控制的丧失"④。

8. 主权的侵犯

主权的侵犯，一个国际法学者说道，是一个国际侵权，受害国有权要求补偿。⑤ 主权的侵犯与主权的限制不一样，后者具有永久性，而前者仅仅具有暂时性。并且如果一个国家承认它侵犯了另外一个国家的主权，就会对后者进行补偿。另一方面，限制或许可以取消，但是限制所已经导致的损失和伤害不会得到补偿。

没有国家能够在另一国家的司法范围内采取一些强制性的行动，除非得到它的许可，否则这样的行动就是对主权的侵犯。⑥ 同样地，如果一个国家在其司法权之外通过刑法的实施去强迫其他国家的人们服从其要求，而这种要求并不符合本地法律的规则，这也是对主权的侵犯。⑦

---

① Scott, *Hague Court Report*, 159～161页。
② Oppenheim, *International Law*, 第1卷, 第203节。
③ Hall, *International Law*, Higgins 主编, 204页, 主编所加的注释。
④ Fenwick, *International Law*, 261页。参考 Fauchille, *Droit International Public*, Ⅰ, Paix, 第339节, 1922。
⑤ W. E. Hall, *Rights and Duties of Neutrals*, 15页。
⑥ Stowell, *Intervention in International Law*, 322页。
⑦ Stowell, *Intervention in International Law*, 322页。

在国际关系史上关于主权的侵犯的指控是非常多的。① 早在1793年，法国驻美大使"公民"热内（Citizen Genet）武装私掠船的激进行为，就侵犯了美国的中立权。② 时任美国国务卿杰弗逊表达了这样的观点："每一个国家都有权利阻止其他国家在其领土上实行主权行为，中立国家的义务就在于阻止这种行为，因为这种行为将伤害到交战者中的一方。"③

在1885年的克兰普顿（Crampton）事件中，由于英国大使劝诱美国的新兵到加拿大去应征参加对俄战争，美国国务卿梅西（Marcy）指责他的这种行为是侵犯了美国的主权。④ 在萨拉热窝事件中，法国政府在海牙仲裁法院（Hague Arbitration Tribunal）上辩称夺取萨拉热窝是对法国主权的侵犯。⑤

在第一次世界大战期间类似事件很多。1914年中国政府谴责了日本对中国胶州湾的侵略，并被认为是对中国主权的严重侵犯。在阿帕姆号事件（the case of

---

① 中立国家的权利的侵犯和与此相关联的所谓干预的事例好像正在增多。Hershey教授说："在战争期间一个独立国家拥有不可剥夺的保持中立的权利。敌对国有尊重这种中立的义务，特别是其领土主权。" *Essentials of International Law*, 445页。Hall说道："就中立而论，所有国家都是主权者。" *Rights and Duties of Neutrals*, 15页。Hall说道："干预是一种敌意的行为，因为它包含对一个独立国家的独立性的侵犯。" *International Law*, 第8版, 337页。"干预无疑是一种敌意的行为，因为它包含对一个独立国家的独立性的侵犯。如果不是被事先同意，就会被看作一种入侵，就像在战争中，其主权受到了损害。" H. G. Hodges, *The Doctrine of Intervention*, 5页。也可以参见Stallybrass, *A Society of States*, 60页。Lawrence, *Principles of International Law*, 172页。

② 此即有名的"公民"热内事件。对于美国人对欧洲战争看法的剧烈分歧，华盛顿颇感忧伤。他还担心法国根据1778年的《法美同盟条约》，要求美国提供军事帮助，尤其是利用美国港口来装备远征军，攻击英国船只和殖民地。华盛顿坚信，对于年轻的合众国而言，卷入欧洲战争无异于自杀。这一看法得到了汉密尔顿和杰弗逊的支持，这两人都敦促美国中立。汉密尔顿还进而声称，1778年条约已不再有效，因为美国是与法国君主，而不是与法国共和国签订该条约的。然而，华盛顿并未公开宣布条约已经失效，而是发布一加中立公告"。在"公告"中，华盛顿要求美国人公正地对待交战国。此时，法国驻美大使"公民"埃德蒙·热内，利用很多美国人的亲法情绪，置华盛顿发布的"中立公告"于不顾，在美国港口内装备私掠船，并派遣其前往攻击英国船只和殖民地。华盛顿担心此举将会把美国卷入场与英国为敌的战争之中，乃下令热内停止此类活动，并且最终要求法国政府将其召回。——译者注。

③ Moore, *International Law Digest*, 第2卷, 446页。就在"热内"事件发生一个月之后，英国大使George Hamond到达美国。他写道："虽然还没有与我正式交流，但我已经对这类投诉准备就绪，我希望这表明我方的立场，我将不保护那些不考虑美国中立立场的英国人的行为。这种中立立场是这个国家的政府所使用的，并迅速建议给其公民，以不卷入法国和其他交战国中。"在这里我必须感谢我的朋友Charles S. Hyneman告诉我这段论述。

也比较 The Brig Alerta诉Moran, (1815), 9 Cranch 359, 365, 3L. Ed. 758, 760—766。

④ Stowell与Munro, *International Law Cases*, 第2卷, 278～295页。也见Stowell, *Intervention in International Law*, 332页的注释。

⑤ Scott, *Hague Court Report*, 279页。Stowell与Munro, *International Law Cases*, 第1卷, 418页。

appam）中①，美国政府也作了同样的谴责。② 这样的例子还有很多，但是已经举出的例子就足以证明对主权的侵犯的观念已经存在很长时间，并且是国际关系中的一个重要特征。

9. 主权的藐视

正如许多国际法的学者指出的，主权的藐视与主权的侵犯有所不同。前者对主权的干涉不如后者对主权的干涉严重。外国代表试图对政府产生间接影响以达到某种目的，就是对主权的藐视的例子。在第一次世界大战期间，德国大使本斯塔夫（Bernstorff）在报纸上警告乘客不要登上路西塔尼亚号（Lusitania）被认为是对美国主权的一种藐视。③

尽管主权的侵犯与主权的藐视有所不同，后者的观念也没有前者复杂，但对主权的藐视的行为也曾被视为是对主权的侵犯。

10. 结论

现在让我们从国际法的角度对主权的主要的观念作一个简要的概括。我们首先要指出的是，有些人希望在全世界范围内只存在一个主权，而也有人坚持要使许多主权同时存在。然而前者没有变成现实，而后者长久以来就已是现实。但这并不表明在未来没有只有一个主权的可能性。无论是理论上还是现实中都表明，每一个主权国家作为国际关系中的单元都可以分成许多主权国家，另一方面，许多主权国家也可以合并成一个主权国家，尽管它还不是世界上唯一的主权。

世界上的每一个主权国家不仅可以分成许多单一的主权，也可以分成对内和对外两部分。每一部分都不必要同时拥有，一部分可以交给一个国家而另一部分可以交给另一个国家。而且，每一个主权可以分成多个部分，而不必非要是对外和对内两部分，这些部分的数量可以是两个或更多。部分主权是完整主权的一部分，所有的部分主权联合在一起就等于完全主权，并且也能够享有完全主权享有的权利。更进一步，几个主权可以对一个地区联合统治。如果在一个领域内有两

---

① 英国的阿帕姆号货轮在运送战利品的途中，因为恶劣天气等原因被迫停靠在中立国港口纽波特纽斯时被一艘德国商船袭击舰截获。当时的国际法学家对此事件展开的讨论是：在战时，滞留在中立国港口的战利品应该给予什么地位？由于各方对此事件存在争议，阿帕姆号被扣留在纽波特纽斯，直至战争结束。——译者注。

② Stowell 与 Munro，*International Law Cases*，第 2 卷，290 页。

③ Stowell，*Intervention in International Law*，323～324 页的注释。1914 年 8 月战争爆发时，路西塔尼亚号被移交给英国海军（Admiralty），并被送往利物浦的加拿大码头（Canada Dock），在那里配备上 12 门 6 英时口径的炮。它被注册为英国海军舰队的后备武装巡洋舰，而它所装备的武器重量超过了在英吉利海峡（English Channel）巡逻的皇家海军（Royal Navy）舰队。1915 年 5 月 7 日（星期五）下午两点十分过后，负重 30396 吨的路西塔尼亚号在没有被事前警告的情况下被一枚鱼雷击中。20 分钟左右它就沉没了，1201 个男人、妇女和儿童失去了生命。在死亡的人数中，有 128 人是美国公民。发射鱼雷的德国潜艇 U20 绕着下沉的船只转了几圈，然后就逃离了现场，于 5 月 13 日回到了其位于威廉港（Wilhelmshaven）的基地。——译者注。

个主权，我们就称之为双重主权。①

从另外的角度看，我们发现主权可以从一个国家转移到另一国家。这种转移从本质上说可以分为两种形式：获得或失去。通过一种方式获得主权，也就可以通过同样的方式失去主权。转移主权的方法有多种。但是为了便于理解，它们被归结为三类：领土的转移、革命、内部改良。同主权可以获得和失去一样，主权也可以中止和恢复。获得和失去与中止和恢复有所不同，前者是永久的，而后者仅仅是暂时的。还要提及的是主权可以被全部或部分地获得、失去、中止和恢复。

进一步的研究表明，主权不仅能联合和分离，获得与失去，中止和恢复，而且也可以被限制、侵犯、蔑视。简单地说，在国际交往中有五种限制国家主权的方式。限制与侵犯的不同主要在于一个特征是永久性的，另一个是暂时性的。侵犯和蔑视不一样，因为前者被认为比后者更为严重。

从上面所说的，我们可以这样总结，从国际关系的角度来看，主权从本质上来说可以联合也可以分离，可以获得也可以失去。可以中止也可以恢复，更进一步，它可以消失也可以增加。最后，它可以被限制，也可以被侵犯，还可以被蔑视。

---

① "双重主权"（double sovereignty）一词在运用到两个以上的主权接合的领土的时候是不合适的；但是还没有学者采用"复合主权"（co-sovereignty）的用法。

第五章 国际关系中的主权 归宿和批评（续）

四、主权的归宿

我们现在从国际关系的角度来看主权归宿的理论。如前所示，尽管主权的本质和主权的归宿彼此不同，但把其中一个作为前提往往能从逻辑上推导出另一个的相应结论。出于这个原因，我们很难在它们之间作一个清楚的区分界线。举例来说，从主权的本质的角度来看，领土的放弃可以作为一种主权从一个国家转移到另一国家的方式。① 但另一方面，如果有人把它看作国际关系发生的形式或机制，则它也可以归于主权的归宿一类。

根据不同的国际惯例，从国际法看主权归宿的观念也有不同的形式。此处试图对那些最重要的观点进行了简要的讨论。

1. 主权与邦联（Confederation）

邦联与联邦（federation）这两个词常常连在一起使用。② 许多学者对它们没有进行区分，就是那些对此做出区分的学者，对于具体的例子也没有一致的意见。③ 不管对它们的使用是如何的混乱，它们之间的区别仍是很明显的。尽管它们的区别仅仅是程度上的，而不是种类上的。

很少有学者坚持认为由成员国家组成的邦联是一个完全的拥有最高主权的联合。另一方面，有学者认为参加邦联的国家是拥有完全主权的国家。这种主张由奥本海（Oppenheim）教授等学者所倡导。奥本海教授认为邦联的主权不影响成员国家的主权④，几个国家同意组织一个联合体只不过是一个国际条约，这个联合体不具有国际关系的人格。⑤

普遍被接受的观点是邦联国家仅仅是部分主权国家。这种观点以劳伦斯教授为代表。他这样说道："邦联是一个分散国家的集合，它们中的每一个保留一些主权的权利，放弃了其他的。相应地，根据国际法，这些国家必须被看作第二层

---

① 这并不意味着作者赞同领土丧失了主权就丧失了的理论。
② 参见以上第二、第三章的内容。
③ 比较 Ferguson 和 Freeman 的分类。
④ Oppenheim, *International Law*, 第三版, 第 1 卷, 156 页。比较 Hall, *International Law*, 28 页; Moore, *Digest*, 第 1 卷, 第 10 节; Garner, *Introduction to Political Seience*, 143～144 页, 1910。
⑤ Oppenheim, *International Law*, 第三版, 第 1 卷, 156 页。

的部分主权国家。它们比一个更大整体的管理区要高级，比主权国家要低级。"①

正如已经指出的，目前不存在邦联。奥本海教授指出的最后一个例子是结束于 1898 年——由三个主权国家组成的中美洲大共和国。我们现在所讨论的问题仅仅是一个历史上的问题。

2. 主权和英联邦自治领（the British Dominions）

近些年来，特别是在第一次世界大战之后，主权问题变得越来越重要，讨论也同英联邦自治领广泛地联系在一起。旧的观念认为在英帝国中只有一个主权。这种观点由一些英国政治哲学家和政治家所坚持②，甚至在 1918 年为加拿大内阁所接受。③

与此相反，也有一些政治家和政治学者坚持认为英联邦自治领不再在英国的主权之下，因为它们各自都是最高主权者。正如已经指出的澳大利亚总理修斯（Hughes）不只一次，而是许多次都强调指出澳大利亚是一个独立的国家。④ 斯马茨（Smuts）将军也表达了同样的观点，他是第一次世界大战中的英国国家英雄，也是一个有创造性思维的人。⑤ 1923 年 9 月，在国联第四次代表会议上成为成员国之后，爱尔兰总统科斯格雷夫（Cosgrave）在演讲中说爱尔兰加入了"一个庄重的同盟，以实施主权者的权力"⑥。

认为英联邦自治领是主权国家的讨论建立在不同的根据之上。第一点，根据国际联盟的协议，只有主权国家才是联盟的成员。既然英联邦自治领被认作是联盟的成员，它们理所当然是主权国家。⑦ 第二点，《国际联盟盟约》的第 22 条宣称："（一）凡殖民地及领土，于此次战争后不复属于从前统治该地之各国，而其居民尚不克服今世特别困难状况下实行自治，则应适用下列原则：即将此等人民之福利及发展视作文明之神圣任务，此项任务之履行，应载入本盟约。（二）实现此原则之最妥善途径，莫如将此种人民之管理，委诸资源上、经验上或地理上足以承担此责任且乐于加以接受之各先进国，该国即以受任统治之资格，为联盟

---

① Lawrence, *Principles of International Law*, 69 页, 第 40 节。

② "Metternich 说过没有主权者能够担当得起放弃他的主权的一微小部分。Pollard 教授明确地表达这样的观点："我们没有放弃主权，只是把它出租给自治领而得到一种很好的回报。" Stallybrass, *A Society of State*, 第 117 页。这种理论也有它的捍卫者，在一篇题为 "Sovereignty Colonies" 的文章中，T. Baty 否认帝国的主权是分离的。"王冠（主权）只有一个且不可分，虽然主权在王国的不同部分由不同的机构以不同的原则执行。" 见 *Harvard Law Review*, 第 34 卷, 837～861 页。

③ 参见 *A History of the Peace Conference of Paris*, 第 6 卷, 343 页。由国际事务研究所（Institute of International Affairs）发行, 1924。

④ Stallybrass, *A Society of State*, 176 页。

⑤ Stallybrass, *A Society of State*, 176 页。

⑥ 国联：*Records of the Fourth Assembly, Plenary Meeting*, 第 24 页。必须提到的是在爱尔兰和英国之间的条约没有被英国方面承认，因为在条约中有"主权"字样。

⑦ 这种观点还可以从加拿大代表是委员会成员这一事实上得到证明。

实行此项管理。"英联邦自治领必须是主权者，否则它们如何能被委托管理殖民地？第三点，派遣和接受大使是主权的内在权利。如果英联邦自治领不是主权国家，它们就不会有这些权利。

但是最重要的是讨论奠定在 1926 年的帝国会议（the Imperial Conference）中的宣言："在大英帝国内的各自治体，地位不分上下完全平等，然因对英王的共同忠诚而联合，而自由结盟成为英联邦的成员。"① 英国是一个主权国家，而如果英联邦自治领又被宣称同英国在地位上平等，则它们一定是主权国家，除非英国也不是主权国家。②

另外一种理论，在特点上是复合的。这种理论认为英联邦自治领是部分主权国家。刘易斯（M. M. Lewis）教授是一个引人注目的代表。在引述了韦斯特莱克的主权是可分的论述之后，刘易斯教授在一篇标题为《英联邦自治领的国际地位》的重要文章里总结道："成为英帝国的成员，就必须行使普通伙伴关系政策。它们有处理对内事务和参与与其他国际关系的权力，但是，它们不是完整的主权国家，因为它们的独立受到成员义务的必要限制。"③

哈佛大学的劳威尔（A. L. Lowell）校长，一个世界知名的学者，他的观点与上述观点略有不同，虽然在表述上不是太清楚。他在说自治领不受英国的控制或不臣属英国的权威的时候，认为英联邦自治领是主权国家。但是他也指出英国人在两种意义上使用"主权"一词。他这样说道："一般而言它是指王权的所有者；但是在政治哲学家中间它意味着权威的终极来源，在这个意义上，大英帝国的主权尽管由议会代表，但它最终属于全体选民，在当前它也在自治领中。"④

3. 主权和被保护国家

最初的被保护国家被认为是主权国家。巴蒂（Baty）教授说："保护，仅仅是担保的一种形式，它不能在任何程度上影响被保护国的主权。"⑤ 这种观点被那些最高权威如格劳修斯、普芬道夫和瓦泰勒（Vattel）等所支持。瓦泰勒说一个弱小的国家为了安全，而处在一个更有力量的国家的保护之下，但是没有放弃它的主权和政府的权利，根据国际法，其主权者之间的地位并没有改变。⑥ 在 1893 年的梅格海（Mighell）诉苏奥坦（Sultan）的案例中，大英帝国的殖民官在回答

---

① *World Peace Foundation Pamphlets*，第 5 卷，第 6 号，1927。

② 参见 J. S. Ewart, "Canada, the Empire and the United States", *Foreign Affairs*, 第 6 卷，127 页，1927。他认为自治领之间的关系的趋势是加拿大将要成为一个人格体。"如果人们继续认为主权国家加拿大的主权者是占据英国王位的人，从国际法来说，她就是一个人格体，旧有的帝国关系也应该随之终结。"

③ *British Year Book of International Law*，1922–1923，40～41 页。

④ A. Lawrence Lowell, "The Imperial Conference", *Foreign Affairs*, 第 5 卷，275 页以下。也可见 *World Peace Foundation Pamphlets*，第 5 卷，第 6 号，581 页。

⑤ Baty, "Protectorates and Mandates", *British Year Book of International Law*, 109 页，1922。

⑥ 参见 Evans, *Cases on International Law*, 63 页。

英国上诉法院询问的时候认为尽管杰哈瑞（Jahore）是英国的保护国，但依然是一个主权国家。① 这种观点已经为法院所广泛采用。

但是上面提到的这种观点随着保护国家控制被保护国家的对外事务的愿望的日益增加而日趋变得与理论不相一致。根据巴蒂（Baty）教授的看法，这在法国大革命发生后已经变成了现实。②

也许我们不必把太多精力放在那些认为被保护国家是主权国家的观点上。更广为接受的观点是被保护国家仅仅是部分主权国家。莫尔教授说，这在某种意义上是真实的，即每一个被保护的主权可以看作一个半主权（semi-sovereign），而一个被保护国家也相应地被归为半主权国家。③

4. 主权和中立国家

一个中立国家被定义为它的独立和统一受其他国家的共同保证，并被禁止参加进攻性的战争的国家。④ 有几种理论关系到中立国家的主权问题。第一种可以提及的是中立国同国际大家庭中独立主权国家一样是完全的主权国家。维斯特里克（Westlake）和奥本海（Oppenheim）是这派理论最为引人注目的代表人物。对维斯特里克来说，中立化"并不意味着国家功能的丧失，它仅仅是不做某事的承诺，在某一特殊事件中不干预的承诺，而不是损害主权……另外，对文明世界的每一部分来说，完整的主权权力是应当存在也是必须存在的"⑤。奥本海说："如果主权就是权威，那么中立国和其他非中立国一样都是完全主权者。"⑥ 阻止一个国家参加进攻性战争的中立条约也就是两个或多个主权国家为禁止它们采取战争且要求将它们的矛盾诉诸仲裁法庭的仲裁条约。⑦ 如果这是真实的，参加仲裁条约就不是对主权国家的损害。同样，加入回避战争行为的条约并不意味着丧失一部分主权。⑧

另一种观点，也许是最为流行的一种，认为中立国家的主权是受到了限制和

---

① Evans, *Cases on International Law*, 205~207 页。
② Baty, "Protectorates and Mandates", *British Year Book of International Law*, 111 页, 1922。
③ Moore, *International Law Digest*, 28 页。
在 1911 年 Statham 诉 Statham 事件中, Gaekwar of Baroda 的国王, 在关于 Baroda 的地位的时候, 如下一段话经常被使用："尽管他的国王不是独立的, 但作为他的国家的统治者他实施主权的多种功能, 包括对内主权, Baroda 的统治者、臣民, 但是英国国王拥有宗主权。" Evans, *Cases on International Law*, 62 页。
④ Garner, *Introduction to Political Science*, 164 页。
⑤ Westlake, *International Law*, 28 页, 也可参考 61 页。
⑥ Oppenheim, *International Law*, 第三版, 第 1 卷, 173 页。
⑦ Oppenheim, *International Law*, 第三版, 第 1 卷, 174 页。
⑧ Oppenheim, *International Law*, 第三版, 第 1 卷, 174 页。他也注意到"中立甚至不会对一个国家的等级产生影响。瑞士是一个拥有崇高声誉的国家, 它的等级不在英国和其他国家之后。""比利时也是使其中立化的条约的一方, 因此它的发动战争的权力与自由受到了严格的限制, 但它的限制是一种自我限制, 因此在条约以及在实践中被看作国家大家庭中的独立成员。" 参见 Stallybrass, *A Socieiy of State*, 67 页。

削弱的阿尔伯特国王（King Albert）。1918年11月22日他在比利时议会发表演讲："比利时要趁着这些国家在战争中伤了元气，从它们强加给它的中立中解放出来，比利时要享受完全的独立。"他继续说："比利时重建它的权利，要根据它自己的抱负和完全主权决定它的命运。"① 在回应奥本海教授的观点的时候，赫尔希（Hershey）教授说道："当一个国家加入一个仲裁条约的时候，并没有失去它主权的任何部分。但像这样只对国际社会中的某些国家加以限制，而其他国家依然保持有参加战争的权利，那这样的国家还是完全主权国家吗？"②

第三种关于中立国家的主权的归宿观点是认为中立国家的主权在保证者手中。这种观点由卢森堡的地方法学家所阐释，他们认为卢森堡不是根据卢森堡人民的意志而中立，而是根据欧洲列强的意愿，当大公想以"所有权力来自于本国"的原则修改宪法时，他们就出来干预了。③

第四种观点认为中立国家的主权是由担保者之一单独拥有的，而不是共同拥有的。这是1920年9月国联任命的由三个成员组成的调解在瑞典和芬兰之间关于阿兰德群岛的管辖权纠纷的调查团（the Commission of the Rapporteurs）的意见。他们认为芬兰对群岛的主权是无可争议的并且"分开它们将是导致它地位的改变，也是剥夺了本来属于它的东西"④。尽管有这样的评论，调查团还是倾向于群岛的中立化和非军事化，而这也是瑞典所希望的，而且芬兰对此也不反对。⑤并且，在否认瑞典对群岛的主权的时候，调查团对当地的瑞典人的诸如语言、学校的利益给予了在芬兰法律之外的保障。

5. 主权和国际联盟下的国际管理区

（1）但泽自由市（Danzig Free City）

关于但泽自由市的主权归属有六种观点。第一种观点认为但泽自由市的主权仍然归德国。这种理论被德国的大多数学者所支持。他们的理论立基于《和平条约》的第192条，认为德国决不会向列强割让她的主权的权利。第二种观点认为主权在主要协约国（the principal allies）的手中。在托管的情况下，德国将有争议地区的主权转给了主要协约国。因此在但泽的事例中也是如此。但是主要协约

---

① 《纽约时报》，1919-11-23。Fenwick 在 *International Law*（1924）第89页的注释中引用。

② Hershey, *Essentials of International Law*。Garner教授也接受这种观念。参见其 *Introduction to Political Science*，164页。"在所有其他方面，一个中立国家是完全主权者和独立的。"

③ Stallybrass, *A Society of State*，67页注释。兰辛也支持这种观点。参见其 On Sovereignty, *American Journal of International Law*，18页以下。

④ Gregory, "The Neutralization of the Åaland Islands", *American Journal of International Law*，第16卷，69页。

⑤ *American Journal of International Law*，第16卷，75页。刚果自由国的中立化在某种程度上比较特殊，因为它的主权被认为是比利时的，但是正如Oppenheim教授所指出的在这个事例中中立化的行为是不完整的。见 *International Law*，第1卷，178～179页。

国从来没有放弃该主权,因为如果它们准备放弃该主权的话,它们就会明确地宣布,就像它们在麦摩尔(Memel)事例中所做的那样,在《和平条约》的第90条,它们就宣布将麦摩尔的主权给予了立陶宛。①

第三种观点认为主权在国际联盟手中,因为国联在这个区域有权威并负责对该城市进行保护与防卫。进一步的讨论认为,正是在国联的监督下,该城市的宪法得以形成,也正是在国联的监督下,宪法才得以保证,宪法的修改也必须得到国联的同意。更进一步,代表国联的高级使团明确表示该城市的实际主权在国联那里。

第四种观点认为主权在于波兰。这主要是波兰学者的观点。他们坚持认为主权意味着在国际关系中的权利。既然处理国际事务的权力在《凡尔赛条约》第104章中给予了波兰,那么但泽就仅仅是波兰的自治区域。

第五种观点认为主权就在但泽自由市自身。大多数但泽的学者认为政治上有组织的领土就不能没有主权。但泽有领土,有司法权,有商业区。所有这些都包含着城市的主权。这种观念更进一步认为波兰与但泽的关系就是两个主权国家之间的国际协议。②

第六种观点认为主权在波兰、国际联盟、但泽自由市之间分离,因为它们都不同程度地行使了一个国家主权者的权力。③

(2) 萨尔(Saar)盆地

在所谓的"三巨头"在解决萨尔盆地问题的时候,主权问题是最重要的问题之一。威尔逊总统,尽管希望把矿产转给法国,但不只一次,而是多次激烈反对对德国在该区域的主权进行改变和悬置。④ 另一方面,法国代表理所当然地反对威尔逊总统的观点,因为如果德国继续保持该区域的主权的话,法国的有关劳工、征兵、工资的法律就不能在该地区实行,而这却正是《巴黎和约》赋予法国的权利。⑤ 法国代表认为执行法律的权利就是主权的权利,给予前者而不给予后者,在本质上是不可能的。英国首相劳合-乔治(Lloyd-George),虽然或多或少地站在法国这一边,但是采取一种中间立场,正如他所说:"我愿意给予萨尔盆地在国联管辖之下的独立性。"⑥

政治学家在萨尔盆地的主权归属上的观点并不一致。奥本海(Oppenheim)

---

① G. Levesque, *La Situation internationale de Danzig*, 113~131 页。

② 这个主题的最好的讨论在 G. Levesque 的 *La Situation internationale de Danzig* 中, 93 页。

③ M. M. Lewis, "Free City of Danzig", *British Year Book of International Law*, 90 页, 1924。

④ 参见 Sidney Osborne, *The Saar Question: A disease Spot in Europe*, 56 页、58 页, 1923。也可参见 Donald, *A Danger Spot in Europe*, 13 页, 1925。

⑤ Sidney Osborne, *The Saar Question. A disease Spot in Europe*, 57 页、59 页, 83 页, 1923。Donald, *A Danger Spot in Europe*, 14 页, 1925。

⑥ Sidney Osborne, *The Saar Question. A disease Spot in Europe*, 57 页, 1923。

认为主权在国际联盟那里，因为各种权利、义务以及权力都归于国际联盟的代理机关——管理委员会。① 而科贝特（Corbett）先生则持另外一种观点，他支持威尔逊总统的意见，认为主权依然保留在德国。他说："德国宣布放弃的不是主权，而是萨尔地区的行政权。"② 在他看来，必须在主权和行政权之间做出区分。法国和联盟执行了主权的权力，但不是主权本身。③ 一些法国学者分享法国代表的观点。还有的人认为主权在萨尔盆地的人民手中，这种观念是基于到了1935年，萨尔盆地的人民有权自己决定他们生活在哪个主权之下。

6. 主权和委任统治制度（Mandate System）

委任统治制度是世界大战后的一个新的产物，是对殖民地的一种新的管理方式。④ 某些人认为它是国际法的最大进步。⑤ 因为这个原因，委任统治的问题就是国际联盟条约中的最大的和最有价值的经验之一。⑥ 简单地说，它是对国际联盟的考验。⑦

也许关于委任统治制度的最重要和最复杂的问题是主权问题。在主权问题上的知名权威兰辛在新的委任统治制度中不能发现主权的归宿。⑧ 当威尔逊总统被兰辛提出的一大堆关于委任统治制度的问题所困窘的时候，他通过说这些问题是法律技术性问题因而是不重要的而把它们放到一边。⑨ 永久委任统治调查团也长时期地为这个问题所困扰。当调查团的成员，M. F. 德·瑞德（M. F. d'Andrade），建议把伊拉克的地位问题提交到秘书处的法律部门解决，罗潘德（Rappard）教授，当时正是秘书处委任统治部门的主任，告诉调查团的成员说如果德·安瑞德的建议得到采用，则法律部门将被置于一个十分尴尬的境地。后者表示他不愿意在现在

---

① Corbett, "What is the League of Nations", *British Year Book of International Law*, 121 页, 1924。
② Corbett, "What is the League of Nations", *British Year Book of International Law*, 127 页。
③ Corbett, "What is the League of Nations", *British Year Book of International Law*, 127 页。
④ 参见 H. W. Harris, *What is the League of Nations?* 104 页, 1925。委任统治制度：第一次世界大战结束后，帝国主义战胜国所建立的通过国际联盟对战败国的殖民地进行再分割和统治的一种制度。《国际联盟盟约》规定，战前（甲）奥斯曼帝国（土耳其）所属近东部分地区、（乙）德国所属非洲殖民地、（丙）德国所属西南非和太平洋诸岛，均由国际联盟委任英国、法国和日本等国进行统治。被统治的殖民地称为委任统治地，受委任进行统治的国家称为受委任国。受委任国的任务，对甲类委任统治地，是给予行政"指导及援助"；对乙类委任统治地，是根据所规定的条件将其作为单独的领土担负地方行政责任；对丙类委任统治地，是按照各种保证将其作为自己领土的组成部分加以治理。在形式上受委任国与委任统治地是一种"保护"关系，受委任国对国际联盟负责，须就委任统治地之情况向行政院提出年度报告。到第二次世界大战结束成立联合国时，甲类委任统治地，如伊拉克、叙利亚和黎巴嫩，均已成为独立国家；而乙类和丙类委任统治地，则被转为联合国托管制度下的托管领土。——译者注。
⑤ Smuts 将军的陈述，*League of Nations, Permanent Mandate Commission Minutes*，第二部分，附录六，91 页。也可参见同上第 92 页，详细内容来自 *Cape Times*, 1920-09-18。
⑥ 国联, "Records of the First Assembly", *30th Plenary Meeting*, Balfour 公爵的陈述。
⑦ Hughan, *International Government*, 229 页。
⑧ Lansing, *The Peace Negotiations*, 151 页以下。
⑨ Lansing, *The Peace Negotiations*, 153 页。

就这个问题发表过多的看法。于是这个讨论也就结束了，不过谜团仍然没有解开。①

在《国际联盟盟约》的第22条，这样写道："凡殖民地及领土，于此次战争后不复属于从前统治该地之各国……"这话已经足够清楚地表明了德国不能再宣布对委任统治的区域拥有主权，宣布主权仍然在德国手中很荒谬，事实上，这种观点已经没有多少人认可了。

格耐维夫·莱维斯克博士（Dr. Genevieve Levesque）关于但泽的主权的理论可以运用到这种情况。② 这种理论是德国将这些地域的主权转移给主要联盟国家，如果后者不将它们转给其他列强的话，那主权就保留在主要联盟国家的手中。这种观点也许不乏支持者，但也有人评论说，总的来说，协约国和同盟国都是时代的产物（它们仅存在于它们所属的那个时期）。对一部分人来说，它不再存在；对另一些人来说，它通过国际联盟表达它的愿望和意愿。

后一种观念导致主权在国际联盟的结论。这种观点为诸如温伯格（Wehberg）和许金（Schucking）的学者所支持。以下所引可以发现其逻辑："这些地区虽然是被协约国或同盟国中的一个或几个国家所征服的，但是从国际法考虑，是作为一个整体的同盟国或协约国所征服的；尽管对这些地区的军事占领是由一个或几个国家完成的，但根据法律，所有的同盟国或协约国都获利，而不是实现军事占领的国家单一地享有主权。正如盟约所说，从前统治该地的主权已经停止，这些地区的主权在所有的同盟国家那里。因此，当它们组成一个联盟的时候，联盟就被它们认为继承了这些主权。因此，非正式的停止或放弃索偿契约是没有必要的，只承认主权让渡给了国联就足够了。"③

从上面的引述来看，可以得出联盟对托管地区的主权必须被看作唯一和真正的主权。国联会在必要的情况下，指定一个文明国家来托管这些未独立的领土，保护它们，以不辜负它们的信任。

而且，从法律角度说，国际联盟对托管地区的主权是不能被质疑的，因为委任统治的转移、终止和修改要求前者的同意。④ 更进一步说，这些区域是通过国际联盟的代理机构即长期托管代表团而进行控制的，虽然这种控制是间接的而不

---

① 国联，*Minutes of the Permanent Mandate Commission*，第七部分，123页。

② Levesque, *La Situation internationale of Danzig*, 121页。参见委员会执行主席致同盟国家首脑的信，1921-06-15。*Official Journal*, 1921-12, 645页。也见 Baty, "Protectorates and Mandates", *British Year Book of International Law*, 117页注释，1922。Snow, *Proceedings of Academy of Political Science*, 第8卷，427页。

③ Snow, "The Mandatory System under the Covenant of the League of Nations", *Proceedings of Academy of Political Science*, 第8卷，427页。

④ 第22章，第h段。

是直接的。①

另一方面，也有一些学者根据不同的理由来反对上述观点。斯马茨（Smuts）将军说："国际联盟与委任统治根本无关，委任统治已经被《和约》作为一种事实而解决，已经跟国际联盟无关。"② 而且，国际联盟不是一个国家，它不拥有领土，不管理臣民，不拥有主权。③ 另外，国联的委员会，这个国联对托管地区的最重要的建议机构，已经明确表明它无权分配托管权④，也没有限制区域的权威。⑤

发现国际联盟对托管地区没有主权，一些学者坚持认为主权在委任统治国那里。罗琳（R. E. Rolin）是这种理论的最重要的阐释者之一。⑥ 从法律的观点看，他坚持认为委任统治制度就是兼并的制度。⑦ 他宣称："殖民地的委任与国内的委任不同，意味着对管理事物的永久权力的承认。在这种视角下，殖民地的委任在本质上就是出让。"⑧ 于是他得出这样的结论：无论委任这个词怎么理解，主权都属于委任统治国。⑨

南非联邦就一再宣称在它托管之下的被托管区域是统一体的不可分割的一部分。如果这样的话，被托管区域就不在永久托管委员会的监督之下。⑩ 在关于南非联邦和葡萄牙边界线的条约中，南非联邦宣称它"拥有西南非洲的主权，因为

---

① 也可见 M. F. d'Andrade 的观点，*Minutes of the Permanent Mandate Commission*，第 1 部分，41 页，1921。

② *Minutes of the Permanent Mandate Commission*，第 2 部分，92 页，1922。在另外的地方，他宣称："在《和约》下，德国已经宣称她的殖民地不是给国际联盟，而是给大国。"第 2 部分，4～5 页。附录 6，92 页。

③ 参见 Larnarde，*La Société des nations*，Paris，1920，也可参见 Leveaque，*La Situation internationale de Danzig*，118 页。

④ Levermore，*Year Book of the League of Nations*，第 2 卷，19 页。也可参见 League of Nations，*Offocial Journal*，第 1 卷，343 页，1920。

⑤ *Minutes of the Permanent Mandate Commission*，第 2 部分，6 页，调查团关于英国和比利时之间的卢旺达边界（Ruanda Boundary）的报告。

⑥ *Minutes of the Permanent Mandate Commission*，第 3 部分，218 页。也可参见 Millot，*Les Mandats internationaux*，107 页以下。参见 *Revwe de Droit international et de legislation comparee* 1920，no. 3～4，350 页。

⑦ *Minutes of the Permanent Mandate Commission*，第 3 部分，218 页。

⑧ *Minutes of the Permanent Mandate Commission*，第 3 部分，219～220 页。

⑨ *Minutes of the Permanent Mandate Commission*，第 3 部分，220 页。他进一步指出："文本不包含其他保护区。委任统治国的法律没有意义但是是实际的主权。这是一个部分运用到全体的例子。并且，'托管区域的完整部分'意思就是兼并。"219 页。

Smuts 将军也认为丙类托管地区实际上就是兼并。参见他在国联时写的一封信：*Permanent Mandate Commission*，第 2 部分，附录六，91 页。

Baty 教授也喜欢这种理论。"在这种状态同兼并区分开来是很困难的。如果你对托管区有完全的管理权，你对它就有了完全的控制。托管区是没有主权的，甚至一点点主权也没有，它不能阻止委任统治国对其控制下的人民任何行为。""Protectorates and Mandates"，*British Year Book of International Law*，1921-1911，117 页。

Lansing 评论委任统治制度为兼并的伪装。

⑩ 国联，*Minutes of the Permanent Mandate Commission*，第 7 部分。

西南非洲的主权不久以前是德国拥有的"①。这里所引用的已经足以表明政治家在考虑关于委任统治制度时主权归宿的观点了。

但是也有一些学者否认主权被转让给委任统治国。这种理论的起点在下面的引文中可以发现："当今被运用的委任统治制度有两个主要的观点：第一，委任统治国被禁止因为自己特殊的目的而获取托管区的资源，无论是通过劳工的形式，还是如矿藏或蔬菜产品等物质财富的形式。第二，委任统治国从精神上和物质上帮助托管区达到自治这个目的。这些最基本的原则排除了在任何时候对托管区的兼并。"②委任统治制度的应用并没有把德国在委任统治国的殖民地包括在内，并不意味着给后者以主权。③

而且，乙、丙类殖民地的委任统治国不具有其托管地的主权。④ 没有哪个委任统治国认为这些托管区是它们自己的，是不可分离的；没有哪个委任统治国认为托管区的人民是它们自己的国民。相反，每一个委任统治国都给与了托管区以财政自治，大多数还保证了它们的管理自治。⑤ 简单地说，正如希克斯（Hicks）所言，委托统治国拥有管辖权，不拥有主权。⑥

因此有一些学者认为主权还是在托管区。即，以前，主权在德国那里，既然德国宣布放弃了，既然主权没有转移给任何国家，那主权就必须存在于托管区。⑦这个观点并非没有理由。这种观点被制宪大会于 1924 年 7 月 10 日通过的伊拉克

---

① 这样运用语词被认为是非常严重的。永久调查团已经再三提出"拥有主权"表述的确切含义的问题。这个问题也在委员会和代表大会中被讨论。参见 *Minutes of the Permanent Mandate Commission*，第 10 与第 11 部分。也可参见 *The Monthly Summary of the League of Nations*，第 7 卷，第 7 期，1927 年 8 月，227 页。

② 国联，*Minutes of the Permanent Mandate Commission*，第 3 部分，217 页。同样的观点也被在叙利亚托管区的法国全权代表 M. de Caix 所表述："委任统治是为了教育托管区的人民，以使之在某一天达到完全自治这个目的。这个前提意味着委任统治将逐步在托管区设立一些本国人管理的机构（native organization），当这完成之后，能够保证这个国家完全可以自治后，如果委任统治国以一种恰当的方式来执行它们的义务，对托管区的干预就是不必要的了。"

③ 国联，*Minutes of the Permanent Mandate Commission*，第 3 部分，218 页。"委任统治国与托管区之间的关系在种类上不同于一个主权国与它的依附国之间的关系。委任统治国在地位上并不具有优先性，它仅仅是受托人。它不能因为自己的利益而实施统治。它是作为国际联盟的代表去实施对托管区居民的权威，它要保护它们的利益，还要对国联所有成员都开放。接受一个托管区，并不能要求兼并的权利。它意味着监护的义务。" W. Rees 所引用，*A Plan for the Government by Mandate in Africa*，7 页。
"'委任统治'这个词意味着新获得其以前没有的权利，但是这些权利是为了管理好被委托国家的利益，而不是为了委任统治国家自己的利益。作为一个受托人，一个委任统治国要履行它的责任，而防止一些权利被占用；另一方面，它必须保护被委托国家的人民的财产，推动其发展，维护其健康，保护其自由及道德和物质福利。" "Colonial Mandates and the League of Nations"，*Preliminary Document of the 12th innter-Parliamentary Conference*，76 页。*Minutes of the Permanent Mandate Commission*，第 3 部分，218 页。

④ 南非政府的例子是一个例外，见 128～129 页。

⑤ *Minutes of the Permanent Mandate Commission*，第 3 部分，218～219 页。也可参见第 2 部分，46、58、68 页。参见 Balfour 的观点，Levermore，*Year Book of the League of Nations*，第三卷。

⑥ Hicks，*New World Order*，125 页。也可参见 *American Journal of International Law*，第 18 卷，308 页。

⑦ 参见 Albert Millot，*Les Mandats internationaux*，巴黎，116～117 页，1924。

《基本法》所支持，《基本法》（或称为宪法）宣称："伊拉克是一个自由和独立的主权国家。它的主权是不可分离的和不可剥夺的。"①

但是这种理论也有它的反对者。如甲类的托管区，尽管盟约称之为"独立国家"，事实上，英国对马来苏丹们的所谓建议，都不是真正的建议，而是苏丹们必须要接受的。② 更不要说乙类和丙类的托管区了，它们跟兼并实际上没有多少差别。③

前文提到的那些大相径庭的观点以及它们在应用中的困难，促使一批思想家提出了另一种理论，虽然这种理论与以前的理论都不同，但它无论如何也算不上一种新理论。持这种理论的人，认为主权不在任一特殊的地方。之所以这样，是因为他们认为把主权放在某一特定地方与事实不符，并且也解决不了难题。Q. 赖特（Q. Wright）教授在对委任统治制度的主权问题进行了详细研究之后，被迫做出了这样的结论："把托管区的主权归于联盟委员会同意下的委任统治行为是达到事实的一种近便方法。"④ 梅洛特（Millot）教授，委任统治制度领域的优秀学者，也持类似的观点，虽然他得出类似观点的途径不一样。

同许多政治学者一样，梅洛特教授把主权区分为对内和对外部分。前者在一个地方，后者在另一个地方。但是在两者之间没有确切的界限。举例来说，甲类的托管区，它的对外主权是由委任统治国家所实施的；但是在某些方面已经转给地方权威。重要的主权都是由委任统治国家执行的，但都是为了顺应地方人民的要求，委任统治国行使主权一般采用与人民的愿望相一致的方式。另外，对内主权一般由地方和委任统治国两个权威的有限合作来行使，而后者又基本上放弃了这种权力。⑤

为了把这种观念表述得更清楚，让我们引述一段一位知名学者的话："被协约国所接管的叙利亚和美索不达米亚（Mesopotamia）的主权，已经被这些国家赋予了叙利亚和美索不达米亚自身。因为临时托管存在的依据是承认这些地区是发展的政治实体，所以与独立和主权相联系的一些权力依然被这些国家保留执行，当然是在国联的监督之下。那种选择会导致协约国对托管区一部分主权的丧失。

---

① 第二章。这一章的表述与委任统治的一些词语是相当不一致的。在 Minutes of the Permanent Mandate Commission 的第 7 部分中，W. Rees 评论道："伊拉克不是被委任统治国统治的国家，也不是某种程度的自治区域。它是一个名副其实的国家，一个在英国政府的某些建议和原则指导下的独立王国。" Minutes of the Permanent Mandate Commission，第 7 部分，12 页，1925。

② Baty, "Protectorates and Mandates", *British Year Book of International Law*, 1921-1922, 117 页。

③ 那些持主权在委任统治国那里和国际联盟那里的人自然的是这种理论的支持者。

④ Wright, "Sovereignty of the Mandates", *American Journal of International Law*, 第 17 卷，698 页。或 13 卷，315 页。

⑤ A. Millot, *Les Mandats Internationaux*, 96 页，巴黎，1924。

然而那些没有转移给托管区人民的权利在委任统治国和国联之间分享。"①

7. 主权和国际联盟

随着国际联盟的建立，世界开启了一个新的时代。它标志着国际或世界组织发展史上的达到的最高水平。我们被告知"国际联盟是许多主权或自治国家为了推动国际合作、达致国际和平与安全而自由参加的组织"②。

但是，国联的产生是否对国家或者其成员国的主权产生影响是当今政治哲学中的一个最有趣味的问题，毫无疑问会引起我们的考察和注意。

没有学者打算承认国际联盟是一个单一的主权者，而其成员国的地位降到法国的一个行政区或英国的一个郡。但是，这种情况也是真实的，无论在过去还是在现在，世界主权的种子已经种下，不久的将来我们就会看到它的实现和出现。早在1920年，瑞士的总统莫塔（Motta）先生在他与国际联盟代表的第一次会面的欢迎演讲中就热情地宣布"联盟不是各政府的联合，它是各民族的联合"③。罗伯特·塞西尔（Robert Cecil）爵士，世界会议的成员都听到过他的声音，在以前说过这样的话："随着时间的推移，联盟将解决所有重要的国际问题。它将在欧洲和世界成为唯一的国际权威。所有希望参加国际事务的国家都将通过联盟这个机构达到它们的目的，因为没有其他更为重要的机制。"④

但是没有谁说过国际联盟是唯一的主权，不少学者断言联盟是世界的主权之一，起码在它的层面上是最高权威。有这样的说法："一个新的拥有全部主权的国际人格诞生了，我们有理由期待……国际和平与安全的保持，通过发展国际法来提升国际合作。"⑤

这种观点得到耶鲁大学教授白德温（Baldwin）的很好的阐发。白德温教授的起点在下述引文中得到了体现："人类社会的一般运动是从简单到复杂。家庭发展到第一个政治组织——部落，族长的意志是行为的规则。逐步地这种意志的运用将在某种程度上被限制。几个部落组成国家……社会在特征上是民族的，但是每一个国家都和另外的国家有某种程度的联系……从家庭的管理到部落的管理再到国家的管理，是一个自然的步骤，因此从国家的管理到国家间关系的管理也不是一个非自然的进程。"⑥

国际联盟仅仅是社会秩序自然发展的结果。既然国家通过缓慢发展的进程获

---

① Corbett, "What is the League of Nations", *British Year Book of International Law*, 130 页, 1924。

② "World Peace Foundation Pamphlets", *Sixth Year Book of the League*, 137 页, 1927（3~4）。

③ *Provisional Verbatim Records*, 卷 1, 4 页, 1920。

④ D. J. Hill 所引的陈述。见 E. S. Rankin, *The Dominion of Sea and Air*, 222 页。参见 H. H. Powers, *The Great Peace*, 111 页。

⑤ 参见 *Political Science Quarterly*, 第 36 卷, 709 页。也可参见 J. E. Harley, *The League of Nations and International Law*, 参见 Oppenheim, *International Law*, 第 3 版, 第 1 卷, 268 页。

⑥ "Vesting Sovereignty in a League of Nations", *Yale Law Review*, 第 28 卷, 209 页, 1919。

得主权，联盟也是如此。根据白德温教授的看法，联盟是主权者，而且只能是它的领域内的主权者，这一主张有三个大的法律学派支持，即历史学派、哲学学派和实用主义学派。

历史事实已经表明国际联盟已经执行了主权者的权力。汉萨同盟（Hanseatic League）、根据《维也纳公约》第105章成立的国家间特别法院（the Interstate Tribunal）、邮政联盟（Postal Union）、德国关税同盟（German Zollverein）、神圣罗马帝国（the Holy Roman Empire），每一个都在一定程度上作为主权国家实施主权权利，实际上每一个也是主权实体。这是真实的，国际联盟的情况也是真实的。

转到哲学学派，白德温（Baldwin）教授发现它的主要理论在主权的权利依靠人民的同意。人民可以放弃一部分主权和保留一部分主权。"如果他们能够分离成部分，一部分被授予积极的机构，另外一部分保存，为什么主权不能分离，从而使整个主权的一部分可以授予一个公共机构，而剩余的部分被授予另外的机构？"① 如果一群个人可以构成一个主权国家，一群国家为什么就不能？作为实用主义学派，他发现这种论据建立在事实之上。美国的实用主义者只要看他们自己的国家就提供了一个一群国家可以组成一个主权者的好例子。在他看来，国际联盟只不过是一个更宽泛意义上的联邦。②

没有上述观念如此大胆，但更为广泛接受的观点是国际联盟成员国的主权受到国际联盟的损害或限制。普罗克（Pollock）教授说，争论作为一个整体的国际联盟在何种意义上可以称为主权者是无用的。但是一个国家的主权可以受到限制，就像一个人的自由要受到婚约的严重限制一样。③ 他又说，国家仅就对内主权来说，是不受任何限制或损害的，但是从对外来说，它是受限制的。④

委内瑞拉的代表，马努尔·迪兹·罗德瑞古兹（Manuel Diaz Rodriguez）博士，在1920年11月20日递交给国际联盟的大会的文件中阐述了这样的观点：由于交通工具的不断发展，不同国家的联系更加紧密了。这带来了利益的国际化。由于"利益的联系变得越来越紧密，导致国家的相互依赖"。他补充说："尽管相互依靠和依赖是不同的，但有时候二者的效果也差不多，需要每个国家实际上放弃主权，以求得在更大范围内实现共同利益。"⑤

已经有评论指出："主权权利不可以被削减的理论是一种含糊不清的理论，这种理论就像一种虔诚的誓言……虽然有些机械论；因为为保持和平，盟约必须

---

① "Vesting Sovereignty in a League of Nations"，*Yale Law Review*，第28卷，217页，1919。
② "Vesting Sovereignty in a League of Nations"，*Yale Law Review*，第28卷，218页。
③ Pollock，"Sovereignty and the League of Nations"，*Fortnightle Review*，第110卷，814页，1918。
④ Pollock，"Sovereignty and the League of Nations"，*Fortnightle Review*，第110卷，813页以下。"只要一个国家在其领域内保存有最高权力的一般特征，并且在其管辖的事务中继续实施权力，则没有明显的理由否认它是一个主权国家。" 814页。
⑤ *Provisional Verbatim*，1920-09-20，第8次会议，5页。

加强对主权的限制。"① 同样的观点在下述引文中也可以发现："没有禁令禁止任何一个国家或统治者去坚守国王或国家的主权，但是一个国际联盟的成功存在可以减少这些理论可能导致的伤害。"②

上面所述的是政治家和学者们的概述。现在我们来看看，在现实中，国联会员国的主权怎样被限制，正如一些学者所说的那样。《国际联盟盟约》第10条宣布禁止对作为独立国家的成员国的征服。这种征服不仅指直接的领土侵犯，也包括对政治独立的侵犯。③

国际法允许每一个主权国家对另一个主权国家宣战。④ 利伯（Lieber）的法案中表达了这种观点。⑤ 当美国的一个参议员宣称战争权不能损害的时候，他是认为它是主权的本质特征。⑥ 但是，在联盟盟约的第十章下，这种权利不存在了。第十一章也有类似的话："任何战争或战争威胁，不论直接影响任何联盟会员国与否，兹特宣告其为与联盟全体有关之事，联盟应采取其认为明智有效之行动，借以确保国际和平。"

在类似的12、15、16和17条，国际联盟的成员都被限制了战争的权利。"很显然签署《国际联盟盟约》的每一个国家通过上述条款放弃了一些重要的主权权利。"⑦ "无论如何否认盟约对国联成员国主权的影响，上面讨论过的条款已经是对主权损害的充分证明。"⑧

另外，在第五次大会上通过的《太平洋国际争端条约草案》中，也提及："对国联成员国的侵犯意味着对国联所有成员国的主权的侵犯，也是最严重的侵犯，因为它牵扯到生死存亡的大事。将决定战争与和平的主权权利从国家议会转移到国际联盟行政院，跟代议政府的基本原则是相反的。这样一个国家可能卷入一场违背自己的意愿和利益的战争中。"⑨

在其他国家卷入战争之后，每一个独立的国家有保持和平的权利是主权国家不可剥夺的权利。⑩ 霍尔（Hall）说道："在战争中保持中立是每一个国家的主权。"⑪ 但是在这里，正如上面已经指出的，国家的中立权利在《国际联盟盟约》

---

① 参见 Duggan, *League of Nations, the Principles and Practice*, 89 页。
② Gildsmith, *A League to Enforce Peace*, 81 页。
③ "国际联盟会员国家承担尊重和保持所有国联会员国之领土完整和现存之政治独立，以防御外来侵略。如遇这种侵略或这种侵略之威胁或危险时，行政院应建议履行这项义务之方法。"
④ Wright, "Effects of the League of Nations Covenant", *Political Science Review*, 第 13 卷，560~570 页。
⑤ U. S. Army, *General Orders*, 第 100 条，第 67 章，1863。
⑥ Lodge, *Senate and the League of Nations*, 407 页。
⑦ Montgomery, *Issues of European Statesmenship*, 123 页。
⑧ Montgomery, *Issues of European Statesmenship*, 124 页。也可参见 *Political Science Review*, 第 13 卷，563 页。
⑨ Montgomery, *Issues of European Statesmenship*, 138 页。
⑩ Wheaton, *Elements of International Law*, 第 8 版，509 页，1866。
⑪ Hall, *Rights and Duties of Neutrals*, 15 页。也可参见 Hershey, *Essentials of International Law*, 445 页。

的第 16 条被取消了:"国际联盟会员国如果不顾盟约第 12 条、第 13 条和第 15 条的规定而从事战争,应视为对联盟所有其他会员国犯有战争行为应予以制裁。其他会员国应该立即与之断绝各种商业上或财政上的关系,禁止其人民与破坏盟约国人民的一切交往,并阻止其他国家人民与该国人民之间的一切交往。如果这些措施未能迫使违反盟约的国家屈服,国联行政院应向会员国建议派遣和组织军队来维护盟约。"①

我们已经阐述了那些认为国际联盟正在成为世界上唯一的主权和国际联盟是一个主权者,至少在其范围内是主权者,国际联盟的建立对其成员国的主权是一个限制的观点。现在让我们看看那种认为国家的主权并不因为成为国际联盟的成员而受到限制的观点。这不是一种新观点。威廉姆·潘(William Penn)在写他的《通向现在和未来和平论文集》的时候就有这种观点。他这样写道:"来看我最后一个问题,主权国家将不再是主权国家了——这是它们绝不能忍受的一件事情。但这也是一个错误,因为在国内它们和以往一样保留主权……如果这被称做是减少它们的权力,那也仅仅是因为大鱼不能把小鱼吃光,每一个主权国家都可以平等地保护它们免受伤害。"② M. 黑曼斯(M. Hymans)在第一次会议的开幕式上的演讲中宣称:"我们必须再次重申,国际联盟不能、决不能成为一个超国家,从而使主权国家成为其奴役。"③ 克容勋爵(Lord Curzon)在国际联盟行政院第一次会议上也表达了同样的观点。④ 这样的观点也为鲍尔吉斯(Bourgeois)所支持。⑤ 这些学者的主要根据在于主权是一个国家的本质特征。只要是国家,就有主权。但是联盟不是一个国家,因为它缺乏成为国家的两个基本要素,也就是领土和人民,因此它不拥有主权。⑥ 正如他们所意识到的,联盟与国家的主权无关,因为它不过是主权国家自由参与的一系列组织之一,它们随时可以在想要退出的时候退出。

---

① 参见 Q. Wright, "Effects of the League of Nations Covenant", *Political Science Review*, 第 13 卷, 571 页。也见 "Sovereignty and Neutrality", *International Conciliation*, 208 页。
W. F. Taft 和 E. J. Bryan, *World Peace, A Written Debate*, 114 页, 1917。参见 J. A. Hobson, *Towards International Government*, 127 页, 1915。
② Pollock 引用, 见 "Sovereignty and the League of Nations", *Fortnightle Review*, 第 110 卷, 818 页, 1918。
③ *Provisional Verbatim*, 6 页, 1920。
④ *Provisional Verbatim*, 6 页, 1920。
⑤ Leon Bourgeois, *L'Ouvre de la societe des nations*, 113 页, 1922—1923。
⑥ M. Larnaude, *La Société des nations*, 巴黎, 1920。"国际社会不是一个与联邦、邦联、同盟或者是其他的所有的非同盟国家相类似的国家社会。它首先是一种全新类型的构成,我们甚至可以专一地说它是一种契约式的构成,在这种构成中,各政府承担某些义务,让其主权保持完整。(国际)社会不是一个超国家;它更多的是像一个协会,像一个多政府工会,像一个多政府的合作社,但是,此外,它有一些特殊的特征,尤其是这些特征超过了契约本身规定的权利。"(原文为法文——译者注)

8. 结论

上面我们从国际关系的视角所谈到的主权归宿的观点并不是全部的观点。我们还可以加上许多条目①，但是就显示主权的归宿的困难和复杂而言，这已经足够了。不同的学者从不同的角度可以将主权放置在这里或那里，但是很少有理论能摆脱困境以及由此而来的批评。

交通能力的增强导致了世界的不同地区的个人与组织的联系比以前更紧密。人类行为和利益的相互依赖不再是一种选择，而是一种必要。相互依赖的加强必然导致国际组织和条约的增加，为了满足需要并适应变化的环境，更多的组织和条约出现，这就导致了主权归宿的问题变得越来越复杂。委任统治制度的产生和国际联盟的建立已经向我们显示了所言不虚。

五、近来对主权观念的攻击

在国际关系领域的应用中，主权观念受到不同角度的攻击。第一，有些人甚至否认在国际关系中"主权"一词的用处。他们坚持认为主权只存在于一个国家的内部，在边境之外就不存在主权了。韦罗贝教授就说："主权在宪法中的地位很重要，但在国际法中却没有适当的位置。"② 另外一位学者指出："把主权观念引入国际法中是徒劳的。"③

有一些人认为研究主权的视角应该是从上向下或从下向上，也就是说它体现了上级与下级之间的关系，但这种关系绝不应该是国家之间的关系，因为后者是站在同一个水平上，被认为是彼此平等的，而无论其强弱、大小和贫富。因此，"一个矮子和一个巨人同样是人，日内瓦和俄国同样是国家"，道理就是这样。

从国际关系的角度看，一个国家的主权通常是指它的独立。④ 从本质上看，独立是否定的、被动的和潜在的而不是积极的、主动的和明显的。⑤ 它仅仅意味着一个国家有其存在的权利，同其他国家一样不受其他国家的限制和控制地处理与其他国家的关系。将一个误认为另一个就意味着把梯子平放到地上从一端走到

---

① 举例来说，海牙仲裁法院、国际永久法院、国际劳工组织等在何种程度上对国家主权构成影响。

② Willoughby, *Fundamental Concepts of Public Law*, 283 页。

③ P. A. Brown 的陈述，参见 *American Journal of International Law*, 第 9 卷, 326 页。也可参见 Garner, "Limitations on National Sovereignty in International Relations", *Political Science Review*, 第 19 卷（1925), 6 页。

④ 参见 Crane, *The State in Constitutional and International Law*, 65 页。"主权"和"独立"因而被一些学者看作同一个事物。Foulke, *International Law*, 69～70 页注释。

⑤ Manning, *Law of Nations*, Amos 修订, 第 93 页。"主权代表肯定方面, 独立代表否定方面。"参见 Brown, *International Reality*, 64～65 页。

另一端，而不是用它来上下，结果不仅是毫无意义的，也是不适当的，甚至是危险的。①

然而，也有另一些学者从另外的观点反对将主权的观点应用到国际关系中。他们说当今的世界已不是过去的世界。他们认为过去的学者和政治家尚可以宣称主权意味着行为的自由和做一切想做的自由，但是霍布斯的时代已经过去了，他的理论和今天的现实情况之间的鸿沟变得越来越大，时间也显示它们之间不再一致，甚至是相冲突的，一个的存在就意味着另一个的灭亡。

这里有一段很雄辩的话语值得引述："随着世界经济变得越来越相互依赖，必须创造新的体制来使政治能适应并控制经济力量。因此17、18世纪，甚至19世纪的主权理论已经不适应今天的实际情况了。有充足理由证明"主权"一词现在已经变成一个很含混的语词。"主权"这个词和观念已经威胁到英国和爱尔兰之间最近条约的最终达成……它产生了什么不同？这或许是我们要问的。《国际联盟盟约》的策划者们面临同样的问题。什么国家可以被承认？他们决定整个地摒弃'主权'这个词。成员国对'自治'的国家自治领或殖民地都是开放的。'世界主权'这个词在整个《盟约》里，只使用了一次，也只是在较小的范围内使用。还有其他从新体制中产生的问题可供佐证，但上面所讲的一切已足以显示"主权"一词已经过时。它仅仅是一种对结果和形式进行分类的理论而不能作为一个给结论提供支持的论据。"②

刚才所引的这段话是才写的，但其中的观点并不新鲜。安吉尔（Angel）先生，所谓的悲观论者，告诉我们对国家主权的崇拜是一个大幻想。他小心谨慎地说道："当现实（迅速的交流导致的信用系统的日趋复杂和精细化）已经使得当今的国际政治与古代相比发生了深刻的和本质上的变化；但是我们的观念却还是非常陈旧的。"③ 他断言："社会是靠利益而不是国家间的分离来自我分类，现代国家已经失去了它的同质性；所有这些多方面的因素导致国家竞争的迅速消失。"④

甚至黑格尔的故乡的思想家们也意识到在商业、工业和保险业及其他多种多样的组织所建立的国际基础上，国家已经发生了完全的变化。国家间的经济上的相互依赖与日俱增。⑤ 作为这种变化导致的结果，"国家已经进入一个通过会议和条约而生存和发展的阶段，这是一种必需，而不是选择。原来意义上的主权观念

---

① 参见 Garner, "Limitations on National Sovereignty in International Relations", *Political Science Review*, 第19卷（1925），2页。也可以参见 R. Pound 在 *Political Theory and International Law* 中的观点，见 Merriam 和 Barnes 的 *Political Theories*, 121页。

② E. D. Hamilton, "In Re Alienation of Sovereignty", *Virginia Law Review*, 第13卷（1927），524页。

③ Angel, *The Great Illusion*, 9页。

④ Angel, *The Great Illusion*, 9页。

⑤ Wehberg, *The Problem of an International Court of Justice*, 1页。

已经受到强烈的冲击，也已经不再合适了；因为国际社会的利益一定会代替单个国家的单独利益"①。

上面所提到的第一种反对主权的观点纯粹是从法律的角度，第二种反对主要是从经济的角度。现在我们看看第三种，它主要是从道德的角度。这种观点来源于人类过去战争的结果，特别是世界大战。

需要提醒的是这种观点的支持者反对主权，除非整个世界只有一个主权。他们认为，假如主权是不可限制的，不会出错的，如果同时有两个以上主权，则一定有冲突、竞争、敌对，最坏的就是战争。他们同但丁的观点一样，认为和平只能通过一个单一权力下的统一政府系统才能得到。因为一个单一的权力，已经没有对手，没有进一步的野心去满足。

凡圭尼（Faguini）说道："现在的战争，在最高和最坏的方面显示了国家主义。除非现在的独立的、单一的主权国家通过成为世界联邦的成员的方式交出它们的主权，否则目前所发生的一定会再次发生。"② D. A. 金斯利（D. A. Kingsley），纽约人寿保险公司的主席，不论他是为了他的客户，还是为了整个人类，他都强调指出："只要世界上存在哪怕两个大的不受限制的主权国家，就不会有持久的和平。"③ 在他看来，如果只有一个主权，全世界的人民就可以愉快与和平地生活，因为"美国已经显示了所谓的主权国家可以融入一个更大的主权国家，而不丧失它的个性和参与的民主原则"。"如果要让当前的不受限制的主权原则得以废弃；如果作为一个国家必须像1789年每一个殖民地放弃的那样放弃，我们应当支持这样做，我们应当发现时间已经到来——正如我们的国父所作的——我们确实仅仅放弃一点点错误的傲慢、一点点仇恨、一点点偏见和一点点恐惧，我们就会进入，我们的殖民地已经进入的和平和幸福的秩序。"④

六、结论

传统论者在我们的时代并不缺乏，但是现在的传统论者同以往的传统论者是不同的。他们中的许多人，不主张主权是毫无条件地不可限制和不可分割的，而是主张主权观念与其说是国际法中的概念，不如说是宪法中的概念。它只存在于一个国家的内部，而不在之外。实际上，他们希望"主权"这个词不再运用到国际关系中。如果这种观点与事实大体相符，则我们所讨论的主题就没有多大价值，仅仅具有历史意义。

---

① Wehberg, *The Problem of an International Court of Justice*, 3页。
② Bigelow 所引用, *World Peace*, 219页。
③ "The World's Fundamental Error", *The Independent*, 第85卷, 153～155页。
④ "The World's Fundamental Error", *The Independent*, 也见第84卷, 376页, 1915。

然而，不必去管刚才提到的那种观点是否合理，看起来现在需要指出现代思想追求的或者已经达到的目标，来对我们的讨论做一总结。无论谁对谁错，对我们来说都已不重要。事实上，主张主权不可分并且不受限制的观念在国际关系中的应用已经被大多数思想家置疑，这种置疑很可能以后还会持续，对这个问题深有研究的一个学者说："承认主权可分的国家主权观念，应被归于一种国际关系理论，因为这种理论已经为许多国际法学者所接受。"① 并且如果麦克白（Markby）教授没有错的话，奥斯丁也算是一个主权可分论的信奉者，起码在国际关系领域中是如此。

---

① Crane, "The State in Constitutional and International Law", *Johns Hopkins University Studies*, 41 页, 1907 (6～7)。

第六章 主权与法律

一、导论

在讨论主权理论在国际关系中的运用时,我们已经简要地指出不同阶段的关于主权与国际法关系的不同观念。但是,正如前文所述,许多学者仍然不承认国际法是严格意义上的法律。即使我们同意许多权威尤其是国际法权威的主张而肯定国际法是法律,前面的讨论也还不够全面。一个简单的理由是:国际法不过是法学领域里的一个分支。因此在本章和下两章中,我们就来讨论主权与法律关系的不同方面,不仅局限在某个特殊领域,而是就法律整体而言。

现在所讨论的主题是一个既古老又新鲜的话题。说它古老是因为它已经在古希腊甚至更早的时候就被讨论。① 说它新鲜是因为最近出现了许多新的表现形式,这包括出现了一些新情况并发现了一些新规律。考察这些极端的观点,我们发现,一方面,有些人坚持认为法律是主权的产物,如果没有主权作支撑,则不能称之为法律;另一方面,有些人坚持认为法律高于主权,因而比主权更为高级没有主权作支撑,法律依然可以存在。②

在这两种极端观点之间,我们发现有许多人坚持认为法律是对主权的一种限制。有人认为二者没有对方的限制都可以存在。有些人认为在政治和法律组织的早期历史中,法律是独立的,是外在于主权的,但是最近的趋势使得法律越来越成为主权的产物。另外,有些人把主权比作是烟囱,而法律是烟;他们说,烟囱是有用的,因为烟是通过烟囱出来的,但事实是如果炉子里没有煤或燃料,就不会有烟。③ 还有些人认为主权不是独立于或者说外在于法律的,可以在法律中找到它;这样法律本身就是主权者,没有法律,就没有主权。

这个主题的重要性不能轻视。说它是法理学中的核心问题,因而是整个政治科学甚至社会科学领域里的一个重要问题,也许都不太为过。自从古希腊开始,特别是在布丹的《国家六论》出现之后,就有很多的学者在讨论它,然而,这个讨论似乎没有穷尽。但是对已有观点的考察并不是徒劳,不仅因为它能引导我们看到未来之曙光,也因为它能使我们了解过去的观点。

---

① 参见 Allen, *International Relations*, 12 页。
② 参见 K. C. Hsiao, *Political Pluralism*, 9 页以下, 1927。
③ 参见 Todd, *Theories of Social Progress*, 1918。

二、分析学派

加纳（Garner）教授说："一个被广泛讨论、并对最近半世纪的法律思想产生重要影响的主权的观念是由分析法学派的法学家所阐明的。"① "分析学派"这个词长久以来与约翰·奥斯丁的名字连在一起，但是必须意识到奥斯丁不是分析学派的唯一学者，也不是阐明这一理论的第一人。为了分析该派关于主权与法律关系的定义，我们来了解一下该派的一些代表人物。

1. 法国的分析法学家

一般而言，分析学派在法国并不受欢迎，但是，正是在法国，我们找到了分析学派的源头。是布丹预示了霍布斯和奥斯丁这两位分析法学派的捍卫者所采用的分析（法学的）方法②，正如已经指出的，根据布丹的看法，主权是高于公民和属民的最高权力，它不受法律的限制。③ 它不受法律的限制，因为法律是主权的命令，也是主权的产物。很难理解主权应当从属于它自己的命令，或从属于由它自身创造的法律。因此他说："一个人可以接受另一个的命令，但没有人会命令他自己。"④

主权者不仅不受他自己法律的限制，也没有一个前任者的法律来约束他。而且，当主权者制定法律的时候，不需要上级、平级或下级的同意，因为"如果需要上级的同意，则很显然君主（主权者）处于一个臣属的地位；如果需要平级的同意，则有其他人分享他的权威；如果需要下级、人民、议员的同意，则他就失去了最高权威"⑤。因此，我们很自然地认识到主权者可以在没有他的属民的同意下废除、修改或替换他所制定的法律，因为正义需要时，就应该完全允许这些行为。然而，这种废除、修改或替代，不能含糊不清，而必须清细地提出。⑥

虽然主权者不受他自己和他的先辈的法律的约束，但他臣属于上帝的法律、自然法、国际法和我们所谓的宪法。布丹说："没有哪个试图废除或削弱上帝的法律和自然法的人能逃脱神圣主权的裁判。"⑦ 在布丹那里，上帝的法律和自然法

---

① Garner, *Political Science and Government*，第 8 章，179 页。也可参见 *Introduction to Political Science*，268 页，1910。

② 参见 Dunning, *Political Theories, from Luther to Montesquieu*，84 页。也可参见 Merriam、Barnes 等 *Political Theories, Recent Times*，146 页。

③ 见前文第一章。

④ *De Republica*, 134 页。英文翻译部分，参见 Coker, *Readings in Political Philosophy*，230 页以下。

⑤ *De Republica*, 240 页。

⑥ *De Republica*, 136 页。

⑦ *De Republica*, 135 页。"如果正义是法律的目的，并且法律是君主的要求，君主又是万能的上帝的影像，则君主的法律与神法是一致的。"同上书，167 页。

之间没有清楚的区别，国际法与二者之间也不应该有区别。因此国际法如果与上帝之法和自然法相违背，则主权者就不必受到它的约束。他说，主权者"不必受国际法的限制，正如它不必受自己制定的法律限制一样，除非前者与自然法和上帝之法一致"。他还补充道："如果国家的某些法律是不公正的，主权者可以废弃它们并禁止他的属民遵守它。这可以从奴隶制中显示出来，这种在许多国家建立起来的制度与每一个国家的法律是相一致的，但是有几个国家的君主颁布了一些有益的法令将它废除，从而与自然法保持一致。"① 最后，"君主不能废弃或修改涉及最高权力的法律。因为它们跟主权是联系在一起的。就像萨利克法典（Salic Law），是我们王国的基础"②。

正如前文所述，主权的首要的作用是制定法律；③ 法律不过是主权的命令。④ 但是如果它既不是主权者意志直接表达也不是隐含的表达，它能称为法律吗？这个问题，布丹并没有清楚地说明。有人这样讲过："制订法律的权力并不是主权的明显标志，除非我们只承认主权者制定的法律；因为一个治安法官也可以在他的司法权辖内对他的属民制订法律，只要他的命令与君主的法律不相违悖。"⑤ 布丹写道："法律的通过和颁布，一般是由代表大会和议院来完成，这并不意味着主权旁落到了立法机构和议会那里，他们仅仅是一种保证国王制定的法律在其死后顺利实施的权威。"⑥

现代法国学者中支持布丹关于主权与法律关系的看法的人很多。他们中间最伟大的也许是埃斯曼（Esmein）教授。在他的著作《宪法》（*Droit constitutionnel*）中，他宣称："国家是民族的法律人格化：它是公共权威的主体和基础。"⑦ "这种权威在其管辖的领域内被认为是最高权力，没有其他权力能与之竞争，因而它被叫做主权。"⑧

"公法的基础体现在，它认为主权独立于并且高于实践它的人，而这些人始终把主权作为一种理想的和永久的主题或象征，而这种象征就是全民族的人格化。这种理想人格就是国家。人们往往把它和它的内在特质即主权等同起来。"⑨

既然主权是一个国家的最高权力，认识到没有更高的权力，因此对它就没有

---

① *De Republica*，167页。
② *De Republica*，139页。萨利克法典（Salic Law），法兰克人古代习惯法汇编，编撰于5世纪末6世纪初，其中以禁止女性后嗣继承王位的条款最为著名。——译者注
③ 参见前文第一章。
④ *De Republica*，167页。也可参见 Dunning，*Political Theories*，第11卷，103页。
⑤ Crane，*State in Constitutional and International Law*，29页。
⑥ *De Republica*，143页。
⑦ Esmein，*Éléments de droit constitutionnel*，第7版，第1卷，1页，1921。
⑧ Esmein，*Éléments de droit constitutionnel*，第7版，第1卷，1页，1921。
⑨ Esmein，*Éléments de droit constitutionnel*，第7版，第1卷，1页，1921。"公法本身的基础包括它给与主权的一切，是在人之外和高于人的。"（原文为法文。——译者注）

任何限制。他这样说道:"主权不受限制,因此国家的权力是无限的。"① 主权是最高的和不受限制的,法律由之产生,赖其支撑,由是主权得到了服从和尊重。② 遵守主权者的法律就是遵守主权者本身。因此他宣称"公民能够拒绝跟他意识相反的国家的法律"就是错误的。③ 他继续说道:"一个公民的首要职责是尊重他的国家的法律。在自由国家的人民尤应如此,因为他们往往可以通过公共舆论来迫使不合理的法律被修改或废除。霍布斯已经指出,那些持这种观点的人是错误的,他们阻碍了人类社会的发展,虽然这是他们的权力。"④

2. 德国的分析法学家

在德国学者中,坚持这种主权观念的是黑格尔和赛德尔(Seydel)等。黑格尔关于主权和法律的观念在上文中已经指出。⑤ 根据赛德尔的看法,一个国家是占有地球表面一部分的一群人在一个最高意志下联合起来形成的事物。⑥ 这种最高的意志,赛德尔认为是属于统治者。统治者的意志不在国家之下,而在国家之上。对于赛德尔而言,正如狄骥教授所说:"任何关于国家的人格、国家的意志、和国家是一个有机体的表述都毫无意义。"⑦ 在国家和国王之间的区别就像是财产和所有者之间的区别。这是很明显的,因为国王可能失去他的"王国"。⑧ 赛德尔说:"这样一来,'国王'的意志一般是在国家之上的意志,而不是国家的意志;因为我们没有意识到这种关系导致了我们认为主权是国家人格(the personality of the state)的幻觉。"⑨

既然统治者的意志是最高的,在本质上它是一个命令性的意志。简单地说,它是主权者的意志。这如何被表达?以法律的形式表达。赛德尔说:"法律,就是统治人类组织、国家的命令性的意志(统治者的意志)的集合。法律渊源因此就是国王的意志。"⑩ 上面所说的,可以归结为:没有独立于或高于或与统治者平等的法律,是一个颠扑不破的事实,法律只有通过统治者而存在。⑪

赛德尔的国家主权和法律关系的观念的逻辑结论使他同意黑格尔否认国际法

---

① Esmein, *Elements de Droit Constitutionnel*, 第7版, 33页, 第1卷。
② 法律必须有主权者的权力作支撑。国际法没有主权者支持,就不能成为真正意义上的法律。"Le droit international public, faute de ce droit de contraitne qui réside dans l'état, est encore un droit incomplètement forme", Esmein, *Elements de Droit Constitutionnel*, 第7版, 39页。
③ Esmein, *Elements de Droit Constitutionnel*, 第2卷, 534页。
④ Esmein, *Elements de Droit Constitutionnel*, 第2卷, 534页。
⑤ 参见 Esmein, *Elements de Droit Constitutionnel*, 第7版, 第三章。
⑥ Duguit, "The Law and the State", *Harvard Law Review*, 第31卷, 150页。
⑦ Duguit, "The Law and the State", *Harvard Law Review*, 第31卷, 153页。
⑧ Seydel, *Grundzuge der allegemein Statslchre*, 5页, 1873。
⑨ Seydel, *Grundzuge der allegemein Statslchre*, 7~8页。
⑩ Seydel, *Grundzuge der allegemein Statslchre*, 13页。
⑪ Seydel, *Grundzuge der allegemein Statslchre*, 14页。

有法的效力的观点。他这样说道："既然法律命令是作为法律渊源的高级意志，在国家之间就没有法律命令。如果这样的一个高级意志存在，那就将有一个世界国家，中世纪的神权高于主权的观念就将实现。"①

因此在国家之间没有法律。在严格的意义上来说，国际法是根本不存在的。国际事务要靠武力解决，而且只能靠武力。② 赛德尔说："统治者们认为，为了维护他们的利益，应当在他们之间制定一些规则。但是只有当国家自愿接受这些规则的约束时，它们才起作用。因此，这样的规则显然不是法律。国家之间没有法律，就像它们之间没有司法权一样。利益冲突的最终解决办法是战争。处理复杂的外部关系是国王的最重要的功能：保护集体的利益不受其他国王的侵犯。既然他可以被迫在最后采用武力保护集体利益，那他就必须使武力处于常备状态。武力就是军队。因此军队就是通过暴力（Zwang）来实现国王内外意志的工具。"③

3. 英国的分析法学家

人们往往将分析法理学家同英国法学家等同起来。④ 这当然是成问题的，但是应当承认分析学派的滥觞之地是英国。早在1651年，布丹的著作出现于75年之后，霍布斯发表了他的《利维坦》。在这本书中，布丹所揭示的关于法的主权观念达到了它的顶点。杜威（Dewey）教授告诉我们，被归于奥斯丁名下的理论，其实不是奥斯丁的，而是霍布斯和刘易斯（Lewis）的。⑤ 毫无疑问，奥斯丁受霍布斯的影响，反过来，霍布斯又受布丹的影响。邓宁教授说："说布丹的著作在霍布斯的哲学思想形成过程中起了一定作用，并不是对他的贬损。"⑥

我们已经指出，在布丹的系统中，主权受上帝之法、自然法，在某种意义上，也受国际法和所谓的宪法的限制。我们也已经指出，在霍布斯那里，没有这类限制。他说上帝之法是所有法律中最高的，但是它不能实现，除非在上帝和凡人之间有一个中介人。他这样说道："有人对于自己不服从主权者一事提出的借口是他们和上帝而不是和人订立了新信约，这也是狡辩。因为不通过代表上帝的人的中介作用就不可能和上帝订约，而代表上帝则只有握有神权的神的代理人才能办到。"⑦ 在霍布斯的观念里，上帝的代理人，就是主权者，也就是君主自身。

霍布斯明确宣称自然法不是法，而是道德准则，因为它不是主权者的命令。他这样说道："这些理性的规定，人们一向称之为法，但却是不恰当的，因为它们

---

① Seydel, *Grundzuge der allegemein Statslchre*, 31~32页。
② Seydel, *Grundzuge der allegemein Statslchre*, 32页。
③ Seydel, *Grundzuge der allegemein Statslchre*, 32页，1873。
④ 参见 Pollock, *A First Book of Jurisprudence*。
⑤ Dewey, "Austin's Theory of Sovereignty", *Political Science Quarterly*, 第9卷，31页。
⑥ Dunning, *Political Theories*, 第二卷，84页。
⑦ Hobbes, *Leviathan*, E. Rhyd 编辑，91页。但是在另外的地方，他又宣称："但我们如果认为这些法则是以有权支配万事万物的上帝的话宣布的，那么它们也就可以恰当地被称为法。"83页。

只不过是关于确定哪些事物有助于人们的自我保全和自卫的结论或法则而已。正式说来,所谓法律是有管辖他人权利的人所说的话。"①

但是一个生活在自然法流行的年代,并且同时又是一个寻求对属民有绝对权威的君主的辩护士的人,会发现在自然法和市民法(civil law)之间有密切的关系,但是他却有意把它们区分开来。他说:"自然法同市民法是互相包容而范围相同的。"② 又说:"市民法和自然法并不是不同种类的法律,而是法律的不同部分;其中以文字载明的部分是市民法,没有以文字载明的部分就是自然法。"③ 并且,"自然法也是各国都有的那部分市民法,反过来说市民法就是那部分必须强制执行的自然法"④。尽管自然法是不成文的,它们仍然应该被所有人遵守。⑤

法律,大体说来,"不是建议,而是命令,也不是任何一个人对任何另一个人的命令,而是一个人给应该服从他的人发布的命令"⑥。于是,法律就是立法者的命令,这个立法者就是国家的主权者。但是主权者的命令可以采取许多形式。它可以通过语言、文字或类似的形式充分表达出来。⑦ 很显然,法律,无论是成文的还是不成文的,都是国家的意志,也就是主权者的意志。在君主制下,主权者是一个人;在民主制下,主权者是多数人组成的议会。⑧ 因此,除了国家的主权者,没有谁能制定法律。⑨

市民法,根据霍布斯的看法,可以这样定义:"市民法对于每一个臣民来说就是国家以文字语言或其他方式发布的,作为人民判断是非的准则;也就是用来区别哪些事情与法规相符、哪些事情与法规相违。"⑩ 从这个定义出发,我们可以推导出如下原则:第一,某物要成为法律,就必须是上级给下级的命令,后者必须服从。第二,主权者是唯一的立法者,也就是说,他是法律的唯一来源。第三,从第一个原则和第二个原则,可以得出第三个原则,主权者不受制于法律,因为它在法律之上。第四,相应地由第三个原则推导出第四个原则,也就是如果没有主权者,就没有法律,因为法律是主权者的产物。如果法律仅仅是主权者的产物,那么就是先有主权者,后有法律。第五,这导致第五个原则,也就是是主权者的

---

① Hobbes, *Leviathan*, E. Rhyd 编辑, 83 页。
② Hobbes, *Leviathan*, E. Rhyd 编辑, 141 页。但是他接着说:"因为自然法是公道、正义、感恩以及根据它们所产生其他道德,这一切在单纯的自然状况下都不是正式的法律,而只是使人们倾向于和平与服从的品质。"
③ Hobbes, *Leviathan*, E. Rhyd 编辑, 142 页。
④ Hobbes, *Leviathan*, E. Rhyd 编辑, 141 页。
⑤ Hobbes, *Leviathan*, E. Rhyd 编辑, 141 页。
⑥ Hobbes, *Leviathan*, E. Rhyd 编辑, 140 页。
⑦ Hobbes, *Leviathan*, E. Rhyd 编辑, 143 页。
⑧ Hobbes, *Leviathan*, E. Rhyd 编辑, 140~141 页。
⑨ Hobbes, *Leviathan*, E. Rhyd 编辑, 140 页。
⑩ Hobbes, *Leviathan*, E. Rhyd 编辑。

意志，而不是它存在的时间，造就了法律的权威。第六，法律，无论是成文法还是不成文法都有国家意志赋予的权威和强制力。第七，法律是由拥有国家最高权力的人发布的指导臣民以后的行动的命令，无论这个最高权力人是国王一个人还是议会里的许多人。①

这些都是霍布斯的市民法定义所包含的原则。然而，它们是彼此相关联的，它们之间的核心观点是法律是主权者的意志以命令的形式的表达。

第二个要提到的英国学者是边沁。在《政府片论》（A Fragment on Government）中，边沁激烈地批评布莱克斯通（Blackstone）的《英国法释义》的"行文保守，逻辑混乱"。他批评后者认为的主权者受上帝之法和自然法限制的观点。对边沁来说，布莱克斯通的看法——如果真有法律允许或要求我们去违反它，那我们就尽管去违反它，否则我们就是既触犯了自然的法律又触犯了神的法律。——对神法来说，这种论调是危险的；并且，"至于自然法，如果它什么也不是，而仅仅是一个术语，如果除了某种行为的有害的倾向之外，再没有其他手段可以证明该行为是对自然法的一种触犯；如果除了某项法律的不适当之外，再没有其他手段去证明该项国家的法律是与自然法相冲突的，除非是某些人的毫无事实根据的非难（他们认为这可以被称为一种证明）；如果一种用来把那些可能与自然法相冲突的法律和那些仅仅是不适当，但并不和自然法相冲突的法律区别开来的检验标准，甚至连我们的学者，或者其他任何人也不曾作为虚构的检验标准提出过；总而言之，任何法律如果为一些人出于那种或这种原因而不喜欢，那么，这种法律很少不会被他们认为和《圣经》的某些内容有矛盾；我看不出有什么补救的办法，除非这种学说的自然倾向是通过良心的力量迫使一个人站出来，用武力反对他偶然发现的不喜欢的法律"②。他还补充道："什么样的政府能够与这种安排相适应，我还得让我们的上帝来告诉我们。"③

对边沁来说，主权不能被上帝的法律和自然法所限制。正如前文所述，这并不意味着没有任何的限制，因为它受习俗的约束。他的观点跟布丹的观点很相近，他宣称主权的本质作用是制定法律。法律就是权威或主权者所制定，社会成员习惯性的服从的东西。法律被认为是政治社会的主权者的意志以命令的形式的表达。④

在一篇被广为引用的文章中，杜威（Dewey）教授说道："对奥斯丁的法理学仔细研究后，我相信那些被归于他名下的理论其实根本不是他的。"⑤ 他进一步指

---

① Hobbes, *Leviathan*, E. Rhyd 编辑，第 26 章。
② Bentham, "A Fragment on Government"，参见 *Works*, J. Bowring 选编，第 1 卷，287 页。
③ *Works*, J. Bowring 选编，第 1 卷，288 页。
④ *Works*, J. Bowring 选编，第 1 卷，285 页，注释（a）。
⑤ Dewey, "Austin's Theory of Sovereignty"，*Political Science Quarterly*，第 9 卷，31 页。

出梅因（Maine）错误地理解了奥斯丁的历史地位，格林（Green）错误地理解了奥斯丁的哲学思想，刘易斯（Lewis），这个奥斯丁的直接继承者彻底颠倒了奥斯丁的观点。① 总之，杜威教授认为，奥斯丁是一个道德家，而不是一个法学家。无论杜威教授的判断是对是错，都是值得讨论的。但是人们普遍承认，那种认为法之为法，必须有主权为之支撑的观点，在奥斯丁的著作中达到了顶点，被淋漓尽致地阐发出来。

在《法理学的范围》（*The Province of Jurisprudence*）中，奥斯丁这样开头："法理学所要考虑的是实证法：即在简单而严格的意义上所说的法律；也即政治上层对政治下层制订的法律。"② 在其他地方，实证法是这样表述的："每一部实证法，或者说每一部简单而严格的意义上的法律，都是由一个人（主权者），或由多人组成的主权实体，为一个独立的政治社会中的成员制订的，而这个主权者或这个主权实体就是这个独立的政治社会的主宰。"③ 他换句话继续写道："法律就是君主或其他掌握主权的实体为服从于它的臣民制定的。"④

很明显，只有主权者的命令才是真正的法律。但这还不是他的理论体系中的唯一诉求，他接着上述引文又写道："即使法律是由其他机构制定的，它也可以'成为'实证法，即严格意义上的法律，但前提条件是，这个机构必须是由握有最高政治权力的现任主权者授权成立，进而来立法的。"⑤ 在开始，奥斯丁是持实证法的观念，后来他又回到了霍布斯的立场。他引述道："立法者不是最先制订法律的权威，而是使法律继续成为法律的权威。"⑥

在这里他给实证法下了一个更精确的定义："实证法一般可以如下定义，或者说实证法与其他法相比有什么本质的不同，一般可以这样来表述……每一部实证法（或每一部严格意义上的法律），是直接由主权者（个人或实体）来制订的，由君主或主权群体，对在一个国家里臣服它的人们制订的。"⑦ 他补充说，这个定义是目前演讲中出现的最完整的定义了，但还不尽完美。⑧

这样来定义法律自然地就把自然法和国际法排除在外了。他说："一个生活在自然状态的人也许可以被施加一个绝对的法律，因为这个人'存在'于自然状态中，但他不能被施加主权者的法律，也不能施加为取得法律权利的法律。并且只有'绝对的'法律才是真正的法律（因为它来自一个'决定性'的渊源），这

---

① Dewey, "Austin's Theory of Sovereignty", *Political Science Quarterly*, 第 9 卷, 33 页。
② Austin, *Jurisprudence*, Campbell 第五版, 第 1 卷, 86 页, 1911。
③ Austin, *Jurisprudence*, Campbell 第五版, 第 1 卷, 220 页。
④ Austin, *Jurisprudence*, Campbell 第五版, 第 1 卷, 220 页。
⑤ Austin, *Jurisprudence*, Campbell 第五版, 第 1 卷, 220 页。
⑥ Austin, *Jurisprudence*, Campbell 第五版, 第 1 卷, 220 页。
⑦ Austin, *Jurisprudence*, Campbell 第五版, 第 1 卷, 330 页。
⑧ Austin, *Jurisprudence*, Campbell 第五版, 第 1 卷, 330 页。

才使法成为适当意义上的法律。因此，主权者的或明或暗的旨意，不是实证法，而仅仅是一种实在道德的原则。"①

因此，一个主权者对另一个主权者颁布的强行法（imperative law），或一个主权政府为另一个主权政府颁布的绝对的法律不是实证法即不是严格意义上的法律。"既然没有一个主权者能让其他的主权者臣服自己，那么它向其他主权者颁布绝对的法律的时候，它不是以立法者的身份出现的，这样的法律也不会是一个信奉法律权利的主权者颁布的，因为法律权利是一个政府赐给臣服于它的臣民的。因此一个主权者给另一个主权者颁布的绝对的法律并不是实证法或者说严格意义上的法律。但是，因为他是'绝对的'（来自于一个'决定性'的源头），从这个意义上说，它也算是一个法律，但实际上它纯粹是实证道德的原则。"②

根据奥斯丁的看法，甚至连宪法，在严格的意义上，也不是法律。"因为宪法和国际法都对君主的主权或者其成员的主权进行的限制，因此它们处于同一个困境中（不能被认为是法律）。"③

奥斯丁费尽力气去确定宪法的真实特征。他认为宪法就是决定一个政府的结构、组织和政体的实证道德和实证法律的结合。用他的话说，宪法就是"决定了一个法人的性格或者一部分法人的典型性格的实证道德和实证法律的结合。在贵族统治的国家中，或者在联邦国家中，宪法就是决定这个主权国家内部各个成员的共性的东西"④。

"实证道德和实证法律的结合"的表述意味着在奥斯丁的观念里，宪法是实证道德和实证法律的结合。它跟自然法和国际法不同，因为它们纯粹是实证道德，也跟实证法不同，因为实证法是主权者创造并支持的。这样宪法一方面具有自然法和国际法的特征，另一方面又具有实证法的特征。

在这里很容易看出奥斯丁把宪法看作部分的实证法，部分的又不是实证法的模棱两可之处。我们也许纳闷为何像奥斯丁这样一个人把自己陷入这样一种暧昧境地。但是有更好的解释吗？如果有，如何解释？为了做到这一点，最重要的，奥斯丁提醒我们注意他所运用的主权的含义。他说："'主权者'，我一般指的是君主，或者是主权群体（a sovereign number）。"⑤他继续说："总的来说，在其特征上，主权群体是最高者和独立的"，因此，"主权者的权力是不能受限制的"。⑥从这个意义上说，从法律上来说，主权者不受宪法的约束和限制，也是在这个意义上，"在抵制一个主权实体的行为上，宪法仅仅是一种实证道德，或仅仅通过道

---

① Austin, *Jurisprudence*, Compbell 第五版，181～182 页。
② Austin, *Jurisprudence*, Compbell 第五版，182 页，1911。
③ Austin, *Jurisprudence*, Compbell 第五版，270 页。
④ Austin, *Jurisprudence*, Compbell 第五版，267 页，1911。
⑤ Austin, *Jurisprudence*, Compbell 第五版，269 页。
⑥ Austin, *Jurisprudence*, Compbell 第五版，269 页。

德制裁来实施"①。

另一方面,"一般而言,组成主权群体的个人和较小的集合也臣服于那个最高的实体,因为他们是其组成部分"②。由于这个实体在法律和政治义务方面的独立性,作为其组成部分的个人或较小集合就要受这个实体所制订法律的约束。③ 这里的逻辑不难理解。全体比部分更重要,部分低于整体。部分如果不联合起来,有些事情就做不成,但不能推导出部分不能做的,全体也不能做。作为一个整体或者说一个拥有完整主权的主权者来反对宪法,就不是不合法的行为,但相反,整体的一个部分违反宪法,那就是违法了。④ 正是在后一种意义上,宪法被看作一种实证法。⑤

奥斯丁的关于法律的主权的概念可以归结如下:法律要成为真正意义上的法律,就必须由主权者直接或间接地制定。从严格意义上说,不受主权者支持的法律,就不是法律。"主权者"有两层含义在第一层含义上,它是不受限制的,因为它是在法律之上而不是在法律之外,因此它不能受其自己的法律限制。另一方面,组成部分应当受到法律限制,在这个意义上,宪法被认为是实证法。但主权者,一般来说都是拥有完整权力的主权者,因此从这个意义上说,宪法纯粹是一种道德原则。

杜威教授说奥斯丁的理论是绕了一个大圈又回到了原地,也许他是正确的。⑥也许还可以说奥斯丁从来没有达到霍布斯的思想高度,也从来没有超越布丹的研究界限。如果说奥斯丁和布丹之间有什么不同,那也是别的方面,而不是在他们的关于主权和法律的关系的定义上。

奥斯丁的理论在何种程度上被后来的学者们接受,是很难说清的。但是说他在英语国家里比在其他国家有更多的继承者,也许更为可信。⑦ 在他的后继者中,刘易斯(G. C. Lewis)值得我们特别注意。前文已经说过,刘易斯已经被认为是奥斯丁的真正解释者和直接继承者,由于他们的亲密关系,他受奥斯丁的影响很深。但是刘易斯不仅仅是奥斯丁主义者,在某些方面,他更像霍布斯。⑧

根据刘易斯的看法,"只要政府存在,掌握主权的一个人或一些人的权力,就在整个社会之上,并且是绝对的和不受限制的"⑨。他继续说:"主权者对社会的

---

① Austin, *Jurisprudence*, Compbell 第五版, 267 页, 1911。
② Austin, *Jurisprudence*, Compbell 第五版, 269 页。
③ Austin, *Jurisprudence*, Compbell 第五版, 269 页。
④ Austin, *Jurisprudence*, Compbell 第五版, 278 页。
⑤ Austin, *Jurisprudence*, Compbell 第五版, 270 页。
⑥ Dewey, "Austin's Theory of Sovereignty", *Political Science Quarterly*, 第 9 卷, 31 页。
⑦ 参见 J. M. Lightwood, *Nature of Positive Law*, 295 页, 1883。
⑧ 参见 Lewis, *On the Use and Abuse of some Political Terms*, Thomas Raleigh 编辑, 40 页, 1898。
⑨ Lewis, *On the Use and Abuse of some Political Terms*, Thomas Raleigh 编辑, 41 页。

每个成员的生命、权利和义务有完全的处置权。他有改组政府结构的权力，他有权修改任何法律。"①

像奥斯丁一样，刘易斯认为法律是主权者的普遍命令，不管它是由主权者直接创造的，还是主权者授权立法机构制定的。② 既然在严格的意义上是主权者的产物，因此后者就不受前者的约束。

但是法律，根据刘易斯的看法，不能跟契约发生混淆。跟布莱克斯通一样，他认为契约是源自自身的一种承诺程序，而法律是对我们自身的一种直接命令。契约是："我愿意或不愿意这样做"，而法律是："你应当或不应当这样做"。在某种程度上像布丹一样，他认为主权应当受与外国签定的契约的限制，因为它是契约的一部分。③

像奥斯丁一样，刘易斯也不认为宪法是真正意义上的法律。对他来说，宪法意味着在一个社会里或一种政府形式下，主权权力（sovereign power）的安置与分配。④ 和他的前辈一样，他从这一点出发，进一步宣称："恰当地说，宪法的内容是现实存在或曾经存在的事物。"⑤ 总之，宪法不过是一个含混的有赞扬意思的字眼。虽然它是被用来欺骗无知的人们，使他们相信制定让他们遵守的规则或法律只不过是恢复古代的制度，因而这种改变是恢复，而不是革新。⑥

霍兰德（Holland）教授是另一个和奥斯丁一样杰出的当代学者。他说："法律可恰当地定义为：由最高的政治权威制定的人类的外在行为的总规则。"⑦ 对此，有人评论道："他没有像奥斯丁那样，用'命令'二字，但这也说明了主权者的命令的表达既可以是隐讳的又可以是公开的。"⑧

可能是受到历史法学派法学家如梅因（Sir Henry Maine）的影响，或有机会领略他们的讨论，霍兰德教授尽力避免奥斯丁著作中的一些含混的观念和难题。谈到自己的立场，他说梅因对主权和法律的本质没有恰当的论断。⑨ 对梅因，他评论道："有一种说法认为，法律的执行，无论何时何地都明显地不受政治权威的制约，如今的英国就是如此，但亨利·梅因爵士成功地证明了，这种说法是不对的。"他自己的立场更加清楚："我们习惯认为，法律是由最高政治权威支持的规

---

① Lewis, *On the Use and Abuse of some Political Terms*, Thomas Raleigh 编辑, 41 页。
② Lewis, *On the Use and Abuse of some Political Terms*, Thomas Raleigh 编辑, 36 页。
③ Lewis, *On the Use and Abuse of some Political Terms*, Thomas Raleigh 编辑, 42 页。
④ Lewis, *On the Use and Abuse of some Political Terms*, Thomas Raleigh 编辑, 20 页。
⑤ Lewis, *On the Use and Abuse of some Political Terms*, Thomas Raleigh 编辑, 20 页。
⑥ Lewis, *On the Use and Abuse of some Political Terms*, Thomas Raleigh 编辑, 20 页。
⑦ Holland, *Elements of Jurisprudence*, 第 12 版, 41 页。
⑧ Patterson 教授的评论，见 Merriam 与 Barnes 的 *Political Theories, Recent Times*, 147 页。
⑨ Holland, *Elements of Jurisprudence*, 第 12 版, 53 页。

则,尽管在有些国家里,我们还不能说法律就是这样的规则。"①

像奥斯丁一样,霍兰德教授认为国际法实质上仅仅是国家间的一种道德原则。② 除了根据他对法律的定义所认定的真正的法律之外,"其他所有的指导人们行动的规则,被叫做法律,仅仅是一种类比;除了这些规则以外,那些指导人类行为的主张被叫做法律,仅仅是一种比喻"③。

4. 美国的分析法学家

现在来看美国的学者,我们发现卡尔霍恩(Calhoun)在他的《论政府》一书中已经"在总体上,采用分析法学的方法,认为国家是完全通过法律来治理的一个组织,在法律上拥有不可分割的全能的主权"④。但是在过去的三十年中,韦罗贝教授是最为杰出的。韦罗贝教授的观点可以在其《国家的本质》(*The Nature of the State*, 1896)、《美国的宪法体系》(*The American Constitutional System*, 1904)和《公法的基本观念》(*The Fundamental Conception of Public Law*, 1924)等书中找到。

在否定了布莱克斯通的自然法和神法高于人类权威的观念之后,韦罗贝教授写道:"如果那样,只有那些获得国家认可的规则,才是有法律效力(legal validity)的规则,从逻辑上来说,既然没有谁能被自己的意志约束,则对最高的政治权力的法律限制也必然是不可能的。"⑤ 主权,根据韦罗贝教授的看法,属于一个国家,是代表国家的意志的最高权力。⑥ 它必须拥有一些权力,如税收、签订条约等。但它不仅仅是一些权力的集合。⑦ 在本质上它是一个整体和不可分割的。⑧ "分离主权在逻辑上是不可能的,正如在同一个实体中有两个最高权力是不可能的一样。"⑨ 权力是可以分的,但意志不能。

主权既不可分,又不受限制。在本质上它是绝对的。在这里卡尔霍恩的风格得到了运用:"用法律去限制它,就是毁灭它。"⑩ 因此,奥斯丁的话在这里被引用:"最高权力受实证法的限制是语词的矛盾。"⑪ 如果一个国家受到法律的约

---

① Holland, *Elements of Jurisprudence*, 第 12 版, 54 页。
② Holland, *Elements of Jurisprudence*, 第 12 版, 134 页。
③ Holland, *Elements of Jurisprudence*, 第 12 版, 42 页。
④ Gettel, *History of Political Thought*, 396 页, 1924。
⑤ Willoughby, *Nature of the State*, 181～182 页。
⑥ Willoughby, *Nature of the State*, 105 页。
⑦ Willoughby, *The Fundamental Concepts of Public Law*, 72 页。*Nature of the State*, 194 页。
⑧ Willoughby, *The Fundamental Concepts of Public Law*, 72 页。*Nature of the State*, 195 页。
⑨ Willoughby, *Nature of the State*, 195 页。
⑩ Willoughby, *The Fundamental Concepts of Public Law*, 76 页。
⑪ Willoughby, *The Fundamental Concepts of Public Law*, 76 页。主权不能为法律所限制。"既然从理论上,国家自己的主权是所有法律的来源,它就不能被法律限制其自身。" *Fundamental Concepts*, 77 页。

束，则不能说这个国家拥有主权。①

更进一步，主权是不可让渡的。他说，一个国家不能让渡它的主权，主权是它的生命和人格。② 但是，必须把让渡和委任区分开来。"理论上讲，一个主权国家可以在某种程度上将其权力的执行委任给其他国家的政府机构，这些政府机构于是就成了执行该主权国家的政府机器的一部分。"③

在对他的主权观念有一个总体认识之后，让我们回到关于法律和主权的关系的观念。他说："一个国家的主权的归因，和作为合法的全能的定义，在实证的或严格法律意义上来讲，国家是法律的唯一渊源。"④ 很显然上述所引表明了韦罗贝教授同意奥斯丁的观点，即要成为严格意义上的法律，必须有一个最高权威支持它。⑤ 根据他的看法，说上帝之法高于人类权威是不正确的，正如已经指出的那样。

对于国际法的特征，他写道："当我们离开宪法或国内法领域进入国际关系领域之后，就不必再理会颁布法律者和服从法律者的关系了。在国际关系领域，没有最高意志，从法律的角度讲，仅仅是平等意志的集合，是独立国家之间的冲突，或者至少是相互影响。"⑥ 从这种观点出发，他进一步清楚地指出不能过于关注这种主权者对臣民的命令的本质特征。⑦ 但是他继续说："但是，这并不意味着……对于国际规则就不能使用'法律'一词，只不过在使用的时候，其含义已经与分析法学家所谈的国内法有很大的不同了。"⑧

因此，韦罗贝教授仅仅是一个奥斯丁式的人。认为"主权"一词在国际法里面的运用与国内法方面的运用不同，他建议"像'独立性'这样的词用起来可能更好"⑨。但是关于宪法与主权的关系，他与奥斯丁有很大不同。我们已经指出，在奥斯丁的理论系统中，宪法不是一般意义上的法律。与此相反，韦罗贝教授认为宪法是真正意义上的法律。在他看来，奥斯丁把宪法作为实证道德的错误在于没有认识到政府与国家之间的区别。⑩ 宪法旨在控制政府，而不是国家，因为它是国家的产物。"⑪ 在这里，韦罗贝教授同伯吉斯教授的观点一致，断定在政府的后面有宪法，在宪法的后面，有最初的主权者，是最初的主权把政府和自由委托

---

① Willoughby, *The Fundamental Concepts of Public Law*, 76～77 页。
② Willoughby, *Nature of the State*, 221 页。
③ Willoughby, *The Fundamental Concepts of Public Law*, 74 页。
④ Willoughby, *The Fundamental Concepts of Public Law*, 129 页。
⑤ 他很坦白地承认他在某种程度上跟随奥斯丁。参见 *Nature of the State*, 183 页。
⑥ Willoughby, *The Fundamental Concepits of Public Law*, 282 页。
⑦ Willoughby, *The Fundamental Concepts of Public Law*, 298 页。
⑧ Willoughby, *The Fundamental Concepts of Public Law*, 298 页。*Nature of the State*, 198～204 页。
⑨ Willoughby, *The Fundamental Concepts of Public Law*, 283 页, 315 页。
⑩ Willoughby, *The Fundamental Concepts of Public Law*, 89 页。也可参 *Nature of the State*, 204 页。
⑪ Willoughby, *The Fundamental Concepts of Public Law*, 84 页, 89 页。*Nature of the State*, 204 页。

给宪法。① 很显然，由于指出了政府和国家之间的区别，韦罗贝教授扩大了实证法的范围，减少了道德对主权的限制。在这方面，韦罗贝教授的主权观念与奥斯丁的主权有很大的不同，而与霍布斯的主权观念比较接近。

也许还要指出，戴雪（A. V. Dicey）教授和里奇（D. G. Ritchie）教授对法律主权和政治主权所作的区分在韦罗贝教授的系统中没有地位。他说："国家的本质特征，即是它有别于其他人类组织而拥有政治主权。政治主权意味着，一方面它有不受法律和其他权力控制的绝对自由；另一方面，对它的公民的法律权利与义务也加以绝对的控制。国家作为最高权力不仅给予所有法律以最终效力，而且它自身也决定它自身的法律权利的范围和它们执行的方式。"②

然后在另外一个地方，我们发现他在谈及里奇教授所作的区分时指出："做出这种区分毫无疑问是正确的。但是对作者来说，不幸的是同一个'主权'被运用到两种截然不同的方面，成为两种不同的力量，尽管有形容词前缀的区分。"③ 他补充说："总之，尽管从法律上说是绝对的，主权也被认为与制度、国民性和其他客观状况相关联。"④ 最后的陈述表明他的观点和奥斯丁更加接近。

与此相关，我们有必要注意一下加纳教授的观点。加纳教授的观点体现在下面这段话中："我们同意佐恩（Zorn）和伯吉斯的观点，即认为主权不仅是国家的本质要素，也是首要的和最高特征；也同意韦罗贝的观点，即认为主权是使国家同其他社会组织相区别的一个特征。"⑤

同韦罗贝教授一样，他不是毫无保留地接受奥斯丁的理论。他认为："奥斯丁的主要错误在于不恰当地片面地强调主权的法律方面，而忽略了成文法背后的力量与影响这是一个法学者很自然犯的错误。"⑥ 他补充说："或许也可以说他的理论不能适用于所有的国家，正如梅因在其《早期制度史演讲》（*Early History of Institutions*）所举的那些例子中一样。"⑦

但是他对这个著名法理学家的褒奖远多于对他的批评。对他来说："作为一个严格法律意义上的主权的本质的概念，在总体上讲，奥斯丁的理论是清楚的和

---

① Burgess, *Political Science and Constitutional Law*, 第1卷, 57页。参见 Willoughby 对 Burgess 在政府与国家之间的区分所作的评论。Wiloughby, *The Fundamental Concepts of Public Law*, 55页以下。
② Willoughby, *American Constitutional System*, 4页, 1904。
③ Willoughby, *The Fundamental Concepts of Public Law*, 112页。
④ Willoughby, *The Fundamental Concepts of Public Law*, 113页。
⑤ Garner, *Introduction to Political Science*, 267~268页, 1910。
⑥ Garner, *Political Science and Government*, 第8章, 181页, 1928。也见 *Introduction to Political Science*, 271页。
⑦ Garner, *Political Science and Government*, 第8章, 181页, 1928。也见 *Introduction to Political Science*, 271页。

合逻辑的，所有对它的批评都是建立在错误理解的基础上的。"①

由于认为奥斯丁的严格法律意义上的主权的本质观念没有错误，加纳教授否认法律主权是受限制的，这也是韦罗贝和刘易斯（Lewis）所否认的。"的确存在对主权的限制"，他承认，但"只要研究一下那些限制，我们就会发现，从法律上来讲，它们根本就不是对主权的限制"②。他宣称："自然法、道德原则、神法、人道和理性的命令、对舆论的顾忌以及其他对主权的相应的限制，都没有法律效果，除非国家选择承认它们并给予它们效力和合法性。"③

加纳不承认不受限制的主权观念有时会导致一个国家的合法的独裁的观点。他说："很难看出主权不受限制的理论与最广泛的自由之间是不一致的。"④ 当国王拥有国家或者说主权的时候，很少有人否认主权不受限制的理论。实际上，他注意到，不受限制的主权，是随着宪政主义的浪潮而发展的。而宪政主义意味着个体权利和自由的保证以及对政府的限制，"它使化解不受法律制约的主权的弊端变得相当容易"⑤。

但是他不满足于此，因为他认为在国际关系中，主权不是不受限制的。在这方面，他不再是奥斯丁理论的支持者，而是同那些反对传统的绝对不受限制的主权理论的人站在同一条战线上。他写道："如果我们检视当今国家间发生的一些事情，在实践上就不能再坚持传统的法律理论，如果这种运用和实践还是国际法的渊源，国家的绝对主权不仅是一个幻想，而且也是应当放弃的非常有害的一种观念，它应当被废弃。"⑥ 他继续说道："考莱（Kohler）、皮利特（Pillet）、奥普汉斯（Aplheus）、H. 斯诺（H. Snow）及其他许多人的理论都支持在当今社会，国际法不仅在事实上高于每一个国家的国内法，而且它的最高权力已经获得法律基础，因为有这个基础，对国家行为自由的限制是法律限制而不仅仅是国家对自我施加的限制。"⑦

在这里，加纳教授的观点同韦罗贝教授，也同奥斯丁的观点有所区别。对奥斯丁来说，正如前文所述，国际法仅仅是一种实证道德。在韦罗贝教授那里，法律这个词可以指代国际规则，"但必须清楚的是，当这样运用它的时候，与它运用

---

① Garner, *Political Science and Government*, 第8章, 181页, 1928。也见 *Introduction to Political Science*, 271页。

② Garner, *Political Science and Government*, 第9章, 184页。"一个不容置疑的结论是，我们对主权合法的限制的努力是徒劳的和无用的。" 185页。

③ Garner, *Political Science and Government*, 第8章, 181页, 1928。也见 *Introduction to Political Science*, 271页。

④ Garner, *Political Science and Government*, 第9章, 184页。"一个不容置疑的结论是，我们对主权合法的限制的努力是徒劳的和无用的。" 187页。

⑤ Garner, *Political Science and Government*, 187页。

⑥ Garner, *Political Science and Government*, 193页。也可参见 *Political Science Review*, 1页以下, 1925。

⑦ Garner, *Political Science and Government*, 193页。

在国内法领域的时候有不同的含义"①。而对加纳教授而言，情况恰恰相反，国际法在国内法意义上也是法律。奥斯丁和韦罗贝教授从实证法学和分析法学的意义上出发，都认为国际法对主权的限制不是法律意义上的限制。② 加纳教授则认为国际法对主权的限制是法律限制。他们三者之间的区分是显而易见的：奥斯丁是国内法的辩护者，韦罗贝是宪法的辩护者，而加纳是国际法的辩护者。

一方面认为法律主权不能受到限制，但是另一方面，国际法对主权的限制也是合法的，这是一个矛盾。为了避免这个两难境地，加纳教授转而否认主权观念可以运用到国际法中，也就是国际关系中。③ 在这一点上，加纳教授又同意韦罗贝教授的观点。但是要提到的是，奥斯丁和韦罗贝的基本理论，即要成为法，必须有主权者作支撑，法是政治主权者对属民的命令，则是加纳教授所反对的。加纳教授说："奥斯丁的观念——在'法律'这个词的严格意义上，国际法不是法，因为它没有国内法所拥有的支撑，因此国际法仅仅是一种国际'道德'或'礼仪'——这种绝不仅仅是定义和术语的争论已经没有多少实际的意义。现在所有的法学家都承认奥斯丁的观念是狭隘的和武断的，因为它过分地强调了武力制裁的因素，而忽视了习惯这个巨大的因素。而习俗绝不是立法机构正式颁布的，但法庭一般却把它当作法律。国际法往往被国家当作法律，并被用于国与国之间的诉讼中，它是通过合法程序由国际会议颁布，并且由资深的法学家阐明并支持，在国内和国际法庭上被广泛运用。它实际上被认为是对国家的约束，如果否认国际法具有法律的特性，那就会得出与国际关系的实践相矛盾的国际法定义。"④

加纳教授的观点的重要性是显而易见的。他的观念被认为是与奥斯丁和韦罗贝理论的背离，是奥斯丁和韦罗贝理论的反对者的信徒。

奥斯丁的理论被加纳教授全部或者说部分地接受，但发展方向实际上已经有所改变。在下面几页中，我们来看一看它的进展如何。这种改变有许多趋势。他们互不相同，有些趋势甚至截然相反，但是他们都承认一点：并不是只有政治上的上级对下级的命令才能成为法律。

---

① Willoughby, *The Fundamental Concepts of Public Law*, 298 页。
② 参见 Garner, "Limitation on National Sovereignty in International Relations", *Political Science Review*, 2 页, 1925。
③ 参见 Lansing, *Notes on Sovereignty*。
④ Garner, *Rencent Development in International Law*, 3~4 页, 1925。与此论题相关的，在美国学者中，Coker 教授的著作"多元理论与对国家主权的攻击"（见 Merriam 和 Barnes, *Political Theories*, 80~119 页），"The Technique of the Pluralistic State", *American Political Science Review*（第 15 卷, 186~213 页, 1921）可能提及。

三、自然法学派

19世纪晚期，布里斯（Bryce）爵士在对自然法的观念的历史作了一个很好的评论之后，写道："除了从大陆的理论家之口，我们现在几乎听不见自然法这个词了。"① 不过他又立即补充道："尽管这种观念不时在意想不到的地方出现。"② 然后他问："一种如此古老而简单的观念，对历史作了如此的改变，产生了如此广泛的影响，难道我们不应该有专门的学科来研究它吗？况且它仍然还摆在人类面前。"③

布里斯爵士的热诚和洞见毋庸置疑，但是也许他没有想过他的设想会如此之快地变为现实，因为就是在他写下这段话的十年之后，一本叫作《自然法的复兴》（*La renaissance de droit naturel*）④ 的书出版了。需要承认的是，自然法的复兴与旧的自然法的观念不同。但是这种不同在于"新观念和原有的旧观念是并存的，而不是取代它"⑤。

根据庞德（Pound）的观点，自然法的复兴有几种形式。第一种是新康德主义的法律理想主义的适用与扩大；第二是法律的新经院哲学；第三是与机械社会学相近的实证社会学哲学。⑥ 我们将在其他的地方讨论这些形式。为了便于当前的讨论，在自然法与主权的关系上，我们将限制在旧的自然法定义。

虽然自然法的观念在古希腊就得到了阐述，但自然法的观念达到它的顶峰是在西塞罗的著作中。根据西塞罗的看法："这种法律，不是它成文的时候而开始存在的，它是天生的，是和神圣的智慧一起存在。因而，真正的法律，首要的法律，能完全命令和限制的法律，是最高存在——朱庇特的真实意愿。"⑦

布里斯爵士说道："从广义上说，对罗马人而言，自然法与理性、人类本质的最好方面、完善的道德、实用的好的理智、一般习惯是相一致的。它是简单的和理性的，恰与造作的和武断的相对；它具有一般性，而不具有地方性和国家性；它高于所有的法律，因为它属于全人类；它是上帝的目的或人类最高理性的表达。"⑧

自然法被认为高于其他一切法律，当然包括人类的主权者所制定的法律，因

---

① Bryce, "Law of Nature", *Studies in History and Jurisprudence*, 第二卷, 604页。
② Bryce, "Law of Nature", *Studies in History and Jurisprudence*, 第二卷, 605页。
③ Bryce, "Law of Nature", *Studies in History and Jurisprudence*, 第二卷, 606页。
④ 这本书的作者是Joseph Charmont。
⑤ *Modern French Legal Philosophy*, Mrs. F. W. Scott, Joseph P. Chamberlain 翻译, 110页。
⑥ Pound, "Jurisprudence", H. E. Barnes, *The History and Prospects of the Social Science*, 456页。
⑦ R. I. Holand, *Natural Law and Legal Practice*, 51~52页。
⑧ Byrce, *Studies in History and Jurisprudence*, 第2卷, 589页。

此自然法的维护者认为人间的君主要受自然法的约束。

这种观念贯穿于整个中世纪并打上了神学的色彩。普罗克（Pollock）教授说："作为最高权威的自然法的原则一直到 16 世纪仍被教士们坚持，普通的法学家，乐得让教士们去苦思冥想，或许并不仅是重复他们的说法。"①

布丹，虽然不是一个自然法的学者，但也认为君主受自然法的限制。格劳修斯也被他的国家的法律原则引入自然法的思想领域，并且他还认为自然法是所有市民法的来源。② 格劳修斯说："自然法，是正确理性的指示，指示出任何行为与理性的自然协调与否，即它是道德的还是不道德的；进而指出这种行为是自然的创造者——上帝掌管或禁止的。"③ 自然法就是上帝自身也不能改变。④ 因此主权者始终都受这种法律的约束。⑤

著名的评论家布莱克斯通赞同西塞罗的观点，宣称"自然法是与人类一致的，是上帝自己的指示，当然比其他任何东西都要高级"，并且，"它在任何时候约束所有的国家；任何法律如果与此相违背都是无效的；所有的法律都从这个根源处获得它们所有的效力和权威"。⑥

分析学派的兴起并没有取代自然法学派，因为自然法的观念仍然有它的拥护者和维护者。一个最近分析学派的批评者写道："如果霍布斯和奥斯丁的理论是正确的，则暴君的任何行为都会是合法的。因为他们二者用同样的话告诉我们，主权者的权力，从其本质来说，是不能被限制的；由于缺乏自然法，没有其他的可以代替它，主权者的权力是完全不受限制的。这样，承认希律王（Herod）是犹太人（Jews）的法律主权者，他有权命令对伯利恒（Bethlehem）的婴儿的屠杀，士兵也必须执行他臭名昭著的命令，这不是我们说的，而是奥斯丁自己说的。我们不准备匍匐在霍布斯的利维坦的脚下；如果这个宏大的理论用于实践，则将毁坏我们每一个人的自由，整个世界会陷入绝对专制。"⑦

自然法的拥护者的观念是很简单的。他们认为，自然法不是主权者创造的。相反，它的地位高于主权者，主权者必须受其约束。

---

① Pollock, *First Book on Jurisprudence*, 26 页。也可参见他的 *Essays in the Law*, 51 页, 1921。
② 参见 James Mackintosh, *A Discourse on the Study of the Law of Nature and Nations*, 23 页。
③ 参见 Coker, *Readings in Political Philosophy*, 267 页。
④ 参见 Coker, *Readings in Political Philosophy*, 268 页。
⑤ 参见 Coker, *Readings in Political Philosophy*, 274 页。
⑥ Blackstone, *Commentaries*, 导论。
⑦ Holaind, *Natural Law and Legal Practice*, 68～69 页。

第七章 主权与法律（续）

四、历史学派

尽管法理学的历史学派出现在 18 世纪甚至更早①，但其达到高峰却在 19 世纪。哈佛大学法学院院长罗斯科·庞德（Dean Roscoe Pound）曾经这样评论道：正是历史学派"打破了法学家们在过去整整一个世纪所持的信念，即法律是主权者的命令"②。这一派的学者很多，但最为引人瞩目的是德国的萨维尼（Savigny）、英国的梅因（Maine）和美国的卡特（Carter）。

1. 萨维尼

早在 1814 年的《论立法和法学之当代使命》（*Von Beruf unserer Zeit fur Gesetzgebung und Reechtswissenchaft*）一书中，萨维尼就提出了被历史学派接受的关于法律的本质和起源的基本原则。这种观念在《现代罗马法之体系：1840—1849》（*System des heutigen Romischen Rechts: 1840—1849*）一书中再次被阐明。在谈及他在法学中的地位时，一位知名的学者说过："他对于法学就像莱辛之于文学、耐波尔（Niebuhr）之于历史学、瑞特尔（Ritter）之于地理学。"③

该学派的名称清楚地表明了这派学者所运用的方法。萨维尼也不例外。历史学派的原则，正如他所说："每一个时代产生它的世界，不是为了其自身，也不是随意的，而是跟整个的过去密切相关。因此每一个时代一定有其独特的事物。并且这又是必然的和不受约束的；说其是'必然的'，是因为它不依赖于现在任何一个意志；说它是'不受约束的'，是因为它几乎不依赖于外部的命令，而是由作为一个不断发展的实体的人民的最高本质产生的。"④

在《当代罗马法体系》一书的前言中，他写道："对法律科学的历史观被完全曲解，人们实际上认为它是主张传统的法律文化是至高无上的，当今和以后的政府都得保留它。"⑤ 他继续说："这种观点的本质，多少考虑到了每一个时代的

---

① 在 16 世纪这个学派的最重要的先驱是 Cujas.
② Pound, *An Introduction to the Philosophy of Law*, 65 页，1922。
③ E. Freund, "Historial Jurists in Germany", *Political Science Quarterly*, 第五卷，473 页，1890。
④ E. Freund, "Historial Jurists in Germany", *Political Science Quarterly*, 第五卷，475 页，1890。
⑤ Savigny, *System des heutigen Romischen Rechts*, 第 1 卷，19 页。W. Holloway 英译，4～5 页。

价值和独立性,但它在很大程度上仅着眼于过去和现在的关系,并且没有意识到,我们对目前的法律状况仅了解皮毛,还没有抓住它的内在本质。"①

在上述想法的基础上,萨维尼提出了一种全新的法学观念。这种观念在19世纪迅速占据了统治地位。事实上,法律被认为是人性和历史知识的现实成果,而不是由伦理或政治分析产生的理论成果。②

法律的起源和发展同其他社会现象,如宗教、语言和国家等的起源和发展是完全一样的。产生法律的力量也同样产生国家,德国学者认为国家在一定程度上与主权是一致的,或至少它们有同样的渊源。③ 但是那种力量是什么?或者更直接地说,法律的渊源是什么?萨维尼认为是一种激励一个民族所有成员的共同精神。因此他这样写道:"实证法存在于人民的普遍意识中,因此我们称它为人民的法律。"④

人民,不是指他们中的特殊部分,而是意味着一个民族的全体人民。他宣称:"决不能认为法律是人民中的一部分成员的任意意志所产生的;在这种情况下,每个人或许会选择同样的法律,但更有可能的情况是他们会选择不同的法律。或许可以说,人民的共同精神普遍地存在于每一个人中,并由此产生了实证法。它代表了每一个人的意识,不是随便的某个人,而是每一个人。"⑤

然而,在人民的共同意识或精神中,法律的形式(Gestalt)不是抽象的规则,而是法律制度之间的根本关系的活的直觉(Legendige Anschaung)。⑥ 法律的信念在人民中存在得越久,它们就植根得越深。⑦ 法律的发展就像一个个体生命的发展。法律不是一个固定不变的整体,而是在不断地发展当中。⑧ 这样,法律经常处在发展之中。要理解今天是什么,就必须明白昨天是什么。它的发展是阶段式的,而不是突进式的。它是一个被发现的东西,而不是一个被创造的东西。

由上可知,法律很显然不是上帝的意志,也不是一个人类主权者的意志的恣意表达。它也不是偶然的产物,也不是"一件称心的衣服,可以随意脱下来和别人交换"⑨。它是民族生活实际的主要部分。它随着民族的产生而产生,随着民族

---

① Savigny, *System des heutigen Romischen Rechts*, 第1卷, 19页。W. Holloway 英译, 4~5页。
② Pollock 与 Maitland, *History of English Law*, 导论, 23页。
③ 参见 J. M. Lightwood, *Nature of Positive Law*, 278页。
④ Savigny, *System des heutigen Romischen Rechts*, 第7部分, 14页。"在民众的普遍意识中, 积极的权力是存在的, 因此我们也把它叫作公民权。"(原文为德文。——译者注)
⑤ Savigny, *System des heutigen Romischen Rechts*, 12页。他在其 *The History of the Roman Law during the Middle Ages* 中写道:"所有的法律更依赖那些遵从它们的人的变化的愿望和观念,而不仅仅是立法者的命令。" E. Cathar 英译本, 第1卷, 前言, 12页。
⑥ Savigny, *System des heutigen Romischen Rechts*, 16页。
⑦ Savigny, *System des heutigen Romischen Rechts*, 16页。
⑧ Savigny, *System des heutigen Romischen Rechts*, 16~17页。
⑨ 参见 Taylor, *Science of Jurisprudence*, 29页, 1908。

的发展而发展。由于每个民族有它自己的特征,而这些特征与其他民族的特征有所不同,法律就是这样的特征。哪里有政治社会,无论是文明的或原始的,哪里就有法律。研究越原始的法律或所有的法律,我们就会越清楚地认识到法律不是主权的命令,而是人民——全体人民,而不是某个个人——的精神或意识的结晶。

2. 梅因

梅因的《早期制度史演讲》的第七讲这样开始:"英国学者广泛接受的历史理论不仅对法律研究,而且也对历史研究造成了巨大的损害。因此,在对新材料进行研究,并对老材料进行重新发掘的基础上找出我们的法律系统的起源和发展的情况是丰富英国知识宝库的当务之急,除了总结出新的法律历史,我们还需要总结出新的法律哲学。"① 无疑,这是梅因关于主权和主权与法律关系的概念的起点。

在对分析法学派的批判中,特别是对奥斯丁的批判中,梅因提出了两个反对意见。他说:"首先,每个社会的全部历史决定了控制社会资源的权力出自哪里。(奥斯丁的)主权理论忽视了产生这种结果的模式。而这种模式可以将波斯大帝、雅典执政官、罗马皇帝、沙皇、英国君主与议会归为一类。"②

他继续说道:"其次,是历史决定了主权者如何行使他的强制权威。所有这些——观念、情感、信仰、迷信和偏见、公共意识,无论是仅属于某个时期的,还是长久的,无论是由习俗产生的,还是由人类本性产生的都为分析法学家们所拒斥。"③

在批判的方面,梅因尽力表明奥斯丁关于法律的定义太狭窄并且它忽略了那些大多不代表主权者意志的法律。肯定方面,梅因认为法律是由公共意见、情感、信仰和诸如此类的社会力量所产生的。要点就是,法律,要成为法律,不需要有主权者作支撑。但这是为什么呢?针对他的体系有一个例子。他说:"我的例子,是印度的旁遮普(Punjaub),即五河国(the country of the Five Rivers)。它在被英印帝国兼并之前作为一个国家存在了大约四分之一个世纪。在经历了明显的无政府阶段和不明显的无政府阶段之后,它进入了一个锡克教的半军事、半宗教的综合的寡头政治。锡克教徒们被迫臣服于兰季特·辛格(Runjeet Singh)的命令。初看一下,没有比辛格更完美的主权的化身了。他是一个绝对的独裁者。除了遥远的边疆地区的偶尔骚乱之外,他能使国家秩序井井有条。他可以命令所有人。任何人如果对他的命令稍有不从,就会被处死或遭肢解;而其绝大多数臣民对这是完全知道的。然而我怀疑他的一生中是否发出过哪怕一次奥斯丁称为法律的命令。他把绝大部分的农产品收归己有。他侵入敢于抗税的村庄,处死了很

---

① Maine, *Early History of Institutions*, 342 页。
② Maine, *Early History of Institutions*, 360 页。
③ Maine, *Early History of Institutions*, 360 页。

多人。他拥有军队,拥有所有的暴力工具,并通过很多方式来使他的命令被贯彻,但是他从来没有制订过一部法律。他管理其庶民的规则有很古老的渊源,这些规则也为村庄—社区的家族的裁判所所采用。奥斯丁的理论(在这里)不能产生多少影响。"①

然而,梅因认为这种政治社会的国家的存在并不意味着奥斯丁的理论的彻底失败,因为这种理论仍然说得通。根据主权者的命令就是法律的原则,在旁遮普有权力做后盾的规则就是法律,因为锡克教默认习俗规则,或村里的长老所制订的规则。因此,这些规则就是他的命令,因而也就成了这个国家真正的法律,就像英国的普通法(the common law),只要君主和议会同意,不管它们是成文的还是不成文的都可被称为法律。但是应该意识到,在英国,君主和议会可以随时随意修改或重新制定普通法,现实中它们也经常这样做,现在更是如此。但同时兰季特·辛格则从来没有想过在他的国家里修改那些让他的臣民遵守的规则。他说:"认为兰季特·辛格制定了那些规则的东方和印度法律理论家,会对奥斯丁的观点感到愤怒。因为这样看来,奥斯丁竟然认为兰季特·辛格的这种行为是合法的。"② 他补充道:"这种理论在某些情况下是真实的,但这种真实性仅仅是理论上的。"③

虽然他承认奥斯丁的名言,即"法律是主权者的命令",并不适用于古代社会或现今的未开化国家,但他还是认为法律由主权者制定是现代社会的趋势。在他看来,历史上这种趋势是很明显的。它起源于罗马帝国时代,当时罗马开疆扩土,并建立了稳固的政治系统,法律制度当然也在其列。这样,正如梅因指出的那样,主权者的命令在历史上第一次成为了法律。在现今,边沁所处的时代甚至霍布斯所处的时代莫不如此。

这种观察和概括使得他总结道,从某种程度上说,这个世界上从古至今只存在两种类型的社会。他说:"在古老的社会,人们的生活规则往往产生自他们的风俗习惯,无论是在乡村还是在都市都是如此,人们有时也会服从一个有绝对权力的统治者的命令。但这个统治者一般只征税,而从不管立法。另一种社会就是我们熟悉的社会,主权者往往根据自己的意志来立法,而不顾当地的风俗和习惯。"④ 他补充说:"在我看来,在这两些政治体制的替换过程中,法律的特征也随之明显改变。"⑤

如果撇开第一种类型的政治社会不谈,而只关注第二种类型的政治社会,我

---

① Maine, *Early History of Institutions*, 380~381 页。
② Maine, *Early History of Institutions*, 382 页。
③ Maine, *Early History of Institutions*, 382 页。
④ Maine, *Early History of Institutions*, 392 页。
⑤ Maine, *Early History of Institutions*, 392 页。

们就会发现，梅因不过是法理学分析学派的支持者。既然世界在逐渐朝向第二种类型的社会发展，梅因的理论也就越来越奥斯丁化了。如果最后第一种类型的社会最终消失，只有第二种类型的社会存在，那么梅因的理论与奥斯丁的理论相左的局面就会成为历史，到那时，梅因也会成为彻底的奥斯丁主义者。也许正是从这个角度考虑，詹姆森（Jameson）认为梅因是分析法学派的支持者。① 正是梅因动摇了分析法学派的根基，但是他又重新给它培土，浇水。

梅因在多大程度上对分析法学派妥协，下面这一段话会给我们一些提示："但是，即使由于分析法理学家忽视了历史，而导致没有认识到许多事实，但他们也至少发现了其他许多事实，这些事实即使在今天也没有被那些完全沉溺于历史的人所认识到。事实上，法律和主权的概念在霍布斯、边沁、奥斯丁的定义的互动过程中才逐步地成型，但它们的雏形在当时已经出现，并渐渐地趋于完美。这样就可以用一个法理学词汇来表述它们，这个词汇一方面与其内涵完全保持一致，另一方面，如果它没有把事实完全表达出来，这种事实的缺失也不会严重到彻底否定它的价值的地步，更不会使其重要性日渐消失。没有一种关于法律和社会的定义能解开这团迷雾。在那些分析法学家看来，主权者的权威的确借助法律发挥了很大的作用，但这种作用中往往包含了含混不清的东西和许多错误遗漏。他们首次认识到，如果它们被全面持久地执行下去，最终它们的作用就会完全体现出来，他们的睿智就会被证明。"②

3. 卡特（Carter）

我们现在来研究一下卡特法官，他是一个在美国法学领域里有影响的学者。庞德在谈到他的观念时说："当卡特还是一个学生的时候，萨维尼的学生就把形上的历史法学的观念原原本本地传授给了他。"在谈到他的主张和他的著作的时候，庞德也指出："卡特最近的理论对十九世纪最后二十五年的美国法院的判决产生了不小的影响，他的遗稿在某种程度上使他的思想得以流传下来。"

在对奥斯丁的理论的批判上，卡特法官和梅因的观点一样。但是，对他来说，梅因还做得不够。他同梅因都认为，在原始社会习惯发挥了重要的作用，法律就是习惯。但是他对梅因认为的主权者的意志将来会成为法律的观点提出强烈质疑。③ 他进一步质疑梅因对奥斯丁的这样一种观点的附和，即主权者的意志不受限制。④ 总之，在批判的方面，他彻底否定了奥斯丁的这样一种观点，即法律就是主权者的命令的观点。⑤

---

① Jameson, "National Sovereignty", *Political Science Quarterly*, 193 页。
② Maine, *Early History of Institutions*, 396~397 页。
③ Carter, *Law: Its Origin, Growth and Function*, 201 页, 1907。
④ Carter, *Law: Its Origin, Growth and Function*, 189 页, 1907。
⑤ Carter, *Law: Its Origin, Growth and Function*, 120 页, 1907。

肯定的方面，他坚持认为法律就是习惯。然而，他指出，不是意味着所有的习惯都是法律。① "有许多人类的行为法律并没有涉及，但这些行为和法律一样，都受习惯的制约。"② 在对其他学者关于法律的定义进行评述之后，他提出法律就是约束人类行为的所有规则。③ 但是在像如达荷美（Dahomey）④、阿散蒂（Ashantee）王国这样的政治组织中，如何约束人类行为呢？他说："这里没有立法机构，主权者没有亲自或通过其大臣对人们的日常生活进行干预。英帝国的殖民地的不同民族，在它们被征服以前就已经有自己的习惯，这些习惯千百年来潜移默化地影响着他们，这种影响一直持续到现在。即便暴君想去改变它们，也奈何它们不得。要改变它们，除非通过时间的流逝，慢慢去影响它们，别无他途。但是他是不愿改变它们的。所有的暴君都乐于保存这些习惯。而他们却凌驾于这些习惯之上，恣意抢劫、杀戮。暴君的统治靠的是恩威并用，社会的和平与秩序并不是他的根本目的。古老的习惯一直被人们所遵守，只有依靠主人苟延残喘的奴隶除外。除此之外，人们还服从于国家的统治，国家是有组织的，即使这种组织相对粗暴，它也有自己的政治体制；主权者和他的大臣们通过效忠于他们的军队来行使权力。当臣民受到伤害，向他们申诉的时候，他们就会对此做出裁决，实施赔偿。对习惯的侵犯都会招致公共权威的惩罚，这样公共权威就开始发挥作用，对私人的侵犯，就会招致公共审判；换句话说，法治社会始具雏形，但一种行为究竟是公共罪行还是仅对私人的侵害，仍通过习惯来判断。"⑤

但这个例子，无非是梅因举出的旁遮普省那个例子的翻版。但就我们已经涉及的范围而言，卡特基本上仍在梅因的圈子里打转。但他对梅因的思想也进行了些许发展。在梅因看来，正如前文所述一个社会在从地方部落向庞大的帝国的转变过程中，法律的性质已经发生了明显的变化。正是因为意识到了这种转化，梅因倾向于认为存在两种类型的社会：①在一种社会中，法律不以主权者的意志为转移；②在另一种社会中，法律就是主权者的命令。

另一方面，卡特的理论体系没有对此做出区别。他认为法律在古时是何种面目，在当今亦是何种面目。他宣称："拿起美国或英国的成文法典，我们会发现几乎里面的所有条文，在司法意义上说，都不是立法者首先创造的，就像我们之前研究过的那样，即使是那部分直接涉及行为管理的部分，尽管是正当和有效的，也很少是立法者的首创。人们在查阅实体法（substantive law）时，往往会忽略它们。它们被形容为普通法的一个'小镶边'。"⑥

---

① Pound, *Interpretations of Legal History*, 34～35 页，1923。
② Carter, *Law: Its Origin, Growth and Function*, 120 页，1907。
③ Carter, *Law: Its Origin, Growth and Function*, 14 页，1907。
④ 17 世纪在今非洲贝宁中部兴起的一个国家。——译者注
⑤ Carter, *Law: Its Origin, Growth and Function*, 24～25 页，1907。
⑥ Carter, *Law: Its Origin, Growth and Function*, 203～204 页，1907。

在英语国家里面是如此，在古代罗马、法国、德国和美洲的国家亦是如此。上述国家的所有法律都明白地显示出了立法者对非成文法或习惯法的最高权威。他说："但是我在这里想指出的是，似乎所有的法律都与当前的讨论联系不大，因为它们只不过是对现存法律的再次立法。所以，由此看来立法的作用不过是对非成文法和习惯法的发现和采用，除此而外，别无他用。所以非成文法、习惯法和立法者制定的法律都是一样的。"①

很明显梅因对奥斯丁的有限辩护是完全错误的。奥斯丁的观点：法律是主权者的命令是完全错误的。法律不过是习惯，因为习惯才是指导人类行为的规则。习惯在当今民主国家发挥的作用和在所谓的野蛮部族或落后国家中发挥的作用是一样的。现代各个国家的立法者所当做的，就是支持习惯发挥作用，而不是用其他东西去取代它。②

习惯，简言之，就是"同一环境下的人们的一致行为"。这种行为上的一致来源于人性。而人性，在任何时间任何地点，对任何人而言都是一样的。他所调查研究的人类包括"原始人、剽悍的游牧民族、刚刚进入定居时代的族群、开始自发地建立起国家的人民、学会书写并制定法律的人民、被统治的底层人民、受强大的异族奴役的人民、人身权利得不到保障的人民、不懈追求建立司法体系以求自身的权利能得到保障的人民、生活在已建立起完善的司法制度的国家的人民、生活在当今文明时代的人民"③。

时代无时无刻不在变化，"人类的本性却不会发生剧烈的变化因此，我们冠之以'法律'这个名字的东西，过去是，将来也永远是习惯"④。对卡特来说，在这个方面，过去、现在和将来都是一样的。在过去和现在如此，在将来也会如此。随着时代的发展，也许会有更多的立法者，通过更多的法案，但是他们所做的，都不过是"法律这个整体的很小一部分而已"。

五、经济学派

我们现在来讨论另一个领域，也就是从经济学的观点得出的关于法律的主权的概念。这有时也被称为"金钱制造法律理论"。这种理论的学者也接受分析学派的观点，即认为法律是主权者的命令。但是，在他们看来，主权者仅仅是一个代言人。"这种观念，是真实的，但它也是无意义的。"⑤ 经济学派的学者仅仅把

---

① Carter, *Law: Its Origin, Growth and Function*, 204 页, 1907。
② Carter, *Law: Its Origin, Growth and Function*, 120 页, 1907。
③ Carter, *Law: Its Origin, Growth and Function*, 119 页, 1907。
④ Carter, *Law: Its Origin, Growth and Function*, 120 页, 1907。
⑤ Commons, "A Sociological View of Sovereignty", *American Journal of Sociology*, 第 5 卷, 355 页。

奥斯丁的"主权者"看作一个代言人，而这种观点对分析法学派理论的破坏更甚于直接反对它。

这种理论可以在哈林顿（Harrington）的著作中找到根源（1656）。"主权就是所有权，"他说，"主权和所有权之间有平稳的关系，这也是英帝国的本质。"① 但是陶兰德（Toland）的名言更为精彩，他说："在任何一个时代，任何一个国家，谁有钱，谁就可以制定法律，并让广大人民拜倒在他的脚下。"② 著名英国学者阿瑟·扬（Arthur Young），也在某种程度上表达了相同的观念。"划分人们的一个重要标准就是有钱或没钱……其实并不应该以人们的财产的多寡来决定他们在选举中的发言权。那些在财产分配中有直接利益的人更应该远离权力中心才是。对于立法来说，一个巨大的难题就是如何既保障有钱人的财产，又保障没有财产的人的自由。"③ 19世纪马克思的著作，虽然不是法律著作，但却对法律哲学产生了重大的影响，并且深深地鼓舞了那些认为经济因素是研究法律制度问题的基础的人。

1. 洛里亚（Loria）

所有的著作中最为重要的，也许是意大利的阿奇瑞·洛里亚（Achille Loria）和美国的布鲁克斯·亚当斯（Brooks Adams）的著作。洛里亚的著作，特别引起我们注意的，是《社会的经济基础》，这本书的基本思想，正如他告诉我们的，是"经济收益是政治主权的基础"④。

国家，在他看来，仅仅是经济统治阶级的政治诉求。⑤ 因而主权是从财产中产生的。洛里亚的观点受到了著名社会学家和法学家塔德（Tarde）的激烈批评。后者坚持认为从逻辑上和历史上说，是政治权力决定经济影响。他还说，如果我们回溯到很远的时期，我们会发现父权（patria potestas）是所有政治的、宗教的和法律的权威的最初来源，它先于财产出现，并且是它导致了财产的出现。⑥ 为了回应塔德的批评，洛里亚说："说父权是政治权威的最初来源是绝对不正确的。因为在父权出现很久以前主权是建立在母权（mother right）的基础之上；并且在那些被认为的父系部落中，在'父权'被承认之前政治权威已经得到了很好的发展。并且，现在对史前状况的研究……已经很清楚地显示'父权'本身是私人财产的结果，在财产共有时期，母系权威占绝对主导地位。"⑦

---

① Harrington, *The Oceana and other Works*（Toland 选编），39 页，1700。Loria 在 *The Economic Foundation of Society*（L. M. Keasbey 翻译）中引述，332 页，1899。
② Loria, *The Economic Foundation of Society*, 334 页，1899。
③ Loria, *The Economic Foundation of Society*, 336 页，1899。
④ Loria, *The Economic Foundation of Society*, 358 页，1899。
⑤ Loria, *The Economic Foundation of Society*, 343 页，1899。
⑥ Loria, *The Economic Foundation of Society*, 359 页，1899。
⑦ Loria, *The Economic Foundation of Society*, 360 页，1899。

如果政治权力是经济收益的产物，则主权行为一定会本能地促进资本收益的增加，并以任何可能的方式为掌握它的人谋取利益。① 主权，从财产产生，自然地成为财产的产物和工具。因为财产集中到少数人手中，主权也变成少数优越和富有的阶层的人用来谋求他们的利益的工具。简单地说，从国家的所作所为中可以一眼看出"政治权威的所有努力都为达到一个目的：确保并扩大资本收益"②。

　　但是在一个国家里，资本家或有产阶级怎样取得最高权力？在洛里亚看来，他们通过两场胜利来获得。首先，他们摧毁了封建地主阶级的政治权威，然后他们又镇压了大众的反抗，而他们最初正是得到了大众的支持才得以胜利。③ 在取得政权之后，为了保护自己，资产阶级"又制定了一系列的制度。这些制度的作用是保护财产权不受侵犯，但这不包括土地所有权"④。这一系列的相关联的制度是什么呢？这正是关键。他说："这些所谓的相关联的制度中最重要的，就是道德、法律和政治。这些重要的社会存在可以被相应地看作是资产阶级财产所有制的有机产物，资产阶级用它们来达到自己的目的。"⑤

　　很显然，为了保护并发展他们自己的既有利益，就必须取得政权，真正的制定法律的权力，因为法律是一种工具——它是保障社会有序和稳定的最为有力的工具，只要国家处于有序、稳定的状态，资产阶级就一直享有他们既有的优先权利。资产阶级用尽千方百计得到了它，并用它来谋取自己想要的东西。并且"正是这种对主权彻底的占有，成就了资产阶级最耀眼的王冠，并谱写了它的历史上最为有趣的篇章"⑥。

　　如果法律仅仅是经济状况的必要结果，如果法律现在成为资产阶级的产物，仅仅是扩大资产阶级利益的一种手段，那么法律是立法者的意志的偶然结果的观念就是错误的。形式上，法律必须通过立法大会，但是立法大会只是一个代言人，因为在立法大会的后面，存在着法律的真正来源，即有产阶级。洛里亚写道："政治学至今为止被这样一种观念统治，即法律完全受立法者的意见所决定——非出自母胎（prolem sine matre creatam）——法律的功能就是根据相互正义原理来规范社会关系。这种观念恢复了法理学以前的声望，也使公法成为社会科学的基础和关键。19世纪确实是这样的，但是如果对社会结构进行更深入的研究，一种新的观念就会应然而生，即法律是经济状况的一种有机产物，而不是立法者意志的结果。"⑦ 总之，法律是资产阶级的法律，由资本家制定，也是为了谋求资产阶级

---

① Loria, *The Economic Foundation of Society*, 206页，1899。
② Loria, *The Economic Foundation of Society*, 206页，1899。
③ Loria, *The Economic Foundation of Society*, 307页，1899。
④ Loria, *The Economic Foundation of Society*, 9页，1899。
⑤ Loria, *The Economic Foundation of Society*, 9页，1899。
⑥ Loria, *The Economic Foundation of Society*, 114页，1899。
⑦ Loria, *The Economic Foundation of Society*, 127页，1899。

的利益的。

耶林（Ihering）的法律定义——"作为集体权威施加于个体之上的一种权力，使个人不致陷入其不可预见的会导致不利局面的暴行之中"——可以这样理解，"资产阶级群体成员之间的关系中，法律确实对这些成员采取了与其实际利益一致的一系列的行为；但是它不能适用于劳动者，因为他们为法律所压迫"①。

不仅仅是分析法学派的耶林的法律观念受到批评，萨维尼的理论（法律是民族意识的产物）和历史学派的理论（法律是人民特殊遗产和习惯的结果）都被质疑。② 法律，不是抽象理性的产物，不是民族意识或种族特性的产物，而仅仅是经济状况的必然要求。③

如果社会始终都存在一个只享受不劳作的阶级和一个只劳作不享受的阶级，如果主权就是前者通过颁布条令来保护其权利、财产、享受、自私的愿望以及对后者实施压榨的机器，则仅仅对这种机器的修正是不会带来正义的维护后者或全体社会成员的利益的法律的。④ 经济状况所派生的法律只能随着经济状况的改变而发生改变。对分析法学家来说，正如我们已经指出的，法律是主权者的产物，只能由主权者改变，至少要得到他的同意。对洛里亚来说，主权者可以继续保留，条件是他只是一个代理人，一个没有实际权力的代理人，但是产生和改变权力的真正动力是经济状况。经济状况是一个必要条件，而不是可有可无。它们随着人类社会的发展变化而变化。

虽然坚持认为法律不是意志的产物，经济状况不能由意志来改变，但他不排除许多经济状况如贫民的卫生状况改善的可能性。这种类型的立法绝不会影响资产阶级的地位。相反，它会给予后者更多的实惠⑤，因为高素质的劳动者带来高质量的服务，高质量的服务意味着更多的利润。这是我们所能做的，也是我们应当做的。为了维护这种主张，我们的学者指出："我们的理论不是导致宿命论，恰恰相反，它是鼓励人类的理性行为。这样可以避免或者至少减少社会转型期的混乱。"⑥

2. 布鲁克斯·亚当斯

庞德这样评论过："布鲁克斯·亚当斯在英国的分析法学理论之后提出了经济决定论。"⑦ 接着他这样概括这位思想家的观点："法律由主权者所制定，或者由它的代理机构公布并实施。但是这些法律的制定、认可和实施仅代表统治阶级

---

① Loria, *The Economic Foundation of Society*, 76 页, 1899。
② Loria, *The Economic Foundation of Society*, 79 页, 1899。
③ Loria, *The Economic Foundation of Society*, 84 页, 1899。
④ Loria, *The Economic Foundation of Society*, 344 页, 1899。
⑤ Loria, *The Economic Foundation of Society*, 334、376 页, 1899。
⑥ Loria, *The Economic Foundation of Society*, 377 页, 1899。
⑦ Pound, *Interpretations of Legal History*, 97 页, 1923。

的私利，因为它最终由经济规律决定。为了进行正式的法理分析，我们需要提到主权者。当我们深入研究时，我们就不能不提到经济冲突。奥斯丁说主权者有发号施令的实际权力，但布鲁克斯·亚当斯使我们明白了，统治者以法律的名义来操纵这些号令，以谋求自己的私利。"①

布鲁克斯·亚当斯在他的《社会革命论》一书中说道："在社会高度集中的情况下，主权权力是如此重要，以至于在社会管理中，有必要对它进行必要的垄断，财产的私有化必然会导致冲突的产生。"② "这些权力被授予某个行政当局，如君主或国王以后，他就将这种权力作为一种信用来为全民的福利服务，至少在西方国家中是如此"。如果国王或皇帝忽视或破坏了这种信任，他就会相应地被废黜或处决，以示惩罚。查理一世（Charles Ⅰ）被处死就是证明这个观点的例子之一。"总之，主权者和臣民之间的关系或建立在契约和相互义务的基础之上，或建立在对命令的绝对服从上；但是无论在哪种情况下，都意味着双方的责任。只有在主人和奴隶之间才会出现将主权交给不负责任的统治者的状况。"③

上面几段从其《社会革命论》所引述的话代表他对主权的一般观念。现在切入主题。在上述最后引文之后，他又迅速说道："虽然如此，应用科学的发展仍将现代资本家置于与其他公民对立、类似封建贵族的位置上。"④ 现在主权者拥有主权的各种权力。⑤ 但是他们是如何得到这些权力的？在亚当斯看来，"他（资本家）认为最高权力是可以被买卖的。他认为，他可以买它们；既然他买了它们，他就可以随心所欲地使用它们"⑥。主权被认为是"管理能量的变量"。在文明社会中，它可以加速积累。⑦

如果最高权力可以买来，自然地，资本家能够使主权者制定他们喜欢的法律，以有利于他们的利益，也可以改变与他们的希望相反的法律。亚当斯这样说道："如果资本家已经买到了一些主权者的功能，而且希望根据他自己的利益来使用它。他认为限制他的法律是对他的宪法权利的一种粗暴入侵，在他独特的观念里，他不能理解主权功能与作为一个整体的国家之间的关系。因此，他认为对一项可以保护公共利益但会有损个人利益的法律的侵犯，非但无罪，甚至是有功的。资本家如果在大选中失利，民选的立法者又不能被收买，通过了令他不满意的法

---

① Pound, *Interpretations of Legal History*，97～98 页。Pound 主要是依据 *Centralization and the Law*（1906）这本书中 Brooks Adams 的文章。遗憾的是我手头没有这本书。
② Brooks Adams, *The Theory of Social Revolution*，13 页，1913。
③ Brooks Adams, *The Theory of Social Revolution*，14 页，1913。
④ Brooks Adams, *The Theory of Social Revolution*，14 页，1913。
⑤ Brooks Adams, *The Theory of Social Revolution*，13 页，1913。
⑥ Brooks Adams, *The Theory of Social Revolution*，209 页，1913。
⑦ Brooks Adams, *The Theory of Social Revolution*，20 页，1913。"也就是说，社会发现或多或少完全地从个体那里撤离的安全性和或多或少严格控制其功能的巨大的变化是它的本质。"

案,他的第一反应就是去找律师,他不是想让律师依法办事,而是让他想办法钻法律的漏洞。如果实在钻不了,他就会设法使法院宣布这个法案违宪,而使之失效。"①

总之,法律是资本家为了谋求私利而制定的,而不是主权者制定的。主权者这个名称仍然被用来指示法律的出处,但他已不是法律的真正出处,因为它只不过是一个没有心肝的傀儡。但这样的情况还会继续吗?不能,这是布鲁克斯·亚当斯的回答。他预言道:"资本家作为统治阶级的美国社会已不能更进一步集中了,既然宇宙中没有绝对静止的事物,如果它不继续集中,它自然要开始分离。"② 在这里,我们需要指出在洛里亚和布鲁克斯·亚当斯之间的分歧。他们俩都重视经济状况在法律制定中的重要性并且都否认主权者是法律的真正来源,但是前者认为经济状况的变化是未来的一个自然结果,但后者进一步认为它们现在已经开始变化。

资本家的最高权力和政府的崩溃是注定的。并且它一旦崩溃,主权就不再是不负责任的了,因为正如前文所述,对主权的行使,意味着承担责任。并且,如果行使主权需要承担责任,那么主权者颁布的法律就不会再被认为是像在主人和奴隶之间的关系中一样的上级给下级的命令,而会被看作是对整个社会公共福祉的责任的履行。在这里我们就涉及了狄骥所提出的观点。我们将在以后的讨论中对此详尽阐述。

3. 康芒斯(John R. Commons)

因为康芒斯教授的观点和法理学的经济学派有关联,因此,需要在这里提上几笔。他的观点在他的长篇巨制《主权的社会学观点》中提出。书名表明,他是从社会学的视角着眼,但是 H. E. 巴恩斯(H. E. Barnes)说他更强调社会中的经济因素。③ 在分析了奥斯丁的主权和法律理论之后,康芒斯教授说:"这种观点当然正确,但它毫无意义,因为他的法律的定义排除了习惯。事实上,这种观念仅意味着习惯被彻底破坏,主权的秩序被搅乱。"④ 主权,像其他社会制度一样,起源于财产私有制,"财产私有制不过是人与人之间强制关系的一种别称。资产阶级通过它来命令其他人为他服务,这也就是主权"⑤。法律是国家的标准,暴君的

---

① Brooks Adams, *The Theory of Social Revolution*, 213~214 页, 1913。
② Brooks Adams, *The Theory of Social Revolution*, 226~227 页, 1913。
③ Barnes, *Sociology and Political Theory*, 131 页, 1924。
④ Commons, "A Sociological View of Sovereignty", *American Journal of Sociology*, 第五卷, 355 页。
⑤ Commons, "A Sociological View of Sovereignty", *American Journal of Sociology*, 第六卷, 87 页。

反复无常的命令不是法律。① 法律如果不是高于，那也至少是优先于主权。因为法律和主权都是经济条件的产物。

六、社会学学派

奥古斯特·孔德的《实证哲学》的出现表明人类思想拓展到一个新的研究领域。这个新的领域就是社会学。在上个世纪（19世纪——译者注）后半段的斯宾塞的著作给了这个新的领域更大的支持。和斯宾塞观点相近的有奥地利的古姆普洛维茨（Gumplowicz），德国的齐默尔（Zimmer）和美国的沃德（Ward）。这些人在社会学领域所作的工作就如同达尔文、瓦兰斯（Wallace）、魏斯曼（Wissman）、门德尔（Mendel）等人在生物学领域所作的工作。

在这些研究方面的进展不仅给人们带来了一门新的科学，也给人类知识的其他领域带来了新的启发，这当然包括法律科学。社会学本身是一种新的科学，但是社会学在法律研究中的应用产生的成果现在已经被认为是法学中的主导观念。由于运用社会学的方式不尽相同，有关法的起源和本质的观念相应地也就不尽相同。

第一，在社会学发展的早期，社会学的解释往往以物理条件为依据。因此法律被认为是物理——地理、气候——自然力的产物。人们认为一种类型的自然条件会导致一种与之对应的法律的产生。主权者是存在的——立法者或法庭——但是他们所作的只是宣布法律，而法律实际上是自然力的产物。

接下来的一段时间，生物学的解释比较盛行。达尔文所提出的生存竞争的理论被分类学家古姆普洛维茨所运用。社会制度被认为是社会冲突的产物。主权和法律也是如此。平等只能在最简单的游牧部落中发现。在那里，没有法律意义上的命令和服从。② 国家被定义为少数人对多数人的有序统治，主权是经常由少数人执行的最高权威。③ 法律由此被认为是统治阶级的产物。"这些统治阶级"，古姆普洛维茨说，"通过他们的议会执行立法的权力，能够通过法律制度进一步通过剥削他人来增加他们自身的利益。"④

---

① Commons, "A Sociological View of Sovereignty", *American Journal of Sociology*, 356页。"主权的首要目标是保护财产。它不是绝对的与不受限制的，它受依然保留在私人手里的强制（coercion）的限制。他否认Burgess教授的主权定义。在他看来，主权有三个组成部分——强制、秩序和权利。强制来源于私人财产。生存的斗争导致这种垄断和集权化的形式。秩序作为主权的组成部分是当主权扩展到很广的区域，以及当自由代替物质和竞争需要、下层民众获得决定主权者权力的时候。"同上书，3页，359页、552页、824页。

② Gumplowicz, *Outline of Sociology*, Moore翻译，124页。

③ Gumplowicz, *Outline of Sociology*, Moore翻译，118页。也可参见Ward, *Pure Sociology*, 30页，205～206页。

④ Gumplowicz, *Outline of Sociology*, Moore翻译，145页。

第二，斯宾塞，作为一个极端的个人主义者，强烈反对国家的权威。在他的《社会学研究》一书中，他甚至谴责议会通过的一项提高人民教育的议案。他批评霍布斯和奥斯丁的认为法律是上级对下级发布的命令的观念。① 他认为奥斯丁混淆了公民权威（civil authority）和军事权威之间的区别。"在他的《法理学的范围》中可以看出这种评论是正确的。"② 因为混淆了这种区分，奥斯丁推导出其法令的有效性，也就是他称为的实证法。"真正的问题是：主权者从哪里开始的？什么是一个人，或一少部分人，或大多数人所给予的对其余人的不受限制的最高权力的保证？"对于这种要求，正如他所看到的，没有回应。③

第三，有一种我们可以称之为对社会学的经济解释的运动。由此而来从经济的角度来解释主权和法律的关系，我们已经在前面的章节中讨论了这一点。

第四，我们来谈谈社会学中的心理学解释。这场运动的最重要的学者是法国社会学家、法学家塔德。塔德（Tarde）反对梅因对现代和古代法律所做出的区分，④ 而坚持认为"法律仅仅是一种人类模仿的模式或成果"⑤。模仿可以从一个人传到另一个人，也可以从一个阶级传到另一个阶级。⑥ 因此通过模仿的进程，法律可以从一个阶级转移到另一阶级或从一个国家转移到另一国家。

德国的学者如基尔克（Gierke）反对这样的观点，即法律是一个国家的主权者意志的表达。他认为心理方面的因素必须考虑到。为了理解基尔克的观点，可以引述下面的一段话："在法律与国家之间存在特别密切的相互渗透的关系。法律内在于国家。二者相辅相成。但是，尽管每一个都自有其存在的理由，但它们都相互促进对方的发展，相互成为对方的补充……现在国家起着立法机构的作用。但是由于那个原因，国家既不能成为法律的终极来源，也不是唯一的立法机构。法律的终极来源在于社会存在的普遍意识中。关于善的普遍观念需要通过一种社会表达把它固定下来，以使它能被外界接受……这种表达通常通过国家的手段来实现。国家在人们的法律意识的形成中扮演着主要的角色。但是除了国家，社会这个有机组织也能制定法律……法律生活和国家生命是社会生命的两个独立的方面。对国家来说，权力是一种必要的条件，因为没有权力的国家就不是一个国家，但是法律的定义表明，它是非物质的，与它有关的权力，存在于其外部。因

---

① Spencer, *Social Statics and Man vs. State*, 378～380 页, 1903。
② Spencer, *Social Statics and Man vs. State*, 380 页, 1903。
③ Spencer, *Social Statics and Man vs. State*, 380 页, 1903。
④ Tarde, *The Laws of Imitations*, Parsons 翻译, 314 页。
⑤ Tarde, *The Laws of Imitations*, Parsons 翻译, 61 页。
⑥ Tarde, *The Laws of Imitations*, Parsons 翻译, 201 页。

此，法律即使没有权力，不被实施，它也依然是法律。"①

美国的学者如埃尔伍德（Ellewood）教授和威廉姆斯（Williams）教授都极力强调心理因素在法律制定中的作用。埃尔伍德教授说："现在的法律源自习俗，那是一种社会习惯。"法律并不是来自社会，而是从社会的心理本质中产生出来的。② 根据威廉姆斯教授的看法，法学家们犯了一个错误，即他们相信法律是政治权威的命令。③ 法理学家是法学家而不是科学家，法学家的职业思维方法是演绎法，而不是科学家的归纳法。④ 真正的法律本质的定义需要合理的社会–心理学假设，这只能通过对社会–心理学的理解来获得。⑤ 现在的法律已经不能再用"发号施令"这个成语来描述了，因为这个成语用在这里就表明法律是主权者赐予的。事实上，法律从本质上说是习惯。因此，在这里不能说法律是指定的。⑥

社会学现在的趋势是由单一学科研究到系统研究。这种运动可以说是发轫于孔德和斯宾塞的著作，在斯莫尔（Small）教授和海耶斯（Hayes）及其他最近的学者的著作中得到发展。在社会学领域里的综合研究，相应地导致了法学领域里的综合研究。庞德说道："在当前这个世纪（20世纪——译者注），法学家们已经意识到在不同社会科学中进行区分是必要的，不是因为事物的本质，而仅仅是因为劳动分工的需要。实际上，除了分析法学家，他们从来没有完全否认法理学与其他社会科学之间的联系。"⑦ 后一种运动中的重要的代表是德国的科勒尔（Kohler），美国的霍姆斯（Holmes）法官和庞德，澳大利亚的萨尔蒙德（Salmond）⑧，而领军人物是法国的狄骥和荷兰的克拉勃（Krabbe）。

1. 科勒尔

在庞德看来，科勒尔无疑是在世的法学家中的佼佼者。⑨ 著名的法律哲学史学者伯罗茨海默（Berolzheimer）也认为科勒尔的法律哲学是继黑格尔之后对法律哲学最重要的贡献。⑩ 像黑格尔一样，科勒尔认为法律就是一种文化现象，但

---

① Gierke, "Die Grundbegriffee des Staatsrechts und die neuesten Staatstheorien", *Zeitschrift fur die gesammate Staatswissenchafte*, 图宾根, 179页, 1874。Daguit 在"The Law and the State"一文中引用, 见 *Harvard Law Review*, 第31卷, 159~160页。

② Ellewood, *Sociology in its Psychological Aspects*, 37页, 1912。

③ Williams, *The Foundations of Social Science*, 210页, 1920。

④ Williams, *The Foundations of Social Science*, 209页, 1920。

⑤ Williams, *The Foundations of Social Science*, 211页, 1920。

⑥ Williams, *The Foundations of Social Science*, 219页, 1920。也可参见他的 *Principles of Social Psychlogy*, 1922。

⑦ Pound, "Sociology and Law", 参见 Ogburn 和 Goldenweiser, *The Social Sciences and their Interrelations*, 323页, 1927。

⑧ 他的理论的有相当的重要性，我们在这里正好有机会论述他的观念。

⑨ 参见 *Harvard Law Review*, 第24卷, 155页。

⑩ Berolzheimer, *The World's Legal Philosophy*, 英文版, 426页。

是他不像黑格尔那样，把法律哲学视作演绎的产物。他用经验主义的方法，在历史和民族学的基础上进行学术研究。① 因此，他同意萨维尼的观点。但是他不仅认为法律是过去产生的，而且认为法律可以被有意识地修改，以适应当前的需求。他说："一个民族的法律只能用它的全部文化来诠释。也就是说，要完全诠释它就不能仅着眼于物质和经济因素，还要考虑受法律影响的民族和宗教观点。法律不是通过对功用的随意领悟而产生的。人生观也影响法律。法律就是从这些重要的文化功用中产生的。法律创造了一系列供文化存在的渠道。这些渠道的本性显示了他们在文化存在中的特征。它们在很大程度上被有关精神生活和生活规则的现实观念所决定。"②

因此，法律是文明的产物。但这还不是全部，因为法律也是实现文明的一种手段。用庞德的话说，"我们必须以三种方式来看它，在过去是文明的产物，在现在是保持文明的手段，在未来是促进文明的手段"③。这样产生的法律跟法律由最高意志所创造的观点是相反的。科勒尔认识到在法律制定中有意志因素的存在，但这并不是说，这是一种上级给下级的法律，它只意味着这种法律的制定或修改是为了保护或增进文明。

2. 霍姆斯

霍姆斯法官有时也被认为是一个历史法学家④，但是早在1891年，他已经表明他不再是那个学派的学者。⑤ 在普罗克和拉斯基给他的感谢函中，已足以清楚地表明了他在法学领域中的观点。⑥ 在出版于1920年的《选集》的一个简单的前言中，在向拉斯基先生收集付印这些文章表达了谢意之后，他说："新一代人已经在进行我将近半个世纪前开创的事业，对于一个老兵来说，最高兴的事情莫过于在不能战斗以后，那些善解人意的年轻士兵仍在战壕里给他保留一个位置。"⑦ 甚至一个外行也容易从这段话中看出这是一场什么战争，他站在哪一边。

一个景仰霍姆斯的著作的学者说他是美国法官中一个伟大的例外。"其他法官都是由生活的经验指导，他则为哲学家的语言和诗人的想象所引导。他希望哲学家成为国王。"⑧ 在某种程度上，霍姆斯更像一位哲学家，而不是法学家。他说："理论是法律条文中最为重要的部分，就像建筑师是参加建筑的人中的最为

---

① Berolzheimer, *The World's Legal Philosophy*, 英文版, 422页。
② Berolzheimer 所引用。同上书, 423页。
③ Pound, *Interpretations of Legal History*, 143页。
④ 参见 Taylor, *Science of Jurisprudence*, 30页, 1908。
⑤ 参见他的选集中的标题为 "Agency" 的文章。
⑥ Pollock, *First Book of Jurisprudence*, 前言; Laski, *Problem of Sovereignty*, 前言。
⑦ Holmes, *Collected Papers*, 前言。
⑧ "Mr. Justice Holmes and the Constitution", *Harvard Law Review*, 第XLI卷, 128页, 1927。

关键的人一样。"①

早在 1881 年，在他的《普通法》一书中，霍姆斯指出了仅仅从形式上思考法律的理论是失败的。他宣称："你可以同霍布斯、边沁、奥斯丁等一样假定所有的法律都是主权者颁布的，甚至说是法官最先颁布了法律，你也可以认为法律是'时代精神'（Zeitgeist）的声音，或者随你怎么说。"②

分析学派的错误，在霍姆斯看来，就是认为只有逻辑才是法律在发展过程中起推动作用的力量。什么是逻辑？它就是法律是主权的产物的断言。但是，"法律的生命从来就不是逻辑，而是经验"③。然而经验是人类过去行为的积累，"法律是一个民族通过几个世纪的发展经历而来，而不是一本数学书中几个原理所能解决得了的"④。

他宣称："事实是，法律只能无限接近，而永远不可能达到。它不停地从生活中吸收新的规则，同时又保留老的规则。只有当它停止发展的时候，才能完全达到它。"⑤ 为了知道它是什么，我们必须知道它曾经是什么和将要成为什么。⑥

3. 庞德

在其《法律与道德》收录的三篇在 1923 年在北卡罗利亚大学发表的演讲中，庞德对法律哲学的历史做了一个总的鸟瞰："希腊人通过自然权利的原则为法律找到了一个理论的道德基础。罗马法学家使自然权利进入自然法之中……中世纪在自然法之下安放神学的基础……17、18 世纪则抛弃了这种神学的基础，而代之以或部分代之以理性的基础……在十八世纪末期康德用形而上学的基础取代理性的基础……只有分析法学家认为法律不需要任何基础……"⑦

庞德在这里所强调的是法律不应当从道德习惯中分离，法律仅仅是主权者的命令的分析学说不应再坚持。对他来说，法律不仅是主权者的意志，实际上远不止此。⑧ 因为法律是个人和社会利益的一种平衡。当我们想起法律的时候，我们不要只想起权利，还要想到利益、要求和需要。⑨ 这是"满足人类需要，保证利益的安全，或以最少的摩擦和最少的消耗满足需求的方式之一，满足的方式则是越多越好"⑩。

---

① Holmes, "The Path of Law", 第十卷, *Harvard Law Review*, 477 页。也可参见其 *Collected Papers*。
② *Collected Papers*, 179 页。*Harvard Law Review*, 465 页。
③ *Common Law*, 1 页。也可参见 Taylor, *Science of Jurisprudence*, 30 页。参见他在 the American Banana Co. 诉 the United States Co. 一案中的观念, 1909, 213 页、347 页、356 页、358 页。
④ *Common Law*, 1 页。
⑤ *Collected Papers*, 36 页。
⑥ *Common Law*, 1 页。也可参见 *Collected Papers*, 185 页。
⑦ Pound, *Law and Morals*, 12~14 页, 1924。
⑧ 参考 Pound, *Law and Morals*, 77~84 页。
⑨ Pound, *Interpretations of Legal History*, 152 页。
⑩ Pound, *Interpretations of Legal History*, 157 页。

在庞德眼中，今天的世界已经不是昨天的世界。随着时间的演进，情况在发生变化。不仅分析法学派的学说已经与事实不相协调，甚至历史学派的理论也不能满足时代的需要。他说："分析法学派和历史学派发展的基础已经不存在了。法学家面临这样的任务：建立新的社会秩序。"① 法律功能的改变不仅是必须的，它已经在改变了，因为现在的趋势是反对少数人的绝对权威，法律是少数人的命令的旧的观念已经一去不返。总之，现在的法律是为了大多数人的福利，而不是为了某一个阶级的福利而牺牲其他阶级的利益。②

4. 萨尔蒙德

萨尔蒙德教授的著作标志着在英国广为接受的主权和法律观念的一个大的分离。他不仅是一个多元主义者，而且是一个狂热的多元主义者。他把传统的主权理论归结为三种主张：①主权是国家的本质；②主权是不可分的；③主权是不受限制的。对于第一种，他彻底赞同。但是他认为第二种和第三种主张没有坚实的基础。③

根据他的看法，主权不仅是可分的，正如"部分主权"一词所显示的那样，而且在一个国家里可以分成许多部分，因为它是由不同的部门所拥有的。这样，在英国，主权就被委任给三个政府部门，也就是立法、行政和司法。在各自的范围内每一个部分都是主权。④

而且，主权不是不可限制的。"在不久以前，"他说，"由英国议会制定的法律如果与理性法和上帝法相冲突，也是无效的。这种规则现在已经被法院放弃，很明显，它从理论上来说，并不是荒谬的和不可能的。然而它已清楚地表示对立法的权力的限制。"他继续说："举另外一个例子，英国议会立法的一个最为明显的特征是英国国会下院（House of Commons）有权延长现届议会的任期。人民选举产生的有限任期的代表，有权延长自己的任期。为什么法院不立法规定议会只在任期内是主权者，并且无权延长自己的任期？在这种情况下，立法者的权力不能被法律限制吗？"⑤

如果议会立法权力的执行需要服从于法律，它受法律的限制就一定是真实的。如果立法权力执行的方式可以由法律来规定，则它的事务也可以由法律来规定。⑥

但是萨尔蒙德教授还不是停留于此。在坚持主权是受法律的限制之外，他进

---

① Pound, *Introduction to the Legal Philosopy*, 57 页, 1922。
② 参见 Pound, "Legislation as a Social Function", *Publications of American Sociological Society*, 第 7 卷, 153~154 页。
③ Salmond, *Jurisprudence*, 第 6 版, 467 页。
④ Salmond, *Jurisprudence*, 第 6 版, 467~474 页。
⑤ Salmond, *Jurisprudence*, 第 6 版, 472 页。
⑥ Salmond, *Jurisprudence*, 第 6 版, 473 页。

一步表明法律是主权的命令以外的东西。法律仅仅是主权的命令的假设不能被接受，因为它建立在错误的观念之上。国家的功能，根据他的看法，是"保持权利、支持正义、保护权利和改变错误"①。它的功能使法律是第二位的和非本质的。

　　法律仅仅是维护正义的一种手段，因此对法律的定义就不能涉及它的目的。②"因此，法律可以定义为由国家在进行司法管理时采用的所有规则，或者更简单地说：法律由法庭所认可和颁布的规则所组成。"③ 从这个定义可以推导出，即便没有法律，司法管理也是完全可能的。他承认，在现代国家，一个人从法庭所得到的是有法律依据的判决，"但是它从本质上来说是判决，而不是法律"④。

---

① Salmond, *Jurisprudence*, 第 6 版, 12 页。
② Salmond, *Jurisprudence*, 第 6 版, 9 页。
③ Salmond, *Jurisprudence*, 第 6 版, 14 页。
④ Salmond, *Jurisprudence*, 第 6 版, 13 页。

第八章 主权与法律（续）

5. 狄骥

在一篇关于狄骥的法学概念讨论的文章中，一个政治哲学学者写道："在十八世纪的法国，卢梭的理论对法律的本质进行了最经典、最精妙的阐释。也是在近代法国，狄骥对卢梭的理论进行了精妙的反驳。"① 另一位法理学学者评论道："在他的《公法的变迁》（*Transformations du Droit Pulic*）中……狄骥对于法律科学就像孔德对于哲学那样，试图使之从神学和形而上学中解放出来。"②

毋庸置疑，狄骥在法学界很有影响，他也是与我们关注的问题有联系的最重要的代表人物。基于此种考虑，我下面将对他的观点进行更详细的探究。

（1）著作

狄骥教授担任波尔多大学的宪法学教授将近三十年。他的第一篇论文《制宪机构的分离和制宪大会》（*La Séparation des Pouvoirs et L'Assemblé Constituante*）（巴黎）早在1893年就出版。第二篇论文《法国的宪法和主要政治阶层》是在1898年与亨利·默里（Henry Monnier）先生合写的。在1901年，他出版了《国家、客观法和实在法》（*L'État, Le Droit Objectif et La Loi Positif*），在这本著作里，他毫不留情地批评了耶利内克（Jellinek）的名著《主观公法体系》（*System der subjektiven öffentlichen Rechte*, 1897），并进而提出了他的关于主权及主权与法的观念。一个学者对此评论说，这本著作，"包含了他的主要理论的精髓，要理解他的关于法律的本质以及法律与国家的关系的基本理念，这是一本最好的著作"③。

按狄骥教授的说法，这本书的目的是推翻一种观念，即说明国家不是被赋予了最高权力的人的，立法者通过的法律体系也不是建立在个人权利或国家全能这样不牢靠的理论基础上，这种抽象思维和凭空想象的产物，一点也经不起事实的检验。④

刚才所提到的这一书的观点在另一本题为《国家、政府及执政者》（*L'État*，

---

① 见 *Political Science Quarterly*, 640页, 1922, W. Y. Elliot 教授的文章。
W. Y. Elliot 对政治多元论展开了系统攻击。他把政治多元论的言论看作是对国家主权的侵蚀。——译者注
② W. J. Brown, "The Jurisprudence of M. Duguit", *Law Quarterly Review*, 第32卷, 168页, 1916。
③ "Modern Legal Philosophy Series", *Modern French Legal Philosophy*, xlix, 1921。
④ Duguit, *L'État, Le Droit Objectif et La Loi Positive*, 1页。也可参见 *Modern French Legal Philosophy*, 238页。

Les Gouvernemants et Les Agents）（1903）的书中得到了补充。在这之后，他写了《论宪法》（*Constitutional Law*）的论文。根据拉斯基的看法，"该论文在透彻分析了埃斯曼（Esmein）的近乎完美的成果的基础上，找到了批驳它的核心的完美切入点"①。

他在高等社会科学学院（École Des Hautes Études En Sciences Sociales）做的演讲中对其论点又做了进一步的阐述，这些演讲冠以《社会权利、个人权利和国家》（*Le Droit Social, Le Droit Individual et L'État*）的书名于1908年出版。在1912年，他对私法进行了研究，进而出版了《拿破仑法典以来私法的普通变迁》（*Les Transformations Générales du Droit Privé*）。在1913年他写了《公法的变迁》。后者可以看作是他全部观念的结晶。在1917年11月份的《哈佛法律评论》上他发表了长篇论文《法律与国家》。在这篇文章里，他重申了自己的观念，也回应了一些对他的批评。

以上简单的介绍足以显示狄骥教授是一个多产的学者，但他的思想观点却始终如一。《国家、客观法和实在法》出版已经25年了，但是那本书中所阐释的原理如今仍然是他的思想体系的基础。1917年，在引用了他写于1912年的话后，他写道："这些战前写就的观点，与当今的现实更加吻合。"②

（2）先驱者

无论在任何领域，若想有所建树，就必然得知道前人的成果。但是知道了他人的成果，在自己未有所见之前，就不免受到前人或同时代人的影响，这可以说是一个普遍现象。狄骥教授也不例外。他继承了许多人的思想。从孔德那样的哲学家那里，他继承了这样的观点："只要权力一成不变地来源于超自然的意志，就只能有一种真正的权力……在不承认神的特权的世俗国家里，权力的观点就绝不会存在。"③ 从涂尔干那样的社会学家那里，他得到了社会连带的观念，而这正是他的法律哲学的灵魂。从政治学者赛德尔（Seydel）那里，他继承了国家的人格是不存在的观念。从法学家基尔克那里，他继承了法律外在于国家的观念。

我们并没有列举出所有对其产生影响或给予他灵感的思想家，而只是限定于其中的几位，他们的理论，狄骥教授进行了深入的研究。早在19世纪的上半叶，罗耶-科拉尔（Royer-Collard），一个法国政治家，就否认主权的观念，而坚持法律的权威。④ 根据罗耶-科拉尔的看法，一个国家也许有主权，但主权就是专制政治，而"专制政治意味着社会的消亡或者至少是组织的无序"。因此主权只能存

---

① *Harvard Law Review*，第31卷，189页。
② *Harvard Law Review*，第31卷，185页。Duguit 教授的另一本书名为 *Souveraineté et liberté*（1922年），遗憾的是我手头没有这本书。
③ Comte 孔德的论述，见 *Systeme de politique positiviste*，1890年版，第1卷，361页。Duguit 所引用。
④ 关于 Royer-Collard 的理论，特别参见 Laski 在 *Authority in the Modern State* 第四章中有关 Royer-Collard 的内容。

在于一个无序的国家里面，它不是政治家和政治学者所企望看到的完美的事物。

如果理想的国家中没有主权，那么，维系个体的本质的东西是什么？答案是"法律"。法律，正如他所认识的，是实际利益的基础，也是一个国家的基石。它源自正义或理性，而不像主权那样建立在暴力的基础之上。①

伯努瓦（M. Charles Benoist）是另一位值得关注的学者。狄骥教授认为他是现实主义国家观念的权威代表。伯努瓦认为主权的观念是不可捉摸的。他说："对我们来说，更为明智和合理的做法就是抛弃主权的观点。当然，它是一种古老而又庄严的观念，但这种观念已经很过时，它在现代政治社会中已经不能再占有一席之地，就像博物馆里面的亚述人（Assyrian）和埃及人的神一样……或像中非的民族崇拜的吃虫的偶像一样……让我们仅仅在社会中活的东西中建立我们的理论。我们应该去发现社会中存在的事物的理论。主权观念在事实上曾经是正确的，并风靡一时，但现在却不再流行。但是主权从现实中消失以后，现代欧洲对主权观念的认同还要持续多久？现在已经没有必要回答，因为西欧诸国目前已不存在主权，以后也不会有。某种能取代它的东西已经到处涌现。"②

但是这种到处涌现出的取代主权的东西是什么呢？他宣称："目前，甚至在西欧诸国中主权也已不存在。与我们的主题有关的，是这样一种东西。它绵绵不绝，势不可当。他过去就已存在，将来也会存在下去。它先于我们存在，我们死后，它还会存在。它不可遏制，它包容一切。它是万物的缩影，它是永恒的，任何人或任何事物都不能阻止它，它不能被分割或摧毁。我们无法衡量它存在的空间和时间。它有至高无上的权力和地位。"③ 由此他指出："这个东西就是国家的生命。国家是不是主权者？这个问题没有意义。它是有生命的。现实中，每个人都生活于国家之中。相应地，每个人都有权利参与政治，只要他们参与政治的手段是合法的。"④

很显然国家生命的观念代替了主权观念的位置。法律不再服从一个主权者，而变成了国家的权威。法律和国家生命是国家的两个最为重要的要素。"我们不仅应该谈论国家生命，还要谈论法律权威；但是，应该说明的是，国家生命是它的永久的来源，也正是通过国家生命，这种权威可以永久的焕发生机，在国家生命里它可以不断凝聚，并从国家生命那里得到不断的活力。所以应将国家生命和

---

① 这是 Royer-Collard 理论的摘要，参见 Duguit, "The Law and the State", *Harard Law Review*, 第 31 卷，165～189 页。

② Charles Benoist, *La Politique*, 41 页, 42 页。Duguit（狄骥）引述，参见 *Harvard Law Review*, 第 31 卷，172 页。

③ Charles Benoist, *Sophismes politiques de ce temps*, 61 页。Duguit 引述，参见 *Harvard Law Review*, 第 31 卷，174 页。

④ Charles Benoist, *Sophismes politiques de ce temps*, 61 页。Duguit 的引述，参见 *Harvard Law Review*, 第 31 卷，174 页。

法律权威这两个事物放在一起来讲。不要仅仅谈生命的观念、法律的观念、秩序的观念,还要谈暴力的观念;主权的立法机构,强制理论,法律所限制的权力,税收,都要归于法律权威。我们应该毫不犹豫地将'主权'这个词从我们的政治词汇里面删除,因为现在是该删除它的时候了。"①

(3) 国家的人格

在对狄骥教授的著作和先驱者做了一个大概的说明之后,我们现在来讲他的理论。一般来说,正统理论的主张是:法律是主权的命令,主权是一个国家的本质特征,国家被认为是一个有独立人格的有机的整体。狄骥教授认为,要证明法律并不是主权者的意志或命令的体现,就得说明主权的定义是错误的,主权并不是国家的内在本质。要证明主权不是国家的内在本质,主权观念已经过时,就得说明国家和个人是不一样的。

许多学者维护国家人格的观念。他们采取许多形式:有人认为国家是一个道德组织。格伯(Gerber)就这样说:"国家的权力就是一种道德组织的权力。这种道德组织的结果,就像人的结构一样。它不是几个单独意志的人为的机械的集合,而是有自我意识的人的全部道德力量。"② 也有人认为国家是一个法人。耶利内克(Jellinek)就说:"国家法人观的理论建立在每个民族都是受某一地域的国家统治的这一不容置疑的自然的,也是历史的事实基础之上……人格是作为权利拥有者的能力——也就是法律能力。它不属于'物自身'的世界;它不是有形存在的事物,而是一种从属关系,一种符合法律秩序的关系……人格不是法律社会的基础,而是它的结果……国家人格观能独立地从法律角度给公法的存在一个令人满意的诠释。这一事实即可证明它的合理性。它也足以让国际法成其为法。"③

狄骥教授认为,这些理论都是无稽之谈④——"国家人格"和诸如此类的其他抽象概念都是虚无缥缈的。所有这些希望对政治权力进行哲学论证的理论,全都是死板的教条。实际上,政治权力本身无所谓合法不合法,它是社会进化的产物。⑤ 只有单个的人才是人。⑥ 国家的人格并不存在。只有个人才会有意志,而没有集体意志之类的东西存在。国家意识一说不过是幻想而已。正因如此,这样的国家与组成它的个人之间没有共性,当然也就不具有人格。⑦

---

① Charles Benoist, *La Politique*, 156 页。Duguit 引述,见 *Harvard Law Review*, 第 31 卷, 176~177 页。

② *Die Grandbegriffe des deutschens*, 218 页, Duguit 所引述:Duguit, *L'État, Le Droit Objectif et La Loi Positive*, 3 页。也可参见 *Modern French Legal Philosophy*, 239 页。

③ Jellinet, *Systemder subjiecktiven of fentlichen Rechto*, 20 页、26 页、27 页、32 页。Duguit 引述于 *L'État, Le Droit Objectif et La Loi Positive*, 3~4 页。也可参见 *Modern French Legal Philosophy*, 240 页。

④ Duguit, *L'État, Le Droit Objectif et La Loi Positive*, 5 页。

⑤ *Manuel de Droit Constitutionel*, 第 3 版, 23 页。

⑥ Duguit, *L'État, Les Gouvernants et Les Agents*, 27 页。

⑦ Duguit, *L'État, Les Gouvernants et Les Agents*, 242 页。

的确有些时候某些人会有相同的观念和愿望，但这也不会导致某个单一意志或意识的产生。即使我们能保证某个团体中的所有人都思考同一件事，并且用同一种方式思维，那也不会导致有别于个人意志或意识的产生。在这一点上，狄骥教授的观点与涂尔干很相近。

　　进一步来说，国家不是一个法人。法律赋予了国家一些人格的特征，并且，只有当国家被看作一个人的时候才能制定法律，因而国家的人格不可能源自法律，但不能因此而说国家是一个人。①

　　狄骥教授问道："如果国家是一个人，那么公法还有可能存在吗？"② 国家人格的支持者坚持认为，要有公法，就必须先有一个主观存在的公共权利，并且由作为一个人的国家掌握这种主观存在的权利。主观存在的权利这个观念很重要。但从实际上讲，这种主观存在的权利并不真的存在。狄骥教授指出，即使耶利内克本人也承认在所谓的国家组织或国家组织系统的背后，其实空无一物。除了组织系统，什么东西也没有。而所谓的组织不过是某些人通过强制手段将自己的意志强加于另一部分人的身上。③

　　（4）国家和政府

　　在否认了国家的人格之后，那么什么是国家？这里我们回到狄骥理论的建设性的方面。狄骥教授说，国家仅仅是一个力量的证明，它可以被定义为"在一个特定的社会里一个人或一些人比其他的人要强，或者是统治者和被统治者的区别这一简单的事实"④。

　　一位政治学学者对这种国家的定义如此解释："这种国家的定义，忽略了一种差别，因为它只看到了国家中统治者与被统治者之间的差别，而没有认识到统治者也可能臣服于更高的权力。这样就无法看到加拿大这样真正的国家和美洲联盟这样的所谓的国家之间的差别。"⑤ 并且，拉斯基教授说："对狄骥来说，国家不过是这样一群人，在他们中间，由于历史环境的改变，而产生了统治者和臣民之间的区别。"⑥

　　这样对国家的定义和观点，部分地与政府的定义联系起来。一个国家是一个统治者和被统治者的联合体，而另一方面讲，政府是某个特定的社会中，掌握垄

---

① Duguit, *L'État, Les Gouvernants et Les Agents*, 79 页。
② Duguit, *L'État, Les Gouvernants et Les Agents*, 7 页。
③ Duguit, *L'État, Les Gouvernants et Les Agents*, 7～8 页。
④ Duguit, *L'État, Les Gouvernants et Les Agents*, 261 页、350 页、519 页。参见 N. Wilde, "The Attack on the State", *Journal of International Ethics*, 第 30 卷（1919—1920），352 页。
⑤ Mathews, "A Recent Political Theory", *Political Science Quarterly*, 第 21 卷，289 页。
⑥ *Harvard Law Review*, 第 31 卷，189～198 页。也可参见 *Law in Modern State* 导论，Laski 翻译。

断武力的阶级或组织体。①

(5) 主权

在其《宪法概要》(Élements de Droit Constitutional) 一书中，埃斯曼 (Esmein) 教授写道："国家是民族的法律人格化；它是公共权威的目标和基础……这种权威天然地排斥高于或与之相配敌的权力，它被叫作主权……主权的所有者是全民的人格化，即道德人格。它的最终的、永久的目标就是国家，国家因此往往被人们与它的内在特征，即主权等同起来。"②

道德人格拥有主权以及将整个国家拟人化是狄骥教授激烈反对的。"没有哪个阶级和政党在19世纪不把国家主权当作宗教教条加以接受的，很少有例外。"③他认为如果这种理论本身适用于现实的话，则反对这种主权理论是没有什么用处的。但情况并不是这样。因为，"所有的事实都表明它与社会和政治的变迁是相矛盾的。随着它的有效性的消失，这种理论甚至变得有很大的危害了"④。

民族主权观念包含的最为本质的原则是：①它给国家和民族之间强行规定了一种关系，而这种关系在现实中并不存在；②从定义上来讲，它是唯一的和不可分的，它对该民族区域内的所有独立的部族实行统治。⑤

但是这样的原则与现实不再一致。因为事实已经显示，在第一方面，目前在国家与民族之间不再彼此等同。有时候，一个政府会统治几个明显互不相同的民族。这些民族之间，许多情况下，还会发生冲突。奥匈帝国就是这样的一个例子。没有人能够说奥匈帝国的意志是唯一的和不可分的，也没有人说奥地利这个国家是奥地利民族在政治方面的表现。这种情况在大不列颠王国也是如此。大不列颠王国毫无疑问是一个国家，但它不是一个民族。⑥

并且，还存在被认为是国家或政府的属民，但不是相应的民族的成员的情况。如不同国家的殖民地的居民就属于这种情况。狄骥教授发现这种情况与那种认为由国家产生的公权只能对其成员发生效力的民族主权理论不相一致。⑦

第二方面，与民族相联系的主权是单一的和不可分的，同一个国家内，只有一个民族能执行和分享主权的主张与事实是不相符的。这从地方分权和联邦主义

---

① Duguit, *L'État, Le Droit Objectif et La Loi Positive*, 311页。当Mathews说Duguit在政府和国家之间没有区分的时候，只是部分的正确。同上书，290~291页。

② Duguit, *Le Transformations du Droit Public*, 16页。Laski译本（Laski将该书译为 *Law in the Modern State*），15页。

③ Duguit, *Le Transformations du Droit Public*, 19页。Laski译本，18页。

④ Esmein, *Élements de Droit Constitutionnel*, 1页。Duguit所引。

⑤ Duguit, *Le Transformations du Droit Public*, 19页。Laski译本，18页。

⑥ Duguit, *Le Transformations du Droit Public*, 19~20页。Laski译本，18~20页。

⑦ Duguit, *Le Transformations du Droit Public*, 20页。

的趋势中可以看出。① 即便是在法国,这种趋势也是很明显的。法国的行政区(French Commune)拥有主权的真正权利,如警察权、税收权和管辖领地内的优先权。②

这还不是全部。为了表明那种主权观念已经走向没落,还可以提到其他的事实。多数统治原则与这种民族主权原则是一致的,但是这个原则在现代民主社会里不再是重要的了。③ 并且,根据那种旧的主权理论,主权者是不能被控诉的,但是这样的观念已经被事实证明为没有根据。更进一步,旧的理论是注定要衰落的,因为那些执行国家的最高权力的人有时不能做他们想做的事情,另一方面,有时他们必须做他们不想做的事情。这意味着对主权有一个限制,而这又是对旧的主权是不能被限制的观念的一种否认。

所有的事实都使得我们相信旧的主权观念已经走向没落。主权的衰退在一定程度上也改变主权与法律关系的观念。我们现在就来考虑法律。

(6) 法律

在旧的理论家看来,主权与法律之间的关系,如赛德尔说,就是没有主权者就没有法律,法律通过主权者而存在。与此相反,狄骥教授说道:"我们认为没有主权者法律也能存在,法律在主权者之上。我们坚定地相信在个人和国家之上,在统治者和被统治者之上有一个法律规则;这种规则对两方面都是强制性的,我们认为如果有一个像国家的主权那样的东西存在,它一定会受到法律规则的限制。"④

如果法律不是主权的产物,那么法律从哪里来?它建立在个人的自然权利上吗?不是的,狄骥教授说。但是为什么呢?因为个人的权利只是一个假说,一个形而上学的断定,而不是一种事实。⑤ 个人的自然权利暗含了社会是由社会契约为基础组成的观点,但社会契约的理论只不过是虚构的。只要人们还生活在一个社会里面,契约的观念就不会出现在人们的观念中的。"是社会产生契约,而不是契约产生社会。"⑥

但是否认个人的自然权利是法律的基础并不意味着"个人自然权利的理论不会在适当的时候出现,和不产生伟大的贡献"。因为正是这个原则宣布了国家的主权是受法律的限制的。这是法国大革命的荣耀,并将永闪光辉。⑦

但是什么是法律,什么是法律的基础?狄骥教授说:"法律既不再是社会的

---

① Duguit, *Le Transformations du Droit Public*, 20 页。对于其联邦主义的观点,参见第三章。
② Duguit, *Le Transformations du Droit Public*, 20 页以下。
③ Duguit, *Le Transformations du Droit Public*, 35~36 页。
④ Duguit, *L'État, Le Droit Objectif et La Loi Positive*, 1~12 页。*Modern French Legal Philosophy*, 247 页。
⑤ Duguit, *L'État, Le Droit Objectif et La Loi Positive*, 12 页。
⑥ Duguit, *L'État, Le Droit Objectif et La Loi Positive*, 13 页。
⑦ Duguit, *L'État, Le Droit Objectif et La Loi Positive*, 11~12 页。*Modern French Legal Philosophy*, 14 页。

权力，也不再是个人的权力。"① 它是客观存在的。简单地说，它是事实的规则②——社会连带的事实的规则。

（7）社会连带——法律的基础

根据狄骥教授的说法，人是社会的动物。因为是社会的动物，他们必须生活在社会里且只能生活在社会里。狄骥教授认为，由许多学者如霍布斯、洛克、卢梭等提出的自然状态的观点，仅仅是一个虚幻。③ 社会不是人类意志的产物。人类一开始，它就开始了。生活在社会里不是一个偶然的选择，而是具有必然性的。"我们不能说社会存在，是因为人们想生活在社会里面。人一直且只能在那种方式下生活。"④ 坚持人是社会的动物的前提，不会推导出没有人，人类社会也能够存在的结论。如果没有人，就没有人类社会。人和社会构成一个事物的两个方面。

作为一个人、一个社会的动物，会同他的同类有某些同样的希望和愿望。也正因为他们有相同的愿望和想法，他们才可以生活在一起而组成一个社会组织。每一个人都希望能尽其所能获得尽可能多的幸福并尽可能避免痛苦。但是如果一个人生活在一个共同体中，他才能遭受最少的痛苦，因为只有通过与其他人生活，他才知道他在遭受痛苦并进而想减少痛苦。⑤ 在意识到不能单独地生活之后，他才意识到共同生活的价值。正是通过这种方式，社会连带才产生。这就是被形象地称为连带的东西。

但是在一个特定的社会里，不是所有人在所有情况下都在同一种方式下思考或想同样的事情。但是在想法上的不同不会导致削弱社会连带的倾向。相反，它们还有增强它的倾向。正因为人们不以同样的方式思考、愿望和行动，劳动的分工才是可能的。劳动的分工使得人与人之间产生相互依赖，这种相互依赖性使得社会中的人联系在一起。

当人们认识到他的需要、想法和愿望跟其他人不一样的时候，他就意识到他的个体性。但是他的个体性不是他自然拥有的个体性，而是与其他人相关的个体性。这样，他不是天生就是一个个体，而是作为社会存在的一个个体。他对自己思考得越多，他对社会思考得也会越多。一个人的渴望和需求越多，为了满足他的需求，他就会尽力多做他所渴望做的事，社会就将越高级。文明的进步意味着劳动分工的加强。狄骥教授说，文明只不过是对个体之间差异性的强调。⑥

---

① Duguit, *L'État, Le Droit Objectif et La Loi Positive*, 11~12 页。*Modern French Legal Philosophy*, 16 页。
② Duguit, *L'État, Le Droit Objectif et La Loi Positive*, 11~12 页。*Modern French Legal Philosophy*, 16 页。
③ Duguit, *L'État, Le Droit Objectif et La Loi Positive*, 37 页。
④ Duguit, *L'État, Le Droit Objectif et La Loi Positive*, 37 页。
⑤ Duguit, *L'État, Le Droit Objectif et La Loi Positive*, 31 页。
⑥ Duguit, *L'État, Le Droit Objectif et La Loi Positive*, 11~12 页。*Modern French Legal Philosophy*, 43 页。

在一个社会里一直存在两种进程：社会化和个体化。社会化的提高与劳动分工成正比，劳动分工的提高与个体化成正比。① 这两个进程是并行不悖的，而且二者都需要对方的帮助。劳动分工，作为二者共有的标准，是社会连带产生作用的方式。这就是涂尔干（Durkheim）所说的通过社会分工产生的连带。②

从上面所说的，我们得出下面的结论："在每一个群体里面，两个因素促成社会联合；这两个因素可以表现为不断变化的形式，但是它们的基础归根到底是一样的。它们是：①需求的相似性，这是他们连带的基础，无论是通过组织依赖还是通过比较；②需求的差异性，这导致他们交换服务的必要性，这是通过个体依赖或劳动分工来实现连带。"③

狄骥教授还补充："因此，从这里，我们就会认识到法律能使自己加诸社会中每一个成员的身上：无论是伟大人物还是平凡者，无论是强者还是弱者，无论是统治者还是被统治者。它告诉人们：不要通过合作或劳动分工做任何可能有损于社会的相互依赖性的事情；而要在力所能及并符合你的地位和特殊条件的范围内，通过合作和劳动分工去做能加强社会相互依赖性的事情。"④

（8）法律的标准和一般特征

法律的标准就是社会连带。如果它是建立在社会连带的基础之上的，它就可以称为法律。⑤ 法律，作为社会连带的产物，打上了连带的烙印。"它有相同的特征。像连带一样，它包括所有的人；也像连带一样，在同一时间它既具个体性，又具社会性。"⑥ 它具有社会性，因为只有人生活在社会中它才存在，既然人已经生活在社会中并仍将生活在社会中，法律也就已经存在并仍将存在。它具有个体性，因为首先它仅仅是一个关于个体的概念，其次，它仅运用于个体。因为它具有个体性，在运用中它是多样化的。在运用中是多样化的，因为人们的需要、愿望和态度是不一样的。个体间的差异越大，法律条文就越具有多样性。

而且，法律施用于所有个体，不管是强者还是弱者，概莫能外。它要求每一个人做有利于增强连带的任何事情而不做任何可能伤害社会连带的事情。个体越

---

① Duguit, *L'Etat, Le Droit Objiectif et La Loi Positive*, 11～12 页。*Modern French Legal Philosophy*, 48 页。
② Duguit, *L'Etat, Le Droit Objiectif et La Loi Positive*, 11～12 页。*Modern French Legal Philosophy*, 48 页。
③ Duguit, "The Law and State", *Harvard Law Review*, 第 31 卷, 178 页。"我们不说在社会连带中人们应该合作，因为合作本身就是好的，但是在社会连带中人们应该合作，因为他是一个人，如此他就不会排除在连带之外。我们不说在连带中合作的行为是好的；我们说，连带的行为有一个社会后果。" *Droit Constitutionnel*, 16 页。
④ Duguit, "The Law and State", *Harard Law Review*, 第 31 卷, 178 页。"我们不说在社会连带中人们应该合作，因为合作本身就是好的，但是在社会连带中人们应该合作，因为他是一个人，如此他就不会排除在连带之外。我们不说在连带中合作的行为是好的；我们说，连带的行为有一个社会后果。" *Droit Constitutionnel*, 16 页。
⑤ Duguit, *L'Etat, Le Droit Objiectif et La Loi Positive*, 105 页。
⑥ Duguit, *L'Etat, Le Droit Objiectif et La Loi Positive*, 91 页。

强大，越能运用他们的权力为增强社会的连带做更多的事情。只有这样做，他们的行为才会符合法律。但是使用权力去增强法律的效力并不意味着法律建立在权力基础之上，因为权力只是一种手段。相反，它意味强者有义务用自己的力量为法律服务。①

更进一步，法律是永久性的和不断变化的。它是永久性的，因为在内容上它是一样的。"每一个社会都是一种社会连带。每个为生活于社会中的人制订的法律条文都要求他们在这种连带中合作，并支持这种劳动分工与合作的社会连带。因此，法律条文的原则和精神是永久的。"② 它是不断变化的，因为社会连带的形式是多样的。家庭、家族、部落、民族无所不在，这些形式在时间上和空间上都有分布。既然法律的基础是社会连带，则社会连带形式的改变也一定会导致法律形式的改变。文明的改变也会导致它的改变。一句话，法律随着客观条件的改变而改变。

很显然，法律的变革源自社会连带的变革。"这种规则（法律）在本质上具有社会性，但在应用中具有个体性。在概念上，因为它具有个体性所以是多样的，而又因为它具有社会性，所以是一般的。它的原则是永久不变的，但其应用方式是不断变化的。"③

（9）法律的定义

在讨论了法律的基础、标准和一般特征之后，让我们来引用他的法律定义作为我们已经讨论内容的结论和进一步讨论的起点。法律被定义为"在永久进化过程中的行为规则，它的产生，源自社会连带的形式的不断改变，它随时间和空间的不断变化而变化"④。

这样，我们又回到了我们开始的地方：法律不是主权的命令，主权不是国家的本质特征，国家不是一个人格。但是狄骥教授没有到此为止。法律，正如所定义的，是客观法，与被看作是主权的命令的所谓的主观的法律相反。他宣称："国家没有命令的主观权利，个人也没有自由或财产的主观权利，所有的统治者和被统治者，都服从于基于社会的相互依赖性的法律规则；通过这种法律规则的应用，所有个体的意志——无论是统治者的意志还是被统治者的意志——发现它们自己被置于某种特定状况，也就是我们称之为客观的或合法的状况。"⑤

服从建立在社会连带基础上的法律也是为了增强社会连带。因此法律不仅是社会连带的产物，也是进一步增强社会连带的方式。根据法律增强连带的活动是

---

① Duguit, *L'État, Le Droit Objectif et La Loi Positive*, 98 页。
② Duguit, *L'État, Le Droit Objectif et La Loi Positive*, 98~99 页。
③ Duguit, *L'État, Le Droit Objectif et La Loi Positive*, 100 页。
④ Duguit, *L'État, Le Droit Objectif et La Loi Positive*, 428 页。
⑤ Duguit, "The Law and State", *Harvard Law Review*, 第 31 卷, 182~183 页。

公共服务。"公共服务"的概念在狄骥教授的理论中的地位就像"公意"在卢梭的理论中的地位一样。在完成对狄骥教授的讨论之前，让我们考察一下公共服务的含义。

(10) 公共服务

狄骥教授告诉我们公共服务这个观念本身不是一个新的观念。它是一个旧的观念，就像公共服务本身一样古老。这种观念，根据狄骥教授的看法，在统治者和臣属者之间的区分产生的时候，它就产生了。虽然公共服务的观念本身不是一个新的观念，但在法律领域里面，则是一个新观念。狄骥教授认为，将这种观念介绍进入现代公法是一个伟大的贡献。狄骥教授反复告诉我们公共服务的观念很快将代替主权的观念。后者赋予了这种规则以一种主权的权利，这种权利是以形而上学和神学为理论基础的。与此相反，前者是依赖于事实或可以知道的事实，也就是社会连带。这是统治和被统治必须也是唯一可以用来实现各自目的的手段。这样，法律不是主权者的法律，而是为公共服务的法律。

可以以这种方式定义公共服务："任何对社会连带的实现与促进而言不可或缺，而必须由政府来加以规范和控制的活动，都是公共服务。因为没有政府的介入，便不能保证它万无一失。"①

随着时间的推移，政府的行为也许增加，历史显示它们已经和正在增加。但是行为的增加并不意味着权力的增加。相反，它意味着责任和义务的增加，那些权力的受托者不再是人们的主人，不能将主权这意志强加于其属民之上，也不能再发布命令。"他们仅仅是国家事务的管理者。他们的事务增加，其责任也就扩大；但是他们是没有控制的权利的，因为没有人再相信它。"②

公共服务的性质和范围并没有被明确地界定。在过去，国防、内卫，维持秩序和坚持正义就是公共职能或公共服务，但是现在，这些已经不是全部了。当代仍有一些思想家坚持认为，政府的职能就是刚刚所列举的那些，但是事实已经不仅如此；当现代的思想家意识到这些事实，他们的态度也会相应地改变。

事实是近些年经济的改变已经产生新的政府职能，因此增加了政府的行为。这种趋势不仅在欧洲的一个国家或多个国家是明显的，在整个世界也是明显的。没有人能够说未来的公共服务仍将会同今天的公共服务是一样的，原因在于"公共服务的内容是经常变化的且处在不断变化之中"③。"甚至很难判明这种变化的一般方向。所能够讲的是，随着文明的发展，与公共需要相关的活动的数量会增加，进而导致公共服务也跟着增加。这是很符合逻辑的。实际上，文明本身就是能在最少的时间内满足各种需要的能力的增强。结果是，政府的干预随着文明的

---

① Duguit, *Le Transformations du Droit Public*, 51 页。Laski 译本，48 页。
② Duguit, *Le Transformations du Droit Public*, 55 页。Laski 译本，51 页。
③ Duguit, *Le Transformations du Droit Public*, 47 页。Laski 译本，45 页。

发展而变得越来越频繁，因为政府本身足以使文明有意义。"①

在简要地指出狄骥教授的公共服务的观念之后，让我们再引述一段狄骥教授一再引述的话来作结尾："现代公法的整个系统的原则可以用这样一句话来概括：那些实事上有权力的人没有拥有公共权力的主观权利；但是他们有义务运用他们的权力来组织公共服务，以保证和控制它的发展。除非他们的行为是为了这个目的，否则，所有的行为都不具强制力或政治价值。公法不再是这样一些应用到不同种类的权利的主体（一些人是统治者，另一些人是属民；一些人有发布命令的权利，另一些人只有服从的权利）的原则的集合。所有的意志都是个体的意志，所有的意志都是平等的。他们的价值只能由其所追寻的目的来决定。那些统治者的意志是没有这样的强制力的，除非他们为一项公共服务的组织和运作发挥作用时，才有价值和强制力。这样，公共服务的观念就代替了主权的观念。国家不再是发布命令的最高权力拥有者；它是一个由个体组成的群体，这些个体拥有自己控制的力量，他们会用这些力量去创造并管理公共服务。因而公共服务的观念就成了现代公法的基本观念。"②

6. 克拉勃（Krabbe）

（1）著作

克拉勃教授有两本重要的著作：①《法律主权学说》（*Die Lehre der Rechtssouveränität*，1906）；②《近代国家观念》（*Die Moderne Staats-idee*，1919）。正如有的评论指出的，前者主要是对国家的观念和它与法律的关系的批判的和历史的分析。③ 后者意图在于解释他的理论的建设性方面。后者已经被萨拜因（Sabine）和夏普德（Shepard）教授翻译成英文。韦罗贝教授认为译者通过解释性的注释而增加了这本书的价值。④

（2）历史上法律主权的理论

克拉勃教授把他自己的理论描述为"法律主权理论"。我们已经了解到这种理论可以追溯到古希腊时期。知名的政治哲学家巴克（Barker）教授这样说过："对希腊人来说，法律是统治的内在本质，也是主权者统治社会的道德和法律依据。"⑤ 在巴克教授看来，只有柏拉图在他的《理想国》中部分地表达了这一观

---

① Duguit, *Le Transformations du Droit Public*, 47 页。Laski 译本, 45 页。

② Duguit, "The Law and State", *Harward Law Review*, 第 31 卷, 184～185 页。也可以参见 *Le Transformations du Droit Public*, 18～19 页。

③ Krabbe, *The Modern Idea of the State*, Sabine 与 Shepard 翻译, 译者导言, 15 页。

④ Willoughby, "The Juristic Theories of Krabbe", *The American Political Science Review*, 第 20 卷, 第 509 页注释, 1926。

⑤ Barker, *Greek Political Theory, Plato and His Predecessors*, 39 页。

念,并且,法律的主权是他的"法律"的基本原则。①

克拉勃教授自己指出,在一定意义上,阿尔图休斯(Althusius)可以看作是这种理论的鼻祖。对阿尔图休斯来说,主权的权威和法律的权威没有不同的基础,因为前者植根于后者。但是另一方面,阿尔图休斯也谈到了社会和主权者之间的契约。正是在这个方面克拉勃教授与阿尔图休斯有所不同。克拉勃教授说:"如果阿尔图休斯更为清楚地意识到在他的政治理论中社会契约的重要性,他也许可以成为法律主权理论的鼻祖,尽管这种主权的基础已不再包括社会契约这种假设。"②

在一定程度上,格劳修斯也可以看作是这种理论的先驱,但是格劳修斯比阿尔图休斯更少清楚地察觉。如果卢梭的理论不是如一般所理解的强调社会契约的观念的话,"现代国家观念"也可以在他的系统中找到,因为他把社会看作是核心事实,一旦有人认识到了这个事实,他自然就会认识到国家权威的基础,也就是法律。③ 克拉勃教授认为,卢梭混淆了法律的权威和主权者的权威,这样就把旧的和新的观念混在一起了。

早期的学者对法律的权威和主权者的权威所作的混淆的原因在于他们所生活的实际情况。但是既然是生活的实际情况产生了这种混淆,那么随着情况的改变,混淆也会远离。随着宪政主义的广泛传播,这种改变发生了。与旧的历史的君主手中的主权相反,产生了人民的代表组成的代表机关。起初,这种由选举产生的机构被认为是一种限制国王的主权,防止其被滥用的合理的政府机构,它的合理性来自分权理论。但是随着近些年来人类活动的各个领域的立法的增加所导致的制定法律的权力的增强,法律的权威逐步地取代了主权者的权威。④

但是宪政主义还远没有被彻底实现。在有的国家,法律没有实际效力,在有的国家里,主权仍然独立于法律。即使我们能保证法律被完全执行,它也仍有待完善。换句话说,在法律的主权的地位确立之后,接着就要考虑法律的内容。从这个角度来看,法律主权的理论既可以被看作一个既成事实,又可以被看作一个有待实现的原则。⑤

(3) 法律的基础

法律本身是主权者。但是法律的约束力量的基础是什么?或者法律什么时候

---

① Barker, *Greek Political Theory, Plato and His Predecessors*, 39页、205页。"法律就是具体形式的共同精神实质,因而也就是一个社会的暴力和主权。"同上书,38页,脚注见 Krabbe, *die Moderne Staats-idee*, 15页。Dunning, *Political Theories*, 第1卷, 71页。

② Krabbe, *The Modern Idea of the State*, 19页。在这和之后都是使用的英文版。原版19~20页。

③ Krabbe, *The Modern Idea of the State*, 28~30页。原版30~32页。

④ 用法律的权威取代主权者的权威仅仅是对过去历史上在很长一段时间内失去的一种重复,因为在实践上和在理论上这种理论都可以回溯到过去。Krabbe, *The Modern Idea of the State*, 36页。原版39页。

⑤ Krabbe, *The Modern Idea of the State*, 40页。原版37页、39页。

能够实际实施？对克拉勃教授来说，不是如以往的理论家所说的在上帝的意志中，或者在一个人类的主权者的意志那里可以发现的，而是在人们的精神生命中，特别是在人们的精神生活中的正义意识（the sense of right）①，即法律意识（Rechtsbewusstsein）中。

（4）意志理论的批评

要对权利意识有一个清晰的认识，就必须指出意志是法律强制权威来源这一观点的一点或几点错误。这种意志为法律基础的观念有两种表现形式：其一是这种权威是来自服从于法律的人们的意志，其二是这种权威是来自作为主权者的统治者的意志。② 根据前者，法律的基础存在于人类之中；而根据后者，它存在于人类之外的上帝或社会的属性那里。③ 前者是错误的，因为法律的目的是控制人类的意志，因此，它自然不能从这种意志中获得强制权威。④ 而后者也是错误的，因为这种认为主权者拥有可以为所欲为的主观权利的说法与事实不符。⑤

（5）正义的感觉或意识

在证明了意志是法律的权威的基础的理论是站不住脚的之后，让我们来考察正义的感觉或意识的观念。第一个需要问的问题是：什么是正义意识？正义意识，克拉勃教授说，"是一种普遍的人类冲动，由此导致对于自身和其他人的行为的一种特殊反应。"⑥ 起源于这种反应的规则，是权力和法律的规则。除正义意识之外，法律没有其他的来源。"正义意识内在于人，在其有意识的生命中占据一席之地，像其他导致价值判断的取向一样。"⑦ 所有的法律，无论是实在法、习惯法或不成文法，都是奠基于其上。⑧

而且，正义意识"意味着正义的观念，它存在于成文法、习惯法和不成文法中，直接用来解决涉及利益的冲突"⑨。这里，也许可以指出，我们来到了克拉勃教授的理论中的一个关键，即在将利益看作正义意识方面，道德和法律有它们共同的来源。⑩

（6）正义意识的进一步研究

更进一步，可以发现正义意识或感觉的力量不仅仅在于它是法律的基础，它

---

① Krabbe, *The Modern Idea of the State*, 41 页。原版 43～44 页。
② Krabbe, *The Modern Idea of the State*, 41 页。原版 43～44 页。
③ Krabbe, *The Modern Idea of the State*, 43 页。原版 46 页。
④ Krabbe, *The Modern Idea of the State*, 44 页。原版 47 页。
⑤ Krabbe, *The Modern Idea of the State*, 36 页。原版 47 页。
⑥ Krabbe, *The Modern Idea of the State*, 46 页。原版 49 页。
⑦ Krabbe, *The Modern Idea of the State*, 47 页。原版 50 页。
⑧ Krabbe, *The Modern Idea of the State*, 47 页。原版 50 页。
⑨ Krabbe, *The Modern Idea of the State*, 50 页。原版 54 页。
⑩ Krabbe, *The Modern Idea of the State*, LXXIII。

也在许多方面显示它自身。是正义意识或感觉的力量导致了暴乱和革命的产生；是它导致了王朝的更替；是它使得君主制向民主制改变，修订宪法和法规。它像暴风雨一样涤荡着污浊的政治空气。①

(7) 对正义意识的观念的误解

为了揭示正义意识的观念的真实情况，需要从正反两方面来进行分析。由此，指出并修正一些对这种理论的误解就是必须的。

第一，正义意识缺乏规范的特征，因为没有人会为他自己的正义感觉或意识所约束，因此它对行动和判断没有强制力。对于这一点，克拉勃回应道，我们的判断、思想与行为都应当与具有规范性特征的意识的感觉保持一致。正如已经指出的，正义意识包含着正义的观念，这种正义的观念不"仅仅是一种玄思，而是为我们的共同经验所证明，是要求我们该去做什么和不该做什么的一种强制力量"②。

第二，有人认为主权者的命令具有法律效力，因此法律的主权仅仅是主权者的命令。但是对于这一点，克拉勃教授坚持认为它不是奠定在一个坚固的基础之上，因为几个世纪以来被作为法律来接受的东西现在已不被当作法律了。所谓的主权者的命令已经被新情况下的新法律所取代。这两种理论之间的差异是显而易见的。在一种理论那里，法律的基础是我们的精神生活；而在另一种理论那里，主权者被赋予了最初的权威，或者说人们很自然地臣服于这个主权者。一个主权者的历史的合法的地位已经结束。再坚持认为它是颁布法律的权威，已与事实相反。③

第三，新的理论被批评为在它的基础上制定的法律没有稳定性。这种批评的错误，克拉勃教授说，是忽略了这样一个事实，法律的内容是不断变化的，"一个人不要能要求本质上缺乏稳定性的东西永恒不变"④。"法律的'稳定性'是一个悖论。"⑤ 只有"法律教皇"颁布的法律具有绝对的稳定性。"当一个人不管法律内容的规律，而一味地去要求它的'稳定性'的时候，他只有在失去它的合法特征的代价下，才能得到。"⑥

第四，正义意识的理论受到攻击因为它是"单方面的，它仅仅涉及了正义，但是暴力的因素也应当考虑在内"⑦。对于这一点，克拉勃回应道："我们的理论并没有否认这一点。它所否认的仅仅是已经存在的国家和法律的观念，这种观念

---

① Krabbe, *The Modern Idea of the State*, 52 页以下。原版 57 页以下。
② Krabbe, *The Modern Idea of the State*, 55 页。原版 61 页。
③ Krabbe, *The Modern Idea of the State*, 56~61 页。原版 61~67 页。
④ Krabbe, *The Modern Idea of the State*, 61 页。原版 68 页。
⑤ Krabbe, *The Modern Idea of the State*, 61 页。原版 68 页。
⑥ Krabbe, *The Modern Idea of the State*, 63 页。原版 70 页。
⑦ Krabbe, *The Modern Idea of the State*, 63~64 页。原版 70 页。

认为应当为主权者对处于臣属地位的人民进行惩罚留下权威的空间，然而与此同时，法律建立了另一种类型的臣属。"①

旧理论的假设包含权力的二元：国家权力和法律权力。② 有人否认二元论，不仅仅因为它是二元论，而是"因为现在已经意识到庶民对主权者的那种自然关系绝对是一种虚构，因为主权的观念仅仅是一种逻辑的建构而与事实不相符合。因为主权权威的基础不存在，也因为，人们不服从这种义务，从现实上说，并不会产生所说的社会会变成一盘散沙的结果，并且这种假设也不会成立"③。

这里，我们可以发现克拉勃教授著作的主题。否定方面，他发现旧的主权观念是跟事实相矛盾的，不过是一个幻想。建设性方面，他尽力表明如果有主权这样的东西，它仅仅是法律主权。④ 法律不再是主权者的意志的表达，而是正义意识或感觉。人们的正义意识不仅仅是法律的来源，也是使法律得以遵守的强制力量。⑤

（8）正义意识和利益——法律的来源和主体

已经指出了正义意识能够产生解决有关利益的现实冲突的正义观念。很显然，法律的基础是正义意识，法律的主体是利益。在这里法律权威的必要性和合理性体现出来了。一个人的利益和其他人的利益也许不同，在一个社会里面，一个人的利益和其他人的利益会发生冲突。法律的目的就是调整这种利益的冲突。但是建立在正义意识基础上的法律如何保证达到调整利益冲突的目的？为了回答这两个问题，必须进一步地说明①正义意识的统一和②正义意识的品质。

（9）正义意识的统一：多数原则

在一个特定的社会中目的统一代表着法律规则的统一。所应用的法律为一个社会中的所有成员的正义意识所支持当然是必须的。拥有一个约束社会所有成员的单一规则的唯一途径就是这个规则被大多数人的法律意识所赞同，但是这种情况很少发生。这样被采用的法律被认为是最好的法律，"因为被大多数人接受的事实表明它拥有比其他规则更高的价值"⑥。在这里，克拉勃教授没有走出卢梭的循环。⑦ 正义意识是大多数人的意识，建立在正义意识上且被看作是主权者的法律只是大多数人的法律。

---

① Krabbe, *The Modern Idea of the State*, 65 页。原版 72 页。
② Krabbe, *The Modern Idea of the State*, 1～2 页。原版 1～2 页。
③ Krabbe, *The Modern Idea of the State*, 65 页。原版 72 页。
④ Krabbe, *The Modern Idea of the State*, 1～2 页。原版 1～2 页。
⑤ Krabbe, *The Modern Idea of the State*, 68～69 页。原版 76 页。
⑥ Krabbe, *The Modern Idea of the State*, 69 页。原版 77 页。
⑦ Krabbe, *The Modern Idea of the State*, 78 页、87 页。也可参见 Willoughby, "The Juristic Theories of Krabbe", *The American Political Science Review*, 第 20 卷, 513 页。

（10）正义意识的品质

正义意识的品质是我们决定谁有制定法律的权利的标准。未成年人和神志不清的人被排除到参与制定法律的人之外，因为他们的自然品质干扰了正义意识的运作。① 但是，这种排除不能包括那些穷人。"因为排除穷人将对由有产者的各种利益所产生的紊乱的正义意识有利，而不能对那些无产者的正义意识带来好处。因此法律应该给予所有的阶级以同样的对待。"②

但是让每一个正常的人都参与制定法律，"并不意味着每一个人应该对社会的'所有'利益的法律价值做出判断"③。"利益的相关'知识'也是必要的。正义意识不必对那些没有被当下意识到的或很少意识到的利益的法律价值做出判断。能够对现存的立法机构加以反对在于这样的事实：人民是出于他们的知识范围以外的利益而立法。"④ 现在，可以很明显地看出正义意识，即法律的基础，为组成共同体的利益所决定。⑤ 一个真实的情况是与权利意识相分离的法律不能被称为法律，但是法律不能与导致人们一起组成一个共同体的利益相分离也是真实的；因为法律代表着利益实际实现的水平⑥，利益的价值是利益正当化的过程。简单地说，一个共同体的法律就是为了使利益正当化的正义意识所派生的法律。

（11）正义意识的扩展——法律的扩展

正义意识的扩展从个人扩展到国际社会。有个体的正义意识，也有一个社会的正义意识，也有国际社会的正义意识。正义意识的扩展导致法律的扩展。这样，从个体的正义意识产生的规则仅仅能控制个人的意志而不能应用到由许多个体组成的群体中去。从群体或共同体的正义意识所产生的规则只能控制群体或共同体的意志。只有世界的正义意识能够控制整个人类的意志。

（12）国家

克拉勃教授以这样方式定义国家："生活在一个共同的社会中，建立在独立的正义意识基础上的人类的一部分，就是一个国家。"⑦ 它不同于其他的共同体，因为"它的功能在于保护公共和私人利益的法律价值"⑧。一个国家"区别于另一个国家，乃是因为应用于利益的法律价值的特殊标准"⑨。它的真实性建立在对法律价值的控制之上。除了对某些利益赋予法律价值，国家没有什么其他功能。克

---

① Krabbe, *The Modern Idea of the State*, 88 页。原版 99 页。
② Krabbe, *The Modern Idea of the State*, 88 页。原版 99 页。
③ Krabbe, *The Modern Idea of the State*, 89 页。原版 100 页。
④ Krabbe, *The Modern Idea of the State*, 89 页。原版 100 页。
⑤ Krabbe, *The Modern Idea of the State*, 特别是第 5 章。
⑥ Krabbe, *The Modern Idea of the State*, LXXIV。也可参见 209 页，原版 236 页。
⑦ Krabbe, *The Modern Idea of the State*, 211 页。原版 289 页。
⑧ Krabbe, *The Modern Idea of the State*, 213 页。原版 240 页。
⑨ Krabbe, *The Modern Idea of the State*, 209 页。原版 236 页。特别是 LXXIV 以下。

拉勃教授宣称："我们必须坚持，国家除了是一个法律共同体之外，什么也不是。也就是说，一部分人类有它自己的初始的法律标准，它自己的法律的最初来源，因此一部分人类有它自己的法律关系的独立实体。因此国家除了对某些利益赋予法律价值之外没有其他功能。国家除了服务于公共和私人利益之外什么也不能做。"①

（13）国际社会——国际法

正如国家的法律是建立在本国的成员的正义意识的基础之上，国际法建立在世界的正义意识之上。从这个前提出发，"国际法不能建立在国家的主权这个不真实的基础之上"②。国际法区别于国内法"不在于它的起点和基础，而在于它适用的范围"③。

如果国际法不是被视为国内法，不是因为"它凌驾于'主权'国家之上，因此它根基于国家的意志"，而是因为趋向于管理文明国家的共同体的权利意识的组织是不完善的。④如果我们看看国际社会的组织，我们仍然生活在中世纪。⑤只有当国际法被一个完善的具有世界正义意识的组织实施的时候，它才会和国内法具有同样的地位。

国际法，如通常所说，实在是一个误称。把它说成是超国家的法律可能更好⑥，因为国际法在事实上是国家之间的宪法⑦。超国家的法律的时代已经来临，"因为法律的每一个分支已经越来越扩展到超国家法律的领域"⑧。"只有当现代国家的观念被完全和清楚地理解，进而主权的观念被摒弃，所有的权威被还原成法律权威的时候，国际法才能提升到真正科学的层次。这样，国际法可以拥有同国内法同样的基础、同样的内容和同样的主体。"⑨

（14）结论

法律主权的理论否认权力的二元论的假设，也就是否认国家权力和法律权力。它坚持认为主权不是独立于法律，不在法律之上和之外，因为法律是本质上的主权者⑩，在法律之外，没有主权者。但是为了成为法律，它必须被正义的意识认可。正义意识不必理解为一个社会的所有成员的正义意识，而是大多数人的。

---

① Krabbe, *The Modern Idea of the State*, 215 页。原版 243 页。
② Krabbe, *The Modern Idea of the State*, 234 页。原版 265 页。
③ Krabbe, *The Modern Idea of the State*, 236 页。原版 268 页。
④ Krabbe, *The Modern Idea of the State*, 236 页。原版 268 页。
⑤ Krabbe, *The Modern Idea of the State*, 237 页。原版 268 页。
⑥ Krabbe, *The Modern Idea of the State*, 245 页。原版 278 页。
⑦ Krabbe, *The Modern Idea of the State*, 246 页。原版 279 页。
⑧ Krabbe, *The Modern Idea of the State*, 247 页。原版 280 页。
⑨ Krabbe, *The Modern Idea of the State*, 248 页。原版 281 页。
⑩ Krabbe, *The Modern Idea of the State*, 232 页。原版 262 页。

法律的目的是调整社会中的不同利益，因此法律不能同社会的利益相分离。这样，法律的标准有两个层面：一是正义意识，一是利益。它们中间任何一个缺失就意味着法律特征的缺失。两者必须手牵手前进。如果一个人不懂得现行法律，他的正常的正义意识也就不是法律的基础。"因此把这样的人排除在法律制定之外，就不能说是否认正义意识是法律的基础。"①

七、结 论

对法律哲学的历史的一个总体上的鸟瞰提醒我们这样一个事实，我们上面所讨论的五种学派绝对没有穷尽法理学的所有派别。但是说它们是主要的，并且对于我们的研究目的来说它们最为重要的，则是可以的。分析学派的法律的格言：在严格的意义上要成为法律，必须有主权者在后面作支撑，主权的主要功能是制定法律。自然法学派坚持认为主权受自然法的限制。历史学派在 20 世纪作为分析学派的对立面而存在，甚至在今天还宣称法律不必是主权者的命令。这样，分析学派的"主权"，在历史学派的眼里，变得一文不值。② 经济学派认为主权只是一个手段，这比直接反对它所产生的破坏作用更大。社会学派，特别是狄骥教授和克拉勃教授，对于旧有的主权观念及其与法律的关系作了激烈的批评。虽然狄骥教授反复宣称用公共服务的观念取代主权观念，但他同时也将公共服务和统治者的权力联系在一起。但是在这样做的时候，他把主权放在法律的权威之下，并且把它分解成几块。克拉勃教授，与此不同，坚持认为法律是主权者，主权不能独立于、外在于或高于法律。这样，对克拉勃教授而言，主权就是法律，法律就是主权。从这个前提出发，一个社区的法律就是一个社区的主权，一个国家的法律就是国家的主权，国际社会的法律就是国际社会的主权。

---

① Krabbe, *The Modern Idea of the State*, 51 页。原版 56 页。
② 这种陈述一定程度上一定要归因于诸如 Maine 这样的学者的理论。

第九章 主权与职能组织

一、导论

根据所谓的古典主权理论,一般地讲,主权是国家的本质特征。国家,只有国家,是这种权威的所有者。不拥有主权,就不能称之为国家,一个实体若不是国家,就不能全部或部分地拥有主权。在一个国家里面,必须有主权,且只能有一个主权。因此,必然推导出在国家边界内的所有社团或组织都在国家的控制之下,因而任由国家摆布。

这种理论一直以来受到一些学者的反对,认为它跟事实相反。事实是,他们说,社团或组织的起源和存在,虽然不是在国家之上,但也是独立于国家的。它们同国家有一样的形成和成长的方式。他们并且坚持认为,人类的利益是多方面的,利益使人类组成不同的组织。通过国家来表达的政治利益仅仅是多方面利益中的一种形式。如果一个国家宣称对其属民有表达和增加其政治利益的权威,为什么一个教会或贸易组织就不能宣称有表达和发展其相应利益的同样权威?不进入细节的讨论,我们将在下面的章节中展现这种新学术思想的一些最为瞩目的代表的重要特征。

二、德国学者

长期以来,法学家的思想被所谓的法人拟制理论(fiction theory)所占据。① 它被德国和法国的学者所接受,它也几乎被英国和美国的所有的法庭所接受,也被这两个国家的大多数法学家所认同。它的支持者认为一个机构组织可以看作是一个人,但是这个人是拟制的,也只能是拟制的。② "它能有专门的权利,但不能像人一样认识、期望、希望或行动。"③

现实主义学派的出现就是为了反对这种理论。这种新的学术思想,梅特兰

---

① 根据 Gierke 教授的看法,是英诺森四世(Innocent Ⅳ)最先使用"虚拟人"(person ficta)一词。但是另一方面,H. A. Smith 坚持认为英诺森四世没有创造这种理论。参见他的 *The Law of Associations*,152~156 页。

② 参见 Holland,*Jurisprudence*,82 页。Freund,*Legal Nature of Corporation*,10~12 页。

③ Maitland,*Introduction to Gierke's Political Theories of Middle Ages*,20 页。

(Maitland)教授说,开始于贝赛勒(Besler)对萨维尼的批评,特别是在基尔克(Gierke)那里,这种理论逐步成型。基尔克在《德意志社团法》(*Das deutsche Genossenschaftsrecht*, 1868, 1873, 1881, 1913)和《社团理论》(*Genossenschaftstheorie*, 1887)两本著作中推翻了法人拟制理论并建立起了一种新的理论。前者是论述德国法律的论文,后者——用菲吉斯教授的话说——是试图显示法人理论是如何在现代生活中的各方面失败的。在德国,尽管浪漫主义的原则得到很好的运用,法庭有时候甚至也被迫将企业团体作为真实的、而不是虚拟的人看待,并且认为这种人格是永久协会的自然结果,而不仅仅是主权这种权力所强加的一个标记。①

基尔克教授研究的着眼点是个体。个体或人类,正如他所意识到的,不仅仅是一种手段,也是它自身的目的。从自身作为目的而言,所有政治的、社会的、宗教的组织都是人们寻求和达到其目的的手段。作为国家的一个成员,一个人仅仅部分地属于它;在国家之外,他还属于其他许多组织,通过这些组织,他的个体性得以实现。他这样写道:"人类的生活不同于动物的生存,他是他自身的存在,同时也是他的目的。我们必须认识到是个体,而不是国家具有优先的本质,他自身存在,并且在其自身中发现其最终的目的。作为国家的一员,个体仅仅是一部分属于国家。剩余的部分是完全独立于国家的集体生活的,这组成了他自由个体的主体。个体的存在与作为国家成员的存在是彼此依存的两个自由生命,二者相互依存、相互补充,但是每一个都无疑有它自身的直接目的。"②

尽管个体被认为是首要的本质,也尽管社团和组织被认为是达到目的的手段,但组织不是个体的产物,也不仅仅是个体一起构成的总和。组织,根据基尔克的看法,是自然的产物。它们的形成就像个体的生成一样。正如每一个个体都有它的意志、精神和意识一样,一个组织也是如此。正如一个组织不是个体的或其成员的总和一样,组织的意志也不是它的成员的意志的简单总和。正如前文所述,组织是一个无意识的产物,因此组织的意志是无意识的社会直觉的结果。但是人是一种社会存在。作为一种社会存在,他只有认识到自己是组织的一部分时,他才会有自我意识。在这种情况下,他的意志、他的精神、他的意识的内容部分地由其自身的意志、精神和意识决定,部分地由他人的意志、精神和意识决定。③

由于组织有它自身的意志,因此它也就有人格。这种人格不是拟制的,而是

---

① J. N. Figgis, *Churches in the Modern State*, 55~56页, 1913。也可参见 Maitland, *Introduction to Gierke's Political Theories of Middle Ages*, 26页。

② Gierke, "Grundbegriffe des Staatsrecht und die neuesten Staatsrechtstheorien," *Zeitschrift fur die gesammte Staatswissenschaft*, Tubingen, 306页, 1874。参见 *Harvard Law Review*, 第31卷, 159页。

③ Gierke, "Grundbegriffedes Staatsrecht und die neuesten Staatsrechtstheorien", *Zeitschrift fur die gesammte Staatswissenschaft*, Tübingen, 1874。

与自然人的人格一样真实。它不是国家或国家法律的虚拟或人工产物。国家或国家法律"没有创造团体,但是发现了它的存在,并授予了它某种法律能力。团体虽然同自然人有同样的基本属性,但二者并非等同,因为它除了有和自然人有关的方面,还有新的特点,它有其存在的独特的一面,有其自身的意志。团体的权利不同于个体的权利,是因为它受这种独特的意志所支配。团体作为不同于它的成员的一个人格而存在,不是拟制的,而是真实的"①。

但是国家必须与其他的组织有所区别,否则它就不能称为一个国家。这些区别是什么?第一,国家与其他组织不同是由于国家是群体生活的政治形式。但这不是本质的不同,因为这就像说贸易组织区别于其他组织是因为它是一个经济组织一样。第二,国家的意志在范围上比其内部的其他组织的意志要广,而这也是最重要的一点。

由于组织有其自身的意志和人格,自然地,它就拥有自身内在的权威或主权。既然意志在内容上没有不同,主权在内容上也就没有不同。因此基尔克教授认为,主权不是一个国家的本质特征,一个国家内的组织也可以拥有主权。正是从这个方面说,基尔克教授被认为是主权多元主义理论的先驱。

但是,由于意志在程度上有不同,故而主权在程度上也可以有不同。由此推导出国家的主权比存在于其间的组织的主权在程度上要大。因此当需要维护大众利益的时候,国家的主权就具有优先的地位。② 在这种情况下,霍布斯的利维坦依然存在,但是它的基础已经被严重地动摇了,因为它不再是仅仅存在于国家里而神圣不可侵犯的了。

三、英国学者

1. 梅特兰

费舍尔(H. A. L. Fisher)教授(梅特兰教授《选集》的编辑者)用这样的语言谈及梅特兰教授:"在编辑部分没有一个注释,因为在过去三十年的时间里,关于社会或法律的历史已经写得很多,但都没有对梅特兰的著作的永久价值产生明显的影响。他早年写作很少,几乎可以说没有写,在晚年还想把他早年所写的

---

① Freund, *Legal Nature of Corporation*, 13~14 页, 1897。"我们德国的团体不是虚构,不是象征,不是国家机器的一个碎片,不是众多个体的集合名词,而是一个活生生的机构和一个真实的人,有其自身的机构、成员和意志。它自身能有意志、行动;它的意志和行动就像一个人样通过其大脑、嘴、手来意志和行动。它不是一个虚构的人,它是一个'集体法人(Gesammtperson)'它的意志是'共同意志(Gesammtwille)';它是一集体人格(group person),它的意志是集体意志(group-will)。" Maitland, *Introduction to Gierke's Political Theories of Middle Ages*, 26 页。

② Gierke, "Grundbegriffe des Staatsrecht und die neuesten Staatsrechtstheorien", *Zeischrift fur die gesammte Staatswissenschaft*, Tübingen, 308 页, 1874。

销毁。他很博学并有自己的原创理论,在绝大多数情况下,他明显是正确的。"①用菲吉斯教授的话说,梅特兰教授被认为是"整个十九世纪历史领域三个最重要的占有史料最多的思想家之一"②。

梅特兰教授受基尔克教授很深的影响。这一点他自己也多次承认。且不提对基尔克的《中世纪政治理论》的翻译本所写的序,也不必提他的《选集》中的一些文章,我们发现《英国法律史》③ 中的一个章节,在初版的时候标题为"虚拟人格",然而在对基尔克的大作《德意志社团法》(*Das Deutsche Genossenschaftsrecht*)进行反复研读后,梅特兰教授将这一章从标题到内容都作了修改。④

像基尔克一样,他强烈反对把法人看作一个"拟制的人"的拟制理论。他说,法人,就是一个人格体,一个实际上的人。它有它自己的人格。它是一个权利与义务的结合体。"但并不是说组织具有和个人完全一样的法律权利。举例来说,它不能结婚;但是在多数情况下,两个实体X、Y的法律地位是相同的,不管X、Y是代表两个人、两个团体,还是团体和个人。"⑤ 一个大学可以买地,租赁建筑物,或从其他的机构那里借钱,从法律的观点看,这些行为都被看作是两个人之间的交往。这该怎样理解呢?它意味着大学是一个权利与义务的结合体。但是这还不是全部,因为交往也可以在团体和它的成员之间发生,这样一个人可以和一个大学订下契约,反之亦然。

那么什么是团体?根据梅特兰教授的看法,它是一个有组织的机构,有它自己的人格,而不仅仅是国家或国家法律的产物。团体表现为许多形式。王国政府(the Crown)是一个团体。"我们的主权者不是一个'唯一的团体',而是一个复杂的高度组织化的'众多团体的集合'的首脑。我认为称呼这个团体为王国政府并无大的危害。但是在最新的条目书中有一个更好的词,这个词就是'英联邦'(commonwealth)。"⑥

美国的一个州可以被看作是一个团体。虽然有所保留,但梅特兰教授还是同意迪伦(Dillon)的这段话:"美国所有的有健全政治功能的州,尽管被称呼为'团体'并不太恰当,但具有许多和团体相同的重要特征,如一个独有的名称,无限期的继承权、私有权利、上诉权,诸如此类的权利。在法典中,'团体'这个

---

① Maitland, *Collected Papers*, 编者前言Ⅶ。
② Figgis, *Churches in the Modern State*, 附录二, "Three Cambridge Historians: Creighton, Maitland, and Acton", 227 页, 1913。也可参见 Holmes 法官的文章, *Law Quarterly Review*, 第 23 卷, 139 页和他的 *Collected Papers*。
③ 这本著作是 Maitland 教授与 Pollock 教授合著的。但著作的主要部分是 Maitland 教授的。参见 Pollock 教授的致谢辞,第 1 版的前言注释。第 1 版出版于 1895 年,第 2 版出版于 1899 年。
④ Maitland 和 Pollock, *The History of English Law*, 第 1 卷, 486 页注释。
⑤ Maitland, *Collected Papers*, 第 3 卷, 307 页。
⑥ Maitland, *Collected Papers*, 第 3 卷, 259 页。

词，并不包括国家，只包括那些依赖国家而存在，并依照法律行事的一般团体。但是，国家像一般团体一样，会和别的实体订立契约，也会犯错误。因此，从这个角度说，国家也会采取一些那些一般团体会采取的行动来维护自己的利益，并纠正错误。"①

殖民地是团体。"我们现在否认一个殖民地是一个团体，但是我们能够——是在实际上而不仅仅是在字面上——不承认新西兰这个殖民地具有单独的人格吗？"② 如果享有某些自治权的市镇（borough）是一个团体，它可以有自己的权利与义务，违反法律和受到惩罚，那么一个县、一个郡、一个镇也应该是这样。③ 因此教会④或者贸易组织⑤也可以被看作是法人。甚至一个早期产生的为保护财产免于被征税的托拉斯的组织，也和团体有紧密的联系。这种联系可以回溯到四个世纪以前。⑥ 目前，已经很难在这两者之间划清界限。

也许还可以问托拉斯的规则与团体的规则有什么关系？"无疑，托拉斯的规则已经成为团体的规则的补充，当有一天《英国史》被写就的时候，将托拉斯和团体合而为一的过程将是最为有趣的传奇之一。"⑦

这样托拉斯这个词在现时代就获得了一个全新的含义。"现在美国的'托拉斯'如果不是总是，也几乎经常是指一个团体。"⑧

考虑到托拉斯几乎就是一个团体，梅特兰教授断言托拉斯，像团体一样，有其自己的人格。他这样写道："定义信托者的方法，可以用来重新定义'团体'，这样可以避免机械的团体理论，并使之不受个体理论的威胁。这样的人格：实体——我这样称谓它——虽然不能为法学家们所接受，但在现实中作为一个整体

---

① Dillon, *Municipal Corporations*, 第 31 章, Maitland 引述, *Collected Papers*, 第 3 卷, 266 页。
② Maitland, *Collected Papers*, 第 3 卷, 262~263 页。
③ Maitland, *The Constitutional History of England*, 54 页。
④ Maitland 和 Pollock, *The History of English Law*, 第 2 版, 486 页以下。
⑤ 当 Balfour 公爵在议会宣称贸易组织是一个团体的时候，一个持反对意见的著名法学家打断了他的讲话，说贸易组织不是团体。Balfour 公爵辩护道："我知道，我是在谈英国，而不是在谈法律。" Maitland, *Collected Papers*, 第 3 卷。
⑥ Maitland, *Collected Papers*, 395 页。关于托拉斯的起源，参见上书, 335 页以下。
⑦ Maitland, *Collected Papers*, 第 3 卷, 272 页。
⑧ Maitland, *Collected Papers*, 第 3 卷, 395 页。

却得到了很好的发展。"①

简单地说，对梅特兰教授来说，法学家也许可以在团体和一个没有联合的组织之间做出区分，但在实际上，它们是一回事。所有有其自身的意志和人格的有组织的群体都可以被称为团体。但是有组织的群体与主权有什么关系？这正是我们想知道的，梅特兰教授这样说："我所说的有组织的群体，应当成为一个主权国家。"②他继续说道："我们称之为 Nunsquamia。和其他许多主权国家一样，我敢保证。"③

但是和他的前辈（基尔克）一样，梅特兰教授没有就此为止。组织同国家有相同的特征，也拥有最高权威或主权。但是国家的主权，在存在的范围上比国家内部的组织要大，因为国家是一个特殊的高级组织体。④

当伯吉斯教授说美国在第一次大陆会议期间获得她的主权的时候，韦罗贝教

---

① 他补充道："从发生的这种事情中，你可以得到一个简单的事实。以前有一段时间，我们在成文法中加进了'非法人团体'这一词。如果一个法国人看到这个词，他会做何感想？'非法人团体：没有灵魂的人'，难怪你们的首相，作为一个哲学家，发现很难用英语来表达法律这个词。"《论文集》317 页，也见 367 页，卷三。"托拉斯在向这个领域渗透的过程中，永远不会满足，直到它渗透到政治权力的所有方面，政治机构的所有机关。打开一份英国报纸，如果你没有看到'托管人'这一词被用来指'王权'或者一些高贵的团体，那绝对是偶然。我不久前刚刚体验到这一点，今天我要说的是，既然德蓝士瓦（Transvaal）没有一部典型的宪法，那么帝国议会就'还是它的托管人'。这里有一个暗喻。那些这样说的人就会承认托拉斯不是任何法庭可以强迫推行的，它只是一种'道德信托'。我认为德国国家科学委员会的学者会对法律隐喻非常感兴趣。尤其是当它们在政治辩论中成为常用语的时候。而要判明这种隐喻从何处开始，也不是件容易的事情。一条法规宣布东印度公司在印度取得的赫沙夫特（Herrschaft），是处在大英帝国的国王的'信托'之下。这不是一个无效的主张，而是对争论的裁定。不久前，美国的法官们还在说，美国是在对古巴的'信托'之下，取得古巴的主权的。"同上书，卷三，403 页。

谈到国家的特征，他写道："我认为法官无权说英国的郡是'非法人'，没有法律特征，只能算是一个'被动的'团体。因为他们并没有确定是否应该对诸如天主教堂（按英国的法律的说法）、卫斯理教派、林肯律师学院、伦敦股票交易所、伦敦图书馆、赛马俱乐部和贸易组织之类的团体加以同样的评论。并且我们也要记住，制造高深的理论从来就不是我们解决问题的关键所在。显而易见的理论有时候往往是不能有助于深入研究的舶来品，而真正不可缺少的理论往往要在不起眼的地方寻找。"同上书，卷三，400～401 页。

也见他翻译的 Gierke 的 *Political Theories of Middle Ages* 译本的序言，27 页。

② Maitland, *Collected Papers*, 第 3 卷, 318 页。

③ Maitland, *Collected Papers*, 第 3 卷, 318 页。

④ Maitland 翻译的 Gierke 的 *Political Theories of Middle Ages* 译本的序言，9 页。"英国人眼中的国家曾经是非常奇怪的单细胞的。在一个变革的时代，他们还没有做好接受这样一些可靠的传统思想的准备。这些思想是与爱尔兰的例子和美国的社区，组织，团体的例子相适应的。而爱尔兰和这些美国社区、团体、组织都是有意志的绝不是虚幻的意志，并最终变成了国家和合众国。中世纪的帝国在一个过于简单的理论的重压下挣扎，因为法学家们一直以来只认识到恺撒是查士丁尼法典的主宰。现代的多细胞的英国，通常被叫作大英帝国，这也没有害处。没有了这个简单理论的束缚，它可能就会繁荣，但这也不是绝对的。如果我们认真对待关于主权的讨论，我们就会无法容忍这种简单的理论。虽然这种理论对罗马帝国来说是适用的，但我们不能借此否认那些作为更大的主权者的组成部分的'自治殖民地'、社区、团体的一个与国家类似的重要特征。" Maitland 翻译的 Gierke 的 *Political Theories of Middle Ages* 译本的序言，10 页。

授告诉我们他言过其实了。但是，在梅特兰教授看来，他言犹不及，因为美国的主权在有组织的团体形成的时候就存在了。只要有组织的群体存在，主权就存在。一个群体的主权，可以在一个更大的整体的主权之内存在，但是在比它大的整体的主权之内存在并不意味着它不再成其为一个主权者实体。只要群体存在，主权就存在。

2. 菲吉斯（Figgis）

早在 1868 年，阿克顿勋爵（Lord Acton）就写道："信奉教皇极权的宗教至上论者（Ultramontanes），因为支持教会反对市民权力而名声大振，但他们支持的不仅仅是宗教的利益，而是代表了一种普遍的规律，因为他们由教会的自由扩展开来，扩展到其他组织的自由。"①

菲吉斯教授在引述了这段话之后说道："现在这正是我所愿意承认的国家的特点。"菲吉斯教授的观点可以在《现代国家的教会》，1921 年 7 月的一系列的演讲集中找到。他所使用的标题和素材都主要是宗教的，但是所采用的原则却"不涉及宗教的优先权或英国国教的特殊地位，而是涉及人类的组织体的本质，因此也就是涉及了国家的本质"②。

他告诉神父们，或者更贴切地说是警告他们："我们不可能把自己的蛋糕吃了以后还占有它。我们不能在主张自己的自由权利的时候，否认他人的自由。我们呼吁世俗权力放弃对婚姻、信条、仪式或宗教内部交流的控制。因为对于一个自由的宗教社会来说，管理这些事务是它存在的必要条件。但同时，我们也应该试图不去干涉那些涉及全体公民的国家政策。"③

这本书的前言中的一段话，对该书的目的，做了更为清晰的说明："作者提出目前这个观点，并不是因为他想维护教会的权利，而是在对奥斯丁的理论以及梅特兰和基尔克对他的最终评价作了长时间的认真思考后，认为它十分荒谬，并且不完整，只不过是一个口头论证。起初，人们往往会认为奥斯丁的理论是不言自明的，等到进行了大量的调查了解后，才会明白，他的整个理论是十分抽象和形而上的。"④ 很显然，菲吉斯教授在否定的方面，否认奥斯丁式的理论，但在肯定的方面，菲吉斯教授又赞同基尔克和梅特兰提出的理论。

根据菲吉斯教授的观点，或多或少体现了古希腊城邦状况的主权理论在罗马帝国那里得到了应用。这个权威是不能分离的，不可剥夺的和不能被限制的，这是近几代法学家的信条。在帝国或王国之内，除了这个已确定的实体之外，没有

---

① Figgis, *Churches in the Modern State*, 110～112 页, 1913。也可以参见 111 页的注释。参见 Acton, *History of Freedom*, 151 页。
② Figgis, *Churches in the Modern State*, 49～50 页, 1913。
③ Figgis, *Churches in the Modern State*, 112～113 页, 1913。
④ Figgis, *Churches in the Modern State*, 前言第 ix～x 页, 1913。

其他的权威。法国最伟大的政治家之一康伯斯（M. Emile Combes）说："除国家的权利之外没有其他的权利，除公共权威之外没有其他的权威。"①

因此，奥斯丁的主权理论并不比古罗马人或古代的政治家和哲学家们提出的主权理论高明多少。②"霍布斯的巨大的利维坦，圣典主义者（canonists）的'全权'（plenitudo potestatis），统治秘术（arcane imperii），奥斯丁的主权，都是同一种东西的不同叫法——国家法律制订者的无限的和不可限的权力，都从这一共同的观念中得来。"③

这种理论的自然的结果是什么？就是：它假设有两个社会实体存在，一个是国家，一个是个体。后者的权利或行为是私人的，前者的权利或行为是公共的。"国家在结构上可以有很多形式，如君主制的，贵族制的，或纯粹集体主义的；但是在所有情况下都被法律所认可，除了不受限制的主权和众多个体之外，没有其他真正的社会实体，也没有真正的权力。"④ 在个体和国家之外，还有其他一些组织——教会、贸易组织、大学等等，但是它们仅仅是法律的产物，是主权者意志的产物，是主权者的恩赐，它们可以被主权者随时随意地取消或修改。

仅仅是因为对一部分法律的习惯性印象和为了给予一个群体行动、拥有财产、上诉和被诉的权利，"把它们看做人就是必要的；因此最高权力就自动给予了这些可以称之为团体的实体，因而使之具有了'拟制的人格'"⑤。这些实体，有可以像人那样去行动的权利，但是它们的权利仅仅是最高权威的代表权利，这也被称为法人团体的特评理论（the concession theory）。⑥

但是上述理论，在菲吉斯教授看来，与实际的社会生活是相反的。为了表明这一点，我们可以引述下面的一段话："整个关于教育的争论中都听到反对私营学校接受公共财政的不公，起码在征税的方式上（因为没有对它们征收所得税）。现在看来这其实（单个人经营的状况除外）是一个完全错误的观念。当然得承认'私有'这个词是与公共管理相对应的，但如果你认为它指的是纯粹的私人管理，那你就错了。这些社会实体同国家一样不仅不是私有的，而且在它们的运行中它们与国家联系得更为紧密。我的意思是说，它是作为一个整体运行的社会中的一份子，而社会中的所有个体成员都要服从于社会。社会成员和社会之间的关系比公民与国家的关系以及个人之间的关系都更密切。很容易理解说大学、院校、贸易组织，律师学院是纯粹私营的，这在某种意义上也是正确的。它们不是国家或其分支机构的代表。但是从根本上说它们其实是公共的。比如说，它们在

---

① Figgis, *Churches in the Modern State*, 56 页, Figgis 所引述。
② Figgis, *Churches in the Modern State*, 38 页。
③ Figgis, *Churches in the Modern State*, 79 页。
④ Figgis, *Churches in the Modern State*, 67~68 页。
⑤ Figgis, *Churches in the Modern State*, 60 页。
⑥ Figgis, *Churches in the Modern State*, 25 页。

组织上是集体的，不是个人的。'公立学校'这个词的通常用法意味着在集体管理下的学校，当然是一种更为合理的和理性的习惯，尽管我认为严格地说这是不合理的。因为很明显的一个事实是所有这类组织都具有公共属性。如果我们认为那些不是国家代表的组织是私有的，而以此标准在公私之间画一条线，那明显就是错误的。实际上，这个世界并不是一方面由国家，另一方面由大批毫无联系的个人组成；而是由大批的团体交织在一起的。这里面包括个人、家庭、俱乐部、贸易组织、大学、各业各行等等。还有，这些团体具有一些带政府特性的功能，它包括立法、行政和司法三个方面；当然这只是针对它的成员而言。对于这样的组织的成员而言，它具有同公立机构一样的公共属性。"①

对社会组织的人格真正人格的误解归因于对社会现实的误解。人是一种社会动物，他天生就是组织的一员。让他成为这样主要不是因为他有什么，而是因为他是什么。他受家庭、学校的影响。这无数的组织，各自都有真正的人格。"正是他们组成了现代世界的生活，无论是从法律理论，还是从经济集体主义的抽象的角度来否认他的实际存在或权力，在我看来，都是与事实根本相反的。"②

社会现实摆在我们面前。不论你是否喜欢他，你都得接受他们。菲吉斯教授这样评论道，"塔夫谷案"（Taff Vale Case）的判决清楚地表明事实是不容回避的。虽然在本案中，法庭仍然认为贸易组织不是团体，但也承认他是有组织的。"且不说其他影响法官的思想的因素，事实上，判决明显地承认这样一个事实，即团体人格，这个生活和行动的共同体是人类为实现某种目的而组织起来的实体的本质特征。他不会仅仅因为人们口头上不承认他，就被长久地否定。换句话说，这种人格是与社会的本质相联系的，并不是最高权威可以随心所欲地承认或否认的简单名词。"③

在教育和经济等方面是如此，在宗教方面也是如此。在题为"自由国家的自由教会"的首篇演讲中菲吉斯教授就详细地论证了宗教实体不是由国家创造的。它们有自己的生命和人格。它们"产生于人类自然的联合的本能，最高权威应该承认它们都有原始的生命，并像对待人那样去管理和指导它们，而不是出于司法目的，把它们的组织能力看作空洞的词条，因为这样看的话，它们只是具有名义上的人格"④。

"最高权威"这个词，在菲吉斯教授看来，意味着国家的权威。如果这是真实的，则菲吉斯教授没有超越基尔克和梅特兰的观点。他认为团体的主权权力和

---

① Figgis, *Churches in the Modern State*, 68～70 页。
② Figgis, *Churches in the Modern State*, 72～73 页。
③ Figgis, *Churches in the Modern State*, 64 页。
④ Figgis, *Churches in the Modern State*, 47 页。德国的文化斗争（Kulterkampi）、法国的法律分离（the Law of Separation）和苏格兰的自由教会（the Free Church）等都放大了干涉宗教团体的国家主权的傲慢。Figgis 教授如此说。

国家主权的权力一样都是真实存在的，国家的权威更为高级，因为国家是一个更大的整体。这样除了国家拥有的主权之外，在国家之内还存在着许多小的主权。主权是最高的权力的旧观念也许还可以被接受，但那些像主权是国家的本质特征，只有国家本身才具有，主权是不可分的、不受限制的观念则被抛弃。

让我们来引用菲吉斯教授这篇演讲的最后一段话作为我们的结论："在演讲中所讲的许多内容是看似司空见惯的，有些也是很明显的。但是很显然这里所提出的原则没有被接受，即使有的被接受，也往往是误解。如果我摆出了这些事实，则它们的目的就达到了：第一，教会和国家之间的关系问题不是孤立的。它引起了所有政治哲学都必须考虑的基本主题，迫使我们面对市民社会的真正本质和人格的含义的整个问题。如果我们在这里提出的观点是正确的，我们就必须根除从来没有正确过的理论，或者在很久以前如城邦时代是正确的，但与现在事实不符的理论。我们必须使我们的理论与人们现在的生活保持一致。我们必须放弃那些抽象的主权理论。总之，我们应该把自由看作高于其他所有目标的政治目标，并且相信在对团体的本质的各种表现形式做出充分的分析之后，就会发现真正的自由。我们不是在只为自己战斗，我们也在为所有的小团体反对集中、争取自由而战斗。这从某种意义上说，也是我们这个时代的最显著的特征。我们自己还有其他人都需要从中世纪的行会制度中学习很多，进而我们要学会在团体社会中承认他人和我们一样，也可以要求自由，并平等地面对我称之为'现代国家的宗教混合体'。最后，我们要看到，英国国教唯一能找得到用来反击天主教的依据和我们现在所要表达的观点是一致的。罗马教廷作为一个宗教政权，仅承认那些从古代一直流传到现代的主权万能的观点。因此，我们不得不从普遍意义上来考虑宗教权威的本质，从整体意义上来考虑个体的生命。"①

3. 巴克（Barker）

一般不认为巴克先生是主权理论领域里的专家，他也不是多元主义的先驱。但说他是站在多元主义的立场上对传统主权理论宣战的第一人，也许并不为过。巴克这方面的文章主要有发表于1915年2月的《政治学季刊》的题为《失信的国家》的文章，还值得注意文章有《英国的政治思想：从斯宾塞到现在》中的一

---

① Figgis, *Churches in the Modern State*, 170～171页。也可参见 Figgis, *The Will of Freedom: Or, the Gospel and Nietzsche and the Gospel of Christ*, 1917。

些章节以及其他一些著作。①

批评性方面，巴克先生同菲吉斯教授和其他主权多元理论的维护者一样，攻击奥斯丁的理论。他说："奥斯丁对于英国法不是太精通，对于罗马法也是浅尝辄止，他可以对'统治权'（majestas）加以理论化，但是把他的主权理论应用到英国政治中的困难就表明他的主权理论在英国本土水土不服。"因为在英国，正如巴克所发现的，国家一般是不被信任的，也很难说有一个单一的主权。黑格尔赞同的，并且德国的理论家也设想的主权和君主国家超越了社会冲突。中立的、调停的、公正的、单一的、不可分的"帝权"（imperium）在英国没有市场。② 在英国，无论是在行政领域，还是在立法领域都没有最高的权威。她所拥有的是"一群相互制衡的官员和一个受社会制约的立法者"③。

这是事实，并且历史和现实也表明它是真实的。1215 年的《大宪章》、1688 年的革命是最显明的例子。这里承认作为天赋权利的个人权利、财产权和工作权，承认存在上帝赋予的自由权利。巴克说："牛津基督圣体学院（Corpus Christi College）的罗伯特·布朗（Robert Brown）对伊丽莎白的国家没有多少用处，卡莱尔（Clare）的亨利·巴罗（Henry Barrow）也是如此。"④

但这些还不是全部。新的情况已经引起新的要求和新的反抗。国家被反抗得越多，对它的不信任就越多，但是反抗在实际生活中，往往不是由个体而是由群体发起的。"理论家或许可以以个人的名义限制国家，但实际上起限制作用的通常是群体的意识。"⑤ 巴克这样写道。在这里，我们发现了巴克是跟随了基尔克、梅特兰和菲吉斯的观点。⑥

但是组织是什么？它有与它的成员不同的人格或意志吗？基尔克教授及其追随者对于这个问题给予了肯定性的答复。我们也会在后面的讨论中发现有一些学

---

① 参见他的论文 "Mediaeval Political Thought"，于 Hearnshaw 的 *The Social and Political Ideas of Some Great Medieval Thinkers*，1 页以下。Coker 在他的 "Pluralistic Theories and the Attack upon State Sovereignty"（Merriam 和 Barnes 的 *Political Theories: Recent Times*，115 页）指出巴克在最近修正了他的理论。但是 Coker 教授所引述的陈述所包含的观念已经在 1915 年就出现了。参见他的 "The Discredited State" 最后的注释，也可参见 Gettell, *History of Political Thought*，462 页注释，1924。也可参见 Barker, *A Comfederation of the Nations*, 1918, 以及他最近出版的 *National Character and the Factors in its Formation*（131 页、276 页，1927）。Nietzsche and Treitschke, *Oxford Pamphlets*, 第 20 卷，1914。

② Barker, "The Discredited State", *The Political Quarterly*, 第 5 卷，101 页，1915。
③ Barker, "The Discredited State", *The Political Quarterly*, 第 5 卷，101 页，1915。
④ Barker, "The Discredited State", *The Political Quarterly*, 第 5 卷，103 页，1915。
⑤ Barker, "The Discredited State", *The Political Quarterly*, 第 5 卷，110 页，1915。
⑥ *Political Thought in England*, 175 页以下。"如果我们现在是个人主义者，我们也是团体的个人主义者。我们的'个人主义'现在变成了群体。我们不再写'人与国家的对抗'而写'群体与国家的对抗'。"同上书，181 页。

者给出了否定性的答复。① 但是巴克先生既不同于前者，也不同于后者。② 对他来说，还有另外一种可能。它是什么？他这样宣称："让我们称它为观念（idea）。"③

但是什么是观念？他说："观念，既是又不是虚幻的；它们有手有脚；但是它们不是人，它们正是虚幻的东西。"④ 我们可以不承认团体的人格和意志——超越的人格和超越的意志。我们可以把国家看作一个建立在法律和秩序的政治观念之上的系统；我们可以把团体看作是一个通过共同的有组织的观念把真实的个体以及它们的意志联系起来的组织系统。我们中的大多数也是许多其他多种的系统的成员和其他多种观念的支持者。这种观念与其他观念相联系；也许它们处于相互竞争的状态。因而，它是观念的竞争，而不是真实的集体人格的竞争。认识到这一点就是一个很大的收获。我们要抛弃这种使国家的真实人格和其他团体的真实人格两败俱伤的战斗。我们不应再剑拔弩张。真正的观念是不可能被杀死的；它们只能是自求灭亡或者因为生命的逐渐衰老而死亡。⑤

但是观念与主权有什么关系？答复是，政治团体的观念产生公共观念，公共观念也可以看作是主权。⑥ 这样巴克转了一个弯，而回到了里奇（Ritchie）教授的立场上了。但是可以进一步问道：团体的观念分等级吗？有可能只存在一种公共观念吗？"绝对不可能，许多人也不希望它变成现实。"⑦ 巴克这样说。社会中有观念冲突是不可避免的。人类的知识越发展，这类冲突的观念就越多。一个人可以认为在亨利八世的时代英国的主权是唯一的，但是"如果现在人们还承认一个披着公共主权论外衣的新亨利八世，那么工团主义者就依然会向资产阶级国家请求对他们的阶级理论给予豁免；民族主义者就会要求去民族化国家对他们的民族观点进行豁免；如果一个教士忘记了耶路撒冷，他的右手就会失去法力"⑧。一个虔诚的天主教徒可以生活在英国，但他效忠的是罗马教廷，而不是西敏寺（Westminster）。⑨

国家观念是更宽更大的综合物，正因为它的宽广，它才是一个不完善的综合物。⑩ 既然观念从来就不是单一的，那么现实中的主权就有多种。奥斯丁的一元

---

① 参见 Barker, *A Confederation of the Nations*，牛津，40 页，1918。
② 见 *Political Thought in England*，180 页。
③ Barker, "The Discredited State", *The Political Quarterly*, 第 5 卷，111 页，1915。
④ Barker, "The Discredited State", *The Political Quarterly*, 第 5 卷，113 页。
⑤ Barker, "The Discredited State", *The Political Quarterly*, 第 5 卷，113 页。
⑥ Barker, "The Discredited State", *The Political Quarterly*, 第 5 卷，114～115 页。
⑦ Barker, "The Discredited State", *The Political Quarterly*, 第 5 卷，115 页。
⑧ Barker, "The Discredited State", *The Political Quarterly*, 第 5 卷，115 页，1915。
⑨ Barker, "The Discredited State", *The Political Quarterly*, 第 5 卷，114 页。
⑩ Barker, "The Discredited State", *The Political Quarterly*, 第 5 卷，116 页。

主义在巴克先生手里变成了多元主义。① 像霍布斯这样的公民可以认为国家是利维坦；但是要看到霍布斯的做法，无非就是和一个教士把教会作为"全权"如出一辙。国家可以成为公民的教育者；教会也可以作为教士的教育者。国家可以有它的西敏寺议会；民族也可以有它的都柏林议会。国家可以成为一个政治行为的领域；贸易组织也可以成为一个政治行为的领域。② 他继续说道："很难说只有经过国家允许，教会才有吸收教众的权利，都柏林才有议会，贸易组织才有政治行为。"③ 如果国家能宣称它有权利去颁布法律，贸易组织也可以；如果贸易组织要受法律的束缚，国家为什么不需要？无论法律是国家的产物或创造者，都没有什么区别。但是，无论在何种情况下，国家处于什么地位，贸易组织或教会也都处于什么地位。④

4. 林赛（Lindsay）

林赛说："观念是由历史条件形成的，对应于历史问题，那些政治哲学家们提出的一些看似不受时间限制的观念一般是国家的清晰标记。人们对自身在政治组织中的定位的有关观念是不断变化的。"⑤ 有了这样的观念，林赛先生指出霍布斯的政治思想与亚里士多德的政治思想不同，并不仅仅因为一个是正确的而另一个是错误的，还因为他们所要面对的政治问题是不同的。⑥

正如霍布斯的理论区别于亚里士多德的理论一样，个人主义也区别于集体主义。但是无论是个人主义还是集体主义，都与现在的事实不一致。除非一种新的理论被提出，否则政治理论将与实际相分离。事实是什么？对林赛先生来说，就是团体生活的发展与扩展。社会组织形式的多样性在现在变得越来越明显，那些忽略了人类的社会属性可以通过多种形式表现出来的事实的理论，也就会忽略政治学中的关键。⑦

真的有什么理论与这样的事实相符合吗？林赛先生说，有的。它就是由基尔克所阐发和梅特兰所强化的理论。它是当前政治实践的反映，它不"仅仅是一种空想的理论，而且是使这种原则在实践中实现的努力"⑧。这种注定会成为主流的

---

① Barker, "The Discredited State", *The Political Quarterly*, 第5卷, 120页, 1915。也可参见他的 *National Character*, 131页, 1927。"现代国家的生命和行为变得越来越复杂。理论家们谈及它的'多元'，并发誓放弃单一中心主权的观念。这种观念确实很受欢迎。除了我们提及的国家团体之外，还有其他的专业团体、职业团体等都宣称它们的连带。"

② Barker, "The Discredited State", *The Political Quarterly*, 119页, 1915。

③ Barker, "The Discredited State", *The Political Quarterly*, 119页, 1915。

④ 关于Barker的理论，还可以注意W. Y. Elliott（艾略特）的文章"Sovereign State or Sovereign Group?", *American Political Science Review*, 第19卷, 475页, 1919。

⑤ Lindsay, "Political Theory", 见F. S. Marvin, *Development in European Thought*, 164页, 1919。也可参见他的早期的文章"The State in Recent Theory", *The Political Quarterly*, 第1卷, 1914; *Proceedings of Aristotelian Society*, 1924-06-16。

⑥ Lindsay, "Political Theory", 见F. S. Marvin, *Development in European Thought*, 165页, 1919。

⑦ Lindsay, "The State in Recent Theory", *The Political Quarterly*, 第1卷, 132页, 1914。

⑧ Lindsay, "The State in Recent Theory", *The Political Quarterly*, 第1卷, 129页, 130页, 1914。

新理论不否认也不能否认人类的社会本质。它所否认的是那种认为人的社会属性只能通过国家这个唯一的组织表现出来的理论。

这种旧的理论承认国家的人格，而否认国家内部的组织也具有人格。林赛先生不能明白为何一个国家能够被作为一个人而有人格，而一个贸易组织或一个教会却不能这样。① 林赛认为，真正的问题不在于从所有在一起工作的人产生的共同意志比他们所有个人的单个意志的总和要多这一意义上承认团体人格的存在，问题在于如何限定团体人格的数量。"既然我们承认了国家是一个人，有它自己的意志，我们就不得不承认团体人格数量是不受限定的，我们必须确定国家如何与其他团体人格区分开来以及国家和它们之间的合理关系应该是什么。"②

另外，那种旧理论还认为只有国家才拥有强制的权力即主权。但是这种观念现在不能再成立，因为没有组织天生就有权力或主权"国家对其成员的权力依赖于成员自身的意志。事实上他们允许国家对他们实行组织权力，这种权力其实只能对个人有管理作用，但对社会没有。因而，国家能够且仅仅能够在公民准备给予这种权力的时候，才能对团体加以控制"③。

国家曾经被认为是一个最大的组织，但是事实不允许我们相信这样一种观念了，因为在许多情况下组织都延伸到国家界线之外。"如果我们从那些我们用来证明它比其他团体高级的原则上来看，则现存的国家说大也大，说小也小。如果我们从公共利益的意识的原则，相互依赖的感觉和关系上看，国家是太大的。在小的、更单纯的实体中，更容易显示忠诚。如果我们从为管理或控制个人的冲突和协会的需要的原则上看，国家还是太小的。"④

5. 柯尔（G. D. H. Cole）

柯尔的著作在近些年来引起了普遍的关注。他的名字与基尔特社会主义联系在一起，尽管他不是这个运动的先驱。⑤ 一般认为基尔特社会主义主要关注经济

---

① Lindsay, "Political Theory", 176 页。
② Lindsay, "The State in Recent Theory", *The Political Quarterly*, 第 1 卷, 131 页, 1914。
③ Lindsay, "The State in Recent Theory", *The Political Quarterly*, 第 1 卷, 134 页, 1914。
④ Lindsay, "The State in Recent Theory", *The Political Quarterly*, 第 1 卷, 136 页, 1914。
⑤ 基尔特社会主义的起源与发展参考 Hobson 的 *National Guilds: An Inquiry into the Wage System and the Way Out*（1919）的前言。与我们的讨论相关的 Cole 的观点可以在如下著作中发现：*The World of Labour*（1915）；*Self-Government in Industry*（1917）；*Labour in the Commonwealth*（1919），*Social Theory*（1920），*Guild Socialism Re-stated*（1920 年或美国版的 *Guild Socialism*）；*The Future of Local Government*（1921）；*Organized Labour: An Introduction to Trade Unionism*（1924）；以及 Everyman 对卢梭 *Social Contract* 的介绍。Cole 的一般观念可以在 Rockow 的 *Contemporary Political Thought in England* 的第七章和 Ellis 小姐的题为"Guild Socialism and Pluralism"的文章（*American Political Science Review*，第 17 卷，584～596 页，1923）。前者主要处理经济组织，后者更多地与 the Nature of State 相关。但是她的文章奠基于 Cole 在 *Self-Government in Industry* 中的一章"the Nature of State"。在这本书中所提出的观念，根据 Cole 的说法，连他自己也不支持。他在 1919 年版的导论中这样说："我对这本书并不满意；但是我不知道如何修改它……我现在不同意在这本书中的几种论述。"也见 147～148 页的注释。

改革，但是我们发现在柯尔的著作中，所讨论的东西已经超过了经济的领域，特别是在他的《社会理论》一书中更是如此。

柯尔的观念随着时间的改变而改变。起初他是一个费边主义者。但是正如被评论的，"窗户后面的人"（man behind a window）的政府的危险使得他加入了一个新的运动（基尔特社会主义）。① 俄国苏维埃体系的出现对柯尔产生了很大的影响，他宣称"苏维埃的观念就是基尔特的观念，或者起码有许多的共通之处"②。从哲学上讲，柯尔已经深受英国的莫瑞斯（William Morris）、德国的马克思和美国的麦基韦的影响。③

否定的方面，柯尔先生认为国家主权无论在理论上还是在实践上都失败了。④ 肯定的方面，他认为主权在个体或共同体的成员手中。⑤ 在这一点上他几乎完全同意卢梭。⑥ 但是他不认为主权是不可让渡的，因为主权可以由社会团体或组织所执行⑦，而人不能生活在孤岛上，他必须成为这些团体的成员，因此在许多情况下，他不能做他想做的一切事情。

因为人类的利益是多方面的，所以组织形式也有许多。这些形式随着时间和空间的差异而不同。⑧ 一般而言，它们可以分为两个大的部分：一种是重要的，一种是不太重要的。⑨柯尔对前者有特殊的兴趣，因为它对有组织的社会具有重要的社会意义。⑩ 组织的重要形式可以根据这些原则来分类：①组织所要追求的利益的内容；②处理相关利益的方法。根据前者，组织形式是政治的、职业的、欲望的、宗教的、深谋远虑的、仁慈的、社会的或理论的。⑪ 根据后者来看，组织的每一种形式都具有管理性或宣传性。举个例子，在宗教组织中，我们可以有像教会那样的管理组织，有像"生命与自由运动"那样的宣传组织。管理组织被认为是首要的而宣传组织被认为是次要的。⑫

从上面所讨论的内容出发，我们来看看国家的地位。国家，根据柯尔的看法，

---

① Lewis Rockow, *Contemporary Political Thought in England*, 150 页, 1925。
② Cole, *Self-Government in Industry*, 1919 年版的导言, 22 页。
③ Cole, *Labour in the Commonwealth*, 181 页。*Social Theory* 第 2 章。
④ Cole, *Social Theory*, 102 页。*Labour in the Commomwealth*, 187 页。*Guild Socialism*（美国版）23 页。参考 *Organized Labour: An Introduction to Trade Unionism*, 149 页。
⑤ 他拒绝使用"公民"这一词，因为它与国家联系得过于紧密。
⑥ Cole, *Labour in the Commonwealth*, 202 页、205 页。
⑦ Cole, *Social Theory*, 133 页。参见他对卢梭的 *Social Contract* 的导论。
⑧ Cole, *Social Theory*, 64 页。
⑨ Cole, *Social Theory*, 65 页。
⑩ Cole, *Social Theory*, 65～66 页。
⑪ Cole, *Social Theory*, 66～72 页。
⑫ Cole, *Social Theory*, 72～73 页。

是一个政治组织。它被定义为在利益共同体中进行政治管理的机构。① 它"绝不是社会中最大的和最持久的组织"②。国家是必要的，但是它的必要如同贸易组织是必要的一样。③ 它没有比其他组织更多的强制权力或主权。④ 他说："每一个组织，仅仅因为它的存在这个事实，就被赋予了强制权力，而在实现它的目标的过程中它实际在使用这种权力。"⑤

现实中存在不同种类的强制力或主权。"有一种强制仅仅影响一个人的钱包或财产，这种强制通过罚款而实现……第二种强制通过限制他的机会和自我表现的范围而影响一个人的行为自由，比如禁止他在某个工厂或行业中工作……第三种强制直接影响到一个人的身体，这通过限制一个人移动的权利、拷问他、囚禁他，或者最后来枪毙他或砍下他的头颅。"⑥

第一种形式在所有的组织中都被运用；第二种在有些组织中被运用，如贸易组织。国家，除了具有第一种和第二种形式之外，还单独具有第三种。国家是否应该继续垄断第三种而同时却与其他组织分享第一种和第二种？对于这一点柯尔给了一个否定的答案。

旧的主权理论认为国家有绝对的权力，且单独拥有它，有这样一个假设，"在它的地域内，国家代表和拥有每一个人，因而相对于在其地域内仅仅拥有一些人的其他组织来说必然要高级"⑦。但是在何种意义上国家代表和拥有每一个人？柯尔问道。"如果我们的代表的功能理论是正确的，它可以拥有每一个人；但是它不包括每一个人的整体；它可以代表每一个人的一些目的，但不能代表每一个人的所有目的。"他继续补充道，且这一点是关键的，"因此，它就不能基于它代表和拥有每一个人这一理论来宣称自己理所当然地拥有主权；因为如果只存在一个主权，它就必须尽可能地代表和包括每一个人的全部"⑧。

如果没有特殊的职能组织，甚至连国家也不能拥有这种优于其他组织的绝对的权力，自然就会导致主权在职能组织之间分享。从这一点说，柯尔是多元主义的强烈拥护者。但这不是全部，不同职能组织之间的矛盾冲突使得困难可能产生。在我们的时代，职能组织在特征上大多是民族的（国家的）⑨，因此有必要在

---

① Cole, *Labour in the Commonwealth*, 50 页。他的国家和共同体的概念，参见 Cole, *Social Theory*, 57 页、216 页。在他看来，一个共同体包括所有的组织，而国家仅仅是一个政治组织。
② Cole, *Social Theory*, 81 页。参见 *Self-Government in Industry*, 119 页。
③ Cole, *Labour in the Commonwealth*, 185 页。
④ 对 Cole 来说，强制权力和主权是同一个事物。参见 *Social Theory* 第 8 章。
⑤ Cole, *Social Theory*, 128 页。参见 *Labour in the Commonwealth*, 191 页。
⑥ Cole, *Social Theory*, 129~130 页。
⑦ Cole, *Social Theory*, 131~132 页。
⑧ Cole, *Social Theory*, 132 页。
⑨ 这两个词都是不充分的。柯尔更喜欢用"共同体"这个词。

国家范围内，为了共同体的整体社会生活而设立一个统一的协调的实体。但是共同体和职能组织的相互依赖的增加使得为了整体世界应该有一个统一体或协调组织。然而无论是世界协调实体还是一个共同体的协调实体，所应用的原则都是一样的。这个协调实体应该是一个代表职能组织的实体。①

为了解决职能组织的冲突，这个协调组织也应当具有一些强制权力。这导致柯尔在职能组织的主权之外发明另一种主权。然而，必须注意的是，这种协调组织不应该与现代国家的机器混为一谈，因为在柯尔的理论系统里，国家仅仅是一种职能组织。②它拥有的主权就如同教会和贸易组织拥有的主权一样。再必须注意的是这种协调机构，"只能是一种联合，不是所有的组织的联合，而是所有重要的组织的联合，能代表社会中各个主要职能的最高实体组成的联合委员会或议会"③。"每一个职能团体都负责与它的职能有关的活动的执行，但是为了不同组织的活动的协调就必须有一个代表它们的联合实体。"④

这样，我们就足以表明柯尔先生在一方面，反对旧的国家主权的理论，但是在另一方面，坚持认为主权应该被、实际上也正在被具有各自独特功能或协调功能的职能组织来执行。现实中存在许多主权，也存在一个主权的联合体。它们都存在，彼此不发生冲突，因为它们每一个都在其自身的范围内执行主权。

但是，柯尔先生并没有在这里止步，因为他认为主权不是职能组织的一个最为重要的东西。相反，它仅仅是社会病的表征。它的出现意味着无序的社会现象的存在。它在社会里消失或至少无用时，则表明那时的社会是和平和有序的。他写道："既然我们知道了一个职能社会里强制权力会于何时出现，我们现在就可以来发泄对它的不满了。我相信来源于对职能组织的完全承认的最重要的结果之一是强制权力在社会中的应用会从根本上即刻减少。因为强迫是社会无序的一个后果，对它的需求很大程度上，不是因为人类的脆弱，而是因为人类不能在一定社会条件下寻求适当的社会服务的方式，不能清楚地认识到社会中的权利和义务。如果我们使我们的社会变得有序，使人们更容易认清他们的社会服务的适当方式，我相信对强迫意志的需要就将迅速而逐步地消失。"⑤

由于我们不准备考虑除柯尔以外的其他基尔特社会主义者的观念，我们可以引用柯尔在1919年版的《工业的自治》的导论中的一些话来说明他本人和霍布森之间的区别。"逐渐地，对于一个基本问题的观点差异，最终变得很明显了。随着其他的基尔特主义者逐渐加入我的阵营，我和S. G. 霍布森先生之间的长期对

---

① Cole, *Social Theory*, 140 页。
② Cole, *Social Theory*, 136 页。
③ Cole, *Social Theory*, 135 页。
④ Cole, *Social Theory*, 135～136 页。
⑤ Cole, *Social Theory*, 139～140 页。

立更加尖锐化了。霍布森先生——跟随他的是奥兰治（Orage）先生和其他新时代（New Age）的作者——坚持认为国家的主权作为基尔特原则的一个重要的方面。他们拒绝把国家在某种意义上当做是消费者的代表或保护者，坚持认为它的主权就是主权的实施，是生产者或消费者的最终代表。他们希望工业的控制应该在生产者的基尔特之手，并且认为在正常情况下，基尔特将同保护生产者一样充分保护消费者的利益；但是他们希望生产方式的拥有者作为国家的最终的权威，国家是代表以公民身份而不是以消费者身份出现的全民的所有者。"①

"一个奇特的立场由此产生。霍布森先生和他的支持者们坚决认为在经济以及其他领域存在国家主权；但是他们却不希望国家在正常运转的工业中发挥作用，也不认为有必要持续表达消费者关于组织的意见。在理论上，他主张国家是终极权威；但在现实中，他却希望国家尽量少干预，它的程度甚至比我们这些主张对国家的权威做出严格的理论限定的人主张的干涉程度还要小。"

"我们那些持另外意见的人则认为工业和服务的组织中有两种角度的观念应当考虑——从生产者或服务的提供者的角度和从消费者或服务的享受者的角度。我认为基尔特——工业的和市民的——代表了前一个方面，而国家（和地方权威）代表了后一个方面。我否认某种形式的组织比其他的组织优越，而坚持认为所有组织彼此是相互补充的。我因而反对国家主权理论，而坚持国家和基尔特在经济领域共享主权（co-sovereignty），其他的实体在社会活动的其他领域中也可能会这样分享主权。"

"我不再相信我是完全正确的，或相应地，认为霍布森先生是完全错误的。我一如既往地强烈反对国家主权理论；但是我不再满意于把国家作为消费者的最高和唯一代表。"②

四、法国学者

1. 涂尔干（Durkheim）

为了清楚地理解涂尔干，让我们从考察他的心理分析开始。③ 根据他的看法，

---

① Cole, *Self-Government in Industry*, 第4版, 4～5页。

② Cole, *Self Government in Industry*, 5～6页。Hobson 的观点可以参见他的 *National Guilds and the State* (1920), *Guild Principles in War and Peace* (1917), *National Guilds: An Inquiry into the Wage System and the Way out* (1919), Orage 编辑, 也可参见 A. R. Orage, *National Guild* (1914), A. J. Penty, *Old World for New* (1917) 和 *Guild and the Social Crisis* (1919)。

③ Durkheim 的观点可以参考他的 *Le Suicide* (1897年) 第434～450页和他的 *De la Division du Travail* (1902) 前言。参考 C. E. Gehike 的 "Émile Durkheim's Contributions to Sociological Theory", *Columbia Studies in History, Economics and Public Law*, 第63卷。H. E. Barnes 的 "Durkheim's Contribution to Political Theory", *Political Science Quarterly*, 第35卷, 236～254页, 1928。还有他的 "Some Contributions of Sociology to Modern Theory", *American Political Science Review*, 第15卷, 487～533页, 1921。

脑细胞之间的相互作用产生感觉，感觉是个人意识的首要要素。感觉的复合产生印象。通过同样的进程，印象可以产生概念，概念的复合产生具体的事物。①

这是个人意识的起点和发展，可以作为个人意识的相互作用的结果。尽管集体意识是个体意识的产物，但集体意识与个体意识绝对不一样。集体意识与个体意识的区别体现在两个方面：第一，它外在于个体意识；第二，它具有约束力。

社会意识的外在性——格尔基（Gehlke）更喜欢用意识或表象——是说导致这种意识的材料来源于外部，说它外在于个体意识是因为它不能由孤立的个体而形成，它必须从其联合和统一体中形成。它具有约束力，是因为社会表象要比个体表象高级。逻辑的运用在这里很简单：整体比部分要大，前者要比后者高级。并且从等级的角度看，由于它是精神层次中最高的，所以它是最为高级的。②

在解释了他的基本概念之后，我们回到他的社会概念。社会，根据他的看法，有两个含义：第一，它意味着一群具体的个体；第二，它是一个精神的整体。但是后一种含义得到了更多的强调。在后一种含义里，个体意识与群体意识的关系的最重要的部分是前者对后者的一般规则和道德行为的服从。这样，个体意识对群体意识的服从就成了社会连带的关键。③ 在人类社会里，社会连带的增加是必须的，只有在职业社会里社会连带才能得到很好的保护；因为正是在这里我们发现一个社会约束，也正是在这里，有人们寻求的共同利益。

近些年来工业和经济变化导致了职能组织的重要性增加，这些变化也证明了在面对目前的工业社会的时候，全能国家的存在是不可能的。如果我们想要生活在一个更好的社会，职业团体应当既作为政治表达的基础，又作为经济管理的资源。国家可以仍然存在，但它的权力应该被分散和受到限制。

那么国家与其他组织之间的关系如何？根据涂尔干的看法，国家应该涉及一般的关系，而细节的应该留给职能组织，以满足它们的特殊的和不同的需要与愿望，这样专业化的和多样化的规则的制定就成了职能组织的首要功能，而这也不应该受到国家的干涉。

由于强调职能组织在现代社会生活中的重要性，职能表现、地理分离的原则在一定的程度上也应当被运用。这样职能组织在范围上可以是地方的，也可以是全国的。每个职业的全国性组织应该给整个国家的该职业以普遍的原则，地方的事务则应该完全留在地方组织手中。

涂尔干对雇主和雇员之间的工业管理特别感兴趣。这导致他坚持认为在雇主

---

① C. E. Gehike, "Émile Durkheim's Contribution to Sociological Theory", *Columbia Studies in History, Economics and Public Law*, 第63卷, 19~27页。

② C. E. Gehike, "Émile Durkheim's Contribution to Sociological Theory", *Columbia Studies in History, Economics and Public Law*, 第63卷, 19~27页。

③ 参考上文讨论的 Duguit 的社会连带的概念。

和雇员那里应该有分离的职能组织。在它的范围内关于它自己的每一个政策都应是彼此独立的。在仲裁机构双方都应该有代表，以服从国家由于行业的特殊需求而对其进行的一般管理。

2. 索雷尔（Sorel）

人们普遍承认 G. 索雷尔是工团主义最著名的代表人物。在给丹尼尔·哈里夫（Daniel Halevy）的一封信中，他说："我既不是教授，也不是博学的人，也不是一个党的领导者。我只是一个自学的人，我将记录我思想的笔记给众人看。"① 但是法国著名学者李·波（Le Bon）在他的《社会主义心理学》（*La Psychologie du Socialisms*）中说索雷尔是"法国最博学的社会主义者"。

索雷尔深受马克思的影响，他自称为一个马克思主义者。② 但是，既然现在的世界已与过去不同，我们碰到的一些事实，马克思没有碰到过，那么对马克思的理论进行修正就是必需的。这种修正的重要性在于，"因为，一方面，马克思不是经常有'好灵感'，并且经常思考过去而不是预想未来；也因为，另一方面，马克思并不可能知道我们现在的所有事实；马克思对资产阶级的发展了解得很清楚，但是并不可能了解已经作为当代社会生活的重要特征的劳工运动的发展"③。

他称自己的理论为"新学派"或革命工团主义，以区别于议会社会主义。根据他的看法，后者承认国家的存在，因而也就是承认政权的存在。他宣称："经验一再表明，革命者一旦取得政权，他们就会承认国家的存在的合理性，他们就会运用政治手段，将司法作为武器来居高临下地打击政敌。议会社会主义者也逃不出这个普遍规律；他们将国家的旧有特征保留下来，因而也就会犯旧的制度和革命所犯的错误。"④

在其他地方，他写道："工团主义者和官方社会主义者根本不可能就此问题达成哪怕最轻微的谅解。后者，嘴里喊着要打碎一切，但是他们实际上反对的是拥有权力的人，而不是权力本身。他们希望掌握国家政权，并且他们也认为，一旦掌握了政府，他们就需要军队，也需要玩外交手腕，最终他们就会反过来赞美为国家作贡献的精神。"⑤

---

① Sorel, *Reflections on Violence*, T. E. Hulme 翻译，3 页。除了这本书之外，他的观点还可见于下列书籍：*L'Avenir socialiste des Sydicats*（1898），*La Decomposition du Maxisme*（1908），*Introduction a Deconomic moderne*（1922）。也可参见 L. Levine, "Syndicalism in France", *Columbia University Studies*, 第 XLVI 卷，1913 年（3）；J. H. Harley, *Syndicalism*, 第六章；J. R. Macdonald, *Syndicalism*, 第三章；Kirkup, *History of Socialism*, 293 页以下；Mott, "The Political Theory of Syndicalism", *Political Science Quarterly*, 第 34 卷，25~40 页，1922。

② Sorel, *Reflections on Violence*, 127 页。

③ L. Levine, *Syndicalism in France*, 143 页。也可参见 Sorel, *Reflections on Violence*, 133 页、155 页。他认为马克思生活在英国是一个错误，他还告诉我们他从贸易联合主义者那里学得了很多。参见 Sorel, *L'Avenir socialiste des Sydicats*, 12 页。

④ Sorel, *Reflections on Violence*, 118~119 页。

⑤ Sorel, *Reflections on Violence*, 123~124 页。

另一方面,"工团主义者如同十八世纪的人们所做的那样不赞成对国家的改革;他们希望毁灭它"①。既然主权与国家密不可分,毁灭国家就意味着毁灭主权。正是这个原因,索雷尔强烈反对主权的观念和卢梭的公意。②

国家,在他看来,不过是一个暴力组织。"国家,"他说,"实际上已经成为征服行动的组织者、赃物的瓜分者和由此获利的统治阶级的'存在理由'(raison d'être)——而这些征服行动的代价却要社会大众来承担"③。但是"神圣国家"(God State)拥有为所欲为的权力的时代已经一去不复返了,因此,国家现在也该消失了。④

这种国家的消失是必须的。我们不能忍受它继续存在下去。他强烈反对持那种观念的人,即认为:"国家最后一定会消失——但那是以后的事,你现在要做的就是适应它作为给政客提供美味珍馐的方式。让国家消失的最好方式就是加强政府的职能。"⑤ 索雷尔说:"这种理由与糊涂虫(Gribouille)的行为比较类似,他为了避免被雨淋湿而跳进水里。"⑥

这样,工团主义者希望毁灭国家,并且是立刻毁灭它,"因为他们希望实现马克思的这种观念,即社会主义者的革命不应该使一些少数统治阶级被另一些少数统治阶级代替"⑦。要毁灭它就要从根本上毁灭它,这样,它就永远不会再存在。

但是如何去毁灭国家?我们应当运用什么方法?根据索雷尔的说法,有效的方式就是总罢工(general strike)。一个学者说道:"总罢工的概念是他对工团主义哲学的首要贡献——但并不是他所有的朋友都承认这一点。"⑧ 根据索雷尔的看法,总罢工是工人阶级渴求解放的"社会奇迹"(social myth),而社会奇迹是社会和道德发展的方式。在每一个革命运动中社会奇迹都是必需的。历史表明这是正确的。耶稣复活的奇迹是早期基督教最有号召力的方面。"必须承认革命的真正发展不像描绘激情澎湃的画卷;但是没有这些画卷,革命能够取得胜利吗?"⑨ 尽管我们知道总罢工是一个奇迹,"但我们仍遵照不误,就像一个对自己的学科充

---

① Sorel, *Reflections on Violence*, 123 页。
② *L'Avenir socialiste des Sydicats*, 45 页。
③ Sorel, *Reflections on Violence*, 190 页。
④ Sorel, *Reflections on Violence*, 116 页。"我们不会比 1793 年的人更好、更人道、对他人的不幸更敏感;我更倾向于认为国家比那个时候更不道德了;我们的父辈因对'神圣国家'的迷信而成了牺牲者,我们不再让国家像以前一样控制了。"
⑤ Sorel, *Reflections on Violence*, 128~129 页。
⑥ Sorel, *Reflections on Violence*, 128~129 页。
⑦ Sorel, *Reflections on Violence*, 123 页。
⑧ H. W. Ladier, *A History of Socialist Thought*, 379 页, 1927。
⑨ Sorel, *Reflections on Violence*, 134 页。

满自信的物理学家那样,尽管他知道他的成果以后会过时的"①。

"工团主义的暴力体现在那些希望推翻国家的无产阶级举行的罢工中,但是不应该像国家宣传的那样,将它与1793年大革命(the Revolutionaries of 1793)中的野蛮行为相混淆,当这些革命者掌握政权后,就用那些统治阶级——教会和君主的手段来镇压教会和君主。"②

但是假如总罢工的奇迹能够发生,国家及其政权就此被毁灭了,下一步该如何做?对许多工团主义者来说,建设性的工作应该展开,但是索雷尔的回答是:我们还没有完成破坏性工作,谈论建设性工作有什么用?并且,"也可以说,威胁工团主义的最大的危险是效仿民主的努力;保持脆弱的和无序的组织一段时间对它来说要更好一些,模仿中产阶层的政治形式会使工团陷入不稳定的境地"③。

这样的理论好像是悲观主义的。但是,索雷尔说,悲观主义"对完成伟大事业来说是必不可少的"④。"'悲观主义'是一种行为的哲学,而不是一种普适理论"⑤;"悲观主义者认为社会现状是由不可消除的铁的定律维系的一个体系,因此这个体系自始至终都是固定的,除非对它从整体上进行破坏,否则它就不会消失。如果这种理论被承认,则让某些无辜的人为社会弊病负责就是荒谬的。由于执着于他的计划中碰到的诸多变数,悲观主义者不会认同乐观主义者的盲目乐

---

① Sorel, *Reflections on Violence*, 167 页。"正是在罢工中,无产阶级显示了其存在。我不能赞成这样的观点,即罢工仅仅类似于买卖李子干的买家和卖家因价格上不能达成一致而导致的商业关系的破裂。罢工是一种战争现象。这样,说暴力是注定要从未来的罢工中消失的偶然事故是一个严重的歪曲。""社会革命是这种战争的一种外延,在其中每一次大的罢工都是一个插曲;这就是为什么工团主义者用罢工的语言来谈论社会革命的原因所在;对他们来说,社会主义就是总罢工,就是对总罢工的期望与准备。就像拿破仑战役一样,总罢工会彻底消除了一个被诅咒的社会制度。""我们可以把议会社会主义者比作拿破仑封为贵族的公务员,他们用旧制度的方式来强化国家机器。而革命工团主义者则能和拿破仑的铁军相提并论,虽然他们知道自己将永远贫穷,他们还是完成了许多英勇的壮举。帝国留下了什么?只有伟大军队的史诗;而当前的社会运动将会留下罢工的史诗。"《为暴力声辩》,参见 *Reflection on Violence*,附录。

② Sorel, *Reflections on Violence*, 152 页。

③ Sorel, *Reflections on Violence*, 204 页。Sorel 强烈反对当今政治家、教授和思想家们所谓的民主。也可参见他的 *Illussions du Progres*,10 页,1911。尽管索雷尔在破坏工作完成之前不讨论建设工作,但是作为一个工团主义者,他确实认为工人的工团主义者们应该处理这种情况。如果仍然还有一种称之为权力或主权的东西,它应该为工团所实施。

④ Sorel, *Reflections on Violence*, 7 页。

⑤ Sorel, *Reflections on Violence*, 10 页。

观;他不会幻想着杀光所有的自私自利的人,以给后代带来幸福"①。

五、美国学者

1. 麦基韦(R. M. MacIver)

在美国学者中,对于我们所讨论的话题而言,最为著名的是麦基韦教授和福利特(M. P. Follett)女士。麦基韦教授的哲学基础体现在他的早期著作《共同体:社会学考察》(1917)一书中。但是他的观点在他近期的著作《现代国家》中得到了充分的发展。后一本著作得到了许多著名学者的高度赞扬。② 斯克斯(Jenks)教授说:"在对主权教条的攻击中,他当然不是先驱。但是很明显,他的支持,或者说他的有价值的论辩发展了这种攻击。"③

麦基韦教授说:"与过去比较,现在的政治思想最大的不同,是它对主权的有限性和相对性有清晰的认识。"④ 过去的教条断言国家的主权是"终极的权力,它应该像全能的上帝的意志那样自由,不受限制地统治人类"⑤。法学家们提出的这种理论"也许在它自己的领域里是足够适用的",但是,"当它被用来解释主权的丰富内涵的时候,它就不仅是不充分的,而是错误的了"⑥。

"从法律上讲,"他写道,"国家是不受限制的,因为它本身就是法律产生的根源;但这样辩解,就像说,教会是不受限制的,因为它是教会法的来源,或者说皇家古代高尔夫球俱乐部(Royal and Ancient Golf Club)是不受限制的,因为它是高尔夫规则的制定者一样,不具有绝对意义。我们不必去缩小政治制度和所有其他社会规则之间的差别。我们只要坚持说政治制度是社会规则中的一种形式就

---

① Sorel, *Reflections on Violence*, 10页。
对于 Sorel 的观念,也可以参见 W. Y. Elliot 教授所写的"The Poltical Application of Romanticism", *Political Science Quarterly*,第 39 卷,234~264 页。对一般工团主义和其他学者的观念,还可以参见下列书籍:Hubert Lagardelle 和其他人的 *Syndicalisme et Socialisme*,巴黎,1908;E. Berth 的 *Les Nouveaux Aspects du Socialisme*,1908;E. Pataud 和 G. Pouget 的 *Syndicalism and the Cooperative Commomwealth*,C. Charles 和 F. Charles 翻译,1913;Emile Fouget 的 *Sabotage*,1913;John Spargo 的 *Syndicalism, Industrial Unionism and Socialism*,1913;J. A. Estay 的 *Revolutionary Syndicalism*,1913;Louis Levine 的 *Syndicalism in America*,1913;F. G. Brooks 的 *American Syndicalism*,1913;P. F. Brissenden 的 *The I. W. W., A Study in American Syndicalism*,1919;F. D. H. Cole 的 *World of Labour*,1917;Sudney Webb 和 Beatrice 的 *What Syndicalism Means*,1912。另外一些鼓吹职能组织的主权的权力的法国学者,特别参见 Paul Boncour 的 *Le Fédéralisme économic* 和 *Les Syndicats de Fonctionnaires*。(根据 Kirkup 的说法,Sorel 在最近已经不再是工团主义的信奉者,*History of Socialism*,294 页,1920。)

② Jenks, "Recent Theory of the State", *Law Quarterly Review*, 188 页, 1927 年 4 月。
③ Jenks, "Recent Theory of the State", *Law Quarterly Review*, 192 页, 1927 年 4 月。
④ MacIver, *The Modern State*, 468 页。
⑤ MacIver, *The Modern State*, 467 页。
⑥ MacIver, *The Modern State*, 467 页。

可以了。国家是众多社会组织形式中的'一种',但与此同时,我们也要承认它的巨大贡献和更大的诉求。"①

国家被定义为:"通过政府颁布法律而赋予了强制权力的社会团体,它维持依据领土划分的共同体内的社会秩序。"② 社会团体被定义为在社会中追求某些共同利益的组织。③ 当一个团体被法律所承认,它就成了法人团体。④ 团体或法人团体的形成如同国家的形成一样。可以说一个团体存在于一个社会之内,但不能说一个团体存在于一个国家之内。⑤ 在这里,麦基韦教授同意基尔克教授和梅特兰教授的观点,认为法人团体外在于国家,因此,法人团体的特征不需要国家行为的许可,国家有义务承认它。他说:"国家有义务承认团体的特征,集体主义团体的权利和责任和被正式承认的国家的特征差别不大。"⑥ 在某种意义上,国家可以解散一个托拉斯或一个团体,这是真实的,但是它"往往又是在改变组织的模式的时候才有效力,即使如此,也存在相当大的困难,并且还要在特定的条件下才能实施"⑦。

但是,同基尔克教授和梅特兰教授不同的是,麦基韦教授否认团体的人格或意志。他写道:"我们不能接受基尔克和梅特兰给团体的'群体意识''群体意志'或'群体人格'的特性。"⑧ 团体是一个联合体,但不是一个整体。它仅仅是一个其成员借以追求共同目的的组织。⑨ 既然否认了团体的人格,他自然也会否认国家的人格。对他来说,认为国家本身具有人格,是不现实的。⑩

既然国家仅仅是组织中的一种,既然团体或组织与国家是在同一个层次上,则组织所行使的主权权力与国家所行使的主权权力是一样真实的;因为主权或权力来自人们的意志,不应该将人们的意志与公民的意志相混淆。根据麦基韦教授的说法,认为权力仅仅是公民的意志的说法是错误的,因为权力是社会存在的意志。⑪

在国家和其他组织之间有什么不同?国家区别于其他组织的地方是它的管理功能:它解决不同团体的利益的冲突和划定"它们的界限以及把它们带入有序的关系中"。但是"它不把它们看作是自己的代理机构,或它发号施令的下属",

---

① MacIver, *The Modern State*, 467~468 页。
② MacIver, *The Modern State*, 22 页。
③ *Communtiy*, 23 页。也可参见 *The Modern State*, 6 页。
④ *The Modern State*, 473 页。
⑤ *The Modern State*, 477 页注释。
⑥ *The Modern State*, 475 页。
⑦ *The Modern State*, 475 页。
⑧ *The Modern State*, 473~474 页。参见第 490 页。
⑨ *The Modern State*, 274 页。
⑩ *The Modern State*, 450~454 页。
⑪ *The Modern State*, 468 页注释。

"它不会也不能决定它们的目的,并且也不会在很大程度上决定它们的行事方式"。① 简单地说,除了当一个群体的利益侵犯了另一个群体的利益,它不会与它们中的任何一个单独发生关系。它不能对贸易组织、雇工协会、教会等颐指气使。这些是绝对主权的特性,但是国家并不具有这些特性。②

正是如此,国家的主权绝不比其他组织的主权高级。也许在范围上,国家的利益要比许多组织的利益大,但这并不带给国家更优越的特征,也不能给予它更多的要求其成员效忠的权利。相反,人们的利益与团体有更为紧密的联系,人们对团体的忠诚一般要超过对国家的忠诚。"考虑到这一点,绝对主权理论,如果在当今的国家真正加以实践,则会对社会生活的和谐产生致命的危害。"③

把国家看作是组织之一,国家和组织与法律的关系也是一样的,麦基韦教授得出了几乎和克拉勃教授一样的论点,即对法律权威的肯定。根据麦基韦教授的看法,国家具有组织的本质特征。如果组织需要服从于法律,国家为什么不需要?他说,与其说国家是法律的制订者,不如说它是法律的官方保护者。④

认识到法律是外在于国家的,把法律看成是社会、连带、公共利益意义的表现以后⑤,麦基韦教授同意狄骥的观点,特别是后者的公共服务的概念。同狄骥一样,麦基韦教授认为国家所执行的权力仅仅是服务的工具。他写道:"它(权力)仅仅能够提供那些它能提供的服务。当然从目的与手段进行分离是可能的。人们很容易陷入那种使他们服从于组织的习惯之中,而这些组织本来应该给他们提供服务的。但是这样他们并没有得到真正的服务。一般来说,只要他们能思考,他们就会以法律或其他组织的结果来判断它们的好坏。没有人认为国家的服务是没有限制的,因此,没有限制的主权观念是一个危险的错误。赋予政府超过其服务能力限制的权力是一个极大的错误,所有的暴政都是在这个错误的基础上产生的。"⑥

2. 福利特

在她的《新国家》中,福利特女士用以下的话开篇:"我们的政治生活是停滞不前的,资本和劳力处于对立之中,欧洲的国家互相争斗因为我们还没有学好

---

① *The Modern State*, 476 页。

② *The Modern State*, 476 页。

③ *The Modern State*, 477 页。"国家的最高权力的主张……经常被成功地反对,但是它从来没有被没有组织起来的个人主义所打败。只有通过个人主义,在国家周围或之内有组织地进入另一个组织。" MacIver, "Supremacy of the State", *New Republic*, 304 页, 1927 年 10 月。在这一点上, MacIver 教授同意 Barker 的观点。

④ *The Modern State*, 478~479 页。参考第 263 页以下。

⑤ *The Modern State*, 481 页。

⑥ *The Modern State*, 468 页。从 J. Dickinson 教授那里,笔者了解到 MacIver 教授已经在 1926 年 11 月的 *Economica* 写了一篇关于主权的重要文章。参见 "A working Theory of Sovereignty", *Political Science Quarterly*, 第 XLII 卷, 524 页, 1927。

如何相处。20世纪必须出现一种新的联系原则。大众哲学、大众管理、大众爱国主义必须产生。大众已经不再满足于以我们为中心了。"

"团体组织将成为政治领域里的新方法，我们的未来的工业体系的基础、国际秩序的基石，将创造一个我们隐约意识到的新世界。因为创造性的力量来自团体，创造性的权力存在于团体生活的活动中。"①

团体组织应该成为我们社会和政治生活的基础，团体组织应该引起我们的注意。但是团体组织主要是指邻里团体（neighborhood group）。她说："我们的主张是人民应该自发组织成邻里团体以管理他们的日常生活，将生活的需要、愿望和灵感拿到桌面上来，这些需要应该成为政治的本质，这些邻里团体也就成了被认同的政治体。"②

邻里团体是需要的和值得拥有的，因为第一，可以实现人们之间完全的了解和真正的理解；第二，邻里团体给经常性的和有规律性的交流提供了机会。③

但是在强调邻里团体的重要性的同时，她并不完全否认职业团体。④ 它们两者都是必要的，因为现在的工业和经济情况要求它们这样。最好能成立一些职能部门使邻里团体将职业团体纳入其中。她坚持认为："我们所有的功能一定被表达，但是有时候必须进行合作，以使它们真正发生作用。"⑤ 因为这个原因，邻里团体和职业团体都必须在国家里面有所反映，无论是独立地来反映，还是一个通过另一个来反映。简单地说，不管是邻里的，经济的还是其他类的团体，她所强调的不是团体的分类，"而是强调，无论是什么性质的团体，都是'真实的团体'"⑥。

"真实的团体"，福利特是指真实的整体。但是一个真实的整体的观念不是仅仅属于团体。一个个体、一个国家、世界都和一个组织一样有一个真实的整体，是真实的整体拥有最高权力或主权。这样，哪里有真实的整体，哪里就有主权。"个人是他自己的主权者，只要他的本质特征是独特的。两个人是他们自己的主权者，只要他们两个能够合为一个整体。一个群体是其自身的主权者，只要它能够将几个或许多人融为一个整体。国家是主权者仅仅因为它有产生一个整体的权力。"他继续说："主权是由具有自我意识的彻底相互依赖产生的。主权是真实的集体意志的必然命令。它不是空想的，而是于他人的实际生活中产生的——我们只能通过群体生活了解它。通过缓慢的相互渗透过程，从分散的主权发展出集中的主权。这样能够也必须通过其存在的规则，群体联合组成更大的群体，这些

---

① Follett, *The New State*, 3 页, 1918。也可参见 *Creative Experience*。
② Follett, *The New State*, 192 页。
③ Follett, *The New State*, 192 页。
④ Follett, *The New State*, 320 页, 1918。
⑤ Follett, *The New State*, 320～321 页, 1918。
⑥ Follett, *The New State*, 323 页, 1918。

更大的群体进而组成一个世界群体。"①

很显然，主权不是绝对的，因为它是由一个完整的相互依赖所导致的。它可以在范围上有所不同，但不是在内容上。个体的主权和组织、国家甚至整个世界的主权一样，都是真实的。这样主权是国家的本质特征的旧观念在福利特女士的体系中找不到容身之地。并且，集体的主权只是有限的主权的产物。有限的主权的统一体是从个体开始的。没有有限的主权，就不会有集体的主权。团体的主权是一种集体的主权，因为它是由许多个体的主权或许多有限的主权所组成的；但是，反过来说，团体的集体的主权也可以被看作是一个有限的主权，因为它可以是一个更大的团体的许多有限的主权之一。根据福利特，或起码根据她的逻辑，只有作为一个整体的世界的集体主权可以不是一个有限的主权。

这样，福利特的整个系统可以归纳为"一"与"多"的问题。通过缓慢的相互渗透的过程，多个主权可以变为一个主权，当然一个主权也可以变为多个主权。她说："一与多是相互转化的。"但是，"当我们说一'来自'多的时候，不意味着一在多'之上'。生命的最为真实的本质是相互关联的双方都是同时产生的。在建设新国家的时候，这一点是必须要清楚地理解的"②。

从上述的引述，我们可以非常清楚地理解福利特的主张。国家的主权可以是许多有限的（个体的或团体的）主权组成的集体主权，但是国家的主权并不在个体的或团体的主权之上，因为个体的或团体的真实的整体的主权和国家的主权是一样地具有相同的分量。

她的主权概念的一个显著的特征是，她把作为一个整体的世界主权与个体的主权联系起来。这样，世界主义、国家主义和个人主义在她的系统中联系在一起了。③

六、结论

上面所提到的所有的学者都反对认为主权是单一的、不可分的、绝对的和不受限制的旧理论，他们也都反对那种认为主权是国家的本质特征的观念。也许除了那些主要目的是完全毁灭国家及其主权的工团主义者之外，所有其他的理论家都在一定程度上承认主权的存在。④ 而且，他们似乎认为主权可以在程度上有所不同，而不是在内容上。更进一步，在他们的观念里，存在一个属于整个世界的完整主权，尽管在现在它还没有实现。

---

① *The New State*，271 页。
② *The Modern State*，284 页。
③ 如果我没有记错的话，Follett 受到了密歇根的 Cooley 教授的很大影响（特别是他的 *Social Organization*）。
④ Cole 先生一定程度上喜欢看见主权的完全消失。

他们都强调团体生活的重要性,因而都重视由团体执行的内在权力。一方面,他们的一些人,如巴克先生和麦基韦教授尽量弱化个体在与国家主权关系中的重要性。另一方面,像福利特女士,认为一个个体的主权和其他团体和国家的主权一样真实。其中一些人如基尔克教授和梅特兰教授,重视团体的人格和意志,主要是认为团体的主权是合理的。但是,一些人像麦基韦教授和柯尔先生,拒绝承认团体意志和人格的观念。他们好像认为,权力对于一个有组织的社会性团体的存在而言是必需的。然而,一个社会团体未必是人类思想的有意识的产物,但这不一定意味着团体有它自己的人格和意志。

上面所提到的理论家的原理一般来讲都是相同的,但是他们获得相同原理的方法却是不同的。大致讲,可以从法律的、宗教的、经济的、心理学的、社会心理学的和社会学的观点来看:梅特兰是从法律的观点,菲吉斯是从宗教的观点,柯尔先生是从经济的观点,基尔克是从心理学的观点,福利特是从社会心理学的观点,麦基韦教授是从社会学的观点。然而,在这里需要指出的是,不应该过分强调这里所作的区分,因为从我们的目的出发,我们首先要关注的是原理,而不是方法。

第十章　拉斯基和其他

一、拉斯基

1. 导论

拉斯基的名字与主权多元主义理论紧密地联系在一起。说他是这个运动中最为突出的代表，也许并不为过。如果主权的多元主义理论不被后人忘记，则拉斯基先生一定会被研究主权观念史的学者永远铭记。

但是拉斯基不是阐述这种理论的第一人。事实上，比较而言，这种理论本身并不是现代的产物。回顾 17 世纪的著作，国际法之父格劳修斯在他的著作《战争与和平法》（*De Jure Belli ac Pacis*）里就有这样一段话："应该看到的是主权本身是一个整体，不可分割。它由我们在前面提到过的几个部分组成，并且不必承担任何责任。但它的所有权可以分割。因此，虽然古罗马的主权只有一个，但所有权经常被分割。由此，可以有一个统治者领有西罗马帝国，另一个领有东罗马帝国，有时候，它甚至会被分成三个部分。还有一种情况，如一个民族可以选出一个国王，但它自己可以先保留一部分权利，而把剩下的权利交给国王。这并不是我们先前说的那种国王被某种契约约束的情况，而是权利被分割后的情况，就像我们刚才说的那样。也不是说，一个天生自由的民族给国王制定一些永久的准则，或者在契约中加入一些内容，以使强迫和惩罚国王变得合理。因为国王的行动就是准则，但也不总是只有国王才强迫别人。因为根据自然法，债权人也可以强迫债务人还债。但臣民是不应该强迫别人的，况且这样的还会引起权利的分割，进而会导致主权的分割。"他补充道："许多人对这种模棱两可的主权观感到无所适从。但在政治领域没有哪种东西能让人完全觉得合适。"①

很显然格劳修斯开始是对主权的可分性产生怀疑，但最后他不得不悲哀地承认主权是可分的。从这个角度来看，这个国际法之父也可以称得上是主权的多元主义理论之父。由格劳修斯所提出的观点在那个世纪并没有随着其论文的问世而大行其道。原因似乎很简单，因为当时国家主义的理论是正处于低谷，而君主的权力又处于顶峰。法国的君主可以向世界宣称"朕即国家"。詹姆斯一世的话——"国王就等于神，因为他们在世俗世界中代行神权"——有许多狂热的支

---

① Grotius, *De Jure Belli ac Pacis*, 第 1 册, 第 3 章, 第 17 节。也可参见第 20 节。这里使用的是英文译本, 参见 Coker 的 *Readings in Political Philosophy*, 275 页。

持者。菲尔默（Filmer）和霍布斯没有全部举出这类例子。

但是在1787年宪法之下建立起来的美国把主权观念的历史带入一个新的时代。1787年宪法的大多数制订者都相信主权是可分的，在美国的国体下，主权可以在州和联邦之间分离。这种观念尤其被美国建立初期的政治家和学者所广泛接受。

美国的理论或者说主权可分论，由托克维尔在他的著名的《论美国的民主》中大力提倡，已经被许多欧洲政治家和学者用来解释瑞士和德国联邦中主权的地位。多元主义理论被欧洲学者所拥护的显著特征是主权可以在程度上受到限制，而不是在内容上。他们认为联邦的成员在其自身的范围内是主权者，联邦也是如此。他们是想说联邦的主权比联邦成员国的主权在程度上要大，但在内容上两者是一样的。基尔克教授正是紧扣这一点，并将它扩大为另一种形式。而这种形式又被其他学者所认同。这些学者我们已经在前面的章节中研究过。

一般说来，那些认为在一个联邦国家中的主权是可以分离的人，是从主权的对外和对内两个方面来谈主权的。他们坚持认为尽管州加入联邦后失去了对外主权，但对内主权却没有失去。这样一来联邦在国际事务中是主权者，而州在国内事务或地方事务中也是主权者。

这种被用来论述联邦国家的观点为国际法学家和论述国际关系的学者所接受。由于主权理论在国际关系中的应用，远比在联邦国家中的运用要复杂，多元主义理论发展为不同的形式。除了对内和对外主权的观点之外，还有与之相关联但又绝对不同的部分主权观念。因为，正如前文所述，尽管所有拥有对内主权的州是部分主权的州，但不是所有部分主权的州仅仅拥有对内主权。所谓的双重主权、对主权的限制、对主权的侵犯、对主权的藐视，尽管不表明"主权"这个词在其严格意义上是分离的，但也距此不远了。

跟主权在联邦国家和在国际关系中可以分离的理论并存的是主权可以在许多形式的国家的政府系统中分成不同的部分的理论。它们可以称为立法、行政和司法主权，因为政府有立法、行政和司法三个分支机构。每一个在其自身的范围内都是主权者。最为清楚地表述这种观点的是亚历山大·汉密尔顿。汉密尔顿用来支持它的历史证据是古罗马共和国的政府系统。这种观点在20世纪初萨尔蒙德教授的著作中得到了充分的发展。

许多思想家认为主权可以在一个国家中被分成几部分，无论它是联邦国家还是邦联。由此可见，他们认为主权对国家很重要。只有国家，他们说，可以拥有主权，是主权使得国家成其为国家。与此相反，正如前面指出的，一群德国学者认为对国家而言最重要的是权利而不是主权。联邦中的州，虽然作为联邦中的成员而失去了它们的主权，但仍然保持着国家的特征，因此仍然应当被看作是国家。

似乎这种观点是在调和那些主张联邦主权论和拥护州主权论的人之间的矛

盾，同时也避免了被指为主权可分论。他们不愿承认主权在州与联邦之间可以分离，但他们也不准备把联邦中的州与法国的省和英国的郡相提并论。

由于从不同的角度进行研究，在基尔克教授的著作中，主权的多元主义的理论和主权不是一个国家的本质特征的观点被有意无意地融合到了一起。他首先否定了团体的法人拟制理论。基尔克教授说，团体的存在方式和国家的存在方式一样。它的形成方式同国家也是一样的。它有它自己的意志和人格，它有在内容上与国家一样的内在权力。这样主权不是只是国家拥有的东西，因为它也可以为自身具有人格和意志的组织所拥有。由于在国家范围内有许多有组织的团体可以拥有它，因此主权在事实上就是分离的，也是可以分离的。

基尔克教授的观点被梅特兰教授介绍到英语国家后，被许多学者从不同的角度加以发展。其中，菲吉斯教授和巴克先生无疑是最为令人瞩目的。也正是在这些著作中，拉斯基找到了他的灵感的源泉。拉斯基对不同国家的众多学者都表示了感谢。在他的《主权问题》的前言中，我们读道："我说不清我借鉴了梅特兰、萨雷利斯（Saleilles）、菲吉斯多少；但是如果读者在看了我的书以后，会再想去看他们（特别是梅特兰）的书，我会感到欣慰。我从我的朋友和同事们的工作中借鉴了很多东西。我从 C. H. 麦韦恩（C. H. McIlwain）的《英国议会及其无上权威》（*The High Court of Parliament and Its Supremacy*）那里获得了一整套有价值的观念。我没有（我希望如此）错过从霍姆斯法官那里学习宪法观念。是从费舍尔（Fisher）先生那里我第一次理解了个人的价值，是从巴克那里我第一次理解了团体的意义。"

在他的《现代国家的权威》的前言中，他写道："在那些逝者中，我最想强调的是我从阿克顿和梅特兰那里学得了很多；他们的著作是我的灵感的丰富宝库。在活着的人中，我欠波尔多的狄骥教授、菲吉斯教授最多，还有戴雪教授，正因为我和他站在不同的立场。我的老导师，新学院（New College）的欧内斯特·巴克（Ernest Barker）先生无疑是我的这本早期著作的无意的担保人……我的同事，庞德（Pound）院长和麦韦恩教授，不断给我鼓励；正是从庞德教授的文集中，我认识到了国家功能观这一实用主义理论的价值。我的新共和的朋友们，特别是弗朗西斯·哈克特（Francis Hackett）先生和赫伯特·克劳利（Herbert Croly）先生，给了我很大的帮助。格拉汉姆·沃拉斯（Graham Wallas）先生给我提出了许多好的建议；而且我还发现他的《伟大社会》对许多研究都有很有价值的指导作用。《伦敦时报》的一个不知名批评家所作的许多评论都很精彩，我从中获益匪浅。"

我们在他的《主权的基础》一文中再次看到，"我深信，任何对目前学科的重建都离不开历史知识的深厚积淀。因此我们不应该仅仅知道梅特兰、基尔克、菲吉斯和霍姆斯法官这些人的名字，还应该了解他们的实际文本。在议会运动中,埃德蒙德·柏克(Edmund Burke)的伟大抱负;宪章运动中的斗争,美国联邦党人的早期历史。我们从加利福尼亚州的约翰·泰勒(John Taylor)身上发现的线索并不比在汉密尔顿这样的大思想家那里获得的少。这并不是说当今的社会科学缺乏建树。在法律领域有庞德和狄骥;在经济学领域有悉尼·韦伯夫妇的伟大理想;在历史学领域有 R. H. 托尼(R. H. Tawney)、霍维尔(Hovell)和哈蒙德(Hammond)夫妇的作品;在管理学领域有格拉汉姆·沃拉斯(Graham Wallas)先生的著作和霍尔丹(Haldane)爵士的评论;在政治学教育学领域,有 F. D. H. 柯尔(F. D. H. Cole)的建议,也许这样说过于笼统。所有这些,总括起来,都是下一个时代将要出现的思潮的标志,它的影响不比一个世纪以前功利主义者的著作所产生的影响小"。

最后,在他的新书即《政治典范》中,他说道:"我的著作的完成获得了朋友们的大力帮助。在我的同事中,L. T. 霍布豪斯(L. T. Hobhouse)和格拉汉姆·沃拉斯教授、塔维尼先生的著作让我获益良多并且他们也给我提供了极大的便利,所有这些帮助都让我获益匪浅;其他人,我特别要感谢哈达尼公爵、霍姆斯法官、约瑟夫·雷德利克(Josef Redlich)博士、菲利克斯·弗兰克福特(Felix Frankfurter)和庞德教授。"

我在这里随便引用这些段落,部分是因为这些引文中被拉斯基所提到的学者,都或多或少地对他产生过影响,可以说是他的思想的来源,部分是因为这里所提到的许多学者的理论前面没有并且后面也不会出现在本书中,尽管他们的主权概念的重要性绝不比我们已经讨论的那些学者的主权概念的重要性小。

2. 著作

我所能找到的拉斯基的第一篇关于主权问题的文章,题为《国家的人格》,它发表在 1915 年 7 月的杂志《国家》上。在这篇文章里提出的观点可以看作是拉斯基的主要思想。他强烈反对主权的一元主义和团体的法人拟制理论。另一方面,他跟随威廉姆·詹姆斯(William James)的多元主义理论和由基尔克教授和他的继承者提出的理论。他的出版于 1917 年的《主权问题研究》,由多篇文章组成。第一篇论文为《国家的主权》。该文在 1915 年 11 月 27 日在哥伦比亚大学举行的第四次法律与社会哲学会议上宣读。在这篇文章中,他主要重述了同上面所提到的文章的观念。接下来的四篇文章都是研究性的,也是菲吉斯教授在他的《现代国家的教会》中所极力推荐的——《1843 年苏格兰教会的混乱》《牛津运动》《英国的教会复兴》《法国大革命之后的法国》,对于后者,德梅思特尔(de Maistre)也是最引人注目的支持者。两篇附录分别为《主权与联邦主义》和《主权与中央化》,在其中,拉斯基提出了主权在本质上是联邦的,并且否认奥斯丁的理论能在像美国那样的联邦国家那里有容身之地。

另一本论文集,题为《现代国家的权威》,面世于 1919 年。这本书,用拉斯基自己的话说,"覆盖了很广的范围,它的主旨是坚持认为主权仅仅是权威的一个特例,这其中隐含了我认为的解决这个问题的主要方法"。第一篇文章的标题就是书名,发展了他的主权论点。对伯纳德(Bonald)、拉美奈斯(Lamennais)和罗亚尔-克劳德(Royer-Collard)的研究是他和德梅斯特尔早期对宗教历史的研究的继续。最后一篇文章为《法国的管理工团主义》,此时进入一个新的研究领域。他倾向于认为发动公务员(functionaire)运动以组织联合企业来反对国家的不受限制的权威是合理的。

第三本书是《主权的基础》,由许多论文组成,这些论文正如他在前言中所说的,"我希望是国家的整体重建的脚手架的一部分",通过这个脚手架,我们最终将会实现对国家的伟大重建。第四本著作题为《政治典范》,他评论说,"这一本更为精妙和全面,因为它试图勾勒出这一理论的全貌,这正是我的研究所迫切需要的"①。

对拉斯基的著作做一个鸟瞰就可以看出他的早期著作主要是破坏性的和批评性的,他最近的著作是建设性的。他主要是从巴克先生那里获得灵感,但是他的理论成型主要得益于菲吉斯教授。最近他好像受到一些社会主义者的影响,这些社会主义者主要企图对社会进行经济重建。简言之,可以说拉斯基用与宗教有关的证据来打击利维坦,他的理论体系还是建立在经济基础之上的。

3. 各种多元理论的结合

正如我们指出的那样,由于拉斯基的著作受到许多学者的影响,因而被看作是多位学者的多元主义理论的糅合。他的观点与那些认为在联邦制国家中主权是分散的学者相同。在谈到美国的主权时,他说道:"如果奥斯丁对美国宪法详加研究,无疑他就会强烈反对这种宪法,无论是在理论上,还是在实践上。除非他承认主权的合法存在……否则我们便不会知道谁是统治者。当然,总统也没有绝对的权力,议会和最高法院也没有不受限制的权力。但是,如果我们再继续混淆本就容易混淆的概念,就会导致否认国家所独有的这种不易说清的主权权利。"②

他与那些我们在讨论主权与国际关系时提到的学者在根本上持相同的观点。在国际上,他宣布,独立主权国家的观念对人类是非常重要的。"国家的日常生活,"他写道,"与国家间的协定息息相关。因此,国际政府在国家的所有行动规划中都起至关重要的作用。国际政府意味着将国家都置于一个权威的控制之下。在这里每个国家都有发言权,但单个国家的意见并不是做出决议的根据。"③

至于主权与法律之间的关系,他同那些反对奥斯丁的观点的人站在同一立场。他尤其受诸如庞德、霍姆斯、狄骥、克劳勃等的影响。像庞德一样,他持法

---

① *A Grammar of Politics*,前言。
② *Studies in the Problem of Sovereignty*,267 页。参见 *A Grammar of Politics*,270 页以下。
③ *A Grammar of Politics*,65 页。也可参见第 6 章。

律实用主义的理论。① 受霍姆斯的影响，他宣称法律是完全得自经验的。② 在某种程度上他同克拉勃一样，坚持认为法律本身是最高的权威。③ 他也同狄骥有同样的主张，认为法律与其说是主权的法律，不如说是公共服务的法律。④ 他宣称："我们认为法律实际上不是国家的意志，国家的意志反而是从法律中派生出来的，无论具有何种道德力量的法律都可以派生出国家意志。很明显，这就避免了定义的简单化。理所当然地，服从的基础存在于社会组织中的各种复杂的现实中，而不仅仅存在于一个组织的现实中。通过愿意将自己限制在某种行为规则中，国家立即成了法律的主人，又成了法律的仆人。由此立即否定了国家主权及其更为精妙的理论。这种理论坚持认为，法律的重要性不是体现在它的命令上，而是体现在这种命令所要达到的目的和达到目的的手段上。它认为国家不是一个主权高高在上的金字塔，而是一种由相互协作的利益团体的组成的系统，而每个利益团体都能在其中实现自己的利益。每个利益团体都将它们自身的道德权利赋予了法律。也就是说，是我们自己的切身经历产生了法律，而不是说，法律本身是独立于我们而客观存在的。几乎不能（根据它出现的频率）来对这些经历进行分类，因为是许多人的经历合在一起才能对社会产生作用。它似乎就是寻求实现目的的手段。它尽力使法律能尽可能地体现自己的需求。它以自己的利益是否被满足来判断法律的好坏。它同样也需要一个能实现它的目标的社会体系，因此在这个社会中也能体现出权利观念的重要性。这就使得法律成为了实现自己的需求的途径。并且，人们在满足自己的需求的同时，也有义务将别人的需求与自己的需求一视同仁。法律也就可以体现出利益的大小和不同利益的混合程度。它是社会整体的工具，而不仅是其中某个方面的工具。它能满足整体社会需求的程度的大小决定了它的权力的大小。"⑤ 熟悉所谓的社会学派法律理论的人不难看出这段话的来源。

现在看来法律不是主权的命令。他在另一个地方说道："奥斯丁所作的所有寻找主权者的努力都将是徒劳的。因为他认为主权者拥有的能力在实际中并不存在。它把一个很重要的词的含义缩小了。而如果坚持这样的话，会对社会造成致命的危害。在政治学中，法律毫无疑问会被认为是国家生活中的重要方面。但是也必须时刻认识到，达到法律本质的方法本身既可能是类似于孟德斯鸠提出的方法，也很可能是那种错误性大于正确性的方法。对政治学者来说，法律建立在整个社会环境之上。它体现了在某些特定时期中，哪些是一个国家必要的社会关

---

① 参见 *Problem of Sovereignty*，64 页。也可参见 *Authority in the Modern State*，前言。
② *A Grammar of Politics*，278 页。
③ 参见 *A Grammar of Politics*，386 页以下。
④ *A Grammar of Politics*，27 页。
⑤ *A Grammar of Politics*，286～287 页。

系。从政治意义上来说,颁布法律的机构的重要性不比使其运作的权力机构的重要性小。"①

很明显,奥斯丁所说的主权根本就不存在。② 所谓的法律主权实际上是毫无意义的。有人指出拉斯基承认法律主权的无上权威,因为他说过:"从法律的角度来说,没人可以否认在每个国家中都有拥有不受限制的权威的机构。"这样的批评实际上有失公允,因为拉斯基在这句话之后,立即补充道:"但是这种法律仅仅是一种逻辑的虚构。"③ 在英国,主权在国王和议会的手里。但是国王和议会能为所欲为吗?拉斯基说不能。拉斯基阐述道,如果英国议会立法禁止英国人成为罗马天主教徒,则一定会失败,④ 因为"主权者不可能在什么方面都拥有不受限制的权威;对无限权威的追求往往会导致限制权威的机制的建立。即便土耳其的苏丹在他权力鼎盛的时候,自身也受到传统法典的限制,他不得不服从它们。在法律上,他可以使社会生活的各个层面改变;但在实际上,他必须放弃追求奥斯丁所主张的那种主权权力,才能生存下去"⑤。

拉斯基否认法律主权理论的有效性,他也认为戴雪教授所提出的区分法律主权和政治主权的方法是不令人满意的。做这种区分,"清楚表明了主权是分离的观点,这与原来的定义是背道而驰的"⑥。同样,奥斯丁所认为的英国的主权在选民那里的观点也是不能被接受的。"因为首先君主和上议院并不是公众的代表,这是明白无误的,当他进一步论证选民可以将自己的权力无条件地委托给代理人的时候,他忘记了这个定义暗含的不可能让渡的含义。如果选民仅仅创造出一种联合体,后者就不是一个主权实体。如果它创造一个主权实体,从奥斯丁的理论的角度来定义这个词,它自身就不再是一个主权者了。"⑦

很明显,在拉斯基看来,主权观念的实际内容比法学家所认为的要多得多;拉斯基对此深信不疑。⑧ 那么,在拉斯基看来,主权的含义是什么?下面的话就是答案,这即使不是整个拉斯基理论中的唯一最重要的观点,也是最重要的观点之一。他宣称:"主权的真正含义不是体现在它拥有的强制权力,而是在于它所代表的美好意志。人们接受它的命令,既因为他们自身的意志在那里部分地得到了表达,又因为他们认为它的意图是良好的,他们甘愿被它驱驰。于是很显然,法律不是命令。它仅仅是方便生活的规则。它的善存在于其结果中。它必须自己

---

① *A Grammar of Politics*,55 页。
② *The Nations*,第 101 卷,116 页,1915。
③ *Foundations of Sovereignty*,236 页。
④ *Problem of Sovereignty*,12 页。
⑤ *A Grammar of Politics*,51 页。
⑥ *A Grammar of Politics*,54 页。
⑦ *A Grammar of Politics*,54 页。
⑧ *Problem of Sovereignty*,16 页。

去证明。那种认为议会从某种特殊意义上来看是全能的观点是不明智的。议会行使的权力不是法律赋予的，而是由决议产生的。但就像一些著名的事件显示的那样，决议往往易于被搁置……当主权占据优势时，国家就会依照人们的决议行事。"①

最终的主权依赖于个体的承认，个体在何种程度上同意服从和认可它，它就在何种程度上是主权者，这可以说是拉斯基理论的主题。因为"主权仅仅是我们给予一个特殊的意志的名称，它可以为了实现自己的目的而运用不同寻常的力量"②。个体在任何时候任何地方都是社会行为的关键。③ 个体是其自身的目的，它不仅仅是达到某种目的的手段。如果个体被认为是目的，则所有社会组织都是手段。国家不是目的。他宣称："国家以其所拥有的权利而被认识。我们判断它的特征的方法首先在于看它对人类幸福的实质贡献。"④ 由于坚持认为个体的幸福是社会组织的目标，拉斯基把他的理论奠定在功利主义的基础之上。"也就是说，个体是社会的中心。否则，在如此广大的世界里，他的呼吁可能被完全忽略。起码从哲学解释的角度来看，国家的起源是为了个体的幸福；因为如果好的生活不能给男女大众带来幸福，它就是没有意义的。因此，我们判断它的作用的大小应该依据人们所得幸福的多少。"⑤

为获得个体的幸福，个体必须有权利得到他认为对他的幸福至关重要的东西。言论自由、基本工资、充分教育、适当的闲适、结社权力，都是作为一个国家成员的个体的主要权利。这些权利不是由国家派生的，而是他们内在的权利。"它们是自然权利，没有它们，国家的目的就不能被实现。它们的合法存在不需要依赖国家。它们是人类永恒的内在价值。如果它们被剥夺了，人们对国家的忠诚就会被毁坏。这些权利对自由而言是必须的，因为没有它们，人们就会犹如身处无法理解的境地，感到茫然不知所措。我们把它们放在国家权力之外；这又意味着对国家主权的限制。"⑥ 也许有人说这种理论赞同无政府状态；但是不公比无政府状态更甚。

个体是社会行为的中心，主权必须奠定在个体的意志之上。为了弄清楚主权是否能够分离，我们首先必须弄清楚意志是否能够分离。这里我们就来讨论拉斯基的多元主义的哲学基础。

在他的《多元的宇宙》中，詹姆斯宣称："用实用主义的观点来解释的多元论的意思是：现实世界的所有组成部分都是通以各种各样的方式与其他部分进行

---

① *Problem of Sovereignty*，12～13 页。
② *Foundations of Sovereignty*，210 页。
③ *A Grammar of Politics*，259 页。
④ *A Grammar of Politics*，89 页。
⑤ *Authority in Modern State*，120 页。
⑥ *Foundations of Sovereignty*，246 页。

外部联系。你能想到的每一事物,不管多么硕大或者无所不包,根据多元论的看法,都有某一种类或者某种程度的真正'外在'的环境。事物都是以诸多方式相互'关联',但是没有任何一个事物包括每个事物,或者统率每个事物。'以及'这个词跟在每个句子的后面。总归有些东西遗漏掉。要想说在宇宙里的任何地方有这种无所不包这种状态,就不得不说成是'任何时候都不十分'。多元论的世界就这样更像一个联邦共和国,而不大像一个帝国或者王国。不管能集合到一起事物是多么的多,不管聚集在意识或者行动的有效中心里的是多么的多,仍会有其他的事物是自主的,没有收集进去的,没有归于一统。"①

读了拉斯基著作的人,会非常容易地发现他受这段话的影响多大。因为他同詹姆斯一样相信,宇宙在本质上是多元的。他拒绝这样的一元主义的观点:"一"先于"多"出现,所有的"多"都来源于"一",并终将归于"一",因此,所有的事务都包含有"多元"和"整体"的特征,只有在"一"控制"多",指导"多",去达到终极目标的条件下"多"的目标才能实现。他宣称:"不能因为国家比它的部分更具整体性而说国家的部分是源自国家,多是源自"一";相反,我认为部分和整体一样真实存在。我在知道纽约和奥尔巴尼(Albany)之前,不知道美国。是由纽约和奥尔巴尼,我才知道了美国。当然,我由纽约和奥尔巴尼知道了美国,只因为它们之间有逻辑的联系。"

对拉斯基而言,多元主义几乎就是实用主义,多元主义不仅是一个事实,它也是一种不断发展的理论。"发展来自多样性的选择,而不是来自对同一性的保留。"为了更清楚地表明一元主义和多元主义之间的不同,让我们来读读这段话:"我们从研究各种各样的冲动入手,它们都是为了追求个人价值的实现。我发现像我国这样的国家只能满足相对少数人的追求……这样就会导致社会中随处可见的压制和相伴而来的是非颠倒。多元主义国家就会从人民的需求出发,用更好的方法来满足人们的追求。在单一国家里,最受重视的是权威,不同意政府的观念就是错误的。多元主义国家通过分散权威来保证自由,这样个人的那种在只有单一的生活方式的社会中不能被满足的需求就能得到实现。总之,单一国家用武力压制人民的意志,而多元主义国家会尽力给人们提供合理的途径去实现自己的个人价值。当然,我们必须仔细研究历史,来发现究竟哪种途径更先进。在社会生活中,我们不可能就任何问题达成完全一致,但是,只要一个法律在少数服从多数的原则下被通过,我们就要将其付诸实施。当然,它会妨碍少数人的利益,但这并不是我们想看到的。也就是说,我们在不断为政治行动寻找合适的实施途径。这些途径不会对个人价值的实现产生压力。并且,有些因素——宗教、职业、政治——作为个人价值的外在表现,其方式是多种多样的。多元主义国家是

---

① James, *A Pluralistic Universe*, 321～322 页。

从结构上解决问题。它不会对任何一个人特别关照,因为它不能在不了解人的行动背景的情况下,给人以优先关注。你也可以说,它否定古典意义上的主权观念,因为这种主权观念明显是提高了一部分人的地位,而让其他人不得不接受一个让人难受的命令。也可以说它毁灭了主权国家,以保证个人价值的实现。"①

这样,在一个多元化的国家里面,古典的主权理论就没有容身之地。主权,正如已经注意到的,必须建立在个体的意志基础之上。由于宇宙是多元的,那么意志也应该是多元的。"因为每一种政治哲学的出发点是人类意志的不可避免的多样性,在它们之间没有连续性……所有的意志会聚集到一个共同的目的上;但是它们在其他所有事情上都是分散的,除非这个事情是许多人都想要做的。"

这种理论很自然地反对卢梭的公意。拉斯基说:"如果意志分散地存在于社会中的每一个个人中,则很明显它不能组成一个单一的共同的意志。其实你要研究现代社会的特征的话,你就会发现它的显著特征就是意志多样性的存在。这种多样性不会产生一个导致其认同的共同的目的。"②

一个人可以向国家屈从他的意志,但他也可以向教会或其他组织屈从其意志,如果他也是它们中的一个成员的话。如果国家宣称对他拥有主权,因为他的意志屈从于它,为什么教会不可以?"在其实施上,主权是意志的行为。在这种意志的背后是保证它实现的权力。现在如果还要强调说某个团体,比如国家能从理论上保证所有人都服从它的行动,是没有价值的,因为我知道在现实中这种做法应该被抛弃。很明显国家的主权和教会、贸易组织的主权没有什么区别。"③

如果个体的意志没有形成一个整体,如果他的意志没有统一并不妨碍个体成为个体,则教会或贸易组织的人格同个体的人格一样真实,尽管教会或贸易组织的意志没有形成一个整体。团体的人格和国家的人格是一样的,因为它们采用同一种方式,具有同样的基础,但是它们彼此互不依赖。"因为一个群体和个体与其他群体和个人相联系,因而它就不被迫与政治体的其他部分相联系。"④ "当一个贸易组织因为其成员拒绝扮演一种政治角色而将其逐出之后,并不因此而和摩门教(Mormon Church)有了什么关系。这样的贸易组织与摩门教没有什么关系;它是自足的。它可以和国家一起运行,但它不必然要这样做。它可以和国家有联系,但这是'跟'而不是'属于'。国家,再次在詹姆斯的意义上使用,是'分散的',而不是'集中的'。那里没有本质的联系。"⑤

我们必须使诸如国家这样的组织人格化,因为人是组织的动物。在人类活动

---

① 参见 *New Republic*,第19卷,148~150页,1919。
② *New Republic*,第19卷,32页,1919。
③ *Problems of Sovereignty*,270页。
④ *Problems of Sovereignty*,10页。
⑤ *Problems of Sovereignty*,10页。也可参见 *Authority in Modern State*,26~27页。

的每一个方面,都存在各种各样的组织。每一个组织都有它自身的目的,以此与其他的组织区分开来,它的目的决定它的人格。他这样写道:"当我们把那些有相同观念和共同目的的人们划归为一些团体的时候,我们可以把它们看作一个整体,一个人。或者复杂一点说,是一种居于其成员之上的人。这个人对我们来说是真实存在的;因为当我们假定它是真实的,这种假定就会自然地显现出生活中的具体不同。"① 这样一个人格化的团体是绝对的自控的实体。它有其自己的政府或机器去实现其复杂的意志。我们随处都能发现团体的主权在挑战国家的权威。简单地说,拉斯基在这里所坚持的就是巴克所称的"多头政治主义(polyarchism)"。② 一个团体可以与国家有关联,但是这并不意味着它必须与国家有关联;因为如果它的形成就与国家没有关联,那么它将独立于国家而存在。它的部分或许在国家之内,但不是所有都在国家之内,因为它有自身的利益、自身的目的和自身的意志,而这些与国家的是不同的。

那么国家的地位是什么?拉斯基说,国家就是一个公共服务团体。"它与其他组织不同,因为第一,加入它是强制性的。第二,它在本质上有限定的统治区域。人们作为消费者利益是息息相关的;在任何地方,它们都需要最大限度地得到满足。并且,在某种程度上,它的成员的利益也是相同的。因为他们都有吃、穿、住、受教育等基本需求。而国家正是这样一个满足这些需求的机构。它维护消费者的利益。在国家面前,所有人都是一样的。他们不再是大律师、矿主,不再是天主教徒和新教徒,也不再是雇主和工人。从社会学理论来说,他们仅仅是需要他们本身不能生产的服务的人。"③

拉斯基还补充道:"很清楚,这种功能,对其他功能具有优先地位。国家管理人的基本生活层面。用管理的术语来讲,一个政府的行为由其成员的共同需要决定。为了满足这些共同需要,它就必须在一定程度上控制其他组织,来保证它们能提供产品满足这些需要。更具体地说这些功能——例如教育,或燃料供应——关系到国家生活的命脉,更应该被控制。也就是说,每一种功能的发挥,都必须以消费者的利益为出发点,以保证人民能享受充分的文明生活。因此就有了为保证人的全面发展而对工作时间的限制,为保障人民的公民权利而涵盖所有人的最低工资保障。国家直接或间接地发挥着管理作用,以保证社会整体的利益被满足。"④

拉斯基的国家是消费者的国家。一个人作为一个艺术家,他的利益与农民或法学家的利益当然会不同;但是,当他作为一个消费者时,前者的利益与后两者

---

① 参见 *The Nations*,第 101 卷,115 页。
② 参见 *Foundations of Sovereignty*,169 页。
③ *A Grammar of Politics*,69~70 页。
④ *A Grammar of Politics*,69~70 页。

的利益基本上是一样的。因为一个艺术家同一个农民一样需要食物、衣服。既然每一个人都是消费者，在某个特定的区域内的所有人都有大致相同的利益。并且人们做工或经商仅仅是保证他的消费目的得以实现的手段。他工作，不是因为他想成为一个工人，而是因为他意识到如果他不工作，他就会遭受饥饿、寒冷，诸如此类。每个人都在寻找幸福；一个人在消费时比在工作时会得到更多的幸福。国家的本质体现在它保护人民的消费利益，因为，现实中，很有必要去保证人民消费他们自身不能提供的服务的权益。但是，研究到此就可以打住了，因为没有生产，就没有享受。

要保护消费者的利益，就需要有一定程度的管理和控制的权力为前提。既然消费者的利益是最重要的，以保护这些利益为目标的机构就需要比其他组织高的权力。这样我们就发现拉斯基认为国家就是利益的联合体。他否认主权是不可分的和绝对的古典主权概念，但是拉斯基也并不认为在国家里面所有的主权都是平等的。因为他认为，国家代表一般利益，一般利益应当比个别利益具有优先性。于是，主权被认为是联邦的①，联邦主义就是多元主义。

很显然代表一般利益的国家是一个协作体。但是拉斯基的协作体与基尔特社会主义者所提出的协作体是不同的。后者，正如我们已经在讨论柯尔的理论的时候就已经指出的，是组织的组织，也就是职能组织的代表机构，但与此相反，拉斯基的观点是一个协作体直接对个体负责，而没有中间的环节。原因很明显，拉斯基更是一个个人主义者，他不希望看见一个协作体离个体的控制太远。②

二、其他学者

说有多少学者就有多少理论也许是不完全正确的，但是如果读过近来的一些著作的人不难意识到学者们的学术理论之丰富。关于主权的理论也是如此。讨论所有的学者的主权理论是不可能的。我们在这里仅简要列举不同国家的同拉斯基先生的思想比较类似的学者。

首先，英国学者中，我们发现格拉汉姆·沃拉斯教授，他多次为拉斯基教授所称赞。沃拉斯教授的理论起点是心理分析。他坚持认为政治不仅仅是有意识的理性的产物，而且大部分是下意识的进程、习惯和直觉的事物，是建议和模仿的产物。并且，在政治领域里面，没有实体存在③，从众多意志中产生公意也是不可能的。可以有一个组织的意志，但是"组织的意志只能在具有必要的社会机构的

---

① *A Grammar of Politics*，特别是第七章。
② *A Grammar of Politics*，72 页以下。
③ Wallas, *Human Nature in Politics*，第 1 部分，第 4 章。

社群中存在"①。我们的时代急需大社会（the Great Society）中的这种机构。他坚持认为未来意志的组织的基础应该是个人主义者、社会主义者、工团主义者所提出的主权的综合。这三者中任何单独的一个都是不充分的。因为个人主义是以财产意识为基础的，财产意识不再被认为与社会价值相协调。社会主义是对19世纪个人主义的一种反动，但是社会主义者所主张的国家对组织完善的机构而言是无效的。工团主义好像是对极端的个人主义和社会主义的调和，然而在实践中，如果我们仅仅根据工团主义的框架，完善的意愿组织（Will-Organization）就不能得到。于是，这三者的综合是必要的。只有通过这种综合，个人财产的意识、整个社会的福利、各行各业的利益才能得以完全维护。② 这种主张的意愿组织毫无疑问对议会制带有敌意，对议会政府的批评也正是沃拉斯理论的关键。表面上看，沃拉斯教授不是在反对主权的战役中的战士，但正是他给在前线的人制造炮弹。

另一个以心理学作起点的思想家是罗素。罗素认为人类的行动不是受理性所决定的，而是受冲动所决定的。有两类冲动：一类是创造性的；一类是占有性的。前者倾向于寻求知识和艺术，而后者倾向于对外部事物的获得。"占有意味着保存某种好的东西以防止其他人享受；创造意味着把一种好的东西公之于众，否则没有人能够享受它。"③

"国家和财产是最大的可以占有的两种东西；正因如此，它们是反生命的，它们往往意味着战争。"④ "国家危害的主要来源是它将权力作为自己的主要目的。"⑤ 在目前，国家的权力受到两方面的限制：一类是内部的；一类是外部的。内部的，是担心受到反抗；外部的，是担心被别国打败。尽管有这两种限制，国家的权力仍然是绝对的。⑥ "国家的过分权力部分体现在对内镇压，但主要的是体现在战争和以战争相威胁，这也是现代世界悲剧的最为主要的原因之一。"⑦

由此认识到只要存在许多主权国家，每个国家都有自己的陆军和海军，战争就不会结束，灾难就不可避免。这样罗素设想了一个世界国家，只有它才能有陆军和海军。因此他写道："在世界上只有一个陆军和海军的时候，战争才能结束。这意味着，只要考虑到国家的军事功能，世界上最终就只存在一个国家。"⑧

另一方面，公民事务也可以由国家来执行。既然公民事务与军事事务是不同

---

① Wallas, *The Great Society*, 7 页, 也可参见 287 页。
② Wallas, *The Great Society*, 第 2 部分, 第 7 章。也可参见他的 *Our Social Heritage*, 1921。
③ Russell, *Principle of Social Reconstruction*, 63 页。
④ Russell, *Principle of Social Reconstruction*, 63 页。
⑤ Russell, *Principle of Social Reconstruction*, 63 页。
⑥ Russell, *Principle of Social Reconstruction*, 64 页。
⑦ Russell, *Principle of Social Reconstruction*, 65 页。
⑧ Russell, *Principle of Social Reconstruction*, 101 页。

的,"这两种不同的功能没有理由都必须由同一个国家来执行"①。在我们的时代,大国在实行公共管理上而言过于庞大。相反,在寻求军事目的上却显得太小,因为它们不是世界范围的。

但是如果许多功能都给予国家,个人自由就会受到侵害。罗素是个人自由的辩护士。为了保护个人自由,根据他的看法,权力和功能要扩大,而不是缩小。他宣称:"有一个方法可以使组织和自由结合起来,这就是保证那些人们自愿加入的团体的权力,他们加入这样的组织因为他们认为这可以帮助他们实现他们认为重要的目的,而不是为了实现别人强加给他们的任务。"②他继续说:"国家,是一个地域组织,不可能成为一个彻底的志愿组织(voluntary organization)。但是正因如此,为了限制它的权力的滥用,必须要有强有力的公共舆论监督。这种公共舆论,在多数情况下,只有由那些有某种相同利益或愿望的人们联合起来才可能得到保证。"③

因此,在一定意义上,罗素是个人主义者、世界主义者和群体主义者。说他是个人主义者,是因为他趋向于限制(如果不是完全否认的话)国家的权力。为了达到这一点,他主张对内,权力应该被分配给志愿组织;对外,应该有一个世界国家,只有它拥有限制国家进攻的武力。④

其他的学者如霍尔丹(R. P. Haldane)坚持认为在英帝国没有不可分的和绝对的主权,因为英联邦的自治领不在英国的议会的绝对控制之下。像拉斯基一样,他认为甚至在英国本土,议会的最高权力也不是绝对的,因为实际上,它有许多事情不能做。但是霍尔丹不是极端的多元主义者。根据他的看法,多元主义和一元主义都是矛盾的,因为"在每一个国家的省里面,主权都可以是多方面的;也就是说,公意自身可以在公共生活的不同领域分别得到实现"⑤。

在美国,像吉丁斯(Giddings)教授一样的思想家从社会学的立场出发,反对古典主权理论。他坚持认为不是政治理论家,而是社会学家对决定主权的实际运作的条件有整体研究和彻底理解。⑥ 根据他的看法,"主权不是,也从来不能是'一个基本的、无条件的、普遍的和不可让渡的权力'"。但是他补充道:"尽管

---

① Russell, *Principle of Social Reconstruction*, 102 页。
② Russell, *Principle of Social Reconstruction*, 71 页。
③ Russell, *Principle of Social Reconstruction*, 71 页。
④ 参见他的 *Political Ideals*(1917 年);*Proposed Roads to Freedom*(1918 年);*The Practice and Theory of Bolshevism*(1920 年);*The Prospects of Industrial Civilization*。
⑤ R. P. Haldane, "The Nature of the State", *The Contemporary Review*,第 117 卷(1920 年 1—6 月),第 771 页。从经济的角度看,H. Belloc 在他的 *Servile State* 中主张一种分配主义。也可参见 R. H. Tawney, *Acquisitive Society*, 1923。
⑥ Giddings, F. H., *The Responsible State*, 45 页。参见他的"Sovereignty and Government"一文,*The Political Science Quarterly*,第 21 卷,7 页。

如此，它确实是一个非常真实和伟大的事物，因为从它的全部形式和表现来看——我们可以用这些词来定义它——它都是人类主要的权力，无论是对个人主义还是多元主义，无论是对与政治有关的人群还是无关的人群都是如此。"①

主权不是绝对的，因为它受宇宙、国际和道德的限制，也还受大众的意愿的限制。他说，主权"服从于宇宙的限制，并且主权既不能超越于宇宙的有序规律，也不能超越环境的限制。主权，正如《宣言》的口号所承认的必须服从人民的意愿。并且，它还服从于人类为它规定的特性。不仅仅是在民主国家，在所有地方，统治者和统治集团通常都由于多数的同意而存在。最后，主权还受理性法则的限制，还在道义上为全人类的知识意识负有责任"②。

根据他对主权历史的研究，他发现主权有四种类型：①个人主权；②阶级主权；③大众主权；④一般主权。这四种类型都以社会环境为存在条件，因而也是受社会环境的制约的。"在政治社会中存在着的这四种类似的主权获得了绝大多数人的服从，只有一种主权是强迫别人服从它，其他的是获得大众的有条件的服从。个人主权作为一种最古老和最普遍的主权，它不是强迫而是要求大众服从。阶级主权是通过宗教或传统对人们的情感的影响而获得，或者是依靠财富来获得，它是激发或者索取人们对它的服从。大众主权是情感稳固的大众的主权，它是一种真正的强迫人们服从的主权，在它存在的时间和影响范围内，它是不可抗拒的。一般的主权是开明人的主权，它通过才智使人们自觉去服从。"③

斯莫尔（A. W. Small）教授在1917年的一次演讲中说："如果我们不彻底把国家的观念与传统的主权观念分开的话，我们就永远不会分清是非。正是传统的主权理论导致了战争这种人类世界灾难的发生。"④

斯莫尔教授的基本理论是他的利益概念。利益被定义为："经过重新安排后实现其预定的条件。"⑤ 有六种类型的利益：健康、财富、社会能力、知识、美和正义。⑥ 每一种利益都倾向于绝对，每一个都寻求它自己的满足而不管其他的。⑦ 这样的结果便导致利益之间的相互冲突。国家的功能就是发展、满足和调节利益。他说："国家就是公民为了推进他们所意识到的所有利益而进行的合

---

① Giddings, F. H., *The Responsible State*, 47～48 页。
② Giddings, F. H., *The Responsible State*, 46～47 页。
③ Giddings, "Sovereignty and Government", *The Political Science Quarterly*, 第 21 卷，12 页。也可参见 Giddings, *Principles of Sociology*（1896 年，1909 年第 3 版），285 页、314 页；*Inductive Sociology*（1914 年），133 页以下；*Descriptive and Historial Sociology*（1906 年），332 页以下。
④ Small, "Americans and the World Crisis", *American Journal of Sociology*, 第 23 卷。
⑤ Small, *General Sociology*, 433 页。
⑥ Small, *General Sociology*, 443 页以下。
⑦ Small, *General Sociology*, 201 页。

作。"① 这样国家变成了一个道德机构。② 如果人民的利益的发展是国家的目的，则与其说国家是权力国家，不如说国家是一个责任国家。③

阿瑟·F. 本特雷（Arthur F. Bentley）和斯莫尔教授观点基本一样，他在其《政府的演进》（1908）中强调说，解读历史的一个重要因素就是团体利益的驱动。主权在现实中的作用是微不足道的。他写道："主权对国家的意义比对大众的意义更大。主权在为现政府的存在进行辩护时，起着至关重要的作用。或者还被用来以人民或其他人的名义对政府进行言语攻击，或为人们的行动提供合法的解释。但它现在已经从法律书籍和政治手册中被剔除出去了。它已经成了一种笑谈。既然我们已经有充足的论据来证明国家存在的必要性，何必再用这种虚无缥缈的证据呢。"④

赫伯特·克劳利（Herbert Croly）指出："无论是所有现代国家中的内耗还是权力国家中的不能确保被用来为大众谋利益的权力都会产生罪恶。"⑤ 他补充道："要么是我错了，要么就是国家应该允许限制并重新分配它的权威。因为这是增加福祉的一个不可缺少的条件。"⑥

沃特·李普曼和拉斯基一样，坚持认为人类的忠诚是可分的，并且也是分开着的，而不是只能由国家占有。为了满足人类的根本需求，必须建立一种新的更加有效的联邦。李普曼在多大程度上认同拉斯基的观点呢？从下面这段话中或许可以找到答案："拉斯基对现代主权的多元主义的言论是对我们的要求的精确解释。他正确地说明了我们生活的世界是怎样的，并认为政治思想应该对政治需求

---

① Small, *General Sociology*, 226 页。
② Small, *General Sociology*, 239 页。
③ Small, *General Sociology*, 240 页。也见他的 *Between Eras, from Capitalism to Democracy*（1913），也参照 E. A. Ross, *Social Control*。
④ Bentley, *Process of Government*, 264 页。在另一个地方，他写道："主权实际上仅仅是一种法律理论……我们不能认为这些理论同主权论一样无足轻重。"同上书，273 页。
⑤ Croly, "The Future of the State", *New Republic*, 第 12 卷, 176 页, 1917 年 9 月。
⑥ Croly, "The Future of the State", *New Republic*, 第 12 卷, 176 页, 1917 年 9 月。也可参见他的 *The Promise of American Life and Progressive Democracy*（1914 年）。特别是后一卷的 "Popular Sovereignty" 章。

的描述和分类给予更多的关注。"①

在法国学者中,像本瑟里曼(Berthelemy)、欧里乌(Hauriou)、坡·班库(Paul-Boncour)和莫里那瑞(de Molinari)这些人都从不同立场上批驳了传统主权观。和狄骥一样,本瑟里曼认为公共服务的观念应该取代主权的观念。因此,在他看来与其说国家的主权是一种发布命令的主观权利,不如说是一种功能。他说:"一个维护秩序的公务员不能行使主权权利。"② 但他又补充道,人们可以把这种功能看作他行使的主权权力。由此,在他看来,人们也会承认这种主权权力这样一个东西的存在。但是,我们必须记住的是,对主权而言,它本身已经不再具有这样主观的、永久的、绝对的并不受任何条件限制的权力了。

欧里乌也认为,公共服务应被看作是现代政治体系的基础。主权已不再是公法领域里的重要概念。③ 他对此这样说道:"一个国家的全部社会组织,无论是经济组织还是政治组织,都是源自众多的社会现状。它们由主权这种强制性的权力保证其稳定性……这种权力的真正功能是创造并保护国家的现状。人们往往没有

---

① Walter Lippmann, "A Clue", *New Republic*, 第 10 卷(1917 年 4 月),317 页。其他的美国学者像 McIlwain, Victor S. Yarros, Richard Roberts, 也从不同观点攻击了经典的主权理论。Laski 高度评价了 McIlwain 教授的 *High Court of Parliament and Its Supremacy*, McIlwain 教授认为英国的议会主权是机械的、虚假的、不符合自然发展规律的,一句话,它是违背历史的。*The High Court of Parliament*(1900 年),320 页。又见 *The American Revolution: A Constitutional Interpretation*,1923。

在一篇名为 "What shall we do with the State" 的文章中(*American Journal of Sociology*, 25 期, 572~583 页, 26 期, 59~72 页)Victor S. Yarros 写道:"战争导致保证。战争毫无宽容性。战争造就了国家主权。另一方面,和平、富裕、机遇、经济平等又会削弱国家。自由和富裕的人们不需要太多的管束。反对贫困、无奈的失业和无意义的痛苦,就是反对现行的国家。就业自由会为更多的政治自由开辟路径。这就是为什么明知的自由主义者并不热衷于对形而上学的国家或政治国家进行学术上的攻击。他们感兴趣的是对特殊利益和垄断的直接攻击,因为他们知道,解决了这些问题,就能消除贫困和由贫困而带来的犯罪、邪恶和腐败。一个人要争取进行经济和社会改革就应争取对个人思想的解放和对国家主权的限制。" 第 23 卷,1920—1921, 68 页。

I. A. Cornelison 和 Richard Roberts 从教会的立场攻击经典的主权论。前者认为主权理论是一种虚幻的理论。据说:"主权,只不过是一种占优势地位的权力。它存在于文明民族中,蒙着一层神秘的面纱,并受一种十分复杂和牢固的制度体系所制约。并没有一种可供王的灵魂——主权存在于其中的事先存在的东西。国家并不是永恒的观念;也不是一个自动产生的东西,像阿弗萝蒂特(Aphrodite)从海中产生一样,从土里产生出来。它存在于所有的政府之上,并将自己的所有权力赋予政府。" *The Relation of Religion to Civil Government*, 202 页, 1895。

他在他的 *The Church in the Commonwealth* 的最后写道:"因为国家主权权威的概念深深植根于世俗的法律中。国家对教会生活的干涉的要求只不过是奥斯丁的主权理论的进一步发展。除了改变国家自身的定义外,没有其他的方式能有效地将教会从国家的权威中解放出来。也许这种改变将随着英联邦内对独立的宗教团体的内在权利的承认而发生。因为这将意味着,要接受一个被削弱的、有限度的权威。这意味着主权国家的终结,这种情况将很快发生。" 102~103 页。参见 William Prall, *The State and the Church*, 1900。"没有教会,国家就会四分五裂。" 259 页。又见 R. E. Turner 的 *America in Civilization*, 第四章, 1925。

② Berthelemy, *Droit Administratif*, 41~42 页(第 10 版, 巴黎, 1923 年)。又见他在 *Revue du Droit Public*(第 32 卷, 1915 年)的文章 "Le Fondement de l'autorité Politique", 662~682 页。

③ Mauric Haurion, *Principles de Droit Public*, 第二版, 1916 年。

仔细去注意研究它的目的，因而认为它仅仅是一种命令……权力的真正功能是创造秩序和稳定……它的功能多少会奏效。当它的目的达到时，这种权力就是合法的。"①

班库从团体或组织的立场攻击传统的主权理论。他像其他团体主义者一样，认为团体是人们为了处理各种利益而应运而生的。这种团体刚开始是自发形成的，但逐渐发展成强制性的，并行使类似国家的权力的组织。既然，组织已经发展到能实现各种利益的程度，那就最好应该由国家去处理普遍利益，而把特殊利益留给组织去处理。他认为这样的话，就自然应该有团体的特殊主权和国家的普遍主权。②

莫里那瑞从个人的立场攻击传统的主权理论。他坚持认为个人的权力应该是未来社会中的政治系统的基础。他认为，个人的主权是可以被代表的，它可以由代表或直接的协定来集中实施。③ 其他的一些学者像马克西诺·乐华（Maxine Leroy）和格吉斯·卡罕（Georges Cahen）都受到了狄骥的影响，他们与后者持多少相同的立场。④

意大利学者若梅诺·德马兹鲁（Ramiro de Maezlu）尽管没有受狄骥的影响，但也和他持大致相同的观点。他认为战争是权威与自由之间的冲突。他认为，在我们的时代，自由与权威都是危害极大的。自由仅仅是个人主义的要求，而个人主义主要来自人类自私的天性。权威就是暴力的使用，而使用暴力是与道德原则是相反的。权威的历史可以被看成是灾难和血腥的历史。如果我们的社会不必建立在自由和权威基础之上，那么它的重建，应该奠基在何处？德马兹鲁认为它应奠基在功能之上。当国家和社会奠基于此的时候，国家就仅仅是一个公共服务组织了。这时我们会发现，这正是狄骥在他的著作中所强调的。他认为国家的人格并不存在，因为那仅仅是拟制的。在这一点上，他也与狄骥教授的看法一致。⑤

比利时的社会学家德格里夫（De Greef）认为正是绝对的主权的观念导致了国际的无政府状态和战争灾难。为了维持和平和秩序，应该创建一个世界联邦，并且传统的主权理论应该被废止。⑥ 德国学者佛朗兹·奥本海默（Franz

---

① Mauric Haurion, *Principles de Droit Public*，第二版，1916，78～79 页。英文翻译是 Laski 的。参见他对 Duguit 的 *Les Transformation du Droit Public* 的翻译。

② Paul-Boncour, *Le Federalisme economique*（1901）和他的 *Syndicats des Fonctionnaires*（1906）。

③ G. de Molinare, *The Society of Tomorrow*，P. H. Lee Warner 翻译，也可参见他的 *Theorie de l'évolution*（1908）。

④ M. Leroy, *Transformation de la Puissance Publique*（1907）和 M. Georgen Cahen 的 *Les Fonctionnaires*。也可参见比利时的社会学家 De Greef 的 *La Structure générale des sociétés*。

⑤ Ramiro de Maeztu, "Liberty", *Authority and Function*，英文版。也可参见 M. A. Vaccaro, *les Bases Sociologiques du Droit et de l'état*（1898）。

⑥ 参见 De Greef, *La Structure générale des sociétés*。

Oppenheimer）认为旧的国家系统正在消失,"未来的国家将成为自治的基尔特"。① 茹多夫·斯坦纳（Rudolf Steiner）,看见了现行的政治系统的缺陷,并提出社会共同体应分成三个部分,即经济系统、政治系统和精神系统。② 奥地利学者如古斯塔夫·拉岑霍费尔（Gustav Ratzenhofer）的立场处于古姆普洛维茨（Gumplowicz）和斯莫尔（Small）之间。③ 俄国学者 J. 诺维考姆（J. Novicow）认为在国际关系领域中不应再坚持绝对主权的观点。在这一点上,他和德格里夫一样。④

---

① Oppenheimer, *The State*, John M. Gitterman 翻译, 275 页。
② Steiner, *The Three Fold State: The True Aspects of the Social Question*, 1922 年, 纽约。
参见如下：Luwig Stein, "Autoritat ihr Ursprung, ihre Begrundung und ihre Grenzen", 在 Schmoller 的 *Jahrbuch fur Rechts-und Wirtschafisphilosphie*, 1907 年 10 月。也参考他的 *Philosophische Stromungen der Gegenwart*, 第 15 章。(这些参考文献应当归功于 H. E. Barnes, 参见他的 *Sociology and Political Theory*, 130 页)
③ Ratzenhofer, *Wesin und Zweckder Politik*, 1893.
④ Novicow, *War and Its Alleged Benefits*, Sektzer 翻译, 1911 年, 也见 *La Fédération de l'Europe*, 1901。
对传统主权理论有敌意的所谓的地方分权主义也应该被提及。参见 Brun, *La Regionalisme* (1911), J. Hennessy, *Recoganization Administrative de la France* (1919)。共产主义和无政府主义理论强烈反对国家,因而也强烈反对国家的权威,这两种理论的著作非常多,没有必要特别提及。

结论：一个观点

　　人们普遍认为在理论和事实之间有一种密切的关系。一方面，一种既存的理论可以影响或改变某种事实；另一方面，某种事实状况也可能导致一种理论的产生。虽然理论和事实相互影响，但历史表明后一种情况好像更为真实。一千年前的思想家提出的许多理论直到今天仍然被拥护，但它们已经或即将与事实不同了。但是，一旦一个事实引起人们注意以后，思想家们就会发表理论以解释或者说证明它，或者干脆批判它，以期它能变得符合我们的愿望。无论我们喜欢不喜欢，我们都必须面对它。

　　对此，主权理论的历史也不例外。中世纪的人习惯于说在他们所能认知的世界内只有一个单一的不可分的主权。萨里斯布瑞的约翰（John of Salisbury）认为主权应该在教会手里；但丁想把主权交给君主；皮瑞·杜·巴斯（Pierre Du Bois）将主权放在法国国王的手中。民族国家的兴起证明统治世界的唯一主权是不存在的。布丹注意到了这一点，但是他告诉我们每一个国家的主权仍然是唯一的和不可分的。于是，霍布斯告诉我们分离利维坦就会使人类回到战争的状态。卢梭意识到路易十四的时代已经过去了，应把主权放在人民的手中。

　　因此，我们知道了，在一个国家内，无论主权掌握在谁那里，它都是且必须是唯一的和不可分的。这样一种理论几个世纪以来一直就没有被质疑过。但是，当联邦国家出现的时候，它开始受到冲击。国家在外部联系中相互依赖的增加，国际组织和机构的发展，团体生活特别是关系到人类利益的团体生活的增加，人类个体的意识的增强以及其他因素都不得不使我们相信，霍布斯的国家不过是一个幻想。

　　从一个角度看，它太大；从另一个角度看，它太又小。正是由于这个以及其他的原因使得一些持激进态度的人们要求立即废止国家。

　　对我们来说，如果国家是这样一种组织，它是为了在政治领域促进人类利益的发展，则我们就没有理由去废除它。但是，在这种观点下，我们必须否定霍布斯的国家，这个国家拥有在其范围内不可分的和统一的主权，它可以控制国家内部的所有事物，并自主发展与其他国家的关系。国家没有理由拥有这样高的权力——单独拥有它。原因很简单，人不仅仅是政治性的动物，因此我们的生活不能仅仅由政治组织所统治。我们不仅仅提倡一个道德原则。我们生活的依据的是目前所存在的所有事实。我们绝不满意于所有现在存在的事实，但是我们必须面对它们。

一些学者告诉我们，主权不同于权力，它不仅仅是权力。他们坚持认为权力是可以分离的，但是主权不能。我们不必去质疑主权是否"应该"和权力有所不同，这样会把自己限定在查找这些人的著作中是否有对此问题满意的解释的框子。

布丹是第一个在主权和权力之间做出区分的学者，但是他从这样的主权定义入手的："（主权是）联合体的绝对的和永久的权力"以及拉丁文本："控制市民和属民的不受法律限制的最高权力。"很难看到这种权力与最高的、绝对的和永久的权力有什么不同。可以肯定的是它们只是程度的不同，而不是种类的不同。如果按布丹所说，既然权力是可以分离的①，为什么最高权力或主权不能呢？

卢梭关于主权与政权的区分最为坚定并经常被引用。卢梭说："政权，可以分离，但意志不能。"在这里，我们不打算考察意志是否可分。让我们来引用下面一段话："这一由其全体成员结合所形成的公共人格，以前称为'城邦'，现在则称为'共和国'和'政治体'；在其被动意义上，它的成员称它为'国家'；在其主动意义上，就称它为'主权者'；为了与其他机构相区别，就称它为'政权'。"②实际上，这段话显示出国家、主权者和政权，其实就是对同一个事物从不同方面进行解释。

在《论美国的宪法与政府》中，卡尔霍恩写道："这样被委任的权力可以分为明显的两个部分：一部分是被各州的人民委任给他们的州的政府的；另一部分是人民自己保留的——没有委任给政府的。这两部分权力中包含有最高主权，通过最高主权人们使这两部分权力得以委任和建立；也是通过最高主权人们可以随时修改、改变或废除这两部分权力。最高主权和其他未授权给国家的权力，是人民自己保留的重要权力。"③

上面所提到的"最高的权力"，无疑是州的主权或州的人民的主权。④ 在卡尔霍恩看来，是唯一的和不可分的。但是当他把这种最高主权放在权力的两个部分中的一个那里，这部分权力掌握在人民手中——没有交给政府时，他就承认了主权是权力，并且承认了，至少是无意识地承认了主权是可分的。但他又用普拉提

---

① Bodin, *De Republica*，143～144 页。
② Rousseau, *Social Contract*，第一卷，第六章，Tozer 翻译本，110～111 页。
③ Calhoun, *Works*，第 1 卷，144 页。
④ Calhoun 坚持认为主权在州的人民的手中，而不是集中起来的。

诺斯的隐喻①，自相矛盾地宣称主权是完整的东西，分离它就是毁坏它。②

卡尔霍恩毫不避讳地承认几个主权可以合并成一个主权。他说："如果州通过宪法放弃自己的主权和人格，加入一个更大的团体或者说国家中去，那么很明显这个整体就会有一个主权。"③ 如果主权是可以联合的，为什么一个主权不能分成多个部分或者说多个小的独立政治实体呢？

韦罗贝教授与卢梭和卡尔霍恩的思想很相近。他宣称："主权不仅仅是权力的集合，也不仅仅是多种单个能力的机械结合。"④ 但是他又补充道："它的确需要控制某些权力——比如，税收、缔约、保持军事力量等等。"然后他又回过来说道："但是又不仅满足于此。它本身是一个实体，代表国家最高的政治权力。"⑤ 我们不需要更进一步地指出韦罗贝教授在他的观念中没有区分清楚主权和权力。就我们的目的而言，光看一下他的《国家的本质》这本书的第四章的标题就足够了，它是这么写的——"国家的权力：主权"⑥。

主张主权和权力之间有区别，并且权力可分而主权不可分的人很多，前面提到几位代表人物并不是所有持这种观点的人，但是这就足以显示他们没有真正弄清二者之间的区别。我们认为没有权力就没有主权。如果权力可以分离，那么主权就也可分离。坚持权力可以分离，而主权不能分离，是滑向了神秘主义。

但是我们听有人说主权是一个法律主体，"法律"的主权是不可分的。我们暂且不论主权是否是一个法律主体，我们发现"法律的"主权是不可分的观点根

---

① "所有存在的事物都是有整体性的——只要它们真的存在，并且是真实的，如果事物没有整体性，还怎么可以存在？没有整体性，我们就不能说事物存在，军队不能没有整体性。房屋、轮船也不能没有整体性，房屋或船舶被解体以后，也就不称其为房屋或船舶了。当事物分开以后，它作为一个整体就不存在了。"Plotinus, *Enneads*, 第九章。此处转引自 Avey 的 *Readings in Philosophy*, 1921。

② "由主权可分的观点引出的一个问题——各国的人民怎么会部分地是主权者，部分地又'不是'主权者，一是保留的权力的主权者，一而又不是授予国家的权力的主权者？不难理解主权的权力是怎样被分开的：一部分授予了代理机构；另一部分留在人民手里，或主权是怎样被一个人或少数人或大多数人享有的。但主权本身——这个最高权力怎么被分开，各国的人民既部分地是主权者，又部分地不是主权者——部分地是至高无上的，部分地又不是至高无上的，这是不可想象的。主权是一个完整的东西——分开它，就是毁灭它。"Calhoun, *Works*, 第一卷，146 页，参考 275 页以下。

③ Calhoun, *Works*, 第一卷，122 页。

④ Willoughby, *Nature of the State*, 194 页。

⑤ Willoughby, *Nature of the State*, 194～195 页。

⑥ 参考 Willoughby, *The Fundamental Concepts of Public Law*, 27 页。Alexander Stephen 试图区分主权和最高权力："主权权力是可分的，而主权本身作为主权权力的来源，自始至终是不可分的。"(*War Between the States*, 第一卷，第 23 页。) 但是他没有对二者的不同做出一个令人满意的解释，他从来没有将主权和权力分开讨论。"我说最高权力，"他说，"是指它是术语政治体或者说联邦的内在的，始终正确的权力或意志——它是所有政治权力的来源和基础；它可以随时收回它给联邦政府或州政府的权力。"(*War Between the States*, 第一卷，24 页) 在另外的地方，他说："主权和忠诚是相互的。公民效忠于哪个政权，哪个政权就有主权。美国人有双重公民身份，如果忠诚是主权的基础，那对前者的分割，自然会造成对后者的分割。"(*War Between the States*, 第一卷，492 页)

本没有分量。相反,它只能显示该理论的弱点。道理很简单,既然一个人坚持认为"法律"的主权是不可分的,那他至少就得承认,除了"法律的"主权,还有其他的主权——政治的、道德的、经济的等——它们中的每一个,都是可分的。换句话说,坚持"法律的"主权是不可分的,就是承认道德的或政治的主权是可分的;而承认后者的可分性的同时又否认前者的可分性,是自相矛盾的。事实上,在法律的、政治的和道德的主权之间做出区分,就等于承认了主权是可分的。

  法律主权不能分离的主张一般被认为是法学家的观点。有人说那些不专门研究法律的人是很难理解国家的主权的含义、意义和统一性的。也许让一个外行去谈法律的本质是不公正的,但是事实是,主权不可分的原理一直没有被立法机构承认,起码在美国是如此。不说州的最高法院,也不说联邦和州的下级法院,单是联邦的最高法院,从它成立之初到现在,已经多次宣称主权在这个国家里是分离的。可分的事物不一定是分离的,但是,分离的事物一定是可分的。美国的最高法院无疑被认为是这个国家的最有权力的法院,我们不能在其他国家找到权力与之相等的法院。事实上,它不仅是法律唯一的来源,也是法律的指导者。它的决定被清晰地理解并被彻底地执行。当它说主权是分离的,这就是以法律的名义说的。除非最高法院关于主权的可分性的决议被推翻,主权不可分的主张,就不仅是违法的,也是与稳固的传统和规则,甚至美国的现实相违背的。①

  主权,正如我们所理解的,绝不仅仅是一个关于法律的事物。如果法学家谈法律主权,那么政治学家可以谈政治主权,道德家可以谈道德主权,如此等等。一个法学家可以认为经济学家、道德家和社会学家没有资格讨论主权,但是主权的观念决不仅仅是一个法律观念。这种观念存在于所谓的原始社会,也存在于所谓的文明社会,既存在于过去,也存在于现在。我们都知道在原始社会和在遥远的过去,劳动的分工仅具雏形。在法律、道德和其他观念之间还没有一个大致的区分。甚至在当今这个高度发达的社会,无论我们能多么迅速地根据事物的本质确定它的概念,我们都得承认我们的概念还有很多的重叠。仅仅认识到这一步,我们就不得不否认那种认为主权仅仅是一个法律概念的主张。

  但是,一些学者告诉我们主权的观念在其严格意义上是一个现代观念。这并不意味着主权仅仅是一个法律的观念或一个政治的观念。即使我们能确定现代主权主要是法律或政治概念,因为它是 16 世纪或 17 世纪法律的或政治的组织的发展的反映,我们也不能得出它仅仅是法律的或政治的观念的结论。原因很简单,如果 16 世纪或 17 世纪的法律或政治组织能够产生一个法律的或政治的主权观念,为什么 19 世纪或 20 世纪的经济组织就不能产生一个经济的主权的概念呢?因此正如我们已经在以前的讨论中指出的,既然我们承认某个时期的某种条件能

---

  ① Bryce 爵士在他的 *Studies in History and Jurisprudence* 中肯定地指出法律主权是可分的。参见 *The Nature of Sovereignty* 中的论文,第二卷,507~510 页、520 页。

够使得一种新的观念兴起,我们就必须承认随着条件的改变,观念也会跟着改变。

因此主权是可分的,历史已经向我们证实这是真实的。从地域上讲,现在的欧洲仍然是几百年前的欧洲。然而,历史显示,在16世纪初,除英国、法国、西班牙和一些意大利的城邦之外,很少有主权国家。但是在17世纪中期,当《威斯特伐利亚和平条约》(*The Peace of Westphalia*)达成后,主权国家的数目开始增加。在18世纪和19世纪,特别是在世界大战之后,更多的主权国家出现。既然主权的增加仍然限定在欧洲范围内,那么这种主权增加的进程也可以看作是主权分离的进程。研究历史的人会不止一次地发现一个主权整体会分成许多部分,并且这些部分自身也变成了主权国家。一个主权国家不是由许多主权国家组成的,但并不意味着它不能分裂成为许多主权国家。当卡尔霍恩说主权是一个整体的时候,他是正确的。当他坚持认为分离主权就是毁坏主权的时候,他也没有错;因为当我们要把一个主权国家分裂成两个或多个主权时,它的完整性当然会被破坏。主权是一个整体,但是它可以分离成两个或多个主权。

主权可分论不仅有历史依据,还有道德上的依据。主权不可分的理论告诉我们主权是一个国家的本质特征;它是最高的、绝对的和绝对无误的。对内,它可以伤害任何人或组织而不负任何责任,对外,它可以做它想做的任何事情。它是侵略战争的发动者。主权不可分论是一个国家把他国的爱好和平而手无寸铁的人们从他们世世代代生活的土地上赶出去的理由。总之,它是鼓励残暴行为的理论。相反,主权可分的理论告诉我们国家不是主权的唯一拥有者;主权被分成不同的部分,或者可以说,在国家的界限之内或之外分成不同的实体。国家和其他组织一样都没有理由宣称可以在自己的领域内为所欲为。国家可以看作是维护和发展人类的某一方面的利益的组织之一。它是手段,而不是目的,它所能做的一切只是保证人们成为它自身的目的。简单地说,国家所拥有的主权不是它可以为所欲为的依据,而是用来发展人类利益的一种权力。

这样的一种理论建立在一个比较合理、充分而牢固的哲学基础之上吗?我们对此问题的答案是肯定的。多元主义在我们的时代是一个广为接受的观念。它建立在实用主义和新实在论基础之上。用詹姆斯的话说它的优点是,"(1) 它更为'科学',对此,它认为,既然主权是一个整体,它就具有明确的倾向连接的结构。这与事物中的倾向于分离的结构具有同等重要的意义。它们两个是事物的相协调的两面,一元论者为了使连接的结构显得比分离的结构更重要,就会不顾现实经验,去支持一种难以分清的整体。(2) 它更能满足生活中的道德和民主诉求。(3) 它不必再附会任何形式的多元主义,因为只要它能发现一丁点儿的事物中存在分离的倾向,它就能彻底打败一元主义。它对一元主义说的只是'并非完全不可分'。一元主义也必须去证明多元主义所主张的绝对不可能是真实的,但这可困难多了"①。

事实上，如果我们打算把这种主权理论建立在形而上学的基础之上，多元主义是唯一我们可以接受的选择。斯宾诺莎及其跟随者所主张的一元主义，并不是那些认为主权是不可分的人所拥护的一元主义。斯宾诺莎告诉我们在宇宙中只有一个东西，这一个东西就是上帝。他是唯一的实体。他写道："只存在一种具有某种属性的物质，并且它依赖于它自身的性质而存在，无论它是有限的还是无限的。但实际上它也不可能是有限的。因为如果它被另一个具有相同属性的东西限制，那么，那个东西也是存在的。这样就有了两个具有相同属性的物质存在。这是荒谬的。因此，它是不受限制的。"②

如果斯宾诺莎的观点被那些认为主权是唯一的和不可分的人所承认，他们就得承认在世界或整个宇宙中只能有一个主权。但是这不是他们所坚持的。他们认为世界分成许多政治实体，它们每个拥有一个不可分的主权，每一个主权与其他的主权都是平等的。一旦他们承认或者说坚持认为在世界上存在许多主权，他们实际上是多元主义者。他们实际上不否认主权是分离的，因而认为主权是可分的。他们所坚持的是一个国家的主权是不分离的，是不可分的。如果主权本身是分离的和可分的，我们就不理解他们如何能够否认一个国家的主权的可分性。

绝对的、最高的而没有任何限制的这种一元主义的观点根本就不是一种合理的观点。③ 如果一个主权是最高的和绝对的，没有限制，那么在整个世界或宇宙就只能有一个主权。既然我们知道在世界上有许多主权，每一个主权就不能在绝对的意义上说是最高的和绝对的，也就更不能说是不受限制的。我们至多只能说在相对的意义上和在其范围内，它是绝对的和最高的。但是承认这一点，就是承认有对主权的限制。承认了对主权限制，起码从主权的范围的角度承认，就意味着对可分性的承认；正是从这个意义上说，限制意味着分离。

同斯宾诺莎一样，黑格尔认为宇宙是一个整体。但是他认为，这个唯一的整体不是上帝，并且它不是静止的。这个终极的整体，在黑格尔看来，从本质上说是运动的，它可以分化成多个表现形式，其中的每一种形式是这个终极的一的本身的部分表达。这样，一变多的原则就暗含着对可分性理论的承认。对我们来说，黑格尔一元主义应用到主权理论中，与主权可分论并不冲突。④

我们知道一元主义在我们的时代已经开始衰退。它并不会给那些坚持主权是不可分的人以支持。一个人可以既是一元主义的拥护者，同时也承认存在主权分离的可能性。换句话说，尽管多元主义暗含着对主权可分理论的承认，但主权可

---

① William James, *Some Problems of Philosophy*, 142~143 页。
② *The Philosophy of Spinoza*, Fullerton 译, 29 页。
③ 参见 Bradiey, *Appearance and Reality*, 140 页。
④ 参见 George S. Morris, *Hegel's Philosophy of the State and of History*, 105 页, 1892 年。

分的理论并不总是多元主义。

在过去的讨论中已经认识到，主权可分的主张是建立在现存的事实、历史证据、普遍被接受的道德标准、比较合理充分的哲学观念的基础上。但是这还不是全部。因为从语源学意义上讲，我们的主张也同样是合理的。我们已经指出，现在已经可以确定"主权"一词最早是由波马诺（Beaumanoir）使用的；但是当他使用这个词的时候，他是在两个意义上使用它：一是每一位男爵在他的领地内是主权者，二是国王在整个王国内是主权者。① 换句话说，除了国王的主权，在王国之内的领地还有许多主权。王国的主权，根据波马诺的看法，在程度上比领地的主权要大，但是它们两者之中一个的存在不会干扰或毁坏另一个的存在。原因很简单，因为他们在各自的领域内是主权者。如果后来对波马诺使用的"主权"一词的理解没有错误的话，则主权是单一的和不可分离的，并且是国家的特征，在国家内没有其他的主权存在的主张就缺乏词源学上的基础。②

"主权"一词据说是从中世纪的拉丁文 *supremitas*，也就是 *supremapotestas*，即"最高权力"派生而来。③ 但是 *supremapotestas* 是国际的或超国家的。它的含义与奥斯丁的主权理论大不相同。奥斯丁理论中的主权，菲吉斯教授说，在中世纪的许多单一国家中是不为人知的。④

前面的讨论已充分证明主权是可分的。在主张主权是可分的同时，我们也主张主权是可以合并的。我们不否认在一个国家或在整个世界有一个主权的可能性。我们所否认的只是主权的不可分性。正如我们所理解的，主权可分论既可以被看作是对现存的情况的一种描述，又是一个我们目前应该遵守的原则。事实现在足以让我们不再相信主权是不可分的以及在一个国家内只能有一个主权。国家从来就不是达到人类生活至善的唯一手段，以后也不会是。许多高尚的人并没有借助国家的作用，那些热爱人类的人从来就没想过让利维坦主义者统治世界。

---

① Beaumanoir, *Les Coutumes du Beauvoisir*, A. Salmon 编辑，第 34 卷，1043 页，巴黎，1899。

② Bryce 评论道："在中世纪，修隐院的负责人有时会被称为'主权者'，在爱尔兰自治区，'主权者'这个词，一直到不久前，还被用来指自治区的负责人。" *Studies in History and Jurisprudence*，第二章，505 页注释；又见 James A. H. Murray, *A New English Dictionary*。据说，法律曾允许丈夫是妻子的"主权者"。见 *Oxford Dictionary*。

③ Meyer, *Lehrbuch des deutschen Statrechts*, 15 页；又见 Skeat, *Etymological Dictionary*；又见 John Macdonell 被收录在 *Encyclopaedia Britannica*（第 11 版）中关于主权的文章。

④ Figgis, *Divine Right of the Kings*, 13 页及注释。Maitland, *Lectures on Constitutional History*, 101～102 页。读这一段："当我们在谈论主权的时候应该注意到现在的理论与中世纪的理论是不同的——他们看待国家和教会的关系的整体方式。尽管他们是由一样的人组成的，尽管每个人在这两个组织中都有位置，但这两个实体仍是不同的。国家有它的国王或皇帝、法律、立法机构、法庭、法官；教会有它的教皇和大主教、宗教会议、宗教法律、宗教法庭。没有人认为教会在任何意义上比国家的地位低，主张国家比教会地位低似乎还有点道理。人们普遍认为，二者是相互独立的，它们都不必从对方那里获得权威。很明显，当人们这样想时，当人们多少按这个理论行事的时候，奥斯丁理论意义上的主权者就不存在。在宗教改革前，奥斯丁的理论是不可能出现的。"

因此，现实要求我们的主权观念必须改变；如果不这样，我们现时代关于在不同的组织里面的主权的归属的争论就永远不会解决。一个具体的例子可以表明这一点。很多人认为托管区的主权在国际联盟那里。另一些人坚持认为它被授予了委任统治国，仍有一些人坚持认为主权保留在托管区。谁是正确的？谁是错误的？我们认为他们都是正确的，同时，他们都是错误的。换句话说，他们都是部分正确，部分错误。很容易看出如果仍坚持主权不可分的理论，则托管的主权只能在一个地方。但是众所周知，国联、委任统治国、托管区三者中的任何一个都不单独拥有这个不可分的主权。除非我们采用主权可分论的观点，否则只要现存的状况还存在，我们关于托管区的主权归属的争论就不会停止。

国际交往的日益频繁表明坚持主权不可分论是不足取的。当认识到这一点的时候，有人认为主权的观念不是国际关系领域的概念。我们不能理解为何它不是一个国际关系的概念。我们不需要指出持这种观点的人的软肋。我们仅仅需要对他们之间的争论稍加考察。尽管奥斯丁与霍布斯的观点非常相近，但是前者却把后者的绝对的、不受限制的主权狭窄化为"市主权"。接着，韦罗贝教授，尽管是一个坚定的奥斯丁主义者，却强烈反对他的老师的关于主权的狭隘观念，并把它扩展为"宪法主权"；但是，他却拒绝再更进一步去接受将主权理论运用到国际关系中！

由于韦罗贝教授认为在国际关系领域没有主权，他建议用"独立"这一词去取代"主权"。在这里我们又不能明白他如何能够仅仅通过改变词汇，就能绕过这个难题。我们认为，困难在于他们误解了观念本身，而不是词语的运用。也许还要说的是，"主权"一词经常被与诸如"独立""司法权""统治""优先权"等这些词混用。① 在许多情况下，这些词语被用来指同一个或者说相同的事物。看起来甚至可以确定地说，"主权"一词从它诞生到现在，从来就没有出现过对它的含义的一致意见。我们所能说的只是主权意味着权力，我们也注意到没有学者在谈及主权的时候不涉及权力的。权力在人类社会中无处不在。否认主权观念在国际关系中的运用就是否认主权观念本身，如果主权观念本身就被怀疑，那就没有国家的主权这样的东西了。在这里，我们要对主权的基础说上几句。主权，我们认为，建立在个体或大众的同意的基础上，此外再无别的基础。那些否认这种观点的人也许认为，比如，一个菲律宾人处在美国的主权控制下，但他不得不这样，这并非出自他的本愿。坚持这样观点的人，毫无疑问，没有触及问题的实质。很难想象一个主权会施加到一个不认可它的人身上。我们在这里不能担保能分析出使他同意生活在美国的主权之下的动机。但是不能否认，如果一个菲律宾人不同意这样做，他可以离开，甚至可以在任何时候以任何方式推翻它。他可以

---

① 参见 W. G. Miller, *The Data of Jurisprudence*, 102 页、113 页、118 页、122 页, 1809。又参见 Dicey, *Conflict of Law*, 38 页。

说服他的追随者跟他去发动革命，他可以离开菲律宾，到其他任何一个地方。如果他不能成功这样做，或如果他不想这样做，那他可以自杀或被杀掉。但是只要他自杀或被杀掉，美国主权对他的控制就立即停止了。

历史是一个储藏室，里面存放着无数可以证明我们的观点的事例。不同时期，不同地域的革命此起彼伏。一个人如果不愿意受其祖国的主权控制，大可以选择到其他国家，并在那里终老。许多事例证明，人们宁愿死，也不愿意向他们不认可的主权屈服。

坚持主权的基础是认可，然而也包含着这样一个认识，也就是主权，究其根本，是个体的主权，并且它是可以被代表的。说个体是主权者，因为它可以独立地以他认为合适的方式行动。根据某时某地的道德标准，一个人的行为或许是错误的，但是如果他执意这样做的话，也没有一个外部力量能阻止他。

但是，在某种意义上，人是一个社会的和社会化的动物。他当然可以成为一个生活在孤岛上，按照其自身的意愿行事的梭罗（Thoreau）①，或者他也可以通过自杀来结束他的社会生活。但是一般地说，他会同意成为某种社会组织的成员。一旦同意成为一个组织的成员，他就将他的主权委托给那个组织。委任主权的方式有多种：委任可以是直接的，也可以是间接的；可以是公开的，也可以是默认的；可以是全部的或是部分的；可以是暂时的或是永久的。然而，需要指出的是，这些方式一般都是彼此交织在一起的。

由个体直接组成的组织一般会行使直接委任的主权。我们不准备像瑞士的总统 M. 莫塔那样前卫，他在 1920 年国际联盟代表大会的第一次会议上宣称国际联盟是民族的联盟。但是既然承认了主权也可以以一种间接的方式委任，我们也同意有些人所持的这样一种观点，即国际联盟在处理其能胜任的事物中拥有主权。

一个出生在某个现存主权国家里的人，通常默许由该主权国家代行其主权。另一方面，新建立起来的组织的主权一般以表达的方式委任。但一个个体同意将他的主权转移到一个特定的组织一小段时间的时候，委任是暂时的，当他同意长时期甚至一生放弃的时候，委任是长久的。

当一个人的主权不是分离的，为了一个特殊的目的委任给一个特定的组织的时候，是完全的委任。这种主张并不否认，举例来说，德国可以有一个统一的、不可分的主权，如果它能够使它所有的公民或其他成员都同意它做它喜欢的事情。如果德国所有的个体都同意放弃他们的家庭、他们的职业以及其他的一切，而仅仅去为所谓的威望、荣誉、德国的主权等而战的时候，主权毫无疑问是单一的和不分的，然而并不是不可分的。我们已经说过，事情是分的，就一定是可分的；事情是可分的，但不一定是分的。但是我们可以意识到如果德国在一种情况

---

① 伯夷和叔齐的事情是另外的特殊的例子。参见《论语》第五篇第二十二章的注释。

下能够有一个统一的可不分的主权,那么一个教会或一个贸易组织可以在同样的条件下拥有同样的东西。

人类的利益是多方面的。一个人可以为了一个且仅仅一个利益而尽其所能,为了提高这种利益而同意放弃他的整个主权给一个组织。但是,一般地说,他有许多利益。他可以是一个教会的成员,同时,也是一个贸易组织的成员。他同意成为每一个机构的忠实成员,或者他对这些机构的忠诚依据他的兴趣是不同的。无论哪种情况,他部分地在一个机构的主权之下,部分地在另外的机构的主权之下。

还可以补充的是,为说明主权的基础是同意,我们可以在根本的主权和委任的主权之间做出区分。根本的主权,严格来说,是个人的主权;委任的主权,是社会组织的主权。[①] 但是应当记住它们是同等重要的,因为一个简单的理由是,当我同意让教会在我之上实施权力时,等于是在说我在对自身实施权力。

---

① 相应地,我们可以这样说,国联成员国的主权是原初的主权,而国联的主权是委任的主权。

参考文献

Acton, J. E. E. D., The History of Freedom and other Easays, edited by J. N. Figgis, 1919.

Adams, B., Centralization and the Law, 1906.

Adams, B., The Theory of Social Revolution, 1913.

Adams, F. O., and Cunningham, C. D., The Swiss Confederation, 1894.

Adams, J. Q., Writings, edited by Worthington Chauncey Ford, 1913.

Adams, Samuel, Writings, edited by H. A. Cushing, 1904.

Advisory Opinion of the Permanent Court of International Justice, Collection of Advisory Opinions, No. 4.

Ahrens, H., Naturrecht oder Philosophie des Reichs and des Staats, 1870.

Allen, S. H., International Relations, 1920.

Angell, N., The Great Illusion, 1913.

Aristotle, Politics, translated by B. Jowett.

Arndt, V. A., Das Statsrecht des Deutschen Reiches, 1901.

Ashley. H. L., American Government.

Austin, J., Lectures or Jurisprundence, edited by R. Campbell, 1911.

Baoer, G. S., First Steps in International Law, 1899.

Baldwin, S. E., "Division of Sovereignty", in International Law, note, July, 1918.

Baldwin, S. E., "Vesting of Sovereignty in League of Nations", in Yale Law Journal, Vol. 28, 1919.

Barker, E., "Political Thought of Plato and Aristotle", 1906.

Barker, E., "The Discredited State", in Political Quarterly, No. 5, 1915.

Barker, E., "Political Thought in England from Spencer to To-day", 1915.

Barker, E., "The Superstition of the State", in London Times Literary Supplement, July, 1918.

Barker, E., Greek Political Theory, Plato and his Predecessors, 1918.

Barker, E., A Confederation of the Nations, 1918.

Barker, E., National Character, 1927.

Barnes, H. E. , "Durkheim's Contribution to Political Theory", in Political Science Quarterly, Vol. 35, 1920.

Barnes, H. E. , "Some Contributions of Sociology to Modern Political Theory", in American Political Science Review, Vol. 15, 1921.

Barnes, H. E. , Sociology and Political Theory, 1924.

Barnes, H. E. , The History and Prospects of the Social Sciences, 1925.

Baty, T. , International Law, 1909.

Baty, T. , "Protectorates and Mandates", in British Year Book of International Law, 1923.

Baty, T. , "Sovereign Colonies", Harvard Law Review, Vol. XXXIV, pp. 837 ff.

Beale, J. H. , "Jurisdiction of a Sovereign State", Harvard Law Review, Vol. 36, January, 1923.

Belloc, H. , The Servile State, 1912.

Benoist, C. , L'Organisation de la Démocratie, 1900.

Bentham, J. , Works, collected by J. Bowring. See particularly Fragment on Government, 1776.

Bentley, A. F. , The Process of Government: A Study of Social Pressures, 1908.

Bernard, M. , A Historical Account of the Neutrality of Great Britain during the American Civil War, 1870.

Berolzheimer, F. , The World's Legal Philosophy, translated by R. S. Jastrow, 1912.

Berthelemy, N. , Droit administratif, 10th ed. , 1923.

Berthelemy, N. , "Le Fondement de l'autorité politique", in Revue du droit public, XXXII, 1915, pp. 662–682.

Bigelow, J. , World Peace: How War Cannot Be Abolished, How it May Be Abolished, 1916.

Blackstone, W. , Commentaries on the Laws of England, 1765–1769.

Blakey, R. , ⟨The⟩ History of Political Literature, 1855.

Bliss, P. , Of Sovereignty, 1885.

Blummer, J. J. , Handbuch des Schweizerischen Bundesstaatsrechtes, 1863.

Bluntschli, J. K. , Das moderne Völkerrecht der Civilisirten als Rechtsbuch Dargestellt, 1872.

Bluntschli, J. K. , Allgemihes Staatsrecht, 6th ed. , 1885.

Bluntschli, J. K. , Theory of the State, English translation, 1892.

Bluntschli, J. K. , Le Droit international, Codifié Traduit d'allemand par M. C. Lardy, 1886.

Bluntschli, J. K., Geschichte der Neueren Staatswissen schaft, 1881.

Bodin, J., De Republica Libri Sex, 1575.

Bonald, de., Théorie du pouvoir politique et Religieux dans la société civile.

Bonjour, F., Real Democracy in Operation, 1920.

Borel, E., Étude sur la Souveraineté et L'État Fédératif, 1886.

Bornhak, C., Preussisches Staatsrecht, 1888.

Bosanquet, B., Philosophical Theory of the State, 1899.

Bourgeois, L., La Solidarité, 1897.

Bourgeois, L., L'Œouvre de la société des nations, 1920-1923.

Bradley, A. C., Aristotle's Conception of the State, Hellenica, edited by Abbott, 1898.

Bradley, F. H., Appearance and Reality: A Metaphysical Essay, 1908 ed.

Brierly, J. L., "The Shortcomings of International Law", in British Year Book of International Law, 1923-1924.

Brie. S., Der Bunderstaat, 1874.

Brooks, J. G., American Syndicalism, 1919.

Brown, I. J. C., English Political Theory, 1920.

Brown, P. M., International Reality, 1917.

Brown, W. J., "The Jurisprudence of M. Duguit", in Law Quarterly Review, April 1916.

Brown, W. J., Austinian Theory of Law, 1906.

Brownson, O. A., The American Republic, 1866.

Brun, C., Le Régionalisme, 1911.

Brunet, R., The New German Constitution, translated by J. Gollamb, 1922.

Bryce, J., The American Commonwealth, 1890.

Bryce, J., "Laws of Nature", in Studies in History and Jurisprudence.

Bryce, J., Modern Democracies, 1921.

Bryce, J., Studies in History and Jurisprudence, 2 volumes.

Buchanan, G., On the Sovereign Power among the Scots, 1579.

Buell, R. L., International Relations, 1925.

Burgess, J. W., Political Science and Comparative Constitutional Law, 1902.

Burgess, J. W., Recent Changes in American Constitutional Theory, 1923.

Burns, C. D., Political Ideals, 1919.

Calhoun, J. C., Works, ed. by R. K. Cralle, 1883. See especially his Disquisition on Government and Discourse on the Constitution and Government of the United States,

Works, Vol. I.

Carter, J. C., Law, Origin, Growth, and Function, 1907.

Carlyle, R. W. and A. J., A History of Mediaeval Political Theory, 1903-1922, 4 volumes.

Centz, P. C. (Bernard J. Sage), The Republic of Republics, 1865.

Charteris, A. H., "League of Nations and the Doctrine of Sovereignty", in Scots Law Times, February, 1920.

Chipman, N., Principles of Government, 1853.

Chipman, W., "Sovereignty", in Canadian Bar Review, Vol. 3, pp. 530 ff. and 607 ff., 1925.

Clark, W. L., Elementary Law, 1909.

Clute, W. K., "Home Rule System of Municipal Government—City Sovereignty versus State Sovereignty", in Central Law Journal, Vol. 77, Nov., 1913.

Cobbett, P., Cases and Opinions on International Law, 1909.

Coker, F. W., Readings in Political Philosophy, 1914.

Coker, F. W., "The Technique of the Pluralistic State," in American Political Science Review, Vol. 15, May, 1920.

Cole, G. D. H., The World of Labour, 2nd and rev. ed., 1915.

Cole, G. D. H., The Meaning of Industrial Freedom, 1918.

Cole, G. D. H., Self-Government in Industry, 1919 ed.

Cole, G. D. H., Labour in the Commonwealth, 1919.

Cole, G. D. H., Chaos and Order in Industry, 1920.

Cole, G. D. H., Social Theory, 1920.

Cole, G. D. H., The Future of Local Government, 1921.

Cole, G. D. H., Guild Socialism, A Plan for Economic Democracy, 1921.

Cole, G. D. H., Workshop Organization.

Cole, G. D. H., Introduction to Rousseau's Social Contract, Everyman's Edition.

Commons, J. R., "A Sociological View of Sovereignty", in American Journal of Sociology, Vol. V, pp. 1 ff., 347 ff., 544 ff., 683 ff., 814 ff., and Vol. 6, pp. 67 ff.

Constant, B., Réflexions sur les constitutions et les garanties, 1814-1818.

Constant, B., Principes potitiques, 1815.

Cooley, T. M., A Treatise on the Constitutional Limitations which Rest upon the Legislative Power of the States of the American Union, 1871.

Cooley, T. M., The General Principles of Constitutional Law in the United States of America, 1880.

Corbett, J., "What is the League of Nations?", in British Year Book of International Law, 1924.

Cousin, Coursd' histoire de la philosophie morale au dix-huitième siècle, 1839-1840.

Cornelison, I. A., The Relation of Religion to Civil Government, 1895.

Crane, R. T., The State in Constitutional and International Law, 1907.

Croly, Herbert, The Premise of American Life, 1909.

Croly, H., Progressive Democracy, 1914.

Croly, H., "The Future of the State", in the New Republic, Vol. XII, September 17, 1917.

Current History, February, 1922.

Curtis, G. T., History of the Origin, Formation and Adoption of the Constitution of the United States, 1861.

Dente, De Monarchia, trans. by A. Henry, 1904.

Davis, G. B., The Elements of International Law, 1916, 4th ed.

Davis, H. W. C., The Political Thought of Heinrich von Treitschke.

Davis, J., Rise and Fall of the Confederate Government, 1881, 2 volumes.

Dealey, J., "Austin's Theory of Sovereignty", in Political Science Quarterly, Vol. IX, pp. 31 ff.

Dewey, J., "Social Absolutism", in New Republic, Vol. XXV, pp. 315-318.

Dickinson, E. D., Equality of States in International Law, 1920.

Dickinson, J., "A Working Theory of Sovereignty", in Political Science Quarterly, December, 1927, and March, 1928.

Dicey, A. V., The Law of Constitution, 1885.

Dicey, A. V., Law and Public Opinion, 1925.

Donald, R., Danger Spot in Europe, 1925.

Douglas, P. H., "Occupational versus Proportional Representation", in American Journal of Sociology, Vol. XXIX, pp. 129-57.

Dowdall, H. C., "The Word 'State'", in Law Quarterly Review, Vol. XXX-IX, January, 1923.

Duggan, S. P. H., The League of Nations, the Principle and the Practice, 1919.

Duguit, L., L'État, le Driot objectif et la Loi positive, 1901.

Duguit, L., L'État, les Governants et les Agents, 1903.

Duguit, L., Le Driot social, le Droit individuel et l'État, 1911, 2nd ed.

Duguit, L., Traite de driot constitutionnel, 1911.

Duguit, L., Les Transformations du driot public, 1913.

Duguit, L., "The Law and the State", translated by F. J. de Slovere, in Harvard Law Review, Vol. XXXI, No. I, Nov., 1917.

Duguit, L., Manual de droit constitutionnel, 3rd ed., 1918.

Duguit, L., Souvereineté et Liberté, 1922.

Duguit, L., "Concept of Public Service", in Yale Law Journal, Vol. XXXI, March, 1923.

Dunning, W. A., Political Theories: Ancient and Medieval, 1902.

Dunning, W. A., Political Theories: From Luther to Montesquieu, 1925.

Dunning, W. A., Political Theories: From Rousseau to Spencer, 1920.

Dunning, W. A., "Jean Bodin on Sovereignty", in Political Science Quarterly, Vol. XI, 1896, pp. 82 ff.

Dunning, W. A., "The Politics of Aristotle", in Political Science Quarterly, Vol. XV, pp. 273 ff.

Dunning, W. A., "Political Theories of Jean Jacques Rousseau", in Political Science Quarterly, Vol. XXIV, 1909, September.

Durkheim E., Le Suicide, 1897.

Durkheim E., De la Division du Travail, 1902.

Elliott, W. Y., "Sovereign State or Sovereign Group?", in American Political Science Review, Vol. XIX, 1919.

Elliott, W. Y., "The Metaphysics of Duguit, Pragmatic Conception of Law", in Political Quarterly, December, 1922.

Elliott, W. Y., "The Pragmatic Politics of Mr. H. J. Laski", in American Political Science Review, May, 1924.

Ellis, E. D., "The Pluralistic State", in American Political Science Review, Vol. XIV, August, 1920.

Ellis, E. D., "The Pluralistic State", in American Political Science Review, Vol. XVII, November, 1923.

Ellwood, Sociology in its Psychological Aspects, 1912.

Esmein, Droit Constitutional, 5th edition.

Estey, J. A., Revolutionary Syndicalism, 1913.

Evans, L, B., Leading Cases in International Law, 2 ed.

Evans, L, B., Leading Cases on American Constitutional Law, 1925.

Ewart, J. S., "Canada, the Empire and the United States", in Foreign Affairs,

Vol. VI, 1927.

    Fauchille, P., Traite de Droit International Public, 1921-1926.

    Fenwick, C. G., International Law, 1924.

    Ferguson, J. H., Manual of International Law, 1884.

    Fichte, J. G., Right, 1796-1896.

    Figgis, J. N., From Gerson to Grotius, 1907.

    Figgis, J. N., Churches in the Modern States, 1913.

    Figgis, J. N., The Divine Right of the Kings, 1914.

    Figgis, J. N., The Will of Freedom, 1917.

    Filmer, R., Patriarcha, or Natural Power of Kings, 1680.

    Filmer, R., Observations Concerning the Original of Government, 1652.

    Foignet, R., Droit International Public, 1915.

    Follet, M. P., The New State, 1918.

    Ford, P. L., The Federalist, 1898.

    Foster, R., On the Constitution, 1895.

    Foulke, R. R., A Treatise on International Law, 1920.

    Freund, E., "Historical Jurists in Germany", in Political Science Quarterly, Vol. V, pp. 473 ff.

    Freund, E., The Legal Nature of Corporations, 1897.

    Freund, E., Empire and Sovereignty, 1903.

    Gareis, K., Alligemein Staatrecht.

    Gareis, K., Volkerrecht, 2nd.

    Garner, J. W., Introduction to Political Science, 1919.

    Garner, J. W., Recent Developments in International Law, 1925.

    Garner, J. W., "Limitations on National Sovereignty in International Relations", in Political Science Review, 1925, Vol. XIX.

    Garner, J. W., Political Science and Government, 1928.

    Gehlke, C. E., Emile Durkheim's Contribution to Sociological Theory, 1915.

    General Orders of the United States Army, No. 100, 1863.

    Gettell, R. G., Introduction to Political Science, 1910.

    Gettell, R. G., Readings in Political Science, 1911.

    Gettell, R. G., Problems of Political Revolution, 1914.

    Gettell, R. G., History of Political Thought, 1924.

    Geza, Englemrnn, Political Philosophy From Plato to Bentham, translated from German by K. F. Geiser, 1927.

Giddings, F. H., The Principle of Sociology, 1896.

Giddings, F. H., Readings in Descriptive and Historical Sociology, 1906.

Giddings, F. H., Inductive Sociology, 1909.

Giddings, F. H., The Responsible State, 1918.

Gierke, O., Die Grundbegriffe des statsrechts und die Neuesten Staatstheorien, Zeitschrift fur die gesammte Staatswissenschafte, Turbingen, 1874.

Gierke, O., Johannes Althusius, 1880.

Gierke, O., Das deutsche Genossenchaftsrecht, 1868–1913.

Gierke, O., Political Theories of Middle Ages, trans. Maitland.

Gilchrist, R. N., Principles of Political Science, 1921.

Gooch, G, P., Political Thought in England from Bacon to Halifax, 1914–1915.

Graham, W., English Political Philosophy, 1899.

Greef, de, La Structure Générale des Sociétés.

Gregory, "The Neutralization of the Asland Islands", in American Journal International Law, Vol. XVII.

Grotius, De Jure Belli ac Pacis, 1625.

Guizot, Du Government de la France depuis la Restauration et du Ministère Actuel, 1821.

Gumplowiez, L., Geschicte der Staatstheorein, 1927 ed.

Gumplowiez, L., Outline of Sociology, trans. by Moore.

Haldane, R. P., "The Nature of the State", in Contemporary Review, CXVII, June, 1920.

Hall, W. E., Rights and Duties of Neutrals, 1874.

Hall, W. E., A Treatise on International Law, 8th ed., 1924.

Halleck, H. W., International Law, 4th ed., 1908.

Haller, L. V., Restauration der Staatswissenschaft order Theorie des Naturalichgeselligen Zustandes der Chimaera des Kunstlichen-burgerlichen entgegensetzt, 1816–1834.

Hamilton, A., Works, edited by J. C. Hamilton, 1850.

Hamilton, E. D., "In Re Alienation of Sovereignty", Virginia Law Review, Vol. XIII, p. 524, 1927.

Hancke, E., Bodin: Eine Studie über den Begriff der Souverainetat.

Hanel, A., Studien zum Deutschen Staatsrechte, 1873r80.

Harley, J. E., The League of Nations and the New International Law, 1921.

Harley, J. E., Syndicalism, 1912.

Harris, H. W., What is the League of Nations, 1925.

Hart, A. B., Introduction to Federal Government, 1891.

Hauriou, M., La Souverainete Nationale, 1912.

Hauriou, M., Principes de Droit Public, 2 ed., 1916.

Hearnshow, E. J. C., The Social and Political Ideas of some Great Mediaeval Thinkers, 1923.

Hearnshow, E. J. C., "The Social and Political Ideas of Some Great Thinkers of the Renaissance and the Reformation", 1925.

Held, J., System des Verfassungsrechts der Monarchischen Staaten Deustchland Mitbesanderer Rucksicht auf den Constitutionalesimes, 1856.

Hegel, G. W., Grundlinien der Philosophie des Rechts, 1821, trans. by S. W. Dyde.

Henderson, A., Washington's Southern Tour, 1923.

Hennessy, J., Récoganization Administrative de la France, 1919.

Hersey, A. S., The Essentials of International Public Law and Organization, Rev. ed., 1927.

Hicks, F. C., The World Order, 1920.

Hill, D. J., World Organization as Affected by the Nature of the Modern State, 1911.

Hill, D. J., The Rebuilding of Europe, 1919.

History of the Peace Conference of Paris, 1924. Issued under the Auspices of the Institute of International Affairs.

Hobbes, T., Leviathan, edited by Rhys.

Hobson, J. A., Towards International Government, 1915.

Hobson, S. G., National Guilds: An Inquiry into the Wage System and the Way out, 1919.

Hobson, S. G. Guild Principles in War and Peace, 1917.

Hobson, S. G. National Guilds and the State, 1920.

Hocking, William E., Man and the State, 1926.

Holaind, R. I., Natural Law and Legal Practice, 1899.

Holcombe, A. N., State Government, 1916.

Holland, T. E., The Elements of Jurisprudence, 12th ed., 1917.

Holmes, O., Common Law, 1881.

Holmef, O., Collected Papers, 1921.

Holt, H., "The Passing of National Sovereignty", in The Independent, 1917, Vol. XCII, pp. 120 ff.

Hotman, F., Franco-Gallia, 1573.

Hsiao, K. C., Political Pluralism, 1927.

Hughan, J. W., A Study of International Government, 1923.

Hurd, J. C., The Theory of Our National Existence, 1881.

Hurd, J. C., The Union State, 1890.

James, I., True Law of Free Monarchies. 1598.

James, W., Pragmatism, 1907.

James, William, A Pluralistic Universe, 1909.

James William, Some Problems of Philosophy: A Beginning of an Introduction to Philosophy, 1911.

James, W., Essays in Radical Empiricism, 1912.

Jameson, J. A., A Treatise on Constitutional Convention, 1866.

Jameson, J. A., "National Sovereignty", in Political Science Quarterly, Vol., pp. 193 ff.

Janet, P., Histoire de la Science Politique.

Jefferson, T., Works, ed. by P. L. Ford, 1892–1899.

Jellinek, G., Lehre von den Statenverbingungen, 1882.

Jellinek, G., Allegemeine Staatslehre, ed.

Jenks, E., "Recent Theories of the State", in Law Quarterly, 1927, April.

Johnston, F., "Some Modern Aspects of the Public Power", in Massachusetts Law Quarterly, Vol. VIII, May, 1923.

Judson, H. P., Our Federal Republic, 1925.

Kaltenborn, C. V. B., Einleitung in das Constitutionalle Verfassungercht, 1862.

Kant, I., Principles of Politics, trans. by Hastie.

Kant, I., Metaphysical First Principles of the Theory of Law, 1796, trans. by W. Hastie.

Kant, I., Perpetual Peace, 1795, trans. by M. C. Smith.

Kelsen, H., Das Problem der Souveranitat und die Theorie des Volkerrechts, 1920.

Kent, J., Commentaries on American Law, 12 ed., 1884.

Kent, J., Commentary on International Law, 1865, ed. by J. T. Abdy.

Kingsley, D. A., "The World's Fundamental Error", in The Independent, Vol. LXXX, pp. 153–155.

Kirkup, T., A History of Socialism, 1920 ed.

Korff, S. A., "The Problem of Sovereignty" in American Political Science Review,

Vol. XVII, August, 1 23.

 Korkunov, N. M., General Theory of Law, trans. by Hastings, 1922.

 Krabbe, H., Die Lehre der Rechtssouveranitat, 1906.

 Krabbe, H., Die Moderne Staatsidee (1919), also English tran lation by G. H. Sabine and W. J. Shepard.

 Kruger, F. K., Government and Politics of the German Empire, 1915.

 Laband, P., Das Staatsreacht des Deustches, 1880-1882.

 Lagordelle, Huberts and others, Syndicalisme et Socialisme, 1908.

 Laing, B. M., "Aspects of the Problem of Sovereignty", in International Journal of Ethics, Vol. XXXII, pp. 1 ff.

 Lansing, R., Notes on Sovereignty: From the Standpoint of the State and the World, 1921.

 Lansing, R., The Peace Negotiation, 1920.

 Larnaude, La Sociétédes Nations, 1920.

 Laski, H. J., "Personality of the State", in the Nation, July, 1915.

 Laski, H. J., Studies in the Problem of Sovereignty, 1917.

 Laski, H. J., Authority in the Modern State, 1919.

 Laski, H. J., Political Thought in England, from Locke to Bentham, 1920.

 Laski, H. J., The Foundation of Sovereignty and other Essays, 1921.

 Laski, H. J., A Grammar of Politics, 1925.

 Laski, H. J., Communism, 1927.

 Laski, H. J., "Democracy at Crossroads", in Yale Review, Vol. IX, pp. 788 ff.

 Laski, H. J., "The State in the New Social Order", Fabian Essays, 1922.

 Lawrence, T. J., International Law, 7 ed., by P. H. Winfield, 1923.

 League of Nations, Provisional Verbatim Records, 1920.

 League of Nations, Records of Plenary Meeting, 1925.

 League of Nations, Records of the 4th Assembly, Plenary Meeting.

 League of Nations, Monthly Summary.

 League of Nations, Official Journal.

 League of Nations, Minutes of the Permanent Mandate Commission.

 League of Nations, Records of the First Assembly, 80th., Plenary Meeting.

 Lee, R. W., "On Sovereignty", in Canadian Law Times August, 1915.

 Le Fur, L., L'État Federal, 1897.

 Le Fur, L., "La Souraineté et le Droit", in La Revue du Droit public et de la Science Politique en France et a L'étranger, No. 3, 1908.

Leroy, M., Transformation de la Puissance Publique, 1907.

Levermore, C. H., Year Book of the League of Nations.

Levesque, G., La Situation internationale de Dantzig, 1924.

Lewis, G. C., On the Use and Abuse of some Political Terms, edited by Thomas Raleigh.

Lewis, M. M., "Free City of Danzig", in British Year Book of International Law, 1924.

Lieber, F., Manual of Political Ethics, 1829.

Lieber, F., On the Civil Liberty and Self-government, 1853.

Lieber, F., The Miscellaneous Writings, 188.

Lightwood, J. M., Nature of Positive Law, 1883.

Lindsay, A. D., "The State in Recent Theory", in the Political Quarterly, 1914, Vol. I.

Lindsay, A. D., "Political Theory", in Marvin's Development in European Thought, 1919.

Lippmann, W., Politics, 1913.

Lippmann, W., "A Clue", in the New Republic, Vol. X, 1917, April.

Liszt, F. V., Das Volkenrecht, 12 ed. 1925.

Levine, L., Syndicalism in America, 1913.

Levine, L., Syndicalism in France, 1913.

Locke, J., Two Treatises of Government, 1690.

Lodge, H. C., The Senate and the League of Nations, 1925.

Lord, A. R., Principles of Politics, 1921.

Loria, A., The Economic Foundation of Society, trans. by M. Keasbey, 1890.

Lowell, A. L., Essays on Government, 1897–1899.

Lowell, A. L., "The Imperial Conference", in Foreign Affairs, Vol. V, pp. 375 ff.

Lucas, W. W., "Legal Status of sovereignty", in Juridical Review, October, 1912.

Lucas, W. W., "The Corporate Nature of English Sovereignty".

MacIver, R. M., Community: A Sociological Study, 1917.

MacIver, R. M., "Society and State", in Philosophical Review, Vol. XX, pp. 30 ff.

MacIver, R. M., The Modern State, 1927.

Mackintosh, J., A Discourse on the Study of the Law of Nature and Nations, 1835.

Madison J., The Writings of Madison J, ed. by Gaillard Hunt, 1900-1910.

MacDonald, J. R., Syndicalism, 1912.

Maeztu, R. de, Authorship, Liberty and Function, 1916.

Maine, H., Ancient Law, 1861.

Maine, H., Early History of Institutions, 1874.

Maine, H., Early Law and Custom, 1883.

Maine, H., Popular Government, 1884.

Maine, H., International Law, 1887.

Maistre, de, Etude sur la Souverainete, 1796.

Maitland, F. W., Introduction to Gierkie's Political Theory of the Middle Ages, 1900.

Maitland, F. W., The Constitutional History of England, 1908.

Maitland, F. W., Collected Papers, 3 volumes, edited by A. L. Fisher.

Manning, W. O., Commentaries on the Law of Nations, 1875.

Mansfield, E. D., The Political Grammar of the United States, 1834.

Markby, W., Elements of Law, 6th ed., 1905.

Martens, G. F., de, Précis du Droit des Gens Moderne de L'Europe, 1788.

Mathews, J. M., "A Recent Development in Political Theory", in Political Science Quarterly, 1909, Vol., pp. 284 ff.

Martin, J., Concepts of State, Sovereignty, and International Law, 1928.

Mallwain, C. H., The High Court of Parliament and its Supremacy, 1910.

Mallwain, C. H., "The High Court of Parliament", 1910.

Mallwain, C. H., "The Political Works of James I", Harvard Political Classics, vol. I.

Mallwain, C. H., The American Revolution, 1923.

McLlaughlin, "Social Compact and Constitutional Construction", in American Historical Review, 1900.

MeNair, A. E., "So-called State Servitudes", in British Year Book of International Law, 1924.

Merignhac, A., Traite de Droit public international, 1905.

Merriam, C. E., A History of American Political Theories, 1903.

Merriam, C. E., American Political Ideas, 1920.

Merriam and Barnes, A History of Political Theories: Recent Times, 1924.

Merraim, C. E., History of the Theory of Sovereignty since Rousseau, 1900.

Mexican Constitution of 1924 and 1917.

Meyer, H. V., Lehrbuch des deutschen Staatsrecht, 1914 ed.

Millot, A., Les Mandats internationaux, 1914.

Modern French Legal Philosophy, Modern Legal Philosophy series, translated by Mrs. F. W. Scott and J. P. Chamberlin.

Mohl, R. V., Encyklopadie der Staatswissenschaften, 1959.

Mohl, R. V., Geschichto und Literatur der Staatswissenschaften.

Molinari, G. de, Théorie de l'évolution, 1908.

Molinari, G. de, The Society of To-morrow, trans. by P. H. Lee-Warner.

Montegomery, B. G., Issues of European Statesmanship, 1926.

Moore, J. B., Intarnational Law Digest, 1906.

Moore, J. B., "Law and Organization", American Political Science Review, Vol, IX.

Morris, G. R. and M., A History of Political Ideas, 1924.

Morris, G. S., Hegel's Philosophy of the State and of History, 1887.

Mott, "The Political Theory of Syndicalism", in Political Science Quarterly, Vol. XXXVII, 1922, pp. 25 ff.

Mulford, E., The Nation, 1872.

Munro, W. B., The Government of the United States, 1919.

Nippold, Die Fort bildung des Verfohrens in Volkerrechlichen Stritigkeiten.

Nippold, The Development of International Law after the World war, trans. by Hershey, 1913.

Nobicow, La Fédération de l'Europe, 1901.

Nobicow, War and its Alleged Benefits, trans. by Seltzer, 1911.

Nys, E., Le Droit International, 1904-1906.

Sppenheim, L. F. 〈L.〉, International Law, 3rd ed.

Sppenheim, L. F. L., The League of Nations and its Problems, London, 1919.

Sppenheim, L. F. L., The Future of International Law, 1921.

Sppenheimer, H., The Constitution of German Republic, 1923.

Sppenheimer, Franz., The State: Its History and Development Viewed Sociologically, trans. by J. M. Gitterman, 1914.

Orage, H. R., National Guild, 1914.

Osborne, S., The Saar Question: A Disease Spot in Europe, 1923.

Panunzio, S., Syndicalisme et Souveraineté, Le Mouvement Socialiste, 34, Nos. 253-254, pp. 59 ff.

Pataud, E. and Pouget, G., Syndicalism, Industrial Unionism and Socialism,

1913.

Paul-Boncour, J., Syndicats des Fonctionnaires, 1906.

Paul-Boncour, J., Le Fédéralisme économique, 2nd, 1901.

Penty, A. J., Old World for New, 1917.

Penty, A. J., Guilds and the Social Crisis, 1919.

Pergler, C., "Sovereignty in Judicial Interpretation", in American Bar Association Journal, Vol. XII, April, 1926.

Phillimore, R. J., Commentaries upon International Law, 1879-1889.

Pollock, F., "Locke's Theory of the State", in Proceedings of British Academy, Vol. I.

Pollock, F., An Introduction to the History of the Science of Politics, 1902.

Pollock, F., A First Book of Jurisprudence for Students of Common Law, 1918.

Pollock, F., "Sovereignty and the League of Nations", in Fortnightly Review, 1918, Vol. CX.

Pollock, F., League of Nations, 1920.

Pollock, F., Essays in Law, 1922.

Pomeroy, J. N., An Introduction to the Constitutional Law of the United States, 1886.

Porter, W. D., State Sovereignty and the Doctrine of Coercion, Association, No. 2, 1860.

Pound, R., "Legislation as a Social Function", see Publications of American Sociological Society, Vol. VII, pp. 153 ff.

Pound, R., "Scope and Purpose of Sociological Jurisprudence", in Harvard Law Review, Vol. 24, June, December 1911, and April, 1912.

Pound, R., The Spirit of Common Law, 1921.

Pound, R., Interpretations of Legal History, 1923.

Pound, R., An Introduction to the Philosophy of Law, 1922.

Pound, R., "Jurisprudence", in Barnes' The Philosophy and Prospects of the Social Science.

Pound, R., "Sociology and Law", in W. F. Ogburn and A. Colderweisser's The Social Sciences and Their Interrelations, 1927.

Pound, R., Law and Moral, 1924.

Pound, R., "Theory and Law", in Yale Law Journal Vol. XXII, pp. 114 ff.

Powers, A. H., The Great Peace, 1918.

Prall, W., The State and the Church, 1900.

Preuss, H., Gemeinde, Staat Reich, 1889.

Pufendorf, S., De Jure Naturae et Gentium, 1672, translated by B. Kennett.

Rankin, E. S., The Dominion of Sea and Air, 1925.

Ratzenhofer G., Wessen and Zweck der Politik, 1893.

Ratzenhofer G., Die Sociologische Erkenntnis, 1898.

Reed, James A., "Encroachment of the Federal Government", Proceedings of Texas Bar Association, Vol. XLVI, October, 1927.

Resch, P., Europaische Volkerrecht, 1885.

Ritchie, D. G., "On the Conception of Sovereignty" in Annals of American Academy of Political and Social Science, 1891, January.

Riviers, A. P. O, Principes du Droit des Gens, 1896.

Roberts, R., The Unfinished Program of Democracy, 1919.

Roberts, R., The Church in the Commonwealth, 1918.

Rockow, L., Contemporary Political Thought in England, 1921.

Roune, L. V., Staatsrecht des Deustche Reiches, 1876-1877.

Root, E., "The Sanction of International Law" in proceedings of American Society of International Law, 1908, pp. 14 ff.

Root, E., Address on International Subjects, edited by J. B. Scott, 1916.

Ross, E. A, Social Control, 1904.

Rougier, A., Les Guerres Civiles et le Droit des Gens, 1903.

Rousseau, J. J., The Social Contract, English translation by Toler.

Russell, B. A. W., The Prospects of Industrial Civilization, 1923.

Russell, Bertrand, A. W., Bolshevism: Practice and Theory, 1920.

Russell, B. A. W., Proposed Road to Freedom: Socialism Anarchism, and Syndicalism, 1919.

Russell, B. A. W., Principles of Social Reconstruction, 1918.

Russell, B. A. W., Political Ideals, 1917.

Ruttiman, P., Das Nordamerikanische Bundesstaat Verglichen mit den Politischen Einrichtungen der Schweiz, 1867-1872.

Ryan, J. A., "Proper Function of the State" in Catholic World, Vol. CXIII, pp. 169 ff.

Sabine, G. H., "The Concept of the State as Power," in The Philosophical Review, July, 1920.

Sabine, G. H., "Pluralism, a Point of View", in American Political Science Review, Vol. XVII, Febuary, 1923.

Salmond, J. W., Jurisprudence, sixth ed., 1920.

Savigny, F. K. V., Von Beruf unserer Zeit fur Gesetzgebung und Rechtswissenchaft, 1814.

Savigny, F. K. V., The History of Roman Law, trans, by E. Cathcart.

Savigny, K. V., System des Heutigen Romischen Rechts, 1840-1849.

Schulze, G. H., System des Deutschen Staatsrechts, 1881-1886.

Scott, J. B., James Madison's Notes of Debates in the Federal Convention of 1787 and their Relation to a more Perfect Society of Nations, 1918.

Scott, J. B., Cases on International Law, 2nd ed., 1922.

Scott, J. B., Sovereign States and Suits before Arbitral Tribunals and Courts of Justice, 1925.

Scott, J. B., The Hague Court Report, 1916.

Seeley, J. R., Introduction to Political Science, 1896.

Seydel, M. V., Xommentar zur Verfassung Kunde fur das Deutsche Reich, 1897.

Seydel, M. V., Grundzuge der Allgemein Staatslehre, 1873.

Small, A. W., Between Eros from Capitalism to Democracy, 1913.

Small, A. W., General Sociology, 1905.

Smith, H. A., The Law of Associations, 1914.

Smith, H. A., Federalism in North America, 1923.

Snow, "The Mandatory System under the Covenant of the League of Nations" in Proceedings of Academy of Political Science, Vol. VII, p. 427.

Sorel, G., Introduction à L'économie Moderne Composition du Maxisme, 1908.

Sorel, G., L'Avenir Socialiste des Syndiactes, 1898.

Sorel, G., Les Illusions du Progres, 1911, 2nd ed.

Sorel, G., Reflections on Violence, translated by T. E. Aulme, 1912.

Spargo, G., Syndicalism, Industrial Unionism, and Socialism, 1913.

Spaight, J. M., War Rights on Land, 1911.

Spencer, H., Man versus the State, 1884.

Spencer, H., Social Statics, 1851.

Stallybrass, W. T. S., A Society of States, 1919.

Steiner, R., The Threefold Commonwealth, 1922.

Stenphens, A. H., A Constitutional View of the Late War between the States, 2 volumes, 1867-1869.

Story, J., Commentaries on the Constitution of the united States, 1883.

Stowll, E. C., Intervention in Intervention Law, 1927.

Stowell and Munro, International Cases, 1916.

Sumner, W. G., Folkway, 1913.

Taft and Bryan, World Peace: A Written Debate, 1917.

Taft, W. H., "The Paris Covenant for a League of Nations" in American Political Science Review, Vol. XIII, 1919.

Tarde, G., The Laws of Imitation, 1903.

Taylor, J., New View of the Constitution, 1822.

Taylor, Science of Jurisprudence, 1903.

Treitschke, Undesstaat und Einheitsstaat, 1864.

Treitschke, H. G. V., Politik, 1899–1900, also English translation by Dugdale and T. de Bille, 1916.

Treumann, R. M., Die Monarchomachen, 1895.

Tucker, G., His Edition of Blackstone's Commentaries

Tuft, J. H., "The Community and Economic Groups", in Philosophical Review, XXVII, pp. 89 ff.

Turner, R. E., America in Civilization, 1925.

Twiss, T., Law of Nations, 1884.

Vaccaro, M. A., Les Bases Sociologiques du Droit et de L'étate, 1898.

Vattel, E. de, Le Droit des Gens, 1863 ed.

Waitz, G., Grundzug der Politik, 1862.

Wallas, Human Nature in Politics, 1909.

Wallas, G., The Great Society: A Psychological Analysis, 1914.

Wallas, G., Our Social Heritage, 1921.

Ward, P. W., Sovereignty: A Study of a Contemporary Political Nation, 1928.

Washington's Writings, Collected and edited by W. C. Ford.

Webb, S. and B., A Constitution for the Socialist Commonwealth of Great Britain, 1920.

Webster, D., Works, 1851.

Wehberg, H., Problems of International Court of Justice, trans. by C. G. Fenwick, 1918.

Westlake, J., International Law, 1904–1907.

Wheaton. H., Elements of International Law, 1899, 3rd edition.

Whitfield, J. B., "Sovereign Power of Constitutional Governments", in Central Law Journal, Vol. XCI, August, 1920.

Wickersham, G. W., "Confused Sovereignty", Illinois Law Review, November,

1916, Vol. XI.

Wilde, N., The Ethical Basis of the State, 1924.

Williams, D. R., "Is Congress Empowered to Alienate Sovereignty of the United States", in Virginia Law Review, Vol. XII, pp. 1 ff., 1925.

Williams, G. H., "Sovereignty", in Central Law Journal, Vol. XCVIII, pp. 385 ff., 1925.

Williams, J. M., The Foundations of Social Science, 1920.

Williams, J. M., Principles of Social Psychology, 1922.

Williams, H. E., Dual Government, in Kentucky Law Journal, March, 1927.

Willoughby, W. W., The Nature of the State, 1896.

Willoughby, W. W., Political Theories of the Ancient World, 1903.

Willoughby, W. W., The American Constitutional System, 1904.

Willoughby, W., "The Juristic Conception of the State", in American Political Science Review, Vol. 12, pp. 192-208.

Willoughby, W. W., "The Political Theories of John W. Burgess", in Yale Law Review, Vol. XVII, May, 1908.

Willoughby, W. W., The Fundamental Concepts of Public Law, 1924.

Willoughby, W. W., The Juristic Theories of Krabbe, in American Political Science Review, August, 1926.

Wilson, J., Works.

Wilson, W, An Old Master and Other Political Essays, 1893.

Wilson, W., The State, 1898.

Wise, B. R., Outline of Jurisprudence, 4th ed., 1925.

World Peace Foundation Pamphlet, 1912.

World Peace Foundation Pamphlets, Sixth Year Book of the League of Nations.

World Peace Foundation Pamphlet, Vol. X, No. 6, 1927.

Wright, Q., "Effects of the League of Nations Covenant", in Political Science Review, Vol. XIII, p. 569.

Wright, Q., "Sovereignty of the Mandates", in American Journal of International Law, Vol. XVII.

Yarros, V. S., "What shall we do with the State", in American Journal of Sociology, Vols. XXV, pp. 572-583 and XXVI, pp. 58-72.

Zane, J. M., The Story of Law, 1927.

译名对照表

Acton, J. E. E. D. 阿克顿
Adams, B. 亚当斯
Adams, F. O. 亚当斯
Adams, J. Q. 亚当斯
Allen, S. H. 阿伦
Althusius, H. 阿尔图修斯
Angell, N. 安吉尔
Aristotle 亚里士多德
Arndt, V. A. 安得特
Ashley, H. L. 阿希莱
Austin, J. 奥斯丁

Baker, S. 贝克
Baoer, G. S. 鲍尔
Baldwin, S. E. 白德温
Barker, E. 巴克
Barnes, H. E. 巴恩斯
Baty, T. 巴蒂
Beale, J. H. 巴莱
Beaumanoir 波马诺
Belloc, H. 贝洛克
Benoist, C. 伯努瓦
Bentham, J. 边沁
Bentley, A. F. 本特利
Berdahl, C. A. 伯代尔
Bernard, M. 贝尔纳德
Berolzheimer, F. 伯罗茨海默
Berthelemy, N. 本瑟里曼

Beseler 贝塞勒
Bigelow, J. 贝格洛
Blackstone, W. 布莱克斯通
Blakey, R. 布莱克
Bliss, P. 布利斯
Blummer, J. J. 布鲁默尔
Bluntschli, J. K. 伯伦知理
Bodin, J 布丹
Bonald, De. 德伯纳德
Bonjour, F. 伯杰尔
Borel, E. 波莱尔
Bornhak, C. 波伦哈克
Bosanquet, B. 鲍桑奎
Bourgeois, L. 鲍尔吉斯
Bradley, A. C. 布拉德雷
Bradley, F. H. 布拉德雷
Brentano, F. 布伦塔诺
Brie, S. 布瑞
Brierly, J. L. 布瑞利
Brooks, J. G. 布鲁克斯
Brown, I. J. C. 布朗
Brown, P. M. 布朗
Brown, W. J. 布朗
Brownson, O. A. 布朗森
Brun, C. 布鲁恩
Brunet, R. 布鲁纳
Bryce, J. 布里斯
Buchanan, G. 布坎南

Buell, R. L. 标厄尔
Burgess, J. W. 伯吉斯
Burke, E. 柏克
Burns, C. D. 伯恩斯
Butler, N. C. 巴特勒

Cahen, G. 卡罕
Calhoun, J. C. 卡尔霍恩
Carter, J. C. 卡特
Carlyle, R. W. 卡莱尔
Cecil, R. 塞西尔
Centz, P. C. 森特兹
Chipman, N. 奇普曼
Chipman, W. 奇普曼
Clark, W. L. 克拉克
Clute, W. K. 克卢特
Cobbett, P. 科贝特
Coker, F. W. 科克尔
Cole, G. D. H. 柯尔
Commons, J. R. 康芒斯
Constant, B. 康斯坦丁
Colley, T. M. 库利
Corbett, J. 柯贝特
Cornelison, I. A. 科耐里森
Crane, R. T. 克兰
Croly, H. 克劳利
Cunningham 坎宁翰
Curtis, G. T. 柯蒂斯

Davis, G. B. 戴维斯
Davis, H. W. C. 戴维斯
Davis, J. 戴维斯
Dealey, J. 第雷
de Maistre 德梅思特尔
Dewey, J. 杜威

Dicey, A. V. 戴雪
Dickinson, E. D. 迪金森
Dickinson, J. 迪金森
Donald, R. 唐纳德
Douglas, P. H. 道格拉斯
Dowdall, H. C. 多德尔
Duggan, S. P. H. 达根
Duguit, L. 狄骥
Durkheim E. 涂尔干

Elliott, W. Y. 艾略特
Ellis, E. D. 埃利斯
Esmein 埃斯曼
Estey, J. A. 埃斯蒂
Evans, L. B. 伊文思
Ewart, J. S. 尤尔特

Fairlie, J. A. 费尔赖
Fauchille, P 佛契莱
Fenwick, C. G. 冯为柯
Ferguson, J. H. 福格森
Fichte, J. G. 费希特
Figgis, J. N. 菲吉斯
Filmer, R. 菲尔默
Fisher, H. A. L. 费舍尔
Fodere, P. 福德瑞
Foignet, R. 富瓦涅
Follett, M. P. 弗里特
Ford, P. L. 福特
Foster, R. 佛斯特
Foulke, R. R. 弗尔柯
Freeman 弗里曼
Freund, E. 弗劳德

Gareis, K. 格瑞斯

Garner, J. W. 加纳
Gehlke, C. E. 格尔基
Gerson, J. 热尔松
Gettell, R. G. 格特尔
Geza, E. 格泽
Giddings, H. 吉丁斯
Gierke, O. 基尔克
Gilchrist, R. N. 吉尔克里斯特
Gooch, G. P. 古奇
Graham, W. 格兰姆
Greef De 德格里夫
Gregory 格列高里
Grimke 葛罗米柯
Grotious 格劳修斯
Gumplowiez, L. 古姆普洛维茨

Hackett, F. 哈克特
Haenel, A. 海内尔
Haldane, R. P. 霍尔丹
Halevy, F. 哈里夫
Hall, W. E. 霍尔
Halleck, H. W. 哈勒克
Haller, L. V. 哈勒
Hamilton, A. 汉密尔顿
Hamilton, E. D. 汉密尔顿
Hancke, E. 汉克
Hane, A. 海恩
Harley, J. E. 哈利
Harrington 哈林顿
Harris, H. W. 哈里斯
Hart, A. B. 哈特
Hauriou, M. 欧里乌
Hayes, E. C. 海耶斯
Hearnshaw, E. J. C. 赫恩肖
Held, J. 赫尔德

Hegel, G. W. 黑格尔
Henderson, A. 亨德森
Hennessy, J. 亨尼西
Hershey, A. S. 赫尔希
Hicks, F. C. 希克斯
Higgins 海因斯
Hill, D. J. 希尔
Hobbes, T. 霍布斯
Hobhouse, L. T. 霍布豪斯
Hobson, J. A. 霍布森
Hobson, S. G. 霍布森
Hodges, H. G. 霍吉斯
Holaind, R. I. 霍莱德
Holcome, A. N. 荷尔卡姆
Holland, T. T. 霍兰德
Holloway, W. 赫乐为
Holmes, O. 霍姆斯
Holmef, O. 霍尔姆夫
Holt, H. 霍尔特
Hotman, F. 霍特曼
Hovell 霍维尔
Hsiao, K. C. 萧公权
Hughan, J. W. 霍安
Hulme, T. E. 休姆
Hurd, J. C. 赫德
Hymans, M. 黑曼斯

Iredell. J. 艾尔德尔
Ihering 耶林

James Ⅰ. 詹姆斯一世
James, W. 詹姆斯
Jameson, J. A. 詹姆森
Janet, P. 珍妮特
Jefferson, T. 杰斐逊

Jellinek, G. 耶利内克
Jenks, E. 靳克斯
Johnston, F. 约翰斯顿
Jowett, B. 乔伊特
Judson, H. P. 贾德森

Kaltenborn, C. V. B. 卡登朋
Kant, I. 康德
Kelsen, H. 凯尔森
Kent, J. 肯特
Kingsley, D. A. 金斯利
Kirkup, T. 柯卡普
Kobler 克布勒
Korff, S. A. 卡尔夫
Korkunov, N. M. 卡尔库诺夫
Krabbe, H. 克拉勃
Kruger, F. K. 克鲁格

Laband, P. 拉班德
Ladier, H. W. 雷德尔
Lagordell 拉格德莱
Laing, B. M. 莱恩
Lansing, R. 兰辛
Larnaude 拉尔诺德
Laski, H. J. 拉斯基
Lawrence, T. J. 劳伦斯
Leacock, S. B. 里柯克
Lee, R. W. 李
Le Fur, L. 乐福尔
Leroy, M. 乐华
Leyermore, C. H. 里耶摩尔
Levesque, G. 莱维斯克
Lewis, G. C. 刘易斯
Lewis, M. M. 刘易斯
Lieber, F. 利伯

Lightwood, J. M. 莱特伍德
Lindsay, A. D. 林赛
Lippmann, W. 李普曼
Liszt, F. V. 李斯特
Levine, L. 莱文
Locke, J. 洛克
Lodge, H. C. 洛奇
Lord, A. R. 罗德
Loria, A. 洛里亚
Lowell, A. L. 劳威尔
Lucas, W. W. 卢卡斯

MacIver, R. M. 麦基韦
Mackintosh, J. 麦金托什
Masison, J. 麦锡逊
Macdonald, J. R. 麦克唐纳
Maezru, R. 麦兹罗
Maine, H. 梅因
Maistre, De 德迈斯特
Maitland, F. M. 梅特兰
Manning, W. O. 曼宁
Mansfield, E. D. 曼斯菲尔德
Markby, W. 马克白
Martens, G. F. 马特恩斯
Mathews, J. M. 马修斯
Martin, J. 马丁
Marvin, F. S. 马尔文
Mallwain, C. H. 麦韦恩
Mattern, J. 马特恩
McClure, M. T. 麦克卢尔
McLaughlin 麦克劳恩
McNair, A. E. 麦克奈尔
Merignhac, A. 迈瑞戈汉克
Merriam, C. E. 梅里亚姆
Meyer, H. V. 麦耶

Miller, W. G. 米勒
Millot, A. 梅洛特
Mohl, R. V. 摩豪
Molesworth, W. 莫斯沃斯
Molinari, G. 莫里那瑞
Montgomery, B. G. 蒙哥马利
Moore, J. B. 莫尔
Morris, G. R. 莫里斯
Moser, J. J. 莫泽尔
Mott 莫特
Mulford, E. 马尔福德
Munro, W. B. 门罗

Nietzsche, F. 尼采
Nipold, O. 内庞德
Nobicow 诺贝考
Novicow, J. 诺维考姆
Nys, E. 努斯

Oppenheim, L. F. L. 奥本海
Oppenheimer, H. 奥本海默
Orage, H. R. 奥兰治
Osborne, S. 奥斯本

Panunzio, S. 帕农齐奥
Pataud, E. 帕陶德
Paul-Boncour, J. 保罗-邦库尔
Penty, A. J. 盘提
Pargler, C. 帕格勒尔
Plillimore, R. J. 普利里摩尔
Pollock, F. 普罗克
Polybius 波利比奥斯
Pomeroy, J. N. 波莫罗伊
Porter, W. D. 波特
Pound, R. 庞德

Powers, H. H. 鲍尔斯
Prall, W. 普劳尔
Preuss, H. 普拉乌斯
Pufendorf, S. 普芬道夫

Raleigh, T. 雷利
Rankin, E. S. 兰肯
Ratzenhofer, G. 拉岑霍费尔
Redlich, J. 雷德利克
Reed, James A. 里德
Resch, P. 里斯奇
Ritchie, D. G. 里奇
Rivers, A. P. O. 里维尔
Roberts, R. 罗伯茨
Rockow, L. 洛克伍
Rodriguez, M. D. 罗德瑞古兹
Rolin, R. E. 罗琳
Root, E. 鲁特
Ross, E. A. 罗斯
Rougier, A. 罗吉尔
Rougier, J. J. 罗吉尔
Roune, L. V. 郎恩
Russell, B. A. W. 罗素
Ruttiman, P. 鲁提曼
Ryan, J. A. 瑞安

Sabine, G. H. 萨拜因
Sainte-Beuve, C. A. 圣佩韦
Saleilles 萨雷利斯
Salmond, J. W. 萨尔蒙德
Savigny, F. K. V. 萨维尼
Schulze, G. H. 舒尔茨
Scott, J. B. 斯科特
Seeley, J. B. 西利
Seydel, M. V. 赛德尔

Small, A. W. 斯莫尔
Small, H. A. 斯莫尔
Sorel, G. 索雷尔
Spaight, J. M. 斯潘特
Spencer, H. 斯宾塞
Stallybrass, W. T. S. 斯塔列布拉斯
Steiner, R. 斯坦纳
Stephens, A. H. 斯蒂芬
Story, J. 斯托尼
Stowell, E. C. 斯托厄尔
Sumner, W. G. 萨姆纳

Taft 塔夫脱
Tat, W. H. 塔特
Tarde, G. 塔德
Taylor, J. 泰勒
Tawney, R. H. 托尼
Tozer, H. J. 图泽
Treitschke, H. G. V. 特赖奇克
Tremann, R. M. 特罗曼
Tucker, G. 塔克
Tuk, J. H. 图科
Turner, R. E. 特纳
Twiss, T. 特威斯

Vaccro, M. A. 瓦克罗
Vattell, E. 瓦泰勒

Waitz, G. 魏茨

Wallas 沃拉斯
Wallsd, G. 沃思德
Ward, P. W. 沃德
Washington 华盛顿
Werb, S. and B. 韦伯夫妇
Webster, D. 韦伯斯特
Wehberg, H. 温伯格
Westlake, J. 韦斯特莱克
Wheaton, H. 惠顿
Whitfield, J. B. 温斯菲尔德
Wielersham, G. W. 维勒夏姆
Wilde, N. 维尔德
Williams, D. R. 威廉姆斯
Williams, G. H. 威廉姆斯
Williams, J. M. 威廉姆斯
Williams, H. E. 威廉姆斯
Willoughby, W. W. 韦罗贝
Wilson, J. 威尔逊
Wilson, W. 威尔逊
Wise, B. R. 怀斯
Wright, Q. 赖特

Yarros, V. S. 雅罗斯
Young, A. 扬

Zane, J. M. 赞恩
Zimmer 齐默尔
Zorn 佐恩

译 后 记

近些年来，"陈序经研究"是学术界一个不大不小的热点。陈序经的著作都在陆续重版。但陈序经于1928年提交答辩、1929年付印的博士论文一直没有引起研究者的注意，实际上这也是陈序经研究难于深化的一个重要原因。我一直想把这本著作翻译出来，以为陈序经研究提供更为坚实的基础。2003年8月到2006年2月，我在中国社会科学院哲学研究所撰写博士后出站报告《陈序经政治哲学研究》（人民出版社2007年版）时，就一直在断断续续地翻译这本书，但译事艰辛，加之心有旁骛，拖至2008年暑假才决定了此一"心结"，不过也只能够交出一份勉勉强强的答卷，实在是非常惭愧！后又经张伟生、金欣两位好友详加校对，避免了若干硬伤。特别需要指出的是，在翻译过程中，我参考了前贤与时贤的一些翻译文本，有些更是直接援引，这里译者深表感谢。

感谢中山大学历史系赵立彬教授为我复印陈序经的原版论文，感谢陈其津先生和陈穗仙女士慨然允许我翻译陈序经的这本著作，感谢高全喜教授和许章润教授为本书出版所提供的方便，感谢本书责任编辑，她们精益求精的编辑使我避免了许多错误。

由于译者水平有限，书中定还有许多翻译上的错误，请读者批评指正。

译者
2010年9月

Politology

CONTENTS[①]

Introduction		559
Chapter 1	Politology	566
Chapter 2	Subject Matter of Political Science	597
Chapter 3	Government and State	623
Chapter 4	Forms of Government and State	647
Chapter 5	State in Primitive Society (Origin of the State)	671
Chapter 6	Origin of the State	695
Chapter 7	Political or Social (State or Society)	723
Chapter 8	State & Other Organizations	747
Chapter 9	Sovereignty	771
Chapter 10	Sovereignty	805
Chapter 11	Sovereignty	830
Chapter 12	State & Law	854

---

① 校按：原文没有目录，编者据书中章节添加。

Introduction

My dear Professor Fairlie:

After having sent to the publisher some writing called *Oriental and Occidental Culture* in commemoration of my father's sixtieth birthday, I am now sending you a small gift to congratulate you on the anniversary ⟨of⟩ your birth. Here in China we think of parents and teachers together, for life can be perfected only through nourishment and education given together. Our parents give us nourishment while our teachers provide us with knowledge. Thus a teacher, according to the Eastern sense of virtue, is honoured equally with one's parents.

Moreover, the sixtieth birthday is the most important one in a lifetime. It is even more important than your jubilee in the West, for one is not only honored for having travelled so far in the journey of life, but also regarded as having been reborn. Our astrologers have made sixty yours into a cycle of life, and to complete a cycle means to begin a new life. By happy coincidence, you were born within a few months of my father, and when have you both have your sixtieth birthday in the same year my happiness as son and pupil is very great indeed.

My father does not read English, and you, I know, have not taken time to study our language. Having written a Chinese treatise for my father, I am presenting you with the following pages in English. The difference in form, i. e. language, does not mean that I am treating you differently, since I have been cultivated on both Chinese and American soil. I shall let my father judge the fruit produced on Chinese soil. You will, I hope, find my humble offering to you worth the patient and kind labours of many years which you spent for my cultivation.

If spirit and character are to be counted more than physical identity, I must confess that I am not a Chinese in the old sense of the phrase.

I have been and shall always be a sincere admirer of Western civilization because it helps so well to fulfil the present needs of China. This is the thesis of my work in Chinese. My father hesitates to share my view. My answer is: "You have spent much time and money and hope in cultivating your seed in both Europe and America, and to expect returns entirely agreeable to the old Chinese taste, would be contrary to your original will."

Now if the little fruit here presented is not that which you have expected and therefore is not perfectly agreeable to your taste, the reason may be that it is a product of a mixed soil under a mixed environment.

When I think of sixty years as a part of our history, I feel that it is so short fleeting that a Chinese historian would not have much to say about it in a college textbook on Chinese history. But this is undoubtedly not the right way of thinking, for in the United States or even in your mother country, Scotland, it is something different. Sixty years occupies almost half of the life history of the United States. Yet this is not all. It is the importance of the moment and event rather than the length of the time that is significant. And if we look back to the last sixty years, we can not help feeling that it surely is the most important epoch in human history. At least this is true if we take it from the standpoint of the social sciences. Darwin's *Origin of Species* published in 1859, may be regarded as a milestone in the development of natural science, and the year 1872 may be considered as having seen the birth of modern social studies.

Thirty years before you were born, August Comte completed his monumental work *Cours de Philosophie Positive (1826-1842)*. It was he who coined the word "sociologie", and it was he who pointed out that social phenomena may be made an independent field of investigation. But Comte, as Professor Giddings remarks, only "predicted sociology; he did not himself create it"; and we may venture to say that before 1872, sociology can hardly be said to have been accepted as an independent discipline. Robert von Mohl, one of the greatest figures in the field of social studies of his time almost failed to mention the name of Comte in 1855 in his voluminous work *Geschictte und Literatur der Staatswissenschaften*.

It is to Herbert Spencer that we must give the credit of laying the corner-stone of sociology. Professor Giddings speaks of his *Social Statics* (1851) as one of the greatest books of sociology, comparable with the *Politics* of Aristotle, and yet it is his *Study of Sociology* (1873) that must be regarded as a formal declaration of the new study. This work although published in book form in 1873, was in fact written and published in the form of fragments in 1872. According to Spencer himself, the book was written by way of introduction to his *Principles of Sociology*, which, whether we like it or not, is nevertheless an epoch-making work not only in the field of sociology, but also in general social studies. It was the *Study of Sociology* that attracted so much attention and received such recognition by the world that sociology is not only a "Wissenschaft" in name, but also a "Wissenschaft" in fact.

To a certain extent the like may be said for economics. Adam Smith's *The Wealth of Nations* was published almost a century before you were born, but at least the term economics can be found only after the seventies of the last century. John Stuart Mill, in whom we find the culmination of the classical political economy, died only a few months after your birth. Karl Marx, a prominent figure in modern economics and the father of so-called scientific socialism, published the first volume of his world-known treatise *Das Capital* only five years before 1972. State socialism, a movement led by prominent scholars such as Albert Eberhard, Friedrich Schäffle and Adolf Wagner, dates only from the Congress of Eisenach in 1872.

When I consider the field of political science, in the study and teaching of which you have been engaged for the last few decades, I find the years 1872 and thereafter to be very important in its history. At the outset, one can even say that from 1872 onwards political chronicles flourished. The people of the United States had not long before that obtained the peace that followed the Civil War. The German unification for which Bismarck had laboured for years was just completed. The republican foundation of France was then laid. China began to be conscious of the need for westernization. Japan had come to a new age with a new emperor. The three emperors of the greatest powers of Europe, i. e. Russia, Austria and Germany, met together in the city of Berlin. Although England had suffered no great political upheaval she was nevertheless undergoing tremendous changes in many respects.

The beginnings of modern systematic political study, as generally recognized, are to be found in Germany. Yet there were only two works mentioned by Treitschke (before 1872) to the audience listening to his lectures on *Politik* at the University of Berlin. One is Dahlmann's *Politik* (1838) and the other is Bluntschli's *Contribution*. He considered the former to be the better of the two although it appeared fifty years before his own lectures on politics. Bluntschli's work was considered to be the "eigentliche systematische Politik", yet according to him, it was coloured with the theory of natural rights and laws (Naturrechtslehre).

We should not believe too much in Treitschke, because he himself was not free from bias. But Bluntschli was considered, as Treitschke told us, the only systematic writer, and indeed the greatest master of Staatswissenschaft, his most systematic and well-known work, although appearing twenty years before 1872, can not, however, be said to have been completed until 1875. I mean here his *Die Lehre vom Modernen Staat*. At first it was published under the title *Allgemeines Staatsrecht* (geschichtlich begrundet) in a single volume. Then gradually it was expanded into two volumes but still under the old title up to the fourth edition of the work (1868). Only in 1875, in its fifth edition, did Bluntschli reorganize the materials under the title *Die Lehre vom Modernen Staat* into three volumes: *Das Allgemeine Staatslehre*, *Das Allgemeine Staatsrecht*, and *Die Politik*. While 1875 was the final date for its publication, it was in 1872 or thereabouts that the author busied himself writing it.

If some other systematic works need to be mentioned, we find that they all fall approximately on the auspicious year of your birth. Georg Waitz, who transfered the American conception of sovereignty and exerted a great influence on his own countrymen through the works of Tocqueville, published his *Grundzuge der Politik* only ten years before 1872. Holtzendorff's *Die Principien der Politik* came still later (1869). To say nothing of Treitschke, Jellinek's *Allgemeine Staatslehre* which is still accepted as the textbook in German universities, quoted frequently by German scholars, and regarded as the best treatise on a general survey of the so-called political science, made its first appearance in 1900. Thus if Buntschli and Jellinek are to be taken as the greatest masters of political study in their respective times, the fruits of their achievement were all produced within the last sixty years.

It is often said that the French people are more or less romantic, and have cared very little about systematic political writings. They even disregard real facts. Thus Montesquieu misunderstood the English political institutions and Rousseau just pictured a state of nature without historical support. Yet we find 1872 was just the year that Paul Janet completed his monumental work, *Histoire de la Science Politique dans ses Rapports avec la Morale* in its present form, although its first edition appeared in 1852. Great masters of law such as Leon Duguit and Esmein by whom the modern French writers have been profoundly influenced appeared on the academic stage much later. And systematic works on the state such as Carre de Malberg's *Theorie generale de l'etat* were not published until a little over ten years ago.

Crossing the Channel, we find that in England, the teaching of political science hardly made any headway before 1872, although England had given to the world a large number of political philosophers. Freeman, for instance, confused politics and history by declaring that history is past politics and that politics is present history. He forgot that much of our history is not political. Somewhat different from Freeman, Seeley maintained that history without political science has no fruit; and political science without history has no root. But the two series of lectures on the *Introduction of Political Science* were delivered by him more than ten years after 1872, and not published until much later. Amos's *The Science of Politics* appeared in 1883 and Sidgwick's *Elements of*

Politics came almost at the end of the last century (1897). Other works of significance such as Maine's *Early Institutions* came just a year before 1872. All of Bryce's works in the field of political study were published after 1872. Even his *The Holy Roman Empire* appeared only a few years before that time.

As early as the seventeenth century, great political thinkers such as Hobbes and Locke enabled England to play a very important role in the history of political philosophy, but systematic political scientists can hardly be found before 1872. Still younger is political science as a study in the English universities. It was true that Bodin's *Six Books of the Republic* was used in Oxford after it was translated into English, but the first professorship for this study was created in 1911. Oxford took the lead and London University followed. Cambridge did not have a chair of political science until 1927.

In the United States political science as a field of study scarcely attracted any attention from the general public. Burgess, the father, if you like, of modern political science in the United States, wrote in 1890 in his classical work, *Political Science and Comparative Constitutional Law* these words: "America has yet to develop her own school of publicists and her own literature of political science. Down to this time, the two names which stand highest in our American literature of political science are Francis Lieber and Theodore D. Woolsey." But he added: "The former was, as every one knows, a European, educated under European institutions, and a refugee from their oppression, as he regarded it. The latter was Lieber's ardent admirer, —we might almost say disciple."

Professor Burgess forgot to mention that Woolsey was himself influenced by German political writers. His two volumes on *Political Science, or the State* was modeled on the German pattern. He wrote: "With regard to the plan of the work the author desires to say a few words. The division into three parts, which somewhat answers to the Naturrecht, Staatslehre, and Politik of the Germans, seemed to be necessary..." Moreover the work, which grew out of lectures delivered between the years 1846 and 1871, as the author told us, [did] was not available until 1877. In fact, according to Professor Seligman in an autobiography written for a German publisher, there was no such thing as political science that one could study in the United States in eighteen-seventies.

When we come to Burgess himself, we find that his admirable work was published in 1890. In 1872 he was just a student studying in Germany where he went only a year before, and then came back to his mother country in the following year. In spite of the fact that his residence in Germany as a student lasted only two years, he was profoundly influenced by German scholars. His *Political Science and Comparative Constitutional Law*, the best book that he wrote, was dedicated to Johann Gustay Droysen, and the contents of the work were full of German characters. Professor Burgess, as we all know, was also the organizer of the first faculty and school of political science in the United States, but again the school of this kind was founded eight years after 1872.

Twenty years after Burgess wrote his monumental work, Professor Garner published his *Introduction to Political Science*. This book, according to Professor Arthur N. Holcombe, contains the most complete lists of references to the literature of political science that are available in any modern work in English. Professor Garner can use French to deliver lectures and to write books, but he is influenced more by the German than by the French writers. The book mentioned above was rewritten by Professor Garner in 1928 under the new title *Political Science and Government* and you are there mentioned as having given him the benefit of your wise criticism. ①

When I come to the study of public and municipal administration, it seems to me that although much attention had been already given by some of the German writers, you are one of those who have paved the way in the New World. It was a fact, as you said about thirty years ago: "Since Bryce's ehlightening work appeared, the attention has been given to methods of legislative procedure and the influence of party and party machinery. But the administrative organization and activities of the government have still been hardly mentioned in most works of a general nature." And you were right to predict that the problems of administration would "receive the attention which in earlier times was given to problems of constitution or organization".

No one will deny now that more attention has to be given to the administrative affairs of the nations, for it is the real corner-stone of the political fabric and the daily need of the citizens. Our daily life will not be affected much if we have no president or foregn minister for a short time, but we simply can not live without an administrative government. This is the reason why men like Professor W. F. Willoughby have come to the conclusion that besides the classical divisions of government, as legislative, executive and judicial, an administrative division should be added. And this is the reason why the British and many other governments have appointed men of high character and intellect to consider the administrative problems of their lands.

Thus Professor Fairlie, you have not only witnessed the development of political

---

① Prof. W. W. Willoughby's *The Nature of the State* (1896) is not mentioned here because it is, as the author himself puts it for the subtitle, A Study in Political Philosophy, rather than a systematic study of political science.

study during the last sixty years, but you have also been a part of it. We in China speak of thirty years as a *generation*, and sixty years are, therefore, two *generations*. Now if the first may be regarded as the preparatory age of modern political study, the second is indeed the growing period. The second part is much more important than the first. And this is the period in which you have devoted yourself to educating the younger generation. Thus the extent of your career is correspondent to the period of the *scientific* study of political development. But how important is it and what will be the outcome? I believe I can do no better than to quote a passage from your presidential address before the American Political Science Association: "A quarter of a century is a brief span in the recorded history of the world. But the first lap of the present century may well be of outstanding importance to those who have witnessed the march of the times, and signs are not lacking that in the future it may be considered one of the great turning points in political development."

What is that great turning point in political development? Let it be a reform of political science as followed in recent years. And may it begin sixty years from the auspicious day of your birth.

Very respectfully yours,
S. C. Chen

Chapter 1
Politology

Tsze-Lu said, "The ruler of Wei has been waiting for you, in order with you to administer the government. What do you consider the first to be done?"

The Master replied, "What is necessary is to rectify names."

"So, indeed!" said Tsze-Lu. "You are wide of the mark! Why must there be such rectification?"

The Master said, "How uncultivated you are, Yu!① A superior man, in regard to what he does not know, shows a cautious reserve.

"If names be not correct, language is not in accordance with the truth of things. If language be not in accordance with the truth of things, affairs cannot be carried on to success.

"When affairs cannot be carried on to success, proprieties and music will not flourish. When proprieties and music do not flourish, punishments will not be properly awarded. When punishments are not properly awarded, the people do not know how to move hand or foot.

"Therefore, a superior man considers it necessary that the names he uses may be spoken *appropriately*, and also that what he speaks may be carried out *appropriately*. What the superior man requires is just that in his words there may be nothing incorrect."②

There are many things in the Master's Analects considered as not up-to-date, but his insistence on "appropriate language" as indicated above still holds the truth that terms should be used to indicate what they really mean.

The writer is by no means unaware of the fact that terms are merely indications of things, but he is deeply convinced that as regards a term which does not indicate really what the thing itself indicates, a change is desirable or even necessary. This is what happens in the case of the so-called political science. The lack of a precise and

---

① Another name of Tsze-Lu.
② *Confucian Analects*, Book Ⅷ, ch. Ⅲ.

generally accepted nomenclature has been recognized by most of the writers in this field and we need only to mention a few of them. Jellinek, for instance, in his well-known text *Allgemeine Staatslehre*, remarks that there is no study which is so much in need of a terminology as that of the state.[1] In his *Modern Democracies*, Lord Bryce writes: "The terms used in the latter (human sciences) lack the precision which belongs to those used in the former (natural science). They are not truly technical, for they do not always mean the same thing to all who use them. Such words as 'aristocracy', 'prerogative', 'liberty', 'oligarchy', 'faction', 'caucus', even 'constitution' convey different meanings to different persons. The terms used in politics have, moreover, contracted associations, attractive or repellent, as the case may be, to different persons. They evoke feeling."[2] The same view is expressed by Professor J. W. Garner. "There is as yet," says he, "no commonly accepted term by which the science of government may be designated."[3] Again he says in another treatise, "It is characteristic of political science that, differing from the natural science, it lacks a precise and generally accepted nomenclature."[4]

These are the opinions of the writers in the field of the so-called Political Science, Yet none of them has made, so far as I know, any attempt to find a better name. It is on that ground and for that purpose that I propose to use the term *Politology*[5], as I use it for the title of this essay, instead of what is known as Political Science, Politics, or any other names which have been employed.

It should be noted at the outset, that the term politology was coined by Professor J. S. Mackenzie in his *Outlines of Social Philosophy*[6]. But it was put in parenthesis and its meaning is, according to Professor Mackenzie, much different from what I understand it. Here is a statement we find in his admirable book: "If anthropology were taken to mean the general study of humanity, it might be divided into two main branches of idiotology and sociology (or politology), each of which would comprise a considerable

---

[1] G. Jellinek, *Das Recht des Modernen Staates. Erster Band. Allgemeine Staatslehre*, Berlin, Zweite Auflage (1905), S. 129. "Die Terminoligie folgt jedoch nicht immer der Logik, Wissenschaftlich ist aber kein Terminus so brauchear wie der des Staates…"

[2] Bryce, *Modern Democracies* (1921), Vol. I, p. 15.

[3] J. W. Garner, *Introduction to Political Science* (1910), p. 7.

[4] *Political Science and Government* (1928), pp. 1–2. President Lowell remarks that the study of politics "lacks the first essential of a modern science—a nomenclature incomprehensible to educated men". *American Political Science Review* (1909), Vol. IV, p. 1. See also Amos, *The Science of Politics*, pp. 56 ff.

[5] I have used this term as Prof. John A. Fairlie preferred to use it. For my part *Politology* would be equally if not more preferable.

[6] Edition of 1918.

number of separate sciences."①

It is obvious that Professor Mackenzie proposed to use the word for what is known as sociology which he seems to consider as a subdivision of anthropology. The word so used does not only need etymological support, but it also leads to a misunderstanding of the whole field of social sciences, and consequently a reconstruction of social sciences would be required. In fact, sociology is not, and can never be, called politology which, as understood by Professor Mackenzie, is to be a branch of anthropology and therefore in contrast to ideology.

It was Professor Jonn A. Fairlie of the University of Illinois, who, as my knowledge goes, first made the suggestion to employ and coin the word *Politology* in lieu of Politics or Political Science. The formal suggestion made by Professor Fairlie may be found in an article entitled "Politics and Science" published in the *Scientific Monthly* some years ago.② Professor Fairlie, although he has occasionally repeated and used the term in his lectures on the Nature of the State given in the University of Illinois during the last few years, did not and does not insist positively upon it, So far as I can recall it, his characteristic expression is this: "Curiously the term politology has not been used by any writer."③ It is proposed, therefore, in this essay to make a positive attempt to apply the term "politology" to the study of what has been inadequately understood as political science, polities, etc.

First of all, it may be remarked that so far as etymology is concerned, there is no objection to using this word. One may still recall that a few decades ago when the term "sociology" was first coined by Comte and used by subsequent writers for the study of social phenomena and relations, a warm discussion was aroused and a strong opposition made against it on the ground that the term is a hybrid, compounded from both Latin and Greek words, as it begins with Latin, but ends with Greek. "C'est donc une sorte de Monstre", so remarked a French writer.④ But there can be no such objection in the case of the present word politology. It is of pure and simple Greek origin, beginning and ending with Greek. It is just like words such as biology and psychology.

But most important of all, as we have already pointed out, none of all the terms

---

① *Outlines of Social Philosophy*, p. 14.
② *Scientific Monthly*, Jan. 1924, Vol. XVIII, pp. 18–37. I feel sorry for not having the article mentioned in hand, although I read it more than once when I was in the United States some years ago.
③ It is to be added that although I read Professor Mackenzie's *Outlines of Social Philosophy* before the appearance of Professor Fairlie's article, the word politology used by the former did not come to my attention until very recently.
④ Rene Maunier, *Introduction a la Sociologie* (1929), Paris, p. l.

which have been generally used and accepted can convey to us the true meaning of the study. In order to show the desirability of employing the new word, it is quite necessary to show, first of all, how the old ones are not precise and comprehensive.

The German word "Staatswissenschaft", or "Staatswissenschaften", has been used by many German writers. But as the term is so vague, it does not give one a precise meaning. Schmitthenner, one of the earlier writers, included in his *Zwölf Bücher vom Staate, oder systematische Encyklopädie der Staatswissenschaften* (1832), [1] almost the whole field of what is now understood as social science. He subdivided the field of Staatswissenschaft into theoretical, practical and cultural, and these in turn included such studies as economics, law, education and even ethnology. Such practice was followed to a certain extent by Robert v. Mohl in his *Geschichte und Literatur der Staatswissenschaften* (1855), and his *Enzyklopädie der Staatswissenschaften* (1859). Statistics, Economics, Politics, and Law and others are considered to be within the sphere of Staatswissenschaft. [2] Even to the present day, such a view is still followed. Thus the department of Staatswissenschaft in the University of Berlin contains almost the most important subjects in the field of social sciences. [3] So is this true in the case of some other universities such as Kiel, Frankfurt, etc.

While Staatswissenschaft is still used to indicate what is known as social science to a certain extent, its true meaning has been essentially changed. What is now meant by Staatswissenschaft is different from what the earlier writers understood it. "Die eine

---

[1] I used the second edition (1839), Gissen. Compare also Friedrich Bülau, *Enzyklopädie der Staatswissenschaft*, 1 Aufl. (1832) and his "Literatur der Staatswissenschaften" in Rotteck und Welcker's *Staatslexikon*. Here Bülau divided Staatswissenschaft into the following categories: Staatsrechtlich-politische, völkerrechtlich-diplomatische, national ökonomische, statistische. See also J. Held's article on "Staatswissenschaften" in Rotteck und Welcker's *Staatslexikon* 3 Aufl. Leipzig (1865). Bluntschli's article "Staatswissenschaft" in Bluntschli und Brater's *Deutsches staatswörterbuch*, Stuttgart and Leipzig (1867). "Staatswissenschaft" in H. Wagener's *Das Stasts-und Gesellschaftslexikon*, Bd. XIX. R. Piloty, "Staat und "Staatswissenschaften" in the second edition of *Wörterbuches des deutschen Staats-und Verwaltungsrechts*, Tübingen (1914). G. Schmoller, *Grundrisz der Allgemeinen Volkswirtschaftslehre*, Leipzig (1900), and his article "Volkswirtschaft, Volkswirtschaftslehre und methode" in *Handwörterbuch der Staatswissenschaften*, 3 Aufl.

[2] H. Rehm, "Politik als Wissenschaft" in *Handbuch der Politik*, Erster Band, S. 9. See also Jelliners, *ibid*. S. 6.

[3] In the Vorlesungsverzeichnis of the University of Berlin (1930), Sommersemester, we find in page 80 a division of Staatsund Sozialwissenschaften belonging to the Philosophische Fakultät, including such courses ss Volkswirtschaftslehre, Nationalökonomie and Gesellschaftslehre. Besides, Das Staatswissenschaftlich-statistischen Seminar is somewhat like a seminar of social science. See also *Zeitschrift für die gesammte Staatswissenschaft* Ester Band (1844), p. 5. "Es sind sämmtliche Staatswissenschaft welche, wir besprechen beabrichtigen. Somit Staatsrecht und Völkerrecht; politische Oekonomie in ihrem ganzen Omfange, Polizeiwissenschaft, Politik; Statistik und Staatengeschichte."

bedeutungsvolle Tatsache," says Professor G. v. Mayr, "dasz man heute in der Regel unter 'Staatswissenschaften' etwass anderes versteht, als zu der Zeit, da Robert von Mohl in der Pflege der Staatswissenschaften führend hervortrat, ist zutreffend hervorgenoben."① The same writer remarks that there is yet no positive attempt to find out the difference in the field of Staatswissenschaft between its old sense and its new sense.② In fact even in such voluminous work as *Handwörterbuch der Staatswissenschaften* one can hardly find an article explaining what is meant by Staatswissenschaft. Nor can one even find such a word in its index.

But generally speaking, it may be said that the meaning of the term Staatswissenschaft in its old sense is more or less confined to the state, and perhaps the state alone; its new sense is somewhat shifted to the study of Economics.③ Thus we find most of the courses offered by the department of Staatswissenschaft in the University of Berlin are largely in economics, while the so-called Staatswissenschaft in its old sense and as understood by the American or English students is to be found in the juristische Fakultät.④ English and American students in particular, who go to Germany to do their advanced studies, used to be surprised at being told that there is no such department as political science in Germany as in their own country, where it is entirely separate from the department of Economics, Sociology, or the like. Thus one who occupies a chair in the staatswissenschaftliche Fakultät may not be a professor of political science. He is presumedly a professor of Economics or Sociology. Staatswissenschaft is not what is known as political science, and it is a mistake to translate staatswissenschaft as political science.⑤

The distinction between Staatswissenschaft in its old sense and in its new sense, according to Professor Mayr, may be regarded as a distinction in the sense of the word

---

① G. v. Mayr, *Begriff und Gliederung der Staatswissenachaften* (1901). I used the fourth edition (1921), pp. 1–2.

② *Ibid.*, p. 2. "Wie aber in der zweiten Hälfte des 19 Jahrhunderts allmählich eine Veranderung des geläufigen Begriffs der Staatswissenschaften sich vollzogen hat, ist nicht erötert. Es fehlt auch der positive Versuch einer schargen Abgrenzung der Wissensgebiete der Staatswissenschaft in jenem älteren und im nunmehr überwiegenden neueren Sinn."

③ "Staatswissenschaften sind der Darstellung der Wirtschaftsorduung gewidmet" see Paul Pasener, *Rechtslexikon*, Zweiter Band. p. 55l, Berlin, 1909.

④ In Kiel University and in many other universities, courses such as Allgemeine Staatslehre are to be found in the juristische Fakultät, while all the courses in economics in staatswissenschaftliche Fakultät. Sociology may be found sometimes in the latter, but sometimes in the philosophische Fakultät.

⑤ The Oxford translation of Bluntschli's *Lehre vom Modernen Stat* translated the word Staatswissenschaft as political science and this has been generally followed. See *The Theory of the State*, 3 ed., p. 1.

(im wörtlichen Sinn) and in the transferable sense (im übertragenen Sinn). ① The former is narrow while the latter is broad. ② While this is true in a sense, it must be added that when the power of the state is at its highest watermark, the study of the state includes the study of other social phenomena, for the state is society and society the state. Thus before 1850 one scarcely spoke of "die Wissenschaft von der Gesellschaft". One knew only "die Wissenschaft vom Staats". When Robert v. Mohl tells us something about "Gesellschaftslehre", he tells us in such a dramatic manner: "Zuerst von Schwärmern und ihren Schulen; dann aber allmählich auch auf der Rednertribüne, in der Schenke und in den heimlichen Versammlungen Verschworener; es wird in entsetzlichen Straszenschlachten als Banner vorangetragen. Jetzt öffneten sich plötzlich die Augen... Die Wiesenschaft der Gesellschaft ist zu begrüngen und zu entwickeln..."③ But whence is it to develop (zu entwickeln)? It is undoubtedly from *die Staatswissenschaft*.

Staatswissenschaft is not only to be objected on the ground that its meaning is too vague, it is also objectionable because of the very word "Staat". We shall discuss this point later, but it is sufficient to remark here that the state is either too big or too small to include the political phenomena. To take the word *Staat* as the subject-matter of the study of political phenomena leads one to disregard many activities and organizations outside of its own field. This objection may be also said against the German term "Staatslehre" which has been commonly employed by modern writers.

"Staatslehre", as we are told by one of its best defenders, is "theoretische Staatswissenschaft". ④ Now it is clear that even if we take it for granted that "Staatswissenschaft" is equivalent to the English term political science, the so-called "theoretische Staatswissenschaft" is only a part of political science (Staatswissenschaft). For besides the "theoretische Staatswissenschaft", there is a "praktische Staatswissenschaft". Jellinek proposed to call the latter Politik. ⑤ Such division was already observed by Bluntschli although he added another division, i. e., "Staatsrecht" besides "Staatslehre" and "Politik". But here we are led to the abyss of confusion.

---

① Mayr, *Begriff und Gliederung der Staatswissenschaften*, p. 25 ff.

② *Ibid.* "Wenn man den Umbreis jener Disziplinen im Sinn hat, welche mit dem Wissen vom Staat sich beschäftigen, das sind die Staatswissenschaft im engeren wörtlichen Sinn. Man spricht aber auch von Staatswissenschaften bei ganz anderer Auslese gesellschaftswissenschaftlicher Disziplinen, wobei das Wissen vom Staat gar nicht im Vordergrund steht..."

③ Mohl, *Geschichte und Literatur der Staatswissenschaften* (1855), p. 71.

④ G. Jellinek, *Allgemeine Staatslehre* (1905), p. 9.

⑤ *Ibid.*, p. 13.

"Politik" as used by Aristotle for the title of his book seems to imply both theoretical and practical aspects of the state. This view is still entertained by many writers.① G. Waitz held, however, that politics is "Staatslehre". He said: "Die Politik fassen wir allgemein als die Lehre vom Staate…"② So Gierke identified "Staatslehre" with "Politik". "Die Staatslehre", he remarks, "fasst alle Vorgänge des staatslebens unter dem Gesichtspunkte einer Zwecktätigkeit auf".③ Somewhat a different view is maintained by Rehm as he declares: "Politik, Staatslehre und Staatswissenschaft besagen der Wortbedeutung nach dasselbe, ihre technischen Bedeutungen dagegen gehen mehr oder weniger stark auseinander."④

Thus the ambiguity of the term "Staatslehre" is no less than that of the word "Staatswissenschaft". Although practice has tended to employ the former instead of the latter, the term "Staatslehre" still remains vague. In short, in the German language, we are still in lack of a precise and generally accepted nomenclature.

The Oxford translation of Bluntschli's *Die Allgemetne Staatslehre* is entitled *Theory of the State* (1892). Just as we protest against the term "Staatslehre", so we are not content with the English translation, in the place of which we prefer to use the word politology. But there is Professor Ernest Barker who, in an inaugural address for the newly appointed chair of political science in the University of Cambridge, chooses to use the term "political theory"⑤ in spite of the fact that the title of the little pamphlet containing the address mentioned above is called *The Study of Political Science and its Relation to Cognate Studies* (1928). Professor Barker remarks that he is not happy about the term science because that term is too closely connected with the exact and experimental study of natural science. "I am not", says the Cambridge Professor, "altogether happy about the term science. It has been vindicated so largely, and almost

---

① Compare Holtzendorff, *Die Principien der Politik* 2 Aufl. (1869), p. 1 ff. He held that "Aristotle schrieb seine 'Politik' als eine Staatslehre oder Staatswissenschaft". p. 1. In another place, he says, "Die all gemeine Staatslehre, enthaltend die überall nachweisbaren Merkmale, Thatigkeitsformen und Rechtsgestalrungen des menschlichen Gesellschaftszustandes, die sich aus dem Wesen und den Zweckbestimmungen des Staates ableiten lassen." p. 4.

② Grundzüge der Politik (1862), p. 1.

③ O. Gierke, "Begriff und Aufgaben der Staatswissenschaft" in Fortbildung in der *Internationalen Wochenschrift für Wissenschaft*, Kunst und Technik 4 (1910), s. 489.

④ H. Rehm, "Politik als Wissenschaft", *ibid*.

⑤ In the first year of our century, Prof. W. A. Dunning published his first volume of his well-known books. The title he used is *A History of Political Theories*. Although the term Political Theory is here employed, [but] the author expressly declared: "While the scope of the work thus is not to be identical with that of political science, it is also to be distinguished from that of political literature." Introduction, p. XVIII.

exclusively, for the exact and experimental study of natural phenomena, that its application into politics may convey suggestions, and excite anticipations, which cannot be justified. If I am to use the designation of political science, I shall use it, as Aristotle used it, to signify a method, or form of enquiry, concerned with the moral phenomena of human behavior in political societies. I should prefer to call such a method or form of enquiry by the name of 'Political Theory' , because I should hope, by the use of that name, to avoid the appearance of any excessive claim to exactitude, and I should be indicating more precisely the nature of the enquiry, as simply a 'speculation' about a group of facts in the field of social conduct, a speculation intended to result in a general scheme which connects the facts systematically with one another and thus gives an explanation of their significance. If that name be adopted, a respectable and honorable antiquity may readily be vindicated for the subject I have to profess. "①

So far as I am aware, Professor Barker seems to be almost the only one who prefers to use the name. And in doing this he is somewhat contradictory to his previous view, for he had defined political theory in this manner: "Political Theory is the speculation of individual minds—political thought is the thought of a whole society. "②

It is generally recognized that political theory is the speculative or philosophical part of the so-called political science, and therefore a branch of the latter. It is hard to conceive how that name can cover the whole field of political phenomena, and the adoption of it would lead to a serious misunderstanding of the true significance of the subject.

We must admit that the name proposed by Professor Barker is somewhat different from the German term "Staatslehre", for the former is more or less broader than the latter since political phenomena are much larger in scope than those of the state. ③ But the objection here lies in the very word theory. The richness and importance of English political theory noone can doubt. Professor Barker may be influenced by the tradition of

---

① *The Study of Political Science and its Relation to Cognate Studies*, Cambridge, 1928.

② Barker, *Greek Political Thought*, Cambridge Classical History, Vol. VI, p. 507. Also his essay on "Mediaeval Political Thought" in Hearnshaw's *The Social and Political Ideas of Some Great Thinkers of the Mediaeval Age*, p. 1 ff. *Political Thought in England: From Herbert Spencer to the Present Day*. "Political theory only deals with political associations, united by a constitution and living under a government. "

③ In 1905 Ludwig Gumplowicz published his *Geschichte der Staatstheorien*, but he seemed to use the term in contrast to what is known as Staatswissenschaft. Although the word Staat used here means something more than a strict sense of the term, Gumplowicz used it loosely with the term social, for this work was written mainly from the sociological standpoint.

his own country and gives preference to that branch of study. But the term is not properly to be applied for the chair to which he is appointed. Twenty years ago, Oxford took the lead by establishing a chair of what is understood as political science in England. Instead of naming the new child political theory which is supposed to be more in accordance with the spirit of Oxford, Professor W. G. S. Adams was honored as Gladstone Professor of Political Theory and Institutions. To be nearer to the truth this is what it ought to be. Now if Professor Barker reminds us that political theory is "simply a speculation about a group of facts", and that consequently it does not overlook the factual aspect of the study, he may be asked: Why is it not called political institutions instead of political theory?

In connection with, but different from, the name political theory is the term political philosophy. ① What is now understood as political science has been for times regarded as political philosophy. In his three heavy volumes on the extensive study of the forms of the monarchical, aristocratic and democratic governments of the world, Lord Brougham employed the term political science② very frequently, but he gave to his work the title *Political Philosophy* (London, 1946). He divided human knowledge into two categories: One is natural or physical philosophy, and the other moral or mental philosophy. The latter consists, in turn, of two great subdivisions. Thus he wrote: "But perhaps the better and more correct division of the whole philosophy is to consider it in two points of view—as it treats of man in his individual capacity, and man as a member of society."③ And he added: "This last branch is termed Political Science and forms the subject of the following discourse."④ In order to make clear what is meant by Political Science, the author remarked in a footnote that political science was derived "from the Greek for city or state—the different communities in Greece having originally been cities and their adjoining territories"⑤.

Our author thus confused terms such as society, state and city, for what is political is different from what is social and municipal. Moreover, it is clear that the three terms, political philosophy, political science and governmental forms, were used indifferently

---

① It may be said that most of the writers do not differentiate political theory from political philosophy. See for instance, Garner, *Political Science and Government*, p. 10. For the contrary view, see J. S. Reeves, "Perspectives in Political Science" in *The American Political Science Review*, Vol. XXIII, No. I, p. 7.

② In the preliminary discourse, the author used the chapter heading as this: "Objects, Pleasures, and Advantages of Political Science."

③ *Political Philosophy*, Vol. I, p. 1.

④ *Ibid.*, p. 2.

⑤ *Ibid.*

by our author. This view was also taken by J. R. Seeley, the well-known English historian and political scientist. "It has been my practice," he says, "ever since I was appointed to this chair—now sixteen years ago—to give instruction in two subjects which are commonly held to be altogether distinct,—in history proper and in that which hitherto in the scheme of our Tripos has been political philosophy, and which it is now proposed to call political science."[1]

As Seeley considered political science as an inductive science, and "inductively pursued, political science would live and move among historical facts"[2], he formulated the often quoted statement that history is the root of political science and political science is the fruit of history. Thus not only political philosophy may be called political science, but also it may, by logical consequence, be considered as history.[3] "What, you are professor of history;" he spoke as if he were a student who would speak, "and yet you tell us that during this year you are not going to lecture on history at all, but on a different subject,—political science or political philosophy."[4]

When Cambridge called political science political philosophy, it was over fifty years ago. But the popular use of the term political science does not make us forgetful of the term political philosophy in its earlier meaning. We have for instance in 1917, Professor H. P. Farrell, who in his *Introduction to Political Philosophy*, still reminded us of it by saying: "Our subject is known indifferently as political philosophy, political science, the science of politics or simply as politics."[5]

Nevertheless, the distinction between political philosophy and political science has been observed by most modern writers. "Political science," says Professor Willoughby, "using the term in its broadest sense, has for its purpose the ascertainment of political facts and the arrangement of them in systematic order as determined by the logical and causal relations which exist between them."[6] On the other hand, political philosophy "deals with generalizations rather than with particulars and seeks to determine essential

---

[1] Seeley, J. R. *Introduction to Political Science*, ed. by Sidgwick, London (1896), p. 1. I used the edition of 1914. The lectures were delivered between 1885–1886.

[2] *Ibid.*, p. 21.

[3] Walter Bagehot in his *Physics and Politics*, p. 11. even considered political economy as a part of political philosophy. "Political economy is the most systematised and most accurate part of political philosophy."

[4] Seeley, *Introduction to Political Science*, pp. 2–3. W. E. H. Lecky, *Democracy and Liberty*, Vol. I, Preface. History is useful for present politics.

[5] H. P. Farrell, *Introduction to Political Philosophy* (1917), p. 1.

[6] W. W. Willoughby, *The Fundamental Concepts of Public Law* (1924), p. 3. See also pp. 6, 7.

and fundamental qualities as distinguished from accidental or unessential characteristics"①.

Another writer attempts to distinguish the difference of the two in the following passage: "Political philosophy is body of ideas, theories② and ideals 'of' the state, whereas political science is an examination or critical study of the state concerning (i) constitutions as well as (ii) doctrines, i. e., theories. Political philosophy is thus the concern of one man, one thinker, one philosopher, whereas political science is essentially descriptive—historical, comparative, universal. Political philosophy is essentially propondistic, ethical or normative; political science, in the main, an objective presentation of all historical facts and theoretical viewpoints, with indication of tendencies."③

The foregoing quotations have given us some idea of the difference between the two terms, but a precise demarcation of their boundary lines between them is hard to conceive. "The distinction between political science (Staatswissenschaft) and political theory or political philosophy (Staatslehre, Staatsphilosophie) is generally observed by the systematic writers on the state, though a precise demarcation of the boundary lines which separate them is difficult, if not impossible", says Professor Garner. ④

It may be remarked that the difference between political science and political philosophy may be traced back to the fundamental difference between science and philosophy. The common saying is: "Science deals with what it is, and only philosophy can deal with what ought to be." But according to Professor Sidgwick, the author of *Elements of Politics*, an opposite view is held. Political science, to this writer, is to deal with what the state ought to be, while political philosophy deals with what it is. ⑤

It may be suggested that the term political philosophy may not only mean anything purely abstract, but also that which is more or less correspondent to what Comte and Spencer used respectively in their *Philosophie Positive* and *Synthetic Philosophy*. But so

---

① W. W. Willoughby, *The Fundamental Concepts of Public Law*, 1924, p. 8. See also his "The Value of Political Philosophy" in the *Political Science Quarterly*, March, 1900.

② "Political theory is not," says J. S. Reeves, "identical with political philosophy, but has always to some extent rested upon it..." *The Am. Pol. Sci. Review*, Vol. XXIII, No. I, p. 7.

③ Sarkar, *The Political Philosophies since 1909*, 1928, p. 3.

④ *Political Science and Government*, p. 10. Cf. Gilchrist, *Principles of Political Science*, 1921, p. 3. "Political Philosophy is in a sense prior to political science since the fundamental assumptions of the former are the basis of the latter."

⑤ *Elements of Politics*, p. 7. Also compare his *Development of European Polity*, p. 2. E. Barker, "Political Philosophy in itself, and apart from other studies, is essentially an ethical study which regards the State as a moral society and inquiries into the way by which it seeks to attain its ultimate moral aim." *Political Thought in England*, p. 12.

far as we understand, no writer has insisted on that point. Professor Willoughby, for example, protests against it. He says, "When a Political Philosophy is spoken of, the word philosophy is not used in its metaphysical or epistemological sense, nor as indicating a synthesis of political conclusions in a sense analogous to that employed by Herbert Spencer when he designated his system of thought a 'Synthetic Philosophy—a Scientia Scientiarum.' ① Nor had the earlier writers such as Brougham been in favor of its being so employed."②

From what has been considered, we may conclude that the term political philosophy has been frequently if not always used to signify that part of political phenomena which cannot be regarded as covering the whole of it, and that the use of the term is so ambiguous that its adoption to mean what is known as political science in the modern sense would lead to a serious misunderstanding.

We come now to the term Politics. It is derived from the Greek words *polis* and *politeia* and has been frequently used by well-known authorities in different countries. Aristotle used it as the title of his famous book. During the nineteenth century, most writers preferred using it. Dahlmann, Waits, Holtzendorff and Freistschke in Germany, Ratzenhofer in Austria, Sidgwick and Amos in England all used the word in the titles of their works. And in our own day, prominent writers such as Laski of England, Stier-Somlo of Germany and Catlin of the United States, still adhere to this term. But while all these writers have employed the same word as the title of their respective works, they did not mean it in the same sense. F. von Holtzendorff long ago remarked: "Mit dem Worte 'Politik' werden noch jetzt fortdauernd verschiedene Vorstellungen und Begriffe verknüpft."③

Thus Aristotle used the word, "politics", to mean the study of the association or community which is formed for the attainment of the supreme Good and embracing the rest of human associations. ④ This is almost correspondent to what is known as the study of society in the modern sense. Dahlmann confined it more or less to the constitution (Staatsverfassung) and administration (Staatsverwaltung) of the different states in different ages. So we find that, in his *Politik*, with the exception of the introduction (Einleitung) consisting of not more than six pages and the chapter on "die Systematik der Staatswissenschaft", the work is mainly devoted to a historical description of

---

① Willoughby, *The Fundamental Concepts of Public Law*, p. 8.
② Brougham, *Political Philosophy*, pp. 1 ff.
③ Holtzendorff, *Die Principien der Politik* (1869), p. 1.
④ See Aristotle, *Politics*, Book Ⅰ, Ch. Ⅰ.

governmental forms and organizations. ① Waitz declared: "We consider Politics in general as the theory of the state."② Holtzendorff seemed to regard it as both "wissenschaftu" and art. ③ Freistchke maintained that all politics is art. ④ Ratzenhofer almost identified it with sociology. ⑤ Sidgwick emphasized the question of what it ought to be in the field of politics. ⑥ Laski was inclined to identify it with political science on the one hand and with political philosophy on the other. ⑦ Stier-Somlo did not make a clear distinction between politics and "Staaslehre". ⑧ Catlin enlarged the field of politics and considered it as somewhat equivalent to what is known as sociology. ⑨

Many other writers used the word in various ways, thus Andre Lichtenbergerin declared that "la politique est proprement l'art de governer un État"⑩. Frank Granger considered politics as historical sociology. ⑪ Bluntschli regarded politics as "more of an art than a *science*"⑫, and Jellinek maintained that it is an applied or practical "Wissenschaft". ⑬ Professor Garner used it "to describe the activities by which public officials are chosen and political policies promoted, or, in a wider sense, the sum total of activities which have to do with the actual administration of public affairs, reserving the term political science to describe the body of knowledge relating to the phenomena of

---

① Dahlmann, "Die Politik", *auf den Grund und as Masz der gegebenen Zustande zuruckgefuhrt*, edition (1847).

② Waitz, *Grundzüge der Politik* (1862), p. 1.

③ Holtzendorff, *op. Cit.*, p. 1. "Am leichtesten verständigt man sich, wenn man zunächst die beiden Hauptbedeutungen unterscheidet, denen zufolge Politik entweder Staatskunst oder Staatswissenschaft bedeutet."

④ Treitschke, *Politik: Vorlesungen gehalten an der Universität zu Berlin*, p. l. "Alle Politik ist Kunst."

⑤ Ratzenhofer, *Wesen und Zweck der Politik* (1893).

⑥ Sidgwick, *The Elements of Politics*, "I therefore propose, generally, to examine what is essentially involved in the terms property, contract, executive etc… But a preliminary discussion of the fundamental conceptions government, law, right, obligation, is, I think, expedient before we discuss the general principles on which Government ought to act…" p. 15, see also p. 7.

⑦ In his *On the Study of Politics* (1926), Mr. Laski seemed to use the terms, Politics, Political Science, indifferently. In one place he declared, "A true politics, in other words, is above all a philosophy of history." p. 10. His *A Grammar of Politics* (1925) may be regarded as a book on political Philosophy rather than political science, and we find the opening sentence declares: "A new political philosophy is necessary to a new world."

⑧ Stier-Somlo used the word for a little work's title, but the substance of the book was also published, as I can recall, in another work entitled "Allgemeine Staatslehre".

⑨ Catlin, *Principles of Politics*. This is conscious on the part of the author as stated in the preface.

⑩ *La Grande Encyclopedie*, Vol. XXVII, p. 123.

⑪ Historical sociology is the subtitle of the writer's *Politics* (1911).

⑫ *Theory of the State*, English tran., pp. 1, 2.

⑬ Allgemeine Staatslehre, p. 13. "Die angewandte oder praktische Staatswissenschaft ist die Politik."

the state"①.

The foregoing definitions cannot be said to exhaust the various meanings of the word politics; ② but enough has been said to show that it is loosely applied and its meaning is uncertain. "The term Politics", as properly remarked by a certain writer, "is open to the objection that it possesses several meanings and, when used without qualification or discrimination, leads to confusion if not misunderstanding."③ In fact, even if it is used with qualification or discrimination, we are still easily led to confusion and even misunderstanding. In order to illustrate our point of view, a passage written by Professor Blackmar of Kansas University may be quoted here: "In the early spring of 1889, the regents of the University of Kansas came to John Hopkins, Baltimore, searching for a man to take charge of a new department to be formed in the University of Kansas. They asked me to take charge of the department and name it. On being told what they wished the department to include, I thought it best to call it History and Politics. Whereupon the regents were very much excited, telling me it would not do to give a department that name, because the people of Kansas would not tolerate a department of Politics in the University, as they had politics enough in the state already."④ The Kansas professor told here how he was compelled to use the term Sociology to name the department, and therefore it became the first one of its kind in the United States; but what interests us particularly is that the term, Politics, is understood by the general public as something undesirable and sinister.

But this is not all. The name Politiques was given to a party formed in France during the sixteenth century. It is thus closely connected with party politics. The term so understood prevails even more widely in our own day. "The term politics", says one writer, "was used by Aristotle as the title of his study of the state; but it is nowadays not altogether a fortunate word, since it is often used in the narrow sense of the party struggle in Parliament; and 'politician' has come to be almost a term of abuse, to indicate a man devoted, not to the broader aims of statesmanship, but to the selfish

---

① *Political Science and Government*, pp. 2 – 3. See also Fröbel, *Theorie der Politik* (1864), where he declared, "Die Politik ist die wissenschaft und Kunst des Lehre im Staat." Vol. I, p. 1. In Eschen's *Hanbuch der praktischen Politik*, it is stated, "die politik soll die staatlichen Einrichtungen im Sinne des Fortschritts entwickeln die kraft und wohlfahrt der Nation heben, nach einer höhern Stude der Cultur struben." Part I, sect. I, p. 11.

② For the various meanings of the word politics, see P. Zorn's article "Politik als Staatskunst"; H. Rehm, "Politik als Wiesenschaft" in *Handbuch der Politik* (1912).

③ Garner, *Introduction to Political Science* (1910), p. 8.

④ Quoted by Small, "Fifty Years of Sociology in the United States" in *American Journal of Sociology*, May 1916, Vol. XXI, p. 706.

interests of one party or to his own private ambition."①

Moreover the term politics, as Ostrogorski has well noted, "is applied to electioneering methods by which publics are chosen and political policies promoted". "The expression politics has become a synonym for election affairs, for the concoction of them, and has almost ceased to be associated with ideas of government and administration."② So remarked the French author. And he added: "The statesman has had to give way to the political machinist, since politics has been lowered to electioneering considerations and the management of the elections has become the first political duty.③

Thus to "play politics" is to do what is not respectable as it is generally understood. It is even worse than to "play tricks". And a politician, a man who is taking part in politics, is almost considered to do something contrary to what a statesman would do. Such a distinction in the use of the words has been observed by most careful writers, and to call a man a politician may be regarded as being impolite to him. Even terms such as "current politics" are supposed to be differentiated from the so-called academic meanings.

It may be suggested that the term "politics" be used in the sense in which Aristotle used it so that the objections made against it may be minimized. As a matter of fact, many recognized authorities who employed the term for the title of their writings seemed to have this view in mind. We may agree, then, with Professor Gilchrist in saying that the term politics when used in its original Greek sense is unobjectionable.④ But still it may be argued that the conditions under which Aristotle wrote his *Politics* were entirely different from our own and what he conceived to be properly belonging to the field of politics may not be true in our own day. It is thus not safe to follow the Greek master. Even Professor Gilchrist himself does not think it proper to go back to the original Greek meaning. "Since modern usage," he says, "has given it a new meaning, it is useless as a scientific term."⑤ Holtzendorff is thus correct in declaring: "Mohl nennt es mit Recht eine unentschuldbar unbegreifliche Begriffsverwirrung, wenn man in unserer Zeit noch

① E. F. Bowman, *An Introduction to Political Science* (1927), pp. XVI ff.
② M. Ostrogorski, *Democracy and the Organization of Political Party* (1903), English translation, Vol. II, p. 564.
③ *Ibid.*, p. 501. A. G. Keller, says: "Politics is the play of local interests." See *Societal Evolution* (1916), p. 121.
④ Gilchrist, *Principles of Political Science*, p. 2.
⑤ *Ibid.* This may be regarded as the reason why the author used the term political science instead of Politics.

einmal auf die ursprunglichen Bezeichungen zurückgehe. "①

Moreover, we have already pointed out that the term politics used by Aristotle is somewhat correspondent to what is now understood as social science or sociology. Thus Paul Barth remarks: "Der name der 'Sociologie' stammt bekanntlich von A. Comte; der Sache nach aber hat sie schon früher bestanden. Sie war nur, wie am Anfange alles Wissens jede Wissenschaft, nicht rein theoretisch, sondern zugleich auf praktische Fragen gerichtet und fünrte den Namen 'Politik'. "② The writer goes on to point out that while this term as used by Aristotle is nothing more than sociology, its essence may be even found in the writings of Plato. ③ Such a view is frequently entertained by the sociologist as he goes to the historical aspect of the subject. ④

Professor Dunning, after completing his scholarly work on the *History of Political Theories* (1902-1922), concludes with these words: "For obviously political theory has been much reduced in scope by the expansion, classification and precise delimitation of various kinds of human knowledge. A Doctrine that was in Aristotle political has since his time been definitively assigned to theology, to ethics, to jurisprudence, to economics and to sociology. This fact gives no basis for judgment on the substance of the doctrine, but is a matter of names only. Every one of the special sciences mentioned goes back to ancient philosophies for substantial elements of its dogma propounded under the name and in the categories of politics. The field of this early speculation was in fact what we think of today as social science in general. That the name given to the ensemble of ideas about social man was 'politics' was due to preoccupation of the Greeks with their particular social unit, the city-state or 'polis'. "⑤

In view of what has been considered, it is safe to conclude that the term politics is objectionable on various grounds and that the use of it will lead us at least to a position of confusion, if not of misunderstanding. For students of the subject, a change of nomenclature is thus desirable and even necessary.

---

① Holtzendorff, *Die Principien der Politik*, s. 4.

② Barth, "Die Philosophie der Geschichte als Soziologie", *Dritte und vierte Auflage* (1922), s. 160.

③ Barth, *op. Cit.*, s. 160 ff.

④ See B. Kidd's Article "Sociology" in *Encyclopedia Britanica*; and E. S. Bogardus, *A History of Social Thought* (1922).

⑤ Dunning, *A History of Political Theories*, Vol. III, p. 115. "The polis was to them (Greeks) primarily a society and only subsidiarily a state. It was ethical, furnishing the norm of right and duty. It was juristic, embodying in its institutions the foundations of law. It was economic, determining the conditions of material prosperity. It was sociological, revealing the principles that produced not only the best man, but also the best form of association among men. It finally was political, solving the problem of authority and liberty—of the control of one human will by another."

When we come to the more popularly accepted term "Political Science"①, we find it is equally unsatisfactory.

This has been generally recognized by careful writers. "The term political science", says Professor Leacock, "has been used with a good deal of latitude, not to say ambiguity, both in colloquial language and in scientific discussion."② Another publicist expresses somewhat the same opinion: "The term 'Political Science' is one of various meanings and consequently of somewhat hazy content."③ We have nowadays books called *Introduction to Political Science*, *Elements of Political Science*, *Political Science*, *History of Political Science*, etc. Mere consideration of these titles perhaps will lead one to think that they mean what the terms indicate, but this will prove to be not the case if a glance is given to the contents of the works. Instancing an article written by Professor Walter J. Shepard,④ we shall understand how much confused is the term thus employed. The article is entitled "Political Science". It is divided into three parts. The first is entitled "Its History" and in turn subdivided into (1) the nature of political thought, (2) Greek and Roman political thought, (3) mediaeval political theory, (4) early modern political thought, (5) political speculation in the seventeenth and eighteenth centuries, and (6) the rise of contemporary political science. We cannot help feeling that these headings cause some confusion by distinguishing political science from political thought, political theory, and political speculation. The editor of the work begins by telling us that "this book consists of articles on the History and Prospects of the social sciences which, so the editor and contributors believe, possess something more than mere esoteric and scholarly significance, namely an immediate practical value for the solution of concrete social problems"⑤. But here is an article mainly devoted to what is really known as the history of political thoughts or theories. It is more or less modelled on the work of Professor Dunning, not only because of a similarity in treatment, but also because so much has been referred to the latter. But what have we

---

① Here we include the French term "Science Politique" and also the term "Science of Politics" although it must be admitted that the latter has been used somewhat different from "Political Science".

② Stephen Leacock, *Elements of Political Science* (1906), second edition (1913), p. 3.

③ W. J. Shepard, "Political Science" in H. E. Barnes' *The History and Prospects of the Social Sciences* (1924), p. 396. The writer goes on to say: "Sometimes it is employed to describe the entire field of the social sciences, and this was indeed the earlier meaning of the term. The division of the social sciences into economics, sociology, jurisprudence, political science and perhaps others, represents a rather advanced state in the development of thought relating to human social institutions. For the men of antiquity no such divisions existed and the early works in the field of politics were concerned with all aspects of society."

④ *Ibid*. Also Garner, *Pol. Scie. and Government*, p. 1.

⑤ Barnes, "Introduction" in *The History and Prospects of Social Sciences*.

learned from Professor Dunning? "A history of *political theories*", "may properly include much that would be out of place in a history of *political science*. The title of this work has been chosen in view of this distinction". And he continues, "Many political doctrines of the utmost historical interest and value have had an origin and a career quite out of relation to any formal body of scientific dogma."①

Confusion as this has been consciously or unconsciously committed by so many writers—and even by careful writers—that space will not allow us to cite them all; but one more example may be taken for illustration. Mr. Robert H. Murray wrote a book on the *History of Political Science* (1926). Being informed of the title, we thought of it as something different from works such as a history of political theories or of political thought. But when we secured the book, we found the full title to run like this: *The History of Political Science from Plato to the Present*. It may be well questioned: Is Plato a political scientist? Mr. Murrey says, "On the principle that first things come first, I concern myself with only the most important thinkers in political science." Then he goes on to tell us, "For my book is essentially a history of 'idées-forces', and not merely of literary ideas." This is what we find in the preface.② And if we run over the book, we feel that it is in fact a treatise which Professor Dunning would name as a history of political theories, different from the so-called political science, had he himself written it or been asked to give it a title.

That terms may be loosely employed is easily found in books on political subjects, and this is enough to prove that there is an urgent need of an adequate name.

Yet this is not the only reason for us to repudiate the term political science. The terms employed by students of different fields of study are single words such as astronomy, geology, physics, chemistry, biology, psychology, sociology, economics, religion, etc. The term political science seems to be the only one describing an outstanding field of study that is composed of two words. In order to be uniform in denomination, a change is indeed desirable; and in proposing this we are by no means alone.

Before the year 1838, what is now known as sociology was called by Comte, social physics. In the fourth volume of his *Cours de Philosophie Politive*③, the term sociology was first coined in its French form as "sociologie". The word which occurs in page 185

---

① Dunning, *A History of Political Theories*, Vol I, p. xvii.

② In another work, Mr. Murry called it *The Political Consequences of the Reformation* (1926). Still another is named by him as *History of English Political Theories*, although the substances of all these are more or less the same.

③ I used the third edition (1869).

of the volume mentioned appears so suddenly that one who reads it cannot help feeling that it comes like a fog or haze suspended in the sky without having a beginning or an end. Comte himself seemed to be conscious of that. So he added in a footnote: "Je crois devoir hasarder, dés à présent, ce terme nouveau, exactement équivalent à mon expression, déjà introduite, de *physique sociale*, afin de pouvoir désigner par un nom unique cette partie complémentaire de la philosophie naturalle qui se rapporte à l'étude positive de l'ensemble des lois fondamentales propres aux phénoménes sociaux."①

It is clear that the explanation here made does not deal with the origin of the term nor the justification of using a hybrid word. It explains only that the new term is equivalent to the old one, and that it is most important, as it seems to me, to use *un nom unique* instead of the term *physique sociale*. We shall explain in the course of our discussion, why we dislike the term political science, and particularly the word *science* in this connection, not only in name, but also in substance. Comte, however, did not oppose the word *physique* in spite of the fact that the word designates already a field of its own, for Comte's sociology is as a matter of fact, social physics. Now if it is only for the sake of employing *un nom unique* that leads Comte to coin the word and consequently make it a common name in our vocabulary, the change of the term political science into *un nom unique* would be more appealable and desirable.

Indeed it is curious that among the principal branches of studies, political science is the only one using the word "science".② The students of natural phenomena, such as astronomy, physics, chemistry, biology, and of the so-called social studies, such as economics, jurisprudence, and even sociology which Comte considers as a complementary part of natural philosophy, do not trouble themselves to use the word "science". Why, may we ask, are the students of political phenomena so persistent in employing it?

It is somewhat absurd and illogical for writers who use the term *political science* ⟨as⟩ the title of their works to discuss at length whether "political science" is a science or not. If the scientific character of the study is still uncertain, the word science should not be used. If it is called a science or is taken for granted that it is a science, its

---

① The sentence in which the word sociology may be found this: "Depuis Montesquieu, le seul pas important qu' ait fait jusqu'ici la conception fondamentale de la *sociologie* (and here a footnote sign is added) est du a l'illustre et malheureux Condorcet…"

② The terms natural science and social science seem to come from what the earlier writers understood as natural philosophy and social philosophy respectively. Social science is used to differentiate from science *natural*, it is simply a common *name* for the field of social studies, it has not yet had a definite data of its own. Some writers identify it with sociology, but this must be rejected.

character as science should not be questioned. Here is a dilemma. The premise is out of harmony with its consequence. And I may confess that, not only once but many times, I have been embarrassed by students in a class of so-called political science on account of this dilemma.

The enunciation of the phrase "political science" is sometimes attributed to William Godwin who lived at the end of the eighteenth century, [1] but the popular and official use of it did not come till the latter part of the nineteenth century. Theodore D. Woolsey's lectures on political science, [2] as he told us, were delivered between the years 1846 and 1871. But the work of two heavy volumes was not published until 1877. Francis Lieber, in order to introduce himself, wrote in a footnote in his *Civil Liberty and Self-Government* these words: "The writer is professor of History and of Political Philosophy and Economy in the State College of South Carolina... In the year 1857, he was appointed Professor of History and Political Science in Columbia College, in the city of New York..."[3] Seeley also noted that what he proposed to call Political Science during the years 1885 and 1886 was called political philosophy before that time. [4] According to Professor W. R. Shepherd, Professor John W. Burgess organized the first faculty and school of political science to be founded in the United States in 1880, [5] although he was already appointed as professor of the newly established departments of history, political science and political economy in Amherst College in 1873.

The gradual and wide adoption of the term political science has led some writers to justify its use. So Professor Catlin tells us in this manner: "Politics is not merely a science in the sense in which we speak of the sense of venery or of pugilistic science. If it were no more than this, the phrase 'political science' which Godwin and Mary Wollstonecraft introduced, should be banished from our vocabulary."[6] We must confess that we can hardly entertain such a point of view. It leads to a blind if not dangerous situation. In fact the statement here quoted seems to be somewhat childish. And it is

---

[1] Godwin, *Enquiry Concerning Political Justice* (1793), Book II, Ch. I and Book IV, Ch. 5.
[2] Woolsey, *Political Science*, Preface, second edition (1886).
[3] Lieber, *On Civil Liberty and Self-Government* (1853), p. vi.
[4] Seeley, *Introduction to Political Science*, p. 1. In 1883, Amos published his *The Science of Politics*. We did not mention the German writers here because the term "Staatswissenschaft" should not be translated as "political science", for neither the word Staat is equivalent to the English word political, nor the word Wissenschaft means the same thing as the English and French word science in the strict sense of the term. Such a distinction of Wissenschaft and science has been sometimes observed by German writers.
[5] H. W. Odum, *American Masters of Social Science* (1927), p. 30.
[6] Catlin, *Principles of Politics*, p. 20.

indeed curious that, defending the phrase "political science" so strongly and devoting so much energy in studying its scientific character as Professor Catlin did, he should fail to use it instead of the term "Politics".

David Hume is supposed to be the first man (thinker? writer?) who suggested that "politics may be reduced to a science"①. He insisted that there is a certain stability in human affairs, and this may be taken as the scientific basis of politics. While this is true to a certain extent, the so-called universal axioms enumerated by Hume in politics are by no means invariable. His best monarchy, aristocracy and democracy formed by a hereditary prince, a nobility without vassals, and a people voting by their representatives cannot be said to have been recognized as infallible axioms. ②

No less modern writers insist that there is a science of politics. Sir Frederick Pollock says that if those who deny the existence of a political science mean that there is no body of rules from which a prime minister may infallibly learn how to command a majority, they would be right as to the fact, but would betray a rather inadequate notion of what a science is. ③ An adequate notion of science, we believe, can only be found in the world of facts. To formulate a set of principles which are not supported by facts is like building a castle in the air. Sir Frederick is thus, it seems to us, taking refuge in mysticism.

The title of Sir Frederick's admirable little book is *An Introduction to the History of the Science of Politics* (1890). But as a matter of fact it is a book on the history of political theory. This is expressly recognized by our author. "Thus", he says, "Political science must and does exist, if it were only for the refutation of absurd political theories and projects. "④ This is the reason why Edward Jenks thinks it desirable to have another complementary part under somewhat the same title, i. e. , *A History of Politics*. "Some ten years ago", says Professor Jenks, "Sir Frederick Pollock published a valuable and interesting little book on the history of political speculation. But the author is not aware that anyone has yet attempted to summarize in a brief, popular form, the record of political action. It has occurred, therefore, to the promoters of this series that such a

---

① Hume, *Essays and Treatise on Several Subjects* (1742), third edition of the first volume. I used the edition of 1809, p. 13.
② *Ibid*.
③ Pollock, *History of the Science of Politics*, p. 2.
④ Pollock, *History of the Science of Politics*, p. 4.

summary might prove interesting, if only by way of comparison. ① Obviously, if politics were considered as the study of political phenomena both in theory and in practice, Sir Frederick Pollock's political science is only a part of it, and consequently the term so used is not comprehensive.

Lord Bryce has been sometimes cited as characterizing politics not as a deductive science but as an experimental science. ② Yet this can only be admitted in a very limited sense. On the other hand, he says definitely, "Experiments can be tried in physics over and over again till a conclusive result is reached, but that which we call an experiment in politics can never be repeated because the conditions can never be exactly reproduced, for, as Heraclitus says, one cannot step twice into the same river. Prediction in physics may be certain: in politics it can at best be no more than probable... However widely and carefully the materials may be gathered, their character makes it impossible that politics should ever become a science in the sense in which mechanics or chemistry or botany is a science."③

The French writer Paul Janet has been also cited as maintaining that politics is a science. The argument is that he used the term "science politique" as the title of his monumental work: *Historie de la Science Politique dans ses Rapports avec la Morale*. ④ But just as Professor Dunning remarked: "Despite the form of the title, Janet includes much more than what is strictly the 'science' of politics in his survey, and thus makes his field include all political theories."⑤ In fact, the title itself explains that it is not a science in the strict sense of the term, but is at best only, as Sir Frederick Pollock says, ⑥ ⟨a science⟩ political in the same sense that there is a science of morals. In the introduction to the first edition, Janet declared: "Il y a donc une science de l'État, non pas de tel ou tel État en particulier, mais de l'État en général, considéré dans sa

---

① Jenks, *A History of Politics* (1900), Preface. "These pages profess to give, then, a brief account of what men have *done*, not of what they have *thought*, in that important branch of human activity which we call politics, or the Art of Government. But if it should be objected that what men do is really always the outcome, more or less perfect, of what they think, the answer is, that we recognize, for practical purposes, a distinction between what the world, in theory at least, believes to be best, and that which it actually succeeds in achieving. And a comparison of the two objects can hardly fail to be instructive."

② Bryce, "The Relations of Political Science to History and to Practice", in *The American Political Science Review* (1909), Vol. III, pp. 1-3.

③ Bryce, *Modern Democracies*, Vol. I, p. 14.

④ I used the cinquième edition.

⑤ Dunning, *History of Political Theories*, Vol. I, p. XXII.

⑥ Pollock, *History of the Science of Politics*, p. 2.

nature, dans ses lois, et dans ses principales formes."① This statement was quoted by a writer to support his contention that politics is a science, but he failed to note the sentences following which give us a very clear notion that the so-called *science politique* is nothing more than *la philosophie politique*. Thus we read from Janet: "C'est cette science que l'on peut appeler la philosophie politique, et dont j'entreprends l'historie."②

Finally we have eminent writers of the so-called systematic political science such as Professor Garner who defends strongly the scientific character of politics. "For our purpose," he declares, "a science may be described as a fairly unified, mass of knowledge relating to a particular subject, acquired by systematic observation, experience, or study, the facts of which have been coordinated, systematized, and classified."③ "The scientific method of examining facts," he adds, "is not peculiar to one class of phenomena or to one class of investigators; it is applicable to social as well as to physical phenomena, and we may safely reject the claim that the scientific frame of mind belongs exclusively to the physicist or the naturalist."④

He goes on to remind us that "the consensus of scientific opinion is in favor of this view"⑤, and to maintain that eminent writers such as Aristotle, Holzendorff and many other systematic writers on the state also took the same point of view.⑥ "We must conclude," he writes, "therefore, that the weight of authority justifies the claim of politics to the rank of a true science. It renders practical service by deducing sound principles as a basis for wise political action and by exposing the teachings of a false political philosophy."⑦ So far Professor Garner holds firmly to what he calls "the

---

① Janet, *Histoire de la Science Politique*, p. lXXV.

② *Ibid.* "Cependant, quoique la philosophie politique soit une science qui ait ses principes propres et ses lois particulières, quoiqu'elle porte sur un ordre de faits oui ne doit être confondu avec aucun artre, il est utile et même necessaire de ne point la séparer d'une autre science à laquelle elle est naturellement unie par mille liens divers, je veux dire la philosophie morale. Les publicistes anciens n'ont jamais mis en doute cette alliance de la morale et de la politique; et les plus grands d'entre eux ont été aussi les plus grands moralistes de leur temps: Platon, Aristote, Ciceron…"

③ Garner, *Political Science and Government*, pp. 11–12.

④ *Ibid.*

⑤ *Ibid.*, p. 13.

⑥ The word "science" used in the English translation of Aristotle's statement that politics is the master "science" in the highest sense should be qualified, for really what Aristotle means here is nothing more than "study". It is the study in the highest sense, not, of course, in the sense of its scientific character, but in the sense that the polis is the means for attaining the highest good. Professor Garner's version in English of Holtzendorff's statement seems to be doubtful. See *Political Science and Government*, pp. 13–14; *Introduction to Political Science*, p. 18.

⑦ Garner, *Political Science and Government*, p. 14.

affirmative view" on the question, as he himself puts it: Is there a science of politics?① We are somewhat sceptical when we read: "as a science it falls short, of course, of the perfection attained by the physical science, for the reason that the facts with which it deals are more complex and the causes which influence social and practical phenomena are more difficult of control and are perpetually undergoing change."② And we go down to the abyss of doubt as when we are told that "as yet it is still probably the most incomplete and undeveloped of all the social sciences"③. How far, it may be asked, is the way from the most complete and developed of all the "natural sciences" to the most incomplete and undeveloped of all the "social sciences"?

The few writers mentioned above do not, of course, exhaust the list of those who consider politics as science and consequently maintain that there is such a thing as political science and the use of the phrase is justifiable; but enough has been said to show that their arguments are not sound and their conclusions are not decisive.

The trouble seems to be this: Man is by nature more or less biased, and this brings him somewhat to a state of exaggeration. Each one claims his own field of study to be the most important and noblest. In order to attract the attention of the public, and to adapt oneself to the current of the time, one is easily led to violate the sacredness of truth. The nineteenth century has been characterized as the age of "science", science in the strict sense of the term. Being influenced by such a spirit as this, we have become accustomed to hearing phrases and terms which we did not have before. Thus Christianity which, as a principle and as a creed dominated almost the whole of the Middle Ages, has been also recently called Christian Science. The same thing occurs in other fields of study. Sir Robert Phillimore, for instance, told us half a century ago that international law was noble science;④ but even in our own day the propriety of calling international law law in the strict sense of the term, to say nothing of its being a science, is still questioned. Indeed the desire to make one's own study a science is admirable, but the truth may be somewhat obscured. Considering any book whose title includes the term political science, one finds that the contents do not remind him of the concept "science". If the opinions or theories therein classified and systematized under one chapter or another may be regarded as scientific in character, then a poem, the thought or feeling of which is expressed in a systematic way, may also be scientific so

---

① Garner, *Political Science and Government*, p. 11.
② Garner, *Political Science and Government*, p. 14.
③ *Ibid.*
④ Phillimore, *Commentaries upon International Law (1878-1889)*, Preface.

that we can have a "poetical science".

A study should not be called a science before it becomes a science, and that which is really a science will be always a science in spite of the fact that it is not called such. Thus chemistry is not called chemical science, yet the scientific character of chemistry has never been questioned. Yet we are now still facing the question whether politics can, by its very nature, become a very science or not!

Politics, it seems to us, is not, or cannot be, a science. This has been supported by the highest authorities and many scholars. Comte, the author of *Système de Politique Positive*, ① did not think that this branch of studies has attained the positive, i. e., scientific, stage for various reasons. In the first place, according to him, there is no consensus of opinion among experts as to its methods, principles, and conclusions. Secondly, it lacks continuity of development. Thirdly, it lacks the elements which constitute a basis of prevision.② The same view was entertained by John S. Mill who declared: "It is accordingly but of yesterday that the concept of a political or social science has existed anywhere but in the mind of an isolated thinker here and there, generally ill-prepared for the realisation."③

"In the present state of knowledge," said Buckle in his well-known work, *History of Civilization*, "politics so far from being a science is one of the most backward of all the arts."④ It is true that Buckle wrote these words more than half a century ago,⑤ but it is equally true that in the present state of knowledge, politics is still too far from being a science and Buckle is still right to say that it "is one of the most backward of all the arts". Sheldon Amos maintained that practical statesmen "immersed in actual business and oppressed by the over-recurring presence of new emergencies almost resent the notion of applying the comprehensive principles of science". "The result is that politics floats in the public mind either as a mere field for ingenious chicanery or as a boundless waste for the evolution of scholastic phantasy."⑥

Even within the last decade the claim that politics is a science has been denied by many writers. Indeed the tendency seems to be that most of the authorities have not been so enthusiastic in regarding politics as a science as it used to be. "A science", says M.

---

① At first this was an essay written when Comte was twenty-four years old. About thirty years later, he developed it into four volumes.
② Comte, *Positive Philosophy* (English trans.), Vol. II, Ch. 3.
③ Mill, *System of Logic*, 8th edition (1906), p. 547.
④ Published in 1857. See Vol. I, p. 361.
⑤ Amos, *The Science of Politics*, pp. 2 ff.
⑥ Quoted by Catlin in his *Principles of Politics*, p. 20.

G. Mosca in his *Elementi di Scienza Politica* (1923), "is the product of a system of observation made on a given order of phenomena, with special care, appropriate methods, and so coordinated as to raise them to the level of an indisputable truth, not apprehensible by ordinary superficial observation... We do not think that political science in its present condition has yet genuinely entered upon the scientific stage."

And so Professor Merriam tells us in an amusing manner: "All types of political social theory conjured with the term, scientific. There was scientific socialism, scientific democracy, scientific aristocracy, scientific anarchism, scientific militarism and scientific pacificism; scientific paternalism, and scientific *laissez-faire*; scientific materialism and scientific spiritualism; scientific selfishness and survival of the fittest and scientific altruism. But on the whole the name and authority of science were more frequently coveted and appropriated than its efficient spirit and objective method which reached for the truth without regard to struggle of interest for power, or without respect to authority or convenience rooted in the past. Of scientific social studies it might truthfully be declared that not everyone who saith, 'Lord, Lord', shall enter into the kingdom."[1]

At most one can share the opinion of Professor Shepard, but with him politics is again not a science if the term science should be used in an adequate way. Thus he writes: "The question is frequently discussed as to whether political science may properly be called a science. There is no doubt that it lacks many of the criteria of the natural sciences. So far from having achieved the exactitude and precision which the physical sciences clearly display, it must be conceded that it has not even advanced to the position which biology or even psychology has attained. But the progress made in the last generation or two constitutes substantial ground for anticipating a perfection in method and in results which will perhaps, in the course of the next half century, entitle it to the dignity of a true science. The scientific method can be resolved into three processes. The first is the accumulation of facts; the second, the linking of these facts together in causal sequences of fundamental principles or laws; and the third... As yet political science has not progressed beyond the second state. If there are any assured principles of politics they are exceedingly few and of the most general sort."[2]

Thus in its present status, politics as a science has not even attained Professor Shepard's second process. We have already pointed out that Professor Shepard, although

---

[1] Merriam, "Recent Tendencies in Political Thought" in Merriam and Bames, *Political Theories: Recent Time* (1924), p. 13.

[2] Shepard, "Political Science" in Barnes' *History and Prospects of Social Science*, p. 427.

himself writing an article on political science, is in fact writing on what is known as political speculation which, it seems to us, has not yet attained even the first process mentioned above.

John Adams, the well known lawyer and statesman of the new world, once expressed in 1813 to Thomas Jefferson the following view: "While all other sciences have advanced, that of government is at a stand, little better practiced now than three or four thousand years ago." Then a hundred and fifteen years later, the same opinion was expressed by a Michigan Professor: "Although political phenomena have been observed, recorded, discussed, theorized upon, and philosophized about for nearly three thousand years, we have even yet no unvarying generalizations akin to natural laws in the physical world."① And Professor William B. Munro, in an article entitled "Physics and Politics—An Old Analogy Revised", although with the hope that politics may reach the objectivity of science, remarks, however, in the following such manner: "Government, as Emerson once said, is 'the greatest science and service of mankind'. Yet the science of government has been probably the least successful of all the sciences in building up a set of principles upon which anybody of men can agree. It has not yet caught up with meteorology, which can fairly be said, I think, to rank as the least exact of all the natural sciences."②

To make the story short, let us conclude with a list of those who are frank enough to say that politics is not a science by presenting briefly the opinion of Professor Charles A. Beard, an eminent writer in the field of social studies. He says, "A genuine political science would deal with known tendencies projected in time; it would be in some indeterminate measure prophetic if it deals only with what is past, and what is, and omits that which is becoming, then it is nothing at all, but merely a part of something."③

And the learned writer rightly adds: "No science of politics is possible; or if

---

① J. S. Reeves, "Perspectives in Political Science"(1903–1928) in *The American Political Science Review*, Vol. XXIII, No. 1, p. 10.

② Munro, "Physics and Politics—An Old Analogy Revised" in *The American Political Science Review* (1928), Vol. XXII, No. 1, pp. 8–9. Cf. the article by Edward S. Corwin, " 〈The〉 Democratic Dogma and the Future of Political Science" in *The American Political Science Review* (1929), Vol. XXIII, No. 3. This writer declares: "That the primary task of political science is today one of popular education, and that therefore it must still retain its character as a 'normative', a 'telic' science, is, then, my thesis…It may not make political science more scientific, but it will make it *appear* to be so…The real destiny of political science is to do more expertly and more precisely what it has always done; its task is criticism and education regarding the true ends of the state and how best they may be achieved. So far as it contributes to this end, the more of scientific method the better." p. 529.

③ Beard, "Political Science" in *Research in the Social Sciences*, edited by Wilson Gee, 1929, p. 273.

possible, desirable. There is no valid distinction between descriptive politics, political science, political theory, or political philosophy. They all represent more or less serious effort to think about a phase of life called political. The method of natural science is applicable only to a very limited degree and, in its pure form, not at all to any fateful issues of politics. What we have, therefore, and can only have is intelligence applied to the political facts of unbroken social organism."[1]

It is clear that Professor Beard does not deny absolutely that there is no such thing as political science at all. It may be a part of "something" as he termed it. In other words, in that branch of study known as political, there may be one part called political science, but this part is only a fraction of the whole. We venture to say that Professor Beard is indeed sound in his assertion. For in the whole field of political "phenomena", by which we mean not only the phenomena in the narrow sense but as Professor Edward A. Ross says, in relation to social phenomena,[2] in preference even to activities and therefore including beliefs, feelings and ideas as well as actions, there is no doubt that so far as the scientific methods employed in the fields of chemistry or physics may be employed in political study it can be called scientific political study, and consequently the term political science may be used. But the part which can be so called has, as Professor Beard points out, decided limitation. The study itself, it must be admitted, is not limited, but limitative and it is impossible to go beyond its chosen field. The recognition of such political science does not mean, to be sure, to go back to the old term political science, for the latter has been used to indicate what Professor Beard would call "something" which is much larger in scope than the former. And to use the one for the other would bring us to a state of misunderstanding.

How should we name that "something"? In the article referred to above, Professor Beard retains the old name, i. e., political science,[3] although he does not favor it.

In order to avoid any misunderstanding as a consequence of the indifferent use of

---

[1] Beard, "Political Science" in *Research in the Social Sciences*, edited by Wilson Gee, 1929, p. 287. See also p. 271. "Natural scientists are always telling us that we can never discover great truth if we passionately seek what we wish rather than that which actually prevails. Given these two inescapable facts—our prejudiced minds and the necessity for disinterested reason in the pursuit of truth, the prospects for a political science are not very hopeful." Huxley is right when he said: "whether there is a political science depends on whether any rational principles can be found to regulate the form of constitutions, the determination of the sphere of the state, which make a complete and systematized branch of knowledge, clearly formulated and understood in their mutual relations."

[2] Ross, *The Foundation of Sociology* (1905), p. 6.

[3] Cf. also Prof. Beard's article, "Time, Technology, and the Creative Spirit in Political Science" in *The American Political Science Review* (1927), Vol. XXI, No. 1, p. 1 ff.

it, we prefer to name it "Politology". It may be added that so far as we know, there ⟨seems to have⟩ no better word. Reasons one after another have been already given in the course of our discussion for supporting the use of the new term; but they are not exhaustive. In order to make it clearer, let us take a case for illustration.

Economics as a separate field of inquiry dates back only to the latter part of the eighteenth century. Sir James Stuart's *Inquiry into the Principles or Political Economy* was published in 1767. Sir James spoke of "what economy is in a family, political economy is in a state". About ten years later, Adam Smith published his monumental treatise on the subject; but instead of using the term political economy, he named his book *The Wealth of Nations*. Smith considered, however, political economy as a branch of the science of a statesman or legislator. James Mill followed his forerunners very closely by declaring that "political economy is to the state, what domestic economy is to the family"①. Thus far we may call political economy a part of the so-called political science. Then we find in the writings of John S. Mill something larger in scope than what his predecessors considered. "Political economy," he wrote in 1848, "properly so called, has grown up almost from infancy since the time of Adam Smith; and the philosophy of society, from which practically that eminent thinker never separated his more peculiar theme, though still in a very stage of its progress, has advanced many steps beyond the point at which he left."②

Then in the latter part of the nineteenth century, when political economy acquired its autonomy from political science, the change of the term became desirable. According to MacLeod,③ Whately proposed to use the term "Catallactics", another proposed "Plutology" and still another proposed "Chrematology". All these terms are preferable to a certain extent, but the simple word "Economics" has been generally and finally accepted. The reasons seemed to be many: In the first place, the word "economic" comes from the Greek word "oikonomos", meaning "house-manager", and consequently it has etymological support. Secondly, when the adjective "political" has been taken away, it cannot be understood to be still a part of political science, and therefore including all the phenomena economic, be it political or domestic or anything else like it. And thirdly, to use a single word to designate certain branch of study is more convenient in vocabulary. It is now generally understood that the phrase political

---

① Mill, *Elements of Political Economy* (1824), 2nd ed., p. 1.
② Mill, *Principles of Political Economy with Some of Their Application to Social Philosophy* (ed. 1875), p. 166.
③ H. D. MacLeod, *The History of Economics* (1896), p. 166.

economy is no longer used, and if it is still heard it is likely to mean something quite different from Economics.

Indeed, it is quite possible, that, as the adjective "political" is being taken away from the phrase "political economy", the word science may be added so as to make that branch of study "economic science". But this has not been generally done, for economists seem to be wise enough in that respect not to tamper with a satisfactory term. For, as we have already remarked, to call it a science before considering whether it is a science or not is illogical, and what is illogical is unscientific.

The introduction of the term "biology" may also throw some light on our understanding. Before the time of Lamarck, what was understood by scholars to comprise field of "natural history" was a group of studies known as zoology, botany, etc. Even Lamarck himself, the inventor of the term, ① did not use it for the title of his well-known treatise *Philosophie Zoologique* (1809). But when it became generally realized that organic matters have certain common characteristics and elements which extended beyond the confines of zoology or botany, the term "Biology" came to be used.

The like may be said of politology. That "something" which Professor Beard pointed out has not been named. And here we see the need of introducing a new name. Sixty years ago, Franz von Holtzendorff was of the opinion that with the growth of the knowledge of the state, it is impossible to put the whole field of the study under the collective title "Staatswissenschaft". ② "Daher kam es," he remarked, "dass an deren Stelle die 'Staatswissenschaften' als eine Mehrheit, in Frankreich die 'sciences morales et politiques' Platz nehmen." Of the same opinion is Professor Garner who writes: "Thus the tendency has been to group them (the distinct political studies) into separate categories and treat them as distinct sciences. The plural form, the 'political sciences', therefore seems to correspond more nearly with the facts and is preferred by many writers."③

The objection to the term "Staatswissenschaft" or "Staatswissenschaften" has been already pointed out, and since the term science in English is objectionable, its plural form "sciences" is equally unsatisfactory.

It is obvious now that all the terms which have been commonly or sometimes employed to designate that branch of social studies known as political, such as we have considered above, are not adequate. None of them is comprehensive enough to include

---

① It is understood that the word was coined simultaneously by Treviranus.
② Holtzendorff, *Die Principien der Politik*, p. 4.
③ Garner, *Political Science and Government*, p. 5.

the whole field; and none of them is proper and precise enough to meet the need of its present conditions. The new term proposed, however, has not only the benefit of etymological support, it has also the advantage of being not understood as to mean something more nor something less than what is known as political. It is broad enough to include terms such as Staatswissenschaft and Staatswissenschaften; Politics, Staatslehre, Political Theory, Political Philosophy and Political Science. Yet it does not pretend to cover the field (which does not belong to its own) in spite of the fact that they are closely related to each other.

Su-Ching Chen

Chapter 2
Subject Matter of Political Science

"Il faut une socience politique nouvelle a un mode tout nouveau. Mais c'est a quoi nous ne songeons guere; places au milieu d'un fleuve rapide, nous nexons obstinement les yeux vers quelques debus qu'on opercoit sur la rivage, tandis que le courant nous entraineet nous pausse a reoulons vers les abimes."

What the author of the monumental work, *La Democratie en Amerique*[①] wrote about a century ago is still true in our age. And Harold J. Laski, one of the most eminent political philosophers of our time, echoes, on the other side of the channel, the French-statesman by declaring, in the opening sentence of *A Grammar of Politics*[②], that "a new political philosophy is necessary to a new world".

A somewhat similar opinion has been expressed by Rudolf Kjellen in a different tone: "Es ist nur éines der Anzeichen in der gleichen allgemeinnen Zeitstroemung, wenn die Aufmerksamkeit hier nun unmitelbar auf die Notwendikeit einer Reform der Staatswissenschaft gelenkt wird: keine Begrenzung mehr durch den Horizont Manchester, kein Zuruecklichen mehr aud eine vergangene Zeit, waehrend die Staatsentwicklung des Abendlandes bereits im Begriff ist, einen neuen und reicheren Inhalt zu offenbaren."[③]

"Political science is in the crucible"; so we are told by Charles Beard. And another writer asserts that political science is at the crossroads. "Its foundations," she says, "have been undermined by the claims of law and jurisprudence, into whose hands it has been deliberately surrendering itself for the half-century or more, and now its chief strongholds are under fire from the neighboring fields of sociology, economics, and ethics. So severe and so persistent have these attacks become that the time has arrived when the political scientist must decide whether he will allow his subject to be absorbed

---

① Alexis de Tocqueville, *La Democratie en Amerique 1838*, Introduction.
② H. J. Laski, *A Grammar of Politics*, 1925, p. 15.
③ R. Kjellen, *Der Staat als Lebensform*, German translation by J. Sandmeier, 1924, p. 12. (The original text is in Swedish 1917.)

in any one or all of these various fields, or will attempt to reestablish it as a distinctive discipline."①

Thus the so-called political science needs a reform: reform not only in its name about which we have already argued, but also in its substance. Indeed, what is more important is the substance rather than the name. Here we come to the vital point of the subject, and here we see the necessity for reconstruction.

What is, then, the substance of the so-called political science? In other words, what is the subject-matter or data of the so-called political science?

The answer given by the so-called traditional scientists is that the state is the subject-matter of political science. Theodore D. Woolsey, for instance, views the state as the subject-matter of political science. This is obvious because his two-volume work is entitled *Political Science or the State*②. So Heinrich von Treitschke declares that "die Politik im sinne der alten is die Lehre vom Staat schlechthin"③. "Political Science" (die Staatswissenschaft), says Bluntschli, "in its proper sense is the science which is concerned with the state, which endeavours to understand and comprehend the state in its conditions, its development. Jellinek also considers the state as the subject-matter of this field of study.④

"In short", so remarks Garner, "political science begins and ends with the state."⑤ And Laski, although departing from his predecessors in many respects, defines, however, political science in almost the same manner: "Political science concerns itself with the life of men in relation to organized states."⑥

---

① Ellen D. Ellis, "Political Science at the Crossroads" in *the American Political Science Review*, 1927, Vol. XXI, November, p. 773.

② Woolsey, *Political Science or the State*, Lectures between the years 1846 and 1871 and published in 1887.

③ I use the Oxford translation. The original text may be quoted here: "Under Staatswissenschaft im eighentlichen Sinne verstehen wir die Wissenschaft, deren Gegenstand der Staate ist, welche den Staat in seinen Grundlegen, in seinem Wesen, seinen Erscheinungsformen, seiner Entwickelung zu Erkennen und zu Begreifen sucht." Bluntschli, *Allgemeine Staatslehre*, 1886 edition, S. 1. It is to be noted that when the Germans call this branch of study Staatswissenschaft, there is no objection to saying that the subject-matter of this branch of study is the state with the understanding that the so-called "Staatswissenschaft" is not to include all things political.

④ Treitschke, *Politik*, p. 2.

⑤ Garner, *Political Science and Government*, 1928, p. 9. See also, for instance, J. R. Seeley, *Introduction to Political Science*, Seeley points out that the scope of political science will be arranged under two heads: "First will come those presented by the internal structure and development of the state itself, the manner in which government enters into it, and the machinery through which government works; then will follow the problems of the interaction of one state upon another, or the external action of the state." p. 18.

⑥ Laski, *On the Study of Politics*, an inaugural lecture delivered at the London School of Economics and Political Science, 1927, p. 6. See also his *An Introduction to Politics*, 1931.

It is safe to say that almost all of the writers of political science for the last hundred years have regarded the state as the sole subject-matter of the so-called political science. In other words, what is known as political science is nothing more and therefore nothing less than the "science" of the state or in the French form "Le science de l'etat", and consequently identical with the German form "staatswissenschaft", although the "wissenschaft", as we have already pointed out, can not be translated, in its strict sense, as science in English.

Thus the identification of the state with what is understood things political, as already said, is a conception which has dominated the minds of the writers in the field of political study, and hardly can we find any thinker who has freed himself from such tradition until very lately. This, undoubtedly, is not right, for the simple reason that neither in the sense of the word, nor in its substance, is political phenomenon identical ⟨with⟩ what [what] is known as state.

It is to be remarked that although there are a few writers who see the need of reconstructing the so-called political science, it seems that none has made a distinction between things political and what is known as concerned with the state. When, for instance, James Q. Dealey remarks that "all bodies politic are not states", we may think that he does make such a distinction. But he continues to [us] tell us: "Throughout the inhabited world there are numerous bodies politic, large and small, each definitely organized for purposes of common defense and welfare, but most of these are in subordination to similar but large organizations. Some of these larger organizations are recognized as independent and sovereign, in which case they are known as national bodies and are called *states*. The subordinate bodies are known by such names as provinces, departments or counties, cities, or municipalities and townships or communes."[①]

Our author is not conscious of, or at least overlooks the rapid growth of the international activities and organizations which are political in nature but not necessarily within the control of a state. Nor does he remember that there were many political organizations in the past and that there are many such organizations in the so-called primitive societies which are neither parts of the state nor created by the latter. Moreover, although he does not regard the smaller political organizations such as provinces, departments, communes, etc. as states and consequently he may be expected to deny the state as the only subject-matter of political science, he defines, the

---

① Dealey, *The Development of the State*, 1909, p. 54.

so-called political science "as the science concerned with the study of the state and the conditions essential to the existence and development"①. Here we see the dilemma: If all bodies politic, as Dealey calls it, may be regarded as the data of political science, and we consider this as the proper way, then political science can not be taken as the science of the state simply. If only the state is viewed as the data of political science, then the so-called bodies politic other than the state should be excluded from the field of political science according to the reasoning of Dealey. As a matter of fact, the difference here made has nothing to do with the subject-matter of political science, for so far as this is concerned, the state remains to include the other bodies politic.

Rudolf Kjellen also sees the necessity of enlarging the scope of political science. He tells us: "Unsere traditionelle Staatswissenschaft muss erweitert verden, wie ein Ring, der zu eng geworden ist fuer den Ginger, den er umschlies sen soll."② And he adds in another place: "Die Selbstbesinnung der Staatswissenschaft hat zu der Einsicht gefuehrt, dass die Grenzen der Wissenschaft einer Erweiterung befuerfen."③

What Kjellen tries to do is to broaden the so-called "rechtwissenschaftliche-staatswissenschaft"④ to a real Staatswissenschaft, because, as he remarks, what belongs to the state is much more than what belongs to the field of law, ⑤ and, in order to call it Staatswissenschaft, attributes which belong to the state such as the social and economical forces as well as legal forces (Rechtskraft), should be also taken into consideration. ⑥

This being his conviction, he comes to the conclusion that a true Staatswissenschaft would consider the state as "Reich" or "Geopolitik", as "Volk" or "Ethnopolitik", as "Haushalt", "Gesellschaft" and "Regierungsgewalt" or "Wirtschaftspolitik", "Soziopolitik" and "Herrschaftspolitik".

Now, a content like this is of course much broader than that of the so-called Verfassungspolitik, or rechtlicher Staatswissenschaft, but it is far from being comprehensive in the field of Staatswissenschaft, and still less in the field of political "science". It tells us mainly the forces making up the state. We may call them the foundations of the state,

---

① Dealey, *The Development of the State*, 1909, p. 51.
② Kjellen, *Der Staat als Lebensform*, p. 12.
③ *Ibid.*, p. 11.
④ *Ibid.*
⑤ *Ibid.* "Weil unser Staat tatsaechlich seinen Wirkungskreis so ueberwiegend auf das Recht eingestellt hatte, bliet unsere Staatswissenschaft eine Rechtswissenschaft."
⑥ *Ibid.*, p. 17. "Die Staatswissenschaft muss der Eigenschaft des Staates Raum geben, neben einer Rechtskraft auch eine soziale und wirtschaftliche Kraft zu sein."

though they are not so much about the state itself. Moreover, we deny that the state is the only subject-matter of political "science", and we certainly can only take the learned author's *Der Staat als Lebensform* as a part of what is known as things political.

Other writers such as A. D. Lindsay and G. E. G. Catlin, also remark that political science needs to be reconstructed, but neither one of them has given a satisfactory solution. Lindsay points out that "it looks almost as though the state as it now exists were either too large or too small". But the standpoint that he here takes is from the whole field of human activities and organizations. In other words, when Lindsay says that the state is either too large or too small, he does not mean in respect to the political organizations alone, but also comparing the state with other kinds of associations such as economical organizations, religious groups and the like. The point advanced here is that the state can no longer hold the position that it used to occupy. The result would be to reform the whole field or political science, but the Oxford Professor here stops.①

Catlin writes: "Political science is not sociological science of everything, a psychological study of all human behavior in all aspects, an anthropological inguiry into miscellaneous human customs, or a form of social organization resulting from one species of political action, or a study only of government and the state properties of law and administration."② Although the writer declares that "political science is not a sociological science of everything", he gives us almost a book on sociology under the name of politics. In the preface of his *Principles of Politics*, we read "It may further be objected that this is a treatise on Sociology, misdescribed as Politics. In the mind of the writer, politics and sociology (according to the most satisfactory definition of this latter) are inseparable and indeed, identical subjects."

To say nothing of the contradiction which Catlin has committed himself to by declaring politics as sociology on the one hand and not as sociology on the other, we think he is here making a serious challenge to the sociologists. We learn, for instance, from Paul Barth that sociology is politics; but what is here meant by Barth is that the origin of sociology is to be found in the past, certainly not in the present. Possibly with the exception of G. Ratzenhofer③, we seldom find a sociologist who maintains that sociology is identical with politics as Catlin has declared, although they are considered

---

① Lindsay, "The State in Recent Theory" in *Political Quarterly*, Vol. I , 1914, p. 136.
② Catlin, "The Delimitation and Measurability of Political Phenomena" in *the American Political Science Review*, 1927, Vol. XXI, No. 2, p. 225.
③ Ratzenhofer, *Wesen und Zweck der Politik*, 1893, also his *Die Sociologische Erkenntnis*, 1898.

as inseparable. Neither Comte nor Spencer considers political science as sociology. The former, besides writing his well-known work *Positive Philosophy* with the chief aim of establishing a new study which he called "sociology", published another two volumes on *Positive Polity*. The latter expresses very clearly in the preface of the first volume of his *Principles of Sociology* that the term "Politics" can not be used in the place of sociology, because it is narrower in scope and therefore can not cover the field which is known as sociology.

It may be safe to say, then, that, as a rule, the sociologists regard political phenomena as narrower in scope than social phenomena, and to identify the two would lead to such confusion that a reform of the whole field of the so-called social sciences would be needed. ①

Politology does not pretend to embrace what is known as the field of sociology. Nor is it, to be sure, content to live within the abode of the state. It is too large a field to include the former and too small to confine itself to the latter. We shall discuss later the relation of politology to sociology, or to speak more properly the relation of things political to things social. It is our purpose to make a clear distinction between the state and what is known as things political in this and the following chapters.

At the outset, it must be noted that the state is one and only one of the political organizations the function of which is to secure a certain definite political end for the interest of human beings, and consequently it can not be regarded as the only subject-matter of what we prefer to call politology. In fact politology itself is only one branch of the social studies. It deals with certain aspects of human interests which may be designated as political, being different from what is understood as economic, religious and the like, although they are closely related to each other and a hard and fast line between them cannot be easily drawn.

Before showing in detail how things political should be differentiated from the state, it is necessary to point out that the subject-matter of politology has changed as conditions changed. The understanding of this point is very important to our understanding of the distinction between the state and things political. It is desirable, then, for us to show how the subject-matter of this branch of study has changed in the course of time.

---

① Catlin, *Principles of Politics*. That politics and sociology are not distinguished by Catlin may be noted in many places. For example, on pages 73 and 74, he says: "It seems to me important that a distinction should be clear between, on the one hand, politics or sociology which as sciences must be abstract and which must aim at such treatment measure—and on the other, social or political philosophy which I would suggest, is concerned with social life as a concrete whole." Note.

We know very well that the earlier writers on the so-called political science, usually if not always, confined themselves, so far as the subject-matter of the study was concerned, either to a certain form of government or to the ruler of the political organization. Thus Plato called one of his works the *Republic* and the other the *Statesman*. But what was more important to Plato were the rulers, particularly what he called philosopher-kings of his ideal political organization or small city. Aristotle, though using the term Politics as the title of his well known work, wrote a treatise mainly concerning the city rather than what we understand as state or body politic in our day. As a matter of fact, the very name politics as used by us comes from the Greek word *polis*, meaning the city.

To the men of the Mediaeval Age, politology was only a branch of theology, and in the language of J. N. Figgis, the state is merely the police department of the church. If we confine ourselves to what is known as things political, we find the personal activities of the emperor or of the kings were the chief subjects for discussion. John of Salisbury, for example, in his *Polycraticus*[①], besides defending the rights of the church and the pope, considered only one form of government, namely the monarchy. "Monarchy is the only form of government," says one writer, "in which John is interested as a working reality, although he seems conscious that there may be other forms."[②] "The king," according to John, "is the minister of the common interest and the bond-servant of equity, and he bears the public person in the sense that he punishes the wrongs and injuries of all, and all crimes, with even-hand equity."[③]

The reason why the king is the most important of all in a political organization is because he occupies a position which is equal to the head of a body. "The place of the head of the body of the commonwealth is filled by the prince, who is subject only to God and to those who exercise His office and represent Him on earth, even as in the human

---

① The title is supposed to mean "The Statesman's Book".
② See J. Dickinson's introduction to *The Statesman's Book of John of Salisbury*, 1927, p. Xl.
③ See Dickinson's translation of *The Statesman's Book of John of Salisbury*, Book Ⅳ, Ch. 2, p. 7.

body the head is quickened and governed by the soul."① So we are told by John.

It may be said that to many writers as well as to John in the twelfth century②, the vital point and therefore the subject-matter of the so-called political science was the monarch, the king, the prince or whatever name you may call him. This was true in the following centuries until almost to the end of the eighteenth century in many countries. So Egidio Colonna's treatise on *Li Livres du Gouvernement des Rois*, published in the thirteenth century, tells us that "monarchy is considered to be the best and that hereditary monarchy is better than elective, because it contains the powerful element of tradition which perpetuates the bonds between king and subjects and acts as safeguard for the established prorogatives of both"③.

Dante Alighieri named his book *De Monarchia*, although his monarch is supposed to be a world monarch who serves as an arbitrate for kings and princes. There were, of course, a group of writers who were called monarchomachs, questioning or repudiating the authority of the king and advocating the theory of popular sovereignty. But the issue raised here was not whether there should be a king or not, but rather where the final authority of a political organization was vested. The monarchomachs insisted that the final authority was in the hands of the people and it was the people who had delegated his power to the king so that he could exercise authority for the good of the people. If he did not do that or misused his authority, then the people would have the right to resist him or even to depose him.

Now it is clear that what the monarchomachs attempted to show was the origin of the final authority and the justification of the people to arm themselves in case the ruler failed in his mission. But the exercise of authority was still in the hands of the monarch,

---

① John of Salisbury, *Policraticus*, Book V, Ch. Ⅱ. He continues: "The place of the heart is filled by the Senate, from which proceeds the initiation of good works and ill. The duties of eyes, ears, and tongue are claimed by the judges and governors of provinces. Officials and soldiers correspond to the hands. Those who always attend upon the prince are likened to the sides. Financial officers and keepers (I speak now not of those who are in charge of the prisons, but of those who are keepers of the privy chest) may be compared with the stomach and intestines, which, if they become congested through excessive avidity, and retain too tenaciously their accumulations, generate innumerable and incurable diseases, so that through their ailment the whole body is threatened with destruction. The husbandmen correspond to the feet, which always cleave to the soil, and need the more especially the care and foresight of the head, since while they walk up on the earth doing service with their bodies, they meet the more often with stones of stumbling and therefore deserve aid and protection all the more justly since it is they who raise, sustain, and move forward the weight of the entire body. Take away the support or the feet from the strongest body, and it can not move forward by its own power, but must creep painfully and shamefully on its hands, or else be moved by means of brute animal." Book V, Ch. 2, p. 65.
② John's Book was completed in 1159.
③ See Introduction to *Li Livres du Gouvernement des Rois*, edited by S. P. Molenaer, 1899.

the king or the prince. In other words, a monarchy still remains although one monarch may be replaced, if necessary, by another. Thus so far as governmental form is concerned there is not much change in the theory of the monarchomachs.

Dissatisfaction with one monarch did not mean the abolition of the system of monarchy. Both those who were for or against a certain monarch all looked to the monarch as the central point of the political problem, and book written on political subjects usually dealt with the conduct of the monarch, king or prince. The so-called political science was, then, as a matter of fact as well as a matter of theory, the "science" of monarch, king or prince.

In order to elaborate this point a little further, we may cite the works of Sir John Fortescue and of Niccolo Machiavelli. Fortescue's *The Governance of England*, otherwise called *The Difference Between an Absolute and a Limited Monarchy* was written between 1471 and 1476. If we look at the titles of different chapters, we find that the book may be regarded as a treatise on the king. Thus the Governance of England may be also called the monarch of England. We know well that in Fortescue's time, the parliament of England was already becoming important and when we look at the title *The Difference Between an Absolute and a Limited Monarchy*, we certainly expect that the author would tell us something about the composition and powers of the Parliament; but Fortescue was silent on these questions. One writer tells us that the reason why he was silent on these questions was that "probably he considered them to be too firmly settled and too well known to require any commentary"[1]. And he continues: "The increase of the power of parliament is indeed too obvious to escape notice." And so states Stubbs: "Never before and never again for more than two hundred years, were the commons so strong as they were under Henry Ⅳ."[2] Yet we must also ask: Is it not that monarchy is a subject too firmly settled and too well known to be considered by him? Yet the author wrote a treatise dealing mainly with the king.

The reason is simple. Although conditions had changed during the time of Fortescue and although parliament had already come into power at that time, political writers were still influenced by the writers of the past, giving more consideration as it used to do, regarding the king as the chief actor on the political stage, and therefore the subject-matter of the so-called political science.

This is particularly true in our day in regard to this field of study. And this is one of the most important reasons for reconstructing our political study with the hope that

---

[1] Charles Plummer's "Introduction" to *The Governance of England*, p. 4.
[2] *Ibid.*, quoted by Plummer.

theories and principles formulated should conform with facts.

There is no question that being in public life and occupying high position in the government such as Fortescue did, he could not be unconscious of the fact that the power of Parliament was rising and that the composition of that body was important to the governance of England. But instead of giving special attention to this obvious fact, he was silent, and proceeded to make the king, and if you like the crown①, the central theme of his book. As a matter of fact, the position of the king was still very important in those days. To say nothing of other countries, this was also true to a large extent in England.

Because the King was still a very important or even the most important figure in politics, his actions became on almost all occasions political actions. We all know that the morganatic marriage of Edward Ⅷ caused his abdication, which although an important event to the Royal family of England, did not disturb the political problems of the country in any serious manner. It was a romantic affair or even a comedy as some people call it. But this would not have been true in the time of Henry Ⅳ. The marriage of Henry to Margaret of Anjou in 1445 was a great misfortune not only to the house of Lancaster, but also to England. And Fortescue was himself involved with the case as a result. Then again the poverty of the king, for instance, according to Fortescue, was disastrous to the country as well as to the king himself. Fortescue devoted much space to the discussion of this problem. ②

Fortescue was conscious of the fact that England was not a country ruled by an absolute or despotic king. He spoke of two kinds of monarchy: one was limited monarchy and the the other absolute. "Ther bith ij kyndes off kyngdomes, of the wich that on is lordship callid in laten *Dominium regale*, and that other is callid *dominium politicum et regale*."③ In the former the king rules above the law and by his own arbitrary discretion and will, in the latter he rules inside the law. France is an example of the former and England of the latter.

Yet in spite of the limitation of law on the authority of the king of England, Fortescue thought more of the king of his country than of other political subjects. ④ It goes without saying that the king of France or of other countries would be more important

---

① The term "Crown" was used by Fortescue in his work.
② Fortescue, *The Governance of England*, Chapter Ⅴ and following Chapters.
③ *Ibid.*, Chapter Ⅰ.
④ See also S. B. Chrimes, *English Constitutional Ideas in the Fifteenth Century*, 1936. "It is true that the theory of the only outstanding political thinker of the century, Fortescue, is essentially a theory of kingship, rather than of the state, and of dominion rather than of kingship…" p. 304.

in view of the fact that the country or countries were ruled by the caprice of the king.

When we come to consider the work of Machiavelli, particularly his *The Prince*, we are led to think that the so-called political science is really the "science" of the prince. Whether a political organization will be in order or in disorder, can be prosperous or not, or can exist at all or not, according to Machiavelli, depends almost entirely on the character of the prince. A strong and efficient ruler is the first condition for the maintenance of a country. In order to attain this end, it is better, so far as the experience of our author goes, to rule by force and craft. He is better to be feared than loved. And even fraud and treachery are tolerable if necessary.

Machiavelli speaks, to be sure, of two kinds of state. One is republic and the other monarchy. Of the latter it may be either hereditary "in which the rulers have been for many years of the same family, or else they are of recent foundation"[①]. But that which Machiavelli prefers is the hereditary monarchy. It is also interesting to note, as Machiavelli tells us, that *The Prince* is entirely devoted to the study of the monarchy. The reason why a hereditary monarchy is preferable is clearly stated by the author: "The difficulty of maintaining hereditary states accustomed to a reigning family is far less than in new monarchies; for it is sufficient not to transgress ancestral usuages, and to adapt one's self to unforeseen circumstances; in this such a prince, if of ordinary assiduity, will always be able to maintain his position, unless some very exceptional and excessive force deprives him of it; and even if he be thus deprived, on the slightest mischange happening to the new occupier, he will be able to regain it."

In another place, Machiavelli tells us "that the kingdoms known to history have been governed in two ways: either by a prince and his servants, who, as ministers by his grace and permission, assist in governing the realm; or by a prince and by barons, who hold their positions not by favour of the ruler but by antiquity of blood. Such barons have states and subjects of their own, who recognize them as their lords, and are naturally attached to them. In those states which are governed by a prince and his servants, the prince exercises more authority, because there is no one in the state regarded as a superior other than himself, and if others are obeyed it is merely as ministers and officials of the prince, and no one regards them with any special affection".

If history supplies only these two kinds of monarchy, it is only natural that a realistic or practical subject-matter of the so-called political science will be the

---

① Machiavelli, *The Prince*, Ch. I.

monarchy, monarchy in the sense of personal ruling rather than institutional authority. This is the reason why Machiavelli has given so much attention to the individual capacity of the king. One case after another has been cited in order to show how a prince should act under different circumstances; but all the numerous cases mentioned are the individual actions of the kings of his own time or of the past. It is, indeed, a treatise on king's craft as well on kingship.

In England, although there were many writers who insisted in the sixteenth century, on the mixed form of government by which it was meant some kind of division of sovereignty between the king and the parliament, political writers still wrote more about the king than about the parliament. This was true, to an even larger extent, in the seventeenth century. Both John Hayward and Thomas Craig gave more consideration to the question of succession. The former wrote his *An Answer to the First Part of a Certain Conference Concerning Succession* in 1603, and the latter wrote his *The Right of Succession to the Kingdom* almost at the same time.

In the writing of Thomas Hobbes, particularly his *Leviathan*, absolute and irresponsible power is strongly advocated, and the destruction of kingship meant, to him the destruction of civil society. Indeed, it is curious to note that the absolute authority of the monarch, in the system of Hobbes, comes from a social contract by means of which all the members of a given society with the exception of the one who is going to be king give up all of their rights in order to form a civil society. This is the point that makes Sir Robert Filmer feel that Hobbes conceded too much when the latter based his absolute sovereign on a social compact. According to Filmer①, there was never a time when men were equal as Hobbes pictures it. Even when there were only two human beings in the world, one was the master and the other subordinate. Thus from the very begining, Adam was the master, first over his wife and then over his children. This is the basic argument of Sir Robert and hence he wrote his *Patriarcha*; or *The Natural Power of Kings*. One might think that both Hobbes and Filmer were wrong in their interpretations of the origin of kingship, and yet the importance of the idea of kingship in the political writings of England in the seventeenth century can not be questioned.

What is true in England is even more true in France in both the sixteenth and seventeenth centuries. Bodin is no less a monarchist than most of his contemporaries. His application of the theory of sovereignty to the monarch strengthens the position of the king in other countries as well as in his own country. Loyseau, the author of *Traite des*

---

① In one of Filmer's writings, Filmer holds that Parliament is an evil.

Seigneuries published in 1608, follows Bodin very closely so far as the theory of sovereignty is concerned. He devotes much of his time and space to classifying and explaining the different kinds of seigneuries. It was a political science of the age, for, at that time, there was perhaps nothing more important in the field of this study than the description of the rulers. And when Louis XIV declared: "L'etat, c'est moi", it was not merely a boast. It contained much truth.

Thus the monarch was the real governor. Government was then his majestic government and state, if there was any, was conceived as the estate of the king. As a matter of fact, as we shall show later, the word state is derived from the word estate.

But if Bodin was the prophet for the absolutism of his own country, Hobbes and Filmer were advocating something of the past in England. Constitutionalism found its expression in the *Magna Carta* in the twelveth century. It was the gradual growth of constitutionalism that led men of farsightedness to conceive the distinction between the monarch and the government. Since England was the first country that introduce the constitutional system in the strict sense of the term, English writers have been in a better position to make such a distinction.

In speaking of the political theories of the fifteenth century in England, one writer tells us: "But there is perhaps one tendency in the political thought of the fifteenth century, a definition of which reflects both these interpretations, and that tendency was towards a change in its subject-matter. Political thought was becoming exclusively a theory of monarchy, and rather more a theory of the state. This tendency is noticeable in many expressions of political concepts made by active politicians, even though theory was still shot through and through with notions of kingship."[①]

It is to be noted that the word "state" used here is objectionable and that it would be more appropriate to use the "government" for substitute. And yet it must be also remembered that although there was a tendency to become "less exclusively a theory of monachy", there was little if any indication of its becoming more a theory of government, not to say of the state. Thus there was a negative denial of the absolutism of the monarch, but there was almost none of the positive reconstruction for a theory of government.

But it was different in the time of the seventeenth century, particularly after the Revolution of 1688. Indeed, England of the seventeenth century was very fruitful in the field of political literature. And when an Englishman wrote in the next century that "on

---

① S. B. Chrimes, *English Constitutional Ideas in the Fifteenth Century*, 1936, p. 304.

the subject of government, no country hath produced writings so numerous and valuable as our own"①, he referred mainly to the political writings of the seventeenth century. It was the century of Hobbes, but it was also the century of Locke. It was the century of Filmer, but it was also the century of Sydney. It was the century of James Ⅰ, but it was also the century of Milton. Then it was the century of James Harrington and many others.

But theories and political theories in particular are always formulated either for the justification of facts already existing or for criticism of the existing conditions with the hope of improving them. This was undoubtedly true of political conditions in England in the seventeenth century. For England, it was a century of unrest, of confusion and of anxiety. "From the time of the differences between James Ⅰ and his Parliament in 1610, to the Revolution of 1688," writes an English writer, "our history and literature contain records of energetic difference about the limit of authority. There was a problem to be solved that touched the interests and stirred passions of men, until some fought, while others reasoned, and all human forces were spent on labour to get the problem solved. It seemed for a [a] while that the right answer was the Commonwealth. But a Commonwealth sustained by the genius of one man was monarchy. After Cromwell's death, it became clear that the answer to the problem had not yet been found. Stuarts were tried again, and Charles Ⅱ, and James Ⅱ served the country most effectually by betrayal of the trusts confided to them. Their shortcomings ensured us against risk of another Civil War. Liberty seemed to be dying, but in the worst signs of disease there was nature at work on her own way of cure."②

John Locke was unquestionably the best interpreter of the Revolution of 1688. But even before the publication of Locke's well known treatise, many writers spoke of government instead of the king or the monarch. Howels wrote *Reflexes on Government* instead of reflexes on king. Marchamont Nedham published a book under a long title without using the word king or monarch: *The Excellencie of a Free-State: Or the Right Constitution of a Commonwealth, Wherein All Objections Are Answered, and the Best Way to Secure the People Liberties Discovered with Some Errors of Government and Rules of Policies* in 1656. Here we find many terms which are more or less new to the time such as "State" and "Constitution" and such as "Commonwealth" and "Government". Yet there was no term such as king or monarch or prince as it was frequently used by writers for the title of the books in the past.

---

① See Richard Baron's preface to Marchamont Nedham's *The Excellencie of a Free-State*, 1656.
② See Henry Morley's Introduction to Locke's *Two Treatises on Civil Government*, 1884 edition.

In his *Discourses Concerning Government*, Algernon Sydney argues that "the English nation has always been governed by itself or its representatives"① and that "the king was never master of the soil"②. He further points out that "the follies with which our author (Filmer) endeavors to corrupt and trouble the world, seem to proceed from his fundamental mistakes of the ends for which governments are constituted; and from an opinion that an excessive power is good for the governor or the diminution of a prejudice; whereas common sense teaches, and all good men acknowledge, that governments are not set up for the advantage, profit, pleasure, or glory of one or a few men, but for the good of society"③.

Sydney wrote this treatise in reply to Filmer's *Patriarcha; or, The Natural Power of Kings*. By holding that the king was never master of the soil and that the nation was always governed by itself or its representatives, he minimized the position of the king and gave more emphasis to the importance of the House of Commons which consists of the representatives of the people. So instead of capitalizing the king or the monarch he used the term government, not only for the title of his oft-quoted book, but also through the whole work. To Sydney, the king became a minor part in the government, not above the government. The king did not have the absolute power which was not originally vested in the hands of the king. And if the end of the government is for the good of society and not for the good of a king or a few, government must be the government of all or of society. Thus it is the government, not the king or the monarch, that is considered as the subject-matter of the so-called political science.

If we compare the work of Fortescue or of Machiavelli on the one hand and that of Nedham or of Sydney on the other, we can easily see that in the former it looks as if it were written not only of the king but also for the king, while in the latter it was the governmental institution which forms the subject-matter for inquiry. Government was gradually becoming a common vocabulary. Nedham spoke of kingly government and of free-state-government. He also mentioned government political. Although terms such as king, government, state and political were not clearly differentiated by the writers of the time, the meaning of government was then definitely regarded as larger in scope than that of the king or monarch. Moreover, it became institutionalized instead of being personified, since the king was only a part and possibly a minor part of the government.

It must be admitted that the English writers of the seventeenth century gave more

---

① A. Sydney, *Discourses Concerning Government*, 1805 edition, New York, Vol. Ⅲ, p. 206.
② *Ibid.*, p. 233.
③ *Ibid.*, Vol. Ⅰ, p. 451.

attention to the question of the origin of government than to the institution of government. But it must be also remembered that it was rather the question of the origin of the government and of the king that led these writers consciously or unconsciously to make a distinction between the king and the government.

This can be well illustrated in the work of Locke, particularly his *Two Treatises on Civil Government* published in 1689. Like Sydney, Locke wrote these treatises in reply to Sir Robert Filmer's work mentioned above. Repudiating the theory of Filmer that the power of the king may be traced back to Adam, first the master of his wife, then, the head of his children and servants and consequently the first ruler of human beings, Locke constructed his civil government on the basis of a social compact.

According to Locke, "To understand political right, and derive it from its original, we must consider what estate all men are naturally in, and that is, a state of perfect freedom to order their actions, and dispose of their possessions and persons as they think fit, within the bounds of the law of nature, without asking leave or depending upon the will of any other man."[①]

And he continues: "A state also of equality, wherein all the power and jurisdiction is reciprocal, no one having more than another, there being nothing more evident than that creatures of the same species and rank, promiscuously born to all the same advantages of nature, and the use of the same faculties, should also be equal one amongst another, without subordination or subjection, unless the lord and master of them all should, by any manifest declaration of his will, set one above another, and confer on him, by an evident and clear appointment, an undoubted right to dominion and sovereignty."[②]

The state of nature is, then, not only a state of freedom, but also a state of equality. But why man, instead of living in the state of nature, comes to live in a political society? According to Locke, in order to protect one's property and to prevent any crimes committed, men have come together and established the civil society. He describes them as "those who are united into one body, and have a common established law and judicature to appeal to, with authority to decide controversies between them and punish offenders, and in civil society one with another"[③].

"And thus," says Locke, "the commonwealth comes by power to set down what

---

① Locke, *Two Treatises on Civil Government*, with an introduction by Henry Morley, 1884, Book II, Ch. 2, p. 192.
② Ibid., pp. 192–193.
③ Ibid., p. 235.

punishment shall belong to the several transgression they think worthy of it, committed amongst the members of that society (which is the power of making laws,) as well as it has the power to punish any injury done unto any of its members by any one that not of it (which is the power of war and peace); and all this for the preservation of the property of all the members of that society, as far as is possible. But though every man entering into society has quitted his power to punish offences against the law of Nature in prosecution of his own private judgment, yet with the judgment of offences which he has given up to the legislative, in all cases where he can appeal to the magistrate, he has given up a right to the commonwealth to employ his force for the execution of the judgments of the commonwealth whenever he shall be called to it, which, indeed, are his own jedgments, they being made by himself or his representative. And therein we have the original of the legislative and the executive power of civil society, which is to judge by standing laws how far offences are to be punished when committed within the commonwealth; and also by occasional judgment founded on the present circumstances of the fact, how far injuries from without are to be vindicated, and in both these to employ all the force of all the members when there shall be need."①

It is to be noted now that Locke speaks of "the original of the legislative and executive power of civil soceity". And it is this power that constitutes the government. So Locke says: "Wherever, therefore, any number of men so unite into one society as to quit every one his executive power of the law of nature, and to resign it to the public, there and there only is a political or civil society. And this done wherever any number of men, in the state of nature, enter into society to make one people one body politic under one supreme government; or else when anyone joins himself to, and incorporates with any government already made."②

Thus, from the point of view of the origin of government, there seems be no place for the king. Nor is he important in the government after its establishment since the government is dominated by the legislative body. "And hence," says Locke, "it is evident that absolute monarchy, which by some men is counted for the only government in the world, is indeed inconsistent with civil society, and so can be no form of civil governmeit at all. For the end of civil society being to avoid and remedy those inconveniencies of the state of nature which necessarily follow from every man's being judge in his case by setting a known authority to which everyone of that society may

---

① Locke, *Two Treatises on Civil Government*, with an introduction by Henry Morley, 1884, Book Ⅱ, Ch. 2, pp. 235-236.

② *Ibid.*, p. 236.

appeal upon any injury received, or controversy that may arise, and which everyone of the society ought to obey. Wherever any persons are ⟨those⟩ who have not such an authority to appeal to, and divide any difference between them there, those persons are still in the state of nature. And so is every absolute prince in respect or those who are under his dominion."①

The government of Locke is dominated by the legislative power "which has a right to direct how the force of the commonwealth shall be employed for preserving the community and the members of it"②. This "power is put into the hands of diverse persons who, duly assembled, have by themselves, or jointly with others, a power to make laws"③. "But because the laws are at once, and in a short time made, have a constant and lasting force, and need a perpetual execution, or an attendance thereunto, therefore it is necessary there should be a power always in being which should see to the execution of the laws that are made and remain in force. And thus the legislative and executive power come often to be separated."④

But there is, according to Locke, another power or department of government which "contains the power of war and peace, leagues and alliances, and all the transactions with all persons and communities without the commonwealth, and may be called federative if anyone pleases"⑤.

The so-called federative power is what we nowadays call the power for dealing with foreign or international affairs. This power, being a part of the executive power, or also shared by the legislative department, in our own day, is regarded by Locke as independent of both the executive and the legislative.

Locke spoke of all these powers and of the government as a whole without referring to the monarch or the king, although he knew very well that there was still a king in his country. Moreover, as we have already pointed out, in the system of Locke, no absolute monarchy can exist. The question that occupies Locke's mind is not that of the character of the monarch, but that of the origin, structure, division and function of the government. When the supreme power of the government is vested with the legislative body, the representative body of the the people, the question of who is going to be the head of the executive is not very important. Although the executive may exercise the

---

① Locke, *Two Treatises on Civil Government*, with an introduction by Henry Morley, 1884, Book Ⅱ, Ch. 2, pp. 236–237.
② *Ibid.*, p. 267.
③ *Ibid.*, p. 267.
④ *Ibid.*, pp. 267–268.
⑤ *Ibid.*, p. 268.

supreme power when the legislative is not in session, this occurs only for a short time, for besides the power of the legislative, there lies also the power of the people. The king, as a matter of fact, becomes only a part of the executive. And if we think of the English king in our own day as an executive head, we can not help feeling that he is nothing more than a mouthpiece through which some other persons make their thoughts known.

It must be said that it is now generally recognized that the social compact upon which Locke builds his government is like a castle built in the air. It lacks historical evidence. But the merit of his theory is that instead of considering kingship as the subject-matter of the so-called political science, he makes the government the subject-matter of this branch of study, and thereby enlarges its scope. As to its practical value, it interprets as well as predicts the increase of the power of Parliament. It is based on the actual condition of the day and points out the tendency in the future.

Thus the separation of the legislative body from the executive department and the increase of the power of the [the] former to its supremacy over the latter in England led the English writers, consciously or unconsciously, to regard the government as an institution rather than as a personal instrument of the king or the monarch. The theory of kingship was, then, changed into a theory of government. Undoubtedly, the process of change from the the former to the latter was gradual and slow, usually unnoticeable if one looks only from a short span of time; but in the long run the change is clear. In the transitional period, terms such as kingly government were employed, but a man of farsightedness like Locke could no longer think of the kingly government. It is true even in our own day, the English officials still speak of His Majestic Government, meaning the English government, but we all know that these are merely words. And when the king of England says: "My government is doing this or that," people also understand that if the king can do no wrong, he can also never do right because he has almost nothing to do with the government.

The English governmental institutions influenced not only English writers, but also writers of other countries. Of the latter Montesquieu was the most notable. His *De L'Esprit des Lois* published in 1748 has become a political classic. Though inclining to retain the Monarchy of France, his chief interest in the political problem is the governmental organization. Political liberty, according to him, can only be secured by a system of check and balance between the three departments of the government, namely the legislative, the executive and the judicial. This is what is known as his well-known theory of the separation of powers. Each power should be exercised by each organ, yet each should check the others so that a balance of powers can be maintained. Although Montesquieu insists on the separation of three powers, i. e. the legislative, executive and the judicial, the separation of the first two is, to him, especially important.

The theory of separation of powers as advocated by Montesquieu is somewhat based on the English governmental system, especially pronounced after Montesquieu's two years' sojourn in England. We know well, at that time, that in England the rise of the Cabinet government already combined the functions of both the legislative and the executive. Montesquieu's interpretation of the English government was not in accordance with facts. But in spite of his misunderstanding of the English governmental system from which he drew his sources of material for formulating the theory of separation of powers, the influence of this theory to the practical governmental institutions as well as [as] to the writers following him cannot be questioned. This theory has definite effect on both the federal and state constitutions of the United States of America. It is said that the fathers of the American Constitution regarded the *Spirit of Law* as a political bible.

But the point that interests us here is that in Montesquieu's work, like in the writings of Locke, it is to the government and governmental institutions rather than the king or monarch that our author gives special consideration, though, as we have already mentioned, Montesquieu preferred to retain the monarchy and the French institution and spirit.

So when D. De Real published his voluminous work, fifteen years after the appearance of Montesquieu's monumental work, he called it *La Science du Governement*. And in Rousseau's *Social Contract*, the revolutionary theory was intended to destory completely the power of the king. If the French Revolution owes a great deal to Rousseau, this must be Rousseau's greatest contribution. It is true that the kingly regime of France was not entirely rooted out by the Revolution, but it is also true that it was the Revolution that served as the dividing line between the old political regime and the new political institutions in France. It marked the passing of the ruling of the kingship and tended toward constitutionalism. It is to be added that the effect of the Revolution was not confined to France alone; it penetrated to every country in Continental Europe and created an undercurrent which gradually forced the supremacy of kingship behind the curtain and paved the way for a new age in political thinking.

If actual political conditions count a great deal in shaping political concepts, the Declaration of Independence of the United States must be regarded as a death-knell to the theory that kingship is the subject-matter of political inquiry. Here we have a new world where Kings only ruled in name and not in fact, where monarchs governed only by proxy and not in person and where royal blood was seldom continued and nobility not deeply rooted. Once the revolution succeeded, old traditions did not mean very much. A new governmental system was set up and the old repudiated. There were jealousies among the states, there were arguments for or against the powers of Congress or of the federal government; but almost none advocated the restoration of monarchy. Nor was there any prince or princess who claimed the title of a king or queen for the ruling of some or all of the colonies.

This being the background, it was only natural that both the fathers of the American constitution and later American writers did not need to write books on kingship and the royal or imperial house, and they were able to give exclusive attention to the governmental institutions. Moreover, the theory of the separation of power as formulated by Montesquieu was very closely applied here, and it was and is a government really governed by law instead of a government by man or by king. Being free from the ruling of kingship, the American writers, taking at first the government as the subject-matter of the so-called political science, have gradually enlarged the scope of this branch of study and made a distinction between the government and the state, a distinction which has been claimed as one of the most distinct contributions of American political ideas and which we shall deal with more fully in the next chapter.

It may be well concluded now that after the publication of Locke's *Two Treatises on Civil Government* and especially after the establishment of the American Republic, kingship has gradually disappeared and government has come to be the central theme for political discussion.

Indeed, it would be hard for us here to exhaust the list of works which deal with government as the subject-matter of this branch of study. A few titles of the works will suffice to show that political concept changed as condition changed. J. Bentham's *Fragment on Government*, 1776; Calhoun's *Disquisition on Government* and *The Constitution and Government of the United States*; N. Chipman's *Principles of Government*, 1853; and many others can be cited if we have the space and time. As a matter of fact, books on the Principles or Government, Introduction of Government, or even Philosophy of Government, are now crowded in our libraries. And even those which do not bear such titles also consider government as the subject-matter of the so-called political science. Brougham, for instance, had written a few volumes on *Political Philosophy*, but if one looks at the contents of the book, one sees immediately that it is a treatise on government rather than on political philosophy.

The distinction between the monarch and the government was clearly shown by

Francis Lieber in his writings. He remarks that "if government is not the monarch, the monarch not the state, if the state will endure although Louis XIV may die, it clearly follows that sovereignty is an attribute of the state and not of monarch"[①].

Lieber does not make a distinction between the government and state in this passage, but he does see that government is distinguished from the monarch, so the monarch may die while the government or the state still endures. In the writings of Lieber, the word "government" and the term "state" are frequently used, and yet it seems to us that he prefers the word government and this can be easily understood if we just look at the title or one of his books which is called *On Civil Liberty and Self-government*.

It may be noted that the saying "the king is dead and long live the king" goes back to the ancient past and that although the first sentence regards the king as a person the second considers him as an institution which means kingship has been institutionalized and therefore the government or the king is not purely a government by man but also a government by law. Being a government by law, it is said, a monarchical form of government can be also regarded as a constitutional government. We must say that there is no question of having a constitutional government, but the question referred here is a question of a successor to the king and therefore it is still a personal rather than a public question and necessarily a problem of the government, for the simple reason that a government can exist without a king.

Robert Blakey, in *A History of Political Literature*, tells us that "all political literature has the nature of government for its theme". And he asks: "What is a government?" "It is," he says, "an embodiment of power and obedience; —power in the hands of rulers, and obedience in the people." "What are the grand purposes of government?" he asks again. "To promote the peace and happiness of mankind. The value of all sound and constitutional governments are estimated by the measure or liberty they confer on the individual members of the state, compatible with the safety and well-being of the whole. These are the leading points of discussion in all literary and scientific treatises on politics as a general system of human knowledge."[②]

Blakey wrote almost a hundred years ago. But even up to the present day there are still many writers who take government as the subject-matter for political inquiry. So we are told that political science deals with government and with government only.[③] Thus a political problem is identical with a governmental problem. And because there has been

---

① Lieber, *Political Ethics*, Vol. I, p. 245.
② Blakey, *History of Political Literature*, Vol. I, pp. XIII–XIV.
③ Compare Leacock's *Elements of Political Science*, p. 3.

always one kind or another of political problem in modern society, government is a subject that receives worldwide attention. In *The Study of Government* published in 1871, George H. Yeaman says: "I have essayed to write an elementary work of government. There is no subject, besides history and religion, upon which so much has been written. There is no subject, unless it be religion, in which men have taken so much interest."①

It must be said that even history of the past was almost nothing more than political history and consequently the record of governmental activities. And religion, unless it is pure and purely theological in nature, has been always mixed with politics. It is hard to understand the European political problems, especially those in the days of or even long after the Reformation without an understanding of the religious background. Conversely, it may also be said that the influence of the former on the latter has been so great that the church or Christianity has been regarded as the church of the state or of government.

Just as a king or a monarch was, at one time, considered as the possessor of sovereign power and could control almost everything within his kingdom, the government became the supreme authority of the state. So the sovereignty of the king became the sovereignty of the government. What was done formerly in the name of the king was done, from the seventeenth century to the nineteenth century, in the name of the government.

Just as king or monarch was identical with the state and therefore with things political, government was then considered as identical with the state and consequently with things political. The scope so enlarged and so fixed has been and still is followed to a certain extent to the present time, as we have already shown that there are still many writers who view government as the subject-matter of the so-called political science.

Some writers even go so far as to identify society with government. Thus civil society has been regarded as civil government. In the writings of those who hold the theory of social contract, seldom do we find a clear distinction between the terms society and government. They are interchangeable and they are usually mixed. And not long ago, one writer says: "Government is society in action; it is the whole people as members of society. There is not, never was, nor ever can be any sovereignty save that of government. While government is both society and people as one organic, the entire severally are neither society or government."[1]

Indeed it takes centuries for the government to separate from the monarch and it is

---

① Yeaman, *The Study of Government*, p. 1.

no wonder that it takes a long time for many writers to make such a distinction even when the government is no longer under the absolute control of the king. But once such a distinction is made, the scope of the so-called political science is larger than it used to be. Few writers if any after the eighteenth century and particularly after the American Declaration of Independence and the French Revolution would still follow the fashion of Machiavelli or Loyseau to confine their political studies purely to the prince or the lords alone. The prince and the lords are, as we have already noted, still considered as parts of political studies in the countries where princes and lords are still existent and yet it may be safe to say that in the latter part of the nineteenth century and especially in our century, prince and lords have become vestiges of the past which, judging from the experiences of recent times, may not last very far into the future. They are something of the past and there is no livelihood for restoration. In fact, countries in which the republican form of government is established prohibit, usually if not always, the grant of titles of notability.

I have dwelt upon this subject, the distinction between king or monarch and government, somewhat in detail, partly because it has not been well observed by the so-called political scientists despite its importance with regard to the change of subject-matter and therefore the nature of political science and partly because an understanding of such a distinction will lead to a clearer understanding of the distinction between the government and the state and particularly the distinction between the state and things political.

Garner also follows Austin and Willoughby by holding that legally sovereignty can not be limited. There are limitations on the sovereignty, he admits, but "an examination of these limitations, however, will show that 'legally' they are not restrictions on sovereignty at all"[1]. "The law of nature, the principles of morality, the laws of God, the dictates of humanity and reason, the fear of public opinion, and other alleged restrictions on sovereignty," he declares, "have no legal effect, except in so far the state chooses to recognize them and give them force and validity."[2]

But like Willoughby, he does not accept the Austinian theory without any qualification. He thinks that "Austin's chief error consisted in unduly emphasizsing the purely legal aspects of sovereignty, and ignoring the forces and influences which lie back of the formal law—a very natural mistake for a lawyer to make."[3] And he adds: "It may

---

[1] Yeaman, *The Study of Government*, p. 184.

[2] *Ibid.*

[3] *Ibid.*, p. 181.

also be said that his theory is probably inapplicable to all states of society, such, for example, as those which Maine described in his work on the *Early History of Institutions.* "①

This is not all. Garner does not think that the sovereignty of the state is unlimited in regard to international dealings. In this respect, he is no longer to be considered as an [an] advocate of the Austinian theory, but standing on the same line with those who attack the traditional theory of absolute and unlimited sovereignty. "If we examine the facts relating to the intercourse of states today," he writes, "no other conclusion is possible than that the practice no longer corresponds to the traditional legal theory, and if usage and practice are sources of international law, it follows as a consequence that the absolute sovereignty of the state in its international relations is not only a legal fiction but a baneful and dangerous dogma which ought to be abandoned, and that the notion should ⟨be⟩ expunged from the literature of international law."② And he says again, "Much indeed may be said in support of the thesis of Kohler, Pillet, Aplheus H. Snow, and various others which today not only is international law superior in fact to municipal law of every state, but its supremacy has even acquired a legal basis, from which it results that the limitations which it sets to the liberty of action of states are legal limitations and not merely self-imposed restrictions."③

Here Garner differs radically from Willoughby and therefore even much further from Austin. To Austin, as pointed out, international law is merely positive morality. To Willoughby the term law may be applied to international rules, "if it be borne in mind that the term when so employed, has a meaning different from that which it has when used by analytical jurists when speaking of municipal laws"④. To Garner, on the contrary, international law is law in the sense of municipal law. Both Austin and Willoughby consider that the limitations laid by international law upon sovereignty are not legal in the sense in which that term is used in positive or analytical jurisprudence. It seems to Garner, it is a legal limitation. The difference between these three writers is obvious. Austin is a municipal lawyer; Willoughby is a constitutional lawyer; while Garner, on the other hand, is an international lawyer.

But it seems that there is a contradiction in maintaining that legally sovereignty can not be limited on the one hand, and that the limitation laid upon sovereignty

---

① Yeaman, *The Study of Government*, p. 181.
② *Ibid.*, p. 193.
③ *Ibid.*
④ Willoughby, *Fundamental Concepts of Public Law*, p. 298.

international law is a legal one on the other. In order to avoid this dilemma, Garner is led to deny that the conception of sovereignty can be applied in international law, and therefore in international relations. In this point, Garner again agrees with Willoughby. But it is to be noted that the fundamental principle of Austin and of Willoughby that in order to be called law, it must be backed by a sovereign and that law is the command given by ⟨a⟩ political superior to a political inferior, is turned down by Garner. "The old controversy," says Garner, "to which Austin's conception gave rise as to whether international law is law in the strict sense of the term, since it lacks certain of the earmarks which municipal law possesses, or whether it is nothing more than international 'morality' or 'comity'—a controversy which has never been much more than a question of definition and terminology—has ceased to have any practical interest. All jurists now admit that the Austinian conception was too narrow and arbitrary, since it unduly emphasized the element of physical sanction, and ignored the large body of custom, which the courts regard as law but which are never formally enacted by a legislative body. To deny the character of law to rules which all foreign offices and governments treat as law and to which they appeal in their controversies with one another, which have developed through judicial precedent or which have been formulated by international congresses, which have been elucidated and expounded by trained jurists, which are applied by national and international tribunals and which states in fact regard as binding upon them, is to adopt a conception of the nature of international law which is in contradiction with the facts of international practice." (Garner, *Recent Development in International Law*, 1925, pp. 3-4)

Chapter 3
Government and State

So far as the subject-matter of the so-called political science is concerned, if it is true that there was a great change when the distinction between the monarch and the government was made as we have already pointed out in the previous chapter, it is equally true that there was another change when the government was distinguished from the state.

Although the distinction between the government and the state may be traced back to the writings of those who held the doctrine of popular sovereignty, especially that which is connected with the theory of a social contract, not until the later part of the nineteenth century was such a distinction clearly made by the writers or the so-called political scientists.

We find, for instance, in the *Two Treatises on Civil Government* of Locke, such a distinction, though it was not explicitly described. "For no man or society of men," Locke pointed out, "having a power to deliver up their preservation, or consequently the means of it, to the absolute will and arbitrary dominion of another, whenever anyone shall go about to bring them into such a slavish condition, they will always have a right to preserve what they have not a power to part with, and to rid themselves of those who invade this fundamental, sacred, and unalterable law of self-preservation for which they entered into society. And thus the community may be said in this respect to be always the supreme power, but not as considered under any form of government, because this power of the people can never take place till the government be dissolved."①②

Again, Locke concluded his famous treatises with these words: "The power that every individual gave the society when he entered into it can never revert to the individuals again, as long as the society lasts, but will always remain in the community; because without this there can be no community—no commonwealth, which is contrary to the original agreement; so also when the society hath placed the legislative in any

---

① Locke, *Two Treatises on Civil Government*, pp. 269–270.
② *Ibid.*, pp. 319–320.

assembly of men, to continue in them and their successors, with direction and authority for providing such successors, the legislative can never revert to the people whilst that government lasts; because, having provided a legislative with power to continue forever, they have given up their political power to the legislative, and can not resume it. But if they have set limits to the duration of their legislative, and made this supreme power in any person or assembly only temporary; or else, when, by the miscarriages of those in authority, it is forfeited; upon the forfeiture of their rulers, or at the determination of the time set, it reverts to the society, and the people have a right to act as supreme, and continue the legislative in themselves or place it in a new form, or new hands, as they think good. "

It seemed to Locke that the body politic, society or community which had been established on the basis of social contract was different from the government which consisted of the legislative, executive and the federative departments. So if we take for granted that what Locke meant by body politic, society or community is equivalent to what is known as the state, then the distinction between the government and the state is recognized here. But to Locke, the supreme power of the people or of the community was given to the legislative body, and if this was not in session, to the executive, and unless some limits were set, the government as represented by the legislative or by the executive and federative was not clearly differentiated from the state or body politic, since the power, the supreme power of the government was not different from that of the people or of society. Only when the government is dissolved, will the power of the government go back to the people. When the power of the government is identical with the power of the people, the organization which represents the people or the community and which is called government is not discriminated from the state or society, as Locke viewed them. Thus they all merge into one. Locke provided a body politic in order to check the government if it went wrong or became tyrannical. Yet if it did not go wrong or become tyrannical, the government was identified with the state. Moreover, as a matter of fact, if the people took back the power of the government, the government was immediately dissolved. Thus in actuality, it is not likely, according to the system of Locke, that both the government and the state can exist at the same time; for either the former goes back to the latter or the latter merges into the former, although in theory the state is prior to the government. It may be said that one is latent and the other active, or that one is abstract and the other concrete, yet it seems that Locke thinks that they are one thing with two aspects.

In spite of what has been said, It must be added that in the mind of Locke there was a distinction between the government and the body politic, or the state, or whatever name you may call it. Vague as such a distinction may have been and hard to draw a line of demarcation as it is when Locke applied it to actual practice, there existed in theory at least a discrimination between them.

Such a distinction seems to be clearer in the writings of J. J. Rousseau. In book Ⅲ of Rousseau's *Social Contract*, the author began by saying: "Before speaking of the different forms of government, let us try to fix the precise meaning of that word, which has not yet been very clearly explained." Rousseau asked: "What, then, is government?" And he answered immediately: "An intermediate body established between the subjects and the sovereign for their mutual correspondence, charged with the execution of the laws and with the maintenance of liberty both civil and political."[1]

Again said Rousseau: "Without embarrassing ourselves with multiplication of terms, let us be content to consider the government as a new body in the state, distinct from the people and from the sovereign, and intermediate between the two."[2] And he continued: "There is this essential difference between those two bodies, that the state exists by itself, while the government exists only through the sovereign."[3]

The distinction made here between the government and the state seems to be clear, clearer than Locke has made it. And it is obvious that the scope of the state is larger than that of the government. Yet in Rousseau, the meaning of the government and that of the state and the relation between the two was not so simple as they appeared to be. "The government," said Rousseau, "is on a small scale while the body politic which includes it is on a large scale. It is a moral person endowed with certain faculties, active like the sovereign, passive like the state, and it can be resolved into other similar relations; from which arises as a consequence a new proportion, and yet another within this, according to the order of the magistracies, until we come to an indivisible middle term, that is, to a single chief or supreme magistrate, who may be represented in the middle of this progression, as unity between the series of fractions and that of the whole numbers."[4]

Now if the government is to be represented as unity of fractions and that of the whole numbers and active like the sovereign, passive like the state, the difference between the government and the sovereign or the state cannot be well observed. Yet this

---

[1] Rousseau, *Social Contract*, Translated by Henry J. Tozer, 1912 edition, p. 150.
[2] *Ibid.*, p. 152.
[3] *Ibid.*
[4] *Ibid.*

is not all. While it is generally recognized that according to the theory of popular sovereignty such as that of Locke and Rousseau the destruction of the government does not mean the dissolution of the state, since the former is established by the latter, it is to be noted that in the writings of Rousseau, the contrary may be also true. "The dissolution of the state," said Rousseau, "may occur in two ways: Firstly, when the prince no longer administers the state in accordance with the laws and effects a usurpation of the sovereign power. Then a remarkable change takes place—the state, and not the government, contracts; I mean that the state dissolves, and that another is formed within it, which is composed of the people nothing more than their master and their tyrant. So that as soon as the government usurps the sovereignty, the social compact is broken, and all the ordinary citizens, rightfully regaining their natural liberty, are forced, but not morally bound, to obey. The same thing occurs also when the members of the government usurp separately the power which they ought to exercise only collectively; which is no less a violation of the laws, and occasion still greater disorder. Then there are, so to speak, as many princes as magistrates; and the state, not less divided than the government, perishes or changes its form. When the state is broken up, the abuse of the government, whatever it may be, takes the common ⟨form⟩ of *anarchy*. To ⟨be⟩ *distinguished*, democracy degenerates into *ochlocracy*, aristocracy into *oligarchy*; I should add that royalty degenerates into tyranny."①

It is possible, then, that the government may still exist while the state is dissolved, although in such conditions, the government is not a legal government or a government of the people as a whole.

But government, according to Rousseau, is confined only to the executive department, and the legislative department is virtually identified with the sovereign or the state. Let us see how Rousseau makes this point clear.

"Every free action has two causes concurring to produce it; the one moral, viz., the will which determines the act; the other physical, viz., the power which executes it. When I walk toward an object, I must first will to go to it; in the second place, my feet must carry me to it. Should a paralytic wish to run, or an inactive man wish to do so, both will remain where they are. The body politic has the same motive powers; in it, likewise, force and will are distinguished, the latter under the name of *legislative power*, the former under the name of *executive power*. Nothing is, or ought to be, done, in it without their co-operation."②

---

① Rousseau, *Social Contract*, Translated by Henry J. Tozer, 1912 edition, pp. 178-179.
② *Ibid.*, p. 149.

And he added: "We have seen that the legislative power belongs to the people, and can belong to them alone. On the other hand, it is easy to see from the principles already established, that the executive power cannot belong to the people generally as the legislative or sovereign, because that power is exerted only in particular acts, which are not within the province of law, nor consequently within that of the sovereign, all the acts of which must be laws."①

"Consequently," said Rousseau, "I give the name *government* or supreme administration to the legitimate exercise of the executive power, and that of Prince or magistrate to the man or body charged with that administration."②

And he says again: "The principle of the political life is in the sovereign authority. The legislative power is the heart of the state; the executive power is its brain, giving movement to all the parts. The brain may be paralysed and yet the individual may live. A man remains an imbecile and lives; but as soon as the heart ceases its functions, the animal dies."③

Thus the difference between the state and the government becomes almost a difference between the legislative and the executive powers or bodies. As a result, the scope of the government of Rousseau is much narrower than what is generally understood, since we often think that the government includes both the executive and the legislative.

But more confusions are encountered when we come to consider Rousseau's conception of the Prince. Although Rousseau tries to make a distinction between the prince and the government as he does in chapter ii of book III in his *Social Contract*, the distinction is not clearly defined, and in many other places, the distinction seems to disappear almost entirely. A prince is defined by Rousseau as "a moral and collective person united by the force of the laws, and as the depositary of the executive power in the state". But the prince may be also considered as a "power concentreated in the hands of a natural person, of a real man, who alone has a right to dispose of it according to the laws. He is what is called a monarch or king"④.

The dominant will of the prince is, or ought to be, "according to Rousseau, only

---

① Rousseau, *Social Contract*, Translated by Henry J. Tozer, 1912 edition, p. 149.
② *Ibid.*, p. 150.
③ *Ibid.*, p. 180.
④ *Ibid.*, p. 163.

the general will, or the law; its force is only the public force concentrated in itself; so soon as it wishes to perform of itself some absolute and independent act, the connexion of the whole begins to be relaxed. And if the prince should chance to have a particular will more active than that of the sovereign, and if, to enforce obedience to this particular will, it should employ the public force which is in its hands, in such a manner that there would be so to speak two sovereigns, the one *de jure* and the other *de facto*, the social union would immediately disappear, and the body politic would be dissolved"①.

"Further, in order that the body of the government may have an existence, a real life, to distinguish it from the body of the state; in order that all its members may be able to act in concert and fulfil the object for which it is instituted, a particular personality is necessary to it, a feeling common to its members, a force, a will of its own tending to its preservation. This individual existence supposes assemblies, councils, a power of deliberating and resolving, right, titles, and privileges which belong to the prince exclusively, and which render the position of the magistrate more honourable in proportion as it is more arduous. The difficulty lies in the method of disposing, within the whole, this subordinate whole, in such a way that it may not weaken the general constitution in strengthening its own; that its particular force, intended for its own preservation, may always be kept distinct from the public force, designed for the preservation of the state; and, in a word, that it may always be ready to sacrifice the government to the people, and not the people to the government."②

And then he says: "Moreover, although the artificial body of the government is the work of another artificial body, and has in some respects only a derivative and subordinate existence, that does not prevent it from acting with more or less vigour or celerity, from enjoying, so to speak, more or less robust health. Lastly, without directly departing from the object for which it was instituted, it may deviate from it more or less, according to the manner in which it is constituted."③

It is clear to Rousseau that the prince may be identified with the government and the government is nothing more than the executive. Being identified with the government, the prince, not only may do what he pleases with the executive body, but also may exercise independent sovereign will or "have a particular will more active than

---

① Rousseau, *Social Contract*, Translated by Henry J. Tozer, 1912 edition, p. 152.
② *Ibid.*, pp. 152–153.
③ *Ibid.*, p. 153.

that of the sovereign". The result of this is that the prince identifies himself with the legislative as well as the executive power. It is true that what the prince has is only *de facto* sovereign, not the *de jure* sovereign, yet this sovereign can exist even the state or the *de jure* sovereign disappears.

Because the prince can represent the government, the executive body, the government of the state, in this sense, becomes the government of the prince, the monarch or the king. And because the legislative body is identical with the sovereign will, the state, the sovereign will or the state, in this sense, is identical with the government, or to be exact, becomes a part of the government as we understand it. Thus the distinction between the government and the state as viewed by Rousseau becomes the distinction between the prince and the government. And even the latter distinction is not clear, since in practice the exercise of the power of the prince at least tends to include the other power or powers. ①

It seems to us that Rousseau is explaining that there ought to be a distinction between the prince or the king and the government and between the government and the state rather than there is or was such a distinction. For as we know, the state, the body politic, the society or the social body which is supposed to come from the social contract lacks, as we have already shown, historical evidence. It is only something in the air; it is something pictured by a group of writers who use it as pretext for vindicating the rights of the people rather than for stating the historical or existing facts.

Yet it must be admitted that if the distinction between the government and the state is still advanced for the men of the eighteenth century to conceive it, the distinction between the monarch and the government is not one that has no factual support. Judging from this respect, Rousseau may be regarded as an interpreter of the political facts of his

---

① In one place Rousseau says: "If the sovereign wishes to govern, or if the magistrate wishes to legislate, or if the subjects refuse to obey, disorder succeeds order, force and will no longer act in concert, and the state being dissolved falls into despotism or anarchy." And "as there is but one mean proportional between each relation, there is only one good government possible in a state; but as thousand events may change the relations of a people, not only many different governments be good for different peoples, but for the same people at different times." p.150. In another place, Rousseau says: "The members of this body (government) are called magistrates or *kings*, that is, *governors*; and the body as a whole bears the name of *Prince*. Those therefore who maintain that the act by which a people submits to its chiefs is not a contract are quite right. It is absolutely nothing but a commission, an employment, in which, as simple officers of the sovereign, they exercise in its name the power of which it has made them depositaries, and which it can limit, modify, and resume when it pleases. The alienation of such a right, being incompatible with the nature of the social body, is contrary to the object of the association." *Ibid.*

time as well as a prophet for the political development for the future, although the distinction either between the monarch and the government or between the government and the state as viewed by Rousseau is not very clear to us.

It is for this reason that Rousseau may be regarded as a forerunner of modern political theory. He predicts the distinction between the government and the state. If the French Revolution did not make political writers [to] see his point, it did make it clear that it is possible to have a government without a king or monarch and that back of the government lies a popular force which is the foundation upon which the government is supposed to be built.

But as political writers are wont to follow what has been said and thought by their predecessors of the past and decline consciously or unconsciously to state or push something which is new, few writers if any besides Rousseau would take the trouble to make or would really see the discrimination between the government and the state. So there is no such a distinction conceived by Montesquieu in his *The Spirit of Law*. Even Blackstone, having the constitutional government of England before his eyes does not make this clear in his widely read treatise *Commentaries on the Laws of England*. As Bentham points out, in criticising this work, "Society, in one place means the same thing as a *state of nature* does; in another place it means the same as *government*." Nor Bentham himself gives us a clear distinction. When Austin, the disciple of Bentham, declares that "if a determinate human superior, not in a habit of obedience to a like superior, receives habitual obedience from the bulk of a given society, that determinate superior is sovereign in that society, and the society (including the superior), is a society political and independent", he simply confuses not only the government and the state, but also the government and the monarch.

Even in the United States where there are many governments, i. e. the different state governments as well as the federal government, in a federal union, the government is seldom differentiated from the state until the latter part of ⟨the⟩ nineteenth century. Terms such as American Republic, American Commonwealth, American nation, or American Federation have frequently been used, but what are these terms different from the government, few care to question it.

In the nineteenth century, no country in the world has produced more treatises on the so-called political science than Germany, yet there, few if any have attempted to distinguish the government from the state. When Dahlmann wrote his *Politics* in 1838, he confined himself mainly to what may be called as *Verfassungspolitik* or the organizations of the government rather the state, although the short introductory chapter of this book is devoted to the origin and nature of the state.

Bluntschli, better known than most of the German political scientists outside of Germany, did sense out the difference between the government and the state, but still it may be said that such a difference is very vague and not very significant to him. "The sovereignty of the state," says he, "is especially that of the law; that of the prince and that of the government or administration. The latter operates where the former is inoperative." The [the] author points out: "A conflict between them is rare in fact and impossible in principle; for it would imply a conflict of the head alone with the head in combination with the rest of the state, and [and] hence a conflict of the same with himself."①

Neither Treitschke nor Jellinek is bothered with the question of such a distinction. Both give a lot of space to deal with the forms of the state; but the forms of the state as conceived by them are also the forms of government. As a matter of fact, they are really the forms of the latter.

What is true to the German writers is also true to the French writers. In fact, the French give more attention to the the constitutional and administrative laws rather than to theory of state.

The same may be said of the English writers in general. When J. R. Seeley delivered his lectures on the *Introduction to Political Science* from 1884 to 1885, he seemed to be unconscious of such a distinction. "Human beings," he says, "as we see them around us, are found to be enrolled or regimented in certain large groups which are organized in a peculiar way, held together by the contrivance known as government and called states."②

But when facts become too obvious to be neglected, men cannot refuse to overlook them entirely and those who have the insight to see things deeper can always sense their true characters. Sheldon Amos, for instance, in his *The Science of Politics*, published in 1883, already noted that the state is different from the government. He writes: ③ "The history of the European State has been seen to presuppose the fact of government. Had

---

① Bluntschli, *Theory of the State*, pp. 503–504.
② Seeley, *Introduction to Political Science*, 1896, p. 30.
③ Amos, *The Science of Politics*, pp. 67–68.

the tribes which overran the provinces of the Roman Empire been essentially anarchical, or had the result of their irruption been to produce limitless and lasting anarchy, no true States could have arisen. There could have no demarcation of national territory; no national self-consciousness based on well-preserved customs commemorative of the past and on more and more luminous anticipations of the future; no cherishing of the dislocated relics of Roman law, municipal institutions, and administrative discipline. But habits of government, however rude, were well formed among the tribes before invasions and a variety of favourable circumstances conspired to rivet and develop these habits, while the amalgamation of native and Roman inhabitants of the newly occupied lands was being effected."

And he says: "Thus the state, at one moment, means the governing authority as opposed to the governed; at another, the secular authorities, legislative and executive, as opposed to the ecclesiastical. Sometimes the state is contrasted with the existing or temporary mechanism for governing the state, that is, with what is called the government. At other times the state implies the body politic, that is, the nation regarded as a subject of government; and this last meaning is most in accord with the results of the historical analysis just concluded, though serious omissions in the full and proper connotation of the term, —as in respect of territorial limits, and of continuous identity in point of time, —are not avoided."

To consider the state as a subject of government is to make the former live in the abode of the latter and this is the traditional concept of the so-called political science, i. e., to view government as the subject-matter of [the] this branch of study which is different from those who regard the state as the subject-matter of political science.

Since the European political writers have been too much influenced by the political conditions and political writings of the past and consequently have not been able to see clearly the difference between the state and the government, the American people have been in a better position to understand such a distinction not only because of their peculiar political institutions, but also because of the less influence of the political writings of the past.

Among the American writers, the man who makes a strong attempt to distinguish the state from the government and at the same time has the greatest influence on the writers following him in this point is John William Burgess. But before speaking of Burgess, it is necessary to point out that as early as 1885, in the case of Poindexter v.

Greenhow, the Supreme Court of the United States insisted on such a distinction. "The state itself," observes the court, "is an ideal person, intangible, invisible, immutable. The government is an agent, and within the sphere of the agency, a perfect representative; but outside of that it is a lawless usurpation."①

Here we see that the state is considered as something abstract and the government concrete. Moreover, the former is larger in scope than the latter. It is pointed out that the state can only act through the government, but if the government is doing something which is not allowed by the constitution or beyond that which is assigned to it, the acts of the government are illegal and these are not the acts of the state. In other words, it is the government, not the state, that acts wrong.

Thus the government is only an agent of the state. It is "a perfect representative" when it lawfully acts. If it is unlawful or illegal, it may be overthrown or changed. But the change of the government does not mean the change of the state, for the state is something not only exterior or above the government, but also behind the constitution which is the fundamental principle upon which the government is based.

In the third chapter of the first volume considering the forms of the state, J. W. Burgess writes in his *Political Science and Comparative Constitutional Law*: "There is no topic of political science concerning which a more copious literature is at hand than this. There is none, again, in regard to which a less satisfactory treatment has been attained than this. A careful student of what has been written upon this subject, both in Europe and America, will, I think, discover that the cause of this unsatisfactory result, upon the part of the European publicists, is the fact that they do discriminate clearly between state and government; upon the part of the American writers, that they copy too closely the European authors."

He continues: "Both of these facts are explicable. In Europe, state and government are actually more or less mingled and commingled. The publicists are confused in their reflections by the confusion in the external object. It will be profitable to dwell upon this point a moment, and inquire how this actual condition of things has come about, which has exercised such a troubling influence upon political science. I think the explanation is to be found in the consequences of the historical development of the state. No great state in Europe, except France, has cut its history into two distinct and separate parts by revolution. We may say then, as the rule, that in European states the form of the state

---

① 114 U. S. 270.

generated in one period of their history laps over upon that developed in the succeeding period or periods. A close scrutiny of this process will disclose the following significant facts, viz; that in the transition from one form of the state to another, the point of sovereignty moves from one body to another, and the old state, becomes, in the new system, only the government, or a part of the government. Take the example of the English history after 1066, to make this clearer. First, the king was the state as well as the government. Then the nobles became the state, and the king became the government only. Then the Commons became state and both king and lords became but parts of the government. Now this change from the old form of state to the new, when it works itself gradually and impliedly, so to speak, does not mark off the boundary sharply and exactly between the old and the new system. Naturally the old state does not perceive the change at all, or at least, not for a long time, and not until after suffering many bitter experiences. It still expresses itself in the language of sovereignty. It still stunts about in the purple, unconscious that the farment is now borrowed. On the other hand, the new sovereignty comes very slowly to its organization. Moreover, it organizes itself, for the most part, in the government, and only very imperfectly outside of and supreme over the government. For a long time it has the appearance of being only a part of the government and, at first, the less important part. For a considerable time it is uncertain where the sovereignty actually is. With such condition and relations in the objective political world, it is not strange that the European publicists have failed, as yet to distinguish clearly and sharply between state and government, not that their treatment of all problems, dependent for correct solution upon this distinction, is more or less confused and unsatisfactory."

Then the professor of Columbia University goes on to point, "In America, on the contrary, existing conditions and relations are far more favorable to the publicists. Our state is but little more than a century old, and rests wholly and consciously upon a revolutionary basis. The organization of the state existing previous to the year 1774 was completely destroyed, and did not reappear in the succeeding organization as a part of the government, holding on to its traditions of sovereignty. We Americans have seen the state organized outside of, and supreme over, the government. We have, therefore, objective aids and supports upon which to steady out reflection and by which to guide our science. The reason why the American publicists have written better upon this subject can not, therefore, be the lack of the proper external occasions for the excitation of thought. It is, it seems to me, as I have already said, the fact that they still copy too closely the European authors, and have not ventured to essay independent work. America has yet to develop her own school of publicists and her own literature of political science. Down to this time, the two names which stand highest in our American literature of political science are Francis Lieber and Theodore D. Woolsey. The former was, as every body knows, a European, educated under European institutions, and a refuge from their oppression, as he regarded it. The latter was Lieber's ardent admirer, —we might almost say disciple. It is not strange that they should have suffered under the power of the old influences, and should have confounded, in some degree at least, state and government in their reflections. The new and the latest generation of American students of political science have been most largely trained in European universities under the direction of European publicists, again, and by means of European literature. It will be an effort for them to make such use of their European science as always to gain advantage. It will be of the greatest service to them if they employ it as a stepping-stone to a higher and more independent point of view, on which will enable them to win scientific appreciation of the distinctive lessons of our institutions. If they fail to do this, however, we can expect little help from them in this attainment of a better and more satisfying treatment of the topic of this chapter."

Let us quote from the author once more: "It is, therefore, with good deal of misgiving that I approach this part of my subject. I know that nothing has, as yet, been written in regard to it which has commanded general assent from the political scientists. I am myself conscious of mental dissatisfaction of the confusion of thought, clearly manifest in the different theories presented, is what I have above indicated; but when I come to the task of making clear and exact the distinction between state and government myself, I find myself involved in the same difficulties against which I have just given the word of warning. The fact is, that the organization of the state outside of, and supreme over, the government is, as yet everywhere incomplete; and that when we assign to it this separate and supreme position, we are, in greater or less degree, confounding the subjective with the objective state, the ideal with the actual state. Nevertheless, I am resolved to make the trial upon this line; content if, upon a single point, I can bring a little more light into this discussion, and make it manifest that a better organization of the state outside of the government would be a great[①] advance in practical politics."[②]

I have quoted so extensively from the Columbia professor for the reason that these statements were written by the so-called father of modern political science in the United States; and that if there is anything which, contributed by Burgess, may be considered as very important, in the field of political studies, and which has exerted a great influence upon the subsequent writers in the same field, it is the attempt to distinguish the state from the government; and that this may throw much light for the understanding of our present study.

The position taken by Burgess in regard to the distinction between the state and the government has been followed by W. W. Willoughby in his *The Nature of the State* published ⟨in⟩ 1896. In the second chapter of this book, Willoughby writes: "The fundamental distinction that must be made, is that between 'state' and 'government'. By the term 'government' is designated the organization of the state, —the machinery through which its purposes are formulated and executed. Thus, as we shall see, while

---

① Burgess, *Political Science and Comparative Constitutional Law*, Vol. I, pp. 57–58: "I think the difficulty which lies in the way of the general acceptance by publicists of the principle of the sovereignty of the state is the fact that they do not sufficiently distinguish the state from the government. They see the danger to individual liberty of recognizing an unlimited power in the government; and they immediately conclude that the same danger exists if the sovereignty of the state be recognized. This is especially true of European publicists, most especially of German publicists. They are accustomed practically to no other organization of the state than in the government; and in spite of their speculative mental character, they, as well as other men, reveal in their reflections a good deal of dependence upon the conditions of the objective world. In America we have a great advantage in regard to this subject. With us the government is not the sovereign organization of the state. Back of the government lies the constitution; and back of the constitution the original sovereign state, which ordains the constitution both of government and of liberty. We have the distinction already in objective reality; and if we only cease for a moment conning our European masters and exercise a little independent reflection, we shall be able to grasp this important distinction clearly and sharply. This is the point in which the public law of the United States has reached a far higher development than that of any state of Europe. Several of the most modern European publicists, such as Laband, Von Holst and Jellinek, have discovered this fact; and their conception of the state has, in consequence thereof, become much clearer. The European states have made great progress towards this condition since the period of the French Revolution. Europe has seen the French state several times organized in constituent convention; and in the years 1848 and 1867 something very like constituent conventions sat at Frankfort and Berlin, to say nothing of the Spanish Cortes and the less important movements of similar character. Such an organization of the state is, however, hostile to independent princely power. It tends to subject the prince to the state. It may leave the hereditary tenure, but it makes the princely power an office instead of a sovereignty. Therefore the princely government disputes the sovereignty of the constituent convention; and the political scientists become confused in their reflections by the din and smoke of the conflict in the objective world. They do not know exactly where the state is; and, therefore, they hesitate to recognize its great and essential attribute of sovereignty. The national popular state alone furnishes the objective reality upon which political science can rest in the construction of a truly scientific political system. All other forms contain in them mysteries which the scientific mind must not approach too closely."

② Burgess, *Political Science and Comparative Constitutional Law*, Vol. I, pp. 68–71.

the term 'state' is, when strictly considered, an abstract term, government is emphatically concrete, More than that, government is purely mechanical and governed by no general laws. Its varying forms are in all cases determined by political expediency, and the examination of its essential character involves no such philosophical considerations as will interest us in our present inquiry. The subject of government thus lies almost wholly without the field of political theory, and is comprehended within the domains off descriptive and historical."[1]

And he adds: "Simple and definite as is this distinction between the state and its governmental machinery (corresponding as it does very much to the distinction between a given person and the material bodily frame in which such person is organized), we shall find it to be one that has been but seldom made. In fact, it has the confusion between these two terms that has led directly or indirectly to a great majority of the erroneous results reached by political philosophers in the past."[2] And again he says: "Variations in governmental organizations and administration are to be considered as merely differences in form that have arisen in response to the demands of time, place and peculiarities of political temperament of the people, but without disturbing the state's fundamental nature."[3]

The distinction made by Willoughby is somewhat similar to that made by the Supreme Court of the United States as we have already noted, i. e. the state being abstract and permanent and the government concrete and changeable. It goes without saying that according to Willoughby the scope of the former is larger than that of the latter.

Since Burgess and Willoughby, most of the American writers have made such a distinction. While not intending to take more time and space to enumerate the distinction made by different writers, I should like to quote one or two more statement from recent authors. "From an examination of types of state and unions of states," Says Garner, "We come to consider the forms and kinds of government, always keeping in mind that the state and its government are, strictly speaking, separate and distinct institutions. The state, as we have seen, is a politically organized community of people independent of external control or nearly so, and sovereign in respect to its internal affairs, or at least possessing so large an autonomy that for all practical purposes it may be regarded as a state. Government, on the other hand, is the organization through which the state

---

[1] Willoughby, *The Nature of the State*, 1896, p. 8.
[2] *Ibid.*, pp. 8-9.
[3] *Ibid.*, p. 15.

manifests its will, issues its commands, and conducts its affairs. While, as pointed out in a previous chapter, all states are alike in their essence, that is in respect to the component elements which enter into their make-up, and, in general, in respect to their ends and objects, and therefore, do not readily lend themselves to differentiation and classification, governments, on the other hand, vary widely in respect to the form of their organization, frequently in respect to their spirit and methods, in respect to the mode in which those who govern are chosen, the nature and extent of the authority with which they are invested, the particular objects which they seek to accomplish, the relations between their legislative, executive and judicial organs, and various other matters. Attempts to classify them have usually, therefore, been more successful than attempts at the classification of states, for the reason that satisfactory criteria can be found upon which various governments can be grouped into one class and others in a different class in such a manner that the distinction between the different classes subserves both practical and scientific end."①

And so a recent writer says: "If the state is an association of embodying some specific common in purposes as other associations, and this association is to be distinguished from institutions that refer to forms of order or control for the achievement of purposes we must draw a distinction between state and government. Political society is the state viewed as an association which expresses a community of will directed to common purposes. Political organization or government is the state viewed in the institutional sense, in the sense of mechanics and organization of control. The institution in federal community existence is therefore merely the agent of the association. The government, both sociologically and legally, is to be viewed as the agent of the state."②

The reason why there must be a distinction between state and the government has been summarized by Harold J. Laski in the following words: "Now it is one of the fundamental axioms of political science that we must distinguish sharply between state and government. The latter is but the agent of the former; it exists to carry out the purposes of the state. It is not itself the supreme coercive power; it is simply the mechanism of administration which gives effect to the purposes of that power. It is not, we are told, sovereign in the sense in which the state is sovereign; its competence is defined by such authority as the state may choose to confer upon it; and it oversteps that authority it may, where such provision exists, be called to account. The idea of a

---

① James W. Garner, *Political Science and Government*, 1928, pp. 303-304.
② Francis Graham Wilson, *The Elements of Modern Politics*, 1936, pp. 54-55.

government responsible for the commission of acts beyond its allotted powers is the central idea or every state where legal rule has replaced arbitrary discretion as the basis of political action. Louis XIV could, not unjustifiably, identify his private purpose with the will of the state; but even a ruler so powerful as the President of the United States must find authority for the exercise of his will either in the Constitution or in some power legally granted to him thereunder by the Congress or his country. There are even countries, of which the United States is itself an example, in which the state expressly forbids its government, by the Constitution under which that government must act, to take certain types of power or to exercise others in certain ways. "①

"The purpose, it is said, of the distinction between state and government is to emphasize the limitation upon the latter so tact that it pay proper regard to the end for which the state exist. That end, however variously defined, is the creation of those conditions under which the members of the state may attain the maximum satisfaction of their desires. The expedients of limitation—a written constitution, a bill of rights, the separation of powers and so forth—are all methods which experience has suggested to prevent abuse of the state's sovereign power by the government which acts in its name. For every government is composed of fallible men. They may deliberately exploit the authority they possess for their own selfish purposes. They may, with the best intentions, but quite unreasonably, mistake the private interest of a few for the well-being of the whole community. They may be ignorant of the position they confront, or incompetent in handling it. Circumstances such as these have occurred in every political society at some period of its history. The value of the distinction between state and government is the possibility it offers of creating institutional mechanisms for changing the agents of the state, that is, the government, when the latter shows itself inadequate to its responsibilities. "②

"Yet, " as Laski points out, "it must be said at once the distinction between state and government is rather one of theoretical interest than of practical significance. For every act of the state that we encounter is, in truth, a governmental act. The will of the state is its laws; but it is the government which gives substance and effect their content. We say that the British state went to war with Germany on August 4, 1914; but those who brought the sovereignty of Great Britain into action on that day were its government. We say that the British state returned to old standard in 1925 and abandoned it in 1931; but in each case it was the government which made the decision. We say that the

---

① Laski, *The State, Theory and Practice*, 1935, p. 11.
② *Ibid.*, pp. 11-12.

Russian state went communist in the November Revolution of 1917; we mean in fact that a body of men became its government who were able to the sovereignty of the Russian state for the purposes we broadly call communist. Whenever a state acts in some given way, it is invariably because those who act as its government decide, rightly or wrongly, to use its sovereign power in that given way. The state itself, in sober reality, never acts; it is acted for by those who have become competent to determine its policies."①

"By those who have become competent; and here we have to ask what, again in sober fact, gives them their competence. We may say that their power derives from the law. But the law, after all, is only a body of words until men give it the substantiality of enforcement. We may say that it is the consent of those over whom they rule which gives them the power to get their obeyed. There is a truth in this view in the sense that Hume emphasized when he insisted that all governments, however bad, depend for their authority upon public opinion. But this cannot be regarded as the whole truth for the effective reason that there are times and places when men are ruled by a state from the policies of which their consent is actively withheld. It is hardly a proper use of language to say that the Tsarist state before 1917, or the state of Fascist Austria today, can be regarded as built upon the consent or their citizens; for, in each case, many or those citizens sought to change the policies of the state by revolt against the responsible for them."②

So Laski concludes: "I think, therefore, that we have to say that, in the last analysis, the state is built upon the ability of its government to operate successfully its supreme coercive power."③

There are some writers who would deny the distinction between the state and the government because they think that such a distinction is nothing more than an artificial product of legal reasoning and logical refinement. Léon Duguit, for instance, does not seem to make such a distinction. When he defines the state as the simple fact of the differentiation between the governor and the governed④, we are not so clear whether the government which represents only the ruling agency and which does not necessarily include those who are governed is identical with the state. But when he views the state as the man or the group of men who in fact in a given society are materially stronger than

---

① Laski, *The State, Theory and Practice*, 1935, pp. 12–13.
② Laski, *The State in Theory and Practice*, p. 13.
③ *Ibid*.
④ Leon Duguit, *L'Etat, Le Dorit Objectif et La Loi Positive*, p. 261.

the others, or the class or body which monopolizes the forces in a given society[1], he definitely does not discriminate the government from the state.

Other writers think that the modern political pluralists, denying the sovereignty of the state, deny also the state itself and consequently they also reject the distinction between the state and the government. This, however, is not entirely true. Because to reject the sovereignty of the state is one thing, and to deny the distinction between the state and the government is another thing. There may be a state without sovereignty as it is in the case of the states in the United State as it is maintained by some such as Wooddraw Wilson or Paul Laband. It is also possible that the sovereignty of the state may be divided either between the different departments of the government, or between the central and the local governments of a state, or between the state on the one hand and the other associations within the state on the other.

Moreover, it must be pointed out that the term "government" is not necessarily confined to a political machinery.[2] Just as the state may have a government, so the church may also have a government. The same may be said of a company or a corporation. For every association needs to have some sort of machinery or agency to carry out its will and to act for it. A church, a company, a corporation or a university is an abstract entity just as we speak of a state as an abstract. Each of these organizations needs an agency or machinery to express its purpose and to conduct its affairs. This agency or machinery may be called a government. The papacy, for instance, is a catholic association. It is a religious entity. So at least in concept it may be distinguished from its governmental organization or organizations. So this is true to a university. It is a learning institution. There are many universities, but the internal organizations of them may not be similar to each other. And the president, deans and many other officials who form the council or committees are the governing people and the totality of these people may be called the government of the university.

It is possible that the government of a university may be similar to the government of a state in their essential aspects. The president of the university is equivalent to the president of the state. Just as there is a legislative body or assembly of the state there may be also such a body in the university which consists of the representatives of the professors. There may be other controlling bodies in the university, such a senate or council serving as advisory or executive capacity for the president or for the university.

---

[1] Leon Duguit, *L'Etat, Le Dorit Objectif et La Loi Positive*, p. 311.
[2] Cf. MacIver, *The Modern State*, p. 41.

And this is not all. There may be a government in a tribe, in the league of nations and in other political associations. And even within a state there are many governments, such as local, municipal, provincial as well as the central government. Then in the federal state, the governments of the several member states, like that in the United States, are not only similar to each other, but also similar to the federal government.

So when we speak of a government, we have to make it clear whether it is a township government, county government, municipal government, state government in a federal state or federal government in a federal state, or it is a government of a church, of a company, or of a university.

Thus no matter how abstract it may be, the state is not only a form of social association, but also a form of political association. In order to differentiate the government of the state from that of other political organizations or social groups, the existence of the state as distinct from that of the government cannot be questioned.

As we know from the standpoint of international law, states are more or less alike or at least they are treated in this way. But governments may be different and indeed radically different from one another, not only monarchy is different from aristocracy and aristocracy is different from democracy; but also each of these may have different forms. Monarchy may be absolute or limited, or it may be a despotic or tyrannical. Aristocracy may become oligarchy. When you say that aristocracy is a government by few, the question still remains to be asked: How few or how many noble men or aristocratic people are there? You may have pure democracy or indirect democracy. You may have a parliamentary form or a presidential form or a councilor form of democracy.

It is true that state has been and still is called monarchical aristocratic or democratic state, but this is looking from the constitutional rather than international standpoint. In the eyes of international law, the state is a unit. A dwarf is equal to a giant. So the United States of America is treated as one state, in spite of the fact that each member state of the American Federation is more or less independent of the federal government and sovereign within its own sphere.

The case of German Reich from 1871 to 1918 is more striking for our illustration. It was a federation, though different from that of the United States. It consisted of big and powerful kingdoms as well as small dukedoms and free cities. Not only the governments of these member states or "lander" as the German called them were different from one another, also the government of the Reich was different from that of the member states. Prussia was undoubtedly the dominating member of the Reich. Besides having the largest votes in the federal council, the king of Prussia was also the Kaiser of the Reich.

Kaiser was generally translated as Emperor in English, but this was not entirely right; because the position of the Kaiser was, as a matter of fact, the president of the Federal Council. The Bundesrat, according to some, was a council of ambassadors sent by different member states. Therefore the representatives who represented their kingdoms or free cities might be recalled at any time. The powers and the terms of the representatives of different member states varied from one another. So the composition of the Federal Council was by no means similar to that of the Senate of the United States. The Kaiser, as the head of this council and therefore the head of the Reich was not a king or monarch in the sense of the term. We may say that so far as the Federal government was concerned, the German Reich during that period was a republic rather than a monarchy. But so far as Prussia and other kingdoms were concerned, their governments were monarchical. Then there were governments of the free cities and dukedoms the composition of which differed in many ways.

So we find that there were many kinds of governments within the German Reich. Yet to the foreign countries, Germany was one state, one unit in her international dealings, although exception must be made in the case of Bavaria in which some powers for international relations were still retained.

It is clear then within one state, besides there are many governments, there may be also different forms of governments as we have shown in the case of Germany. Moreover, different forms of governments do not confine alone to the different member states or the federal government, there are different forms of governments in different cities. In this respect, the case of the United States is a good example. Here in the cities, one may find what is known as mayor form, councilor form, or manager form, existing in different places at different times or at the same time.

Nor the powers of the state is necessarily centered in one government. In the federal state, as in the case of the United States, the power of the federal government is delegated while that of the state government is reserved. What is not delegated to the federal government is reserved to the several states. Not only the federal government exercises its powers within its own sphere, also each of the several states is supreme within its own sphere. Externally speaking, there is only one government, competent to deal with the international affairs, but internally speaking, there are many political entities, each having its own government and power, power which can not be taken away or encroached upon by the federal government.

Even within the sphere of the federal government, the three departments which compose it may not be unified in the dealing of affairs, domestic or foreign. As the head of the executive department, Wilson might enunciate the League of Nations and sign the Treaties of Versail, but one branch of the legislative, i. e. the senate, might not ratify it. Congress may pass some laws while the court may declare them unconstitutional.

Thus, the governments of a state are not only numerous in number, but also different in forms and sometimes various and sometimes equal in powers. Government or governments can not be said to be identical with the state, since in such cases no one government can be said to represent the whole state. Only where there is an absolute government, can we say that it is identified more or less with the state. But even in such case, government is not state; because in a state, besides the government, there are people and many other social organizations.

The laws of the state which prescribe the composition and powers of the government or governments may also prescribe the structure and functions of the other social organizations, or the rights of the people. The government or governments can be only regarded as parts of the state and not whole of the state. We speak of governmental actions within a state, we also speak of non-governmental actions within a state. It may be said that the sphere of this latter is much larger than that of the former. Many things go on without either the help or the interference of the government. Government is mainly referred to the ruling class or institution of a state rather than the people. Those who are ruled are overwhelmingly large in number. It is not infrequent to speak of the government and the people as the antithesis. The same may be said of the government and the church and many other social organizations.

This being true, it is only natural that one or a group of people may be very critical toward or hostile to the government; yet at the same time he may be very loyal to the state. The overthrow of the government by the revolutionary group in order to establish a new governmental regime is based on the theory that there is a distinction between the state and the government.

It may be argued, as Laski does, that the distinction here made is rather one of theoretical interest than of practical significance, but it has to be remembered that theoretical interest may be translated into practical significance. The effect of the revolutionary theory on the French Revolution, the communistic idea of Karl Marx on the Soviet Russia, the theory of the separation of powers of Montesquieu on the American constitution or the Three Principles of Sun Yat-Sun on the Chinese government are some of the well-known instances, showing that once a theory becomes influential, it has not only the negative force which maybe served as a check on certain practical institution, but also the positive power to modify the existing conditions or to create certain new institution. Thus it is the anti-monarchical theory that checks the absolutism of the monarch, and it is the theory of popular sovereignty that is chiefly responsible for the development of the modern representative system.

We do not mean to magnify the importance of the theoretical interest, but to admit the truth of the cases just mentioned is to admit that facts are very closely related to theories and that which is theoretical in one place or at one time may become fact in another place or at another time.

Coming back to the question under consideration, the distinction between the state and the government is more than, we may say a theoretical interest. If we recognize, a church, a company, a university or a town, a county and a province are facts, social facts in term of social phenomena, then we can not deny that the state is a social fact, a social phenomenon. It is one or the political organizations and at the same time of the social associations.

Moreover, in certain sense, it is even more concrete than the government. When I cross the border of Germany from Belgium, I feel I travel from one state to another state much more than I feel that I go from the jurisdiction of one government to another government. The state as it is now existing has a territorial limit, has its people as citizens. I think more of France as a state than as a government when I look at the map of the world or take a trip through the country. I think more of a Frenchman as a citizen of a state than as a subject of a government. The simple truth is that the geographical setting and the characteristics of the people are those physical elements which characterize the state rather than the government. And if we follow those who think that land, people and government are the essential characteristics of a state, the government is only one of the three elements; yet this is the most abstract element among the three. I can see the land of France, I can talk to the people of France almost everywhere in France, but I cannot see or talk to the government, unless I go to the place where the government is situated. In fact it is somewhat figurative when I say I see or talk to the government, because the government is an abstract thing, much more abstract than the land and the people. So if I say I see or talk to the government, it is the governmental building that I see and the governmental officials to whom I talk. In this sense, government is not as concrete as the state. It is only one of the parts which constitute the state.

To summarize what we have said, generally speaking, the state seems to be abstract while the government concrete, the former seems to be negative while the latter positive. But in certain sense the state is more concrete than the government and the former is no less positive than the latter.

But the most important distinction lies in the fact that the government is only an agency, a machinery or a part of the state. And because of this fact that the concept of the state is larger than that of the government. It is the former includes the latter not the latter embraces the former. So when the so-called political scientists make the states instead of the government as the subject-matter of the political science, they have thereby enlarged the scope of this branch of study.

I have discussed the distinction between the state and the government in detail, in order to show that in the historical development of political studies, many concepts which were not differentiated in the past are now well distinguished, mainly due to the change of the political conditions. As we know, there was a time when terms such as monarch, government, state and many others were more or less mixed together. For one time, the monarch is identified with the government and the state, so he was the subject matter of the so-called political science. At another time, although the monarch was considered as part of the government, but the latter was not discriminated from the state, and then government became the subject-matter of the political study. But as times changed and conditions changed, not only the monarch was clearly differentiated from the government, but also the government has been discriminated from the state.

It is now obvious that they are different in extent. The monarch is only a part of the government and in turn the government is only a part of the state. How important the parts may be is another question, but few if any would deny that monarchy is narrower in scope than government and that government is narrower in scope than the state. It is true, generally speaking as we have already pointed out, that the state is more abstract than government and government is more abstract than monarchy; but this is only natural; because the more general one is always more abstract and because it is general so that it can be more comprehensive in order to include the others.

Here we come to the vital point of our study. As a political concept, it is to be borne in mind, the state can no longer [to] be considered as comprehensive enough to include that which is known as political. Just as monarchy is part of the government and government is a part of the state, so the state, in turn, may be regarded as a part of things political. As a matter of fact, to understand the distinction between what is state and what is political is much more important than the differentiation between the monarch and the government and that between the government and the state in the field of political research.

Chapter 4
Forms of Government and State

In connection with the distinction between the government and the state, the question of and particularly the differentiation between the forms of government and that of the state deserve our due consideration.

If we take a general survey of the works on the so-called political science we shall find that writers of this subject have spent a lot of inks and papers in considering the forms of government and that of the state. While the earlier writers such as Aristotle, Polybius, Cicero, Machiavelli, Bodin, Thomas Smith, Hobbes and many others gave special attention to the forms of the government, modern writers such as Burgess, Willoughby and Garner were somewhat confused in distinguishing the forms of the government and that of the state.

We have already pointed out that the earlier writers did not make a distinction between the government and the state, since the conception or even the name of the state did not appear until the modern period. Government, as we have already shown, was for a long time identified with the king, the monarch or the prince and to distinguish the government from the state is still a recent thing. And yet such a distinction is still not very clear to many writers, especially to the European writers, at least this is particularly true in its application to the forms of the government and that of the state.

This being so, it is only natural that the so-called classification of government not only is confused with the so-called classification of the state, but also, in many cases and particularly in the earlier political writings means as a matter of fact classification of kings, monarchs, princes and of lords or barons. The *Prince* of Machiavelli, for instance, begins with a classification of the various kinds of princes. Although the word "Prince" has been used by many writers to mean both the prince as a person and the prince as an institution, as it is used by Rousseau, the difference between the two has not been well observed by writers in general. Nor the word "Prince" even when it is meant something institutional is broad enough to include what the word "government" embraces. Thus when the English speak of His Majestic Government, it means something more and much more than His Majestic the King of England or the Emperor of the Dominions and Colonies of the four seas. So even the word "Crown", institutionalized as it is, can not take the place of the word "government". The former is only the symbolic link of the British Empire or the British Commonwealth as some prefer to use it, the latter embraces many branches of governmental institutions to which the King himself is only a part, and indeed a very minor part.

But when government was considered as the subject-matter of the so-called political science, the classification of government became one of the most important problems in this field of study. Brougham's *Political Philosophy* may be regarded as an interpretation of the various kinds of government. So Treitschke devoted almost one third of his two volumes on *Politics* to consider this question.

Just as government for a long time was not differentiated from the prince, so the state for a long time was not distinguished from the government. Hence the classification of the forms of the two has been always confused. Jellinek devoted about fifty pages in one chapter in his *Allgemeine Staatslehre* to describe the historical leading types of the states (Die geschichtlichen Haupttypen des Staates) and almost seventy pages in another chapter in the same work to consider the forms of the state (Die Staatsformen)

Although Jellinek speaks of the forms and types of the state, the distinction between state and government can hardly be found in his writings. What he means by forms of the state may be also meant by others as the forms of government. This is true to many of the European writers.

Even those who make an attempt to discriminate the government from the state, they fail to make clear such a distinction when they come to the differentiation between the forms of the former and that of the latter. John W. Burgess, as we have already noted not only realizes the difficulty of making such a distinction, but also gets confused when he comes to the topic himself. Burgess points out that: "In my book upon the state I endeavored to show that the conception of the forms of state is vitiated, and current nonmemclature employed to give expression to the conception rendered almost useless, by the confounding of the ideas of state and government. The same criticism must be made as regards the usual and orthodox notions of the forms of government. The absence of the clear and correct distinction between state and government is fatal in the latter case as in the former. In consequence of its absence in the literature of this subject, I am compelled to break new ground in this case, as in the former, or even more completely than in the former. I am compelled also to create, in large degree, a new nomemclature upon this topic, which may appear, in some respects, clumsy, but which

I hope to make clear."①

Does he make himself clear? We think that he is not. Let us see how he approaches the subject. He writes: "The great classic authority upon this topic is Aristotle. Every student of political science is acquainted with his noted distinction of states, as to form, into monarchies, aristocracies, and democracies. Not every student reflects, however, that the Greek states were organized wholly in their government; i. e. completely confounded with them. This fact made the question far more simple than it is at present. We of today have a double question instead of a single one. We must determine, first, the forms of the state, and then, the forms of the government. It is perhaps natural that the state and its government should harmonize in this respect; but it is not always a fact they do, and it is always desirable that they should completely coincide in form. It is difficult to see why the most advantageous political system, for the present, would not be a democratic state with an aristocratic government, provided only the aristocracy be that of real merit, and not of artificial qualities. If this be not the real principle of the republican form of government, then I must confess that I do not know what its principle is. Now, it seems to me that the Aristotelian proposition contains the true solution of the whole question for the Hellenic politics, and for all systems in which the state and the government are identical; and that it is the true and complete principle of distinction in regard to the forms of state, but not of government, in those systems where state and government are not identical, but exist under more or less separate organization. I accept the Aristotelian proposition, therefore, as to the forms of state, and reserve the discussion of the forms of government to later part of this part of this work."②

Then after criticising the classifications of the forms of the state and therefore the government as rendered by some of the eminent writers such as Robert von Mohl, and particularly Bluntschli, he concludes by saying that "my contention is, therefore, that the classification of states, as to form, into monarchies, aristocracies, and democracies, is both correct and exhaustive; that no additional forms can be made of a combination of these, or a union out of several states; and that the notion that there can be proceeds from the confounding of state and government in the treatment of the subject"③.

But Burgess also tells us that "under this modification, the principle of Aristotle must be explained somewhat differently from what he himself intended. He undoubtedly had government in mind more than state when he invented this classification. He spoke

---

① Burgess, *Political Science and Comparative Constitutional Law*, Vol. II, p. 1.
② *Ibid.*, Vol. I, pp. 71-72.
③ *Ibid.*, Vol. I, p. 81.

of monarchy as the *rule* of one, of the aristocratic form as the *rule* of the minority, and of the democracy as the *rule* of the masses. In limiting his proposition strictly to the state, as distinguished from the government, I must define the monarchy to be the sovereignty of a single person, the aristocracy to be the sovereignty of the minority, and the democracy to the soveriegnty of the majority"①.

Before considering the validity of the classification of the state as proposed by Burgess, we may quote a statement made by a keen writer in this point. "Set opposite to all these various forms of so-called psychical interpretation, we have a dead political science. It is a formal study of the most external characteristics of governing institutions. It loves to classify governments by incidental attributes, and when all is added and done it can not classify them much better now than by lifting up readily Aristotle's monarchies, aristocracies and democracies which he found significant for Greek institutions, and using them for measurements of all sorts and conditions of modern government. And since no body can be very sure but that the United States is really a monarchy under the classification or England really a democracy, the classification is not entitled to great respect. Nor do the classifications that make the fundamental distinction between despotism and republic fare much better. They lose all right of the content of the proves in some trick point about the form."②

Now, besides being unable to do better than Aristotle for more than two thousand years ago, if it was government that Aristotle had in mind for such a classification, to take his classification of the government for that of the state would easily mislead us to confuse the government and the state, to say nothing of the misinterpretation of what was invented by Aristotle. Moreover, this classification of forms of government has been followed and adopted by so many writers in the field of the so-called political science, it is hard, if not impossible, to disassociate such a classification from the government and to think in terms of the state, unless we admit that the government is identical with the state and therefore that the classification for one will be also good for the other, or at least unless we think that Aristotle is wrong to classify the government in such a way and that it is only right to apply it for the state. In other words if there is nothing wrong for Aristotle to classify government into monarchies, aristocracies and democracies and unless there is no distinction between the state and the government, to change one thing for another is merely to give more confusion rather than clarification. This does not mean that we are in favor of Aristotle's classification of the government, nor does it mean that

---

① Burgess, *Political Science and Comparative Constitutional Law*, Vol. I, p. 72.
② Arthur F. Bentley, *The Process of Government: A Study of Social Process*, 1908, p. 162.

there is nothing better than that of Aristotle. As a matter of fact, the change of the political conditions for the last two thousand years and especially for the last few hundred years has already made it impossible to retain the Aristotelian classification, although there have been still many writers who have followed Aristotle in this point. We shall elaborate this point in our later discussion, suffice it to show here that Burgess's proposed modification is to make it more confusing.

But this is not all. Defining "the monarchy to be sovereignty of a single person, the aristocracy to be the sovereignty of the minority and the democracy to be the sovereignty of the majority", Burgess has done damages to his conception of sovereignty which is really the corner-stone of his whole political idea. Sovereignty is defined by him as the "original, absolute, unlimited, universal power over the individual subject and over all associations of subjects". Moreover, while government is distinguished by him from the state, sovereignty is to him identified with the state. "Back of the government," says he, "lies the constitution; and back of the constitution the original sovereign state, which ordains the constitution both of the government and of the liberty."① In another place he declares: "Really the state cannot be conceived without sovereignty; i. e. without unlimited power over its subjects."② And he continues: "That is its very essence."

Besides, if sovereignty is so essential to the state and in fact identical with the state as it is called sovereign state which lies behind the government, and if sovereignty is the original, absolute, unlimited, universal power, how can it be in the hand of single person, of minority and of majority, unless we admit that the state and consequently the sovereignty are identical with the single person, the minority and the majority. In making a distinction bewteen the government and the state, all that the single person, the minority or even the majority can represent is the government, not the sovereignty or the sovereign state, for the state is not only something more, much more than the single person or the minority, but also something more than the majority, since even the majority is only the major part of the state, not the whole of the state.

Moreover, by thinking that sovereignty can be in the hands of one single person, of minority or of majority, Burgess identifies, consciously or unconsciously, the state and the government, since sovereignty is here not only essential to and identical with the state, but also essential to and identical with the government. This is easy to understand because in the system of Burgess, the one, the minority or the majority who is or are sovereign is or are undoubtedly the governmental agency or agencies, different from the

---

① Burgess, *Political Science and Comparative Constitutional Law*, Vol. I, p. 57.
② *Ibid.*, p. 56.

sovereignty of state which is original, absolute, unlimited and universal power, and which just as the state is all-comprehensive, exclusive and permanent.

It is impossible to think then that such a sovereignty, original, unlimited, absolute, universal, all comprehensive, exclusive and permanent as it can be in the hands of one, few, or majority. It is also unimaginable that such a sovereignty can be changed from the hands of one to the hands of the few or the hands of the majority, or vice versa as it has been the case in our history. For to classify states in accordance with whether sovereignty is in the hands of one, few, or majority would be, in the last analysis and as a matter of fact, a classification of the government, not of the state; unless one is willing to admit that state is identical with government. But to identify the state with the government is not only to make Burgess's classification of state become meaningless, but also to destroy his attempt of distinguishing the state from the government; a distinction which is essential and vital in his political concept.

Writers such as Garner seem to see the point here made. He says: "The most common and most satisfactory classification of states is therefore that which is based upon the similarities and differences of their government. But in the last analysis such a classification is nothing more than a classification of *government* and not of *states*. Modern political science and consequently a classification of states on the basis of forms of government rests upon a confusion of the two. Consistency and scientific logic therefore require that such classifications be placed in their category and labeled as classifications of 'governments' and not of 'states'."①

And he says in another place: "In their legal character, in their essence, and in their primary ends and purposes all states are essentially alike and cannot therefore be differentiated one from another in the same way that natural organisms, physical objects, or chemical elements may be distinguished. The things which differentiate one state from another are not differences of constituent elements but rather external phenomena or characteristics. The most important of these latter are the forms and character of their governmental organization."②

Yet curious enough, in spite of what has been said, Garner follows Burgess and particularly Jellinek very closely. "The proposed classifications of both Jellinek and Burgess," says Garner, "possess the great merit of simplicity; they are meticulously logical and they represent an effort to differentiate forms of state upon the basis of a single, consistent jurisdical principle or criterion. But even the classifications which

---

① Garner, *Political Science and Government*, p. 241.
② *Ibid.*, p. 240.

they propose are not entirely satisfactory nor are they wholly free from the objections which they themselves urged against various previous classifications. Their criterion of differentiation and classification is largely quantitative, arithmetical, or numerical and not of principle. The line of demarcation between a state in which the sovereignty rests with a bare majority and one in which the sovereignty minority especially if it be a large one, may be shadowy, in which the distinction between a democracy and an aristocracy becomes very slight, so that they can hardly be assigned to separate categories. Jellinek was more logical than Burgess when he placed democracies and aristocracies in the same class and treated them as different varieties of a common form, republic."①

In order to avoid the difficulty encountered by Burgess and therefore by Garner, Willoughby insists firmly that while governments are different and may be classified into various forms, states are all alike. He points out that: "The character of political sovereignty is no more bound up with the manner in which its power is exercised than is man's nature determined by the form of his physical frame. When, therefore, we consider the nature of the state we do not need to be concerned with its form. We have to do with its ontology, not its morphology. At the same time, to such extent are governmental terms used in all political treaties and discussions, that one of the main objects of this work, which is to render political phraseology more definite, would not be performed, did we not stop to examine the nomenclature ordinarily employed in distinguishing the various forms of political organizations."②

And he continues: "To one who has pursued the arguments of the preceding pages it need not be said that there can be no such thing as a classification of states, as states. In essence they are all alike, —each and all being distinguished by the same sovereign attributes. Hence it follows that the only manner in which states may be differentiated is according to the structural peculiarities of their governmental organizations."③

For the reason stated above, Willoughby, instead of making any attempt to classify the forms of the states, devotes his attention only to the classification of governments.

It is to be remembered that although Willoughby refuses to admit that there is such a thing a classification of states, he maintains, as both Burgess and Garner do, that the state is different from the government and therefore that a distinction between the two should be made. It is to be noted also that although the three writers, Burgess, Garner and Willoughby, agree in general that there is a distinction between the state and the

---

① Garner, *Political Science and Government*, p. 255.
② Willoughby, *The Nature of the State*, p. 351.
③ *Ibid.*, pp. 351-352.

government, that sovereignty is essential to the state and that this supreme authority is indivisible, they are different not only in regard to the relations between the state and the government, as already shown in the last chapter, but also with reference to their conceptions of forms of the state and that of the government.

Burgess applies the Aristotelian classification of the government for the forms of the state and tries to advance a new ⟨a⟩ classification of forms of government. Willoughby repudiates that there is such a thing as classification of forms of state and confines himself to consider only the forms of government. Garner, though agreeing with Willoughby that all states are alike and realizing the difficulty of Burgess's application of Aristotelian classification of the forms of government for the forms of the state, accepts, nevertheless, to a large extent, both the classifications of the forms of the state and that of the government as proposed by Burgess.

I have taken the view points of these three writers in order to show that although ⟨the⟩ state is distinguished from the government, a lot of confusions and difficulties arise when further scrutiny is made. And this ⟨is⟩ particularly true as we come to the question of the forms of the government and that of the state. It is to be remarked that the confusions made and the difficulties faced by these writers are also connected with their conceptions of sovereignty. We have already shown how Burgess is confused and runs into difficulty when he classifies states according to the sovereignty vested in the hands of the number of persons. Willoughby tries to avoid such confusions and difficulties by refusing to recognize the forms of the states, since he conceives that the sovereignties of the states are all alike and therefore each remaining as an entity in each state and being essential to or even identical with the state. In short, Willoughby tries to solve the question by separating the sovereignty from the governmental organizations. Just as a man's nature is not determined by the form of his physical frame, so sovereignty is not bound up with the manner in which its power is exercised.

But it seems to us that Willoughby is no more successful than Burgess by doing so. While endeavoring to separate the sovereignty from the governmental power in order to discriminate the government from the state, Willoughby's contention that "at all times the state is wholly organized in its government" makes it hard for us to see the real significance of the distinction between the government and the state as we have already pointed out in the last chapter.

Nor is his contention that there is no such thing as forms of the state is correct. But in order to make this point clear, it is necessary for us, first of all, to consider the forms of government, and then proceed to see whether there is such a thing as the forms of the state.

A clear classification of the forms of the government may be said to begin with Aristotle in his book *The Politics*. We know well that Aristotle classifies governments into monarchical, aristocratic and democratic forms. Aristotle also thinks of another form, that is, the mixed form which it seems to him to be an ideal form. The principles upon which Aristotle applies for analysing the forms of the government are two: one is according to the number of persons in whom the power is vested; and second, according to the end to which the government is directed. Both are, to be true, interrelated. According to the first, if the power of the government is in the hands of one person, it is monarchical almost one that Vtto Bluntschli's theory of the state is devoted to the forms of the state. If it is in the hands of few, it is aristocracy; and if it is in the hands of many, it is polity. Monarchy, aristocracy and polity are supposed to be good governments. When monarchy corrupts, it becomes tyranny; when aristocracy corrupts, it becomes oligarchy; and when polity corrupts, it becomes democracy. Democracy, a word though panegyrized by most of the modern writers and statesmen, is considered by Aristotle and by the ancient Greeks in general as nothing more than a government by mob.

We have already noted the two principles upon which Aristotle classifies the forms of government are interrelated. As a matter of fact, the second principle may be said to be derived from the first. If we use the Aristotelian classification of the forms of government without referring to be good or bad, we may follow the ordinary way of saying that there are, according to Aristotle, three fundamental forms of government, namely, monarchy, aristocracy and democracy. The mixed form is merely a combination of the three forms, or if you like, any two of the three forms.

The classification enunciated by Aristotle is not necessarily to be logical, but it is rather a reflection of the political institutions of the ancient period and consequently of the ancient Greek cities. At those days, it is to be remembered, political institutions are much simpler than what we have at present. The Greek cities are not exceptional to this rule. How much is a Greek city, say Athen, more complex than a primitive tribe in political organization is hard to tell. But we can be sure that the Greek city is not too much advanced from a highly political organization in the so-called primitive society. It is true that the Greeks attained the crescendo of civilization of the ancient world, but equally is it true that the ancient Greeks were not too far away from their primitive ancestors. Attention is called to this fact, because it will lead us to understand the reason why Aristotle classified governments in such a way. When governmental organization is simple, one or few good men count a great deal. And in a small city like that the ancient Greece with so small a population all of whom, as Aristotle tells us, can be seen from a high place of the city, it is not hard to have a majority to come to a place together in order to hold a meeting to consider the public affairs of the city.

In such a political organization, somewhat similar to a tribe or a small urban city in our day, it is easy for one man or a few or even many of them to handle the so-called political affairs of the whole community. If we bear in mind that human wants are few and simple in those days, much too few and much too simple in comparison with ours in modern period, it is possible to have one man to take care of the public affairs. This man will be called monarch and the government viewed as an institution is monarchy. It is also possible to have all the legitimate citizens of the city to discuss and to decide their common affairs. So it may be called polity or to use the modern word democracy. It is only logical too that the whole city may be administered by a few men.

This being the conditions of the world of the ancient Greece, it was easy for Aristotle to group the governments into a few categories and say this is ruled by one and that is ruled by few or many. And if the city is ruled by one with some help from a few and occasionally from many, it may be called a mixed government.

Although political institutions have become more and more complex, political writers still follow the phraseology and terminology of Aristotle without paying much attention to the change of political conditions. George Cornewall Lewis, in his *Remarks on the Use and Abuse of Some Political Terms* pointed out very clearly that the Aristotelian classification was not in accordance with the actual political facts many decades ago. "The fact is," says he, "that, by common agreement, we call all governments of which a king is chief, monarchies; which agreement is solely derived from historical recollections, and is not founded on the actual state of things. There was a time when the kings of France were truly monarchs, or absolute princes; there was a time when the kings of England were, in practice, nearly absolute, and when the crown was by far the most important part of the constitution. The King of England is always, in solemn language, styled 'our sovereign lord'. Yet the king of England possesses only a part, and that the least important part, of sovereign power. With the regard to the administration of laws, and the declaration of peace and war, he is sovereign; but the entire legislative sovereignty he shares with two deliberative bodies, altogether forming a parliament, which alone possesses the power of making laws. To this arrangement of the supreme power Gibbon has adapted his account of Monarchy when he says, that the obvious definition of a monarchy seems to be that of a state in which a single person, by whatsoever name he may be distinguished, is intrusted with the execution of the laws, the management of the revenue, and the command of the army."①

Again he says: "According to this usage, therefore, monarchy would signify, not only a government in which the whole sovereign power is possessed by one, but all governments in which the head of the state is called king, prince, or emperor, although he may only be part of the sovereign body." ②

As to Aristocracy, he remarks: "Aristocracy signifies a government in which the sovereignty is shared by several persons, being less in number than half the community. Such are the government of England, France, Bavaria, the United States of America, etc." But, "it also signifies a certain class in a state, whatever may be the form of its government. Thus we speak of the French aristocracy, when the government was a monarch; or the aristocracy of Rome, when the government was democratic; and many writers have called the English government an aristocracy; and a class of persons in England, the aristocracy"③.

"The ambiguity of this word," he says in another place, "has been turned to great account by modern writers and speakers, who shift from one sense of it to another, as it suits their purpose, and having succeeded in raising a prejudice against one class transfer and direct it against another, by merely confounding them under one name. Substantially, however, 'aristocracy', as the name of a class in England, is synonymous with 'the rich' in the widest sense; and any measure tending to increase the power of the rich is considered aristocratic; and any measure tending to increase the power of the poor is considered anti-aristocratic."④

When we come to democracy, Lewis points out that it "properly signifies a government in which a majority of the whole nation or community partake of the sovereign power. Such were, at one time, the governments of Athens, Rome, and many other Grecian and Italian states as well as of some of the Italian and German cities in the Middle Ages, in which all the male adult citizens had a voice in the supreme legislative assembly"⑤. "It also used to signify a government in which either a majority or a large portion of the people have, by means of the right of election, an influence on the appointment of the members of the supreme power. In this sense the federal government

---

① Lewis, *The Use and Abuse of Some Political Terms*, pp. 59-60.
② *Ibid.*, p. 60.
③ *Ibid.*, p. 72.
④ *Ibid.*, pp. 73-74.
⑤ *Ibid.*, p. 75.

of the United States, as well as the government of the several states, are called democracies; ① although, both in the one and in the others, the sovereign power resides in a very small minority of the whole people." ②

Then he continues: "Even during the rule of the multitude in the French Revolution, at the worst periods of the reign of terror the sovereignty was never shared by a large part of the population of France. The government was really in the hands of the lower orders of Paris, and hence it was termed a democracy. This agrees with the definition of Aristotle, who says that democracy is not, according to common opinion, a government in which the many govern but a government in which the poor govern. It so happens (he adds) that the rich are always the minority, the poor the majority of the people; and hence accidentally a democracy is a government where the many rule."③

It is clear that democracy is not necessarily to be a government ruled by majority. This has been also well observed by J. Bentham, as noted by Lewis. "What is curious," says Bentham, "is, that the same persons who tell you (having read as much) that democracy is a form of government under which the supreme is vested in all the members of a state, will also tell you (having also read as much) that the Athenian Commonwealth was a democracy. Now the truth is, that in the Athenian Commonwealth, upon the most moderate computation, it is not one tenth part of the inhabitants of the Athenian state that ever at time partook of the supreme power: women, children and slaves, being taken into the account."④

Lewis also notes that: "Mr. Mill, in his *Essay on Government*, appears to follow the common use of this word, not assenting to Mr. Bentham's remark; for he says that 'in Greece, not withstanding the defects of democracy, human nature ran a more brilliant career than it has ever done in any other age or country.' Now if we take from the rolls of democracy the illustrious name of Athens, and give to the cause of aristocracy the splendid achievement of her sons in every department of literature, science, and art, there will be little ground for extolling the renown of Grecian democracy. Indeed there was no republic in Greece which, according to this phraseology, would not have had an aristocratic government."⑤

Lewis shows not only the impossibility of having the purely monarchical,

---

① It is to be noted that Lewis also regards the United States as aristocratic government.
② Lewis, *The Use and Abuse of Some Political Terms*, p. 75.
③ Ibid., pp. 75-76.
④ Bentham, *A Fragment on Government*, p. 180, note 3.
⑤ Ibid., pp. 77-78.

aristocratic or democratic governments, but also the difficulty of the so-called mixed form of government. "A mixed government," says he, "is opposed to a *pure* or *simple* government, belongs to a classification of governments upon a different principle from any hitherto examined; though what that principle may be, or in what manner it is connected with the theory of the *balance of power* in a state, to which it is always linked, cannot be very readily or satisfactorily determined. The common notion, appears to be, that there are three pure forms of government, viz. monarchy, aristocracy, and democracy, in which there is no balance of powers: but that by combining any two of these forms of government, or all three together; a mixed government is formed in which a balance of powers exists; that is to say, in which the elementary parts of the compounded constitution mutually check and counterpoise one another."①

But he goes on to tell us: "This notion is subject to the obvious difficulty, that as the triple division of governments is strictly accurate and logical, it must be exhaustive, and its members must be opposed to one another; whence it follows, that there can be no form of government which is not one of these three, and that a combination of any two of them, much more of all three, is as inconceivable as that a number should be odd and even at the same time; inasmuch as the notion of one excludes that of any other. For example: monarchy is the government of one, aristocracy of more than one; therefore, as a state cannot be governed both by one person and by several persons, it cannot, at the sametime, be both a monarchy and an aristocracy. Aristocracy is a government of less than half, democracy of more than half the community: therefore, as a state cannot, at the same time, be governed by more and less than half its members, it cannot be, at the same time, a democracy and an aristocracy. Still less can it be governed by one, by a minority, and a majority of its members, all at once."②

"To call this a classification of governments," he adds, "is therefore not less an abuse of language, than to call the offence of one man a conspiracy; it is, in effect, a denial of all classification, an abolition of all distinction between different classes of governments, which are thus joined together in one undistinguished heap."③

Lewis's criticism against the so-called mixed form of government is from the legal standpoint which is different to what he calls the moral standpoint. "No classification of government," he maintains, "can be serviceable which turns on moral influences, and not on the construction of the sovereign body, or some permanent attribute of the

---

① Bentham, *A Fragment on Government*, p. 79.
② *Ibid.*, p. 80.
③ *Ibid.*, p. 96.

established constitution. The one principle affords a precise and definite ground of distinction, about which no two persons can disagree. The other depends on an uncertain opinion as to the comparative moral and political influence of certain persons and parties in the state, an influence which may be exercised in the most various ways, and is liable to fluctuate from year to year, and almost from day to day... Legally, there can be no competition between different powers in the same state, as the sovereign power is supreme and undivided; nor can any other power, according to law, enter into competition with it."①

"But," as he continues to tell us, "the acts of the persons composing the sovereign body may be influenced by the wishes, interests, and proceedings, as well of each other as of other persons and classes in the community. So that, although a legal balance of powers is impossible, a moral balance must always exist."②

Thus, according to Lewis, although, morally speaking, there may be a mixed form of government, from the legal point of view, there is no such. The reason why it is impossible to have a mixed government from this latter point of view is because of the assumption that legally sovereignty is one and can not be divided. Since sovereignty is indivisible, it must be either in the hands of the monarch or of the aristocratic class or of the democratic group. It can not be shared by each of these and mixed together.

The contention that there can be no mixed form of government, because sovereignty can not be divided, is also held by J. K. Bluntschli. "By a mixed state," he remarks, "may be understood one in which monarchy, aristocracy, or democracy are moderated or limited by other political factors, e. g. a monarchy may be limited by the formation of an aristocratic Senate or upper House, and of a primary or representative assembly of the people. In that case it is true that such a divided constitution is better than when an individual, or a few, or the majority, rule absolutely and without restraint. But such a mixture as this does not create a new form of state, for the supreme governing power is still concentrated in the hands of the monarch, or of the aristocracy, or of the people."③

"Moreover," he declares, "it is generally forgotten that the principle of Aristotle's division does not rest on the nature and composition of the legislative power; for in any advanced state this is usually representative of the chief elements of the whole nation. On the contrary, it depends on the antithesis between the government and the governed,

---

① Bentham, *A Fragment on Government*, pp. 96–97.
② *Ibid.*, p. 97.
③ Bluntschli, *Theory of the State*, translation, p. 312.

and upon the question to whom the supreme administrative power belongs. This latter cannot be divided, not even between a king and his ministers, for this would create a diarchy or triarchy, and would be opposed to the essential character of a state, which, as a living organism requires unity. In all living beings there is a variety of powers and organs, but in this variety there is unity. Some organs are superior and other inferior, but there is always one supreme organ, in which the directing power is concentrated. The head and the body have no separate and independent life, but they are not equal. So also for the state, a supreme organ is a necessary condition of its existence, and this cannot be split into parts, if the state itself is to retain its unity."①

Bluntschli concludes by saying that: "there is not, therefore, any such fourth form of state as has been called a mixed state; and so far as mixture is possible, it is amply treated in a consideration of the three simple states enumerated above."②

Now it is clear that the reason why writers refuse to admit that there is such a thing as mixed form of government is, as already noted, because of the belief that sovereignty is divisible. We shall show, in our later discussion of the question of sovereignty, that sovereignty is indivisible and that even legally sovereignty can be divided. Suffice it to point out here that Lewis's statement that a state can not be governed, at the same time, by one person, by few persons and by more than half of the community and therefore a state can not, at the same time, be called monarchy, aristocracy and democracy, seems to be only a play of words; because when it becomes a mixed government, it can no longer be called either a monarchy, or an aristocracy or a democracy. It is somewhat like a house which is built of stone and wood; but when you look at the house you no longer call it stone or wood, but house. It is true that a mixed government is composed of the elements or rather characteristics of the monarchy, aristocracy and democracy, yet it is by itself a form which is different from each of these.

Take the English government for illustration. There is still a monarch; there is still a House of Lords which represents the aristocratic class; and then there is the House of Commons which represents the majority of the people. When you hear and indeed often hear that the English government is "His Majesty Government", you certainly think that it is a monarchical form of government. But there is also a group of aristocratic people whose influence in political affairs cannot be entirely overlooked. And if you think of the power of the House of Commons, you say that the English government is a democratic government. It is true that in our own day, the House of Commons is the dominating

---

① Bluntschli, *Theory of the State*, translation, pp. 313–314.
② *Ibid.*, p. 314.

body in the government; but if we take a glance at the history, we shall find that not only there was a time when the king was very powerful and that there was a time, say, even before 1911, when the House of Lords had also a share in governing the country, but also there was time that these three bodies were more or less equal in strength in the matters of government. Under such a condition, you can not say that it was or even is a pure monarchy or a pure aristocracy or a pure democracy. Looking from this angle one may say that most, if not all, of the governments in the history were mixed governments. Lewis himself puts the government of the United States of America under both the form of aristocracy and that of democracy as example for both of these forms of government. If both are right as Lewis thinks, then, the United States has also a mixed government, a mixture of both aristocracy and democracy. If this being not the case, how can the United States, the government of the United States, according to Lewis's logic, be taken as an example for both aristocracy and democracy at the same time.

The reason why Lewis takes the government of the United States of America as an example for both aristocracy and democracy seems to be very doubtful. If he thinks that after all that the government of the United States is governed by few, minority or less in number than half the community, then this would be true to practically all of the governments. But at the same time he admits that the government of the United States is an example of democracy, meaning that "a majority or a large portion or the people have, by means of the right of election, an influence on the appointment of members of the supreme power". Thus the government of the United States is at once an aristocracy and a democracy. Yet, this, it seems to Lewis, is impossible. Is it not then that Lewis is here self-contradictory?

But this is not all. If it is true that sovereignty is indivisible and that in order to preserve its unity it must be in one place or rather in the hands of one, then in the last analysis, there can be only one form of government, namely monarchy. Because to say that sovereignty is in the hands of few, in an aristocracy, or in the hands of many, in a democracy, there is already an assumption that sovereignty is divided between or shared by the few or the many. Here we have the theory of divisible sovereignty.

Take again the House of the Commons for example. There are more than six hundred members of the house. Each individual is a self-centered and self-conscious entity, no matter how a unity of the House can be reached, you have to secure the consent of each and to count them one by one in order to make the unity. And not only there may be an even vote for an issue, but also there may be a majority of 51 to 49. In each of these cases, the sovereignty is not a unity.

As a matter of fact, even taking for granted that sovereignty is indivisible, there is still a possibility of having a mixed form of government. W. W. Willoughby, though holding that sovereignty is one and indivisible, inclines, however, to see this point. Referring to Bluntschli's denial of the mixed form of government, he writes: "While agreeing fully with Bluntschli as to the essential unity of the state (without accepting the 'organic' manner in which it is conceived by him), it will nevertheless be observed that his argument is not to the point, being directed rather to the nature of the state than to the character of government. The reasoning is good as against the mediaeval and early modern writers who introduced an essential duality into the state itself, by a prediction of a contract, and of an opposition, between the 'rights' of the people and those of the Grown; but is not valid as against those who distinguish between the state and its government, and who recognize the state's personality, and identify sovereignty with its supreme will:—who, in other words, distinguish between the supreme power itself, which is essentially a unit; and the exercise of that power, which may be distributed among several organs. Thus, because of the failure to make this distinction, Bodin held absolute monarchy alone as possible, while Althusius maintained a like ground for democracy. Hobbes, also, though holding either monarchy, aristocracy, or democracy possible, yet denied the possibility of a union of two or more. But all were alike at fault in identifying the agent with the state itself, whose will the agent merely utters."①

While history supplies numerous cases of the mixed form of government, it seems to have been declining in our century. Monarchy has been disappearing, and aristocracy in the sense of nobility shares the same fate with the former. Even titles of nobility are prohibited in many of the countries in our own day. The so-called royal families or noble bloods do not mean so much as they used to be. They have been and are in the wane. If Aristocracy is regarded as "any measure tending to increase the power of the rich", we must say that on the whole the world current is directed against such a tendency. Even in the so-called capitalistic countries such as the United States and Great Britain, the movement for equalization of wealth is a telling fact, the heavy taxes on large incomes, on inheritance and the like are important checks on the rich to become richer. On the contrary, many measures have been and are being taken in order to set up a minimum standard of living for even the poorest. Democracy, besides signifying the principle of political equality, comes to mean more and more the institution of economic equality.

If aristocracy means simply the rule of the few or the minority, it may be said that

---

① Willoughby, *The Nature of the State*, pp. 370–371.

in the last analysis no governing body can be composed of the whole or even the majority of the population. Government consists of the so-called ruling people who in opposition to people in general are always in a small number. Since there is no pure democracy which means that all of the people can participate the governmental affairs, government, in terms of the number of people who run it, is always in the hands of a few or a minority. But this can not lead us to call all governments aristocratic, if the supreme authority of a state is taken into consideration. Because although the government may be run by a small group of people, the supreme authority may not be in their hands. In a democratic country, these people are simply the agents nay, the public servants of the people. They can hold their positions only with the consent of the people. Unless they do according to what the people wish them to do, their positions in the government will not be secure. By the right of election or that of revolution the people can change the personels of the government. And if we say that a government is aristocratic because it is composed of a few or a minority without considering the location of the supreme authority or sovereignty, then as already noted all governments are aristocratic. But this would be somewhat meaningless, for in such a case, aristocracy is not merely a form of the government but the only form of government. Yet a government which is either ruled directly or indirectly by the people, the majority of the people, is also called a democratic government, in spite of the fact that it is composed of the few or minority of the people. One may say that this is a mixed government, because looking from one angle it is a government of the few while looking from another angle, it is a government ⟨of⟩ the many or of the majority. Only when the sovereignty of the state is also in the hands of the few or the minority can we say that its government is an aristocracy. So aristocracy as a form of government can hardly be found in the present day, if it is used in the strict sense of the term which implies the meaning not only of the rule of the few or minority, but also of the noble, rich and sovereign few or minority.

Not satisfied with the Aristotelian division of the forms of government into monarchy, aristocracy, democracy including the mixed form of government, many writers classify the government into two main forms: "one is monarchy and the other republic. The latter is subdivided into two again, namely aristocracy and democracy. Machiavelli, in his *The Prince*, remarks that all the governments and forms of dominion that have had and now have rule over men [over men] have been and are either republican or princely."[①] Montesquieu, although speaking of three species of government,

---

① Machiavelli, *The Prince*, Chapter 1.

republican, monarchical and despotic, seems to think that the last two belong to one group and subdivides the first into two classes. "A republican government," says he, "is that in which the body, or only a part of the people, is possessed of the supreme power; monarchy, that in which a single person governs by fixed and established laws; a despotic government, that in which a single person directs everything by his own will and caprice."[1] And he says again, "When the body of the people is possessed of the supreme power, it is called a democracy. When the supreme power is loged in the hands of a part of the people, it is then an aristocracy.[2] G. C. Lewi holds that "when the whole sovereign power over a community belongs to one person, the government is called a monarchy; when it belongs to several, it is called a republic or commonwealth. In a commonwealth, if the sovereign power belongs to a minority of the nation, the government is called an aristocracy; if to a majority, a democracy. Such appears to be the division of governments most consistent with the received phraseology, formed on the number of the persons who possess the sovereign"[3]. G. Jellinek, after criticizing a long list of the classifications of the forms of government proposed by writers before him as being arbitrary, unscientific, confusing or valueless, concludes that there are only two main divisions of the forms of government; that is monarchy and republic. "Monarchie," says he, "is der von einem physischen Willen gelenkte Staat."[4] A republic, on the other hand, is that which the sovereign will rests not with a single person, but with a group of persons. While admitting that politically or socially there is a difference between the wills of the few and that of the many or majority, juridically speaking there is no such distinction. Thus the so-called difference between the aristocracy and democracy as different forms of republic is not a juridical distinction.

While there are many modern writers who prefer to follow the twofold division of the government, there are also those who strongly oppose such division. Roscher points out that the difference between aristocracy and democracy is greater than that between monarchy and the other forms.[5]

As a matter of fact, the term republic is ambiguous. Lewis writes: "According to the custom already noticed of identifying royalty with monarchy, or of calling all states in which a King rules, monarchical, it is usual to class England and France with

---

[1] Montesquieu, *The Spirit of Laws*, Book II, Chap. 1.
[2] *Ibid.*, Chap. 2.
[3] Lewis, *The Use and Abuse of Some Political Terms*, p. 53.
[4] Jellinek, *Allgemeine Staatslehre*, p. 612.
[5] Roscher, *Politik*, pp. 3 ff.

monarchies, and not with commonwealths or republics, to which, in strictness, they belong. The interval in English history, between the death of Charles the First and the Restoration, is commonly known by the name of the Commonwealth: although, during part of that time, the state was more absolutely under the rule of one individual than it has ever been since the Restoration, or, at any rate, since the Revolution. By the writers, indeed, of the age which preceded the Civil War, the English government (as Mr. Mitford has remarked) is often called a commonwealth: but they appear to use this term as nearly synonymous with state, or *res publica*. This is the sense in which Locke uses the word in his treatise on government: and such he considers to be genuine signification. Unquestionably, however, since the end of Charles the First's reign, it has received the narrower meaning of a republic (thus, at the end of the seventeenth century, a commonwealth's man signified what a republican does now); although, even now, it occasionally obtains its wider acceptation. And hence, in such passages as that where Mr. Hallam calls the Kings of England, the chiefs of the English commonwealth, it is uncertain in what way the term should be understood. Probably, however, noone would call an absolute monarchy by this name, would speak, for example, of the Turkish commonwealth, or the French commonwealth under Louis the Fourteenth."[1]

Besides the confusions as pointed out by Lewis, it may be added that when Bodin used the word Republic for the title of his book, he employed it to include monarchy and other forms of government. He considered monarchy to be the most stable form of government and preferred to have the monarchy rather than any other form. It would be more properly, it seems to us, to call his work *The Monarch* instead of *The Republic*.

Moreover, the word Republic has sometimes been used as opposit to the word democracy. Thus Madison distinguishes between a democracy, in which the people meet and exercise the government in person, and a republic, where they administer it by their representatives and agents.[2] Then there are others who identify republican with democratic. As Lewis points out that "Crabb, in his *Dictionary of Synonyms*, says, that 'governments are divided by political writers into three classes—monarchical, aristocratic, and republican' "[3].

Lewis identifies commonwealth with republic. Thus he says: "Commonwealth or republic, is a general name for all governments in which the sovereign power resides in

---

[1] Lewis, *The Use and Abuse of Some Political Terms*, pp. 69–70.

[2] *Federalist*, No. XIV.

[3] Lewis, *ibid.*, p. 69.

several persons, whether they be few or many." ① Yet this may be true. As we know Commonwealth comes from common weal. W. Cunningham, in his *The Common Weal* published ⟨in⟩ 1917 tells us the origin of the term in the following passage: "The term takes us far back, for it has been associated with the projects of the Kentish Peasants who agitated, once and again, for better government. The insurrection of which we know most was that under Wat Tyler in 1381, and it was the striking outcome of widespread discontent with the existing order in church and state; there is real difficulty in getting at the root of the troubles. We are fortunate, however, in being able to discern, at least dimly something of the positive aims of the insurgents. They were aiming not merely at the redress of their own particular grivances, whatever they may have been, but at the common weal of the nation as a whole—all of localities and of all classes, and so they were ready to follow the king when he adroitly took the place of their dead leader at Mile End and shouted, 'I will be your leader.' The particularism of the mediaeval England was the root of every sort of evil. The malcontents had had enough of the jealoucies of different towns, of the quarells of different guilds and the ambitions of privileged classes, of the disputed customs of different estates, the disabilities of the serfs and the claims of the free labourers, —and they were ready to look to the king, as one who, by his position was raised above these rival forces and might be expected to have regard for the common weal of the nation as a whole."②

It is clear then that there may be a king or monarch in a commonwealth. This is true even up to the present day. The British Empire is now called as the British Commonwealth and this was officially declared in the Imperial Conference of 1926. Yet in the British Commonwealth, there is a king, the monarch of the whole Commonwealth.

As a matter of fact the term commonwealth is now used to identify the state rather than the government. So the word Republic has been employed in the sense of the state rather than the government, although the word republican is usually referred to a certain form of government rather than state.

From what has been said, we may conclude that the twofold division of the forms of government into monarchy and republic is by no means satisfactory.

And if we make a general survey of the governments of our own days, such a division is even more absurd, partly because the monarchical form of government is becoming more and more absolute and partly because the word republic may be used for

---

① Lewis, *The Use and Abuse of Some Political Terms*, p. 68.
② W. Cunningham, *The Common Weal*, pp. 1-2.

many forms of government.

Since the First World War, governments have been classified by many writers into two groups: one is democracies and the other dictatorships. It is also generally recognized that the Second World War is fought between democratic governments and dictatorial governments, although a scrutiny into the governmental organizations will reveal the facts that not all the allied nations which fight against the aixed countries are democratic; nor are the latter all dictatorial in the real sense of the term as in the case of Japan where the Emperor symbolizes the governmental regime.

If we attach closely to the existing facts, that governments may be divided into democracy and dictatorship cannot be denied. It is true that there are still many monarchs surviving in many countries particularly in Europe, but they are, as a matter of fact, only figured heads and merely historical remains which have very little to do with the actual administration of the political affairs or governmental policies. We all know well that both in England and in Italy, king still remains; but the government of England is regarded as democratic, while that of Italy, under the administration of Mussolini, as dictatorial. Thus if a government is under the caprice of one man who does not get his position by inheritance and at the same time who does not assume the name of king or a monarch is balled dictatorship whereas a government, though retaining a king or a monarch, is called democracy if the power of the government is in the hands of the people.

But here again, we must admit that dictatorial government is only a temporary form of government unless a state is under the control of dictators in succession for many years. Few if any dictators have dictated through their own life times and none, it seems to us, has succeeded in giving his position to another dictator. Neither Hitler nor Mussolini had a happy end. The dictatorial system, if the word system can be used, ended in both Germany and Italy when both of the dictators died. In fact, the dictatorship of Italy collapsed before the death of Mussolini.

Temporary as it is, dictatorship does not end with the death of Hitler or Mussolini. Nor history lacks examples of this kind of government. Cromwell and Napoleon were dictators.

But since dictatorship is, after all, a temporary form of government, to say that government may be classified into dictatorship and democracy would be also a temperory classification. For such classification is undoubtedly true since the First World War until even to the present day; but to maintain that dictatorship will still remain for a considerable period is very doubtful.

In order to have a comprehensive and concise classification of the forms of government, I propose to divide governments into two classes: One may be called constitutional government and the other may be called personal government. The former may be considered as government by law and the latter as government by man. The phrases such as these have been used by numerous writers but, so far as I am aware, their distinctions as applied for the classification of the forms of government have not, or at least seldom, been employed by political writers. Although the distinction between government by law and government by man signifies respectively the distinction between constitutional government and personal government, the two are somewhat different. The reasons are obvious. In the first place, law is different from constitution. Strictly speaking, while constitutionalism is a modern thing, law is an old institution. No government, how crude it may be, is run without law or some kind of rules of law; but almost all of the governments of the past particularly before the modern period in our history and many governments of the present day are governed without constitution. It is true that it is hard to draw a clear distinction between law in general and constitutional law, particularly when we come to a country which has an unwritten constitution. But in general it may be said that law may be issued by government itself while constitution is rather a limitation on government and a protection for the rights of the people as against the abuse of the power on the part of the government. So although constitutional law may be considered as a kind of law, it is nevertheless different from law in general.

Secondly, personal government as a term is more preferrable than the term government by man. If we say government by man in its singular form, one may think that it is a government run by one man. It is possible that the government may be run by a few or many men. Unless you phrase it as "government by man or men", it is not clear. The term "personal government" has the advantage of avoiding this ambiguity. Moreover, when you say that it is a government by man or men, you may also be led to think that such government has no law at all. This is not true as we have already indicated above, since the man or men who take charge of the government may also give law to his or their subordinates or subjects. It is possible that with the exception of this man or these few men, the rest of the men, be they subjects or officials, are all ruled by law.

On the contrary, the term "personal government" merely means the government is a personal thing either to one person or a few. While theoretically it is possible to have a personal government which is run by many, historical fact shows that it has not happened in that way. Under personal government we may subdivide into monarchy and dictatorship. While both monarchy and dictatorship are supposed to be government by one, it is also possible to have a personal government by few. But since human nature tends to get power, governmental or otherwise in the hands of one aristocracy becomes merely a theoretical possibility. It seldom occurs in practice. Even it does occur, it is always a temporary phenomenon. So it may be said that personal government is almost always a government by one man, be he a monarch or a dictator.

Although there has been such a thing as constitutional monarch, constitutional government is mainly a democracy. It is generally recognized that modern democracy develops as constitutionalism develops. The reason why there has been such a thing as constitutional monarchy is because of the fact that there has been a transitional period from the absolute monarchy to the modern democracy. When the process was still going on, there was a mixture of monarchy and democracy and this has been called as mixed form of government. But definitely the tendency has been toward democracy, since, as already noted, constitutionalism is, negatively speaking, a check upon the power of the government including of course that of the king or monarch and, positively speaking, the protection of the rights of the people.

It may be suggested that the term democracy may be used for the term constitution. In other words, instead of calling it constitutional government, it may be called democratic government. But it is to be remembered that the word democracy has been also used by the ancient Greek writers to denote a government by poor people and at the same time a government by mob. Thus what we call democratic government in the nineteenth and twentieth centuries has been and is really a constitutional government.

Historically speaking, it may be said that government has been in general developing from personal to constitutional. But this is not entirely true, because dictatorship occupies a very important chapter in the history of government in the twentieth century, although the day of the monarch has been already gone. For this reason, personal government is a thing of the present as well as of the past.

Chapter 5
State in Primitive Society (Origin of the State)

The distinction between the state and things political may be, at the outset, put in this way: Although the state is a political concept, what is political is not necessarily to be the state. In other words, the state is simply one of the political organizations or entities. It is true that from the time of Reformation to the present day, the state has been the most important political organization or entity; but equally it is true that the importance of the state is only momentary and after all temporary in our history. It is not existing at all in the so-called primitive societies. And if the [the] primitive societies existing in our day in different parts of the world are nothing more than the vestiges of the earliest human societies, it is only logical to say that the state did not exist in our earliest history. Nor was it present, in the strict sense of the term in the ancient world, the ancient world of Egypt, of China, of Greece and of Rome. Still less was it to be found in the Mediaeval Age. And judging from the experience of the past and that of the present, we may say that it is doubtful that it will retain its supremacy in the future.

While some political writers, like Gustav von Struve, in almost a hundred years ago, might declare that "Der Staat is ein Verein, welcher so alt is, als die Geschichte und sich ueber die ganze Erde verbreit"[①], modern anthropologists and sociologists and other research workers in social studies have proved that in many primitive societies there is not only no state but also no political organization of any sort which is significant for our consideration.

Herber Spencer, in 1879, already noted that "the Greelanders are entirely without political control; having nothing which represents it more nearly than the deference paid to the opinion of some old man, skilled in seal-catching and the sign of the weather"[②]. And "of one of the Columbian tribes we read that the Salish can hardly be said to have any regular form of government", and "among the Bodo and the Dhimals, whose village heads are simply respected elders with no coercive powers, those who offend against

---

① G. v. Struve, *Grundzuege der Staatswissenschaft*, 1847, Book I, p. 1.
② H. Spencer, *Principles of Sociology*, Vol. II, Part I, section 465, p. 319.

customs are admonished, fined, or excommunicated, according to the degree of the offence". ①

In another place, he writes: "When Rind asked the Nicobarian who among them was the chief, they replied laughing, how could he believe that *one* could have power against so many?" I quote this as a reminder that there is, at first, resistance to the assumption of supremacy by one member of a group—resistance which, though in some types of men small, is in most considerable, and in a few very great. To instances already given of tribes practically chiefless may be added, from America, the Haidahs, among whom "each sovereign in his own right as a warrior;" and from Asia the Angamies, who "have no recognized head or chief, although they elect a spokesman, who, to all intents and purposes, is powerless and irresponsible". ②

Again, "groups of Esquimaux, of Australians, of Bushmen, of Euegians are without even that primary contrast of parts implied by settled chieftainship. Their members are subject to no control, but such as is temporarily acquired by the stronger, or more cunning or more experienced"③. And, as a matter of fact, Spencer even doubts that there is any social, not to say of political, organization in some of the primitive societies. Thus he points out that "naturally in a state like that of the Cayaguas or Wood-Indians of South America, so little social that 'one family lives at a distance from another', social organization is impossible; and even where there is some slight association of families organization does not arise while they are few and wandering"④.

So Henry Sidgwick remarks that these groups mentioned by Spencer "lack what we regard as an essential characteristic of political society, though they can hardly be excluded from the range of sociology or social science". And he continues to say: "Since the majority of mankind are, and have been in historical times members of political or governed societies, still we know of inferior races who only exhibit this characteristics doubtfully and imperfectly."⑤

As we know well, results of recent social research reveal that what Spencer said more than half century ago is still true in many ⟨of⟩ the so-called primitive societies in our day. For instance, recent reports on the Yurok⑥ and their neighbors have clearly

---

① H. Spencer, *Principles of Sociology*, Vol. II, Part I, section 465, p. 319.
② *Ibid.*, p. 311.
③ Spencer, *Principles of Sociology*, Vol. I, Part II, section 228, pp. 471-472.
④ *Ibid.*
⑤ Henry Sidgwick, *The Elements of Politics*, 1891, pp. 579 ff.
⑥ T. T. Watepman, *Yurok Ethnology*, 1931; *Yurok Geography*, 1910.

shown that among these people, not only there is no such a thing as state, but also there is little if anything that can be called political in its nature. In order to make this point clear, let us give a little more attention to these people.

The Yurok lived in the Northwest of California. They are called as such not because they formed a tribe or a community, but because they spoke the same language. Among the Yurok, it is said, not only there was no state or political organization, but also there was no court, no military organization, no war chief, no religious organization, no priesthood, no head shamen ships, and curiously enough even no family organization in the ordinary sense of the term.

Nor was there anything like a tribe or community having a council consisting of elder people or representatives from different clans or families to discuss and conduct its affairs among the Yurok. Nor even was there anything like a chief or chiefs who were recognized by all or majority of the people as their leaders in the political sense among these people. Although economically speaking there were rich and poor and the former enjoyed a kind of social prestige in the community, but as social distinction is closely connected with wealth, it lost when the wealth was lost. So socially speaking, to say nothing of political, there was no titles, no ranks, no prerogatives, and no offices.

Although there were customs guiding the conducts of the people but there was no court or organization to enforce the customs. It is said that "there is no offense against the community, no duty owing to it, no right or power inhering in it". The individuals observed the customs as individuals and damages were payable only from and to individual litigants. To get compensation from offender, one was usually backed by alliance with his kin, the alliance with his kin was by no means to form an organization. As a matter of fact, there was no ceremonialized or public punishment of any kind. It was by alliance with his kin and made the offender feel that it was necessary for him to pay the damages.

If there was anything to be called war, it was mainly a kind of temporarily organized band of relatives and friends which was formed in order to seek revenge for injury. But there was no war chief nor any title or prestige related to war.

There were men who specialized ⟨in⟩ magic, but this was just as some ones specialized in other professions and the specialization of certain magics could be learned by anybody. Thus a specialist in this field did not attain a higher social position than others on account of his practice of magic. There were some sweathouses which were sacred, but there were no altars in them nor were there any priest attached to them. The so-called communal religious ceremonies were absent except some sort of temporary dancing might be performed in certain localities without having religious significance.

We have said that among the Yurok there was hardly even a family organization, not because there was no marriage or no care of the children, but because the family was so loosely organized that it can hardly be called family as we generally understand it. It is reported that husband and wife did not live together for most part of the year. During the winter half of the year there was no sexual relation between men and women and even during summer time, men and women having sexual relations did not sleep at home or indoors, but rather outdoors. While women lived with children at home, men lived in men's clubhouse or sweathouse where women were forbidden to come in.

Since every adult individual in Yurok is a sovereign by himself or herself, so this may be said as true to husband and wife. Neither one had the rights over the other. Even between husband and wife, property in land was owned by each; so there was no common property in land for the family. A husband's lands might be in one place and the wife's lands might be in another place. Sometimes they were located in different villages.

Although these families lived in the villages, but each village was by no means a well organized community nor could it considered as an economically sufficient unit. Lands in the village were usually owned by people of other village or villages. Just as there was no family territory, there was also no village territory. There might be some of social relations between villages such as some sort of dances which were handed down from the ancestors, but this was a kind of informal and temporary affairs. Consequently, neither inter-villages' sentiment, nor village feeling was strong among these people. One can not say that they were anarchical, because they lived not only peacefully, but also orderly. An it was seldom that they had some sort of violent conflicts as we have had or have among the different nations.

There are still many other primitive societies which are more or less similar to the Yurok, either in America or in other parts of the world; but enough has been shown that there are societies in which no state or even no political organization can be found.

It is not true, then, as Struve says that the state is as old as history and widespread over the whole world. Nor is it true as Aristotle says that man is by nature a political animal, since we have already pointed out that there are people who live without political organization. Some writers have suggested that what Aristotle speaks of man as a political animal is nothing more than a social animal. Undoubtedly there will ⟨be⟩ no objection if Aristotle really means that, for a social animal is entirely different from a political animal. Although what is political is always social, what is social is not necessarily political. But concerning this point, we shall discuss later.

It is to be remarked, however, that there are many writers who maintain that the germ of the state is to be found in the family. In other words, the state is originated in the family. In the western world, from Aristotle to the present day, many people entertain such view point. Treitschke speaks of the ancient family as the ancient state. ① The Chinese sages used to regard the family as the foundation of the state or empire. Some even insist that the state or empire is nothing more than the enlargement of the family and they maintain that the principles which are employed for managing the family may be also applied for the administering of the state or empire. This being the case, it is said, the family is politically very significant, even though it may [be] not be regarded as a state.

We have already shown that in the primitive societies, there are many people who neither live in the state nor subject to political control. While the Yurok family can not be called family in the ordinary sense of the term, there are many families, in the strict sense of the term, in many of the primitive societies in which there is no political organization. If the primitive societies themselves are not political in character, it is hard to see how the families within these societies would have political significance.

It may be argued that in the family, the children are under the control of the parents and such a relationship may be considered as a relationship between the governor and the governed or ruler and the ruled. Therefore, those families in which the mothers are the heads are called matriarchal authority and those in which the fathers are the heads are called partriarchal authority. In China, the emperor or the governors used to think themselves and to be considered as the parents of the people and the latter are called their children. So it may be argued that the family is the miniature of the state.

Yet in spite of what has been said, we must be led to think that either the family is the state or the latter is originated from the former, or it has political significance. The relationship between the parents and the children is entirely different from that between the ruler and the ruled in a state. For in the former, the relationship is based on love and on affection; while in the latter, it is based on authority and obedience, authority on the part of the ruler and obedience on the part of the ruled. The reason why a family cannot be considered as a political group or a state will be dealt with later in this work, it is sufficient to state here that state is not a family or originated from the family is just as it is not a church, a company or a school or originated in these social groups.

---

① Treitschke, *Politik*.

Is the state originated from a clan or a sib? Some writers answer yes; but we think that it is not. The reason why the state is said to have its origin in a clan is because of the fact that in the clan a chief is sometimes to be found and he is considered as the ruler of the clan. But it is to be noted that although a chief is usually found in a clan, he is by no means a political leader. A clan is a kinship group. It consists of a group of families. While the family is bilateral, the clan is unilateral. A family consists of a relationship between a man and a woman, the former being called father and the latter mother by their children. The clan traces kinship through one of the parents without thinking of the other. The head of the clan is usually an aged man attaining his position chiefly as a magician. Thus he is usually one and the same chief and magician. While the clan is usually a totemic group, it is thought that the magical powers intrinsic to the clan are concentrated in its chief. Only by proving his magical power he can maintain or increase his authority. If he fails to do that or someone in the clan can do that better than he, his position as the chief will be questioned or overthrown. Not infrequently, a clan chief has to give up his position, because he has lost the magical power.

It is clear, then, that a clan is a religious as well as a kinship group, and it is not going too far to say that a clan is different from the family in that the latter is mainly a kinship group, the former may be regarded as a religious group mixed with blood relationship. The political function of a clan can hardly be found. It is a non-political organization of kinship based by and surrounded with that mysterious totemic system with its totemic taboos as rules of law for the control of the conducts of the members of the group.

As a matter of fact political significance can seldom be found in a close kinship group such as family or clan. "We have little evidence," says W. H. R. Rivers, "concerning the exertion of authority in the kindred. In the case I know best, that of Eddystone Island in the Solomons, the group has no member in whom any kind of authority is vested, the older members being probably the more influential if any problem arises which needs the exertion of authority."[①]

And he adds: "Authority in the clan is also a subject about which our information is defective. Occasionally the clan may have a headman, but usually there is no one person in the clan who exerts more authority than the rest, except as the result of age or prestige."[②]

---

① Rivers, *Social Organization*, 1924, p. 160.
② *Ibid.*

Both George Frazer① and W. J. Perry have advanced a theory that the state and political chief are evolving from what is known as gerontocracy, a term used by W. H. R. Rivers for the ruler of the elders, through the rise to power of the public magician. It is beyond question that both the old men and the medicine men in the primitive society are very influential. Whether political authority is gradually developed from religious power is a question which we shall not discuss here. We shall concern ourselves to the question whether or not the state and political authority come from the system of gerontocracy in the primitive society.

The old men in the primitive society in general are men who are supposed to know more about the history and customs of their clans or groups. They are respected for having more experience in life but they are not to have what is known as political powers unless we interpret germs of political powers are closely mixed wherever there are social forces. But even it is so interpreted we can not call a clan a state or political organization, for a clan, as already said, are dominated by both kinship and religion.

"Gerontocracy," as pointed out by MacLeod, "we must emphasize, is not a form of the state. The gerontocrates, as we have seen in our African case study, are not political officials. They are mere custodians of tradition, advisers of the people, old men possessed of prestige, controlling their people in a sense, but not in political sense, being possessed of no power actually to judge of guilt, to execute, or to legislate."②

Two or more clans may form a tribe. In a sense, a tribe is also a kinship group, because, as we know, one of the cardinal principles making for growth into and consciousness of tribal unity is the practice of clan exogamy. A clan member can not marry within the clan. A man seeks his wife from another clan and a woman seeks her husband outside of her own clan. If there were only two clans, then all the women of one clan must marry men from the other clan or all the men of one clan must marry women from the other clan. As a result, these two clans are tied together by blood relationship and they are relatives to one another. Even there are more than two clans, it is still possible that all of clans will be related directly or indirectly one another by matrimonial relations. Thus a tribe consisting of many clans is still based on blood-relationship.

But a tribe is more than a kinship group. The role of religion in the tribe is no less important than that in a clan. But we shall not go on to that subject. What interests us is its political function. Some writers think that a tribe is the beginning of the state and the

---

① Frazer, *Golden Bough*, 1905.
② W. C. MacLeod, *The Origin and History of Politics*, 1931, p. 80.

difference between the tribe on the one hand and family and the clan on the other is because of the fact that the authority of the former over the individual, is essentially political. One writer, for instance, remarks: "The tribe as distinguished from the clan or the family, is thus viewed as the natural beginning of the state, since the authority of the tribe over the individuals is essentially political. It is very probable that the very first subject of men to authority contained something of the political in it, but is difficult to say just what the authority was or how primitive man viewed it."①

And then he says: "The authority of the tribe was impersonal in that its object was primarily defense and aggression; its leadership became impersonal in that the leader in war was required to gain success; it was impersonal in that religious and family authority tended to be excluded. The impersonal authority of the tribe did not grow out of the control of the family. The authority of the tribe is different in nature from the family authority, although even in modern times we find some relics of the patriarchal theory in the divine right of the kings, which taught that God had selected a particular family to rule over the state."②

It must be said that the tribe plays a very important role in primitive society and its relation to political origin, not necessarily to be the origin of the state, is a subject which we are here taking special interest. As we know, the ruling body of a tribe consists of the chief and the council of men of age or of prestige. Here we may say that there exists what may be called government. Yet it is to be noted that such a government is not necessarily to be essentially political. For instance, "the tribal council of the Dieri consisted of the heads of local divisions, the medicine men, the influential old men and the fighting men. From time to time, they met in council, the deliberations being held secret; in fact, whosoever was guilty of revealing to an outsider the subject of a council's deliberations, was doomed to die. The usual topics of discussion at councils were death by magic, other forms of murder, breaches of moral code, especially with reference to marriage regulations and the revealing of council secrets to women or the uninitiated"③.

Referring ⟨to⟩ the tribe, another writer has pointed out that "even in the case of superior races, in a primitive condition, it is often difficult to find anything that can be properly called government—except during the time of war. Thus Burckhart (note on the Bedouins, 1. pp.115–116) tells us that though 'every Arab has its chief sheikh, and every camp is headed by a sheikh or at least by an Arab of some consideration', still

---

① F. Wilson, *Elements of Modern Politics*, p. 80.
② *Ibid*.
③ A. A. Goldenweiser, *Early Civilization*, 1921, p. 274.

'the sheikh has no actual authority over individuals…his commands would be treated with contempt, but deference "may be" paid to his advice' " ①.

Results of recent investigations conform the statement mentioned above. "Among the Germanic tribes, the Galla, and Somali, this body (the council) composed of mostly assortment of freemen. Chieftainship is not purely hereditary. Among the Germans and the ancient Romans the leader was usually elected. Among the Rurdic-Tarars the bey was not a hereditary office. We have already noted that the Falla had a series of temporary chiefs for eight years each, but they were generally elected. The Somali and the Danakil have a hereditary chieftain, but he maybe set aside and a new one elected. Paulitschke was impressed by the utter lack of respect these two tribes showed their chiefs. Democratic customs prevailed among Arabs also, so that the leader's authority was practically restricted to the time of war. During peace time, however, the sheik of a camp of tribal division must use all the artifices of political popularity and intrigue to hold the tribe together, for each and every family group is at liberty to leave its own tribe and join another at any time. In this regard Wellhausen writes of Arabian sheiks, that their duties are considerable greater than their privileges and that they possess no means of coercion. Seldom does a chief make the final decision in any important matter, since the partriarchal heads of the families control tribe. Their control of the economic welfare of the tribe."②

It is obvious, then, that not only politically, the function of the tribe is very vague, but also militarily the leader's authority in a tribe is very much limited.

Nor is it entirely true that the authority of the tribe is impersonal, because in the tribe neither the religious and family authority is excluded, nor the military ability for defense or aggression is essential to a chief as already mentioned.

As a matter of fact, the insignificance of the tribe as a political group in the primitive society has already pointed out by Morgan in his *Ancient Society* about seventy years ago. As H. Lowie puts it, "According to Morgan's atomistic theory, primitive society differed fundamentally from civilized society in that it lacked *political* organization founded upon territorial contiguity. Primitive tribes, he contended, deal with an individual as a member of a sib, i. e. of kinship group, and accordingly through his personals; the civilized state deals with him through his territorial relations, as a member of a township, county or larger spatial unit. This political organization in the narrow sense is, according to Morgan, a relatively recent development at a very high

---

① Henry Sidgwick, *Elements of Politics*, p. 597, note.
② S. A. Sieber and F. H. Mueller, *The Social Life of Primitive Man*, 1941, pp. 295-296.

cultural level. He denies that it was achieved by the Aztec of Mexico and his follower Cunow denies its existence in ancient Peru. Primitive tribes might have combinations of sibs into major sibs, they might even organize confederacies of the Iroquois pattern, yet the duties of individual remained bound up with his kinship status. This was the original condition of ancient Greece, including Athens, until Cleisthenes about 509 B. C. divided Attica into a hundred demes or townships."①

What Morgan means by political organization in the narrow sense is what we understand as things political at the present day. Contrary to this is the political organization in the broad sense which is really meant that which is politically vague and that authority of the tribe is also personal, since it is still bound up with kinship, and not with territory.

Even taking for granted that such a bond is territorial, the political significance of the tribe is usually found during the time of war. "A Buin chief who erects a council-house and gathers about him the men of his settlement in a man's club, is in so far forth disrupting the ties of the family or sib, or rather is creating a new bond which by its very existence restricts the dominion of the kinship motive. The nature of that bond is territorial since it units men of the same locality and of different lineage; and it is invested with political significance as soon as the assemblage of fellow-villagers no longer contents itself with common festivities but undertakes joint expeditions against a neighboring encampment. As already hinted, it is not necessary that all inmates of the settlement should actively participate in the association."②

In speaking of the political function of the tribe, W. H. R. Rivers has made a very comprehensive study in his *Social Organization*. To make our point clearer, a few passages quoted from this well-known book are desirable.

"It is in connexion with the tribe that the subject of authority becomes of special importance, and takes a form which justifies us in speaking of government. In tribal societies we can discern, at first sight, three main varieties of government: one in which authority is vested in one or two persons, giving us the institution of chieftainship or kinship, single or dual, the powers of which may, or may not, be limited by some kind of council; a second, in which authority is vested in a council; and a third, in which authority is in the hands of a few, who may be either a body of hereditary nobility, or may attain their prominent position by age or wealth. When we learn to know these various forms of government in simple societies, we find, in many cases, a state of

---

① Robert Lowie, *Primitive Society*, 1921, p. 376.
② Lowie, *Primitive Society*, p. 380.

affairs in which such words as 'chief' and 'government' mean something very different from that which they ordinarily bear. It will be the principal task of this chapter to try to make clear the nature of the institution we call chieftainship in many human societies, and the nature of the process of government in the absence of any definite person in whom authority is vested."①

"As a characteristic example of the kind of institution which is found in many parts of the world, I may take the chieftainship of Eddystone Island in the Solomons, which I have already mentioned on several occasions. This island is the seat of an institution which, at first sight, seems to correspond closely with concept of chieftainship, and has, as a matter of fact, been thought so to correspond by the British protectorate of the islands. There are certain persons called *bangara* occupying a prominent position, which they transmit to their children, who are regarded with respect, if not even with reverence, by the society in general. In other words, the island appears at first sight to provide a characteristic example of hereditary chieftainship. On investigation, however, it was found that these so-called chiefs exerted none of the social functions which we ordinarily associate with chieftainship. It is question whether these 'chiefs' had anything to do with government in the sense in which we understand the term. They held no courts before which offenders were brought, nor had they any special position in connexion with the administration of justice. They had important functions in connexion with war, in that they had the chief voice in deciding when a head-hunting expedition should be organized, but they were not the leaders in the expedition, when it set out. Even if a *bangara* accompanied an expedition, he was not expected to be its leader. It was only in connexion with the more ceremonial or religious aspects of warfare that the 'chief' was important, and this gives the clue to his special position, for it was in the ordering of ceremonial, and in the arrangement or the feast which formed important features of this ceremonial, that he was especially prominent."②

"This aspect of a chief's function was well exemplified by the chief with whom we had most to do in Eddystone. Though his proper name was Rembo, we found that he was habitually called Kikere, or bad, and we were told that he was definitely regarded as a bad chief. We expected to hear tales of his injustice or cruelty, of his arbitrary ways of government or of the severity of the punishments he inflicted, but in place of these we heard only the complaint that he gave few feasts, and these lacking in quality. The social function which stood out prominently in the people's minds was the

---

① Rivers, *Social Organization*, pp. 160-161.
② *Ibid.*, pp. 161-162.

arrangement and provision of feasts. "①

"These features of Eddystone society may be summed up in the statement that its chieftainship was a religious rather than a political institution, and when we pass from Melanesia to Polynesia we find that the sacred character of the chief or kind is so pronounced that it seems to be impracticable for him to exert such of his functions as would bring him into contact with the common people, so that another kind of chief, especially associated with war, is associated with him, producing the dual chieftainship characteristic of many parts of Polynesia... A dual chieftainship similar to that of Polynesia occurs in some parts of New Guinea. Thus, among the Medeo people, each clan possesses two chiefs, the high chief and the war chief, while, among the Roro peoples, the high chief was associated with another, whose business it was to see that the orders of the high chief were obeyed. In these cases the functions of the high chief were mainly of a sacred kind. He could impose taboos, and was able to bring about peace in case of war, but entirely by religious or magico-religious means, such as the scattering of lime or the waving of a bough of a dracaena tree; while the ordering of feasts formed, as in Eddystone, an important part of his functions. "② Rivers also points out that "in North America, despite many superficial differences, the position of the chief appears not to have been very different from that of Melanesia. "③

Our author's conclusion is: "The general result of this survey is to show that, in many parts of the world, the institution called chieftainship or kingship is unaccompanied by the exertion of real authority or of political functions such as associate with government in our own country, at any rate, so far as the administration of justice is concerned. The divine right of kings, and the religious aspect of kingship, which long survived, if they do not still survive, in our own society, form the essence of the chieftainship of such regions as Melanesia and Polynesia, as well as of many parts of Africa and America. "④

The political significance of the tribe has been somewhat exaggerated. And the reason why it is so is explained by Rivers in the following words: "Before I leave the subject of chieftainship, I should like to point out that no other feature of simple society suffers such rapid modification under the external influence of the European, which is now permeating all parts of the world. The European official who visits a new region will

---

① Rivers, *Social Organization*, p. 162.
② *Ibid.*, pp. 162–163.
③ *Ibid.*, p. 164.
④ *Ibid.*, p. 165.

at once ask for the chief, by which he means a person with whom he can negotiate, and who will act as an intermediary between the people and himself. Sometimes the real chief steps forward, when he comes to wield powers of which till then he had not dreamed, so that the whole institution of chieftainship, as well as the mode of government, soon suffers great modification. In other cases, in response to the demand of the stranger, the place of the chief is taken by some other man, who is thus vested with an authority wholly foreign to the people. In Melanesia authority may thus fall into the hands of one whose position depends on his having paid a visit to Sydney, and his having acquired some pidgin-English, with the result that the representative of the British Government is one who has little prestige, and conducts, his business apart from those whom the people regard with reverence."①

If the observation of Rivers is correct, the real and original tribe, not being influenced by the European institutions or misinterpreted by the modern investigators, is chiefly a religious group, having little if any to do with political function, to say nothing of the state. This, to be sure, is not to deny that the germs of political functions are to be found in the tribe, since the chief and particularly the tribal council reveal some sort of political functions which we can hardly find in the family or in the clan. But this can only be said as the beginning of such functions and it seems that the role which it plays in the tribe is not important except during the time of war. Therefore, we can not say that a tribe is a political group, still less can it be called a state, because this latter is a modern association the development of which requires a higher level of culture. When ⟨there is⟩ a distinction between the state and the political organization or things political, it is easy to see that the origin of political organization or rather things political does not necessarily mean the origin of the state, since the state is not only the recent form, but also merely one form of political organizations or institutions.

We must also point out that the modern tribes in the primitive societies seldom develop into state or states. Even tribes which come together to form a league like the Iroquois in North America did not develop into a state. It is possible that some of the modern states did come from a tribe or many tribes, but it is open to question whether all states are originated in that way. Even it is true that all of the states did come from this way, still it is not true that all tribes have become or will become state or states. Consequently, the study of the tribe as a political subject can not be included under the name of the state.

---

① Rivers, *Social Organization*, p. 165.

The same may be said of a league of tribes which, though very significant in political aspect, is not a state. For this reason we can not agree with the Aristotelian logic that the state, evolving from the family, tribe and other organizations, is a natural growth; that the family, tribe and other organizations are merely preparatory stages for the ultimate completion of the state; and that, consequently, the latter is to embrace and absorb all of the former and becomes the organic whole for the realization of the highest good.

Thus if there are social organizations such as family, clan or tribe which have existed and are still existing without becoming a state, the Aristotelian reasoning that these organizations exist merely for the sake of the state just as hands and legs exist for the sake of a man and that the state is prior to the family, clan and tribe and the like is not sound at all. For historical as well as our modern knowledges show that on the one hand a clan or a tribe can exist without becoming state and on the other the state has become and is tending to become more and more a group which is not self-sufficient. Hence it can hardly be regarded as an organization, as Aristotle thinks, not only to live, but to live well.

The reason is simple. As conditions changed the state becomes either too big or too small. One can not live well in a social group which is too big; nor can one live well in one which is too small. Aristotle would never dream of a closely correlated world like ours and it would be hard for us even to subsist were we living in a small city as pictured by him.

Instead of saying the state is prior to the family, clan or tribe, we maintain that the latter are prior to the former. While the tribe may be considered as the beginning, though it must be said that this is very vague, of the political functions, the so-called primitive societies in general have very little to do with political functions. "Thus it is justifiable to speak of the primitive state as a society," says Edward Jenks, after a general survey of the primitive societies, "for it was simply a band of warriors under a military leader."[①] We should add that the so-called primitive state is a misuse of the term "state". Although it is true as Jenks says that the so-called primitive state is justified to call society, it is open to question whether such a society is "simply a band of warriors under a military leader", because, as already pointed out, the tribe is chiefly a religious group and not necessarily to be a military band.

One can call the tribal council together with its chief as a government, but

---

① Edwards Jenks, *The State and the Nation*, p. 133.

government, it is to be borne in mind, is not necessarily to be political, nor it must mean the government of the state. R. M. MacIver is right when he says: "It might be generally stated, without exaggeration, that the activities of early government are scarcely political at all."[①] He says again: "The display of leadership and the exercise of authority is found wherever society exists. It gives form and character to an urchin club as well as to a cabinet committee; to a gang of thieves as well as to a convocation of clerics. But no one would call such leadership and authority 'political', and neither should we say that wherever we find a 'head' in a savage tribe we are in the presence of the state."[②]

To quote again: "The ancient rule of retaliation—'an eye for an eye', 'a tooth for a tooth'—obviously goes back to the prepolitical stage. It was the injured man or his group that found satisfaction in that primitive revenge, and we must in fact remember that 'revenge' is a personal and not a political category. 'The avenger of blood himself shall slay the murderer: when he meeteth him, he shall slay him.' (Num. XXXV, 19) It is above all the kinsman's duty sanctioned by custom and often enforced by the dreadful shapes of expiatory divinities. Orest must avenge on his own mother his father's death. Vengeance belongs to the kin, not to the state. Its mode is often prescribed in most meticulous form. The curious rigour of this barbaric logic is seen in such a case as the following. 'A boy who had climbed a tree happened to fall down right on the head of his little comrade standing below. The comrade died immediately; and the unlucky climber was in consequence sentenced to be killed in the same way as he killed the other boy, that is, the dead boy's brother should climb the tree in his turn, and tumble down on the other's head till he killed him.' In other cases revenge is modified into the milder expiation of fine, embodying the idea of 'damages' later translated, for an entirely different type of offence, into a principle of the 'civil' code. Thus it is still characteristic of Chinese society that an appeal to the family of the offender is made for compensation. But in such cases the relation of the state to the act is not yet envisaged."[③]

We must conclude now that in the primitive society, be it modern or ancient, there is no state. If there is anything which is political in its character, it is closely mixed up with other social functions and it seems that it exists only after the tribe comes into being. If we think how widespread this primitive society prevails in our own day and how long it occupies our history before the existence of the state, we cannot help feeling that

---

① Seer, *The Modern State*, p. 41.
② MacIver, *The Modern State*, pp. 41–42.
③ *Ibid.*, pp. 42–43.

the state to which we are accustomed was and is unknown to millions and millions of our ancestors and our contemporaries.

But the essential point that we want to make clear is what is political is not necessarily to be state, though the state is always a political organization. You may find political functions in the tribe, but you cannot find a state there. You may find political functions in a league of tribes, but even here you cannot find a state. Thus things political, besides having existed long before the state, is much larger in scope than the state. This point is important to the so-called political scientist, because without making such a distinction, we are easily led to think where things political begin, there we have the state, or in other words wherever things political present, there we see the state. We seem to forget that there were people and there are people who live without the state or even political organizations. We seem to forget that there were and are people who might live within some sort of political control without living in a state. Again, we seem to forget that the state is only a momentary or temporary phenomenon, which important as it was and still is was and is not known to many people.

Thus the primitive people do not make use of the state; they really don't know of the state. Yet we can not say that there is nothing political in the primitive society, though its significance is not clear to us.

It is to be noted that while the fruitful results of the recent researches in the different fields of social studies have convinced some writers to realize the fact that primitive people can live without state or political organization and that there is a distinction between state and things political, there are also many writers who have overemphasized the political significance of the primitive society talked of primitive state, thinking that the primitive people also live in state as we live in our own. It must be said that both of these people are wrong. A clear understanding of the political significance in the primitive society is the vital clue for the understanding of the subject-matter of the so-called political science.

Yet it is regretful that the materials which have been presented ⟨by⟩ the social investigators, especially the anthropologists, have not been adequately utilized by the students of political studies, for they are still deeply imbued with the terms and concepts of the traditional writers.

I have confined myself so far to the world of primitive people in order to show that there is no state in the primitive society; that even political functions are not clearly defined in such society although it cannot be denied that things political are present in the tribe; and consequently that things political are not only different from the state but also prior to and larger in scope than the latter. If we take a brief survey of human history from the ancient period to the time of Reformation, the same conclusion may be reached in regard to the point that we have just considered.

W. J. Perry, in his various writings, [1] contends that the state originated only once in the history and according to him it [was] happened in predynastic Egypt. His main thesis is that agriculture was invented and developed by the Egyptians of the Nile Valley before about 5000 B. C. The agriculture of Egypt was closely related to irrigation, because of the flood of Nile.

The first kingship was established in the predynastic Egypt, when the public magician was able to use his magical power to control irrigation in order to develop irrigated agriculture. Thus agriculture was first initiated by the Egyptians and it was from Egypt that agriculture was gradually diffused, first to the neighboring people and then to the furthest corner of the earth.

Just as agriculture was spreaded out from Egypt, the state was also diffused from this place to different parts of the world. In short, it was the Egyptians who invented the state, other people merely followed them to develop their states.

The underlying theory of Perry for maintaining that the state was originated in predynastic Egypt was cultural diffusionism. He holds that Egypt was the cradle of world culture. Culture, as he sees it, can be originated but once. He repudiates the theory of independent creation in different places of the world by different people and argues that all the cultures of the world may be directly or indirectly traced back to the ancient Egypt. State, as he views it, is one aspect of human culture and cannot be exceptional to this rule. Moreover, the origin of the state was very closely related to the growth of agriculture and other aspects of the Egyptian culture and therefore it must find its origin in that region.

Without questioning whether there was any state in predynastic time in Egypt or even much later period, the general thesis of Perry's cultural diffusion has not yet been adequately proved. Although the old theory of independent creation of culture as advanced by Herbert Spencer and others have been somewhat discredited, the arguments of the diffusionists can hardly be accepted without reservation. Unless we are assured that God selected Egypt as the original center for human culture, or unless we are convinced that the Egyptians were born to be superior biologically and mentally, so that they could invent the different or fundamental aspects of culture, what the Egyptians

---

[1] See W. J. Perry, *The Origin and Growth of Civilization*, 1925; *The Children of the Sun*, 1923.

could do could also be done or created by other people.

Even at the present day, with the wonderful means and facilities of communication to bring all the people of the world so closely united together, invention of one thing or another has been claimed by many inventors. It is possible for one thing to be invented only once, but equally it is possible that may be invented more than once at the same or different times. It is true that agriculture developed very early in history of Egypt, but this does not warrant us to conclude that they Egyptians were the sole inventors of agriculture. If political talent, if there is such a thing, is to be counted for political achievement, the Egyptians are by no means specially gifted in this respect.

The so-called kingship in the predynastic Egypt was nothing more than, or as a matter of fact, something less than, the chieftainship of a tribe in the primitive society. It was deeply coloured with religion, magic or if you like superstition. We even doubt whether it had any political significance and it would go too far to assume that there was state present in such a period. We may venture to say that even in much later period or up to the recent time whether Egypt could be called a state in the strict sense of the term is still open to question. It was, in many respects, predominantly a religious entity rather than a political group. It was ruled by priests rather than by king. Therefore to maintain that the predynastic Egypt had already formed a state is to talk of a state which is entirely different from what we understand as state. It is to be added, however, that to deny that there was any state at that time does not mean that there was no political significance whatsoever at the same time.

China, as it is generally recognized, attained a high political system long before the occidental world, but here nowhere could one find a state in the strict sense of the word. Even during the time of the so-called Warring States between about 400 B. C. and 200 B. C., there were no states in existence. There were what is known as seven feudal lords or dukedoms fighting against each other for power. Five of them in succession became the leaders of these dukedoms, each leading for a time, though the importance and time of the role played by each of them are different. Some were very powerful and some weak; some occupied the leading position much longer than the others; but none of them succeeded in unifying the whole empire until the rising power of the Tsin dynasty. It was true that the dukedoms during these periods were more or less independent from each [each] other, but it was also true that the imperial house of Chou dynasty was still regarded as the legitimate authority. The slogan used by the powerful dukes to assume their leading roles conformed to the statement made above; for they all proclaimed that they assumed the leading position in order, in the first place, to show loyalty and respect to the emperor and in the second place to defend against the aggressiveness of the so-called barbarian countries outside of the Middle Kingdom. So we find that even the most powerful feudal lords never dared to declare themselves emperors, in spite of the fact that the imperial house of Chou Dynasty was so that it could be easily overthrown by any one of these powerful lords. Indeed the latter might utilize the name of the imperial house for their own selfish purposes, but legally speaking, they did not proclaim themselves as independent entities.

Thus the conception of the universal empire was deeply rooted in the Chinese minds and this has remained until the modern period when the door of China was knocked by the western powers. It is safe to say that a system of states, equal in name and before law if not in power or size was practically strange to the Chinese before the contact of the China and the west. The Chinese besides thinking in term of universalism looked down the other nations as inferior to their own. "It is better for China to have no ruler than the barbarian countries to have a king or a chief." So declared Confucius, the sage of China. It was hard, then, for Chinese to conceive that there would be a country equal to China. China was the universal empire and so she should be in that way even though in time of chaos she might break into pieces. For the chaos, to the Chinese, were not only temporary but also merely the exceptions to the general rule and at most the preparatory stage through which the normal condition was attained. The normal condition was the universal empire which included the soil of the world and the people of the four corner of the earth. She was considered to be situated in the center of the universe and named as the Middle Empire. When M. Ricci came to China and presented the map of the world to the Chinese, he had to put China in the center of world in order to fit the Chinese traditional conception so that no contempt of the position occupied by China would be shown and so that no feeling of antagonism against the Jesuits would be resulted.

The foundation of the Chinese fabric was considered to be the family the final and natural development of which was the universal empire. If there was anything that might be called state or somewhat like the state, it would be nothing more than an enlargement of the family or an undeveloped and premature miniature of the empire. The modern concept of state based on the theory of equality of a group of political entities was absent in the Chinese ideology. There were provinces and districts or other subdivisions of imperial administration, but they were not states. When one dynasty changed into another, there might be, as already hinted, some war lords equal in power for a time, but they would not give up fighting until the whole empire was unified by the strongest, because in the Chinese conception, nothing should stand between the universal empire and the family.

So neither theory nor fact could demonstrate to us that there was a state or many states in the history of China. On the contrary, the whole political history of China was a history of the universal empire which was founded on the family. The difference between the family and the empire was not on the principle upon which they were regulated, but rather on the extent in which they were controlled. The empire was larger in extent than the family, but the principle which managed the family might also be applied for the administration of the empire.

Here we see again, there was a political entity or organization, but there was no state. In a sense, the universal empire may not be regarded as a purely political organization, because, being an enlargement of the family, it was regarded as a big family.

Nor do we find any state in the Babylon world. While the Chinese were controlling and thinking of universal empire, the Babylonians were living in the city. "Nineveh, Babylon," says Francis Lieber, "were mighty cities that swayed over vast dominions as mistresses, but did not form part of a common state in the modern term."①

With the Greeks of the ancient time, we find only the small and self-sufficient cities. It is true that the *Republic* and the *Politic* of Aristotle are still studied in our universities and that there are some political problems which, being fundamental to the Greek cities, are also important in our days; but we should not be misled to conclude that the Greek cities are states. The Greeks did not develop a system of states either from the international or national standpoint. There were, of course, many inter-cities relationships, but such relationships were religious rather than political in their characters. We shall show in our later discussion that Greek life is still predominantly religious and that Greek cities were originated by religious motives rather than by political interests. But looking from the political aspect, the Greek city is by no means equivalent to our state. Nor is it similar to our city. The Greek city, occupying a small area of territory and composing of a small number of population, is very much like a village of our own. This is the background of the ideal world of both of Plato and Aristotle, for according to them, an ideal political unit is that which surrounded by a city wall and composed of a few thousand population can be seen from the tower of the city. If Plato be considered as the father of systematic political philosophy and Aristotle the father of the so-called political science, they would be more properly called fathers,

---

① Francis Lieber, *On Civil Liberty and Self-Government*, pp. 48–49.

respectively, of the philosophy and "science" of municipal government.

It can not be denied that both Plato's *Republic* and Aristotle's *Politics* are two of the most important political treatises in the history of political literature, but at the same time we should not forget that their achievements and ideas were the products of the very few of the Greek people in the time of the past. The general public of the ancient Greece were far below the intellectual level of these chosen few and what was thought by the latter might not and could not represent what was thought by the former.

Moreover, that which were presented in the *Republic* or the *Politics* were what both Plato and Aristotle thought to be what ought to be rather than what they were. Although both these works reflected more or less the actual conditions of the Greek cities, to read these works alone does not give us the real and complete picture of the Greek life, political or otherwise.

While the Greek city can not be regarded as state, it has nevertheless, political significance which is much clearer and more important than that in a tribe or any other groups in the primitive society. Here, again, we see that which is political is not necessarily to be a state, although, may we repeat again, that which is state is always political.

With the Romans, and this is also true in many respects with the Greeks, the starting point of their political organization has been considered as the family. Families, it was viewed, were combined into a tribe and in turn tribes were formed into city or republic. The Roman city or republic has been regarded by some written as state, but this is undoubtedly wrong. For, in the first place, neither the city nor the republic had the essential characteristics required in order to become a state in our sense, and secondly, the so-called city or republic was a transitional stage in the Roman political development. As soon as the republic or city came into existence, the empire was making its head way from the gradual extension of territories by means of conquering one city after another. Rome, for instance, according to Francois Pierre Guillaume Guizot, the well known French historian, "in its origin was a mere municipality, a corporation". "The Roman government", so the learned writer adds, "was nothing more than an assemblage of institutions suitable to a population enclosed within the walls of a city; that is to say, they were *municipal* institution: —this was their distinctive character."

"This was not peculiar to Rome." Guizot continues, "If we look, in this period, at the part of Italy which surrounded Rome, we find nothing but cities. What were then called nations were nothing more than confederation of cities. The Latin nation was a confederation of Latin cities. If we follow her history, we shall find that she conquered or founded a host of cities. It was with cities she fought, it was with cities she treated, it was cities she sent colonies. In short, the history of the conquest of the world by Rome is the history of the conquest and foundation of a vast number of cities."①

The Roman Empire is thus "a vast number of cities". And if Polybius' *History of Rome* be regarded as a treatise on the so-called political science, it is rather a treatise on an empire or the cities than on the state, because Polybius himself stated clearly that the purpose of writing the history was to explain the greatness of Rome, to trace the steps by which she became the ruling power in the world, and to describe the manner in which control over her vast dominions was exercised. Cicero, instead of using the word state, named his work *De Republica*. And by republic according to him, "est respublica res populi; populus autem non omnis hominum coetus, quoquo modo congregatus, sed coetus multitudinis iuris consensu et communione utilitatis sociatus."② The so-called common sense of right and a community of interest cannot be regarded as the characteristics of the state; it may be applied to any kind of social organizations formed for iruis consensu et communione utilitatis.

It is clear, then, that to the Romans, there were either cities or empire. Looking from standpoint of city the political organizations of the Romans is like that of the Greeks; and looking from the standpoint of the empire, the political institutions of the Romans is like that of the Chinese. To think of the state in the Roman period is to misunderstand the political conditions of that period.

Still less can we find such thing as the state in the Middle Ages. The empire or, to speak correctly, the temporal world was not a state. Much less so was the church. It has been often said that the mediaeval age is non-political. This is, of course, not true. Yet equally it would be wrong to assure that there were states during this period. Politics was deeply coloured with religion and it has been declared that it was a branch of theology.

It can not be questioned that there many political groups in the mediaeval age, ranking from the local unit up to the imperial house. Lords, dukes, barons, princes, kings and emperor were all there, but there was no state or even something like the state.

"In the Middle Ages, the omnipotent internal state, treated as a person and the co-equal of other states, was non-existent. It might be a dream, or even a prophecy, it was nowhere a fact. What we call state was a loosely compacted union with rights of property and sovereignty everywhere shading into one another and the central power struggling for

---

① Guizot, *The History of Civilization*, Vol. I, Lecture II.
② Cicero, *De Republica*, Vol. I, 25.

existence."① So writes Figgis. Then he goes on to tell us: "Neither Normandy nor Burgundy, neither the dominions of Henry the Lion nor those of a Duke of Aquilaine, formed a state in the modern sense. Yet how far can their rulers be regarded as in any real sense subjects?"② "Yet even granting the king of France or Germany was a true sovereign in his temporal dominions, the power of the church and the orders was a vast inroad on governmental authority. It is to be noted that Suarez and others developed a doctrine of extra-territoriality out of the rights preserved by the universities and monastic orders of the church."③

Now it is obvious that while there was no state during the period under consideration, there was by no means a lack of political institutions and ideas. If this were not the case, there would be no such conflict as that between the king and the pope, and neither the drama of Canossa nor the tragedy of Avignon would have been performed. A group of political entities equal both in name and before law was unknown to the medievalists. Their political system was hierarchical originating from the will of God down to the individuals. You can hardly call it *a* state, for besides itself, there was no other state. Nor can you call it the state because to do so you would identify it with the temporal world in opposition to the spiritual world both of which are created by God to govern both the soul and the body of human being.

Indeed, the church, for a time, seemed to symbolize the universalism of the Middle Ages; but while in practice it did exercise a lot of powers which were supposed to be the powers of the temporal heads, in theory it was not denied that things belonging to Peter should give to Peter and that things belonging to Caeser should give to Caeser. As a result, the conflict between the spiritual world and the temporal one did not end until both were broken into pieces.

We can not leave the Middle Ages without giving a little attention to the feudal system. But here again it is not a state. "The feudal system," says Lieber, "is justly called a mere system; it was not state."④ It can not be doubted that there was some political significance in this system; but to what extent it was coloured with things political is still open to question. Edwards Jenks suggests that this system is something between a patriarchal and a political system. Thus he says: "Feudalism represents a compromise between purely patriarchal and purely political society. It is the result of a

---

① John N. Figgis, *Studies of Political Thought from Gerson to Grotius*, second edition, 1931, p. 13.
② *Ibid.*
③ Figgis, *From Gerson to Grotius*, p. 14.
④ Francis Lieber, *On Civil Liberty and Self-Government*, p. 49.

conflict between the principles of the two systems, in which neither is completely victorious, and historically speaking, it bridges the gulf between the two systems."① But he also remarks: "Nevertheless, the usefulness of feudalism has narrow limit; and it is difficult, if not impossible, for real political progress to be made while feudal ideas hold sway."②③

While admitting the political significance of the feudal system, our author is also conscious of its limitation in this respect. His last statement indicates that the modern state or what he calls the real political progress has not much to do with feudalism. It had its usefulness in political development, but it was a negative rather than a positive force for that purpose. On the contrary, were it not destroyed, it would be a hindrance to the development of the state. Here we see not only the distinction between what is political and what is state, but also the conflict of the two concepts.

---

① Jenks, *The State and the Nation*, pp. 135–136.
② *Ibid.*, p. 150.
③ Giovauni Boteri, "Della Ragione di Stato", *Milano*, 1596.

Chapter 6
Origin of the State

We have already shown, in the previous chapter, that although there are things political in the primitive society and there were political organizations or institutions in the ancient world and in the mediaeval age, there is no state in such society and there was no state during or before the mediaeval age. When did the state, then, come into existence? It may be asked. The state, we may say, came into being only after the Refomation. In other words it merged only with the dawn of modern period. It is a modem institution and it is a modern invention.

While, for a time, the state claimed to include almost every aspect of political and even social life, it has never become as such in fact. It has been and is, as a matter of fact, only one of the many political organizations or institutions viewed either from national or international standpoint. It has, as already hinted, either too big or too small and can hardly fulfill the mission or purpose which it has ostensibly claimed.

Thus, there are many political organizations or institutions which can fulfill the political needs and interests of human being much better than the state can do and the development of which has tended to minimize the importance of the latter and has compelled us to change our concept of the state and to reconstruct the field of the so-called political science. Let us consider this point a little more fully in order to understand the true subject-matter of the so-called political science or as we prefer to call it as politology.

We say that the state is a modern institution. This can be proved not only from the fact and the concept of the state but also from the name of the state.

We know very well that the Greek word "polis" means really city and different radically from the word "state".① Moreover, the word "polis", as used by the Greek philosophers and statesmen, was confined mainly to the Greek city and they were not willing to apply to the world outside of their own, since the foreign country was considered as the world of barbarism.②

The state, etymologically speaking, is derived from Latin, and, therefore, it is taken for granted by some writers that the state in its technical sense, that is, politically speaking, may be found during the Roman world of the past. Obviously this is wrong. The Romans did not use the word state to denote a political organization as we have used it. They spoke of "Status nostras civitatis", but the word "status" signifies simply state or condition in its general application, without referring to any political significance. The word "civitatis" has been, of course, frequently used by political writers in political sense, but its real and original meaning, however, is simply to denote a city somewhat in the same sense as the Greeks used the word "Polis", a place where a civic community dwelt, or a body of men politcally united in a community. Speaking of the Roman terminology in connection to our discussion, Jellinek says: "Der Staat is die civitas, die Gemeinde der Vollbuerger oder die res publica, das dey Volksgemeinde Gemeinsame, dem greichischen Ausdruck emtsprechend. Italien und die Provinzen sind zunaechst nur Bundesgenossen und abhaengige Landschaften der einen Stadt. Volles Buergerrecht wird nur dem in der Stadtgemeinde Aufgenommenen zu teil, der civis Romanus is und bleibt roemischer Stadtbuerger."③

Still less is the word "natio" to denote any political sense. "It rather referred those bodies of men," to quote from Woolsey, "who were brought together by birth and other co-operating causes. Cicero speaks of the nation of the Greeks who never had political nationality, and it is not, I believe, used of Rome in the early writers."④

We have already stated that in the middle ages there was no state. Nor do we find the word "state" used in political sense at that time. "In the strict sense or the term," says Figgis, "there is no sovereign in the Middle Ages; only as we find even a little later

---

① So Jellinek writes: "Den Griechen hiess der Staat, war daher ihentisch mit der Stadt, – einer der Hauptgruedne, weshalb die griechische Staatswissenschaft sich auf dem Boden des Stadtstaates bewegte, den Land- order Flaechenstaat jedoch niemals zu erfassen vermochte. Wird von solchen Staaten gesgrochen so werden sie nur als Inbegriff der Bewohner bezeichnet, irgend eine Bezeichnung jedoch, welche die Beziehung der Bewohner zum Territorium zun Ausdruck breachte, hat niemals groessere Bedeutung gewinnen koennen." Georg Jellinek, "Das Recht Des Modern" en Staates, Erster Band, *Allgemeine Staatslehre*, third edition, p. 123.
② See Aristotle's remark in his *Politics*, Book Ⅲ, on the meaning of the word Polis, B. Jowett's translation.
③ Jellinek, *Allgemeine Staatslehre*, p. 124.
④ Theodore D. Woolsey, *Political Science or the State*, 1877, Vol. Ⅰ, p. 140.

in France, there is an etat which belongs to the king; but there is also an etat de la Republique, while even a lawyer in the Paris Parlement has his etat. Only very gradually does state come to mean the organization of the nation and nothing else. The change is probably due to the influence of Italian life and Machiavelli its exponent."[1]

It must be added that although the word "state" was first used by the Italians in the later part of the middle ages and by Machiavelli at the beginning of the sixteenth century in its political sense, neither the writers before Machiavelli nor Machlavelli himself used the word in the sense that we employ it. Machiavelli spoke of "stati" in the first sentence of the first chapter of his well known trestise *The Prince* written in 1513 and published about twenty years later. The word "stati" is a plural form and its singular form is "stato". While Michiavelli identified the term with the word "prince" and also with the term "dominion", other writers used it in somewhat a vague way. It should be also pointed out that the word was not very common even in Italy until the later part of sixteenth century.

Thanks are due particularly to Botero who popularized the term in his work entitled *Le Ragione di Stato* which was published 1583. While the Italian writers deserved the honour of being the first to give to the world the word "state" in its modern sense, Italy, as a state in our sense, was not actualized, as already hinted in our previous discussion, until very much later, for neither in the day of Machiavelli nor at the time Botero was there any state existing in Italy. The political entities existing at that time properly were cities rather than states.

In France, as Figgis remarks, the etat belonged not only to the king but also to the lawyer in the Paris Parlement at the later part of the middle ages. In the fifteenth century, there was also etat de Paris (1413). So there was etat provincianx in France. Even when J. Bodin published his momumental work, *Les six livres de la republique* (1577), the term etat was not in current use. Bodin himself used the word etat occasionally in his writings, but in most cases he employed it in the sense of constitution or class. Instead of employing the word etat, he used the term republique for the title of his. It was possible that he might have l'etat de la republique in his mind, but this was not clearly expressed. There is only one place where we find that Bodin employed the term etat somewhat similar to our sense[2]; but here again it should be regarded as an exceptional case.

Montaigne has been supposed to be the first who used the word in the modern

---

[1] John N, Figgis, *Studies of Political Though from Gerson to Grotius*, p. 10.
[2] Bodin, Les six livres de la republique, (ed. 1580), Book I, Chapter 8, p. 99.

sense, but in his own time, officially it was still used in a very narrow sense. The French knew more, for instance, the "conseil d'etet" than the state in its abstract or general sense as they understand it now. Even in the seventeenth century, L'état wes identified with the roi. "It was no metaphor", says James Brown Scott, "when Louis XIV identified himself with the state, for the state was his; he was in fact its sovereign, and his will was undoubted law."① The same writer remarks that "not long ago state and estate were in fact concertible terms, both forming the domain of the king, princeling, or potentate who governed or misgoverned one or the other, according to the bent of his mind or the extent of his ability or incapacity. Too often he ruined his state, as he squandered his estate, and though less of the former than he did of the latter."②

In Germany, the word "Staat" or "Stat" was used in the seventeenth century, but here again it was not meant in the sense as we know it. C. E. Loehneys, for instance, employed the word in a book entitled *Hof-Staats und Regierungskunst* (1622), but as Edgar Loening pointed out the word Staat can not be found in any place except for the title.③ V. L. von Sechendorff used the term as early as 1655 in his *Fuerstenstaat* and used it frequently, but in 1685 in the preface to his *Christenstaat*, he declared that he felt sich to employ the word. However, he continued to use it mainly in the sense of condition or class (Stand). He remarked, in one place, that he did not like the word Stand, because it indicated more a personal relation or nature rather than political significance.

J. E. Kessler was supposed to be the first in Germany to employ the term in the sense somewhat similar to the word stato used by the Italians, but the time was still too earlier for adopting it in the general vocabulary. It was the beginning of the eighteenth century that we find the term "Staatsrecht" was adobpted instead of "publicum". And this we find in writers like Zschakwits whose work was entiled *Einleitung zu dem Teutschen iure publico oder Staatsrecht* published in 1711. It is to be noted, however, that officially the word staat scarcely occurred in any document in the eighteenth century.

It may be safe to say that the term Staat has attracted every little attention among the German speaking people. To denote the federal or the confederate body, the term Reich was usually adopted, and to signify the individual parts which composed the

---

① Scott, *Sovereign States and Suits*, 1925, p. 6.
② *Ibid.*, Jellinek remarks that Loyseau used the word Etat in the same sense as Machiavelli.
③ Loening, "Der Staat", in *Handwoerter buch des taatswissenschaften*, Zweite Auflage, Sechster Band, S. 908.

union, the word Land is preferable. Even at the National Assembly of 1919 the word Staat, although suggested by some framers of the constitution, was objected by the majority on the ground that, in the first place, it can not indicate the true meaning of the word Reich or Land, and in the second place, it is not familiar to the German usage.①

The word "state" in English is undoubtedly originated from the word "estate". In 1399 Thirning, J., told Richard Ⅱ that he was deposed and deprived of the "Astate of Kyng", and of all the lorship, dignity, worship and administration belonging thereto.② The phrase "prerogative or estate royal" was also used very often. Fortescue, in his *Governance of England*, spoke of the "estate of the king". He wrote: "Though the king's estate be the highest estate temporall in the erthe, yet it is an office in which he mynestrith to his resume defence and justice."③

One recent writer summarizes the conception of the estate of king in the fifteenth century in the following passage: "The estate of king, in the fifteenth century, was thus conceived to be inseparable from the king's own person. To him belonged lordship and power, rule and empire, and all the honour and highness on that estate; the divine facour on him was displayed by marvellous healing powers; to him were given will, liberty, and grace, that the laws might be upheld and the peace maintained. The king was indispensable; but the rules by which he succeeded to his estate were not precise. In so far as the kingdom was real property, it seemed that he inherited it in much the

---

① "In Deutschland schwankt die Bedeutung von status lange Zeit. And fang des 17. Jahrhunderts ist zuerst vom status reipublicae die Rede, der abgkuert als der ganze "status" im Gegensatz zum Hof, Kriegs-, Kammerstaat den gesammten Zustand der allgemeinen Angelegenheiten des Landes bezeichnet. Spaeterhin wird auch wohl vom status pyblicus gesprochen. Lange aber ist die Terminologie noch sehr unsicher und es wird mit demselben Wort der Hof oder die Kammer des Fuersten bezeichnet. Erst im Laufe des 18. Jahrhunderts knosolidirt sich, wohl unter dem Einfluss der Staatswissenschaftlichen Literatur, der Ausdruck in der weise, dass er ohne jeden Beisatz das gesammte politische Gemeinwesen bezeichnet. Erst in den letzten Decennie des 18. Jahrhunderts ist dieser Process beendigt, ensprechend der im allgemeinen Bewusst sein sich vollziehenden Umwandlung der Territorien in Staaten. Noch aber haftet dem Worte Staat ein Dopelsinn an, dessen. Staat heisst naemlich auch Provinz oder Landschaft mit besonderer Ver fassung. In diesem Sinne wird officiell von den koeniglich preu ssischen Staaten gesprochen, als Laendern eines Fuersten, der zugleich Koenig von Preussen war. Noch heute werden die preussichen Gesetze in der 'Gesetz-Sammlung fuer die Koeniglichen preussischen Staaten' verkuendigt."

Ebenso aber ist in Oesterreich in dem Patent vom 11. August 180 durch welches Franz Ⅱ. den Titel eines erblichen oesterreichis chen Kaisers annimmt, von dem "unzertrennlichen Besitz Unserer unabhaengigen Koenigreiche und Staaten, so wie von". Unserer unabhaengigen Koenigreche und Staaten die Rede, was in der heutigen officiellen Sprache nichts Anderes als "Koenig reiche und Laender 'bedeutet', wie klar aus der weiteren Bezeichi ung der damals noch im Verbands des Deutschen Reiches stehenden deutschen Erblands als 'Erb-Staaten' hervorgeht. Es ist."

② See S. B. Chrimes, *English Constitutional Ideas in the Fifteenth Century*, p.3.

③ Fortescue, *The Governance of England*, chapter Ⅷ.

same that the land was commonly inherited; in as much as the kingship was an office, he was called to occupy it by divine vocation, and God might make his choice known through the voice of the nobles and estates."①

Edwards Jenks, in a recent book, remarks that "at any rate, from the early years of the sixteenth century, the word 'estate', being familiar to the English public as denoting a particular interest, or class of interest, in land, began to be specially associated with cermonies and symbols of the King's court. Perhaps to distinguish it from the legal interests in land just alluded to, the initial letter was dropped and the word 'state' took its place"②. Jenks also points out that "by the end of the sixteenth century, there appears the Queen's Principal Secretary of State (or estate) and, though the Commonwealth Constitution of 1653, rejected the royalist associations of the term 'privy Council', it did not hesitate to set up a 'council of state'".③

It seems clear that although the word state was used by many writers, its meaning for indicating things political was still vague, because it was mixed up with estate the meaning of which is mainly confined to property and land. And it may be added that there was state of the town and state of the city as well as state of the king. The New English Dictionary cites two examples from writings of the sixteenth century. "Every of the statte of this town, when they are warnid to come to the courte housse, shall sit every man according his degre and callinge." (1516). And in 1575, we find that "they have commytted agaynst Mr. mayor and the state of thys cytie."

Even in the seventeenth century, it can hardly be said that it was popularized. Thomas Hobbes, for instance, told us that Augustu Caesar changed the state into a monarchy.④ The so-called state as used by Hobbes here is opposite to monarchy and may be regarded as identical to republic. This practice has been followed until very much later.

It may be also remarked that both Hobees and Locke in the seventeenth century were not familiar with the word state in the sense that we use. They speak, to be sure, of the state of nature; but this state is not meant the state political. On the contrary, it is an anthesis to that. Terms such as society, civil society, political society, body politic and government and commonwealth were used very frequently by Locke and other writers. But seldom, do we find the word state in the political sense. Edwards Jenks

---

① Chrimes, *English Constitutional Ideas in the Fifteenth Century*, p. 61.
② Jenks, *The Ship of State: The Essential of Political Science*, 1939, p. 12.
③ *Ibid.*
④ Hobbes, *Leivathan*, Ⅳ, ⅩⅣ 365.

tells us that "indeed, the word state gained at the expense of what looked, at one time, to be a formidable rival, viz. The 'commonwealth', which at the restoration of the monarch in 1660, became suspect for its Puritan flovour, and has only within the present century regained something of its former popularity as a democratic description of the British empire."[1] And he adds: "But it was not until the ministers of the crown, in the debates which ensued on the introduction of the official Secret Act of 1889, had succeeded in dissipating the suspicion that, in seeking to protect the interests of the state, they were really seeking to protest their own interests, that the word state may be regarded as having received its official batism in England."[2]

It is true that the word commonwealth has regained its popularity in recent years in the English speaking people. Lord Bryce called his fomous book *The American Commonwealth* published more than fifty years ago. In England, people use this word to denote the whole empire while the word dominion is used to indicat certain parts of British Empire such as Canada, Australia, and South African Union. And this is clearly expressed by the Imperial Conference of 1926 which declares: "They (the dominions) are autonomous communities within the British Empire, equal in status, in no way subordinated one to another in any respect of their allegiance to the Crown, and freely associated as members of the British Commonwealth of Nations."

But it is to be pointed out that it was not enitrely true that the word state has become officially baptized and gained its popularity in the United Kingdom, for officially the British people have not used the word so frequent as other terms such as Empire, commonwealth, kingdom, dominion and colony.

It seems that only some of the so-called political scientists and possibly also some of the social scientists within the last hundred years have adopted the word state in the sense that we use it. Austin still spoke of political society. Herbert Spencer in his early writings was fond of using the word government and so this was true to John S. Mill. Only in the later part of the nineteenth century, the word was used frequently in poiltical treatise. Spencer named his book *The Man versus the State*. Political scientists, regarding the state as the subject-matter of the political science has done more to popularize the word; yet it has not been and is not generally employed by the general public.

In the United States the word state was used in the Declaration of Independence. However, most of the writers and documents adopted the term to indicate mainly the

---

[1] Jenks, *The Ship of State: The Essential of Political Science*, 1939, p. 13.
[2] Ibid.

individual states or the colonies which composed the United States. Adam spoke of the "royal authority in the state of Massachusetts", ① and Hamilton mentioned "a treaty—between the Court of France and the States of America". ② "The practice in our country of using the word states both of the United States and of esch state," says Woolsey, "creates a poiltical difficulty which cannot be removed but by some term for the Union in general, such, for instance, as Nation, Republic, or Commonwealth. The want of a term to distinguish the Union as being in reality a state in the unitary sense, is an evil that goes beyond the mere use of words; it confuses or colors thoughts. Thus we often have to say 'the general government,' as if it were the United States; thus exalting the organ, the administration, or the law-making and executive powers above their true place; and, on the other hand, giving the impression that there is no state, besides those states which composed the Union. This, and the word sovereignty, as an attribute of both, have been the means of no small amount of evil."③

Yet this is not all. Washington, for instance, wrote in 1796 "From the office of state you will receive every thing that relate to business."④ The word state used here is referred to the secretary of State. The secretary of state, as we know well, is in fact the minister of foreign affairs in other countries. In the United States it is only one department of the executive department. It is, it may be said, the secretary of the president.

But in spite of the difficulty as pointed by Woolsey, Woolsey himself was, I believe, the first writer who attempted to employ the term state. His two volumiuous work of *Political Science* published in 1887 had as its substitle *The State*. The reason for his adoption of this word is expressed in the following passage: "State has this advantage over other words that have been used in English to denote a political union, that it is more comprehensive. Thus we cannot speak of a political union embracing several natlonalities, and call it a nation, for it is not one; there being no tie of birth or common descent to bind it together, and perhaps no common language. Hence, the kingdom of the Netherlands, as constituted by the treaties of 1814–1815, was a state, but not a nation, since the inhabitants differed territorially in religion, language (speaking Dutch, Flemish, and French), and past history… . The characteristic which attaches to the nation is a sense of union springing out of inner causes, while a state need imply nothing

---

① Adam, in *Farmer Letters*, 1776.
② *Works*, 1886, Vol. Ⅶ, p. 487.
③ Woolsey, *Political Science or the State*, 1877, Vol. , p. 141.
④ *Washington Letters*, 1892, Vol. ⅩⅢ, p. 213.

more than an external connection… . On the other hand, two nations may subsist, speaking the same language and having the same institutions, but there is a want of one binding force, of a common government or constitution ot being them together. Still further, there are forms of political life where neither nation nor state can be said to be found, save in a very rudimentary form. Such were the parts of Europe, particularly France, after the feudal system came in. The feudal barony was not a state nor a nation; the general country under the suzerain could be called in some sort a state, although quite an imperfect one, but not a nation in any true sense. The United States are a state, and are a nation also; yet the essential character of the union of states under different laws and constitutions is such that the separation of the parts is absolutely vital, and the name of nation is not a sage one to us. On the whole, state is the only scientific term proper for a treatise on politics."[1]

The word state as proposed by Woolsey has been used and popularized by Burgess and many others. Burgess identifies the word state with the word sovereignty. W. W. Willoughby develops the idea of state in his *The Nature of State* and W. W. Wilson names his book *The State*. All these appeared at the end of the nineteenth century. Many other American writers follow then in our own century and state has been regarded as the subject-matter of political science.

Yet it must be also said that terms such as nation, republic and commonwealth have been also widely used. Mulford named his book *The Nation* in 1872 and he preferred this word instead of the word state. In our common vocabulary, we speak more of the nation than the state. So we have the League of Nations instead of the League of States. This is not only true in English but also true in French. The German calls it as the Voelkerbund which really means the league or union of people, although it would be more appropriate to call it the Staatenbund.

So the term republic is also often employed. Brownson entitled his work as *American Republic* in 1866. There are many other writers prefer to use the word republic, for example, the South American Republics or the Republic of China although the term here used indicates also the form of the government which is different from the monarchy.

The term commonwealth seems to be even more popularized in recent years. We have already pointed out that James Bryce, for instance, used the word for his well known book, *The American Commonwealth*, although it is to be added that English writers have been very familiar with this term. Besides the Commonwealth of Crowell,

---

[1] Theodore D. Woolsey, *Political Science* or *the State*, 1877, Vol. I, pp. 141-142.

many English writers used it. Locke, in his *Two Treatises on ⟨Civil⟩ Govermment* speaks of the forms of a commonwealth.① But he says: "By commonwealth I must be understood all along to mean not a democracy, or any form of government, but any independent community which the Latins signified by the word *civitas*, to which the word which best answers in our language is 'commonwealth' and most properly expresses such a society of men which 'community' does not (for there may be subordinate communities in a government), and 'city' much less. And therefore, to avoid ambiguity, I crave to leave to use the word 'commonwealth' in that sense, in which sense I find the word used by King James himself, which I think to be its genuine signification, which, if anybody dislike, I consent with him to change it for a better."② Recent English writers incline more to use this word than any other word for indicating the whole empire as we have already stated above.

So Arthur N. Holcombe, in "an introduction to the study of th science of government", prefers, to put the title of his work like this: *The Foundations of the Modern Commonwealth*, 1923. And it may be well said that the term Commonwealth seems to be always preferable when one comes to the real nature and the relation of the political institutions of the United States. The fact is that the word state has by usuage monopolized the separate and individual parts of the Republic, and there is as yet a common name which can be used to indicate the united whole of the same. The word state in the phrase of "The United States" is undoubtedly used to mean the state of New York or Illinois, not the united whole. It is more proper, to say that "The United States of America *are*..." than to say "The United States *is*....", if we are going to follow the common usuage. But technically speaking, the United States of America are, as a matter of fact or as a matter of law—particularly in the sense of international law—*a state*, and consequently it seems to be equally proper to call the united whole a state, and a state it *is*. Yet the dilemma remains: The Americans may be either regarded as grammatically wrong in using the word *is* for the plural noun or they have misused one thing for another.

We may also remark that in our common vocabulary, the word country is more frequently used than the word state. I used to say that China is my country instead of my state. When you ask an American that for whom he is fighting in the Pacific, he will answer that he is fighting for his country, instead of saying that he is fighting for his state.

---

① Locke, *Two Treatises on Civil Government*, Bk. II, chapter X.
② *Ibid.*

It is clear, then, that the word state was not used before or during the mediaeval age, and that although it has been used by some of the political writers in modern period, it has not become a common vocabulary even in our own day.

What is true with term is also true with the theory and the fact concerning the state. The theory of the state, even admitting that it has been advanced by writers such as Machiavelli, Bodin, Hobees and many others, is still a modern theory. We have shown that the mediavalists did not have a theory of the state, although they had theories concerning other forms of political organization or institutions and their relations to the church.

The state has come into existence with the tide of nationalism. But nationalism is itself mainly a product of religious conflict and racial difference. We all know the Reformation was a religious movement, aiming at reforming the Roman Catholic church. But the protest against the universal church for its curruptions and absolutism was utilized by the the princes and kings who represented more or less the nationalist sentiment of each nation. Protestants thus became pro-nationalism. As a result, the national church came into being. And the separation of the national church from the Roman Catholic church means also the separation of the national entities from the universal empire. It started with a religious movement, but it ended with nationalistic movement, a movement which leads to the development of the modern state system. While the protestant countries declared definitely their independence from the church at Rome, the Catholic nations tried to dominate the latter for their self-interests. Religiously speaking, there the countries in Europe were divided into protestanism and catholicism; but politically speaking, all the countries became nationalistic. Thus both France and Spain, though still recognizing the pope as the head of the Roman Catholic church, were no less nationalistic than England or some of the German states.

It was the downfall of the Roman Catholic church, then, made it possible for the rise and the development of the system of modern states. But the rise and the development of the system of the modern states did not make the states absolutely independent from one another. On the contrary, the growth and increase of international relations made the states dependent on one another. The process of such interdependence develops as the means of communication becomes easier and easier. It is evident now that no state can keep a close door policy so that there will be no dealings with other states. There were states trying to maintain such a policy. China tried it once and again. But in spite of the fact that she was economically self-sufficient and geographically far away from the occidental world, she had to open her door in order to deal with the other nations; but once the door was open, it was open for ever, for, it is impossible for her to close the door again.

The growth of interdependence of the nations of the world has compelled and is still forcing the states of the world, not only to have international dealings, but also to set up numerous international organizations and institutions, politica or otherwise.

It is to be noted at the outset that international relations go far beyond and deep beneath their public character. The field which characterizes as conflicts of law or private international law embraces almost the whole range of human activities. A marriage between citizens of one country and of another, a law suit between two or more persons of two or more nationalities, the sending of a relgious mission from one state to another, the selling of commercial goods from one nation to another, the travelling of a person crossing the border of one sovereign power to another and many other business which an ordinary person would think as private affairs are as a matter of fact international dealings.

It is true that common citizens would never or seldom ask the question how a watch in his pocket or how a piece of goods in his room has come from a country which he knows nothing about. It is also true that common people would never or seldom ask the question how a letter that he drops in the letter box in China would get through many countries and reach [to] their friends abroad. Yet all these are internationally very significant.

Take another example for illustration. It is, perhaps, easy for one to make love with a girl or a man who is a citizen of another state. But when one comes to the question of marriage, many questions are likely to be involved. One has to know whether the girl would lose her citizenship of her own country immediately after the marriage or not and how long it takes her to acquire her citizenship of her husband's country. If the marriage takes place at the girl's country and if she would lose her citizenship as soon as the the ceremony of the marriage is over and at the same time if she can not obtain the citizenship of the country of her husband unless she lives in the latter's homeland for certain period or unless she has to wait for certain time in order to get it, a lot of difficulties will be involved in such case. When one asks why it is so complicated in such a private affair as marriage, it is because of international marriage. It involves a dealing between two states and such a dealing involves many questions that would not occur to a man and a girl who are citizens of the same state.

Because many problems are international in character, therefore, they are more complicated than many of the so-called national questions. A Chinese who lives in the border close to Indo-China knows well that it takes more time and more difficulties for a letter to get through to his friend in Sinkiang than to send one to his friend in Hanoi, yet he has to pay more stamps for the latter than the former. Why it is so. Because it is international in character, so he has to pay more.

While nations can not live without having intercourse with one another, some sort of international organizations or institutions have come into existence.

The regular channels through which the international affairs are conducted are the diplomatic agencies. These include the embassies and consulates. These may be regarded as the earliest and most regular means for dealing or settling international affairs. Unless countries are at war, diplomatic relations are to be maintained. One country sends diplomatic envoys to another and even a country which for some reasons do not have diplomatic representatives in a certain country will be represented by a third state.

But the increase of international relationship requires state to have many other international organizations for the execution of international business. Here belongs a wide range of so-called international administrative bureaus or functionaries. The Central Rhine Commission of 1804, the Danube Commission of 1856, the Telegraphic Bureau of 1868 and the Postal bureau of 1875 may be cited as those for dealing with questions of international communications. Then there international commissions dealing with commercial and financial problems such as the Bureau for the Publication of Customs Tariffs. In connection to international bodies dealing with the questions of health and morals, we have many examples such as the Sanitary Council of Constantinople of 1838, the Penitentiary Commission of 1880. In respect to international organizations dealing with educational or scientific research, the Committee for the Exploration of the Sea of 1899, the International Institute of Seismology of 1903 and the Pan-American Scientific Commission of 1907 may be cited as examples.

These are only some of the earlier international administrative bureaus. The last few decades have added many to our list and the tendency has been and is to have more and more of these kinds of bureaus or commissions. While in the past many of these bodies are created for collecting data for distributing to members, recent tendency has been and is to fix rules for the members or even to carry out these rules in the actual affairs of the world. Thus gradually, these bureaus have become not only an informative or advisory bodies, but also an executive bodies in international business.

The calling of the Hague Conference in 1899 demostrated to the world that many international questions can be discussed and possibly settlled by gathering the representatives of different nations together and having face-to-face talks instead of sending their envoys from one capital to another in order to deal something which concerns not only two or three nations but most or all of the states of the world. The relative success of the first Hague Conference anticipated the second Hague Conference in 1907. Moreover, the Hague Conferences were by no means temporary international conferences. The establishment of the Court of Arbitration for settling international disputes, for example, has pointed toward the organization of international justice. The Permanent Court of International Justice created after the First World War might be regarded as having its origin in the Court of Arbitration.

There have many international conferences held since the Hague Conferences. These are well-known to the general public of the world. According to statistical reports, there has been almost a thousand private international organizations existing in our own day. A reflection of the development of these organizations shows that the nations and their citizens are drawing more and more closely together. It has been pointed out that between 1840 to 1849, there were ten meetings of private international organizations. The next decade increased eight and between 1860 to 1869, there were sixty-four of these meetings. The two decades following 1870 increased to 272 and the last ten years of nineteenth century had 475. From 1900 to 1910, there were 985 meetings of this kind, more than twice as many as the decade before. The five years after 1910 still had 458. Although the period during the First World War made a setback, there have been more international gatherings, private or otherwise, after the war.

If we think of the many international conferences held during the time of this World War, we can easily imagine that the number of such meetings will undoubtedly increase after the defeat of both Germany and Japan.

While international relations seldom cut off except during the time of war under the system of modern states, the arising and paticularly the ending of the war usually intensifies the human desire for peace. Such a desire for peace urges men to think more of international security. The so-called peace conferences were, as a matter of fact, the results of the war. While peace has been concluded by belligerents, the tendency has been to include also states which have not been at war. The peace conference at Westphalia in 1648, at Vienna in 1815, at Paris in 1856, in 1919, and at San Francisco in 1945 are only some of the conspicuous examples.

Why even a peace conference after the war has included states other than the belligerents? The reason is obvious. Because of the close relationship of the nations to one another, a war between two or three states always affects those who are not at war.

It is hard, if not impossible, for any nation nowadays to stand aloof without being entirely affected, if any two countries are at war. Moreover, one war at one place or at one time may also bring another war at another place or at another time. We may say that the the present European war is closely linked with the last European war as well as the war between China and Japan. The Germans never forgot their defeat in 1918; but the Japanese occupation of Manchuria in 1931 without being checked by the powers who pledged to garantee the territorial integrity of China certainly inspired the ruthless actions of Fascist and Nazi in North Africa and in Europe. Had Japan been checked in 1931, the Aixes in Europe might not dare to challenge the world at large. When things went from bad to worse and to worst, even the United States was drawn into war. One may say that the United States fights against Japan, because Japan declared war against her. But why should the United States fight against Germany and Italy and even send more men and more materials to the European theater of war? It is not purely because Japan is allied with Germany and Italy; rather it is because the war of the west and of the east are one. To defeat one would lead to defeat the other; for the menace of Germany is no less than that of Japan to the United States, although the latter was not hitted by Germany at the beginning.

Thus the interests of the nations of the world are interwoven in time of war as well as in time of peace. The world, we may say, has become one. It is because many nations would not recognize this fact that many troubles have been resulted. Yet history shows that after each catastrophe, an advanced step has been taken in order to find a better means for international security. This has been the general trend of our history. The more men have suffered from the war of the past, the more men have been looking to the peace of the future.

The development of the means of communication and the invention of the new techniques have brought the world into close contact. About a hundred years ago, it took a Chinese student almost five months to come from China to the United States. In 1944, one can travel the same distance by airplane, if without stop, in two and half days. The speed of flying is going to be quicker and faster and the distance will mean less and less. In terms of technology, modern technology, the world of our day is much shorter in distance than a courtry, a small country if you like, [in] fifty years ago.

The closer the contact of the nations, the more will they deal with one another. Consequently there will be more international organizations which are necessary and essential to the existence of the states. As a result, the state can neither be regarded as the largest political organization nor be considered as an inclusive political entity which can exist or live by itslf.

The state is not a political entity which can live alone, because modern economic and other relationship has made the states dependent on one another. Even countries such as the United State and Russia possessing rich and various resources can not boast that they can exist without the other states. If a state is predominantly agricultural, she needs to import many industrial goods from other countries. If she is predominantly industrial, she need to find markets in other countrtes in order to sell her goods and at the same time to import raw materials outside of her own boundaries. Seldom do we find a state self-sufficient in her economic and other aspects of life.

Even a state is self-sufficient, she still can not live at peace unless the world at large is at peace. For as we have already pointed out [that], she may be invaded or involved if there are other countries fighting with each other. The isolation of the American Continent seems to be free from being attacked or affected by war, but the experience of the last and this world war has made it clear that no country is absolutely independent.

As a matter of fact, every kind of international relations is a limitation upon the independence and therefore the so-called sovereignty of the state. An independent and sovereign state as conceived by Hobees and his followers does not exist in our present world. It was a myth even during the time of Hobbes.

Nor the state is the largest political organization which includes all other political organizations or institutions. Every international organization or institution transcends the boundarie of a state, and ⟨is⟩ therefore, in a sense, larger in scope than the latter. It is true that no all the international organizations or institutions are political in character; yet there have been and are many international political organizations and institutions. It is not a place here to enumerate all these organizations and institutions, but it is desirable to mention a few of them in order to illustrate our point.

The most striking example for our consideration was the League of Nations established after the First World War. It was undoubtedly a political organization. Some writers maintained that it was a state while others even considered it as a "super-state". The League, it was argued, had a seat or capital. It had its own buildings and grounds over which it had the authority of absolute control. When it was brought into existence in January, 1920, it had a membership of eighteen states and other political entities. In 1934 its membership consisted of 59 states, including all the the so-called independent states of the world with the exception of Afghanistan, Arabia, Brazil, Costa Rica, Egypt and the United States. Although the League of Nations had no direct control over the citizens of the member states, it could control them by indirect means, that is through the member states and many of the commissions which were working in one way or another in direct contact with the people in different parts of the world.

Moreover, the League of Nations had a government consisting of departments just as the government of any state. The council of the League was regarded as an executive body. This body consisted of one delegate from each of the member states entitled to be represented in the council. These include six permanent members. Then there were ten more members elected annually by the assembly from among the other members of the League. The Council was presided over by a President who was chosen in alphabetical rotation from among the delegates of the members represented in the council when the latter met. This is undoubtedly something like the federal council of Switzerland.

There was a permenent Secretariat and many affiliated organizations serving as the administrative agency of the League. The head of the Secretariat was the Secretary-General assisted by two Deputy Secretaries-General and three Under Secretaries-General each with assistants, secretaries. The Secretariat was divided into twelve sections under the following designations: Political Information; Legal; Economic Relations; Financial; Communications and Transit; Minorities Questions and Opium; Health; International Cooperation.

The representative body of the League was the Assembly which consisted of not more than three representatives of each member state, who, however, cast only one vote for each member state. This might be regarded as a legislative body. Like the legislative body of a state, this body was subdivided into six standing committees and also several special committees, dealing with such questions as constitutional and legal, technical organizations; armaments; budget and financial; humanitarian and general problems; and political problems.

There was also a Permanent Court of International Justice. This might be regarded as the judicial department of the League. It was composed of fifteen judges elected, as it was understood regardless of nationality for a term of nine years by the Council and the Assembly of the League of Nations. Those who were chosen were chiefly jurists rather than diplomatic people. They were supposed to represent the major legal systems of the world. There was a president and a vice president for the Court. The Court was also subdivided into three special chambers, dealing with the following questions: summary procedure, labor and transit and communications. As we know that there were many cases presented to the court either for decision or for advisory opinions since its creation. On the whole it might be said that the decisions and the opinions rendered by the court were well observed.

The League was connected with many other international organizations such as the International Labor Organization. It is also argued by some that it had sovereignty over, for instance, the Saae basin and the territories under mandate; it had the power of intervention for the protection of minorities in certain states and it had the power of a protectorate over the free city of Danzig.

Moreover, it was pointed out that it had the right of legation. Some states had sent permanent quasi-diplomatic envoys to the League and the latter did send temporary missions to other states. The representatives sent to or by the League were entitled to diplomatic privileges and immunities as stated by Article 7 of the covenant of the League when they were engaged on the business of the League. Furthermore, it had, as pointed out by some, the power of declaring war and concluding peace.

The League of Nations was thus regarded by some as a state or the super-state. It must be said that although the League had many of the essential characteristics of a state, it seems to be clear that it was not *a* state in the sense as its member-states. Nor can it be called the *super*-state, because it had not the coersive to force an issue within its member states. It might be called the state of states; but this is also not satisfactory, because that would make the league as nothing more than a state, assuming that it stood on the same footing as its member states. Of course one might call it as a confederation of the states; but it must be borne in mind that a confederation is not a state, as it is evidenced by the fact there have been in the past many confederacies which have not been regarded as states.

As a matter of fact, if the League becomes a state or the state or the super-state, then, the character of its member states [and] would be affected or even destroyed, since a state as conceived by the traditional writers is a sovereign body both internally and externally. If the League is state, the member states composing it would become states within state. This, according to the traditional theory, is absurd. In other words it is illogical to have a state consists of many states. States there can and must be when they are equal in status and at the same time not to live within or under other state or states.

If the League of Nations can not be regarded as state, it is, nevertheless, a political organization, an organization which is much larger in scope than a state or any state of the world, though not necessarily superior in power to these states.

I have taken the League of Nations as an example for illustration. In fact, there have been and are many political organizations and institutions which transcend the boundaries of one or many states and which can not be regarded as states. The mandatory system, the international administrative areas in connection to the League of Nations, the confederacies, the alliances and many international administrative bureaus or commissions which are politically significant are all not states. Yet politically speaking, their importance can not be overlooked. While the number of these political bodies are increasing in the course of time, particularly as the means of communication become easier and easier, their influences are not merely on the external life of the states; for they go deeply into the daily and inner life of the people of every state. In fact, these international political organizations and institutions become parts of the life of the people of different states.

It may be argued that the so-called international political organizations or institutions are nothing more than the creatures of state or states and therefore may be considered as merely parts of the states. This, however, is not true. Even take for granted that they are created by the states, they are not parts of any state or of all the states that create them; because they are exterior if not superior to any or all of the states. Take the League of Nations, for example. Although it was created by some states, the state or states which created it or which joined it after its creation were left free to leave the League by notification. There were some states withdrawn from the League; but the withdrawal of one or a few states from it, did not mean the dissolution of the League. The League remained while its members might join or get out. If all the members withdrew from the League, then there would be no League. So long ⟨as⟩ the League remained, the League did not live on one or a few of the states. W. Wilson was really the creator ⟨of⟩ the League of Nations, but in spite of the fact that the United States never did become a member of it, it was created and it did exist for a long time—until the Second World War broke out. We may think that the Second World War killed the League; but is it not true that either the League of Nations will continue to function or another League of Nations will be created? Is it not true that the statesmen and representatives of the nations of ⟨the⟩ world who met in Dambarton Oak or in San Francisco were laboring for a world organization? We may say then: The League is dead and long live the League.

The League, it has to be borne in mind, is only one, though it may be the largest international organization of the world. Even the San Francisco failed to create a league or to use the form league, some sort of international organizations need to be organized; for the nations of the world are so closely related to each other that to exist without having some sort of international cooperation becomes almost impossible. So no matter what name it takes or how is it to be organized, the nations at our day can not go on without some sort of international organizations or institutions.

It is true that had such a league been proposed a hundred years ago, or fifty years ago or even before 1914, possibly no nation would like to create one; but the world of 1919 was so different from the world before 1914 and much more so before 1900, or before 1850, just as if the worlds before and after the Reformation were different from each other. Before the Reformation there was no such thing as the system of modern states, while after this, there came the states as the result of the change of conditions. So the conditions before and after 1914 were different. And the same may be said of the conditions before and after 1945. If the League of Nations created in 1920 did not fulfill its mission as we are now expecting, it only means that it was not strong enough to prevent the nations from fighting with each other and consequently that we need more a league, a league that is strong enough and competent enough, to deal with international conflicts. Unless this [will be] ⟨is⟩ done, we will face another catastrophe which, mostly likely, will be much worse than what have experienced in this war, and which no sensible human being would like to see it again.

This being the case, we can see clearly that there will be not only one international political organization or institution, but many of them and that these organizations or institutions will become even more important than those we have had in the past or we are having at present and that the states would not, as they used to be, the largest political organizations nor would they be still so powerful and important as they were in the past.

From what we have considered, we may conclude that the state is only one of the many political organizations and that to understand the state does not mean to understand things political; for as we have already stated again and again that the state is different from things political.

Thus from the necessity of modern political organization, the state is not large enough to deal with current political problems—problems interwoven with many other aspects of human life as well as many states. Just as modern men can not confine their political activities within a tribe, so we can no longer close the door of our state and live politically within the boundaries of one state.

As a matter of fact, it is evident that even to confine our political activities to an isolated continent such as the New World is not enough. Those who elaborate what is known as Pan-Americanism know it well that Pan-Americanism can not be divorced from the universalism of the twentieth century.

If it is true that the state is not large enough for conducting our political activities, equally is it true that it is not small enough for the realization of our political interests. Here we come to another point which is very striking in the field of the so-called political science; i. e., the realization of the importance of the so-called local political organizations within a state.

According to the traditional theory of the political science the so-called political organizations such as the county, commune, province, canton or city are nothing more than the creatures of the state. This is not true. We have already shown that the city existed long before the state came into being. There were cities in Babylon world, in Greek period, in Roman Empire and in the Mediaeval age.

The importance of modern city can hardly be doubted. Cities like New York, London, Paris or Berlin, not only have more population but also richer than many of the states. Nor should their positions in their respective countries be overlooked. When a revolution starts in Paris, the whole France will be affected. History shows many cases like this. So the occupation of Paris symbolized the downfall of France. If we think that in many countries more than half of their people live in the cities, we can see easily that the dominance of the urban life in the national life. Even where cities are few and rural population are overwhelmingly large, cities still play the leading role in politics. As a matter of fact civilization means almost urbanization.

The movement of local autonomy for the last few decades only shows the realization of the real importance of the local political organizations. The chief principle of democracy is to be ruled from the bottom to the top rather than from the top to the bottom. The representatives of the people who are entrusted to make laws and to formulate national policy are elected from the local districts.

Yet this is not all. It is the small local political unit which is close to the daily life of the people and it is here that democracy is at work or experimented. As a resident of my district or county, I know more the political activities and organizations of the county than I understand what is going on in the capital of my state, for here is the place where I vote for not only the men to whom I trust any daily political affairs, but also the men who take charge of the national affairs at large. I shall feel much happier to see my old friend Mr. Smith who used to sit with me at a table in the tea house opposite to my own house get elected as member of the local council than to hear Mr. Jones who has been elected as a member of the senate in Washington, unless Mr. Jones is also one of my friends who, like Mr. Smith, used to sit with me in the same tea house. But even here there is a difference, because as soon as Mr. Jones has been elected as senator, the social distance between him and myself will become wider and my interest in relation to him is likely less than to Mr. Smith. Of course, I am supposing here that my occupation is so established that I am more or less to be a permanent resident of the same locality; and this, as I am sure is generally true of most people.

I am thus born a man with trusts or distrusts, likes or dislikes, more interested that which I am personally taking part in or have directly experienced than in that which I know or experience very little of. Therefore for a simple, practical, common, and self-content person as I am, what I care most is the nearest to me.

If I am a man of high ideal and ambition, and of good ability and character, and am wishing to care for something and somebody outside of the circle within which I am closely related to or know personally well, I shall not be satisfied to care for only the circle which is so artificially, so unnaturally organized as the state like ours at the present day. To be a traveller, I like to see the world at large, and not merely my own country or much less for that. To be an ambitious man in intellectual investigation I am not satisfied with reading my national language; I like to understand as many kinds of languages as possible. And to be a true pacifist, I seek to secure the peace and welfare of the whole of mankind. "As a pacifist, you are traitor." So a group of Nazi students accused a very well known professor when he spoke pacifism in a meeting that the writer happened to attend in Germany before Hitler came to power. "By reasonable, Gentlemen! I love my own fatherland no less, or even more, than you do, but you must think and think thoroughly that Germany is not the only state in the world nor can she stand alone if she is left to be alone." The answer of the professor did not calm the mob-like excitement, but the truth stated remains eternal. And when we see the death of Hitler and the collapse of Germany with our own eyes, we have to deny that the state is all mighty.

Now if the facts did tend to show, and theories asserted that the world was consisting of numerous states each of which, internally, possesses an absolute authority over all the subjects and things and externally is independent of all limitations and restrictions, then facts and theories can also demonstrate to us that a state like is not very easy to be found in the modern world.

"It is perhaps not an untrue saying," so remarks Mrs. Ernest Barker, "that the state has generally been discredited in England… A sovereign and majestic state, a single and undivided imperium, lifted above the conflicts of society, neutral mediatory, imperial such as Hegel conceived and such as German theorists still postulate—this we have not known. Our state is on its executive side a bundle of officials, individually responsible for nothing and serves chiefly as a bracket to unite an indefinite series of 1-

1-1-1-1. Our state on its legislative side, as Hegel told us a hundred years ago, is no pure state, emancipated from society; it is trammelled in the bonds of buergerliche Gesellschaft; and our legislative, composed of members of this society, 'sacrifices objective freedom or rational right to mere formal freedom and particular private interests'. With a bracket-enclosed bundle of officials, and a socially trammelled legislatiure, we can not have a state, a German will say; or if we have a state, it can only be discredited."①

But here we have learned something only within a circle. Going beyond the boundary lines of England, we find the situation is still complicated. Shall we call the British Empire a state in the sense of Hobbes? Certainly it is not, for we have learned from the Imperial Conference of 1926, as already remarked, that all the parts composing the whole are "equal in status, in no way subordinated one to another in any respect of their domestic or external affairs." Shall Canada be considered as a state? From the Crown's standpoint, it may be doubtful, yet from the eyes of international law, since the last war and particularly after this war, there is no question of her statehood. Yet she is one member of the British Empire.

Not only is the Empire internally not a state, but to take the empire as united whole in its external relations, it is not a state in the sense of Hobbes. For as we have already shown that the empire taken as a whole is so bound up with the international treaties concluded, the international conventions held between herself and the other powers that she can hardly act as she wishes, and consequently the so-called absolute independence from the external limitations is merely a phantom.

What is true to the British Empire is, to a large extent, true to the United States. And in France, long ago Rehm in his *Geschicht der staatsrechtswissenschaft* (1896) has shown well that if the French monarchs did fulfill the will of Bodin, they did that much later than the days of Bodin, and indeed only momentarily. In our time, Leon Duguit tells us that the French Comme is a very obvious example of a local and decentralized group holding real rights of sovereign character: it has a police power, it can levy taxes, it has the privilege of eminent domain. This according to Duguit is just contrary to the conception of a unified and indivisible national, personally-exercised sovereign power of the state. ②

---

① Barker, "The Discredited State", in *Political Quarterly*, 1915, p. 101.
② Barker, "The Discredited State", in *Political Quarterly*, 1915, p. 101.

What shall we say about Germany? Here is the home of Hegel who spoke of England as no pure state. Undoubtedly both William Ⅱ and Hitler have tried to make Germany a pure state, or to use a modern term, a totalitarian state. But as already said Germany under William Ⅱ was something less than a federation, though more than a confederation. It may be argued that Prussia was a state, but as a constituent part of the German Reich, she could not be regarded as a state, at least from the standpoint of international law. When Hitler tried to purify Germany in order to make her a state in the sense of Hegel, Germany was destined to be what she is now, being devided into different parts and occupied by the four powers: Great Britain, The United States, Russia and France. It is true that for time that it seemed that Germany was going to be a Hegelian or Treitschkean state, but the price that the German people are now paying or going to pay is too big for the dream of the Fuehrer.

It may be added that in order to get rid of Hitler's totalitarian state, the so-called democratic countries, in order to mobilize for war, have been also in their highest watermark in term of state. State seems to be everything and individual is nothing. Yet, as we have already shown, history tends toward international organizations rather than nationalistic aggression and toward international cooperation rather than national or regional isolation. And after each catastrophe, a further step has been usually taken in order to work for international peace.

From what has been considered, it may be safe to say that the state as clearly expressed by the Philosopher Hobbes or his followers is very incomplete and imperfect in practice and that if there has been any state like this, though we seldom have seen one it is, nevertheless, momentary even in the modern period. Having clarified this, we shall be easily in the position to understand that the result of taking the state as the subject-matter of the so-called political science would lead us, as a matter of course, either to leave or to neglect the largest part of political phenomena from the earliest period down to the present day a blank and to confuse a city or a church for a state, or to ignore the rapid growth of the importance of modern local political as well as the international political organizations and institutions.

It is to be repeated that the reasoning so advanced is by no means to minimize the importance of the state. The state occupies an important and indeed very important chapter in our politology, for, besides being momentary in our history, though that which is political may not be the state the state is always political. But once admitting that it is momentary and once the differentiation is so drawn, the importance of the political organizations and institutions other than the state can not be overlooked. And consequently the need for the reconstruction of the so-called political science which has long made the state as its subject-matter is obviously evident.

In Chapter IV of his *The Modern State in Relation to Society and the Individual*, Paul Leroy Beaulieu speaks of three errors on the subject of the state and the individual: "It is not true that the state is to the social body what the brain is to the human body not is it true that the individual and the state are the only two forces in the field, since society produces with a marvellous fertitlity and an infinite number of free intermediate associations; it is not true that the individual obeys one sole motive of action, namely, pecuniary interest; there is in him another tendency which urges him, outside of all considerations of material interest, to occupy himself with collective needs and with the sufferings of others." (English Trans. by A. C. Morant, p. 62)

It is the second that we give special attention. With this the author writes: "Another error, quite as wide-spread and quite as pernicious as the last, consists in confusing the state with the society. There are some philosophers who have been guilty of this mistake, and the common herd have followed suit. Yet the two terms are far from being synonymous.

"The common practice is to contrast the state with the individual as if there were no intermediate organization between these two forces. Certain theorists would lead us to suppose that we have on the one hand 40 or 50 millions of isolated individuals, scattered and having no bond of union among themselves, incapable of spontaneous combination, of voluntary concerted action, of free co-operation in pursuit of ends which are beyond their individual reach; and on the other hand, confronting this shifting waste of sand, we have the state, the only force which can group together all these thinking molecules and give them cohesion amongst themselves. Humanity is, therefore, required to choose between the intrusion of the state into every branch of economic life, and the simple instinctive movement, the so-called incoherent efforts of 40 or 50 millions of men; each one acting for himself, without concert or mutual understanding, without knowledge or concern of one another.

"Nothing can be more false than this conception. The whole of history contradicts it, and the present even more than the past. We must not confuse the free regions of the surrounding social medium, the society with its spontaneous movement, ever creating new combinations with an inexhaustible fertility; we must not, I say, confuse this with that apparatus of force and coercion which is called the state.

"Society and the state are two different things. We have not only in society the state on the one side, and the individual on the other: it is puerile to set the action of the former against the sole action of the latter. To begin with, there is the family, which is the first group, having marked characteristics of its own and an existence whose limits transcend those of the individual.

"We find, besides this, an unlimited number of other groupings some stable, others variable, some formed by nature or custom, others by an established concert, others again the result of chance encounters. The laws of combination in accordance with which human beings unite, become associated together, then subsequently separate and become isolated, are at least as numerous and as complicated as those which chemistry is able to prove and to catalogue among purely material molecules. " (p. 51)

"Side by side with the political organization of collective forces, proceeding by way of injunction and restraint, that is, the state, there arise on all sides other spontaneous forms of collective force, each created with a view to a precise and definite end, and acting with various degrees of energy, sometimes very intense, but altogether without coercion. There are the various associations which answer to some sentiment or interest, some requirement, or some illusion, the religious and philantlropic societies, civil, commercial, and financial companies. They simply swarm: the crop is inexhaustible. " (pp. 52-53)

"Man is a being with a natural taste for association, not association of the fixed, immovable, rigid sort imposed from without, and embracing his whole existence, like the instinctive assiaciations of bees, ants, and beavers, but association of a flexible and variable kind, and in every possible form. This natural taste has been still further developed in man by education and experience. Most of the ancient associations—for instance the church, continue to exist, and as each day sees the creation of new ones, the number will end by defying all calculation. " (p. 52)

"You speak of the isolated individual! But where do you find such a thing as an isolated individual? I find groupings of every order and kind, associated persons and associated capitals: I see 300 millions of persons united into a single church, altogether without reference to any State: in money matters altogether apart from the national budget I see free societies by thousand controlling hundreds of thousands of pounds sterling: I see them by the hundred controlling hundreds of millions. I examine what we are all agreed in calling the great achievements of contemporary civilization: and I find that three-fourths, if not nine-tenths of them have been effected by these various collective energies wielding no coercive force of any kind. " (pp. 52-53)

"Suppose that I who write these lines, and you who read them were to reckon up— if that be possible—the number of groupings of which we form a part, and of societies to which we belong either with our hearts or our minds, on our bodies, and of those to which we periodically give some portion of our time, or of our means: or let us count if we can the number of men to whom by virtue of some special link of free association we can give the name of comrade or of colleague." (pp. 53-54)

"We shall then begin to realize how the life of each one of us is intertwined in this enormous network of combinations formed for various purposes which touch upon our profession, our fortune, our opinions, our tastes, our relaxations, our general conception of the world, and our particular conceptions of the arts, literature, the sciences, education, politics, the work of helping others, and so on. How many are the opportunities we have of meeting each other of discussing, and deliberating, and acting in common! What were the necessary repasts or *symposia* of the Spartans to all our periodical or occasional banquets, which serve constantly to bring together men of differing opinions, professions, and social standings, so that by virtue of the marvellous fecundity of private association, we can always find some point of contact, some common ground with the great number of our fellow-men." (p. 54)

"Some thinkers of today have invented a special term, a somewhat barbarous one, to designate these manifold and freely formed connections of individuals among themselves; they call it *interdependence*, and speak with emotion of the growing progress of this phenomenon." (p. 55)

"It can not be said that the peasant or the working man escape from these combinations. He also, in almost all cases, belongs to some Mutual Aid Society, some industrial or agricultural associations, or some kind of syndicate, while, if he has any means, as in a healthy country like France is usually the case, he belongs to a round half-dozen societies, financial and commercial.

"It is evident, therefore, that all kinds of collective requirements are not within the domain of the state. Let us hear no more from our philosophers of any such abstraction as the isolated individual; let them no longer ask us, as they sometimes do with an almost touching simplicity, how we should be able to have Banks, Saving Banks, Hospitals, etc., if the state will not condescend to use its coercive power in the creation of these institutions." (p. 55)

State and society

"In conclusion it is plain that there is no historical or logical basis supporting the extreme claims of those who attempt to boycott the state as an unworthy social instrument, or to deify the state as the earthly lord of human destiny, or to decree priorities in competing controls. Neither the proposition that the state soils whatever it touches nor the counterpropostion that the state sanctifies and saves whatever it touches has any sound basis in experience or reflection. These are merely the battle cries of competing groups, having symbolic value rather than rational validity." (p. 58)

"A sounder principle is that the role of various groupings, their techniques, personnel, values, the family, the state, the church, the industrial and the cultural, shifts with shifting trends of civilization from one period to another, with the types of presure groups, the technologies, the value systems and the urgency for new forms of social control place a heavier emergency burden on the state than in the preceeding cycle of western development. But it must be noted that this involves a change in the broad framework of society, rather than in the fundamental function of the state. Other types of control may later develop more widely and more vigorously in the new framework set up by the now emerging twentieth-century society." (Charles E. Merriam: *The Role of Politics in Social Change*, pp. 58-59)

Political Society. *The Elements of Politics* by Henry Sidgwick 1891.

"In the first place, it means to me earverment and in accordance with usage I draw a distinction—which is sometimes overlooked—between "politics" and "social science", or as it is now more commonly called sociology I take the former study as having a narrower scope than the latter: sociology, as I conceive it, deals with human societies generally; Politics with governed societies regarded as governing government, —that is societies of which the members are accustomed to obey, at least in certain matters, the directions given by some persons or body of persons forming part of the society. The difference between the two subjects is not indeed great if we merely consider the number of human beings included in either case; since the great majority of mankind are, and have been, in historical times, members of or/a government societies."

Still, we know of inferior races who only exhibit their characteristic doubleicty or imperfectility quotical sphere. (1897 ed., p. 2)

Treilitarlae Politik.

Wie Politik un Scine der alten vir die Lehre von Staatschlectthin.

Chapter 7
Political or Social (State or Society)

In the foregoing chapters, we have made it clear that there is a distinction between what is state and what is political. We have also pointed out that the latter is larger in scope than the former and that, consequently, although what is state is always political, what is political is not necessarily state. Furthermore, we have hinted that the state is either too small or too large for the execution of its functions in the present world and the recognition of this fact will force us to feel that there is a need for the reconsideration of the functions of the state and that there is a need for the reconstruction of the so-called political science.

While admitting that the state is not large enough to include all things political, it does not mean that hereafter we should add more functions which are political to the state, nor does it mean to include functions which are not political by character to the political organization or to the state.

In order to clarify this point, a distinction between what is political including, of course, the state and what is social or society is necessary. For by making such a distinction, we can see clearly, not only the difference or differences between things political and social, but also the true character and real nature of each of these concepts by itself. It is to be borne in mind, however, that the recognition of such a distinction in concept does not mean that they are unrelated to each other.

At the outset, it may be noted that from the time of Aristotle to the beginning of nineteenth century, distinction between what is social and what is political or state has been seldom made. Aristotle begins his well-known book, *The Politics*, by telling us that although every city, or the city state as it is usually translated or called by modern writers, is a community and every community aims at some good, it is the city or city state aims at the highest good and therefore it is the city which embraces all the other communities. The other communities, according to Aristotle, are merely the prepartory stages through which the city develops just as childhood is the preparatory stage for manhood; for man is born not only to live but to live well. While a village or other communities may be sufficient for our material necessity, it is the city in which we can live well and live for a life which is complete.

Thus a family, a household or any other communities are simply parts of the city just as a leg, a hand or other organs are merely parts of a human being. Just as parts of human body develop in order to make man as a man, as parts of the city develop in order to make the city as a city. A city can not be a city without family or other necessary parts just as a man can not be a man without legs and other necessary parts.

Since man is by nature a political animal, it is the city that fulfills his political need. He can live without a city, unless he is a beast or a god. In other words, he would not be a political animal if he does not live in a city. As a man, he must be a political animal. If he is not a political animal, he can not be a man, and consequently he must be either a beast or a god.

Thus the individual together with his family, village and possibly tribe are merely the constintuent parts of an inseparable and complete whole, the city. Although the understanding of this inseparable and complete whole, according to the Aristotelian philosophy, may be obtained through the understanding of the [its] parts, the parts remain to be means rather than the ends by themselves, for the whole is the end.

Moreover, since the whole is greater than its parts, the whole must be superior. Hence the Greek city becomes a world by and for itself. We may go so far as to say that what belongs to man belongs to the city. The city, not only represents all aspects of human life, but also provides the complete life of human being. In fact only in the city can we find such a life.

Social life is thus submerged to the city life or political life. To separate one from another would be unthinkable, for the former is only the means, the parts of, and the subordination to the latter. This is the reason why some of the modern writers have thought it more proper to translate the Greek word polis as social and insisted that what Aristotle means a political animal is nothing more than or less than a social animal. So we are told by Mr. Warde Fowler that "The πολις was in fact, in most respects though not [ib] all, a more perfect form of social union than the modern State, and its history, if we were more exactly informed about it, would be relatively easier to understand."①

Many other writers have entertained the same opinion advanced above, and expressed more explicitely. Prof. Charles Howard McIlwain says that the Greek city "was a community, a *res publica*, or in good old English, a true common weal or

---

① Fowler, W., *The City-State of the Greeks and Romans*, p. 9.

commonwealth... The vividness of the feeling of community, the approximation of neighborliness and citizenship, the living realization of a true *res publica* or common weal, this was probably the deepest root from which the ancient polity drew its life. We need not inquire into its history, nor touch on the mooted question whether its unity originated in kinship or in contiguity. It was there, and the exceptional vigor of its political life was heightened by circumstances probably more favorable than have ever existed in the world before or since."①

The learned scholar goes on to say: "Never has there been so close an approximation as in the Greek city-state of the 'political man', in the sense in which the Utilitarians created their 'economic man', never has man been so completely a 'political animal'. He had fewer temptations than we have to be anything else. Religion and worship did not, as they must now, draw him away from the affairs of his city, they involved for him no division of his loyalty between 'church and stat'; they were, on the contrary, probably more inseparably connected with his 'political' life and activity than any other part of it, for the gods he worshiped—at least in the period when civic life remained most vivid—were not 'strange gods' but divinities who presided over his own fireside and his own city. We can not think truly of Athena without thinking of Athens, nor can we understand Athens without Athena. The very establishment of their city and the constant preservation of [of] its distinctive character and welfare the citizens attributed to the particular divinity who presided over it, and for that very reason the common worship of that divinity naturally came to be in their eyes at once the most striking manifestation of the common life they lived within their little commonwealth and the surest means of preserving its distinctive character and institutions."②

"But it was not religion alone that bound the citizen to his city. The *polis* was in a sense his home, for he never, at least in the later period of Greek development, allowed his household to draw him away from the everyday association with his fellow citizens. For him there was nothing quite comparable with the English love of home to keep him from the market-place where his real life was to be lived, and it was there that his days were actually passed.... Politics at all times have personal and must always to 'a great extent remain so, however large the state'. It was Aristotle's view that it becomes too large just so soon as these personalities can no longer be based on immediate personal contact. In a sense its very 'pettiness' is its chief merit; and it [it] is borne in mind that the Greek was no mere satrapy of a far away king, but an independent self-

---

① McIlwain, C. H., *The Growth of Political Thought in the West*, pp. 6-8.
② *Ibid.*, pp. 8-9.

governing whole, we begin to see why the greatest political thinkers of all time were educated in such a school, small as it was; we fully understand for the first time what Aristotle really means when he says there can be no government where friendship is impossible and no political life where no leisure exists, and we can appreciate his feeling that if a state becomes too large it ceases really to be a state. For to the Greek, the city consisted primarily in the union of its citizens. It was far more than that. The government was no less than the sum of the political activities of its citizens, and Aristotle was warranted in calling it, as he did 'a life'. The life of the citizens was its life, and that life was more nearly the whole of their than men in the varied distractions of our modern time can appreciate without an effort. To a Greek audience there seemed no straining for effect in Plato's famous figure in which he finds the mind of man depicted in the larger letters of the 'constitution' of the state. None but a modern man could dismiss this ⟨as⟩ a mere 'parallel' or 'analogy'. It was something far deeper. The mind of the state and the mind of the its citizen are identical—the macrocosm and the microcosm. The citizen is simply the counterpart of the state, nor the state of him. He is the state in little. The life of the state is the life of the men composing it. There is some idealization here, of course, but to the Greek it was certainly neither meaningless nor absurd as it seems to have been to the utilirarian mind of Grote."[1]

I have quoted the above paragraphs in order to show that to the ancient Greeks, city life is a unique. It embraces all what we would call the whole sphere of social life including political life. But what is social means nothing more or less than political to the Greeks.

It is clear then that to the Greeks political life is city life which includes all aspects of social life. Here we see that not only there is no distinction between city, state and things political, but also there is no distinction between city, state and things political on the one hand, and society or things social on the other hand.

It must be said that the ancient Greeks, though attaining a higher civilization in the ancient world, were not entirely free from the life of the primitive people. Social life on the whole was simple. When Plato would limit the number of the population of the city to 5040 citizens and when Aristotle thought of its territory as a place that one could see across it with his own eyes, they reflected the actual size of the Greek city. Undoubtedly there is nothing to compare with our modern cities like New York or London or even a city of very small size. Possibly it is more proper to call it a village in the modern sense

---

[1] McIlwain, C. H., *The Growth of Political Thought in the West*, pp. 10-11.

of the term. The streets were dark at night and dirty everywhere. There was no city planing; nor was there any special administrative machinery such as our municipal government; nor was there any need for having such a machinery, for the government of the city was, in a sense, the municipal government and the the king the mayor. It never did develop into a state; nor did it become so complex as many of our political institutions. Yet at the same time it include practically all aspects of life, simple as it was, of the ancient people.

"The Romans formed their empire by conquering one city after another and established a dominating and universal empire in the western world. Politically speaking, they enlarged the horizon of the Greek city into a gigantic whole which was never dreamed of by the Greeks. Although Cicero declared that this whole world must be thought of as one political organization common to gods and men as contrary to the Aristotelian idea that those who live out of the city are either or beasts, he did not think that there were social organizations outside of the political fabric. We know very well that the Roman jurists made a lot of contributions in the field of jurisprudence, but according to Carlyle, the Roman jurists were not, properly speaking, philosophers, or even political philosophers."[1] Still less, we must say, were they to be considered as social philosophers. Social organizations, whatever forms they might be, were, as the Greeks, regarded as integrated parts of the political organizations. The empire was an enlargement of the city and the city the family. There find the hierarchical relationships, but not horizontal divisions.

The [the] influence of Christianity made it possible for the church to stand besides the empire. But the separation of the church from the empire from the later part of the Roman period through the whole mediavel ages was a matter of fact rather than that of theory. In theory, both the pope and the emperor or the kings claimed their authority from God and none thought of being subject to other. While it was said that things belong to Caesar should give to Caesar and things belong to Peter should give to Peter, neither in theory nor in pratice was this worked out in the Mediaeval period.

It was true that in the middle ages many and powerful social organizations developed beside the political institutions such as economic guilds and particularly the church. It was also true that many modern writers, notably Otto v. Gierke, have derived a whole fund of pluralistic ideas from the social organizations of the mediaeval ages. But this is the modern interpretations of mediaeval facts. Gierke, in his well known book,

---

[1] R. W. Carlyle and A. J. Carlyle, A History of Mediaeval Political Theory in the West, Vol. I, p. 35.

Johannes Althusius says: "The properly medieval system of thought started from the idea of the whole and of unity, but to every lesser unit down to and including the individual it ascribed an inherent life, a purpose of its own, and an intrinsic value within the harmoniously articulated organizm of the world-whole filled with the divine Sprit. Thus in accordance with the medieval scheme of things it attained a construction of the social whole which in effect was federalistic through and through. While it postulates of the visible unity of mankind in Church and Empire, yet by reason of the dualism of the two Swords it not only starts throughout from the idea of two allied Orders, but it limits even this unity to those relations in which joint action is demanded by the general purpose of all mankind. Thus for it the unity is neither absolute nor exclusive, but forms the overarching dome of a social structure organized as an independent whole. And this principle is repeated in its various gradations down to the smallest local, vocational and domestic groups. Everywhere in the Church and in the State the unitary total body consists of living member-bodies, each of which, though itself a whole, necessarily requires connection with the larger whole. Each has a purpose of its own, and consists of parts which it procreates and dominates, and which in their turn are wholes. Between the highest Universality or 'All-Community' and the essential unity of the individual there is a series of intermediate unities, in each of which lesser and lower units are comprised and combined. The political theories endeavor to set up a definite scheme descriptive of this articulation of mankind; for the church they follow the existing hierarchical system and for secular societies they set up a parallel system by enlarging the Aristotelian gradation of communities."[①]

Thus if the mediaeval organizations are mainly the enlargement of "the Aristotelian gradation of communities," the unity of the whole must be more emphasized than the unity of the parts. It may be well concluded now that in spite of the fact that facts showed that there were social organizations which were not only outside of but also superior to the political structures during the middle ages, theorists seldom made a clear distinction between social and political institutions.

The publication of Jean Bodin's *Six Books of Republic* intensified the theory that the state is everything and society nothing. Instead of building the state on an ethical basis as the Ancient Greeks did, Bodin tried to explain his political fabric on the so-called

---

① Otto v. Gierke, Johannes Althusius, English translation by Bernard Freyd under the title: The Development of Political Theory, 1939, New York, pp. 257–258. "To be sure, the prevalent doctrine made a large reservation in adopting the idea that the state is simply 'human society'. It confined this universality of the political society to that aspect of human life which is concerned with temporal welfare, and secured to the Church."

legal foundation. The keynote of his theory is sovereignty. Sovereignty is defined as supreme power over citizens and subjects unrestrained by the laws. We shall have more occasion to speak of Bodin's theory of sovereignty. It suffices to say here that he makes the sovereignty as the highest authority, absolute and indivisible. It is essential to the political entity, the state and its will is law. It is only natural then that other social organizations as well as citizens and subjects are under the control of the state.

Writers following Bodin such as Hobbes and Rousseau have made the sovereignty of Bodin more absolute and indivisible and aggrandized the position of the state. As a result, organizations within the state become the creatures of the latter. Both Hobbes and Rousseau believe in a pre-political condition which is called the state of nature. The procedure through which the state or political organization is established is the social contract. The social contract is prior to the state. In term, the word "social" as used here seems to be different from the word "political", yet to both Hobbes and Rousseau, what is meant by social is nothing more than political. And once the state is established it becomes all-mighty within its own sphere and therefore the creator of all the organizations therein. It is to be added that although that there are many important points that both Hobbes and Rousseau do not agree, they do essentially agree in regard to the relation of the state to other social organizations.

It may be remarked that the term "society", though used very often during the seventeenth and eighteenth centuries, was usually if not always, in connection with political organization or institution. "Civil society", "political society" and even the so-called natural society were terms similar to terms such as body-politic or state. Even in the later part of nineteenth century, when Spencer published his first volume of *The Principles of Sociology*, he still remarked that the word politics was used by some in the place of sociology.

Yet the condition of the nineteenth century has gradually forced man to admit that there is a distinction between what is political and what is social. The German writers are wont to trace the idea of society *Gessellschaft* to the writings of Hegel.① In his *Philosophy of Rights*, Hegel speaks of the buergerliches Gesellschaft which according to him stands between the individual and the state. Paul Vogel, the author of Hegels Gesellschaftsbegriff, 1925, remarks that "der Gesellschaftsbegriff Hegels wurdedie Beute des Nationaloekonomen, des Soziologen und des Juristen... . Von Hegel ueher

---

① O. v. Gierke speaks of Johannes Althsius as the forerunner for expounding the idea of society; see his *Johannes Althusius*.

Stein bis zu Lassalle fuehrt eine in sich gesch-lossene Gedankenbewegung."① We think that Vogel has somewhat exergerated the influence of Hegel in regard to the distinction between state and society. Robert von Mohl rightly says: "Hegelian 'civil society' (buegerliches Geselschaft) is no real being, no organism standing outside the state, but is rather only part of a logical process."②

Other German writers such as J. F. Herbert and F. J. Stahl③ realized the fact that between the individual and the state, there are many groups each of which has its own purpose as different from that of the state, but to Herbert and Stahl they are all complementary part and therefore under the control of the state. For the state alone has the supreme authority both internally and externally.

In considering the modern conception of society, particularly before the middle of nineteenth century, the contributions of the French writers should not be underestimated. Besides the distinctive contributions made by Augustine Comte, the so-called socialists in France should also be credited for advancing this concept.

From 1838 to 1842, Comte published his Positive Philosophy in six volumes. The chief purpose of his work was to create a new science, namely sociology. And this is the reason why he devoted the last three volumes for the study of sociology. Comte viewed society as a united whole although it may be studied from two aspects: one is the dynamic and the other static. The former is to deal with the growth or development of society and the latter the order and organization of society.

The study of the so-called political science or politics, as we know, included almost all the fields known as social sciences during the first part of nineteenth century. Law was considered as the command of the state and economics as it is generally used at our own day was then called political economy. If all the social sciences could be studied under the name of political science, there would be no need to have a new social science. But when Comte wanted to have new study which he first called social physics and afterward sociology, he certainly had in mind that this is something entirely different from the so-called political science. Otherwise he would not take the trouble to establish

---

① Paul Vogel, *Hegels Gesellschaftsbegriff*, 1925, p. 122.
② Herbert.
③ Stahl, *Philosophie Des Rechts*, pp. 1829–1838.

"Political organization is to be understood as that part of social organization which constantly carries on derective and sustaining functions for public ends. It is true, as already hinted, and as we shall be presently, that the two kinds are mingled in various ways—that each ramifies through the other more or less according to their respective degrees of predominance. But they are eventually different in origin and nature." pp. 245–246. Spencer, *Principles of Sociology*, Vol. II, Part I, § 441.

a new branch of study.

Sociology, according to Comte, is the science of social phenomena just as biology is the science of biological phenomena. It is the science of society in general as it is different from the so-called special sciences such as economics law and politics. Here again an analogy between sociology and biology may be noted, since the latter is the science of living matter in general as it is different from the sciences of zoology and botany.

It is beyond question that to Comte the social phenomena must be larger in scope than the political phenomena. In one chapter of his Positive Philosophy in which he traced the history of social sciences. Although he paid a lot of tribute to men like Aristotle and particularly Montesqueur and considered them as the forerunners of social sciences, he was fully aware that the sociology which he was to create, or as someones prefer to put it, predict was something new in the field of social studies.

The new study created or predicted by Comte has been advanced by many sociologists for the last century and it has already become a well-established field of social studies. Although sociologists are still different in opinions in regard to the subject matter of sociology, it may be said that they agree that sociology deals with society in general and as a whole. Since the time of Comte, not only the concept of society has been well interpreted and defined, but also its relations to and differences from things political have become very clear.

Herbert Spencer, who has done more than any body in laying the foundation of sociology, maintained, in his *Study of Sociology* published in 1872, that sociology deals with the origin, growth, structure and function of society. Society is here considered as an organism consisting of different aspects of human life to which the political institution is only one of them. It is clear to him that the subject matter of politics is much narrower in scope than that of sociology and the former is regarded as a differentiated part of the latter. [1] It is for this reason that he strongly opposed to use the term polities for substituting the term sociology, because, as he says, "to use, as some suggested, the word politics, too narrow in its meaning as well as misleading in its connotations, would be deliberately to create confusion for the sake of avoiding a defect of no practical moment."[2]

It is safe to say that sociologists in general entertain the view that society is larger in scope than what is known as political including the state. Prof. E. A. Ross says that

---

[1] See F. H. Giddings, *Principles of Sociology*, 1896, p. 28.
[2] H. Spencer, *Principles of Sociology*, Volume I, Preface to the first edition, 1876.

"in fact, the political is simply imbedded in the social...Political organization is only a part of social organization ... Government is becoming functional to society, and if political science remains distinct, it will be because the breadth of the field calls for specialist, and not because these are well defined natural boundaries marking it off from sociology."① Other writers in this field may be also cited in order to show that they share the view expressed by Prof. Ross in the statement just mentioned above, but enough has been said in regard to the scope of society and state or political organization.

Besides considering the scope of society is larger than that of political organization, many sociologists also point out that society is the foundation of political organization and consequently the principles and laws underlying the social activities and regulating the social conducts are essential and fundamental to political institutions. L. Gumplowicz declares that "the state is a social phenomenon consisting of social elements behaving according to social laws."② Giddings tells us that "to teach political economy and the theory of the state to men who have not learned these first principles of sociology, is like teaching astronomy or thermodynamics to men who have not learned the Newtonian laws of motion."③

Thus the concept of society which, to the earlier political scientists, is embraced in the concept of state or political organization extends much larger in scope than the concept of state and things political. Now, to the sociologists, it even includes the state or things political within its abode. The rapid development of sociological study and great influence of the sociological concept for the last century in the different fields of social studies have made the students in these latter fields including the so-called political scientists to change their social concepts and in particular in their relations to their own particular fields.

It is to be noted that such a change is not simply a change in concept alone. It is a change in fact. We may venture to say that the change of concept is rather a reflection of the change of fact. Here we need a new approach of political study and here we need a reconstruction of political science.

It must be added also that sociologists together with the anthropologists, by putting the state within the cloak of society and tending to limit the scope and actions of the state, have also enriched the field of political study from the results of their research in the so-called primitive political institutions which though seldom known or noticed by the

---

① E. R. Ross, *Foundations of Sociology*, 1905, pp. 21-22.
② L. Gumplowicz, *Outlines of Sociology*, 1885, p. 116.
③ F. H. Giddings, *Principles of Sociology*, p. 33.

earlier political scientists have thrown much light on the early development of political institutions. Moreover, by their comparative study of the historical and contemporary societies, the sociologists are able to give an impartial and comprehensive view point not only on the difference between what is political and what is not political, but also on the interrelations and interactions of political institutions and the other social institutions.

While sociologists mainly inquire into the nature of society and its relations to other specific social organizations, the socialists give more emphasise to the problems arising out from social injustice or inequality. Being anxious to solve the social problems which they have in mind, they also take interest in studying different aspects of social life. From the beginning of 19th century many writers took interest in social reforms. Instead of looking to the state for such reforms, they proposed voluntary cooperation among workers and industrial circles to establish one kind or another of associations for promoting social welfare. Thus instead of calling his book *A New View of State*, Robert Owen named it *A New View of Society*. The new society which he proposed to establish is built on an economical basis rather than on political power. So the new society is to be different from the system of state or old political organization. Charles Fourier outlined in detail a program for a system of "phalanxes" or co-operative communities. According to him, each of these communities is to be composed of a group of workers and technicians assured of a minimum income, and sharing the surplus on an equitable basis. Here again, it is a kind of society which is different from the old regime of political organization. It is a new society, not only different from, but also, in many ways, antagonistic to the state.

Lorenz von Stein, deeply influenced by the socialistic movement of France and the socialist ideas of such men as Saint-Simon, Fourier and Proudhon, has contributed a great deal to German political thought by making a distinction between state and society. It was he who paved the way for the German thinkers to formulate their social theories based on actual social facts and conditions, in spite of the fact that he himself was imbued with the Hegelian metaphysics.

Stein maintained that the state, being dominated by the ruling class, is in fact under the caprice of that class. The power of the state is the power of that class. Thus the ruled class is ruled by the ruling class under the name of the state. This ruling class is to Stein a form of society which although closely connected with the state in many ways is different from the latter in concept and in pratice.

Both state and society are viewed as organism by Stein. While the purpose of the latter is the highest development of each individual as a member of the society, an ideal state should stand above and apart from the societies which are usually in conflict with each other in their interests. Here we see the supremacy of the state. Here we see the influence of Hegelian thought on our author. Yet at the same time, Stein would never allow his state to be absolute in power, because the state, according to him, is justified for its function for maintaining the law and keeping the balance of power between the different groups within itself. ①

By limiting the power and function of the state, the dignity of the state is greatly degraded by Stein. On the contrary, he lifts the position of society which finds no such a place in the Hegelian system. As already remarked, Stein leaves the abode of Hegelian metaphysics and builds his social theory on actual social facts and conditons. Here we see that he forms a bridge between Hegal and Karl Marx and F. Engels.

"The modern state," so declares the Communist Manifesto of 1848, "is but an executive committee for administering the affairs of the whole bourgeois class." The state is here merely a tool used by the ruling class to exploit the proletarian class. Society is thus divided into two conflicting classes: one is the bourgeois and the other proletarian. Historically speaking, the feudalistic society gave its place to capitalistic society. As to the future, there will be a communistic society takes the place of capitalistic society. The change from one society to another is due to the change of the economic facts and conditions, particularly to the methods of production. It was handicraft that produced the feudalistic society and it was machine industry that produced the capitalistic society. When capital accumulates in the hands of few, the rich become richer and the poor poorer. The instrument used by the capitalists to suppress the poor or the workers is the state. State is therefore not only different ⟨from⟩ the proletarian society, but also different from the bourgeois society.

Marx and Engels advocate a proletarian revolution in order to destory the capitalistic society. Although the state may be still used by the proletarian society in order to serve its own purpose, it is not viewed as a permanent institution; for according to Marx and Engels, as soon as proletarian revolution is complete and capitalistic society is destroyed, the state is no longer needed. It is clear then that the state, in the mind of Marx and Engels, is only a transitional organization. It is the free society of workers of the world which will take the place of the state in the future.

It is obvious now that the expounders of communism, after degrading the state as an instrument of economic society, want to destroy it in the long run.

---

① See Stein, *Das Socialismus und Comunismus des heutigen Frankreichs*, 1842. Also his *System der Staatswissenschaft*, Bd. Ⅱ: Die Gesellschaftslehre, 1856.

The syndicalists agree with the Communists by denouncing the state as an instrument for protecting the economic interest of the dominant groups, and perpetuating social injustice and legal exploitation of the worker. In a sense, the syndicalists are non-political. They oppose all forms of government and refuse active participation in politics. Here they are like the anarchists. It is their belief that society can exist without the state, although it must be said that by society they mean essentially the economic society.

The ideal society which they propose to create is the *syndicate*, an organization of producers managing its own affairs without the help or interference of the state. In contrast to the state as a compulsory organization, it is a voluntary association. Although the syndicalistic theory is mainly destructive, it proposes not only local unions of producers, but also in favour of a general society made up of federated and self-governing industries.

There are other socialists who differentiated society from state; but enough has been said in this point. It may be remarked that it was the industrial revolution and economic development of the nineteenth century that give rise to the socialistic movement. While different or even conflicting view points are prevalent among the socialists themselves, by giving more emphasis to the social and particularly the economic reforms, they see the importance of the social groups. Besides being different from the state, society performs a function which is not only close to the heart of human being, but also nearer to the justice of mankind. To the socialists this is an ideal to be realized rather than a fact to be stated. Here we see the difference as well as the similarity between the sociologist and the socialist. To the former, society is differenciated from the state either as a historical fact or as existing condition. To the latter, it is more an ideal for realization. Of course, such a difference should not be overemphasized; for the sociologist will not be satisfied by merely presenting the fact and the socialist has usually used fact as evidence for assuring the need of realization of his ideal society. Again to the sociologist, besides the state or political organization, there are many types of social organizations which can be differentiated indefinitely; but to the socialist the non-political group which draws his special attention is economic in nature. It is true that with the exception of the political organization, the economic institution and problem plays a special role in our age; yet to ignore the other social factors in human life will easily lead us to misunderstand our social problems and to have more difficulties in solving them. We protest against political determinism; but should also beware of economic determinism. There is no question that this is one of the most important problem that we are now facing; but this is not the place for us to discuss. What we want to show here is with the development of sociology and socialism, man has come to understand that society is not a creature of the state; that it has a life of its own, each by itself; and that it is different from, and sometimes in conflict with, the interest of the state or political organization, and yet it is closely related to, and much larger in scope to include, the state or political organization.

As a matter of fact, even writers on history in the modern age have not failed to see the distinction between what is social and what is political. E. A. Freeman once remarked that history is past politics and politics is present history. There were and are writers still confining the scope of history to political events and to political events alone, but as early as 1859, when Thomas Buckle wrote his *Introduction to the History of Civilization* in England, he already pointed out that history should not deal with political events alone. What he had in mind was a history which attempts to include the civilization of mankind. It can not be doubted that such a history would embrace the whole range of social activities including though the political activity, for civilization is composed of social as well as material and spritual elements. So this is true with Spencer when he attacked the history of his own day as too narrow in scope because it only deals with political and military affairs. ①

Modern historians call this political history the old history and history that deals with the whole range of social activities the new history. Karl Lamprecht, one of the best expounders of the new history has pointed out the difference of these kinds of history as well as the development from old history to the new history in following words: "It was a time of almost purely political activity; the nation yearned with every fibre of its soul for the long-coveted political unity. Such works as the political history of the old German empire by Giesebrecht, or Droysen's 'History of Prussian Polity,' may be cited as important phenomena in this connection. Why should they not have preferred political history which to a certain extent, was the individual psychologic method, to all other forms of history? This explains for the most part the fact that the advance in the socio-psychological interpretation of events, made in the meantime by other people, e. g. the French in the philosophy of Comte, met with small acceptance in Germany."

And he continues: "But the last decades of the nineteenth century brought the rebound. The years 1870 and 1871 released men from their great anxieties concerning the national life and unity; the development of internal culture comes prominently now to

---

① Spencer, *On Education*.

the front. And that happened at the very dawn of a new period of modern psychic existence. The rise of political economy and technology, the rapid development of freedom of trade all over the globe, the victories of science in the realm of nature, even to the penetrating into the confines of the inner life: all this and a host of other less important phenomena yielded an untold amount of new stimuli and possibilities of association, and with that unheard-of extension of psychic activity as then existing. But of this more in another lecture. The result was a marked differentiation of intellectual activity, and with it the renewed and determining advance of the socio-psychic elements. This was evident along the whole line of scientific endeavor, especially in the rise of sociology and anthropology during the last decades, with their far-reaching consequences and accompanying phenomena. In the domain of history, this meant a fresh start in the writing of histories of civilization in so far as the development of method was energetically taken in hand; description alone was no longer the watchword, but an intelligent comprehension."[1]

Lamprecht refers here to the historical development of Germany in its relation to the change of historical method and scope. According to him, Herder "was the first to admit the importance of the socio-psychic demands for the proper historical comprehension of the most important of all human communities, —nations, —and to draw from these the necessary conclusions."[2]

In short, to Lamprecht, "history is primarily a socio-psychological science. In the conflict between the old and the new tendencies in historical investigation, the main question has to do with social-psychic, as compared and contrasted with individual-psychic factors; or, to speak somewhat generally, the understanding on the one hand of conditions, on the other, of heroes, as the motive powers in the course of history. Hence, the new, progressive and therefore aggressive point of view in this struggle is the

---

[1] *Alte und neue Richtungen in der Geschichtswissenschaft*, Berlin, 1896. I use the English translation under the title: What is History; translated by E. A. Andrews, 1905, pp. 23–25.

[2] *Ibid.*, pp. 19–20. But Lamprecht continues: "Herder's enthusiastic grasp of the socio-psychic elements of history does not stand alone. It is the property of the whole epoch and dominates the characteristic movement of the time—Romanticism. The advance step in all this was a clearer view of the vast combinations of the phenomena of the *mass-psyche*—an advance which brought one to describe vital points poetically, in part or wholly so. But there was not the clear comprehension of the constituent elements of the *mass-psychic* or even of the elementary disentangling of combined phenomena."

"It has been reserved to the so-called history-of-civilization method to attempt the description of socio-psychic phenomena, and Freytag, Riehl, even Burckhardt, devoted themselves to this task. Since the last decade of the last century, however, this method has gradually grown out of date."

socio-psychological, and for that reason it may be termed modern."①

It must be added that socio-psychological approach of history is not only in conflict with the individual psychological approach, but also different from the so-called political approach, an approach which, as Lamprecht has pointed out, is narrower in scope than the new history.

Other German scholars such as E. Berheim and Paul Barth stood on the same line with Lamprecht. Berheim remarks that "Die Geschichte is die Wissenschaft von der Entwicklung der Menschen in ihrer Betaetigung als sozialer Wesen."② Paul Barth points out that the institutions of family, marriage, property and national economy may be also considered as the subject matter of history. So he tells us that "geschichtlich ist dasjenige, was fuer eine menschliche Gesellschaft wichtig ist, Damit diese Wichtigkeit so objektiv also moeglich bestimmt werde, kann sie nur rein quantitativ bemessen werden. Das Lebenswichtige kann nur durch das Leben selbst offenbart werden. Was also der Erhaltung und reicheren Entfaltung oder der zerstoerung und Verkuemmerung des Lebens einer Gesellschaft dient, das is Sache der Feschichte."③

"Es ist zunaecht offenbar", says Barth, "Das Object der Geschichte ist nicht der einzelne Mensch, nicht das Ereignis, das den Einzelnen betrifft, sondern es ist die menschliche Gesellschaft, oder, genauer ausgedrueckt, es send die menschlichen Gesellschaften."④ It is clear to Paul Barth as it is to Lamprecht that individual is not the object of history. Moreover, history, to Barth, deals not only society, but also societies.

The same position was taken by E. Gothein in his *Die Aufgaben der Kulturgeschichte*,⑤ when he proposed cultural history for substituting the so-called political history or the history of the state. Gothein opposed the contention of D. Schaefer that history deals with the state or political organization.⑥ According to him, the activity of the state can hardly be understood without an understanding of the other cultural elements to which the state is a part and by which the activities of the state are

---

① Lamprecht, *Alte und neue Richtungen in der Geschichtswissenschaft*, p. 3.
② Bernheim, *Lehrbuch der historischen Methode*, 2nd. Ed., 1894, p. 5.
③ Paul Barth, *Die Philosophie Der Geschichte als Soziologie*, 2nd. Edition, pp. 76–77.
④ Ibid., p. 77.
⑤ Gothein, *Die Aufgaben der Kulturgeschichte*, 1899, p. 10.
⑥ See D. Schaefer, *Das eigentliche Arbeitsgebiet der Geschichte*, 1888, p. 23. The problem of the historian, according to Schaefer, is "den Staat zum Verstaendnis zu bringen, seinen Ursprung, sein Werden, die Bedingungen seines Seins, seine Aufgaben. Hier war, hier ist, hier bleibt der einigende Mittelpunkt fuer die unendliche Fucile der Einzelfrage, die historischer Loesung harren." p. 23. He also points out that each aspect of human culture will be dealt with by historian so far as it is related to the state. p. 27.

conditioned. Hence a history which merely takes the state or political institutions into consideration will not give a complete picture of the history.

To Gothein, culture is composed of religion, state, arts, law and economic life.① But these are all related to each other and form the unity of culture. We may say that what Gothein means by different aspects of culture is nothing more than the different aspects of society. If the subject matter of history is to be enlarged from the political history or the history of the state to social history or the history of society, the significance of the social factors other than the state or political institutions can be easily understood. Nor do we fail to see the difference and relation of the state to the society. The state is only a part of society and therefore conditioned by society.

In the United States, James H. Robinson and H. E. Barnes have made a lot of contributing by enlarging the field of history from political study to social activity. Robinson criticized the old historians for giving too much emphasis on political events to the exclusion of "other matters of greater and narration of extraordinary episodes not because they illustrate the general tendencies of a particular time, but because they are conspicuous in the annals of the past."② Barnes has followed Robinson very closely and expounds this idea through his numerous writings.

Other writers such as Guglielmo Ferrero of Italy also points out that the old history was written in an age in which it was still contended over forms of government and that it is necessary to widen our points of view in order to adapt to the moral and social needs of the day.③

What is the content of the new history? To answer this question we can do no better than to quote the following passage: "That which constitutes History, properly so called, is in great part omitted from works on the subject. Only of late years have historians commenced giving us, in any considerable quantity, the truly valuable information. As in past ages the king was everything and the people nothing; so, in past histories the doings of the king fill the entire picture, to which the national life forms but an obscure background. While only now, when the welfare of nations rather than of rulers is becoming the dominant idea, are historians beginning to occupy themselves with the phenomena of social progress. The thing it really concerns us to know is the natural history of society. We want all facts which help us to understand how a nation has grown and organized itself. Among these, let us of course have an account of its government;

---

① Gothein, *Die Aufgaben der Kulturgeschichte*, p. 6.
② Robinson, *The New History*, 1912.
③ Ferrero.

with as little as may be of gossip about the men who officered it, and as much as possible about the structure, principles, methods, prejudices, corruptions, etc., which it exhisbited; and let this account include not only the nature and action of the central government, but also those of the local governments, down to their minutest ramifications. Let us of course also have a parallel description of the ecclesiastical government—its organization, its conduct, its power, its relation to the state; and accompanying this, the cermonial, creed and religious ideas, —not only those nominally believed, but those really believed and acted upon. Let us at the same time be informed of the control exercised by class over class, as displayed in social observances—in titles, salutations, and forms of address. Let us know, too, what were all the other customs which regulated the polular life out of doors and in-doors: including those concerning the relations of the sexes, and the relations of parents to children. The superstitions, also, from the more important myths down to the charms in common use, should be indicated. Next should come a delineation of the industrial system; showing to what extent the division of labour was carried; how trades were regulated, whether by caste, guilds, or otherwise; what was the connection between employers and employed; what were the agencies for distributing commodities; what were the means of communication; what was the circulating medium. Accompanying all which should be given an account of the industrial arts technically considered: stating the processes in use, and the quality of the products. Further, the intellectual condition of the nation in its various grades should be depicted; not only with respect to the kind and amount of education, but with respect to the progress made in science, and the prevailing manner of thinking. The degree of aesthetic culture, as displayed in architecture, sculpture, painting, dress, music, poetry, and fiction, should be described. Nor should there be omitted a sketch of the daily lives of the people—their food, their homes, and their amusements. And lastly, to connect the whole, should be exhibited the morals, theoretical and practical, of all classes; as indicated in their laws, habits, proverbs, deeds. These facts, given with as much brevity as consists with clearness and accuracy, should be so grouped and arranged that they may be comprehended in their *ensemble*, and contemplated as mutually-dependent parts of one great whole. The aim should be so to present them that men may readily trace the *consensus* subsisting among them; with the view of learning what social phenomena co-exist with what other. And then the corresponding delineations of succeeding ages should be so managed as to show how each belief, institution, custom, and arrangement was modified; and how the *consensus* of preceding structures and functions was developed into the consensus of succeeding ones. Such alone is the kind of information respecting past times which can be of service to the citizen for the regulation of his conduct. The only history that is of pratical value is what may be called Descriptive Sociology. And the highest office which the historian can discharge, is that of so narrating the lives of nations, as to furnish material for a comparative sociology; and for the subsequent determination of the ultimate laws to which social phenomena conform."①

We may not agree with Spencer by calling history as descriptive sociology, because by descriptive sociology it may mean descriptive sociology of the present time or contemporary age. Although what we describe now may become history in the future, history, after all concerns more on the past and descriptive sociology is not necessarily to deal with the past.

When history widens its scope to deal with social facts, it studies the same things that the sociologist, and in a certain sense, the socialist are taking interest, although each approaches them from a different angle. The historian looks to the facts of the past, the sociologist seeks the fundamental principles of both the past and the present and the socialist cares more about the problems of the present. But they view society as a whole and in its different aspects, not as they are separate from each other but rather related to each other, although it must be said that the socialist is somewhat different from the sociologist and the historian in this connection.

The important point is that they all make a distinction between society and state or between things social and things political and that they all view the latter as a part of the former. It is not, however, simply an accident that they have come to agree on these points, since they are different in many respects, in their methods of approach as well as their ideas of looking things, in their training as well as their sentiments.

Yet they agree on the points under our consideration. It is mainly, we think, because that their view points are the reflections of the actual facts and conditions of the time. As a matter of fact, we may say that the both sociology and socialism are the products of these facts and condition, while history having confined itself to what is known as history of the state or political history when the state's power was at its zenith has been forced to change its concept and scope as facts and conditions have changed.

Under the influence of the change of conditions as well as the writers on new history, sociology and socialism or other subjects of social studies, even political scientist and jurist have come to realize that there is a distinction between state and

---

① Herbert Spencer, *Essays on Education*, Everyman's Library Edition, pp. 27-29.

society or between things political and things social.

As early as 1839, Heinrich Ahrens, in his writings①, already pointed out that there were many social groups each of which is an organic whole and has an end by itself. He further pointed out that some of these groups are found to be within the boundaries of the state and some extend beyond the jurisdiction of the state. The state is only one form of these social groups which in their interrelationships form the concept of society of Ahrens. The different forms of society or social groups, though closely related to the state, are by no means absorbed by the state either functionally or territorially, because besides having the ends of their own they may not be within the boundaries of the state.

In spite of what has been said, Ahrens, considering the state as an organization for maintaining the harmony of the different social groups and for protecting the interest of each of these groups remains supreme in the realm of law. But such supremacy of the state is radically different from what is understood by Hegel, for in the system of Ahrens political absolutism is unhealthy so the state should not be given the absolute power to control the other social groups. Instead of an absolute, and indivisible whole which is characterized as the state, he proposed to have federalistic system of social groups with the state as a legal order for developing a haromony between the different groups.

The theory advanced by Ahrens has been followed by Robert von Mohl in an article published in 1851 under the title Gesellschaftswissenschaft und Staatswissenschaft in the Zeitschrift fuer die gesammte Staatewissenschaft.② To Mohl as to Ahrens, there are many social groups which are independent of the state and only externally controllable by the laws of the state. Of these groups Mohl mentioned such as family, religious community, economic organizations, estates and many others. They belong to the concept of society in contrast to the concept of state. The interests of social groups are different from that of the state. They are so real and vital to the individuals that the latter may be absorbed by the these groups much more than they are absorbed by the state. On the other hand, no matter how much the state may claim from the individuals, there always remains a lot of activities of the individuals for the groups and the inner lives of these groups can seldom be disturbed by the change of political fabrics.

To maintain the unity of the state Mohle would leave to the state to decide the sphere of activity of its own. Here the supremacy of the state is again conceded, though not in the Hegelian sense.

---

① H. Ahrens, *Naturerecht*, pp. 304–305.
② This article was incorporated into his book: *Die Geschichte und Literatur der Staatswissenschaften*.

But besides contending that society is different from the state, Mohle proposed to establish a new field of study which he called "Gesellschaftswissenschaft" or social science. Some of the modern sociologists claim Mohl as one of the forerunners of sociology on account of that. Positively speaking, whether Mohl can be regarded as a sociologist remains to be asked. But negatively, he strongly denied that political science or Staatswissenschafte is capable to include all the social groups within its own scope. Social facts and conditions demanded a new study which was different from the so-called political science, because they were not things political in their nature. Just as the state can not absorb all the social groups, political science can not absorb the social science. If Mohl can not be regarded as one of the founders of sociology, he at least predicted sociology. Mohl remained to be one of the most outstanding political scientists in the nineteenth century in Germany; but he admitted a science of society or to speak more adequately in his words, die gesellschaftswissenschaft standing side by side with political science or Staatswissenschaft.

Mohl's proposal of establishing a science of society has been challenged by Heinrich von Treitschke in his *Die Gesellschaftswissenschaft: Ein kritischer Versuch*, a doctor dissertation published in 1859. Contrary to Mohl, Treitschke held that all the social groups mentioned by Mohl as independent of the state were not only related to the state but also under the control of the state. Therefore, the so-called political science was adequate enough to include what was known as the science of society.

In spite of Treitschke's protest, the science of society, or sociology if you like, has so rapidly developed during the later part of nineteenth that Treitschke could see with his own eyes. It is to be added that Treitschke stood almost alone in this connection.

In 1862, Otto Baehr, in his *Der Rechtsstaat*, although recognizing the state as the most important form of social groups and its law as the supreme and the most highly developed form of the laws of association (Genossenschaftsrecht), maintained that the state was not adequate to control all the activities of the social groups and that its law was not different in kind from the laws of the social groups.

Somewhat the same position was taken by Rudolf von Gneist.[①] He insisted that society was not identical with the state; its interests being different, in many ways from, and therefore not subject to the complete control of, the state. He recognized, however, that the interest of the state was permanent and general in nature while that of the society or social groups was immediate and particular. The tendency of the social interests was

---

① Gneist, *Der Rechtsstaat*, 1872.

not only in conflict with each other but also in opposition to the interest of the state, in the sense that the social groups were constantly struggling for the powers of the state in order to develop their own interests. It was the purpose of the state, then, to seek a balance of forces of the social groups and to maintain its position for the promotion of the permanent and general interest.

Even Georg Jellinek①, strict to the juristic viewpoint of the state, did not fail to see that there was a social viewpoint of the state. There were social functions which being deeply rooted in human beings were the expressions of the inner lives. The sciences of human relations were founded upon the recognition of these facts.

So W. W. Willoughby distinguished society from the state and sociology from political science. "To distinguish then," say he, "the domain of political science from the larger field of sociology; and from the other special departments of knowledge embraced therein, we say that political science deals with society solely from its organized standpoint, —that is, as effectively organized under a supreme authority for the maintenance of an orderly and progressive existence."

And he continues: "We thus distinguish between the conception of an aggregate of men as politically organized—as constituting a body politic—and the same community of men as forming merely a group of individuals with mutual economic and social interests. The body politic is the social body plus the political organization. An aggregate of men living together and united by mutual interests and relationships we term a society…When this society becomes organized for the effectuation of certain general, or, as they are called, political interests, and with a magistracy into whose hands is entrusted the exercise of its controlling authority, it assumes a political form, and a state is said to exist; and the rules defining the contents of this authority and the manner of its exercise are collectively termed its constitution."②

Whether it is true that "the body politic is the social body plus the political organization." or not, we shall not discuss here. What we want to show is that even representative of the juristic school like Willoughby can not disregard of the distinction between society and state, although the state with its sovereignty remains to be the supreme authority over society or rather societies which are found within the boundaries of the state. It may be also remarked that, like Gneist, he regards political interests as the general interests.

Other scholars such as Prof. Garner speaks of the distinction, not only from the

---

① Jellinek, *Allgemeine Staatslehre*, 1900, pp. 153 ff.
② Willoughby, *The Nature of the State*, pp. 2–3.

functional viewpoint but also from the territorrial viewpoint. According to him: "The state, as we have seen, is an association of human beings. It is not, however, the only such association. Within the territorial limits of every highly civilized state are to be found an almost bewildering number of other associations, such as churches, labor unions, political bodies, learned societies, associations of public functionaries, and countless others. One of the striking facts of modern life, in fact, has been the tendency of men to unite themselves into group associations for the advancement of common social, scientific, religious, educational, political economic, and other interests, with the result that today society is a veritable network of such associations. The state is no longer a mere" sand heap of individuals, all equal and related, except to the state. "Some of these associations embrace within their membership a large proportion of the adult population of the state; many of them are international in scope, cutting across boundary lines and including in their membership persons of many countries. Large numbers of men and women are members of more than one such association. All of them are organized; many of them have treasuries and budgets, own property both real and personal, have statutes, by-laws, and rules of discipline, and exercise a certain control over their members. Many of them have a charters of incorporation from the state and therefore possess what the lawyers call a personality, but whether they have been thus recognized by the state or not, they have according to some writers a real as contradistinguished from a hypothetical or fictitious personality. Some of them, such as religious, charitable, and educational bodies, are occupied with interest in the advancement of which the state is itself concerned. Indeed, in some cases the state recognizes the fact that they are, in a sense, cooperating partners with it in the pursuit of a common task and aids them by means of subventions from the public treasury."[1]

But Prof. Garner also points out that the most fundamental difference between the society and state is that the former is a voluntary group while the latter is the compulsory association. Being voluntary it "lacks the legal power of coercion—the supreme power to command and enforce obedience—in short, the power of sovereignty."[2] Because "the state possesses the sovereignty, all voluntary associations are subject to a certain control and regulation on the part of the state, even the churches and religious bodies...It is sufficient to say that from the standpoint of law they are subject to the control of the state equally with individuals; they can exist only with the consent of the state; and their activities may be regulated and controlled by it in the interest of and for the protection of

---

[1] J. W. Garner, *Political Science and Government*, 1928, pp. 61–62.
[2] *Ibid.*, p. 64.

the rights of the community."①

Most of the so-called political scientists or jurists mentioned above are considered as monists in the field of political philosophy, because they believe that sovereignty is essential to the state and that sovereignty is indivisible. Yet they all believe that society is different from the state and that it is larger in scope than the latter.

It is the modern political pluralists who have not only made a distinction between society and state, but also questioned the state as the sole possessor of sovereignty. As to their standpoints we shall discuss under the topic of sovereignty. Before concluding, it is desirable to quote a passage from MacIver's *The Modern State*, in order to show that the distinction between what is social and what is political is essential to the understanding of either society or state. "To identify the social with the political is to be guilty of the grossest of all confusions, which completely bars any understanding of either society or the state. It is perfectly obvious, if only we look at the facts of the case, that there are social forms, like the family or the church or the club, which owe neither their origin nor their inspiration to the state; and social forces, like custom or competition, which the state may protect or modify, but certainly does nor create; and social motives like friendship or jealousy, which establish relationships too intimate and personal to be controlled by the great engine of the state. The state exist within society, but it is not even the *form* of society. We see it best in what it does. It achievement is a system of order and control. The state in a word regulates the outstanding external relationship of men in society. It supports or exploits, curbs or liberates, fulfils or even destroys, the social life over which it is invested within control—but the instrument is not the life."②

---

① J. W. Garner, *Political Science and Government*, 1928, pp. 64-65.
② R. M. MacIver, *The Modern State*, 1926, pp. 4-5.

Chapter 8
State & Other Organizations

We have already shown, in the last chapter, that students in the fields of social studies such as sociologist, historian and the so-called political scientist and social reformers have come to realize that there is a distinction between state and society or rather between political and social and that the former is, narrower in scope than, and consequently only a part of, the latter. The understanding of such a distinction is very important to the so-called political science as well as to other social studies. The development of sociology and other special social studies, it may be said, is chiefly due to the understanding of such a distinction. For if things social are not differentiated from things political as it was usually thought and maintained by political writers of the past, then there is no need to have other social studies such as sociology or economics besides political science, since the latter would embrace the former or at most the former would be only the branches of the latter just as economics was long considered as a part of politics and even when it has divorced from politics, it has been still called political economy.

The recognition of such a distinction made it possible for not only the development of sociology and other special social studies, but also the reconstruction of some old social studies such as history and jurisprudence.

It is clear, then, that the distinction so made between what is social and what is political is a change and indeed a radical change in the field of social studies and particularly in the field of the so-called political science. On the one hand, we may say that from the domain of political science a lot has been taken away by the other social studies. But on the other hand, many of the things which are political in nature and which were either unknown to the students of political science or not existing in the past may now be also included into the province of political science. For instance, the results of the sociological, historical, and anthropological researches have thrown much light on the question of the origin and early development of political institutions and the rapid growth of the international political activities has added into the field of political studies many new factors or phases which were never dreamt of by the political scientists of the past. All of these are recent results and new changes. Whether such a gain can be made up what is lost is still open to question. But it can not be doubted that there is a gain as well as there is a loss.

Now, if a lot of old things were taken away from and at the same time a lot of new things were added into the domain of political science, as we have pointed out, we can not help wondering how many things which were once considered as essential and inherent to what is known as political science are still left to this field of study. It is only natural that changes must be made and reconstruction is needed. Yet it is to be noted that there are still many students in the field of political science treating their subject as if it were treated by men of the past, such as Aristotle or Hobbes.

To understand what properly belongs to the field of political study is to understand the scope, nature, or subject matter of political science. But in order to understand this, it is necessary to understand how the distinction between the state and society or rather what is political and what its social has come to exist. We have shown in the last chapter that such a distinction has been made by men in the different fields of social studies and men of social movements. It is to be borne in mind, however, that the distinction as conceived by these scholars or reformers is mainly the reflections of the changes of actual facts and conditions.

The causes of the changes of the actual facts and conditions in connection to the subject under consideration are many; but it is sufficient to state here both the economic and political revolutions in the latter part of eighteenth century may be regarded as the chief factors for the changes. There are many writers who think that the economic or rather the industrial revolution is the only factor for the changes of political as well as social facts and conditions since the later part of eighteenth century. It is true that the economic factor is more important than the political one, yet to neglect the political revolution and its effect on our political and social outlooks is to ignore the whole truth.

The political revolution in France and particularly in the United States has made men feel sure that king or monarch is different from government and that government is different from state. But most important of all is that it has made man feel sure that he is the master and not the slave of the political fabric and that he is an end by himself and not the means of the state. On the contrary, it has made him feel that the state, the government, and the monarch or the king, not to say the president, are the means or instruments by which he and his fellow citizens are using to attain their own ends. This idea is well defined in the Declaration of the Rights of Man as well as in the Declaration of Independence. Government is no longer consdiered to be the government of the king, for the king and by the king. It is declared, in the language of Lincoln, to be government of the people, for the people and by the people.

Indeed, it takes a long time for men to realize the importance of the individuals in their relations to the state. Even in the later part of nineteenth century, Herbert Spencer still wrote essay on Man versus the State. But once the idea spreads, it has effects not only [on] in the field of political philosophy, but also in human thought in general.

Now if government is the means for attaining the ends that the people or individuals are seeking, the government or the political machinery that is nearer or more close to, the people and at the same time can serve them better would naturally be considered as more important to them than that which is far away from them or that which is very indirectly concerned their daily life. Here we come to the principle as well as the movement of self-government, a term referred here mainly to the autonomy of the local government in contrast to the central government. In other words, instead of governing a country from the top to the bottom, it is now ruled from the bottom up to the top. And because it is ruled from the bottom to the top, that which is nearer or more close to the bottom is regarded as the foundation of the political fabric.

Since the local governments, rural as well as urban, are nearer or more close to the people and at the same time can serve them better in their daily life, it is only natural that they should have played a very important role in the arena of modern politics. We shall not elaborate this point, because we have already dealt with in one of the foregoing chapters. What we want to emphasize here is that government being ruled from bottom up, its gravitation has shifted from the central to the local. So besides man versus the state, we have also seen local government versus the central government. This is not only true in a federal state, but also true in the so-called unitary state.

What is true in the arena of politics is also true in other aspects of social life. Just as local political machinery which is more important to men, because it is nearer or more close to them, so other social groups are more important to men, because they are nearer and more close to them. And since men are the ends by themselves and institutions, political or otherwise, are only means for realizing the ends, those institutions which are nearer or more close to them and at the same time can serve them better will be considered as more important to them than anything else. It is the industrial revolution that brings men to form many new social groups other than the political organizations and makes them realize that there is a distinction between what is social and what is political and that the latter is only a part of the former. It makes man see clear that either within or beyond the boundaries of the state, there are many social organizations which are not political in essence or in nature. Thus the horizon of society is extended and that of the state or political organization becomes narrower until it is considered as a part of the former.

Such a change of conception, important as it is, has not been well observed particularly by students of the so-called political science. And this is the reason why political science, being the oldest social science, is larging behind and far behind many of the social studies.

It is to be borne in mind, however, that although it was the political revolution and particularly the industrial revolution that made the man realize the distinction between state and society, this does not mean that before the political or industrial revolution, there was no social groups existing besides or before the state or political institution. As a matter of fact, just as men lived in the governments, such as town, country, province or city long before they lived in the state, so men lived in other social groups long before they lived in the state or political organization. Even when the state was glorified as the Levithan and considered to monopolize every aspect of human life, it was not true in fact, because even then, there were still many social groups existing either within or beyond the boundaries of the state, each retaining its own entity and to a large extent carrying its own affairs without being interferred or encroached upon by the state.

An understanding of this fact will give us an understanding, not only the distinction between what is social and what is political, but also the proper function or functions of the state and its relation to other social groups. So it is necessary for us to examine this point somewhat in detail.

It is generally recognized that the earliest and the most universal social organization is the family. Even among the Yurok, as we have already noted, there are family organizations, although they are very loosely organized. Being the earliest social organization, family existed long before the state or political organization was known to men. Being the most universal organization, there are still many places where we find families without having the state or political organization. Thus family is exterior as well as prior to the state or political organization. Nor can we say that the state is originated from the family as we have already stated in one of the previous chapters.

This being the case, it is clear that family, as a social organization, is an entity by itself, having its own existence, its own life and its function entirely different from that of the state. With the development of the state or political organization, those families which are within the boundaries of the state, though closely related to or even strictly controlled by the latter, still retain its own entity, its own existence, its own life and its own function.

There are political philosophers like Plato, who would like to destroy the system of family in order to solidify the unity of the state. According to Plato, the family is the anthesis to the state. It divides a man's loyalty and interest. It makes man feel that besides the state, there [there] is still something of his own, there is something for him to take care of and there is something that makes him selfish. If every citizen of the state would think more of his own wife, his own children, and his own family, so the Platonic logic goes, then, they will care less and or none at all for the state. In order to preserve the unity of the state, it is necessary to get rid of the family. When no one would have his own wife, his own children and his own family, he will devote his whole interest for the state. Although Plato confines himself to the denial of the family life to a small group of people known as the governors of the state, his argument can be carried out to a larger extent.

The inadequacy of Plato has been already pointed out by his own student, Aristotle. We shall not go into the detail of the disciple's criticism. It is sufficient to point out that Aristotle is right when he says that the abolition of the family ties would narrow the scope of human activities and prevent the development of social bonds necessary and valuable to human beings.

That the state can not take the place of the family is obvious; because the function of the latter is entirely different from the former. How they are different in this respect needs our explanation.

A family is an organic whole. Although the word may be used in a broad sense to include a group of people who are closely connected together by blood relationship, it consists, in the strict sense of term, of parents and children. There are different forms of the family, but we are here dealing chiefly with its function or functions. It has the function of satisfying human sexual desire, but it has also the function of satisfying the desire for offsprings. But a family is something more than that. It is the home of human beings. When we speak of home, we mean something which is very close to our heart. To be at home or to make oneself at home is to make oneself at ease without being formal. One may be far away from home, but home is always in his heart and the desire of going home is always present in his mind. As a matter of fact, to leave home is something unusual to him or her. No matter where he goes and no matter where he works, he always wants to have his home with him, or at least near to him. Unless he is at home, he usually considers himself a guest, a stranger. To say that a man or a woman is harmless means something miserable or pitiful. Generally speaking, it's the family or the home that demands most of the time of one's lifetime, it is the family or home that requires most of one's service and responsibility. In short, it is family or home life that dominates one's own life. In general, we may say that one lives and rests at home, works and cares for home, and so far as children are concerned they are born in and brought up by the family or home.

If a man is so much a man of home, we can easily imagine how much would be left for him to be a citizen of the state. And this is not all. Besides being a member of the family and as a citizen of the state, he may be a member of the church, a worker of the factory or a manager of a company or a teacher of a college and at the same time a member of many other associations or clubs. Unless he is a statesman, a politician or an employer of the government so that he would take more interest in politics or political affairs, his own profession as a worker, a manager, or a teacher requires him to give more time and more attention. As a result, he would not have much time to think or to deal with politics. In other words, besides being a family man, he is a man of profession, we may say that he thinks of his career no less than of his family, yet from his childhood until his death, a normal, or rather a common person is likely to spend more of his time and give more attention to his family. Nor should we neglect to mention his hobby or his belief. He may be a good tennis player, a very religious man, so he joins tennis club and goes to church whenever he can spare his time.

This being the case, it is possible that he does not take interest in political problem at all or that he may forget entirely that he is a citizen, unless he is asked to elect his president or his representative in the legislature, or he has to get a passport for going abroad for a trip. Perhaps it is not going too far to say that he cares the most for the family and the least for the state. And it is because of that he is willingly to give all his monthly salary for the monthly expenses of his family, and in case of necessity, he is willingly to be in debt or to work harder in order to prevent his wife and his children from hunger, from sickness or from death. It is only seldom, as we know, that he will do that for his fellow citizens and for the state. As a matter of fact, he usually complains of tax on his house, on his income, and on his business even the tax is not too high and even he makes a lot of money. Thus he is not only born in the family, but he is also born for the family. This is the reason why he usually feels obliged to do what the family expects and hostile to what the state asks from him.

It is true that modern state exercises certain control over the family, for instance, concerning the marriage in its monogamous form or with one's close relative, regarding divorce and inheritance and relating to the care of children and wives. But equally is it true that one can not have a few wives or husbands at one time, he or she can marry to different women or different men respectively by the process of divorce from time to time. So it is true that if one does not like to leave all of his money to his wife or children, he can always dispose his money by one way or another. A family is not a mechanical organization which can be set up or broken like a machine. It is an organic unity. Its relationship goes much deeper than its blood or sexual relationship. It builds its foundation on love, on affection, and on mutual understanding and cooperation all of which are beyond the realm of law and can not be controlled by the state. All that the state can do is to lay some rules for regulating its external aspect which is not the essence of the family.

When a family becomes a broken home, the state may send the children to its own institution or orphanage so that they can be still taken care of. Yet it is generally recognized that such an institution can never substitute for a home. Instead of going to such an institution, people prefer to find an adopted home for the children. Even then we have to admit that no matter how much we may love our adopted daughter or son, there is always a difference between our love to our own children and our love to our adopted children.

It is clear then that at most that a state can do for a family is to regulate it in a negative way. Its function is to prepare for the worst. It deals with abnormal family rather than normal. And whenever the state puts its fingers on a family, we always think that this means something bad in and for the family.

Moreover, there is always a limit for the state's control. The state may not issue a license of marriage to an underaged couple, but it can not prevent them from making love to each other or getting married afterward. A state may find no reason to render a divorce to a couple, but it can not make them love each other if they don't love each other. A family is a social organization, but it is something more than that. It is an expression of the innermost life of human beings. And perhaps, one's real identity can be found only when he is at home. But a home is not simply a collection of individuals, each expressing its own individuality, it is a common life, a super-organic as well as an organic unity.

The function of the family is so closely connected with the essence of the family that unless the very life of itself is destroyed its function can not be separate from it. In other words, no other social groups can perform the function of the family and the state is the least to be qualified for doing that. In short, to take away the function of the family is to destroy this human institution.

Furthermore, it may be said that to destroy family life means almost to destroy life itself, because, as we have already noted, our life is chiefly dominated by family life. Human beings lived for a long time and still live in many places until very recently without the state, but seldom they lived or live without family. Being the earliest as well as the most universal social group of human society, we don't believe that it will cease to exist in the future, nor do we believe that its function will be taken over by other social groups including the state itself.

It may be well concluded now that the family, although existing within the boundaries of the state, it has a world of its own, performing a kind of function which not only is different from that of the state, but also can not be performed by the state.

On the contrary, the stability of the political organization or the state depends, to a large extent, on the family system. Men and women who form a family and have children have in general more sense of stability. Being responsible to the family, particularly to his or her children, he or she does not only usually think of them more than himself or herself, but he or she also think of them into a long future. One does not only think of the health of one's children, he thinks also of their education. One does not only wish one's own children to have education, but he also wishes them to have higher education and the best education. The long years that require a parent to do these things usually occupy the whole, or beyond the span of one's married life. So if the children are still young and he or she is already old, he or she would have to provide means for them to live and to get educated if he or she would die earlier. This is the sense of permanence as well as the sense of responsibility. The reason why many of the enterprising organizations prefer to employ married man instead of unmarried one has a lot to do with what we are saying.

If we admit that the chief function of the state is to maintain order and peace, the family is one of the most important factors for maintaining order and peace. The order and peace of a state can not ⟨be⟩ viewed as something different or separate from the order and peace of society. Unless society is in order and in peace, a state can hardly have peace and order. Family is the foundation of society and so it is the foundation of the state. Looking from this standpoint, we may say that the existence of the state would be endangered if the system of family is destroyed. In fact, there were some families without state, but we have not seen a state without family.

In his *Politics*, Aristotle told us that families may unite into village and villages may form a state. Thus historically speaking, the family came first and then the village. The state came after the village. But we must also note that according to Aristotle, the state is prior to the village and the family, because both the village and the family are only parts of the state and they come into existence merely for the completion of the state. Thus at least in concept, if it is not for the development of the state, there would be no family and no village. Before nature creates family and village, it has first the state in mind.

We have already pointed out that there were families long there were states and that until recently there were many families existing in different parts of the world without being under the jurisdiction of the state. This is also true to the village. It is apparent then that Aristotle's contention that the state is prior to the family and the village is not true.

But what we want to point out here is that he puts the village between the state and the family and it is in the middle stage through which the family develops into the state. Either from the standpoint of time or from the standpoint of space, the village plays a very important role. Although the family alone can exist, it is not sufficient enough, only in the village man will have all he wants for his material needs. And it is in the state that man can live well. It seems to Aristotle that without the village, neither the family can get enough to exist, nor the state can be originated.

While the so-called political scientists in the past have given a lot of attention to the family and its relation to the state, and until recently, after being influenced by the anthropology and sociology, have realized the political significance of the tribe or even the clan; they have seldom taken the village into consideration.

Even up to the end of nineteenth century, there were many writers, still asking the question whether village is a primitive institution or a modern institution and whether village existed before the state or a creature of the latter. Mr. G. L. Gomme, for instance, wrote in 1890 with these words: "The village community is thus presented to us as a primitive institution, having a prominent position among the backward races and a subordinate position among the advanced races of the world, and it is suggested that the latter of these two phases is survival from the former."[①]

And then he says in another place: "If, as I suggest, the village community can be proved to be a primitive institution, this must have a most important bearing upon its history in Britain. It means that the village community originated at a stage of social development long prior to the political stage, and that hence its appearance among the

---

① G. L. Gomme, *The Village Community*, 1890, London, p. 116.

local institutions of Britain is of the nature of a survival from prehistoric times."①

Had our author believed the actual historical development of the village as already suggested by Aristotle, he would not need to write a book in order to prove that the village community originated at a stage of social development long prior to the political state. Nor is it to be doubted that at the present world, the village community is still playing an important role particularly in the oriental states and societies.

It seems to be very curious that the political scientists in the western world, being influenced so much by the Politics Aristotle which indeed is regarded as the bible for their political science and which is still being used by some of their universities as text book, have almost entirely disregarded the importance of the village as conceived by Aristotle in their political writings. Yet at the same time, they have given much attention to Aristotle's conception of family in its relation to the state, assuming that the state is originated from the family and thinking that the family is an integrated part of the state.

Sir Henry Maine who has done more than anyone else to introduce the Indian village institution to the western academic circle has noted the similarities between the Indian village and English Township. He says: "The village community of India exhibits resemblances to the Teutonic township which are much too strong and numerous to be accidental; where it differs from the township, the difference may be at least plausibly explained. It has the same double aspect of a group of families united by the assumption of common kinship; and of a company of persons exercising joint ownership over land. The domain which it occupies is distributed, if not in the same manner, upon the same principles; and the ideas which prevail within the group of the relations and duties of its members to one another appear to be substantially the same. But the Indian village community is a living, and not a dead institution."②

We shall not go to the question whether township resembles exactly to the Indian village or villages in other parts of the world, but we agree with Maine that the Indian village community is a living and not a dead institution. As a matter of fact, not only in India, but also in China, in Japan and in many other places, the village community is a living and not a dead institution. Moreover, the village community is just as old as the family organization. It can be found among the primitive societies and it can be traced back to ancient China or as Mr. Gomme has pointed out to the prehistoric times in Britain and other parts of Europe. And even in Europe it does not disappear entirely in

---

① *Ibid.*, p. 2.
② *Ibid.*, p. 2.

our own day.

While in Europe the village community has long been merged into the other local institutions, in the east and particularly in China, only recently it has been fully utilized as a local unit for the administration of the government. In regard to many of the primitive societies, it may be said that it still retains its original character, having little if any to do with political functions. Here villages may combine to form a tribe which, as we have said, has political significance. The villager or villagers may represent its or their village or villages in the tribal council and therefore having something to do with things political. But we have to remember that the village itself is not a political organization, its function being nonpolitical.

It is true, as Aristotle tells us, that a village is an economic self sufficient unit; but it is something more than that. Its origin may be traced back to kinship and it is composed, as Aristotle suggests, of families. It is also possible that these families may be related to each other by blood relationship. It is even possible that these families come from one family. At least this is true to many of the Chinese villages where we find each of them has its own ancestral temple. Here we may say that there is a religious function.

But the essential characteristic of the village community is its communal life, life in its spiritual and social as well as material aspect. The village occupies a definite piece of territory. The villagers are chiefly dependent on the products of the soil, although the farms are not necessarily to be all surrounding or close to the village. Men are tied here not only by kinship or a common supernatural being, but also by land. Land may be owned privately by each family, but there are also lands common to and used by all the members of the village. This is also true to other kinds of property. But what we want to emphasize is those things which are common to or owned by all the members of the village, for these are the things that constitute the communal life of the villagers. Besides different kinds of lands such as used for cultivation, for grass or for grave which are common to and used by all the villagers, there are common well or wells, common temples, common feast, common school and many other things. In certain respects, it may be considered as an enlargement of the family. It is this communal life that makes its life a super-organic as well as organic whole. There is esprit de corp. There is a village sentiment. It has its inner life as well as its exterior life. It is a self sufficient unity in different aspects of life.

Since there are still many villages existing without having any political function or being much controlled by state or political organization, and since village existed long before the state or political organization came into being, village life is not only exterior but also prior to political life, or the life of the state.

Although the recent tendency has been to utilize these villages for administrative units of the state, but the life of the village retains, in many parts of the world, its own identity. China, for instance, has more than eighty percent of her population live in the villages. How much the state may try reorganize its political structure and in the villages, it would take a long time for the state to change the life of the village. Even when it is changed in order to serve the political purpose, it still retains its nonpolitical functions which are the essential characteristics of it. Just as the state can only exercise certain control on the exterior aspect of family, so it can only do so to the village. "Work when the sun rises; Rest when the sun sets; what do I care for the imperialistic power." This was [and] the song of the villager in China. The change of time has changed the attitude of the Chinese villager, yet the function of the state can not substitute for the function of the village.

What is true to the family and village is also true to the religious organization or the church. The so-called secret societies among the primitive or modern people are chiefly the religious organizations. W. H. R. Rivers has shown that all the theories concerning the origin of the secret societies are connected with religion, religion in the broad sense of the term. He says: "One is that they arose as the means of practising religious rites which had been forbidden by rulers, a motive which seems to have been definitely present in the case of many of the secret societies of China, while has also been supposed to have been the motive of witches' organizations which are said to have been widespread in Europe. In each case the societies embody an early religious cult which has been thrust into the background by rulers, who had either brought a new religion into there from elsewhere, or had adopted a new religion. According to this view the witches' cult of our own in other European countries is the survival of a pre-Christian religion. A different view, for which I am responsible, was put forward especially to explain the nature of the organizations of Melanesia. It is that Melanesian secret societies embody the religious cults of immigrants who, coming in small numbers among an alien people, pratised their religion in secret, and only gradually admitted the indigenous people to participation in their rites."①

Hutton Webster, in his well known book, *The Primitive Societies*, maintains that secret societies are originated from totemic clans. Rivers, although noting that "it is a

---

① Rivers, *Social Organization*, 1924, p. 133-134.

striking fact that, wherever secret societies exist in Melanesia, totemism is absent, or of a very indefinite kind, admits that "that there is a relation between totemism and the organizations which I have been describing seems to be fairly certain." ①

Even secret societies which are not regarded as having religion as their essential characteristic, the process of initiation is always religious. While the process of initiation is a very important feature of secret societies, particularly in the primitive societies, secret societies are always strongly coloured with religious character. In order to make this point clear, a few more passages may be quoted from Rivers' *Social Organization*.

"In the New Hebrides the practice that only men of one rank may eat together is definitely connected with the fire. Each grade has its own fire, and the essential rule is that a man may only eat food cooked at a fire of his rank, at which no other food may be cooked. This feature has been only recorded with certainty in the New Hebrides, but is probably an essential feature of all the graded societies of Melanesia. The place thus taken by fire in the rules of the organization almost certainly has a religious character, and this is quite certain in the case of the next feature of the societies, that according to which the whole organization is connected with a cult of ancestral ghosts. Many features of the ritual of initiation depend on the belief that, at this time, the initiate and the group as a whole come into relation with the ghosts of dead ancestors."

"Thus, in the island of Ambrim in the New Hebrides, an image is made as a part of the ceremony of initiation into several of the higher ranks, and it is believed that the ghost of the grandfather of the initiate enters this image in order to watch over the career of his descendant. In another part of Melanesia, the Banks Islands, there are special societies distinguished from, though related to, the graded organization, which are called ghost societies, and are connected with ancestral ghosts."

"Certain widespread features of secret associations, which have attracted much attention, are definitely connected with cults of ghosts. The masks, which form prominent objects in our museums, are, in many cases, intended to represent ghosts. In Melanesia these masks are worn especially when the members leave their secret place of meeting, and serve to keep up the general belief of the community that the organization embodies a cult of ghosts. The masks serve as one of the means by which the secrecy of the proceedings is secured. Another means to this end is the production of certain mysterious sounds, of which that produced by swinging a bull-roarer is the most widespread. This and other sounds are believed by the uninitiated to be the voices of the

---

① Rivers, *Social Organization*, 1924, p. 135.

ghosts. In Melanesia hats take a prominent part in the ritual of the secret societies. The relation of these hats to masks is doubtful, but it is probable that the hat is only a special form of mask, and that the emphasis of that part of the mask which covers the head is connected with the sanctity of that part of the body."①

The importance of the secret societies among the primitive people is beyond question, for besides, the family, clan or those groups which are still more or less related to them such as village or tribe, almost all of the other social groups in the primitive societies may be called secret societies. These societies, as we know, exist side by side with the primitive family and the clan and they may be found in the primitive village and tribe. Just as the family and the village, they existed not only prior to the state, but also exterior to the state.

Even in our modern society, secret societies having religious significance are usually exterior and sometimes antagonistic to the state. They are exterior to the state, not only because each of them has an inner life of its own, but also because it may be an international organization which is beyond the boundaries of a state. The so-called Three Points Organization, founded by the Chinese, for instance, had not only local chapters in different parts in China, but also branches in different parts of South Sea Islands and other parts of the world. Although this organization is strongly coloured with political purpose, its religious character can hardly be doubted.

The secret societies are antagonistic to the state, partly because some of them are organized for political purpose, but chiefly because they are secret and therefore suspected by the political machineries. The state demands organizations within its boundaries make known their purposes and sometimes requires them to get registered in the governmental agencies. To keep something secret is always intolerable to the state, even such society has nothing whatsoever to do with politics and purely confines itself to religious activities.

When we come to the church such as that of Christianity in the history or even in our day, we shall see more clearly that religious organization, besides being prior and exterior to the modern states, has been and to a certain extent still is one of the largest as well as the most powerful human organizations. No modern state has yet attained to such a position. Nor will there be likely to have such a state in the future. While political fabric such as Roman Empire was large and powerful so far as political organization is concerned, it becomes somewhat insignificant in comparison with the

---

① Rivers, *Social Organization*, pp. 123-124.

christian church during the middle ages. For the church, besides being large in size and powerful in force, has penetrated into the bottom of human heart and into the routine of his daily life. Thus the mediavel church, though utilizing the Roman Empire as a model for its external extension, it went beyond the boundaries of Roman Empire, not only in its exterior aspect, but also in its spiritual life. It is said that the church of the middle ages was the ghost of the Roman Empire coming out from the grave. Even this is true, it must be added that the ghost was more magnificent and more influential than the Roman Empire itself. Moreover, while the Roman Empire was dead long ago, the church is still living, living almost as it used to be in the old World and extending its sphere of influence in the Orient as well as in the New World.

The rising of the modern states did not begin until the Reformation. It is clear that the church, the Christian church existed long before the state. If we say that there were political organizations before the church, then we may also say that there were religious organizations such as the secret societies before the political society. Our present knowledge assures us that there are secret societies among some of the primitive people who do not organize into a tribe in which, as we have already remarked, we find, for the first time, the germs of political activities.

It is safe to say then that the religious group existed before the political organization and that the church existed before the state. While religious and political activities can hardly be distinguished among the primitive people or in the early history of mankind, the difference between the church and the state has been constantly insisted upon by modern writers. It must be said that although many writers have interpreted the mediaeval society in term of church and state, there was no state in the strict sense of the term during that period. There were, of course, political organizations and institutions. But there more or less subordinate to the church. This is also true, to a large extent, to the earlier as well as to the primitive societies where religious influence has been always the major factor in shaping the different aspects of human life.

It is after the reformation that the conception of state begins to be worked out gradually. It is interesting to note that the Reformation, being religious in its origin and in its character, has turned out to be a political issue and hence given rise to the system of modern states. And although, it was never dreamt of by the leader, M. Luther, of the Reformation when he first started the movement, he was forced to take refuge in the political regime in order to carry out his program. Emperor, kings, princes and lords, after having been long under the yoke of the church and its pope, did not hesitate to utilize the opportunity to revolt against the pope and the hierarchical regime of the church. It was a first group of political entities hostile to the pope and the Roman church, then came the national state which demanded not only its separation from the church, the Roman church, and its pope, but also the supremacy over the church within its own boundaries.

For a time, it looked as if the church were going to collapse, breaking into pieces and never coming into life again. But history did not go that way. The reason is simple enough. For while man of political ambition did not like pope and the church in which he was the head, no one dared to question the existence of God or the necessity of the church. God there must be and so it is with church. The question that men during and after the time of Reformation were arguing was who should be the representative of God in order to ⟨be the⟩ head of city of God, namely the church. When the king claimed that he should be the head of the church, he claimed that not because he was the king, the head of a political organization or a state, but because he was sanctioned by God to do that. Thus the theory of the divine right of the King was a timely invention, insisting that it was the king, not the pope, who was the vicar of God. This theory had its mediaeval origin, but it was put into practice until after the Reformation. In a sense, it did a lot of harm to the pope and the Roman church. But if we look from another angle, politics was thereby even more strongly coloured with religion. It was different from the time of middle ages. At least in theory it was then thought that things belong to Caesar should give to Caesar and things belong to Peter should be given to the Pope. Now even in theory this was disregarded. It can not be doubted that the king was using God and the church as a pretext for his own political interest. But if we ask why he had to use God and the church instead of using something else, then we can not but admit that God was still faithfully believed and church strongly supported. Thus if God or church had no longer the power to check the king for utilizing him or it for his own selfish purpose, the king did not have the power to denounce him or to destroy it respectively.

Here we see the potential force of the church and God. But we are considering here the relation of the church to the state in the so-called protestant countries. If we look at the Catholic countries, although politically speaking each country was considered as an independent entity, religiously speaking, they were and still are under the control of the pope. It was true that the pope and Roman church lost his and its control in the protestant countries, but they have gained and are still gaining new forces outside of European countries. With the effort of members of the Jesuit order and of other Catholic organizations, Catholicism has been widely spreading into the four corners of the earth. Look at the Congo State of Africa or other parts of that continent, look at the Phillippine or Indo-China or other parts of Asia, or look at South America or even in the United States and Canada, Catholicism, being interpreted as Medievalism by some, is still living and expanding. It not only remains to be the rival to Protestantism, but even menaces the latter. It is not merely a religious belief; it has also political significance. So when Al Smith was nominated as the candidate for presidency sometimes ago, the protestants of the United States were afraid that if he would become the president of the United States, instead of listening to the will of the people of his country, he might become a tool for the pope, because, it was thought, a Catholic was always loyal to his religious superior.

As a matter of fact, we may say that the pope himself is an international politician. He talks and acts very frequently beyond his religious capacity, in spite of the fact that by an express declaration in 1929, "the Holy See announced its intention of remaining aloof from all temporal disputes between nations and of refraining from participation in international congress convoked for the settlement of such disputes, except upon special appeal from the contending parties."①

In connection to this, ⟨a⟩ question has been raised in regard to the status of the Papacy. According to Prof. J. W. Garner, "Prior to 1870 the Holy See was a state and the Pope was a temporal sovereign, as well as the ecclesiastical head of the Roman Catholic church. In that year, however, the papal territories were secularized and incorporated in the new kingdom of Italy and thus the temporal sovereignty of the pope came to an end." He concludes by saying that "the better opinion, however, is that while the papacy was treated somewhat as if it were an international person, it was not such in fact and that it was still less a state according to political science. It was not invited to send plenipotentiaries to either of the two Hague Peace Conferences or to other international conferences later convoked. Moreover, the diplomatic representatives appointed by or accredited to the Vatican were charged only with interests of a religious character, and the concordats to which the papacy was a party dealt only with such matters."②

We agree that the papacy is not a state, although to be a state it is not necessary to have representative in the two Hague Peace Conferences or in other international conferences, nor is it true that the representatives appointed by or accredited to the Vatican were charged only with interest of religious character as suggested by Prof. Garner. Moreover, as we see it, the papacy is not a state, not because it does not have

---

① See J. W. Garner, *Political Science and Government*, pp. 60–61.
② See J. W. Garner, *Political Science and Government*, pp. 60–61.

the so-called essential characteristics such as sovereignty, government, territory and people since the pope not only has the highest authority over his subjects within the Vatican ground, it has also a governmental organization and judicial court of its own. It is true the subjects within the Vatican territory are not large in number. It is also true that the territory over which the pope rules is small in size. But is it not true that in the eyes of international law, states are all alike and equal without considering how large or how small they may be?

But when we say that the papacy is not a state, we are looking to the essential function of the one as it is different from the other. For the essential function of the papacy is religion and that of the state is politics. Originally and fundamentally the papacy is a religious entity while the state is a political organization. Just as the state of our day goes beyond its own function to attempt to control the church, so the church of the medieval period went beyond its function to get hold of political or temporal powers. But as a church, we understand it as a religious institution and as a state we understand it as a political organization.

Being a religious entity, the papacy, has not only a history that may be traced back to the medieval age, a history longer than most of the modern states, but also a life of its own, a life clearly expressing in its external as well as it spiritual aspect. The pope is the spiritual head of Catholicism. But he is also the temporal, though not political, head of the Vatican City, a small territory of 160 acres inhabited by a few hundred person. This city, though surrounded by the territory of Italy, or, to be exact, the city of Rome, is entirely independent of Italy. It is also interesting to note that it was under the control of Mussolini, the dictator of Italy a treaty was concluded between the papacy and Italy in 1929 to the effect that the sovereignty or exclusive jurisdiction of the Holy See over the Vatican City was recognized by Italy.

But the influence of the Holy See goes far beyond its own city and the territories of Italy. It has the right to send and receive diplomatic representatives to and from different states of the world respectively according to the general rules of international law. It has the right to appoint or dismiss the bishops or its subordinate officials of the Catholic churches in any country on earth.

But most important of all is the loyalty and respect that the Catholic people give to their churches and their religious head among whom the pope is the highest. The homage which the Catholic subjects pay to the pope is the most solemn, both in form and in spirit, that human beings give to their superior.

When we come to this point, we may say that not only the Catholics but also the protestants or believers for other religion usually give more loyalty and respect to their religious superiors than to their other superiors. For it is thought that the religious superiors are either representatives of Gods or the ones who transmit or interpret the words of Gods. The belief of God or Gods, though many of us would think it as merely superstitious, is something which can hardly be explained in term of reason. It is emotional, ultra-rational and so close to many of our hearts that we seldom take the trouble to ask why we believe in him or in them. It is true that many of us believe God or Gods simply because our parents or our ancestors believed. But even this is taken for granted, we can still ask why should we follow our parents or ancestors in doing this while at the same time we do not follow them in doing so many other things. It is also true that the people of our age do not believe God or Gods so strongly as the people of the past; but equally it is true that such a belief has not been entirely washed away from the hearts of human beings. So long it still remains in the hearts of human beings, there remains also religion, and hence the church.

Western history has supplied us so many examples in regard to the conflict between the church and state. The latter, assuming to have the supreme authority over everything including the church within its own boundaries, has again and again attempted to suppress the church by one way or another for the last few hundred years. Yet the church are still surviving. Even antagonistic and hostile as the Nazi in Germany and the Communist in Russia have not succeeded in destroying the church in their respective countries. The Kaiser was gone, the house of Hohenzollern was gone. The Csar was gone, the regime of monarchy was gone. But the church, though not powerful as the monarchical regime for one time and though severely suppressed by the state again and again, is still alive and it is still living.

Why it is so? It is because men still believe in God or Gods and therefore religious life is still a part of men's inner life, close to their hearts and latent in their minds. The state may, as it did many times in history, close the church or even destroy it, prohibiting its service to be held and bell to be sounded; but it can not prevent the belief of human heart or the inclination of human mind either toward God or Gods or hostile to the state.

Just as religious life is prior and exterior to the state or political life, economic life is also prior and exterior to the latter. Although it was the industrial revolution that gave rise to many economic organizations and problems which led men to question the capability of the state or political organization to handle adequately the economic affairs of modern age and consequently to develop the so-called political pluralism for the last few decades, the history of economic organization may be traced back to the time, when economic life began. So it is safe to say that economic organization is prior and exterior to the state and political organization.

Among the primitive people and in the earliest societies, economic organization, though it may be very loosely organized, may be found. Thus among the Yurok, as already noted that there was hardly even a family organization, we find, however, that there was economic cooperation and organization. William Christie MacLeod gives us the following description of the economic organization[①]: "Economic interrelations, in fact, appear to have had no concern for village limitations. The Yurok and their neighbors, for example, established business cooperations which are almost comparable to our modern joint-stock companies. They had developed the practice of selling and renting part interest in fishing places and other productive properties. As a result, eight men, say, from separate villages, might possess shares in a fishing hole, one with the exclusive right to take eels there; another with the exclusive right to take salmon there, and so on; or one with the exclusive right to fish there on certain days, while the others also possessed certain rights as to time. Even primitive 'shares of stock,' of a sort, existed. In the case of whales stranded on a beach, the individual's claim in the whale was evidenced by a pack strap, the relative length of the straps determining their relative amount of interest in the whale. Comparable practice existed in the joint ownership of sealeries. Trading in the shares of interest was by means of selling the strap or other evidence of one's interest in the joint stock, these primitive 'shares' being sold far from the location of the land in which interest was held."

Group hunting is a common phenomenon among the primitive people. Since wild game can not be handled by one man or even very few, it is necessary to have collective action. Experienced and skillful man would take the lead and those who are not would follow him. The ultimate aim of seeking food is distributive and for the individuals or their families, but the way of getting the food is collective. Such an economic group is usually seasonal and sporadic. Once the purpose is achieved, it desolves automatically. Nevertheless, it is the germ of economic organization.

The so-called nomadic tribe may be regarded as an economic group rather than a political group. For here it is the interest of the cattle that holds men together. Even in agriculture which is usually described as an occupation of the family is developed in a collective way which is by no means confined to the members of the family alone among

---

① MacLeod, *Origin and History of Politics*, 1931, p. 29.

the primitive people. Men and women of different families help each other to cultivate the land or to plant the seed when the work is too much for the members of one family to carry on. No reward is given here except sometimes meal is provided for those who help or the same help will be given back when it is needed.

Thus no matter how loosely or sporadically the economic organization of the primitive societies might be organized, it can not be denied that there were economic organization long before the political organization came into existence. It was the material needs that drove men to form economic groups and so long the needs are present, there will be groups of some sort to fulfill these needs. The guilds of the Medieval ages, the trade companies of the sixteenth or seventeenth century after the sea route of the world was open, and the huge and complicated economic corporations of our own days have developed to meet the human needs. They are by no means the creatures of the state. As a matter, many of them have grown in spite of the hostile or antagonistic policy of the state. The Chinese government, for instance, for centuries has prohibited her people to go beyond her own boundaries to do business particularly in the South Sea Islands such as Java and Singapore, yet the Chinese people in those parts of the world have built up an economic foundation which, though in turn having been restricted and assaulted by the colonial governments and the Thai government, still remains to be one of the dominating economic factors in these regions. The Chinese Chamber of Commerce in Bangkok has been long regarded as an obstacle by the Thai Government's anti-Chinese policy. But since Siam does not allow China to send her diplomatic envoys to Siam, the Chinese Chamber of Commerce becomes the most convenient organization that the Thai government can deal with the Chinese in a collective way. Is it not a pity on the part of the state to retain something that is bitterly hated by it or sometimes hostile and antagonistic to it?

We all know that many modern states live on their colonies. British Empire, for instance, has controlled the largest colonial territories of the world. But colony, a term, though often used by the so-called political scientist, finds its origin rather in economic expansion. The East India Company, and many others in the Far East were originally motivated by the economic desire rather than political ambition. So it was the discovery of the New World. The Declaration of Independence was motivated by economic no less than political freedom, and it is going too far to say that economic factor anticipated political revolution.

It is true that industrial revolution has gradually destroyed the autonomy of the local economic units such as village, county or province within the state and the state has become the owner of many economic enterprises or it has controlled, directly or indirectly, these enterprises. But we should not forget that at the same time industrial revolution has made it almost impossible for any state in the present world to exist economically without any help from other state or states. Even such a state as the United States has to transport so many daily necessities from different parts of the world. Here we see, one of the most, or rather the most highly industrialized and highly developed agricultural state, yet it needs economic help from other countries. Even the United States can get all the raw materials that she wants for her industry and her people, she still needs to find markets outside of her own territories.

With the rapid development of the means of communication on the continent, on the sea and in the air, distance, in the geographical sense, means almost nothing to human beings. The commercial and industrial centers of the different states are going to be linked by the fastest means of communication. It is possible that it will take one less time to go from New York to Shanghai than to go from New York to one of the country place within the United States itself. Nor will it be surprising to us that men of New York will know more about Shanghai than about the city of Claremont in California, to say nothing of the red Indians in the western states. When an American tells me that he comes from Berlin, it is more natural for me to think that he comes from Berlin in Germany rather than from Berlin in Connecticut or from Berlin in Oregon. When you say that you live in Paris, it is more natural for me to think that you live in Paris of France rather than in Paris of Illinois. When we say New York, we refer more frequently to the city of New York rather than the State of New York and it can not be doubted that there are people who know only the city of New York and know nothing or never heard of the state of New York, in spite of the fact that New York city is politically under the control of New York state. Even many of us know well that Albany is the capital of New York State and therefore is the political superior to New York City, few of us would care to know what is going there.

It is commerce and industry that make New York great and important. No one will question the political significance of Washington, D. C., yet in population and in wealth, it has little in compare with New York. And as a city, Washington, D. C. is smaller than many of the American cities. In a sense, urbanization typifies our modern civilization, but why it is so? This can not be answered unless rapid growth of commercialization and industrialization is taken into account.

It is to added also that although both commerce and industry are spoken of as anthesis to agriculture, the development of commerce and particularly industry for the last two or three centuries has quickened the development of agriculture. The application of scientific method and mechanical instrument in the farms is, in a sense, the result of industrialization. Hence industrial revolution may be well called as agricultural revolution. It revolutionalizes the method of cultivation as well as the method of industrial production.

Thus the whole of economic life of the modern age has turned to a new leaf and the mechanism which is responsible for the development of such a life may be called the economic organization. Its origin may be traced back to the fishing or hunting group, long before the appearance of political organization, to say nothing of the state. Its sphere of influence has long been beyond the jurisdiction of the state. It expresses in numerous forms, both in content and extent, and penetrates into almost every aspect of human life. It challenges the authority of the state and even tends to take its place.

No one can understand the significance of modern life, unless he understands the significance of modern economic organization.

We have mentioned four kinds of social organizations other than the political organization or the state in order to show that no one of them finds its origin later than or in the state or political organization. They are all prior and exterior to the state and political organization. They are not only the essential factors of the primitive or earlier life of human beings, but also the main pillars of modern and civilized life. Their functions are not only different from that of the state, but also incapable to be performed by the state.

It is needless to say that there are still many other organizations, academic, artistic, moral and the like, each of which expressing each aspect of the inner life of human beings has a life of its own. Like the life of the family and that of religion, it is close to men's hearts and latent in men's minds. The state may use its force to close the school, to destroy the art gallery and to check moral conduct, but all it can do is in a negative way. Even here the control is very superficial. Because the school may be closed, I can still pursue my knowledge in social laboratory and in natural phenomena. Because the art gallery may be destroyed, the talent and genius of an artist can never be destroyed. [Because] The outward moral conduct may be checked, but if I don't intend to do good, I shall always remain bad.

Thus social life, in its exterior as well as in its inner aspect, is too big and too complicated a world for the state to embrace in its [w] bosom.

Objection of the Word Sovereignty

"The word sovereign, with the abstract term sovereignty would be well enough if confined to its use in international law, as signifying independence, equality with independent states; but [is] it is full of mischief as usually applied to the inter-relations of federal states.

"The uncertainty of the term is an objection to its use upon any occasion. Words applied to political science. Contest chiefly arises from the use of different lexicons, or because of long-accustomed but blind terms, which have become so consecrated that we hardly dare question their propriety. And thus we fight over shadows. The term sovereign or sovereignty—a comparison merely as applied to modern states—is seldom used by two speculative writers as embodying the same notion, and it is oftener used to supply the absence of distinct notion. To say that the absolute prince or the voting people is sovereign is the most certain of its uses; and yet this but puts them in the place of the suzerain, —a place for centuries unknown in constitutional law. Sovereignty is necessarily personal, if at all definite; and, to prevent the use of the term in support of arbitrary government, Lieber, Guizot, and others make it intangible—the one giving us sovereiegnty without sovereigns, and the other giving personality to the obligations which rest upon rulers. The conceptions of both are worthy the elaborate care given them; that of Guizot, which enthrones justice, reason as the sovereign, commands our reverence. Yet in effect it is but a denial that sovereignty can exist among men; it destroys the word by giving it to an obligation; it is not a figment of the imagination, like that ⟨of⟩ social contract; it is a metaphor—a sublime one, but of little use in our present inquiries." (pp. 171–172)

Philemon Bliss, *Of Sovereignty*.

Chapter 9
Sovereignty

Why the state claims to embrace in its own bosom all the other social as well as political organizations? Because the state and the state alone possess the sovereignty. So, this is the answer given by the traditional political scientists. "Every book on political science," declares by Sir John Macdonell, "from the *Republic* of Plato and the *Politics* of Aristotle, has dealt with or touched sovereignty."[1] While it is true that the conception of sovereignty was not clearly defined or presented by the earlier writers, it can not be denied that it has been the heart and corner-stone of the so-called political science; for, sovereignty, according to most of the traditional political writers, is almost and sometimes always identified with the state, and the state being considered as the subject-matter of political science. Rousseau, for instance, tells us in this manner: "This public person, which is thus formed by the union of all individual members, formerly took the name of 'city', and now takes that of 'republic' or 'body politic', which is called by its members 'state' when it is passive, 'sovereign' when it is active, 'power' when it is compared to similar bodies."[2] If what is active is more important than what is passive, then we may say that the sovereign is more important than the state, since, as Rousseau points out, the former is active and the latter is passive. It may be also remarked that the recent attack on the state and hence political science is mainly aiming at the conception of sovereignty and such phrase as "political science at the crossroads" which has been used by a writer as the title for an essay is, as a matter of fact, to be phrased as "sovereignty at the crossroads"[3].

Thus, sovereignty is not only essential, but also identical to the state. But what is sovereignty? Bodin declares it as the supreme power over citizens and subjects unrestricted by law.[4] Although Bodin himself sets many limitations upon sovereignty,

---

[1] See Macdonell's article on sovereignty in *Encyclopedia Britannica*, 14th Edition.
[2] Rousseau, J., *Social Contract*, English translation by H. J. Tozer, Bk. I, p. 10.
[3] See Article by Ellis, in *The American Political Science Review*, 1927, November issue, pp. 733 ff.
[4] Bodin, J., *Six Books of Republic*, 1576, Chapter VIII.

such as the law of God, the law of nature, the law of nations and the fundamental law of France, many writers after him go far beyond his definition, considering the power of sovereignty so absolute that it seems that no power on earth is higher than that. Neglecting or disregarding Bodin's limitations on sovereignty, from Thomas Hobbes to J. Rousseau including a group of the so-called traditional theorists of sovereignty have overemphasized the character of absoluteness of sovereignty.

Being absolute, sovereignty, we are told, is indivisible. That is to say that it can only be possessed by the state, not any other political organizations, nor any other social groups. Where there is a sovereignty, there is a state. Where there is not a sovereignty, there is not a state. Sovereignty is thus identical with the state.

Although this group of writers maintains that there are many characteristics of sovereignty, indivisibility is really the keynote of it. Because it can not be divided, it must be in the hands of one, i.e., the state. Because it can not be divided, it can not be shared by others, political or social entities. Because it can not be divided, it always remains to be supreme and absolute, and consequently the state is always superior to all that are within its boundaries.

This being the case, it is not hard to see how the state is distinguished from other organizations, political or otherwise. Nor is it hard to understand why the state claims to embrace in its own bosom all the other social as well as political organizations. For the state is the sovereign body, while others are not.

It is our purpose to point out, in this chapter and also in the subsequent one, that the theory of indivisible sovereignty enunciated by Bodin and developed by subsequent writers such as Hobbes and Rousseau, is not only contrary to the facts of both the past and the present, but also not entertained by many of political writers.

We contend that sovereignty is divisible. And how can it be divided is not hard to be demonstrated.

Although writers on the history of political thought are wont to trace the idea of sovereignty back to the time of ancient Greece or even earlier,[①] the word "sovereignty" or "sovereign", so far as we know now, was not coined until the later part of Mediaeval Age. Not only the meaning of sovereignty was never defined in the sense of Bodin and still less so in the sense of Hobbes or Rousseau, but also the system of the so-called sovereign states, numerous in number and presumingly equal in status was foreign to the

---

① See Coker, F., *Readings in Political Philosophy*, 1923; also Lowie, R., *The Origin of the State*, 1929.

ancient Greek, Roman and the earlier mediaevalist. ①

It is now generally recognized that the term sovereignty or sovereign was enunciated, or at least used in political sense, by Beaumanoir at the later part of the thirteenth century. In a work entitled *Les Coutumes du Beauvoisir* (1283), Beaumanoir wrote: "Pour ce que nous parlons en cest livre, en pluseurs liurs, du souverain, et de ce qu'il puet et doit fere, li aucun pourorient entendre, pour ce que nous ne nommons conte ne dur, que ce fust du roi; mais en tous les lieus la ou li rois n'est pas nommés, nous entendons de ceus qui tienent en baronnie, car chascuns barons est souverain en sa baronie. Voirs est que le rois est souverains par dessus tous, et a, de son dorit la general garde de tout son roiaume, par quoi 11 puet fere teus establissemens comme il li plest pour le commun pourfit, et ce qu'il establist doit estre tenu. Et se n'i a nul si grant dessous li qui ne puist estre tre en sa court pour defaute de droit ou pour faus jugement et pour tous les cas qui touchuent le roi. Et pour ce qu'il est souverain par desseus tous, nous le nommons, quant nous parlons d'aucune souverainet qui a li apartient."②

Thus, both the French forms "souverain" and "souverainetè" appear in this passage. The term so applied is undoubtedly used in two senses: one is that every baron is the "souverain" in his own barony and the other is that the king is "souverain" in the whole kingdom. In other words, besides the sovereignty of the king of the Kingdom, there are many sovereignties of the baronies within the Kingdom.

Some writers, like R. H. Carlyle and A. J. Carlyle, incline to think that Beaumanoir is here speaking for the sovereignty of the king rather than for the barons. "Beaumanoir is careful", says Carlyle, "to point out that while every baron, is 'souverain' in his own barony, the king is 'souverain' in all the kingdom, and therefore he can make such 'establissemens' as he thinks well for the common good. The words represent an important development of the conception of the national monarchy, and they attribute the supreme legislative power to the King; but it should be noticed that the holds the power because he is responsible for the care of the whole kingdom, and

---

① See Jellinek, G., *Allgemeine Staatslehre*, 1900, p. 398. "So wie den Griechen war aber auch den Roemern die Vorstellung des souveraenen Staates fremd geblieben."

Commentary of Previous Work

A. Haemel, *Archiv fir Pfentliches Recht*, 1890, 5Bd, pp. 468–469.

He remarks that the word "sovereign" from philosophiocal standpoint, expounds merely a comparative conception, and is wrongly used to indicate an imperative or absolute".

② Beaumanoir, *Les Coutumes du Beauvoisir*, edition by A. Salmon, Paris, 1889, Section XXXIV, 1013.

exercises it not for his own ends, but for the common good."① In another place, it is remarked: "Beaumanoir asserts very emphatically that the king is supreme over all jurisdictions and over all persons. In one passage of great importance which we have already discussed he explains the sense in which he uses the word 'souverain', and says that while every baron is 'souverain' in his own barony, the king is 'souverain' overall, and has the charge of the whole kingdom, and therefore can make 'establishments' which are binding everywhere. No one is so great that he can not be called before the king's court, 'pour defaute de droit ou pour faus jugement.' "②

While it may be true that Beaumanoir is here advocating the rising tide of the national monarchy then started, it should not be forgotten that during the fourteenth century, instead of reducing the authority of the feudal lords, the power of the latter were considerably extended. In England, as we know, the influence of feudalism, never strongly established, gradually disappeared. But this does not mean that the king concentrated the powers of the feudal lords into his hand. Because before the king could do so, the common people with the help of the privileged classes rose up to revolt against the king, forcing him to give more liberty to the people. The Magna Carta, may be regarded as the crystalization of this movement for it guarantees the liberty of the people. And the parliament, as a representative body of the people, gradually merges into power, acting as a check upon the royal authority. This [was] happened as early as the thirteenth century. Beaumanoir could not fail to notice that.

Even in the continental Europe, the king was by no means supreme over all jurisdictions and over all persons. Only at the close of the fifteenth century, after centuries of warfare with one another and with the Mohammedans, the Spanish feudal lords were able to get rid of the Moors and to establish a national government with a monarch.

Both the Germans and the Italians have not succeeded their national unity until very recently, although the dream of the Holy Roman Empire has been never realized. The papal authority in Italy, the local lords in Germany, and the numerous free cities in both

---

① Carlyle, *A History of Mediaeval Political Theory in the West*, 1928, Vol. Ⅲ, p. 50.

"Sovereign (From French, a word to be found in all the idioms of Latin origin, as if from *Suprerauus*) meant, originally, highest, excellent and was the same with supreme. It was applied therefore to the monarch, as highest, chief, especially in the feudal times, When the king of prince was not monarch in the sense in which we take the word, but the chief one, the leader, frequently *primus inter pases*. Thus, prince, from princeps, the fair, chief one, the German Furk, the Swedish Färrte, Danish Fyzrte, and the Dutch Vorst, all lead to the same original idea." F. Lielier, *Pol. Ethics*, Vol. Ⅰ, p. 246.

② *Ibid.*, p. 84.

of these two countries were too strong for the German or the Italian king to put the crown on his head in order to rule each country with a single hand.

What was the French situation during the time when Beaumanoir wrote or in the centuries following his own? It can hardly be said that the French king was powerful enough to make his orders well observed through the whole kingdom at the later part of thirteenth century. It was true that the French King, in the tragedy of Avinon, did put the Pope, the head of the Mediaeval church and the so-called vicar of God, into his pocket. But here he was dealing with a declining power which was not a temporal authority. But equally was it true that he was fighting hard even up to the beginning of fifteenth century in order to make his own position secure. As a matter of fact, not until the French Revolution, did the feudal lords in France begin to disappear.

Generally speaking, only some of the powers of the feudal nobles in Europe were encroached upon at the close of the fifteenth century, some still remained in the following one. It was the introduction of gun-powder, the rise of the standing armies and the ceaseless wars such as Hundred Years' War and the Wars of the Roses, together with system of national taxation and many other factors that the authority of the kings in different countries were gradually strengthened and the that of the feudal nobles were reduced.

Now when facts are clear to us, we can easily understand that Beaumanoir was expressing the hope rather than stating the facts of his own day, if his words, as Mr. Carlyle thinks, have led us to assume that he "asserts very emphatically that the king is supreme over all jurisdictions and over all persons."

It must be conceded, however, that looking either from the standpoint of mediaeval universalism or from the standpoint of mediaeval sectionalism, the rising of the monarchical power in the time of Beaumanoir was a salient feature. But that does not warrant us to come to the conclusion that the king was very powerful in fact.

We have to keep constantly in mind these facts, because they guide us from being tempted to believe theories, no matter what they are, are merely reflections of facts, because there are many writers whose ideas, instead of reflecting the facts, may be different or even contrary to the actual conditions of their own times.

But Beaumanoir was by no mean merely expressing his hope without basing on any fact. When he said that each baron was sovereign in his own barony, he was telling us the fact. Nor was he entirely wrong when he said that the king was sovereign over all. This was also the fact.

It was clear to the mind of Beaumanoir that so far as each barony was concerned, the baron was supreme for conducting the affairs therein. But we can also easily understand here that not all the barons were equal in power, nor all the baronies were equal in size. There were some more powerful and some less powerful. There were some bigger and some smaller in the territories over which they controlled. There might be differences in many other respects also. It seemed that there was a hierarchical or rather federalistic in power perhaps more in extent than in content, although it was possible also that some barons were more or less equal in many respects. Moreover, even the king himself was considered as a baron for sometimes. But with the rising tide of the nationalistic movement, when both universalism and sectionalism were showing signs of decline, some barons or kings came into power gradually and claimed to rule over an area which was known as kingdom or nation.

It was for the sake of common welfare rather than for the sake of the kings themselves that they were in a position to execute something which were general in nature and which were inconvenient or unable to be carried out by each baron or by some barons only. Here we find the rise of the national monarchy of the age.

But, for our present purpose, the vital point in Beaumanoir's passage quoted above is that sovereignty of the kingdom is divided—devided between the king and the barons on the one hand and between the barons and barons on the other. It means also that besides the sovereignty, of the king, there would be as many sovereignties as there were barons. You may say that there are sovereignties within sovereignty; but it may be more proper to say that there are more than one sovereignty or there are many sovereignties within one kingdom, since the sovereignty of the king may not be higher in content than that of the barons, although it is larger in extent than that of the latter.

If sovereignty is divided within a kingdom, it must be divisible in its nature; for, although that which is divisible may not be divided, that which is divided is always divisible. Now if the foregoing interpretation of the term sovereignty as used by Beaumanoir, its enunciator or inventor if you like, is not mistaken, the proposition that sovereignty is divisible is strongly supported by historical facts as well as by etymological basis.

This theory of sovereignty is not only different from but also contrary to what Bodin and his followers, particularly men like Hobbes and Rousseau, have advocated, insisting that sovereignty can not be divided and indivisible. To them there can be one and only one sovereignty within a kingdom or a state. One French writer[①] even goes so

---

[①] De Rèal, *La Science du Gouvernement*, 1765, Vol. IV, p. 113.

far as to declare that to divide sovereignty is to destroy it. "Partager la souverainetè," says he, "c'est la dètruire." If John Calhoun has been frequently quoted for being stubborn in insisting that to divide sovereignty is to destroy it, he was merely following what De Rèal had said long ago.

It may be safe to say that that sovereignty is indivisible is sound neither in theory nor in fact. Theoretically speaking, the more we analyze, the more we are compelled to believe that pluralism is the only one that we can accept in interpreting the theory of sovereignty. Monism, as advanced by Spinoza and defended by his followers, is not the monism that is advocated or maintained by those who hold that sovereignty is indivisible. We are told by Spinoza that there is only one thing in the universe, and this one thing is God. He is the only real substance. So Spinoza writes: "There does not exist more than one substance with a given attribute and it belongs to the nature of that one to exist. It must, therefore, belong to its nature to exist either as finite or as infinite. But not as finite. For it would have to be limited by another of the same nature, and this, also would necessarily have to exist. There would, then, be two substances with the attribute, which is absurd. It, therefore, exists as infinite."①

If the view of Spinoza were to be adopted by those who hold that sovereignty is one and indivisible, they would have to insist like many of the mediaeval writers have insisted that there can be only one sovereignty for the world or for the whole universe. But instead of following these mediaeval theorists to struggle for the realization of one sovereignty for the world as a whole they seek their indivisible sovereignty from among the multitude of nations or states the existence of which is not only the indication of the disintegration of, but also in opposition to, the universal empire, be it spiritual or temporal, of the mediaeval ages. Thus they have tried to reconstruct a new political system which is really contradictory in logic.

Why it is so? Because they refuse to commit themselves to the position taken by the

---

① *The Philosophy of Spinoza*, translated by Fullerton, p. 29.

M. De Réal, *La Science du Gouvernement*, Vol. 4, Chapter second, Dec. LXV Section Premiere, p. 113.

"Partager la Souverainete, c'est La détruire Ce qu'ou appelle Souveraineté, ou Pent le denigen aussi par la norn de majeste." p. 121. "La majeste est la souverainete méine; c'est cette Puissance au dessus de laquelle mulle autie Puissance recommende, c'est la Puissance absolue qui s'exerce les majeste." p. 122.

Yet De Réal has a section devoted to the "souveraineté imparfailēs": Un Prince pent pater une Couraune saus être un vrai souvarain, car une souverainet pent être imparfaite de qartre mavieres (1) quand elle n'est pas pleine et eutiere, c'ert-a-dire larsque le souverain n'exerse pas tous les actes de la souveraineté, (2) quand elle est obligée á la foi et hommage lige envers un supremier, (3) quand elle est tributaire, (4) quand elle est rous la protection d'une actre souveraineté.

mediaeval advocates on the one hand, and admit the existence of many political entities on the other. That is to say that although they are dreaming of an absolute, supreme, and, in particular, an indivisible sovereignty, they recognize that the world is divided into many political sovereignties. But to accept that there are many sovereignties existing within the whole world at the same time means to accept, in the last analysis, a pluralistic view of sovereignty. When you start your premises by saying that the whole world is divided into many sovereignties, and then you conclude by saying that within each kingdom or state, to which belongs a piece of territory of the whole world, sovereignty is indivisible, this is unthinkable. It is equal to say that the whole is divided into certain parts, or to be exact, the changeable parts, yet the parts can not be divided. To put it in another way, it means to say that the divided parts can not be divided or the changeable parts can not be changed. This is absurd. This is self-contradictory.

Thus, in admitting or rather maintaining that there are many sovereignties in the world, the so-called monistic writers already presuppose a theory of pluralism. By doing so, they start with a pluralistic point of view, but deny it afterward and end with monism. They live in the pluralistic world and take refuge in its abode; yet they are led to destroy it by their monistic belief.

If there are many sovereignties and sovereignty is divided, sovereignty is divisible. Consequently, the theory that the sovereignty of the state can not be divided must be rejected, for if sovereignty itself is divided and divisible, we don't see why it can not be divided within a state.

The argument of De Rèal and Calhoun that to divide sovereignty is to destroy it may be likened to say that to divide a man is to destroy or to kill him. There are many political scientists who view the state as an organism. So, the argument of De Rèal and Calhoun and many of those who hold that sovereignty is identical with state and that sovereignty is indivisible may apply the organismic theory in the field of biology to the field of political science in order to prove the theory of indivisible sovereignty. But we should not forget that a state is after all not an organism. One may compare an organism and a state and find out that there are similarities between the two. But still you can not call a state an organism.

Herbert Spencer has done more than anyone else to interpret human society and the state from the biological view point. He considers society as an organism and so is the state. Government is compared with the brain and both the upper and lower houses of the legislature are regarded as similar to the two sets of the brain. The blood circulation system resembles the communication system of a country, and so with many other things. But in spite of all the similarities, there are, according to Spencer, striking differences and the differences seem to be more important than similarities. In an organism, Spencer points out, there is only one center of consciousness, while in human society, there are many centers of consciousness, each individual being a center of consciousness. Moreover, the parts composing the whole organism have their fixed and unchangeable places in the living body, while those constitute a society are free to move from one place to another. Besides, the life of each individual organism has certain limit and therefore may be shorter than that of a society.

I say that the differences are more important than the similarities, because it is the former that makes an organism entirely distinguished from a society or a state that shows that a state is really not an organism, while the latter only giving us some hints for the understanding of the outward features of the two things. This may also explain the reason why Spencer, being a celebrate interpreter of the organismic theory of society and state, has become an extreme defender of individualism, thinking that the quality of society is determined by the quality of the [the] individuals and that society is only the means for attaining the ends of the individuals.

Since the state is not an organism, nor is its sovereignty as such, to divide the state or its sovereignty is by no means to destroy as it is in the case of organism. A state can be divided into two or many and this has been frequently done in the past. What is true to a state is also true to a sovereignty. Instancing the case of the United States, we can easily understand the point here elaborated. Before the Declaration of Independence, the Thirteenth colonies in the New World were under the sovereignty of the Great Britain. According to the monistic interpretation, there was only one sovereignty within the British Empire at that time. If the sovereignty of Great Britain would be divided, it would be also destroyed, since sovereignty, as it is said, can not be divided. But after the Declaration of Independence, or after the British recognition of the Independence of the United States if you like, besides the sovereignty of Great Britain, there has been and is a sovereignty of the United States. Is it not that the sovereignty of the Great Britain was divided so that a part of it becomes the sovereignty of the United States? Indeed, it may be argued that Great Britain still retains its sovereignty intact, one and undivided or indivisible. But if this is the case, then, it may be asked: where did the sovereignty of the United States come from? Or where did the thirteen sovereignties of the thirteen colonies come from? You may say that it came or they came naturally. Yet this is not the answer. For before the Declaration of Independence, there was no such thing as sovereignty of the United States. Nor were there sovereignties of the thirteen colonies. If something can not be made out of nothing, the only explanation for the existence of the sovereignty of the United States or that of the thirteen colonies is that it comes or they come from the British Empire. Since the British Empire does not lose all her sovereignty, all that she gives away in order to form what is known as the sovereignty of the United States or that of the thirteen colonies can only be part or parts of the sovereignty of the Great Britain. Here we have the sovereignty divided. And that which is divided is divisible.

It is to be added that few if any would deny that the dominions such as Canada, New Zealand, Australia and South African Union are not sovereign bodies. But did each of them possess sovereignty about thirty or fifty years ago? Here are cases unlike that of the United States where there was a formal declaration or formal recognition for the establishment of a new sovereign power. Yet the sovereignty of each of these dominions has come into existence, not through violence, nor even through the mutual consent. One may think that the Imperial Conference of 1926 has lifted the status of the dominions into sovereign nations, since it declares that they are equal in status both in internal and external affairs within the British Empire. But this can not be interpreted as a declaration of independence, because they are still within the British Empire and tied together by the Crown almost as they used to be.

Where came, then, the sovereignty of each of these British dominions? It came, undoubtedly, from the British Empire. But, as already noted, unlike the United States, the manner in which the sovereignty of each of these dominions came is a gradual and slow process. Moreover, the process is a continuous one. It is hard to demarcate the dividing line between that which is not sovereign and that which is sovereign, or even between that which may be called partial or half sovereign and full sovereign, yet the whole process is a process of division, a process of division which is not only occurred in one place, say in Canada, but also in other places such as Australia, New Zealand, South-African Union and which, we believe, is also being occurred in India and in many other places.

Thus, it is a process of division both in time and in space. In time, some take longer period than others and some shorter than others. India takes a long time. Even up to the present, she is not considered as a sovereign body, though we see clearly, she is in the process of realizing this. If we call India as a partial sovereign nation, we again have a divided sovereignty. If we don't like to call her in that way, she has been and still is in the process of dividing anyhow. When that process of dividing is complete, we call her a sovereign body or, if you please, a full sovereign body. Yet even she is a sovereign, a full sovereign body, from the standpoint of the process of development and from that of Great Britain, she is a dividing part. How much is that part in proportion to the part owned by Great Britain or to that owned by other dominions is open to question. But by common sense alone, you can always tell which of them is enjoying more sovereign rights and which of them is enjoying less sovereign rights. This, however, is not the main issue that we are considering here. What we are taking special interest is that no matter from what angle you look at the British Empire, you see the process of division of sovereignty both in time and in space.

I have taken the British Empire as an example for illustrating the divided sovereignty, showing us that sovereignty is divisible and that the monistic viewpoint that sovereignty within a state or a kingdom is not divided or indivisible is not only contrary to fact, but also illogical in theory. Example like this may be multiplied indefinitely. But enough has been shown that sovereignty is indivisible is absurd.

Nor can the monistic reasoning that a sovereignty is absolute and supreme without any limitation whatsoever be accepted as a sound argument. Here again we must say that if a sovereignty which is absolute and supreme without being limited, there can be only one sovereignty for the whole world or universe. As long as we recognize that there are many sovereignties in the world, no sovereignty can be said to be absolute and supreme in the strict sense of the terms. Because every other sovereignty is a condition to one sovereignty. The condition itself is a limitation. In the world of many sovereignties, each sovereignty is limited by other sovereignty or sovereignties either geographically or otherwise. The most we can say is that it is absolute and supreme within its own sphere. But this is a relatively absolute and supreme sovereignty. And to admit that sovereignty is relatively absolute and supreme is to recognize that there is a limitation. The recognition of a limitation upon sovereignty, at least from the viewpoint of the extent of sovereignty, involves a recognition of divisibility; and in this sense, limitation means division.

Although the monistic theory of sovereignty may be traced, and as a matter of fact it is usually traced back to Bodin, Bodin has set many limitations upon sovereignty. In fact, Bodin himself is contradictory in this point, the vital point of his theory of sovereignty. On the one hand, he declares that sovereignty is the supreme power over citizens and subjects unrestricted by law; but on the other hand, he admits that sovereignty is limited or restricted by law, not only the law of God, of nature and of nation, but also the fundamental law of a state which is known now as constitutional law.

To many of us in the twentieth century, the so-called law of God may mean something of no value or at least something impractical and insignificant to our life. This was not true to Bodin; for he, being born in a time which was not far from, or, if you like, still a part of, the Middle Ages, could not free himself from the theological atmosphere and the dogma that human power is an emanation of God. So, the law of God was very important, practical and significant to him. Moreover, it may be said that all other laws can not be contrary to the law of God. To Bodin, there is no clear distinction between the laws of God and the law of nature, nor that both of these are or should be different from the law of nations. Accordingly, the sovereign is not bound by the nations if it is contrary to the law of God and of nature. The sovereign, says he, is no "more bound by the law of nations than by his own laws, except in so far as the former are in agreement with laws of nature and of God."[①]

Since the law of God is the highest law, "No one", according to him, "who attempts to abrogate or weaken the law of God can escape the judgement of divine sovereignty."[②] Just as the sovereignty is limited by the law of God, so it is limited by the law of nature, the law of nations and the fundamental laws of the Kingdom. "As to the laws concerning the supreme power," Bodin tells us, "the prince can not abrogate or modify them, since they are attached to the very sovereignty with which he is clothed; such is the Salic law, which is the foundation of our Kingdom."[③]

We can see now how narrow is the sphere of Bodin's sovereignty. It is not only restricted by something high above the earthly world such as the divine law and something naturally surrounding us such as the natural law, but also something just beyond as well as within the boundaries of a kingdom. That which limiting the sovereignty of a kingdom just beyond its jurisdiction of is the international law and that which limiting the sovereignty of a kingdom within its jurisdiction is the Salic law, the fundamental law of the kingdom.

Every legal order or every order of law has a sphere of its own in spite of the fact that it may be closely related to other orders of law or something else. Bodin speaks of "divine sovereignty" which we may consider either, as the source of divine law or the sphere in which the divine law is found. If we follow this logic of Bodin, we may speak of the "natural sovereignty" and the "international sovereignty" in contrary to the

---

① Bodin, *De Republica*, p. 134.

② *Ibid*.

③ *Ibid*., p. 139.

"national sovereignty" which is really the sovereignty of the kingdom at that time. Thus we have here many spheres of sovereignty in which the sovereignty of the kingdom is one of them. If the sovereignty of the kingdom, as Bodin sees, is limited by all the other spheres of law or, if you like, of sovereignty, the sphere of the sovereignty of the kingdom seems to be the smallest sphere which is within the other spheres and which can hardly be regarded as standing side by side with the other sphere, because just as the sphere of sovereignty of the Kingdom is smaller than that of international sovereignty and that of natural sovereignty, both of the latter are smaller than the divine sovereignty. Since the divine sovereignty is the highest, all the other sovereignties are existing below as well as within the sovereignty of God. Here we see a division of sovereignty, though hierarchical and federalistic in order.

But this is not all. Within the boundaries of the kingdom, the sovereignty of the Kingdom is also limited by the Salic law, a kind of fundamental law of the kingdom. This legal order, like the other legal orders must have either a sovereignty behind it or a sovereignty within its own sphere. This sovereign power exists within the boundaries of the kingdom. From the geographical standpoint, there is sovereignty within sovereignty and therefore it may be said that either the sovereignty within this area is divided or there are two sovereign orders. But looking from another standpoint, as a limitation upon the sovereignty of the kingdom, the Salic law must be, like the divine law, natural law and international law, independent and indeed outside of the sovereignty of the kingdom. In this sense the sovereignty of the Salic law is larger in sphere and higher in power than that of the kingdom.

To Bodin, "The first and principle function of sovereignty is to give law to the citizens generally and individually."[1] In the language of Dunning, "Legislation, then, is not only the chief function of the sovereign; it is practically the sole and all inclusive function."[2] Now if the law that the sovereignty of the kingdom makes is limited by and therefore inferior to the Salic law, this law is nothing more than what we call municipal law in our day and the sovereign behind it is not a sovereignty outside of, but under the Salic law. The sovereignty of the Kingdom of Bodin is nothing more or even something less than the legislative body of the United States which is only a constituent part of the United States government. In the language of J. W. Burgess, it would not be a sovereignty at all; because back of the government, there is a constitution and only back

---

[1] Bodin, *De Republica*, pp. 240–243.
[2] Dunning, W. A., *Political Theories: From Luther to Montesquieu*, p. 103.

of the constitution there is a sovereignty. ①

Yet to Bodin, this power of legislation, limited as it is, is the sovereignty. When Bodin prefers to give this power to the king, we may call it the sovereignty of the king which, as a matter of fact, may be also regarded as the sovereignty of government at his day.

We have elaborated Bodin's conception of limitation of sovereignty to some length, because this conception of limitation of sovereignty implies, in the last analysis, the theory of division of sovereignty. We have already pointed out that the recognition of a limitation upon sovereignty, at least from the viewpoint of the extent of sovereignty, involves a recognition of divisibility. If a foreign country will force the United States to limit its sovereign power within the eastern part of Mississippi River or not beyond the western part of that river, it is equal ⟨to⟩ say that the sovereignty of the United States will be divided. So, limitation, in this sense, means division and things which are limitable are things which are divisible.

Even in our daily language, limitation usually means division. When one says to me: don't go over that limit, he has in mind that there is a dividing line to which I can go and beyond which I can or should not go. The limit of a campus, the limit of a county, the limit of a province or the limit of anything else implies a division. Thus, where there is a limit, there is a division.

Moreover, as we have already noted, Bodin speaks of the sovereignty of God besides the sovereignty of the King. Anyone who reads Bodin's *Six Books on the Republic* can not fail to notice that there are two kinds of sovereignty constantly occurring in his mind: one is the divine sovereignty and the other the princely sovereignty. Generally speaking, the princely sovereignty is to be found ultimately from the divine sovereignty for the latter is not only superior to the former, but also regarded as the source of all powers, be that human or natural. But in some places, Bodin thinks that the sovereignty of the monarch is originally in the hand of the people. The conception of popular sovereignty clearly recognized by our author may be considered as the starting point of his theory of sovereignty.

Bodin favors the princely sovereignty. This can not be doubted. But to favor something is simply to express his own hope. He does not think that originally the king or prince has this supreme authority. Sovereignty is, therefore, inherent to the people rather than to the king. How the king comes to have this sovereign power? It is the

---

① Burgess, J. W., *Political Science and Comparative Constitutional Law*, 1902, Vol. I, p. 57.

people who give to him. The influence of ideas of popular sovereignty during the later part of the mediaeval age can not be questioned here. Because the sovereignty is originally in the hands of the people, it is possible that the people may not give it to the king, although it is desirable or sometimes necessary to do so as Bodin sees it. It is also possible that if the people do not give the sovereignty to someone or a few for a considerable period of time, the sovereignty is still in the hands of the people. Bodin states very plainly this point with the following words: "But suppose that supreme power, unlimited by laws, and without protest or appeal, be granted by the people to someone or few, shall we say that the latter have sovereignty? For he has sovereignty who, after, God, acknowledges no one greater than himself. I hold that sovereignty resides not in such person, but in the people, at whose pleasure they hold their power, or to whom they must return their authority at the expiration of the period designated. The people can not be considered as having divested themselves of their power when they entrust supreme authority, unrestrained by laws, to one or a few, if the commitment is for a certain period of time, or at the pleasure of the people; for in either case the holders of the supreme authority must render account of their doings to the prince or people, who, being sovereign, are required to give account to no one, save immortal God."①

On the contrary, "If the power is given unlimited by laws, and without the name of magistrate, deputy, governor, or guardian, and not at the pleasure of anyone, certainly it must be confessed that sovereign rights have despoiled to such a one. The people in such case have despoiled themselves of their authority, in order to give to another all the privileges of sovereignty, without conditions; in like manner as anyone might by pure gift surrender to another the ownership and possession of his property; such a perfect donation contains no conditions."②

It is obvious, then, that the sovereignty is not only originally vested with the people, but also to be given with or without conditions as the people see fit.

There are, really, three kinds of sovereignty, namely that of God, that of the people and that of the king, although to Bodin the last two kinds can not exist at the same time within one kingdom. It can not be doubted, however, that there is a divine sovereignty and that there is a temporal sovereignty which includes both the sovereignty of the people and that of the king. Here again is a division of sovereignty: the divine one and the temporal one. It may be said that the latter is limited by the former, just the sovereignty of the king is limited, in a sense, by the sovereignty of the people, yet the

---

① Bodin, *De Republica*, p. 126.
② Bodin, *ibid.*, p. 128.

existence of two or even three kinds of sovereignty are very certain, the sovereignty of God and that of either king or people can exist at the same time in one kingdom, while both the sovereignty of people and that of the king may exist in two different states.

We have spoken of the mediaeval influence on Bodin. Here we have another instance. The separation of the spiritual authority from the temporal authority prevailed through almost the whole mediaeval age. They are separate not only in theory, but also in fact. Things which belong to Caesar give to Caesar, and things which belong to Peter give to Peter. Bodin has been, consciously or unconsciously, influenced by this conception.

It is interesting to note that when the sovereignty of God becomes insignificant to the writers after Bodin, instead of separating the divine sovereignty from the temporal sovereignty, many writers try to make a distinction between the sovereignty of the people and that of the king, and instead of following Bodin to think that sovereignty of the people and that of the king can not exist at the same time in one kingdom, they hold that the former may be delegated to the king or the government. Thus what the king or the government possess is a delegated sovereignty, while the ultimate sovereignty is still in the hands of the people.

John Locke, in his *Two Treatises of Government*, though not using the term sovereignty, strongly entertains this viewpoint. He thinks of two kinds of sovereignty; one may be called acitve and the other latent sovereignty. When the sovereignty of the people is delegated to the government, the former becomes latent and the latter active. But even within the government, the delegated sovereignty may be also regarded as active or latent. The legislature, being the representative body of the people, is the sovereign body. When the legislature is in secession, its sovereignty is said to be active. When it is not in cession, the executive department of the government may be also regarded as a body to exercise the sovereignty rights and the sovereignty of legislature becomes latent. But can the sovereignty of the people be active. Yes, according to Locke. It becomes active in the time of revolution. The separation of the sovereignty of the people and that of the government and the separation of the sovereignty of legislature and that of the executive may be also regarded as a division of sovereignty. And so when it is divided between the active sovereignty and the latent sovereignty.

Besides the conception of active and latent sovereignty, the distinction between the real and ideal sovereignty as advanced by Immanuel Kant may be also considered as a division of sovereignty. Kant agrees with Rousseau that out of the social contract comes the state or political organization, and that a sovereign general will come into being as soon as the political organization is established. But Kant is radically different from Rousseau in that while the state and its sovereignty, in the mind of the latter are nothing more than creatures of human beings, they are, in the mind of the former, truly ideal or divine. Thus, to Kant, in an ideal state, there may be a political organization and sovereignty created arising out from a compact, but this does not happen in an actual state. Criticizing those who hold that there are states arising out from social contract in an actual state, Kant says: "Where these is no record of anything like a compact actually proposed to the commonwealth, or accepted by the sovereign, or sanctioned by both, these thinkers have assumed the idea of an 'original contract' which is always involved in reason, as a thing which must have 'actually' happened; but thus they supposed that the right was always reserved to the people in the case of any gross violation of it in their judgement, to resile from it at pleasure."①

In short, Kant makes a distinction between the ideal state and sovereignty and the actual state and sovereignty. In the former sovereign power rests on the union of the will of all, while in the latter, it is in the hands of those who hold actual power. We may say that Kant starts with the premise of Rousseau, but ends like Hobbes. Like Hobbes, he attributes this practical sovereignty to the head of the state—the monarch. He says: "The origin of the supreme power is practically inscrutable by the people who are placed under its authority. In other words, the subject need not reason too curiously in regard to its origin in the practical relation, as if the right of the obedience due to it were to be doubted (jus controversum). For a people, in order to be able to adjudicate with a title of right regarding the supreme power in the state, must be regarded as already united under one common legislative will, it can not judge otherwise than as the present supreme head of the states (summoms imperans) wills."②

We can not deny here that sovereignty is divided into actual and ideal ones, for they are entirely different from each other: one being real in our life and one being found in our reason or ideal. But this does not mean that they are not related to one another. Admitting the existence of the actual sovereignty, Kant, as an idealist, thinks more of his ideal sovereignty. According to Kant, there is a tendency toward the realization of the ideal state and sovereignty. In other words, the actual sovereignty tends to be idealized and when the process of idealization is complete, what Rousseau postulates in regard to the social contract from which the sovereignty comes into being will become true.

---

① Kant, *Principles of Politics*, translated by Hasti, p. 53.
② Kant, *Philosophy of Law*, p. 174.

But what we are interested in is that so long the actual sovereignty is not completely idealized, there remains a division of sovereignty. For before the completion of the process of idealization, there will be always a dividing line between the actual sovereignty and the ideal sovereignty, a dividing line changing in the course of the time as the process of idealization is going on.

It is true that this is a sequence of division chiefly referring to time rather than to space or sphere, but equally is it true that both the actual sovereignty and the ideal sovereignty may exist at the same time and during the process of idealization, the sovereignty is partly actual and partly ideal. One may say that this is a mixture of both ideal and actual sovereignty, yet a distinction can be clearly perceived, for they are two entirely different things. On when the actual sovereignty completely disappears and the ideal sovereignty is completely realized, they will be, then, only one sovereignty. But, then, the so-called ideal sovereignty does not exist in our reason or idea alone, because it exists, at same time, in the actual world in which we live.

It may be well concluded now that the distinction between the actual and ideal sovereignty may be also considered as a division of sovereignty. At least we have to admit that it is a conceptual division.

The distinction between actual and legal sovereignty implies also a division of sovereignty. Such a distinction has been elaborately discussed by James Bryce in an article entitled "The Nature of Sovereignty".[①] According to Bryce, "the term sovereignty is used in two senses, legal supremacy and practical mastery", and the difference or differences between the two are set forth in the following passage: "Legal sovereignty exists in the sphere of law: it belongs to him who can demand obedience as of right. Practical sovereignty exists in the sphere of fact: it is the power which receives and can by the strong arm enforce obedience. The legal sovereign in any state is ascertained by determining the person (or body) to whom the law assigns in the last resort the right of issuing general rules or special orders, or of doing acts without incurring liability therefor. The practical sovereign is ascertained by determining who is the person (or body) whose will in the last resort prevails (or in case of conflict, will be likely to prevail) against all other wills."[②]

Then he continues: "Legal sovereignty does not depend upon the obedience actually rendered; for the law assumes obedience to be always enforceable. Obedience paid is not a note characterizing the legal sovereign but a postulate of his existence. That the

---

① Bryce, J., *Studies in History and Jurisprudence*, 1901, Vol. II, Essay X, pp. 503-555.
② *Ibid.*, p. 520.

legal sovereign does in fact exercise his rights under the influence of another person (or body) makes no difference. He is nonetheless a legal sovereign. A Midado is legal sovereign though the Shogun may rule in his name."①

Here we have a sovereignty which is divided into two aspects, one being legal and the other actual. For although the Japanese Emperor or the Midado is legal sovereign over the Japanese empire, the actual sovereignty is exercised by the Shogun. Cases like this are numerous, particularly in international relations. The Chinese still claim her legal sovereignty over Manchuria, while the actual sovereignty is exercised by the Japanese for many years. So says Bryce: "Where a legal sovereign exists, there are sometime particular persons or groups who stand out as able to control the state."②

And he says again: "Sovereignty *de jure* and sovereignty *de facto* have a double tendency to coalesce; and it is this tendency which has made then so often confounded. Sovereignty *de facto*, when it has lasted for a certain time a shown itself stable, repens into sovereignty *de jure*. Sometimes it violently and illegally changes the pre-existing constitution, and creates a new legal system, which, being supported by force, ultimately supersedes the old system. Sometimes, the old constitution becomes quietly obsolete, and the customs formed under the new *de facto* ruler become ultimately valid laws, and make him a *de jure* ruler. In any case, just as possession in all or nearly all modern legal system turns itself sooner or later through prescription into ownership—and conversely possession as a fact is aided by title or reputed title—so *de facto* power, if it can maintain itself long enough, will end by being *de iure*… Sovereignty *de iure* in its turn tends to attract to itself sovereignty *de facto*, or, in other words, the possession of legal right tends to make the legal sovereignty actually powerful. Hence a ruler *de facto* is always anxious to get some sort of *de iure* title, and Louis Napoleon, who had seized power by violence in 1851, thought himself, and doubtless was, more secure after he had got two (so-called) plebiscites in his favor in 1852, recognizing him first as president for ten years and then Emperor."③

Whatever the case may be, it is clear that unless both the legal and actual sovereignties are combined into the hands of one person or one body, there remains a division of sovereignty. If we analysize deeply into the actual working of the sovereignty of modern period or in our own time, we can always discover that there are some discrepancies between the legal sovereignty and the actual sovereignty and in such case

---

① Bryce, J., *Studies in History and Jurisprudence*, 1901, Vol. Ⅱ, Essay Ⅹ, p. 520.
② *Ibid.*, p. 512.
③ *Ibid.*, p. 516.

or cases we may say that sovereignty is more or less divided.

Not only is sovereignty divided into legal and actual aspects, but also legal sovereignty or actual sovereignty can be divided. "Legal sovereignty," says Bryce, "is divisible: i. e. different branches of it may concurrently vested in different persons (or bodies), or co-ordinate altogether (pope and Emperor), or co-ordinate partially only (president and congress), though acting in different spheres."①

In regard to practical sovereignty, according to Bryce it may also be divided, although he thinks that the case of dividing is not as so obvious as the legal sovereignty. He writes: "Practical sovereignty seems indivisible, for by its definition it can belong to one person (or body) only, viz. that which is actually the strongest (though perhaps not known to be the strongest) in the state. But it may be so far divided that men obey one ruler in one sphere of action and another in another sphere. In the fourteenth century, for instance, all Christians obeyed the Pope in spiritual matters, their secular government in temporal, and this whether the latter was only *de facto* or also *de iure*. There might course be much dispute as to what were spiritual matters, but no one denied that in matters which were really spiritual the church alone should obey."②

Somewhat different from, but very closely related to the distinction made above is that there may be a sovereignty in name and a sovereignty in fact. The former may be called actual sovereignty and the latter titular sovereignty. Thus in England, and in other monarchical form of government, the king is still called sovereign, while actually the actual sovereignty is in the hands of parliament or some other bodies. The British government is still addressed or addressing as his majestic government and whatever is done by the government is under the name of the the king. But the king has no actual sovereignty and if we follow the prevalent theory that in England the legal sovereignty is

---

① Bryce, J., *Studies in History and Jurisprudence*, 1901, Vol. II, Essay X, pp. 520–521.
② *Ibid.*, p. 521.

In the discussions on the "partition of Rights", the lords proposed to add a clause reviewing "the sovereign power" of the kings. This was objected to in the commons city Pym. Su Edward Coke, Sir T. Wentworth, Enoy, Seeden and others. Sir Ed. Coke, in particular, said, "I know that perogative is part of law; but 'soveriegn power' is no parliamentary word. In my opinion, it weakens magna charte, and all the statutes; for they are absolute without any saving of 'soveriegn power', and should we now add it, we shall weaken the foundation of law, and then the building must needs fall... if we grant this, by implication, we give a 'sovergin power' above all laws."

In consequence of the objections made by the Commons the proposed clause was withdrawn (2 Paul. Hust, pp. 355, 371) nevertheless, the king of England is commonly called the "soveriegn", and even in legal phraseology is denominated "our sovereign lord; not in the sense of the clause condemned by the House of Commons in 1628, but as signifying supreme rank and dignity in the state". p. 90 fartrid.

G. C. Lewis, a treatise on the methods of observation and reasoning in Politics.

vested with the Parliament, the king is even not the legal sovereign. It is to be admitted, however, that at first the king was regarded as sovereign in both practical sense and legal sense, but when the actual sovereignty has been transferred to the parliament, the legal sovereignty of the kings has gone with it. But the king is still called sovereign and a sovereignty in name is still something sovereign or, if you like, a part, indeed the unimportant part, of sovereignty. How unimportant this part may be, it can not be doubted that the king still retains something in sovereignty, and hence the sovereignty of England is still divided, unless the king can no longer be called as sovereign.

Finally, there is still another distinction of sovereignty which implies also a division of sovereignty. This is what is known as legal sovereignty and political sovereignty. The leading exponent of this theory is A. V. Dicey. He tells us in the following passage: "It should, however, be carefully noted that the term 'sovereignty', as long as it is accurately employed in the sense in which Austin sometimes uses it, is a merely legal conception, and means simply the power of law-making unrestricted by any legal limit. If the term 'sovereignty' be thus used, the sovereign power under the English constitution is clearly 'parliament'. But the word 'sovereignty' is sometimes employed in a political rather than in a strictly legal sense. That body is 'politically' sovereign or supreme in a state the will of which is ultimately obeyed by the citizen of the state. In this sense of the word the lectors of Great Britain may be said to be, together with the Crown and the Lords, or perhaps, in strict accuracy, independently of the King and the Peers, the body in which sovereign power is vested. For, as things now stand, the will of the electorate, and certainly of the electorate in combination with the Lords and the Crown, is sure ultimately to prevail on all subjects to be determined by the British government. The matter indeed may be carried a little further, and we may assert that the arrangements of the constitution are now such as to ensure that the will of the electors shall by regular and constitutional means always in the end assert itself as the predominant influence in the country. But this is a political not a legal fact."[①]

In another place he says: "At this point comes into view the full importance of the distinction already insisted upon between 'legal' sovereignty and 'political' sovereignty. Parliament is, from a merely legal point of view, the absolute sovereign of the British Empire, since every Act of Parliament is binding on every Court throughout the British dominions, and no rule, whether of morality or of law, which contravenes an Act of

---

① Dicey, A. V., *Introduction to the Study of the Law of the Constitution*, 1927, eighth edition, pp. 70-71.

Parliament, binds any Court throughout the realm. But if parliament be in the eye of the law a supreme legislature, the essence of representative government is, that the legislature should represent or give effect to the will of the political sovereign, i. e. of the electoral body, or of the nation. That the conduct of the different parts of the legislature should be determined by rules meant to secure harmony between the action of legislative sovereign and the wishes of the political sovereign, must appear probable from general considerations. If the true ruler or political sovereign of England were, as was once the case, the King, legislation might be carried out in accordance with the King's will by one of two methods. The Crown might itself legislate, by royal proclamations, or decrees; or some other body conformed to the will of the Crown. If the first plan were adopted, there would be no room or need for constitutional conventions. If the second plan were adopted, the proceedings of the legislative body must inevitably be governed by some rules meant to make certain that the Acts of the legislature should not contravene the will of the Crown. The electorate is in fact the sovereign of England."[①]

It is clear then that there are two sovereignties existing at the same time in England as Dicey sees it. The one is the legal and the other the political. The legal sovereignty is vested in the parliament while the political sovereignty is vested in the electorate. The former may be called the sovereignty of law, while the other may be called the sovereignty of the people.[②] The sphere of the former is smaller than the latter. In this sense, it may be also said that there is a sovereignty within sovereignty, since the political sovereignty is really the ultimate sovereignty of the British Empire.

There are other writers who make the distinction between the legal sovereignty and the political sovereignty.[③] It is not our purpose here to give the viewpoints of different writers, but rather to show that such a distinction involves a division. Sidgwick, H., for instance, has pointed out that this is a recognition of a dual sovereignty in the state. Being a true follower to Austin, he refuses to admit that sovereignty is divisible, and therefore, opposes the distinction between legal sovereignty and political sovereignty. But the truth remains to him, and undoubtedly to many others, that a distinction like this is to divide sovereignty.

It may be remarked that those who doubt such a distinction means a recognition of

---

① Dicey, A. V., *Introduction to the Study of the Law of the Constitution*, 1927, eighth edition, pp. 424–425.
② *Ibid.*, p. 426.
③ See Ritchie, D. G., "The Conception of Sovereignty", in *The Annals of the American Academy of Political and Social Science*, 1891, January. Also see McKechnie, *The State and the Individual*, p. 131. "The will of the legal sovereign is or should be the authorized embodiment or manifestation of the will of the political sovereign. If the popular will is accurately expressed by the legal sovereign, the power of the people is effective, otherwise it is not."

division has overlooked the real nature of the distinction. Prof. J. W. Garner, for example, does not think to differentiate legal sovereignty from political sovereignty implies the recognition of division. He holds that "a little reflection, however, will show that the distinction between legal and political sovereignty does not rest upon the principle of a divided sovereignty, but rather upon the distinction between two different manifestations of one and the same sovereignty through different channels." But he adds: "As has been said, the one may not harmonize with the other, that is, the expressed will of the legal sovereign may not be that which the political sovereign has commanded, in which case the legal sovereign ought to be reorganized or reconstituted by a new election, otherwise the will of the electorate can not be made effective. This is nothing more than saying that law ought to conform to public opinion when properly expressed; that the legislature ought to obey the mandate of the electorate; and that when it does, the electorate and the legislature are out of harmony."①

Professor Garner further remarks that "where the system of pure democracy exists, the possibility of divergence between the will of the legal and political sovereigns is eliminated, for under such conditions the two are identical. In a pure democracy, the expressed will of the electorate is not mere opinion or mandate, but law itself. Ordinarily, however, the legal sovereign is organized separate and distinct from the political sovereign, and is either some determinate organ like the British Parliament or a constituent body called into existence for the specific purpose of formulating and expressing the sovereign will."②

No one will deny that both the legal and political sovereignty may coincide with each other and form one and an undivided sovereignty. But, just as Prof. Garner has said, not only "the one may not harmonize with the other," but also "ordinarily, the legal sovereign is organized separate and distinct from the political sovereign". In such cases, we can not but agree that the sovereignty is divided. Nor do we find, in our present world, that there is any pure democratic state, not even in the case of England, the so-called home of democracy. If the so-called pure democracy has not been realized, it would be hard to have legal sovereignty coincident with political sovereignty. And so long as things now stand, there we have a division of sovereignty.

As a matter of fact, the recognition of the possibility of making a distinction between legal sovereignty and political sovereignty presupposes a division of sovereignty. The question is whether there is a possibility for dividing the sovereignty. It is beyond

---

① *Ibid.*, p. 162.
② *Ibid.*, p. 162.

doubt that it is possible to have an undivided sovereignty. Whether it is divided or not is a question of fact rather than a question of opinion or of law.

Sovereignty, then, is divisible. It is divisible, because, the very word "sovereignty" was originally used to signify a division within a kingdom; it was divided even when Bodin insisted that it was not divisible; because facts demonstrated that it was divided and because the theory of limited sovereignty of Bodin implies a division of sovereignty. Nor is this all. It has been divided into spiritual and temporal aspects, into latent and active aspects, into ideal and actual aspects, into legal and actual aspects, into titular and actual aspects and into legal and political aspects.

Sovereignty is divisible: F. C. Montague's *Introduction to Bentham's A Fragment on Government*, 1900, Oxford.

"Sovereignty is a complex fact admitting of endless gradation not a mathematical quantity admitting of definition at once abstract and useful." (p. 75)

"These observations apply to the unity as well as to the extent of sovereign power. The definitions which we have been discussing suggest that sovereign power is indivisible. The sovereign of Hobbes is so unreservedly absolute as to imply a perfect singleness of authority. The sovereign of Bentham may be limited by express convention, but only by express convention with other sovereigns. The sovereign of Hobbes [and] is characterized by no less a degree of unity. But, as a matter of fact, the unity of sovereign power, like the extent of sovereign power, admits of many degrees. Its most perfect unity is seen in the government of an able and popular and well-served despot. A unity less perfect but still striking is seen in the government of one compact, disciplined and homogeneous assembly. In singleness of purpose and contrivance such an assembly can not equal an individual, but it surpasses the complex sovereign of a constitutional monarchy and the still more complex sovereign of a federal state. In these last forms of government, the separation of powers is something more than a mere fiction of publicists. Although the ultimate supremacy may be lodged in the hands of some one person or body of persons, it may be a supremacy not recognized by law or a supremacy which does not admit of continuous enforcement. The ordinary work of government is performed by a machine composed of many parts, subject to much friction and liable to occasional stoppage. In such a machine the power is great but the movement is slow, because the work done is the product of a complex system of forces." (pp. 75-76)

"In a constitutional monarchy the sovereign powers are at least in appearance divided upon two distinct principles. First, there is an apparent division of legislative power between the monarch and each of the two houses of parliament. Secondly, there is an apparent separation between the legislative, the executive and the judicial authorities, respectively represented by the monarch with his parliament, the monarch with is ministers, and the highest courts of justices. This apparent division of authority was regarded in the last century as a momentous fact, may more, a contrivance of the highest wisdom. " (p. 76). Montague goes on to say that although "in our own century its existence has very generally been denied, it must be remembered that the relative importance of these three powers has fluctuated incessantly through a long course of years.

"But if the separation of sovereign powers has not yet lost every vestige of meaning in England; if it were once incomparably more real than we can suppose it now; there must be now, there must always have been a possibility of conflict between the partners in sovereignty; and in case of such a conflict, it may be asked, where could an arbiter be found. The only possible arbiters the nation itself, or the most influential part of the nation. This then, it may be said, is the true, the ultimate sovereign. As a figure of speech, the expression may be allowed; but for purposes of accurate discussion, it is inadmissible. An uncertain and varying proportion of the whole people, a crowd without unity, fixity or organization, can not be sovereign either in the legal or in the practical sense. If the mere dread of its interpretation moves one of the parties legally invested with power to submit to the others, there need be no breach of formal law. If its actual interposition becomes necessary, this amounts to a revolution. Sooner or later a new governing power, a new sovereign, whether a single person or a determinate body of persons, will emerge; but until its emergence political society is dissolved, and the citizens are in a state of anarchy. " (pp. 79-80)

"In a federal state the separation of sovereign power is still more striking than in a constitutional monarchy. Under a written constitution, the sovereign powers may be divided into many parcels and every parcel will be held by the same equal title. Thus in the United States, the Federal and the State governments are equal as regards their title, although unlike in the extent of their powers. Within the Federal government the president, the senate, the house of Representatives and the Supreme Court hold their prerogatives by the same charter and within their respective provinces are still independent. But since these various authorities derive their jurisdiction from the written constitution, the authority which can modify the constitution may be regarded as the ultimate sovereign. It was thus that Austin reconciled the facts of the American polity with his axiom that sovereignty is indivisible. The unwieldly legislature which can amend the constitution of the United States corresponds, according to Austin, with the

Parliament of the United Kingdom. In a certain sense this may be true; but in another sense it is misleading. The authority which can revise the constitution of the United States is an extraordinary authority, capable only of extraordinary acts. The parliament of the United Kingdom is a standing authority which transacts the ordinary business of the state. In the United States the Federal and State authorities are supreme, until the extraordinary authority can be set in motion and as soon as it has ceased to move. They may disagree to any extent short of that which would call the dormant sovereign into action. In the United Kingdom every inferior authority is constantly reminded of its subordination to the Imperial Parliament. If two such authorities are legally entitled to counterwork each other, a new statute disposes of the difference at once. Within the Imperial Parliament such conflicts are also possible; but there they are less likely to occur, because the possible parties are so few and less likely to be prolonged, because the possible parties are so unequal in point of strength." (pp. 80–81)

"Obscure as is the unity of the sovereign authority in a constitutional monarchy or in a federal state, it is still more obscure in such a body politic as the British Empire. The sovereign power of the Queen in Parliament legally comprises the whole Empire and certainly comprises the United Kingdom, India, and the Crown Colonies. Whether it practically comprises the self-governing colonies is a question which might tax all the resources of casuistry. If, for example, we consider the colony of Victoria we find that it obeys laws made by two different legislatures, by the Imperial Parliament and the Victorian Parliament. Inasmuch as the Imperial Parliament created the Victorian Parliament and endowed it with the powers which it now enjoys, the Victorian Parliament might appear to be merely the delegate of the Imperial Parliament. But in fact it is much more than a delegate. It is obeyed by the Victorian people not because it represents the Imperial Parliament, but because it represents themselves. It would be obeyed by them even if its enactments were to clash with the enactments of the Imperial legislature. It would have their armed support if the dispute came to the arbitrament of force. Evidently the Victorian legislature and the ministers whom it appoints have a real and ample share of sovereign power. Full sovereign power they do not indeed possess. On some few subjects the law obeyed by Victoria is made by the imperial legislature. For some few purposes the executive government of Victoria is in the hands of the British ministry of the day. But whilst Victoria is not actually the same with the sovereign state, neither is she a really subordinate community. The sovereign authority in Victoria is not actually the same with the sovereign authority in the United Kingdom." (p. 81)

"When several self-governing colonies unit to form a federal body such as the

Dominion of Canada, the problem becomes still more complicated. To the difficulties which occur when we try to state the real political relations of two such communities as the United Kingdom and Victoria are added the difficulties which occur when we try to describe the political organization of the United States. These difficulties have no weight for the lawyer who finds in his books that the Judicial Committee of the Privy Council and the Imperial parliament are entitled to decide every constitutional question affecting the colonies. But they must have the greatest weight with the political enquirer who knows that a devision of the Judicial Committee which was unpalatable to the people of the Dominion would at once be overruled by an act of parliament, and that an Act of parliament would not be obeyed by the people of the Dominion if it conflicted with the will of their own legislature." (pp. 81-82)

"Here again we must repeat that the types of political, like the types of animal, organization are manifold and slide one into another. In every type of political organization a different degree of unity is achieved. In none can absolute unity be found, for absolute unity in the state would annul the diversity of individual wills. More or less of unity may be found in all, for even the laxest league causes or furthers joint action for certain objects. Thus political unity, the unity of sovereign power, is infinitely variable in mode and quantity. To seek to define it as one would define a straight line is to misconceive its nature. We may say that in discussing the unity, as in discussing the extent of sovereign power, Austin embarrassed himself as well as his readers by a method unsuitable to his matter. He took for his subject sovereignty in fact, not sovereignty in law, but he discussed it in the spirit of lawyer. Legal conceptions may be treated by [by] a method of rigorous dichotomy, by holding fast to unqualified Yea or Nay; but political facts can not be treated by this abstract method; they can be described only by a series of balanced and mutually qualifying proportions." (p. 82)

Sovereignty Divided

The Unity Argument. "To premise: in order to form a federal state from states hitherto independent, there must be an irrevocable transfer of a class of powers to the state thus formed. This involves a division of sovereign powers; and the federal state and the local states, as to classes of powers, become thereby subordinate. Properly, a sovereign state can have no superior; it must supreme as to all powers. If this partition of powers is revocable at the will of the several states, then there is no transfer of sovereignty—the local is still supreme, federal jurisdiction is but loaned. And if the federal state may, without the consent of the local states, add to its powers, then the federal state becomes, —it is a consolidation, and not a federal union. A divided sovereignty involves then an absolute division, not to be changed except at the will of both the federal and the local states.

"To the transfer of sovereignty it is objected, as we have seen: First, that it can not be divided; and, second, that neither in whole nor in part—certainly in part—can it be transferred, especially to a state created *eo instanti*, with the division and transfer. To divide sovereignty involves a transfer of a part, to transfer a part involves division; and the two things may be considered together." (pp. 111–112)

"I will not now speak of the more comprehensive claim, that sovereignty can not be ceded at all, further than to say that, as I understand the claim, it contradicts the facts of history, —the fact that the states have voluntarily united with, have become merged in or subordinate to other states; and I may venture to say that what has been done can be done." (p. 112)

"Would, then, such a division of supreme powers that neither party could thereafter exercise the full powers of a single sovereignty, be a division of sovereignty itself? Certainly not, say the unitarians, because it must from its nature exist in a single person or determinate class of persons. Such a division of powers does not affect the location of sovereignty itself. It may be distributed in exercise, yet it must by held somewhere in unity. To cut it in two would kill it, as is said; for the sovereign to consent would be suicide, as is also said. It would be like dividing globe would cease to be a globe. To distribute its powers, as among counties and towns in an ordinary state, would certainly not be a division; neither. say the, would it be a division so to distribute as to make them irrevocable, for the reason that such division would destroy the single sovereignty." (p. 112)

"To illustrate: a state—and, to avoid any question as to pre-existing independence, I will instance Texas, or Corinth of the Achaian League—freely enters a federal union, one which has important powers, with ample governmental machinery, and which is declared to be supreme in the exercise of its powers, By the terms of the paper marking future political relations, certain sovereign powers are surrendered. This state would seem to have parted with its sovereignty, or part of it: it has certainly parted with important powers; in respect to many things it has become subordinate. Yet it is claimed that the state is still sovereign, and for reason that whatever it may do, whatever the language used to define its new federal relations, its sovereignty is still presverved. It has not surrended this essential attribute of a state, not because it has not in fact become subordinate, not because it did not do all to that end that corporate action could do, but because the surrender is impossible." (pp. 112–113)

Divided by a division of Powers. "Can this claim to unity be reconciled with the racts in federal society? If sovereignty, aside from its sense in international law, means the political supreme jurisdiction as it exists in fact, it is not a unit in federal states; for in such states there is in fact a division of supreme powers, —not a distribution at the will of a superior, as some say, but an absolute endowment of different bodies politic. As a fact, in federal states, each citizen is under the jurisdiction of two governments, two states, each with full machinery; and one is supreme as to one thing, and the other is supreme as to another. Each citizen, in respect to one class of subjects, is governed by and knows only the federal state, and, in respect to another class of subjects, is governed and knows only his own local state. In spite of speculation the great fact remains that powers are permanently divided between distinct bodies politic; and what is sovereignty without its powers?" (p. 113)

"The inference may be avoided by saying that this division is not permanent, —that it is no division, in fact, of the aggregate people of the federal body, or the aggregate people of the several local bodies in union, and others say at the (p. 113) will of the separate people of each local body. I assume, and shall presently more fully show, that in the United States the aggregate people can not change the division of powers; and I shall consider the claim that [he] several people may each lawfully withdraw from federal jurisdiction, and thus achieve supremacy in all things. I need now but barely refer to our present legal relations; and according to them neither the federal people nor the local people can make any change; to so requires substantially the same action taken in effecting the present division, —that is, the action of a the federal state and of the several local states, each in its own sphere. There is no one sovereignty, or one sovereign, or aggregate of peoples, that can make the change." (p. 114)

"This inference in respect to a division of sovereignty is also sought to be avoided by saying that the powers do not imply its location in their holder. That may depend upon what they are: if powers do not imply sovereignty, power does, or shows where it lies. Powers intrusted to a special agency, even to a people, and subject to be recalled, show no sovereignty in such people. But power to say what that agency may or may not do, whether it can be a people or a body of officials, does involve sovereignty in those who possess it. The inability to dictate or regulate the exercise of the powers held by such agency negatives the possession of sovereignty in respect to such powers. Sovereignty involves the full law-making power so far as it exists. To speak of it as held by a people or by a state without such power is nonsense. If sovereignty is not in the maker, the controller, of powers, it is nowhere, it is but a dumb idol. But the federal state can neither create nor change powers, nor can the local. In neither, then, is there sovereignty. As a unity it no longer exists". (p. 114) "Like the divided manmal, it is killed. It matters not whether we say that it is in fact destroyed by such division, or whether we so define it as to predicate it of both the federal and the local state, though neither is supreme in all things; that is, each is sovereign *pro tanto*. I am willing to treat it as destroyed or divided. It is more reasonable to say either than to enthrone in full regalia a something, —a puppet like the native princes under the East India Company, —and with the tinsel and court ceremonies of sovereignty, while many of its essential attributes belong to another. I only insist that in a true federal state, upon any definition that can make it attach to a people or a state, sovereignty does not exist in unity, —it is divided, and in part transferred." (pp. 114–115) (Philemon Bliss, *Of Sovereignty*, 1885. Professor of Law in the State University of Missouri, Boston)

Sovereignty divided as legal, political and ethical

"It can not be said that Austin was so successful in elucidating the theory sovereignty as he was in elucidating the theory of law or in defining the province of jurisprudence. He was successful in his delimitations of law and jurisprudence because he was able to distinguish more clearly than any of his predecessors the sphere of legality from the sphere of morality. He was less successful in his attempts to define sovereignty because not able to distinguish with sufficient clarity between three separate and distinct forms of sovereignty—namely, the legal, the political, and the ethical. The only question which he, as a hurist, was called to answer was the legal question: What is the ultimate or supreme authority recognized by the law-courts as the source of positive law? But he confused this simple, straightforward, and easily answered question with the more complicated and difficult political question: What, as a matter of fact, is the ultimate or supreme power which actually controls or governs the State? Nor did he wholly keep these legal and political questions from confusion with the still more disputable ethical question: Where ought the ultimate and supreme sovereignty to reside?" (F. J. C. Hearnshaw, *Some Great Political Idealists of the Christain Era*, London, 1937, p. 227)

"That Austin confused the legal sovereign with the political sovereign and with the ethical sovereign is no doubt due to the fact that his predecessors had done the same. Bodin, the first thinker of deal systematically with the subject, had accurately, if not adequately defined sovereignty, as a legal conception, in the statement: Majestas est summa in civies ac subditos legibusque soluta potestas. But his further discussion of majestas showed that his prime concern was the political problem—where in France an actual sovereignty resided—and the ethical problem—as to whom the ultimate loyalty of Frenchmen was properly due. Similarly Hobbes, the second great theorist to treat sovereignty, had dealt with the matter almost wholly from the political point of view...He vehemently maintained on prudential grounds the political supremacy of the state, and on utilitarian grounds its ethical claims to ascendency. Finally, Jeremy Bentham, Austin's immediate predecessor and master, had been primarily a law-reformer, and not a legal theorist. His 'Gragment on Government' (1776), which is mainly an essay on sovereignty, had been devoted to destructive attack upon the introductory sections of Blackstone's *Commentaries*, wherein Blackstone had eulogised the English constitution as almost flawless; had exalted English law as ideal; had deprecated changed; and had attributed the virtues of the English system of government precisely to that division and separation of the sovereign powers of legislation, administration, and adjudication whose division and separation Hobbes had declared to be impossible. Bentham had demolished Blackstone and reaffirmed with striking emphasis the necessary indivisibility of sovereignty. But it (pp. 227-228) had been political, not legal, sovereignty of which he had treated." (p. 229)

"Since all Austin's great predecessors had treated sovereignty from the political or ethical point of view, rather than from the legal point of view, it is not astonishing that Austin did the same. Nevertheless it is a misfortune that he was not able to emancipate himself from the influence of his masters, because, since he had determined the province of jurisprudence, it was essential for the completion of his system of thought—his philosophy of positive law as he called it—that he should consider and define sovereignty purely as a legal conception, without any reference to either politics or ethics. His problem was simply, as we have remarked: What is the ultimate or supreme authority recognized by the law-courts—the authority from which these is no legal appeal?" (p. 229)

"Moreover, fourthly, legal (though not political) sovereignty is capable of division, and in Great Britain is actually divided. Montesquieu and Blackstone were not, in this matter of separation, so completely mistaken as Bentham and Austin supposed them to be. The legal sovereign in Great Britain is, as we have noted, the King in Parliament—that is to say, King, Lords, and Commons. But the King is the supreme executive, and the House of Lords is the supreme judicature. He, although no doubt the King in Parliament can legally do what it likes with both monarchy and peerage, nevertheless every legislative Act of Parliament requires for its sovereign efficacy the consent of the King (the supreme executive) and of House of Lords (the supreme judicature), and *in the sphere of law* there is no reason why either of them should give it. Of course, in the sphere of pratical politics... but we are not treating of that at present. In the sphere of law, or any rate of legal theory, Great Britain seems to have developed a specimen of that jurisdical rarity, a divided sovereignty. " (p. 231)

After citing the definition of sovereignty of Austin, Hearnshaw says: "Here, it is obvious, is a hopeless confusion between the legal and the political sovereign—a confusion due, apparently to the baseless assumption that the two are identical. The legal sovereign must be a 'determinate human superior': the law courts must know precisely from whom emanate the commands which they precluded from treating as invalid. The political sovereign, however, —that is, the power which actually exercises supreme control in a state—need not be determinate, and, in fact, very rarely is so. As the American jurist J. C. Cray well says, 'The real rulers of a political society are undiscoverable. They are the persons who dominate over the wills of their fellows.' " (*The Nature and Sources of Law*, 1921, p. 79). (pp. 232-233)

"If we ask what are the distinguishing marks of the political sovereign—that is, of the actual controlling power in the state, as distinct from the legal sovereign—the answer is that the political sovereign, as distinct from the legal sovereign, (a) is generally indeterminate; (b) is generally incapable of precise location; (c) can not be in abeyance, any more than a mass can be devoid of a centre of gracity; (d) is incapable of division, just as the centre of gracity of a mass can not be divided; but (e) is subject to all kinds of effective limitations and restrictions. " (p. 233)

"The last is, perhaps, the only point that calls for explication. Is not a limited or restricted sovereignty a contradiction in terms? No; in the sphere of politics it is not. For political sovereignty—the actual control of a state—is a shifting, unstable impermanent thing. A stroke may incapacitate Lenin, a shot may remove Mussolini, a mistake in tactics may overthrow a trade union or newspaper oligarchy, a parrot-cry or a panic may revolutionize public opinion. Hence there are certain things which no political sovereign-of-the-moment dare do, if he wishes to remain sovereign. Political sovereignty is always precarious. Not even Lenin dared to take the land from the Russian peasants. Not even Mussolini dared to break with the Papacy and occupy the Vatican. No political sovereign in short, however highly exalted above all subjects he may be, can hope to retain supreme authority unless he recognizes that there are certain things he cannot do, certain sphere into which he must not enter. The penalty for the ignoring of these restrictions and limitations is that he ceases to be sovereign. That is to say he ceases to receive that 'havitual obedience from the bulk of a given society' which Austin might have correctly noted as a mark of the political sovereign, even it had no relevance to the legal sovereign to whom he seemed to apply it." (pp. 233-234)

"If no constitutional means exist for keeping the legal sovereign in harmony with and—outside the law-courts, wherein alone it is supreme—in subjection to the political sovereign, a revolution is likely ensue. In Great Britain the electors are assumed to be political sovereign, and periodical general election are the device adopted for the maintenance of harmony between them as a body and the legally sovereign Parliament. But the precise seat of political sovereignty, as we have already observed, is extremely difficult to locate, and the assumption that it resides in the electors as a body is by no means unchallenged. In 1926, for instance, it was challenged by the trade union, or, rather, by a certain of trade-union officials, syndicalists, and communists, who acted in the name of the unions. If their general strike had been successful and they had destroyed Parlamentary government in this country they have been compelled to institute a new legal sovereign a new system of law-courts, and a new body of law. By some means or other, in short, the conventional sovereign within the law-courts must be kept in harmony with, and in subordination to, the politic sovereign who actually exercises dominant authority in the world outside of the law-courts." (p. 235)

"What, finally, is to be said concerning the ethical question, where ought supreme power to reside in a community? We have already remarked that the political sovereign, however great his power, is practically restricted by numerous limitations of a prudential kind. In other words, there are certain things which no despot, however autocratic, could possibly do with any hope of being allowed to retain his place and power. As David Hume well observed, 'It is on opinion only that government is founded; and this maxim extends to the most despotic and most military governments, as well as to the most free and most popular.' (Essay on the First Principles of Government, 1741). Political sovereigns who abuse their power are faced by rebellion, which, if it is sufficiently widespread, deprives them of their sovereignty and sets up another sovereign in their stead. And just as there are certain things that they can not or dare not do, so there other things which (on moral or religious grounds) they *ought* not to do. These things, no doubt, vary from age to age as ethical standards change. At the present time it could perhaps be generally agreed that the political sovereign *ought* not to persecute its subjects in the matter of religious belief, and, on the other hand, that it *ought* to seek so far as its power extends to secure 'the greatest happiness of the greatest number', of those within the scope of its authority." (p. 236)

"But, since political sovereignty can not divided, the problem remains, when all has been said concerning moral and other limitations of sovereignty, where in the last resort *ought* this supreme authority reside? This is the problem that Austin discusses in his *Plea for the Constitution* (1859). He solves it in a conservative sense; but he is emphatic as the most convinced democrat that the ultimate sovereignty must reside, and ought to reside, in the state. For the state represents the community as a whole, and, as the world is at present constituted, it is the only institution that does so. Hence, however large an autonomy, the state may leave to churches, to trade unions, to universities, and to other voluntary associations of a sectional kind, in the last resort its authority must, in the interest of the community as a whole, override them all. So long as the primary division of mankind is the present division into nations, so must each nation, organized as a state and acting through its government, be supreme within the territorial limits of its jurisdiction in all causes and over all persons. Political sovereignty can not be partitioned. There cannot within one and the same territorial area be more than one authority employing the sanction of physical force. The conduct of international deplomacy and the power of waging war and making peace also demand a central and a final authority. The right of levying taxes by compulsion can not reside in multiple hands." (pp. 236-237)

Chapter 10
Sovereignty

Since the time of Beaumanoir, sovereignty has been regarded as divisible, not only in the manner in which we have already described in the last chapter, but also in many other ways if further analysis will be made. A book would be needed were we to mention the defenders of exponents of the doctrine of division of sovereignty from the time of Beaumanoir to our own days. While this is not intended to be a historical or an exhaustive study of this theory, suffice it to say that the theory has been approached from and developed along by, roughly speaking, four directions. The first one which may be mentioned is what may be called departmental division of sovereignty. Sovereignty is here conceived to be divided between the different departments of the government. It may be divided with reference either to executive, legislative and possibly judicial, or to the central and local governments. Secondly, sovereignty is thought to be divided between the federal union and the several states, lander, cantons or whatever it may be called, in a federal state. Thirdly, that sovereignty is divisible has been generally accepted in its application to international relations. Fourthly, sovereignty may be divided or shared by the functional groups other than the state.

The last line of thinking will be discussed in the next chapter. In this one, we shall deal with the other three directions pointing to the theory that sovereignty is divisible.

Let us begin from the first in order, namely that sovereignty may be divided between the different departments of the government.

It may be said that, during and long after the time of Beaumanoir, sovereignty considered to be divided between the temporal and spiritual heads was still prevailing. And it is needless to say that the conception of Beaumanoir in regard to the divided sovereignty held its truth for the fourteenth and fifteenth centuries and has been survived in modified forms after the eighteenth century in both the federal and unitary states.

It has been already noted in the writings of Beaumanoir, the development of the monarchical system may be traced. But while both the spiritual heads and the temporal barons were gradually deprived of their sovereign powers, the kings were by no means happy by taking over these powers which were enjoyed either by the church or by the baron. The decline of the sovereign powers of church and the baron marked, of course, the increase of the sovereign powers of the kings. But it is to be remembered that it marked the growth of the so-called popular sovereignty. Instead of finding the ultimate authority from the supernatural being, God, men tried to argue that it was originally vested in the hands of the people. The difference here is very obvious. On the one hand, it is maintained that sovereignty comes from above, above human beings, including kings themselves. On the other hand, it is advocated that it comes from below, below the God and the king. Thus the king's sovereign powers were considered to be delegated either by God, higher above him, or by the people under his control. There were, to be sure, a theory holding the divine rights of the king; but chiefly, this theory defended the rights of the king on the ground that it was God who gave him the power. So even when James the First declared "kings are justly called gods", he added immediately these words: "for they exercise a manner of resemblance of divine power upon earth." It is clear then that he dared not to say that he is god in the sense that he takes the place of God in heaven. The words "justly", and particularly, "resemblance" should not be overlooked here. They may be looked like, or even called as, Gods; yet they are not Gods.

This will bring us to an understanding of the fact that when God was no longer regarded as a limitation on the sovereignty of the kings, it was the sovereignty of the people that checked their authority.

It is generally recognized that in spite of some writers such as Bodin and Hobbes advocating the indivisible sovereignty of the king, limited monarchy was really the prevailent system proposed even when the time the power of the king was at its zenith. If it was recognized that the ultimate authority came from God, the power of the monarch would be limited either by the divine law or by the vicar of God, the pope. If it was believed that this authority was originally in the hands of the people, the representative body of the people, the parliament would be considered as a rival factor to the king. As England was the home of modern constitutionalism, the theory of limited monarchy was developed there earlier than that in other continental European countries. "None of the English Elizabethan writers," says one writer, "are willing to admit, or do actually conceive, that any absolute and unlimited authority exists."① The authority here referred is that of the king. But what is meant by limited monarchy is generally understood as a mixed form of government. In other words, it is not a pure and simple monarchical form of government. And the so-called mixed form of government is, as a matter of fact, a mixed sovereignty which is shared by or divided between at least two persons or bodies.

John Ponet, one of the most celebrated advocates of limited monarchy, in his *A Short Treatise of Politicke Power*②, written at the middle of sixteenth century, regards the mixed form of government is a government in which the sovereignty is divided between the king and the parliament. J. W. Allen, has very well summarized his position in the following words: "Ponet was strongly of opinion that no wise people would establish monarchy pure and simple. Far preferable is the 'mixed' form of government 'which men by long continuance have judged to the best sort of all'. By the mixed government he understood some kind of division of sovereignty between a prince and some sort of parliamentary body. Such a constitution, he imagined, existed in England, France and Germany."③

Nor Ponet was alone in this contention. Sir Thomas Smith, in his *De Republica Anglorum*, was of the same opinion. This work of Sir Thomas's is very important. F. W. Maitland, in the preface to Smith's *De Republica Anglorum*, remarks that "Sir Thomas Smith's discourse on the Commonwealth of England is a famous and in some sort a well-known book. No one would think of writing about the England of Elizabeth's day without paying heed to what was written about the matter by her learned and accomplished Secretary of State. His little treatise comprises some sentences touching the powers of Parliament which have been quoted and transcribed times without number, and which will be quoted and transcribed so long as men take any interest in the history of the English Constitution."④

Both Maitland and Sir Frederick Pollock thought that Smith was advocating the sovereignty of the parliament and that he defined sovereignty somewhat after the fashion

---

① J. W. Allen, *A History of Political Thought in the Sixteenth Century*, 1932, p. 269.
② See also W. S. Hudson, *John Ponet*, 1942, pp. 154 ff.
③ Allen, *ibid.*, p. 119.
④ Smith, T., *De Republica Anglorum, A Discourse on the Commonwealth of England* edited by L. Alston, 1906, p. vii.

of Bodin①, but this has strongly opposed by recent writers②. Smith did not employ the term "sovereignty" in his work, although he used the word "sovereignty". It is true that Smith regards sovereignty as the supreme and highest authority. "To rule", he says, "is understoode to have the highest and supreme authoritie of commandment. That part or member of the common wealth is said to rule which doth controwle, correct, and direct all other members of the common wealth. That part which doth rule, define and commaund according to the forme of the government, is taken in everie common wealth to be just and lawe."③ But to him, such ruling part of the sovereignty is consisting of many persons or bodies, because there is always a mixed, not pure, simple and absolute government. The position of the Smith is clearly stated in the following passage: "Now although the governments of common wealthes be thus divided into three, and cutting ech into two, so into sixe: yet you must not take that ye shall finde any common wealth or governement simple, pure and absokute in his sort and kinde, but as wise men have divided for understadninges sake and fantasied iiij. Simple bodies which they call elementes, as fire, ayre, water, earth, and in a mans bodies foure complexions or temperatures, as cholericke, sanguine, phlegmatique: not that ye shall finde the one utterly perfect without mixtion of the other, for that nature almost will not suffer, but understanding doth discerne ecj nature as in his sinceritie: so seldom or never shall you finde common wealthes or governement which is absolutely and sincerely made of any of them above named, but always mixed with an other, and hath the name of that which is more and overruleth the other alwayes or for the most part."④

We have already noted that a mixed government, to the writers of the sixteenth

---

① See particularly Pollock, *History of the Science of Politics*, "In the *De Republica Anglorum* or *English Commonwealth* of Sir Thomas Smith, first published after the author's death in 1583, we find something much more like a forerunner of Hobbes. Indeed, so clear and precise are Smith's chapters on sovereignty that one is tempted to think he must somehow have had knowledge of Bodin's work. At the outset he defines political supremacy in a manner by no means unlike Bodin's. When he comes to English institutions in particular, he states the omnipotence of Parliament in the most formal manner, and so far as I know for the first time, as if on purpose to contradict Bodin's argument that the monarchy of England is really absolute." p. 54. It must be pointed out, however, that Smith's book was said to ⟨be⟩ written about 1562.

Smith speaks of absolute king (p. 16), but also speaks of absolute parliament (p. 48).

"The most high and absolute power of the realme of Englande, consisteth in the parliament Bk Ⅱ, Chapter Ⅰ, p. 48, which in Bk. Ⅰ, Chap. 8, p. 16, he speaks of absolute king, if each is absolute in its own sphere, the sovereignty is divided.

② See the Introduction to Smith's work written by L. Alston, particularly pp. XXX ff. See Also J. W. Allen, *A History of Political Thought in the Sixteenth Century*, pp. 264-265.

③ Smith, *De Republic Anglorum*, Ch. Ⅰ, p. 9.

④ Smith, *De Republic Anglorum*, Ch. Ⅵ, p. 14.

century, is a government in which sovereignty is divided. Smith is not an exception to this. This point is very well stated by J. W. Allen. One or two passages quoted from him will illustrate clearly what we have insisted. "It must be remembered that he (Smith) was not concerned with what may be and little with what should be. He was asking simply how England was actually governed. He found that it was governed by the prince, but, that normally at least, the prince made law and imposed taxes only in parliament. He explains that while the making of law and the providing of money is done by the prince in parliament, the management of foreign relations and of official appointments is by the prince alone. He never explicitly says that the prince can neither make law nor impose taxes of his own will simply. He was not, I think, prepared to say what the prince could not do. He might have said that what really relies is custom; but he did not say so… Sir Thomas never uses the word 'sovereignty' and, had he been asked where sovereignty lay in England, he would have said it was in prince… But to sovereign to sir Thomas is not the law maker and in his view ought not to be. He associates 'absolute' monarchy definitely with tyranny, saying that 'uncontrolled authority', necessary in war, is in peace very dangerous both to monarch and people and asserting that 'for the most part they have had absolute power' have become very tyrant. Sir Thomas seems to have seen no reason why law-making should not be the function of a specially constituted body completely impotent in many relations."[1]

And he continues: "Sovereignty, in fact, ought to be divided and commonly is. To say that such a division of power cannot exist is mere nonsense, for it evidently does exist, talk about sovereignty as you will. Sir Thomas was looking at very complex thing, compounded of law and custom, tradition, habit, institutions and detailed arrangements and he tried to describe it as it was. He did so with a sense that it was quite admirably adapted to its purpose. To say that in a well-ordered state there must a sovereignty power, *legibus solutus*, definitely vested somewhere, struck him, if he ever thought of it at all, as simply untrue."[2]

Not only in England sovereignty was conceived as divided between or shared by the parliament and the king, or the legislative and the executive departments of the government, but also in France the same conception was entertained by many writers. As a matter of fact, this was the common view in the sixteenth century. The Catholic League, for instance, formed in France under the influence of the Duke of Guise in 1576, "tended to adopt a constitutional theory and to claim sovereignty, or at least a

---

[1] J. W. Allen, *A History of Political Thought in the Sixteenth Century*, 1932, pp. 264–265.
[2] Allen, *ibid.*, p. 265.

share in sovereignty, for the Estates of the realm."①

Even Bodin himself, the so-called enunciator of the theory of indivisible sovereignty inclined to admit, when he wrote his *Methodus ad facilem historiarum cognitonem* in 1566, that the Parliaments had a real share in sovereignty, particularly through the power to veto the royal edicts. Only in his *Six Books of Republic* did he change his view point in this respect. But still he lay many limitations on the sovereign monarch as we have already dealt with in the previous chapter.

But the change of Bodin's view point did not, to be sure, change the common view of the time. The view of the Catholic League was formulated in the same year when Bodin published his *Six Books of Republic* in 1576. As to the time before that, Allen writes: "France in 1560 was even further from accepting the doctrine of unlimited sovereignty in the king than it had been in 1540. Before that idea, even in a form not quite absolute, could be accepted, many obstacles had to be removed. The idea of law of nature limiting all governmental action, the idea of the sacredness of customary rights, the claim of the parliaments to veto royal edicts, the conception of States-General as sharing in sovereignty all stood in the way."②

Nor the theory of divisible sovereignty in its application to the different departments of the government disappeared after the publication of Bodin's work on the *Six Books of Republic*, although, we are told, this work was used by the University of Oxford for teaching after its appearance. We find, for instance, at the beginning of seventeenth century, both John Hayward and Thomas Craig accepted the conception of mixed government and therefore, the theory of divisible sovereignty③, although both of them thought that it was possible for the sovereignty to be in the hands of one person or body. In fact, they believed this is the natural government, in contrast to the less natural one to which the mixed government belongs. Thus it is possible for many wills to combine into one will and form one sovereignty; yet this is not usually the case. As a result, "the more they are who join in government the less natural is their union and the more subject to dissipation."④

Even Robert Filmer, according to Algernon Sydney, admitted the possibility of a

---

① J. W. Allen, *A History of Political Thought in the Sixteenth Century*, 1932, p. 344.

② Allen, *ibid.*, p. 291.

③ Hayward, J., *An Answer to the First Part of a Certain Conference Concerning Succession*, 1603. Thomas Craig, wrote a work in Latin at the same time, but this was not published until the publication of an English translation of his work under the title: *Concerning the Right of Succession to the Kingdom* in 1703.

④ Hayward, *An Answer to the First Part of a Certain Conference Concerning Succession*, I. B. See also Allen, *ibid.*, p. 256.

divided sovereignty.① And to John Locke, as we have already noted, sovereignty is divided between the legislative and the executive departments. In fact, the theory of separation of powers as presented by Locke and later developed by Montesquieu, means really the separation of sovereignty.

In his *Commentaries on the Law of England*, William Clackstone although defining sovereignty, after the fashion of Bodin, as supreme, irresistible, absolute, uncontrolled authority②, admits, consciously or unconsciously, that it is divided among the different department of the government. He tells us that on the one hand the "law ascribes to the king the attribute of sovereignty, or pre-eminence"③ and on the other hand the British parliament is "the supreme and absolute authority of the state."④ This is almost equal to say that both the king and the parliament are sovereign. But in another place he speaks very clearly of divided sovereignty particularly in England, and regards that public liberty can be secured only in a country where sovereignty is divided. Let us quote the following statement: "In all tyrannical government the supreme magistracy, or the right both of *making* and of *enforcing* the laws; is vested in one and the same man, or one and the same man, or one and the same body of men; and wherever these two powers are united together, there can be no public liberty. The magistrate may enact tyrannical laws, and execute them in a tyrannical manner, since he is possessed in quality of dispenser of justice, with all the power which he as legislator thinks proper to give himself. But, where the legislative and executive authority are in distinct hands, the former will take care not to entrust the latter with so large a power, as may tend to the subversion of its own independence, and therewith of the linerty of the subject."

And then he continues: "With us, therefore, in England this *supreme power* is divided into two branches; the one legislative, to wit, the parliament, consisting of king, lords, and commons; the other executive, consisting of the king alone!"⑤

I have italicized the phrase "supreme power", because it cannot be doubted that it means sovereign power, for sovereignty is defined by Blackstone as "supreme authority" which means nothing more than supreme power. Besides, Blackstone speaks of "sovereign legislative power"⑥, which is in contrast to what he calls the sovereignty of

---

① See Sydney, *Discourses Concerning Government*, 1698, Chapter Ⅱ, section XXX, p. 247.
② Blackstone, *Commentaries on the Law of England*, 1765, edited by W. G. Jones, p. 85.
③ *Ibid.*, p. 361.
④ *Ibid.*, p. 250.
⑤ Blackstone, *ibid.*, pp. 249-250.
⑥ *Ibid.*, p. 362.

the king. Moreover, Blackstone does not insist that sovereignty is indivisible, although he speaks of sovereignty as supreme, absolute, irresistible and uncontrolled. Thus either from the positive standpoint or from the negative side of his position, he is, as we have said, consciously or unconsciously, admitting that sovereignty is divided between the legislative and executive departments.

Alexander Hamilton, one of the fathers of the Constitution of the United States, besides arguing that sovereignty is divisible between the federal union and the several states, inclines to admit that sovereignty can be also divided in the central or federal government in its different departments. He even cites the case of the Roman Republic in order to show that sovereignty may be shared by the two bodies of the legislature. He says: "It is well known that in the Roman Republic the legislative authority, in the last resort, resided for ages in two different political bodies—not as branches of the same legislature, but as distinct and independent legislatures, in each of which an opposite interest prevailed, in one, the patrician; in the other the plebeian."①

If it is true that the federal system of the United States in the latter part of eighteenth century was a new invention, equally is it true that the separation of powers of the three departments, namely the executive, the legislative and the judicial was also a new creation. Each department, having a function and sphere of its own, checks against and keeps balanced with the others. No one can claim supremacy over others, or subjects to others. Each is independent within its own sphere. This is really a division of sovereign powers, although some writers would hold that a division of powers does not mean a division of sovereignty.

It may be remarked by passing that the distinction between sovereignty and power as conceived by some writers has never been well founded. The earlier writers on the theory of sovereignty seldom made such a distinction. Although Rousseau declares that power may be divided, but not will, he himself does not make it clear when he says that the body politic is "sovereign when it is active, power when it is compared to similar bodies." So it may be well concluded as one of the writers points out that the theory of separation of powers as applied in the United States "was simply an attempt to set up three sovereign instead of one."②

That sovereignty is divided between two or more governmental departments is well defended by recent writers. James Bryce, in an article entitled "The Nature of

---

① See *Federalist*, edited by Ford, p. 207.
② See George W. Walthew, *Philosophy of Government*, 1898, p. 5.

Sovereignty"[1] considers the sovereignty, the legal sovereignty as he calls it, is divided between the president and the congress in the United States[2]. And this may be applied to other countries. "Let it be noted," he says, that "where sovereignty is divided between two or more authorities, one of those (or possibly even more than one) may have executive functions only. Where there is but one sovereign person or body, that person or body will evidently have both legislative and executive powers, i. e. will be entitled to issue special commands as well as to prescribe general rules. But a division of sovereignty may assign legislative functions to one authority, executive to another. In the United States, for instance, the President is, by the constitution, sovereign for certain executive purposes (e. g. the command of the army) and the legislature cannot deprive him of that sovereignty. If congress were to pass an act taking the command of the army from him, that act would be void. So in England four centuries ago, although Parliament was already beginning to be recognized as sovereign for legislative purposes, the king had, in some departments, an executive sovereignty which the two houses of Parliament did not dispute; and he laid claim in the time of the first two Stuarts to a sort of concurrent legislative sovereignty, which is required first a civil war and then a revolution finally to negative and extinguish."[3]

Perhaps the ablest defender of this theory is Sir John Salmond. His conception on this point is well set forth in an article entitled "The Theory of Sovereignty"[4]. This article aims at criticizing the theory of sovereignty of Bodin and Hobbes. He points out that the theory of Bodin and Hobbes may be reduced to three fundamental propositions: That sovereign power is essential in every state; that sovereign power is indivisible; and that sovereign power is unlimited and illimitable. Although he seems to concede to the first proposition, he denies flatly the other two.

For our purpose, it is the second proposition that we are taking interest. But to illustrate his view point, we can do no better than to quote his own words: "Every state, it is said, necessarily involves not merely sovereignty, but a *sovereign*, that is to say, one person or one body of persons in whom the totality of sovereign power is vested. Such power, it is said, cannot be shared between two or more persons. It is not denied that the single supreme body may be composite, as the English Parliament is. But it is alleged that whenever there are in this way two or more bodies of persons in whom

---

[1] In Bryce's *Studies in History and Jurisprudence*, vol. Ⅱ.
[2] *Ibid.*, p. 521.
[3] Bryce, *ibid.*, p. 508.
[4] See Appendix Ⅱ in his *Jurisprudence*, ninth edition, 1937, pp. 680–687.

sovereign power is vested, they necessarily possess it as joint tenants of the whole, and cannot possess it as tenants in severalty of different parts. The whole sovereignty may be in A, or the whole of it in B, or the whole of it in A, and B jointly, but it is impossible that part of it should be in A and the residue in B. "①

After stating the argument of the theory of indivisible sovereignty, he begins to test it in its application. "We may test," says he, "this doctrine by applying it to the British constitution. We shall find that this constitution in no way conforms to the principles of Hobbes on this point, but is on the contrary a clear instance of divided sovereignty. The *legislative* sovereignty resides in the Crown and the two Houses of Parliament, but the *executive* sovereignty resides in the Crown by itself, the Houses of Parliament having no share in it. It will be understood that we are here dealing exclusively with the law or legal theory of the constitution. The practice is doubtless different; for in practice the House of Commons has obtained complete control over the executive government. In practice the ministers are the servants of the legislature and responsible to it. In law they are the servants of the Crown, though whom the Crown exercises that sovereign executive power which is vested in it by law, independently of the legislature altogether. "②

"In law, then, the executive power of the Crown is sovereign, being absolute and controlled within its sphere. This sphere is not indeed unlimited. There are many things which the Crown cannot do; it can not pass laws or impose taxes. But what it can do [it does it] with sovereign power. By no other authority in the state can its powers be limited, or the exercise of them controlled, or the operation of them annulled. It may be objected by the advocate of the theory in question that the executive is under the control of the legislature, and that the sum total of sovereign power is therefore vested in the latter, and is not divided between it and the executive. The reply is that the Crown is not merely itself a part of the legislature, but a part without whose consent the legislature can not exercise any fragment of its own power. No law passed by the House of Parliament is operative unless the Crown consents to it. How, then, can the legislature control the executive? Can a man be subject to himself? A power over a person, which cannot be exercised without that person's consent, is no power over him at all. A person is subordinate to a body of which he is himself a member, only if that minority, for example, may be subordinate to the whole assembly. But this is not the position of the Crown."

"The English constitution, therefore, recognizes a sovereign executive, no less

---

① Salmond, *Jurisprudence*, ninth edition, 1937, p. 681.
② *Ibid*.

than a sovereign legislature. Each is supreme within its own sphere; and the two authorities are kept from conflict by the fact that the executive is one member of the composite legislature. The supreme legislative power is possessed jointly by the Crown and the two Houses of Parliament, but the supreme executive power is held in severalty by the Crown. When there is no Parliament, that is to say, in the interval between the dissolution of one Parliament and the election of another, the supreme legislative power is non-existent, but the supreme executive power is retained unimpaired by the Crown."①

Salmond even goes a step further to assert that judicial department in the British Empire was also sovereign in its own sphere. He adds: "This is not all, however, for, until the passing of the Parliament Act, 1911, the British Constitution recognized a supreme judicature as well as a supreme legislature and executive. The House of Lords in its judicial capacity as a Court of final appeal was sovereign. Its judgements were subject to no further appeal, and its acts were subject to no control. What it declared for law no other authority known to the constitution could dispute. Without its own consent its judicial powers could not be impaired or controlled, nor could their operation be annulled. The consent of this sovereign judicature was no less essential to legislation than was the consent of the sovereign executive. The House of Lords, therefore, held in severalty the supreme judicial power, while it shared the supreme legislative power with the Crown and the House of Commons."②

I have quoted some writers extensively and at the same time dealt the question somewhat longer, partly because the subject has seldom explored and partly because the conception of sovereignty having, in the past, become somewhat mysterious, has been

---

① Salmond, *Jurisprudence*, ninth edition, 1937, p. 682.
② Salmond, *ibid.*, p. 682.
Sidiey. He speaks of sovereign *majority*, Ⅶ, p. 146.
"But unless the light of reason had been extinguished in him (Filmer 8), he might have seen that though no law could be made without a supreme power, that supremacy may be in a body consisting of many men, and several aders of men. If it is true, which perhaps may be doubted, that there have been in the world unique monarchies, aristocracies, or democracies, legally established, it is certain, that the most part of the governments of the world (and I think all that are or have been good) were mited. Paul—if the power has been conferred upon the king, or the magistrates that represented him, and rank upon the senate and people, as has been assumed in relation to the governments of the Hebrews, Spartans, Roamns, Venetians, Germans and all those who live under that which is usually called the gothic politics. If the single person participating of this divided power dislikes either the man he bears or the authority he has, he may renounce it; but no reason can be from there down to the prejudice of nations, who give so much as they think consistent with their good and reserve the rest to themselves, as to such other offices as they please to establish." (sur [主权在罗马] people, Vol. Ⅱ, 112) pp. 147-148, Vol. Ⅲ, Chapter Ⅲ, Section ⅩⅩⅠ.

regarded by some writers as if it were entirely divorced from the governmental organization. They hold that what the government possesses is power, but not sovereignty, because, as their reasoning goes, back of the government, lies the constitution and back of the constitution lies the sovereignty. Sovereignty is not only the ultimate source of governmental powers, but it lies so far away from the latter that their relationship becomes very indirect and that seem to be entirely different from one another.

I have already pointed out that, in general, writers, particularly those in the earlier period, did not make a clear distinction between what is power and what is sovereignty, so these two things are interchangeable. But this may be considered as a theoretical question. It may be said that it is liable for man to argue it from one way or another. But if we look to the real facts, we don't see how people can deny that sovereignty can not be possessed by governmental organization. It is generally recognized that, in England, the Parliament is the sovereign body. Is it not that the English Parliament is a governmental organization or a department of the government? To this question no one seems doubtful. Yet if the parliament, as a department of the government can be regarded as a sovereign body, why not an executive department of the government can not be vested with sovereign powers. As a matter of fact, before the parliament has come into power, power which is called sovereignty, it was the head of the executive department, the king or the monarch who was regarded as the possessor of sovereignty. Even up to the present day the king of England is still addressed as the sovereign of that country. It would be absurd to say that only the head of the executive department of the government, the king or the monarch, or that only the parliament, one of the governmental department, can possess sovereignty, while the executive, as a governmental department can not possess sovereignty.

If we admit that the head of the executive department or the executive department as a body by itself was sovereign before the parliament is sovereign, then we must also admit that in the English history, there has been a change of the location of sovereignty from one place to another. But to admit that there has been a process of transferring of the sovereignty from one governmental department to another usually if not always implies a process of division of sovereignty. This is particularly true in the case of English sovereignty. Because the process of changing the sovereignty is very slow. Revolutionary movements there have been in England. And monarch has been killed also. But on the whole, the change of sovereignty or rather sovereign powers did not occur overnight. It took hundred and hundred of years to complete the process.

Sometimes the change was noticeable while sometimes it was so slow and indeed so slight that even men of the inner circle of the government were not conscious of it.

But every change, how slow and how slight it might it (be), implied a decrease of the sovereign powers of one department and an increase of these powers of another. This process of increase or decrease, means really a division of sovereignty. Until one department is completely sovereign or become an undivided, though not indivisible, sovereignty, the sovereignty of England is divided disregard of the fact whether or not the process of transferring the sovereignty from the executive to the legislative departments keeps on going or stands still. Thus the sovereignty of the executive has been and possibly still is taken away by the legislative or the parliament bit by bit in a long course of time, not however, once for all. To take something in fragments is to divide it. In this sense, the process of change is a process of division.

This being clear, we may well conclude that sovereignty is not only attached or incorporated into governmental departments, but also may be divided between these departments. What is true to the executive and legislative departments may be also true to the judicial department or other departments if there are such in parallel to the executive or legislative. And what is true in England may be also true to other countries if the governmental departments of these countries are more or less independent from each other.

When we come to the division of sovereignty between what is known as central government and what is known as local government, we find that this is not only true in fact, but also supported by numerous writers. It may be remarked that the divided sovereignty as conceived by Beaumanoir is the germ of this kind of division of sovereignty. His sovereignty of the king may be considered as the sovereignty of the central government, and his sovereignty of the barons as the sovereignty of local government, although it has to be borne in mind that he attaches sovereignty to persons, while we refer to institutions.

What is true to Beaumanoir is also true to Thomas Smith, although the latter refers to the earliest development of political powers rather than to his own time. He relates: "By olde and ancient histories that I have read, I do not understand that our nation hath used any other general authoritie in this realme neither *Aristocratical*, nor *Democratical*, but only the royal and kingly majesty which at the first was divided into many and sundrie kinges, each absolutely reigning in his countrie, not under the subjection of other, till by fighting thone with thother, the overcommed always falling to the augmentation of the vanguisher and overcommer, at the last the realme of England grew into one Monarchie. Neither any one of those kinges, neither he who first had all, tooke any investure at the hand of Themperour of Rome or of any other superiour or fouuaine prince, but helde of God to himselfe, and by his sword his people and crowne, ackowledging no prince in earth his superiour, and so it kept and holden at this day."①

Thus the growth of the monarchy in England did not come at one time and it may be said the absolutely reigning powers of the many and several kings was one by one and by and by augmentated into the hands of overcomer. The kings Smith here speaks of are equivalent to the barons of Beaumanoir, and the relations between these kings and the monarch are somehow like the relations between the barons and the king.

Concerning this point, the writers in France in the sixteenth century could see more clearly and their viewpoints are worth to be considered. In the *Roveile Matin des Francais*, a work supposed to be written by several authors between 1573 and 1574, we find the theory of divisible sovereignty between the local and central governmental agencies is clearly stated. The starting point is that sovereignty was originally vested in the people. It was given to the king not without conditions, nor to him alone. He is given the power for promoting justice. But besides the sovereignty was conferred to him, [it] part of it was conferred to many of the magistrates who are subordinate to the king.②

The same opinion was expressed in a work entitled *Du Droit* about the latter part of sixteenth century. The author of this work contends that the officers of the kingdom share in the sovereignty with the king. By offciers he means all dukes, counts, viscounts, barons and chastelains. Sovereignty is thus divided between the king and those who administer the territories considered as parts of the kingdom. The relations between the king and his subordinate administrators are institutional rather than personal. So the magistrates are the magistrates of the kingdom rather than that of the king. The sovereign rights exercised by the local or subordinate magistrates do not come from the king, for

---

① Smith, *De Republica Amglorm*, Bk. I, Ch. 9, p. 19. See also Ch. 8, p. 17. "For at first, all kings ruled absolutely, as they who were either the jeads and most ancient of their families, derived out of their ow bodies, as Daam, Noa, Abraham, Jacob, Esau, reigning absolutely over their own children and bondmen as reason was: or else in the rude world amongest barbarous and ignorant people, some one them who God had endewed with singular wisedome to invent thinges necessary for the nourishing and defence of the multitude, and to administer justice did so farren excell other, that all the rest were but beastes in comparison of him, and for that excellencie willingly had this authortie given him of the multitude, and of the Gentils when he was dead and almost when he was yet living, was taken for a God, of other for a Prophet."

② See J. W. Allen, *A History of Political Thought in the Sixteenth Century*, pp. 311-312.

both these rights of the king and that of the magistrates are delegated by the people. If the king is tyrannical, these magistrates can resist him and if necessary they can do that by force. "Il y a un mutuelle obligation entre un Roi et les officiers d'un Royaume: duquel Royaume tou le gouvernement n'est pas mis entre les mains du Rol, ains seulement le souverain degre de ce gouvernement, comme aussi les officiers inferieurs y ont chacun leur part selon leur degre et le tout a certaines conditions d'une part et d'autre."① Thus if the officiers are obliged to do something for the king, the latter is also obliged to do something for the former. It is "un mutuelle obligation" between them, since they share the sovereign powers delegated by the people and since each is sovereign within its own sphere so far each is related to other.

Speaking of the conception of sovereignty of the Huguenot in France in the sixteenth century, Allen points out that "The Huguenot writers claim a share in active sovereignty for the aristocracy of the towns also."②

Even in the eighteenth century, when J. L. De Lolme declared that "England was not, like France, an aggregation of a number of different sovereignties: it fomed but one state, and acknowledged but one master, one general title"③, he had in mind also that in France sovereignty is divided between the central and the local governments.

There were many German writers holding that sovereign powers may be divided between the central and the local governments. For instance, Nettlbladt and Puetter are prominent expounders. In his *Elementa juris publici Germanici* published in 1754, Puetter speaks of "forma mixta, in der einige Souveraenetaetsrechte conjunctim bei Kaiser und Staenden, andere unter di letzteren getheilt sind."④ And when he published his *Beytraege zum Teutschen Staatsund Fuestenrecht*, he declared that there were two sovereign powers in Germany, one central and the other local.⑤ Somewhat the same idea was held by Nettelbladt.⑥

Modern writers like Leon Duguit in France incline to think that the local government is also vested with sovereign powers, therefore the sovereignty of a state is divided between the central and the local government.

It is thought that many of the local government, not only exercise the sovereign rights inherent to them, but also had these rights before the state came into existence.

---

① Quoted by Allen, *ibid.*, p. 325.
② *Ibid.*
③ De Lolme, J. L., *The Constitution of England*, 1784, p. 19.
④ Otto v. Gierke, *Johannes Althusius*, 1880, p. 249, note 59.
⑤ Puetter, *Beytraege*, Book I, p. 25 ff.
⑥ Gierke, *ibid.*, p. 249, note 60.

Thus local political groups are prior to the state. Many people lived in the town, in the county or other local units before they lived in a state. After the growth of the state, the state may utilize them for its administrative units, but the latter are by no means the creatures of the former. They have their own rights which may be traced back to hundreds and thousands of years ago. The state may by force or by other means take some of their powers away, but there are always some of these power left to them.

Even in the case of those which are created by the state, powers are given to them for the administration of their own affairs. It may be argued that these powers are not sovereign powers, because the powers of the state are supreme to them. Yet we should not forget that the so-called sovereign powers are prescribed by law. They are supreme only within their own spheres. It can not do what it pleases. Still less is the central government whose powers are usually prescribed by the constitution.

What we have said in regard to the theory of divisible sovereignty in its application to the central and local government maybe also applied to the federal state, although in the latter case the divided sovereignty becomes much clearer and more definite. And there are numerous expounders of this theory. While a book would be needed to expound the theory of divisible sovereignty in its relations to the federal state, we can only present it in a very brief way. ①

Federal state, in its strict sense of the system, may be said to have been first founded in the United States. So it is in the United States that we find the full expression of the theory of divisible sovereignty. We may doubt the saying of James Madison, the champion of the theory, that this theory as applied to the federal state was an American creation, but we must, at least, admit that it is the most characteristic feature in the history of American political thought. The theory under consideration has been advocated, maintained and defended by different kinds of men; but for our purpose, only a few representatives will be presented in the following pages.

Looking back to the fathers of the Constitution and the earlier statesmen, we find Hamilton, though expecting to have created a thoroughly centralized and aristocratic union, and trying, with all of his efforts, to extend the powers of the federal government, admitted that sovereignty was divided between the several states and the union. Samuel Adams, in a letter to R. H. Lee, when the constitution was still in preparation, praised the division of sovereignty between the several states and the union as a means for the people to govern themselves more easily, the laws of each state being

---

① Bryce, J., *Studies in History and Jurisprudence*, p. 505, note. "The name sovereign was down till very recent times used to describe the heads of a municipality in several Irish Boroughs."

well adapted to its own genius and circumstances and the liberties of the United States more secure than they would be otherwise.① John Adams also remarked that "the government is an attempt to divide a sovereignty—a fresh assay at imperium in imperio."② When Thomas Jefferson said that "the states are foreign to each other, in the portion of sovereignty not granted, as they were in the entire sovereignty before the grant," he no longer spoke as a defender of the absolute sovereignty for the several states.③

But the ablest exponent of this theory among the fathers of the Constitution is James Madison. The difficulty for those who do not see the possibility of dividing sovereignty, according to Madison, lies in the fact that they do not see clearly in their mind "that all power in just and free government is derived from compact, when the parties to the compact are competent to make it."④

The parties to this compact, as he pointed out, was not, as Webster would say, the people of the United States as a whole, but the people of the several states. By state, he meant the "people thereof respectively in their sovereign character, and they alone."⑤ And by people, he meant the majority of them rather than all. Sovereignty, as he conceived it, is the will of the people, i. e. the will of the majority of the people in a given society. At this point, a question presents itself: how far can the will of a majority of the society, by virtue of its identity with the will of society, divide, modify or dispose of the sovereignty of society?⑥ This, according to Madison, may be answered under two ways: in the first place, "the majority has not only naturalized, admitted into society by actually dividing the society itself into distinct societies equally sovereign."⑦ The separation of Kentucky from Virginia, and Maine from Massachusetts, may be cited as examples of this operation.⑧ Secondly, if it is true that the sovereignty can be divided into two, when a state divides into two, it is equally true that two sovereign states may combine into one sovereignty. Thus sovereignty is a thing which in its nature can be divided or combined whenever the majority of the people of a society so desired.

Based on what has been said, it follows that "if two states, could thus incorporate

---

① Samuel Adams, *Works*, Vol. IV, pp. 324-325.
② Jonn Adams, *Works*, Vol. IX, p. 564.
③ See Madison, *Works*, Vol. IX, p. 352.
④ Madison, James, *Works*, Vol. IX, p. 569, also pp. 383-394.
⑤ *Ibid*, p. 352, also pp. 600-602.
⑥ Madison, *Works*, Vol. IX, p. 571.
⑦ *Ibid*.
⑧ *Ibid*.

themselves into one by a mutual surrender of the entire sovereignty of each; why might no a partial incorporation, by a partial surrender of sovereignty, be equally practicable if equally eligible."①

What is true as to two states is also true to ten or twenty or more states, so the reasoning goes.② The possibility of dividing sovereignty is not only logical, but also in conformity with fact. "Thus a division of sovereignty is illustrated by the exchange of sovereign rights often involved in treaties between independent nations, and still more in the several confeferacies which have existed, and particularly in that which preceded the present constitution of the United States."③

But this is not all. Here we come to his main point. Even under the present constitution of the United States, "sovereignty is in its nature and in fact divided between the states in their united and the states in their individual capacities that as the states, in their highest sovereign character, were competent to surrender the whole sovereignty as form themselves into a consolidated state, so they might surrender a part and retain, as they have done, the other part, forming a mixed government with a division of its attributes as worked in the Constitution."④

This being the case, it is difficult, then, to argue intelligibly concerning the compound system of government in the United States without admitting the divisibility of sovereignty.⑤

This theory of divisible sovereignty has been entertained by the Supreme Court of the United States. As early as 1793, in his dissenting opinion in the case of Chisholm v. Georgia, Justice Irodell said: "Every state in the union in every instance where its sovereignty has not been delegated to the United States are in respect to the powers surrendered. The United States are sovereign as to all powers of government actually surrendered. Each state in the union is sovereign as to all powers reserved. It must necessarily be so, because the United States have no claim to any authority but such as the states have surrendered to them, Of course the part not surrendered must remain as it did before."⑥ Even Chief Justice Marshall, while trying with all his efforts to the extend the powers of the federal government, expressly declared, in the case of McCullock vs. Maryland, that "in America the powers of sovereignty are divided

---

① Madison, *Works*, Vol. IX, also Vol. IV, pp. 420-421.
② *Ibid.*, pp. 571-572.
③ *Ibid.*, pp. 568-569.
④ *Ibid.*
⑤ *Ibid.*, p. 572.
⑥ Dallas, p. 419, 435.

between the government of the union, and those of the states. They are each sovereign with respect to subject committed to them. "①

And so this is the opinion expressed by President Monroe in a message to Congress in 1822: "There were two separate and independent governments established over our union, one for local purposes over each state by the people of the state, the other for national purposes over all the states by the people of the United States. The whole power of the people, on the representative principle, is divided between them. The state governments are independent of each other and to the extent of their powers are complete sovereignties. The national government begins where the state governments terminate…. This government is also, according to the extent of its powers, a complete sovereignty. "②

There are some writers who think that the Civil War cleared the dispute between the sovereignty of the federal government and that of the several states and affirmed the theory of indivisible sovereignty. But this has not been the case. We shall not go into detail here to present the view points of the defenders of doctrine of divisible sovereignty. It suffices us to point out that even the courts and the judges of the United States have not adhered to the traditional theory of sovereignty. In the leading case of Collector vs. Day, decided in 1870, it was held that two sovereignties may exist in the same territorial limit: "They are distinct and separate sovereignties acting separately and independently of each other, within their respective spheres. "③

The theory under discussion was presented more clearly in the work of Judge T. M. Cooley. Sovereignty, in its full sense, is here defined as "supreme, absolute and uncontrollable power by which any independent state is governed." While this may sound like what Bodin or Hobbes would say, the learned Judge tells us: "In American constitutional law a peculiar system is established; the powers of sovereignty being classified, and some of them appointed to the government of the United States for their exercise, while others are left with the states." "Under this apportionment", he continues, "the notion is possessed of supreme, absolute and uncontrollable power in respect to certain subjects throughout all the states, while the states have the like unqualified power, within their respective limits, in respect to other subjects. "④

Even as late as 1922, Chief Justice Taft expresses the same opinion in the case of

---

① 3 Dallas 232.
② *Writings of Monroe*, Vol. VI, p. 223.
③ 11 Wallace, p. 113, 124.
④ Cooley, *The General Principles of Constitutional in the United States*, third edition, 1898, pp. 21–22.

Panzi vs. Fessenden et al, in the name of the Court: "We live in the jurisdiction of two sovereignties, each having its own system of courts to declare and enforce its laws in common territory. "①

This theory of divisible sovereignty has not been advocated by the American writers alone. It has been introduced into Europe by A. de Tocqueville and strongly supported by G. Waitz and many other European writers. "The principal aim of the legislators of 1789, " says Tocqueville, "was to divide the sovereign authority into two parts. In the one they placed the control of all the general interests of the union, in the other the control of special interests of the component states. " ② The difference between the sovereignty of the central government and that of the several states is stated in the following statement: "The sovereignty of the union is an abstract being, which is connected with but few external objects; the sovereignty of the states is hourly perceptible; easily understood, constantly active, and if the former is of recent reaction, the latter is coeval with the people itself. The sovereignty of the union is factious, that of the states natural and derives its existence from its own simple influence, like the authority. "③

The theory of G. Waitz was set forth in an article entitled "Das Wesen des Bundesstaates", published in Allgemeine Monatsschrift fuer Wissenschaft und Literatur, 1853. This article was later reprinted in his *Grundzüge der Politik*, 1862. He strongly denies sovereignty as the highest power in the state and therefore indivisible both in respect to sphere and objects. He makes a distinction between *Staatenbund* and *Bundesstaat*. In the former, sovereignty remains in the several states, while in the latter, it belongs exclusively to neither center nor parts, but inheres in both within their respective spheres. He declares that only the extent, not the content, of sovereignty is limited, "Nur der umfang, nicht der Inhalt der Souveraenetaet is beschraenkt. "

Even Treitschke while maintaining that the sovereignties of all other member states in Germany had been swallowed up in that of the Reich, was forced to admit that Prussia still retained her sovereignty. Thus by implication if not by express recognition he committed to the theory of divisible sovereignty by reason of his belief that there would be two sovereignties existing in the Reich. "What would happen to Germany if Prussia should cease to be?" He asked. "There could be no more German Empire. Out of this follows a truth, unpleasant to most people, but which contain no insult to a non-

---

① 258 U. S. 254.
② Tocqueville, *Democracy in America*, translated by Henry Reeve, Vol. I , p. 122.
③ *Ibid*.

Prussian—namely, that Prussia is the former state within the German Empire who has preserved her sovereignty."[1] "Prussia, too", he went on, "is the only German state which is secure from any diminution of the limits of its sovereignty."[2] This to be proved by the fact that Prussia had seventeen votes in the federal council (Bundesrat) which is more than enough "to hinder any curtailment of her sovereign rights."

It is clear then that sovereignty in the federal state is divided. Without going any further we may conclude this particular subject by quoting a passage from James Bryce's article on the "Nature of Sovereignty".

"Another class of cases arises in a federal state, where the powers of government are divided between the central and the local legislatures, each having a sphere of its own determined by the constitution of the federation. In such a state the power of making laws belongs for some purposes to the Central, for some to the local legislatures. Thus in the United States, while Congress is everywhere the supreme legislative power for some subjects, the tariff, for instance, or copyright, or interstate commerce, the legislature of each state is within that state supreme for other subjects, the law of marriage, for instance, or of sale, or of police administration. Each legislature therefore (Congress and the state legislature) has only a part of the sum total of supreme legislative power; and each is moreover further limited by the fact that the constitution of the United States also. These complication however, do not affect the general principle. In every country, the legal sovereign is to be found in the authority, be it a person or a body, whose expressed will binds others, and whose will is not liable to be overruled by the expressed will of any one placed above him or it. The law, may, in giving this supremacy, limit it to certain departments, and may divide the whole field of legislative or executive command between two or more authorities. The sovereignty of each of these authorities will then be, to the lawyer's mind, a partial sovereignty. But it will none the less be a true sovereignty, sufficient for the purposes of the lawyer. He may sometimes find it troublesome to determine in any particular instance the range of action allotted to each of the several sovereign authorities. But so also is it sometimes troublesome to decide how far a confessedly inferior authority has kept within the limits of the power conferred upon it by the supreme authority. The question is in both sets of cases a question of interpreting the law, which defines in the one case the sphere of power, in the other case the extent of delegation actually made; and this difficulty nowise affects the truth that legal sovereignty is capable of being divided between co-ordinate

---

[1] Henry Treitschke, *Politik*, English translation, Vol. II, p. 373.
[2] *Ibid.*, p. 374.

authorities, or of being from time to time interrupted, or rather overridden, by the action of power not regularly at work. It will be understood that I am now dealing with legal sovereignty only, and not at this stage touching the question of whether, from the point of view of philosophic theory, sovereignty is capable of division."①

That sovereignty is divided in the federal state is also elaborated by Bryce in his well known works, *The American Commonwealth*, (1888) and *The Modern Democracy* (1922). I have quoted this passage, because he treats the subject from the legal view point. As we know, to the so-called analytic school of law, sovereignty is incapable of division. It is incapable of division, because it is *legally* incapable of division. Yet from what Bryce has said it is rather legally that sovereignty is divisible and it is divided in the federal state between the federal union and the several states.

When we approach the theory of sovereignty from the standpoint of international relations, we find again there is a general recognition that sovereignty is divisible. The lituratures in this respect are so rich that what we can do is give a few illustrations.

To begin with, we must say that from the international view point there are many sovereignties. This is the principal assumption of international law. But if we look from the historical as well as geographical standpoint, we are compelled to recognize that the existence of many sovereignties involves a division of sovereignty. This sounds curious. But it is a truth. It is a fact.

Take, for instance, Europe since the sixteenth century. We understand very well that within the same span of time and at the same time within the same territorial area, the number of the states has been increased manifold. Here again, we have a process of the increasing of sovereignties or sovereign states. At the beginning of the sixteenth century, besides England, France, Spain and, possibly, although it is doubtful, some of the Italian city states, few if any could be called, according to the prevailing opinion of the international lawyers, as sovereign states. But the list of sovereign states or sovereignties has been increased by the middle of the seventeenth century when the peace of Westphalia was concluded.

Then, more sovereignties came into existence in the eighteenth and nineteenth centuries. After the First World War at the beginning of our century, many more sovereignties have added into the the so-called international community.

The same may be said of the New World. There was none, in the eyes of international law, sovereign state until the later part of the eighteenth century when the

---

① Bryce, *Studies in History and Jurisprudence*, Vol. II, pp. 506–508.

Declaration of the United States was proclaimed. For before that time, there were colonies. Even the colonial powers were not many. Spain, England, France and Netherland would exhaust the list of these powers. While the colonial powers are undoubtedly sovereign states, the colonies themselves are not. But after the establishment of the American Republic, i. e. the United States of America, for quite a long while there was none sovereign state other than this. With the collapse of the Spanish colonial empire in the south America, sovereignties merged one after another until there are twenty South American Republics. And as already pointed out that Canada has already become a sovereign state.

We can not deny that within the same historical and at the same time within the same geographical surface the increase of sovereignties means a division of sovereignties. It means, many time, one sovereign state has been split into two or more sovereign states or one sovereignty has been divided into many sovereignties. The case of the Austrian Empire after the First World war and in many other cases illustrate the principle here advanced. There was one sovereignty before, but there were many sovereignties after that war. Yet they have been more or less still confined to the same area. Sovereignty is thus divided within the boundaries of the former Austrian empire. And as we know, before the German invasion, Austria still retained her own sovereignty. Now if the sovereignty of Austria was not divided where did the sovereignty of Czechoslovakia and where did the sovereignty of Hungary come from?

Thus no student of history can fail to see that not only once, but many times, a sovereignty unity was divided into two or many parts, each of which, usually if not always, in turn became a sovereignty itself. On the contrary many sovereignties might and did combine together and form one sovereignty. In the eyes of international lawyer, all sovereignties are equal. It does not make any difference whether a sovereignty was originally composed of many sovereignties or a sovereignty is only one of the fragments all of which formed one sovereignty before it was broken into pieces. While sovereignty "is" not sovereignties, it does not mean that it "may" not become sovereignties. Thus Calhoun is grammatically right when he says that sovereignty is one. Nor De Real is wrong, in certain sense, when he insists that to divide "sovereignty" is to destroy "it"; because it is only natural that the "original entity" must be destroyed if we are going to make two or more out of it. But to destroy the "original entity" of sovereignty does not mean to destroy sovereignty entirely. It means to divide it into many parts some of which may become full sovereignties and some may be swallowed into another sovereignty.

Sovereignty is one; but one may be divided into two or many. The question that we take special interest is not so much as to whether sovereignty is actually divided or not but rather whether it is divisible or not. And it is to be remembered that which is divided is always divisible, although that which is divisible is not necessarily divided.

What we have just said is only a general consideration of the possibility of division of sovereignty. If we come to some of the general principles of international relations, we will find that sovereignty is divisible is common rule of international dealings. International lawyer speaks of full and partial sovereignty. By partial sovereignty it is meant either more than or less than half or just half of the sovereignty. So the so-called partial sovereignty is really a division of sovereignty. As a matter of fact the term "half sovereignty" is often used in international relations in referring to a state which has lost part of its sovereignty, although the part which is lost or retained may not be exactly half.

Then the distinction between the external and internal sovereignty implies also a division of sovereignty. A state may retain its internal sovereignty, yet it may lose its external sovereignty. Many of the so-called protected states lose their external sovereignty, though it still retain its internal sovereignty. Internal or external sovereignty may be called partial sovereignty, although partial sovereignty may be external or internal sovereignty; for a state may lose part but not whole of its external sovereignty. It is also possible that a state may lose the whole of its external and part of its internal sovereignty. All these can be called partial sovereignty, not necessarily to be internal or external sovereignty. It is also a general pratice to call a state half sovereign state when it loses its external sovereignty or even part of its internal sovereignty, although the part it retains may not be half at all.

There is also "double sovereignty" or "co-sovereignty" in international pratice. This occurs in an area where it is under the control of two or more sovereignties. The case of Trieste which was once under the joint sovereignty of Austria and the German Federation may be cited as an example. It is true that the sovereignty of each controlling state is by no means divided here; but it is also true from the standpoint of Trieste, there were two sovereignties within the same territorial sphere. It is logical to say that the sovereignty of Trieste was divided between the German Federation and the Austrian Empire. In this sense, the double sovereignty or co-sovereignty is a divided sovereignty.

Then there are many limitations on sovereignty in international relations. Limitation, as we have said, involves, in certain sense, division. Besides the so-called violation of sovereignty or contempt of sovereignty means doing damage to sovereignty, even though in such case sovereignty is not divided.

It may be well concluded that international lawyers as well as other writers on the subject of international relations have generally accepted the theory of divisible sovereignty in its application to international dealings, not necessarily because they like to advocate this theory as such, but rather because the undeniable facts of international relations compel them to do go.

Chapter 11
Sovereignty

Sovereignty is thus divisible. And because it is divisible, it is not necessarily essential to the state. It may be shared by many other political units or organizations. It may be divided either between the executive and the legislative or even the judicial or between the central and the local governments. Moreover, it is divided between the federal union and the several states in a federal state and it is usually divided between different political entities in international relations.

But such a division of sovereignty is still limited within the sphere of political organizations, not organizations which are not political in their nature. The question remains to be asked, then, is: Can other social organizations also possess sovereignty?

If the answer is negative, it may be said that although sovereignty is not essential to the state, it is still essential to political organizations. And since the state is still the most important political organization, the sovereignty of the state is therefore more important than that of other political organization.

If the answer is affirmative, it has to be admitted that sovereignty is not only shared by political organizations other than the state, but also shared by other social organizations.

But neither answer will be accepted by the so-called traditional theorists of sovereignty, for according to them, sovereignty is essential to the state and only the state can possess sovereignty. Therefore, neither other social organizations nor political organizations other than the state can possess sovereignty. It is indivisible, they say, because it is essential to the state. In other words, the reason why the state is distinguished from other political organizations or social organizations is because the state is sovereign while the others are not.

We have already shown that besides the state other political organizations may also possess or share the sovereignty and consequently sovereignty is divisible. This is undoubtedly the pluralistic view point of sovereignty. But pluralistic view point of sovereignty goes beyond that. It contends that sovereignty is divisible, divisible not only among political organizations other than the state but also among other social organizations. This is really the vital point of the recent pluralistic view point of sovereignty and we propose to consider it in this chapter.

That sovereignty is divided among or shared by the social organizations other than the state or political organizations is not, however, a recent discovery. Edward Jenks remarks: "Like the word state itself it (sovereignty) is an instance of the specialization, for a particular purpose, of a term which once had a wide connotation. Philologically, the word 'sovereign' is merely an adoption of a Latin word 'supremus' which signified little more than primacy or pre-eminence. In the later middle ages, it was freely applied to any conspicuous or important person. For example the heads of colleges in Oxford or Cambridge are described in some law reports as sovereign."① James Bryce also points out that "The heads of monasteries seem to have been sometimes familiarly described as sovereigns in the Middle ages."②

And one writer even declares: "The fact of the matter is that the word 'sovereignty' can be used to prove pratically anything and therefore proves nothing, having in the cause of time been employed in so many senses, and still being equivocally used. It was originally a relative term. 'Sovereignty' (from the Mediaeval Latin supreranus and superanitas) means the highest authority in a particular field."③

It is clear then that sovereignty was not originally owned by the state or political organization alone. If the heads of the colleges of a university or of the monasteries could be called sovereign, it is possible that the heads of other social organizations might be called in the same way.

But the important point is that sovereignty was not essential to the state or political organization. Nor was it indivisible. This does not mean that sovereignty may not be regarded as the supreme power, but supreme within its own sphere. It admits that every social organization including the state has a supreme power of its own in order to control the affairs within its own limit which is prescribed either by law or by custom. It also admits that the supreme power of one organization may not be equal to another as a matter of fact, for this is also true in the case of the states themselves. No two states can be said to be exactly equal in power, yet every state is considered as sovereign, sovereign within its own sphere.

It may be added by passing that the difficulty of applying the monistic theory of

---

① Jenks, Edward, *The Ship of State*, 1939, p. 15.
② Bryce, James, *Studies in History and Jurisprudence*, Vol. II, p. 505, note.
③ Kranenburg, R., *Political Theory*, trans. by R. Barregaard, 1939, p. 163.

sovereignty in both the federal state and international community has even forced some of the traditional writers to consider that sovereignty is not essential to the state and to maintain that there can be state without having sovereignty. Paul Laband, for instance, holds that it is possible to have non-sovereign state.① In a federal state, according to him although the sovereignty of each of the several states is merged into one sovereignty which is vested in the federal union, each of the several states does not cease to be a state simply because it becomes a member of the federal state. For each of the several states has its own inherent right, the right of rule or Herrschaft. Thus it is right of rule that is essential to the state. This inherent right is the right to command and to receive obedience from the subjects of the state. Laband admits that other associations may also possess such right, but the right of these associations is always at the grace of the state. This view of Laband's has been followed by some writers. Wilson, is one of them. He says: "In the federal state, self-determination with respect to their law as a whole has been lost by member state. They can not extend, they cannot even determine, their own powers conclusively without appeal to the federal authorities. But they are still states because their powers are original and inherent, not derivative; because their rights are not also legal duties; and because they can apply to their commands the full imperative sanctions of law. But their sphere is limited by the presiding and sovereign powers of a state superordinated to them, the extent of whose authority is determined under constitutional forms and guarantees by itself."②

In international relations, "it is futile," says one writer, "to introduce the conception of sovereignty."③ Even men like Willoughby is forced to admit that "the idea of sovereignty as it is found in constitutional, can find no proper place among international conceptions".④

It is proposed, therefore, by many writers that instead of using the word "sovereignty" we should employ the term independence. According to this conception, the sovereignty is only essential to its internal aspect, but not its external aspect.

It must be said such a theory is to destory sovereignty entirely from the state; for if the member states of the federal state can still retain their statehood without possessing sovereignty, it can not be denied that it is possible that federal union can be regarded as state without having sovereignty. Again, if a state can still retain its statehood without

---

① Paul Laband, *Das Staatsrecht des deutschen Reiches*, 1876-1882, Vol. I , pp. 59, 69.
② W. Wilson, *An Old Master and other Essays*, pp. 93-94.
③ State made by P. A. Brown, see *American Journal of International Law*, Vol. IX, p. 326.
④ W. W. Willoughby, *Fundamental Concepts of Public Law*, p. 283

external sovereignty, there is no reason why it should not be called state without internal sovereignty.

Yet it is curious to say that while conceding that sovereignty is not essential to the state these writers would still insist that sovereignty is indivisible.

We have mentioned this theory, the theory that there can be state without sovereignty, because on the one hand it takes away the essential characteristic of the state which, according to the traditional theory of sovereignty, and which alone makes the state distinguish from other associations, and on the other hand, it concedes that other associations, like the state, may have the inherent right.

Such a theory, different as it is from the pluralistic theory of sovereignty, is, however, similar to the latter in that both recognize the inherent right of the other organizations as well as the state, although, as already pointed out, according to Laband, the inherent right of the state is still superior to that of other organizations. Here we come to the starting as well as the essential point of the pluralistic theory of sovereignty as advocated by recent writers.

It is said that Otto Gierke is the forerunner of the recent pluralistic theory of sovereignty. This is not, however, true, because he neither expressly believes that sovereignty is divisible nor consideres that it is shared by other social organizations. But it is chiefly he who inspires directly or indirectly to insist that sovereignty is not vested by the state alone, but also by other social organizations. This being so, before considering the recent pluralistic theory of sovereignty, it is desirable for us to give a little attention to the basic theory of Gierke. But before presenting the theory of Gierke, a few words would be said of Georg Beseler, the pioneer of the Genossenschafttheorie; for Gierke himself was deeply influenced by Beseler, although the theory as advanced by Gierke is much more fruitful than that of his predecessor and goes far beyond what Beseler has achieved.

As early as 1843, Besler, in his *Volksrecht und Juristenrecht* already devoted a whole chapter on "Das Recht der Genossenschaft", and pointed out that the Genossenschaft which has a life and personality of its own is by no means absorbed by the state. Beseler was mainly dealing with the German social groups and he was approaching the subject from the legal standpoint. Legally speaking, the social groups other than the state were vested with independent legal personality. And in the broad sense of the term, the state and the commune (Gemeinde) may be included in the conception of Genossenschaft. In this sense, the state is not only one of the social groups or Genossenschaften, but also smaller in compare with the latter.

There are, according to Beseler, many kinds of Genossenschaft. In the first place, there are Genossenschaften which have direct political significance. To this belongs the German Union (DeutscherBund), the ruling house of the country. Secondly, there are Genossenschaften of landed possessor of a definite district such as the old Markengenossenschaften or the dike and sewer unions (Deichund Siehlverbaende). Then there are Genossenschaften of Church, for commerce and industry, for the means of communication, for common defense (gegen gemeinschaftliche Gefahr), for religious, moral, scientific, artistic, economic and social purposes. And finally there are Genossenschaften in the family such as that of higher or lower noble families. ①

Genossenschaft comes into being either as a result of a definite act of reation or as a result of historical development. The former is a legal process. The latter originates from the needs and the urge deeply rooted in the spirit of association (Associationsgeiste) from which the individual members of a group have gradually come to identify the purpose of each to that of whole so that an independent personality of the group has come into existence. ② It is an organic whole.

Beseler repudiates the fiction theory that such group can only come from the highest authority of the state. On the contrary, he considers the state comes from the same way as the group does. He says: "Gewoehnlich behauptet man, jede juristische Person sey als solche eine Fiction, und koenne deswegen nur durch die hoechste Gewalt im Staate zur Existenz kommen. Allein Beides is nicht richtig. Die Genossenschaft nameentlich und die Gemeinde sind so wenigeine Fiction, als der Staat es selber ist; es liegt in der so geordneten Gesammtheit ein organisches Leben, eine Persoenlichkeit, deren Bedeutung man ganz missversteht, wenn man sie bloss im Gegensatz zu der des einzelnen Menschen auffasst, so wie es auch nicht richtig ist, wenn man is ausschliesslich auf den civilrechtlichen, freilich besonders wichtigen Punct der Vermoegensfaehigkeitbezieht!" ③

---

① Beseler, *Volksrecht und Juristenrecht*, Chapter Ⅵ, pp. 165–168.

② *Ibid.*, p. 169.

③ *Ibid.*, p. 173. He continues however: "Das aber ferner eine solche Persoenlichkeit, die immerhin als eine juristische bezeichnet werden may, nur durch den Staatswillen soll enstehen koennen, is einfach eine *peitiio principii*, welche durch die Geschichte und das Rechtsleben der germanischen Voelker widere legt wird. Auch is schon aud den Widerspruch aufmerksam gemacht worden, dessen sich diejenigen schuldig machen, welche dem ausdruecklichen Staatswillen die stillschweigende Anerkennung und Duldung substituiren. Es verhaelt sich damit, wie mit der aelteren Theorie von der Entstehung des Gewohnheitsrechts: weil man sich das Gesetz als die auschliessliche Quelle des Rechts dachte, so liess man das Gewohnheitsrecht nur durch die ausdrue-ckliche oder stillschweigende Genehmigung des Staats entstehen, und nahm, um ein falsches Princip aufrecht zu erhalten, zu Fictionen seine Zuflucht." pp. 173–174.

The influence of Beseler on Gierke is, indeed, great and Gierke has repeatedly admitted his indebtedness to his predecessor. Besides following the example of Beseler to give his own students pratice in research in the sources of mediaeval law, he succeeded the chair occupied by Beseler in the University of Berlin, after the death of the latter.

But most important of all is that it was Beseler who inspired Gierke to devote almost all of his academic life to the study of the Genossenschafttheorie. And it is this theory that gives Gierke a high position in the academic world and that influences, in turn, many of the followers both in Germany and particularly in the English speaking countries.

The starting point of Gierke's theory is that man is at once a member of a collective association as well as an individual. "We proceed," he says, "from the firmly-established historical fact that man everywhere and at all times bears within himself the double character of existing as an individual in himself and as a member of a collective association. Neither of these characteristics without the other would have made human beings unman beings. Neither the particularity of the individual nor his membership in the generality can be thrown away without denying the nature of man. Thus we not only accept it as naturally established fact, but set it down as a conceptual characteristic of man that he has his existence partly in himself alone and partly in an association standing above him. In agreement with this, we assert as well founded a twofold tendency of human consciousness and instinct. Man can have no self-consciousness without *at the same time* recognizing himself as a particular and as a part of a generality. His will receives content and direction only partly from himself; he is also partly determined by other wills. And in so far as we attribute purpose to existence, individual human life is neither mere self-purpose nor a mere means of the demands of the association; but we believe that the individual and the generality exist for themselves and at the same time for each other, and that the task of mankind lies in the establishing of harmony between the mutually complementary factors of the particular and the generality. ①

"From this point of view," he continues, "we must attribute to the human individual as well as to the human association full reality and a unitary character. For us, the individual existing for himself alone and drawing upon himself is a natural and real like-unit. But we find just as natural and just as real a unity of life in every human

---

① Gierke, "die Grundebegriffe des staatsrechts und die neuesten Staatsrechtstheorien" in *Zeitschrift fuer gesammte Staataswisssenschaft*, XXX, 1874, pp. 153 ff. The English translation is rendered by John D. Lewis in Appendix D in his *The Genossenschaft-theory of Otto von Gierke*, p. 169.

association which, by partially absorbing their individuality, binds a group of individuals together into a new and independent whole. For the significance of human existence could as little be created by a mere totaling of the lives (Lebensinhalt) of all individuals as it could expressed by the picking out of single elements of associational life. Thus we find above the level of individual existence, a second, independent level of existence of human collective associations. Above the individual spirit, the individual will, the individual consciousness, we recognize in thousandfold expressions of life the real existence of common spirit, common will, and common consciousness. And not figuratively, but in the most real sense of the word we speak of 'communities' (Gemeinwesen) over single individuals. "①

The social group as well as the individual must, then, have a personality which is not only real but also above the individuals who compose the group. Here we see the superiority of the groups.

Although social groups are composed of individuals, each of the social groups is not only above but also exterior to the individuals. Gierke explains this point very clearly in the following passage: "Since communities arise from individuals this all occurs in and through individuals. But the individuals, in so far as their activity is connected with the social institution, are controlled by physical and intellectual influences which flow from their membership in the institution. To be sure, we observe that single, dominant individuals play creative roles, and by qualities which come from themselves alone transform the community. But this is possible only when the community cooperates and takes over as its own what is introduced by the individual. It is possible to hold widely differing opinions upon the question of how far the active influence of the whole or of the individual is responsible for great changes in social life. But whether one embraces a one-sided cult of hero worship or revels in a one-sided collective picture of history, still one can never overlook the fact of a continual interaction between the two factors. At all events, the community is something active. But then the activities which we must attribute to the community are such that they can not be explained as arising from a mere sum of individual forces. For they can not be produced in part by any isolated individual, so that the whole result might be considered similar in kind to the partial results and only quantitatively larger; on the contrary, they are of a particular type. Organization of force, law morals, national economy, speech—these are phenomena which promptly come to mind. The active community, therefore, can not be identified

---

① Gierke, "die Grundebegriffe des staatsrechts und die neuesten Staatsrechtstheorien" in *Zeitschrift fuer gesammte Staataswisssenschaft*, XXX, 1874, pp. 169-170.

with the sum of its active individuals. We are still in the domain of external experience when we induce the existence of a real social unity from the facts of cultural history. And we are justified in applying the concept of such a unity, induced by abstracting the real content of our findings, as a scientific basis concept in the whole field of social science."

"Moreover," He continues, "what we learn by external experience is verified by internal experience. For we find the reality of the community in our personal consciousness as well. The association of our ego with a social institution of a higher order is a personal experience of us. We feel ourselves to be self-sufficient beings, but we also feel ourselves to be parts of a whole which lives and acts within us. Were we to think away our membership in particular people and state, a religious community and a church, a professional group, a family, and numerous other societies and associations, we should not recognize ourselves in the miserable remainder. But when we think over all this, it becomes clear that is not a matter merely of external chains and bonds which bind us, but rather a matter of psychological relation which, reaching deep within us and integrating us, form constituent elements of our spiritual being. We feel that part of the impulse which determines our action comes from the community which permeates us. We become conscious that we are living a social life. If then we fashion from our inner experience the certainty of the reality of our being, this certainty is not based solely upon the fact that we form individual living entity. The higher living entity can not, to besure, be found in our consciousness. For since we are only parts of the whole, we can not contain the whole within ourselves; and so from inner experience we can learn directly only of the existence and not of the nature of the social unit. Indirectly, however, we can conclude from the effects of the community upon ourselves that the social entities are of physical-spiritual nature. For these effects exist in physically mediated psychic invidents. For this reason we speak not only of social bodies and their members, but also of the soul of the people, the national consciousness, popular conviction and popular will, of class spirit, of fraternity spirit, of family spirit, and so forth. We designate thereby very lively psychic forces, of whose reality we are not the least conscious when, making use of our individuality, we revolt against them. Self-observation may convince us every day of the existence of these spiritual forces. But there are hours in which the community spirit manifests itself with primitive force in almost tangible form and so fills and dominates our inner being that we are scarcely conscious of our single existence as such. Such a sacred hour I experienced here in

Berlin *Unter den Linden* on 15 July, 1870. "①

Having understood the nature of social groups, we may come now to the relation of the state and other social groups. It is clear to Gierke that the state is one of these social groups. And as one of the social groups, the state may be viewed as one of those either in the process of historical development or in the process of functional differentiation. Historically speaking, "as the forward march of world-history is inevitably realized, there appears in an unbroken ascending arch the noble structure of those organic associations which in ever greater and more interpendence of all human existence, unity in its multi-colored variations. From marriage, the highest of those associations which do not outlast their members, grow forth in abundant gradations families, races, tribes and clans, 'Gemeinde', states and league of states; and for this development one can imagine no other limit than when, sometime in the distant future, the whole of mankind shall be drawn together into a single organized community, which shall visibly demonstrate that all are but members of one great whole."②

Functionally speaking, "human communal life is continually dividing and branching out according to content and purpose. Originally the purely physical associations, the family, race, nation, fulfilled the whole task of human communal existence. They realize at the same time in unitary and exclusive manner community of speech, morality, belief, economics, laws and political life. But more and more, in the course of time, the unitary associational organizations split up into a great number of independent associational organisms, each of which dealt with only a single side of human communal life. Although originally these specialized associations simply grew up unconsciously and spontaneously upon a physical basis, the human spirit, when developed to the point, undertook the conscious and deliberate creation of related associations for definite purposes extending beyond the lives of individuals."③

The state is thus in the midst of multifold associations. It is certainly not the smallest, yet it is or will be not the largest, because from the standpoint of historical development, there has been already league of states and there will be an organized world community. From the standpoint of functional specialization, the state performs

---

① The few passages quoted above are taken from his inaugural address upon assuming rektorate at the University of Berlin, 15 October 1902 on the subject *Das Wesen der menschlichen Verbaende*. The English translation may be found in Appendix C in John D. Lewis, *The Genossenschaft-theory of O. von Gierke*, 1935.

② See the Introduction to Volume Ⅰ of *Das Deutsche Genossenschaftsrecht*, 1868, pp. 1–14. English translation by J. D. Lewis in Appendix A in his *The Genossenschaft-theory of Otto von Gierke*, p. 113.

③ See Lewis, *ibid.*, p. 170. Gierke, *Grundebegrirfe des Staatsrecht und die neuesten Staatsrechtstheorien*, in *Zeitschrift fuer die sesammte Staatswissenschalt*, XXX, 1874, pp. 153 ff.

only one of the many functions. This is a very important point and Gierke has explained it more fully in the following passage:

"The state is, of course, generality (Allgemeinheit), but it is by no means, as a widely published doctrine teaches, *simply human society*. It is only one among the associational organisms of mankind, and only one definite side of human social life represented by it. It is possible, to be sure, that, with a particular and at a particular time, the state should take over all or a large number of the functions of social life; but in higher stage of culture and in the modern world above all, the non-political sides of human associational life find expression in special institutions which are in no way to be confused with the state organization. Although the physical associations of blood, speech, and habitation are to be a certain degree the undeniable basis for the growth of the state, they can theoretically exist as easily without the state as the state can exist without them. And even when the state approaches its ideal of becoming the political organ of a single and united people, still the natural and political comcepts of people can not be fully amalgamated. Thus the communal life of a people creates for the political as for all other association the most important, but by no means the only natural center."①

And this is not all. "There still exist below the united people (Volkseinheit) the race, the 'Gemeinde', and the family, above it the international community of culture-peoples, and finally mankind in general, as narrower and wider human associational institutions with special spheres of life. And so far as a political organization corresponds to these narrower and wider associations they can, on the one hand, possess a certain independence as against the state, and, on the other hand, they can, like the state, the oretically divest themselves of their natural corollary. Furthermore, the ethical-social, the relgious, the artistic and literary, the economic communal experiences all create, at different levels, their own special organisms, all of which have an independent existence as opposed to the state, whether they develop naturally or are consciously directed, whether they are formally proclaimed as unities or exist only as latent forces, whether they are as permanent as the church or as ephemeral as many clubs."②

Even the individual, according to Gierke, does not give the whole of his being to the state. He tells us: "But, since human existence is not exhausted in associational life, but is at the same time purpose itself, we must recognize over against the state the

---

① Gierke, *Grundebegrirfe des Staatsrecht und die neuesten Staatsrechtstheorien*, in *Zeitschrift fuer die sesammte Staatswissenschalt*, XXX, 1874, Lewis, *The Genossenschaft-theory of Otto von Gierke*, pp. 173–174.

② *Ibid.*, Lewis, *ibid.*, p. 174.

individual as an original reality, existing for himself and bearing a purpose within himself. For it is only with part of his being that the single man belongs to the state as a member; the rest of his being remains completely untouched by the communal life of the state, and is the stuff of his free individuality. Thus state and individual existence stand side by side as two independent spheres of life, of which neither, to be sure, can exist without the other and each points toward the other as its complement, but both of which, for all that, have their immediate purpose in themselves."①

So far we may say that Gierke is a strong advocate of pluralistic view point. And it is aspect of his political theory that exerts a tremendous influence on the later writers and therefrom we have the school of political pluralism. But Gierke does not stop here, for he sees the difference or differences between the state and other associations. Here we see the difficulty of the theory of Gierke, because tending to follow the traditional writers in considering the state as the highest and the most powerful organization, he is forced to be in a position of self-contradiction. Let us see what he says:

"But if", says he, "in the face of such a wealth of non-state social life, the state must abandon the pretension of being simple human society, it is indeed still simply society for those social relations the realization of which constitutes its nature. And thus, in so far as it deals with common relations of authority (Gemeinheitliche Machverhaeltnisse), all other collective realities even when they are for their own spheres political institutions with their own spheres of authority, are in relation to the state only particular institutions whose political authority is in the last instance ordered by and subordinated to the authority of the state. Thus, indeed, the living *political* element of all other social as individual entities finds its final definition of purpose and definitive boundary in the state, which as the sovereign organism of social authority, alone among all organisms has no institution above it to limit its power, which, as the political whole, is alone not a part of another political whole. To be sure, the question of how far the domain of the state reaches is not one to be fixed for all time, but depends upon the positive separation by time and circumstances of the political functions of life from the other social functions of life. But, in some way or other, the problems and competence of political authority will always project themselves into every sphere of human social life. For in general the consideration of how far a general interest requires for its realization the authoritative (machtvolle) carrying out of general will will always be decive in bounding the political sphere. But to a certain point in all periods and in

---

① Gierke, *Grundebegrirfe des Staatsrecht und die neuesten Staatsrechtstheorien*, in *Zeitschrift fuer die sesammte Staatswissenschalt*, XXX, 1874, Lewis, *The Genossenschaft-theory of Otto von Gierke*, p. 173.

all cultural environments, all social functions, in order to develop fully and without hindrance, will assigned to the protection and care of a power capable of coercing opposing wills. And so the state, even though theoretically it includes but one specific side of social life, is, according to its reason for existence, not an organization founded for a specific single purpose, but its functions correspond with the cultural functions of human society (Gattung), because and in so far as the highest power (Macht) must exist for their realization..."①

In another place, he says: "The nature of the 'state' union is to be found that in the fact that it has as its purpose the carrying out authoritatively (machtvolle) of the common will. It is the association of political action. Its substance is the general will, its manifestation is organized authority (Macht), its function purposive action. Political associational life of this sort has always existed; but one speaks of a true state only when an original and distinct organism for state life appears. The isolated tribe, the roaming horde, the wandering clan fulfill state functions, to be sure, but here the state has not yet achieved independent existence. When the latter occurs, political functions can be undertaken by numerous narrower and wider organizations, by graduated political 'Gemeind', corporations, and unions. They are all of state nature, but that one authoritative union (Machtverband) whose authority from above is limited by similar authority, and from below is superior to all similar authority, must exhibit a specific character, and a set of qualitative differences from all other political organizations. For an authority which is the highest distinguishes itself from every other authority by the specific characteristic, that it is, through and through, authority (Macht) that is distinguished from every other will, as a sovereign, simply general, will, determined by itself alone. For this reason, among the political organizations, although they are state-like (staatlich) only the actually highest power-organization may be termed 'stat'."②

Gierke is thus tending to the traditional theory of state, viewing the state as the sole possessor of sovereign power which is the essential characteristic of the state and by which the state is distinguished from other social organizations.

Because he assigns the sovereign to the state and to the state alone, and at the same time advocates the importance of the Genossenschaft, Gierke has been self-contradictory. For logically speaking, if the state is only one of the social groups, each of which comes into existence for the fulfillment of its own purpose, the state can have no more rights than the other social groups. Still less can it possess the highest power

---

① Gierke, *ibid.*, Lewis, *ibid.*, pp. 174–175.
② Gierke, *ibid.*, Lewis, *ibid.*, pp. 171–172.

which is different from that of the latter. With the appearance of the association as a "public personality and as universal in relation to its own members," says one of the modern writers in refering to Gierke, "the unique position of the state tended to vanish with it the state's a *priori* claim to sovereignty. If the state were no more than one association among, many, whence did it derive a rightful claim to sovereign power at once all-absorbing and all-creating? Once the opening wedge of pluralism has been inserted, how is unity under a single sovereign to be rewon?"[①]

Gierke faces even more difficulty when he applies the theory of sovereignty to the federal state. Sovereignty, to him, is essential to the state. Yet in the federal state, there are states without sovereignty. It is interesting to note that according to Gierke the quality of the state (das Staatliche) is divided in the federal state. In other words, the states in the federal states are not states in the full sense of the term. The federal union has some qualities of the state, and so with the member states; so both can be regarded as states. Thus the state is divided. But the division of the state does not mean the division of sovereignty; for neither the federal union alone nor the several states individually can possess the sovereignty. Rather it is the organic interrelation (Organische Zusammenfassung) of both the federal union and the several states posseses the sovereignty.[②] As a result, it may be said that there are three kinds of state in the federal state: one with sovereignty; and two without sovereignty. The last two are states, states not in the full sense, for they have been divided. An indivisible sovereignty in a divided state or in the midst of many partial states is what Gierke has in mind!

It must be said that Gierke is by no means unaware of the fact that sovereignty has been divided in history. He himself points out that the growing influence of the conception of state sovereignty broke the mediaeval theory and planted the "seeds of the later natural rights system of ruler sovereignty, popular sovereignty and divided sovereignty—with their partly centralized and partly atomistic but in all cases simply mechanic construction of the state legal subjectivity."[③]

Here we have a divided sovereignty. Yet being influenced by the monistic theory of sovereignty, Gierke will not concede that sovereignty is divided either in the federal state or among the social groups. Hence we have the dilema: a pluralistic theory of state with a monistic theory of sovereignty.

---

① Rupert Emerson, *State and Sovereignty in Modern Germany*, 1928, pp. 136-137.
② Gierke, *Das deutsche Genossenschaftsrecht*, Ⅱ, p. 854.
③ Gierke, *Das deutsche Genossenschaftsrecht*, Vol. Ⅲ, p. 609. See also Maitland's translation of part of his work under the title *Political Theories of the Middle Age*, p. 45. And also S. Mogi, *Otto von Gierke*, pp. 201-203.

This aspect of the theory of Gierke is somewhat like the theory of Laband and many other writers, holding that there may be state without sovereignty, although according to the judgment of Laband the sovereignty is vested in the federal union in the federal state.

But to maintain that there can be state without sovereignty is to destroy the very weapon of the traditional theory of sovereignty, because it holds that sovereignty is the essential characteristic of the state, that, as a matter of fact, the two are identical and to have one without the other is equal to destroy both, since if it is possible to have a non-sovereign State, the state can hardly be distinguished from other social groups.

I have given more space for quoting and explaining Gierke, because his writings form the store house from which the recent political pluralists draw their sources of materials and because his theory, the theory of Genossenschaft has become the chief weapon as well as the starting point of those who advocate the pluralistic theory of sovereignty.

It seems that it is desirable, at this point, to make a distinction between political pluralism and the pluralistic theory of sovereignty, for the simple reason that those who are regarded as defenders of political pluralism may not necessarily be those who advocate the pluralistic theory of sovereignty. Gierke himself is a good example here. He is the founder of recent political pluralistic school, yet he inclines so much to the traditional theory of sovereignty, the theory of indivisible sovereignty that leads some people to think that he has destroyed the very foundation that he has built.

It must be said that such a distinction is, in a sense, a contradiction by itself as we have already pointed out in the case of Gierke. But there are many people who have committed the mistake that Gierke has committed, although they have damaged the state of Hobbes no less than Gierke did, for however much they want to retain or incline, consciously or unconsciously, the theory of indivisible sovereignty, once they admit that the state is only one of many social groups and that it stands side by side with the state, they injure seriously the supremacy of the state and the sovereignty thereof. Sovereignty is considered by the traditional theorist as essential characteristic of the state and therefore the former is usually if not always identified with the the latter. It is impossible to injure one without doing damage to the other.

Gierke fails, consciously or unconsciously, to see the correlation of the two. And those who fail to see this or follow Gierke more or less along such trend of thought are compelled to commit the same error.

But it is the pluralistic, not the monistic, Gierke that exerts more influence and although Gierke himself does not divide the sovereignty of the state, he does more damage to the traditional theory of sovereignty than those who propose to divide it, partly because he views the state as nothing more than one of the social organizations and largely because to divide the state into many parts in a federal state he is forced to declare that sovereignty is not essential to the state. In other words there can be state without sovereignty. And to take out the sovereignty from the state means to destroy the state of the traditional theorists.

We do not intend to present all or even most of the writers's view points of this school. It is desirable, however, to give a general survey of leading exponents in order to show that the pluralistic theory of sovereignty, as applied to the functional groups, has been well received in recent years in different countries.

As early as 1889, Hugo Preuss already published his well known book on *Gemeinde, Staat, Reich als Gebietskörperschaften*, advocating the Genossenschaftstheorie. It must be said that so far as the Genossenschaftstheorie is concerned, especially in regard to the personality and organic nature of the social groups, Preuss does not go beyond what Gierke has already done. But Preuss is different from Gierke in many respects. Mainly responsible for the drafting of the German Constitution of 1919, instead of adhering to Gierke's state of constitutional monarchy, Preuss insists on democratic republicanism. ① And in contrast to Gierke, he inclines to the socialistic idea, although he himself can hardly be regarde as a socialist.

But most important of all that he holds a very different view point from Gierke in regard to the theory of sovereignty. Being still influenced by the traditional theory of sovereignty, Gierke, although conscious of the gradual development of international organizations, does not think that such organizations are above the sovereign states. Nor international law, to him, has the character of public law. Instead, he considers this category of law as having only the character of private law. ② On the contrary, Preuss sees very clearly that the modern states are, as a matter of fact, merely the highly dependent members of the community of states (Staatengemeinschaft). The development and expansion of different kinds of international organizations would lead to a world organization binding the states together. As a result, the supremacy of the states can no longer be maintained. ③

Preuss also criticizes Gierke's solution of the problem of sovereignty in the federal

---

① Preuss, *Staat, Recht und Freineit*, 1926, p. 427.
② Gierke, *Deas deutsche Genossenschaftsrecht*, Vol. I , p. 834.
③ Preuss, *Gemeinde, Staat, Reich als Gebietskörperschaften*, p. 207.

state as the most difficult and complicated one. Preuss can not see how a sovereignty which is neither in the federal union nor in the member states in a federal state can exist as it is advanced by Gierke.

As a matter of fact, within a state, the different kinds of genossenschaften, existing side by side with the state, are blows to the sovereignty of the state. The theory of Preuss means to destroy the sovereignty of the state. Preuss even goes so far to show that Jellinek's auto-determination is in fact a denial of sovereignty, because its exercise implied an act of auto-limitation. Although auto-limitation is self-imposition, it is a limitation. Sovereignty, according to the traditional theory is illimitable. To limite it, then, is to deny it.

While Gierke still can not free himself from the influence of the old theory of sovereignty, Preuss is very positive in attacking it, although positively he does offer a satisfactory theory of sovereignty. This is the reason why A. Haenel remarks that Preuss gives an entirely new meaning to the word sovereignty which is different from what has been used to understand it and which is purel subjective and wholly arbitrary. ①

Yet it must be said that the position of Preuss is very important in that he may be regarded as connecting link between Gierke and those who follow him, so far as the theory of sovereignty is concerned. The reason is simple. Gierke, after giving a big blow to the traditional theory of sovereignty at its heart retains its outward form. It leaves to Preuss to clean what is still left in the system of Gierke, and thus opens the way toward the theory of divisible sovereignty in the functional school of political pluralism.

In Germany, the pluralistic conception of the state and sovereignty of Gierke and Preuss has been somewhat followed by Walther Rathenau and Kurt Wolzendorff. Rathenau in his *Der Neue Staat*, published in 1919, points out that, as an imperialist state, the modern state has come to an end in the course of the last World War. The so-called military sovereignty of the state would be destroyed eventually. Part of it, as Rathenau though, would be taken away by the League of the Nations. The rest of it would be destroyed by the social revolution.

Rathenau insists that in a new age the state is not a mere state. Besides the political, military and legal organizations, we have also the cultural, educational, commercial and the economic organizations. It is hard for the state, in the midst of all these organizations, to control adequately the complex social activities both from the territorial and functional aspects. So the ideal social organizations would be to have a

---

① Haenel's Comment in *Archiv für öffentliches Recht*, 1890, Bd., pp. 468–469.

series of self-governing bodies based on local or vocational elements with proper representative organs. In other words, the old system of representation should be replaced by functional basis. In stead of having only one political state, there should be a series of 'functional' states each of which should be headed by a minister in order to look after the affairs of its 'state'. In the matter of common concern, there will be a general parliament for all, but the important point is that each functional state should have the greatest possible freedom for administering its own affairs.

Somewhat the same opinion is expressed by Wolzendorff in his *Der Reine Staat*, published in 1921. Here it is also proposed to have many non-political organizations in intellectual, economic and other social functions, each independent in its own sphere. The state is thus one of the social organizations. According to Wolzendorff, the true German conception of the state has always been genossenschaftlich. "In diesem Gedamken," he says, "is aber die Anthithese von Volkssouveraenitaet und Fuerstensouveraenitaet ueberhaupt nicht moeglich, weil es nur ein gibt: das der Gemeindienlichkeit als rechtlich-politischen Masstabes aller Macht, aller Pflicht und aller Befugnis."

Thus the pure state of Wolzendorff is to have a dencentralized state. The state, as a political organization, will remain to function and play an important role for co-ordinating the different social functions within the state. On in such a state the conflict between the popular sovereignty and princely sovereignty will be avoided.

Outside of Germany, Frederic William Maitland was the first one to introduce Gierke Genossenschaftstheorie. In 1900, Maitland published a part of his translation of Glerke's *Das Deutsche Genossenschaftsrecht* under the title *Political Theories of the Middle Age*.[①] The translator added to this book a long introduction in which it may be said that he explains his own theory of corporation as well as he introduces the Genossenschaftstheorie of Gierke.

Like Gierke, Maitland denies strongly the fiction theory which regards a corporation as a "persona ficta". The corporation, says he, is a person and is a person in fact. It is a right-and-duty-bearing unit. Corporation, to Maitland, is an organized group which has a personality of its own and is not merely a creature of the state or the law of the state. He points out that "not all the legal propositions that are true of man will be true of a corporation. For example, it can neither marry nor be given in marriage; but in a vast number of cases you can make a legal statement about X and X which will hold good whether these symbols stand for two men or for two corporations, or for a

---

① This may be found in the third volume of Gierke's work under the title *Die publicistischen Lehren des Mittelalters*.

corporation or a man."①

A university is a corporation according to the definition of Maitland. A university can buy land, hire buildings, or borrow money from another corporation and these acts are treated, from the eyes of law, as if there were transaction between two men. What do we mean by this? It means that the university is a right-and-duty-bearing unit. But this is not all, for a transaction may also take place between a corporation and one of its members on any one outside of it. Thus one can contract with a university or vice versa.

Maitland's conception of corporation include not only the social groups other than political organizations or institutions, but also the latter. So the Crown is a corporation. "Our sovereign lord is not a 'corporation sole', but is the head of a complex and highly organized corporation 'aggregate of many'—of very many."② Even the member states of the federal state are corporations. "Each one of the United States in its organized political capacity, although it is not in the proper use of the term a corporation yet it has many of the essential faculties of a corporation, a distinct name, indefinite succession, private, power to sue, and the like... Like corporations, however, a state, as it can make contracts, and suffer wrongs, so it may, for this reason and without provision, maintain in its corporate name actions to enforce its rights and redress its injuries."③

So a colony is a corporation. "We deny nowadays," says he, "that a colony is a corporation—but can we—do we really and not merely in words—avoid an admission that the colony of New Zealand is a person."④ And "if the borough is a corporation, and may be spoken of as having rights and duties, as breaking the law and being punished, this is also true of the county, the hundred and the township."⑤

If political organizations are also corporations, the traditional theory of sovereignty as it is applied to the British empire is absurd. Maitland tells us: "The state that English know was a singularly unicellular state, and at a critical time they were not too well equipped with tried and traditional thoughts which would meet the case of Ireland or of some communities, commonwealths, corporations in America which seemed to have wills—and hardly fictitious wills,—of their own, and which became States and United States. The medieval Empire laboured under the weight of an incongruously simple theory so soon as lawyers were teaching that the Kaiser was the Princeps of Justinian's

---

① Maitland, *Collected Papers*, Vol. Ⅲ, p. 307.
② Maitland, *Collected Papers*, Vol. Ⅲ, p. 259.
③ *Ibid.*, p. 266.
④ *Ibid.*, pp. 262–263.
⑤ Maitland, *The Constitutional History of England*, p. 54.

law-books. The modern multicelullar British State—often and perhaps harmlessly called an Empire—may prosper without a theory, but does not suggest and, were we serious in our talk of sovereignty, would hardly tolerate, a theory that is simple enough and insular enough, and yet withal imperially Roman enough, to deny an essentially state-like character to those 'self-governing colonies', communities, commonwealths, which are knit and welded into a larger sovereign whole. The adventures of an English joint-stock company which happened into a rulership of the Indies, the adventures of another English company which while its charter was still very new had become the Puritan commonwealth of Massachusett's Bay should be enough to shew that our popular English Staatslehre if, instead of analyzing the contents of a speculative jurist's mind, it seriously grasped the facts of English history, would shew come inclination to become a Korporationslehre also."①

It is clear that the state is also one of the corporations. "For, when all is said, there seems to be genus of which State and Corporation are species. They seem to be permanently organized groups of men; they seem to be group-unit; we seem to attribute acts and intents, rights and wrongs to these groups, to these units. Let it be allowed that the State is a highly peculiar group-unit; still it may beasked whether we ourselves are not the slaves of a Jurist's theory and a little behind the age of Darwin if between the State and all other groups we fix an immeasurable gulf and asked ourselves no questions about the origin of species."②

If the state is nothing more than a corporation the right of sovereignty which owned by the state may also owned by other corporations. "My organized group," says Maitland, "shall be a sovereign state."③ And he continues: "Let us call it Nunsquamia. Like many other sovereign states, it owns money."④

Since Maitland's translation of Gierke's work, there have been, in the English-speaking world, many writers approaching the subject more or less along the same line that Gierke has worked. J. N. Figgis, for instance, attacks the traditional theory of the state and sovereignty from the standpoint of the church, although he concedes that the church is only one of the social groups. He says: "The author has been led to his present views not by the desire to defend church rights, but by long brooding over the Austinian doctrine and the perception forced on him at last through Maltland and Gierke; that it is

---

① Maitland, *Introduction to Political Theory of the Middle Age*, pp. x–xi.
② Maitland, Introduction to Gierke's *Political Theory of the Middle Age*, p. ix.
③ Maitland, *Collected Papers*, Vol. Ⅲ, p. 318.
④ *Ibid.*

either fallacious or so profoundly inadequate as to have no more than a verbal justification. One begins by thinking Austin self-evident, one leans that many qualifications have to be made, and finally one ends by treating his whole method as abstract and theoretic."①

And he says again: "We must distrust abstract doctrines of elaborate sophistry. Above all, we must be willing to put liberty above other ends as political goal, and to learn that true liberty will be found by allowing full play to the uncounted forms of the associative instinct. We are fighting not only our own battle but that of the liberty of all smaller societies against the tendency to mere concentration, which in one way is a marked feature of our time. Much has to be learned both of 'ourselves and others from the mediaeval guild system. Further we must learn to allow to others that liberty we claim for ourselves as a corporate society, and fairly face the fact which I have called 'the religious heterogeneity of the modern state'. Lastly, we shall see that the only basis on which a true defence of the English church against Rome can be founded is precisely the same as that which we have been expounding. For Rome, as a church polity, simply embodies those seeming notions of omnipotent sovereignty which we saw had passed over from the antique state to the modern world. And thus we are forced to consider something of the nature of religious authority in general and of life of the part in the whole."②

The Austinian theory of sovereignty which is supreme and indivisible is also severely criticized by Earnest Baker. "Austin," says he, "who, one is told, was not particularly skilled in English law, and could blunder shockingly in Roman law, may have theorized about 'majestas'; but his own difficulties in fitting his theory of sovereignty into the framework of English politics seem to show that it is fairly remote from the 'genius loci'. For in England, as Barker sees, the state has been generally discredited and there one can hardly find a singularly unicellular sovereignty. A sovereign and majestic state, a single and undivided 'imperium', lifted above the conflicts of society, neutral mediatory, impartial, such as Hegel conceived and such as 'German theorists' still postulate—this we have not known."③

One may argue that the sovereignty of England is unique in the day of Henry Ⅷ, but "if to-day some may see a new Henry Ⅷ in the guise of a sovereign public opinion, the syndicalist will none the less claim exemption from the bourgeois state for his idea of

---

① J. N. Figgis, *Churches in the Modern State*, preface, pp. Ⅸ-Ⅹ.
② *Ibid.*, pp. 170-171.
③ E. Baker, "The Discredited State", *The Political Quarterly*, No. Ⅴ, 1915, p. 101.

class, the nationalist will claim immunity from the denationalized state for his idea of the nation, and the right hand of the churchman will lose its cunning if he forgets Jerusalem."①

A. D. Lindsay, another English writer, tells us that "the power of the state over its members depends upon the will of the members themselves, and on the fact that they allow the state to organize force which can indeed coerce individuals, but cannot coerce the whole community. The state, therefore, can have control over the corporations within it only if and in so far as the citizens are prepared to give such power."②

Again he declares: "It looks almost as though the state as it now exists were either too large or too small, for any principle in which we may try to rest its supremacy over other associations. If we choose the principle of consciousness of common interest, the feeling of mutual interdependence and relations, the state is too large. Intense loyalties are easier in smaller, more homogeneous bodies. If we choose the principle of the need for regulating or controlling conflicting individuals and associations the state is too small."③

As to the English guild socialists' view points, G. D. H. Cole's writings deserve our special attention. In speaking of the difference of the opinion of his own and that of other guild socialists, Cole says: "Mr. Hobson and his supporters were firm in their insistence on state sovereignty in the economic as well as in other spheres; but they did not desire that the state should play any part at all in the normal conduct of industry, or recognize the need for any continuous representation of the consumer's point of view in relation to the organization. Theoretically, they claimed for the State an unlimited authority; but actually they wanted it to intervene considerably less than those of us who desire a strict limitation upon its theoretical sphere of authority."④

And then he says: "those of us who took the other side urged that in the organization of the communnal industries and services there were two distinct points of view to the considered—the point of view of man as a producer or renderer of services, and the point of view of man as a consumer of enjoyer of the services rendered. I argued that the guilds—industrial and civil—represented men in the former aspect, while the state (and the local authority) represented them in the latter. I denied that either form of organization could be regarded as superior to the other, and insisted on the co-

---

① E. Baker, "The Discredited State", *The Political Quarterly*, No. V, 1915, p. 115.
② A. D. Lindsay, "The State in Recent Theory", *Political Quarterly*, Vol. I, 1914, p. 134.
③ *Ibid.*, p. 136. Farki—On Sovereignty.
④ Cole, *Self-Government in Industry*, 4th edition, pp. 5–6.

sovereignty of the Guilds and the State in the economic sphere, a co-sovereignty possibly to be shared with other bodies in other spheres of social action."①

Although Cole declares that "I no longer believe that I was completely right, or that Mr. Hobson was completely wrong, in the controversy; he tells us that "I am strongly opposed as ever I was to the theory of state sovereignty; but I am no longer satisfied with the state as the final and only representative of the consumers."②

In America, there are also many writers hold the pluralistic view of sovereignty. Miss M. P. Follet, in her *The New State*, emphasizes not only the importance of occupational groups, but particualrly the need of what she calls the neighborhood groups.

"Our proposal," she says, "is that people should organize themselves into neighborhood groups to express their daily life, to bring to the surface the needs, desires and aspirations of that life, that these needs should become the substance of politics, and that these neighborhood groups should become the recognized political unit."③

Neighborhood groups are both necessary and desirable, because in the first place, it is there that fuller acquaintance and more real understanding between the people are possible and secondly neighborhood organization gives opportunity for constant and regular intercourse. ④

While emphasizing the importance of neighborhood groups, she does not ignore the occupational groups. Both of these groups are necessary, because the present industrial and economic conditions make them so. But it is better, however, to work out some machinery by which the neighborhood group can include the occupational groups. "All functions," she insists, "must be expressed, but somewhere must come that coordination which will give them their real effectiveness." It is for this reason that both the neighborhood, be it economic or otherwise, but the point that she emphasizes is that it is not the kind of group, "but that the group whatever its nature shall be a genuine group."⑤

By "Genuine group", Miss Follet means the genuine whole. But the idea of a genuine whole does not belong to the group alone. Thus there is a genuine whole of an individual, of a state and of the world as well as that of a group. And it is the genuine

---

① Cole, *Self-Government in Industry*, 4th edition.
② *Ibid*.
③ M. P. Follet, *The New State*, 1918, p. 192.
④ *Ibid*.
⑤ *Ibid*., pp. 320-323.

whole that possesses the supreme power or sovereignty. Thus wherever there is a genuine whole there is a sovereignty. "The individual," says Miss Follet, "is sovereign over himself as far as he unifies the heterogeneous elements of his nature. Two people are sovereign over themselves as far as they are capable of creating one out of two. A group is sovereign over itself as far as it is capable of creating one out of several or many. A state is sovereign only as it has the power of creating one in which all are."①

"Sovereignty," she continues, "is the power engendered by a complete interdependence becoming conscious of itself. Sovereignty is the imperative of a true collective will. It is not something academic, it is produced by actual living with others—we learn it only through group life. By the subtle process of interpenetration a collective sovereignty is evolved from a distributed sovereignty. Just so can and must, by the law of their being, groups unite to form large groups, these larger to form a world group."②

It is obvious, then, that sovereignty, according to the reasoning of Miss Follet, is not absolute, for it is engendered by a complete interdependence. It may be different in extent, but not in content. The sovereignty of an individual is just as real as that of a group, of a state or even of the world state. The state is not the only group possesses sovereignty. It is not even the largest group, for above it, there is a world group or state as Mis Follet calls it.

Other writers such as R. M. MacIver, after explaining the state as one of the many social organizations, concludes by saying "Let us remember in the first place that the state does not regulate the internal affairs of the other corporations; it does not and cannot determine their purposes or for the most part their methods. It marks their boundaries and brings them into relation within a common order. It does not treat them as its own agencies, as subordinates which it commands. Except as one group of interests encroaches on another, it does deal with any of them in isolation from the rest. It does not say to the trade union, Go, and to the employers' association, Come, and to the church, Do this. These are the attributes of absolute sovereignty, and the state does not possess them. True it stands for the common interest; but only so far as the common interest is sufficiently unified to admit of political expression, and only so far as it sufficiently externalized to admit of legal regulation. True, it stands for the common interest; but not for the whole of the common interest. There is a common interest in customs, but it is not guarded by the state. There are common interests, such as that in

---

① M. P. Follet, *The New State*, 1918, p. 271.
② *Ibid.*

the economic welfare of a country, which depend at least as much on the specific activity of various associations as on the general activity of the state. The common interest is no simple objective, attainable in its entirety by an inclusive authority. The partial interests of a thousand associations, cultural and economic, are also parts of the common interest."[1]

Not only associations of thousand kinds set limits on sovereignty, custom and usage never allow the sovereignty to be absolute. "Owing to the peculiar character of political power," says MacIver, "it (the state) claimed to dominate the whole system within which it arose. This proud claim was never in fact realized for custom and usage set sheer bounds in every direction to the exercise of sovereignty. But the significance of this fact only appeared when, as the interests of men grew more complex and varied, distinct associations took shape to promote objects which the state was itself not capable of securing, or which made an appeal only to particular groups." (*Ibid.*, p. 472)

---

[1] R. M. MacIver, *The Modern State*, 1926, p. 472.

Chapter 12
State & Law

According to the traditional concepts of the so-called political science, the state, besides being the sole possessor of sovereignty, is also the creator of law. We have already noted in the last few chapters that sovereignty is divisible and divisible within the state and consequently that sovereignty is not necessarily essential to the state. We shall come now whether or not law is the creature of the state.

At the outset, it is to be remarked that the reason why law has been regarded as the creature of state is because the state is the sovereign body, that is the sole possessor of sovereignty and that law is the command of the sovereignty. In other words, the reason why the state is the creator of law is also because of its sovereignty. As a matter of fact, according to some traditional writers, sovereignty is identified with the state. And when they say that law is created by the state, they mean really that law is created by the sovereignty.

That law is the command of and created by the sovereign is the keynote of the so-called analytical school of jurisprudence. And it is this school of thought which represents mainly the traditional concepts of the so-called political science for the last hundred years. "A conception of sovereignty," as pointed out by J. W. Garner, "which has been the subject of wide discussion and which has exerted an important influence upon the legal thought of the last half century is that enunciated by the analytical school of jurists."[①]

It is our purpose in this chapter to examine the validity of the theories as expounded by the writers of the analytical school particularly in regard to the relation of sovereignty to law. The term "analytical school has long been connected with the name of John Austin, yet it has to be borne in mind that Austin is not the only writer in the analytical school, nor is he the first one who enunciated the doctrine.

The forerunner of this school is Jean Bodin. We have already pointed out that

---

① Garner, *Introduction to Political Science*, 1910, p. 268.

sovereignty is defined by Bodin as the supreme power over citizens and subjects unrestrained by law. It is unrestrained by law, because law is the creature of the sovereignty. In fact, the chief function of sovereignty is to give law to all his subjects in general and to every one of them in particular. And since law is the command of the sovereign, it is difficult, then, to conceive that the sovereign should be subject to the command of his own or to the law which is made by him. "One may receive a command from another," says he, "but no man can command himself."①

Not only is the sovereign unrestrained by his own law, but also he is bound by no laws of his predecessor.② Moreover, no consent of superiors, equals, or inferiors is required when the sovereign makes law, for "if the consent of superiors is required, then, the prince (sovereign) is clearly a subject; if he must have the consent of the equals, then others share his authority; if the consent of inferiors—then, he lacks supreme authority."③

"This being so, it is only natural for Bodin to think that the sovereign may abrogate, modify, or replace a law made by himself and without the consent of his subjects, for such action is fully permissible where justice seems to demand it; but the abrogation, modification, or substitution, however, must not be obscure of ambiguous, but must set forth in clear detail."④

"Under this supreme power of ordaining and abrogating law," says Bodin, "it is clear that all other functions of sovereignty are included; so that it may be truly said that supreme authority in the state is comprised in this one thing—namely, to give laws to all and each of the citizens, and to receive none from them. For to declare war or make peace, though seeming to involve what is alien to the term law, is yet accomplished by law, that is by decree of the supreme power. It is also the prerogative of sovereignty to receive appeals from the highest magistrates, to confer authority upon the greater magistrates and to withdraw it from them, to allow exemption from taxes, to bestow other immunities, to grant dispensations from the laws, to exercise power of life and death, to fix the value, name and form of money, to compel all citizens to observe their oaths: all of these attributes are derived from the supreme power of commanding and forbidding—that is, from the authority to give law to the citizens collectively and individually, and to

---

① Bodin, *Les Six Livres de la republique*, 1576; The English translation by Richard Knolles, London, 1606, under the title: *The Six Books of Commonwealth*, chapters 8 and 10.
② *Ibid*.
③ *Ibid*.
④ For the English version, see Coker, F. W., *Readings in Political Philosophy*, 1938 Edition, p. 380.

receive law from no one save immortal God. A duke, therefore, who gives laws to all his subjects, but receives law from the emperor, Pope, or king, or has a co-partner in authority, lacks sovereignty."

Thus the function to make laws includes almost all the essential functions of the sovereignty. Law is, therefore, the most important instrument of the sovereign to rule the subjects and citizens.

While the sovereign is not bound by the law of his own or of his predecessor, he is nevertheless subject to the laws of God, of nature, of nations and what we call the constitutional law of the state. "No one," says Bodin, "who attempts to abrogate or weaken the laws of God and of nature can escape the judgement of divine sovereignty."① It seems to Bodin that there is no clear distinction between the laws of God and that of nature, nor that both of these are or should be different from the law of nations. Accordingly, the sovereign is not bound by the law of nations of it is contrary to the laws of God and of nature. The sovereign, says Bodin, is no "more bound by the law of nations than by his own laws, except in so far as the former are in agreement with the laws of nature and of God." And he adds: "If certain of the laws of nations are unjust, the prince may abrogate them and forbid his subjects to follow them. This we showed in relation to slavery; this institution was established in many states, by pernicious examples, yet in accord with the law of almost every nation; but through salutary decrees of several princes it has been abolished, in conformity to the laws of nature."② Finally, "as to the laws concerning the supreme power, the prince can not abrogate or modify them, since they are attached to the very sovereignty with which is clothed; such is the Salic law, which is the foundation of our kingdom."③

It is clear, then, that sovereignty is not only limited by the law of God, of nature and of nations or what we call international law, but also limited "par les lois qui concernent l'Etat droyaulme et l'establishment d'iceluy, d'autant qu'elles sont annexees et unies avec la couronne... le Princce n'y peut deroger, comme est la loi salique."④

It must be said, now, that, supreme and absolute as the sovereignty of Bodin, it has its limitations. And although sovereignty is defined as the supreme power over citizens and subjects unrestrained by law, it is limited by the law of God, of nature, of

---

① Bodin, *Les Six Livres de la republique*, 1576.
② *Ibid*., "If justice is the end of law, and law is the command of the prince, and the prince is the image of the almight God, the laws of prince should bear the stamp of divine law."
③ *Ibid*.
④ *Les Six Livres de la republique*, chapter 10.

nations and the loi salique. Here we see that Bodin is self-contradictory. He starts by saying that sovereignty is not restricted by law, then, he proceeds to enumerate that the sovereignty is limited by many kinds of law, law of God, of nature, of nations and of the kingdom.

There are some writers who may think that those laws mentioned by Bodin as limitations on sovereignty are not laws in the strict sense of the term. They are, according to Austinian logics, not positive laws, but moral principles. This, however, is the right way to interpret Bodin's conception of law. The reason is very obvious. To Bodin, there is no such distinction. On the contrary, the divine law is the source of all law, and it is even more lawful than other laws.

It was Hobbes who insisted that sovereignty could not be limited by any kind of law. Although Hobbes speaks of law of God as the highest of all, but that can not be realized unless these is a mediator between God on the ⟨one⟩ hand and the individuals on the other. Thus he declares: "And whereas some men have pretended for their disobedience to their sovereign, a new Govenant, made, not with men, but with God; this also is unjust; for there is no covenant with God, but by mediation of some body that representeth God's person; which none doth but God's lieutenant, who hath the sovereignty under God."[1] The so-called God's lieutenant, in the mind of Hobbes, is none other than the sovereign or the king himself.

Hobbes also expressly declares that the law of nature is not law, but moral rule, because it is not the command of the sovereign. So he says: "These dictates of reason, men use to call by the name of laws; but improperly: for they are but conclusions, or theoremes concerning what conduceth to the conservation and defence of themselves; whereas law, properly is the word of him, that by right hath command over others."[2]

But living in an age in which the notion of the law of nature prevailed, and being an apologist of the king or kings who seek to have an absolute authority over the subjects within their dominion, he tells us that there is a close relation between the law of nature and civil law, though he makes, at the same time, an attempt to distinguish the one from the other: "The law of nature," says Hobbes, "and the civil law contain each other, and are of equal extent."[3] Again he says: "Civil and natural law are not different kinds, but different parts of law; whereof one part being written, is called

---

[1] Thomas Hobbes, *Leviathan*, edited by E. Rhys, p. 91.
[2] *Ibid.*, p. 83.
[3] *Ibid.*, p. 141.

civil, the other unwritten, natural."① Moreover, "The law of nature is a part of the civil law in the commonwealth of the world. Reciprocally, the civil law is a part of the dictates of the law of nature."② Although the laws of nature are not written laws, they are equally obligating on all mankind if they be generally observed in all the provinces of a dominion, and no iniquity appear in the use thereof. ③

Here we the absolute Hobbes becomes somewhat unabsolute. If the law of nature may be considered as a part of the civil law, the contention that law is the command of the sovereign becomes meaningless, since the natural law is not the command of the sovereign.

Nor Hobbes's differentiation of civil and natural as written and unwritten respectively is clear in his mind. For according to him, even the civil law, that is, the command of the sovereign may take many forms. It may be by voice, writing or some other sufficient argument of the same. Thus it is not necessarily for the civil law to be written.

We have already noted that Bodin makes the divine law as the source of all laws including the civil law; that is, he views the law from top down as well as from outside in. Hobbes tries to turn it inside out, thinking that civil law, as the command of the sovereign is the real law; while the so-called law of God, of nature and of nations are not laws. ④ But Hobbes does not succeed in doing this; for once he admits the natural law as a part of civil law; it is hard to see how can he deny that both the law of God and that of nations are not parts of the civil law, since both of them are almost inseparable from the law of the nature as they were so considered by the men of his age.

As a matter of fact, the social contract upon which, Hobbes construct his sovereignty is only a phantom. It lacks common sense as well as historical evidence. Men who have pratically no experience in political affairs can hardly come together at once and for all to form a Leviathan, a sovereignty by means of social contract. Never in

---

① Thomas Hobbes, *Leviathan*, edited by E. Rhys, p. 142.
② *Ibid.*, p. 141.
③ *Ibid.*
④ F. J. C. Hearnshaw, *Some Great Political Idealists of the Christian Era*, 1937, remarks: "He (Hobbes) nominally accepted classification of the schoolmen⋯. The jus divinum, he said (professing profound veneration), applied solely to the other world beyond the grave; the *jus gentium*, in Grotius's sense of the term, was non-existent, since nations in respect of one another were in a state of nature—that is, of chronic war; the *jus nature* consisted merely of the dictates of common sense tending towards self-preservation, and as such was devoid of all ethical or jurdical character; only the *jus civile* remained in any way imperative. The will of Leviathan is the only source of valid law on earth, and 'no law can be unjust'." p. 222.

history do we find such instance. If the origin of the sovereignty as construed by Hobbes is to be rejected, the law which is interpreted by Hobbes as the command of the sovereignty, the creature of the sovereignty, will be left without foundation. This is, of course, a theoretical discussion. When we come to the actual state of things, we find that history shows that few laws have been made by the so-called sovereign, particularly in the earlier history and primitive society of mankind. We shall see this point more clearly when we come to discuss the historical school of jurisprudence in the later chapter. But enough has been shown that Hobbes's interpretation of sovereignty in its relation to law is unsound.

Jeremy Bentham follows Hobbes more closely than Bodin, but his interpretation of sovereignty in its relation to law is even less absolute and less clearly than that of Hobbes. In his *A Fragment on Government*, he vigorously attacks the "conservative tempe and logical fallacies" of Blackstone's *Commentaries*. He criticizes the view of the latter that a sovereign is limited by the law of God and of Nations. To Bentham, the statement made by Blackstone that "if any human law should allow or enjoin us to commit it, we are bound to transgress that human law, or else we must offend the natural and the divine," is dangerous so far as the Divine Law is concerned; and "as to the law of nature if it be nothing a phrase; … if, in a word, there be scarce any law whatever but what those who have not liked it have found, on some account of another, to repugnant to some text of scripture; I see no remedy but that the natural tendency of such doctrine is to impel a man, by the force of conscience, to rise up in arms against any law whatever that he happens not to like."① And he adds: "What sort of government it is that can consist with such a disposition, I must leave to our author to inform us."

Sovereignty, to Bentham, can not be limited, then, by the laws of God or of nature. But this does not mean, that there is no limitation whatsoever; because it is bound by express convention. "Let us avow then, …that the authority of the supreme cannot, unless where limited by express convention, be said to have any assignable, any certain bounds. —That to say there is any act they cannot do, —to speak of any thing of their's as being illegal, —as being void; —to speak of their exceeding their authority. (whatever be the phrase) —their power, their right, —is, however common, an abuse of language."②

Bentham refers this express convention to the case "where one state has upon terms

---

① Bentham, *A Fragment on Government*, collected by J. Bowring, Vol. i, p. 287.
② *Ibid.*, edited by F. C. Montague, p. 218.

submitted itself to the government of another or where the governing bodies of a number of states agree to take directions in certain specified cases from some body or other that is distinct from them all; consisting of members for instance appointed out of each."①

And Bentham adds, "To say, in short that not even by convention can any limitation be made to the power of that body in a state which in other respects is supreme, would be saying, I take it, rather too much: it would be saying that there is no such thing as government in the German Empire; nor in the Dutch Provinces; nor in the Swiss Cantons, nor was of old in the Achaean league."②

"In this mode of limitation," he continues, "I see not what there is that need surprise us. By what is it that any degree of power (meaning political power) is established? It is neither more nor less, as we have already had occasion to observe, than a habit of, and disposition it is as easy, or I am much mistaken, to conceive as being absent with regard to one sort of acts; as present with regard to other. For a body them which is in other respects supreme, to be conceived as being with respect to a certain sort of acts, limited, all that is necessary is, that this sort of acts be in its description distinguishable from every other."③

"By means of convention then we are furnished with that common signal which, in other cases, we despaired of finding. A certain act is in the instrument of convention specified, with respect to which the government is therein precluded from issuing a law to a certain effect: whether to the effect of commanding the act, of permitting it, or of forbidding it."④

The express convention as viewed by Bentham is mainly international in character. That is to say that the sovereignty of Bentham may be limited by express convention with other sovereignties. Bentham who enunciates the term "international law" thinks more of the law of nations which according to Hobbes is non-existent, since nations in respect of one another were in a state of nature—that is, of chronic war.

The effects of the conditions of times of these writers including Bodin are very striking. Bodin, living in an age which is more closely to the Medieaval period, was deeply imbued with the medieaval theory, theory which insisted that God is the source of all powers and that all laws civil or otherwise emanated from the law of God. Hobbes, writing in a time when theory of natural law was prevailing as the powers of the pope,

---

① *Ibid.*, quoted by Montague, p. 70.
② *Ibid.*, p. 223.
③ *Ibid.*, p. 223.
④ *Ibid.*, p. 223.

the vicar of God and his Roman church were declining and somewhat forgotten, thought more of the natural law and less of the divine law. Thus the law of God was becoming something of past in the time of Hobbes while the law of nations was still too earlier to make him feel significant in spite of the effort of Grotius. It was only natural that natural law was the only thing that characterized the legal thinking of the time and that he was unable to free himself from it.

With Bentham, we can be safe to say as Hobbes would did [say] that Jus divinum could only be applied to the other world beyond the grave. While natural law has been accepted as a matter of course in the eighteenth century and reached its highest water mark in the writings of Rousseau and many others and therefore found its climax in the French Revolution, the tide for ebbing was also very strong. Bentham noticed the current. So when Blackstone still moved in the midst of both divine and natural law, Bentham made him as a target for rejecting what he disliked and for vindicating what he believed.

But if the divine law was already in the grave and if the natural law was showing sign of declining, the law of nations has just appeared into the arena of international politics. Grotious had already made a systematic study of it and many writers in the seventeenth and eighteenth centuries advocated for it. But most important of all was ⟨that⟩ the relationship of the nations of the world became more and more close and more and more frequent as a result of the discovery of the new world and the opening of the sea route between the west and the far east.

The law of nations has become more and more important as the relationship of the nations of the world has increased. Unless there are some rules of law regulating the conducts of the members of the family of nations, chaos and even catastrophe will be resulted. The law of the nations might not be so effective as the civil or municipal law in the eighteenth century, but the need of it could not be doubted. Bentham did not fail to see that. So he even coined the term "international law" which, since his own day has been used not only by international lawyers but also by writers in other fields of study.

It is true that the express convention as spoken of by Bentham is nothing more than the moral principle pledged by the sovereigns of the world in order to maintain peace and order among themselves. It is, nevertheless, a kind of limitation. It may be argued that since such a limitation is not legal in character it can not be regarded as a limitation at all. For according to some, when the sovereign is not legally bound by something, he can do what he pleases. The express convention is accepted by his own will and it can also be abrogated by his own will. Yet it must be said that this is not true in fact. Since no nation in the world can live alone without having any contact with other nations, no nation can be free to do anything she pleases. The pressure laid upon a nation to fulfill its obligations is more real than we think and history supplies numerous examples to demonstrate that usually it is the external pressure that influences or instigates the internal problems of a nation.

Further scrutiny will make us realize that the sovereignty as viewed by Bentham as well as both Hobbes and Bodin is not a legal sovereignty at all. Although Bodin defines sovereignty as supreme power over subjects and citizens unrestricted by law (Majestas est summa in cives ac subditos legibusque soluta potestas). Bodin does not stake to this definition when he comes to the questions of the origin as well as the location of sovereignty.

Sovereignty was, as Bodin thinks, originally in the hands of the people and he even goes so far as to assert that if the people do not give their sovereignty to someone or few for a considerable period of time, the sovereignty is still in the hands of the people. Only after the people give this supreme authority to the king or the prince for a long period, can the latter claim to have the sovereignty. And only when the sovereignty of the people is given up for a long period, can it be said that the sovereignty of the people is transferred to the king or prince and that only then the people are no longer sovereign.

Now it must be said that the sovereignty which was originally in the hands is the same sovereignty which is held by the king or prince after the process of transferring or delegating. We can say that the sovereignty of people is a legal one. It seems that it does not even occur to Bodin that the chief function of sovereignty is to make law when it is still in the hands of the people. Because, according to the logic of Bodin, the people can not make laws over themselves. "One may receive a command from another, but no man can command himself." So reasons Bodin. Hence so long the sovereignty still remains in the hands of the people, it seems that it is impossible for it to make laws. If the people make law in such case it would mean to command themselves. And this is absurd in the reasoning of Bodin. Moreover, there would be no subjects or citizens, since all the people or the people as whole are sovereign. But here comes the difficulties of the Bodinian system.

In the first place, how can the same sovereignty make laws in one case but not in the other. In other words, it is absurd to say that the same sovereignty when it is vested with the people it can not make laws, but when it is given up by the people to the prince, it can make laws.

Secondly, since the sovereignty of prince or king is the same sovereignty which was originally in the hands of the people, then it follows that if the sovereignty of the people is not legal in character, the same must be said in regard to the sovereignty of the king or prince. Unless Bodin admits that the sovereignty of the people is also a legal sovereignty, he can not say that the sovereignty of the king or prince is legal sovereignty. But so say this would lead him back to the difficulty just mentioned in the first case.

Thirdly, as a matter of fact, in the system of Bodin, as we have already noted, besides the sovereignty of the king or of the people, there is also a sovereignty of God which is the highest and the most original of all. Later writers do not recognize the sovereignty of God as legal sovereignty, yet to Bodin the command given by divine sovereignty is the source of all laws, civil or otherwise. In fact, to him, divine law is much more a law than the other laws including, of course, the civil law. Thus according to Bodin, the scope of law embraces not only what Austin would call positive law, but also the divine law. It is a divine, moral, political as well as legal sovereignty. Bodin does not make such a distinction. They are all the same to him. Yet when it comes to make laws, the sovereignty of people does not seem to have this function.

Finally, although Bodin considers the law-making function as the chief or almost the sole function of the sovereignty, his advocacy of the sovereignty of the king or prince goes much beyond the law-making function of the sovereignty. It was the national unity the [of] France that Bodin was looking forward. Sovereignty is, then, only the means for attaining this national unity. It is used as a pretext in order to control the feudal lords in France. He wants to make sure that the position of the French king is higher than that of the barons and that the obedience of the latter to the former is necessary. It is more a political problem than a legal question although political unity may be achieved, as Bodin thinks, by legal means. Yet if the fundamental laws, the loi salique, of France can not be changed by the sovereign, we don't see how the aged long rights of the barons or feudal lords can be taken away by the sovereign in the name of law.

To put so many limitations, limitations of salic, international, natural and divine laws, is to reduce his supreme, absolute, irresponsible, and indivisible sovereignty into a very inferior position which if we still call it sovereign, it is sovereign only in a much limited sphere and a smaller degree. It is, as we have already noted, a sovereign within many sovereignties which are different in gradation and in extent. Because beyond the kingly or princely, there is a sovereignty of salic law; and beyond the sovereignty salic law, there is a sovereignty of international law; and beyond the sovereignty of the international law, there is a sovereignty of natural law; and beyond the sovereignty of natural law, there is the sovereignty of divine law which is the highest and most original of all.

Although Hobbes tries to free himself from the limited sovereignty of Bodin, he does not succeed in doing this. We have already pointed out that his conclusion of natural law as a part of civil law destroy the rigidity of his logic and allows his law to have an abode much larger than what is known by the writers of analytical school as law in the strict sense of the term. Thus he goes beyond the so-called legal range to interprete his sovereignty.

When we come to his conception of the origin and location of sovereignty, his sovereignty becomes even less legal and more abstract than that of Bodin. Sovereignty is identified there with the monarch or king. This is Bodinian. But sovereignty is also identified here with the commonwealth and with the whole body of the people. Yet sovereignty comes from the people by the act of social contract. The curious thing here is the one or who receives the sovereignty is not in the contract. It seems that the people must have someone to be sovereign before the sovereign comes into being; therefore the one who will receive the sovereignty is excluded from the contract. This is really illogical. If one, be it a person or a body of persons, is excluded before the contract is made, he must be considered as sovereign before the conclusion of the social contract. What then is the use of having the act of social contract by means of which everyone in the community is to give up his own right in order to form the sovereignty of the whole. On the other hand, if this person or a body of persons who is not sovereign before the act of social contract and therefore it is necessary to have such an act in order that he may have the sovereignty, then he must up to the time of the conclusion of the act is no more than an ordinary person among those who are going to perform the act. This being the case, how can he be taken as a special person who is excluded from the participation in the contract.

Even taking for granted that it is possible for him to stand outside until the act is concluded, the origin of his sovereignty is not merely a legal sovereignty. It comes from a social act. Its origin is not even a political sovereignty. Because those who conclude the social contract are those who come directly the state of war, the state of nature, as Hobbes calls it, in which there is no political as well as legal institution or organization. It may be argued that out of the social contract comes the legal sovereignty. But this is to say that the social contract is the foundation for the legal sovereignty. Since we have already shown that such a foundation is groundless and unhistorical, the legal sovereignty which is founded on the social contract must be also like a castle built in the air.

Moreover, when a sovereign is free to do what he likes, the so-called law will be entirely under his caprice. As a result, it will be hard to draw a line between what is lawful and what is not lawful. This, of course, is an ethical question as the writers of the analytical school would call it. Yet neither Hobbes nor Bodin has confined himself to what is known as legalistic view point of sovereignty and its relations to law.

Nor Bentham adhers himself to the so-called legal standpoint of sovereignty. Bentham's chief concern is things political rather than legal. He even goes beyond the political society. He writes: "The idea of a natural society is a negative one. The idea of a political society is a positive one... When a number of persons (whom we may style subjects) are supposed to be in the *habit* of paying *obedience* to a person, or an assemblage of persons, of a known and certain description (whom we may call governor or governors) such persons altogether (subjects and governors) are said to be in a state of *political* society."[①]

And he continues: "The idea of a state of *natural* society is, as we have said, a negative one. When a number of persons are supposed to be in the habit of conversing with each other, at the same time that they are not in any such habit as mentioned above, they are said to be in a state of *natural* society."[②]

The difference between the natural and political society is to be found in the fact that while in the latter we find the presence the habit of obedience in the former we do not find such habit of obedience. The habit of obedience is, then, the foundation of sovereignty as well as that of political society. The one or those who receive the habit of obedience are sovereign and those who render the habit of obedience are subjects.

Now if the habit of obedience is the keynote of political society and therefore of sovereignty, we have to ask what is the habit of obedience. Is the habit of obedience a legal behavior?

Undoubtedly it is not. One may say that it is a political behavior. But it is something more than political and much more than political. Christians who habitually obey the head of the church or Catholics who habitually obey the pope do not necessarily constitute a state or a political society. Nor students who render habit obedience to their teacher make the school a political society. Nor children who pay habit of obedience to their parents make the family a political society.

It is clear that the habit of obedience is a social habit in its multifold aspects no less

---

① Bentham, *A Fragment on Government*, F. C. Montague's edition, p. 137.
② *Ibid*.

than in its political aspect. If the habit of obedience is the foundation upon which sovereignty is established, then there can be sovereignty other than what is known as political. This being the case, we can easily see that from the standpoint of the nature of sovereignty as well as from the standpoint of the origin and the location of sovereignty, it has almost nothing to do with law. Only when the sovereignty commands, then we have the law. But law in a political society is somewhat irrelevant; because the purpose of having laws is to make the subjects obey. Since in a political society there has already been formed a habit of obedience before the sovereign commands or even before the sovereignty comes into being, the function of law becomes insignificant, and indeed very insignificant.

It may be argued that law is necessary in such a political society, lest the subects may not habitually obey. But this, to be sure, is detrimental to the premise of Bentham; for if the subjects do not habitually obey, it would be hard to have a political society, to say nothing of sovereignty. It is more or less meaningless when Bentham insists that law is the command of sovereignty.

I have discussed the theories of Bodin, of Hobbes and of Bentham and pointed out their mistakes somewhat in detail, because generally speaking what have been criticized against the theories of these three writers may be also applied to the theory of Austin, the so-called champion of the analytical school or jurisprudence. And it may be added that Austin never reaches the point which Hobbes attains and the does not go beyond the line where Bodin stops. Bentham is his immediate predecessor and he is influenced more by Bentham than by other writers.

The keynote of Austin's theory of sovereignty is to be found in the so-called and often quoted definition which reads: "If a determinate human superior not in a habit of obedience to a like superior, receive habitual obedience from the bulk of a given society, that determinate superior is sovereign in that society, and the society (including the superior), is a society political and independent."①

A comparison between this definition of political society and sovereignty and that of Bentham mentioned above reveals the fact that they are essentially identical with the difference in certain words. Enough has been said about the definition of Bentham and it is not necessary for us to dwell on this definition since the criticism set forth against Bentham is applicable to Austin.

But it is to be remarked that since the publication of Bentham's *A Fragment of*

---

① Austin, John, *Lectures on Jurisprudence*, Vol. I, p. 221.

Government in 1776, conditions of the world have changed much more radically than the change of the conditions from the time of Bodin to that of Bentham. Both the American and French Revolutions came after the appearance of this work of Bentham. While constitutionalism and constitutional system already well developed in England, the written constitution, in the strict sense of the term, did not appear until 1789 when the Constitution of the United States was ratified by the member states of the union. Many written constitutions were drawn in France after the French Revolution. And this was not all. The industrial Revolution took place at the end of eighteenth century and at the beginning of the nineteenth century. The invention of machine and its application to railway and steamship shortened the distance of the world and nations of the four corners of the earth were thus brought so close together that neither Bodin nor Hobbes could ever dream of.

Thus, after the political revolutions of France and America and the Industrial Revolution in England, constitutionalism became a vogue and internationalism rapidly developed. Austin could not fail to recall what [was] happened. Besides accepting his master's conception of sovereignty and its relation to law, Austin had to face some of the facts which Bentham did not have a chance to see them before he published his *A Fragment on Government*. Although Bentham's later writings also noticed the radical changes, but his fundamental ideas concerning sovereignty and its relation to law are still to be found in this work. Austin, being in the current of the changes, had to give more attention to the two streams of thought mentioned above, i. e. constitutionalism and internationalism.

And these led him to give more thought to the scope of law or the province of jurisprudence as he called it.

It is to be noted, however, that if both constitutionalism and internationalism attracted the attention of Austin, both and particularly the latter were still in a stage of making if not in a state of infancy. There was a constitution in England, consisting of some historical documents and some laws passed by the parliament together with a great mass of customs, the common law as the English call it. It has been called unwritten constitution, because so much of the customs were to be found in it. Then there was a constitution, written constitution of the United States of 1789. While there were some people regarding it as a wonderful invention of the New World, there were many people, particularly those defended the rights of the member states of the federal union insisting that it was something like the international treaty concluded by the independent and sovereign states. Again, before the publication of Austin's *The Province of Jurisprudence*

Determined in 1832, France produced quite a few constitutions, one superseding another. While some of the principles incorporated in the constitutions were accepted by men of the age as inherent and eternal rights of men as citizens and members of political society, it also gave the impression to the world at large that constitution was something that could be produced, drawn or written just as essays could be handed in by students in their classroom.

Again, while internationalism was making its head way as a result of the change of the means of communication, the status of international law was still very doubtful. This is true even to our own day.

It was in such atmosphere that Austin tried to "determine the province of jurisprudence. When we look at the subtitle of the *Lectures on Jurisprudence* which reads: *The Philosophy of Positive Law*, we can easily see that his main task is to point what is positive law and what is not positive law?

But before explaining the questions just set forth, it is desirable to give a moment's attention to Austin's classification of law. With the development of the constitutional law, the old fourfold classification of law by the schoolmen into divine, natural, "international" and civil laws seemed to be outworn. Austin classifies the laws into two main categories: laws set by God and laws set by men.

"A law," says Austin, "in the most general and comprehensive acceptation in which the term, in its literal meaning, is employed, may be said to be a rule laid down for the guidance of an intelligent being by an intelligent being having power over him. Under this definition are concluded, and without impropriety, several species. It is necessary to define accurately the line of demarcation which separates these species from one another: as much mistiness and intricacy has been infused into the science of jurisprudence by their being confounded or not clearly distinguished. In the comprehensive sense above indicated, or in the largest meaning which it has, without extension by metaphor or analogy, the term *law* embraces the following objects: —Laws set God to his human creatures, and laws set by men to men."[①]

Austin does not make a clear distinction between the law of God and that of nature and he prefers to include the latter under the name of the former. He writes: "The whole or a portion of the laws set by God to men is frequently styled the law of nature, or natural law: being, in truth, the only natural law of which it is possible to speak without a metaphor, or without a blending of objects which ought to be distinguished broadly.

---

① Austin, *Lectures on Jurisprudence*, Vol. I, Lecture, p. 86.

But, rejecting the appellation Law of Nature as ambiguous and misleading, I name those laws or rules, as considered collectively or in a mass, the *Divine law*, or the law of God. "①

As a matter of fact, when law of nature is defined by many writers as the dictate of reason, it is something different from the law of God which is imposed or commanded by a super-natural being. In short the difference between the divine law and the natural law can be easily drawn from the fact that one is super-natural and the other natural.

"Laws set by men to men," according to Austin, "are of two leading classes: "② Some "are not established by political superiors, or are not established by political superiors, in that capacity or character. "③ "Closely analogous to human laws of this… class, are a set of objects frequently but improperly termed laws, being rules set and enforced by mere opinion, that, by the opinions or sentiments held or felt by an indeterminate body of men in regard to human conduct. Instances of such a use of the term law are the expressions—'the law of honour'; 'the law set by fashion'; and rules of this species constitute much of what is usually termed 'international law'. "④ Both that which are not established by political superiors and that which improperly but by close analogy termed laws are classified by Austin under a common class and denoted by the term positive morality.

The second class of the laws or rules which are set by men to men "are established by political superiors, sovereign and subject: by persons exercising supreme and subordinate government, in independent nations, or independent political societies. The aggregate of the rules thus established, or some aggregate forming a portion of that aggregate, is the appropriate matter of jurisprudence, general particular. To the aggregate of the rules thus established, or to some aggregate forming a portion of that aggregate the term *law*, as used simply and strictly, is exclusively applied. "⑤

It is the second class of law that Austin takes special interest and calls it positive law. In fact his Lectures on the province of jurisprudence is dealing mainly with the positive law. In the first lecture on this subject, Austin begins by declaring "that the matter of jurisprudence is positive law: law, simply and strictly so-called: or law set by political superiors to political inferiors. "⑥ In another place, we find that positive law is

---

① Austin, *Lectures on Jurisprudence*, Vol. I, Lecture, p. 86.
② Ibid.
③ Ibid., p. 87.
④ Ibid., p. 87.
⑤ Ibid., pp. 86–87.
⑥ Ibid., p. 86.

defined in this manner: "Every positive law, or every simply and strictly so called, is set by a sovereign or person, or sovereign body of persons, to a member of the independent political society wherein that person or body is sovereign or supreme."① To change the expression, "it is set by a monarch, or sovereign number, to a person or persons in a state of subjection to its author."②

It is obvious, then, that, in order to be called law proper, it must be the command of or the emanation of a sovereign. But this is certainly not the final appeal of his system, for he adds immediately to the statements just quoted above that "even though it springs directly from another fountain or source, it *is* a positive law, or a law strictly so called, by the institution of that present sovereign in the character of a political superior."③

It seems that at the beginning Austin defines positive law in a very strict sense, namely only that which is commanded by the sovereign can be called positive. Yet the tone becomes soft in the course of his discussion. For whatever is permitted by the sovereign may be also called law. In the language of Hobbes, our author quotes, "the legislator is he, not by whose authority the law was first made, but by whose authority it continues to be a law."④

Here is a more accurate definition of positive law: "A positive law may be defined generally in the following: or the essential difference of positive law (or the difference which severs it from a law not a positive law) may be stated generally in the following manner—Every positive law (or every law simply and strictly so called) is set, directly or circuitously, by a sovereign individual or body, to a member or members of the independent political society wherein its author is supreme. In other words, it is set, directly or circuitously, by a monarch or sovereign number, to a person or persons in a state of subjection its author."⑤ "This definition," he adds, "of a positive law is assumed expressly or tacitly throughout the foregoing lectures. But it is only approaches to a perfectly complete and perfectly exact definition."⑥

The definition of positive law so stated naturally excludes many other laws as they are generally accepted to laws. In order to understand what is positive law, it is better to approach from the reversed way, i. e. what are not positive laws?

---

① Austin, *Lectures on Jurisprudence*, Vol. I , Lecture, p. 220.
② Ibid.
③ Ibid.
④ Ibid.
⑤ Ibid., p. 330.
⑥ Ibid.

Can we call divine law positive law? We have already pointed out that Austin identifies natural law with divine law, the former being grouped under the name of the latter. In another place, he calls it religious duties in contrast to human laws. He says: "As distinguished from violations of duties imposed by human laws, duties imposed by the divine laws may be called religious duties."[1] He also speaks of Divine law as religious sanctions. So he says: "As distinguished from sanctions annexed to human laws, the sanctions annexed to the Divine laws may be called religious sanctions."[2] But in another place, he remarks that "the Divine laws or laws of God, are laws or rules, *properly* so called."[3]

Although the last quotation leaves some doubts in regard to the positive character or the divine law as he uses the word "properly" to speak of divine law as law while at the same time he considers divine law as religious duty or sanction, his conception of both the law of nature and that of nations is very clear. To him both the law of nature and that of nations are not positive laws, but as rules of positive morality.

"A man living in a state of nature," says he, "may impose an imperative law: though, since the man *is* in a state of nature, be can not impose the law in the character of sovereign, and can not impose the law in pursuance of a legal right. And the law being 'imperative' (and therefore proceeding from a 'determinate' source) is a law properly so called: though, for what of a sovereign author proximate or remote, it is not a positive law, but a rule of positive morality."[4]

It is clear that from the passage quoted above, law of nature is not positive law. Since the word 'properly' is also used here and since the law of nature is a part of the law of God, we may conclude that divine law as well as natural law are not positive laws.

So an imperative law set by a sovereign to a sovereign, or by one supreme government to another is not a positive law or law strictly so called, "since no supreme government is in a state of subjection to another, an imperative law set by a sovereign to a sovereign is not set by its author in pursuance of a legal right; for every legal right is conferred by a supreme government, and is conferred on a person or persons in a state of objection to the granter. Consequently, an imperative law set a sovereign to a sovereign is not a positive law or law strictly so called. But being 'imperative' (and therefore

---

[1] Austin, *Lectures on Jurisprudence*, Vol. I, Lecture, p. 104.
[2] *Ibid*.
[3] *Ibid*., p. 103.
[4] *Ibid*., pp. 181–182.

proceeding from a 'determinate' source) it amounts to a law in the proper signification of the term, although it is purely or simply a rule or positive morality."①

Thus, the so-called international law is not positive law. In fact, we have already noted in his classification of law, international law is classified in the same group with the law of honour and the law of fashion.

Even constitutional law, according to Austin, can not be called law in the strict sense of the term and it is somewhat in the same status with international law in a certain sense. "Against a monarch properly so called," he remarks, "or against a sovereign number in its collegiate and sovereign capacity, constitutional law and the law of nations are nearly in the same predicament."②

Austin certainly takes pains to decide the real character of constitutional law. And this is one of the most important controversial issues even among the analytical writers themselves. In fact, when we come to the question of the true character of constitutional law and look at the arguments of the analytical jurists among themselves, we see one of the most important weaknesses of the theory of the analytical school. Curiously enough, though it is not a slightest surprise to us at all, is the fact that these jurists encounter the same trouble in considering the true character of international law in recent years, as we shall see it in the course of discussion.

Austin tries to solve the question of the true character of constitutional law by declaring it as the compound of positive morality and positive law for determining the structure, organization or constitution of a given government. To quote his own words, constitutional law is defined as "the compound of positive morality and positive law, which determines the character of the person, or the respective character of the persons, in whom, for the time being, the sovereignty shall reside: and, supposing the government in question an aristocracy or government of a number, which determines moreover the mode wherein the sovereign powers shall be shared by the constituent members of the sovereign number or body."③

The expression "the compound of positive morality and positive law," may be meant that the constitutional law is partly positive morality and partly positive law, or it may be meant that to some ones it is positive morality, while to others it is positive law. In the former case, it may be said that it is different from the laws of nature and of nations which are purely positive morality and it is different from the positive law in that

---

① Austin, *Lectures on Jurisprudence*, Vol. I, Lecture, p. 182.
② *Ibid.*, p. 270.
③ *Ibid.*, p. 267.

the latter is a thing which is given and backed by a sovereign. In this sense, constitutional law involves both the characteristics of the laws of nature and of nations on the one hand and of the positive law on the other.

If this is what Austin has in mind, it is difficult for us to determine what part is positive morality and what part is positive law. The ambiguity of such a viewpoint is obvious. But this may not be the case in the mind of Austin. Rather he means that constitutional is to some ones positive morality while to others positive law. To understand this, we must go back to his conception of sovereignty. "By sovereign," he says, "I always mean a monarch properly so called, or a sovereign number in its collegiate and sovereign capacity."[1] "Considered collectively," he continues, "or considered in its corporate character, a sovereign number is sovereign and independent;" and therefore, "the power of a sovereign is incapable of limitation."[2] It is in this sense that a sovereign is not legally bound or limited by constitutional law, and it is in this sense that "against a sovereign body in its collegiate and sovereign capacity, constitutional law is positive morality merely, or is enforced merely by moral sanction."[3]

On the other hand, "considered severally, the individuals and smaller aggregates composing that sovereign number are subject to the supreme body of which they component parts."[4] Consequently, "though the body is independent of legal or political duty, and of the individuals or aggregates whereof the body is composed may be legally bound by laws of which the body is the author."[5] The logic here is very simple. The whole is greater than the parts, so the parts are inferior to the whole. There are things that the compenent parts of the sovereign can not do in the capacity of not being united together, but it does not follow that which the parts severally can not do the whole also can not do. To violate the constitution in the capacity of the whole, i.e., a sovereign in its collegiate capacity, is not an illegal act.[6] On the contrary, a breach of it by the component part would not be legal. It is in the latter sense that a constitution is regarded as positive law.[7]

Constitutional law is thus a compound of both positive morality and positive law,

---

[1] Austin, *Lectures on Jurisprudence*, Vol. I, Lecture, p. 269.
[2] *Ibid.*, p. 269.
[3] *Ibid.*, p. 267.
[4] *Ibid.*, p. 269.
[5] *Ibid.*
[6] *Ibid.*, p. 278.
[7] *Ibid.*, p. 270.

not necessarily in the sense that part of it is positive morality and that part of it is positive law, but rather in the sense that to some people it is positive morality that to others it is positive law. We think that the latter interpretation is even more illogical and ambiguous than the former explanation, not only because in its application there are many difficulties, but also because of the fact that to make a distinction between the sovereign in its collegiate capacity and the sovereign in its individual capacity is to divide the sovereign and this is very detrimental to the indivisible sovereignty of Austin. Unless the individual capacity of the sovereign is not sovereign, although this would be illogical and ambiguous, the sovereignty is divided when a sovereign can act individually as component parts. But if it is admitted that the act of the component parts is also sovereign, then the constitutional law would not be a positive law at all; for how can, in the system of Austin, a sovereign be limited by the law which he makes. On the other hand, to say that the sovereign in its individual capacity is legally limited by the constitutional law and particularly that constitutional law is positive law, it means that it is and must be the command of the sovereignty. In this case it is impossible to think that the command of the sovereign would be considered as positive morality and not positive law.

Austin's doubt for the true character of constitutional law as positive law is strongly protested by many of the analytical writers themselves. W. W. Willoughby, for instance, does not agree with Austin in this point, although the former is an ardent advocate for the juristic theory of the latter. "As is well known," says Willoughby, "John Austin refused to recognize that constitutional law has a 'positive' legal character. That which gives to them force, he said, is public regarding their expediency and morality, —in fine, that they belong to the class of moral rather than of legal rules. In so holding he was clearly wrong, and his error is traceable to his failure to distinguish between the state and its government. He was controlled by the view that constitutional laws purport to control the state itself, which, according to his conception of sovereignty, as well as according to the one accepted in the present treatise, is a logical impossibility. He did not appreciate that constitutional laws operate only as a limitation upon the organs of government."[①]

It is obvious that by pointing out the distinction between the government and the state, Willoughby thus enlarges the scope of positive law which to Austin is mainly confined to what is known as municipal or civil law, and narrows the limitations, be

---

① Willoughby, *The Fundamental Concepts of Public Law*, 1924, p. 89, see also *The Nature of the State*, p. 204.

moral or whatever else one may call it, on sovereignty. In this respect, Willoughby brings the notion of sovereignty farther away from that of Austin and closer to that of Hobbes.

As to the character of international law, Willoughby is almost completely in accord with Austin. He writes: "When we forsake the field of constitutional or municipal law and enter of international relations we no longer have to deal with legal superiors and legal inferiors. Here we find no supreme will, but, legally speaking, a collection of equal wills, and the conflict, or at least the interplay, of independent powers. This is the fundamental premise of those who attempt the systematic statement of the principles which govern the relations of states to one another. It is true that the more developed and civilized states of the world are spoken of as forming a 'family of nations', and that from this fact it is quite proper to argue that *ubi societas, ibi jus est*. But the *jus* which is thus brought into being has not the same essential character as has that of municipal life. Especially is this shown in the origin of international law, although the manner in which it is determined and enforced is not without significance."①

And he continues: "As regards their origin, the laws governing international relations do not find their birth in the mandatory utterances of supreme wills declaring to inferior perior persons what for them shall be deemed legally right and legally wrong. Instead, they derive their force from the fact that they have been accepted by those political persons—the states—whose actions they regulate. This acceptance may, indeed, be one which, for the most part, the states may not find it practicable to avoid, even should they so desire, and thus, in fact the rules of international intercourse may, *arguendo*, be admitted to be as definite, and in general, as uniformly conformed to as are the provisions of the municipal law of the most orderly state. This, however, does not change the essential character of those international laws as tules which obtain between equals rather than as commands addressed by a superior legislative will to persons who are conceived of as subject to its control."②

In short, according to Willoughby, international law is not positive law, because "it lacks the essential quality of embodying commands issued by political superiors to political inferiors."

This being so, it is not proper to apply the idea of sovereignty in international relations. "It would plain appear," he says, "then, that the idea of sovereignty, as it is found in constitutional law, can find no proper place among international conception.

---

① Willoughby, *The Nature of the State*, pp. 282-283.
② *Ibid.*, p. 283.

The word, indeed, generally used in the literature of international jurisprudence, but, when thus employed, it has a meaning which is so different from that which it has in the municipal field that it is most unfortunate that it should ever have obtained this currency. It would have been far better if some such term as Independency had been employed. This word, far better than sovereignty, would indicate the fact that, regarded from the point of view of positive law, complete individualism prevails in the international field. Socially, economically and morally there may be a family of nations, —a *societies maxima*, —but, looked at from the point of view of the constitutional jurist, international life is atomistic, non-civic, individualistic. Thus regarded, nations are, as individuals, in that 'state of nature' in which Hobbes, Locke, Rousseau, and the other natural law writers placed primitive man. Even when, by formal treaties, independent states have established rules by which with reference to the matters specified, their future dealings with one another are to be regulated, there has been no creation of law in a positive or Austinian sense, for, as to those matter, the contracting parties remain subject only to their own wills and not to that of an outside or foreign power." As Jellinek briefly puts it: "Der staatenvertrag bindet baer er unterwirft nicht."①

We can hardly agree with our author in many points made in this passage, but here it is sufficient to point out that Willoughby's conception of international law is not accepted even by many of those who profess to be sympathetic with the writers of analytical school including Willoughby himself.

In connection to this, it is desirable to give a little attention to the position taken by J. W. Garner for illustration. Garner tells us: "We agree with Zorn and Burgess that sovereignty is not only an essential element, but the first and the highest conceivable mark of the state; and with Willoughby that it is one characteristic which serves to distinguish the state 'in toto genere' from all other human associations."

Garner accepts Austin's conception of legal sovereignty. He declares: "As a conception of the strict legal nature of sovereignty, Austin's theory is, on the whole, clear and logical, and much of the criticism directed against it has been founded on misapprehension and misconception."②

---

① Garner, *Introduction to Political Science*, 1910, pp. 267-268.
② Garner, *Political Science and Government*, 1928, p. 181.